2019

Guidebook to
PENNSYLVANIA
TAXES

Charles L. Potter, Jr., JD

James W. Forsyth, JD, LLM, CPA

Sheldon J. Michaelson, CPA

Wolters Kluwer

Wolters Kluwer Editorial Staff

Reviewing Editors . . . . Marlia Berg, Andrew Soubel

Production Coordinator . . . . Ravikishore M, Shashikant G

This publication is designed to provide accurate and authoritative information in regard to the subject matter covered. It is sold with the understanding that the publisher is not engaged in rendering legal, accounting, or other professional service and that the authors are not offering such advice in this publication. If legal advice or other expert assistance is required, the services of a competent professional person should be sought.

ISBN 978-0-8080-5053-7

PREFACE

This *Guidebook* is designed for practitioners and students of Pennsylvania state and local taxes. It explains the background and operation of each tax and provides many helpful hints to practitioners to help solve their everyday tax problems. Because of this design, the *Guidebook* can be used as both a textbook for students and as a tool for the tax practitioner.

The authors have over 90 years of combined experience in the practice of Pennsylvania taxation, and fully appreciate the frustrations when answers to Pennsylvania tax questions are either ambiguous or difficult to find. Thus, they have attempted to provide as many examples, hints, cautions, and answers as possible to the commonly encountered real life problems, while stressing areas for tax planning.

The administration of taxes and the appeals process are complex in Pennsylvania. In many instances, a taxpayer with a valid claim for tax relief is denied such relief because of a failure to follow the proper procedures. For this reason, the *Guidebook* stresses the appropriate procedures to be followed, and gives practical tips toward obtaining appropriate relief.

All 2018 legislative amendments received as of press time are reflected, and references to Pennsylvania and federal laws are to the laws as of the date of publication of this book.

The emphasis is on the law applicable to the filing of income tax returns in 2019 for the 2018 tax year. However, if legislation has made changes effective after 2018, we have tried to note this also, with an indication of the effective date to avoid confusion.

The *Guidebook* is not designed to eliminate the necessity of referring to the law and regulations for answers to complicated problems, nor is it intended to take the place of detailed reference works such as the CCH PENNSYLVANIA TAX REPORTS. The *Guidebook* is able to provide a concise, readable treatment of Pennsylvania taxes that will supply a complete answer to most questions and will serve as a time-saving aid where it does not provide the complete answer.

In addition, we have provided the reader with the sources of authority to consult whenever a problem arises that may need further clarification. We strongly encourage the reader to consider the original source before making important tax decisions.

SCOPE OF THE BOOK

This *Guidebook* is designed to do three things:

1. Give a general picture of the impact and pattern of all taxes levied by the state of Pennsylvania and the local governmental units.

2. Provide a readable quick-reference work for both the major and minor taxes levied in Pennsylvania. As such, it explains what the Pennsylvania law provides and indicates whether the Pennsylvania provision is the same as federal law.

3. Analyze and explain the differences (especially corporate net income and personal income taxes), in most cases, between Pennsylvania and federal law.

HIGHLIGHTS OF 2018 PENNSYLVANIA TAX CHANGES

The most important 2018 Pennsylvania tax changes received by press time are noted in the "Highlights of 2018 Pennsylvania Tax Changes" section of the *Guidebook*, beginning on page 11. This useful reference gives the practitioner up-to-the-minute information on changes in tax legislation and recent relevant judicial decisions.

LOCAL TAXES

The *Guidebook* also features several sections on local taxation. Included in these sections are chapters regarding taxes relevant to Philadelphia, Pittsburgh, and other jurisdictions, as well as the Allegheny County sales and use tax.

FINDERS

The practitioner may find the desired information by consulting the general Table of Contents at the beginning of the *Guidebook*, the Table of Contents at the beginning of each chapter, or the Topical Index at the end of the *Guidebook*.

The Topical Index is a useful tool. Specific taxes and information on rates, allocation, credits, exemptions, returns, payments, collection, penalties, and remedies are thoroughly indexed and cross-referenced to paragraph numbers in the *Guidebook*.

November 2018

ABOUT THE AUTHORS

James W. Forsyth, J.D., LL.M., C.P.A. is a member of the Cozen O'Connor law firm resident in the Pittsburgh office. He works primarily with business and corporate tax matters, the taxation of pass-through entities and international tax matters. Jim is the author of BNA Tax Management Portfolios 765-4th "Stock Rights and Stock Dividends - Sections 305 and 306" and 711-3rd "Partnerships –Formation and Contributions of Property or Services." Bloomberg Tax portfolios are often cited in federal tax cases as containing the most persuasive thinking on cutting edge topics. He has also written articles appearing in national publications, including "Handling the Problems of Forming a Partnership or Limited Liability Company" in the Journal of Partnership Taxation and "Compensatory Transfers of Partnership Interests" in Vol. 42, No. 12 of the BNA Tax Management Memorandum periodical. He serves on the Corporate Taxation Advisory Board and also the Pass-Through Entities Advisory Board of Bloomberg Tax. Mr. Forsyth is a frequent speaker at various federal and state tax seminars on a number of subjects. In addition, he is a Certified Public Accountant. Jim has garnered an AV® Preeminent distinction, the highest available mark for professional excellence from Martindale-Hubbell's Peer Review Ratings. Additionally, Mr. Forsyth is recognized in Pittsburgh's Top Rated Lawyers (2012 through 2018 editions) for Business, Corporate and Taxation law by The Legal Intelligencer and has also been selected for inclusion in The Best Lawyers in America© 2017 and 2018 list. A graduate of the West Virginia University College of Law, Mr. Forsyth was selected to the Order of the Coif upon graduation. At the WVU College of Law, he served as an adjunct lecturer for eight years subsequent to graduation. He holds a master's degree in taxation from the University of Florida College of Law and a bachelor's degree, with the highest honors, from West Liberty State College.

Charles L. Potter, Jr., J.D., C.P.A., is an attorney in the Pittsburgh, Pennsylvania, office of Tucker Arensberg, P.C. Mr. Potter represents businesses and individuals in federal, state, and local tax matters, as well as corporate matters. Mr. Potter has more than 38 years of experience as a lawyer, and he is a Certified Public Accountant. He received a Bachelor of Arts in business and accounting from Monmouth College in 1968 and a Juris Doctor from the University of Pittsburgh in 1973. He received his Certified Public Accountant Certificate from Pennsylvania in 1978. Mr. Potter is a member of the American, Pennsylvania, and Allegheny County Bar Associations, the Estate Planning Council of Pittsburgh, the American and Pennsylvania Institutes of Certified Public Accountants, and the Pennsylvania and Pittsburgh Chamber of Commerce Tax Committees.

Sheldon J. Michaelson, C.P.A., received a Bachelor of Science degree in Accounting from Drexel University, where he also served as an adjunct professor. He is a tax partner at Deloitte & Touche LLP and has been with the firm for more than twenty years. He is a member of the American and Pennsylvania Institute of Certified Public Accountants, has served as Chairman of the Pennsylvania State Tax Conference Committee and the Committee on State Taxation, and is a member of the Tax Section of the Philadelphia Chamber of Commerce. He is a frequent speaker on federal and state tax topics and has published numerous articles in various tax periodicals.

CONTENTS

HIGHLIGHTS OF 2018 PENNSYLVANIA TAX CHANGES

Important statutory changes enacted in late 2017 and 2018 received by press time are noted below as well as noteworthy court cases.

In *South Dakota v. Wayfair, Inc.*, 138 S. Ct. 2080, 201 L. Ed. 2d 403 (June 21, 2018), the United States Supreme Court ruled that out-of-state online retailers can be required to collect use tax from their customers without the retailers having a physical presence in the state. In so holding, the Supreme Court overturned the physical presence requirement that had been previously established by it in the *Quill* case.

In 2016, South Dakota enacted a law which required remote out-of-state e-commerce sellers to collect and remit sales tax on sales to South Dakota residents. A remote seller was caught by the South Dakota law (and, therefore, required to collect and remit tax to South Dakota) if it met either of the following conditions: (1) On an annual basis, the remote seller delivered more than $100,000 of goods or services into South Dakota; or (2) the remote seller engaged in 200 or more separate transactions for the delivery of goods or services into the State. This South Dakota law was specifically designed to test the physical presence requirement of the US Supreme Court's *Quill* case.

The Court found that the physical presence test was flawed for three reasons. First, the substantial nexus requirement under the *Complete Auto* case did not necessarily mandate a physical presence. Second, the physical presence test created market distortions rather than eliminated them. Finally, the physical presence test imposed an arbitrary formalistic distinction inconsistent with modern Commerce Clause precedents. The Supreme Court concluded that rejecting the physical presence requirement was necessary to ensure that artificial competitive advantages were not created by the Court's prior case law precedents.

Notwithstanding the elimination of the physical presence requirement, the Court explained that a substantial nexus with the taxing state is still required under the Commerce Clause, which continues to forbid a state from imposing undue burdens on interstate commerce. The Supreme Court remanded the case back to the South Dakota state court system asking the state courts to determine whether the South Dakota statute violated the Commerce Clause given that the physical presence test was no longer applicable. The Supreme Court identified several features in South Dakota's law that could avoid a finding that the Commerce Clause was violated. First, the South Dakota law contains a safe harbor for those entities that transact only limited business in South Dakota. Second, there was no obligation for a taxpayer to remit sales tax retroactively. Third, South Dakota had adopted the Streamlined Sales and Use Tax Agreement ("Streamlined Agreement") with uniform definitions of products and services, standardized tax rate structures, and other uniform rules to reduce administrative and compliance costs. The Court intimated that these features should be considered on remand. See ¶722.

Sales, Use and Hotel Occupancy Tax

In *Downs Racing, LP v. Commonwealth of Pennsylvania* __ A.3d __, (Pa. October 25, 2018), the Pennsylvania Supreme Court determined that a closed circuit horse racing simulcasting system was subject to sales and use tax. The court also found that royalties paid for intellectual property used in operating video poker machines in the race track operator's casino resort were exempt.

The race track operator contracted with a service provider that supplied the necessary simulcasting system equipment. The operator rented the equipment from the service provider. The service provider supplied the employees to operate the rented equipment. In some cases, equipment rented with an operator is not subject to tax. This exemption requires that the work be controlled by the person providing the equipment and the operator. In this case, the race track operator directed the service provider's employees in their use of the equipment. Furthermore, charges for the equipment rental and related services, and for the various types of labor, were not separately stated. Therefore, all charges for the simulcasting system were subject to tax.

The race track operator paid royalties for intellectual property used in operating video gaming machines at its casino resort. These fees applied to the right to use trademarks, copyrights, and patented methods of play owned by third parties. The royalties were not payments for purchases of gaming machines or software needed to operate the machines. There were separate agreements for the use of software and for the use of intellectual property. Furthermore, the operator incurred the royalty charges on a daily basis. These charges were separate from charges to purchase the machines, operating software, and software licenses. Since the royalties were not payments for tangible personal property, they were not subject to tax.

In *Victory Bank v. Cmwlth.*, 190 A.3d 782 (Pa. Commw. 2018), the Commonwealth Court addressed a situation where a financial institution had claimed a sales tax exemption relating to the purchase and installation of computer hardware, canned computer software, and services. The bank had purchased the disputed items from three sellers and used all of the hardware and software for the bank's protection in conducting financial transactions. The bank maintained that the purchases were exempt from tax because of a regulation issued by the Pennsylvania Department of Revenue ("PA DOR") exempted purchases of property used "for its protection or convenience in conducting financial transactions" under the Financial Institution Security Equipment Regulation (FISE regulation). The PA DOR maintained, that at the time the FISE regulation was promulgated, there was no statutory definition of what constituted a "construction contract" so that the exemption for financial institutions applied based on the definition of "installation" as provided in the FISE regulation. Since the promulgation of the regulation, however, the term "construction contract" had since been statutorily defined as "a written or oral contract or agreement for the construction, reconstruction, remodeling, renovation or repair of real estate or a real estate structure" in 72 P. S. §7201(nn). The PA DOR maintained that the subsequent statute trumped the administrative agency's regulation and the court agreed. Since there was no other exemption applicable to the sale of computer hardware, canned software, and related services, the items were taxable by the seller. See ¶703 and ¶715.

The PA DOR issued Sales and Use Tax Bulletin 2018-02 (issued July 27, 2018, revised October 1, 2018, and effective July 1, 2019). This Bulletin is titled Taxation of the Sale of Malt or Brewed Beverages in Pennsylvania by Manufacturers. The purpose of this Bulletin is to clarify when sales tax must be collected and remitted by manufacturers of malt or brewed beverages specifically, and is not applicable to any other type of liquor licensee. Generally, a manufacturer is required to collect sales tax on sales of malt or brewed beverages to any person for any purpose, with the exception of sales made to importing distributors or distributors. In contrast, sales of malt or brewed beverages by retail liquor licensees or retail dispenser licensees are not subject to sales tax. The Bulletin details the taxability of sales by manufacturers holding a variety of licenses issued by the Pennsylvania Liquor Control Board (PLCB). The PLCB issues more than 70 types of licenses and permits which has created significant confusion as to when sales are taxable. A "manufacturer of malt or brewed beverages" is any person licensed by the PLCB to engage in the manufacture, transportation and sale of malt or brewed beverages. A manufacturer of malt or brewed beverages also includes any person engaged in the legal manufacture of malt or brewed beverages within the United States, even if the beverages are manufactured outside Pennsylvania but within the US. When a manufacturer sells its own product under its brewery (G) license, brewery pub (GP) license, or brewery storage (GS) license, the sale is taxable (unless the sale is to a distributor or importing distributor). The PA DOR announced that it will allow a manufacturer (selling under a manufacturing license) to include the sales tax in the advertised purchase price of its own product, instead of separately stating and charging its customers sales tax. However, if a manufacturer selling its own products under its manufacturing license elects not to include the sales tax in the advertised purchase price of its products, the manufacturer must collect and remit tax on each individual sale of its own product, whether the sale is for on-premises or off-premises consumption. Additionally, if that manufacturer sells the products of other manufacturers, it must collect sales tax on the purchase price of those sales as well and should provide the other manufacturer with a resale exemption certificate claiming a sale for resale exemption. See ¶702.

The PA DOR issued Sales and Use Tax Bulletin 2018-01 Marketplace Sales on January 26, 2018. The Bulletin provides guidance related to marketplace sales based on Act 43 of 2017. Act 43 generally requires certain marketplace facilitators, remote sellers and referrers who do not maintain a place of business within the Commonwealth (but who had aggregate taxable sales in Pennsylvania worth at least $10,000 in the prior twelve months) to make an election to either: (1) register to collect and remit sales and use tax; or (2) comply with tax notification and reporting requirements by March 1, 2018. These terms are defined in the Bulletin. Pennsylvania customers should begin receiving information notices from businesses who have elected not to collect sales tax beginning April 1, 2018. The information notice will identify the purchases made and the purchase price of products for which sales tax was not collected by the seller. Following the enactment of Act 43, Amazon announced that it would begin calculating, collecting and remitting sales tax in Pennsylvania as of April 1, 2018 for all transactions it facilitates for out-of-state sellers.

Act 43 of 2017 also:

- provides that (effective October 30, 2017) support services for digital and electronically delivered products and separately invoiced help desk and call center support services for canned software are not subject to sales and use tax;

- provides that kegs used to contain malt or brewed beverages are exempt from sales and use tax (effective October 30, 2017);

- imposes a fee on carsharing, ranging from 25 cents for less than two hours to $2 for four hours or more on each rental of a motor vehicle. Carsharing is defined as a membership based service that provides an alternative to personal car ownership and which meets the following conditions: (1) does not require a trip-specific written agreement each time a member rents a vehicle, (2) does not require an attendant to be present at the beginning or end of a rental, (3) offers members access to a dispersed network of shared vehicles 24-hours per day, 7 days per week, 365 days per year, (4) allows a vehicle to be rented on a per minute, per hour, per day, or per trip basis, and at per mile or per kilometer rates, which typically include fuel, insurance and maintenance; and

- imposes a 12% tax on consumer fireworks (effective October 30, 2017), in addition to the sales and use tax.

Act 108 of 2018 makes booking agents responsible for collecting Pennsylvania state and local hotel occupancy taxes on rent they charge for a room. This includes taxes on accommodation fees and any other amount charged by the booking agent. Under Act 108, hotel operators are not responsible for collecting hotel occupancy taxes on a booking agent's accommodation fees.

Personal Income Tax

Act 43 of 2017 generally requires taxpayers that bring out-of-state independent contractors into Pennsylvania and pay over $5,000, and entities making rent and royalty payments on Pennsylvania property to nonresidents over $5,000, to withhold personal income tax. The PA DOR issued online guidance to help taxpayers understand the change in Pennsylvania law in regard to certain withholding requirements in connection with nonresidents. Under Section 316.2 of the Tax Reform Act of 1971, Pennsylvania businesses must withhold taxes at the applicable income tax rate (currently 3.07 percent) on payments to a nonresidents on non-wage Pennsylvania source income attributable to services performed in Pennsylvania (PA source income). The guidance includes an overview of key terms, a detailed explanation of the Pennsylvania source income rules, and directions regarding a payor's obligations. Payors who fail to comply with the withholding requirement may be liable for the amount that should have been withheld, plus penalties and interest, and payors who are unsure of the total amount of payments that will be made during the year are encouraged to withhold and remit income tax from all payments made. Generally, for nonresident withholding to apply to a payor, all of the following must be present: (a) the payor is making payments of non-wage income from Pennsylvania sources (for example, commercial leases, royalties, services rendered); (b) payments will exceed $5,000 per payee in the calendar year; (c) payments are made to a resident of another state. The nonresident withholding requirement does not apply to wages paid to employees, payments for goods and materials, or payments related to residential rental agreements or residential lease payments, or related to sales of real estate located outside Pennsylvania. Nonresident withholding is also not required when the payee is a corporation, a partnership or multi-member liability company, a nonresident with no Pennsylvania source income, or a disregarded entity owned by a corporation or partnership. See Pennsylvania Tax Update No. 197 June/July 2018. See ¶302.

In Information Notice Corporate Taxes and Personal Income Tax, 2018-1 (issued April 20, 2018), the PA DOR announced that the Repatriation Transition Tax (RTT) will not be treated as a taxable dividend for personal income tax purposes because it is not considered an actual dividend under Pennsylvania's eight classes of income. The PA DOR explained that the RTT is a deemed dividend for federal purposes, not an actual dividend. However, when earnings and profits related to the RTT is ever actually distributed, it will then be a taxable dividend for personal income tax purposes.

Corporation Tax

On October 18, 2017 the Pennsylvania Supreme Court handed down its decision in *Nextel Communications of the Mid Atlantic v. Cmwlth.*, 171 A.3d 682 (Pa. 2017). In this decision, the Court held that, as it was applied in 2007 to a Pennsylvania corporate net income taxpayer, a statutory limitation on the net loss carryover deduction violated the Uniformity Clause of the Pennsylvania Constitution. (Pa. Const. art. VIII § 1). Thus, the Court determined it was required to sever the $3 million flat deduction but it left in place the percentage based deduction cap in the statute. See ¶1003.

The tax provision at issue gave taxpayers with a net loss carry forward a deduction equal to the higher of 12.5% of the current year's taxable income, or $3,000,000. The lower court (Commonwealth Court) had ruled that the $3,000,000 limitation was unconstitutional and that the deduction should be unlimited. The Pennsylvania Supreme Court ruled that the $3,000,000 provision was unconstitutional and the only deduction available was 12.5% of the taxpayer's taxable income for the year.

The court's ruling means that taxpayers who had relied on the $3,000,000 provision now find that their losses are limited to 12.5% of their taxable income for the year. Most taxpayers have used the $3,000,000 deduction rather than the deduction based on 12.5% of taxable income. This means that most taxpayers claimed a net loss deduction in excess of what this decision allows.

The taxpayer's petition for a writ of certiorari to the U.S. Supreme Court was denied on June 11, 2018 (2018 BL 204767).

In response to *Nextel*, the legislature passed Act 43 of 2017 which amends the net loss deduction by removing the $5 million hard net loss cap and increasing the percentage cap to 35% in 2018 and 40% in 2019 and thereafter. The change was to take effect after the PA DOR published a notification that all or a part of the net loss deduction has been deemed unconstitutional as a result of a decision by the Pennsylvania Supreme Court. This notice was published on January 27, 2018 by the Secretary of Revenue following the Pennsylvania Supreme Court's denial of reargument. Thus, the Pennsylvania net loss deduction is limited to 35% of taxable income for tax years beginning after December 31, 2017 and to 40% of taxable income for tax years beginning after December 31, 2018. The PA DOR has announced in Corporation Tax Bulletin 2018-02 (May 10, 2018) that for tax years after 2006 through 2016, it will allow a net loss deduction equal to the greater of the flat dollar net loss deduction applicable to any such year and the percentage cap as authorized by statute. See ¶ 1003.

In *Mission Funding Alpha v. Cmwlth.*, 173 A.3d 748 (Pa. 2017) the Pennsylvania Supreme Court ruled that in the case of a taxpayer who had paid its tax on the April 15 due date, but later filed its tax report in September, the three-year refund period began on the date on which the tax was required to be paid, not the date on which the tax report was filed. The taxpayer had made installment payments of tax during the year and paid the balance of its tax liability on April 15. The relevant refund statute required that a refund petition be filed within three years of actual payment of the tax, interest or penalty. 72 P.S. § 10003.1(a). The Court held that the actual payment of the tax means the date on which a payment is made with respect to a particular liability. Since the statute required payment on April 15th, that date began the refund period, notwithstanding that the report filed later stated the taxpayer's calculation of its liability. The taxpayer argued that until the report was filed, there was no tax amount due to the PA DOR. Consequently, any payment on April 15th could not be considered to have been an actual payment of tax but instead was merely a deposit. The court rejected that argument (and the Commonwealth Court's reasoning) on the grounds that the statute by its terms required payment of tax liability on April 15th, and charged interest if the payment was late. Thus, statutory liability was imposed on April 15th. See ¶ 1207.

Act 72 of 2018 decoupled the state's corporate net income tax law from the bonus depreciation provided in the federal Tax Cuts and Jobs Act of 2017. Act 72 was signed into law by Governor Tom Wolf on June 28, 2018. Administratively, the PA DOR had first stated that a taxpayer was entitled to zero depreciation following the 2017 federal tax changes for qualified property. Corporation Tax Bulletin 2017-02 (December 22, 2017). That Bulletin disallowed all depreciation on assets subject to 100 percent federal bonus depreciation placed in service after Sept. 27, 2017. Further, cost recovery equal to the full acquisition cost of the asset would be allowed only at the time the asset was sold or otherwise disposed of. Following Act 72 (becoming law in June of 2018), however, the PA DOR issued Corporation Tax Bulletin 2018-03, which superseded Bulletin 2017-02, and effectively adopted the Modified Accelerated Cost Recovery System (MACRS) of depreciation as the PA DOR's policy and announced that for property placed in service before September 28, 2017, Corporation Tax Bulletin 2011-01 would continue to apply. Consequently, depreciation for corporate net income tax purposes is thus calculated under the federal MACRS provisions for property acquisitions on or after September 28, 2017. A corporation may deduct any unused bonus depreciation in the tax year in which the corporation sells or disposes of the assets subject to bonus depreciation. See ¶ 1002.

Act 131 of 2018 adopted special apportionment factors for air freight forwarding companies. Act 131 was signed into law by Governor Tom Wolf on October 24, 2018 and the changes apply to tax years beginning after 2016. Air freight forwarding companies will apportion business income to Pennsylvania by multiplying the income by a fraction: the numerator is the taxpayer's total revenue miles in Pennsylvania during the tax year; and the denominator is the taxpayer's total revenue miles everywhere. A "qualified air freight forwarding company" engages in the air freight forwarding business, uses an airline with which it has common ownership and control, and uses the revenue miles of the airline for apportionment. See ¶1114.

In Information Notice Corporate Taxes and Personal Income Tax, 2018-1 (issued April 20, 2018), the PA DOR announced that the Repatriation Transition Tax (RTT) in the federal Tax Cuts and Jobs Act of 2017 is included in federal taxable income tax for purposes of the Pennsylvania Corporate Net Income Tax, notwithstanding that the RTT is not actually included in line 28 of the Federal Form 1120. The PA DOR explained that 61 Pa. Admin. Code § 153.11 provides for a different interpretation of "taxable income" in certain instances. The PA DOR also determined that the RTT deduction applies for purposes of the corporate net income tax as well as for the dividends received deduction because it is Subpart F income. Although federal law permits the RTT liability to be paid over eight years, the deferral is a federal election that is not available under Pennsylvania law. See ¶1002.

Tax Credits

The Pennsylvania Commonwealth Court, in *Vetri Navy Yard, LLC v. Dept. of Community and Economic Dev.*, 189 A.3d 1137 (Pa. Commw. 2018), ruled that the application of the Keystone Opportunity Zone ("KOZ") recapture provisions is not limited to situations where the qualified business physically relocates outside of the KOZ. The taxpayer had constructed and operated a restaurant in the Philadelphia Navy Yard KOZ in 2013 and was granted KOZ benefits. The taxpayer sold the restaurant to a third party on January 30, 2016. Under § 902a of the Keystone Opportunity Improvement Zone Act (Act), when a "qualified business" "relocates" outside a KOZ within a certain period of time, KOZ benefits are subject to recapture. 73 P.S. § 820.902(a). The Commonwealth Court noted that the Act did not define the terms "relocation outside of the zone" but nevertheless determined that the taxpayer's cessation of business through a sale resulted in the equivalent of a relocation outside of the zone - notwithstanding that the purchaser continued to operate a restaurant on the exact same premises. The court's interpretation of the terms "relocation outside of the zone" would logically necessitate a finding that a taxpayer's bankruptcy (another type of cessation of business in a KOZ) would likewise require a recapture of KOZ benefits, thus seemingly making entrepreneurs less likely to attempt development in a blighted area. See ¶1004 and ¶1013.

The PA DOR issued Restricted Tax Credit Bulletin 2018-01 which addressed a variety of issues relating to the use and sale of restricted tax credits. The PA DOR explained that a completed tax report must be filed for the period in which the tax credit was approved before the credit may be passed through, carried forward, sold, or assigned. The sale or assignment of a restricted credit will not be approved if the seller has any unpaid state taxes. Consequently, a seller must file all state tax reports and returns and paid all state tax liabilities as of the date the PA DOR is asked to review the seller's records as a part of the process to approve the sale of a credit. Additionally, in order to request a pass-through of a credit, an entity must complete the credit claim form attached to the credit certificate or include a list of the shareholders, members or partners and the amount of the credit to be passed through to each on the business's letterhead, signed by an authorized representative. The Bulletin also explains that buyers of restricted credits must use the credit in the year in which the purchase or assignment is made. Such a credit is prohibited from being carried forward, carried back, refunded, sold or assigned. This Bulletin indicates that it replaces Corporate Tax Bulletin 2014-04. See ¶1004.

Act 39 of 2018, effective July 1, 2018, increased the aggregate amount of all credits that may be approved for contributions from business firms to scholarship organizations, educational improvement organizations and pre-kindergarten scholarship organizations to $160 million (previously $135 million) per fiscal year. No less than $110 million of that amount must be used to provide tax credits to scholarship organizations. For more information regarding the educational improvement tax credit program, see the Department of Community and Economic Development website at https://dced.pa.gov/download/educational-improvement-tax-credit-program-eitc-guidelines/?wpdmdl=84406. See ¶1011.

Governor Wolf signed Act 42 of 2018 which provides that (1) for fiscal year 2018-19 only, the number of tours that may be awarded tax credits for qualified rehearsal and tour expenses is increased to 10 tours and provides that the Department of Community and Economic Development, in consultation with the PA DOR, may advance the award of tax credits for qualified rehearsal and tour expenses incurred or to be incurred to a maximum of two additional tours in fiscal year 2018-19; and (2) adds a definition of "entertainment business financial management firm" related to qualified businesses operating in neighborhood improvement zones to enable the contracting authority to identify the responsible party required to fulfill reporting compliance on behalf of a qualified business, for concerts or other performances in a facility in the zone in connection with concert rehearsal and tour credits. See ¶1030.

Act 100 of 2018, effective July 1, 2019, increased the aggregate amount of all credits available under the Neighborhood Assistance Partnership Program. The total amount of credits available to all participants each year is now $36 million (previously $18 million) per fiscal year. See ¶1005.

Gross Premiums Tax

On April 24, 2018 the PA DOR issued Corporation Tax Bulletin 2018-01 Credits Against the Gross Premiums Tax Liability Under the Provisions of the Pennsylvania Life and Health Insurance Guaranty Association Act of 1992. In this Bulletin, the PA DOR explained the proper method to calculate the Pennsylvania insurance premiums tax credit available to insurance companies. Key to the availability of a credit is the manner in which the credit is permitted to be claimed. The PA DOR explained how to calculate the proportionate part of an assessment which may be claimed as a credit for each type of assessment. Critical to the calculation of the credit is the amount of guaranteed premiums that an insurance company receives. Guaranteed premiums are those premiums in which the premium rates are guaranteed during the continuance of a policy without a right exercisable by the company to increase the premium rate. 40 P.S. § 991.1711(b). The PA DOR did not provide any advice, however, in regard to when it will consider premiums to be guaranteed premiums. It is this area that is generating significant litigation in Pennsylvania. The PA DOR's historic position is that premiums related to group accident and health insurance policies are not to be included in the numerator of the proportionate part calculation. See ¶2213.

Public Utility Gross Receipts Tax

In *American Electric Power Service Corp. v. Cmwlth.*, 184 A.3d 1031 (Pa. Commw. 2018), the Commonwealth Court *en banc* affirmed the decision of a panel of the court which had considered the effects of the Electricity Generation Customer Choice and Competition Act ("EGCCA"). In 1996, the EGCCA was signed into law and allowed consumers to purchase electricity from any supplier and have that electricity delivered by the local utility in the purchasing customer's area. Companies like American Electric Power ("AEP") were, thus, permitted to make sales of electricity in Pennsylvania even though they were not registered as public utilities.

AEP sold electricity on a wholesale basis to the Letterkenny Industrial Development Authority ("LIDA"). LIDA was formed in 1997 under the Pennsylvania Economic Development Financing Law when the Letterkenny Army Depot was closed by Franklin County. AEP first argued that it was not subject to the gross receipts tax because it was not a public utility and was not subject to the jurisdiction of the Pennsylvania Public Utility Commission. In the alternative, AEP argued that it was entitled to the resale exemption for the sales for resale to LIDA.

The Commonwealth Court determined that the licensure of a seller of electricity from the Pennsylvania Public Utility Commission was not determinative as to whether a business was engaged in the electric light business and, therefore, subject to the gross receipts tax relying on *Hanley & Byrd v. Cmwlth*, 590 A.2d 1382 (Pa. Commw. 1991). *Hanley & Bird* determined that the function a taxpayer performs, rather that PUC jurisdiction, gives rise to application of the tax. The taxpayer was an electric distribution company because the EGCCA provides that the phrase "engaged in electric light and power business" used in the gross receipts tax includes the direct or indirect engaging in business for the purpose of establishing or maintaining a market in the sales of electric energy.

The Commonwealth Court also found that the resale exemption was not applicable. LIDA was found to be a political instrumentality of the Commonwealth. Thus, it was not a private corporation and not subject to the gross receipts tax itself. Because LIDA was not subject to the tax, the resale exemption could not be applicable to AEP.

Act 52 of 2018 revised the Pennsylvania gross receipts tax to clarify that sales of telephones, modems, tablets and related accessories, including cases, charges, holsters, clips, screen protectors and such are not subject to the gross receipts tax in regard to telephone and mobile telecommunications companies. The PA DOR then issued guidance regarding the receipts from telecommunications businesses that are subject to utility gross receipts tax under Article XI of the Tax Reform Code (72 P.S. § 8101). Corporation Tax Bulletin 2018-04 (dated August 20, 2018) provides a general discussion of the application of the gross receipts tax and the clarifications of the tax as provided by the Pennsylvania Supreme Court in *Verizon Pennsylvania, Inc. v. Cmwlth*, 127 A.3d 745 (Pa. 2015). The Bulletin also provides a sampling of sales of services and equipment that give rise to taxable receipts, and a detailed list of authorized deductions. See ¶ 2402.

Public Utility Realty Tax Act

In *Lehigh Valley Rail Mgmt. LLC v. County of Northampton*, 178 A.3d 950 (Pa. Commw 2018), the Commonwealth Court remanded an appeal to the trial court to identify the portions of an 85 acre tract that were subject to the Public Utility Realty Tax Act Tax ("PURTA Tax"). PURTA subjects Pennsylvania utility real property to the PURTA tax instead of the local real property tax. PURTA exempts certain items from its reach as taxable property. Any exempted property does not then become part of the formula for the distribution of PURTA taxes to localities. The 85 acres at issue were used by the taxpayer generally for intermodal facilities. Intermodal facilities enable the railroad to move rail-ready containers from a train to a truck, a truck to a train, or between trains. The court ruled that such facilities are indeed taxable for PURTA purposes because such facilities are part of the real estate necessary for the operation of the railroad on a 24-hour basis. However, certain portions of the 85 acres were used for a driveway, parking lot and an office trailer. The court directed the lower court to identify and quantify the acreage that was devoted to such purposes, and to eliminate those portions from the PURTA exemption. See ¶ 2502.

Uniformity Clause Violations

In *Chester Downs and Marina LLC v. Pa. Dept. of Rev.*, __ A.3d __, (Pa. July 18, 2018), the Pennsylvania Supreme Court dismissed a request for a refund of a taxpayer's local share assessment levied on gross slot machine revenue under the Race Horse Development and Gaming Act (Gaming Act) because no retroactive relief was available for taxes paid prior to the Court's decision in *Mount Airy #1, LLC v. Pa. Dept. of Rev.*, 154 A.3d 268 (2016). In regard to any claims for a refund of taxes paid after the *Mount Airy #1* decision, the Court lacked original jurisdiction to entertain those claims. The taxpayer apparently petitioned the Supreme Court seeking a refund of the local share assessment taxes under the court's exclusive jurisdiction to hear constitutional challenges to the Gaming Act. See 4 Pa. C. S. § 1904. The Court's decision in *Mount Airy #1* held that the local share assessment imposed under the Gaming Act was a non-uniform tax prohibited under the Uniformity Clause of the Pennsylvania Constitution and severed the local share assessment provision from the Gaming Act. The *Chester Downs* ruling prohibited a refund in the case at bar because Supreme Court decisions invaliding a state tax statute are effective as of the date of the decision, and cannot be applied retroactively. See ¶ 3307.

Refund Period

The Commonwealth Court denied the refund of an overpayment of slot machine tax because the claim for refund was not filed within the three-year limitations time period. The refund claim was based on an Pennsylvania Supreme Court decision, *Greenwood Gaming and Entertainment, Inc. v. Cmwlth.*, 90 A.3d 699 (2014) (*Greenwood II*), reversing a Commonwealth Court decision which held that a casino and racetrack operator was not entitled to a deduction for cash and non-cash awards distributed to casino patrons holding Players Cards in determining gross terminal revenue (GTR) for purposes of the gaming tax, and remanded the matter for determination of the refund due for tax years 2007 and 2008. The casino taxpayer subsequently filed a petition for refund of slot machine taxes based on deductions of cash and non-cash awards from January 1, 2009, through January 4, 2011. That refund claim was denied because it was filed outside the three-year period for filing refund claims mandated under 72 Pa. Stat. Ann. § 10003.1(a). The taxpayer argued that the three-year limitations period was inequitable and violated its due process rights because the prior Commonwealth Court opinion (*Greenwood Gaming and Entertainment, Inc. v. Cmwlth.*, 29 A.3d 1215 (2011) (*Greenwood I*)) was the controlling law during that three-year period. Consequently, it would have been futile and improper for the taxpayer to seek a refund during that time. However, the Pennsylvania Commonwealth Court held that a voluntary payment of taxes can be subsequently recovered only as a statute provides, and statutory time limitations must be strictly enforced. Therefore, the taxpayer's failure to file the refund request within the statutory period extinguished its right to a refund and neither the PA DOR, nor the court may rely on equitable principles to revive the taxpayer's statutory right to request a refund. Taxpayer's assertion that filing a timely refund would have subjected it to liability under sections of the Judicial Code commonly referred to as the Dragonetti Act was also rejected because those sections do not apply to taxpayers who have a reasonable belief and probable cause to initiate a judicial proceeding. *Greenwood Gaming and Entertainment, Inc. v. Cmwlth.*, Pa Commw. Ct. Dkt. No. 609 F.R. 2015, 09/06/2018 2018 BL 320987 (unreported). See ¶ 4611.

Property Tax

The Commonwealth Court held that property owned by the Erie-Western Pennsylvania Port Authority and leased to a partnership that operated two private marinas was not immune from taxation in *Bay Harbor Marina Limited Partnership v. Erie County Board*, 177 A.3d 406 (Pa. Commw. 2018). The Port Authority was formed pursuant to the Third Class City Port Authority Act. The court first held that the lessee of the property had standing to appeal an assessment of the property and that the Port Authority was a proper party to the proceedings. In regard to the substantive legal issues, the court affirmed that significant portions of the property was not immune from taxation. Because the Port Authority was a public body, the property was immune unless it could be shown that it was not used for the Port Authority's authorized purposes. The burden was on the taxing authority to prove that the use was not as authorized. The court easily found that the Port Authority's authorized purpose was to operate port facilities. The operation of private marinas did not fall within that purpose. Nevertheless, some portions of the property were open to the public and the court remanded the matter for a determination of the extent to which there was a public use of the property. See ¶3403.

In an unreported decision, the Commonwealth Court held that property owned by a transit authority and used as part of a public transit facility was immune from real property taxation. *In re Appeal of City of Lancaster ex rel. Property of Red Rose Transit Authority*, No. 665 C.D. 2017 (Pa. Commw. Jan. 3, 2018). The Transit Authority was a municipal authority formed under the Municipality Authorities Act of 1945. The parcel involved in the litigation was used by the Transit Authority for various purposes, such as a waiting area for passengers, a parking garage, bus bays, and a roadway for bus entry and exit. The parcel was used as a part of the Transit Authority's Queen Street Transit Center. The decision found that the property was immune from local real property taxation as governmental property. Because the property was used for a public purpose that was within the authorized purpose of the Transit Authority, the property could not be subject to local real property taxes. See ¶3403.

The Commonwealth Court, in *In Re Appeal of Springfield Hospital, ex rel. Prospect Crozer, LLC*, 179 A.3d 632 (Pa. Commw. 2018), held that the assets of a charitable hospital became taxable upon the date of a sale of the property in Delaware County, Pennsylvania to a for-profit entity, not on the first day of the forthcoming tax year. The court noted that, under the general common law rule, a change in the tax exempt status of an entity takes effect on the first day of the coming tax year, not on the day of the change. However, amendments to the General County Assessment Law (GCAL) in 1978 changed this general rule in many counties to provide for an immediate change in the tax exempt status of the property. The court determined, however, that GCAL was not applicable to a second class county and found that the tax assessment day rule remains applicable for Delaware County which is a second class county. Therefore, a change in tax status of a taxpayer becomes effective on the first day of the next year, not on the date of the change. The majority nonetheless held that the effective date of the transfer of the nonprofit hospital's assets on July 1st to a for-profit entity was the applicable date on which the property became subject to real estate tax, not January 1 of the coming tax year due to the existence of a PILOT agreement in effect with respect to the subject realty. The court held that a judicial order enforcing a PILOT agreement modified what would otherwise be the tax assessment day rule. See ¶3502.

In an unreported decision of a panel of the Commonwealth Court, in *Helping Enjoying and Loving People, v. Del. County Bd. of Assessment Appeals*, Pa. Commw. Dkt. No. 558 C.D. 2017, (July 9, 2018) a nonprofit corporation that owned a community center and provided a variety of services, including free coats, free food, free computer classes and free computers, failed to qualify for a property tax exemption because the nonprofit did not meet the criteria for being a purely public charity under *Hospital Utilization Project v. Cmwlth.*, 487 A.2d 1306 (Pa. 1985). The taxpayer established that it advanced a charitable purpose; donated or gratuitously rendered a substantial portion of its services; and that it operated entirely free from a profit motive (3 of the 5 HUP tests), but failed to demonstrate that (i) benefited a substantial and indefinite class of persons who are legitimate subjects of charity (the third prong of the HUP test), or (ii) relieved the government of some of its burden (the fourth prong of the HUP test). In regard to the third prong of the HUP test addressed by the Commonwealth Court in *Helping Enjoying and Loving People*, the court looked to its prior decision in *Appeal of Sewickley Valley YMCA*, 774 A.2d 1 (Pa.

Commw. 2001) holding that in order to meet the third prong of the HUP test an entity must show that it makes a bona fide effort to service those persons who are unable to afford the usual fee or for whom the fee is outside of their financial reach. The taxpayer provided no evidence whatsoever regarding whether the recipients of goods and services under its various programs were unable to pay. Therefore, the court could not find that the taxpayer benefited a substantial and indefinite class of persons who are legitimate subjects of charity and denied the taxpayer an exemption from real estate taxes. See ¶ 3505.

In *Lehighton Area School Dist. v. Carbon County Tax Claim Bur.*, 187 A.3d 280 (Pa Commw. 2018), the Commonwealth Court found that the trial court erred in holding that school districts that hired a private entity to collect delinquent property taxes was not entitled to second priority status in the distribution of proceeds from the sale of properties for delinquent property taxes. The Tax Claim Bureau sold the properties at a judicial sale. The Bureau then filed petitions for confirmation of the sales and prepared schedules for distribution of the sales proceeds. The school districts were not included on the distribution schedule. When the school districts filed a protest, the Bureau argued (and the trial court agreed) that by hiring a private party to collect delinquent property taxes on behalf of the school districts (as permitted under the Tax Liens Act), the school districts had opted out of the Bureau's collection services under the Tax Sale Law; thereby causing any sale proceeds due to the districts to no longer be considered "taxes" entitled to treatment as second priority claims under the Tax Sale Law. The Commonwealth Court disagreed with the Bureau and trial court, ruling that both the Tax Liens Act and the Tax Sale Law establish that all taxes levied on property by any taxing district are considered a first lien on the property, subordinate only to tax liens imposed by the Commonwealth. The court determined that the Tax Liens Act and Tax Sale Law are not mutually exclusive, but instead their provisions are designed to operate in conjunction with one another. Thus, when possible, the courts should give effect to the provisions of both. See ¶ 3510.

Act 42 of 2018 that provides that, effective for claim year 2018 and thereafter, retired federal civil service employees receiving benefit payments from the Civil Service Retirement System (CSRS) who did not have to contribute to Social Security for that equivalent period of employment will be able to exclude 50% of the average annual Social Security benefit amount from their property tax rent rebate income on claim forms reporting their eligibility income for Property Tax and Rent Rebate purposes by amending the definition of income. See ¶ 3512.

Local Tax Enabling Act

Act 18 of 2018, effective July 3, 2018, amended provisions of the Local Tax Enabling Act, 53 P.S. § 6924.101 et seq., relating to local earned income tax. The amendments generally (i) add definitions for "contingent fee audit" and "private collection agency;" (ii) update the definition of "nonresident," "nonresident tax," and "taxpayer;" (iii) prohibit second class cities from using contingent fee audits by private collection agencies as part of an effort to collect payroll taxes; (iv) provide that an individual who does not meet the domicile requirements for purposes of determining and paying tax under the Tax Reform Code will be deemed not to meet the domicile requirements for purposes of local earned income tax; and (v) provide that for purposes of collecting earned income taxes (and for crediting purposes), the terms "earned income" and "net profits" will include all taxes on earned income or net profits whether authorized by the Local Tax Enabling Act or any other Pennsylvania law, unless the law specifically provides otherwise. This act also allows taxpayers who have paid pay earned income tax to avoid penalties for late payment provided that the taxpayer has made timely estimated tax payments (in four equal instalments) that at least equal the taxpayer's previous year's tax liability, or amount to 90% of the current year's tax liability (less withholding). See ¶ 3607.

Tobacco Products Tax Act

In *East Coast Vapor, LLC. v. Pa. Dept. of Rev.*, 189 A.3d 504 (Pa. Commw. 2018), the Commonwealth Court ruled that e-cigarette devices and the e-liquids used in such devices are not subject to the Tobacco Products Tax Act ("TPTA"). The TPTA imposes a 40% tax on tobacco products, which includes electronic cigarettes, or e-cigarettes. As an initial matter, the court rejected the PA DOR's argument that the case should be dismissed because the taxpayer had failed to exhaust its administrative remedies. Instead, the court found that the taxpayer had raised a substantial constitutional challenge to the TPTA which could not have been decided by an administrative agency. The court's preliminary finding was that there was a rational basis for including e-cigarette devices and e-liquid in the definition of tobacco products under the TPTA because the General Assembly was concerned that young people who started using e-cigarettes would become addicted to nicotine and turn to cigarettes. However, the plain language of the TPTA did not support authorizing the PA DOR to tax separately packaged component parts of an e-cigarette that may be considered "integral" to, or an "integral component" of, an e-cigarette. The plain language of 72 P. S. § 8201-A defined "tobacco products" to include "electronic cigarettes." Electronic cigarettes were further defined as an electronic oral device, such as one composed of a heating element and battery or electronic circuit, or both, which provides a vapor of nicotine or any other substance, the use or inhalation of which simulates smoking. The statutory language did not, however, extend the reach of the tax to items that were "integral" pieces of an e-cigarette or to its "component parts."

In light of the decision in *East Coast Vapor, LLC*, in an unreported decision, the Commonwealth Court granted a request for a declaration that integral component parts were not subject to tax under the TPTA. The court noted that it would serve no useful purpose to dismiss the taxpayers' petition and require them to exhaust their administrative remedies when the issue had been decided in *East Coast Vapor*. Consequently, the court issued summary judgment stating that the PA DOR's interpretation of the TPTA to include separately packaged component parts of an e-cigarette as taxable was unsupported by the plain language of the TPTA. *Kingdom Vapor and Smoke 4 Less, LLC v. Pa Dept. of Revenue*, (Pa. Dkt. 697 M.D. 2016, unreported June 22, 2018) (2018 WL 3078891).

Following *East Coast Vapor* and *Kingdom Vapor*, the PA DOR issued guidance on the application of tobacco products tax as it relates to electronic cigarettes and components of electronic cigarettes. Pennsylvania Tobacco Products Tax Bulletin 2018-01, issued July 20, 2018 and amended August 15, 2018. In this Bulletin, the PA DOR advises that electronic cigarettes, any liquid or substance placed in or sold for use in the electronic cigarette (regardless of whether the liquid or substance contains nicotine), and any component not sold separately from the electronic cigarettes, are subject to the tobacco products tax. Components such as, but not limited to, coils, batteries, and reservoirs, are not subject to the tax if sold separately. The PA DOR finds that the tobacco products tax should not be collected on separately packaged components from and after June 22, 2018. See ¶ 3303.

Philadelphia Beverage Tax

On July 18, 2018 the Supreme Court of Pennsylvania upheld the Philadelphia sweetened beverage tax (aka soda tax) in *Williams, et al. v. City of Philadelphia*, 188 A.3d 421 (Pa. 2018). This Philadelphia beverage tax applies broadly to sugar-sweetened beverages and is a tax paid by a registered distributor. The tax is imposed on the distribution of sugar-sweetened beverages on a per ounce basis and legal liability to pay the tax is on the distributor. The Pennsylvania Supreme Court found that the tax was authorized under the Sterling Act and was not duplicative of any other tax as contended by the plaintiffs. The Court ruled that the subject matter of the tax, the non-retail distribution of sugar-sweetened beverages for sale at retail in the city, and the measure of the tax, per ounce of sugar-sweetened beverage, are distinct from the sales tax imposed under the Sterling Act upon the retail sale of the sugar-sweetened beverage to the ultimate purchaser. The Court declined to determine whether duplicative taxation was present through an examination of where the economic incidence of the tax fell. See ¶4014.

Philadelphia Business Income and Receipts Tax and Net Profits Tax

The Philadelphia Department of Revenue announced changes to the treatment of bonus depreciation as applied to Business Income and Receipts Tax (BIRT) and Net Profits Tax (NPT) on July 31, 2018. The Tax Cuts and Jobs Act of 2017 (TCJA) modified federal tax law to allow businesses to immediately deduct the cost of various assets placed in service between September 28, 2017 and December 31, 2022, but the Commonwealth of Pennsylvania decoupled from the federal changes. By law, the City of Philadelphia is required to follow the Commonwealth's treatment of bonus depreciation, so Philadelphia announced that it is also decoupled from changes made by the TCJA. Pennsylvania Act 72 became law in June of 2018 and requires taxpayers to add back any federal bonus depreciation taken. Pennsylvania and Philadelphia taxpayers are permitted to take normal depreciation as determined under IRC § 167. See ¶3907.

Philadelphia Realty Transfer Tax

The rate of Philadelphia Realty Transfer Tax was increased from 3.1% to 3.278% effective July 1, 2018. The rate was set to decrease to 3.178% after 2036. Ordinance of June 20, 2018 (Bill No. 180167). Thus, the combined City and state tax rate is 4.278%.

Effective July 1, 2017, Philadelphia amended the ordinances relating to the imposition of realty transfer tax relative to transfers of interests in real estate companies. The transfer tax applies when there is a transfer of 75% or more of the ownership interests in a real estate company (previously, the threshold was 90%) thereby thwarting the 89% - 11% transactions. For purposes of determining whether there has been a transfer of 75% of more of the ownership interests in a real estate company, all transactions within a six-year period (formerly a three-year period) are be aggregated. If transfer tax arises, there is a presumption that the value of the property will be based on the actual consideration paid for the interests in the real estate company for purposes of computing the tax liability, not the computed value of the real estate owned by the real estate company. The presumption may be rebutted. Finally, the definition of a real estate company was amended to make the gross receipts test and assets test relative to the ownership of the real estate or an interest in the real estate.

The Ordinance of May 17, 2017 (Bill No. 170205) excludes from Philadelphia realty transfer tax a transfer to the Philadelphia Land Bank by gift, dedication or deed in lieu of condemnation or deed of confirmation. This ordinance also excludes from transfer tax a conveyance to a municipality, township, school district, land bank or county of property tax that was acquired as a tax delinquent property at a sheriff's sale or tax claim bureau sale. Another Ordinance of May 17, 2017 (Bill No. 170016) excludes from Philadelphia realty transfer tax transactions involving the transfer of property between a stepparent and stepchild, or the spouse of a stepchild.

Effective April 18, 2018, transfers between the Philadelphia Housing Authority (PHA) and a Pennsylvania limited partnership whose general partner is owned and controlled by PHA are excluded from Philadelphia realty transfer tax. Ordinance of April 18, 2018 (Bill No. 180096). The exclusion includes a transfer from PHA to the Pennsylvania limited partnership and any subsequent transfer from such limited partnership to PHA, and a transfer from PHA or a Pennsylvania limited partnership controlled by PHA to a wholly owned subsidiary of PHA. See ¶4001.

Miscellaneous Taxes

For taxes administered by the PA DOR, the periods for certain petitions to the DOR and the Board of Finance and Revenue (BFR) have been shortened from 90 days to 60 days each. The following appeals must be filed within 60 days after:

- the mailing of the notice of assessment, for a petition for reassessment;
- a notice of adjustment from the DOR, for a petition for review of a tax adjustment not resulting in an increase in liability;
- the mailing of a DOR notice of decision and order, for review of the decision or order by the BFR; and
- the mailing date of a DOR notice of its failure to timely dispose of a petition, for a petition to the BFR of denial by the DOR's failure to act.

The changes are applicable to petitions for refunds, petitions for reassessments, and petitions for redeterminations filed with the DOR on or after December 29, 2017. Act 43 (H.B. 542), Laws 2017, effective October 30, 2017. See ¶4604 and ¶4605.

PART I

TABLES

TAX RATES

¶1 Personal Income Tax

(Resident and Nonresident Individuals and Estates and Trusts)

The tax is levied at a flat rate of 3.07% on specified classes of income.

Personal Exemptions

There are no exemptions or exceptions.

Withholding of Tax

Withholding of tax by employers maintaining an office or transacting business within Pennsylvania is required on compensation paid to resident and nonresident individuals performing services on behalf of such employer within Pennsylvania. There are no withholding exemptions. However, under certain reciprocal agreements, Pennsylvania employers are not required to withhold tax from employees who work in Pennsylvania and are taxed in their home states. Pennsylvania has reciprocal agreements with Ohio, Maryland, West Virginia, Indiana, Virginia, and New Jersey.

¶5 Corporate Net Income Tax

The tax rate is 9.99% on Pennsylvania taxable income. This rate is imposed on the basis of a calendar year or a fiscal year commencing within such year. See ¶905.

¶25 Banks and Other Financial Institutions Tax

Bank and trust companies shares tax: 0.95% upon the book value of total bank equity capital determined by the Reports of Condition at the end of the preceding calendar year. See ¶1906.

Title insurance companies shares tax: 1.25% per dollar of taxable amount of capital stock. See ¶2105.

Mutual thrift institutions tax: 11.5% of taxable net income. See ¶2004.

¶30 Property Taxes

The real property tax rates vary among local jurisdictions (see ¶3506 for maximum allowable rates).

The personal property tax may be imposed by a county at a rate not to exceed four mills (0.004) on each dollar of value.

The realty transfer tax is imposed at a rate of 1% of the value of the real estate transferred. See ¶3304 for more rate information.

¶35 Sales and Use Taxes

The sales, use, and hotel occupancy taxes are imposed by the Commonwealth at the rate of 6%. Consumer fireworks are subject to an additional tax at the rate of 12%. See ¶505 for more Commonwealth rate information. Prior to October 8, 2009 the City of Philadelphia imposed a 1% rate of tax for sales, use and hotel occupancy within the City. Currently, the sales and use tax rate is 2%. Hotel occupancy tax is 1%. See ¶4008 for more Philadelphia rate information. Allegheny County also imposes an additional 1% rate of tax for sales, use, and hotel occupancy within the County (see ¶4504).

New tire fee: Every sale of a new tire for highway use is subject to a $1.00 fee. See ¶726 for more fee information.

Motor vehicle lease tax: An additional 3% tax rate is included on the lease of motor vehicles. See ¶727 for more rate information.

Motor vehicle rental and carsharing fees: A $2.00 fee is added to the rental of motor vehicles for each day or part of day of rental. Carsharing rentals are subject to a fee ranging from 5 cents for less than two hours to $2 for four hours or more. See ¶728 for more fee information.

Vehicle rental tax: A 2% tax is imposed on the purchase price of vehicle rentals (in addition to the $2.00 rental fee). See ¶730 for more rate information.

¶40 Inheritance Tax

The inheritance tax is applied separately to the value of each beneficiary's share of the property transferred (see ¶2904). The rates are fixed and depend on the relationship of the beneficiary to the decedent.

Surviving spouse: There is no tax on inherited spousal assets.

An additional estate tax ("pick-up" estate tax) is imposed in the event a federal estate tax is payable and state death taxes are less than the federal credit. See discussion at ¶2907.

¶45 Miscellaneous Taxes

Gross receipts tax: The gross receipts tax on utilities, except for electric suppliers (light companies, water power companies, and hydroelectric companies) is levied at 50 mills on each dollar of gross receipts (45 mills with a five-mill surtax). The rate on electric suppliers is 44 mills per dollar of gross receipts plus 15 mills revenue neutral reconciliation. See ¶2403 for more rate information.

Public Utility Realty Tax (PURTA) (72 P.S. §§ 8101-A et seq.): The PURTA tax rate is set annually to raise required Realty Tax Equivalent revenue (an amount calculated by the Department of Revenue). See ¶2503 for more rate information.

Gross premiums tax: The gross premiums tax of 2% is imposed on insurance companies doing business in the Commonwealth. See ¶2204 for more rate information.

Cigarette tax: Effective August 1, 2016, the cigarette tax is $.13 per cigarette ($2.60 per pack of twenty cigarettes). The cigarette tax is an excise tax imposed on the sale or possession of cigarettes. See ¶3303 for more rate information.

Malt beverage tax: See ¶3302 for specific rate table information.

¶55 Tax Credits

CREDIT	AUTHORITY	TAXES CREDITED[1]	¶ REFERENCE
Alternative energy production tax credit	H.B. 1, § 703(a)	P, C, CF	1019
Call center credit[2]	72 P.S. § 7206(b)	S	513
City Revitalization and Improvement Zones (CRIZ)	72 P.S. § 8801-C et seq.	C, CF, BT, S, P, MB	1026
Community-based services tax credit	72 P.S. § 8701-I et seq.	P, C, CF, BT, I, M	1024
Credit for Assessments Paid to Pennsylvania Life and Health Insurance Guaranty Association	40 P.S. § 991.1711(a)	I	2213
Credit for Assessments Paid to Pennsylvania Property and Casualty Insurance Guaranty Association	72 P.S. § 7902.1	I	2212
Credit for job creation in a strategic development area	72 P.S. § 9939–C	P, C, CF	1017
Credit for tax liability attributable to business activity in strategic development area	72 P.S. § 9911–C	C	1018
Credit for tax on messages and services paid to other states[3]	72 P.S. § 8101(a.1)	GR	2404
Educational improvement tax credit (EITC)	24 P.S. § 20-2001-B, et seq.	C, CF, BT, T, I, M	1011
Educational opportunity scholarship tax credit	72 P.S. § 8701-G.1, et seq.	P, C, CF, BT, T, I, M, SL	1022
Employment incentive payment credit (EIPC)	72 P.S. § 8702-A et seq.	C, BT, T, M, P	1006
Entertainment production tax credit	72 P.S. § 8701-C et seq.	P, C, CF, BI, I	1012
First class cities economic development district tax credit	53 P.S. § 18200.101 et seq.	C, P, S, U	1020
Historic preservation incentive tax credit	72 P.S. § 8701-H et seq.	P, C, CF, BT, T, I, GR, M	1023
Innovate in PA tax credit	72 P.S. § 8801-F et seq.	I	1027
Job creation tax credit (JCTC)	72 P.S. § 1801-B et seq.	C, CF, I, GR, BT, M, T, P	1007
KIZ credits	12 Pa.C.S. § 3706	P, C, F[4]	4623
KOZ credits	73 P.S. § 820.514 et seq.	P, C, CF, BT, M, I	201, 1013, 1014, 1329, 1908, 2007, 2213
KOZ job creation tax credits	73 P.S. § 820.519	P, C, CF	1014
Malt beverage credit	72 P.S. § 9010	MB	3302
Mobile telecommunications broadband investment tax credit	72 P.S. § 8801-E et seq.	C	1028
Neighborhood assistance credit	72 P.S. § 8901-A et seq.	BT, C, CF, I, M, T	1005
Organ or bone marrow tax credit	Organ and Bone Marrow Donor Act	P, C, CF, BT, T, I, M	1015
Philadelphia credit	53 Pa.C.S. § 8713(b)	P	127
Property purchased outside Pa.	72 P.S. § 7206(a)	S	513
Research & development credit	72 P.S. § 8702-B	P, C, CF	1008
Resident credit	72 P.S. § 7314(a)	P	127
Residential visitability design tax credit	Act No. 132 of 2006 (S.B. 1158), § 4(b)	Property tax	3509A

Resource enhancement and protection tax credit	72 P.S. § 8703–e	P, C, CF, BT, T, I, M	1016
Resource manufacturing tax credit	72 P.S. § 8701-G, *et seq.*	P, C, CF, BT, I	1021
TPPR credit	61 Pa. Code § 58.11	S	513
Use tax credit	72 P.S. § 7206(a)	U	722
Volunteer Responder credit	72 P.S. § 8803-D	P	127
Waste tire recycling equipment grants	35 P.S. § 6115	Reimbursement of cost[5]	1009

[1] BT = bank and trust company shares tax
C = corporate net income tax
CF = capital stock/franchise tax
E = employment tax
I = insurance premiums tax
GR = gross receipts tax
M = mutual thrift institutions tax
MB = malt beverage tax
N = any new tax
P = personal income tax
S = sales tax
SL = surplus lines tax
T = title insurance tax
U = use tax

[2] Available to be used against sales tax on telecommunications services.

[3] Available to telegraph or telephone companies or providers of mobile telecommunications.

[4] Purchasers/assignees of KIZ tax credits can use the credits against P, C, F, BT, T, I, and M.

[5] This, technically, is not a credit. It is a grant can be used to offset qualified costs, not qualified taxes.

PART II

PERSONAL INCOME TAX

CHAPTER 1
TAX RATE, RETURNS, COMPUTATION OF TAX

INTRODUCTION

¶101 History, Sources of Authority, and Administration

The Pennsylvania personal income tax provisions were enacted in 1971 as part of the Tax Reform Code of 1971 (TRC). These provisions are found in the Tax Reform Code of 1971 [Act of March 4, 1971, P.L. 6, No. 2, Part III, as amended by the Act of August 31, 1971, P.L. 372, No. 93, Article III; 72 P.S. §§ 7101 *et seq.*]. Earlier attempts by the Commonwealth to tax income had been unsuccessful because the laws were found to violate the "Uniformity Clause" of the Pennsylvania Constitution that required all Commonwealth and local taxes to be uniform upon the same class of subjects [Pennsylvania Constitution, Article VIII, § 1]. This clause has been interpreted by the Supreme Court of Pennsylvania to prohibit graduated rates, personal exemptions, and deductions. (See, for example, *Kelly v. Kalodner*, 181 A 598 (Pa. 1935).)

In 1971 a new personal income tax was enacted as part of the Act of March 4, 1971. This law was an attempt to "piggyback" on the federal individual income tax by imposing a flat Commonwealth rate on federal taxable income. However, the Pennsylvania Supreme Court held this tax to violate the Uniformity Clause of the Pennsylvania Constitution because the exclusions, deductions, and exemptions reflected in federal taxable income resulted in different effective rates for taxpayers with equal gross incomes [*Amidon v. Kane*, 279 A.2d 53 (Pa. 1971)]. As a result of the *Amidon* decision, a new personal income tax law was enacted to replace the earlier 1971 act, and this law, as amended by later acts, is currently in effect [Act of August 31, 1971, No. 93]. Even though exemptions and deductions are prohibited, tax provisions for special tax relief for low-income taxpayers are possible because of a 1968 Constitutional amendment authorizing the Pennsylvania General Assembly to establish low-income taxpayers as a separate class for taxation purposes [Pennsylvania Constitution, Article VIII, § 2(b)(ii)]. The Tax Reform Code, as amended, remains the statutory authority for the Pennsylvania personal income tax. Certain administrative provisions pertaining to the personal income tax are part of The Fiscal Code. Personal income tax regulations are in Title 61 of the Pennsylvania Code. The personal income tax is administered and collected by the Department of Revenue of the Commonwealth of Pennsylvania, Harrisburg, Pennsylvania.

References to the Internal Revenue Code (IRC)

For personal income tax purposes, any reference to the Internal Revenue Code of 1986 means the internal Revenue Code of 1986, as amended to January 1, 1997, unless the reference contains the phrase "as amended" and refers to no other date, in which case the reference is to the Internal Revenue Code of 1986 as it exists at the time of application [72 P.S. § 7301]. This provision is applicable to taxable years beginning after December 31, 2002 [Act 40 of 2005 (H.B. 176), § 24(2)]. In order to establish the correct reference for Internal Revenue Code sections cited in this *Guidebook*, the wording of the specific Pennsylvania statute containing the citation must be consulted.

• *Revenue information*

According to Department of Revenue regulation [61 Pa. Code § 3.4], informational materials are issued to provide general information that will assist individuals or organizations.

Revenue information material is issued for informational purposes only and should not be relied upon or used in tax appeals. Examples of revenue information are the Pennsylvania Tax Updates, forms, pamphlets, tax bulletins, or information notices provided to taxpayers. Instructions on tax forms and instructional booklets accompanying forms also fall within this category.

- *Obtaining revenue information electronically*

The Pennsylvania Department of Revenue maintains a web site at www.revenue.state.pa.us from which taxpayers can obtain revenue information and forms. The guide is quite detailed and covers many areas of the Pennsylvania personal income tax.

¶102 Outline of Tax—Imposition, Base, and Rate

The Pennsylvania personal income tax is a flat-rate tax imposed on the privilege of receiving eight specified classes of income. Resident individuals, estates, and trusts are taxed on their world-wide income; nonresident individuals, estates, and trusts are subject to tax only on their Pennsylvania-source income. Individuals are natural persons, including members of partnerships and associations. Applicable to taxable years beginning after December 31, 2000, the word "association" is defined as any form of unincorporated enterprise that (1) is subject to the corporate net income tax or (2) is required to make a return under IRC § 6042 (relating to paying and receiving dividends). Partnerships and investment companies are not associations [72 P.S. § 7301(b)]. Prior to the amendment of 72 P.S. § 7301(b), "association" was defined as "any form of unincorporated enterprise other than a partnership." A resident trust is (1) a trust created by the will of an individual who at the time of his or her death was a resident of Pennsylvania or (2) any trust created by, or consisting in whole or in part of property transferred to a trust, a person who at the time of creation or transfer was a resident of Pennsylvania [72 P.S. § 7301(s)]. A nonresident trust is a trust that is not a resident trust [72 P.S. § 7301(n)]. The term *trust* (resident or nonresident) does not include charitable trusts or pension or profit-sharing trusts [72 P.S. § 7301(n), (s)]. See ¶ 105 for discussion of filing requirements for taxpayers.

Comparison to Federal

The Pennsylvania personal income tax does not conform to the federal income tax. No income is taxed at preferential rates for Commonwealth purposes; no personal exemptions or personal-type (as opposed to business) deductions are allowed; progressivity is constitutionally prohibited. Most items that are not recognized for federal income tax purposes must be recognized for Pennsylvania personal income tax purposes. The definitions of income and "deduction" items that have common names in both federal and Commonwealth personal income taxation are often different.

- *Base*

The base (taxable income) for the computation of an individual's Pennsylvania personal income tax liability is the sum of the eight statutorily specified classes of income received or accrued by an individual during a taxable period. Income that does not fall into one of the eight specified classes is exempt. For example, alimony, which is taxable to the recipient for federal income tax purposes, is not taxable for Pennsylvania personal income tax purposes because it does not fall into one of the eight classes of taxable income (discussed in Chapter 2).

Negative Income

A taxpayer cannot use negative income from one class of income to offset positive income of another class. See the example at ¶ 125.

- *No "deductions"*

The Pennsylvania personal income tax laws did not allow deductions before October 30, 2017 when Act 43 of 2017 created an ABLE Savings Account deduction. Certain employee business expenses, however, have been held to be excludable from compensation (see ¶ 203). These are commonly referred to as "deductions for employee business expense," even though they are exclusions. And two classes of income are defined to be net of costs and expenses: (1) net profits from a business, profession, or other activity, and (2) net gains from the sale or other disposition of property [72 P.S. §7303(a)(2), (3)]. These exclusions from gross income to determine net income in these classes are also commonly called deductions. There are also special provisions for forgiveness of part or all of the income tax liability of a taxpayer whose economic circumstances meet the statutory definition of poverty (see ¶129).

Caution: Commonwealth vs. Federal

The Uniformity Clause of the Pennsylvania Constitution bars the adoption of many federal principles. Often new federal income tax changes *do not apply* to the Pennsylvania personal income tax. The elements of the Pennsylvania personal income tax must be determined under the provisions of the laws and regulations of the *Commonwealth.*

• *Rate*

The Pennsylvania personal income tax is levied at the rate of 3.07% of taxable income on both resident and nonresident individuals, estates, and trusts [72 P.S. §7302]. The tax rates for current and prior years are as follows:

Year	Rate
2004 and thereafter	3.07%
1993—2003	2.80%
1992	2.95%
1991	2.60%
Prior to 1991	2.10%

When the rate changes during the year, the rate of tax to be used is the monthly weighted average of the rates applicable during the year.

• *Credits against the tax*

For a discussion of credits allowed against the personal income tax, see ¶127.

• *Reciprocal agreements*

The Pennsylvania Department of Revenue is empowered to enter into reciprocal exemption agreements with other states that impose income taxes. Under these agreements, neither state that is a party to the agreement taxes the income of the other state's residents. To date Pennsylvania has reciprocal agreements with New Jersey, Ohio, West Virginia, Indiana, Maryland, and Virginia. Taxpayers are also allowed credits for estimated tax payment amounts withheld from compensation and the Employment Incentive Payment Credit.

¶103 Definitions

In order to provide a guide to the important personal income tax terms, a glossary is provided in this paragraph for quick reference. Some definitions specific only to certain situations are defined in context when discussing the situation.

Except where the context clearly indicates a different meaning, the following words, terms, and phrases when used in the personal income tax statutes have the following meanings.

• *Accepted accounting principles and practices*

"Accepted accounting principles and practices" means (unless explicitly provided for personal income tax purposes) those accounting principles or practices (including the installment method of reporting) that are acceptable by standards of the accounting profession and are not inconsistent with the regulations of the Department of Revenue [72 P.S. §7301(a)].

¶103

- *Association*

An "association" means any form of unincorporated enterprise that (1) is subject to the Pennsylvania personal income tax or (2) is required to make a return under §6042 of the Internal Revenue Code of 1986. Partnerships and investment companies are not associations [72 P.S. §7301(b)].

- *Business*

A "business" is any enterprise, activity, profession, vocation, trade, joint venture, commerce, or any other undertaking of any nature when engaged in as commercial enterprise and conducted for profit or ordinarily conducted for profit, whether by an individual, partnership Pennsylvania S corporation, association, or other unincorporated entity.

- *Charitable trust*

A "charitable trust" is trust operated exclusively for religious, charitable, scientific, literary, or educational purposes [72 P.S. §7301(c.1)].

- *Claimant*

A "claimant" is a person who is subject to the personal income tax, is not a dependent of another taxpayer for purposes of §151 of the Internal Revenue Code of 1986, but is entitled to a claim under the poverty tax provisions [72 P.S. §7301(c.2)]. The poverty tax provisions are discussed at ¶129.

- *Compensation*

The word "compensation" means salaries, wages, commissions, bonuses, and incentive payments whether based on profits or otherwise, fees, tips, and similar remuneration received for services rendered, whether directly or through an agent, and whether in cash or property [72 P.S. §7301(d)]. Effective for taxable years beginning after December 31, 2004, the term "compensation" includes distributions from plans described in IRC §409A(d)(1) (*i.e.*, nonqualified deferral compensation plans) attributable to an elective deferral of income, regardless of whether the distribution is paid during employment or after retirement. Compensation is discussed in more detail at ¶202.

- *Corporation*

See definition of "small corporation." For purposes of applying the provisions of 72 P.S. §7303(a) with respect to a "reorganization" as defined in that section, the term "corporation" includes (1) a business trust to which Chapter 95 of 15 Pa.C.S. (relating to business trusts) applies, (2) a common-law business trust, or (3) a limited liability company that for federal income tax purposes is taxable as a corporation [72 P.S. §7301(d.1)]. Note, however, that a Pennsylvania partnership cannot be a party to a merger with another corporation, even if it has elected to be taxed as a corporation for federal tax purposes.

- *Department*

"Department" means the Department of Revenue of the Commonwealth of Pennsylvania [72 P.S. §7301(e)].

- *Dependent*

A dependent is a child who is the dependent of a claimant for purposes of §151 of the Internal Revenue Code of 1986 [72 P.S. §7301(e.1)].

- *Dividends*

The word "dividends" includes any distribution in cash or property made by a corporation, association, business trust, or investment company with respect to its stock out of current or accumulated earnings and profits. The term "dividends," however, does not include (1) a distribution of the stock of a corporation made by the corporation originally issuing it to its own stockholders if the distribution is not treated as personal income tax for federal individual income tax purposes or (2) a distribution made by an investment company out of earnings and profits derived from interest that is statutorily free from state and local taxation [72 P.S. § 7301(f)].

• *Employee*

An "employee" is any individual from whose wages an employer is required under the Internal Revenue Code to withhold federal income tax [72 P.S. § 7301(g)].

• *Employer*

An "employer" is individual, partnership, association, corporation, governmental body or unit or agency, or any other entity who or that is required under the Internal Revenue Code to withhold federal income tax from wages paid to an employee [72 P.S. § 7301(h)].

• *Fiduciary*

A "fiduciary" is guardian, trustee, executor, administrator, receiver, conservator, or any person acting in any trust or similar capacity, whether domiciliary or ancillary [72 P.S. § 7301(i)].

• *Health savings account*

"Health savings account" has the meaning given in IRC § 223(d) [72 P.S. § 7301(i.1)].

• *Income*

"Income" for a resident individual, estate, or trust is the same as the eight classes of taxable income enumerated and classified under 72 P.S. § 303 [72 P.S. § 7301(j)]. See Chapter 2.

• *Income from sources within this Commonwealth*

"Income from sources within this Commonwealth" for a resident individual, estate, or trust is the same as the eight classes of income enumerated and classified under 72 P.S. § 303 (discussed in Chapter 2) that are earned, received, or acquired from the following sources within Pennsylvania [72 P.S. § 7301(k)]:

(1) By reason of ownership or disposition of any interest in real or tangible personal property in Pennsylvania.

(2) In connection with a trade, profession, or occupation carried on in Pennsylvania or for the rendition of personal services performed in Pennsylvania.

(3) As a distributive share of the income of an unincorporated business, Pennsylvania S corporation, profession, enterprise, undertaking, or other activity as the result of work done, services rendered, or other business activities conducted in Pennsylvania (except as allocated to another state).

(4) From intangible personal property employed in a trade, profession, occupation, or business carried on in Pennsylvania.

(5) As income from gambling activity in Pennsylvania, except for prizes of the Pennsylvania State Lottery (effective for tax years beginning after December 31, 2003).

Federal Form W-2G Required

Any taxpayer who is required to file a Form W-2G (relating to certain gambling winnings) with the U.S. Treasury Department from sources within Pennsylvania must also file a copy of the form with the Pennsylvania Department of Revenue by March 1 of each year or, if filed electronically, by March 31 of each year [72 P.S. § 7335(e), effective for taxable years beginning after December 31, 2003].

Nonresidents: "Income from sources within this Commonwealth" for a nonresident individual, estate or trust does not include otherwise taxable items of income received from an investment company registered with the Federal Securities and Exchange Commission under the Investment Company Act of 1940 [72 P.S. § 7301(k)].

• *Individual*

An individual is a natural person, including members of a partnership or association and the shareholders of a Pennsylvania S corporation [72 P.S. § 7301(l)].

• *Installment sales method of reporting*

The "installment sales method of reporting" is the method by which a taxpayer reports the gain upon the sale of tangible personal property or real property when at least one payment is to be received in any taxable year following the taxable year of the sale [72 P.S. § 7301(l.1)]. Installment sales are discussed at ¶ 206.

• *Internal Revenue Code*

Unless specifically provided otherwise, any reference to the Internal Revenue Code means the Internal Revenue Code of 1986 (P.L. 99-514, 26 U.S.C. § § 1 "et seq.") as amended to January 1, 1997, unless the reference contains the phrase "as amended" and refers to no other date, in which case the reference is to the Internal Revenue Code of 1986 as it exists as of the time of the application of Article III of the Tax Reform Code [72 P.S. § 7301].

• *Investment company*

An "investment company" is any incorporated or unincorporated enterprise registered with the Federal Securities and Exchange Commission under the Investment Company Act of 1940 [72 P.S. § 7301(l.2)].

• *Nonresident estate or trust*

A "nonresident estate or trust" is any estate or trust that is not a resident estate or trust. However, the term "nonresident estate or trust" does not include charitable trusts, pension plans, or profit-sharing trusts [72 P.S. § 7301(n)].

• *Nonresident individual*

A nonresident individual is any individual who is not a resident of Pennsylvania [72 P.S. § 7301(m)].

• *Partnership*

The word "partnership" means a domestic or foreign general partnership joint venture, limited partnership, limited liability company, business trust, or other unincorporated entity that is classified as a partnership for federal income tax purposes [72 P.S. § 7301(n.0)].

• *Pennsylvania S corporation*

A "Pennsylvania S corporation" is any "small corporation" (see below) that does not have a valid election under 72 P.S. § 7307 in effect. A qualified Subchapter S subsidiary owned by a Pennsylvania S corporation is treated as a Pennsylvania S corporation without regard to whether an election under 72 P.S. § 7307 has been made with respect to the subsidiary [72 P.S. § 7301(n.1)]. See discussion in ¶ 1802 and ¶ 1803.

• *Person*

The word "person" means any individual, employer, association, fiduciary, partnership, corporation, or other entity, estate or trust (resident or nonresident) and the plural as well as the singular number [72 P.S. § 7301(o)]. For the purpose of determining eligibility for special tax provisions (discussed at ¶ 129), the term "person" means a natural individual.

• *Poverty*

"Poverty" is an economic condition wherein the total amount of poverty income is insufficient to adequately provide the claimant, the claimant's spouse, and the claimant's dependent children with the necessities of life [72 P.S. § 7301(o.1)].

• *Poverty income*

See ¶ 129.

• *Qualified Subchapter S subsidiary*

A qualified subchapter S subsidiary is a corporation (domestic or foreign) that for federal income tax purposes is treated as a qualified Subchapter S subsidiary as defined in IRC § 1361(b)(3)(b), as amended to January 1, 2005 [72 P.S. § 7301(o.3)].

• *Resident individual*

A "resident individual" is an individual (1) who is domiciled in Pennsylvania unless she or he maintains no permanent place of abode in Pennsylvania and does maintain a permanent place of abode elsewhere and spends in the aggregate less than 31 days of the taxable year in Pennsylvania or (2) who is not domiciled in Pennsylvania but maintains a permanent place of abode in Pennsylvania and spend in the aggregate more than 183 days of the taxable year in Pennsylvania [72 P.S. § 7301(p)]. On May 24, 2013, the Pennsylvania Commonwealth Court decided the McNeil case *Robert L. McNeil Jr. Trust v. Commonwealth*, 67 A3d 18 (May 24, 2013). In this case, the taxpayer challenged Pennsylvania filing rules concerning resident trusts. The trust was formed by the grantor when he was a Pennsylvania resident. All of the trust's activities took place outside Pennsylvania. In spite this Pennsylvania law required that the trust file as a resident trust. The taxpayer, citing Complete Auto Transit (*Complete Auto Transit Inc. v. Brady*, 430 US 274 (1977)) stated that the normal 3 factor apportionment formula should control the extent of the taxpayer's activity that is to be reported in Pennsylvania. The trust proved that it did not have sufficient physical presence in Pennsylvania, to have substantial nexus there. The trust's only contact with Pennsylvania was the residence of the grantor where the trust was created, and the Pennsylvania residence of certain beneficiaries. The court held that these contacts were not sufficient to show that the trust has substantial nexus. This is the first test set out in the Complete Auto case. If the tax fails this test, it may not be imposed. The Commonwealth has not appealed this case to the Pennsylvania Supreme Court. The holding in this case could provide taxpayer's with an opportunity to claim refunds for past years and modify reporting strategies for future years.

• *Received*

For the purpose of computing taxable income "received" means "received, earned, or acquired" and should be construed according to the method of accounting required by the Department of Revenue for computing and reporting income subject to the Pennsylvania personal income tax.

• *Resident estate*

A "resident estate" is the estate of a decedent who at the time of his or her death was a resident individual [72 P.S. § 7301(r)].

• *Resident trust*

A "resident trust" is (1) a trust created by the will of a decedent who at the time of his or her death was a resident individual and (2) any trust created by, or consisting in whole or in part of property transferred to a trust by a person who at the time of the trusts' creation or transfer was a resident [72 P.S. §7301(s)]. The term "resident trust," however, does not include charitable trusts, pension trusts, or profit-sharing trusts.

• *Small corporation*

The term "small corporation" means any corporation that has a valid election in effect under Subchapter S of Chapter 1 of the Internal Revenue Code of 1986, as amended to January 1, 2005 [72 P.S. §7301(s.2)]. The term "corporation" for this purpose includes a business trust to which Chapter 95 of 15 Pa.C.S. (relating to business trusts) applies and that for federal income tax purposes is taxable as a corporation.

• *Special tax provisions*

The term "special tax provisions" means a refund or forgiveness of all or part of a claimant's liability for the Pennsylvania personal income tax. See ¶129 [72 P.S. §7301(s.1)].

• *State*

The word "state" means any state or Commonwealth of the United States, the District of Columbia, the Commonwealth of Puerto Rico, any territory or possession of the United States, and any foreign county [72 P.S. §7301(t)].

• *Tax*

The word "tax" includes interest, penalties, and additions to tax, as well as the tax required to be withheld by an employer on compensation (unless a more limited meaning is disclosed by the context) [72 P.S. §7301(u)].

• *Taxable year*

The term "taxable year" means the taxable period on the basis of which a taxpayer or claimant is required to file his or her federal income tax return [72 P.S. §7301(v)]. If a person is not required to or does not file a federal income tax return, the person's "taxable year" is the calendar year.

• *Taxpayer*

A "taxpayer" is any individual, estate, or trust subject to the Pennsylvania personal income tax, any partnership having a partner who is a "taxpayer," any Pennsylvania S corporation having a shareholder who is a "taxpayer," and any employer required to withhold tax on compensation paid [72 P.S. §7301(w)].

RETURNS AND PAYMENT OF TAX

¶105 Who Must File Returns

The following is a discussion of personal income tax liability as it applies to individuals, estates and trusts, partners and partnerships, and military personnel.

• *Individuals*

An individual whose tax liability is less than $1.00 does not have to file a Pennsylvania personal income tax return [61 Pa. Code §121.1(f)]. Thus, the minimum amount of income required for filing at the current rate of 3.07% is $33.

• *Deceased individuals*

A return of a decedent with total Pennsylvania gross taxable income in excess of the minimum for the taxable year must be filed by his or her executor, administrator, or other personal representative charged with caring for his or her property, even if no tax is due with the return [72 P.S. §7331(e)]. The return of the decedent covers the period beginning with the taxable year in which his or her death occurred and ends with the date of decedent's death.

• *Surviving spouses*

During the year in which a spouse dies, a surviving spouse may file his or her return for the year jointly with the final return of his or her deceased spouse if the joint return could have been filed if both spouses were living for the entire taxable year. If a personal representative, executor, or administrator, or other fiduciary is appointed on behalf of the deceased spouse before the deceased spouse's tax return is filed, the surviving spouse may not file a joint return without the consent of the fiduciary. If a joint return is filed, both the fiduciary of the deceased spouse's estate and the surviving spouse must sign the joint return [72 P.S. § 7331(e.1)(2)].

A surviving spouse may file the final tax return of his or her deceased spouse if the decease spouse did not previously file a return for that taxable year and if a personal representative, executor, or administrator has not been appointed by the time the return is filed. If the surviving spouse files a final return for the deceased spouse under this condition, a fiduciary who is later appointed for the deceased spouse may supersede the final return filed by the surviving spouse by filing a separate return for the deceased spouse. Any joint return improperly filed by the surviving spouse or superseded by the fiduciary will be treated as void, in which case the surviving spouse is required to file a separate return within 90 days of the filing of the fiduciary's return [72 P.S. § 7331(e.1)(2)].

• *Minors or other individuals unable to file*

Returns for minors or other taxpayers unable to file because of disability who have total Pennsylvania gross taxable income in excess of the minimum must be filed by the appropriate person (e.g., guardian, committee, fiduciary) [61 Pa. Code § 117.6]. Illness or absence from the Commonwealth does not relieve an individual of the obligation to file. In such cases a taxpayer may grant power of attorney to an agent who can file his or her return [61 Pa. Code § 117.6].

Reminder: Children Must File

Pennsylvania law does not provide any exemption from filing for minor children or any other persons who are required to file a return. Children who have total Pennsylvania gross taxable income in excess of the minimum must file a Pennsylvania return without regard to any federal provisions that may excuse them from filing a federal income tax return. Persons who are responsible for the care of minor children must file personal income tax returns for them.

• *Estates and trusts*

Resident and nonresident estates and trusts receiving taxable income must file returns regardless of the amount of the income received by the trust. The fiduciary must file the return of an estate or trust. The income of an estate or trust consists of the income or gains received by it that has not been distributed or credited to its beneficiaries [72 P.S. § 7305]. If there is more than one fiduciary, any one of the appropriate fiduciaries may file the return [61 Pa. Code § 117.5(a)].

Caution: Commonwealth Does Not Follow Federal Grantor Trust Rules

Pennsylvania does not follow Federal rules for grantor trusts, but instead requires income to be reported by the grantor trust.

¶105

• *Partners and partnerships*

Effective January 1, 2014, authorizes actions by the department to improve tax compliance and administrative efficiency for pass-through entities such as partnerships, limited liability companies and S corporations. Provisions include:

- Authorizes assessment at the entity level for understatements of income in excess of $1 million by partnerships with eleven or more partners, or having at least one partner that is a corporation, limited liability company, partnership, S corporation or trust, or that elects to be subject to this provision. A similar provision applies to S corporations. These provisions do not apply to publicly traded partnerships.

- Requires partnerships to maintain accurate lists of partners and addresses.

- Requires estates and trusts to withhold Pennsylvania tax on PA-source income from nonresidents.

- Requires nonresident estates and trusts to file Pennsylvania returns if they have Pennsylvania beneficiaries or PA-source income.

- Clarifies that filing of PA-20S/PA-65 returns (pass-through information returns) and RK-1s and NRK-1s is mandatory.

A partnership is a domestic or foreign general partnership, joint venture, limited partnership, limited liability company, business trust, or other unincorporated entity that for federal income tax purposes is classified as a partnership [72 P.S. § 7301(n.0)]. A partnership *as an entity* is not subject to the Pennsylvania personal income tax; members of partnerships are taxable on their shares of partnership income, whether or not distributed, for its taxable year ending within or with the members' taxable years [72 P.S. § 7306]. Partnerships, however, are required to file returns for the partnership taxable year. (See ¶ 107.) Filing is required for partnerships engaged in a trade or business within Pennsylvania or having Pennsylvania-source income, whether or not its principal place of business is in Pennsylvania and whether or not all of its members are nonresidents. The return must be made for the taxable year of the partnership, irrespective of the taxable years of the partners [61 Pa. Code § 117.17(a)]. If a Commonwealth resident is a partner in a partnership with no Pennsylvania-source income, he or she must file a return, which must state specifically the items of partnership gross income and allowable deductions, the names and addresses of all resident partners, and the amount of the distributive shares of income, gain, loss, deduction, or credit allocable to each resident partner [61 Pa. Code § 117.17(c)].

Comment: Commonwealth vs. Federal

It is possible for the taxable income of a partnership, estate, or trust to be different for Pennsylvania personal income tax purposes than for federal income tax purposes because Pennsylvania does not have an all-encompassing concept of income like that found in IRC § 61. (For an explanation of classes of income, see Chapter 2.) For example, for Pennsylvania personal income tax purposes, sole proprietorships, partnerships, and Pennsylvania S corporations can claim charitable contributions as a business expense in the determination of net business income if the contributions are made publicly and from the entity's checking account. Under these circumstances, charitable contributions are considered an expense of the business entity rather than an itemized deduction of the shareholders. Taxation of pass-through entities is discussed in Chapter 18.

• *Unincorporated entities with single owners*

Unless an unincorporated entity with a single owner is subject to the corporate net income tax, it is disregarded as an entity separate from its owner [72 P.S. § 7307.21].

• *Military personnel*

Whether or not military pay is included in compensation depends on two factors: (1) residency status and (2) place of assignment. In general, the military pay of all Pennsylvania residents is taxable, and the military pay of nonresidents stationed in Pennsylvania is not taxable. However, income items other than military pay are taxed in the same manner as for nonmilitary personnel; and spouses and household members who are not themselves members of the armed forces are treated as any other nonmilitary individuals [61 Pa. Code § 121.12]. A Pennsylvania resident who becomes a member of the armed forces must file a Pennsylvania Form PA-40 and pay the tax due in the same manner as any other resident individual unless he or she satisfies all three of the following conditions [61 Pa. Code § 121.12(a)]:

(1) He or she had no permanent place of abode in Pennsylvania during the taxable year.

(2) He or she maintained a permanent place of abode outside Pennsylvania during the entire taxable year.

(3) He or she did not spend more than 30 days in Pennsylvania during the taxable year.

A serviceman who lives on a military installation or in assigned or rented government quarters is not considered to be maintaining a permanent place of abode. However, it will generally be recognized that a serviceman does maintain a permanent place of abode if he leases, rents, or buys a dwelling place near his station of duty and occupies it with his family if his duty assignment is of an indefinite nature [61 Pa. Code § 121.12(b)].

• *Refund claimant*

Individuals who have prepaid more tax in the form of withholding or estimated taxes than the amount of tax due are entitled to a refund. Refund petitions must be made to the Department of Revenue. See ¶ 4604 for rules governing refunds and reassessments.

¶106 Filing Status

The concept of filing status does not have the same importance in the Pennsylvania personal income tax system as in the federal income tax system because there are no exemptions, itemized deductions, standard deductions, or progressive rates in the Pennsylvania personal income tax. Thus, the filing status confers no tax benefits in the form of reduced tax. However, the concept of filing status is not meaningless. For example (1) an individual's withholding and estimated tax payments can be applied to his or her spouse's liability; (2) an individual's eligibility for the exclusion of gain on the sale or exchange of a principal residence can depend on the spouse's age; and (3) spouses are treated as one shareholder for purposes of determining the number of shareholders in a Pennsylvania S corporation.

Common-Law Marriages

It is important for tax practitioners to ascertain the correct marital status of individuals seeking to file joint returns. Pennsylvania law is silent with respect to common-law marriages (*i.e.*, they are neither specifically permitted nor specifically prohibited). In a recent decision, the Commonwealth Court overruled the concept of common-law marriage [*PNC Bank Corporation v. WCAB (Stamos)*, No. 860 C.D. 2002 (Pa.Commw. 2003)]. Prior to the *PNC Bank* decision, common-law marriages were recognized by Pennsylvania courts under certain circumstances. See, *e.g., Dowd v. Dowd*, 418 A.2d 138 (1980); *Van Brakel v. Lanuze*, 438 A.2d 992 (1981); *Desanto v. Barnsley*, 476 A.2d 952 (1984). In the *PNC Bank* decision the Commonwealth Court stated that it will, henceforth, recognize as valid only those Pennsylvania marriages entered into pursuant to the Marriage Law procedures. Those recognized as valid prior to the *PNC Bank* decision will still be recognized.

¶107 Return Forms—Individuals

- *Use of federal schedules*

Pennsylvania laws do not always follow federal rules. If either federal law or Pennsylvania law requires an adjustment or election that the other does not permit, taxpayers must provide a PA schedule. Read the line instructions carefully to determine whether or not a federal schedule may be used.

Federal Form 1099-MISC

The following must file a copy of Federal Form 1099-MISC to the Department and send a copy of Form 1099-MISC to the payee by the Federal filing deadline each year [72 P.S. § 335(f)]:

(1) Any person who makes payments of income from sources within Pennsylvania.

(2) Any person who makes payments of Pennsylvania-source nonemployee compensation or payments under an oil and gas lease to a resident or nonresident individual, an entity treated as a partnership for tax purposes, or a single-member limited liability company (effective July 2, 2012 and applicable to 1099-MISC forms issued for the 2012 tax year). If payor is required to file electronically for Pennsylvania employer withholding purposes, the Form 1099-MISC must be filed electronically.

(3) Any person who is required to make a Form 1099-MISC to the United States Secretary of the Treasury with respect to the payments.

If the payer is required to perform electronic filing for Pennsylvania employer withholding purposes, the Form 1099-MISC must be filed electronically with the Department of Revenue.

- *School Code and School District Name*

On their Pennsylvania personal income tax returns, taxpayers must enter the five-digit code and name of the school district where they lived on December 31 of the taxable year, not the school district where they work or live if they moved after December 31. The Department provides this information to the Department of Education, and using an incorrect school district code may affect the funding of a taxpayer's school district. Nonresidents as of December 31 should enter 99999 as the school code.

- *Amended returns*

Pennsylvania does not have a special form for filing an amended return. An individual filing an amended return must use a new Form PA-40 for the year being amended (*e.g.*, use a 1999 Form A-40 to amend a 1999 return) and clearly mark the new return "Amended Return" [61 Pa. Code § 121.25(a)]. This is done by completely filling in the oval for an Amended Return at the top of the form or, if there is no oval, writing "Amended Return" at the top of a PA-40 for the tax year being amended. A paper amended return must be filed, even if the original return was filed using PA/ IRS e-file, TeleFile, or Pa.direct.file. The time limit for filing amended returns is three years from the due date of the original return [61 Pa. Code § 121.25(b)]. Caution on amended return does not toll the running of the statute of limitations only petitions filed with the Board of Appeals accomplish the tolling of the statute of limitations.

The Pennsylvania Supreme Court recently decided the Mission Funding Alpha case (*Mission Funding Alpha* 2 MAP 2016 5-22-2017). The court reversed a Commonwealth Court decision. That decision had held that the three year time period for filing a refund claim relating to a tax return with the Board of Appeals began when the return was actually filed. This was true even though some of the monies involved were paid more than three years from the time that the refund claim was filed. These monies would include estimated payments and amounts paid with extension requests. The Supreme court held that refund claims involving estimated payments and amounts paid with extension must be filed within three years of the original due date of the return.

This ruling is contrary to the federal rules and the rules in many states. An amended return can be filed three years from the extended due date of the return. Although the Department of Revenue may process this return. If it involves refund claims it is beyond the statute of limitations and is not a timely refund claim. If the Department of Revenue refuses to process the return, no further appeal is available.

The only exception to these rules is for corporate net income tax returns. A denial of a refund claim made via an amended return can be appealed to the Board of Appeals.

• *Electronic filing*

Pennsylvania offers three alternative electronic or telephone methods for filing an individual income tax return:

(1) *Pa.direct.file:* Taxpayers can file returns over the Internet free at the Pennsylvania Department of Revenue web site. Pa.direct.file gives taxpayers 24-hour, 7-day-a-week access to file their Pennsylvania personal income tax returns. Pa.direct.file performs all calculations on schedules and returns and also offers direct deposit of refunds and an electronic method to pay any taxes due electronic transfer using the ACH Debit Method (see ¶4617). To use Pa.direct.file, taxpayers use 5-digit account numbers assigned by the Department of Revenue.

(2) *E-file (electronic file):* Both federal and state returns can be filed through an approved tax preparer or from home PCs using approved software. Taxpayers can use e-file to file their Pennsylvania personal income tax returns even if they have had their federal returns rejected or they do not need to file federal returns [*Pennsylvania Tax Update No. 101*, Pennsylvania Department of Revenue, September/October 2002].

Effective for tax years beginning on or after January 1, 2013, the department will no longer support the CD rom option of submitting the PA Schedules RK-1 and NRK-1. Entities with 100 or more PA Schedules RK-1 and NRK-1 are required to file their PA Form PA-20S/PA-65 electronically through the Modernized e-Filing platform rather than by CD rom. (Personal Income Tax Information Notice 2013-02, issued May 20, 2013).

(3) *TeleFile:* Taxpayers can file returns using a touch-tone telephone. TeleFile is free. Taxpayers who use TeleFile need the information from the insert in the Fast File booklet that contains Form PA-V and a label [*Pennsylvania Tax Update No. 102*, Pennsylvania Department of Revenue, November/December 2002].

Third-Party Preparer E-File Mandate

A third-party preparer who prepares 50 or more Pennsylvania personal income tax (PIT) returns is now required to electronically file (e-file). See discussion below.

• *Third-party preparers required to e-file*

Requirement to e-file: For all calendar years following a calendar year in which a third-party preparer prepares 50 or more Pennsylvania personal income tax (PIT) returns, the third-party preparer is required to electronically file (e-file) all personal income tax returns in the manner prescribed by the Department. Once a third-party preparer is subject to this filing mandate, the third-party preparer continues to be subject to the mandate regardless of how many PIT tax returns he or she prepares during a calendar year. A third-party preparer who is subject to this filing mandate must have tax software that is compatible with Department e-filing requirements [Pennsylvania Department of Revenue, Notice, 41 Pa.B. 4726, August 27, 2011]. This requirement applies to all tax years beginning on or after January 1, 2012.

Third-party preparer defined: For this purpose, a third-party preparer is any natural person, fiduciary, corporation or other entity who or that prepares for remuneration, or who employs one or more persons to prepare for remuneration, any return for a tax administered by the Department or is assigned a Preparer Tax Identification Number (PTIN) by the Internal Revenue Service. None of the following, however, are considered third-party preparers for remuneration: (1) tax return preparers who voluntarily prepare the returns of others for no pecuniary benefit; (2) persons who merely provide mechanical assistance such as typing; (3) regular employees of an employer who prepare returns for other regular employees of the employer or the employer's officers and regular employees; or (4) fiduciaries who prepare returns for the trusts or estates that they serve.

Penalty: A third-party preparer who fails to file a PIT return by e-file is subject to a penalty of 1% of the tax due on the improperly filed return up to a maximum of $500, but not less than $10.

Penalty waiver: The Department of Revenue will waive the penalty applicable to a return that is not e-filed in the following situations:

(1) The taxpayer has specifically directed the third-party preparer to file the return pursuant to a different filing method than e-file. The taxpayer's directive must be indicated on the return.

(2) The preparer's tax software does not support e-filing of a required attachment to the return.

(3) The Department of Revenue, at its discretion, may waive the penalties applicable to returns not e-file if the Department of Revenue determines the mandate to e-file constitutes undue hardship of the third-party preparer. The third-party preparer must submit a written request for the waiver (clearly explaining why e-filing causes an undue hardship) for every calendar year. A request for a waiver must be mailed to the Department of Revenue, Bureau of Individual Taxes, Director's Office, DEPT 280605, Harrisburg, Pennsylvania 17128-0605.

• *Estates and trusts*

Fiduciary returns are filed on Form PA-41. To file an amended return, a fiduciary files a new Form PA-41 clearly marked "AMENDED RETURN." Use a PA-41 from the same tax year that is being amended. For example, to amend for 2001, use a new 2001 PA-41. It is not necessary to attach a complete copy of the original PA-41 to the amended return.

• *Partners and partnerships*

The partnership return Form PA-65 has been replaced by Form PA-20S/PA-65, which is used by both partnerships and corporations. It must be filed by (1) partnerships located in Pennsylvania, (2) partnerships that derive income from sources within Pennsylvania, and (3) partnerships that have partners who are Pennsylvania residents. See ¶ 1816.

• *New form reporting intangible drilling cost deduction*

The Department of Revenue has adopted a new form—Schedule I to be used by partnerships and S corporations to report their intangible drilling cost deductions. The form is to be used for tax year commencing in the 2014 calendar year.

• *S corporations*

Pennsylvania S corporations are not subject to the corporate net income tax or the personal income tax. Instead, shareholders in a Pennsylvania S corporation must include their distributive shares of Pennsylvania S corporation income as if it were directly realized by them [72 P.S. §7307.8]. Pennsylvania S corporations must file an information return, Form PA-20S/PA-65, which replaces both the old PA-20S and the old PA-65. See ¶1809 for discussion of Pennsylvania S corporation returns.

• *Check-offs for personal income tax refunds*

Taxpayers who receive personal income tax refunds can make voluntary contributions to various causes by checking spaces provided on the face of their personal income tax returns (called check-offs). Any amounts designated as a check-off are deducted from the tax refund to which an individual is entitled and do not constitute additional tax due to the Commonwealth. The Pennsylvania personal income tax statutes provide for the following check-offs:

Check-Off Item[1]	Authority	Scheduled To Expire
Breast and cervical cancer research in the Department of Health.	72 P.S. §7315.2(a)	No expiration
Wild Resource Conservation Fund	72 P.S. §7315.3(a)	Jan. 1, 2014
Governor Robert P. Casey Memorial Organ and Tissue Donation Awareness Trust Fund	72 P.S. §7315.4(a)	Jan. 1, 2014
Korea/Vietnam Memorial National Education Center.	72 P.S. §7315.6(a)	Dec. 31, 2005
Juvenile diabetes cure research	72 P.S. §7315.7(a)	No expiration
Fund for military family relief assistance	72 P.S. §7315.8(a)	Jan. 1, 2014

[1] The check-off for contributions to the U.S. Olympics Committee has been eliminated for taxable years beginning after Dec. 31, 2004.

¶108 Due Dates and Payment of Tax

• *Due date*

Pennsylvania personal income taxpayers and partnerships are required to file return on or before the date when the taxpayers' federal income tax returns are due or would be due if federal filing were required [72 P.S. §7330(a)]. The Commonwealth follows the federal practice of extending the due date to the next business day if the statutory due date falls on a Saturday, Sunday, or holiday. A return is considered timely filed if it is postmarked by the United States Postal Service on or before the due date.

Presentation of a receipt indicating that the report or payment was mailed by registered or certified mail on or before the due date is evidence of timely filing and payment [72 P.S. §7336]. Any other postmark (*e.g.*, one from a private postage meter) is not controlling upon the Department of Revenue [61 Pa. Code §119.28].

• *Payment*

Payment of the tax due (except for combat participants) must be made by the statutory filing date to avoid penalties and interest. However, if the amount due is less than $1.00, no payment is required [61 Pa. Code §121.20]. Even if a taxpayer receives an extension of time to file a return, taxpayers must pay, on or before the original due date, the amount reasonably estimated as tax due to the Commonwealth [61 Pa. Code §121.18(c)].

Payment by Credit Card

Taxpayers can use their credit cards to pay their taxes due [*Pennsylvania Tax Update No. 97,* Pennsylvania Department of Revenue, January/February 2002] by phone or over the Internet by using the following credit card service provider:

Official Payments Corp.

Phone: 1-800-2PAYTAX (1-800-272-9829)

Internet: www.officialpayments.com

Mastercard, American Express, Discover/Novus, and Visa credit cards are accepted. Official Payments Corp. charges a 2.5% convenience fee ($1.00 minimum). The convenience fee and the tax payment will appear as two separate charges on a credit card statement. Payment made by credit card will be effective on the date charged. Payments are not approved until taxpayers are given a confirmation number, which must be retained as proof of payment. Transactions can be confirmed by calling the Official Payments Corp. customer service number: 1-866-621-4109. Note that authorized payments cannot be cancelled.

• *Treasury offset program for collection of delinquent state taxes*

The Internal Revenue Service Restructuring and Reform Act of 1998 permits the federal Treasury Department to offset state tax liabilities against federal income tax refunds. The Internal Revenue Service will intercept federal income tax refunds for delinquent Pennsylvania income tax liabilities. The Department of Revenue will notify delinquent taxpayers about its intention to intercept their federal refund and allow them 60 days to pay their liabilities [PA-40 Instructions].

• *State tax refund offset program for collection of delinquent child and spouse support*

Federal law requires Pennsylvania to establish an income tax refund offset program for delinquent child and spouse support. The Department of Revenue, in cooperation with the Dept of Public Welfare (DPW), intercepts Pennsylvania personal income tax refunds of taxpayers who are delinquent in child support The intercepted funds are transferred to the Pennsylvania Child Support Enforcement System (PACSES).

NOTE: A married person who is liable for child and spouse support must file a separate Pennsylvania personal income tax return even if his/her spouse has no Pennsylvania taxable income.

• *Amnesty Program*

Pennsylvania has adopted an amnesty program. The program will abate $1/2$ the interest and all penalties on qualifying returns that are timely filed under the amnesty program. Returns must be filed between April 21, 2017 and June 19, 2017. Detailed information is available on the Department's website.

¶109 Extensions of Time

The Department of Revenue can grant an extension of time for the filing of any income tax document required by law, but the extension cannot exceed six months (except for a taxpayer who is out of the country) [72 P.S. § 7334]. A taxpayer who is granted an extension of time for filing his or her federal income tax return will automatically be granted an extension for filing his or her Pennsylvania personal income tax return equivalent to the extension period granted by the Internal Revenue Service. A copy of the letter or form granting the federal extension must accompany the taxpayer's Form PA-40 [61 Pa. Code § 121.18(a)].

No Extension for Payment

Payment in full of the tax reasonably expected to be due must accompany a taxpayer's return. There will be no underpayment penalty if at least 90% of the tax actually due is paid by the original due date and the remaining balance is paid with a timely filed return. Interest on any amount not paid by the original due date, however, will carry interest from the original due date.

• *State extension*

Taxpayers who receive no federal extension must apply for a Pennsylvania extension [61 Pa. Code § 121.18(b)]. This extension cannot exceed a period of six months except for a taxpayer who is outside the United States. Use Form REV-276 to apply for an extension of time to file your Pennsylvania personal income tax return. If you owe money, it is a good idea to file Form REV-276, even if such filing is not required, to ensure proper crediting of the remittance of tax to your account.

• *Extensions for members of armed forces serving in combat zones*

Members of the armed forces serving in an area designated by the President of the United States as a "combat zone," as defined in IRC § 7508, are entitled to an extension of time for filing or paying income tax [72 P.S. § 7330(b)(1)]. The definition of "combat zone" was amended by § 9 of Act 46 of 2003 (H.B. 200) to conform to IRC § 7508, retroactive for taxable years beginning after December 31, 2001. Thus, after 2001, members of the armed forces serving in qualified hazardous duty areas that are deemed combat zones will have additional time to file and pay any Pennsylvania personal income tax. The qualified hazardous duty areas include the former Republic of Yugoslavia (*i.e.*, Bosnia, Herzegovina, Croatia, & Macedonia).

Service in Combat Zones

Members of the U.S. Armed Forces serving in qualified Hazardous Duty Areas that are deemed Combat Zones have the same additional time to file and pay Pennsylvania personal income tax and take other actions with respect to the personal income tax that they have for federal purposes [*Pennsylvania Personal Income Tax Guide*, Pennsylvania Department of Revenue, Chapter 5, p. 2].

The period of service in a combat zone, plus the period of qualified continuous hospitalization attributable to injuries sustained in such service, plus 180 days shall be disregarded in determining the time for filing and paying tax [72 P.S. § 7330(b)(1)]. The filing and payment activities covered by 72 P.S. § 7330(b)(1) include filing of returns, payment of tax, interest, penalties, additions, determination of and filing for refunds, filing for redetermination of tax liability, determination of and claims for credits, assessment of tax, giving notice by the Department of Revenue, and bringing suit by the Commonwealth. These provisions apply to the spouse of any qualified individual for any taxable year beginning with one year after the date of termination of combatant activities in a combat zone [72 P.S. § 7330(b)(2)]. If a qualified individual is killed while serving in a combat zone, the tax liability of the decedent for both the year of death and the immediate prior year is waived [72 P.S. § 7330(b)(4)]. These provisions also apply to individuals in a civilian capacity serving outside Pennsylvania in support of combat forces [72 P.S. § 7330(b)(1)].

¶110 Accounting Periods and Methods

A taxpayer's Pennsylvania taxable year is the same as his or her federal taxable year. If the taxpayer is not required to or does not file a federal return, his or her taxable year is the calendar year [72 P.S. § 7301(v)]. The State Treasurer and the Secretary of Revenue jointly prescribe by regulation the method of payment of obligations due the Commonwealth [72 P.S. § 9].

- *Accounting methods*

In general, income must be computed under the method of accounting on the basis of which the taxpayer regularly computes income in keep books. If the Department determines that no method has been regularly used or the method used does not clearly reflect income, the computation of income must be made under a method which, in the opinion of the Department, clearly reflects income [72 P.S. § 7303(a.1)].

- *Depreciation methods*

In computing income, a depreciation deduction is allowed for the exhaustion, wear and tear, and obsolescence of property (1) employed in the operation of a business or (2) held for the production of income. The deduction must be reasonable and computed in accordance with the property's adjusted basis at the time placed in service, reasonably estimated useful life, and net salvage value at the end of its reasonably estimated useful economic life under the straight-line method or other method prescribed by the Department [72 P.S. § 7303(a.2)].

Exception: A taxpayer may use any depreciation method, recovery method, or convention that is also used by the taxpayer in determining federal net taxable income if, when placed in service, the property has the same adjusted basis for federal income tax purposes and the method or convention is allowable for federal income tax purposes at the time of the earlier of (1) the time the property is placed in service or (2) under the Internal Revenue Code of 1986, as amended to January 1, 1997.

Bonus Depreciation Decoupling

By requiring Pennsylvania personal income taxpayers to compute depreciation deductions as they would have under the Internal Revenue Code of 1986 as amended to January 1, 1997, Pennsylvania has decoupled from the provision of the federal Job Creation and Worker Assistance Act of 2002 (P.L. 107-146) that authorizes taxpayers to deduct a 30% bonus depreciation under IRC § 168(k) for certain eligible assets acquired after September 10, 2001, and before September 11, 2004 and the Tax Cuts and Jobs Act of 2017 depreciating provisions.

Taxpayers who take this bonus depreciation for federal tax purposes must (1) reduce the depreciation expense on federal Schedule C or federal Schedule F (or use the PA Schedule C-F Reconciliation); or (2) reduce the depreciation expense on the Pennsylvania Schedule M that is provided with the PA-20S/Pennsylvania Information Return.

No recovery of disallowed federal bonus depreciation is permitted in the form of carryovers or add-backs in future years.

Taxpayers who took this bonus depreciation on their 2001 Pennsylvania personal income tax returns must file amended returns.

Basis adjustment: The basis of property must be reduced (but not below zero) for depreciation by the greater of the following:

(1) The amount deducted on a return and not disallowed, but only to the extent the deduction results in a reduction of income.

(2) The amount allowable using the straight-line method of depreciation computed on the basis of the property's adjusted basis at the time placed in service, reasonably estimated useful life, and net salvage value at the end of its reasonably estimated useful economic life, regardless of whether the deduction results in a reduction of income.

NOTE: Determination of the original basis of an asset is discussed at ¶ 206.

¶110

• *Sec. 179 property*

The cost of property commonly referred to as Sec. 179 property may be treated as a deductible expense only to the extent allowable under the earlier of (1) the version of IRC § 179 in effect at the time the property is placed in service or (2) the Internal Revenue Code of 1986 as amended to January 1, 1996 [72 P.S. § 7303(a.3)].

The basis of Sec. 179 property must be reduced (but not below zero) for costs treated as a deductible expense. The amount of the reduction must be the amount deducted on a return and not disallowed, regardless of whether the deduction results in a reduction of income [72 P.S. § 73039(a.3)].

• *Intangible drilling costs*

Current expensing of intangible drilling costs associated with the creation of wells, as permitted in IRC § 59(e)(2), is not allowable or deductible. As long as the taxpayer or entity is engaged in the active conduct of a business and business activities have begun (beyond the exploration stage), and the drilling costs are reasonable in amount, the direct expenses may be amortized over the life of the wells [*PIT Guide*, Chapter 11, § IV.1.g.].

Under generally accepted accounting principles (GAAP) there are two acceptable methods of accounting for oil and gas exploration and development (E & D) costs— the successful effort method and the full cost method. These methods may be used for Pennsylvania personal income tax purposes consistent with the requirements of *PIT Bulletin 2010-04*, Department of Revenue (December 2010). For taxable years beginning in 2010, the Department of Revenue will permit taxpayers to elect to use an allowable default method described in *PIT Bulletin 2010-04*, Department of Revenue (December 2010) if they do not use either the successful effort method or full cost method for financial accounting or regulatory purposes on a regular and consistent basis. For details see *PIT Bulletin 2010-04*, Department of Revenue (December 2010).

Effective beginning with tax year 2014, permits a taxpayer to recover intangible drilling costs as defined by federal rules by using either a 10-year amortization period or an election to currently expense up to one-third of the allowable costs and amortize the remaining costs over 10 years for personal income tax (Act 52 of 2013). In Notice 2013-04, the Department of Revenue has taken the position that all IDC, capitalization expense elections must be made at the entity level. At the federal level, these decisions are made at the partner level. This notice sets out the Department's current policies concerning the deductions of intangible drilling cost.

¶111 Recordkeeping Requirements

In general, taxpayers must keep permanent books of accounts including inventories, sufficient to establish the amount of gross income, deductions allowable, credits or other matters required to be reported [61 Pa. Code § 117.15(a)]. However, individuals whose gross income include salaries, wages or similar compensation for personal services rendered are required only to keep the records to enable the Department to determine the correct amount of income subject to tax; they are not required to keep the books of account or records required by the general rule [61 Pa. Code § 117.15(b)].

Taxpayers must retain records sufficient to substantiate all items on a personal income tax return for at least four years after the later of the return due date or the date the tax is paid. During this period the records must at all times be available for inspection by the Department of Revenue. Any taxpayer claiming a refund, credit, or abatement must keep supporting documents for at least three years from the filing date of the claim [61 Pa. Code § 117.15(i)]. The *minimum* requirement for retention of records is four years. In some cases, however, the three-year requirement for retention after a claim for a refund may extend the minimum period beyond four years. One rule does not negate the other.

Example: Ted Taxpayer timely filed and paid Pennsylvania personal income tax for 2001 (due on April 15, 2002). He is required to retain records until April 15, 2006. If he files a claim for a refund on October 15, 2002, the three-year retention rule does not shorten the minimum retention period to three and one-half years; he still must retain his records until April 15, 2006. However, if Ted files a claim for refund two years later, on April 15, 2005, the three-year retention rule operates to extend the total minimum retention time to five years—to April 15, 2008.

Pennsylvania does not require a particular form for keeping records but simply requires that taxpayers must use forms and systems of accounting that will enable the Department to ascertain the fact and amount of tax liabilities [61 Pa. Code § 117.15(e)]. Federal income tax records, therefore, are sufficient for Pennsylvania income tax purposes if they contain all the information necessary to determine Commonwealth income tax liability. However, for Commonwealth purposes, taxpayers must keep copies of any return, schedule, statement, or other document they are required to file [61 Pa. Code § 117.15(f)].

• *Confidentiality of tax information*

Criminal penalties are imposed on officers or employees of the Commonwealth who disclose income tax information in any way not authorized by law. The authorized disclosures are for records required by courts or for certified copies of returns to be delivered to a taxpayer, a taxpayer's authorized representative, or to the Pennsylvania Higher Education Assistance Agency if authorized by the applicant or the applicant's parents or guardians [72 P.S. § 7353(f), (g)].

¶112 Amended Returns

If, after filing a final return, a taxpayer discovers new information that would increase taxable income and/or income tax liability, the taxpayer must file an amended return (see ¶ 107) and remit the additional tax in full within 30 days from the date the increase is determined. A statement setting forth the events or facts causing the increase must be attached to the return. The Regulations give the following examples of events that might cause an increase in taxable income and/or income tax liability [61 Pa. Code § 117.9(a)]:

(1) Reimbursements for business expenses previously deducted.

(2) Gains or losses from disposition of property acquired before June 1, 1971, calculated using the June 1, 1971, basis.

(3) Credits for taxes paid to other states when the income tax liability in the other state is later reduced, for whatever reason.

(4) Any other increase in any of the eight classes of income.

¶113 Applications for Refunds

A petition for a refund may be filed for any tax with the Board of Appeals (1) within three (3) years from the date of payment [72 P.S. § 1003.1(a)] or (2) six (6) months of the mailing date of a notice of assessment, determination, settlement, or reappraisal [72 P.S. § 1003.1(d)].

Federal/Commonwealth Difference

An extension of time to file for Pennsylvania purposes does not extend the statute of limitations for filing a refund claim as it does for federal income tax purposes.

• *Refund period*

Comment: Refund Claims Within Three Years

In order to make a timely claim for a refund of Pennsylvania personal income tax purposes, a claim must be filed within three years of the date the tax in question was paid. There is no extension of this three-year period even for statutes later found to be unconstitutional or erroneously interpreted. A proper refund claim can only be made by filing a petition with the Board of Appeals. An amended return will not toll the Statute of Limitations. If the amended return is not processed there is no appeal. Decisions of the Board of Appeals can be appealed all the way to the Pennsylvania Supreme Court. The Supreme Court recently held that payment is generally deemed to be made on April 15, even if the return is extended. The Supreme Court held that the date that the payment was made, not the date that the return was filed, begins the running of the three year refund period. The lower court held that the refund period commenced on the date that the return is actually filed (*See Mission Alpha Funding* 2 MAP 2016 5-22-2017).

• *Direct deposit for electronic filers*

As part of the Federal/State Electronic Filing Program, the Department of Revenue offers direct deposit of refunds, which provides a safe, convenient, and faster alternative to receiving paper checks in the mail. Direct deposit is not available for refunds from paper tax returns. For more information on electronic filing, see ¶107.

RESIDENT TAXPAYERS

¶115 Individuals

Pennsylvania residents are taxed on their worldwide incomes. A resident individual for this purpose is one of the following:

(1) An individual who is domiciled in Pennsylvania. However, an individual domiciled in Pennsylvania may be classified as nonresident for tax purposes if (a) the individual does not maintain a permanent place of abode in Pennsylvania; (b) the individual does maintain a permanent place of abode outside Pennsylvania; and (c) the individual spends no more than 30 days, in the aggregate, in Pennsylvania. Thus, an individual can be a Pennsylvania resident for some purposes (*e.g.*, voting) but not for personal income tax purposes.

(2) An individual who, although not domiciled in Pennsylvania, maintains a permanent place of abode in Pennsylvania and spends, in the aggregate, more than 183 days in Pennsylvania. The 183-day rule does not apply to taxpayers domiciled in Pennsylvania [72 P.S. § 7301(p)].

• *Domicile and abode*

Domicile and abode do *not* mean the same thing. A "domicile" is the place that an individual intends to be his or her permanent home and to which he or she intends to return whenever absent [61 Pa. Code § 101.1]. The domicile of a taxpayer, once established, does not change until the taxpayer moves to a new location with the bona fide intention of making a *permanent* home in the new location. Domicile is determined without regard to citizenship. It is a taxpayer's *intention* of maintaining a permanent place of abode that determines domicile. A "place of abode," on the other hand, is merely a dwelling place maintained by an individual whether or not owned by the individual. To qualify as a permanent place of abode, the dwelling must be used on a regular basis. For example, a vacation home does not qualify as a permanent place of abode [61 Pa. Code § 101.1]. If a member of the armed services lives on a military installation or in assigned or rented government quarters, he or she is not considered to maintain a permanent place of abode. However, a member of the armed forces who leases, rents, or buys a dwelling place near his or her duty station and occupies it with his or her family is considered to maintain a permanent place of abode if the duty assignment is of an indefinite nature [61 Pa. Code § 121.12].

• *NESTOA agreement on residency and domicile*

The members of the North Eastern States Tax Officials Association (NESTOA) have signed an agreement on residency and domicile [*News Release*, Pennsylvania Department of Revenue, October 28, 1996]. The agreement addresses the tax problems created for a person who is considered to have established primary residency in more than one state at the same time and a person who maintains a primary home in one state but is considered a resident for tax purposes of another state. NESTOA includes the following states: Maine, New Hampshire, Vermont, Massachusetts, Connecticut, Rhode Island, New York, New Jersey, *Pennsylvania*, Delaware, Maryland, and the District of Columbia.

The NESTOA agreement on residency and domicile provides for incorporation of the following concepts in state tax policy:

(1) Application of uniform primary criteria for determining a taxpayer's domicile or residency.

(2) Implementation of an informal appeals process that would be available to taxpayers involved in a domicile dispute with multiple member states.

(3) Application of uniform rules in the sourcing of income and the calculation of credits for taxes paid to other states.

(4) Establishment of a system of intrastate sharing of data and compliance techniques in the area of domicile and statutory residences.

(5) Publication of an informational pamphlet outlining the agreement and contact persons in each state's tax administration agency.

• *Current Residency Discovery*

The Department of Revenue, through its Pass Thru Business Office conducts a program where it seeks out taxpayers who qualify as residents who have not been filing returns. In most instances these taxpayers have taken the steps necessary to move their domiciles to a state other than Pennsylvania. The problem is that they still maintain a residence here and have not maintained the records necessary to show that they are not present in Pennsylvania for 183 days during the tax year. This results in them being taxed, as a resident, for that year. Taxpayers that fall into this situation need to keep a diary, during the tax year that keeps track of their days spent and manage those days to make sure they are outside of Pennsylvania for 183 days each tax year.

If taxpayers in this situation have not been filing Pennsylvania returns, the Department of Revenue will normally assess tax for the six years prior to the current year. The taxpayer will then enter the appeals process to resolve the assessments.

A series of residency and domicile decisions rendered by the Board of Finance and Revenue can be found at the Boards website (www.patreasury.gov). They include:

Anna Mac Gray BF&R Docket No. 1523834 (1-25-17)

William Mifflin Large Jr. BF&R Docket No. 1604817 (1-19/17)

Jack Linzer BF&R Docket No. 1321180 (1-19-17)

David C. Rippy BF&R Docket No. 1603217 (1-19-17)

¶116 Estates and Trusts

Estates and trusts are subject to tax on all taxable income they receive during the taxable year after deductions for amounts that have been distributed or credited to its beneficiaries. Resident estates and trusts are taxable on income from all sources; nonresident estates and trusts are taxable on Pennsylvania-source income.

A "resident estate" is the estate of an individual who was a Pennsylvania resident at the time of death [72 P.S. § 7301(r)].

A "resident trust" is one of the following: (1) a trust created by the will of a decedent who was a Pennsylvania resident at time of death; (2) any trust created by a Pennsylvania resident; or (3) any trust that has a corpus consisting, in whole or in part, of property transferred to the trust by a Pennsylvania resident [61 Pa. Code § 101.1]. The term "resident trust" does *not* include charitable trusts or pension or profit-sharing trusts [72 P.S. § 7301(s)]. The recently decided McNeil case (635 A3d 135 (2013)) throws into question arbitrary rules concerning resident trusts. If a resident trust has no contacts with Pennsylvania this case may provide a way for the trust to avoid filing in Pennsylvania.

Recent Board of Finance and Revenue decisions involving trust residency status can be found at www.patreasury.com. They include:

Matthew L. Pincas Family Trust Under Will of Theresa Pincas.

BF&R Docket No. 1601309 (1-25-17)

Caution: Commonwealth Does Not Follow Federal Grantor Trust Rules

The recent Commonwealth Court decision *McNeil* holds that the location of the trust activity must be taken into account in determining residency.

Pennsylvania does not follow Federal rules for grantor trusts, but instead requires income to be reported by the grantor trust.

NONRESIDENTS AND PART-YEAR RESIDENTS

¶120 Taxation of Nonresidents

The term "nonresident" is defined by exception. A nonresident individual is one who is not a resident individual. For definitions of "resident individual" see ¶115. A nonresident estate or trust is one that is not a resident estate or trust (but does not include charitable trusts or pension or profit-sharing trusts) [72 P.S. § 7301(m), (n)]. For definition of "resident estate" and "resident trust" see ¶116.

Nonresidents are taxed at the same flat rate and on the same eight classes of income as residents. However, nonresidents are taxed only on income from sources within Pennsylvania. Income acquired in the following ways is considered Pennsylvania-source income:

(1) By reason of ownership or disposition of any interest in real or tangible property in Pennsylvania. The ownership could be held by another entity. See *Wirth et al., v. Cmwlth.*, 85 MAP 2012, where a nonresident who was a limited partner in a Connecticut partnership that owned a building in Pittsburgh, Pennsylvania, was held subject to the Pennsylvania personal income tax on Pennsylvania-source income.

(2) In connection with a trade or business carried on in Pennsylvania, including compensation as an employee.

(3) As a distributive share of the income of an unincorporated business, Pennsylvania S corporation, profession, enterprise, undertaking, or other activity as a result of work done or services rendered in Pennsylvania.

(4) From intangible personal property employed in a trade, profession, occupation, or business carried on in Pennsylvania.

• *Intangible Income*

In general, Pennsylvania does not tax interest or dividends of nonresidents. Income from intangible personal property is Pennsylvania-source income only if the property is used in a trade or business. Income from an investment company registered with the Federal Securities and Exchange Commission is *not* Pennsylvania-source income [72 P.S. §7301(k)]. Residents of states with which Pennsylvania has a reciprocal agreement are exempt from withholding and payment of tax on Pennsylvania-source compensation.

• *Allocation and apportionment*

When a nonresident has income from sources both within and outside of Pennsylvania, and the portion of the income that is Pennsylvania-source income is not reasonably ascertainable, the nonresident taxpayer must allocate and apportion part of the income under rules specified by the Regulations. See ¶128 for an explanation of allocation and apportionment rules.

• *Deferred compensation*

For any year that a taxpayer spends fewer than 183 days in Pennsylvania and does not constructively or actually receive deferred compensation while a resident of Pennsylvania, the taxpayer is not liable for Pennsylvania personal income tax on that deferred compensation. The taxpayer, however, is liable for Pennsylvania personal income tax for any Pennsylvania-sourced income that falls under any of the eight classifications of income subject to the personal income tax and is earned and received during that year [*Personal Income Tax Bulletin 2005-18*, October 3, 2005].

¶121 Taxation of Part-Year Residents

A "part-year resident" is one who is a resident of Pennsylvania for only part of the year [61 Pa. Code §121.7]. A taxpayer who spends part of the year in another state has not had a change of domicile unless the taxpayer's permanent residence has been changed to a place outside Pennsylvania (*i.e.*, the taxpayer must intend to reside in the other state indefinitely). A part-year resident is subject to the Pennsylvania personal income tax in two capacities: (1) as a resident for the part of the year domiciled in Pennsylvania and (2) as a resident for the part of the year domiciled outside Pennsylvania. A part-year resident follows two sets of rules but files only one return—Form PA-40 [61 Pa. Code §121.8(b)]. Allocation and apportionment may be required for the nonresident portion of the taxable year.

COMPUTATION OF THE TAX

¶125 What Is Involved in the Computations

How to compute the tax after determining the amount of the eight separate classes of income is simple. (For explanation of classes of income, see Chapter 2.) The taxpayer first totals the income, but cannot offset the gains of one class of income against losses in another.

Example: Jonathan has the following items of income for 2005:

Item	Amount	Class
Salary	$100,000	Compensation
Loss on sale of stock	(10,000)	Gain/loss from property
Gain on sale of stock	5,000	Gain/loss from property
Partnership loss	(10,000)	Net loss from a business
Dividends	3,000	Dividends

Jonathan's taxable income is $103,000 ($100,000 compensation + $3,000 dividends).

Note that he cannot use the net loss from property transactions or the net loss from a business to offset income in other classes. He can, however, offset the gain on the sale of stock against the loss on sale of stock because they are in the same class of income.

The taxpayer next applies the flat rate to the entire amount of taxable income and then applies any allowable credits to reduce the gross income tax liability. The result of this last operation is either (1) the amount of tax still payable to the Commonwealth or (2) an overpayment that may be refunded to the taxpayer (or at the taxpayer's option credited to estimated tax payments). Taxpayers who qualify for the Special Tax Provisions for Poverty determine the amount of refund or forgiveness in accordance with the rules explained at ¶ 129.

Always Round to Whole Dollars

All amounts on the Form PA-40 must be entered in whole dollars. Round amounts of less than 50¢ down to the whole dollar; round amounts of 50¢ or more up to the next dollar.

¶126 Deductions and Exemptions

The Tax Reform Code made no provisions for deductions or exemptions before Act 43 of 2017, which created a deduction for donations to Pennsylvania Achieving a Better Life Experience (ABLE) account. Net profits and net gains, however, are defined as income net of expenses. Some items commonly called deductions (*e.g.*, employee business expenses) are allowable as exemptions or exclusions from certain classes of income:

Unreimbursed employee business expenses: Taxpayers may reduce taxable compensation for allowable actual unreimbursed employee business expenses directly related to the taxpayer's occupation and employment that are ordinary, necessary, reasonable. Unreimbursed employee business expenses are discussed at ¶ 203.

Medical Care Savings Accounts: Taxpayers may establish Medical Savings Accounts (MSAs) for eligible medical, dental, eye, Medicare supplemental insurance, and longterm care expenses. Contributions to, interest earned on, and funds reimbursed to account holders for eligible medical expenses are exempt from the Pennsylvania personal income tax [72 P.S. § 3402-A(3)].

Cafeteria plans: Payments made by an employer or labor union or elective contributions deemed to be made by an employer under a cafeteria plan for a nondiscriminatory health, accident or death plan are excluded from compensation (and thus not subject to withholding) [61 Pa. Code § 101.6(c)]. Employee payments and contributions for other benefits, including dependent care and contributions to an IRC § 401 plan, are not excludable from Pennsylvania taxable compensation [*Pennsylvania Personal Income Tax Guide* (Pennsylvania Department of Revenue), Chapter 7, p. 23]. See, also, *Legal Letter Rulings PIT 03-010* and *03-024.*

Special Tax Provisions for Poverty: Individuals whose incomes are low enough to qualify for the Special Tax Provisions for Poverty are entitled to forgiveness of all or part of the Pennsylvania personal income tax liabilities. "Special Tax Provisions for Poverty" are discussed at ¶ 129.

Personal use of employer-owned property: Payment in the form of personal use of employer-owned property (*e.g.*, housing, day care facilities, cars, parking facilities) is not taxable if the following two requirements are met: (1) the property belongs to, or is held under a lease by, the employer at the time of the use; and (2) no title, interest, or estate in the property is conferred upon, or vested in, another person [61 Pa. Code § 101.6a(a), (b)].

Personal use of employer-provided services: Payment in the form of personal use of services (*e.g.*, eating facilities, commuter highway vehicles, parking, education) is not taxable as compensation if either of the following two requirements is met: (1) the service is provided directly by the employer or a co-employee; or (2) rights to the service were procured beforehand by the employer [61 Pa. Code § 1016a(c), (d)].

Achieving a Better Life Experience (ABLE) account: An amount contributed to an ABLE account is deductible from the taxable income of the contributor in the year it is made. The total amount that can be deducted cannot exceed the federal dollar amount allowed. Further, undistributed earnings and amounts distributed from an account that are not included in federal income are exempt from taxation. [Sec. 7 Act 43 of 2017]

¶127 Credits Against the Tax

Pennsylvania residents subject to the personal income tax may use the following credits against their Pennsylvania personal income tax:

(1) Credit for estimated payments of income tax or income tax withheld from compensation (see below).

(2) Resident's credit for taxes paid to other states and countries. Effective January 1, 2014, the resident credit for personal income tax paid to foreign countries is eliminated. (Act 52 of 2013) (see below).

(3) Employment incentive payment tax credit (explained at ¶1006).

(4) Job creation tax credit (explained at ¶1007).

(5) Waste tire recycling grant (formerly the waste tire recycling equipment tax credit) (explained at ¶1009).

(6) Research and development credit (explained at ¶1008). This credit is also available to shareholders of Pennsylvania S corporations that receive a research and development tax credit.

(7) Film production tax credit (explained at ¶1012).

(8) Organ and bone marrow donor tax credit (see ¶1015).

(9) Resource enhancement and protection tax credit (see¶1016)

(10) Credit for job creation in strategic development area (see ¶1017).

(11) Volunteer responder tax credit (see below).

(12) Alternative energy production tax credit (see ¶1019).

(13) First class cities economic development district credit (see ¶1020).

(14) Keystone special development zone tax credit (see ¶1014A).

(15) Resource manufacturing tax credit (see ¶1021).

(16) Educational opportunity scholarship tax credit (see ¶1022).

(17) Historic preservation incentive credit (see ¶1023).

(18) Community-based services tax credit (see ¶1024).

KOZs and KIZs

Certain businesses located in a KOZ are entitled to a KOZ job creation tax credit (see discussion at ¶1014). KIZ companies are entitled to a KIZ tax credit (see discussion at ¶4623).

Pennsylvania allows no credit for income taxes paid to other taxing authorities *within* Pennsylvania (*e.g.*, the Philadelphia city wage tax) or for income taxes levied by local authorities in other states, *except* for the Philadelphia credit discussed below. This prohibition has been challenged and found to be constitutional [*Somma v. Cmwlth.*, 405 A.2d 1323 (Pa.Commw. 1979)].

• *Philadelphia credit*

Taxpayers who reside in a school district that levies the earned income/net profits tax authorized by Act 50 and work in Philadelphia are entitled to a credit against their Pennsylvania personal income tax equal to 0.2756% of their salaries, wages, or other compensation [53 Pa.C.S. §8713(b)]. This credit is available only to residents of school districts who are also subject to Philadelphia's earned income/net profits tax as nonresidents. Other provisions of the Taxpayers' Local Control Act (Act of May 5, 1998, No. 50, S.B. 669) are discussed at ¶3405. This credit is available only if the local government adopts the provisions of the Taxpayers' Local Control Act. See ¶3405 for explanation of the Taxpayers' Local Control Act.

• *Nonresident partners, members, shareholders or holders of beneficial interests*

Nonresident partners, members, shareholders, or holders of beneficial interests are allowed a credit for their share of the withholding tax paid by the partnership or Pennsylvania S corporation. The credit may be taken in the taxable year in which (or with which) the taxable year (for which the tax was withheld) of the partnership or Pennsylvania S corporation ends [72 P.S. §7324.2]. Taxation of partnerships is discussed in Chapter 18. Prior to January 1, 1998, holders of beneficial interests were not included in eligibility for this credit.

• *Residents' credit for taxes imposed by other states*

A resident taxpayer is entitled to a credit against Pennsylvania personal income tax for the amount of any income tax, wage tax, or other tax on or measured by gross or net earned or unearned income imposed on him or her (or on a Pennsylvania S corporation in which he or she is a shareholder to the extent of his or her pro rata share) by another state on income that is also taxable in Pennsylvania [72 P.S. §7314(a)]. The term "another state" for this purpose includes other states of the United States, the District of Columbia, the Commonwealth of Puerto Rico, any territory or possession of the United States. There is no provision for a resident credit for taxes paid to political subdivisions of other states. There may be, however, local provisions for tax credits against local earned income taxes paid to political subdivisions of other states. See discussion at specific local tax.

Computation of the credit: To compute the resident tax credit, multiply Pennsylvania tax by a fraction, the numerator of which is the amount of taxable income subject to tax in the other jurisdiction and the denominator of which is the taxpayer's entire taxable income. Note that the credit is based on Pennsylvania's personal income tax rate, not the other state's rate. See examples below. The credit is also nonrefundable (*i.e.*, it can reduce Pennsylvania personal income tax due to zero but not below zero) [72 P.S. §7314(b)]. It is possible for the resident tax credit to reduce Pennsylvania personal income tax due to zero if the only source of income is taxed by another state. If the resident tax credit reduces Pennsylvania personal income tax due to zero, the taxpayer must file a Pennsylvania personal income return in order to claim the credit. Note that if the taxpayer also has income not subject to tax in another state, he or she will owe some Pennsylvania personal income tax regardless of how much tax was paid to the other state. No credit can be taken with respect to compensation received in states with which Pennsylvania has reciprocal agreements (see ¶301). However, credit may be taken for taxes imposed on the other classes of Pennsylvania taxable income.

Effective beginning with tax year 2014, permits a taxpayer to recover intangible drilling costs as defined by federal rules by using either a 10-year amortization period or an election to currently expense up to one-third of the allowable costs and amortize the remaining costs over 10 years for personal income tax (Act 52 of 2013). In Notice 2013-04, the Department of Revenue has taken the position that all IDC, capitalization expense elections must be made at the entity level. At the federal level, these decisions are made at the partner level. This notice sets out the Departments current policy on the deduction of tangible drilling cost.

Federal/Commonwealth Difference

Pennsylvania residents do not have the option of a deduction for taxes paid to another jurisdiction (as is the case for federal individual income tax purposes). They can, however, take a resident tax credit for income taxes paid to other jurisdictions even though they took those taxes as federal itemized deductions.

¶127

The following examples illustrate the computation of the credit:

Example 1: Joe Jones, a Pennsylvania resident, earned $10,000 of wages in New York and had taxable interest and capital gains of $5,000. Joe was allowed $2,000 of deductions for New York purposes. Joe paid New York income tax of $500. Joe's Pennsylvania personal income tax liability for 2008 (before credits) is $461 (.0307% of taxable income of $15,000). Joe, however, is entitled to a credit for taxes paid to other jurisdictions of $280 [($10,000 ÷ $15,000) × $461]. The remaining $154 is the amount of his Pennsylvania income tax after the credit for taxes paid to New York. The deductions permitted in another state have no effect on the allowable credit for taxes paid to other jurisdictions [61 Pa. Code § 111.4(b)].

Example 2: John and Jane Peet (Taxpayers) filed both Delaware and Pennsylvania personal income tax returns. Delaware's income tax, unlike that of Pennsylvania, uses graduated rates; and Delaware first uses a taxpayer's total income (regardless of source) to establish a tax rate. Then Delaware, using the tax rate derived by using total income, applies that rate only to the income derived in Delaware to determine tax liability in Delaware. Taxpayers claimed a credit for the entire amount of tax paid to Delaware, claiming that their entire income was subject to income in Delaware. The Department of Revenue and the Commonwealth Court did not agree. Although using entire taxable income to determine a progressive rate might not be taxpayer-friendly, said the court, it is not the same as taxing entire income. The total credit for Delaware taxes paid was not $5,299 (100%), but $2,514 (28%), derived by dividing their total taxable Delaware income of $85,204 by their entire taxable income of $303,297). For details, see *John Peet Jr. and Jane Peet v. Cmwlth.,* 705 A.2d 497 (Pa.Commw. 1998).

Caution: Credit Applied State by State

Credits must be applied on a state-by-state basis. For example, consider a Pennsylvania resident with income in Pennsylvania, State X, and State Y. State X has an income tax rate of 2%; State Y has an income tax rate of 4%. In 2005, taxpayer has taxable income of $10,000 in State X and $10,000 in State Y. In addition, Taxpayer has $10,000 of Pennsylvania-source income. Taxpayer's 2005 Pennsylvania personal income tax on $30,000 of taxable income is $921. Taxpayer's credit for taxes paid to other jurisdictions is $507, not $600. Taxpayer's credit for taxes paid to State X is not 1/3 of $921, but $200 because this credit is limited to the amount of tax actually paid the other state. Taxpayer's credit for taxes paid to State Y is not $400 but $307 (3.07% of $10,000) because this credit is limited to Pennsylvania's rate of 3.07% for 2005.

Proof required: Taxpayers are required to provide proof of the amount of tax paid to another state. The mere fact that tax was withheld (*e.g.,* a Form W-2 issued by another state) is not sufficient to establish eligibility for this credit. When claiming a credit for taxes paid to another state, a taxpayer must file with his Pennsylvania return a copy of the tax return filed with the other state and this copy is considered *prima facie* evidence of the amount paid to another state [61 Pa. Code § 111.5]. Prior to February 18, 2006, taxpayers claiming a credit for taxes paid to another state had to submit a *signed* copy of the tax return filed with the other state.

• *Volunteer responder credit*

Authorization: A taxpayer who is certified as an active volunteer within Pennsylvania is eligible for a volunteer responder credit against the Pennsylvania personal income tax [72 P.S. § 8803-D]. An "active volunteer" for purposes of this credit is a volunteer for a volunteer ambulance service, volunteer fire company, or volunteer rescue company certified as meeting the criteria of 72 P.S. § 8807-D [72 P.S. § 8801-D].

Amount of credit: A qualified taxpayer may claim a tax credit of $100. If the taxpayer is not an active volunteer for the entire tax, year, the amount of the tax credit is prorated according to the number of months during which the taxpayer was an active volunteer. The credit is rounded to the nearest $5. Volunteering for any part of a month is considered volunteering for the entire month [72 P.S. § 8803-D].

Carryover and carryback: If a taxpayer cannot use the entire amount of the tax credit for the taxable year in which the taxpayer is eligible for the credit, the excess may be carried over for no more than three taxable years. No carryback is allowed. A tax credit approved by the Department of Revenue in a taxable year must first be applied against the taxpayer's current personal income tax liability before it can be applied in succeeding years [72 P.S. § 8804-D].

How Is Total Amount of Credit Applied?

The total amount of authorized volunteer responder tax credits cannot exceed $4,500,000 [G.S. § 105-8806-D]. However, the statute does not say how the $4,500,000 is to be allocated among claimants if the total exceeds $4,500,000. Is it prorated over all claimants? Is it on a first-come-first-served basis? Or some other method? At this time it is unknown how it will be allocated.

¶128 Allocation and Apportionment

If a nonresident taxpayer has income attributable to sources both within and outside Pennsylvania, the taxpayer must allocate the appropriate portion of income to Pennsylvania and pay Pennsylvania personal income tax on that portion of total income. The law requires that a taxpayer allocate income to Pennsylvania under rules prescribed in the Regulations [72 P.S. § 7310]. A nonresident partner's share of Pennsylvania income from a partnership that conducts activities both in Pennsylvania and in other states is determined at the partnership level. It does not matter whether the partner performed services in Pennsylvania or outside Pennsylvania. Even if the partner performed services entirely outside of Pennsylvania, the partner's income from the partnership will include some Pennsylvania income if the partnership had Pennsylvania income.

Nonresidents must allocate their earnings to Pennsylvania in proportion to days worked in Pennsylvania in the same manner used for withholding purposes. As for withholding purposes, the earnings of a salesman or other individual whose compensation is a function of volume of business transacted by the employee are apportioned by a fraction based on volume of business transacted in Pennsylvania, rather than by working days in Pennsylvania. See the explanation of apportionment fractions at ¶302.

Apportionment vs. Foreign Tax Credit

Note that apportionment rules for taxpayers who receive income attributable to sources both within and outside the Commonwealth apply only to nonresidents (see ¶120). Pennsylvania residents may claim the resident's credit for income taxes imposed by other states (see ¶127).

• *Business carried on partly in and partly out of state*

The Regulations provide that income can be allocated to Pennsylvania (1) by exact accounting in the books of the taxpayer or (2) by an apportionment formula [61 Pa. Code § 109.5(b), (c)]. If the books of the business do not reflect the accurate allocation of income to Pennsylvania to the satisfaction of the Department of Revenue, the taxpayer must determine the income attributable to Pennsylvania sources by multiplying total net profit by a decimal figure that is an average of three fractions, called factors [61 Pa. Code § 109.5(c)]:

(1) A property factor, based on the value of tangible property.

(2) A payroll factor, based on wages, salaries, and commissions.

(3) A sales factor, based on sales or receipts.

¶128

The decimal figure is determined as follows:

Decimal figure = (Property factor + Payroll factor + Sales factor)/3.

After you calculate the decimal figure, you compute the income to be apportioned to Pennsylvania as follows:

Pennsylvania income = (Decimal figure) × (Total net profit)

- *Property factor*

The property factor is a fraction the numerator of which is the average value of real and tangible personal property owned or rented by the taxpayer and used in the taxpayer's trade or business within Pennsylvania and the denominator of which is the average value of the real and tangible personal property owned or rented by the taxpayer and used in the taxpayer's trade or business both within and outside of Pennsylvania [61 Pa. Code § 109.5(c)(1)]. Average value is determined by adding the value at the beginning of the year and the value at the end of the year and dividing the sum by two. If the Department of Revenue considers it necessary to reflect true average value, an average of monthly values may be required.

Property owned by the taxpayer is valued at original cost with no allowance for depreciation. Property rented by the taxpayer is valued by multiplying the gross annual rental rate by eight. The gross annual rental rate is the rent paid during the year and does not include property subleased and not used to carry on the business. Gross rents also do not include (1) payments or credits to the business proprietor or to a partner in a partnership conducting the business for the use of real property; (2) amounts paid as separate charges for electricity or water furnished by the lessor; or (3) payments for storage unless the taxpayer has specifically rented space for storage.

- *Payroll factor*

The payroll factor is a fraction the numerator of which is total compensation paid in Pennsylvania for the year and the denominator of which is the total compensation paid both within and outside Pennsylvania during the year [61 Pa. Code § 109.5(c)(2)].

Compensation is considered paid in Pennsylvania if *one* of the following conditions is met:

(1) The individual's service is performed entirely within Pennsylvania.

(2) The individual's service is performed outside Pennsylvania, but the service is incidental to work performed within Pennsylvania.

(3) Some of the service is performed within Pennsylvania and the base of operations (or the place from which the service is directed or controlled) is within Pennsylvania.

(4) Some of the service is performed within Pennsylvania and the base of operations (or the place from which the service is directed or controlled) is not in either Pennsylvania or in any state in which some part of the service is performed and the individual to whom the compensation is paid is a Pennsylvania resident.

An individual's base of operations is the fixed center from which the individual works. It may be a business office, a place to which employees go to receive instructions, or a place where an individual maintains business records.

- *Sales factor*

The sales factor is a fraction the numerator of which is total sales within Pennsylvania during the year and the denominator of which is total sales both within and outside Pennsylvania for the year [61 Pa. Code § 109.5(3)].

Sales of tangible personal property are considered to be in Pennsylvania if one of the following conditions is met:

(1) The property is delivered or shipped from outside Pennsylvania to Pennsylvania, regardless of f.o.b. point or other sales conditions (unless the purchaser is the U.S. Government).

(2) The property is shipped from Pennsylvania to any place and the purchaser is the U.S. Government.

(3) The property is shipped from Pennsylvania to any other state and the taxpayer is not taxable in the state of the purchaser.

Sales of Derivatives

According to the Department of Revenue, to the extent they are not classified as a security, net gains of the sale of derivatives (*e.g.*, futures, options, and swaps) are used in computing the sales factor [*PICPA Questions for the Department of Revenue*, June 30, 2011]. However, the Department of Revenue notes that there is a question as to whether these items are a security excluded from the sales factor.

A person is taxable in another state if in that state the taxpayer is subject to one of the following taxes: a net income tax, a franchise tax measured by net income, or a business privilege franchise tax. The other state need only have the jurisdiction to subject the taxpayer to such taxes; the taxes need not be actually imposed [61 Pa. Code § 109.5(c)(3)(iii)].

Throwback Rule—Differs from Corporate Net Income

The third condition listed above (property shipped to any other state) in effect requires you to use a "throwback" rule to determine the numerator of the sales factor. This differs from the determination of the sales fraction for corporate net income tax purposes.

Example: Trevor Jennings operates a business in Philadelphia and makes sales in three states: Pennsylvania, State X, and State Y. Jennings is taxable in State X. State Y, however, does not have the jurisdiction to tax Jennings. All of Jennings's sales made in State Y must be included in the numerator of Jennings's sales factor, even though delivery of the goods was made in a state other than Pennsylvania.

Sales of property other than tangible personal property are considered to be in Pennsylvania under either of the following two conditions:

(1) The activity producing the income is performed within Pennsylvania.

(2) The activity producing the income is performed both within and outside Pennsylvania, but more of the activity is performed within Pennsylvania than outside Pennsylvania (based on costs of performance).

Income and deductions connected with rental of real property and gain or loss from disposition of real property are not subject to allocation under 72 P.S. § 7310. These items are deemed entirely derived from or connected with the state in which the real property is located.

Example of allocation and apportionment: Taxpayer S owns and operates a sales company as a sole proprietor. S is a resident of New Jersey, and S's main office is in Camden, New Jersey. However, S also maintains a sales office in Philadelphia. The pertinent facts for the computation of S's apportionment fraction are as follows: S owns the office building in Camden, bought at a cost of $100,000 ten years ago. No capital additions have been made since acquisition. Other tangible and/or real property used in the business in Camden was bought at various times at a cost of $10,000. The office in Philadelphia is rented at a cost of $1,000 per month. Other property owned and used in the business in Philadelphia was bought at a total cost of $5,000. One year ago the values of property, other than offices, were $8,000 for the Camden property and $3,000 for the Philadelphia office. The rent for the Philadelphia office last year was $800 per month. Total compensation paid in New Jersey was $90,000; and total compensation paid in Pennsylvania was $50,000. Total New Jersey sales were $1,200,000; and total Pennsylvania sales were $800,000. Taxpayer S does not have adequate records to support exact apportionment. S apportions total taxable income of $200,000 by using the apportionment formula provided by the regulations.

Property factor numerator = Average value of property used in Pennsylvania =

$[(8 \times \$9,600) + \$3,000] + [8 \times \$12,000) + \$5,000]/2 = \$90,400.$

Average value of property used in Camden =

$[\$100,000 + \$8,000] + [\$100,000 + \$10,000]/2 = \$109,000.$

Property factor denominator = Average value of all property used in the business =

$\$90,400 + \$109,000 = \$199,400.$

Property factor = $\$90,400/\$199,400 = 0.453360.$

Payroll factor = $\$50,000/\$140,000 = 0.357143.$

Sales factor = $\$800,000/\$2,000,000 = 0.40.$

Decimal figure = $(.453360 + 0.357143 + 0.40) /3 = 0.403501.$

Income allocated to Pennsylvania = $0.403501 \times \$200,000 = \$80,700.$

• *Other methods of allocation*

When the methods of allocation and apportionment prescribed by the regulations under 72 P.S. §7310 do not result in a fair and equitable apportionment and allocation, the Department of Revenue may require a taxpayer to use a method of allocation and apportionment that does result in a fair and equitable apportionment [61 Pa. Code §109.9].

¶129 Special Tax Provisions for Poverty

Article VIII, §2(b)(ii), of the Pennsylvania Constitution authorizes the General Assembly to establish special class(es) of taxpayers who, because of age, disability, infirmity or poverty are determined to be in need of tax exemption or of special tax provisions. In accordance with this provision, the General Assembly enacted provisions for the special treatment of taxpayers who meet the criteria for poverty [72 P.S. §7304]. This special treatment is generally referred to as the poverty income exemption.

• *Poverty*

"Poverty" for this purpose means an economic condition wherein the total amount of *poverty income* is insufficient to adequately provide the claimant, his or her spouse and dependent children with the necessities of life [72 P.S. §7301(o.1)]. Taxpayers (claimants) who meet the statutory test for poverty are entitled to a special tax benefit called a poverty income exemption [72 P.S. §7304(c)]. "Claimant" means a person who is subject to the Pennsylvania personal income tax, is not a dependent of another taxpayer for purposes of §151 of the Internal Revenue Code of 1986 but is entitled to the poverty exemption [72 P.S. §7301(c.2)].

Federal Tax Rebates Not Eligibility Income

The Department of Revenue has announced that federal tax rebates are not eligibility income for Pennsylvania tax forgiveness purposes.

• *Poverty income*

"Poverty income" is defined as all moneys or property (including interest, gains or income derived from obligations which are statutorily free from State or local taxation under any other act of the General Assembly of the Commonwealth of Pennsylvania or under the laws of the United States) received *of whatever nature and from whatever source derived* [72 P.S. § 7301(o.2)]. The following are examples of income that must be included in poverty income: use of employer-provided property and services, foster parent payments, exempt payments to IRC § 125 plans, interest (whether taxable or nontaxable), realized capital gains (whether taxable or nontaxable), child support, alimony, life insurance proceeds, gifts, educational stipends, military pay for services outside combat zones, prizes and awards, lottery winnings, inheritances, and any other income not specifically excluded (see below).

NOTE: The definition of poverty income is a broad, inclusive definition of income, unlike the definition of taxable income (which includes only eight classes of income). See ¶ 102 and ¶ 201.

• *Exclusions from poverty income*

The following items of income are specifically excluded from the definition of poverty income:

(1) Combat pay: Combat pay received by members of the United States armed forces.

(2) Expenses: Reimbursement of actual expenses.

(3) Health care payments: Payments made by employers or labor unions for programs covering hospitalization, sickness, disability or death.

(4) Public assistance: Public assistance payments.

(5) Retirement benefits.

(6) Sickness and disability: Periodic payments for sickness and disability other than regular wages received during a period of sickness or disability.

(7) Social security benefits.

(8) Strike benefits.

(9) Unemployment: Unemployment compensation payments by any governmental agency and supplemental unemployment benefits.

(10) Worker's compensation: Disability, retirement, or other payments arising under worker's compensation acts, occupational disease acts, and similar legislation by any government.

• *Poverty exemption*

The poverty income exemption is based on both income and number of dependents. It is a basic allowance of $6,500 for a single claimant and $13,000 for a married claimant if the joint poverty income of the claimant and the claimant's spouse during an entire taxable year is $13,000 or less, with an additional income allowance of $9,500 for each dependent of the claimant [72 P.S. § 7304(d)(1)].

A claimant is not considered to be married for this purpose if the claimant and spouse file separate returns *and* the claimant and spouse live apart at all times during the last six months of the taxable year or are separated pursuant to a written separation agreement [72 P.S. § 7304(d)(1)].

If a claimant's poverty income does not exceed the poverty income exemption limit (see below), the claimant is entitled to a full forgiveness of tax. If any tax has been prepaid (*e.g.*, withholdings), the claimant is entitled to a refund of the tax paid. [72 P.S. § 7304(d)(1)]. The percentage of forgiveness decreases as a claimant's poverty income exceeds his or her poverty income exemption, phasing out altogether when total poverty income exceeds the poverty income exemption limit by more than the specified statutory amount. The phase-out table is found in 72 P.S. § 7304(d)(2).

• *Estimated tax*

If a claimant is required to file an estimated tax return, he or she may use the special tax provisions in computing the amount of estimated tax.

PERSONAL INCOME TAX

CHAPTER 2

INCOME AND EXCLUSIONS

¶201   "Income" Defined

The Pennsylvania personal income tax is levied on "the privilege of receiving" each of eight statutorily defined classes of income [72 P.S. §7302.2]. The Tax Reform Code does not mention gross income, adjusted gross income, or taxable income. In the Pennsylvania personal income tax system, an item is either income or it is not. As there are no deductions or exemptions in the Pennsylvania system, there is no technical distinction between gross income, adjusted gross income, or taxable income. Yet, the Pennsylvania personal income tax forms and regulations use the phrase "taxable income" to refer to the total base to which the tax rate is to be applied, and in practice the term "deduction" is used to refer to items of expense that are not included in the statutory definition of "income." So, it is not meaningless to speak of "taxable income" and "deductions," although the terms have no statutory meaning.

• *Eight classes of taxable income*

The eight classes of income subject to the personal income tax in Pennsylvania are as follows [72 P.S. §7303(a)]:

(1) Compensation.

(2) Net profits.

(3) Net gains or income from disposition of property.

(4) Net gains or income derived from or in the form of rents, royalties, patents, and copyrights.

(5) Dividends.

(6) Interest and any amount paid out of the Archer medical savings account (Archer MSA) or health savings account that is includable in the gross income of an account beneficiary for federal income tax purposes.

(7) Gambling and lottery winnings.

(8) Net gains or income derived through estates or trusts.

Except as otherwise provided and without regard to IRC § 220(f)(4) and IRC § 223(f)(4), the requirements of (1) subsections (b) and (d) of IRC § 106 (relating to employer contributions to health and accident plans; (2) IRC § 220 (relating to Archer MSAs); and (3) IRC § 223 (relating to health savings accounts), as amended to January 1, 2005, are applicable [72 P.S. § 7303(a.6)].

• *Keystone opportunity zone (KOZ) exemptions*

Qualifying persons and businesses (see ¶4622) in a subzone (*i.e.,* a keystone opportunity subzone, keystone opportunity expansion subzone, or keystone opportunity improvement subzone) are entitled to an exemption for the following:

(1) Compensation received during the time period when the person was a resident of a subzone [73 P.S. § 820.512(a)(1)].

(2) Net income from the operation of a qualified business received by a resident or nonresident of a subzone. Apportionment is required if a business operates both within and outside a subzone [73 P.S. § 820.512(a)(2)].

(3) Net gains/losses derived by a resident or nonresident from the sale or exchange of real or tangible personal property located in a subzone [73 P.S. § 820.512(3)]. This exemption applies to net gains or losses from the sale or exchange of intangible personal property or obligations issued on or after February 1, 2994, by the Commonwealth or its political subdivisions. Allocation is required if the property was not located within the subzone for the entire time the zone was in effect or, in the case of intangibles, if the property was not held by a resident of the subzone the entire time the zone was in effect.

(4) Rents received by a resident or nonresident of a subzone from the rental of real or tangible personal property located in a subzone [73 P.S. § 820.512(4)].

(5) Dividends received by a resident of a subzone [73 P.S. § 820.512(5)].

(6) Interest received by a resident of a subzone [73 P.S. § 820.512(6)].

(7) The part of the income or gains received by an estate or trust for its taxable year ending within or with the resident beneficiary's taxable year that is required to be distributed currently or is in fact credited to the resident beneficiary and would that been exempt if received by the resident beneficiary [73 P.S. § 820.512(7)].

Exceptions: Except for dividends, any portion of net income or gain that is attributable to operation of one of the following companies cannot be used to calculate a KOZ exemption [73 P.S. § 820.512(c)]:

(1) Railroad, truck, bus, or airline companies.

(2) Pipeline or natural gas companies.

(3) Water transportation companies.

(4) Entities that would qualify as regulated investment companies for corporate net income tax purposes.

(5) Entities that would qualify as holding companies as defined for capital/stock franchise purposes.

Tax credit for certain excepted companies: Railroad, truck, bus or airline companies, pipeline or natural gas companies, and water transportation that are subject to special apportionment rules (see ¶1112) and that are qualified businesses may apply for a KOZ job creation tax credit, discussed at ¶1014.

¶201

Pass-through entities: Members of partnerships/associations are entitled to KOZ personal income tax exemptions (whether distributed or not) of the partner/member's share (whether or not distributed) of income received by the partnership/association for its taxable year [73 P.S. § 820.512(a.2)(1)]. Shareholders of Pennsylvania S corporations are entitled to the KOZ personal income tax exempts of their pro rata shares (whether or not distributed) of the corporation's income or gain received by the corporation for its taxable year ending within or with the shareholders' taxable years [73 P.S. § 820.512(a.2)(2)]. A partnership/association (resident or nonresident) may not apply an exemption from income under the KOZ Act for any class of income against any other classes of income or gain and may not carry back or carry forward any KOZ exemption from year to year. The exemption cannot exceed the personal income tax liability of the taxpayer for the tax year [73 P.S. § 820.512(b)].

Expiration: Zones expire in 2008, 2010, 2013, 2018, and as late as 2025. Check with the specific Zone Coordinator for each property deadline. For information calculation of credit in year of expiration, see *Corporation Tax Bulletin 2010-01*, Pennsylvania Department of Revenue, August 25, 2010.

Tax Planning

It is possible for an item of income to fit into more than one of these eight statutory classes. If this happens, you should consider available alternatives carefully in order to minimize taxes.

NOTE: Watch Out for These Items!

• Allowable costs and expenses may be subtracted in the computation of compensation, business or farm income, income from the disposition of property, and income from rents, royalties, patents, and copyrights. However, you cannot deduct costs and expenses attributable to the following classes of income: dividends, interest, gambling and lottery winnings, and income from estates and trusts.

• You may use losses only to offset gains in the same class of income. If you have a net loss in one class of income, you should enter the word "loss" on the appropriate line of your Form PA-40. This is treated as zero (0) in computing taxable income [61 Pa. Code § 121.13(a), (b)]. The Form PA-40 Instructions also state that you must attach an appropriate schedule to your Form PA-40, even if you incur a loss.

• Spouses cannot use each other's losses [61 Pa. Code § 121.15(d)]. On a joint return, one spouse cannot use a loss in one class of income to offset a gain of the other spouse in the same class of income. If one spouse has a net loss in one class of income and the other spouse has a net gain, the total amount of income to be reported for that class is the amount of the gain. The loss is counted as zero (0).

• Losses not used in one year are not available in any other year. You cannot carry losses back or forward from year to year [61 Pa. Code §§ 103.1, 103.2].

• If an item of income falls within the definition of more than one class of taxable income, you should include it in only one class [72 P.S. § 7303(a)(8)]. For example, interest income (or any other item of income) derived from an estate or trust retains the same character in the hands of the ultimate beneficiary as in the hands of the estate or trust. If you include distributions of interest from a fiduciary in your interest income, you should not include them in the class of income defined as income from an estate or trust [61 Pa. Code § 103.18(a)].

• *Income from discharge of indebtedness*

The Department of Revenue takes the position that income from discharge of indebtedness is taxable when the discharge is a direct substitute for a taxable class of income. For example, if a business debt is discharged, the amount of the forgiveness is included in the business's net income or loss from operations. However, if the business debt is discharged as a result of bankruptcy proceedings, the cancellation is not taxable. In the case of an individual, if the cancellation is in return for an agreement to perform services for the lender, the forgiveness is taxable as compensation. Therefore, cancellation of an employee's loan would ordinarily be considered compensation. The Pennsylvania Supreme Court recently ruled in Wirth, 95 A3d 822 (2013) that forgiveness of an accrued interest in a partnership foreclosure proceeding was taxable income for Pennsylvania Personal Income Tax purposes. Chapter 24 of the Personal Income Tax Guide covers forgiveness of Indebtedness. This issue is discussed in Chapter 27 of the Pennsylvania Personal Income Tax Guide. The Guide can be found on the Department's website.

• *Federal/commonwealth difference*

Internal Revenue Code § 61 provides that all income "from whatever source derived" is subject to the federal income tax unless specifically excluded. Pennsylvania has no such "catchall" provision. If an item of income falls within one of the statutory classes, it is included in income for Pennsylvania personal income tax purposes. If it does not, it is not taxable in Pennsylvania; thus, Pennsylvania taxable income is not necessarily the same as federal taxable income. Many items that are taxable for federal income tax purposes are not taxable for Pennsylvania income tax purposes (*e.g.*, alimony). Conversely, some items that are not recognized for federal purposes are recognized for Pennsylvania purposes (*e.g.*, interest on obligations of other states).

The lack of a "catchall" taxing provision in the Pennsylvania personal income tax system also means that determining whether an item of income is taxable or not demands a frame of reference that is different from that used in considering the taxability of items under the Internal Revenue Code. In the federal system, you must consider an item taxable unless you can find a specific exclusion for it. On the other hand, in the Pennsylvania system you must consider an item not taxable unless you can find a specific inclusion—a taxable class of income. Thus, in the federal system gifts and bequests are not taxable because IRC § 102 excludes them, while in the Pennsylvania system gifts and bequests are not taxable because they do not fall within one of the eight statutory classes of income subject to the tax.

• *When to include items in income*

Pennsylvania follows the federal rule of taxing an item of income to an accrual-basis taxpayer in the year in which all events have occurred to fix the right to receive the income *and* the amount of income can be determined with reasonable accuracy. An item of income to a cash-basis taxpayer is taxed in the year in which it is actually or constructively received [61 Pa. Code § 101.7(a)]. See 61 Pa. Code § 101.7(c) for the Pennsylvania definition of "constructive receipt." For examples of constructive receipt, see 61 Pa. Code § 107.(d).

Special rule for decedents: A decedent's taxable year ends on the date of death, and only amounts property includable under the decedent's method of accounting are included in taxable income on decedent's last return. However, if the taxpayer used an accrual method of accounting, amounts accrued only by reason of death may not be included in computing taxable income for the year. If the decedent used no regular accounting method, only amounts actually or constructively received during the year shall be included [61 Pa. Code § 107(b)].

¶201

• *Partnership income*

Classification of income from a partnership is made at the partnership level. A partnership determines each partner's share of income (loss) as if the partner realized it directly from the same source and in the same manner that the partnership realized it. Each partner receives a Form RK-1 (resident partners) or a Form NRK-1 (nonresident partners) that shows the amount of partnership income that falls into each class of income.

Guaranteed payments: In the case of guaranteed payments to partners, the partnership is responsible for informing the partner of the classification of the income from which guaranteed payments are made. The guaranteed payment is identified as the class of income from which the payments were made. Whether or not the partner can offset any loss against the guaranteed payment depends upon whether the guaranteed payment and the loss are from the same class of income.

Federal/Commonwealth Difference

Pennsylvania does not follow federal rules for taxation of guaranteed payments. For Pennsylvania personal income tax purposes, if a guaranteed payment is paid for services or for the use of capital, it is classified as follows:

(1) A withdrawal proportionately from the capital of all partners.

(2) A gain from the disposition of the recipient's partnership interest and a loss from the disposition of the other partners' partnership interests, to the extent derived from the capital of the other partners.

(3) A return of capital by the recipient to the extent derived from the recipient's own capital.

Dividends and interest: In general, Pennsylvania does not tax dividends and interest received by nonresidents. Only if the income-producing property is used in a trade or business in Pennsylvania is the interest or dividend considered Pennsylvania-source income. In the case of interest or dividends received by a partnership, the ordinary interest or dividends not received in the operation of a business are not taxable to nonresident partners. In fact, there are no lines on Schedule NRK-1 to report ordinary dividends and interest.

• *Income in respect of a decedent*

The taxable year of a decedent ends on the date of his or her death [61 Pa. Code § 117.3]. In computing taxable income for the year ending on the date of death, only amounts properly includable under the decedent's method of accounting are included in taxable income on the decedent's final return. If the decedent used the accrual method of accounting, amounts accrued only by reason of his or her death are not included in computing taxable income. For a cash-basis taxpayer, only amounts actually or constructively received are included in taxable income [61 Pa. Code § 101.7]. "Income in respect of a decedent" is income to which the decedent had a right but that was not includable in taxable income under the decedent's method of accounting at the date of death. Under § 691 of the Internal Revenue Code, such items must be reported on the individual income tax return of anyone who receives "income in respect of a decedent." However, Pennsylvania has no statutory provision like IRC § 691. Therefore, income in respect of a decedent is *not* taxable to recipients for Pennsylvania personal income tax purposes *unless* it falls within one of the eight classes of taxable income. For example, Adrienne Arnold, a Pennsylvania resident, died on November 10, 2001. Adrienne was a cash-basis taxpayer. When her last paycheck from her employer is received by her estate on November 15, 2001, it is not taxable to the estate because it does not fall within one of the eight classes of taxable income. It is not compensation to the estate. However, property-based income (*e.g.,* gain on the sale of property; rents; royalties; dividends; interest) and business income (*e.g.*, profits from a decedent's business while being operated by decedent's representative) are more likely to be taxable to the recipient because they usually fall within one of the eight classes of income. For example, Jerry Jamison, a Pennsylvania resident, died on November 1, 2001. Jerry, who was a cash-basis taxpayer, owned a rental house on which the rent was due the first of each month. Jerry's estate received a rent check from the tenant on November 5, 2001. In this case, because the estate owned the house at the time the rental income was received, the estate must include the rent in its gross income. Rent falls within one of the eight classes of taxable income.

Inheritance Tax—Decedent Income

Income of a decedent must be reported on a resident decedent's Pennsylvania inheritance tax return even if it is not required to be reported for personal income tax purposes. See Chapters 29—32 for explanation of the Pennsylvania inheritance tax.

¶202 Compensation

The Tax Reform Code defines the term "compensation" as follows:

"Compensation" means and shall include salaries, wages, commissions, bonuses and incentive payments whether based on profits or otherwise, fees, tips and similar remuneration received for services rendered, whether directly or through an agent and whether in cash or in property, except income derived from the U.S. government for active duty outside Pennsylvania as a member of its armed forces and income from the United States government or the Commonwealth of Pennsylvania for active state duty for emergency within or outside the Commonwealth of Pennsylvania, including duty ordered pursuant to 35 Pa.C.S. Ch. 76 (relating to Emergency Management Assistance Compact [72 P.S. § 7303(a)(1)].

The Department of Revenue is examining returns and if the compensation shown on the return is less than Medicare Wages shown on Form W-2, they are issuing an assessment. This can be avoided in this situation by filing Form PA-40 W-2 RW with the return. This form reconciles the differences.

Active State Duty for Emergency

The provision for exemption of personal income tax on compensation earned by National Guard members who respond to active state duty for emergencies within or without the Commonwealth is effective for tax years beginning after December 31, 2006.

Note that this definition is all inclusive with respect to items of income received for services rendered. For example, fees received by corporate directors are classified as compensation. Note that for federal purposes directors' fees would be reported on Schedule C, while for Pennsylvania personal income tax purposes they would be reported with all other items of compensation. The taxpayer would be entitled to claim unreimbursed employee business expenses for Pennsylvania purposes. See ¶203 for discussion of unreimbursed employee business expenses.

Clarification of terminology: In response to comments from the Independent Regulatory Review Commission (IRRC) that the terminology "taxable compensation" is redundant and that it should be changed to "compensation" to be consistent, the Department of Revenue amended 61 Pa. Code §§ 101.1, 101.6, 101.6a and 101.7 to replace the phrase "taxable compensation" with "compensation" [30 Pa.B. 3938]. This usage is followed in this *Guidebook.* "Compensation" is always taxable for Pennsylvania personal income tax purposes.

Distributions From Nonqualified Deferred Compensation Plans

Effective for taxable years beginning after December 31, 2004, compensation includes distributions from plans described in IRC § 409(d)(1) (*i.e.*, nonqualified deferred compensation plans) attributable to an elective deferral income, regardless of whether the distribution is paid during employment or after retirement [72 P.S. § 301(d)]. This provision applies to appeals arising before or after the enactment of this provision [Act 40 of 2005 (H.B. 176), § 24(6), (7)]. Deferrals to nonqualified deferred compensation plans are not includible in compensation. This rule, enacted as part of Act No. 50 of 2005 (H.B. 176), legislatively reverses *Ignatz v. Cmwlth.*, No. 136 F.R. 2003 (Pa.Commw. May 12, 2004), in which the Commonwealth Court held that executive compensation deferred under a nonqualified compensation plan was constructively received in the year deferred for Pennsylvania personal income tax purposes.

Compensation includes the following items [61 Pa. Code § 101.6(a)]:

(1) Salaries.

(2) Wages.

(3) Commissions.

(4) Bonuses.

(5) Stock options.

(6) Incentive payments.

(7) Fees.

(8) Tips.

(9) Dismissal, termination, or severance payments.

(10) Early retirement incentive payments and other additional compensation contingent upon retirement (including payments in excess of the scheduled or customary salaries provided for those who are not terminating service).

(11) Rewards.

(12) Vacation and holiday pay.

(13) Paid leaves of absence.

(14) Payments for unused vacation.

(15) Tax assumed by the employer.

(16) Casual employer signing bonuses.

(17) Amounts received under employee plans and deferred compensation arrangements.

(18) Other remuneration received for services rendered.

Certain Employer Leave-Based Donation Programs

The Department of Revenue will not assert that cash payments an employer makes to IRC § 170(c) organizations in exchange for vacation, sick, or personal leave that its employees elect to forgo constitute compensation of the employees if the payments are (1) made to the IRC § 170(c) organizations for the relief of victims of Hurricane Katrina and (2) paid to the IRC § 170(c) organizations before January 1, 2007. The Department also will not assert that the opportunity to make such an election results in constructive receipt of compensation for employees or that an employer is not permitted to deduct these cash payments as an ordinary business expense [*Personal Income Tax Bulletin 2005-1*, Pennsylvania Department of Revenue, September 27, 2005].

• *Constructive receipt*

With certain exceptions, the constructive receipt rules for cash basis taxpayers for Pennsylvania personal income tax purposes are the same as the federal constructive receipt rules [72 P.S. § 7303(a)(1)(ii), effective for taxable years beginning after December 31, 2002, and applicable to appeals that arise before or after July 7, 2005]. The following rules are Pennsylvania exceptions to federal constructive receipt rules:

(1) Amounts lawfully deducted, not deferred, and withheld from employee compensation are considered to have been received by the employee as compensation at the time the deduction is made [72 P.S. § 7303(a)(1)(ii)(A)].

(2) Contributions to an employees' trust, pooled fund, or other arrangement that is not subject to the claims of creditors of the employer made by an employer on behalf of an employee or self-employed individual at the election of the employee or self-employed individual pursuant to a cash or deferred arrangement or salary reduction agreement are deemed to be received by the employee or individual as compensation at the time the contribution is made, regardless of when the election is made or a payment is received [72 P.S. § 7303(a)(1)(ii)(B)].

(3) Contributions to a plan by, on behalf of, or attributable to a self-employed person are deemed to be received at the time the contribution is made [72 P.S. § 7303(a)(1)(ii)(C)].

(4) Employer contributions to a Roth IRS custodian account or employee annuity are deemed received, earned, or acquired only when distributed, when the plan fails to meet the requirements of IRC § 408A or when the plan is not operated in accordance with such requirements [72 P.S. § 7303(a)(1)(ii)(E)].

(5) Employee contributions to an employee's trust, pooled fund, custodial account, contract, or employee annuity cannot be deducted or excluded from compensation [72 P.S. § 7303(a)(1)(ii)(E)].

Rules for employees other than employees of exempt organizations and State and local governments: For purposes of determining when deferred compensation of employees other than employees of exempt organizations and State and local governments is required to be included in income, the following apply: (1) the rules of IRC § § 83 and 451; and (2) the rules of IRC § 409A [72 P.S. § 7303(a)(1)(iii)]. Note that the application of IRC § 409A is effective for taxable years beginning after December 31, 2004 [Act No. 50 of 2005 (H.B. 176), § 24(7)(ii)].

Rules for employees of exempt organizations and State and local governments: For purposes of determining when deferred compensation of employees of exempt organizations and State and local governments is required to be included in income, the following apply: (1) the rules of IRC § § 83, 451, and 457; and (2) the rules of IRC § 409A [72 P.S. § 7303(a)(1)(iv)]. Note that the application of IRC § 409A is effective for taxable years beginning after December 31, 2004 [Act 40 of 2005 (H.B. 176), § 24(7)(ii)].

• *Scholarships, stipends, grants, and fellowships*

Scholarships, stipends, grants, and fellowships are taxable as compensation if services are rendered in connection with them [61 Pa. Code § 101.6(b)]. Scholarships, grants, awards, and other types of student aid that require no past, present, or future services in return for receipt of the funds are not taxable [61 Pa. Code § 101.6(b)(2)].

Graduate awards based on need or academic achievement: In general, fellowship awards or stipends made to graduate students enrolled in a graduate degree program at a university chartered by a state or foreign country that are based on need or academic achievement for the purpose of encouraging or allowing the recipient to further his/her education are not taxable. However, if the awards are made as compensation for past or present employment or in expectation of future employment services, they are taxable as compensation [61 Pa. Code § 101.6(b)(3)].

¶202

Teaching/research assistants: Fellowship awards and stipends for research, creative work, or some other project or skill are taxable as compensation for Pennsylvania personal income tax purposes unless the recipients can show that the recipient is a candidate for a degree and the same activities are required of all candidates for that degree as a condition to receive that degree [61 Pa. Code § 101.6(b)(4)].

Post-doctoral research fellows: Payments to post-doctoral research fellows for conducting research are taxable as compensation unless the recipients all of the specified conditions in 61 Pa. Code § 101.6(b)(5).

Examples: The following are examples of scholarship taxability rules based on the regulations [61 Pa. Code § 101.6(b)]:

> *Example 1:* Jennings has a high school diploma and is currently employed at XYZ Corporation. XYZ promises to pay for Jennings's college tuition, room, and board for four years if Jennings agrees to return to work for XYZ for four consecutive years after obtaining his degree. Jennings's grant-in-aid is taxable as compensation for Pennsylvania personal income tax purposes.

> *Example 2:* Trevor is employed by DEF Company and agrees that he will work for them for one year without receiving any salary. In return, after that year Trevor will attend EFG College, and DEF Company will pay his tuition, room, and board for the entire year. The payment of Trevor's tuition, room, and board by DEF is taxable as compensation for Pennsylvania personal income tax purposes.

> *Example 3:* Stephen is employed by ABC Corporation, which has established a scholarship program for its employees' children. The program does not qualify as an employer scholarship program for federal income tax purposes. When Stephen's child, Stephanie, receives a scholarship from the program to attend college, its fair market value is taxable as compensation to Stephen for Pennsylvania personal income tax purposes.

> *Example 4:* Ashley is in her first year of a three-year graduate degree program. PHM Company enters into an agreement with Ashley to pay the remaining expenses (*i.e.,* tuition, room, board) necessary to finish her graduate degree. In return, Ashley promises to work for PHM for four years after she graduates. Ashley has income taxable as compensation for Pennsylvania personal income tax when she receives the school expenses payments from PHM.

> *Example 5:* Sydney is enrolled in a graduate degree program in education at OPQ University. All graduate education degree students are required to teach an undergraduate education course for five hours a week to obtain their degrees. If Sydney does not perform additional services for OPQ University, her payment for teaching the required course is not taxable as compensation for Pennsylvania personal income tax purposes.

> *Example 6:* Jay is a post-doctoral research fellow at RST Cancer Research Institute. Jay is required to spend half of his time assisting RST's employees on their own research projects as a condition for receiving his stipend. Jay's post-doctoral research fellowship stipend is taxable as compensation for Pennsylvania personal income tax purposes, even though his payments meet all of the other conditions of 61 Pa. Code § 101.6(b)(5). See 61 Pa. Code § 101.6(b)(5)(xi).

EITC Scholarships

A scholarship received by an "eligible student" under the educational improvement tax credit (EITC) provisions is not considered to be taxable income for Pennsylvania personal income tax purposes [24 P.S. § 20-2006-B(e)]. The EITC provisions are discussed at ¶ 1011.

Definition of terms: For this purpose the following words have the following meanings:

(1) *Fellowship, stipend, or fellowship award:* A fixed sum of money paid periodically for services or to defray expenses to a graduate student who is enrolled in a graduate degree program at a university [61 Pa. Code § 101.6(b)(1)(i)].

(2) *Grant-in-aid:* Financial support given by a public agency or private institution to further the individual's education [61 Pa. Code § 101.6(b)(1)(ii)].

(3) *Post-doctoral research fellowship stipend or post-doctoral research fellowship award:* A fixed sum of money paid periodically for services or to defray expenses of an individual who has obtained a doctoral degree at a university and is conducting research at a research facility [61 Pa. Code § 101.6(b)(1)(iii)].

(4) *Scholarship:* A grant-in-aid to a student [61 Pa. Code § 101.6(b)(1)(iv)].

• *Employee contributions to pension benefit plans*

Employee contributions to pension benefit plans are taxable and subject to income tax withholding for purposes of the Pennsylvania personal income tax. This is true even though the employee contributions may be tax-deferred for federal income tax purposes under § 401(k) of the Internal Revenue Code. See *AMP Products Corporation v. Cmwlth*, 593 A.2d 1 (Pa.Commw. 1991), and discussion of contributions to employers' pension or profit-sharing plans (below).

• *Military personnel*

Military pay received by members of the armed forces serving in combat zones is statutorily excluded from the definition of compensation [72 P.S. § 7303(a)(1)]. Military pay received while on active duty outside Pennsylvania is not compensation subject to the Pennsylvania personal income tax [61 Pa. Code § 121.10(c)(8)]. According to the Form PA-40 instructions, Reservists and National Guardsmen ordered to active duty for training at a two-week summer encampment pursuant to Title 10 or Title 32 of the U.S. Code are presumed to be on federal active duty. Therefore, their pay for such training is excludable from compensation if the active duty training is performed outside Pennsylvania. The Form PA-40 instructions also indicate that the burden of establishing that military pay was received while on active duty is on the taxpayer. However, the Department of Revenue will accept the authority section of the taxpayer's orders as proof. For example, if authority for the active duty is based on a federal statute (*e.g.*, 32 U.S.C. § § 316, 502, 503, 504, 505), federal active duty will be presumed; but if authority for active duty is based on a Pennsylvania statute (*e.g.*, 51 P.S. § 508 or § 3102), state active duty will be presumed.

This exemption, however, does not extend to items falling within the other seven classes of income. An individual domiciled in Pennsylvania when entering the armed services does not cease to be a Pennsylvania resident because of being absent from the Commonwealth while on duty. Therefore, military personnel who are Pennsylvania residents must file a Form PA-40 and pay any tax due just as other resident individuals [61 Pa. Code § 121.12(a)]. Under certain circumstances, individuals, although domiciled in Pennsylvania, may be taxed as nonresidents. See ¶ 115 for an explanation of these conditions.

Under the provisions of the Soldiers and Sailors Civil Relief Act of 1940 (50 U.S.C. § 501 *et seq.*), military pay of nonresident servicemen is not subject to Pennsylvania personal income tax. However, income other than military pay earned in Pennsylvania, as well as income of spouses and/or other household members who are not members of the armed forces, is taxable in Pennsylvania [61 Pa. Code § 121.12(a)].

• *Members of the clergy*

Much controversy has surrounded the question of whether members of the clergy receive compensation as employees or have earnings from self-employment. Whether a clergyman is an employee or a self-employed individual depends upon the facts and circumstances of the individual's case. The Department of Revenue's

¶202

position is that churches or congregations should apply the common-law rules in determining whether an employer-employee relationship exists [Dept. Revenue Release 2-5-81]. The terms "employer" and "employee" are explained at ¶301.

The answer to the question of whether the value of a parsonage furnished to a clergyman by a congregation is excludable from compensation depends on two conditions: (1) whether the clergyman is an employee or a self-employed person and (2) whether the parsonage is furnished for the convenience of the congregation [Dept. Revenue Legal Bur. Chief Counsel Opinion; 1-27-82]. Regulations provide that the value of meals and lodging furnished an employee for the convenience of the employer is not compensation [61 Pa. Code § 101.6(c)(7)]. If the clergyman is an employee *and* the parsonage is furnished for the convenience of the employer, the value of the parsonage is not compensation to the clergyman; otherwise, it is taxable [Dept. Revenue Legal Bur. Chief Counsel Opinion; 1-27-82]. Cash allowances for a parsonage are taxable to clergymen.

• *What is not compensation*

For Pennsylvania personal income tax purposes, the term "compensation" has a specific meaning. In order to be considered Pennsylvania compensation, an item must fall within the statutory meaning of "compensation." Certain amounts received by taxpayers for services rendered may not fall into the statutory definition of compensation for one of three reasons: (1) the individual is not an "employee" within the meaning of the Tax Reform Code, (2) the item is statutorily excluded from the class of income called compensation, or (3) the item in question is not really for services rendered but is intended to cover certain business expenses of the employee. When an individual is clearly an employee, the individual obviously receives compensation. But this is only the first step in the determination of compensation for purposes of the Pennsylvania personal income tax. There are many situations in which compensation of taxpayers is not equal to their salaries. This is because certain items of compensation within the commonly accepted meaning of that term are not compensation within the meaning of the Pennsylvania Tax Reform Code. The following items are specifically exempt from the definition of "compensation" for Pennsylvania personal income purposes [72 P.S. § 7301(d)]:

(1) Periodic payments for periods of sickness or disability other than regular wages. This includes payments made by third-party insurers for periods of sickness or disability. The Department of Revenue has ruled that periodic payments paid to a taxpayer from either a pension or an Individual Retirement Account (IRA) on or after disability are not subject to personal income tax [Pennsylvania Department of Revenue, *Letter Ruling PIT-05-017*].

(2) Disability, retirement or other payments arising under workmen's compensation acts, occupational disease acts and similar legislation by any government. See discussion of "Retirement benefits" below.

(3) Payments commonly recognized as old age or retirement benefits paid to persons retired from service after reaching a specific age or after a stated period of employment. This does not include severance payments to an employee who terminates without retiring. Severance payments are compensation to the extent they exceed the employee's contribution to any plan from which the payments are made. See, for example, *Bickford v. Cmwlth.*, 533 A.2d 822 (Pa.Commw. 1987), in which payments under an employer's special incentive compensation plan were not excludable. Because the plan allowed distribution on termination of employment and was written as a management incentive plan rather than a retirement plan, the payments did not qualify as old age or retirement benefits. See discussion below.

¶202

No Golden Handshakes

The Department of Revenue takes the position that in order to be excludable, retirement benefits must not discriminate against employees before retirement age. This means that employees who are given extra benefits in return for taking early retirement (the so-called golden handshake) receive compensation to the extent their actual benefits exceed the normal benefits for retirement at that age.

No Double Dipping

Taxpayers who retire from one job and then take another or start a business have excludable retirement payments from the first position. However, if the taxpayer is not actually retired, or if the "retirement" plan in question looks like a severance payment rather than a retirement plan, the taxpayer may be liable for tax on payments from the "pension."

(4) Payments commonly known as public assistance, or unemployment compensation payments by any governmental agency.

(5) Payments to reimburse actual expenses of an employee.

(6) Cafeteria plans. A "cafeteria plan" is a plan qualifying under IRC § 125 [61 Pa. Code § 101.1]. See discussion at ¶ 204.

(7) Any compensation received by U.S. servicemen serving in a combat zone or for active duty outside the Commonwealth of Pennsylvania as a member of its armed forces.

(8) Foster care payments. Compensation does not include payments received by a foster parent for in-home care of foster children from an agency of the Commonwealth or a political subdivision thereof or an organization exempt from federal tax under § 501(c)(3) of the Internal Revenue Code that is licensed by the Commonwealth, or a political subdivision thereof, as a placement agency.

(9) Payments made by employers or labor unions for employee benefit programs covering social security or retirement.

(10) Medical care savings accounts. For a medical care savings account established in compliance with the federal Health Insurance Portability and Accountability Act of 1996 (P.L. 104-191), the contribution to and interest earned on an account and account funds reimbursed to an account holder for eligible medical expenses are exempt from the Pennsylvania personal income tax [72 P.S. § 3401a-3].

• *Retirement benefits*

Amounts distributed to an individual from a plan are included in income to the extent that contributions were not previously included in income except for one of the following: (1) distributions made upon or after retirement from service after reaching a specific age or after a stated period of employment; or (2) distributions transferred into another plan, when the transferred amounts are not included in income for federal income tax purposes. A retirement plan includes individual retirement plans [IRAs, Simplified Employee Pension Plans (SEPs)], Keogh plans, and federally qualified employee pension plans.

The issue of the taxability of retirement is an important and regularly recurring issue, particularly in the case of highly compensated executives. The Department of Revenue has consistently maintained that not all benefits labeled retirement benefits are nontaxable. For its position the Department relies on statute, regulations, and judicial decision [*Bickford v. Cmwlth.*, 533 A.2d 822 (Pa.Commw. 1987)]. In *Bickford*, the court held that certain "retirement payments" received from a Special Incentive

¶202

Compensation Plan by retired employee-directors of Bethlehem Steel were taxable. The court found the following facts persuasive: (1) the plan allowed payment after voluntary termination with the consent of the corporation, not just after termination of employment for death, disability, or retirement; (2) the stated purpose of the plan was to "provide an incentive to increased and profitable management," not to provide retirement income; (3) the participants in the plan received a right to cash payments whenever the corporation declared a cash dividend to its stockholders. As a result, the participants' income rights were held to resemble more closely those of shareholders than those of retirees. Because of the numerous differences among retirement plans, no general rule with respect to the taxable status of a particular "retirement payment" can be formulated. Each situation must be analysed on a case-by-case basis.

IRAs and Keoghs Not Excludable

Self-employed individuals may not take a deduction for contributions in their own behalf to IRA and Keogh plans [*Kalodner v. Cmwlth.*, 615 A.2d 900 (Pa.Commw. 1992)]. However, contributions made on behalf of employees are deductible in the computation of net profits from the operation of a business [61 Pa. Code § 101.6(c)].

• *Contributions to employer-provided pension and profit-sharing plans*

Employer contributions: Employer contributions to pension and profit-sharing plans are not taxable to the employees when the contributions are made [*Legal Letter Ruling No. PIT-04-204*, Pennsylvania Department of Revenue (October 26, 2004)]. This is because they are not constructively received by the employees, since the employees' control of the amounts contributed by the employer is subject to substantial restrictions. Because it is currently re-evaluating the position with respect to Employee Stock Ownership Plans and the retirement pay exemption, the Department of Revenue, in *Legal Letter Ruling No. PIT-04-024*, declined to issue an opinion on whether employer-matching contributions made in the form of company stock are taxable.

Employee contributions: There is, however, no statutory basis for the exclusion of employee contributions to any retirement plan. Therefore, the following items are not excludable from compensation:

(1) Employee contributions to annuity contracts tax-sheltered under IRC § 403(b) that are bought by an educational institution or charitable organization.

(2) Employee contributions to IRC § 401(k) plans (commonly called salary reduction plans), whether elective or nonelective.

(3) Civil Service employee contributions to Civil Service pension plans. See *Bernknopf v. Cmwlth.*, 425 A.2d 880 (Pa.Commw. 1981), *aff'd per curiam* 442 A.2d 693 (1982).

(4) Employee contributions to profit-sharing plans. Employee contributions to pension or profit-sharing plans are not excludable even if withheld from the employee's pay. The employee contributions are considered to be constructively received by the employee before contribution to the fund. See also *AMP Products Corporation v. Cmwlth.*, 593 A.2d 1 (Pa.Commw. 1991).

Withholding: The Department of Revenue has ruled that employers are required to withhold Pennsylvania personal income tax on the stock's fair market value when incentive stock options are exercised, unless the underlying stock is subject to a substantial limitation or restriction [*Legal Letter Ruling No. PIT-04-039*, Pennsylvania Department of Revenue (November 5, 2004)].

• *Cost recovery method*

The cost recovery method must be used to determine compensation from distributions from pension and profit-sharing plans. Distributions are considered a tax-free return of capital until all employee contributions have been exhausted. Then distributions become totally taxable. Keep in mind, however, that distributions qualifying as retirement pay are completely tax free and that retirement because of disability is considered retirement for these purposes. Remember, also, that interest on the assets retained in the plan is not taxable [61 Pa. Code § 101.6(c)(3)]. See ¶ 209 for an explanation of taxation of interest income.

¶203 Compensation—Unreimbursed Employee Business Expenses

When the Tax Reform Code was adopted, there was no provision for "deduction" or exclusion of any items of employee business expenses except those actually incurred by the employee and for which the employee received specific reimbursement from the employer. However, taxpayers attacked the Department's strict interpretation of the statute, and the disallowance of unreimbursed employee business expenses as an offset against compensation was found to be a violation of the Uniformity Clause of the Pennsylvania Constitution. See *Cmwlth. v. Staley*, 381 A.2d 1280 (Pa. 1978), *rev'g* 344 A.2d 748 (1975), and *Ritz v. Cmwlth.*, 432 A.2d 169 (Pa. 1981), *rev'g* 412 A.2d 1114 (Pa.Commw. 1980).

Federal/Commonwealth Difference

If an employee business expense is deductible, it is 100% deductible. There are no provisions in Pennsylvania law for expense and percentage accounting limitations and thresholds like the federal limitations (*e.g.*, 50% of meals and entertainment, 2% of adjusted gross income).

• *Allowable employee business expense*

For Pennsylvania personal income tax purposes, an allowable employee business expense must meet *all* of the following criteria [61 Pa. Code § 101.6(c)(5)]:

(1) They must be unreimbursed. For example, an expense reported to and reimbursed by an employer is not an allowable employee deduction.

(2) They must be ordinary, customary, and accepted in the industry or occupation in which the taxpayer is employed.

(3) They must be actually incurred in performing the duties of employment. For example, a fixed mileage allowance or a per diem expense allowance included in an employee's income by neither employer nor employee is not an allowable expense.

(4) They must be reasonable in amount.

(5) They must be necessary to enable an employee to properly perform the duties of employment.

(6) They must be directly related to the performance of the duties of employment.

Filing tips for Schedule UE can be found on the Department's website (UE-489). There is also a link on the Department's website that provides further information.

Comment

Technically, there are no deductions in the Pennsylvania personal income tax. These expenses are not deductions, they are *exclusions* to be used in arriving at total Pennsylvania compensation. However, mathematically they operate as deductions and are commonly called deductions. The authors follow this usage.

• *Examples of disallowed employee business expenses*

The following are examples (not an exhaustive list) of expenses that are not allowable deductions (even if they meet all the above criteria) for Pennsylvania personal income tax purposes:

(1) Dues to fraternal organizations or professional societies.

(2) Subscriptions to publications (even if related to trade or business).

(3) Political contributions.

(4) Charitable contributions.

(5) Commuting expenses.

(6) Cost of meals while working late (unless out of town overnight on business).

(7) Taxes.

(8) Child or elderly care expenses.

(9) Insurance premiums.

(10) Contributions to pension plans.

(11) Legal fees (except to recover back wages).

(12) Bribes, kickbacks, or other illegal payments.

(13) Job-hunting expenses.

(14) Moving expenses (unless for the convenience of the employer).

(15) Educational expenses (except when required by law or by the employer).

• *Audits of schedule UE expenses*

The Department of Revenue has undertaken a program involving the audit of Schedule UE expenses taken by taxpayers. The Department has arbitrarily disallowed expenses without correspondence to taxpayers. Practitioner groups and legislators are questioning this approach, but it still continues. Any taxpayers that are assessed tax or denied refunds should consider filing a timely petition with the Board of Appeals. This is the only way to force the Department to provide a valid explanation for the denial of the deduction.

Board of Finance & Revenue decisions concerning Schedule UE deductions can be found at the Board's website www.patreasury.gov under the Compensation/UE category.

The Department of Revenue provides a template for an employer letter in support of deductions (REV-757) on the Department's website.

¶204 Compensation—Employee Benefits

• *Employee welfare benefit plan*

An "employee welfare benefit plan" is a plan established or maintained to provide benefits to eligible employees or their beneficiaries [61 Pa. Code § 101.1]. The term includes benefits such as the following:

(1) Medical, surgical, or hospital care or benefits in the event of sickness, accident, or disability.

(2) Death benefits.

(3) Scholarships.

(4) Personal expense reimbursements, advancement, or allowances (*e.g.*, rental vehicle, dependent care, and food or housing allowances).

¶204

The term "employee welfare benefit plan" does not include (1) plans that offer a benefit that defers the receipt of compensation or operate in a manner that enables participants to defer the receipt of compensation; or (2) plans established or maintained to provide fringe benefits in the form of use of property or services.

Discriminatory employee welfare benefit plans: The entire cost of employer-provided coverage provided to a highly compensated participant under any discriminatory employee welfare benefit plan is taxable as compensation [61 Pa. Code § 101.6(a), (j)]. A *"discriminatory plan"* is a plan that treats highly compensated participants more favorably in coverage, contributions, or benefits. In determining whether a cafeteria plan is discriminatory, the special rules of IRC § 125(g) apply [61 Pa. Code § 101.1].

Benefits paid in noncash form: Compensation paid in a medium other than cash is valued at its current market value. Compensation paid in the form of employer-provided coverage under an employee welfare benefit plan is valued at cost. The cost is the total amount of payment made during the year by the employer on account of the plan and plan participant, except in the following situations [61 Pa. Code § 101.6(e)]:

(1) In the case of self-insured insurance plans, the cost is the annual cost for financial accounting purposes.

(2) The amount of compensation paid in the form of federally taxable noncash fringe benefits is determined in the same manner as is prescribed by the Internal Revenue Service under federal statutes and regulations.

(3) In the case of cafeteria plans, amounts specified in the plan document as being available to the participant for the purpose of selecting or purchasing benefits, when so used, are included in the total amount of payment made during the year by the employer on account of the plan and plan participant.

Present economic benefit: An amount paid as a contribution shall be considered as received if an employee receives rights, such as coverage under a plan, that are the following [61 Pa. Code § 101.7(e)]:

(1) Of a value that can in no event fall materially below the amount of the contribution.

(2) Presently belonging to the employee.

(3) Unequivocally provided for the ultimate benefit of the employee under whatever contingency and whatever circumstance the occasion for the benefit should arise.

Caution: Commonwealth Does Not Follow Federal

Even though a Pennsylvania cafeteria plan must qualify under IRC § 125, Pennsylvania does not follow all federal rules for cafeteria plans pursuant to IRC § 125. Payments will constitute compensation for Pennsylvania personal income tax purposes if they would be taxable under the Pennsylvania personal income tax if made by an employer outside a cafeteria plan. For example, although not taxable under the Internal Revenue Code, coverage under a dependent care plan providing for the reimbursement of expenses for household or dependent care services would constitute compensation under the Pennsylvania personal income tax because it would be taxable if made by an employer outside a cafeteria plan [61 Pa. Code § 101.6(i)(2)].

• *Cafeteria plans*

Payments made for employee welfare benefit plans under a cafeteria plan will be deemed to be an "employer contribution" for Pennsylvania personal income tax purposes if the following apply [61 Pa. Code § 101.6(i)(1)]:

¶204

(1) The payments were not actually or constructively received, after taking IRC § 101 into account.

(2) The payments were specified in a written cafeteria plan document as being available to the participant (a) for the purpose of selecting or purchasing benefits under a plan and (b) as additional cash remuneration received in lieu of plan coverage.

(3) The benefits selected or purchased are nontaxable under the Internal Revenue Code when offered under a cafeteria plan.

(4) The payments made for the plan would be nontaxable under the Pennsylvania personal income tax if made by the employer outside a cafeteria plan.

If these four requirements are satisfied, cafeteria plan contributions are taxed under the rules for employer payments for employee welfare benefit plans. However, if the benefits are taxable for federal income tax purposes when offered under a cafeteria plan, the payments will also constitute compensation for Pennsylvania personal income tax purposes. Payments also will constitute compensation if they would be taxable under the Pennsylvania personal income tax if made by the employer outside a cafeteria plan. For example, although not taxable under the IRC, coverage under a dependent care plan providing for the reimbursement of expenses for household or dependent care services would constitute compensation under the Pennsylvania personal income tax because it would be taxable if made by an employer outside a cafeteria plan [61 Pa. Code § 101.6(i)(2)].

Wage and salary deductions: In general, any amount lawfully deducted and withheld from the remuneration of an employee and accounted for as part of the employee's total remuneration is considered compensation [61 Pa. Code § 101.7(f)(1)]. However, an amount is not considered to have been paid to the employee if the amount is specified in a written cafeteria plan document as being available to the participant for the purpose of selecting or purchasing benefits under a plan or as additional cash remuneration received in lieu of coverage under a plan. Whether an amount is specified in a cafeteria plan document as being available to a participant shall be determined using federal rules [61 Pa. Code § 101.7(f)(2)].

> *Example:* Landry Corporation is a manufacturing company located in Pennsylvania. Under its collective bargaining agreement with a union, all nonmanagement personnel must contribute $15 per week from their gross salary toward the purchase of medical insurance coverage and $3 per week toward the purchase of group life insurance. The plan is not a federally qualifying cafeteria plan. Landry Corporation must withhold Pennsylvania personal income tax from the $18 contributed by each nonmanagement employer for these benefits.

Contributions to IRC § 401(k) plans: In general, cafeteria plans can offer nontaxable 401(k) plan benefits. However, if an employee can unilaterally elect to have the employer make payments either (1) as contributions to a 401(k) plan or other plan on behalf of the employee or (2) to the employee directly in cash, the payments are not excludable from the employee's compensation [61 Pa. Code § 101.6(k)].

Nondiscriminatory health, accident, or death plans: Compensation does not include payments made by an employer or labor union or elective contributions deemed to be made by an employer under a cafeteria plan for a nondiscriminatory health, accident, or death plan [61 Pa. Code § 101.6(c)(6)]. These payments are excludable from Pennsylvania compensation even if the cafeteria plan is not a federally qualifying cafeteria plan.

> *Example:* C & B is a partnership engaged in providing accounting services. On a nondiscriminatory basis it offers the following fringe benefits to both employees and partners of the firm:

(1) Blue Cross/Blue Shield medical coverage.

(2) Dental and eyeglass coverage with a deductible.

(3) Group-term life insurance with coverage up to the equivalent of the employee's annual salary.

C & B pays the premiums on behalf of all employees and partners for all medical, dental, eyeglass, and insurance coverage directly to the insurance carrier or benefit provider. C & B does not add the premium costs for the benefits to any employee's gross wages, and it accounts for the benefit costs as nonsalary fringe benefit expenses (*i.e.,* the value of the benefits are not shown as an addition to any employee's wages on the paystubs furnished to employees). This is not a federally qualifying cafeteria plan, but the benefits that are paid to employees are excludable from compensation for Pennsylvania personal income tax purposes. However, the premiums paid on behalf of the partners are not deductible or excludable from the income of the partnership or the partners.

• *Fringe benefits in the form of use of employer-provided property*

Remuneration for services received in the form of personal or business use of property is not taxable as compensation if both of the following requirements are met [61 Pa. Code § 101.6a(a)]:

(1) The property belongs to (or is held under a lease by) the employer at the time of use.

(2) No title, interest, or estate in the property is conferred upon, or vested in, another person.

The following are examples of property that is excludable from tax if both of the requirements of 61 Pa. Code § 101.6a(a) are met [61 Pa. Code § 101.6a(b)]:

(1) Aircraft or watercraft.

(2) Athletic facilities or equipment.

(3) Construction or recreation vehicles.

(4) Day care facilities.

(5) Eating facilities.

(6) Educational or training facilities.

(7) Entertainment facilities or equipment.

(8) Housing or clothing.

(9) Office facilities or equipment.

(10) Parking facilities.

(11) Passenger cars and commuter highway vehicles.

(12) Recreational facilities or equipment.

(13) Tools, equipment, or supplies.

• *Fringe benefits in the form of use of employer-provided services*

Remuneration for services received in the form of personal or business use of services is not taxable if either of the following requirements is met [61 Pa. Code § 101.6a(c)]:

(1) The service is provided or supplied directly by the employer or a co-employee.

(2) Rights to the service were procured beforehand by the employer.

The following are examples of services that are not taxable if one of the requirements of 61 Pa. Code § 101.6a(c) is met [61 Pa. Code § 101.6a(d)]:

(1) Air or rail transportation of passengers or cargo.

(2) Day care services or assistance.

(3) Dependent care assistance.

¶204

(4) Eating facility, operation of.

(5) Education or training.

(6) Legal, medical, accounting, or other professional or technical services or assistance, including adoption assistance.

(7) Parking.

(8) Transportation in a commuter highway vehicle.

(9) Tuition reduction provided to an employee or his/her dependents or to a teaching and research assistant.

• *Fringe benefits in the form of consumption of a consumable*

Remuneration for services received in the form of consumption of a consumable (*e.g.*, food and supplies) is not taxable as compensation [61 Pa. Code § 101.6a(e)].

Certain Fringe Benefits Not Taxable Even If Discriminatory

Remuneration in the form of use of property, services, and consumables is not taxable even if the use or service is offered on a discriminatory basis or the employer incurs substantial additional cost (including forgone revenue) in providing the use or service [61 Pa. Code § 101.6a].

¶205 Net Profits

The second class of income subject to taxation is the net income from the operation of a business, profession, or other activity, after provision for all costs and expenses incurred in the conduct thereof, determined either on a cash or accrual basis in accordance with accepted accounting principles and practices (see below) but without deduction of taxes based on income [72 P.S. § 7303(a)(2)]. To constitute net profits, *all* of the following must apply [61 Pa. Code § 103.12(b)]:

(1) The gross profits must be derived from (a) the marketing of a product or service to customers on a commercial basis or from securities employed as working capital in the business operations; (b) accounts and notes receivable from sales of products or services sold in the ordinary course of the business operations; or assets that serve an operational function in the ordinary course of business operations.

(2) The marketing activity must be conducted with the manifest objective of achieving profitable operations.

(3) The marketing activity must be conducted with regularity and continuity and cannot be limited or exclusive.

• *Accepted accounting principles and practices*

"Accepted accounting principles and practices" means those accounting principles, systems, or practices (including the installment method of reporting) that are acceptable by the standards of the accounting profession and that are not inconsistent with Regulations of the Department of Revenue [72 P.S. § 7301(a)]. This means that taxpayers do not have to use federal rules if generally accepted accounting principles (GAAP) differ. For example, for Pennsylvania personal income tax purposes, the Department will *allow* the use of federal uniform capitalization rules for inventory valuation, but the use of these rules is not mandatory. If a taxpayer prefers, the taxpayer may use the rules prescribed by GAAP. Taxpayers may also use GAAP to determine bad debt reserve account and vacation pay accrual account. Consult the instructions to the Form PA-40 for more details.

• *Reporting net profits*

Except for nonresidents, part-year residents, or taxpayers who file jointly for federal purposes and separately for Pennsylvania purposes, taxpayers may use federal profit and loss statements (Schedule C or Schedule F) for reporting net profits from a business. However, there are some significant differences between federal and Pennsylvania tax treatment of some business deductions, for which adjustments to the federal statements may be required. Taxpayers who submit a Federal Schedule C or F must itemize and show adjustments for Pennsylvania purposes.

• *Deductions*

Allowable deductions: Under Pennsylvania personal income tax law, taxpayers may deduct ordinary, necessary, and reasonable expenses currently paid or incurred during the taxable year that are directly related to and necessary for the production and marketing of their products, goods, and services *in the marketplace.*

Commercial Enterprise Test

The requirement that goods or services be offered to others in a marketplace is referred to as the "commercial enterprise test" [*Pennsylvania Personal Income Tax Guide,* Ch. 11, p. 2].

Disallowed deductions: In computing net profits, deductions are not allowed for any item of cost, expense, or liability derived or incurred in connection with, or attributable to, any of the following [61 Pa. Code § 103.12(c)]:

(1) Ownership or disposition of assets that are held for investment purposes or otherwise serve an investment function.

(2) Trading in securities for personal purposes and not for customers' accounts.

(3) Sale, discontinuation, or abandonment of a business or a business segment.

(4) Any tax imposed on, or measured by, gross or net earned or unearned income.

(5) An isolated or nonrecurring transaction that is not a normal or routine business activity.

• *Federal/Commonwealth differences*

The federal computation of net profits is usually acceptable for Pennsylvania personal income tax purposes [*Pennsylvania Tax Update No. 72,* Pennsylvania Department of Revenue, November/December 1997]. Effective January 1, 2014, aligns Pennsylvania with federal rules to allow for a $5,000 start-up business deduction in the year a new business is established. (Act 52 of 2013). However, there are some significant differences between federal and Pennsylvania tax treatment of some business deductions.

The Department's auditors have been reviewing returns for the possibility of moving certain active rental activity from the Net Profits Income Category to the Rental Income Category. This is done when a loss from the rental activity is used to offset income from the net profits category.

To avoid this treatment, the taxpayer must show that the rental activity meets the Commercial Enterprise test. Board of Finance and Revenue decisions can be found at the Board's website (www.patreasury.org) under Commercial Enterprise.

Mandatory adjustments to federal profit and loss statements: If using a federal profit and loss statement for a business or form, the following adjustments *must* be made:

¶205

(1) The federal labor hires deduction or federal wage deduction does not apply for Pennsylvania personal income tax purposes. If claimed for federal purposes, these deductions must be added back to the wage expense.

(2) If claiming the Pennsylvania Employment Incentive Payment Credit (EIPC) and/or the Pennsylvania Jobs Creation Tax Credit, the total wage expense must be reduced by the amount of the credit.

(3) Contributions made as a self-employed individual to one's own pension plan (*e.g.*, IRA, Keogh plan).

(4) Federal, state, and local taxes may be deducted, but not taxes based on gross or net income, such as the federal income tax; taxes paid to other states or foreign countries based on income; estate, inheritance, legacy, succession, and gift taxes; and assessments for improvements. The one-half deduction of the self-employment tax allowed for federal purposes is not deductible for Pennsylvania personal income tax purposes. The Philadelphia Business Privilege tax is an allowable deduction, if not already deducted on the federal schedule.

(5) If claiming the Pennsylvania Research and Development Tax Credit or the Pennsylvania Waste Tire Recycling Investment Tax Credit, the direct business expense must be reduced by the amount of the expenses incurred in the activities that qualified the claim for the credit(s).

(6) Intangible drilling costs may be deducted in the year of investment for Federal purposes, but Pennsylvania's policy is that this deduction must be taken ratably over the life of the well. (See Notice 2013-04) The Department of Revenue has allowed taxpayers, in settlements in the Commonwealth Court, and at the Board of Finance and Revenue to follow the rules set out in Information Notice Personal Income Tax 2013-04 for years prior to 2014.

• *Intangible Drilling Cost Deductions for Tax Years Prior to 2014*

The Department of Revenue is currently allowing taxpayers who have claimed IDC deductions based in the federal law and who have appealed their assessments to settle their cases by following the provisions of the law that apply to tax years 2014 and subsequent.

The taxpayer will take 40% of the IDC deduction the first year and the remainder ratably over the next nine years. These procedures are set out in Information Notice 2013-04 Personal Income Tax.

Currently, the taxpayer must have his case before the Board of Finance and Revenue or the Commonwealth Court to receive this type of settlement.

Effective beginning with tax year 2014, permits a taxpayer to recover intangible drilling costs as defined by federal rules by using either a 10-year amortization period or an election to currently expense up to one-third of the allowable costs and amortize the remaining costs over 10 years for personal income tax. In a draft bulletin, the Department of Revenue has taken the position that all IDC, capitalization and expense elections must be made at the entity level. At the federal level, these decisions are made at the partner level. (Act 52 of 2013).

Optional adjustments to federal profit and loss statements: If using a federal profit and loss statement for a business or farm, the following adjustments *may* be made:

(1) The federal percentage limitations on business meals and entertainment do not apply. Pennsylvania allows 100% of these expenses to be deducted.

(2) Sales tax on depreciable business assets may be a current expense for Pennsylvania personal income tax purposes. On disposition, the Pennsylvania basis and the federal basis will be different.

(3) Charitable contributions made from a business account that the recipient publicly acknowledges are allowable deductions for Pennsylvania personal income tax purposes. Personal charitable contributions are never allowable for Pennsylvania personal income tax purposes.

(4) Any capitalization rules established by the trade, profession, or industry may be used under its generally accepted accounting principles and practices. Once elected, this method must be consistently used.

(5) Any generally recognized or currently accepted depreciation method for business or farm activity (including IRC § 179) may be used. Once elected, this method must be consistently followed.

(6) Itemized ordinary and necessary business expenses that are directly related to the production of goods or services and reasonable in amount that are allowable under GAAP or Financial Accounting Standards Board (FASB) rules may be taken even if limited by the IRS.

Employee Fringe Benefits

Because of recent statutory changes many benefits that used to be taxable under Pennsylvania law are no longer taxable (*e.g.*, personal use of employer's property; see ¶ 204). The Department of Revenue has issued a brochure (Form REV-634) that explains these changes.

• *Depreciation*

Depreciation on assets employed in the operation of a business or in the production of rents or royalties is deductible for personal income tax purposes if the following criteria are met [*Pennsylvania Tax Update No. 50*, Pennsylvania Department of Revenue, May/June 1994]:

(1) The assets render services in the production of income from the operation of a business or from rents, royalties, patents, and copyrights;

(2) The cost is spread over the reasonably expected useful life of the asset in such a way as to allocate it as equitably as possible to the periods of service obtained from the use of the assets; and

(3) The depreciation deductions are obtained through the use of a formula acceptable by the standards of the accounting profession.

Depreciable basis: The depreciable basis of an asset is its adjusted basis for the purpose of determining gain or loss on the sale, exchange, or other disposition for personal income tax purposes (see ¶ 206) at the time the property is placed into service, less its reasonably estimated net salvage value at the end of its reasonably estimated useful economic life.

Revised service lives or salvage values: Revisions in the service life or salvage value of an asset must be made whenever facts are discovered or events occur that would change earlier estimates. Such changes affect only the remaining useful life of the asset; adjustments of prior depreciation deductions are not required or allowed.

Use of federal guidelines: Service lives and salvage values determined under the Federal Class Life ACR System and IRC §§ 168 and 169 may not be appropriate for Pennsylvania personal income tax purposes. Nevertheless, taxpayers may use these federal rules as a convenience for Pennsylvania personal income tax purposes, but only on the condition that they are also used for federal income tax purposes.

Basis adjustments: The basis of depreciable assets must be reduced (but not below zero) each year by the greater of the following:

(1) The amount actually deducted on a Pennsylvania return and not disallowed (but only to the extent the deduction resulted in a reduction of income).

(2) The amount allowable using the straight-line method of depreciation without regard to whether the deduction would result in a reduction of income.

¶205

• *Partnership income*

A partner is taxed on his or her share of partnership income, whether or not it is distributed [72 P.S. §7306]. In general, the amount of partnership income to be reported by a partner is his or her allocation under the partnership agreement. However, the partnership agreement will be disregarded if the allocation does not have substantial economic effect. See Instructions for Form PA-65. The Department of Revenue uses the federal definition of "substantial economic effect" to determine whether the partnership agreement should be used or disregarded. A key to this concept is that the allocation must have substantial economic effect independent of any tax consequences in order for the partnership agreement to be used. Classification of income is made at the partnership level. See discussion of partnership income at ¶1817. Not all income from a partnership, however, is business income. See ¶1817.

Partnership Income Not Automatically Net Profits

Choosing to form a partnership or to associate with others does not of itself make the income of the partnership, entity, or associates net profits [61 Pa. Code § 103.12(d)]. If the income from a partnership does not satisfy the statutory requirements as net profits, the income will not be classified as net profits.

• *Guaranteed payments to retired partners*

Guaranteed payments to a retired partner are taxable as compensation on the same basis as deferred compensation is taxed to former employees of a partnership if the following conditions apply:

(1) The retired partner rendered no services with respect to any trade or business carried on by the partnership or its successors during the taxable year, ending within or with the partner's taxable year in which the amounts were received.

(2) No obligations, whether certain in amount or contingent on a subsequent event, exist during the taxable year of the partnership or its successors, ending within or with the partner's taxable year in which the amounts were received except with respect to retirement payments under the plan.

(3) The partner's share of the capital of the partnership has been paid to the partner in full before the taxable year of the partnership or its successors, ending within or with the partner's taxable year in which such amounts were received.

However, if amounts received by a retiring partner pursuant to a written plan of the partnership that provides (1) for guaranteed payments on account of retirement to partners generally or to a class or classes of partners and (2) for the payments to continue at least until such partner's death, the amounts are excludable retirement benefits if (a) the these requirements are met and (b) the plan otherwise constitutes a qualifying retirement benefit plan.

Other payments received in liquidation of the interest of a retiring partner will be considered as (1) a distributive share of partnership income if the amount thereof is determined with regard to the partnership income, (2) a guaranteed payment, or (3) a distribution made in exchange for the partner's interest in partnership property (including the partnership's unrealized receivables and goodwill, unless the partnership agreement provides otherwise) [*Pennsylvania Personal Income Tax Guide*, Pennsylvania Department of Revenue, Chapter 6, pp. 28-29].

See ¶ 201 for discussion of guaranteed payments to nonretired partners.

¶205

• *Securities transactions*

Only the following participants in the stock, securities, options, derivatives, futures, or commodities market are engaged in the marketing of a product or service to customers [61 Pa. Code § 103.12(e)]:

(1) Those who maintain or provide a marketplace or facilities for bringing together purchasers and sellers of financial investment products.

(2) Those licensed to act as customers' agents who charge a negotiated commission for executing transactions, without taking title to the particular positions they buy or sell.

(3) Investment counselor as defined in 61 Pa. Code § 103.12(e)(3).

(4) Licensed dealers who meet all of the conditions of 61 Pa. Code § 103.12(e)(4).

(5) Underwriters who facilitate initial sales of financial investment products by acting either as licensed dealers in a principal capacity or as brokers in an agency capacity.

Only that portion of a person's securities activities that involve operations as a market establishment, broker, investment counselor, or dealer produces income classified as net profits [61 Pa. Code § 103.12(f)].

¶206 Net Gains or Income from Disposition of Property

The third class of income subject to taxation is net gains or net income, less net losses, derived from the sale, exchange or other disposition of property, including real property, tangible personal property, intangible personal property, obligations issued by the federal government, or obligations (issued on or after February 1, 1994) by Pennsylvania, any public authority, commission, board or other agency created by the Commonwealth, any of its political subdivisions or any public authority created by its political subdivisions. Net gains or income from disposition of property are determined in accordance with accepted accounting principles and practices [72 P.S. § 7303(a)(3)]. This rules does not apply to depreciable tangible property used in a trade or business. See "Business property," below.

• *Reorganizations*

The exchange of stock or securities in a corporation that is a party to a reorganization in pursuance of a plan of reorganization, solely for stock or securities in such corporation or in another corporation that is a party to the reorganization, and the transfer of property to a corporation by one or more persons solely in exchange for stock or securities in such corporation is not a sale, exchange or other disposition for Pennsylvania personal income tax purposes if immediately after the exchange such person or persons are in control of the corporation [72 P.S. § 7303(a)(3)(iv)]. The taxpayer's basis for the stock or securities received in a reorganization is the same as the taxpayer's actual or attributed basis for the property surrendered in exchange for the stock [72 P.S. § 7303(a)(3)(iv)(f)].

• *Common trust funds*

A transfer of all or substantially all of its assets by a common trust fund as defined in § 584 of the Internal Revenue Code of 1986 (transferee) to another company or companies described in § 851 of the Internal Revenue Code of 1986 in exchange for stock or units of beneficial interest in the transferor(s) does not result in a taxable gain or loss if no gain or loss is recognized for federal income tax purposes. The basis of the beneficial interest received by transferee is the actual basis of the assets transferred [72 P.S. § 7303(a)(3)(v)]. This provision took effect January 1, 1997.

- *Disposition of going concern*

Gain from a disposition of a sole proprietor's proprietary interest in a going concern is earned, received, or acquired from sources within Pennsylvania if the gain is attributable to the disposition of real or tangible property with a situs in Pennsylvania (including inventoriable or operational items) and intangible personal property employed in the trade, profession, occupation, or business carried on by the sole proprietor in Pennsylvania. Gain derived from a disposition of a proprietary interest in a corporation, investment company, or investment partnership, a partner's interest in a partnership, a member's interest in a limited liability company, or a shareholder's share in a Pennsylvania S corporation or business trust does not constitute income from sources within Pennsylvania for a nonresident. For more detail, see *Personal Income Tax Bulletin 2005-02*, December 15, 2005.

- *Partnership interests*

A transfer of an interest in an enterprise treated as a partnership for personal income tax purposes for an interest in another such enterprise does not result in taxable gain or loss for Pennsylvania personal income tax purposes unless the gain or loss is taxable for federal income tax purposes. Gains and losses from a liquidation made in connection with such enterprises or an exchange made pursuant to a statutory merger, consolidation, or division are also not taxable for Pennsylvania purposes unless taxable for federal income tax purposes. The taxpayer's basis for the interest received in such transactions is the same as the taxpayer's actual or attributed basis for the interest surrendered in the transaction [72 P.S. § 7303(a)(3)(vi)].

- *Business property*

Gains or losses on the disposition of depreciable tangible personal property held for productive use in a trade or business should not be reported as net gains or income from disposition of property but as net income from a business, trade, or profession (see ¶ 205) if the sale proceeds are used to acquire property to replace the business property sold.

If the proceeds from the sale of property used in the trade of business is reinvested in the business than the gain can be excluded from tax. (See PIT Guide Chapter 12, pages 5 and 16)

- *Like Kind Exchanges*

Section 1031 of the Internal Revenue Code allows certain exchanges of property to be treated as tax free exchanges. Since the Pennsylvania Personal Income Tax Law is decoupled from the federal tax law, Pennsylvania follows the rules set out in generally accepted accounting principles. The Department has taken the position that a taxpayer must keep his books on a GAPP basis to be entitled to tax free exchange treatment. (See Chapter 12 of the PIT Guide), though PIT Bulletin 2006-7 does not contain this requirement. Although the accounting profession has recognized the use of the tax basis of accounting (OCBOA SAS62) the Department of Revenue has been unwilling to allow taxpayers on the tax basis of accounting to receive the benefits of like kind exchange reporting.

There are several well written dissenting opinions on this issue that can be found at the Board of Finance and Revenue website.

- *Partnership distributions*

Distributions to partners in excess of basis are considered gains from the sale of a partnership interest.

• *Division and transfer of interests in oil and natural gas*

If a mineral rights estate owner sells the mineral rights, the consideration less the owner's basis in the mineral rights and other costs associated with the sale is taxable. If the owner owns the entire fee simple interest in the real estate, the owner must allocate a portion of the basis to the mineral rights. A mineral rights owner who is the lessor under an oil or gas lease may sell and assign the rights to income from future production payments, including royalties, under the lease. For Pennsylvania personal income tax purposes, the sale and assignment are treated as an anticipatory assignment of income. A donative transfer of income from production payments under an oil or gas lease is also an anticipatory assignment of future income. For details see PIT Tax Bulletin 2011-XX, (Department of Revenue, January 2011).

The Pennsylvania Department of Revenue (DOR) has issued a notice regarding the property, realty transfer, and personal income tax treatment associated with the division and transfer of interests related to oil and natural gas. Rents and royalties, conveyance of mineral rights, estate by sale or gift, and assignment of an oil or gas lease through donation or sale are discussed in the context of personal income tax [*Informational Notice 2012-04*, Pennsylvania Department of Revenue, October 10, 2012].

• *Capital gains distributions*

Capital gains distributions from mutual funds or other regulated investment companies are classified as dividends, not gains from disposition of property. See Form PA-40R Instructions.

Federal/Commonwealth Differences

Federal income tax law allows optional adjustment to basis (see IRC §§734 and 743). Pennsylvania law has no provisions allowing these adjustments for Pennsylvania personal income tax purposes. Furthermore, there is no Pennsylvania election like that allowed by IRC §732(b). See general discussion of basis, below.

• *Transfers incident to divorce*

Property transferred incident to divorce is not taxable for Pennsylvania personal income tax purposes to the extent the gain or loss is not recognized for IRC §1041 purposes. Some private letter rulings from the Office of Chief Counsel have classified such transfers as gifts, not exchanges.

The questions that generally arise with respect to net gains or income from disposition of property concern (1) determination of basis, (2) method of reporting gains, and (3) nonrecognition of gains or losses.

• *Basis*

Ordinarily, the basis of inherited property is fair market value at the date of decedent's death, and the basis of property acquired in any other manner is cost [61 Pa. Code §103.13(b)]. The Tax Reform Code provides that the basis of property acquired before June 1, 1971, shall be the fair market value on June 1, 1971. However, in *Cmwlth. v. Ringling*, 509 A.2d 936 (Pa.Commw. 1980), the Commonwealth Court ruled that in some cases this requirement, strictly interpreted, would lead to absurd and unreasonable results. As a result, the statute is interpreted to allow taxpayers to use a basis equal to the *higher* of acquisition cost or June 1, 1971, value for property acquired prior to June 1, 1971. The Department of Revenue later issued regulations that incorporate this judicial interpretation.

Property acquired prior to June 1, 1971: The basis for determination of gain or loss on property acquired prior to June 1, 1971, is as follows [61 Pa. Code §103.13(f)]:

(1) The basis for determination of gain is the greater of cost or fair market value on June 1, 1971.

(2) The basis for determination of loss is cost or other adjusted basis without reference to the fair market value on June 1, 1971.

(3) If the selling price is greater than cost but less than fair market value on June 1, 1971, the taxpayer has no gain or loss.

Federal/Commonwealth Differences

Pennsylvania generally follows the federal rules on basis for property acquired by gift or by inheritance, with two exceptions: (1) a joint tenancy interest acquired from a joint tenant by survivorship does not receive a stepped-up basis for Pennsylvania purposes as it does for federal purposes, and (2) there is no alternate valuation date for Pennsylvania purposes. In Pennsylvania if you use the selling price of the asset as its date of death value for inheritance tax purposes, its inheritance tax value can be used as its tax basis if its inheritance tax value was accepted by the Department of Revenue [*Pennsylvania Personal Income Tax Guide*, Chapter 12, p. 15; Pennsylvania Department of Revenue, http://www.revenue.state.pa.us/revenue/lib/revenue/pitguide_chapter_12.pdf].

The fair market value of property on June 1, 1971, is one of the following: (1) the opening price on June 1, 1971; (2) the price of the last sale during the preceding week if it was not traded on June 1, 1971; or (3) the average of the high and low price or the average of the bid and asked quotations on June 1, 1971, which is appropriate, if it was not traded on or during the week preceding June 1, 1971 (see *Income Tax Pamphlet Number 3*, "Gain or Loss on Property Acquired Prior to June 1, 1971").

• *Tax benefit rule*

The Department of Revenue takes the position that, in the case of individuals, the basis of depreciable property (*e.g.*, rental property) must be reduced by a minimum of straight-line depreciation even if the straight-line depreciation provided no tax benefit (*e.g.*, the rental property generated losses that could not be used). If the taxpayer used accelerated depreciation and received no tax benefit, the taxpayer may reduce the basis only by the difference between straight-line and accelerated depreciation. This treatment for individuals is not consistent with the treatment afforded S corporations and partnerships. In *Wirth et al. v. Commwlth.*, 82-85 MAP 2012 the Pennsylvania Supreme Court held that a nonresident taxpayer could exclude income from forgiveness of interest if that interest was deducted in the taxpayer's return in prior years.

Federal/Commonwealth Difference

Frequently a taxpayer will receive a federal tax benefit but not a Pennsylvania tax benefit. This is true because of the Commonwealth prohibition against offsetting between or among classes of income (see ¶201). In such cases, the Pennsylvania basis will be different from the federal basis (see ¶205 for examples of other situations in which Pennsylvania basis differs from federal basis).

• *Method of reporting gains*

In general, all gains or losses in this class of income are reported in full as ordinary taxable income. However, Pennsylvania allows the installment sales method of reporting upon the sale of tangible personal property or real property. The installment method is disallowed for the sale of intangible personal property, for transactions the object of which is the lending of money or the rendering of services, or the sale of a principal residence where the taxpayer elects to exclude gain [72 P.S. §7301(1.1)]. Therefore, the sale of securities, partnership interests, or accounts receivable cannot be reported on the installment sales method. The installment sales method can be used if the seller is to receive at least one payment after the end of the tax year in which the sale took place. Dealers in tangible personal property who regularly sell on the installment plan can still report on the installment sales method on a Pennsylvania Schedule C, even though for taxable years beginning after January 1, 1988, they generally cannot report on the installment method for federal income tax purposes. If a Pennsylvania S corporation uses the installment sales method for book purposes, it can use the installment sales method for personal income tax purposes. Any adjustments should be made on Schedule CF and should include an adequate explanation [*Legislative Alert* (PICPA), Vol. VIII, Issue 2, July 31, 1989, pp. 4-5]. If you elect the installment method, you allocate the gain in equal proportion to each payment to be received.

NOTE: Interest that is directly from the installment sale contract or agreement is reported as gain from the disposition of property. See Form PA-40R Instructions.

Federal/Commonwealth Differences

The Department of Revenue does not follow the practice of requiring you to recapture depreciation in the year of sale in the event of disposition of installment obligations. Note, also, that for Pennsylvania personal income tax purposes, the installment method does not apply unless you elect it, while for federal income tax purposes the installment method applies if all criteria are met unless you *elect out* of the installment method.

• *Nonrecognition of gains or losses*

The Pennsylvania Tax Reform Code provides for nonrecognition of gain or loss in only three situations:

(1) Corporate reorganizations.

(2) Transfers to controlled corporations.

(3) Gains on the disposition of obligations exempt from the Pennsylvania personal income tax if these obligations were issued before February 1, 1994. Gains on government obligations issued on or after February 1, 1994, are taxable. See discussion of exempt obligations, below.

• *Exempt obligations*

In general, all obligations, interest on obligations, and income from obligations issued by the Commonwealth of Pennsylvania, any public authority, commission, board, or other agency created by the Commonwealth, or any political subdivision of the Commonwealth, or any public authority created by any political subdivision of the Commonwealth are free from taxation for state and local purposes. However, the Tax Reform Code specifically provides that these obligations are subject to the inheritance and estate tax and that profits, gains, or income derived from the sale, exchange, or other disposition of state and local obligations issued on or after February 1, 1994, are taxable. Gains on state and local obligations issued before February 1, 1994, continue to be exempt [72 P.S. § 7901]. Federal law exempts obligations issued by or on behalf of the U.S. Government [31 U.S. C. § 742].

Gains in Other States

Gains from the disposition of obligations of other states and countries are taxable. Remember, although you can use losses to offset gains *within* a class of income, you cannot use a net loss in one class to offset a new gain in another class. A net loss that cannot be used in the year incurred can never be used because there are no carryback and carryforward provisions for capital gains in the Pennsylvania personal income tax system.

• *Exclusion of gains from the sale or exchange of a principal residence*

All gains or losses from the sale, exchange or other disposition of a taxpayer's principal residence are excluded from Pennsylvania taxable income [72 P.S. § 7303(a)(3)]. A principal residence is property that has been owned and used by the taxpayer as his or her principal residence for periods aggregating at least two years during the five-year period ending on the date of the sale, exchange or disposition. If a taxpayer, during the required five-year period, has used only a portion of the residence as his or her principal residence, only the gain attributable to the portion used as a principal residence can be excluded. No gain or loss can be excluded if there was a prior sale, exchange, or disposition by the taxpayer of a principal residence *unless* the disposition was because of a change in employment, health or, to the extent provided in regulations, unforeseen circumstances.

The Department of Revenue has taken the position that an installment sale of a principal residence qualifies for the 100% exclusion and that a previous nonresidential use will disqualify a property from the 100% exclusion only if the taxpayer rented or used the property with the intention to realize a profit. If a taxpayer did not have a profit motive, the sale qualifies for exclusion (*e.g.*, rental of home during period of trying to find a buyer where no depreciation allowances were claimed against the rental income).

NOTE: For more details about the computation of net gains and losses from disposition of property, see 61 Pa. Code § 103.13.

¶207 Net Gains or Income from Rents, Royalties, Patents, and Copyrights

The fourth class of taxable income is "net gains or income derived from or in the form of rents, royalties, patents and copyrights" [72 P.S. § 7303(a)(4)]. Pennsylvania statutes and regulations are silent with respect to the method to be used to compute net gains or income from these sources. In general, federal rules are acceptable in the computation of net income from this class of income. Nonresidents pay tax only from the use of property located or used in Pennsylvania. For more details, see the Instructions to Form PA-40.

¶208 Dividends

The fifth class of taxable income is dividends [72 P.S. § 7303(a)(5)]. Dividends are any distribution in cash or property made by a corporation, association or business trust out of accumulated earnings and profits, or out of earnings and profits of the year in which such dividend is paid. Dividends do not include a return of premium [61 Pa. Code § 101.1].

• *"Dividends" of certain financial institutions*

Certain financial institutions (*e.g.*, savings and loan associations, mutual savings banks, cooperative banks, some credit unions) refer to credits to depositors' accounts as "dividends." These are, however, in actuality interest on the funds deposited in these accounts and are, therefore, includible as interest, not dividends.

• *Exempt interest dividends*

The term "exempt interest dividends" means income received from a mutual trust that is attributable to obligations that are excludable from the Pennsylvania personal income tax. However, whether or not income from a mutual fund is excludable depends on the organization of the mutual fund as well as the underlying assets producing the income. If the mutual fund is organized as a business fund, all income from the fund is taxable. If a mutual fund is organized as a fixed portfolio investment trust, the portion of the income from the trust attributable to Pennsylvania exempt obligations is excludable; the rest is taxable.

¶209 Interest

The sixth class of taxable income for Pennsylvania personal income tax purposes includes interest derived from obligations that are not statutorily free from state or local taxation under any act of the General Assembly of Pennsylvania or under the laws of the United States and (effective for taxable years beginning after December 31, 2004) any amount paid under contract of life insurance or endowment or annuity contract that is includible in gross income for federal income tax purposes [72 P.S. §7303(a)(6)].

Exchange of Life Insurance Annuity Contracts

The requirements of IRC §1035 apply to the taxability of an exchange of life insurance annuity contracts [72 P.S. §7303(a.5)]. Under federal rules, an exchange is not taxable if no cash is involved. If the exchange involves cash, the amount of cash received is taxable as interest income.

Generally, interest includes any charge for the use or detention of money or for a forbearance from enforcement of a debt that is due (whether or not payable as such or as principal) including (for taxable years beginning on or after January 1, 1993) any excess of a publicly offered obligation's stated redemption price at maturity over the first price at which a substantial amount of the obligations included in the issue is sold to the public. For this purpose, the public does not include underwriters or wholesalers. In general, interest received by or credited to the taxpayer is fully taxable [61 Pa. Code § 103.16(a)].

Taxable interest includes the following:

(1) Interest on savings or other bank deposits.

(2) Interest on coupon bonds.

(3) Interest on open accounts, promissory notes, mortgages, and corporate bonds or debentures.

(4) Interest portions of condemnation awards.

(5) Usurious interest (unless state law classified it as payment of principal).

(6) Interest on legacies.

(7) Interest on life insurance proceeds held under an agreement to pay interest thereon.

(8) Interest on tax refunds.

Caution: Federal/Commonwealth Difference

You cannot assume that if an obligation is exempt from the federal income tax it is also exempt from the Pennsylvania personal income tax. The exclusion for U.S. tax-exempt obligations does not automatically extend to those obligations whose sole statutory basis for exclusion is the Internal Revenue Code.

• *Bonds*

If a taxpayer purchases bonds where interest has accrued but has not been paid, interest that is in arrears but has accrued at the time of purchase is not taxable interest. If subsequently paid, the payments are returns of capital that reduce basis. Interest that accrues after the purchase date is taxable interest income for the year in which it is received or accrued, depending on the taxpayer's method of accounting [61 Pa. Code § 103.16(b)]. If bonds are sold between interest dates, part of the sale price represents taxable interest accrued to the date of the sale [61 Pa. Code § 103.16(c)].

• *Annuities*

Interest does not include amounts received under an annuity contract [61 Pa. Code § 103.16(d)].

• *Unstated or imputed interest*

Unstated or imputed interest for a taxable year beginning on or after January 1, 1993, including interest derived from government obligations, is computed in the same manner as it is required to be computed for federal income tax purposes [61 Pa. Code § 103.16(f)].

• *Interest on federal and Pennsylvania obligations*

Not all interest on U.S. or Commonwealth obligations retains its tax-exempt status for Pennsylvania personal income tax purposes when it passes through a regulated investment company to an individual taxpayer. Currently, the Department of Revenue takes the position that only those investment companies that have established fixed portfolio unit investment trusts to hold governmental obligations can pass nontaxable interest through to their shareholders. Interest received from open-ended or closed-ended diversified management companies is taxable. Note that the issue is the taxability of interest from U.S. and Pennsylvania obligations. Interest from obligations of other states, municipalities of other states, GNMA or FNMA certificates, or repurchase agreements are never considered exempt. Remember, too, that any *gain* from the disposition of the underlying shares in the trust or fund is a taxable gain from the disposition of property.

• *Interest on repurchase agreements*

An entity may invest its cash with a bank or other financial institution overnight and over the weekend in what are commonly referred to as repurchase agreements ("repos"). Quite often this "investment" is secured by U.S. government instruments that the bank has purchased. If the investment is merely secured by the U.S. government instrument (collateralized borrowing) the interest income is not considered to be from a U.S. government instrument. However, if the entity actually purchases the U.S. security and then resells it to the bank under the "repo" agreement, the interest received is from a U.S. security. The key is the transfer of ownership. The Pennsylvania Department of Revenue has taken the position that interest on repurchase agreements is not tax-exempt interest from U.S. obligations; it is taxable interest (*i.e.,* collateralized borrowing). The U.S. Supreme Court agreed in *Nebraska Dept. of Revenue v. Loewenstein*, 513 U.S. 123 (1994).

• *Loss from fraudulent investment scheme*

Pennsylvania requires that losses from fraudulent investment schemes be taken as a loss from a sale or exchange. There is Federal authority [*Burnet v. Logan*, 283 U.S. 404 (1931)]that would allow refund claims to be filed on all interest reported from the fraudulent investments.

¶210 Gambling and Lottery Winnings

The law establishes a seventh class of taxable income that comprises gambling and lottery winnings. All gambling and lottery winnings, other than prizes of the Pennsylvania State Lottery, are taxable [72 P.S. § 7303(a)(7)]. Taxable winnings include gains arising from gambling and lotteries. In calculating gains, you may deduct gambling and lottery losses (other than losses on the Pennsylvania State Lottery), but you cannot deduct the costs and expenses incurred in connection with gambling and lottery activity. In addition to the recordkeeping requirements under Article III of the Tax Reform Code (see ¶ 111), taxpayers must maintain detailed records substantiating gambling and lottery losses. The burden of proof is on the taxpayer to prove that gambling losses have occurred [61 Pa. Code § 103.17].

Federal Form W-2G Required

Any taxpayer who is required to file a Form W-2G (relating to certain gambling winnings) with the U.S. Treasury Department from sources within Pennsylvania must also file a copy of the form with the Pennsylvania Department of Revenue by March 1 of each year or, if filed electronically, by March 31 of each year [72 P.S. § 7335(e)].

¶211 Net Gains or Income Derived Through Estates or Trusts

The eighth class of income is income "derived through estates or trusts" [72 P.S. § 7303(a)(8)]. A "trust" for this purpose does not include any trust that can be revoked or a real estate investment trust for federal income tax purposes [61 Pa. Code § 105.1]. An estate or trust is an independent taxable entity and may establish a taxable year different from the taxable years of beneficiaries. A beneficiary's income from an estate or trust is his or her portion of income for the tax year of the fiduciary ending within or with the beneficiary's tax year. Whether or not the income is taxable to the beneficiaries depends on the terms of the trust and the actual distributions made to beneficiaries and on the residency status of the parties involved. Resident beneficiaries must report *all* estate or trust income received during the year. Nonresident beneficiaries must report only that portion of estate or trust income received during the year that is attributable to sources within Pennsylvania [61 Pa. Code § 105.4(c)(1), (2)]. In general, the situs of intangibles is considered to be at the taxpayer's place of residence. Therefore, interest, dividends, and gains on intangibles from a trust are excludable for a nonresident taxpayer, even if the trust is administered in Pennsylvania. However, gains on tangible personal property and real property are taxable to a nonresident if the trust is administered in Pennsylvania.

Caution: Separate Class of Income

According to regulations, income retains the same character in the hands of the beneficiary that it had in the hands of the fiduciary [61 Pa. Code § 103.18(a)]. Income derived through estates and trusts is a separate class of income that cannot be offset against or combined with other classes of income. Thus, a beneficiary's income from an estate or trust should be reported as a one-line item as one class of income of the beneficiary's Form PA-40. The beneficiary's K-1 may have items in separate classes of income, but these should be aggregated to a single line of the beneficiary's return.

• *Crime victim awards*

Awards received by crime victims from the Pennsylvania Bureau of Victims' Services are not considered compensation taxable as income for Pennsylvania personal income tax purposes [18 P.S. § 11.708].

Reparation awards for victims of Nazi persecution: Awards received in reparation for the seizure, theft, requisition, or involuntary conversion of the income or property of victims of Nazi persecution receive special treatment for Pennsylvania personal income tax purposes [61 Pa. Code § § 125.41—125.43].

¶212 S Corporation Distributions

The following are guidelines in determining the treatment of one's distributive share of Pennsylvania S corporation income:

(1) The character of any item of income or losses included in a shareholder's pro rata share is determined as if it were realized directly by the shareholder from the source in which it was realized by the corporation. Income or loss is prorated daily for assignment to shareholders during the taxable year [72 P.S. § 7307.9].

¶211

(2) Any deduction (except a net loss deduction) that was disallowed when a corporation was subject to the corporate net income tax is allowed in years in which the corporation is a Pennsylvania S corporation to the same extent and in the same manner that the deduction would have been allowed if it had remained subject to the corporate net income tax [72 P.S. § 7307.8(e)]. However, nonresident shareholders are allowed these "previously disallowed deductions" only to the extent they would have been considered Pennsylvania-source income [72 P.S. § 7307.9(d)].

(3) The aggregate amount of losses taken into account cannot exceed the sum of the adjusted basis of the shareholder's stock in the Pennsylvania S corporation and the shareholder's adjusted basis of any indebtedness of the Pennsylvania S corporation to the shareholder before adjustment. Any losses that cannot be used are lost. Loss carryovers are not allowed [72 P.S. § 7307.10(b)]. However, a year in which a Pennsylvania S election is in effect is considered a taxable year for purposes of the three-year net loss carryover period under the corporate net income tax [72 P.S. § 7401(c)(4)(d)-(f)].

(4) Both resident and nonresident shareholders must make estimated tax payments with respect to their distributive shares of income from a Pennsylvania S corporation.

(5) Resident shareholders may take a credit for income taxes paid by the corporation to other states with respect to their pro rata share of the S corporation's income (subject to the limitations provided by law) [72 P.S. § 7314(a)].

(6) The Department of Revenue takes the position that nonresident shareholders are taxable on their share of income from Pennsylvania S corporations, even if they have no other connection with Pennsylvania. However, remember that nonbusiness income derived from outside Pennsylvania is not taxable to nonresident shareholders because it is allocated to another state. (See ¶ 128 for explanation of allocation and apportionment.)

(7) Your stock basis must be increased by your share of corporation income (including nontaxable income), decreased by distributions not included in your income, and decreased by your share of corporate losses (to the extent you got a tax benefit from the loss deduction). However, you can never reduce your basis below zero.

• *Distributions from S corporations*

If the corporation has no accumulated earnings and profits, a distribution to you will not be included in your income if it does not exceed your adjusted basis in your stock. If the distribution is greater than your basis, treat it as a gain from the sale or exchange of property [72 P.S. § 7307.12(a)]. If the corporation has accumulated earnings and profits from non-Pennsylvania S years, a distribution is taxable to you as a dividend to the extent of the earnings and profits. Treat any distribution in excess of earnings and profits as a reduction in your adjusted stock basis and then as a gain from the sale or exchange of property when your adjusted basis reaches zero. [72 P.S. § 7307.12(b)]. See Chapter 18 (¶¶ 1801—1812) for more details on Pennsylvania S corporations.

Distributions from accumulated adjustment accounts: The term "earnings and profits" refers to accumulated earnings and profits from non-Pennsylvania S years. If you receive a distribution from an accumulated adjustments account (*e.g.*, upon termination of the corporation's Pennsylvania S election), the distribution is a nontaxable return of capital to the extent of your basis in your stock. Distributions from an accumulated adjustments account in excess of basis are taxable as gains from the sale or exchange of property. Terminations and accumulated adjustments accounts are explained at ¶¶ 1806 and 1808.

Basis adjustments: Basis in the stock of a Pennsylvania S corporation is increased by a taxpayer's share of the corporation's income (including nontaxable income). Basis is decreased (but never below zero) by (a) any corporate distribution not included in the shareholder's income and (b) by the shareholder's share of the corporate losses (to the extent the losses reduced income subject to either the Pennsylvania personal income tax or to a tax on or measured by income imposed in another state). If stock basis is reduced to zero, losses in excess of basis are used to reduce the shareholder's basis (but never below zero) in any indebtedness of the Pennsylvania S corporation to the shareholder. Reduction in basis of indebtedness must be restored before stock basis can be increased [72 P.S. § 7307.11].

Tax-exempt income of a Pennsylvania S corporation: If income is not taxable to a Pennsylvania S corporation, it retains its tax-exempt status for the shareholder, and losses from tax-exempt obligations cannot be used to offset other taxable income on the individual shareholder's Form PA-40. However, you must adjust your basis for the corporation's nontaxable income. See above.

No Pennsylvania At-Risk Rules

Pennsylvania does not have at-risk rules like those of IRC § 465 that restrict deductibility of pass-through losses.

¶213 Differences in Federal/Commonwealth Personal Income Tax Rules for Deductions

• *Contributions made to organizations*

For federal income tax purposes, a business deduction is denied for contributions to organizations that conduct nondeductible lobby activities with respect to matters of direct financial interest to the donor. However, since the General Assembly has not specifically denied this deduction, such a contribution may still be claimed for Pennsylvania personal income tax purposes if it is an expense incurred in the conduct of the taxpayer's business and is in accordance with generally accepted accounting principles and practices. These contributions, however, cannot be claimed as an unreimbursed employee business expense.

• *Club dues*

For federal income tax purposes, club dues paid or incurred are not deductible. However, since the General Assembly has not specifically denied this deduction, club dues may still be claimed for Pennsylvania personal income tax purposes if it is an expense incurred in the conduct of the taxpayer's business and is in accordance with generally accepted accounting principles and practices. These dues, however, cannot be claimed as an unreimbursed employee business expense.

• *Entertainment*

For federal income tax purposes, the maximum deduction for business meals and entertainment is 50% of the qualifying amount. For Pennsylvania personal income tax purposes, business meals and entertainment are 100% deductible.

• *Moving expenses*

For federal income tax purposes, deductible moving expenses are deductible for the computation of adjusted gross income (*i.e.,* above-the-line) and are limited to the cost of (1) transportation of household goods and effects and (2) travel (including lodging but not meals) to the new residence. The federal distance test is 50 miles. For Pennsylvania personal income tax purposes, deductible moving expenses may only be claimed as a Schedule UE expense (unreimbursed employee business expenses) and are limited to (1) transportation of household goods and effects and (2) travel (including lodging *and* meals) to the new residence. Only expenses incurred in moving from one official work station of an employer to another official work station of the same employer at the request or direction of the employer are deductible. The Commonwealth distance test is also 50 miles. See ¶203 for explanation of unreimbursed employee business expenses. A moving expense deduction still may not be claimed by new employees or self-employed individuals.

• *Business travel with spouse*

For federal income tax purposes, expenses paid or incurred for a spouse, dependent, or other individual accompanying the taxpayer on a business trip are not deductible unless the person accompanying the taxpayer is an employee of the taxpayer, the travel of such persons serves a bona fide business purpose, and the expenses are otherwise deductible. For Pennsylvania personal income tax purposes, travel expenses for a spouse, dependent, or other individual accompanying the taxpayer on a business trip are not allowed as a business expense deduction unless such person is an employee of the person paying or reimbursing the expenses or the travel of such a person serves a bona fide business purpose.

• *Office in the home*

The Department of Revenue follows the analysis of the U.S. Supreme Court decision in *Commissioner of Internal Revenue v. Soliman* (113 SCt 701, 506 U.S. 168 (1993)) with respect to determining the deductibility of home office expenses. A taxpayer, therefore, is entitled to a deduction for an office in the home only if it is his or her principal business location. In addition, Pennsylvania will follow the federal rule of denying individuals a business deduction for basic local telephone service charges on the first line in their residence even when they claim an office-in-the-home expense.

• *Keogh or IRA contributions, self-employment taxes, and health insurance premiums*

For federal income tax purposes, self-employed individuals may claim above-the-line deductions for their Keogh or IRA contributions, 50% of their self-employment social security tax payments, and some of their health insurance premiums (70% in 2002; 100% in 2003). These are not deductible for Pennsylvania personal income tax purposes.

• *Tax credit arising from employee tips*

For federal income tax purposes, an employer in the food and beverage business may claim a nonrefundable income tax credit for part of the employer's share of social security taxes paid or incurred after 1993 on employee cash tips. For Pennsylvania personal income tax purposes, no such credit exists.

Getting More Information

A taxpayer who has additional questions on how federal tax legislation or court decisions affect the Pennsylvania treatment of the same item should write to PA Department of Revenue, Office of the Chief Counsel, Dept. 281061, Harrisburg, PA 17128-1061.

¶214 Exclusions for Health Savings Accounts

Special provisions, called the Health Savings Account Act, apply to health savings accounts established in Pennsylvania pursuant to IRC §223 [Act No. 48 of 2005 (H.B. 107), §2]. Terms are defined below. These special provisions provide for exclusion from the Pennsylvania personal income tax for the following items:

(1) Any income of a health savings account [Act No. 48 of 2005 (H.B. 107), §4(a)(1)].

¶214

(2) Any amount paid or distributed out of a health savings account that is used exclusively to pay the qualified medical expenses of the account beneficiary [Act No. 48 of 2005 (H.B. 107), § 4(a)(2)].

(3) Any amount paid or distributed out of a health savings account that is used exclusively to reimburse an account beneficiary for qualified medical expenses [Act No. 48 of 2005 (H.B. 107), § 4(a)(3)].

• *Taxable distributions*

The following distributions are taxable and must be included in the income of an account beneficiary:

(1) Any amount paid or distributed out of a health savings account that is used for any purpose other than to pay the qualified medical expenses of the account beneficiary [Act No. 48 of 2005 (H.B. 107), § 4(b)(1)].

(2) Any excess contribution distribution that has not previously been included in the account beneficiary's income [Act No. 48 of 2005 (H.B. 107), § 4(b)(2)].

(3) Any amount of the account beneficiary's income attributable to an excess contribution distribution [Act No. 48 of 2005 (H.B. 107), § 4(b)(3)].

• *High-deductible health plans*

General rule: A health insurance policy that would qualify as a high-deductible health plan under IRC § 223(c)(2) is subject to any provision of law mandating a minimum health insurance benefit or reimbursement [Act No. 48 of 2005 (H.B. 107), § 5(a)].

Exception: A health insurance policy that would qualify as a high-deductible health plan under IRC § 223(c), when offered in conjunction with a health savings account, is not subject to any provision of law that restricts or limits deductibles for mandated minimum health insurance benefits or reimbursements except to the extent such provision mandates benefits for preventive care, as determined by the standards set forth by the Internal Revenue Service [Act No. 48 of 2005 (H.B. 107), § 5(b)].

• *Effective date and applicability*

The Health Savings Account Act is effective September 12, 2005, and applies to taxable years beginning after December 31, 2004 [Act No. 48 of 2005 (H.B. 107), §§ 6 and 7].

• *Definition of terms*

Account beneficiary: The individual on whose behalf the health savings account was established [Act No. 48 of 2005 (H.B. 107), § 3; IRC § 223].

Excess contribution distribution: A distribution described in IRC § 223(f)(3). An "excess contribution" is any contribution (other than a rollover contribution described in paragraph (5) or IRC § 220(f)(5)) that is neither excludable from gross income under IRC § 106(d) nor deductible under IRC § 223. The term "excess contribution distribution" does not include amounts of income attributable to such distribution [Act No. 48 of 2005 (H.B. 107), § 3; IRC § 223].

Health insurance policy: An individual or group health, sickness or accident policy or subscriber contract or certificate issued by an entity subject to any one of the following [Act No. 48 of 2005 (H.B. 107), § 3]:

(1) The Insurance Company Law of 1921 [Act of May 17, 1921 (P.L. 682, No. 284)].

(2) The Health Maintenance Organization Act [Act of December 29, 1972 (P.L. 1701, No. 364)].

¶214

(3) The Individual Accident and Sickness Insurance Minimum Standards Act [Act of May 18, 1976 (P.L. 123, No. 54)].

(4) 40 Pa.C.S., Ch. 61 (relating to hospital plan corporations).

(5) 40 Pa.C.S., Ch. 63 (relating to professional health services plan corporations).

Health savings account: A trust created or organized in the United States as a health savings account exclusively for the purpose of paying the qualified medical expenses of the account beneficiary, but only if the written governing instrument creating the trust meets the requirements of IRC § 223(d)(1) [Act No. 48 of 2005 (H.B. 107), § 3; IRC § 223(d)(1)].

Qualified medical expenses: With respect to an account beneficiary, amounts paid by such beneficiary for medical care (as defined in IRC § 213(d)) for the individual, the spouse of the individual, and any dependent (as defined in IRC § 152) of the individual, but only to the extent such amounts are not compensated for by insurance or otherwise [Act No. 48 of 2005 (H.B. 107), § 3; IRC § 223(d)(2)].

¶215 Deduction for Depletion

Applicable to taxable years beginning on or after January 1, 2005, a reasonable allowance for cost depletion in the case of mines, oil and gas wells, other natural deposits, and timber is allowed as a deduction in computing income. If it is determined as a result of operations or development work that the recoverable units are greater or less than the prior estimate, the prior estimate (but not the basis for depletion) must be revised and the depletion allowance for subsequent taxable years must be based on the revised estimate [61 Pa. Code § 125.51(a)]. The basis on which depletion is computed is the adjusted basis for the purpose of determination of gain upon the sale or other disposition of the property [61 Pa. Code § 125.51(c)(5)]. "Recoverable units" are the number of units (e.g., tons, pounds, ounces, barrels) of resource in the ground and economically worth extracting, estimated according to the best available information and industry standards [61 Pa. Code § 125.51(b)].

Leases: In the case of a lease, the depletion deduction must be apportioned between the lessor and the lessee in accordance with federal income tax requirements [61 Pa. Code § 125.51(c)(1)].

Life tenant and remainderman: The depletion deduction is computed as a life tenant were the absolute owner of the property and is allowed to the life tenant [61 Pa. Code § 125.51(c)(2)].

Property held in trust: The depletion deduction must be apportioned between the income beneficiaries and the trustee in accordance with the pertinent provisions of the trust instrument or (in the absence of these provisions) on the basis of estate income allocable to each [61 Pa. Code § 125.51(c)(3)].

Property held by estate: The depletion deduction must be apportioned between the estate and the heirs, legatees, and devisees on the basis of income allocable to each [61 Pa. Code § 125.51(c)(4)].

• *Percentage Depletion*

A deduction for percentage depletion is allowed only in the following set of circumstances [61 Pa. Code § 125.52]:

(1) The deduction is allowable in computing federal taxable income.

(2) Insufficient information is available to estimate the amount of recoverable units in accordance with industry standards.

(3) The cost of the recoverable units is fixed an certain.

(4) The cost of the recoverable units has not been fully recovered.

¶216 Deduction for Tuition Program Contributions

A deduction for personal income tax purposes is authorized for contributions if tuition programs qualified under IRC § 529(b)(1), subject to an annual limitation not to exceed the exclusion threshold for gifts under IRC § 2503(b) and not to reduce the tax liability below zero [72 P.S. § 7303(a.7)]. Distributions and rollovers from a qualified tuition program that is not taxable under IRC § 529(c)(3)(B) and undistributed earnings on a qualified tuition program are excluded from Pennsylvania personal income tax. A change in a designated beneficiary is not a taxable event.

¶217 Strategic Development Areas

• *Overview*

Exemptions are allowed for the following items of income related to a strategic development area:

(1) Net income from the operation of a qualified business received by a resident or nonresident of a strategic development area [72 P.S. § 2932-C(1)].

(2) Net gains or income (less net losses) derived by a resident or nonresident of a strategic development area from the sale, exchange, or other disposition of real or tangible personal property located in a strategic development area [72 P.S. § 2932-C(2)(i)].

(3) Net gains (less net losses) realized by a resident of a strategic development area from the sale, exchange, or disposition of intangible personal property or obligations issued on or after February 1, 1994, by the Commonwealth, a public authority, commission, board, or other Commonwealth agency, political subdivision, or authority created by a political subdivision or by the federal government [72 P.S. § 2932-C(2)(ii)].

(4) Rents received by a person (whether resident or nonresident of a strategic development area) to the extent that income or loss from the rental of real or tangible personal property is allocable to a strategic development zone [72 P.S. § 2932-C(3)].

(5) Dividends received during the time the person was a resident of a strategic development area [72 P.S. § 2932-C(4)].

(6) Interest received during the time period the person was a resident of a strategic development area [72 P.S. § 2932-C(5)].

(7) The part of the income or gains received by an estate or trust for its taxable year ending within or with the resident beneficiary's taxable year that, under the governing instrument and applicable state law, is required to be distributed currently or is in fact paid or credited to the resident beneficiary and that would have been exempt if received by a resident beneficiary directly [72 P.S. § 2932-C(6)].

Strategic development areas

Strategic development areas are areas of economic distress. They are defined geographic areas comprising one or more political subdivisions or portions of political subdivisions designated by the Department of Community and Economic Development [72 P.S. § 2903-C]. The Governor may, on or before September 30, 2007, by executive order, designate not more than four strategic development areas in Pennsylvania, each of which shall not be less than 10 acres of land nor more than 1,500 acres, and the strategic development areas in the aggregate shall not exceed 5,000 acres [72 P.S. § 2911-C(b)]. Qualified persons and businesses within a designated and approved strategic development area are entitled to the specific exemptions listed above for a 15-year period beginning on the later of (1) January 1, 2007, or (2) the date of approval by all political subdivisions as required in 72 P.S. § 2913-C [72 P.S. § 72 P.S. § 2911-C(c)].

Qualified businesses

In order to qualify for the benefits related to strategic development zones, businesses must own or lease real property in a strategic development area on which the business actively conducts a trade, profession, or business involving energy, bioscience, or manufacturing, or a related activity and meet one of the following criteria [72 P.S. § 2912-C]:

(1) Create or maintain a minimum of 500 jobs within the first three years of full operation within the strategic development area.

(2) Invest a minimum of $45,000,000 in capital investment in the property located in the strategic development area within the first three years of full operation.

PERSONAL INCOME TAX

CHAPTER 3

WITHHOLDING, ESTIMATED TAX PAYMENTS, AND INFORMATION RETURNS

WITHHOLDING

¶301 General

Employers who maintain an office or transact business in Pennsylvania and pay compensation to employee(s) must withhold Pennsylvania personal income tax from all wages paid to residents (whether for services performed inside or outside Pennsylvania) and from all wages paid to nonresidents for services rendered inside Pennsylvania [72 P.S. §7316]. For an explanation of what constitutes compensation, see ¶202.

Interstate Carriers

Interstate carriers are subject to special withholding rules.

• *Employer*

An "employer" is an individual, partnership, association, corporation, governmental body or unit or agency, or any other entity who or that is required under the Internal Revenue Code to withhold federal income tax from wages paid to an employee [72 P.S. §7301(h)]. The term "employee" has the same meaning for Pennsylvania withholding purposes as for federal withholding purposes [72 P.S. §7301(g)]. For Pennsylvania personal income tax purposes, the terms "employee," "employer," and "wages" have the same meanings as in IRC §3401 *et seq.* [61 Pa. Code §101.1]. Note, however, that the term "compensation" has a specific Pennsylvania definition (see ¶202).

Credit Against Taxes Withheld from Wages

The coal degasification tax credit authorized by the "Coal Waste Removal and Ultraclean Fuels Act" is available to offset employer's tax withheld from employees' wages [72 P.S. § 8803-AJ(b)(2)]. This credit is explained at ¶ 1010.

• Employer withholding tax accounts

The Department of Revenue assigns to employers 8-digit numbers to identify their Employer Withholding Tax accounts. The account number is on the pre-printed forms in the employer withholding coupon booklets and is *in addition to* the federal Employer Identification Number (EIN). The EIN identifies the entity; but an entity may have multiple accounts for various taxes (*e.g.*, sales tax, employer withholding). An entity needs additional account numbers to identify its various tax accounts [*Pennsylvania Tax Update No. 78*, Pennsylvania Department of Revenue, November/December 1998].

• Wages not subject to withholding

An employer need not withhold tax from compensation paid to an employee who gives the employer a Form REV-419 (Non-Withholding Application) certifying (1) that his or her Pennsylvania personal income tax liability for the preceding year was zero and (2) that he or she anticipates owing no tax for the current year [61 Pa. Code § 113.15].

Promoting Employment Across Pennsylvania Act

A new jobs incentive authorized by the "Promoting Employment Across Pennsylvania Program" is available that allows an employer to retain tax or receive a rebate in the amount withheld from employees' wages. This program is explained at ¶ 1025.

• Excess withholding

An employee may request withholding in excess of the current rate pursuant to a written agreement between employer and employee. Additional withholding is subject to all requirements applicable to regular withholding [61 Pa. Code § 113.3(b)].

Caution: Watch Excludable Items

Take care that any items excludable from compensation for Pennsylvania purposes do not appear in the base for computing Pennsylvania withholding. The Department of Revenue encourages, but does not require, employers to withhold tax on noncash fringe benefits that are taxable for federal purposes.

• Withholding rates

Prior to August 4, 1991, the rate of withholding on Pennsylvania compensation was determined by the tax rate in effect. See ¶ 102 for discussion of the personal income tax rates. No withholding tables were needed. An employer simply multiplied Pennsylvania compensation by the current rate to determine the amount of withholding. However, the part of 72 P.S. § 7302.1 that tied the withholding rate to the personal income tax rate was repealed by the Act of August 4, 1991. Now the withholding rates are set by the Department of Revenue. The current withholding rate is 3.07%.

• Information statements

Employers use Form W-2 (or one that conforms to it) to report to employees [61 Pa. Code § 113.4(a)]. Employers must furnish information statements to employees on or before January 31 of the year succeeding any year in which compensation is paid.

¶301

If an employee's employment is terminated before the close of the year, the employer must furnish the employee with a statement no later than January 31 of the year succeeding the year of termination unless the employee requests, in writing, an information statement at an earlier time. If a written request is made and there is no reasonable expectation on the part of both employer and employee of further employment, the employer must furnish the statement on or before the later of the 30th day after the date of the request or the 30th day after the last date on which wages were paid [72 P.S. § 7317].

- *Transacting business*

"Transacting business" for Pennsylvania withholding purposes includes having or maintaining within Pennsylvania (directly or indirectly) an office, distribution house, sales house, warehouse, or other place of business, or operating within Pennsylvania by an agent or other representative under the authority of the employer or its subsidiary without regard to whether such presence in Pennsylvania is permanent or temporary or whether the employer is licensed to do business in Pennsylvania [61 Pa. Code § 113.1].

- *Reciprocal agreements*

Pennsylvania has reciprocal agreements with Indiana, Maryland, New Jersey, Ohio, Virginia, and West Virginia. These agreements provide that employers in these states withhold Pennsylvania tax from wages paid to Pennsylvania residents and remit it to Pennsylvania. Pennsylvania employers, in turn, do not withhold Pennsylvania tax from wages paid to residents of reciprocal states. Instead, they withhold the reciprocal state's income tax and remit it to the reciprocal state. On September 4, 2016 Governor Christy of New Jersey rescinded New Jersey's personal income tax agreement with Pennsylvania. The Agreement allowed Pennsylvania residents working in New Jersey to be taxed at Pennsylvania's lower rates. The rescission will take effect January 1, 2017. This means that Pennsylvania residents working in New Jersey will be subject to New Jersey's higher rates of tax.

Advice to Employees

Pennsylvania employers are required to withhold a reciprocal state's income tax only if the nonresident employee files with the employer a Form REV-420 (Employees Statement of Nonresidence in Pennsylvania and Authorization to Withhold Other State's Income Tax). If no Form REV-420 is filed with the employer, the employer will withhold Pennsylvania income tax. This can present a problem to employees who must then file a return in Pennsylvania to get a refund of the Pennsylvania tax that they do not owe. Not all Pennsylvania employers automatically inform their nonresident employees that they are not subject to withholding in Pennsylvania. If you are a resident of a reciprocal state, be sure to file a Form REV-420 with your employer.

- *Philadelphia city wage tax*

An employer having a place of business within Pennsylvania who employs one or more persons who are residents of a city of the first class (*i.e.*, Philadelphia) must register with the revenue commissioner of that city and withhold tax imposed by that city. The employer must remit returns and tax in accordance with the time frames established by 72 P.S. § 7319. See ¶ 303. Annually, on or before February 28, employers who have filed returns of tax withheld and remitted the tax through the year must file an employer's annual reconciliation of wage tax withheld, along with a copy of Form W-2 of the IRS for each employee [72 P.S. § 7359(c)]. See also ¶ 3808.

¶301

¶302 Apportionment of Compensation When Services Are Performed Both Within and Outside Pennsylvania

When an employee performs services both inside and outside Pennsylvania, and the compensation for services performed outside Pennsylvania is not taxable, the employer must compute the amount of compensation attributable to services inside Pennsylvania. There are two methods of apportionment—the working-day method [61 Pa. Code § 113.2(1)(iii)(B)(1), (2)(ii)(A)] and the total-volume method [61 Pa. Code § 113.2(1)(iii)(B)(II), (2)(ii)(B)]. The working-day method is more commonly used. The total-volume method is for employees whose compensation is a function of business volume transacted (*e.g.,* traveling salesperson).

• *Compensation of nonresidents*

Employers may determine Pennsylvania compensation for nonresident employees on the basis of the preceding year's experience or on an estimate made by the employer or the employee. However, the employer must make, during the year, any adjustment necessary to assure proper withholding [61 Pa. Code § 113.2(2)(iii)]. Act 43 (H.B. 542) of 2017 and Informational Notice-Personal Income Tax 2017-1 requires withholding by entities making rent and royalty payments on Pennsylvania property to nonresident individuals and disregarded entities over $5,000 and companies that bring out-of-state independent contractors into Pennsylvania for work in excess of $5,000.

Keep Records

If you do not maintain current records adequate to determine with reasonable accuracy the amount of Pennsylvania compensation, you must withhold on *all* compensation paid to a nonresident who works both inside and outside Pennsylvania [61 Pa. Code § 113.2(2)(iv)].

¶303 Withholding Returns and Filing Dates

Employers paying compensation must file (on a semimonthly, monthly, or quarterly basis) signed deposit statements on forms provided by the Department of Revenue and forward a remittance in payment of the Pennsylvania personal income tax required to be withheld. The frequency of filing depends on the aggregate amount of tax expected to be withheld for the quarter.

• *Payment by electronic funds transfer (EFT)*

Payments made by electronic funds transfer (EFT) are discussed at ¶4617.

Payment by Credit Card

Businesses can now pay employer withholding tax by credit card if electronic funds transfer (EFT) is not required [*Pennsylvania Tax Update No. 102*, Pennsylvania Department of Revenue, November/December 2002]. Credit card payments can be made online or by telephone. American Express, Discover, MasterCard, and Visa cards are accepted. Taxpayers can access the credit card payment option by going to the PA PowerPort at www.state.pa.us (PA Keyword: "credit card").

Credit card payment of sales and use tax is made through the following credit card service provider:

Official Payments Corp.
Phone: 1-800-2PAYTAX (1-800-272-9829)
Internet: www.officialpayments.com

Official Payments Corp. charges a 2.5% convenience fee ($1 minimum) for processing the credit card transaction. The convenience fee and tax payment will appear as two different charges on credit card statements. Payments are effective on the date they are charged. Note that authorized payments cannot be cancelled.

- *Weekly filing*

    Weekly filing is required if the total tax withheld for a calendar year is expected to be $20,000 or more. The tax is due on the Wednesday after payday if the payday is Wednesday, Thursday or Friday, and on the Friday after payday if the payday falls on any other day.

- *Semimonthly filing*

    Semimonthly filing is required if the total tax withheld during the quarter is expected to be $1,000 or more. Effective May 31, 2010, semimonthly filing is required if the total tax withheld for a calendar year is expected to be between $4,000 and $19,999. Semimonthly filers must file within three banking days after the 15th day and the last day of the month.

- *Monthly filing*

    Monthly filing is required if total tax expected to be withheld during the quarter is at least $300 but less than $1,000. Effective May 31, 2010, monthly filing is required if the total tax withheld for a calendar year is expected to be between $1,200 and $3,999. Monthly filers must file on or before the 15th day of the succeeding month for all months except December. December filing is due on or before the next January 31.

- *Quarterly filing*

    If you expect to withhold less than $300 during a quarter, you may file on a quarterly basis. Effective May 31, 2010, quarterly filing is permitted if the tax withheld during a calendar year is expected to be less than $1,200. Quarterly filings are due on or before April 30, July 31, October 31 and January 31 for the quarters ending on March 31, June 30, September 30, and December 31.

    Remittances and deposit statements should be forwarded in accordance with instructions issued by the Department of Revenue. The place of deposit for each employer is included in the information the Department forwards to all employers. If your packet of forms is lost or damaged, a request for duplicate forms, listing the name and identification number of the employer, should be sent to the Department. Employers who have never received a packet of these preprinted forms should obtain the proper forms from the Department of Revenue.

    NOTE: Form REV-415 provides detailed instructions for withholding returns.

- *Reconciliation returns*

    Employers are required to reconcile their accounts quarterly on or before the last day of April, July, October, and January, for the quarters ending on the last day of March, June, September, and December. For this purpose use Form PA501/W-3 (Employer Quarterly Deposit Statement and Return of Income Tax Withheld). Submit with the Reconciliation Statement copies of all W-2 forms furnished to employees. In addition, submit an adding machine tape listing the amount of Pennsylvania personal income tax withheld from each employee as shown on the W-2s [Form REV-417EX+, Instructions for Filing Form PA W-3 Reconciliation Return]. Do not attach the W-2 forms of any employee covered by a reciprocal agreement. Instead, send the W-2 forms of any employee covered by a reciprocal agreement to the employee's state of residence. Employers in other states having employees covered by a reciprocal agreement with Pennsylvania should file a Form PA W-3 with Pennsylvania.

    NOTE: See Form REV-417EX for complete instructions for filing reconciliation forms.

• *Employers paying no compensation for a period*

Employers who are still in business but pay no compensation for a period (*e.g.*, seasonal employers) continue to file Deposit Statements, entering "None" for income tax withheld [Form REV-415 (Withholding Instructions for Employers)].

• *Extensions of time*

If an employer submits a written application showing good cause, the Department of Revenue may grant a reasonable extension of time for filing Form PA-501 or Form PA W-3 [61 Pa. Code § 113.10].

• *Change in filing date*

NOTE: The Regulations have not yet been amended to incorporate the statutory changes that are effective May 31, 2010.

An employer can change to a less frequent basis only at the beginning of a calendar year. Changes to a more frequent basis of filing must be made at the beginning of any quarter that follows a quarter in which the $300 or $1,000 limit is exceeded. Notification of such changes must be made in writing to the Department of Revenue [61 Pa. Code § 113.6(6)].

• *Final withholding*

An employer who discontinues business or ceases to pay compensation must file a final withholding return within 30 days after the end of the month in which business or payment of wages ceases, regardless of the usual reporting period due date [61 Pa. Code § 113.6(7)].

• *Correcting mistakes*

If an employer overpays or underpays tax, the mistake is corrected in one of the following ways [61 Pa. Code § 113.7]:

(1) *Correct amount withheld but incorrect amount remitted:* Make the proper adjustment, including payment of interest due, within the same quarter on the first deposit or later deposits filed after the error is discovered.

(2) *No tax or too little tax withheld from an employee (other than on tips):* Withhold the amount of the undercollection from later payments to the employee. The employer must remit the correct amount with his or her deposit statement and is liable for any underpayment, plus interest and penalties. Arrangements for reimbursement are a matter to be settled between employer and employee.

(3) *Too much tax withheld:* Make an appropriate adjustment in withholding for subsequent periods in the same quarter. If the overwithholding is not offset by the last quarterly period, the employee reports the amount actually withheld on his or her return.

• *Records to be kept*

Employers must maintain and make available for examination and inspection by the Department of Revenue all the information required by regulation [61 Pa. Code § 113.8].

• *Use of prescribed forms*

Employers must use forms prescribed by the Department of Revenue. You will not be excused from filing a return simply because you have not received your forms [61 Pa. Code § 113.9(a)].

Check Your Calendar

Ordinarily, the prescribed forms are furnished regularly without your having to request them. However, be sure to apply for the forms if you have any reason to believe that you have been skipped. Do it in plenty of time to file timely. If, for some reason, the forms are not available, you may file a statement disclosing the amount of taxes due, accompanied by remittance of the tax. This will be accepted as a tentative return and will relieve you from liability for additions if you file a return on a proper form without unnecessary delay [61 Pa. Code § 113.9(b)].

¶304 Employer's Liability and Penalties

Required withholdings are considered a special fund in trust for the Department of Revenue. An employer required to withhold Pennsylvania personal income tax is liable for the payment of the required withholding, whether or not the employer collects it from his or her employees. If the employees actually pay the taxes due rather than having them withheld by the employer, the employer is no longer responsible for payment of the tax. However, the employer remains liable for any interest, additions, or penalties. The penalty for failure to collect or truthfully account for any income tax is equal to the amount of tax evaded or not collected or not accounted for and paid over [61 Pa. Code § 119.24]. There are other penalties (*e.g.*, penalties for failure to provide an employee with a withholding statement) [61 Pa. Code §§ 119.25 and 119.26].

If an employer fails to withhold or truthfully account for taxes withheld, fails to file a deposit statement, or fails to remit taxes withheld, the Department of Revenue may serve notice and make the employer withhold and deposit taxes in a bank designated by the Department in a separate account in trust for and payable only to the Department [61 Pa. Code § 113.11(a), (b)].

¶305 Bulk and Auction Sales

The bulk sale provisions apply when an employer sells or causes to be sold at auction or sells or transfers in bulk at least 51% of any stock of goods, wares, or merchandise of any, kind, fixtures, machinery, equipment, buildings, or real estate held by or on behalf of the employer. The Department of Revenue has interpreted the bulk sales statute disjunctively with respect to each asset classification and as applicable only to assets located within Pennsylvania. Therefore, a taxpayer must secure a clearance certificate when 51% or more of any of the listed assets are sold [REV-1076]. An employer who engages in a bulk sale must comply with the provisions of § 1403 of the Fiscal Code [72 P.S. § 7321.1(a)]. The bulk sale provisions are discussed at ¶4621.

Sales or Transfers Under Court Order

These provisions do not apply to sales or transfers made under any court order [72 P.S. § 7321.1(b)].

¶306 Partnerships, Associations, and S Corporations

See Chapter 18 for discussion of withholding rules for pass-through entities.

ESTIMATED TAX PAYMENTS

¶310 Declarations of Estimated Tax

All individuals, estates, and trusts (resident and nonresident) who expect more than $8,000 of income (other than compensation subject to withholding) attributable to sources within Pennsylvania must file declarations of and pay estimated tax [72 P.S. § 7325]. For estates and trusts this means the receipt of $8,000 of Pennsylvania taxable income that is not to be distributed to beneficiaries. Only one declaration of estimated tax is required for a given year, but a taxpayer may pay the estimated tax in more than one installment, as explained at ¶ 311.

• *Estates and trusts*

The estimated provisions apply to estates and trusts as well as resident and nonresident individuals.

• *Amount of estimated tax*

The estimated tax is the personal income tax rate in effect for the taxable year times the taxpayer's estimated taxable income less allowable credits. As in the computation of final taxable income, losses in one class of income cannot offset gains in another class, and items of income are included in only one class, even if they fall within the definitions of more than one class. If there are any changes in estimated taxable income, adjustments must be made in later payments.

• *Joint declarations*

Spouses may make a joint declaration of estimated tax even though one spouse expects no income [72 P.S. § 7325(c); 61 Pa. Code § 115.5]. If spouses file a joint declaration, their liability for the estimated tax is joint and several. The filing of a joint declaration, however, does not preclude the filing of separate final returns. If spouses file a joint declaration of estimated tax but file separate final returns, the credit for estimated tax paid will be allocated between them in the manner they choose. Spouses *cannot offset gains* of one spouse against losses of the other spouse either in the same class of income or separate classes of income.

• *Corrections to estimated tax accounts*

Form REV-459B (Consent to Transfer, Adjust or Correct PA Estimated Personal Income Tax Account) can be used to make corrections to estimated payment accounts. It can be used to move payments from a joint account to separate accounts or from separate accounts to a joint account. This may be necessary in the case of divorce or separation, death of a spouse, or a requirement to file separate accounts. It can also be used to transfer payments from separate accounts into a joint account in case of reconciliation, marriage between two individuals with separate accounts, or being relieved of the requirement to file separate returns. Form REV-459B may be completed and mailed separately before the Pennsylvania income tax return(s) is/are required to be filed or may be attached to the return(s) [*Pennsylvania Tax Update No. 18*, Pennsylvania Department of Revenue, December/January 2006].

¶311 Due Dates for Filing Declarations

The due date for filing a declaration of estimated tax depends on when a taxpayer determines that income on which no tax has been withheld can reasonably be expected to exceed $8,000 in the taxable year [72 P.S. § 7325(d)], as follows:

Determination Made	Due Date for Declaration
On or before April 1	On or before April 15
After April 1 but before June 2	On or before June 15
After June 1 but before September 2	On or before September 15
After September 1	On or before January 15 of the following year

Exceptions: Persons with Estimated Tax of $100 or Less

The declaration of an individual with estimated gross income from farming for the taxable year that is at least two-thirds of his or her total estimated gross income for the taxable year may be filed at any time on or before January 15 of the succeeding year. If the farmer, however, files a final return and pays the entire tax by March 1, the final return may be considered his or her declaration due on or before January 15. A declaration of estimated tax of an individual, trust, or estate having a total estimated tax for the taxable year of $200 or less may be filed at any time on or before January 15 of the succeeding year [72 P.S. § 7325(f)].

- *Amended declarations*

An individual, trust, or estate may amend a declaration of estimated tax [72 P.S. § 7325(e)]. If the estimated tax is substantially increased or decreased after a declaration is filed, an amended declaration should be filed on or before the next date for payment of an installment of estimated tax and the remaining unpaid installments should be proportionately increased or decreased as required to reflect any increase or decrease in the amount of estimated tax. If an amended declaration is filed after September 15 and on or before the following January 15 and shows an increase in estimated tax, the increase must be paid at the time the declaration is filed. If, however, the taxpayer files an annual income tax return with full remittance of tax due by January 31, no amended declaration is required [61 Pa. Code § 115.7].

Watch for This

Remember that the Special Provisions for Poverty apply when estimating taxable income.

¶312 Additions for Underpayment

Failure to pay all or any part of an installment of estimated tax will result in an addition to tax based on the amount of the underpayment for the period of the underpayment but not beyond the 15th day of the fourth month following the close of the taxable year. The addition to tax is a specified percentage of the underpayment, and the appropriate percentage is the rate set by the Department of Revenue pursuant to the authority of § 806 of the Fiscal Code. No underpayment is deemed to exist with respect to an installment otherwise due on or after a taxpayer's death or, in the case of a decedent's estate or a trust created by the decedent to receive the residue of the decedent's estate and, applicable to payments made after June 30, 2006, for a period of two years after the decedent's death [72 P.S. § 7352(d)(1)].

- *Amount of underpayment*

The amount of underpayment for an installment is the excess of 90% of the tax shown on the final return over the amount actually paid on or before the due date for the installment. In the case of a decedent, no underpayment is deemed to exist with respect to an installment due on or after the taxpayer's death [72 P.S. § 7352(d)(1)].

Underpayment rules are applied on a quarterly basis. Even if the total amount of estimated tax paid is 90% of the final tax due, the taxpayer may incur additions for underpayment in one or more periods. For example, a taxpayer whose final income tax is $1,000 must have prepaid at least $900. If the taxpayer met the filing requirements before April 1, the taxpayer must have prepaid at least $225 on each installment date. In this case, if it is assumed that the taxpayer in 1992 made estimated tax payments of $100, $225, $225, and $350, respectively, he or she, although meeting the overall 90% requirement, is still liable for underpayment additions for the first period's underpayment of $125.

- *Safe harbors*

The statute provides the following *two* "safe harbors" for protection against underpayment additions [72 P.S. § 7352(d)(2)]:

(1) Prepayment of an amount equal to the tax computed by applying the rate for the current year to the taxable income of the prior year. Effective January 1, 2013, this prepayment is based on the amount equal to the tax after consideration of the special tax provisions for poverty.

¶312

(2) Prepayment of at least 90% of the tax computed, using the rate applicable to the taxable year, on the basis of actual income for the months in the taxable year ending before the month in which the installment is required to be paid. In the case of a trust or estate, prepayment of an amount equal to 90% of the applicable percentage of the tax for the taxable year as determined pursuant to IRC § 6654(d)(2)(C)(iii) at rates applicable to the taxable year, computed on an annualized basis in accordance with U.S. Treasury regulations, based upon the actual income for the months of the taxable year ending with the last day of the second preceding month prior to the month in which the installment is required to be paid.

If a taxpayer qualifies under the 90% rule or under one of the safe harbors, Pennsylvania will impose no additions for underpayment of estimated tax. The safe harbor rules are applied on a period-by-period basis, just as for the overall 90% rule.

Federal/Commonwealth Difference

The federal income tax law provides a safe harbor from underpayment penalties based on annualized income. Pennsylvania income tax law does not provide a safe harbor based on annualized income.

INFORMATION RETURNS

¶315 General

Any person who makes payments to a taxpayer of more than $10 from a pension or profit-sharing plan for any reason other than death, disability, or retirement must file (on or before February 28 of each year for distributions of the preceding year) an information return if the distribution to the taxpayer exceeds the taxpayer's contributions [61 Pa. Code § 117.18]. You must make a separate return for each person. "Person" means individuals, employers, associations, fiduciaries, partnerships, corporations or other entities, and estates and trusts—whether resident or nonresident, singular or plural [61 Pa. Code § 101.1].

Information returns must be made in a way that substantially conforms to IRS Form 1099R. If you get approval from the Department of Revenue, you can use magnetic tapes or computer printouts in lieu of copies of Form 1099R [61 Pa. Code § 117.18].

PERSONAL INCOME TAX

CHAPTER 4

PROCEDURE, ENFORCEMENT, ASSESSMENT, AND REVIEW

¶401 General

The Department of Revenue is responsible for enforcement of the Pennsylvania personal income tax and is authorized to prescribe, adopt, and promulgate rules and regulations with respect to it [72 P.S. § 7354].

¶402 Communication Function

The communication function is critical. You must communicate to the Department of Revenue all the information it needs to determine that your return is accurate. If you have any unusual items on your return, make sure all necessary information is there to support your position. If the Department contacts you to ask for clarification or additional information, provide it promptly and in an understandable form. See ¶4608.

¶403 Collection of Tax

Ordinarily, the tax is collected when taxpayers remit tax with personal income tax returns. In other situations the Department of Revenue collects the personal income tax (including interest, penalties, and additions) as follows [61 Pa. Code § 119.10(a)]:

(1) Immediately in cases of bankruptcy, receivership, assignment, judicial sales, and clerical errors or mistakes on returns.

(2) Immediately if a jeopardy assessment notice has been issued unless the taxpayer has filed a petition for reassessment and posted the required bond within 10 days after the mailing date of the jeopardy assessment notice.

(3) After 60 days from the mailing date of an assessment notice unless the taxpayer has timely filed a petition for reassessment.

(4) After 60 days from the mailing date of a decision by the Department on a petition for reassessment unless the taxpayer has timely filed a petition for review with the Board of Finance and Revenue.

¶403

(5) After 120 days from the mailing date of notice by the Department that it failed to dispose of the petition for reassessment unless the taxpayer has timely filed a petition for review with the Board of Finance and Revenue.

(6) After 30 days from the mailing date of notice of a decision by the Board of Finance and Revenue on a petition for review unless the taxpayer has perfected an appeal to the Commonwealth Court within that period and has filed with the prothonotary of the Commonwealth Court appropriate security in the amount of 120% of the amount of unpaid tax.

(7) After 30 days from the last day the Board of Finance and Revenue should have disposed of the petition for review if no decision was made unless the taxpayer has perfected an appeal to the Commonwealth Court within that period and posted appropriate security, as explained above.

(8) Immediately upon a final order of the Commonwealth Court or the Pennsylvania Supreme Court.

Pursue All Available Administrative Remedies

In any proceeding for the collection of tax due (including interest, penalties, and additions), a taxpayer against whom an assessment has been made cannot set up any ground of defense that could have been presented to the Department of Revenue, the Board of Finance and Revenue, or the Commonwealth Court if he or she had properly pursued available administrative remedies [61 Pa. Code § 119.10(b)].

- *Attachment of wages, commissions, and other earnings*

The Department of Revenue has the authority to attach wages, commissions, and other earnings of a taxpayer to collect delinquent taxes [72 P.S. § 10003.15(a)].

Written notice and demand: Upon presentation of a written notice and demand certifying that the information contained within is true and correct and containing the name of the taxpayer and the amount of delinquent state tax due plus the Department's costs, the Department of Revenue may demand, receive, and collect the amount from any entity (1) employing persons owing delinquent state taxes; or (2) having in its possession unpaid commissions or earnings belonging to any person owing delinquent state taxes [72 P.S. § 10003.15(a)].

Entity defined: For purposes of 72 P.S. § 10003.15, the term "entity" means the United States, the Commonwealth of Pennsylvania or any of its political subdivisions, a corporation, an association, a company, a firm, or an individual [72 P.S. § 10003.15(e)].

Wages defined: For purposes of 72 P.S. § 10003.15, the term "wages" means any wages, commissions, or earnings of an individual employee (1) that are currently owed to the individual employee; (2) that become due within 60 days of receive of a written notice and demand (see above); (3) any unpaid commissions or earnings of an individual employee in the entity's possession; or (4) any unpaid commissions or earnings of an individual employee that come into the entity's possession within 60 days of receipt of a written notice and demand [72 P.S. § 10003.15(e)].

Deducting and remitting taxes: Upon receiving a written notice and demand from the Department of Revenue, an entity must deduct from the wages of an individual employee the amount shown on the notice and forward the amount to the Department within 60 days after receipt of the notice [72 P.S. § 10003.15(b)]. However, no more than 10% of the wages of an individual employee who is a delinquent taxpayer may be deducted at any one time for delinquent state taxes and costs [72 P.S. § 10003.15(c)].

Entity's collection costs: An entity is entitled to deduct from the amount collected from the individual employee the costs incurred by the entity for the extra bookkeeping necessary to record the transactions. This deduction, however, cannot exceed 2% of the amount collected from the individual employee [72 P.S. § 10003.15(c)].

Failure of entity to deduct or remit: If an entity fails to deduct or forward a required amount within 60 days, the entity must pay the amount of the delinquent state tax for each individual employee who is a delinquent taxpayer subject to a demand in addition to a penalty in accordance with 72 P.S. § 7352(h), discussed at ¶ 411. An entity paying delinquent taxes, costs, and a penalty does not have the benefit of any stay of execution or exemption law [72 P.S. § 10003.15(d)].

The Department may file citations with magisterial district judges against taxpayers not remitting employer withholding tax (Act 52 of 2013).

• *Tax liens*

If any person who owes tax (including interest, penalties, and additions) neglects or refuses to pay it when it is due, the tax owed is a lien in favor of the Commonwealth against the taxpayer's real *and personal property* [61 Pa. Code § 119.11(a)].

Writ of execution: The Department may issue a writ of execution directly upon a personal income tax lien without the issuance and prosecution to judgment of a writ of *scire facias* if a notice of the filing and effect of the lien is sent to the taxpayer at the last known post office address by certified mail not less than 10 days before issuance of execution of the lien. The lien has no effect upon inventory or merchandise regularly sold or leased in the ordinary course of business by the taxpayer unless and until a writ of execution has been issued and a levy made upon the goods [72 P.S. § 7345(b)].

Priority of tax liens: Personal income tax liens have priority over any other obligation, judgment, claim, lien, or estate arising after the filing and docketing of the personal income tax lien and are subordinate only to the following [72 P.S. § 7345(b); 61 Pa. Code § 119.11(c), (d)]:

(1) Mortgages against the realty duly recorded before the tax lien.

(2) Cost of the writ and the judicial sale.

(3) Real estate taxes on the real estate [61 Pa. Code § 119.11(c), (d)].

NOTE: Tax liens no longer have to be renewed every five years to maintain their priority (see ¶ 4618).

Comment: Tax Lien Filing

Even though unpaid taxes create a lien against you, the lien is not perfected until filed by the Department of Revenue with a prothonotary of the Commonwealth Court and the prothonotary has docketed the lien [61 Pa. Code § 119.11(a)(2)]. The Commonwealth cannot take any action against you (*e.g.*, publish the lien in the newspaper, start action to take your property) until the lien is perfected. Make sure you are complying with all requirements to contest the tax in order to prevent perfection of the lien.

¶404 Assessments

The Pennsylvania personal income tax is a self-assessed tax (*i.e.*, taxpayers determine their own income tax liabilities), but the Department of Revenue is authorized to examine returns and assess additional taxes if the return is not correct [72 P.S. § 7338(a)].

A notice of assessment issued by the Department must be mailed to the taxpayer, setting forth the basis of the assessment [72 P.S. § 7338(d)].

Failure to file a return: If a taxpayer fails to file a return, the Department can make an *estimated assessment* (based on available information) of the tax owed by the taxpayer. A notice of an estimated assessment must be mailed to the taxpayer, and the tax is due in 90 days unless the taxpayer has filed a petition for reassessment (explained at ¶ 407) [72 P.S. § 7338(c)].

For appeal of assessments issued after December 31, 2007, the petition must be made pursuant to the provisions of Article XXVII of the Tax Reform Code (discussed at ¶4604).

False or fraudulent return: If the Department determines that a taxpayer has filed a false or fraudulent return or that the tax reported on the return is less than the tax the Department's examination discloses, the Department will assess the tax and send a notice of assessment to the taxpayer's last known address. An item of income is not considered omitted from income if information sufficient to enable the Department to determine its nature and amount is included in the return or in any schedule or statement attached to the return [61 Pa. Code § 119.2(c)]. Any taxes that were assessed with respect to a false or fraudulent return must be paid within 90 days of the date of the notice unless the taxpayer files a petition for reassessment (explained at ¶407) [61 Pa. Code § 119.2(e)].

Clerical error: If the Department discovers that a taxpayer has made a clerical error or mistake in the preparation of a return (understating the tax), the Department will notify the taxpayer and request payment of the tax (plus any interest, penalties, or additions) within 30 days of receiving the notice. Reassessment procedures do not apply to notices of clerical error or mistake [61 Pa. Code § 119.2(d)].

• *Statute of limitations*

In general, assessments must be made by the Department within three years after returns are filed. A return that is filed before the final due date or before the last day of any extension is considered filed on the final due date (including extensions) [72 P.S. § 7348(a)].

Omission of income: If a taxpayer omits from income an item that is greater than 25% of the income reported, the Department can make an assessment, or instigate court proceedings, at any time within six years after the return was filed [61 Pa. Code § 119.15].

Failure to file a return: If a taxpayer does not file a return, or does not file an amended return when required to, the Department can make an assessment at any time (*i.e.,* there is no statute of limitations for assessment) [72 P.S. § 7348(c)].

False or fraudulent returns: There is no statute of limitations for assessments with respect to false or fraudulent returns (*i.e.,* the Department can make assessments at any time) [72 P.S. § 7348(d)].

Willful evasion: In the case of a willful attempt to evade personal income taxes, the Department may make an assessment or instigate court proceedings at any time (*i.e.,* there is no statute of limitations) [61 Pa. Code § 119.16(b)].

Refunds: An assessment to recover any refund or credit erroneously made or allowed can be made by the Department within three years from the grant or within the period in which an assessment (or reassessment) could have been filed, whichever period occurs last [72 P.S. § 7348(e)].

• *Extension of limitation period*

A taxpayer can, before a limitation period expires, consent (in writing) to extend the statute of limitations on assessments. There is no limit to the number of times a taxpayer can consent to extensions. If a taxpayer consents to extension of the statute of limitations, the Department can make an assessment at any time during the extended period [72 P.S. § 7349].

¶404

¶405 Jeopardy Assessments

If the Department of Revenue believes that delay on its part will jeopardize the assessment or collection of any deficiency, it can notify a taxpayer of its finding and demand immediate payment [72 P.S. § 7339(a)].

If the Department believes that a taxpayer intends to leave or remove property from Pennsylvania or to do anything that would jeopardize the collection of tax, it can declare the taxpayer's tax period immediately terminated. It must notify the taxpayer of the termination of the tax year and can demand immediate payment of tax attributable to the short tax year, even if the usual time for filing and payment of tax has not expired [72 P.S. § 7339(b)].

A jeopardy assessment is immediately due and payable, and proceedings for collection may be begun at once. The taxpayer may, however, postpone collection and prevent finalization of the jeopardy assessment by filing (within 10 days after the date of notice of jeopardy assessment) a petition for reassessment. The petition for reassessment must be accompanied by bond or security considered necessary by the Department of Revenue, but the Department cannot require security greater than twice the amount of the assessment (including interest and penalties and additions) [72 P.S. § 7339(c)]. The Department considers certified checks on any state or national bank within Pennsylvania, satisfactory negotiable municipal bonds, or negotiable U.S. securities acceptable security [61 Pa. Code § 119.5(c)(2), (3)]. If the value of security decreases, the Department may require additional security to cover the assessment [61 Pa. Code § 119.5(d)]. If a petition for reassessment is not made within 10 days, a jeopardy assessment becomes final [72 P.S. § 7339(d)].

Taxpayers (in petitions for reassessment) may request oral hearings for themselves or their authorized representatives [72 P.S. § 7339(e)]. If no oral hearing is requested, the Department will consider the petition for reassessment without a hearing.

The Department will notify the taxpayer of its decision after the oral hearing (if one is requested) and after considering the petition for reassessment.

The Department's decision as to the validity of the jeopardy assessment is final, unless the taxpayer within 90 days after notification of the Department's decision files a petition for review to the Board of Finance and Revenue authorized under 72 P.S. § 7341 (prior to January 1, 2008) or 72 P.S. § 9704 (after December 31, 2007) [72 P.S. § 7339(f)].

The burden of proof in any case of jeopardy assessment is on the taxpayer [72 P.S. § 7339(g)].

¶406 Bankruptcy or Receivership

The law provides for immediate collection of the Pennsylvania personal income tax in the case of bankruptcy, receivership, assignment, or judicial sale [72 P.S. § 7344(4)].

In the case of bankruptcy or receivership, the Department of Revenue will immediately assess the tax due and begin collection proceedings. The Department may use any available information and can examine a taxpayer's books to determine the amount of tax due [61 Pa. Code § 119.3(a)].

¶407 Reassessments

Any taxpayer against whom an assessment is made may petition the Department for a reassessment. Petitions for reassessment of assessment issued prior to January 1, 2008, must be made pursuant to 72 P.S. § 7340; petitions for reassessment of assessments issued after December 31, 2007, must be made pursuant to the provisions of Article XXVII of the Tax Reform Code (discussed at ¶4604). A petition for reassessment is a request to review the assessment and may be filed by taxpayers who do not agree with the Department's original assessment. A separate petition should be filed for each year in dispute [61 Pa. Code § 119.6(b)]. A petition for reassessment must state specifically the reasons the petitioner believes a reassessment is warranted and must be supported by affidavit that it is not made for the purpose of delay and that the facts in the petition are true [72 P.S. § 7340]. Such petitions must be filed within 60 days of the mailing date of the assessment. Petitions may be filed electronically on the board of Appeals Website.

The Department of Revenue requires, by regulation, petitions for reassessment to contain the following information [61 Pa. Code § 119.6(b)]:

(1) The taxpayer's name, address, and employer identification number or social security number.

(2) The assessment notice number.

(3) A detailed statement of the facts and reasons upon which the petition is based, with a separate paragraph for each separate allegation or reason.

(4) Whether or not an oral hearing is desired.

(5) A signed statement by the taxpayer that the petition is not filed for purposes of delay and that all the facts in it are true and correct.

The Department may also request additional information if it needs it to make its determination [61 Pa. Code § 119.6(c)].

Any taxpayer against whom an assessment is made may petition the Department for a reassessment. For appeals of assessments issued after December 31, 2007, the petition must be made pursuant to the provisions of Article XXVII of the Tax Reform Code (discussed at ¶ 4604). Reassessment procedures for reassessment for assessments issued prior to January 1, 2008, were made pursuant to 72 P.S. § § 7340-7342. See ¶ 412 for explanation of petitions for review.

¶408 Refund or Credit of Overpayments

All petitions for refund of taxes, penalties, fines, additions to tax, and other moneys collected by the Department are made to the Department of Revenue. See ¶ 411 for discussion of penalties and additions.

• *Interest*

The Department of Revenue must pay interest on any overpayments that are not credited or refunded within 75 days of the later of (1) the return due date or (2) the actual filing date [72 P.S. § 7806.1(a)(5)]. The provisions for interest on overpayments is explained in detail at ¶ 4612.

¶409 Fiduciaries

The administrative provisions of the Tax Reform Code apply to fiduciaries in the same way they apply to any taxpayer except that assessments or claims are asserted against fiduciaries in their representative capacities, not against them personally. Satisfaction of assessments or claims are limited to the property held by fiduciaries in their representative capacities unless they have committed some act that creates a personal liability [61 Pa. Code § 119.4].

The fiduciary, executor, administrator, or other person who may have any liability for income tax due from a decedent or a decedent's estate may ask the Department of Revenue to determine the tax. If the fiduciary then pays the amount of tax (plus appropriate penalty and interest), he or she is relieved of personal liability for any deficiencies that may be found [61 Pa. Code § 119.27].

¶410 Investigation and Audit

The Department of Revenue, or any of its authorized agents, can examine the books, papers, and records of taxpayers to verify the accuracy of returns. It may require taxpayers to provide copies of their federal income tax returns. The Department can examine people under oath with regard to taxable income and can compel the production of books, papers, and records, as well as the attendance of persons with knowledge of such income. The procedures for hearings and examinations are governed by The Fiscal Code (FC) [72 P.S. § 7355]. These powers are explained in Chapter 46.

¶411 Penalties, Additions, and Interest

Pennsylvania personal income tax law makes provisions for both penalties and additions to tax. The distinction is important. A penalty is not deductible for federal income tax purposes, but an addition to tax is. The explanation of penalties and additions in this paragraph indicates whether a particular "penalty" is in fact a penalty or an addition to tax. Under certain circumstances, additions or penalties can be waived (see below).

- *Tax evasion*

A person found guilty of willfully attempting in any manner to evade or defeat any tax (or payment thereof) imposed by the Pennsylvania personal income tax provisions (a misdemeanor) is subject to a fine up to $25,000, or a prison term up to two years, or both (in addition to other penalties provided by law) [72 P.S. § 7353(a)].

- *Failure to file*

Failure to file a return (except for reasonable cause) results in an *addition to tax*. The addition is 5% per month (or fraction of a month) of the net tax due up to a maximum of 25%. The minimum addition for failure to file is $5 [72 P.S. § 7352(a)]. A person convicted of failure to file a personal income tax return (a misdemeanor) is subject to a fine of up to $5,000, or a prison term up to two years, or both [72 P.S. § 7353(c)].

- *Fraudulent returns and documents*

A taxpayer convicted of submitting a return containing a written declaration that it is made under penalties of perjury, knowing that it contained false information, is guilty of a misdemeanor punishable by a fine up to $5,000, or a prison term up to two years, or both [72 P.S. § 7353(d)]. This provision also applies to preparers of returns. Anyone who willfully delivers or discloses to the Department of Revenue any list, return, account, statement, or other document, knowing it was fraudulent as to any material matter, is subject to the same punishment [72 P.S. § 7353(c)]. A *penalty* of $250 is imposed on any person required by regulation to furnish an information return who furnishes a false or fraudulent return [72 P.S. § 7352(f)(2)].

- *Failure to pay*

Willful failure to pay personal income tax is a misdemeanor punishable by a fine up to $5,000, or a prison term up to two years, or both.

- *Underpayment of tax*

Underpayment of tax due to negligence or intentional disregard of rules and regulations (but without intent to defraud) results in an *addition to tax* equal to 5% of the underpayment [72 P.S. § 7352(b)(1)]. If any underpayment of personal income tax is due to negligence or intentional disregard of rules and regulations (but without intent to defraud) *and* the underpayment is more than 25% of the amount shown on the taxpayer's return, an additional tax equal to 25% of the underpayment is imposed [72 P.S. § 7352(b)(2)]. If any part of the underpayment is due to *fraud,* the "penalty" is an *addition to tax* of 50% of the underpayment. This addition is in lieu of any additions imposed for underpayment due to negligence [72 P.S. § 7352(c)].

• *Failure to pay estimated tax*

Failure to pay any or all of an installment of estimated tax results in an *addition to tax* equal to 9% of the underpayment for the period of underpayment. The underpayment period begins on the day after the due date and ends when the tax is paid but cannot extend beyond the 15th day of the fourth month following the close of the taxpayer's tax year [61 Pa. Code § 119.23(b)]. No additions are imposed if a taxpayer, on or before the last payment date for each installment, meets one of the "safe harbors" (explained at ¶ 312).

• *Failure to remit taxes collected*

A person required to collect, account for, and remit personal income taxes who willfully fails to collect the tax or truthfully account for and remit the tax, or who willfully attempts to evade the tax, is subject to a penalty equal to the total amount of the tax evaded, not collected, accounted for, or remitted (in addition to other penalties that may be provided by law) [72 P.S. § 7352(e)]. In addition, a person found guilty of willfully failing to collect or truthfully account for and pay income tax (a misdemeanor) will be sentenced to pay a fine of up to $25,000, or a prison term up to two years, or both [72 P.S. § 7353(b)]. These provisions apply to failure to withhold income tax from employees or failure to pay withheld taxes to the Commonwealth. If this penalty is imposed, no penalty for underpayment due to negligence or fraud (see above) or for late filing of a quarterly withholding return (see "Employee taxes," below) will be imposed. A "person" for this purpose includes an officer or employee of a corporation (or a member or employee of a partnership), who is under a duty (as an officer, employee, or member) to collect, account for, and remit these taxes [72 P.S. § 7352(e)].

• *Employee taxes*

An employer who willfully furnishes a false or fraudulent statement to an employee or who willfully fails to furnish a statement as required is subject (for each failure) to a penalty of $50 per employee [72 P.S. § 7352(f)(1)]. If an employer required to file quarterly withholding returns does not remit the withholdings on or before the due date for the quarterly return (determined without regard to extensions), there shall be added to the tax and paid to the Department of Revenue each month 5% of the underpayment for each month or fraction thereof for the period beginning with the due date and ending with the date the tax is paid. The underpayment will (for purposes of computing the addition for any month) be reduced by the amount of any part of the tax paid by the beginning of that month. The total additions imposed shall not exceed 50% of the amount of tax due with the return reduced by any amount paid by the return due date and by any credit against the tax that may be claimed on the return [72 P.S. § 7352(h)].

• *Information returns*

A taxpayer who filed a false or fraudulent information return is subject to a penalty of $50 per failure [72 P.S. § 7352(f)(2)]. A Pennsylvania S corporation that files a false or fraudulent return, or that fails to file the return in the manner and at the time required under 72 P.S. § 7330.1, is subject to a penalty of $250 per failure.

• *Defective returns*

If a taxpayer (individual, estate, or trust) files what purports to be a return but which does not contain sufficient information to judge the correctness of the self-assessment or contains information that on its face indicates a substantially incorrect self-assessment and the self-assessment is due to a frivolous position or a desire to

¶411

delay or impede the administration of the tax, the taxpayer is subject to a *penalty* of $500 (in addition to any other penalty imposed by law) [72 P.S. § 7352(i)].

• *Federal Form 1099-MISC*

Any person required to file a Federal Form 1099-MISC (to the Department or to an employee) who willfully furnishes a false or fraudulent form or who willfully fails to file in the manner required is subject to a $50 penalty per failure [72 P.S. § 7351(f)(4), (5)].

• *Flow-through entities*

If any amount of tax required to be withheld and remitted by a partnership, association, or Pennsylvania S corporation is not paid on or before the prescribed due date, there shall be added to the tax and paid to the Department of Revenue each month 5% of the underpayment for each month or fraction thereof for the period from the due date to the date paid. The underpayment (for purposes of computing the addition for any month) is reduced by the amount of tax paid by the beginning of the month. The total of additions under this provision cannot exceed 50% of the amount of the tax [72 P.S. § 7352(j)].

• *Bad checks*

When the Department of Revenue receives uncollectible checks from taxpayers, it charges a fee of 10% of the face amount plus all protest fees to the *presenter* of the check, in addition to the interest and penalties otherwise provided by law. The *additions to tax* imposed by this provision shall not exceed $200, nor be less than $10 [72 P.S. § 7352(g)].

• *Failure to keep records or supply information*

Failure to keep required records or supply required information is a misdemeanor punishable by a fine up to $5,000, or a prison term up to two years, or both [72 P.S. § 7353(c)].

Interest on underpayments is governed by the general provisions of the Fiscal Code (FC) and is explained at ¶ 4612.

• *Waiver or abatement of additions or penalties*

Upon the filing of a petition for reassessment or for review by a taxpayer (other than an employer), the department may waive or abate additions or penalties of $300 or less if the taxpayer has acted in good faith, with no negligence or intent to defraud [72 P.S. § 7352.1].

¶412 Review by Board of Finance and Revenue

CAUTION! New Procedures

This discussion of the procedures of the Board of Finance and Revenue applies to appeals of assessments issued prior to January 1, 2008. For Board of Finance and Revenue procedures for appeals of assessments issued after December 31, 2007, see ¶ 4604. Effective April 1, 2014 the Board has been reconstituted and has adopted new rules and procedures. These changes are clearly set out on the Board's website. Anyone who practices before the Board should carefully review the Boards newly adopted interim operating rules. Some highlights include:

1. All evidence must be submitted within 60 days of the filing date of the petition.

2. Offers in compromise must be submitted within 30 days of the filing of the petition.

3. All written communications with Board staff must be shared with the Department of Revenue.

4. The Department of Revenue must be given the opportunity to attend any meetings held by practitioners with Board staff.

Taxpayers have the right to file a petition for review with the Board of Finance and Revenue when they are dissatisfied with reassessments made by the Department of Revenue. Ordinarily, petitions for review must be filed within 60 days (90 days, prior to October 30, 2017) after the mailing date of notice by the Department of its action on a petition for reassessment. However, if the Department fails to notify a taxpayer of its decision within six months, the petition is considered denied. In such a case, the taxpayer has 120 days after the mailing date of written notice of the Department's failure to dispose of the petition with six months to file a petition for review with the Board of Finance and Revenue [72 P.S. 9702].

A petition for review must specifically state the reasons upon which the petitioner relies or incorporate, by reference, the petition for reassessment in which the reasons are stated and must be supported by affidavit that it is not made for the purpose of delay and that the facts in it are true [72 P.S. 9702].

The Board of Finance and Revenue must dispose of petitions for review within six months after they are received. The period can now be extended for an additional six months at the discretion of the Board. The Board may uphold the Department's action on the petition for reassessment, or it may reassess the tax involved based on its interpretation of the law. If the Board does not act within six months, the action of the Department of Revenue (on the petition for reassessment) is considered sustained. The Board of Finance and Revenue must mail notice of its action to both the taxpayer and the Department of Revenue [72 P.S. 9704]. See ¶4605 for a detailed explanation of the operation of the Board of Finance and Revenue.

¶413 Judicial Review

If the Commonwealth or the taxpayer involved in a case before the Board of Finance and Revenue is dissatisfied with a decision of the Board, the next step in the appeal process is a court proceeding. The first court involved in the process is the Commonwealth Court of Pennsylvania. Commonwealth Court decisions may be appealed to the Supreme Court of Pennsylvania [61 Pa. Code § 119.8]. Appeal from decisions of the Pennsylvania Supreme Court must be made to the U.S. Supreme Court.

The judicial review process is explained at ¶4607.

PART III

SALES AND USE TAXES

In This Part

CHAPTER 5

INTRODUCTION, TAX RATE, AND COMPUTATION OF TAX

INTRODUCTION

¶501 General

Pennsylvania sales and use tax is excise tax imposed on the sale at retail of tangible personal property (unless exempt), hotel occupancy, and certain services. The sales tax is collected by the vendor and remitted to the Department of Revenue. The use tax is imposed on property used in Pennsylvania on which sales tax has not been paid. The use tax is the responsibility of the user. The Pennsylvania use tax is discussed at ¶722 and ¶723.

The sales and use taxes (including the hotel occupancy tax) are governed by Article II of the Tax Reform Code of 1971 [72 P.S. §§7201—7282]. Sales and use tax regulations are contained in Title 61 of the Pennsylvania Code [61 Pa. Code §§31.1—39.13], and sales and use tax rulings are contained in Title 61 of the Pennsylvania Code [61 Pa. Code §§41.1—58.13].

Sales and use taxes are administered by the Department of Revenue, Harrisburg, Pennsylvania [72 P.S. §7270]. The Department handles registrations and applications for licenses, collects the tax, makes rules and regulations, and conducts examinations and investigations necessary to administer and enforce the tax.

• *Revenue information*

According to a Department regulation [61 Pa. Code § 3.4], informational materials are issued to provide general information that will assist individuals or organizations. Revenue information material is issued for informational purposes only and should not be relied upon or used in tax appeals. Examples of revenue information are the *Pennsylvania Tax Update,* forms, pamphlets, tax bulletins, or information notices provided to taxpayers. Instructions on tax forms and instructional booklets accompanying forms also fall within this category.

Streamlined Sales Tax Project

The Streamlined Sales Tax Project (SSTP) is a project created by participating state governments and the District of Columbia. Its mission is to develop measures to design, test, and implement a sales and use tax system that radically simplifies sales and use taxes.

• *Pennsylvania participation in the Streamlined Sales Tax Project*

Pennsylvania is a participating state in the SSTP but is not an implementing state. "Participating states" are those states that support the mission of the SSTP and for which an elected official or body of elected officials has committed the state to participate in the SSTP. An "implementing state" is one that has the right to vote on the terms of the Interstate Agreement among the states (*i.e.*, the Streamlined Sales and Use Tax Agreement (SSUTA)).

• *Internet Tax Freedom Act*

The federal Internet Tax Freedom Act (ITFA) (P.L. 105-277, 112 Stat. 2681, 47 U.S.C. Sec. 151 note, amended by P.L. 107-75, P.L. 108-435, P.L. 110-108,. P.L. 113-164, P.L. 113-235, P.L. 114-53, P.L. 114-113, and P.L. 114-125) bars state and local governments from imposing multiple or discriminatory taxes on electronic commerce and taxes on Internet access.

A state or local government may continue to tax Internet access if the tax was generally imposed and actually enforced prior to October 1, 1998. However, this grandfather clause does not apply to any state that, prior to November 1, 2005, repealed its tax on Internet access or issued a rule that it no longer applies such a tax. The ITFA grandfather clause authorizing certain states to continue to tax Internet access is effective through June 30, 2020.

"Internet access" means a service that enables users to connect to the Internet to access content, information, or other services. The definition includes the purchase, use, or sale of telecommunications by an Internet service provider to provide the service or otherwise enable users to access content, information, or other services offered over the Internet. It also includes incidental services such as home pages, electronic mail, instant messaging, video clips, and personal electronic storage capacity, whether or not packaged with service to access the Internet. However, "Internet access" does not include voice, audio or video programming, or other products and services using Internet protocol for which there is a charge, regardless of whether the charge is bundled with charges for "Internet access."

The ITFA allows the taxation of otherwise exempt Internet access service charges that are aggregated (i.e. bundled) with and not separately stated from charges for telecommunications services or other taxable services, unless the Internet access provider can reasonably identify the charges for Internet access from its books and records kept in the regular course of business.

¶501

TAX RATE

¶505 Imposition and Rate

The sales tax is imposed on each separate sale at retail of tangible personal property and specified services within Pennsylvania at the rate of 6% of the purchase price and must be collected by the vendor [72 P.S. §7202(a)]. The use tax is imposed upon the use in Pennsylvania of tangible personal property and specified services purchased at retail if the sales tax has not been paid [72 P.S. §7202(b)]. The use tax is paid by the user (purchaser).

Consumer fireworks are also subject to an additional tax at the rate of 12%. [Act 43 (H.B. 542), Laws 2017, Section 43 (Sec. 2412)]

For detailed explanation of taxable property and services, see Chapter 7.

• *Bracket system of tax*

The Tax Reform Code provides a bracket system for computing sales and use taxes, as follows [72 P.S. §7203]:

Purchase Price	Tax
10¢ or less	No tax
11¢ but less than 18¢	1¢
18¢ but less than 35¢	2¢
35¢ but less than 51¢	3¢
51¢ but less than 68¢	4¢
68¢ but less than 85¢	5¢
85¢ but less than $1.01	6¢

On sales of $1.01 or more, the tax is 6% of each whole dollar plus the above bracket amount for fractions of a dollar.

Vending Machine Sales

The Commonwealth Court has held that computing tax on the gross receipts from the sales of products through vending machines results in double taxation. In *CRH Catering Co., Inc. v. Cmwlth.*, 539 A.2d 38 (Pa.Comm. 1988), the court held that gross receipts included the purchase price plus collected sales tax, since there is no practical way to collect sales tax on vending machine sales without including tax in the price indicated on the machine. To the extent that regulations impose tax on gross receipts, they are invalid. In *CRH Catering*, the taxpayer computed sales tax by dividing its gross receipts by 1.06 and then multiplying the result by 6%.

¶506 Registration and Licenses

Anyone who maintains a place of business in Pennsylvania selling or leasing taxable services or property must, prior to the beginning of business thereafter, apply to the Department (on a form prescribed by the Department) for a license. If a taxpayer maintains more than one place of business in Pennsylvania, the license will be issued for the principal place of business in the Commonwealth [72 P.S. §7208(a)]. There is no registration fee. Licenses are nonassignable [72 P.S. §7208(b)].

Condition for issuance of license: The issuance of the license is conditional upon the filing of all required Pennsylvania tax reports and payment of any Pennsylvania taxes not subject to a timely perfected administrative or judicial appeal or subject to a duly authorized deferred payment plan [72 P.S. §7208(b)].

Renewal of license: Any license issued after April 30, 1992, is valid for a period of five years [72 P.S. §7208(b)].

Refusal, suspension, or revocation of license: If an applicant for a license or a taxpayer holding a license has not filed all required tax reports and paid all taxes due, the Department may refuse to issue a license or may suspend or revoke an existing license. The Department must notify the applicant or licensee of any refusal, suspension, or revocation, and the applicant or licensee may file an appeal [72 P.S. §7208(b.1)]. The Department of Revenue is in fact revoking sales and use tax licenses for failure to file all required tax reports and pay all taxes.

Publication of Refusal, Suspension, or Revocation

When the Department of Revenue notifies an applicant or licensee of refusal, suspension, or revocation of license, the notice must contain a statement that the refusal, suspension, or revocation may be made public [72 P.S. §7208(b.1)].

Appeals: See ¶4602 for explanation of administrative appeals. If a taxpayer appeals a suspension or revocation, the taxpayer's license remains valid pending a final outcome of the appeals process [72 P.S. §7208(b.1)]. Note that effective July 1, 2013 the period for appealing a license suspension or revocation has been reduced from 90 days to 30 days.

Disclosure of refusal, suspension, or revocation: If no appeal is taken or if an appeal is taken and denied at the conclusion of the appeal process, the Department may disclose, by publication or otherwise, the identity of a person and the fact that the person's license has been refused, suspended, or revoked. Disclosure may include the basis for refusal, suspension, or revocation [72 P.S. §7208(b.1)].

• *Failure to get a license*

Failure to obtain a license prior to maintaining a place of business in Pennsylvania for the purpose of selling or leasing taxable services or property is a summary offense. The offering for sale or lease of any service or tangible personal property the sale or use of which is subject to the Pennsylvania sales and use tax, during any calendar day, constitutes a separate violation. The Secretary of Revenue is authorized to designate employees to cite taxpayers for making taxable sales without a license [72 P.S. §7208(c)

Penalties for failure to register: A person convicted of failure to register is subject to a fine of not less than $300 nor more than $1,500. If the fine is not paid, the sentence is imprisonment of not less than five days nor more then 30 days. This fine or imprisonment is in addition to any other penalties imposed by the statute [72 P.S. §7208(c)].

No License Does Not Mean No Tax Due

Failure to get a license does not relieve one of the responsibility to collect and remit the sales and use taxes on transactions subject to tax [72 P.S. §7208(d)].

• *Transient vendors*

Transient vendors must register (no fee) with the Department before beginning operation in Pennsylvania. This registration must be renewed and updated annually [72 P.S. §7248(a)]. Registration as a transient vendor is in addition to the general registration requirement discussed above [61 Pa. Code §39.2(a)]. Application for a transient vendor certificate must conform to all requirements prescribed by regulation [72 P.S. §7248(a)]. These requirements are specified in 61 Pa. Code §39.2. A transient vendor must possess the certificate at all times when conducting business in Pennsylvania and must show it upon demand by authorized employees of the Department or any law enforcement office [72 P.S. §7248(c)]. A transient vendor conducting business in Pennsylvania with a suspended or revoked license is, if convicted of the offense, subject to a fine of up to $2,500 for each offense [72 P.S. §7248.4]. If a transient vendor fails to exhibit a valid certificate upon demand by

¶506

authorized employees of the Department, those employees have the authority to seize, without warrant, the tangible personal property and the vehicle used to transport it [72 P.S. § 7248.3].

Upon registration, a transient vendor must post a bond of $500 with the Department of Revenue. After a period of demonstrated compliance (or if the transient vendor provides the license number of a promoter who has notified the Department of a show), the Department may eliminate or reduce the amount of bond [72 P.S. § 7248.1(a)]. A promoter for this purpose means a promoter of a show or shows in Pennsylvania who annually files an application for a promoter's license as required by 72 P.S. § 7248.6.

Who is a transient vendor? A "transient vendor" is any person who (1) brings taxable property into Pennsylvania (by automobile, truck, or other means of transportation) or purchases taxable property in Pennsylvania, or comes into Pennsylvania to perform taxable services, (2) offers or intends to offer taxable property or services for sale at retail within Pennsylvania, and (3) does not maintain a place of business (*e.g.,* established office, distribution house, sales house, warehouse, service enterprise, residence from which business is conducted) in Pennsylvania. The following are not transient vendors for purposes of Pennsylvania sales and use taxes: (1) persons who deliver tangible personal orders that were solicited or placed by mail or other means; or (2) persons who handcraft items for sale at special events (*e.g.,* fairs, carnivals, art and craft shows, and other festivals and celebrations within Pennsylvania) [72 P.S. § 7201(t)]. A "handcrafted item" is one predominately made or created by hand. Handicrafting generally consists of giving new shapes, new qualities, or new combinations to matter [61 Pa. Code § 39.1].

¶507 Multistate Sales

Vendors engaging in business in more than one state (*i.e.,* in interstate commerce) may be subject to taxation in more than one state. The restrictions of the Commerce Clause of the U.S. Constitution apply to state taxation of interstate commerce. The criteria for determining the constitutionality of a tax on interstate commerce are those set forth by the U.S. Supreme Court in the *Complete Auto Transit* case. See ¶913 for discussion of the *Complete Auto Transit* case. A state tax on interstate commerce is constitutional if it meets all of the following four criteria:

(1) The tax is applied to an activity that has a substantial nexus with the taxing state.

(2) The tax is fairly apportioned.

(3) The tax does not discriminate against interstate commerce.

(4) The tax is fairly related to the services provided by the state.

Election requirement for remote sellers and other entities: Beginning in 2018, certain remote sellers, marketplace facilitators, and referrers are required to either (1) comply with existing sales and use tax laws or (2) notify Pennsylvania purchasers regarding their potential sales and use tax responsibilities and report certain information regarding purchasers or remote sellers to the Department of Revenue. If they elect to comply with the notice and reporting requirements, the remote sellers and marketplace facilitators must also provide reports to purchasers regarding their purchases, and referrers must also provide reports to remote sellers. The election requirement applies to remote sellers, marketplace facilitators, and referrers with aggregate sales of tangible personal property subject to Pennsylvania sales and use tax of $10,000 or more in the previous 12-calendar-month period. The election must be made by March 1, 2018, and by June 1 of each subsequent calendar year. [Act 43 (H.B. 542), Laws 2017, Section 4 (Secs. 213—213.6)]

• *Maintaining a place of business within Pennsylvania*

The critical question of nexus involves the determination of whether or not a vendor is maintaining a place of business within Pennsylvania. A vendor maintaining a place of business within Pennsylvania is required to comply with all the provisions of the Tax Reform Code, including the requirement to pay or to collect and remit sales and use taxes [61 Pa. Code § 56.1(a)]. This includes out-of-state vendors who come within the taxing jurisdiction of Pennsylvania by maintaining a place of business in Pennsylvania. The term "maintaining a place of business" in Pennsylvania is broadly defined [72 P.S. § 7201(b)] and includes the following:

(1) Having, maintaining, or using within Pennsylvania (directly or through a subsidiary, representative, or agent) an office, distribution house, sales house, warehouse, service enterprise or other place of business; or any agent of general or restricted authority, or representative, irrespective of whether the place of business or agent is located in Pennsylvania, permanently or temporarily, or whether the person or subsidiary maintaining the place of business, representative, or agent is authorized to do business in Pennsylvania [72 P.S. § 7201(b)(1)].

(2) Engaging in any activity as a business within Pennsylvania by any person (either directly or through a subsidiary, representative, or agent) in connection with the lease, sale or delivery of tangible personal property or the performance of services thereon for use, storage or consumption or in connection with the sale or delivery for use of the services described in subclauses (11) through (18) of clause (k) of 72 P.S. § 7201. This includes (but is not limited to) having, maintaining or using any office, distribution house, sales house, warehouse or other place of business, any stock of goods or any solicitor, canvasser, salesman, representative or agent under its authority, at its direction or with its permission, regardless of whether the person or subsidiary is authorized to do business in Pennsylvania [72 P.S. § 7201(b)(2)].

(3) Regularly or substantially soliciting orders within Pennsylvania in connection with the lease, sale or delivery of tangible personal property to or the performance thereon of services or in connection with the sale or delivery of the services described in subclauses (11) through (18) of clause (k) of 72 P.S. § 7201 for residents of Pennsylvania by means of catalogues or other advertising, whether the orders are accepted within or without Pennsylvania [72 P.S. § 7201(b)(3)].

(4) Entering Pennsylvania by any person to provide assembly, service, or repair of tangible personal property (either directly or through a subsidiary, representative, or agent) [72 P.S. § 7201(b)(3.1)].

(5) Delivering tangible personal property to locations within Pennsylvania if the delivery includes the unpacking, positioning, placing, or assembling of the tangible personal property [72 P.S. § 7201(b)(3.2)].

(6) Having any contact within Pennsylvania that would allow the Commonwealth to require a person to collect and remit tax under the Constitution of the United States [72 P.S. § 7201(b)(3.3)].

(7) Providing a customer's mobile telecommunications deemed to be provided by the customer's home service provider under the Mobile Telecommunications Sourcing Act [4 U.S.C. § 116], within the meaning of the Mobile Telecommunications Sourcing Act [72 P.S. § 7201(b)(3.4)]. See ¶ 720.

• *Vendor Enforcement Program (VEP)*

Enabling legislation: Out-of-state vendors or their subsidiaries, agents, or representatives who enter Pennsylvania for the purpose of delivering, assembling, servicing, or repairing tangible personal property are "maintaining a place of business within Pennsylvania" and are thus subject to the Pennsylvania sales and use tax [72

P.S. § 7201(b)(3.1)]. This provision enabled the Pennsylvania Department of Revenue to establish a Vendor Enforcement Program (VEP) that enhances its ability to collect Pennsylvania taxes (*e.g.,* sales tax, corporate net income tax, personal income tax) from out-of-state vendors.

Implementation: The implementation of the VEP involves the establishment of roadside stops to interview truck drivers to determine whether their business activities within Pennsylvania subject them or the persons for whom they act as agents, representatives, or subsidiaries, to the payment of Pennsylvania sales, corporate, or personal income taxes. The Department of Revenue conducts this program at PennDOT weight stations throughout Pennsylvania and relies on the Pennsylvania State Police to stop and temporarily detain the vehicles. Once the vehicles are stopped, Department of Revenue personnel interview the truck drivers and inspect shipping documents, bills of lading, and invoices to determine if taxes are owed to the Commonwealth. If appropriate, the inspecting agent will issue a jeopardy assessment.

Jeopardy assessments: The statutory definition of "maintaining a place of business within Pennsylvania" contained in 72 P.S. § 7201(b)(3.1) also authorizes the Department of Revenue to issue jeopardy assessments to vendors who have not paid tax properly owing to the Commonwealth and to seize property as a means of compelling security for payment of tax. If a jeopardy assessment is issued by the inspecting agent, the truck driver vendor (company) will either pay the jeopardy assessment, post a bond, or register for a license. If the truck driver (company) refuses to comply, the Department of Revenue now has the authority to require security by seizing both the vehicle and the goods. All jeopardy assessments and supporting documentation will also be forwarded to the Discovery Unit of the Department of Revenue for further review and disposition [*Pennsylvania Tax Update No. 103,* Pennsylvania Department of Revenue, January/February 2003].

• *Exemption for commercial printers*

For purposes of defining the phrases "doing business in this Commonwealth," "carrying on activities in this Commonwealth," "having capital or property employed or used in this Commonwealth," or "owning property in this Commonwealth" as used in the corporate net income and capital stock/franchise statutes, the following activities are excluded [72 P.S. § 10003.10]:

(1) Owning or leasing of tangible or intangible property by a person who has contracted with an unaffiliated commercial printer for printing, provided that (a) the property is for use by the commercial printer; and (b) the property is located at the Pennsylvania premises of the commercial printer.

(2) Visits by a person's employees or agents to the premises in Pennsylvania of an unaffiliated commercial printer with whom the person has contracted in connection with the contract.

(3) Owning of printed matter and other items packaged therewith by a person who has contracted with an unaffiliated commercial printer for printing on the premises of an unaffiliated commercial printer prior to deliver of the property regardless of to whom or by whom the printer matter is delivered or mailed.

NOTE: This provision allows Pennsylvania printing firms to do business with out-of-state customers without making the customer liable for Pennsylvania corporate net income or capital stock/franchise taxes merely by reason of doing business with a Pennsylvania firm. However, an out-of-state customer might be liable for Pennsylvania taxes by reason of some other activity that establishes nexus.

The provision with respect to powder metallurgy parts (discussed below) also allows Pennsylvania firms deal with out-of-state customers without making them subject to Pennsylvania taxes. However, the powder metallurgy manufacturer might incur Pennsylvania nexus by reason of some other activity.

• *Exemption for powder metallurgy parts*

For purposes of defining the phrases "doing business in this Commonwealth," "having capital or property employed or used in this Commonwealth," or "owning property in this Commonwealth" for corporate net income tax and capital stock/ franchise tax purposes, the following activities are excluded [72 P.S. § 10003.19]:

(1) Owning or leasing of intangible and tangible property (including dies, molds, tooling, and related equipment) by a person who has contracted with an unaffiliated manufacturer of powder products for manufacturing, provided that (a) the property is for use by the powder metallurgy product manufacturer; (b) the property is located at the Pennsylvania premises of the powder metallurgy product manufacturer; and (c) the products manufactured using such property are incorporated into products produced outside Pennsylvania by the owner or lessor of the property.

(2) Visits by a person's employees or agents to the premises in Pennsylvania of an unaffiliated powder metallurgy product manufacturer with whom the person has contracted for manufacturing in connection with the contract.

(3) Owning of manufactured powder metallurgy products and other items packaged therewith, by a person who has contracted with an unaffiliated powder metallurgy products manufacturer for manufacturing of products, on the premises of the unaffiliated powder metallurgy products, on the premises of the unaffiliated powder metallurgy products manufacturer prior to delivery of the property.

• *Mail-order sales*

One area in which it has been difficult for states to demonstrate sufficient nexus to require collection of use tax by vendors is the mail-order business. See ¶ 722 for discussion of the taxation of mail-order sales.

• *Interstate travel*

The U.S. Supreme Court upheld an Oklahoma sales tax on the full purchase price of a bus ticket from Oklahoma to another state (sold by a Minnesota-based interstate carrier). The reasoning of the Court was that the tax satisfied the four-pronged test of *Complete Auto Transit* (see ¶ 913). The issue was whether the tax was fairly apportioned (the second prong of the *Complete Auto Transit* test). The purchase of the ticket could occur only in Oklahoma. Thus, no apportionment was necessary. The tax had a substantial nexus with Oklahoma because the ticket was purchased in Oklahoma and the service originated in Oklahoma. There was no discrimination against the interstate commerce because the tax was imposed on both the intrastate and the interstate portions of the travel. The tax was found to be reasonably related to the services provided by Oklahoma. In the Oklahoma case, the tax was imposed on the purchaser of the ticket, who could purchase the ticket only in Oklahoma. The Court distinguished the Oklahoma case from another case in New York in which the tax was imposed on the carrier, which was potentially subject to tax in other states [*Oklahoma Tax Commission v. Jefferson Lines, Inc.*, 514 U.S. 175 (1995)].

Sales and Income Taxes Differ

Imposition of taxes on or measured by net income is restricted by P.L. 86-272; imposition of sales and use taxes is not. See the explanation of P.L. 86-272 at ¶ 913. Therefore, nexus for purposes of the imposition of sales and use taxes is "thinner" than nexus for corporate net income tax purposes. For example, employment of "missionary salesmen" in a state is sufficient nexus for sales and use tax purposes but not for corporate net income tax purposes. See the explanation of the *U.S. Tobacco* case at ¶ 913.

COMPUTATION OF TAX

¶510 Purchase Price

Sales and use tax is imposed on the purchase price of each sale at retail at the rate of 6%. See ¶505 for an explanation of rates. "Purchase price" means the total value of anything paid or delivered, or promised to be paid or delivered, whether in money or otherwise, in complete performance of a sale at retail or purchase at retail, but does not include a rental or license to use. There is no deduction on account of the cost or value of the property sold, cost or value of transportation, or cost or value of labor or service, interest or discount paid or allowed after the sale is consummated, any other taxes imposed by Pennsylvania, or any other expense, except gratuities or separately stated deposit charges for returnable containers [72 P.S. §7201(g)(1); 61 Pa. Code §33.1].

• *Trade-ins*

A deduction from the purchase price is allowed for the value of tangible personal property taken in trade or exchange in lieu of the whole or any part of the purchase price. The amount allowed to the customer is considered to be the value of the property [72 P.S. §7201(g)(2)].

• *Purchase price deemed to be inaccurate*

If, because of affiliation of interests between the vendor and purchaser or (without regard to affiliation) for any other reason, the purchase price declared by the vendor or taxpayer is not, in the opinion of the Department, indicative of the true value or fair price of the article or service, the Department may determine the amount of constructive purchase price for purposes of computing the tax. In the case of a transaction between a parent and a subsidiary, affiliate or controlled corporation of a parent corporation, there is a rebuttable presumption that the transaction is not at arm's length [72 P.S. §7201(g)(3)].

• *Full consideration included in purchase price*

When there is a transfer or retention of possession or custody (whether termed a rental, lease, service or otherwise) of tangible personal property (including but not limited to linens, aprons, motor vehicles, trailers, tires, industrial office and construction equipment, and business machines), the full consideration paid or delivered to the vendor or lessor is considered the purchase price, *even though such consideration is separately stated and designated as payment for something other than the tangible property* (*e.g.*, processing, laundering, service, maintenance, insurance, repairs, depreciation). If a vendor provides an employee to operate tangible personal property, the value of the employee's labor may be excluded *if separately stated*. If a lessee pays a person other than the lessor for maintenance, insurance, or repair of tangible personal property which the lessee has possession or custody of under a rental contract or lease agreement, the value of such payments are included in the purchase price [72 P.S. §7201(g)(4)].

• *Exceptions*

The following are exceptions to the rule that the sales tax is imposed upon the original purchase price:

(1) *Vehicle dealers:* If any person actively and principally engaged in the business of selling new or used motor vehicles, trailers or semitrailers, and registered with the Department in the "dealer's class," acquires a motor vehicle, trailer, or semitrailer for the purpose of resale, and prior to such resale, uses the

motor vehicle, trailer or semitrailer for a taxable use, that person may pay a tax equal to 6% of the fair rental value of the motor vehicle, trailer, or semitrailer during the taxable use. This election does not apply to the use of a vehicle as a wrecker, parts truck, delivery truck, or courtesy car [72 P.S. § 7205(a)].

(2) *Commercial aircraft operator:* A commercial aircraft operator who acquires an aircraft for resale or lease, making a valid claim for exemption at the time of purchase, and who subsequently makes taxable use of the aircraft may elect to pay a tax of 6% of the fair rental value during taxable use [72 P.S. § 7205(b)].

(3) *First taxable use in Pennsylvania:* If the user of tangible personal property purchased it at least six months before its first taxable use in Pennsylvania, she/he may elect to pay tax on the fair market value of the property at the time and place of its first taxable use in Pennsylvania [72 P.S. § 7201(g)(5)].

• *Employment agency services and help supply services*

The purchase price of employment agency services and help supply services is the service fee paid by the purchaser to the party who supplies the service. The service fee is the total charge or fee of the supplier minus the following direct costs of supplying the employee: wages; salaries; bonuses and commissions; employment benefits; expense reimbursements; and payroll and withholding taxes, to the extent that these costs are *specifically itemized or, in the aggregate, stated in billings from the supplier* [72 P.S. § 7201(g)(6)]. For an explanation of taxation of these services, see ¶ 703.

• *Premium cable service*

Unless the vendor *separately states* that portion of the billing that applies to premium cable service, the total bill for the provision of all cable services is subject to sales tax [72 P.S. § 7201(g)(7)]. For an explanation of premium cable service, see ¶ 719.

¶511 Cancellations, Returns, Allowances, and Exchanges

The following is a discussion of how sellers and purchasers must account for sales tax on purchases involving cancellation, returns, allowances, exchanges, repossession, and bad debt.

• *Tax not remitted*

If a tax has been returned to a purchaser (or the purchaser's account has been credited for the tax), a seller may deduct a sale or allowance from the amount of gross and taxable sales if, during the same reporting period as a taxable sale was made, one of the following occurs [61 Pa. Code § 33.3(a)]:

(1) The contract of sale is canceled.

(2) The property is returned.

(3) An allowance is made by reason of merchandise being defective.

(4) An exemption certificate is presented by the purchaser to the seller.

• *Tax remitted*

If a tax has not been returned to a purchaser or credited to the purchaser's account, the purchaser may file a claim for credit or refund with the Department of Revenue. If the tax has been returned to the purchaser or credited to the purchaser's account, the purchaser may assign his/her rights to file for refund or credit to the seller, and the seller may file a claim for refund or credit for the tax [61 Pa. Code § 33.3(b)(1)].

If the sale amount and corresponding amount of tax has been returned to the purchaser or credited to the purchaser's account, the seller may deduct the amount of the sale or allowance from the amount of gross and taxable sales for a succeeding reporting period, if it was reported as a taxable sale in a prior reporting period and one of the following applies:

(1) The contract of sale is canceled.

(2) The property is returned.

(3) An allowance is made by reason of merchandise being defective.

(4) An exemption certificate is presented by the purchaser to the seller [61 Pa. Code § 33.3(b)(1), (2)].

The seller claiming the credit must maintain records of the transactions for which the credit is claimed that show the name and address of the person to whom the tax was returned, the reason for the return, and the amount of tax returned [61 Pa. Code § 33.3(b)(3)].

• *Repossession*

Repossession of property by a seller is not considered a canceled or return sale. Therefore, sales tax is due on the full original purchase price within 30 days of sale, whether or not the property was later repossessed by the seller [61 Pa. Code § 33.3(c)].

• *Bad debts*

A seller cannot take a sales tax credit for bad debts or uncollectible accounts but must remit sales tax upon the original purchase price of the property sold [61 Pa. Code § 33.3(d)].

¶512 Credit and Lay-Away Sales

A "credit sale" is a sale in which the purchaser pays part of the total purchase price after the time of purchase. A sale is considered to be on credit whether it is made by open credit (including the use of a credit card) or secured transaction, such as a chattel mortgage, conditional sales, or bailment lease [61 Pa. Code § 33.1].

When sales are made on credit (wholly or partly), the vendor must require the purchaser to pay the total amount of sales tax due on the entire purchase at the time the sale is made, or within 30 days thereafter, and remit the tax to the Department (regardless of whether the vendor received payment from the purchaser) with the next return required to be filed [72 P.S. § 7246].

A "lay-away sale" is a transaction in which a seller agrees to transfer title and possession of tangible personal property to a purchaser for an agreed price, with the transfer of title and possession being conditional upon payment of the agreed price in a series of deposits to be made within a specified period [61 Pa. Code § 33.1].

The sales tax on a lay-away sale is due when the seller appropriates the tangible personal property for the purposes of sale. The seller must collect the full amount of sales tax (as measured by the full agreed purchase price) at the earlier of the time of the first payment following such appropriation or within 30 days of the appropriation. If, during the same reporting period, the purchaser fails to make the agreed payment or otherwise forfeits his right to acquire title and possession under the terms of the agreement and receives a refund of the purchase price, the purchaser is also entitled to a refund of any sales tax paid. However, if the purchaser fails to receive any portion of the purchase price from the seller, the purchaser is not entitled to a refund of the sales tax applicable to that portion not returned to him [61 Pa. Code § 33.4(b)].

¶513 Credits Against the Tax

The following explanation discusses various credits that are allowed against sales and use taxes.

• *Property purchased outside Pennsylvania*

The law provides that a credit against sales and use taxes is allowable with respect to taxable property and services purchased for use outside Pennsylvania equal to a similar tax paid to another state if the other state grants a substantially similar tax relief from Pennsylvania sales and use taxes [72 P.S. § 7206(a)].

• *TPPR (Taxes Paid-Purchases Resold) credit*

There are times when a vendor pays sales or use tax on property included in inventory because at the time of purchase the vendor considers him/herself as the ultimate consumer. If, however, the vendor later sells or leases the merchandise on which the sales tax has been paid in the regular course of business, the vendor is entitled to a credit for "Taxes Paid-Purchases Resold." The credit can be claimed by writing TPPR beside the word "Credit" on the credit line of the return and listing the amount of the credit. The credit can never be greater than the amount of tax remitted with the return, but any excess can be carried over to subsequent returns if the taxpayer retains documentation supporting the credit. If the credit cannot be recovered within three years of the original payment of tax on the item resold or leased, a timely filing of a petition for return must be made to recover the remainder of the tax [61 Pa. Code § 58.11].

• *Call center credit*

Prior to July 1, 2013, call centers were entitled to a credit against the sales and use tax for gross receipts tax paid by a telephone company on the receipts derived from the sales of incoming and outgoing interstate telecommunications services to the call center [72 P.S. § 7206(b)]. The call center credit was repealed effective July 1, 2013.

• *Reciprocal tax credits on motorboats*

Pursuant to a reciprocal agreement with the Maryland Department of Natural Resources, Pennsylvania grants a credit for excise taxes imposed on motorboats in Maryland. Maryland imposes a 5% excise tax on motorboats; Pennsylvania imposes a 6% sales and use tax on motorboats. Both taxes are based on the purchase price of the boat. The maximum credit allowed by Pennsylvania against its 6% sales tax is 5% (the amount collected by Maryland). Maryland, however, will not grant credit for Pennsylvania sales tax paid unless the boat was previously registered or numbered in Pennsylvania prior to being registered in Maryland. Taxpayers who purchase boats in Pennsylvania with the intention of registering them in Maryland should either have the boat delivered directly to Maryland or register with the Pennsylvania Fish Commission prior to taking the boat to Maryland. The biannual fee for registration depends on the length of the boat and ranges from $20 to $40 [*Pennsylvania Tax Update No. 40*, Pennsylvania Department of Revenue, September/October 1992].

• *Discount for prompt payment*

If a licensee timely files a return and pays the tax due less any discount, the licensee is entitled to apply as a credit against the tax due a discount of 1% of the amount of tax collected by him/her [72 P.S. § 7227].

• *Coal degasification tax credit*

Vendors may claim the coal degasification tax credit authorized by 72 P.S. § 8803-A in an amount equal to all sales and use taxes related to the operation and construction of the facility as defined by statute. This credit is explained at ¶ 1010.

• *First class cities economic development district act*

Residents of and qualified businesses located in first class cities economic development districts are entitled to exemptions from sales and use tax. This credit is explained at ¶ 1020.

¶513

¶514 Certificates of Exemption

Exemption certificates are certificates provided by purchasers to vendors to obtain goods and services without paying sales tax that would otherwise be due. Form REV-1220 (Sales and Use Tax Exemption Certificate) is used for both unit exemptions (*i.e.*, for single sales or leases) and for blanket exemptions (*i.e.*, for a series of transactions between the same parties) [61 Pa. Code § 32.2(d)(1)]. Form MV-4 ("Vehicles Sales and Use Tax Return") is used for all claims for exemption with respect to the purchase or lease of a motor vehicle, trailer, semitrailer, or tractor required to be registered with the Bureau of Motor Vehicles [61 Pa. Code § 32.2(d)(2)].

Exemption Certificates Must Be Regular and Complete

Be sure that exemption certificates received from customers are in good form and filled out correctly. Irregular and incomplete exemption certificates are not valid [*Bruce & Merrilees Electric Co. v. Cmwlth.*, 530 A.2d 994 (Pa.Commw. 1987)].

• *When exemption certificates are required*

A person who is required to collect tax on sales or rentals of tangible personal property or a taxable service is required to have an exemption certificate that was accepted in good faith in every case in which tax was not collected. In lieu of an exemption certificate, the vendor may present documentary evidence in the following situations: (1) the property sold or rented is not tangible personal property or a taxable service; (2) the customer is the United States or an instrumentality thereof, the Commonwealth, or a political subdivision or instrumentality of the Commonwealth; (3) the vendor was required to deliver the property sold, rented, or serviced to a destination outside Pennsylvania for use outside Pennsylvania and in fact did so [61 Pa. Code § 32.2(a)].

Qualified Businesses in a KOZ/KOEZ/KOIZ

Qualified businesses in a KOZ/KOEZ/KOIZ must obtain sales tax exemption numbers and present exemption certificates (REV-1220) when they make purchases of tangible personal property and services [*Retailers' Information Booklet* (REV-717), § 17].

Vendor relief from liability: Vendors who accept, in good faith, an exemption certificate disclosing a proper basis for exemption upon its face are relieved of collection or payment of tax for transactions covered by the certificate [72 P.S. § 7237(c)]. The certificate must be in the physical possession of the seller or lessor, and available for Departmental inspection, on or before the 60th day following the date of the sale or lease to which the certificate relates [61 Pa. Code § 32.2(b)(2)(iii)].

Representation of buyers insufficient: If a vendor *receives* an exemption certificate in good faith but cannot later produce it, a vendor may establish that the sales were tax-exempt through means other than an exemption certificate. If, however, a vendor does not first obtain an exemption certificate, the vendor cannot produce other evidence that the transactions are exempt from tax. In the absence of proof the transaction will be deemed taxable [61 Pa. Code § 32.2(b)(2)(iii)]. Thus, a vendor that never demanded or received exemption certificates but relied on the representations of its buyers was not relieved of collection or payment of tax [*Scholastic Services Organization, Inc. v. Cmwlth.*, 721 A.2d 74 (1998)]. Exceptions were filed, and the Court denied the exceptions for the reasons stated in its original opinion [Pa.Commw., No. 549 F.R. 1995 (April 11, 2002)]. However, in a footnote, the Court said the following:

"We are denying the exceptions and therefore reaffirming our previous order even though the Department of Revenue now admits, *inter alia*, that, where an exemption certificate is not received within 60 days or if no certificate is otherwise available for inspection, the Department will accept a **detailed** customer statement outlining the specific information regarding the sales transaction. According to the Department, a sufficient customer statement can be provided at any level of the proceedings—the Bureau of Audits, the Board of Appeals, the Board of Finance and Revenue, or on the stipulated record before us." [Respondent's Brief in Response to Exceptions, p. 16]

NOTE: This seems to conflict with the Department's position in the original case that a vendor cannot produce other evidence that a transaction is exempt unless the vendor first obtains a valid exemption certificate.

• *Penalties for misuse of exemption certificates*

The making of false or fraudulent statements on an exemption certificate by *anyone* (*e.g.*, seller, lessor, buyer, lessee, any representative or agent) is a misdemeanor punishable (upon conviction) by imprisonment up to one year, a fine up to $1,000, or both, plus costs of prosecution [61 Pa. Code § 32.2(c)].

No institution may claim an exemption from sales and use taxes as an institution of purely public charity unless it has received an order from the Department of Revenue approving and authorizing the exemption [10 P.S. § 381]. The Institutions of Purely Public Charity Act is discussed in more detail at ¶705 and ¶3505.

SALES AND USE TAXES

CHAPTER 6

RETURNS, PAYMENT OF TAX, AND RECORDS

RETURNS

¶601 Who Must File

Every person who is required to pay sales and use taxes or to collect and remit such taxes to the Department of Revenue must file returns [72 P.S. § 7215].

• *Returns by purely public charities*

The report must be in a form approved by the Department of Revenue and must include the following:

(1) A copy of the annual return filed or required to be filed with the IRS.

(2) The date the institution of purely public charity was organized.

(3) Any revocation of tax-exempt status by the IRS.

(4) Information of affiliates, including (a) the name and type of organization, (b) whether the affiliated group is organized on a for-profit or nonprofit basis, and (c) the relationship of each affiliated group to the institution making the report.

¶602 Returns

The Department of Revenue distributes forms to taxpayers. Reporting for the sales tax, the use tax, and the hotel occupancy tax is combined on one form. Returns may be filed by a duly authorized agent of the licensee. Any return not fully disclosing the required information is considered incomplete and may be rejected by the Department. If a taxpayer receives a notice that an incomplete return has been rejected, the taxpayer must immediately complete the return and file it. If a return in acceptable form is not filed before the due date, additions and interest will be added to the tax due. The Department of Revenue may also require information in addition to that provided for on the form [72 P.S. § 7216].

• *Report all sales*

Licensees should report on the basis of all sales made during the reporting period, reporting for credit transactions as required by regulation [61 Pa. Code § 34.3(b)(2)]. See ¶ 512 for an explanation of reporting for credit sales.

• *Where to file—Collection of use tax*

Returns should be submitted to the Pennsylvania Department of Revenue, Bureau of Receipts and Control (S&U), P.O. Box 2444, Harrisburg, PA 17105-2444. County treasurers (except in Philadelphia County) are authorized to receive payment of use taxes [72 P.S. § 7226].

Payment by Electronic Funds Transfer

Payment by Electronic Funds Transfer (EFT) is discussed at ¶ 4617.

• *Amended returns*

There is no statutory provision for amended sales and use tax returns. Taxpayers who have underpaid sales and use tax should remit the additional amount owed on their next returns. The underpayments may be subject to interest (see ¶ 4612) and penalties (see ¶ 4613).

• *Sales tax vendor discount*

For sales tax returns for periods ending after August 1, 2016, the sales tax vendor discount is capped at the lesser of one percent of the amount of sales tax collected or $25 on a monthly return, $75 on a quarterly return or $150 on a semi-annual return.

¶603 Due Dates

• *Monthly returns*

Monthly returns are required for licensees with liabilities of at least $600 but less that $25,000 [72 P.S. § 7217(a)(2)]. With respect to licensees whose actual tax liability for the third calendar quarter of the preceding year equal or exceeds $25,000 but is less than $100,000, the licenses must, on or before the 20th day of each month, file a single return including all of the requirements of 72 P.S. § 7217(a)(2) (effective October 1, 2012).

• *Quarterly returns*

All licensees whose total tax liability for the third calendar quarter of the preceding year was less than $600 but more than $75 must file quarterly returns. New licensees also file on a quarterly basis. The due dates for quarterly returns are as follows [72 P.S. § 7217(a)(1)]:

Returns	Due Date
First quarter	April 20
Second quarter	July 20
Third quarter	October 20
Fourth quarter	January 20

• *Semiannual returns*

Licensees whose total tax liability does not exceed $75 annually and who obtain authorization from the Department of Revenue may file semiannual returns. The due dates for semiannual returns are as follows [61 Pa. Code § 34.3(a)(3)(iii)]:

Returns	Due Date
January 1 to June 30	August 20
July 1 to December 31	February 20

¶603

• *Annual returns*

No annual returns may be filed unless required by rules and regulations of the Department promulgated and published at least 60 days prior to the end of the year with respect to which the returns are made. If annual returns are required, they cannot be required to be filed prior to the 20th day of the year succeeding the tax year [72 P.S. § 7217(b)].

• *Nonlicensees*

Any person, other than a licensee, liable for use tax must file a use tax return on or before the 20th day of the month succeeding the month in which the taxable use began. However, nonlicensees are not required to file negative returns for months in which no taxable use occurs. Licensees report use tax liability on their regular returns [72 P.S. § 7217(c)].

• *Timely mailing treated as timely filing*

The Department of Revenue considers all returns with a U.S. Postal Service postmark on or before the due date timely filed. Presentation of a receipt indicating that the report or payment was mailed by registered or certified mail on or before the due date is evidence of timely filing and payment [72 P.S. § 7220]. However, if the postmark is printed by use of a postage meter licensed by the U.S. Postal Service, the return will be presumed filed late if it is received by the Department of Revenue more than five days after the due date of the return [61 Pa. Code § 34.3(a)(2)(iv)].

¶604 Collection by Sellers

Every person maintaining a place of business in Pennsylvania must collect sales or use tax on taxable transactions at the time of the transaction and remit the tax to the Commonwealth, unless such collection and remittance is otherwise provided for in the sales and use tax provisions [72 P.S. § 7237(b)(1)]. Collection of sales and use taxes on motor vehicles, trailers, or semitrailers needing registration with the Pennsylvania Department of Transportation are subject to special collection provisions. See the explanation below.

De Facto Owners Responsible

A person may be liable for collection and remittance of sales taxes and for the filing of returns, even though that person is not the formal owner. See ¶ 808.

• *Property delivered to a Pennsylvania location*

A person not otherwise required to collect Pennsylvania sales and use tax that delivers tangible personal property to a location within Pennsylvania and that unpacks, positions, places, or assembles the tangible personal property is deemed to be selling or leasing taxable property or services. That person must, therefore, collect the tax from the purchaser at the time and delivery and remit the tax to the Department of Revenue if (1) the person delivering the tangible personal property is responsible for collecting any portion of the purchase price of the tangible personal property delivered and (2) the purchaser has not provided the person with proof that sales and use tax has been or will be collected by the seller or that the purchaser provided the seller with a valid exemption certificate [72 P.S. § 237(b)(1.1)].

• *Out-of-state sellers*

The definition of "maintaining a place of business" is broad enough to include out-of-state sellers who sell or lease taxable property or services in Pennsylvania. See ¶ 506 and ¶ 507 for an explanation of what constitutes "maintaining a place of business" in Pennsylvania.

• *Taxes in trust for Pennsylvania*

All sales and use taxes collected by any person from purchasers in accordance with this article and all sales and use taxes collected by any person from purchasers under color of the sales and use tax provisions that have not been properly refunded by such person to the purchaser shall constitute a trust fund for the Commonwealth. Such trust shall be enforceable against such person, his representatives and any person (other than a purchaser to whom a refund has been made properly) receiving any part of such fund without consideration, or knowing that the taxpayer is committing a breach of trust. However, any person receiving payment of a lawful obligation of the taxpayer from such fund shall be presumed to have received the same in good faith and without any knowledge of the breach of trust. Any person, other than a taxpayer, against whom the Department makes any claim under this section shall have the same right to petition and appeal as is given taxpayers by any provisions of this section [72 P.S. § 7225]. All taxes collected must be retained within Pennsylvania and cannot be sent outside Pennsylvania without the consent of the Department of Revenue [61 Pa. Code § 34.2(f)(1)].

• *Responsible party*

Generally, "trust fund" taxes (*e.g.,* the sales and use taxes; see above) are exceptions to the general rule that officers, employees and shareholders of a corporation are insulated from personal liability for the financial obligations of the business. An officer or employee of a corporation who is responsible for or had the duty to collect sales tax and possesses actual or implied control over funds and tax accounts will be personally assessed for collected sales tax that is not remitted. Generally, the Bureau of Business Trust Fund Taxes will issue an assessment against the chief operating and financial offers of a corporation if the facts of the particular case disclose that these individuals are involved in the day-to-day operation of the business and retain decision-making authority over financial matters. A responsible person need not be an officer of the corporation. Managers whose duties include authority and control over financial decisions may be held responsible. The Department presumes that the person who signs the sales tax return is the responsible party unless the facts of the particular case do not support that inference. Therefore, if the signator is an officer of the corporation, it is likely that an assessment will be made. On the other hand, if the person is a clerk or a tax practitioner without control over the funds of the business, no assessment will follow [*Pennsylvania Tax Update No. 75,* Pennsylvania Department of Revenue, May/June 1998].

Liability of Corporate Officer

Taxpayer (Brown) was charged by the Department of Revenue with personal liability for payment of corporate sales and withholding taxes collected by a bank but not forwarded to the state. The Commonwealth Court ruled that Brown was not liable for the taxes collected by the bank because the bank had taken possession of all of the corporation's assets due to a loan default. Brown, however, was held personally liable for taxes not paid over to the state while he was still in control of the company [*Brown v. Cmwlth.,* 670 A.2d 1222 (Pa.Commw. 1996)].

• *Exemption certificates*

Vendors must collect the tax at the time of sale of taxable property or service and remit the tax collected to the Department of Revenue. Any vendor required to collect tax from another person who fails to collect the proper amount of tax is personally liable for all of the tax that should have been collected. A vendor need not, however, collect the tax from a purchaser with an exemption certificate. The law provides that a purchaser or lessee must furnish the vendor an exemption certificate indicating that the sale is not taxable. Exemption certificates are explained at ¶ 514 [72 P.S. § 7237(c)].

Universal Exemption Certificate

Pennsylvania businesses may now use, as an alternative to Pennsylvania's Form REV-1220 (Sales and Use Tax Exemption Certificate), the Multistate Tax Commission's (MTC) Sales and Use Tax Exemption Certificate for resale purposes only. See ¶709 for more detail.

• *Direct payment permits*

Tax also is not collected by vendors on sales to customers with direct payment permits [72 P.S. § 7237(d)]. Direct payment permits are explained at ¶606.

• *Absorbing the tax*

It is illegal for a vendor to advertise, hold out, or state to the public or to any purchaser or user (directly or indirectly) that (1) any or all of the sales and use taxes will be absorbed by the vendor, (2) it will not be added to the purchase price, or (3) if paid, it will be refunded other than as part of a refund of the purchase price on account of return of the merchandise. This offense is a misdemeanor punishable by a fine (not to exceed $1,000) and costs of prosecution or imprisonment (not to exceed one year), or both. However, any person maintaining a place of business outside Pennsylvania may absorb the tax with respect to taxable sales made in the normal course of business to customers present at the place of business without being subject to fines and penalties [72 P.S. § 7268(b)].

Exception for Prepaid Telecommunications

Advertising tax-included prices is permissible (if provided by a service provider) for (1) prepaid telecommunications services not evidenced by the transfer of tangible personal property and (2) prepaid mobile telecommunications services [72 P.S. § 7268(b), as amended by Act 89 of 2002 (H.B. 1848), § 6]. See ¶719 through ¶721 for discussion of sales and use taxation of telecommunications services.

• *Failure to collect tax*

Any person who willfully fails or refuses to collect the tax from the purchaser and remit it to Pennsylvania is guilty of a misdemeanor and, upon conviction, is subject to the same punishment as that for absorbing the tax (explained above) [72 P.S. § 7268(b)(2)].

• *Precollection of tax*

The Department of Revenue may authorize or require particular categories of vendors selling tangible personal property for resale to precollect from the purchaser the tax that such purchaser will collect upon making the retail sale of the property. However, the Department may not require a vendor to precollect tax from a purchaser who purchases for resale more than $1,000 worth of tangible personal property from the vendor per year [72 P.S. § 7239]. Exemption of property purchased for resale is explained at ¶709.

Purchasers who prepay taxes on property for resale may be relieved of the duty to get a license (see ¶506) if the only reason the duty arises is by reason of the sale of the tangible personal property on which the prepayment of tax has been made. When a purchaser (who is also a vendor) later resells the property on which tax has been prepaid, the vendor must separately state at the time of resale the proper amount of tax on the transaction and reimburse him/herself for taxes previously paid.

¶604

• *Motor vehicles*

Payment of the applicable tax on taxable transfers of vehicles is prerequisite to obtaining a Certificate of Title. If a purchaser permits another party to pay the tax and that party's check is uncollectible, the purchaser is personally liable for the tax. All transfers for registration must be accompanied by a Form MV-4ST ("Vehicle Sales and Use Tax Return") [61 Pa. Code § 51.4(c), (d)].

No Certificate of Title: If there is a taxable transfer of a motor vehicle by a registered dealer who knows or has reason to know that a Certificate of Title will not be obtained or required, the dealer must collect and remit the tax. Failure to have evidence that established the securing of a Certificate of Title for or by the customer presumptively makes the dealer liable for the tax [61 Pa. Code § 31.43(b)].

PAYMENT OF TAX

¶605 General

All sales and use taxes are due and payable on the day the return must be filed [72 P.S. § 7221]. All taxes collected by licensees must be remitted with the return, even though the money collected is in excess of 6% of the vendor's total sales [61 Pa. Code § 34.3(b)(1)].

• *Payment by electronic funds transfer (EFT)*

Payments of $10,000 or more must be made by electronic funds transfer (EFT). See ¶ 4617.

Payment by Credit Card

Businesses can now pay sales and use tax by credit card if electronic transfer (EFT) is not required [*Pennsylvania Tax Update No. 102*, Pennsylvania Department of Revenue, November/December 2002]. Credit card payments can be made online or by telephone. American Express, Discover, MasterCard, and Visa cards are accepted. Taxpayers can access the credit card payment option at www.state.pa.us (PA Keyword: "credit card").

Credit card payment of sales and use tax is made through the following credit card service provider:

Official Payments Corp.

Phone: 1-800-2PAYTAX (1-800-272-9829)

Internet: www.officialpayments.com

Official Payments Corp. charges a 2.49% convenience fee ($1 minimum) for processing the credit card transaction. The convenience fee and tax payment will appear as two different charges on credit card statements. Payments are effective on the date they are charged. Note that authorized payments cannot be cancelled.

• *Prepayment of tax*

Whenever a vendor is forbidden by law or governmental regulation to charge and collect the purchase price in advance of or at the time of delivery, the vendor must prepay the tax. If the purchaser fails to pay the vendor for the purchase, the vendor can get a credit or refund of the tax paid on account of the uncollectible account. If the purchase price is later entirely or partly collected, the amount collected must first be applied to payment of the tax, which must be remitted with the first return filed after collection [72 P.S. § 7247].

¶606 Direct Payment Permits

Holders of direct payment permits may purchase property without paying sales tax to their suppliers. Instead, they later pay the tax directly to Pennsylvania. A tax

¶605

status determination must be made when the property or service is actually put to specific use or designated for specific use, or when its proposed use becomes known. Authorization to remit tax via a direct payment permit is limited to taxpayers who acquire tangible personal property or services under circumstances that make it impossible at the time of acquisition to predict the manner in which such property or services will be used and, therefore, impossible to determine whether the use will be taxable or exempt [61 Pa. Code § 34.4(a)].

• *Requirements*

In order to receive a direct payment permit, a taxpayer must meet all of the following requirements [61 Pa. Code § 34.4(b)]:

(1) An application for the permit must be filed with the Department on its special form.

(2) The taxpayer's business activities must include, in a substantial amount, acquisitions of tangible personal property or services, the use of which is impossible to determine at the time of acquisition.

(3) The taxpayer must substantiate the adequacy of its recordkeeping system with respect to the accumulation, recording, and reporting of purchases and the remittance of tax incurred.

(4) A taxpayer's business classification must be of such a nature and size that a direct payment permit is prerequisite to economical and efficient accounting for tax incurred.

(5) Permit holders must, as a condition of receiving a direct payment permit, give the Department access to any and all records maintained to account for the tax due.

• *How to use direct payment permits*

Direct payment permits must be inserted on a certificate of exemption and issued in the same manner as any certificate of exemption in lieu of paying the tax at the time of purchase. Certificates of exemption are explained at ¶514. However, direct payment permits can never be used in conjunction with the following transactions [61 Pa. Code § 34.4(c), (e)]:

(1) Purchase of any motor vehicle, trailer, semitrailer, or tractor that must be registered with the Pennsylvania Bureau of Motor Vehicles.

(2) Purchase of prepared food or beverages at any eating place.

(3) Purchase of occupancy or accommodations subject to the hotel occupancy tax.

A tax status determination, and a recordation thereof, must be made with respect to a purchase on the earlier of (1) the date when the proposed use is known or designated or (2) the date when the use actually occurs. However, it is expected that a tax status determination will be made within one year from the date of acquisition. If a tax status determination has not been made by that time, the Department of Revenue may, upon examination, consider the purchase taxable [61 Pa. Code § 34.4(c)].

• *Revocation of direct payment permits*

The Department of Revenue may revoke a direct payment permit for failure to comply with the conditions under which the permit was granted or for other reasons constituting misuse of the authority of the permit [61 Pa. Code § 34.4(d)].

• *Action after notice of revocation*

When a taxpayer receives a notice of revocation from the Department of Revenue, he/she must, within 30 days after receipt, do all of the following:

¶606

(1) Give notice to each supplier with whom the taxpayer has transacted business that no further claim for exemption will be made.

(2) Create and maintain records that all suppliers have received such notice.

(3) Return the permit certificate to the Department of Revenue.

• *Unilateral discontinuation*

When a taxpayer unilaterally discontinues direct payment authority due to cessation of business activities, corporate reorganization, corporate merger, or similar reasons, the Department of Revenue may waive any of the above requirements if the taxpayer makes a written request, stating the specific reasons for which special consideration is asked.

¶607 Extensions of Time

The Department of Revenue may grant a reasonable extension of time for filing a return, but the extension cannot exceed three months. Requests for extensions must be made in writing, showing good cause [72 P.S. §7218; 61 Pa. Code §34.3(a)(3)(iv)].

RECORDS

¶610 Recordkeeping Requirements

Persons liable for sales and use taxes, or for the collection of such taxes, must keep records as required by the regulations of the Department of Revenue [72 P.S. §7271(a), (c)]. Records must be maintained for at least three years from the end of the calendar year to which the records relate [61 Pa. Code §34.2(e)(3)].

• *Form of records*

The Department of Revenue considers the microfilm, including microfiche, re-production of general books of account and their supporting records of detail as acceptable books and records if they have been approved by the IRS. However, vendors must make available all codes and equipment needed to enable the Department of Revenue to audit the books and records [61 Pa. Code §34.2(g)]. As a minimum, vendors must maintain sales tax records that are amenable to a three-point audit. The requirements for a three-point audit are explained in 61 Pa. Code §34.2(a)(2).

• *Persons engaged in separate businesses*

A person who has a retail business and other businesses that do not involve taxable sales must keep records to show taxable sales separately from nontaxable sales. Failure to do this results in liability for tax on all sales from all of the taxpayer's businesses [72 P.S. §7271(d)]. For example, a person operating a retail business and a construction business may be required to pay sales tax on sales from both businesses if insufficient records are kept.

• *Segregation of tax*

Vendors must keep records that show the amount of tax separate from the total sales. This requirement is met by vendors who keep full-time memoranda of sales showing the amount of tax and the amount charged to the purchasers [61 Pa. Code §34.2(d)(1)(i)] or vendors who use a register that lists each tax collection on a tape retained by the vendor or who make such a list or record manually, using proper accounting and business practices, and keep it for departmental audit [61 Pa. Code §34.2(a)(1)(ii)]. However, vendors who give no sales memoranda or use registers showing only total sales must adopt some method of segregating tax from sales receipts and keep records of this segregation. A vendor desiring to use such a collection and recording procedure must apply for permission from the Department, describing in detail the procedure to be adopted [72 P.S. § 7271(d)].

• *Accessibility of records*

All records required to be kept must be dated, legible, written in English, and maintained and preserved so as to disclose in readily accessible and verifiable detail the basis of accuracy of vendor's or user's tax returns [61 Pa. Code § 34.2(e)].

• *Large number of mixed sales*

The Department recognizes the burden that would be placed on vendors whose businesses involve a large number of mixed sales if they had to maintain complete records of the tax incurred on every individual sales transaction. Therefore, vendors are allowed to keep records of tax incurred on a sample basis pursuant to the standards established by regulations [61 Pa. Code § 34.2(b)(1)].

Sampling System

A vendor should apply for authorization to use a sample recordkeeping system. A vendor may set up a sampling system without prior authorization, but in doing so the vendor proceeds at his/her own risk. Upon audit, the Department of Revenue and subsequent reviewing bodies may find the sampling technique inadequate. If there is no prior agreement by the Department, the records speak for themselves upon examination. If they are found inadequate, the vendor will be in the same position as any other vendor who lacks adequate sales tax records.

• *Purchasers*

Purchasers must keep all purchase invoices, requisitions, documents, and other records of their acquisition of taxable property and services. If purchasers pay the tax to vendors, they must maintain records of payment. If purchasers have not paid the tax to vendors, they must keep records showing why they considered the purchase nontaxable and information concerning the nature, use, price and dates of purchases and use of the property. This information must be adequate to enable the Department of Revenue to ascertain, with reasonable ease, whether or not use tax is due and, if so, how much [61 Pa. Code § 34.2(a)(1)].

SALES AND USE TAXES

CHAPTER 7

TRANSACTIONS SUBJECT TO SALES AND USE TAXES AND OTHER RELATED TAXES

SALES TAX

¶701 Transactions Subject to Sales Tax

The Pennsylvania sales tax is imposed upon each separate sale at retail of tangible personal property or specified services within the Commonwealth [72 P.S. §7202(a)].

• *Sale at retail*

"Sale at retail" is defined as follows [72 P.S. §7201(k)]:

(1) Any transfer for a consideration (whether absolute or conditional and by whatever means effected) of the ownership, custody, or possession of tangible personal property, including the grant of a license to use or consume. "Tangible personal property" is defined at ¶702.

(2) The rendition of the service of printing or imprinting of tangible personal property for a consideration for persons who furnish (directly or indirectly) the materials used in the printing or imprinting. See also ¶702 and ¶720.

(3) The rendition for a consideration of the following services:

(a) Washing, cleaning, waxing, polishing, or lubricating of motor vehicles of another, whether or not any tangible personal property is transferred in conjunction with the service.

(b) Inspecting motor vehicles pursuant to the mandatory requirements of The Vehicle Code [Title 75 of Pennsylvania Consolidated Statutes, 75 Pa.C.S. §§101—9805].

(4) The rendition for a consideration of the following services:

(a) Repairing, altering, mending, pressing, fitting, dyeing, laundering, dry-cleaning or cleaning tangible personal property other than wearing apparel, shoes, or diapers. Such services, however, do not apply to services performed in the preparation for sale of new items excluded from the sales and use tax under 72 P.S. §204(26) (primarily clothing).

(b) Applying or installing tangible personal property as a repair or replacement part of other tangible personal property except (i) wearing apparel, shoes, or diapers or (ii) when rendered in the construction, reconstruction, remodeling, repair, or maintenance of real estate. Such services, however, do not apply to services performed in the preparation for sale of new items excluded from the sales and use tax under 72 P.S. §204(26) (primarily clothing). See ¶716 and ¶717 for further discussion of sales and use tax issues with respect to construction contracts.

(5) Any retention of possession, custody, or a license to use or consumer tangible personal property or any further obtaining of described in items (2), (3), and (4), above pursuant to a rental or service contract or other arrangement other than as security.

(6) The rendition for a consideration of the following (discussed in more detail at ¶703):

(a) Adjustment, collection, or credit reporting services.

(b) Secretarial or editing services.

(c) Employment agency services.

(d) Help supply services.

(e) Lawn care services.

(f) Lobbying services.

¶701

(g) Mobile telecommunications services. The term "mobile telecommunications service" means commercial mobile radio service, as defined in 47 CFR § 20.3, as in effect on June 1, 1999. See ¶721 for more information about mobile telecommunications services.

(h) Pest control services.

(i) Self-storage services.

Listing of Taxable and Nontaxable Items

"Sale at retail" is any transfer for consideration of the ownership, custody, or possession of tangible property. Therefore, the sale of any item defined as tangible personal property is taxable and the resulting list of items within a category of taxable or exempt property is extensive and includes numerous items not specified in 72 P.S. § 201(k). The Department of Revenue publishes (in the *Pennsylvania Bulletin*) a list of taxable and exempt property at least once every three years. In addition, it quarterly publishes notice in the *Pennsylvania Bulletin* of additions, deletions, or revisions to the list. A ruling on unusual transactions or on property or services not included in the list may be obtained upon written request to the Department of Revenue, Office of Chief Counsel, Dept. 281061, Harrisburg, PA 17128-1061 [61 Pa. Code § 58.1]. The Department also prepares a *Retailers' Information Booklet* (REV-717) that provides procedural information and reproduces the list of taxable and nontaxable items published in the *Pennsylvania Bulletin*. To obtain a copy of the *Retailers' Information Booklet* call the 24-hour answering service numbers for forms ordering: in Pennsylvania, 800-362-1050; outside Pennsylvania and within the local Harrisburg area, 717-787-8094; for the hearing impaired: TTD 717-772-2252. Be sure to consult these resources if there is any doubt about the taxability of any item.

• *Dual-use property or service*

When tangible personal property or services are used both for purposes constituting a "sale at retail" and for purposes excluded from the definition of "sale at retail," it is presumed that the tangible personal property or service involved is taxable unless the user proves to the Department that the predominant purpose for which the tangible personal property or services are used does not constitute a "sale at retail" [72 P.S. § 7201(k)(9)].

• *Transactions in keystone opportunity zones (KOZs)*

Otherwise taxable sales at retail of services or tangible personal property (other than motor vehicles) to a qualified business landowner or lessee, for the exclusive use, consumption, and utilization of the property or service at the qualified business's, landowner's, or lessee's facility located within a subzone are exempt from sales and use tax. For contracts entered into prior to September 8, 2008, the exemption for sales to a construction contractor pursuant to a contract with a qualified business is limited to "building machinery and equipment." [73 P.S. § 820.511(b)]. For contracts entered into on or after September 8, 2008 the exemption is no longer limited. All property installed for the exclusive use, consumption and utilization by a qualified business is exempt [73 P.S. § 820.511(b)]. Sales conducted in a subzone prior to its designation as a subzone are not exempt [73 P.S. § 820.511]. See ¶4622 for discussion of subzones.

For contracts entered into prior to September 8, 2008, the exemption for sales to a qualified business, landowner, or lessee was limited to "building machinery and equipment" [73 P.S. § 820.511(b) (repealed)]. For contracts entered into on or after September 8, 2008, the exemption is no longer limited. All property purchased for the exclusive use, consumption, and utilization by a qualified business, landowner, or lessee is exempt [73 P.S. § 820.511].

¶701

¶702 Taxable Property

All tangible personal property is taxable unless specifically exempt. See ¶706 for an explanation of exempt property.

- *"Tangible personal property" defined*

"Tangible personal property" means corporeal personal property and includes (but is not limited to) the following [72 P.S. §7201(m)]:

(1) Electricity for nonresidential use.

Practitioner Comment: Delivery Charges

Electricity distribution, transmission, and transition charges were subject to Pennsylvania sales tax, even though the electricity was purchased from a supplier and delivered by an entity other than the supplier. A regulation that excludes delivery charges from the purchase price, when the delivery charges are made by a person other than the vendor, did not apply to electricity sales because electricity generation and delivery must be bundled for the electricity to reach its destination [*Spectrum Arena Limited Partnership v. Cmwlth.*, 983 A.2d 641 (Pa. 2009), *aff'g* 951 A.2d 1226 (Pa.Commw. 2008)].

---

(2) Goods, wares, and merchandise.

MRI and PET/CT Scans Are Tangible Personal Property

The Pennsylvania Supreme Court has held that magnetic resonance imaging (MRI) and positron emission tomography/computerized tomography (PET/CT scan) systems are tangible personal property subject to Pennsylvania sales tax [*Northeastern Pennsylvania Imaging Center v. Pennsylvania*, 35 A.3d 752 (Pa. 2011)].

---

(3) Premium cable or premium video programming service.

(4) Spirituous or vinous liquor.

(5) Malt or brewed beverages.

(6) Soft drinks.

(7) Steam and natural and manufactured and bottled gas for nonresidential use.

(8) Telecommunications:

(a) Interstate telecommunications service originating or terminating in Pennsylvania and charged to a service address in Pennsylvania. Any charge paid through a credit or payment mechanism that does not relate to a service address (*e.g.*, bank, travel, credit, or debit card, but not prepaid communications) is deemed attributable to the address of origination of the telecommunications.

(b) Intrastate telecommunications service with the exception of (i) subscriber line charges and basic local telephone service for residential use and (ii) charges for telephone calls paid for by inserting money into a telephone accepting direct deposits of money to operate. The service address of any intrastate telecommunications service is deemed to be within Pennsylvania or within a political subdivision regardless of how to where billed or paid. Any charge paid through a credit or payment mechanism that does not relate to a service address (*e.g.*, bank, travel, credit, or debit card, but not prepaid communications) is deemed attributable to the address of origination of the telecommunications.

(c) Prepaid communications.

(9) Videos, photographs, books, any other taxable printed materials, applications (commonly known as apps), games, music, any other audio such as

satellite radio service, and canned software, regardless of whether they are electronically or digitally delivered, streamed, or accessed and whether they are purchased singly, by subscription, or any other manner. Maintenance and updates are included. For canned software, support services are also included, except for separately invoiced help desk or call center support.

NOTE: The taxation of telecommunications services is discussed in more detail at ¶721.

Property vs. Service

Note that interstate and intrastate telecommunications services and prepaid telecommunications services are classified as tangible personal property under 72 P.S. §201(m). Mobile telecommunications service, however, is defined as a service under 72 P.S. §201(k)(19). All of these telecommunication services are treated as services in this *Guidebook* and are discussed at ¶721.

• *Electricity for residential use—Unbundled charges*

The Electricity Generation Choice for Customers of Electric Cooperative Act [66 Pa.C.S. §2804 *et seq.*] gives retail customers the choice of an electric generation supplier [66 Pa.C.S. §2804] and gives the Pennsylvania Public Utility Commission the authority to require unbundling of electric utility serves, tariffs, and customer bills to separate charges for generation, transmission and distribution. Tax will be imposed on each separate charge for the generation, transmission, or distribution of nonresidential electric utility services and all related charges, services, or costs for the generation, production, transmission, or distribution of electricity whether or not the total amount charged is billed as a single charge by one vendor or billed separately by more than one vendor [61 Pa. Code §60.23(d)].

• *Bulk and auction sales*

The bulk sales provisions apply when a person sells or causes to be sold at auction, or sells or transfers in bulk, 51% or more of any stock of goods, wares or merchandise of any kind, fixtures, machinery, equipment, buildings, or real estate involved in a business for which the person is licensed or required to be licensed under the Pennsylvania sales and use tax provisions or is liable for filing use tax returns [72 P.S. §7240]. The Department of Revenue has interpreted the bulk sales statute disjunctively with respect to each asset classification and as applicable only to assets located within Pennsylvania. Therefore, a taxpayer must secure a clearance certificate when 51% or more of any of the listed assets are sold [REV-1076]. A person that engages in a bulk sale must conform to the requirements of §1403 of the Fiscal Code (discussed at ¶4621).

Protection for Buyer

When a taxpayer purchases assets in a bulk sale, and the seller is later found to have a sales tax liability, the buyer has assumed that liability. The way for a buyer to protect himself/herself against such an unknown liability is to have a tax indemnification provision in the purchase agreement, in which the seller agrees to pay any past tax liability that may later be found to be due.

Disaster Recovery Services

The Tax Reform Code of 1971, as amended, provides for the imposition of a sales and use tax on the retail sale of tangible personal property and certain services. 72 P.S. §7202(a). Disaster recovery is not one of the specified taxable services. However, the sale or lease of disaster recovery equipment, such as that offered by Taxpayer, is subject to tax.

Accordingly, Taxpayer is required to collect sales tax on the fee for the declaration of a disaster and the daily usage fee. These fees must be a reasonable charge for the rental of such equipment. Taxpayer is also responsible for remitting tax on its use of the equipment. If Taxpayer does not pay sales or use tax on the total purchase price of the equipment, Taxpayer is required to pay use tax based on the fair market value of the equipment during any period of which sales tax is not being charged.

¶703 Taxable Services

The following services, if rendered for consideration, are taxable, whether or not any tangible personal property is transferred in connection with the services:

- *Adjustment, collection, or credit reporting services*

The rendition for a consideration of adjustment services, collection services, or credit reporting services is taxable [72 P.S. §7201(k)(12)]. "Adjustment services" includes activities performed by a collection agency relating to the reconciliation or settlement of a debt on behalf of a creditor [61 Pa. Code §60.10(a)]. "Collection services" includes an activity relating to the collection of a debt that involves a collection agency, a creditor, and a debtor [61 Pa. Code §60.10]. See 61 Pa. Code §60.10 for details on taxation of these services. "Credit reporting services" means the providing of credit information by hard copy, electronic media, verbal, or another method of transferring credit information [61 Pa. Code §60.11(a)]. For details on taxation of credit reporting services, see 61 Pa. Code §60.11.

- *Building maintenance or cleaning services*

The rendition for a consideration of building maintenance or cleaning services is taxable [72 P.S. §7201(k)(14)]. The term "building maintenance or cleaning services" does not include the following [72 P.S. §7201(aa)]:

(1) Repairs on buildings and other structures.

(2) Maintenance or repair of boilers, furnaces, and residential air conditioning equipment or parts thereof.

(3) Painting, wallpapering, or applying other like coverings to interior walls, ceilings or floors; or the exterior painting of buildings.

"Building maintenance services" means the performance of routine and periodic services upon a building that keep a building in a satisfactory operating condition. The term includes cleaning, oiling, greasing, and replacing parts but does not include building repair services [61 Pa. Code §60.1(a)].

"Building cleaning services" means the performance of services that include the removal of dirt, dust, grease, or grime on a building or inside of a building and the keeping of the building and its contents in a clean, neat, polished, or orderly appearance. The term includes the following:

(1) Janitorial, maid, or housekeeping services.

(2) Office or building cleaning.

(3) Window cleaning.

(4) Floor waxing.

(5) Chimney cleaning.

(6) Acoustical tile cleaning.

(7) Venetian blind cleaning.

(8) Cleaning or degreasing service stations.

(9) Cleaning enclosed telephone booth.

"Interior office building cleaning services" are cleaning services performed in an "office building." These services are only taxable on the service fee (gross fee less separately stated employee costs) [61 Pa Code § 60.1 (b)].

For details on taxation of building maintenance or building cleaning services, see 61 Pa. Code § 60.1.

• *Car wash services*

The rendition of the service of washing, cleaning, waxing, polishing, or lubricating of motor vehicles of another is a taxable service, whether or not any tangible personal property is transferred in connection with the service [72 P.S. § 7201(k)(3)(i)].

Compressed Air Vending Machines

Sales of compressed air through vending machines are not taxable services [*Air-Serv Group, LLC v. Commwlth*, 18 A.2d 448 (April 14, 2011)].

• *Computer hardware and canned software*

Computer hardware and canned software, as well as services thereto, are subject to the sales and use tax. See 61 Pa. Code § 60.19 for details of the taxation of computer hardware and software. Custom software is not subject to tax. "Computer hardware" means assembly of physical equipment that is united and regulated by interaction or interdependence to accomplish a set of specific computer system functions. Examples of computer hardware are personal computers, external hard drives, portable disk drives, scanners, monitors, keyboard, mouses, and microphones. For more examples, see 61 Pa. Code § 60.19(b). "Canned software" is computer software that does not qualify as custom software (discussed below). Canned software includes updates, enhancements, and upgrades, as well as customer software that is transferred pursuant to a sale at retail to a person other than the original purchaser. Adaptation or modification of canned software to meet the specific needs of a particular customer does not convert the canned software to custom software. Charges for custom software or modifications must be reasonable and separately stated to be exempt from tax. For more details on taxation of canned software, see 61 Pa. Code § 60.19(c)(2).

• *Canned software transmitted electronically*

A three-judge panel of the Commonwealth Court has held that fees paid to renew a company's licenses to use canned software programs were subject to Pennsylvania sales tax. The court adopted the "essence of the transaction test" and determined that canned software was tangible personal property, regardless of the method of delivery, because it took up space on a hard drive and could be physically perceived by checking the computer's files [*Graham Packaging Co. v. Commonwealth of Pennsylvania*, Pa.Commw., No. 652 F.R. 2002, September 15, 2005]. The Court concluded that the sale of all canned software, whether transmitted electronically or on a physical medium, is taxable as the sale of tangible personal property. As a result of the decision, effective for invoices dated on or after November 1, 2005, canned software is taxable regardless of the method of delivery [*Sales Tax Bulletin 2005-04*]. This position has been upheld by the Pennsylvania Supreme Court [*Dechert, LLP v. Cmwlth.*, Pennsylvania Supreme Court, No. 12 MAP 2008, July 20, 2010].

Exemptions for certain entities: The sale or use of canned software and computer hardware is exempt if it is purchased by qualified charitable organizations, volunteer firefighters' relief association, or volunteer fire companies, religious organizations, and nonprofit educational institutions, unless the software is used in an unrelated trade or business; by the Federal government; or by the Commonwealth of Pennsylvania, its instrumentalities, or political subdivisions (including public school districts) [61 Pa. Code § 60.19(d)(1)].

Manufacturing and other exemptions: The manufacturing, research, mining, processing, public utility, farming, dairying, agriculture, horticulture, or floriculture exemptions from tax apply to the purchase of canned computer software and computer hardware predominantly and directly used in these operations [61 Pa. Code § 60.19(d)(2)].

Canned software manufacturers: The manufacturing and research exemption applies to a person engaged in the business of manufacturing or researching canned software if the property is predominately and directly used by the purchaser in the manufacture or research of canned software. The creation of custom software does not qualify as manufacturing or research; when a purchaser uses the property to both manufacture canned software and create custom software, the purchaser has the burden of establishing that the tangible personal property is predominately used in the manufacturing or research of canned software [61 Pa. Code § 60.19(d)(3)].

Resale exemption: The sale of canned software and computer hardware to a vendor who will resell it in the ordinary course of business is exempt from tax as a sale for resale. If a vendor uses canned software or computer hardware to produce a separate computer product for resale, the hardware or canned software does not qualify as a sale for resale. Use of canned software or computer hardware to provide a service does not qualify as a resale [61 Pa. Code § 60.19(d)(4)].

• *Custom software*

The sale at retail or use of custom software is considered a purchase of a nontaxable computer programming service [61 Pa. Code § 60.19(b)(2)(i)]. "Custom software" is computer software designed, created, and developed for and to the specifications of an original purchaser [61 Pa. Code § 60.19(b)]. Adaptations and modifications of canned software are not considered custom software. The following items are not taxable:

(1) The sale at retail or use of multiple copies or licenses of custom software to the original purchaser.

(2) The sale at retail or use of:

(a) Custom software installation.

(b) Custom software repair and maintenance.

(c) Custom software updates, enhancements, and upgrades that constitute custom software.

Authors' Comment

Prior to the repeal of the computer service tax, including the tax on custom software, the definition of custom software was found 61 Pa. Code § 60.13, which defined custom software as "a program which has been developed or modified to *any* extent for a specific purchaser" (emphasis added). Thus, under this definition, canned software that had been adapted or modified to the specific needs of a particular customer fell within the definition of custom software. However, in 61 Pa. Code § 60.19 (the current pronouncement), the Department made a radical change in the definition of custom software (see definition above). The authors believe that issuing a pronouncement that attempts to tax what had long been defined as custom software as canned software is contrary to the legislative intent and that the Department exceeded its authority in changing the definition of custom software.

• *Employment agency services*

The rendition for a consideration of employment agency services is taxable [72 P.S. § 7201(k)(15)]. "Employment agency services" means the service of attempting to procure or procuring employment (temporary or permanent) for prospective employees or employers (*e.g.,* executive placing services, labor contractor employment agencies) [61 Pa. Code § 60.5(a)]. Procurement of employees who will report to work in Pennsylvania is taxable; procurement of employees who will report to work outside Pennsylvania is not taxable, unless the employee is assigned to work in Pennsylvania. If the employee is located in Pennsylvania, it is presumed that the employment agency service is taxable unless documentation supports the reporting to a location outside Pennsylvania [61 Pa. Code § 60.5(b)].

Examples of taxable employment agency services: The following examples (adapted from 61 Pa. Code § 60.5) illustrate taxable employment agency services.

> *Example 1:* Nancy, a resident of New York City, contacts an employment agency in New York City and is placed with an employer located in Philadelphia. This is a taxable service.

> *Example 2:* Nathan, a resident of Pittsburgh, contacts an employment agency in Cleveland, Ohio, and is placed with an employer located in Pittsburgh. This is a taxable service.

> *Example 3:* Noble Corporation, located in Scranton, contacts an employment agency in Virginia and accepts an employee for its location in Scranton. This is a taxable service.

> *Example 4:* Natalie, a resident of Philadelphia, contacts an employment agency in Pittsburgh and is placed with an employer in Pittsburgh. This is a taxable service.

> *Example 5:* Noel Corporation, a Philadelphia employment agency, paid on an hourly rate, interviews and recommends a potential employee to an employer. This is a taxable service.

Examples of nontaxable employment agency services: The following examples (adapted from 61 Pa. Code § 60.5) illustrate nontaxable employment agency services.

> *Example 1:* Dave, a resident of Pittsburgh, contacts a Pennsylvania employment agency and is placed with an employer located in Cary, North Carolina. This is not a taxable service.

> *Example 2:* Don, a resident of Philadelphia, contacts a New York City employment agency and is placed with an employer located in New Jersey. This is not a taxable service.

> *Example 3:* Dorothy, a resident of New York City, contacts an employment agency located in Wilkes-Barre and is placed with an employer located in New York City. This is not a taxable service.

> *Example 4:* Denion Corporation, located in Pittsburgh, contacts a vendor in Florida and accepts an employee for its out-of-state location in Miami. This is not a taxable service.

Purchase price subject to tax: The purchase price of taxable employment agency services is the service fee (see below) paid by the purchaser to the vendor or supplying entity [72 P.S. § 7201(g)(6)]. If the purchase price is canceled or renegotiated, tax is due on the adjusted purchase price. If a price adjustment results in an adjustment to the tax, the vendor may offset the adjustment against current tax liabilities [61 Pa. Code § 60.5(e)(3)]. If the purchase price is paid on an installment basis, the tax is imposed on the full purchase price and is payable at the time the purchaser accepts the contract or within 30 days of acceptance of the contract [61 Pa. Code § 60.5(e)(4)].

Gross fee: "Gross fee" is the total amount charged by the seller excluding sales tax [61 Pa. Code § 60.5(a)].

Service fee: "Service fee" is the total charge or fee of the vendor or supplying entity minus the costs of the supplied employee, which costs are wages, salaries, bonuses and commissions, employment benefits, expense reimbursements, and payroll and withholding taxes, to the extent that these costs are specifically itemized or that these costs in aggregate are stated in billings from the vendor or supplying entity. To the extent that these costs are not itemized or stated on the billings, then the service fee shall be the total charge or fee of the vendor or supplying entity [72 P.S. §7201(g)(6)].

Employee costs: "Employee costs" are payments made or withheld by a vendor to an employee, including wages, salaries, bonuses, commissions, employment benefits, expense reimbursements, payroll and withholding taxes, employer-paid FICA tax, or federal and Pennsylvania unemployment taxes. Employee recruiting, training, liability insurance, bonding expenses, and other costs are not employee costs [61 Pa. Code §60.5(a)].

Exclusions: The following employment agency services and tangible property used in the performance of employment agency services are exempt:

(1) *Nonprofit organizations:* Employment agency services purchased by qualified charitable organizations, volunteer fire companies, religious organizations, and nonprofit educational institutions are exempt unless they are used in an unrelated trade or business [61 Pa. Code § 60.5(f)(1)].

(2) *Governmental agencies:* Employment agency services purchased by the federal government or its instrumentalities or by the Commonwealth of Pennsylvania, its instrumentalities, or subdivisions (including public school districts) are exempt [61 Pa. Code § 60.5(f)(1)].

(3) *Theatrical employment agencies:* Employment agency services provided by theatrical employment agencies are exempt [61 Pa. Code § 60.5(f)(2)].

(4) *Motion picture casting bureaus:* Employment services provided by motion picture casting bureaus are exempt [61 Pa. Code § 60.5(f)(2)].

(5) *Farm labor:* Farm labor is exempt [61 Pa. Code § 60.5(f)(3)].

(6) *Resale exemption:* A vendor of employment agency services may claim the resale exemption upon its purchase of tangible personal property that is transferred to its purchaser or a third party in the performance of its employment agency services. The vendor may also purchase employment agency services from another provider for resale to its customer. For details, see 61 Pa. Code § 60.5(f)(4). A vendor cannot claim a resale exemption for administrative supplies or the purchase of another taxable service that it may use in the performance of its employment agency services.

(7) *Manufacturing and other exemptions:* The manufacturing, mining, processing, public utility, farming, dairying, agriculture, horticulture, or floriculture exclusion does not apply to employment agency services [61 Pa. Code § 60.5(f)(1)].

For more details on taxation of employment agency services, see 61 Pa. Code §60.5.

• *Help supply services*

The rendition for a consideration of help supply services is taxable [72 P.S. §7201(k)(15)]. "Help supply service" means the providing of an individual by a vendor to a purchaser whereby the individual is an employee of the vendor and the individual's work is supervised by the purchaser [61 Pa. Code §60.4(a)]. Help supply services include the type of service provided by labor and manpower pools, employee leasing services, office help supply services, temporary help services, usher services, modeling services or fashion show model supply services. The term "help supply services" does not include farm labor, home health care, human health-related services (including nursing and personal care). Personal care includes providing specified assistance to persons with limited ability for self-care (*e.g.,* dressing, bathing, feeding, supervising self-administered medication, transferring a person to or from a bed or wheelchair, routine housekeeping chores provided in conjunction with and supplied by a personal care provider) [61 Pa. Code § 60.4(a)]. If delivery or use of help supply service occurs in Pennsylvania, it is subject to tax [61 Pa. Code § 60.4(b)].

> *Example 1:* A purchaser in Rye, New York, requests a vendor's employee to report to work at her mother's home in Harrisburg, Pennsylvania. This is a taxable transaction.

> *Example 2:* A purchaser in Philadelphia requests a vendor's employee to report to work at his mother's home in Akron, Ohio. This is not a taxable transaction.

See 61 Pa. Code § 60.4(b) for more examples of the sourcing rules. See 61 Pa. Code § 60.4(d) for examples of taxable help supply services and 61 Pa. Code § 60.4(e) for examples of services that are not help supply services.

Professional Employer Organization Services Not Taxable

Fees charged by a professional employer organization (PEO) for providing human resource services (PEO services), through the mechanism of placing clients' employees on the payroll of the PEO, were not subject to Pennsylvania sales tax because the PEO services did not fall within the definition of taxable "help supply services." The definition requires that the supplying entity provide personnel who work under the supervision of the purchasing entity. The PEO did not provide any employees to its clients, and the PEO services were performed solely by the PEO's employees, and not by clients' employees transferred to the PEO's payroll. In addition, the PEO, rather than its clients, supervised the employees performing PEO services [*All Staffing, Inc. v. Pennsylvania,* 38 A.3d 796 (Pa. Commw 2012)].

Purchase price: There are three methods to compute the purchase price subject to tax: (1) the gross fee method; (2) the service fee method; and (3) the average employee cost or average service fee method. These methods are explained at 61 Pa. Code § 60.4(c)(2).

Exclusions: The following help supply services and tangible property used in the performance of employment agency services are exempt:

(1) Help supply service purchased by qualified charitable organizations, volunteer fire companies, religious organizations, and nonprofit educational institutions unless they are used in an unrelated trade or business [61 Pa. Code § 60.4(f)(1)].

(2) Help supply services purchased by the federal government or its instrumentalities [61 Pa. Code § 60.4(f)(1)].

(3) Help supply services purchased by the Commonwealth of Pennsylvania and its instrumentalities or subdivisions (including public school districts) [61 Pa. Code § 60.4(f)(1)].

Resale exemption: The vendor of help supply services may claim the resale exemption upon its purchase of tangible personal property that is transferred to its purchaser or a third party in the performance of its help supply services. The vendor may also purchase from another provider help supply services that the vendor resells to its customer. The vendor may not claim the resale exemption upon its purchase of administrative supplies or the purchase of other taxable services that it may use in the performance of its help supply services. A vendor may not, however, claim a resale exemption for the purchase of administrative supplies or the purchase of other taxable services that it may use in the performance of its help supply services. For details, see 61 Pa. Code § 60.4(f)(2).

Manufacturing and other exemptions: The manufacturing, mining, processing, public utility, farming, dairying, agriculture, horticulture, or floriculture exemption does not apply to help supply services [61 Pa. Code § 60.4(f)(2)].

• *Inspecting motor vehicles pursuant to the mandatory requirements of "The Vehicle Code"*

Chapter 47 of 75 Pa.C.S. sets forth requirements for mandatory safety inspection of motor vehicles. The sale at retail or use of these inspection services is subject to sales and use tax [72 P.S. § 7201(k)(3)(ii)].

• *Labor or services billed by a vendor for delivering, installing, or applying tangible personal property*

Rendition for a consideration of labor or services billed by a vendor for delivering, installing, or applying tangible personal property is taxable, even if separately stated [72 P.S. § 7201(g)(1)]. For example, if a dealer delivers and installs a gas range that the dealer has sold, the charges for delivery and installation, as well as the price of the range, are taxable. The delivery and installation charges are taxable whether or not they are invoiced separately from the price of the range [61 Pa. Code § 31.5(a)(3)].

• *Lawn care services*

The sale at retail or use of lawn care services performed in Pennsylvania is subject to tax [72 P.S. § 7201(k)(17)]. "Lawn care service" means providing services for law upkeep (*e.g.*, fertilizing, lawn mowing, shrubbery trimming, or other lawn treatment services). A "lawn" is an area maintained with grass adjacent to a building. The term does not include athletic fields, cemeteries, golf courses, fields, parks, and public utility or highway rights-of-ways [61 Pa. Code § 55.6(a)]. For details and examples of taxable and nontaxable services, see 61 Pa. Code § 55.6.

Exemptions: Lawn care services are not subject to tax if purchased by the following entities:

(1) Qualified institutions of purely public charity, charitable organizations, volunteer fire companies, religious organizations and nonprofit educational institutions, unless the services are used in an unrelated trade or business [61 Pa. Code § 55.6(f)(1)].

(2) The federal government or its instrumentalities.

(3) The Commonwealth of Pennsylvania, its instrumentalities or subdivisions (including public school districts).

Manufacturing and other exemptions: The manufacturing, mining, processing, public utility, farming, dairying, agriculture, horticulture, or floriculture exemptions do not apply to lawn care services [61 Pa. Code § 55.6(f)(1)].

Resale exemption: The vendor of lawn care services may claim the resale exemption for its purchase of tangible personal property that is transferred to the purchaser or a third party in the performance of the lawn care services. The vendor may also purchase lawn care services from another provider and subsequently resell the services to a purchaser. The vendor may not, however, claim the resale exemption for its purchase of administrative supplies or the purchase of other taxable services that it may use but not transfer in the performance of its lawn care services [61 Pa. Code § 55.6(f)(2)].

• *Lobbying services*

The rendition for a consideration of lobbying services is taxable [72 P.S. § 7201(k)(11)]. The term "lobbying services" means to advocate (1) the passage or defeat of legislation to members or staff of the General Assembly, or the approval or veto of legislation to the Governor or his staff or (2) to officers or employees of a Commonwealth agency that the agency take or refrain from taking formal action, or that an agency engage in lobbying services [61 Pa. Code § 60.6(a)]. A "lobbyist" is a natural person registered under the Lobbying Registration and Regulation Act [46 P.S. § § 148.1—148.76]to perform lobbying services.

¶703

Purchase price: The purchase price of lobbying services means compensation, expense, or obligation, whether in money or property, paid or due to a lobbyist for the performance of lobbying services. Salary or wages paid by an employer to an employee to perform lobbying services solely for the employer are not taxable. See 61 Pa. Code § 60.6 for more details.

Exempt purchases: Lobbying services are exempt if purchased by qualified charitable organizations, volunteer fire companies, religious organizations, and non-profit education institutions unless used in an unrelated trade or business. The services are also exempt if purchased by the Federal government or its instrumentalities; or the Commonwealth, its instrumentalities or subdivisions (including public school districts) [61 Pa. Code § 60.6(f)(1)].

Resale exemption: The vendor of lobbying services may claim the resale exemption with respect to (1) the purchase of tangible personal property that is transferred to the purchaser of its service in the performance of lobbying services; (2) the purchase of lobbying services from another lobbyist that the purchasing lobbyist resells to its purchaser. The resale exemption does not apply to (1) the transfer of property to the individual to whom the lobbying services are directed; (2) the purchase of administrative supplies; or (3) the purchase of other taxable services that the lobbyist may use in the performance of lobbying services [61 Pa. Code § 60.6(f)(2)].

Manufacturing and other exemptions: The manufacturing, printing, publishing, processing, farming, dairying, mining, or public utility exemptions do not apply to lobbying services [61 Pa. Code § 60.6(f)(1)].

• *Mobile telecommunications service*

The rendition for a consideration of a mobile telecommunications service constitutes a "sale at retail" and is taxable [72 P.S. § 7201(k)(19), applicable to mobile telecommunications services billed by home service providers after August 1, 2002]. For more information see ¶ 721.

• *Pest control services*

The rendition for a consideration of disinfecting or pest control services is subject to tax [72 P.S. § 7201(k)(14)]. "Disinfecting" means the performance of services to property that destroys or sanitizes harmful microorganisms. Deodorizing is a disinfecting service. "Pest control" means the performance of services to trees, shrubs, animals, buildings and other property that neutralizes, exterminates, traps, recovers, or prevents pests. Fumigation is a pest control service. See 61 Pa. Code § 60.3 for examples of taxable and nontaxable disinfecting and pest control services.

Sourcing: The sale at retail or use of disinfecting or pest control services is subject to tax when these services are (1) performed on real property located in Pennsylvania; (2) performed on tangible personal property located in Pennsylvania unless the property is to be delivered outside Pennsylvania; or (3) performed on tangible personal property outside Pennsylvania if the property is delivered to a Pennsylvania location [61 Pa. Code § 60.3(b)].

Exclusions: Disinfecting or pest control services are exempt if they are purchased by qualified charitable organizations, volunteer fire companies, religious organizations, and nonprofit educational institutions unless they are used in an unrelated trade or business. Services are also exempt if purchased by the Federal government or its instrumentalities; or the Commonwealth, its instrumentalities, or subdivisions (including public school districts) [61 Pa. Code § 60.3(f)(1)]. Fumigation of agricultural commodities or containers used for agricultural commodities and the spraying of trees that are harvested for commercial purposes for gypsy moth control are not taxable [72 P.S. § 7201(z)].

Resale exemption: The vendor of disinfecting or pest control services may claim the resale exemption with respect to its purchase of tangible personal property that is transferred to its purchaser or a third party in the performance of its disinfecting or pest control services. A resale exemption may also be used when a vendor purchases disinfecting or pest control services from another provider to resell to its customer. The vendor may not, however, claim a resale exemption for the purchase of administrative supplies or the purchase of other taxable services that may be used in the performance of its disinfecting or pest control services [61 Pa. Code § 60.3(f)(2)].

Manufacturing and other exemptions: The manufacturing, mining, processing, or the public utility exemptions do not apply to disinfecting and pest control services [61 Pa. Code § 60.3(f)(1)].

For more details on the taxation of disinfecting and pest control services, see 61 Pa. Code § 60.3.

• *Premium cable service*

Premium cable service is discussed in more detail at ¶719.

• *Printing*

Printing or imprinting of tangible personal property for persons who furnish, either directly or indirectly (through an agent), the materials used in the printing or imprinting [72 P.S. § 7202(k)(2)]. Printing services are taxable whether the person for whom they are rendered or the person's agent supplies the materials. When the person for whom taxable services are rendered fails to pay the tax to the person rendering the taxable services, the Commonwealth may collect tax from either party [61 Pa. Code § 31.5(a)(5)]. Printing, when engaged in as a business, is included in manufacturing under the Tax Reform Code, and regulations applicable to manufacturers are also applicable to printers [61 Pa. Code § 32.36(a)(1)]. For an explanation of the printing exemption, see ¶720.

• *Repair or replacement parts*

Installing tangible personal property as a repair or replacement part of other tangible personal property (except wearing apparel or shoes) is a taxable service [72 P.S. § 7201(k)(4)]. For example, if a garage employee merely replaces an old tire on an automobile with a spare belonging to the car owner, the installation is taxable. If the garage employee replaces a tire on an automobile with a new one, both the installation charge and the price of the new tire are subject to tax [61 Pa. Code § 31.5(a)(2)].

• *Repairing, altering, mending, pressing, fitting, dyeing, laundering, dry-cleaning or cleaning services*

The rendition for a consideration of the services of repairing, altering, mending, pressing, fitting, dyeing, laundering, dry cleaning or cleaning tangible personal property other than clothing or footwear is taxable [72 P.S. § 7201(k)(4)]. For example, if a bookcase is taken to a carpenter to have a defective shelf repaired, the charge for the repair is subject to tax [61 Pa. Code § 31.5(a)(1)].

Clothing or footwear: Charges for repairing, altering, mending, pressing, fitting, dyeing, laundering, dry cleaning or cleaning clothing or footwear are exempt from tax [72 P.S. § 7201(k)(4)]. For example, if a shoe is taken to a shoe repairperson to have a heel fixed, the charge for the repair is not subject to tax [61 Pa. Code § 31.5(a)(1)].

Coin-operated laundries: Charges for the services of repairing, altering, mending, pressing, fitting, dyeing, laundering, dry cleaning or cleaning of clothing and household goods by means of coin-operated, self-service laundry equipment are exempt from tax [61 Pa. Code § 35.1(b)]. Laundry equipment includes washing and dry-cleaning machines. Included within this exemption are services performed on the following types of property: clothing, sheets, towels, rugs, drapes, or other household goods. However, when these services are performed by a laundry, the charges are subject to tax.

¶703

Coin-operated car washes and similar equipment: Charges for equipment similar to laundry equipment used in conjunction with motor vehicles are subject to tax [61 Pa. Code § 31.5(b)].

• *Secretarial or editing services*

The rendition for a consideration of secretarial or editing services is taxable [72 P.S. § 7201(k)(13)]. "Secretarial services" include preparing correspondence or performing routine and detailed office work, letter writing, proofreading, resume writing, typing, word processing, or telephone answering services. The term does not include separately stated charges for notary seals, completion of forms, mail-processing services, stenographic services, or court reporting services [61 Pa. Code § 60.8(a)]. "Editing services" include services performed upon written material, film, videos and audiotape, including altering, adapting, refining, proofreading or confirming, reviewing for clarity, authenticity and meaning, and assembly by cutting or rearranging [61 Pa. Code § 60.8(a)]. For lists of examples of taxable and nontaxable secretarial and editing services, see 61 Pa. Code § 60.8(c) and (d).

Sourcing: Services performed for a purchaser located in Pennsylvania are presumed to be subject to tax. Services performed for a purchaser located outside Pennsylvania are presumed not to be subject to tax [61 Pa. Code § 60.8(b)(2)].

> **Example 1:** A Maryland resident purchases the services of a Pennsylvania secretarial service company to type a resume to be delivered in Maryland. The service is exempt from tax, even if some of the letters would be received by Pennsylvania residents.

> **Example 2:** A Pennsylvania resident purchases services from a Pennsylvania secretarial service company to type 100 letters and mail them to individuals throughout the country. The total charge, including charges for mail processing, is taxable.

Incidental services: The sale at retail or use of secretarial or editing services provided in conjunction with the performance of a nontaxable service is taxable unless the secretarial or editing service being provided is incidental to the nontaxable service [61 Pa. Code § 60.8(b)(3)].

> **Example:** Andrews Company receives 1,000 pamphlets, envelopes, and labels from Cordell Company. Andrews is to fold and stuff the pamphlets into envelopes and affix the mailing labels. This is a nontaxable service. Andrews also is to type and insert a letter in every 200th envelope indicating that the recipient has won a prize. This is a secretarial service, but the typing of the letter is nontaxable because it is incidental to the nontaxable service of folding, stuffing, and attaching labels.

Purchase price: The total amount charged for performing secretarial and editing services is subject to tax. If a taxpayer fails to state separately the charge for taxable secretarial and editing services from other nontaxable charges on the invoice, the total amount of the invoice is taxable. Charges for delivery of a secretarial and editing service are also subject to tax (*e.g.,* postage, handling, insurance) [61 Pa. Code § 60.8(e)].

Exclusions: The following secretarial and editing services and tangible property used in the performance of these services are exempt:

(1) Secretarial and editing services purchased by qualified charitable organizations, volunteer fire companies, religious organizations, and nonprofit educational institutions unless they are used in an unrelated trade or business [61 Pa. Code § 60.8(f)(1)].

(2) Secretarial and editing services purchased by the federal government or its instrumentalities [61 Pa. Code § 60.8(f)(1)].

(3) Secretarial and editing services purchased by the Commonwealth of Pennsylvania and its instrumentalities or subdivisions (including public school districts) [61 Pa. Code § 60.8(f)(1)].

(4) Tangible personal property purchased for resale. A vendor of secretarial and editing services may clam the resale exemption upon the purchase of tangible personal property that is transferred to the purchaser or a third party in the performance of the services. The vendor may also claim a resale exemption on the purchase of secretarial and editing services from another provider of secretarial and editing services if the vendor resells the services to its customer. The vendor may not, however, claim the resale exemption on the purchase of administrative supplies or another taxable service that it may use in the performance of its secretarial and editing services [61 Pa. Code § 60.8(f)(2)].

Manufacturing and other exemptions: The manufacturing, processing, printing, publishing, farming, dairying, mining, or public utility exemption does not apply to secretarial and editing services [61 Pa. Code § 60.8(f)(1)].

• *Self-storage service*

The rendition for a consideration of a self-storage service at a location in Pennsylvania is taxable [72 P.S. § 7201(k)(18)]. "Self-storage service" means the providing of a building, a room in a building, or a secured area within a building primarily for the purpose of storing personal property with a separate access for each purchaser of self-storage service [61 Pa. Code § 60.12(a)].

Purchase price: The total amount charged for providing self-storage services is subject to tax. Charges associated with the cost of self-storage (*e.g.,* utilities insurance, pickup, delivery, locks, keys) are part of the taxable purchase price. If the primary use of a facility is not for self-storage services, the provision of an area for storage is not taxable unless there is a separate charge for the storage area [61 Pa. Code § 60.12(e)(1)].

Exclusions: The following self-storage services and tangible personal property are exempt:

(1) Self-storage services purchased by qualified charitable organizations, volunteer fire companies, religious organizations, and nonprofit educational institutions unless used in an unrelated trade or business [61 Pa. Code § 60.12(f)(1)].

(2) Self-storage services purchased by the federal government or its instrumentalities.

(3) Self-storage services purchased by the Commonwealth of Pennsylvania, its instrumentalities or subdivisions (including public school districts) [61 Pa. Code § 60.12(f)(1)].

(4) Safe deposit boxes rented from financial institutions [61 Pa. Code § 60.12(f)(2)].

(5) Storage of property in refrigerator or freezer units [61 Pa. Code § 60.12(f)(3)].

(6) Charges for storage of property in commercial warehouses [61 Pa. Code § 60.12(f)(4)].

(7) Rental or lease of a facility for goods distribution [61 Pa. Code § 60.12(f)(5)].

(8) Rental of lockers in airports, bus stations, museums, or other public places [61 Pa. Code § 60.12(f)(6)].

(9) A vendor's purchase of tangible personal property that is transferred to its purchaser or a third party in the performance of its self-storage services. Storage racks, bins, covers, tarpaulins, padlocks, and keys are examples of

tangible personal property that may be purchased exempt for resale. A vendor may not claim a resale exemption with respect to its purchase of administrative supplies or other taxable services that it may use in the performance of its self-storage services [61 Pa. Code § 60.12(f)(7)].

(10) A vendor's purchase of self-storage services from another provider that it resells to its customer. Rental of a building for the primary purpose of subleasing it to another is an example of a nontaxable service [61 Pa. Code § 60.12(f)(7)].

Manufacturing and other exemptions: The manufacturing, mining, processing, public utility, farming, dairying, agriculture, horticulture, or floriculture exemptions do not apply to self-storage facilities.

For details on taxation of self-storage services, see 61 Pa. Code § 60.12.

• *Telecommunications services*

Telecommunications services are discussed in more detail at ¶ 721.

Miscellaneous General Provisions

• *Tangible personal property belonging to third parties*

Vendors must collect tax from the person who pays for taxable services, even though the property on which the services were performed does not belong to the person paying the charge. For example, if an insurance company has a car repaired for a policy holder, the vendor must collect the tax from the insurance company [61 Pa. Code § 31.5(d)].

• *Service or maintenance agreements*

Entering into service agreements to render taxable services is a taxable transaction, regardless of how the agreement is designated (*e.g.,* "inspection," "maintenance"). For example, entering into an agreement with a serviceman to have office equipment inspected, repaired, and cleaned is a taxable transaction [61 Pa. Code § 31.5(e)].

• *Services on property to be used by nonresidents outside Pennsylvania*

Whether or not services performed in Pennsylvania on tangible personal property to be used by nonresidents outside Pennsylvania are taxable depends on where the property is to be delivered after the services are performed [61 Pa. Code § 31.5(g)].

If the property on which the services have been performed is delivered to the purchaser (or the purchaser's agent) in Pennsylvania, the services are taxable, even though the purchaser will later use the property outside the Commonwealth. For example, Angela Harrison, who is not a resident of Pennsylvania, had her car repaired in Pennsylvania while on vacation. Angela must pay sales tax on this transaction if she picks up the car in Pennsylvania. However, if she directs that the car be delivered to her out-of-state residence, the services are not taxable.

If the agreement between vendor and purchaser requires delivery of the property to a destination outside Pennsylvania for use outside Pennsylvania, the service performed on the property is not taxable. For example, Buzy Laundry, located in Pennsylvania, picks up soiled drapes from Wendy Horne, a resident of Maryland, and delivers the cleaned drapes to Wendy's residence in Maryland. This transaction is not taxable.

• *Equipment and materials used in taxable services*

Persons who render taxable services are considered consumers of tangible personal property that they use but do not transfer to their customers. Therefore, all machinery, equipment, tools, supplies, materials, etc. (or services performed on them) purchased for use in rendering taxable services are taxable, but tangible personal property that is to be transferred to customers is not taxable because it is considered purchased for resale. See ¶709 for explanation of the resale exemption [61 Pa. Code § 31.5(i)].

> *Example 1:* Eazy Furniture Repair Shop purchases sandpaper and paint brushes for use in refinishing furniture. These are taxable. Eazy also buys finishing nails and varnish for use in refinishing and repairing furniture. These are incorporated into customers' furniture and are not taxable. Eazy may submit a resale exemption certificate on such purchases.

> *Example 2:* Kwik Auto Repair Shop buys brushes, sand paper, masking tape, and other equipment and supplies to use in its repair business. These items are taxable, but paint, parts, and other property that is transferred to the customer as part of the repair service are not taxable. Kwik may submit a resale exemption certificate for these items.

• *Situs—Cloud computing*

On May 31, 2012 the Department of Revenue released a redacted version of private letter ruling SUT-12-001. The ruling established a new policy for taxing canned software. Canned software will be taxed based on the location of the users rather than the location of the software. Thus, canned software loaded onto a server located in Pennsylvania will only be taxed to the extent that the users are located in Pennsylvania. Likewise, canned software located outside Pennsylvania will be taxed to the extent that users are located within Pennsylvania.

Query

> This is a reversal of the previous policy to tax canned software base on the location of the server. Since there has been no underlying change in law, will this policy be applied retroactively?

• *Taxation—Sales, use, service and gross receipts taxes—transactions taxable in general—services taxable*

A closed circuit horse racing simulcasting system was subject to sales and use tax. A service provider rented the simulcasting system equipment to the race track operator and provided employees to operate the equipment. In some cases, equipment rented with an operator is not subject to tax. This exemption requires that the work be controlled by the person providing the equipment and the operator. In this case, the race track operator directed the service provider's employees in their use of the equipment. Furthermore, charges for the equipment rental and related services, and for the various types of labor, were not separately stated. Therefore, all charges for the simulcasting system were subject to tax. *Downs Racing, LP v. Commonwealth of Pennsylvania* __ A.3d __, (Pa. October 25, 2018)

¶704 Rentals and Leases

Rental or lease of tangible personal property is taxable. For example, when a machine shop grants to another the right to use its machinery on weekends for a fee, the transaction is taxable. Similarly, the rental or lease of an electronic computer is taxable [61 Pa. Code § 31.4(a)].

¶704

Lease of Cargo Containers

In *Itel Containers International Corp. v. Huddleston, Commissioner of Revenue of Tennessee,* 507 U.S. 60 (1993), the U.S. Supreme Court held that Tennessee's tax on the lease of cargo containers delivered to lessees in the state did not violate the Supremacy, Commerce, or Import-Export Clauses of the U.S. Constitution. The tax was not a tax on importation but an allowable tax on the transfer of title or possession of property within Tennessee. The tax did not impose a substantial risk of international multiple taxation because it was imposed on discrete transactions occurring within Tennessee, and a credit was allowed for any tax imposed on the same transaction by another jurisdiction, whether foreign or domestic.

If a person furnishes equipment together with the services of an operator to another person who is given the right to use or direct the use of such equipment, the transaction is taxable. For example, if a company furnishes motor vehicles with drivers to a customer on a time, mileage, or load basis, the transactions are taxable if the customers have the right to control the use of the vehicles. Similarly, if an owner of a crane furnishes a crane with an operator to a construction contractor, although the technical operation and maintenance of the crane are under the control of the operator, the transaction is taxable because the contractor has the right to direct the use of the crane. However, if the labor charge for the operator is separately stated in the billing or document of the transaction *at the time of rental,* it may be deducted in computing the purchase price on which tax is imposed [61 Pa. Code § 31.4(a)(1)].

If equipment furnished with an operator consists of tools of the operator's trade and the value of the use of the tools is insignificant in relation to services performed, no taxable transfer has occurred. For example, when a neighborhood gardener cuts lawns and provides other gardening services, the rakes, shears, and other hand tools used are not considered to be transferred [61 Pa. Code § 31.4(a)(3)].

When equipment is furnished with the services of an operator, it is presumed that the transaction involves a transfer of the right to use or direct the use of the equipment. This presumption may be rebutted by establishing that the use of the equipment is under the exclusive control of the person who furnished the equipment and operator [61 Pa. Code § 31.4(a)(2)].

• *Exemptions*

Purchase of tangible personal property for the predominant purpose of renting or leasing it to others is not taxable (resale exemption). Purchase of repair parts or taxable services for this property is exempt, but purchase of equipment or supplies used in connection with the service or care of rental property is taxable [61 Pa. Code § 31.4(b)]. Rental or leasing of tangible personal property for use in any exempt activity is exempt. See the paragraphs that follow for an explanation of exemptions.

NOTE: For rentals and leases taxable under the Public Transportation Assistance Act, see ¶ 725.

¶705 Exempt Persons

Sales of tangible personal property or services to the following persons are not taxable:

(1) Charitable organizations (including volunteer firemen's organizations, nonprofit educational institutions and religious organizations).

(2) Governmental entities [72 P.S. § 7201(10), (12)].

(3) Veterans' organizations (for purchases used for benevolent, charitable or patriotic purposes).

These are discussed in more detail below. The term "person," for purposes of sales and use taxes, means any natural person, association, fiduciary, partnership, corporation, or other entity, including the Commonwealth of Pennsylvania, its political subdivisions and instrumentalities and public authorities. When used in connection with the imposition of penalties, fines, or imprisonment, the term "person" includes the members of an association and the officers of a corporation [72 P.S. § 7201(e)].

Entities Must Satisfy Both Constitutional and Statutory Criteria

An entity seeking a statutory exemption for taxation must first establish that it is a "purely public charity" under Article VIII, Section 2 of the Pennsylvania Constitution before the question of whether that entity meets the qualifications of a statutory exemption can be reached. See, for example, *G.D.L. Plaza Corp. v. Council Rock Sch. Dist.*, 526 A.2d 1173, 1175 (Pa. 1987) and *Community Options, Inc. v. Allegheny County Board of Property Assessment, Appeals and Review*, 813 A.2d 680 (Pa. 2002). The Pennsylvania Supreme Court set forth a five-prong test for determining whether an entity qualifies as a "purely public charity" under the Pennsylvania Constitution in *Hospital Utilization Project*, 487 A.2d 1306 (Pa. 1985). The *Hospital Utilization Project (HUP)* criteria are also discussed at ¶ 3505.

If an entity satisfies the constitutional requirements, it must then comply with the provisions of the Institutions of Purely Public Charity Act [Act of November 26, 1997, P.L. 55, referred to as Act 55]. The Institutions of Purely Public Charity Act is also discussed at ¶ 3505.

Charitable Organizations

The sale at retail to or use by (1) any charitable organization, volunteer firemen's organization, volunteer firefighters' relief as defined in 35 Pa.C.S. § 7412, or nonprofit educational institution, or (2) a religious organization for religious purposes of tangible personal property or services is exempt from sales tax. If the Department has issued sales tax exempt status to a volunteer firefighters' organization or a volunteer firefighters' relief association, the sales tax exempt status may not expire unless the activities of the organization or association change so that the organization or association does not qualify as an institution of purely public charity (in which case the organization or association must immediately notify the Department of the change). If the Department ascertains that an organization or association no longer qualifies as an institution of purely public charity, the Department may revoke the sales exempt status of the organization or association [72 P.S. § 7204(10)].

The origin of the charitable exemption under 72 P.S. § 7204(10) is Article VIII, Sec. 2(a)(v), of the Pennsylvania Constitution, which authorizes the General Assembly to provide by law for the exemption from taxation of "[i]nstitutions of purely public charity, but in the case of any real property tax exemptions only that portion of real property of such institution which is actually and regularly used for the purposes of the institution." The legislature is, therefore, constitutionally limited to exempt only those charitable organizations that are purely public charities. There is no constitutional authorization for the exemption of any organization that is not a purely public charity [*Hospital Utilization Project (HUP) v. Cmwlth.*, 487 A.2d 1306 (Pa. 1985)]. The term "charitable organization," therefore, is synonymous with "purely public charity."

Prior to the 1997 passage of the Institutions of Purely Public Charity Act [10 P.S. § 372 *et seq.*, amending Article II of the General County Assessment Law], there was no statutory definition of the term "purely public charity." The benchmark *Hospital*

Utilization Project (HUP) case set forth five criteria for identifying purely public charities. See ¶3505 for further discussion of the *HUP* criteria.

• **HUP** *criteria*

In *HUP*, the Pennsylvania Supreme Court stated that an entity qualifies as a purely public charity if it possesses the following five (5) characteristics:

(1) It advances a charitable purpose.

(2) It donates or renders gratuitously a substantial portion of its services.

(3) It benefits a substantial and indefinite class of persons who are legitimate subjects of charity.

(4) It relieves the government of some of its burden.

(5) It operates entirely free from private profit motive.

An institution seeking a tax exemption must meet all five prongs of the *Hospital Utilization Project* test.

HUP and Institutions of Purely Public Charity Act

The HUP test and the Charity Act are not mutually exclusive and operate concurrently, with the Charity Act codifying the purely public charity test of HUP and expounding upon the requirements thereof. See *Church of the Overcomer v. Delaware County Board of Assessment Appeals*, Pa.Commw. No. 269 C.D. 2010 (March 17, 2011), footnote 4.

• *Criteria of The Institutions of Purely Public Charity Act*

The Institutions of Purely Public Charity Act sets forth five statutory requirements that an entity must satisfy in order to qualify as an institution of purely public charity. This Act (also known as Act 55) is discussed in more detail at ¶3505. The five statutory criteria of Act 55, which essentially codify the five criteria of *HUP*, are as follows:

(1) The institution must advance a charitable purpose.

(2) The institution must operate entirely free from private profit motive.

(3) The institution must donate or render gratuitously a substantial portion of its services.

(4) The institution must benefit a substantial and indefinite class of persons who are legitimate objects of charity.

(5) The institution must relieve the government of some of its burden.

• *Limitations*

The exemption for charitable organizations does not apply to sales of property or services used in any unrelated trade or business carried on by the organization or to sales of materials, supplies and equipment used by and transferred to the organization in the construction, reconstruction, remodeling, renovation, repairs and maintenance of any real estate structure (other than building machinery and equipment). Materials and supplies purchased for routine maintenance and repairs are exempt.

• *Application for exemption from sales and use taxes*

All applicants applying for exemption status under 72 P.S. § 7204(10) are required to complete the revised Form REV-72 as well as supply all necessary supporting documentation [*Pennsylvania Tax Update No. 73*, Pennsylvania Department of Revenue, January/February 1998]. Questions about tax exemption issues should be directed to the Department of Revenue's Sales Tax Exemption Unit at 717-782-5473 or 717-722-6922.

• *Annual reports*

An institution of purely public charity that does not register with the Department of State under the Solicitation of Funds for Charitable Purposes Act [Act of December 19, 1990, P.L. 1200, No. 202] must file an annual report. This includes institutions exempted from registration under §6 of the Solicitation of Funds for Charitable Purposes Act [10 P.S. §379(a)]. The Department will retain reporting information for three years from the due date of the report [10 P.S. §379(g)].

The annual report must be in a format approved by the Department and must include the following items:

(1) A copy of the annual return filed (or required to be filed) with the IRS. For an institution not required to file an annual federal return, the institution's annual financial statement with reported income constitutes its annual return.

(2) The date the institution of purely public charity was organized.

(3) Any revocation of tax-exempt status by the IRS.

(4) Information on affiliates: (a) name and type of organization; (b) whether the affiliated is organized on a for-profit or nonprofit basis; (c) the relationship of each affiliated to the institution making the report.

(5) The relationship of the institution of purely public charity with any other nonprofit corporation or unincorporated association if the relationship involves formal governance or the sharing of revenue.

Due date: An annual report is due within 135 days after the close of the institution's fiscal year (unless an extension is granted).

Filing fee: Institutions required to file reports under 10 P.S. §373 must pay an annual filing fee of $15, which may be adjusted by the Department by regulation.

Exemption from filing: The following institutions of purely public charity are exempt from the reporting requirements:

(1) A bona fide, duly constituted religious institution and separate groups or corporations that form an integral part of a religious institution that is also exempt from filing an annual federal return.

(2) Institutions that receive contributions of less than $25,000 per year and also have annual program service revenue of no more that the rebuttable presumption amount. Effective July 1, 2011, a charitable organization that possesses a valid Pennsylvania sales and use tax exemption is entitled to a rebuttable presumption that it meets the criteria of a purely public charity if its annual program service revenues are less than $11,404,743 effective July 1, 2012. Under the Institutions of Purely Public Charity Act, the Department of Revenue is required to increase the rebuttable presumption amount by 1% each year [*Notice*, Pennsylvania Department of Revenue, June 25, 2011]. "Program service revenue" is income earned from the provision of goods or services, including government fees and contracts associated with the institution's charitable purpose, that is reported on the annual return [10 P.S. §373].

Paperwork reduction: The Department shall allow an institution to certify that the required information has not changed since the prior report in lieu of providing the same information in a new annual report.

Administrative penalty: The Department may impose an administrative penalty not to exceed $500 for either of the following [10 P.S. §379(i)]:

(1) Knowingly failing to file a required annual report.

(2) Knowingly making a false statement that is material in a required report.

¶705

CAUTION

Some of the cases discussed below were decided prior to the passage of the Institutions of Purely Public Charity Act (Act 55). They satisfy the minimum constitutional requirements for exemption as a purely public charity but may not satisfy the requirements of Act 55.

Cases—Do Not Qualify as Purely Public Charities

Prior to the passage of the Institutions of Purely Public Charity Act, the accepted criteria for identifying a purely public charity were those of *Hospital Utilization Project (HUP) v. Cmwlth.*, 487 A.2d 1306 (Pa. 1985). The *HUP* criteria are the same as the new statutory criteria listed above. The cases discussed below were decided under the *HUP* criteria. See ¶ 3505 for a discussion of the other cases.

Accounting organization: Community Accountants is a not-for-profit corporation registered as a charitable organization with the Commonwealth and recognized as a tax-exempt entity by the Internal Revenue Service. Its charitable purpose is to provide free accounting and financial management services to small nonprofit organizations, sole proprietors, and small businesses unable to pay for such services. Recipients of services pay a small fee or no fee at all. Community Accountants also receives funding from such organizations as the United Way. Analyzing the facts within the framework of *Hospital Utilization,* the court found that this organization advances a charitable purpose, donates or renders gratuitously a substantial portion of its services, and operates entirely free of a private profit motive. However, it does not benefit a substantial and indefinite class of persons who are legitimate subjects of charity; it directs its services at a large, but definite, class of beneficiaries—only small businesses, sole proprietors, and small nonprofit organizations with limited resources—and it is not entitled to exemption from the sales and use taxes [*Community Accountants v. Cmwlth.*, 655 A.2d 652 (Pa.Commw. 1995), *aff'd per curiam* 676 A.2d 194 (Pa. 1996)].

Foundation for education and research: The PICPA Foundation for Education and Research was established exclusively for the advancement and encouragement of education and research in accounting. Its seminars are open to all interested parties regardless of an individual's profession or affiliation with the PICPA. The court held that the Foundation exists primarily or predominantly to benefit individuals who have a professional or occupational interest in accounting, not to benefit an indefinite number of people (*i.e.,* the public). The Foundation was, therefore, denied status as a nonprofit educational institution (*i.e.,* a purely public charity) [*PICPA Foundation for Education and Research v. Cmwlth.*, 634 A.2d 187 (Pa. 1993), *aff'g* 598 A.2d 1078 (Pa.Commw. 1991)].

Nonprofit corporation providing administrative services: Sacred Heart Healthcare System (SHHS) was formed to serve as the parent corporation of a hospital and two other corporate entities and was designed to perform *administrative* functions for all the affiliated corporations, one of which is a hospital. SHHS itself is a not-for-profit corporation. However, merely because an organization is a not-for-profit corporation does not automatically qualify it for a tax exemption as a purely public charity, and it is irrelevant whether an organization is recognized as an exempt charity for federal income tax purposes. SHHS does not satisfy all five prongs of the *Hospitalization Utilization Project (HUP)* case (see above) and therefore does not qualify for a sales and use tax exemption as a purely public charity. SHHS satisfies only one prong of *HUP*: it advances a charitable purpose. It fails the other four tests for qualification as a purely public charity [*Sacred Heart Healthcare System v. Cmwlth.*, 673 A.2d 1021 (Pa.Commw. 1996)].

Publisher of scientific materials: Biosciences Information Service was a not-for-profit corporation engaged in the business of producing abstracts of biological sciences literature from around the world. This scientific literature was made available to government agencies, medical schools, research laboratories, hospitals and individual doctors for a fee. The Commonwealth Court held that this taxpayer did not meet the criteria of HUP. It did not advance a charitable purpose because its services were not directed to the general public, which received only secondary benefit from the taxpayer's services. It did not render a substantial portion of its services without consideration. It did not benefit a substantial and indefinite class of persons who are legitimate subjects of charity: It benefitted a definite class of persons who are not legitimate subjects of charity, and it did not relieve the government of any of its burden. It did not operate entirely free of private profit motive [*Biosciences Information Service v. Cmwlth.*, 551 A.2d 672 (Pa.Commw. 1988), 551 A.2d 672 (Pa.Commw. 1988), *aff'd* 569 A.2d 927 (Pa. 1999)].

Governmental Entities

• *U.S. Government*

Sales to the U.S. Government and U.S. Government agencies are exempt [61 Pa. Code § 32.22]. Sales of tangible personal property or services to a regular department of the U.S. Government (*e.g.,* Defense, Interior, Agriculture, Post Office, Commerce) are not taxable. However, sales of tangible personal property by persons doing business in a federal area within the borders of Pennsylvania are not exempt by this regulation. These sales are exempt only if specifically exempt by other regulation or statute (*e.g.,* purchase for resale).

Banks: Federal Reserve Banks and their branch banks are exempt, but not commercial banks that are merely member banks of the Federal Reserve System. The only banks in Pennsylvania entitled to this exemption are the Federal Reserve Bank of Philadelphia, District No. 3, and the Pittsburgh Branch of the Federal Reserve Bank of Cleveland, District No. 4.

Nonexempt agencies: The following government agencies are not exempt: national banks, federal savings and loan associations, joint stock land banks, national park concessionaires, The Atomic Energy Commission, federal licensees such as warehouses and stockyards, and construction contractors engaged in the improvement of real estate such as buildings, roads, structures, bridges owned by an exempt federal agency, and similar corporations, companies, institutions, or persons.

Federal credit unions: Federal law prevents state and local jurisdictions from imposing taxes (except taxes on real or tangible personal property) on federal credit unions [12 U.S.C. § 1768]. Federal credit unions organized under the provisions of the Federal Credit Union Act (Act of June 26, 1934, P.L. 86-385) and Pennsylvania credit unions formed and incorporated under the provisions of the Credit Union Act (17 Pa.C.S. § 101 *et seq.*) are exempt from sales and hotel occupancy tax. Other federal and state credit unions are presumed taxable unless they are agencies of the U.S. government or an exemption is extended to the organization by the law under which it is created [61 Pa. Code § 48.4].

Foreign diplomats: Sales to ambassadors, ministers, and other diplomatic representatives of foreign governments properly accredited to the U.S. are not taxable. A person entitled to the diplomatic exemption from tax must apply to the Office of Foreign Missions, U.S. Department of State, which will issue a Tax Exemption Card to qualifying individuals. The Department of Revenue recognizes the exemption from tax granted to these individuals in accordance with the restrictions provided on the tax exemption card [61 Pa. Code § 32.24].

• *Commonwealth of Pennsylvania*

Sales to the Commonwealth of Pennsylvania and its instrumentalities or political subdivisions are not subject to sales and use taxes [61 Pa. Code § 32.23]. Transactions are exempt only when the sale is made and invoiced directly to the exempt entity. Sales to individual employees (*e.g.*, teachers, school principals) are taxable.

Instrumentalities: Instrumentalities include all departments, boards, commissions of Pennsylvania and public authorities created under the Municipality Authorities Acts of 1945 [53 P.S. § § 301—322]. Other public authorities claiming exempt status must apply to the Department of Revenue, Office of Chief Counsel, Dept. 281061, Harrisburg, PA 17128-1061.

Political subdivisions: Political subdivisions include any county, city, borough, incorporated town, township, school district, vocational school district, and county institution district.

Sale at retail: The sale at retail of personal property is taxable. These entities are permitted to purchase items for resale using the "resale" exemption, and they must register with the Department for the charging, collecting and reporting of tax.

State credit unions: State credit unions that are not formed or organized under the Credit Union Act [17 Pa.C.S. § 101 *et seq.*] are presumed to be subject to sales, use and hotel occupancy tax unless an exemption is extended to the organization by the law under which it is created. However, a state credit union that is an agency of Pennsylvania or its political subdivisions (but is not formed under the Credit Union Act) is exempt from sales and use taxes but not the hotel occupancy tax [61 Pa. Code § 48.4(c)].

Veterans' Organizations

Any branch, post, or camp of honorably discharged servicemen or servicewomen (or an affiliated organization) is exempt from sales and use taxes for all purchases used for benevolent, charitable, or patriotic purposes [51 Pa.C.S. § 9301(a)(1)]. An affiliated organization for this purpose is one defined as an affiliated organization in § 461.1(b) of the Liquor Code [Act of April 12, 1951 (P.L. 90, No. 21)]. Note, however, that the purchase of alcoholic beverages is not exempt. An exemption for veterans' organizations is also authorized for property tax purposes. See ¶ 3504.

¶706 Exempt Property

Some Exempt Property Taxable Under PTA

Some property exempt under sales and use taxes are subject to tax under the Public Transportation Assistance Act (PTA) [74 Pa.C.S. § § 1301 et seq.]. See ¶ 725.

Even when sold at retail, the property explained in this section is exempt from Pennsylvania sales and use taxes. 72 P.S. § 7204 is entitled "Exclusions from tax." These provisions, however, have been generally interpreted to be exemptions (which are strictly construed against the taxpayer) rather than exclusions (which are construed against the taxing jurisdiction). The exemptions discussed in this paragraph are those provided for by 72 P.S. § 7204.

Listing of Taxable and Nontaxable Items

The list of items within a category of exempt property listed below is extensive. The Department publishes (in the *Pennsylvania Bulletin*) a list of taxable and exempt property at least once every three years. In addition, it quarterly publishes notice in the *Pennsylvania Bulletin* of additions, deletions or revisions to the list. A ruling on unusual transactions or on property or services not included in the list may be obtained upon written request to the Department of Revenue, Office of Chief Counsel, Dept. 281061,

Harrisburg, Pennsylvania 17128-1061 [61 Pa. Code §58.1]. The Department also prepares a *Retailers' Information Booklet* (REV-717) that provides procedural information and reproduces the list of taxable and nontaxable items published in the *Pennsylvania Bulletin*. *Retailers' Information Booklet,* is available on the Department's website (www.revenue.pa.state.us). Taxpayers may also call the 24-hour answering service numbers for forms ordering: in Pennsylvania 800-362-1050; outside Pennsylvania and within the local Harrisburg area 717-787-8094; for the hearing impaired: TDD 717-772-2252. Be sure to consult these resources if there is any doubt about the taxability of any item.

• *Aircraft parts, components and services*

Parts and components for, and services performed on fixed wing aircraft, powered aircraft, tilt-rotor or tilt-wing aircraft, glider or unmanned aircraft are excluded from tax [72 P.S. 7204(69)].

• *Airline food*

The sale at retail to or use of food and nonalcoholic beverages by an airline that will transfer the food or nonalcoholic beverages to passengers in connection with the rendering of the airline service is not taxable [72 P.S. § 7204(61)].

• *Alcohol*

Ordinarily, alcoholic beverages when purchased in a Pennsylvania liquor store are taxable, but a religious organization may purchase beverages for use in religious services if it furnishes the liquor store with a proper religious organization exemption certificate. In order to be exempt, the purchase must be made and paid for directly by the religious organization through an authorized representative. Purchases made by private individuals are taxable, even if they intend to donate the beverage to a religious organization [61 Pa. Code § 48.3(b)].

• *Building machinery and equipment*

The sale at retail or use by a construction contractor of building machinery and equipment and services thereto that are (1) transferred pursuant to a construction contract for any charitable organization, volunteer firemen's organization, nonprofit educational institution or religious organization for religious purpose, provided that the building machinery and equipment and services thereto are not used in any unrelated trade or business or (2) transferred to the United States or the Commonwealth or its instrumentalities or political subdivisions are exempt from sales and use taxes [72 P.S. § 7204(57)]. This provision does not apply to fixed-price construction contracts entered into prior to July 1, 1998, or entered into under the obligation of an unalterable, formal written bid issued prior to July 1, 1998. For definition of "building machinery and equipment," see ¶ 717.

Keystone opportunity zones (KOZs): The exemption also applies to building machinery and equipment for the exclusive use, consumption, and utilization by a qualified business at a facility in a KOZ. KOZs are discussed at ¶ 4622.

NOTE: See ¶ 716 and ¶ 717 for discussion of the rules for pre-July 1, 1998, contracts and post-June 30, 1998, contracts.

• *Building supplies and materials*

The sale at retail to or use by a construction contractor, employed by a public school district pursuant to a construction contract, of any building supplies and materials that, during construction or reconstruction, are made part of any public school building utilized for instructional classroom education within Pennsylvania is exempt if the construction or reconstruction (1) is necessitated by a disaster emergency as defined in 35 Pa.C.S. § 7102 and (2) takes place during the period when there is a declaration of disaster emergency under 35 Pa.C.S. § 7301(c) [72 P.S. § 7204(64)].

¶706

• *Candy and gum*

The sale at retail or use of candy and gum is exempt from sales and use taxes regardless of the location from which it is sold. Under prior law, candy and gum were taxable when sold from an establishment that sold ready-to-eat food [72 P.S. § 7204(53)].

• *Caskets, burial vaults, tombstones*

The sale at retail or use of caskets and burial vaults for human remains and markers and tombstones for human graves is exempt [72 P.S. § 7204(31)].

• *Charitable organizations*

Sales and use taxes do not apply to tangible personal property or services sold to or used by any (1) charitable organization, volunteer firemen's organization or nonprofit educational institution or (2) a religious organization for religious purposes. Property or services pursuant to a construction contract are not exempt. Neither exemption applies to property or services used in any unrelated business or to materials, supplies and equipment used and transferred to the charitable organization in the construction, reconstruction, remodeling, renovation, repairs and maintenance of real estate structures (except building machinery and equipment). Machinery and supplies purchased by an organization or institution for routine maintenance and repairs are exempt [72 P.S. § 7204(10)]. This provision is not applicable to fixed-price construction contracts entered into prior to July 1, 1998, or entered into under the obligation of an unalterable, formal written bid issued prior to July 1, 1998.

• *Clothing*

The sale at retail or use of all vesture, wearing apparel, raiments, garments, footwear and other articles of clothing, including clothing patterns and items that are to be a component part of clothing, worn or carried on or about the human body is exempt [72 P.S. § 7204(26)].

Exceptions: The following items are *not* exempt: accessories; ornamental wear; formal day or evening apparel; articles made of fur on the hide or pelt or any material imitative of fur and articles of which such fur (real, imitation, or synthetic) is the component material of chief value (but only if the value of the fur is more than three times the value of the next most valuable component material); and sporting goods and clothing not normally used or worn when not engaged in sports.

• *Coal*

The sale at retail or use of coal is not taxable [72 P.S. § 7204(18)].

• *Construction contractors*

See "Building machinery and equipment," above.

• *Contract farming*

The sale at retail or use of tangible personal property or services that are directly used in farming, dairying, or agriculture when engaged in as a business enterprise is not taxable whether or not the sale is made to the person directly engaged in the business enterprise or to a person contracting with the person directly engaged in the business enterprise for the production of food [72 P.S. § 7204(62)].

• *Direct mail advertising*

The sale at retail or use of mail order catalogs and direct mail advertising literature or materials, including electoral literature or materials, such as envelopes, address labels, and a one-time license to use a list of names and mailing addresses for each delivery of direct mail advertising literature or materials, including electoral literature or materials, through the United States Postal Service is exempt from

Pennsylvania sales and use taxes [72 P.S. §7204(35)]. The Pennsylvania Commonwealth Court has held Pennsylvania sales and use tax does not apply to fees paid for the printing and distribution of publications that contained cover stories, feature stories, employment opportunities, and advertising for targeted industries because the publications constituted exempt direct mail advertising literature or materials. The Pennsylvania Department of Revenue contended that the exemption could only apply to advertising materials sent directly from vendors to prospective purchasers, rather than from a publisher to prospective purchasers. However, a plain reading of the statute did not support the Department's construction. In addition, the Department's claim was inconsistent with the exemption for printed advertising materials circulated with periodicals or publications because those materials do not emanate directly from vendors to prospective purchasers. The court concluded that the exemption applies to advertising literature and materials that are delivered directly to the intended recipient after placement in the United States mail, and that advertisements do not have to be mailed by the vendor [*Merion Publications, Inc. v. Cmwlth.*, No. 792 F.R. 2003 (Pa.Commw., January 11, 2006); aff'd per curium, 911 A.2d 917 (Pa. 2006)].

• *Disposable diapers and personal hygiene items*

The sale at retail or use of the following items is not taxable: disposable diapers; premoistened wipes; incontinence products; colostomy deodorants; toilet paper; sanitary napkins; tampons or similar items used for feminine hygiene; and toothpaste, toothbrushes, or dental floss [72 P.S. §7204(4)].

• *Electric vehicles*

The net purchase price of the sale at retail or use of electric vehicles, hybrid electric vehicles, and zero-emission vehicles (see "Zero-emission vehicles," below) is exempt from sales and use taxes. Net purchase price is the difference between the purchase price of such a vehicle and the average retail list price of a comparable vehicle. In the case of a passenger car, a passenger truck, or a van, comparable vehicle means the overall average list price in the United States. The Department of Revenue has the authority to promulgate rules and regulations to enforce this exemption and determine the average retail list price on an annual basis. In the case of a qualified motor vehicle other than a passenger car, passenger truck, or van, the Department of Revenue shall determine the average list price of a comparable vehicle classification [72 P.S. §7204(47)].

• *Farming*

The term "sale at retail" does not include transfer of property or rendition of services to be used by the purchaser directly in the operation of farming. The term "farming" includes agriculture, horticulture, floriculture, dairy farming, fur-ranching, propagation of game birds, propagation of aquatic animals and propagation of horses to be used exclusively for commercial racing activities [72 P.S. §7201(k)(8)(B); 61 Pa. Code §32.1]. The farming exemption is explained at ¶712. See also "Contract farming," above.

• *Firewood*

Retail sale or use of firewood is exempt when used as fuel for cooking, hot water production or heating a residential dwelling [72 P.S. §7204(44)].

• *Fish feed*

The sale at retail or use of fish feed is exempt *if* it is purchased by a sportsmen's club, fish cooperative, or nursery approved by the Pennsylvania Fish Commission [72 P.S. §7204(39)].

¶706

• *Flags*

The sale at retail or use of flags of the United States and Pennsylvania is exempt [72 P.S. § 7204(32)]. The sale or use of all other flags is taxable. However, accessories that are purchased or used in connection with any flag are subject to tax, and if a U.S. or Pennsylvania flag is sold with accessories and the purchase price of the flag is not separately stated, the entire purchase price is taxable [61 Pa. Code § 58.12(c)]. A flag of the United States means any flag adopted by a law passed by the U.S. Congress as an official flag. A flag of Pennsylvania means any flag adopted through legislation passed by the General Assembly of Pennsylvania as an official flag. Accessories include any poles, ropes, or other hardware used in display of a flag [61 Pa. Code § 58.12(c)].

• *Food and beverages*

In general, the sale at retail or use of food and beverages for human consumption is not taxable [72 P.S. § 7204(29)].

Accessory items: Accessory items (*e.g.,* disposable plastic or wooden eating utensils, napkins, straws) supplied to retail customers by an operator of cafeterias and vending machines and catering services are subject to use tax. These items are not a "critical element" of the retail sale and therefore are not entitled to a resale exemption [*Covenco Inc. v. Cmwlth.,* 579 A.2d 434 (Pa.Commw. 1990), *aff'd per curiam,* 607 A.2d 1077 (Pa. 1990)].

Confections: Prior to the amendment of § 201(m) by 72 P.S. § 9101 *et seq.,* the exclusion for food and beverages included "confections." "Confections" are not taxable. This led to court decisions ruling that certain prepackaged products (*e.g.,* ice pops) sold from ice cream trucks were "confections" and therefore not taxable but that hand-dipped ice cream was taxable [*O'Boyle's Ice Cream Island, Inc. v. Cmwlth.,* 553 A.2d 1033 (Pa.Commw. 1989)]. The repeal of the exclusion for "confections" means that all such items (including ice cream) are taxable. Candy and gum are still not taxable.

Eating establishments: The following are not considered eating establishments for purposes of this exemption except for the sale of meals, sandwiches, food from salad bars, hand-dipped or hand-served iced-based products (including ice cream and yogurt), hot soup, hot pizza and other hot food items, brewed coffee and hot beverages:

(1) Bakeries.

(2) Pastry shops.

(3) Donut shops.

(4) Delicatessens.

(5) Grocery stores.

(6) Supermarkets.

(7) Farmer's markets.

(8) Convenience stores.

(9) Vending machines. For details on vending machine sales, see 61 Pa. Code § 31.28.

Food and beverages that are taxable: The food and beverage exemption does not apply to the following items (*i.e.,* these items are taxable):

(1) Soft drinks. For this purpose soft drinks are considered beverages, but malt and brewed beverages and spirituous and vinous liquors are not.

(2) Malt and brewed beverages and spirituous and vinous liquors.

¶**706**

(3) Food or beverages (whether sold for consumption on premises or off premises or on a take-out or to-go basis or delivered to the purchaser) when they are purchased from caterers.

(4) Food or beverages (whether sold for consumption on premises or off premises or on a take-out or to-go basis or delivered to the purchaser) when they are purchased from eating establishments. "Eating establishment" includes, but is not limited to, the following: restaurants; cafes; lunch counters; private and social clubs; taverns; dining cars; hotels; night clubs; fast food operations; pizzerias; fairs; carnivals; lunch carts; ice cream stands; snack bars; cafeterias; employee cafeterias; theaters; stadiums; arenas; amusement parks; carryout shops; coffee shops; and other establishments (whether mobile or immobile).

Food stamps: The sale at retail or use of tangible personal property purchased in accordance with the Food Stamp Act [P.L. 95-113, 7 U.S.C. § § 2011—2029] is exempt under 72 P.S. § 7204(46).

Management fees for operation of employee cafeteria: A taxpayer paid a management company, an independent contractor, to operate and manage its employee cafeteria. The management company collected and remitted sales tax on the prices paid for the food sold in the cafeteria. The Department contended that the management fee was taxable because it represented a contract for the sale and delivery of taxable items. The Commonwealth Court disagreed, holding that the prices paid by the cafeteria patrons represented the only and the full taxable purchase price paid by anyone for the transfer of the food; the management fee represented the amount paid by the taxpayer for the operation of the cafeteria and was not subject to sales and use taxes [*M&M/Mars, Inc. v. Cmwlth.,* 639 A.2d 848 (Pa.Commw. 1994), *aff'd per curiam,* 658 A.2d 797 (Pa. 1995)].

Schools and churches: The sale at retail of food and beverages at or from a school or church in the ordinary course of its activities is not taxable.

Sports programs: The sale at retail or use of food and beverages by nonprofit associations that support sports programs is not subject to sales and use taxes [72 P.S. § 7204(49); *Policy Statement 60.17,* Pennsylvania Department of Revenue, July 2, 2011].

• *Gasoline and other motor fuels*

The sale at retail or use of gasoline and other motor fuels subject to the liquid fuels and fuel use taxes is exempt [72 P.S. § 7204(11)]. The liquid fuels and fuel use taxes are discussed in Chapter 26.

• *Governmental entities*

The sale at retail or use of tangible personal property or services made to the United States, Pennsylvania or its instrumentalities or political subdivisions is not taxable [72 P.S. § 7204(12)]. See also ¶ 705.

• *Helicopters and rotocraft*

The sales or use tax of helicopters and similar rotocraft sold, leased or used in Pennsylvania, including repair or replacement parts, installation of parts, and over-hauling or rebuilding of helicopters or similar rotocraft is excluded from tax [72. P.S. § 7204 (67), (68)].

• *Historical memorials*

The sale at retail or use of materials used in the construction of objects purchased by nonprofit organizations for purposes of commemoration of historical events is exempt, provided the commemorative objects are erected upon publicly owned property or property to be conveyed to a public entity upon commemoration of the historical event [72 P.S. § 7204(45)].

• *Horses delivered out of state*

Sales and use taxes are not imposed on the sale at retail of horses if, at the time of purchase, the seller is directed to deliver the horse to an out-of-state location. It does not matter who pays the shipping charges. The seller must get a bill of lading, either from the carrier or from the purchaser (who obtained it from the carrier), reflecting delivery of the horse to an out of state address. If the seller delivers the horse to a party within Pennsylvania before it is shipped out of state, the seller must get bills of lading for both deliveries. The seller must then execute a "Certificate of Delivery to Destination Outside of the Commonwealth," attaching all bills of lading [72 P.S. § 7204(38)].

• *Horses for commercial racing activities*

Sales and use taxes are not imposed on the sale at retail of horses to be used exclusively for commercial racing activities and the sale at retail and use of feed, bedding, grooming supplies, riding tack, farrier services, portable stalls and sulkies for horses used exclusively for commercial racing activities [72 P.S. § 7204(55)].

• *Investment metal bullion and coins*

Sales and use taxes are not imposed on the sale at retail or use of investment metal bullion and investment coins [72 P.S. § 7204(65), effective August 4, 2006]. "Investment metal bullion" means any elementary precious metal that has been put through a process of smelting or refining, including, but not limited to, gold, silver, platinum, and palladium, and that is in such state or condition that its value depends upon its content and not its form. "Investment metal bullion" does not include precious metal that has been assembled, fabricated, manufactured, or processed in one or more specific and customary industrial, professional, aesthetic, or artistic uses. "Investment coins" means numismatic coins or other forms of money and legal tender manufactured of metal and of the United States or any foreign nation with a fair market value greater than any nominal value of the coins. "Investment coins" does not include jewelry or works of art made of coins or commemorative medallions.

• *Isolated sales*

The sale at retail or use of tangible personal property or services sold by or purchased from a person not a vendor an in isolated transaction or sold by or purchased from a person who is a vendor but is not a vendor with respect to the tangible personal property or services sold in such transaction is not taxable [72 P.S. § 7204(1)]. This exemption does not extend to the following:

(1) Inventory and stock in trade.

(2) Motor vehicles, trailers, semitrailers, motor boats, aircraft, or other similar tangible personal property required under either federal or Pennsylvania law or laws to be registered or licensed.

"Isolated sales" are discussed in more detail at ¶ 708.

• *Magazine subscriptions*

The sale at retail or use of a magazine subscription is not subject to sales and use taxes. A "magazine" for this purpose is a periodical (1) published at regular intervals not exceeding three months, (2) circulated among the general public, (3) containing matters of general interest and reports of current events published for the purpose of disseminating information of a public character, or (4) devoted to literature, the sciences, art, or some special industry. This exclusion also applies to any printed advertising material circulated with the magazine regardless of where or by whom the printed advertising material was produced [72 P.S. § 7204(50); 61 Pa. Code § 31.29].

• *Mail order catalogs*

See "Direct mail advertising," above.

• *Manufacturing*

The sale or use of property or services to be used directly in the manufacture of tangible personal property is not taxable [72 P.S. § 7201(k)(8)]. The manufacturing exemption is explained at ¶ 710.

• *Medicines and medical supplies*

The sale at retail or use of the following is exempt: medicines (prescription or nonprescription), drugs or medical supplies; crutches and wheelchairs for the use of handicapped individuals; artificial limbs, artificial eyes, and artificial hearing devices when designed to be worn on the person of the purchaser or user; false teeth and materials used by a dentist in dental treatment; or eyeglasses when especially designed or prescribed by an ophthalmologist, oculist, or optometrist for the personal use of the owner or purchaser. Also exempt are artificial braces and supports designed solely for the use of crippled persons or any other therapeutic, prosthetic or artificial device designed for the use of a particular individual to correct or alleviate a physical incapacity, including but not limited to hospital beds, iron lungs, and kidney machines [72 P.S. § 7204(17)].

• *Molds and related mold equipment*

The sale at retail or use of molds and related mold equipment used directly and predominantly in the manufacture of products is not taxable, regardless of whether the person that holds title to the equipment manufactures a product [72 P.S. § 7204(59)].

• *Motor vehicles*

The sale at retail or use of motor vehicles, trailers and semitrailers, or bodies attached to their chassis, sold to a nonresident of Pennsylvania to be used outside of Pennsylvania *if* they are registered in another state within 20 days of delivery is exempt [72 P.S. § 7204(24)].

• *Newspapers and newspaper advertising materials*

The sale at retail or use of newspapers is exempt; and this exemption extends to any printed advertising materials circulated with newspapers regardless of where or by whom it was produced [72 P.S. § 7204(30)]. The term "newspaper" is defined to include a "legal newspaper" or a publication containing matters of general interest and reports of current events that is a "newspaper of general circulation" qualifying to carry a "legal advertisement" as defined in 45 Pa.C.S. § 101. A magazine is not a newspaper and is taxable unless sold by subscription [*Magazine Publishers of America v. Cmwlth.*, 618 A.2d 1056 (Pa.Commw. 1992), *aff'd*, 654 A.2d 519 (Pa. 1995); 72 P.S. § 7204(50)].

• *Nonresidents' out-of-state purchases*

The use of tangible personal property purchased outside Pennsylvania for use outside Pennsylvania by a nonresident natural person or a business not doing business in Pennsylvania is not subject to Pennsylvania use tax. However, if this person or business later brings such tangible personal property into Pennsylvania in connection with his or her establishment of a permanent business or residence in Pennsylvania, the use of the property is subject to Pennsylvania use tax *unless* it was purchased more than six (6) months prior to the establishment of a permanent Pennsylvania residence or business [72 P.S. § 7204(3)].

Exception: This exclusion does not apply to tangible personal property temporarily brought into Pennsylvania for the performance of contracts for the construction, reconstruction, remodeling, repairing, and maintenance of real estate.

¶706

• *Official documents*

The sale at retail or use of copies of an official document sold by a government agency or a court is excluded [72 P.S. § 7204(66)].

• *Prebuilt housing, used*

The sale or use of used prebuilt housing is not taxable [72 P.S. § 7204(60)]. See "Construction (Prebuilt Housing)" at ¶718 for further explanation of the prebuilt housing provisions.

• *Processing*

The sale or use of property and services to be directly used in processing is not taxable [72 P.S. § 7201(k)(8)(D)]. The processing exemption is explained at ¶711.

• *Public utilities*

The sale or use of property or services to be used directly in the producing, delivering or rendering of a public utility service, or in constructing, reconstructing, remodeling, repairing or maintaining the facilities directly used in producing, delivering or rendering such service, is not taxable [72 P.S. § 7210(k)(8)(C)]. The public utilities exemption is explained at ¶713.

• *Rail transportation equipment*

The sale at retail or use of rail transportation equipment used in the movement of personalty is not taxable [72 P.S. § 7204(36)].

• *Religious articles*

The exemption for sales of Bibles and religious articles provided in 72 P.S. § 7204(28) was held to be unconstitutional by the Commonwealth Court [*Haller v. Cmwlth.*, 693 A.2d 266 (Pa.Commw. 1997)]. Specifically, the court said that 72 P.S. § 7204(28) and 61 Pa. Code § 31.3(22) violate the First Amendment to the U.S. Constitution (the Establishment Clause) and Article I, § 3, of the Pennsylvania Constitution. On appeal, the Pennsylvania Supreme Court agreed, and the U.S. Supreme Court has refused to hear the case [*Haller v. Cmwlth.*, No. 49 M.D. Appeal Docket 1997 (April 21, 1999); *cert. den.*, U.S. Supreme Court, Dkt. 99-154 (October 12, 1999)].

Since the *Haller* decisions, the Department of Revenue has deleted 61 Pa. Code §§ 48.2 and 48.3, amended 61 Pa. Code §§ 31.3 and 31.29, and added "religious articles," as taxable, to its listing of taxable and nontaxable items (see above). Religious publications are no longer exempt. "Religious publications" for this purpose are religious commentaries and other publications primarily devoted to religious instruction, promotion, or information [61 Pa. Code § 31. 29(a)]. See ¶702 for a discussion of taxable items.

• *Resale*

The sale or use of property for resale is not taxable [72 P.S. § 7201(k)(8)]. The resale exemption is explained at ¶709.

• *Residential utilities*

The following are exempt from tax *when purchased directly by the user thereof solely for his own residential use:* the sale at retail or use of steam, and bottled gas (natural and manufactured), fuel oil, electricity, or intrastate subscriber line charges, basic local telephone service, or telegraph service when purchased directly by the user thereof solely for his own residential use, and charges for telephone calls paid for by inserting money into a telephone accepting direct deposits of money to operate [72 P.S. § 7204(5)]. The purchase of these items by anyone other than a residential purchaser for the purchaser's own residential use is presumed to be made for a commercial use and is taxable unless the purchaser is entitled to an exemption (*e.g.*, resale) [61 Pa. Code § 32.25(b)(2)]. The purchase of electricity and gas by a landlord

¶706

for use by tenants is not exempt because the purchase is not directly made by the ultimate user [*Adelphia House Partnership v. Cmwlth.,* 719 A.2d 833 (Pa.Commw. 1998)].

"Residential use" for this purpose is the use or consumption within that portion of a structure used as a home, dwelling, private residence, condominium, housing cooperative, mobile home, camper, summer home, motor home or similar place of abode. The term includes the use or consumption by a condominium association or housing cooperative association that acts on behalf of residents who are using the units as their personal residence. "Commercial use" is use that occurs within a portion of a structure or other area that is used for other than a residential purpose [61 Pa. Code § 32.25(a); *Summit House Condominium v. Cmwlth.,* 523 A.2d 333 (Pa. 1987)].

Mixed use: If these utilities are purchased by a residential purchaser for both his/ her own residential use and for commercial use, the entire purchase is presumed to be made for commercial use (*i.e.,* taxable) unless the purchaser tenders a valid "Sales and Use Tax Exemption Certificate" (Form REV-1220). This certificate should indicate at "other" on the reverse side the annualized percentage of total residential usage. The vendor may accept such a certificate in good faith and charge tax only for the commercial portion of the sale [61 Pa. Code § 32.25(b)(3)].

Equipment and supplies: The purchase, use, lease, repair or maintenance of equipment and supplies (*e.g.,* propane tanks, wire, meters, panel boards, switch gear) is taxable (to both residential and commercial users) unless the purchaser is entitled to an exemption (*e.g.,* resale exemption) [61 Pa. Code § 32.25(d)].

See the regulations for examples of the application of this exemption [61 Pa. Code § 31.25].

• *Ride-sharing arrangements*

Money received by a driver as part of a ride-sharing arrangement is exempt from the sales tax [Act of December 14, 1982, No. 279, § 6].

• *School buses*

The sale at retail or use of buses to be used exclusively to transport children for school purposes is exempt [72 P.S. § 7204(43)].

Exclusive Use Interpretation

It is not clear whether the "exclusive" rule will be strictly interpreted. If school buses are occasionally used for other purposes (*e.g.,* transporting senior citizens), a strict interpretation of the law would deny this exemption for those buses. However, this may not be in the best interests of local jurisdictions; thus, this statute may be interpreted more broadly.

• *Stair lift devices*

Sales or use tax is not imposed on the sale at retail or use of tangible personal property or services used, transferred or consumed in installing or repairing equipment or devices designed to assist persons in ascending or descending a stairway. This exemption is available only if the equipment or devise is installed in the disabled person's residence and the physical disability has been certified by a physician [72 P.S. § 7204(56)].

• *Steam and other utilities*

Steam, natural, manufactured, and bottled gas, fuel oil, electricity or intrastate subscriber line charges, basic local telephone service or telegraph service are not taxable when purchased directly by the user solely for his or her own residential use [72 P.S. § 7204(5)]. See "Residential utilities," above.

¶706

• *Telephone calls*

Telephone calls paid for by inserting money into a telephone accepting direct deposits of money to operate are not taxable [72 P.S. § 7204(5)].

• *Textbooks*

The sale at retail or use of textbooks for use in schools, colleges, and universities (public or private) is exempt when purchased for or by the educational institution if the institution is recognized by the Department of Education [72 P.S. § 7204(33)]. This exemption applies to students and faculty [61 Pa. Code § 58.9].

• *Tourist promotion materials*

The sale at retail of supplies and materials is not taxable *if* made to tourist promotion agencies receiving grants from the Commonwealth *and* the materials are to be distributed to the public as promotional material. The use of the supplies and materials by tourist promotion agencies is exempt *if* the use is for promotional purposes [72 P.S. § 7204(41)].

• *Trout*

The sale or use of brook trout, brown trout, or rainbow trout is not taxable [72 P.S. § 7204(42)].

• *Tourists' out-of-state purchases*

The use of tangible personal property purchased by a nonresident person outside Pennsylvania and brought into Pennsylvania for use in Pennsylvania for a period not to exceed seven (7) days, or for any period of time when the nonresident is a tourist or vacations and, in either case, not consumed within Pennsylvania is not taxable [72 P.S. § 7204(2)].

• *UCC fees (separately stated)*

The sale at retail or use of separately stated fees for filing UCC financing statements or obtaining copies of UCC records is not taxable [72 P.S. § 7204(63)].

• *Utilities*

See "Public utilities" and "Residential utilities," above.

• *Vessels*

The following are exempt: (1) The sale at retail or use of vessels designed for commercial use of registered tonnage of 50 tons or more when produced by the builders thereof upon special order of the purchaser [72 P.S. § 7204(14)]; (2) the sale at retail or use of property or services used or consumed in building, rebuilding, repairing and making additions to or replacements in and upon vessels designed for commercial use of registered tonnage of 50 tons or more upon special order or the purchaser, or when rebuilt, repaired or enlarged, or when replacements are made upon order of or for the account of the owner [72 P.S. § 7204(15)]; or (3) the sale at retail or use of tangible personal property or services to be used or consumed for ship cleaning or maintenance or as fuel, supplies, ships' equipment, ships' stores or sea stores on vessels designed for commercial tonnage of 50 tons or more to be operated principally outside Pennsylvania limits [72 P.S. § 7204(16)].

• *Water*

The sale at retail or use of water is exempt [72 P.S. § 7204(25)].

• *Wearing apparel*

See "Clothing," above.

• *Wrapping supplies*

The sale at retail or use of wrapping paper, wrapping twine, bags, cartons, tape, rope, labels, nonreturnable containers, all other wrapping supplies, and kegs used to contain malt or brewed beverages, when the use is incidental to the delivery of any personal property, is exempt [72 P.S. § 7204(13)]. This exemption does not apply to sales of wrapping supplies in the ordinary course of business, unless the property wrapped or packaged will be resold by the purchaser of the wrapping or packing services [72 P.S. § 7204(13); 61 Pa. Code § 32.6(b)]. If a vendor charges for wrapping, the vendor is considered to have sold the wrapping supplies and must collect sales tax [61 Pa. Code § 32.6(c)].

Rented wooden pallets: The Pennsylvania Commonwealth Court has held that the wrapping supply exemption is applicable to rented wood pallets because the pallets are not containers, a receptacle, or a covering [*Procter & Gamble Paper Products Co. v. Cmwlth.*, 29 A.3d 1221 (Pa.Commw. 2011)].

• *Zero-emission vehicles*

The net purchase price of the sale at retail or use of zero-emission vehicles is exempt [72 P.S. § 7204(47)]. A "zero-emission vehicle" is one that produces no emissions of any criteria of pollutants under any operational mode and under any conditions and that meets the applicable federal motor vehicle safe standards [75 Pa.C.S. § 102]. See "Electric vehicles," above, for definition of "net purchase price."

¶707 Exempt Services

The following services are exempt by statute:

(1) Repairing, altering, mending, pressing, fitting, dyeing, laundering, dry cleaning, or cleaning of wearing apparel or shoes.

(2) Applying or installing tangible personal property as a repair or replacement part of wearing apparel or shoes.

(3) Services performed by means of self-service laundry equipment for wearing apparel or household goods.

(4) Services rendered in the construction, reconstruction, remodeling, repair, or maintenance of real estate [72 P.S. § 7201(k)(4)].

(5) Separately invoiced help desk or call center support services for canned software.

(6) Certain services exempt because of use. These services are explained at ¶706.

In addition, the regulations provide that services rendered by certain persons are exempt [61 Pa. Code § 31.6(a)]:

(1) Services rendered by the learned professions.

(2) Barber-beautician services (except those performed on wigs, falls, or other hairpieces).

(3) Funeral director services.

(4) Stenographic services.

(5) Construction or repair services to realty.

(6) Hauling and transportation services.

• *Office cleaning services, help supply services, and employment agency services*

The sale at retail or use of interior office building cleaning services, help supply services, and employment agency services are exempt but only as relates to the costs of the supplied employee. These costs are wages, salaries, bonuses and commissions, employment benefits, expense reimbursements, and payroll and withholding taxes, to the extent that these costs are specifically itemized or that these costs in aggregate are stated in bills from the vendor or supplying entity [72 P.S. §§7201(g)(6); 7204(51)].

• *Property and services used in business*

Persons who render nontaxable services are considered consumers of taxable property and services that they use in their businesses and are, therefore, taxed on the property and services. Also, if persons who render nontaxable services regularly sell, rent, or otherwise transfer or grant customers a license to use or consume taxable services, they are considered vendors with respect to the property and/or services and must register for a license and collect and remit sales tax on the property or services [61 Pa. Code §31.6(b)].

¶708 Exempt Transactions

In addition to the specifically exempt property and services, certain transactions are exempt from sales and use taxes, even if the property or service would otherwise be subject to the tax. These exempt transactions (isolated sales and sales in interstate and foreign commerce) are explained below.

• *Isolated transactions*

Sales and use taxes are not imposed on tangible personal property or services sold by or purchased from a person who is not a vendor in an isolated transaction or sold by or purchased from a person who is a vendor but is not a vendor with respect to the property or service involved in the isolated transaction [72 P.S. §7204(1)]. The following sales are considered isolated sales:

(1) Infrequent sales of a nonrecurring nature made by someone not engaged in the business of selling tangible personal property (*e.g.*, sale of a used vacuum cleaner by a household resident; isolated sales by executors, administrators, trustees, and other fiduciaries in the liquidation of an estate; sales or execution sales pursuant to court order or by a court officer) [61 Pa. Code §32.4(a)(1)].

(2) Infrequent sales of a nonrecurring nature of tangible personal property not sold in the regular course of a person's business and originally acquired for the seller's own use or consumption (*e.g.*, sale of a typewriter by an insurance company that does not regularly sell typewriters; sale of used machinery and equipment by someone in a manufacturing or retailing business if not sold in the regular course of business; sale of an entire business by the owner except that the value of any motor vehicle, trailer, semitrailer, motor boat, or similar property involved in the sale is not exempt) [61 Pa. Code §32.4(a)(2)].

The following are examples of transactions that are not isolated sales [61 Pa. Code §32.4(b)]:

(1) Sale of property held primarily for sale to customers in the ordinary course of a trade or business.

(2) Sale of stock in trade or other property of a kind that would properly be included by a manufacturer, wholesaler, retailer, jobber, or other vendor in inventory, even if infrequent and providing only an insignificant fraction of total business.

(3) Sales constituting an integral part of a business, even if the sale of the tangible personal property is not the primary business of the seller (*e.g.*, sale of repossessed property by a finance company).

(4) Sale of by-products, waste, and scrap by someone engaged in a business, even if regularly made to dispose of these items.

(5) Sale of food for on-premises consumption by a company operating an employee cafeteria.

(6) Sale of property by a charitable, volunteer firemen's or religious organization or nonprofit educational institution as a fund-raising activity if one of the following applies:

(a) the sale or series of sales is conducted more than three times a year or more than seven days during one year; and

(b) the organization makes sales of taxable property other than food or beverages sold at or from a school or church, on the same premises in competition with other vendors required to collect tax.

(7) Sale of motor vehicles, trailers, semitrailers, motor boats, aircraft, snowmobiles, or other similar tangible personal property required to be registered or licensed under federal or Pennsylvania law.

(8) Sale of any tangible personal property on the same premises in competition with vendors required to collect tax, even though the sale would otherwise qualify as an isolated sale.

(9) Certain sales by auctioneers. In most cases, sales by auctioneers are taxable transactions. Auctioneers who sell their own tangible personal property must collect and remit sales tax. If the sale at auction takes place on the auctioneers' premises, the auctioneers must collect and remit tax, even if the property belongs to another person [61 Pa. Code § 31.23(a)].

Auction Sales

When an auctioneer is involved in the sale of tangible personal property owned by other persons at a place other than on the premises of the auctioneer, the auctioneer is not responsible for collection of tax; the owner is. If the owner is regularly engaged in selling the property, the transaction is taxable.

A sale by an auctioneer is nontaxable only if the owner is not regularly engaged in selling the property and the transaction does not take place on the auctioneer's premises [61 Pa. Code § 31.23(b)]. If these two conditions are met the transaction is considered an isolated sale [61 Pa. Code § 32.4(c)].

The residency of the owner of auctioned property is irrelevant; if the property is sold in Pennsylvania (and it is an otherwise taxable transaction), it is taxable [61 Pa. Code § 31.23(c)].

• *Interstate and foreign commerce*

Federal constitutional restrictions prevent the taxation of sales in interstate and foreign commerce. See ¶ 507 for explanation of constitutional issues and Pennsylvania regulations with respect to sales in interstate commerce.

• *Convention Center exemption*

Effective September 11, 2016, the sale at retail or use of services related to the setup, teardown, or maintenance of tangible personal property rented by an authority to exhibitors at the Pennsylvania Convention Center and the David L. Lawrence Convention Center is exempt from sales and use tax.

• *Royalty payments*

Royalty payments for intellectual property are not subject to sales and use tax when the payments are made for the right to use trademarks, copyrights, and patented methods owned by third parties. The royalties are not considered payments for tangible personal property. *Downs Racing, LP v. Commonwealth of Pennsylvania __ A.3d __, (Pa. October 25, 2018)*

¶709 Resale Exemption

The law provides that the term "sale at retail" shall not include any transfer of tangible personal property or rendition of services for the purpose of resale [72 P.S. § 7201(k)(8)]. The term "resale" is defined in 72 P.S. § 7201(i) to include the following:

(1) Any transfer of ownership, custody or possession of tangible personal property for a consideration, including the grant of a license to use or consume

and transactions where the possession of the property is transferred but where the transferor retains title only as security for payment of the selling price, whether such transaction be designated as bailment lease, conditional sale or otherwise [72 P.S. § 7201(i)(1)].

Purchase for Renting or Leasing

Persons who purchase tangible personal property for the predominant purpose of renting or leasing it to others can get a resale exemption. They are also entitled to a resale exemption on purchases of repair parts or otherwise taxable services for rental property, but purchases of equipment or supplies used in conjunction with the service or care of rental property are taxable.

---

(2) The physical incorporation of tangible personal property, as an ingredient or constituent, into other tangible personal property that is to be sold in the regular course of business or the performance of those services described in subclauses (2), (3) and (4) of clause (k) of 72 P.S. § 7201 upon tangible personal property that is to be sold in the regular course of business or where the person incorporating such property has undertaken, at the time of purchase, to cause it to be transported in interstate commerce to a destination outside this Commonwealth [72 P.S. § 7201(i)(2)]. The services referred to in 72 P.S. § 7201(k)(2), (3), and (4) are printing or imprinting, washing, cleaning, waxing, polishing, lubricating, or inspecting motor vehicles, and repairing, altering, mending, pressing, fitting, dyeing, laundering, dry cleaning or cleaning of tangible personal property. These are explained at ¶ 703.

(3) Telecommunications services purchased by a cable operator or video programmer that are used to transport or deliver cable or video programming services sold in the regular course of business [72 P.S. § 7201(i)(2)].

(4) Tangible personal property purchased or having a situs within Pennsylvania solely for the purpose of being processed, fabricated or manufactured into, attached to or incorporated into tangible personal property thereafter transported outside Pennsylvania for use exclusively outside Pennsylvania [72 P.S. § 7201(i)(3)].

(5) The physical incorporation of tangible personal property as an ingredient or constituent in the construction of foundations for machinery or equipment the sale or use of which is excluded from tax under the provisions of paragraphs (A), (B), (C) and (D) of subclause (8) of clause (k) and subparagraphs (i), (ii), (iii) and (iv) of paragraph (B) of subclause (4) of clause (o) of 72 P.S. § 7201, whether such foundations at the time of construction constitute tangible personal property or real estate [72 P.S. § 7201(i)(5)].

Exclusion for Alcoholic Beverages

The term "resale" does not include any sale of "malt or brewed beverages" by a retail dispenser or any sale of liquor or malt or brewed beverages by a person holding a retail liquor license within the meaning of the Liquor Code [72 P.S. § 7201(i)(4)].

• *Disposition by means other than resale*

Someone who purchases property for resale and later disposes of it in any other manner than by resale becomes the ultimate consumer of the property and must pay use tax on it [61 Pa. Code § 32.3(b)].

• *Presumption of taxability*

Every sale of tangible personal property is presumed to be taxable; therefore, a purchaser claiming the resale exemption must prove that the specific property purchased is to be resold [61 Pa. Code § 32.3(b)].

• *Use by vendor*

A vendor who consumes or otherwise uses tangible personal property in the conduct of his/her business is the ultimate consumer or user of the property. Sales made to a vendor for this purpose are subject to sales tax [61 Pa. Code § 32.3(c)].

• *Withdrawal from inventory*

When vendors withdraw tangible personal property held for resale for their personal use, the property is no longer held for resale and becomes subject to use tax [61 Pa. Code § 32.3(d)].

Universal Resale Exemption Certificate

Pennsylvania businesses may now use, as an alternative to Pennsylvania's Form REV-1220 (Sales and Use Tax Exemption Certificate), the Multistate Tax Commission's Sales and Use Tax Exemption Certificate *for resale purposes only*. To be valid, the certificate must be fully completed with the Seller's sales tax license number. For businesses that resell in another jurisdiction and collect that state's tax, the license number will satisfy the requirement.

NOTE: The use of the MTC certificate is an option, not a requirement. Pennsylvania businesses may continue to use Form REV-1220 [*Pennsylvania Tax Update No. 88*, Pennsylvania Department of Revenue, August 2000].

¶710 Manufacturing Exemption

The law provides that the term "sale at retail" shall not include rendition of services or the transfer of tangible personal property to be used or consumed *directly* in the manufacture of tangible personal property [72 P.S. § 7201(k)(1)]. Direct use is the key to the manufacturing exemption. Direct use is explained in detail below. See ¶514 for explanation of exemption certificates.

Exemption Not Applicable to Certain Services

The manufacturing exemption does not apply to the taxable services enumerated in 72 P.S. § 7201(k)(11) through (18) and 72 P.S. § 7201(w) through (kk). These services are explained at ¶703.

• *"Manufacture" defined*

"Manufacture" means the performance of manufacturing, fabricating, compounding, processing or other operations engaged in as a business that produces any tangible personal property in a form, composition or character different from that in which it is acquired whether for sale or use by the manufacturer [72 P.S. § 7201(c)].

• *Statutory manufacturing operations*

72 P.S. § 7201(c) specifically includes the following operations in the definition of manufacturing:

(1) *Production and packaging:* Every operation, commencing with the first production stage and ending with the completion of personal property, having the physical qualities (including packaging, if any, passing to the ultimate consumer) that it has when transferred by the manufacturer to another. For this purpose, "operation" includes clean rooms and their component systems. A

"clean room" is a location with a self-contained, sealed environment with a controlled closed air system independent from the facility's general environmental control system [72 P.S. § 7201(c)(1)]. Machinery used in packaging candy bars was held to be used in manufacturing [*M&M/Mars, Inc. v. Cmwlth.*, 639 A.2d 848 (Pa.Commw. 1994), *aff'd per curiam*, 658 A.2d 797 (Pa. 1995)].

Who Is the Ultimate Consumer?

The manufacturing exemption does not apply to packaging equipment or returnable containers unless the packaging or returnable container passes to the ultimate consumer [61 Pa. Code § 32.6]. A taxpayer (AMP) argued that its "ultimate consumers" were the manufacturers and distributors to whom it shipped parts that were packaged at its distribution center. The position of the Department of Revenue is that the "ultimate consumer" is the purchaser at *retail*. The Commonwealth Court, in an unreported decision, agreed with the Department of Revenue that the ultimate consumer is the purchaser at retail, and the Pennsylvania Supreme Court has affirmed [*AMP Incorporated*, 814 A.2d 782 (*opinion not reported*), *aff'd*, 852 A.2d 1161 (Pa. 2004)].

---

(2) *Publishing and printing:* The publishing of books, newspapers, magazines and other periodicals, and printing [72 P.S. § 7201(c)(2)]. Printing is considered manufacturing when engaged in as a business [61 Pa. Code § 32.36(a)(1)]. Details regarding printing and related businesses are found in the regulations [61 Pa. Code § 32.4(c)]. See ¶ 720 for a further explanation of the printing exemptions.

(3) *Extracting:* Refining, blasting, exploring, mining and quarrying for, or otherwise extracting from the earth or from waste or stock piles or from pits or banks, any natural resources, minerals and mineral aggregates, including blast furnace slag [72 P.S. § 7201(c)(3)]. This is called the mining exemption. Details about the mining exemption can be found in the regulations [61 Pa. Code § 32.35]. The drilling of water wells is considered mining [*Cmwlth. v. Tyger & Karl Complete Water Systems Co., Inc.*, 5 Pa.Commw. 154 (1972)]. The Department has promulgated rulings governing water well drillers [61 Pa. Code §§ 43.1—43.6]. For applicability of the mining exemption to oil and gas fracturing services, see *Pennsylvania Sales and Use Tax Ruling No. SUT-10-003* (Department of Revenue, September 15, 2010). The Department recently issued Sales and Use Tax Information Notice 2014-02 (Department of Revenue, September 22, 2014). This notice further refines the Department's position on the application of the sales and use tax mining exemption to natural gas mining operations and related activities.

(4) *Commercial vessels:* Building, rebuilding, repairing and making additions to, or replacements in or upon, vessels designed for commercial use of registered tonnage of 50 tons or more, when produced upon special order of the purchaser or when rebuilt, repaired or enlarged, or when replacements are made upon order of, or for the account of, the owner [72 P.S. § 7201(c)(4)].

(5) *Research:* Research having as its objective the production of a new or an improved (1) product or utility service or (2) method of producing a product or utility service, but in either case not including market research or research having as its objective the improvement of administrative efficiency [72 P.S. § 7201(c)(5)]. The research exemption is explained in detail in Ruling 41.9 [61 Pa. Code § 41.9].

(6) *Motor vehicle remanufacturing:* Remanufacture for wholesale distribution by a remanufacturer of motor vehicles from used parts acquired in bulk and using an assembly line process that involves the complete disassembly of such parts and integration of the components with other used or new components of parts (including the salvaging, recycling or reclaiming of used parts by the remanufacturer) [72 P.S. § 7201(c)(6)]. The Commonwealth Court has held that a

company that produces diesel engines by acquiring used engine blocks, breaking them down, salvaging some of the parts, and combining them with new parts to make a usable engine is engaged in remanufacturing within the meaning of this statute [*Cmwlth. v. Mack Trucks, Inc.*, 629 A.2d 179 (Pa.Commw. 1993)].

(7) *Remanufacture or retrofit of defense-related vehicles:* The term "manufacturing" includes the remanufacture or retrofit by a manufacturer or remanufacturer of aircraft, armored vehicles, or other defense-related vehicles having a finished value of at least $50,000 [72 P.S. § 7201(c)(7)]. For this purpose aircraft means fixed-wing aircraft, helicopters, powered aircraft, tilt-rotor or tilt-wing aircraft, unmanned aircraft, and gliders. "Armored vehicles" include tanks, armed personnel carriers, and all other armed track or semi-track vehicles. "Other defense-related vehicles" means trucks, truck-tractors, trailers, jeeps, and other utility vehicles, including any unmanned vehicles.

(8) *Remanufacture of locomotive parts (by a remanufacturer):* The term "manufacture" includes the remanufacture by a remanufacturer of locomotive parts from used parts acquired in bulk by the remanufacturer using an assembly line process that involves the complete disassembly of the parts and integration of the components of the parts with other used or new components of parts, including the salvaging, recycling, or reclaiming of used parts by the remanufacturer [72 P.S. § 7201(c)(8)].

• *Manufacturing exemption court decisions*

The decisions discussed below illustrate the application of the manufacturing exemption provisions.

(1) Asphalt manufacturing

— *Union Paving Co. v. Cmwlth.*, 611 A.2d 360 (Pa.Commw. 1992). In this case the Commonwealth Court held that wheel loaders used to mix, blend, and transport the ingredients used in the manufacture of asphalt are directly used in manufacturing. Therefore, the wheel loaders, their replacement parts, and the fuel oil used to operate them are exempt from sales and use taxes under the manufacturing exemption. In *Union Paving*, the court found that the Department's contention that each stage of the manufacturing process must result in a form different from the form in which it was acquired was inconsistent with the inclusion of product packaging within the definition of manufacturing in 72 P.S. § 7201(c) because packaging does not change the form, composition or character of the product.

— *Golden Eagle:* Taxpayer is a manufacturer of asphalt for both retail sale and use in its highway construction business. At issue in this case is whether Taxpayer is liable for payment of use tax on its purchases of stone and oil for the manufacture of asphalt that it subsequently uses in its contracts with the Pennsylvania Department of Transportation. The Commonwealth Court concluded that it is liable for use tax because the manufacturing exemption does not apply to materials consumed in construction where those materials become affixed to real estate. The imposition of use tax upon construction contractors who purchase stone but not upon those who use their own stone is not a violation of the Uniformity Clause of the Pennsylvania Constitution because a sales and use tax is triggered by a purchase at retail, and there is no "purchase" when a contractor uses its own stone [*Golden Eagle Construction Co., Inc. v. Cmwlth.*, 813 A.2d 13 (Pa.Commw. 2000), *aff'd per curiam*, 834 A.2d 1103 (Pa. 2003)]. This decision has been appealed to the Pennsylvania Supreme Court.

(2) *Cellular radio telecommunications service:* The Pennsylvania Commonwealth Court has held that providers of cellular telecommunications service do not qualify for the manufacturing exemption because they do not transform

tangible personal property into something new. The Legislature and the Pennsylvania Supreme Court have confined the subject matter of the manufacturing exemption to tangible matter. The inclusion of "telecommunications service" in the definition of "tangible personal property" [72 P.S. §201(m)]merely makes telecommunications service subject to the sales and use tax; it does not extend the manufacturing exclusion to intangible property [*Bell Atlantic Mobile Systems, Inc. v. Cmwlth.*, 799 A.2d 902 (Pa.Commw. 2002), *aff'd*, 845 A.2d 762 (Pa. 2004)]. Since this decision the statutes have been amended to specifically include "mobile telecommunications service" in the definitions of "sale at retail" [72 P.S. §7201(k)(19)], "use" [72 P.S. §7201(o)(18)] and "maintaining a place of business" in Pennsylvania [72 P.S. §7201(b)(3.4)] and to remove "mobile telecommunications service" from the definition of "telecommunications service" [72 P.S. §7201(rr)]. See ¶701 for discussion of "sale at retail" and ¶721 for discussion of "telecommunications service" and "mobile telecommunications service."

(3) *Compilation and analysis of statistical data—Hospitalization Utilization Project:* The Pennsylvania Commonwealth Court has held that providing health care data processing and reporting services through compilation and analysis of statistical data is not manufacturing [*Hospital Utilization Project v. Cmwlth.*, 487 A.2d 1306 (Pa. 1985)].

(4) *Distribution center:* Taxpayer, a manufacturer, constructed a distribution center to receive production output from its facilities located in Pennsylvania and Virginia. It purchased shelves, forklifts, conveyors, and packing equipment for its distribution facility. None of the products was manufactured at the distribution facility; the products were wrapped and shipped to the distribution center and stored until used to fill customers' orders. The products were weighed and inspected on arrival at the distribution center and, in some cases, rewrapped. At no time were the products changed. The Court held that the manufacturing exemption did not apply to assets purchased for use in the distribution center because they were not directly used in manufacturing; the activities of the distribution center most closely resembled post-production activities described in 61 Pa. Code §32.32(a)(3)(iii)(1) [*AMP Inc. v. Cmwlth.*, 814 A.2d 782 (Pa.Commw. 2002), *aff'd*, 852 A.2d 1161 (Pa. 2004)]. The Court also held that the packaging was not part of the manufacturing process because the product was not transferred to the "ultimate consumer." See also discussion of "Production and packaging" under "Statutory manufacturing operations," below.

(5) *Icemaking:* Icemaking has been held not to be manufacturing [*Marweg v. Cmwlth.*, 513 A.2d 525 (Pa. Commw. 1986)].

• *Statutory exclusions from definition of "manufacturing"*

The term "manufacturing" does not include (1) altering, servicing, repairing or improving real estate, (2) repairing, servicing or installing tangible personal property, (3) cooking, freezing, or baking of fruits, vegetables, mushrooms, fish, seafood, meats, poultry or bakery products, or (4) the producing of a commercial motion picture [72 P.S. §7201(c)].

• *Photography and photofinishing*

Photographers, photofinishers, and photo-refinishers are vendors of products and services purchased by customers, even if they are produced to the special order of the customer. These products and services are taxable [61 Pa. Code §32.37(a)]. However, photography and photofinishing operations are considered manufacturing operations. Photographers and photofinishers (but not photo-refinishers) may claim the manufacturing exemption for materials, equipment, and supplies purchased and directly used in photography or photofinishing operations [61 Pa. Code §32.37(b)].

¶710

• *Materials incorporated into manufactured or processed products*

The sale of personal property that will be physically incorporated into a manufactured or processed product is a sale for resale. These materials may be purchased by the manufacturer or processor free of tax upon presentation of an exemption certificate. If a manufacturer is not licensed with the Bureau, he is required to explain on the reverse side of the certificate why a sales tax number is not required [61 Pa. Code § 32.23(b)]. Resale exemptions are explained at ¶ 709. Exemption certificates are discussed at ¶ 514.

Photographers, photofinishers, and photo-refinishers may also claim the resale exemption on purchases of tangible personal property that they directly resell or incorporate into products sold to customers [61 Pa. Code § 32.37(b)(4)]. The resale exemption is explained at ¶ 709.

Processing

Always review your options. If your business cannot be classified as a manufacturing operation, it may still qualify as a processing operation. See ¶ 711 for an explanation of processing.

• *Direct use*

The manufacturing exemption for sales and use purposes is available only if the property or services are used or consumed *directly* in manufacturing. This differs from the requirements for the manufacturing exemption for corporate tax purposes. For purposes of the capital stock-franchise tax, the manufacturing exemption is available if the property is merely "used" in manufacturing; this includes such items as working capital. For sales tax purposes, however, the property or service must be *directly* used in manufacturing; this excludes such items as working capital.

Factors: The following factors are considered in determining whether property is directly used [61 Pa. Code § 32.32(a)(1)]:

(1) The physical proximity of the property in question to the production process in which it is used.

(2) The proximity of the time of use of the property in question to the time of use of other property used before and after it in the production process.

(3) The active causal relationship between the use of the property in question and the production of a product. The fact that particular property may be considered essential to the manufacturing process because its use is required by law or practical necessity does not, of itself, mean that the property is directly used in manufacturing.

In *Oberg Manufacturing Co., Inc. v. Cmwlth.*, 486 A.2d 1047 (Pa.Commw. 1985), the Pennsylvania Commonwealth Court ruled that engineering supplies used to prepare design drawings, prints, tapes, and charts were not excludable from sales and use tax provisions because they were not used directly in manufacturing. They were used in a preliminary stage *prior to* the commencement of the first production stage. In addition, the court held that the property was not *predominantly* used in even these pre-production activities because the supplies were not used more than 50% for these purposes. Likewise, in *W.M. Dambach, Inc. v. Cmwlth.*, 488 A.2d 96 (Pa.Commw. 1985), the Commonwealth Court held that a computer used in the preparation of production schedules was used in pre-production activities and therefore was not an integral part of the production process. The computer was held to be subject to use tax.

¶710

The purchase or use of certain property predominantly (but not entirely) directly used in manufacturing is exempt. "Predominantly" in this context means over 50% of the time [61 Pa. Code § 32.32(a)(2)]. This includes the following:

(1) *Machinery and equipment:* Machinery, equipment, parts, and their foundations therefor, and supplies used in actual production or to transport, convey, handle, or store products from the first production operation to the time the product is packaged for the ultimate consumer. This also includes repair parts that are installed and become an integral part of the property.

(2) *Pollution control devices:* Equipment, machinery, and supplies designed and used to control, abate, or prevent air, water, or noise pollution generated in manufacturing or processing. It is not necessary that pollutants be recycled or used in any way. This exemption is available in certain cases, even if the taxpayer is not engaged in manufacturing or processing. For example, the Commonwealth Court has allowed exemption under this provision for a waste disposal business (landfill operator) for the equipment used to dispose of hazardous industrial wastes generated by clients [*Kelly Run Sanitation, Inc. v. Cmwlth.*, 587 A.2d 58 (Pa.Commw. 1985), *aff'd per curiam*, 514 A.2d 1370 (Pa.1986)].

(3) *Testing and inspection:* Property used to test and inspect products throughout the production cycle. Testing and inspecting during production is manufacturing, even if it is carried out by someone other than the manufacturer [*Lancaster Laboratories, Inc. v. Cmwlth.*, 631 A.2d 739 (Pa.Commw. 1993)].

(4) *Cleaning of returnable containers:* Property used to clean or inspect returnable containers before refilling (if they are to be delivered to the ultimate consumer).

(5) *Packaging:* Packaging equipment used to package products for the ultimate consumer.

(6) *Research:* Property directly used in research activities. This does not include market research. See definition of "research," above.

(7) *Timberling Exclusion:* Effective July 1, 2017, property and services directly and predominately used in timbering operations are exempt from sales and use tax when purchased by a company primarily engaged in the business of harvesting trees. Timberling does not include the harvesting of trees for clearing land for access roads.

The following property is not considered to be directly used in manufacturing or processing [61 Pa. Code § 32.32(a)(3)]:

(1) Real estate.

(2) Maintenance facilities.

(3) Managerial, sales, or other nonoperational activities. See 61 Pa. Code § 32.23(a)(3)(iii) for details.

Direct Causal Relationship Exception

If you can establish a direct causal relationship to your manufacturing or processing operation, utilities qualify for the manufacturing exemption. For example, if you have lamps attached or built into production machines for illumination while the machine is being used, the cost of the electricity to operate the light (as well as the cost of the electricity to operate the machine) is directly used in manufacturing.

¶710

Consult Rulings

The Department of Revenue issues a list of activities and products classified as manufacturing or processing and rulings with respect to specific activities and products. You should consult the rulings carefully to see if any of them apply to your activity or product.

¶711 Processing Exemption

The law provides that the term "sale at retail" shall not include rendition of services or transfer of tangible personal property to be *directly* used or consumed by the purchaser in the operation of processing of personal property [72 P.S. §7201(k)(d)]. "Direct use" is explained at ¶710. Exemption certificates are explained at ¶514. The processing exemption does not apply to the taxable services enumerated in 72 P.S. §7201(k)(11)—(18) and 72 P.S. §7201(w)—(kk), except that the exclusion for farming, dairying and agriculture applies to disinfecting and pest control services. See ¶703 for explanation of these services.

"Processing" is specifically defined by statute to include only the following activities when engaged in as a business enterprise [72 P.S. §7201(d)]:

(1) *Animal or poultry feed:* The preparation of animal feed or poultry feed for sale [72 P.S. §7201(d)(6)].

(2) *Baking:* The cooking or baking of bread, pastries, cakes, cookies, muffins and donuts sold at locations that do not sell ready-to-eat food and beverages. For purposes of this clause, a bakery, a pastry shop and a donut shop shall not be considered an establishment from which ready-to-eat food and beverages are sold [72 P.S. §7201(d)(13)]. Note the absence of pizza and pizzerias, often the subject of court decisions and prior statutory amendments.

(3) *Beverages, nonalcoholic:* The production, processing and bottling of nonalcoholic beverages for wholesale distribution [72 P.S. §7201(d)(7)].

(4) *Broadcasting:* The broadcasting of radio and television programs of licensed commercial or educational stations [72 P.S. §7201(d)(12)]. This includes cable television systems engaged in broadcasting [*Suburban Cable TV Co., Inc. v. Cmwlth.*, 570 A.2d 601 (Pa.Commw. 1990)].

(5) *Coffee:* The cleaning and roasting and the blending, grinding or packaging for sale of coffee from green coffee beans or the production of coffee extract [72 P.S. §7201(d)(14)].

(6) *Eggs:* The collecting, washing, sorting, inspecting, and hatching of eggs [72 P.S. §7201(d)(18)]. Tangible personal property used directly and predominantly in the processing of eggs is exempt from the sales and use tax.

(7) *Fertilizer:* The preparation of dry or liquid fertilizer for sale [72 P.S. §7201(d)(15)].

(8) *Fibers, yarns, and fabrics:* The scouring, carbonizing, cording, combing, throwing, twisting or winding of natural or synthetic fibers, or the spinning, bleaching, dyeing, printing or finishing of yarns or fabrics before sale to the ultimate consumer [72 P.S. §7201(d)(2)].

(9) *Flour or meal:* The milling for sale of flour or meal from grains [72 P.S. §7201(d)(9)].

(10) *Fruit or vegetables:* The processing of fruits or vegetables by cleaning, cutting, coring, peeling, baking or chopping and treating in order to preserve, sterilize or purify and substantially extend the useful shelf life of the fruits or vegetables, when the person engaged in such activity packages such property in sealed containers for *wholesale distribution* [72 P.S. §7201(d)(1.1)].

(11) *Honey, fruits, vegetables, mushrooms, fish, seafood, meats, or poultry:* The filtering or heating of honey, the cooking, baking or freezing of fruits, vegetables, mushrooms, fish, seafood, meats, poultry or bakery products, when packaged in sealed containers for wholesale distribution [72 P.S. § 7201(d)(1)].

(12) *Ice:* The production, processing, and packaging of ice for wholesale distributions [72 P.S. § 7201(d)(16)].

(13) *Lubricating oils, used:* The processing of used lubricating oils [72 P.S. § 7201(d)(11)].

(14) *Meat:* The slaughtering and dressing of animals for meat to be sold, or to be used in preparing meat products for sale, and the preparation of meat products including lard, tallow, grease, cooking and inedible oils for wholesale distribution [72 P.S. § 7201(d)(10)].

(15) *Metal, ornamental or structural:* The fabrication for sale of ornamental or structural metal, or of metal stairs, staircases, gratings, fire escapes or railings (not including fabrication work done at the construction site) [72 P.S. § 7201(d)(5)].

(16) *Metals:* The blanking, shearing, leveling, slitting or burning of metals for sale to or use by a manufacturer or processor [72 P.S. § 7201(d)(3.1)].

(17) *Metals and plastics:* The electroplating, galvanizing, enameling, anodizing, coloring, finishing, impregnating or heat treating of metals or plastics for sale, or in the process of manufacturing [72 P.S. § 7201(d)(3)].

(18) *Metals, ferrous and nonferrous:* The rolling, drawing or extruding of ferrous and nonferrous metals [72 P.S. § 7201(d)(4)].

(19) *Mobile telecommunications services:* The producing of mobile telecommunications services [72 P.S. § 7201(d)(17), effective for sales at retail and uses after June 30, 2004].

(20) *Saw mill or planing mill:* The operation of a saw mill or planing mill for the production of lumber or lumber products for sale. Saw mill or planing mill operation begins with the unloading, by the operator, of logs, timber, pulpwood, or other forms of wood material that are to be used in the mill operation [72 P.S. § 7201(d)(8)].

(21) *Tobacco:* The aging, stripping, conditioning, crushing or blending of tobacco leaves for use as cigar filler or as components of smokeless tobacco products for sale to manufacturers of tobacco products [72 P.S. § 7201(d)(9.1)].

Consult Rulings

The Department of Revenue issues a list of activities and products classified as manufacturing or processing and rulings with respect to specific activities and products. You should consult the rulings carefully to see if any of them apply to your activity or product.

¶712 Farming Exemption

The law provides that the term "sale at retail" shall not include the rendition of services or transfer of tangible personal property to be *directly* used or consumed by the purchaser in farming, dairying, agriculture, horticulture or floriculture when engaged in as a business enterprise. The term "farming" includes the propagation and raising of ranch-raised, fur-bearing animals, the propagation of game birds for commercial purposes by holders of propagation permits issued under "The Game Law," propagation of fish and other aquatic animals for commercial use as a food or food product by holders of propagation permits issued under 34 Pa.C.S. (relating to game), and the propagation and raising of horses to be used exclusively for commercial racing purposes [72 P.S. § 7201(k)(8)(B); 61 Pa. Code § 32.1]. Exemption certificates are explained at ¶ 514.

Contract Farming

The sale at retail or use of tangible personal property or services that are directly used in farming, dairying, or agriculture when engaged in as a business enterprise is not taxable whether or not the sale is made to the person directly engaged in the business enterprise or to a person contracting with the person directly engaged in the business enterprise for the production of food [72 P.S. § 7204(62)].

• *Direct use*

In determining whether property is directly used, consideration is given to the following factors [61 Pa. Code § 32.33(a)(1)]:

(1) The physical proximity of the property in question to the production process in which it is used;

(2) The proximity of the time and use of the property in question to the time of use of other property used before and after it in the production process; and

(3) The active causal relationship between the use of the property in question and the production of a farm product. The fact that particular property may be considered essential to the conduct of the business of farming because its use is required either by law or practical necessity does not, of itself, mean that the property is used directly in farming operations.

• *Predominant use*

If a single unit of property is put to use by a farmer in two different activities, one of which is a direct use and the other of which is not, the property is not exempt from tax unless the farmer makes use of the property more than 50% of the time directly in farming operations [61 Pa. Code § 32.33(2)].

• *Property not directly used*

Property in the following categories is not considered directly used and is subject to sales and use taxes [61 Pa. Code § 32.33(a)(3)]:

(1) *Real estate:* The term "farming" does not include the construction, reconstruction, alterations, remodeling, servicing, repairing, maintenance or improvement of real estate. The purchase or use of tangible personal property by a farmer for such purpose is subject to tax, even though the structure may house or otherwise contain equipment or other facilities used directly in farming. Constructing, remodeling, repairing or maintaining buildings (including houses, garages, barns, stables, greenhouses, mushroom houses and storehouses), fences and stanchions permanently affixed to real estate, dams, roads, spillways and other improvements to real estate is not a farming operation, and property used in the work shall be taxable. Activities such as land reclamation, forestry, land clearing, landscaping and similar activities, which are intended to improve or preserve real estate, are not farming operations.

(2) *Maintenance facilities:* Maintenance, service and repair work is not a farming operation. Maintenance facilities, including tools, equipment and supplies predominantly used in performing the work (*e.g.,* chain hoists, tire spreaders, welding equipment, drills, sanders, wrenches, paint brushes and sprayers, oilers, absorbent compounds, dusting compounds, air blowers and wipers) are subject to tax. However, replacement parts that are used to replace worn parts upon exempt machinery and equipment (*e.g.,* motors, belts, screws, bolts, cutting edges, air filters or gears) and operating supplies that are actively and continuously used in the operation of exempt machinery and equipment (*e.g.,* fuel, lubricants, paint and compressed air)

are exempt from tax. Equipment and supplies, including soaps and cleaning compounds, brushes, brooms, mops and similar items, used in general cleaning and maintenance of farm property shall be subject to tax.

(3) *Managerial, sales or other nonoperational activities:* Property used in managerial, sales or other nonoperational activities is not directly used in farming and, therefore, is subject to tax. This category includes, but is not limited to, property used in any of the following activities:

(a) *Farming management and administration.* Office furniture, supplies and equipment, textbooks and other educational materials, books and records, and other property used in farming, recordkeeping, and other administrative and managerial work, are subject to tax. The property includes, but is not limited to, supplies used to record the quality and quantity of work in production or goods in storage, the flow of work, the results of inspection or the instruction of workers in routing work or other production activities.

(b) *Selling and marketing:* Property used in advertising farm products for sale, or in marketing, transporting the products to a market or to customers, or selling the products, is not within the scope of the farming exemption.

(c) *Exhibition of farm products:* Property used in the exhibition of farm products or of farming operations is subject to tax (*e.g.,* blankets, halters, prods, leads, harnesses, dressing, ribbons, clippers and similar show grooming and display equipment).

(d) *Safety and fire prevention:* Property used to prevent or fight fires and equipment and supplies used for programs as safety, accident prevention, or fire prevention is subject to tax, even though such equipment or property is required by law, except for drugs, medicines, and medical supplies exempt under 72 P.S. § 7204(17).

(e) *Employee or personal use:* Property used for the personal comfort, convenience, or use of the farmer, the farmer's family, the farmer's employees or persons associated with him or her is subject to tax (*e.g.,* beds, mattresses, blankets, tableware, stoves, refrigerators and other equipment used in conjunction with the operation of a migrant labor camp or facilities for farm employees). However, protective equipment (*e.g.,* face masks, helmets, gloves, coveralls, goggles) worn by farming personnel is exempt from tax.

(f) *Space heating, cooling, ventilation and illumination:* Property, including machinery, equipment, fuel or power used to ventilate buildings, lighting for general illumination or air conditioning and refrigeration, space heating and similar property, is subject to tax, unless its use is required in order to preserve the health of productive animals or to prevent spoilage of farm products, prior to package passing to the ultimate consumer.

(g) *Prefarming activities:* Property used to transport personnel or to collect, convey, or transport property, and storage facilities or devices used to store property prior to its use in the actual farming operation, is subject to tax.

(h) *Property used during farming operations:* Property used in managerial, sales, or other nonfarming activities is subject to tax even though it is used during farming operations. Examples of such property are safety, heating and ventilation equipment, planking or grating for crosswalks or platforms, and maintenance equipment or facilities.

(i) *Postfarming activities:* Property used to transport or convey the farm product after the final farming operation that includes but does not extend beyond the operation of packaging for the ultimate consumer, and storage and refrigeration facilities or devices used to store the product, are not used directly in farming and are taxable (*e.g.,* equipment that loads packaged products into cases or cartons for ease of handling in delivery). Machinery, equipment, supplies and other property used to convey, transport, handle or store the packaged product is also taxable.

(j) *Additional processing of farm products:* Property used in making butter, sausage, pasteurized milk, canned goods, jellies, flour, juices, cheeses, ice cream, and other items that are not "farm products" is not exempt from tax under the farming exemption. "Farm products" for this purpose are the final natural products of farming operations while they are on the farm premises and in an unprocessed state [61 Pa. Code § 32.1]. Products like butter, sausage, pasteurized milk, flour, canned goods, jellies, and juices are not "farm products." They may, however, be "manufactured products" [61 Pa. Code § 32.1].

• *Exemption certificates*

A farmer who purchases exempt property under the farming exemption is required to present a properly executed exemption certificate to the vendor [61 Pa. Code § 32.33(b)].

¶713 Public Utility Exemption

General rule: The law provides that the term "sale at retail" shall not include the rendition of services or the transfer of tangible personal property (including, but not limited to, machinery and equipment and parts therefore) and supplies to be used or consumed by the purchaser *directly* in the producing, delivering, or rendering of a public utility service or in constructing, reconstructing, remodeling, repairing or maintaining facilities that are *directly used* in producing, delivering, or rendering a public utility service.

Exceptions: This exemption does not apply to the following: (1) construction materials, supplies or equipment used to construct, reconstruct, remodel, repair or maintain facilities not used directly in the production, delivering, or rendering of public utility service; (2) construction materials, supplies, or equipment used to construct, reconstruct, remodel, repair or maintain a building, road or similar structure; or (3) tools and equipment used but not installed in the maintenance of facilities used directly in the production, delivering or rendition of a public utility service [72 P.S. § 7201(k)(8)(C)].

Exemption Not Applicable to Certain Services

The public utility exemption does not apply to the taxable services added by 72 P.S. § 9101 *et seq.* (those enumerated in 72 P.S. § 7201(k)(11)—(18) and 72 P.S. § 7201(w)—(kk)). These services are explained at ¶703.

• *Public utility*

A person engaged in the performance of public utility service (see below) [61 Pa. Code § 32.1].

Utility Must Be User

Purchase of machinery, tools, and supplies used by a contractor in the construction of water mains, sewers, and manholes for public utilities (but not transferred to the public utility) was not exempt under the public utility exemption because the items were not used by the public utility itself and were not affixed to the real estate [*Glenn Johnston, Inc. v. Cmwlth*, 726 A.2d 384 (Pa.Commw. 1998), *aff'd*, Pa. Sup. Ct., Nos. 108 & 109 MD 1998 (March 26, 1999)].

• *Public utility service*

The performance of services for compensation for the general public, without discrimination, which is subject to regulation by a governmental agency rather than determined by contract with the person for whom the services are performed; provided that the services so performed shall be effected with a public interest [61 Pa. Code § 32.1].

• *Direct use*

The following criteria are used to determine whether a particular structure or article is used directly in producing, delivering or rendering a public utility service:

(1) The physical proximity of the items while in use and the proximity of time of their use to the production, rendition and delivery of the utility service [61 Pa. Code § 32.34(a)(1)(i)].

(2) The causal relationship between the use of the item and the production, delivery and rendition of the utility service [61 Pa. Code § 32.34(a)(1)(ii)].

(3) The character of the item (*i.e.,* whether it is in the nature of a general improvement to the premises that would serve various users or is particularly designed or constructed for public utility use). The fact that particular property may be considered essential to the rendering of a public utility service because its use is required either by law or practical necessity does not, of itself, mean that the property is used directly by a public utility [61 Pa. Code § 32.34(a)(1)(iii)].

• *Predominant use*

If tangible personal property or services are used for both taxable and nontaxable purposes, it is presumed that the tangible personal property or services are used for taxable purposes unless the user proves to the Department of Revenue that the *predominant purposes* for which the property or services are used do not constitute a "sale at retail" [72 P.S. § 7201(k)(9)]. When a unit of property is put to use in two different activities, one of which is a direct use and the other of which is not, the property is not exempt unless the public utility makes use of the property more than 50% of the time directly in public utility operations [61 Pa. Code § 32.34(a)(2)].

The purchase or use by a public utility of property in the following categories, when predominantly used directly in rendering a public utility service, are exempt from tax:

(1) *General:* Machinery, equipment, parts and foundations therefor, and supplies which are used in the actual producing, delivering, or rendering of a public utility service shall be considered to be directly used in public utility operations. Repair parts which are installed and become an integral part of the property are also exempt from tax [61 Pa. Code § 32.34(a)(2)(i)].

(2) *Pollution control devices:* Equipment, machinery and supplies designed and used to control, abate, or prevent air, water or noise pollution generated in the rendering of the public utility services are deemed to be directly used in the rendition of a public utility service and, therefore, are not subject to tax. In order for property to qualify as exempt pollution control devices, it shall not be necessary that the pollutants be recycled or used in any manner [61 Pa. Code § 34.32(a)(2)(ii)].

(3) *Realty construction—materials, tools and equipment:* Construction materials, tools, and equipment used to construct, reconstruct, remodel, repair or maintain facilities that are used directly in the production, delivery, or rendition of a public utility service are deemed to be directly used and therefore are exempt from tax. However, tools and equipment used to maintain the facilities are exempt only if installed as a part of the facility [61 Pa. Code § 34.32(a)(2)(iii)].

(4) *Research:* Property that is used directly in research activities by a public utility shall be exempt from tax, provided that the object of the research is the production of a new or improved product or utility service or method of producing a product or utility service. The exemption does not apply to property used in market research or in other research that is conducted with the objective of improving administrative efficiency [61 Pa. Code § 32.34(a)(2)(iv)].

Predominant Use vs. Exclusive Use

The Pennsylvania Supreme Court has ruled that the public utility exemption is available when property or services are "predominantly used" by a public utility, overruling its previous ruling that the property or service must be "exclusively used" by a public utility to qualify for the exemption [*City of Philadelphia v. Cmwlth.,* 803 A.2d 1262 (Pa. 2002)].

Philadelphia city contractors used materials to construct a baggage claim facility, a taxiway, and a tunnel at Pennsylvania's airport, Philadelphia International, which is not a public utility. Because these facilities were not constructed for the exclusive use of the airport's common carriers, the Pennsylvania Commonwealth Court, in an unreported decision, held that the city was not entitled to a public utility exemption [*City of Philadelphia v. Cmwlth.,* Nos. 636, 809, & 958, F.R. 1998 (April 30, 2001), *Opinion Not Reported*]. The Commonwealth Court, in ruling that exclusive use was required, relied on the Pennsylvania Supreme Court's decision in *Cmwlth. v. Public Constructors, Inc.,* 248 A.2d 29 (Pa. 1968).

On appeal, however, the Pennsylvania Supreme Court overruled the Commonwealth Court and its own decision in *Public Constructors.* "The statutes are clear. If a sale or use is for the predominant purpose of public utility service, it is not taxable. There is no requirement in the statutes that the sale or use must be exclusively for the purpose of public utility service." [*City of Philadelphia. v. Cmwlth.,* 803 A.2d 1262 (Pa. 2002)].

Therefore, the public utility exemption applied to these contractors' materials because the airport facilities are "predominantly used" by public utilities (passenger and cargo airlines).

- *Property not directly used*

Property in the following categories is not directly used in public utility operations, and the purchase or use of such property is taxable [61 Pa. Code § 32.34(a)(3)]:

(1) *Real estate:* Construction materials, tools, and equipment used to construct, reconstruct, remodel, repair, or maintain facilities not used directly in the production, delivery or rendition of a public utility service are subject to tax. The purchase or use of property for use in construction, reconstructing, remodeling, repairing, or maintaining a building, road, or similar facility, regardless of its purpose, is subject to tax. The term "building" does not include machinery and equipment and parts for machinery and equipment, whether the property is designated as real estate or not. Structures such as railroad watchmen's shacks, bus terminals, warehouses, and toolsheds are considered buildings. However, the machinery and equipment used as signal towers, water and fuel tanks, and railroad tracks are not considered buildings [61 Pa. Code § 32.34(a)(3)(i)].

(2) *Maintenance—tools and equipment:* Tools and equipment used but not installed in the maintenance of facilities directly used in the production, delivery, or rendition of a public utility service are subject to tax. Tools and equipment used in the maintenance of nonexempt facilities are subject to tax whether or not they are installed so as to become a component of the nonexempt facilities [61 Pa. Code § 32.34(a)(3)(ii)].

(3) *Managerial, sales, or other nonoperational activities:* Property used in managerial, sales, or other nonoperational activities is not directly used in the production, delivery, or rendition of a public utility service and is therefore taxable [61 Pa. Code § 32.34(a)(3)(iii)]. This category includes, but is not limited to, property used in any of the following activities:

¶713

(a) *Management and administration:* Office furniture, supplies and equipment, textbooks and other educational materials, books and records, and other property used by a public utility in recordkeeping and other administrative and managerial work are subject to tax. The class of property includes, but is not limited to, supplies used to record the quality and quantity of work in production or goods in storage, the flow of work, the results of inspection or the instruction of workers in routing work or other production activities.

(b) *Selling and marketing:* Property used in advertising, marketing, or selling public utility services or products is not within the scope of the public utility exemption.

(c) *Public utility exhibitions:* Property used in the exhibition of public utility products or services is subject to tax.

(d) *Safety and fire prevention:* Property used to prevent or fight fires and equipment and supplies used for programs of safety, accident prevention or fire prevention are subject to tax, even though the equipment or property is required by law, except for drugs, medicines and medical supplies exempt under 72 P.S. § 7204(17).

(e) *Employee use:* Property used for the personal comfort, convenience, or use of employees, is subject to tax. Protective equipment worn by production personnel (*e.g.,* face masks, helmets, gloves, coveralls, goggles) is exempt from tax.

(f) *Space heating, cooling, ventilation and illumination:* Property, including machinery and equipment, fuel or power used to ventilate buildings, lighting for general illumination, air conditioning and other space cooling, space heating and similar property, is subject to tax unless it is established that the use of the property bears an active causal relationship to the production, delivery or rendition of a public utility service.

(g) *Activities prior to production, delivery or rendition of services:* Property used to transport personnel or to collect, convey, or transport other property, and storage facilities or devices used to store or hold property prior to its use in the production, delivery or rendition of a public utility service that is delivered as a public utility service is directly used and therefore is subject to tax.

(h) *Property used during production, delivery or rendition of services:* Property used in managerial, sales, or other nonoperational activities is subject to tax even though it is used during the production operation. Examples of this class of property are safety, heating and ventilation equipment, and planking or grating for crosswalks or platforms.

(i) *Activities subsequent to production, delivery or rendition of services:* Property used to transport or convey personnel or property following the production, delivery, or rendition of a public utility service, and storage facilities or devices used for that purpose, are not used directly by a public utility and are subject to tax.

(j) *Waste disposal:* Property used in waste handling and disposal of pollutants is not deemed to be directly used and is subject to tax unless the property qualifies for exemption under 61 PA Code § 32.34(a)(2)(ii). For purposes of this subsection, ash handling equipment used by a public utility electrical generation station is not considered as property used in waste disposal.

¶713

• *Exemption certificates*

A public utility purchasing property under this exemption must deliver to the vendor a properly executed exemption certificate. Exemption certificates are explained at ¶514.

Details on Public Utility Exemption

The Department of Revenue has issued detailed regulations [61 Pa. Code §32.34] and several rulings interpreting the public utility exemption [61 Pa. Code §§45.1—45.3].

The public utility exemption has been held to apply to facilities directly used in rendering public utility service, whether or not they are real estate [*Cmwlth. v. Equitable Gas Co.*, 483 A.2d 1021 (Pa.Commw. 1984); *aff'd per curiam* 512 A.2d 337 (Pa. 1986)]. This exemption has also been held to be available to contractors that install utilities for municipalities and municipal authorities (*e.g.*, sanitary sewer systems, storm sewer systems, water systems). This exemption is available for materials used in burying pipelines and restoring ground surfaces (but not tools, equipment, and supplies used but not installed in the construction of public utility facilities) [*Ernest Renda Contracting v. Cmwlth.*, 532 A.2d 416 (Pa. 1987); *rev'g* 504 A.2d 1349 (Pa.Commw. 1986)]. A taxpayer who installed sewage connection lines for a sanitary sewer system and a water system for a public golf course operated by a municipal authority was denied a public utility exemption because the public golf course was not a public facility [*Vincent Construction, Inc. v. Cmwlth.*, 668 A.2d 289 (Pa.Commw. 1995)].

Keep Adequate Records

It is important to maintain all records required by law in order to protect your right to take an exemption. A taxpayer who did not keep adequate records to show its entitlement to the public utility exemption was denied the exemption by the Commonwealth Court [*Fiore, t/a Fiore Trucking and Contracting v. Cmwlth.*, 668 A.2d 1210 (Pa.Commw. 1995)].

SALES TAX SPECIAL SITUATIONS

¶714 Advertising

• *Advertising agencies*

Materials used or consumed by advertising agencies in rendering professional services (*i.e.*, marketing and public relations counseling, copywriting, art or creative direction, placement and supervision of media and graphic arts purchases on behalf of specific clients) are taxable [61 Pa. Code §31.21(a)(2)]. Any claim for exemption for tangible personal property purchased on behalf of specific clients must originate with the client. If a client furnishes the agency with written evidence of the basis on which exemption is claimed, the agency may inform suppliers on the client's behalf and provide them with duly executed exemption certificates [61 Pa. Code §31.32(a)(2)].

• *Materials purchased for resale*

Materials purchased for resale are exempt. For example, if an advertising agency prepares and sells items (*e.g.*, signs, mats to be delivered to the client) to a client, it must collect tax on the purchase price but is entitled to claim a resale exemption on materials that become part of the items [61 Pa. Code §31.21(a)(3)]. Sale of direct mail advertising materials is exempt, but property used or consumed in producing them is taxable unless it qualifies for the printing or resale exemption [61 Pa. Code §31.21(b)(3)].

• *Charges for professional services*

Charges for professional services (*e.g.,* consultant fees, market research fees) are exempt. See ¶ 707 for an explanation of exempt services. However, if an agency sells tangible personal property (*e.g.,* circulars, posters) to a client along with professional services, the entire charge is taxable *unless* the professional services are separately stated. If no tangible personal property is transferred to the purchaser (other than samples for approval), charges for preparing and placing advertising with the media are exempt [61 Pa. Code § 31.21(b)(1)]. "Professional services" do not include labor performed in the preparation of tangible personal property sold at retail (*e.g.,* fees paid to a commercial artist) [61 Pa. Code § 31.21(b)(2)].

• *Printing exemption*

The major issue within the context of advertising agencies is the application of the printing exemption. Printing engaged in as a business is considered manufacturing. The Department of Revenue maintains that advertising agencies are not eligible for the printing exemption unless they are actually engaged in the business of printing [61 Pa. Code § 31.21(a)(4)]. The problem lies in how to determine what constitutes "engaging in the business of printing." In *Westinghouse Electric Corp. v. Board of Finance and Revenue,* 417 A.2d 800 (Pa.Commw. 1980), the Commonwealth Court held that an in-house printing operation that produced sales and publicity materials for the taxpayer was eligible for the printing exemption; the regulations have been amended accordingly [61 Pa. Code § 32.36].

¶715 Computers

Computer hardware and canned software, as well as services thereto, are subject to the sales and use tax. See 61 Pa. Code § 60.19 for details of the taxation of computer hardware and software. Custom software is not subject to tax. "Computer hardware" means assembly of physical equipment that is united and regulated by interaction or interdependence to accomplish a set of specific computer system functions. Examples of computer hardware are personal computers, external hard drives, portable disk drives, scanners, monitors, keyboard, mouses, and microphones. For more examples, see 61 Pa. Code § 60.19(b)]. "Canned software" is computer software that does not qualify as custom software (discussed below). Canned software includes updates, enhancements, and upgrades, as well as customer software that is transferred pursuant to a sale at retail to a person other than the original purchaser. Adaptation or modification of canned software to meet the specific needs of a particular customer does not convert the canned software to custom software. Charges for custom software or modifications must be reasonable and separately stated to be exempt from tax. For more details on taxation of canned software, see 61 Pa. Code § 60.19(c)(2).

Canned Software Delivered Electronically

A three-judge panel of the Commonwealth Court held that the sale of all canned software, whether transmitted electronically or on a physical medium, is taxable as the sale of tangible personal property. The court adopted the "essence of the transaction test", and determined that canned software was tangible personal property, regardless of the method of delivery, because it took up space on a hard drive and could be physically perceived by checking the computer's files [*Graham Packaging Co. v. Commonwealth of Pennsylvania,* Pa.Commw., No. 652 F.R. 2002, 882 A.2d 1076 (2005)]. As a result of this decision, effective for invoices dated on or after November 1, 2005, canned software is subject to tax regardless of the method of delivery [Sales and Use Tax Bulletin 2005-04]. This issue is being relitigated in *Dechert LLP v. Commonwealth of Pennsylvania,* 942 A.2d 210 (2008).

Exemptions for certain entities: The sale or use of canned software and computer hardware is exempt if it is purchased by qualified charitable organizations, volunteer fire companies, religious organizations, and nonprofit educational institutions, unless the software is used in an unrelated trade or business; by the Federal government; or by the Commonwealth of Pennsylvania, its instrumentalities, or political subdivisions (including public school districts) [61 Pa. Code § 60.19(d)(1)].

Manufacturing and other exemptions: The manufacturing, research, mining, processing, public utility, farming, dairying, agriculture, horticulture, or floriculture exemptions from tax apply to the purchase of canned computer software and computer hardware predominantly and directly used in these operations [61 Pa. Code § 60.19(d)(2)].

Canned software manufacturers: The manufacturing and research exemption applies to a person engaged in the business of manufacturing or researching canned software if the property is predominately and directly used by the purchaser in the manufacture or research of canned software. The creation of custom software does not qualify as manufacturing or research; when a purchaser uses the property to both manufacture canned software and create custom software, the purchaser has the burden of establishing that the tangible personal property is predominately used in the manufacturing or research of canned software [61 Pa. Code § 60.19(d)(3)].

Resale exemption: The sale of canned software and computer hardware to a vendor who will resell it in the ordinary course of business is exempt from tax as a sale for resale. If a vendor uses canned software or computer hardware to produce a separate computer product for resale, the hardware or canned software does not qualify as a sale for resale. Use of canned software or computer hardware to provide a service does not qualify as a resale [61 Pa. Code § 60.19(d)(4)].

- *Custom software*

The sale at retail or use of custom software is considered a purchase of a nontaxable computer programming service [61 Pa. Code § 60.19(b)(2)(i)]. "Custom software" is computer software designed, created, and developed for and to the specifications of an original purchaser [61 Pa. Code § 60.19(b)]. Adaptations and modifications of canned software are not considered custom software. The following items are not taxable:

(1) The sale at retail or use of multiple copies or licenses of custom software to the original purchaser.

(2) The sale at retail or use of:

(a) Custom software installation.

(b) Custom software repair and maintenance.

(c) Custom software updates, enhancements, and upgrades that constitute custom software.

- *Situs —Cloud computing*

On May 31, 2012 the Department of Revenue released a redacted version of private letter ruling SUT-12-001. The ruling established a new policy for taxing canned software. Canned software will be taxed based on the location of the users rather than the location of the software. Thus, canned software loaded onto a server located in Pennsylvania will only be taxed to the extent that the users are located in Pennsylvania. Likewise, canned software located outside Pennsylvania will be taxed to the extent that users are located within Pennsylvania.

¶715

Query

This is a reversal of the previous policy to tax canned software base on the location of the server. Since there has been no underlying change in law, will this policy be applied retroactively?

• *Electronically or digitally delivered items (often called digital downloads)*

The sales and use tax specifically extends to items delivered to a customer electronically or digitally or by streaming unless the transfer is otherwise exempt. This includes music or any other audio, video such as movies and streaming services, e-books and any otherwise taxable printed matter, apps and in-app purchases, ringtones, online games, and canned software, as well as any updates and maintenance of these items. Canned software support services are also taxable, except for separately invoiced help desk or call center support.

• *Zappers and sales suppression devices and software*

Effective immediately, the possession, sale or distribution of zappers or sales suppression software with the intent to evade taxes is deemed an offense and individuals could be fined up to $10,000 and one year in prison.

• *Taxation—Sales, use, service, and gross receipts—transactions taxable in general—transactions taxable in general—information technology*

Service sold to internet service provider (ISP), providing infrastructure, including local dial network and modems to ISPs desiring to outsource the remote access to their network or the internet, constituted "internet access," an enhanced telecommunications service, and not a basic "telecommunications service," and was, therefore, exempt from sales and use tax under Pennsylvania Tax Code, where the service provided a Point of Presence (PoP) for the ISP's end-users' connection to the internet.

¶716 Contractors and Building Trades (Pre-July 1, 1998, Contracts)

• *General rules*

Generally, construction contractors are required to pay tax on all purchases or use of tangible personal property that is to become a permanent part of real estate, in the fulfillment of a construction contract. This is true whether the contract is performed for a governmental agency, public utility, manufacturer, charitable or other organization, person, or entity. Contractors may not claim an exemption based upon the Direct Payment Permit of their customers or any other statutory exemption to which their customers may be entitled. Contractors must pay tax on all tools, equipment, and supplies used in performing their contract services. See ¶703 for discussion of building maintenance or cleaning services. A contractor may claim a tax exemption upon the purchase of equipment, machinery, or parts that upon installation, are used directly by the purchaser in manufacturing, processing, mining, dairying, farming, or public utility operations [*Retailers' Information Booklet,* § 10].

• *Construction contracts in keystone opportunity zones (KOZs)*

Sales at retail of services or tangible personal property (other than motor vehicles) to a qualified business for the exclusive use, consumption, and utilization of the tangible personal property or service by the qualified business at its facility located within a subzone, improvement subzone or expansion subzone are exempt from sales and use taxes [73 P.S. § 820.511(a)]. For contracts entered into prior to September 8, 2008, the exemption for sales to a construction contractor pursuant to a contract with a qualified business is limited to "building machinery and equipment" [73 P.S. § 820.511(b)]. For contracts entered into on or after September 8, 2008, the exemption is no longer limited. All property installed for the exclusive use, consumption and utilization by a qualified business is exempt [73 P.S. § 820.511(b)]. For purposes of the subzone, improvement subzone, or expansion subzone exemption, building machinery and equipment shall include distribution equipment purchased for the exclusive use, consumption and utilization in a subzone, improvement subzone, or expansion subzone facility [73 P.S. § 820.511(b)]. See discussion of KOZs at ¶ 4622.

Two Sets of Rules

The rules governing construction contracts entered into before July 1, 1998, are different from the rules governing construction contracts entered into on or after June 30, 1998 (discussed at ¶ 717). According to Act 89 of 2002, the post-June 30, 1998, provisions [72 P.S. § 7201(qq)] that treat "building machinery and equipment" as real estate apply only to construction contracts (1) entered into with an organization that qualifies for a sales and use tax exemption as a purely public charity or as a governmental entity and (2) entered into after June 30, 1998. Presumably, therefore, the pre-1998 rules continue to apply to contracts with non-exempt entities. There is a question, however, as to whether Act 89 of 2002, which was characterized as a "clarification," applies retroactively, or whether contracts with non-exempts after June 30, 1998, but prior to the clarification were governed by the post-June 30, 1998, rules. This is an area of great confusion and controversy. Taxpayers with a construction contract issue should consult their tax advisers.

For pre-July 1, 1998, contracts (*i.e.,* contracts entered into prior to July 1, 1998, or entered into under the obligation of an unalterable, formal written bid issued prior to July 1, 1998), construction contractors may be involved in both construction and sales activities.

Construction activities: A "construction activity" is one resulting from an agreement or contract under which a contractor attaches or affixes tangible personal property to real estate so that it *becomes a permanent part* of the real estate (*e.g.,* painting a building, installing cabinets, excavating a cellar, repairing a roof, installing built-in appliances) [61 Pa. Code § 31.11]. Contractors whose activities are confined strictly to construction activities must pay tax directly to suppliers. A use tax license number is available to those who purchase from vendors not required to collect sales tax or not registered with the Department. This permits the contractors to remit tax directly to the Department [61 Pa. Code § 31.12(a)(2)].

Construction contractor as ultimate consumer: A construction contractor is considered the ultimate consumer of property furnished and installed in the performance of construction activities [61 Pa. Code § 31.12(a)]. In other words, the contractor is the last person to use or consume such property while it is still tangible personal property. After installation this becomes real property and, thus, is no longer taxable. The contractor, therefore, must pay sales tax on the property. For example, if Contractor C, as part of a contract for construction of a house, agrees to install a built-in dishwasher, C must pay sales tax on the purchase price of the dishwasher. C does not charge sales tax to his customer and may include the tax paid in his bid (but *not* as a separately stated item) [61 Pa. Code § 31.12(a)(1)]. The contractor must pay tax on the dishwasher because the contractor is the final consumer of the dishwasher *as tangible personal property.* After installation it becomes real property, no longer taxable.

Sales activities: A "sales activity" is one resulting from an agreement or contract under which a contractor transfers tangible personal property or performs services upon tangible personal property belonging to another person and *installs it so as not to become a permanent part of the real estate* (*e.g.,* furniture, home appliances that are not built in, carpeting, portable lamps) [61 Pa. Code § 31.11].

¶716

Contractor is vendor, not ultimate consumer: A construction contractor who performs sales activities (tangible personal property or services) is considered a vendor and must register with the Department and collect tax from customers. See ¶506 for explanation of registration. In other words, the contractor transfers the tangible personal property to a customer, and, after the transfer, the property is still tangible personal property. The contractor, therefore, is not the final consumer.

Construction Activity vs. Sales Activity

The distinction between construction and sales activities is critical. Because of the resale exemption, sales and use taxes are imposed on the final consumer of tangible personal property. Ordinarily, the final consumer of tangible personal property is a person who purchases property for his/her own use, not to be transferred by resale (*e.g.*, a book to read, a new stove for one's kitchen). Construction contractors, however, often purchase tangible personal property and install it in realty in such a way that it becomes a part of the real estate, no longer tangible personal property. Contractors are considered to be the final consumers of tangible personal property that, after it is installed, becomes real property, even though they sell the property to someone else and do not "use" it themselves in the ordinary sense of the word "use." For example, if a contractor purchases a kitchen range and builds it into the kitchen of a house to be sold later, the contractor made the final use of the range as tangible personal property, even though the contractor did not "use" the stove for cooking (the ordinary sense of the word "use" with respect to a stove). The critical fact is that the stove is no longer tangible personal property when the contractor sells it; after installation the stove becomes real property.

In trying to decide whether property becomes a part of the real estate, a taxpayer should consider the ordinary understanding of the nature of the property after installation. However, that is not enough. A taxpayer must also consider the relationship between the item after installation and the property as a whole. In order to do this, how the property is attached and whether (and how much) removal of the property will damage either the real estate or the property in question must be considered. See, *e.g., Clayton v. Lienhard*, 167 A 321 (Pa. 1933).

- *Exemptions for property/services used/consumed in construction activities*

A contractor may claim an exemption for property or services used or consumed in construction activities (as opposed to sales activities) only in the following limited cases:

(1) The property installed will be *directly used* by the customer in one of the following operations: manufacturing, processing, farming, public utility [61 Pa. Code § 31.13(b)]. These exempt operations are explained at ¶710, ¶711, ¶712, and ¶713, respectively.

(2) The service is performed on property that will be *directly used* by the customer in an exempt operation [61 Pa. Code § 31.13(c)].

(3) The property is purchased in Pennsylvania solely for the purpose of being processed, fabricated, or manufactured into, attached to, or incorporated into personal property to be delivered to a location outside Pennsylvania and exclusively used outside Pennsylvania [61 Pa. Code § 32.5(c)(3)(i)]. See ¶507 for an explanation of multistate sales. These exemptions and the procedures that must be followed are explained in detail in the regulations [61 Pa. Code § 31.13].

When purchasing property to be used in sales activities (*i.e.*, for resale), a contractor may use a resale exemption certificate and then collect the tax from the customer [61 Pa. Code § 31.12(a)(4)]. The resale exemption is explained at ¶709.

- *Refunds*

Refunds must be made to the person, his/her heirs, successors, assigns or other personal representatives who actually paid the tax [72 P.S. § 7252].

¶716

¶717 Contractors and Building Trades (Post-June 30, 1998, Contracts with Exemptions)

As a general rule, for post-June 30, 1998, contracts (*i.e.*, contracts entered into on or after July 1, 1998, and not pursuant to an unalterable, formal written bid issued prior to July 1, 1998), a construction contractor must pay tax on tangible personal property or services provided to tangible personal property that will be used pursuant to a construction contract, whether or not the tangible personal property or services are transferred [72 P.S. §7201(o)(17)]. For post-June 30, 1998, contracts with any other entities, the rules in ¶716 continue to apply.

• *Construction contract*

A "construction contract" for this purpose is any written or oral contract for the construction, reconstruction, remodeling, renovation, or repair of real estate or a real estate structure [72 P.S. §7201(nn)]. This term, however, does *not* apply to the rendition or the obtaining, for a consideration, of disinfecting or pest control services, lawn care services, building maintenance services, or cleaning services.

• *Real estate structure*

A "real estate structure" for this purpose is a structure or item purchased by a construction contractor pursuant to a construction contract with (1) a purely public charity or (2) a governmental entity and includes the following [72 P.S. §7201(qq)]:

(1) Building machinery and equipment (see discussion below).

(2) Land (developed or undeveloped).

(3) Streets, roads, highways.

(4) Parking lots.

(5) Stadiums and stadium seating.

(6) Recreational courts.

(7) Sidewalks.

(8) Foundations.

(9) Structural supports.

(10) Walls, floors, ceilings, roofs, doors, canopies.

(11) Millwork.

(12) Elevators.

(13) Windows and external window coverings.

(14) Outdoor advertising boards or signs.

(15) Airport runways.

(16) Bridges, dams, dikes.

(17) Traffic control devices (including traffic signs).

(18) Satellite dishes.

(19) Antennas.

(20) Guardrail posts.

(21) Pipes, fittings, pipe supports and hangers, valves.

(22) Underground tanks.

(23) Wire, conduit, receptacle, and junction boxes.

(24) Insulation.

(25) Ductwork and coverings thereof.

(26) Any structure similar to any of the above, whether or not the term constitutes a fixture or is affixed to the real estate or whether or not damage would be done to the item or its surroundings upon removal.

• *Snack Food Packaging*

Effective immediately, returnable corrugated boxes used to deliver snack food products when purchased by a manufacturer are exempt from the sales and use tax.

Plum Borough, 860 A.2d. at 1159-60. Given the holdings in *Plum Borough* and in *Kinsley*, and our conclusion that these Road Signs are not BME, we cannot accept **Strongstown's** arguments that it is exempt from use tax because the Road Signs are tangible personal property and sales for resale.

Imaging Center Equipment

An imaging center was not subject to Pennsylvania sales tax on a purchase of magnetic resonance imaging (MRI) and positron emission tomography/computerized tomography (PET/CT scan) systems because the systems were real estate structures. The equipment fell into the category of property that could be considered tangible personal property or realty. In this case, the evidence showed the equipment was sufficiently attached to be considered realty. In addition, numerous structural, electrical, and mechanical improvements made to the building to accommodate the systems would serve no function without the systems themselves. Accordingly, the systems were essential to the ongoing use of the property as an imaging center. Finally, the systems were installed with an intention that they would become a permanent part of the real estate [*Northeastern Pennsylvania Imaging Center v. Pennsylvania,* Pa.Commw., 978 A.2d 1055 (Pa.Commw. 2009)]. An appeal has been filed with the Pennsylvania Supreme Court.

• *Building machinery and equipment*

The term "building machinery and equipment" for this purpose means generation equipment, storage equipment, conditioning equipment, distribution equipment, and termination equipment and is *limited* to the following [72 P.S. § 7201(pp)]:

(1) Air conditioning (limited to heating, cooling, purification, humidification, dehumidification, and ventilation).

(2) Alarms (limited to fire, security, and detection).

(3) Cathodic protection system.

(4) Communications (limited to voice, video, data, sound, master clock, and noise abatement).

(5) Control system (limited to energy management, traffic and parking lot and building access).

(6) Electrical.

(7) Furniture, cabinetry, and kitchen equipment. This term includes boilers, chillers, air cleaners, humidifiers, fans, switchgear, pumps, telephones, speakers, horns, motion detectors, dampers, actuators, grills, registers, traffic signals, sensors, card access devices, medial devices, floor troughs and grates, and laundry equipment together with integral coverings and enclosures, *whether or not the item constitutes a fixture or is otherwise affixed to the real estate; whether or not damage would be done to the item or its surroundings upon removal; or whether or not the item is physically located within a real estate structure.* This term, however, does not include guardrail posts, pipes, fittings, pipe supports and hangers, valves, underground tanks, wire, conduit, receptacle and junction boxes, insulation, ductwork and coverings thereof.

(8) Laboratory system.

¶717

(9) Medical system (limited to diagnosis and treatment equipment, medical gas, nurse call, and doctor paging).

(10) Plumbing.

Sound Barriers

The Court has held that Pennsylvania sales and use tax applied to a contractor's sales of sound barrier panels and I-beams to the state because the panels and I-beams were not included in the statutory definition of exempt "building machinery and equipment" [Kinsley Construction, Inc. v. Cmlth., 894 A.2d 832 (Pa.Commw. 2006); aff'd per curium, 915 A.2d 639 (Pa. 2007)]. See, also, Hempt Brothers, Inc. v. Cmwlth., 909 A.2d 298 (Pa. 2006), decision unreported.

NOTE: This list is substantially the same as what the administrative boards had determined as *not* permanently affixed under pre-July 1, 1998, rules.

CAUTION

What is the status of property that is not specifically enumerated as building machinery and equipment or a real estate structure? The Department of Revenue's position is that an exemption is available only for building machinery and equipment. Therefore, the purchase of everything else by a contractor is taxable. In *Plum Borough School District v. Cmwlth.*, 849 F.R. 2001 (October 29, 2004), the Pennsylvania Commonwealth Court has held that the only sales and use tax exclusion for construction contractors [72 P.S. §7204(57)]is limited to building machinery and equipment transferred to a political subdivision. This case has been affirmed by the Pennsylvania Supreme Court.

- *Exemptions*

Building machinery and equipment: A construction contractor may purchase building machinery and equipment free from tax when the construction contract is with one of the exempt purchasers identified in 72 P.S. §7204(57). See "Building machinery and equipment" at ¶706.

Contracts in keystone opportunity zones (KOZs): For contracts entered into prior to September 8, 2008, the exemption for sales to a construction contractor pursuant to a contract with a qualified business is limited to "building machinery and equipment" [73 P.S. §820.511(b)]. For contracts entered into on or after September 8, 2008, the exemption is no longer limited. All property installed for the exclusive use, consumption, and utilization by a qualified business is exempt [73 P.S. §820.511(b)]. See discussion of KOZs at ¶4622.

- *Refunds*

A taxpayer is entitled to a refund of all taxes, interest, and penalties when a tax to which the Commonwealth is not entitled is paid [72 P.S. §7252]. Prior to January 1, 2008, refunds are made pursuant to the provisions of §§7253 and 7254. After December 31, 2007, refunds are made pursuant to the provisions of Article XXVII of the Tax Reform Code (see ¶4204).

- *TPPR (Taxes Paid—Purchases Resold) credit*

The TPPR is a credit against the sales tax due on a contractor's sales tax return. If a contractor pays sales tax on an item and later resells it to a nonexempt customer (from whom tax must be collected), the contractor may claim a credit against the tax collected equal to the amount originally paid the contractor's supplier, provided the original purchase took place within three years of resale. To claim the TPPR, the contractor must disclose the amount of tax paid on items resold that is being credited against tax collected from customers [61 Pa. Code §31.14(a)].

¶717

The following example, adapted from the regulations, illustrates the application of the "TPPR" [61 Pa. Code § 31.14(b)]:

> *Example:* Susan Corporation purchased 100 sinks at $70 each and paid tax on them at the time of purchase because Susan Corporation had no good reason to know whether all (or any) of them would be resold. Later Susan Corporation installed 60 of these sinks in homes it constructed and sold 40 of them over-the-counter at retail at a price of $100 per unit. Susan Corporation collected $240 (40 × $100 × .06) sales tax when they were sold.

When Susan Corporation files its sales tax return, it will show the following information regarding the sinks that were resold:

Total gross sales	$4,000.00
Total nontaxable sales	-0-
Net taxable sales	4,000.00
Total amount of tax collected	240.00
Less 1% commission	2.40
Net amount of tax collected	237.60
Amount of use tax	-0-
Total tax due	$237.60
Less "TPPR"	$168.00
Amount to be remitted	**$69.60**

The "TPPR" is computed as follows: 40 × $70 × .06=$168.

NOTE: These TPPR rules apply to both pre-July 1, 1998, contracts and post-June 30, 1998, contracts.

¶718 Prebuilt Housing

The Pennsylvania prebuilt housing provisions were enacted as part of Act 23 of 2000 (Act of May 24, 2000, P.L. 106) and apply to agreements entered into after June 30, 2000.

• *Definition of terms*

The phrase "prebuilt housing" means either of the following [72 P.S. § 7201(vv)]:

(1) Manufactured housing (including mobile homes) that bear a label as required by and referred to in the Act of November 17, 1982 (P.L. 676, No. 192), known as the "Manufactured Housing Construction and Safety Standards Authorization Act."

(2) Industrialized housing as defined in the Act of May 11, 1972 (P.L. 286, No. 70), known as the "Industrialized Housing Act."

"Used prebuilt housing" means prebuilt housing that was previously subject to a sale to a prebuilt housing purchaser [72 P.S. § 7201(ww)].

Used Prebuilt Housing Exempt

Used prebuilt housing is exempt from the Pennsylvania sales and use tax [72 P.S. § 7204(60)].

"Prebuilt housing purchaser" means a person who purchases prebuilt housing in a transaction and who intends to occupy the unit for residential purposes in Pennsylvania [72 P.S. § 7201(zz)].

"Prebuilt housing builder" means a person who makes a prebuilt housing sale to a prebuilt housing purchaser [72 P.S. § 7201(xx)].

"Prebuilt housing sale" means a sale of prebuilt housing to a prebuilt housing purchaser, including a sale to a landlord with respect to whether the person making the sale is responsible for installing the prebuilt housing or whether the prebuilt housing becomes a real estate structure upon installation. Temporary installation by a prebuilt housing builder for display purposes of a unit held for resale is not considered occupancy for residential purposes [72 P.S. § 7201(yy)].

"Purchase price of prebuilt housing" is 60% of the manufacturer's selling price. If, however, a manufacturer of prebuilt housing precollects tax from a prebuilt housing builder at the time of the sale to the prebuilt housing building, the manufacturer shall have the option to collect tax on 60% of the selling price or on 100% of the actual cost of the supplies and materials used in the manufacture of the prebuilt housing [72 P.S. § 7201(g)(8)].

• *Imposition, collection, and payment of tax*

Tax on sales of prebuilt housing is imposed on the prebuilt housing builder at the time of the prebuilt housing sale within Pennsylvania and must be reported and remitted to the Department of Revenue as required. However, a manufacturer of prebuilt housing may opt to precollect the tax from the prebuilt housing builder at the time of sale. In any case where prebuilt housing is purchased and the tax is not paid or precollected by the manufacturer, the rebuilt housing purchaser must remit tax directly to the Department if the prebuilt housing is used in Pennsylvania, without regard to whether the prebuilt housing becomes a real estate structure [72 P.S. § 7202(f)].

Exemption certificates: Prebuilt housing manufacturers are not required to obtain exemption certificates from prebuilt housing dealers. Unless the prebuilt housing manufacturer elects to precollect the tax, the prebuilt housing builder is obligated to remit the tax on its sale of prebuilt housing to a prebuilt housing purchaser. No exemptions apply [Sales Tax Bulletin 2003-01].

Prefabricated Housing

The application of tax on charges made for the repair and maintenance of prefabricated housing is governed by the provisions of 61 Pa. Code § 31.11 [Sales Tax Bulletin 2003-01]. Prefabricated housing was governed by the provisions of a Pennsylvania Department of Revenue policy statement, "Sale and Installation of Prefabricated Housing" [61 Pa. Code § 60.18]. This policy statement applies only to a contract entered into prior to July 1, 1998, or an obligation of an unalterable, formal bid issued prior to July 1, 1999.

⟫⟫→ *CAUTION: Telecommunications services, premium cable services, and prepaid telecommunications, although included in taxable services in this* **Guidebook,** *are technically included in the definition of "tangible personal property" in 72 P.S. §201(k).*

¶719 Premium Cable Service

• *Premium cable or premium video programming service*

"Premium cable or premium video programming service" means that portion of television services, community antenna television services, or any other distribution of television, video, audio or radio services that meet both of the following criteria (*e.g.,* Home Box Office; Cinemax; Showtime; Prism; The Disney Channel; commercial music service) [72 P.S. § 7201(ll); 61 Pa. Code § 60.9]:

(1) It is transmitted with or without the use of wires to purchasers.

(2) It consists substantially of programming uninterrupted by paid commercial advertising, including but not limited to (a) programming primarily composed of uninterrupted full-length motion pictures or sporting events, (b) pay-per-view, and (c) paid programming.

• *Taxable purchase price*

Charges for the following are included in the purchase price of premium cable service:

(1) Installation.

(2) Repair.

(3) Upgrade to include additional premium cable service.

(4) Downgrade to exclude some or all premium cable service.

(5) Addition of premium cable outlets in excess of 10 for an individual customer.

(6) Franchise fees relating to premium cable service.

(7) Any other charges related to premium cable service.

Charges Should Be Separately Stated

If the charge for cable service includes a charge for both premium and nonpremium cable service and the charge for nonpremium cable service is not separately stated, the entire charge is taxable. Nonpremium cable service is that portion of cable service that does not qualify as premium cable service.

• *Exemptions*

The statute specifically exempts the following from the sales and use taxes [72 P.S. § 7201(ll)]:

(1) Transmissions by public television.

(2) Public radio services.

(3) Official federal, state, or local government cable services.

(4) Local origination programming that provides a variety of public service programs unique to the community.

(5) Programming that provides coverage of public affairs issues that are presented without commentary or analysis, including proceedings of the U.S. Congress proceedings (*e.g.*, C-SPAN).

(6) Religious programming.

(7) Subscriber charges for access to a video dial tone system (excluded from definition of telecommunications service).

(8) Charges by a common carrier to a video programmer for the transport of video programming (excluded from definition of telecommunications service).

¶720 Printing

• *Printing defined*

The term "printing" includes the following [61 Pa. Code § 32.1]:

(1) The performance of an integrated series of operations engaged in as a business that is predominantly and directly related to the production of multiple copies (*i.e.*, 50 or more copies) of substantially similar printed matter upon which a sales or use tax is due or for which an exemption exists.

(2) When part of an integrated series of operations, the process of organization and arrangement of graphic material into page or other final format, whether by manual operation, computer operation, or otherwise. It does not include data processing, word processing, photocopying, or automatic typewriters, except where the activities are part of the integrated series of operations.

Printing of Telephone Bills Not Printing

The printing of telephone bills does not fall within the definition of "printing" because every telephone bill is unique. Therefore, EUR cannot meet the requirement of 61 Pa. Code §32.1 that it produce multiple copies of substantially similar printed matter [*EUR Systems, Inc. v. Cmwlth.*, 664 F.R. 2006 (December 8, 2008].

• Duplicating

Persons engaged in the process of accurately duplicating, reproducing, or forming a durable medium for the reproduction of original documents are vendors of tangible personal property purchased by their customers, whether or not the copies are produced to the special order of the customer [61 Pa. Code §31.22(a)]. "Duplicating" includes the production of photostatic copies or blueprints. Sales tax applies to all charges for the duplicating of documents furnished by the customer, without reduction for expenses incurred (*e.g.*, equipment rental, salaries or wages paid to assistants) whether or not the expenses are itemized in billings to customers.

Resale exemption: Vendors may claim the resale exemption on purchases of tangible personal property (*e.g.*, toner, paper) that is transferred to the customer in connection with the sale of a duplicated document. Repair services do not qualify for the resale exemption [Proposed amendment to 61 Pa. Code §31.22(b); 27 Pa.B. 933].

Duplicating and the Printing Exemption

In its proposed amendment to 61 Pa. Code §31.22(b), the Department of Revenue states that the purchase of supplies and equipment (*e.g.*, chemicals, film, proof paper, developer units, or similar items) used or consumed in the process of duplicating, reproducing, or forming a durable medium for the reproduction of an original is subject to tax, unless the vendor is entitled to claim a printing exemption [27 Pa.B. 933]. The Department does not, however, give any indication of the circumstances under which duplicating would qualify as printing.

• Printing exemption

When engaged in as a business, printing and related businesses is a manufacturing activity [72 P.S. §7201(c)(2); 61 Pa. Code §32.36(a)]. The sales and use tax manufacturing exemption is discussed at ¶710. In order for tangible personal property or services to exempt from the sales or use taxes the property or service must be used by the manufacturer (1) during the production stages, (2) directly, and (3) predominantly in manufacturing [*Oberg Manufacturing Co., Inc. v. Cmwlth.*, 486 A.2d 1047 (Pa.Commw. 1985)].

Related businesses: The printing exemption also applies to those businesses related to the printing industry that, although they are themselves not printing, are "manufacturing" within the meaning of 72 P.S. §7201(c) and are thus not subject to the multiple copy requirement. These "related businesses" include trade binding, engraving, silk screening, typography (including advertising typographers), plate making, color separating, stereotyping, electrotyping, gravure cylinder making, photographic processing, and the business of manufacturing page mechanicals, camera ready copy, image carriers, or related or component items for sale to printers for use in their printing operations [61 Pa. Code §32.36(a)(2)].

Direct use: "Direct use" for sales and use tax purposes is explained at ¶710.

Predominant use: Based upon a 12-month period, property is "predominantly used" in printing when multiple copies (*i.e.*, 50 or more) are produced for 50% or more of the time or the total copies of printed matter, divided by the number of orders for substantially similar items, exceeds 50 or more copies [61 Pa. Code §32.1].

¶720

Mixed-Use Property

If equipment is used for both exempt and nonexempt purposes, the predominant use test determines its tax status [61 Pa. Code § 32.1].

- *In-house printing*

If the normal business of an entity is not printing, but the entity also provides its own full service printing requirements, an in-house printing operation will qualify for the manufacturing exemption if the following criteria are met [61 Pa. Code § 32.36(a)(3)]:

(1) The in-house printing is conducted in a separate and distinct location (utilizing separate and distinct machinery and supplies) devoted predominantly to printing activities.

(2) The printing is the responsibility of employees assigned to in-house printing and whose duties are predominantly related to printing activities.

(3) Separate accounting or interdepartmental billing is provided to reflect the cost of operating in-house printing activities and to charge these costs against other business activities conducted by the taxpayer.

(4) In-house printing activities are separate and distinct from other business activities and are not an integrated part of general data processing, word processing, copying, or other business activity of the taxpayer.

(5) In-house printing activities are of sufficient size, scope and character that they could be conducted on a commercially viable basis separate and distinct from other business activities of the taxpayer.

- *Machinery, equipment parts, and supplies used directly in printing*

Equipment, machinery (including components of a computer system), accessories, parts, and supplies for equipment and machinery that are used predominantly and directly in the business of printing (regardless of the technology involved) are exempt from the Pennsylvania sales and use tax. If equipment is used for both exempt and nonexempt purposes, the predominant use test determines its tax status. Foundations used to support equipment, machinery, and parts used directly in printing are exempt from tax [61 Pa. Code § 32.36(a)(1)]. Note, however, that purchases involving improvements to real estate are not exempt from sales and use tax.

> *Example 1:* Herron Company operates a print shop has a separate profit center reproducing multiple copies of substantially identical printed matter. The tangible personal property in this print shop that is predominantly used in printing qualifies for the sales tax exemption.

> *Example 2:* Horne Company has a computer printer and photocopy machine that predominantly supports administrative operations. Neither its printer nor its photocopier qualify for the sales tax exemption.

- *Materials*

The purchase of personal property that will be physically incorporated by the printer as an ingredient or constituent of printed and that will be sold in the regular course of business is a purchase for resale and may be purchased free of sales tax upon presentation of a valid exemption certificate [61 Pa. Code § 34.36(a)(3)]. The resale exemption is discussed at ¶ 709.

- *Sales of printed matter not qualifying as direct mail advertising and materials*

In general, printers must collect sales tax on the sale at retail of taxable printed matter and charges for printing services [61 Pa. Code § 32.36(b)(1)]. The term "printed matter" includes (but is not limited to) books, booklets, letterheads, billheads, printed envelopes, folders, printed packages and packaging materials, advertising circulars, programs, newspapers, magazines, periodicals, and similar items [61 Pa. Code § 32.1].

• *Items included in taxable purchase price*

Generally, unless printed matter qualifies as mail order catalogs or direct mail advertising literature or materials, printers must include charges for service or labor pertaining to the printing or preparing of the printed matter in the purchase price. Charges for printing, imprinting, engraving, mimeographing, multigraphing, typesetting, addressing folding, enclosing, packaging, and selling are included in the taxable purchase price. Even if separately stated, charges made by the printer for the mailing or delivering of the finished product to the customer (or a designee) are included as an element of the purchase price [61 Pa. Code § 32.36(b)(2)].

• *Postage*

When the finished product involves the use of the United States postal cards or stamped envelopes purchased by the printer, the tax does not apply to the amount of the United States postage imprinted upon the postal card or enveloped purchased by the printer if the printer is not required to mail the printed matter to the customer's designee. However, if the printer is required to mail the printed matter to the customer's designee, the value of the postage is taxable because it constitutes a charge for the delivery of the postal cards or stamped envelopes [61 Pa. Code § 32.36(b)(2)].

> *Example 1:* Paprika Printing Company imprints stamped envelopes and brochures not qualifying as direct mail advertising literature or materials for Cayenne Company, a customer. Paprika furnishes stamped envelopes and paper for the brochures. The contract between Paprika and Cayenne requires Paprika to return the envelopes and brochures to Cayenne, who in turn will mail them to its customers. Paprika must collect sales tax upon its services for the envelopes, paper, printing charges, and cost of delivering the envelopes and brochures to Cayenne. Paprika may separately state the costs of the postage stamps, which are not subject to tax.

> *Example 2:* Paradox Printing Company imprints stamped envelopes and brochures not qualifying as direct mail advertising materials or literature for Contrary Company, a customer. Paradox furnishes the stamped envelopes and paper for the brochures. The contract between Paradox and Contrary requires Paradox to mail the envelopes and brochures to Sydney's customers. Paradox is required to collect sales tax upon the charges for the envelopes, paper, printing charges, and stamps. The value of the stamps represent the delivery charge in conjunction with the sale.

• *Tear sheets, clippings, reprints, and extra proofs*

Tear sheets, clippings, reprints, and extra proofs are subject to tax [61 Pa. Code § 32.36(b)(2)].

• *Sales of direct mail advertising and mail-order catalogs*

The sale at retail or use of mail-order catalogs and direct mail advertising literature or materials, including electoral literature or materials, such as envelopes, address labels, and a one-time license to use a list of names and mailing addresses for each delivery of direct mail advertising literature or materials (including electoral literature or materials) through the United States Postal service [72 P.S. § 7204(35)]. Also exempt are (1) a charge incidental to the sale of mail-order catalogs and direct mail advertising; and (2) a charge for the delivery postage or mailing of the items to the customer or the customer's designee [61 Pa. Code § 32.36(b)(3)].

• *Printing services*

The exemption relating to the purchase of direct mail advertising literature or materials is confined to transactions in which the printer provides both the printing services and the material to be imprinted. If the printer performs printing services

¶720

upon paper, cardboard, or other material furnished by the purchaser of the services or a third party, the charges are subject to tax even though the finished product qualifies as direct mail advertising literature or material or a mail-order catalog [61 Pa. Code § 32.26(b)(4)].

> *Example:* Perry Printing Company prints letters for Cape Company, a customer, on paper supplied by the customer. The letters are advertisements that will be mailed directly to Cape's customers. This printing service does not qualify for the direct mail advertising exemption; so Perry must collect and Cape must pay sales tax on the total purchase price of the printing services.

• *Copy matter supplied by customer*

Copy, artwork, photographs, plates, separations, and other preparations and image carriers supplied by a customer will not cause a charge for printing to be taxable as long as the customer does not supply the material that receives the printing image [61 Pa. Code § 32.36(b)(4)].

> *Example:* Preston Printing Company prints letters for Conway Company, a customer. Preston supplies the paper, and Conway supplies the plates and artwork. The letters are intended to promote business and will be mailed directly to Conway's customers. This material qualifies for the direct mail advertising exemption, and Conway is exempt from tax on all the charges by Preston.

• *Commercial printers soliciting out-of-state business*

The term "maintaining a place of business in this Commonwealth" does not include the following [72 P.S. § 7201(b)(4)]:

(1) Owning or leasing of tangible or intangible property by a person who has contracted with an unaffiliated commercial printer for printing, provided both of the following conditions are met:

(a) The property is for use by the commercial printer.

(b) The property is located at the Pennsylvania premises of the commercial printer.

(2) Visits by a person's employees or agents to the premises in Pennsylvania in connection with a contract for printing.

NOTE: This provision allows Pennsylvania printing firms to do business with out-of-state customers without making the customer liable for Pennsylvania sales or use taxes. There is a similar provision that applies to corporate net income and capital stock/franchise taxes (see ¶ 507).

⟫⟫➔ *CAUTION: Telecommunications services, premium cable services, and prepaid telecommunications, although included in taxable services in this* **Guidebook,** *are technically included in the definition of "tangible personal property" in 72 P.S. §201(k).*

¶721 Telecommunications Services

• *Telecommunications service defined*

"Telecommunications service" includes any one-way transmission or any two-way interactive transmission of sounds, signals, or other intelligence converted to like form, that effects, or is intended to effect, meaningful communications by electronic or electromagnetic means via wire, cable, satellite, light waves, microwaves, radio waves or other transmission media [72 P.S. § 7201(rr)].

Caution: These Services Are Property

Although the term "tangible personal property," in its ordinary meaning, refers to property that has a tangible and corporeal existence, within the framework of Pennsylvania sales and use taxation, the term "tangible personal property" refers to anything specifically defined as tangible personal property by statute. Telecommunications services and premium cable services are specifically included in the definition of "tangible personal property."

The term "telecommunications service" includes all types of telecommunications transmission, such as the following:

(1) Cellular telecommunications service.

(2) Local, toll, wide-area or any other type of telephone service.

(3) Paging service.

(4) Personal communications system service.

(5) Private line service.

(6) Radio repeater service.

(7) Specialized mobile radio service.

(8) Stationary two-way radio service.

(9) Telegraph service.

(10) Wireless communications service.

Services and Equipment Purchased to Provide Internet Access

A taxpayer, an internet service provider (ISP), purchased data transport services and equipment (including routers, services, and modems) to be used in providing Internet access to customers. The data transport services meets the definition of "telecommunications services" because the taxpayer used the lines to transmit by wire digital signals containing the customer's message or information. Thus, the data transport services and equipment are subject to the Pennsylvania sales and use tax [*Concentric Network Corporation v. Cmwlth.*, 877 A.2d 542 (April 4, 2005); aff'd per curiam, 65 MAP 2006 (Pa. 2007)].

• *Exclusions*

The term "telecommunications service" does not include the following:

(1) Subscriber charges for access to a video dial tone system [72 P.S. §7201(rr)].

(2) Charges to video programmers for the transport of video programming [72 P.S. §7201(rr)].

(3) Charges for access to the Internet. The Internet is the international nonproprietary computer network of both federal and nonfederal interoperable packet-switched data networks [72 P.S. §7201(ss)]. "Access to the Internet" does not include (a) the transport over the Internet or any proprietary network using the Internet protocol of telephone calls, facsimile transmissions, or other telecommunications traffic to or from end users on the public switched telephone net, if the signal sent from or received by an end user is not in an Internet protocol or (b) telecommunications services purchased by an Internet service provider to deliver access to the Internet to its customers [72 P.S. §7201(rr)].

(4) Mobile telecommunications service [72 P.S. §7201(rr)].

(5) Enhanced telecommunication services [61 Pa. Code §60.20(a)]. See discussion of enhanced telecommunication service below.

• *Mobile telecommunications service*

Background: The federal Mobile Telecommunications Sourcing Act of 2000 [P.L. 106-252] provided a standardized way for states to tax mobile telecommunications services, with sourcing rules based on a caller's place of primary use, and mandated that states comply with these provisions by August 1, 2002. In Act 89 of 2002 (H.B. 1848), the Pennsylvania General Assembly adopted the federal law, replacing the current taxing structure with the new, uniform system.

Imposition of tax: The sale or use of mobile telecommunications services is subject to tax at the rate of 6% of the purchase price. The tax must be collected by the provider of the service and remitted to the Commonwealth if the customer's place of primary use is located within Pennsylvania, regardless of where the mobile telecommunications services originate, terminate, or pass through [72 P.S. § 7202(g)].

Definition of mobile telecommunications service: The term "mobile telecommunications service" means a mobile service that meets the following criteria or is the functional equivalent of such a service [72 P.S. § 7201(aaa); 4 U.S.C. § 116; 47 CFR § 20.3]:

(1) It is provided for profit (*i.e.,* with the intent of receiving compensation or monetary gain.

(2) It is an interconnected service.

(3) It is available to the public, or to such classes of eligible users as to be effectively available to a substantial portion of the public.

Sourcing rules for mobile telecommunications service: The sale or use of mobile telecommunications services that are deemed to be provided to a customer by a home service provider under § 117(a) and (b) of the Mobile Telecommunications Sourcing Act is taxable in Pennsylvania for sales and use tax purposes if the customer's place of primary use is located within Pennsylvania, without regard to where the mobile telecommunications services originate, terminate, or pass through. The term "home service provider" means the facilities-based carrier or reseller with which the customer contracts for the provision of mobile telecommunications services [4 U.S.C. § 124(5)].

Place of primary use: The term "place of primary use" means the street address representative of where the customer's use of the mobile telecommunications service primarily occurs, which must be (1) the residential street address or (2) the primary business street address of the customer and within the licensed service area of the home service provider [4 U.S.C. § 124(8)]. The home service provider is responsible for obtaining and maintaining the customer's place of primary use [4 U.S.C. § 122(a)].

• *Enhanced telecommunications services*

Caution

Part of the discussion below is based on 61 Pa. Code § 60.20. The Department of Revenue has announced that it will soon update this policy statement to reflect the federal *Internet Tax Nondiscrimination Act* and *the Mobile Telecommunications Sourcing Act,* as well as *Pennsylvania Act 23 of 2000* and *Act 89 of 2002 [Sales Tax Bulletin 2005-03,* Pennsylvania Department of Revenue, September 30, 2005]. In *Sales Tax Bulletin 2005-03* the Department also provided a list of examples for both enhanced and nonenhanced telecommunications services to clarify the meaning of these terms. These are discussed below.

Defined: Enhanced telecommunications services are services, offered over a telecommunications network, that employ computer processing applications that include one or more of the following [61 Pa. Code § 60.20(a)]:

(1) Acts on the format, content, code, protocol, or similar aspects of the purchaser's transmitted information.

(2) Provides the purchaser additional, different, or restructured information.

(3) Involves the purchaser's interaction with stored information.

Examples of enhanced telecommunications services: The following are examples of enhanced telecommunications services [Sales Tax Bulletin 2005-03, Pennsylvania Department of Revenue, September 30, 2005]:

(1) *Data processing:* the processing and preparation of reports from data supplied by the customer or specialized service that utilized a telecommunication service to transmit the data processing to its customer.

(2) *Information retrieval service:* the purchase of the right to retrieve data or information through a computer from either an on-line or remote computer or peripheral equipment upon request and the service includes charges for fees for connection, computer time, usage transmission or content of information.

(3) *Video on demand:* a pay-per-view video service in which a viewer can order a program from a menu and have it delivered instantly to the television set or computer screen.

(4) *Video programming service:* video or information programming, whether in digital or analog format, that is provided by a cable television operator, or is of the type that would generally be considered comparable to programming provided by a cable television operator, and upon which the cable television operator pays a franchise fee. The term does not include on-line, interactive information services to the extent that access to these services is accomplished through the use of a dial-up or telephone line, or a wireless or direct-to-home satellite transmission.

(5) *Voice mail:* an electronic communication system enabling the recording and storage of voice messages that can be subsequently retrieved by the intended recipient.

(6) *Telephone information line:* the purchase of an information service that offers telephone callers the opportunity to obtain a wide variety of recorded or live information and entertainment, and where the charge is always greater than the cost of simply transmitting the message, (*i.e.,* medical, sports, weather, psychic or adult lines).

Examples of nonenhanced telecommunications services: The following are examples of nonenhanced telecommunications services [*Sales Tax Bulletin 2005-03,* Pennsylvania Department of Revenue, September 30, 2005]:

(1) *Analog-to-digital transmission (or digital-to-analog):* the conversion of voice or data from analog traffic into digitized or packetized traffic, that may or may not increase the speed, reliability, security, etc., of the transmission, but does not change the actual substance of the voice or data being transmitted.

(2) *Asymmetric digital subscriber line (ADSL):* a group of digital subscriber line technologies that reserve more bandwidth in one direction than the other, which is advantageous for users that do not need equal bandwidth in both directions.

(3) *Asynch-ronous transfer mode (ATM):* a method of data transportation whereby fixed length packets are sent over a switched network. The ability to ensure reliable delivery of packets at a high rate makes it suitable for carrying voice, video and data.

(4) *Broadband integrated services digital network (BISDN):* a second-generation integrated services digital network technology that uses fiber optics for a network that can transmit data at speeds of 155 megabits per second and higher.

(5) *Broadband transmission:* large-capacity networks, such as cable, fiber optics, wireless, power lines, etc., that are capable of carrying multiple services of voice, data and video at the same time.

¶721

(6) *Circuit-switched network:* a type of network in which a continuous link is established between a source and a receiver. Circuit switching is used for voice or video to ensure that individual parts of a signal are received in the correct order by the destination site.

(7) *Digital subscriber line (DSL):* a data communications technology that transmits information over the copper wires that make up the local loop of the public switched telephone network. It bypasses the circuit-switched lines that make up that network and yields much faster data transmission rates than analog modem technologies.

(8) *Direct broadcast satellite (DBS):* a broadcast technology that uses satellites orbiting the Earth to broadcast television or data signals to a dish antenna.

(9) *Frame relay:* a high-speed packet switching protocol used in wide area networks (WANs), often to connect local area networks (LANs) to each other, with a maximum bandwidth of 44.725 megabits per second.

(10) *G.lite:* a kind of asymmetric digital subscriber line technology, based on discrete multi-tone modulation, that offers up to 1.5 megabits per second downstream bandwidth, 384 Kilobits per second upstream, does not usually require a splitter and is easier to install than other types of digital subscriber line.

(11) *Intranet transmission:* transmissions to, from or within a network serving a single organization or site that is modeled after the Internet, allowing users access to almost any information available on the network. Unlike the Internet, intranets are typically limited to one organization or one site, with little or no access to outside users.

(12) *Integrated services digital network (ISDN):* a circuit-switched communication network, closely associated with the public switched telephone network, that allows dial-up digital communication at speeds up to 128 kilobits per second.

(13) *Local area network transmission:* transmission to, from or within a network connecting a number of computers to each other or to a central server so that the computers can share programs and files.

(14) *Multiplexing:* transmitting multiple signals over a single communications line or computer channel. The two common multiplexing techniques are frequency division multiplexing, which separates signals by modulating the data onto different carrier frequencies, and time division multiplexing, which separates signals by interleaving bits one after the other.

(15) *Packet-switch network:* a network that allows a message to be broken into small "packets" of data that are sent separately by a source to the destination. The packets may travel different paths and arrive at different times, with the destination sites reassembling them into the original message. Packet switching is used in most computer networks because it allows a very large amount of information to be transmitted through a limited bandwidth.

(16) *Plain old telephone service (POTS) splitter transmissions:* transmissions utilizing a device that uses filters to separate voice from data signals when they are to be carried on the same phone line, required for several types of digital subscriber line service.

(17) *Primary-rate integrated services digital network (PRI-ISDN):* the primary-rate integrated services digital network interface provides 23 64 Kb/s channels (called B channels) to carry voice or data and one 16 Kb/s signaling channel (the D channel) for call information.

(18) *Protocol-to-protocol conversion:* the conversion of voice or data traffic from one computer protocol to another computer protocol, which may or may

not increase the speed, reliability, security, etc., of the transmission, but does not change the actual substance of the voice or data being transmitted.

(19) *Rate-adaptive digital subscriber line (RADSL):* a variation of DSL that uses carrierless amplitude phase modulation, divides the available frequencies into discrete sub-channels and also maximizes performance by adjusting the transmission to the quality of the phone line while in use.

(20) *Router transmissions:* transmissions utilizing a central switching device in a packet-switched computer network that directs and controls the flow of data through the network.

(21) *Symmetric digital subscriber line:* This technology provides the same bandwidth in both directions, upstream and downstream. SDSL provides transmission speeds within a T1/E1 range, of up to 1.5 Mbps at a maximum range of 12,000:18,000 feet from a central office, over a single-pair copper wire.

(22) *T-1 line:* a dedicated digital communication link provided by a telephone company that offers 1.544 megabits per second of bandwidth, commonly used for carrying traffic to and from private business networks and Internet service providers.

(23) *T-3 line:* a dedicated digital communication link provided by a telephone company that offers 44.75 megabits per second of bandwidth, commonly used for carrying traffic to and from private business networks and Internet service providers.

(24) *Time division multiplexing (TDM):* a digital data transmission method that takes signals from multiple sources, divides them into pieces that are then placed periodically into time slots, transmits them down a single path and reassembles the time slots back into multiple signals on the remote end of the transmission.

(25) *Transmission control protocol/Internet protocol (TCP/IP):* a method of packet-switched data transmission used on the Internet. The protocol specifies the manner in which a signal is divided into parts, as well as the manner in which "address" information is added to each packet to ensure that it reaches its destination and can be reassembled into the original message.

(26) *Vertical services:* related telecommunications services purchased as part of a telecommunications service plans (*e.g.,* caller ID, three-way calling, call forwarding, call waiting).

"Port Modem Management" Service and Data Transmission Service

America Online, Inc. (AOL) purchased a "Port Modem Management Service" and data transmission service from Sprint. AOL filed a petition for refund of tax paid on the purchase of these services, arguing that these were purchase of enhanced telecommunication services. The Pennsylvania Commonwealth Court denied the petition for refund, ruling that, by definition these services are not enhanced telecommunications services. See *America Online, Inc. v. Commonwealth*, 621 F.R. 2004, ____ A.2d ____ (Pa.Commw. January 30, 2008)]. An appeal has been filed with the Pennsylvania Supreme Court.

• *Voice Over Internet Protocol (VOIP)*

It is the position of the Pennsylvania Department of Revenue that VOIP is a taxable telecommunication service subject to the Pennsylvania state and local sales tax because it falls under the statutory definition of "telecommunications service" and does *not* come within the enhanced telecommunication service exclusion from sales and use tax. See *Sales Tax Bulletin 2005-2.*

VOIP defined: VOIP is real-time audio or data transmitted and/or received in a digital format through the use of Internet Protocol data packet transmission, or any similar or successor protocol transmission. Calls may be made between users of the same VOIP service as well as between VOIP users and those with landline or mobile telephone service. Some VOIP services work only over a computer or special VOIP telephone, but others allow the use of a traditional telephone with an adapter [*Sales Tax Bulletin 2005-02*].

• *Prepaid telecommunications*

The term "prepaid telecommunications" means a tangible item containing a prepaid authorization number that can be used solely to obtain telecommunications service and includes any renewal or increases in the prepaid amount [72 P.S. §7201(uu)].

Surcharge

Effective July 1, 2011, prepaid telecommunication services and wireless telephones is subject to a prepaid wireless Emergency-911 surcharge (prepaid E-911 surcharge) at the rate of $1 per retail transaction. This surcharge is collected on each retail transaction regardless of whether the service or pre-paid wireless telephone is purchased in person, by telephone, through the Internet or by any other method. The prepaid E-911 surcharge is to be charged and collected by the retailer in addition to any other charges or fees, but is not to be included for purposes of calculating sales tax. Pre-paid E-911 surcharges are to be reported on the sales tax return, which will include a separate line-item to report the surcharge. Retailers collecting and reporting the pre-paid E-911 surcharge must file electronically using the department's online filing system, e-TIDES, or by TeleFile, 1-800-748-8299. For more information on the pre-paid E-911 surcharge, visit the department's Online Customer Service Center at www.revenue.state.pa.us [*Tax Update No. 155*, Pennsylvania Department of Revenue, April/May 2011, p. 3].

Inclusion of Tax in Advertised Price

This election permits the service provider to include Pennsylvania sales and use tax in the advertised price for prepaid mobile telecommunications services not evidenced by the transfer of tangible personal property.

Prepaid telecommunications evidenced by transfer of tangible personal property: The sale or use of prepaid telecommunications evidenced by the transfer of tangible personal property is subject to the Pennsylvania sales and use tax at the rate of 6% of the purchase price and is deemed to occur at the purchaser's billing address [72 P.S. §7202(e)(1), (2)].

Prepaid telecommunications not evidenced by transfer of tangible personal property: The sale or use of prepaid telecommunications service not evidenced by the transfer of tangible personal property is also subject to tax at the rate of 6% of the purchase price unless the service provider elects to collect the tax at the rate of 6% of receipts from prepaid telecommunications. If the service provider elects to collect sales or use tax at the rate of 6% of receipts, the provider must notify the Department of Revenue of its election and collect tax on receipts until it notifies the Department otherwise [72 P.S. §7202(e)(3)]. This election permits the service provider to include Pennsylvania sales and use tax in the advertised price for prepaid telecommunications services.

• *Prepaid mobile telecommunications service*

The term "prepaid mobile telecommunications service" means mobile telecommunications service that is paid for in advance and enables the origination of calls using an access number, authorization code, or both (whether manually or electronically dialed) if the remaining amount of units of the prepaid service is known by the service provider on a continuous basis [72 P.S. §7201(ccc), applicable to services billed by a home service provider after August 1, 2002]. The term does not include the advance purchase of mobile telecommunications service if the purchase is pursuant to a service contract between provider and customer and if the service contract requires the customer to make periodic payments to maintain the mobile telecommunications service.

Prepaid mobile telecommunications service evidenced by transfer of tangible personal property: The sale or use of prepaid mobile telecommunications service evidenced by the transfer of tangible personal property is subject to sales and use taxes at the rate of 6% of purchase price [72 P.S. § 7202(e.1)(1); 72 P.S. § 7202(a), (b)].

Prepaid mobile telecommunications service not evidenced by transfer of tangible personal property: The sale or use of prepaid mobile telecommunications service not evidenced by the transfer of tangible personal property is also subject to tax at the rate of 6% of the purchase price [72 P.S. § 7202(e.1)(2)] unless the service provider elects to collect the tax at the rate of 6% of receipts from prepaid telecommunications. If the service provider elects to collect sales or use tax at the rate of 6% of receipts, the provider must notify the Department of Revenue of its election and collect tax on receipts until it notifies the Department otherwise [72 P.S. § 7202(e.1)(3), applicable to mobile telecommunications services billed by a home service provider after August 1, 2002].

Inclusion of Tax in Advertised Price

This election permits the service provider to include Pennsylvania sales and use tax in the advertised price for prepaid mobile telecommunications services not evidenced by the transfer of tangible personal property.

USE TAX

¶722 Transactions Subject to Use Tax

The use tax is imposed on the use (within Pennsylvania) of tangible personal property and certain services purchased at retail when the sales tax has not been paid to the vendor. The use tax is levied at the rate of 6% of the purchase price [72 P.S. § 7202(b)]. Purchase price is explained at ¶510. Tangible personal property and taxable services are the same for use and sales tax purposes. Taxable property is explained at ¶702 and taxable services are explained at ¶703.

• *"Use" defined*

"Use" for purposes of the Pennsylvania use tax includes the exercise of any right or power incidental to the ownership, custody, or possession of tangible personal property, including but not limited to, transportation, storage, or consumption [72 P.S. § 201(o)(1)]. Tangible personal property is defined at ¶702. For a list of goods and services specifically included in the definition of "use," see 72 P.S. § 7201(o).

• *Imposition rules*

Imposition of the Pennsylvania use tax conforms to the following rules [72 P.S. § 7204(2), (3); 61 Pa. Code § 31.7]:

(1) If tangible personal property or services are purchased outside Pennsylvania, the purchaser incurs use tax liability if the property or services are afterward used or consumed in Pennsylvania and no sales tax is paid to the vendor at the time of purchase.

(2) The use tax does not apply to the use of tangible personal property purchased by a nonresident outside of Pennsylvania and brought into Pennsylvania for a period of seven days or less or for any period of time if the nonresident is a tourist or vacationer.

(3) The use tax does not apply to property purchased outside Pennsylvania for use outside Pennsylvania by a nonresident natural person or business entity not actually doing business within Pennsylvania who later brings the property, if the property was purchased more than six months prior to the date first brought, into Pennsylvania or prior to the establishment of such business or residence, whichever comes first.

(4) Tangible personal property temporarily brought into Pennsylvania for the performance of contracts for the construction, reconstruction, remodeling, repairing, and maintenance of real estate are subject to the use tax.

(5) If someone purchases tangible personal property or taxable services within Pennsylvania, but no sales tax was paid to the vendor at the time of purchase, the purchaser is liable for use tax.

(6) Licensees must report and pay use tax at the time their regular sales tax return is due. See ¶ 603.

(7) Non-licensees must report and pay use tax on or before the end of the month following the month in which the tax was incurred.

(8) Licensed purchasers pay use tax directly to the Department.

(9) Purchasers who reside outside Pennsylvania pay use tax directly to the Department.

(10) Purchasers who reside in Pennsylvania (except those who reside in Philadelphia County) have the option of (i) paying use tax directly to the Department or (ii) paying use tax to the treasurer of the county in which they reside.

NOTE: The obligation of out-of-state vendors in the mail-order business to collect use tax from Pennsylvania residents is discussed below.

• *Examples*

The following examples illustrate transactions subject to the use tax (assuming the vendor has not collected sales tax):

Example 1: Norman Jones, a Pennsylvania resident, purchased a radio in New York City while there for a weekend visit. When Norman brings his radio back to Pennsylvania, or has it shipped to him, he incurs use tax liability on it.

Example 2: James Shanks, a Pennsylvania resident, purchased a radio in Philadelphia. The vendor forgot to collect sales tax from James. James is liable for use tax on this radio.

Example 3: Eerie Company has offices in Chicago and Scranton. Eerie Company purchased office equipment in New York City and sent it to its Scranton office. Eerie Company incurs use tax liability on this equipment sent to Pennsylvania.

Example 4: Yankee Doodle Corporation is a Connecticut firm that has salesmen soliciting orders in Pennsylvania. Yankee Doodle purchased advertising displays in Connecticut to use for promotional purposes, some of which are used in Pennsylvania. Yankee Doodle Corporation incurs use tax liability on the displays used in Pennsylvania.

Example 5: Hardwood Furniture Corporation purchased lumber from Handy Lumber Supply Corporation. Since Hardwood intended to use the lumber in the manufacture of furniture, it presented a resale exemption certificate and did not pay any sales tax on the lumber. Later, Hardwood's office floor was damaged in a storm, and Hardwood used some of the lumber purchased from Handy to repair it. Hardwood incurs use tax liability on the lumber used to repair the floor.

Example 6: Roy Meadows, a Pennsylvania resident, had his truck repaired in North Carolina. When Roy brings his repaired truck back to Pennsylvania, he incurs use tax liability for the repairs.

Example 7: Kate Sartin, a Pennsylvania contractor, purchased plumbing materials from a Trenton manufacturer to install in houses she is building in Pennsylvania. Kate incurs use tax liability on the materials.

Example 8: Mae Dill, an Ohio contractor, brings equipment and materials into Pennsylvania to use or consume in constructing an office building. She incurs use tax liability on this equipment and materials.

- *Purchase at retail*

The acquisition for a consideration of the ownership, custody, or possession of tangible personal property or of taxable services if the purchase is made for the purpose of consumption or use, regardless of whether the acquisition is absolute or conditional or the means by which the acquisition is effected is a purchase at retail. An acquisition made for the purpose of resale is not a purchase at retail. Acquisition of a license to use or consume and the rental or lease of tangible personal property (other than for resale) is considered a purchase at retail [72 P.S. § 7201(f)(1)]. See ¶ 704 for an explanation of rentals and leases. Purchase at retail also includes the obtaining for a consideration of the taxable services added by the Act of August 4, 1991, § 1. See ¶ 703 for a discussion of these services.

- *Use tax credit*

A credit against use tax is allowed with respect to tangible personal property purchased for use outside Pennsylvania equal to the amount of similar tax paid to another state if the other state grants substantially similar credits [72 P.S. § 7206(a)].

- *Alternate imposition*

Ordinarily, use tax is imposed on the original purchase price of tangible personal property, but there are two situations in which the original purchase price of tangible personal property may not be the basis for imposition of the use tax:

(1) If property was purchased at least six months before its first taxable use in Pennsylvania, the taxpayer may elect to pay tax on a substituted basis (fair market value at the time of its first taxable use). For this purpose the fair market value is the prevailing market price of similar tangible personal property at the time and place of first taxable use. An election to pay tax on a substituted basis must be made at the time of filing a tax return, which must be done within six months from the date the return for the first taxable use is due [72 P.S. § 7201(g)(5)]. Prior to August 4, 1991, this election could be made within one year of the due date for the return for the first taxable use.

(2) If a dealer of certain vehicles uses a vehicle originally purchased for resale for a period no longer than one year, the dealer may elect to pay use tax on its fair rental value for the period of use. Vehicles included in this category are motor vehicles, trailers, or semitrailers (but not wreckers, parts trucks, delivery trucks, or courtesy cars) [61 Pa. Code § 31.7(c)(2)].

- *Reports and payment of tax*

Licensees report and pay use tax at the time their regular sales tax return is due [61 Pa. Code § 31.7(a)(2)]. See ¶ 603 and ¶ 605 for an explanation of due dates for reports and payment of sales tax. Non-licensees report and pay use tax on or before the 20th day of the month succeeding the month in which the liability for the tax is incurred and are not required to file returns for months in which no use tax liability is incurred [61 Pa. Code § 34.3(a)(5)]. Purchasers licensed by the Bureau and nonresident purchasers pay the tax directly to the Bureau of Sales and Use Tax [61 Pa. Code § 31.7(a)(3)]. Purchasers who reside in Pennsylvania (except those who reside in Philadelphia County) have the option (1) to pay use tax directly to the Bureau or (2) to pay use tax to the treasurer of their county of residence [61 Pa. Code § 31.7(a)(3)].

¶722

Mail-Order Sales

• *Obligation to collect use tax*

One area in which it has been difficult for states to demonstrate sufficient nexus to require collection of use tax by vendors is the mail-order business. Constitutional challenges to the use tax usually involve the obligation of out-of-state vendors to collect tax on sales to a state's residents.

• *National Bellas Hess*

In the landmark mail order case *National Bellas Hess, Inc. v. Department of Revenue*, 386 U.S. 753 (1967), the U.S. Supreme Court held that the requirement that out-of-state vendors collect use tax is unconstitutional when the vendor did no more than communicate with customers by mail or common carrier (*i.e.*, did not have a substantial nexus with the taxing state). The *National Bellas Hess* case has not ceased to be controversial since the day it was decided. States have continued strong efforts to establish that the regular exploitation of markets (*i.e.*, economic presence) within their states constitutes sufficient nexus to require the collection of use taxes by mail-order vendors.

• *Quill Corporation*

The North Dakota Supreme Court found sufficient nexus to justify the state's requirement of collection of North Dakota use tax by a Delaware corporation that sold its products through advertising (in catalogues, flyers, advertisements in nationally distributed publications) and through telephone solicitation, pointing out that "the direct marketing of the 1990s bears little resemblance to the mail order of the 1960s." The U.S. Supreme Court, however, reversed the North Dakota decision, ruling that the bright-line test of physical presence required by *National Bellas Hess* is necessary in order to satisfy the requirements of the Commerce Clause [*Quill Corp. v. North Dakota*, 504 U.S. 298 (1992)]. "Physical presence" is ordinarily understood to be offices, property, or employees within a state.

The U.S. Supreme Court, however, overturned *Bellas Hess* to the extent that it requires a physical presence for purposes of the Due Process Clause, thus establishing a *minimum contact requirement for the Due Process Clause and a substantial nexus requirement for the Commerce Clause*. The "economic presence" found to exist in the *Quill* case (*i.e.*, extensive solicitation through various media) was more than sufficient to satisfy the Due Process requirement that there be some minimum connection between a state and a taxpayer and that the tax be related to state benefits received by the taxpayer. However, requiring out-of-state vendors who have no physical presence in a state to withhold the state's use tax violates the Commerce Clause of the U.S. Constitution. In the *Quill* case, a lack of physical presence was found, even though the taxpayer retained title to licensed software present in North Dakota. Since the Supreme Court abandoned the Due Process nexus with respect to mail-order sales, leaving only the protection of the Commerce Clause, Congress is now able, if it chooses, to pass legislation that changes the result of *National Bellas Hess*.

In anticipation of Federal legislation relating to remote sellers, the Independent Fiscal Office will be required to provide a report on revenues to be collected if such legislation is enacted. That report will be due 90 days after notice is published in the Pennsylvania Bulletin that Federal legislation has been enacted.

• *L.L. Bean*

In 1986 the Commonwealth Court ruled that an insufficient nexus exists to impose the requirement to collect use tax even where the company, L.L. Bean, sells to a Pennsylvania outlet, retains (once) an attorney to represent its interest in a bankruptcy hearing, maintains an "800" number in Pennsylvania, accepts payment by credit cards issued by Pennsylvania banks, and sends employees to the Pennsylvania outlet to assure that there is no improper use of its trademark. The court held that the Pennsylvania outlet was not a representative of L.L. Bean [*L.L. Bean, Inc. v. Cmwlth.*, 516 A.2d 820 (Pa.Commw. 1986)].

• *Bloomingdale's By Mail*

This 1989 case involved mail-order sales made in Pennsylvania by a mail-order affiliate (Bloomingdale's By Mail, Ltd.) of a retailer (Bloomingdale's) that makes retail sales in Pennsylvania. Bloomingdale's By Mail (By Mail) is incorporated in New York and conducts its nationwide mail-order business from locations in Virginia and Connecticut. All written or telephone purchase orders are received at these facilities, and merchandise is shipped from these facilities by common carrier or U.S. mail. By Mail has no retail stores, distribution house, sales house, warehouse, business location, office, or employees in Pennsylvania. By Mail makes direct solicitations of sales in Pennsylvania only through its catalogs that refer customers to By Mail's fulfillment center in Connecticut for customer assistance, merchandise return or exchange, or other services. Bloomingdale's operates retail stores in Pennsylvania and employs personnel to make sales to Pennsylvania customers. The court ruled that the mere existence in Pennsylvania of retail stores that are affiliated with a mail-order business does not support a finding of sufficient nexus to impose use tax collection obligations upon By Mail [*Bloomingdale's By Mail, Ltd. v. Cmwlth.*, 567 A.2d 773 (Pa.Commw. 1989)].

• *House of Lloyd*

In a 1996 case, the Pennsylvania Commonwealth Court ruled that the maintenance of a significant sales force in the Commonwealth satisfied the substantial nexus requirement of the *Complete Auto Transit* test. House of Lloyd was a Missouri corporation selling its products in Pennsylvania through a network of home party hostesses. Its sales distribution system consisted of a hierarchy of district managers (who had contracts with House of Lloyd), supervisors, demonstrators, and hostesses. District managers, supervisors, and demonstrators received sample kits (retail value, $500 each) from House of Lloyd to be used in promoting and selling its products. The court ruled that, even though House of Lloyd may have no facilities, real property, or regular employees in Pennsylvania, it directed and controlled a very large sales force in Pennsylvania dedicated exclusively to promoting and selling its products. It equipped its sales force with sample products, catalogs and order forms; trained its salespeople how to recruit, how to promote its product, and how to close sales; and maintained constant communication with its salespeople at all levels. It awarded prizes to distributors and hostesses as a reward for successful sales and promotional activities. These activities constituted a substantial nexus in Pennsylvania; therefore, the sample kits, catalogs, order forms, and prizes were held to subject to the Pennsylvania use tax [*House of Lloyd v. Cmwlth.*, 684 A.2d 213 (Pa.Commw. 1996), aff'd, 708 A.2d 806 (Pa. 1998)].

Sales and Income Taxes Differ

Imposition of taxes on or measured by net income is restricted by P.L. 86-272; imposition of sales and use taxes is not. See the explanation of P.L. 86-272 at ¶913. Therefore, nexus for purposes of imposition of sales and use taxes is "thinner" than nexus for corporate net income tax purposes. For example, employment of "missionary salesmen" in a state is sufficient nexus for sales and use tax purposes but not for corporate net income tax purposes. See the explanation of the *U.S. Tobacco* case at ¶913.

¶723 Exemptions

In general, the exemptions for use tax purposes are the same as those for sales tax purposes. Generally, a purchaser who is not subject to tax on the "sale at retail" to him of property or services is not subject to tax on their use *except* (1) a nonexempt purchaser who acquires taxable goods or services from an out-of-state vendor or (2) an exempt purchaser who makes a use inconsistent with his/her exemption [61 Pa. Code § 31.7(d)(1)]. Exemptions are explained at ¶ 705—713.

There are two additional exemptions for use tax purposes:

(1)   *Establishment of permanent business or residence in Pennsylvania:* If a nonresident person or business entity not actually doing business in Pennsylvania brings property into Pennsylvania in connection with the establishment of a permanent business or residence, no use tax is due if the property was purchased at least six months before it was brought into Pennsylvania or before the establishment of the business or residence in Pennsylvania (whichever occurs first). This provision does not apply to tangible personal property temporarily brought into Pennsylvania for the performance of contracts for the construction, reconstruction, remodeling, repairing, or maintenance of real estate [61 Pa. Code § 31.7(d)(2)].

(2)   *Property brought into Pennsylvania by nonresidents:* If a nonresident purchases tangible personal property outside Pennsylvania and then brings it into Pennsylvania for use for a period no longer than seven days (or for any period of time for tourists or vacationers), the property is not subject to use tax in Pennsylvania. The seven-day period is calculated on a cumulative basis within any 12 consecutive months [61 Pa. Code § 31.7(d)(3)].

HOTEL OCCUPANCY TAX

¶724 Hotel Occupancy Tax

A 6% excise tax is imposed on the rent for occupancy of a room or rooms in a hotel in Pennsylvania. This tax must be collected by the operator from occupants [72 P.S. § 7210]. Occupancy of a room includes, but is not limited to, sleeping rooms, living quarters, housekeeping accommodations, sample rooms, display rooms, function rooms, meeting rooms, banquet and dining rooms, ballrooms, theaters, auditoriums, kitchens, offices, lobby space, garage facilities, and commercial establishments) [61 Pa. Code § 38.1(c)]. Rent includes charges for services, facilities or accommodations. Services and accommodations available to the general public as well as occupants are not considered rent if hotel occupants pay the same rate as the general public and the charges are separately stated.

Effective January 22, 2019, booking agents are responsible for collecting state and local hotel occupancy taxes on rent they charge for a room [72 P.S. § 7210]. This includes taxes on accommodation fees and any other amount charged by the booking agent [72 P.S. § 7201]. Hotel operators are not responsible for collecting hotel occupancy taxes on a booking agent's accommodation fees [72 P.S. § 7210].

• *Enabling legislation and administration*

The hotel occupancy tax is imposed under the authority of the Pennsylvania Tax Reform Code [72 P.S. § 7201] and is administered by the Pennsylvania Department of Revenue.

• *Meals*

Meals sold for on-premise consumption are subject to sales and use taxes, not the hotel occupancy tax.

• *Exemptions*

The hotel occupancy tax does not apply to the following [61 Pa. Code § 38.2]: permanent residents; diplomatic representatives of foreign governments; the U.S. government, its agencies, and their employees if occupancy is for official purposes; credit unions; Pennsylvania public authorities; cooperative agricultural associations subject to the corporate net income tax; electric cooperative corporations formed under the Electric Cooperative Corporation Act; and organizations exempt from sales and use taxes if they have received approval. Sale of meals to a religious or charitable organization or nonprofit educational institution are exempt if the conditions of the regulations are met [61 Pa. Code § 38.1(e)(2)].

The Commonwealth Court has held that the exemption for the U.S. government does not require direct billing to the U.S. government. When employees of the federal government pay for the rooms but are reimbursed by the federal government, the persons are functioning instruments of the federal government and therefore exempt [*Egner v. Cmwlth.*, 557 A.2d 1157 (Pa.Commw. 1989)]. The Department of Revenue takes the position that this exemption does not apply to food, beverages, or other purchases and that in order to claim the exemption, the employee must submit a Sales and Use Tax Exemption Certificate with a copy of his or her orders or a letter from his or her supervisor attached. If a copy of orders or a supervisor's letter is not presented, the hotel operator is required to collect the tax [*Pennsylvania Tax Update No. 31*, Pennsylvania Department of Revenue, May/June 1990].

• *Entities not exempt*

Occupancy by employees or representatives of the Commonwealth, its instrumentalities or political subdivisions is not exempt from hotel occupancy tax, regardless of the nature of their business. Occupancy by employees or representatives of State credit unions is not exempt. Exemption from the Pennsylvania sales and use tax granted to persons, organizations, or institutions (including religious, charitable, educational, and like institutions) are not applicable to the hotel occupancy tax; and those persons, organizations, or institutions must pay tax upon their occupancy of hotel rooms [61 Pa. Code § 38.2(f)].

Not Taxable for Hotel Room Rental Tax Purposes

The Department of Revenue has made it clear that the regulations under Chapter 38 of the Pennsylvania Code apply only to the hotel occupancy tax; they do not apply to the hotel room rental tax. Therefore, 61 Pa. Code § 38.2(f) cannot properly be cited as a basis for a county government to impose a hotel room rental tax upon a Commonwealth official or employee staying overnight in a hotel in the course of performing official Commonwealth business [61 Pa. Code § 38a.1(d)(2)].

• *Innkeepers—Licenses and taxes*

Overnight accommodations provided by religious organization during its retreats did not amount to a "hotel" under ordinance defining a hotel as a structure that was available to provide overnight lodging, and thus accommodations were not subject to 3% county tax for hotel room rentals, where organization held itself out as a religious facility and did not provide lodging to persons merely seeking over accommodations. *Susquehanna County Commissioners v. Montrose Bible Conference* 138 A.3d 142 (2016).

PUBLIC TRANSPORTATION ASSISTANCE ACT

¶725 Public Transportation Assistance Fund Taxes and Fees

Act No. 26 of 1991, as amended, established a special fund known as the Public Transportation Assistance Fund [74 Pa.C.S. § 1814]and imposed taxes and fees that must be deposited into the Public Transportation Assistance Fund to be used for funding urban common carrier mass transit [72 P.S. § 9301(a); 74 Pa.C.S. § 1310].

There are three Public Transportation Assistance Fund taxes and fees: (1) a new tire fee (discussed at ¶726); (2) a motor vehicle lease tax (discussed at ¶727); and (3) motor vehicle rental and carsharing fees (discussed at ¶728). The Public Transportation Assistance Fund taxes and fees are in addition to sales or use tax and are excluded from the computation of tax for sales and use tax purposes [61 Pa. Code § 47.19(a)(5)].

- *Registration*

Persons who make sales, rentals, or leases subject to a Public Transportation Assistance Fund tax or fee are required to apply for a Public Transportation Assistance Tax License Number on a form prescribed by the Department [61 Pa. Code § 47.19(a)(2)]. This registration is separate from registration for sales tax purposes (discussed at ¶506). Registration can be done by completing a paper PA Enterprise Registration Form (PA-100) or by registering on-line using the PA Open for Business Web site at www.paopen4business.state.pa.us. Paper registration forms (PA-100) and instructions may be obtained (1) by telephoning the toll-free FACT & Information Line 1-888-PATAXES (1-888-728-2937); (2) downloading the form from the Internet at www.revenue.state.pa.us; or (3) contacting the Taxpayer Service & Information Center at (717) 787-1064; Service for Taxpayers with Special Hearing and/or Speaking Needs 1-800-447-3020 (TT Only) [www.revenue.state.pa.us/revenue/cwp/view.asp?A=299&QUESTION_ID=209030].

- *Returns and payment of taxes*

Returns must be made on forms prescribed by the Department (currently PA-4) [61 Pa. Code § 47.19(3)]. The Department distributes returns for the convenience of the licensee. However, no licensee is excused from liability for failure to report and pay the Public Transportation Assistance Fund taxes and fees because of failure to receive a return.

Payment: All taxes and fees are due and payable concurrently with the return. The due date for each period is preprinted on the return.

- *Sales and use tax statutes and regulations apply*

Sales and use tax statutes [72 P.S. §§ 7201—7282]and sales and use tax regulations apply to the Public Transportation Assistance Fund taxes and fees [61 Pa. Code § 47.19(a)(8)].

- *Direct payment permits*

A direct payment permit issued under 61 Pa. Code § 34.4 (discussed at ¶606) may be used in conjunction with the Public Transportation Assistance Fund taxes and fees [61 Pa. Code § 34.4].

¶726 New Tire Fee

A tire fee is imposed at the rate of $1.00 per tire on each sale in Pennsylvania of new tires for highway use. "Sale" for this purpose means a transfer of the ownership of new tires for a consideration (whether absolute or conditional) and by whatever means effected. The term "sale" does not include a rental or lease [61 Pa. Code § 47.19(b)(1)]. "Highway use" means the use of a tire on a vehicle that is required to be licensed for highway use. If a tire is of the type used on a vehicle normally required to be licensed, it is presumed to be for highway use [61 Pa. Code § 47.19(b)(1)]. The sale of new tires in conjunction with the sale of other property is taxable [61 Pa. Code § 47.19(b)(2)].

- *Collection of tire fee*

The tire fee is collected by the seller from the purchaser and remitted to the Department of Revenue [72 P.S. § 9301(c)]. If the vendor fails to collect, report, or remit the tire fee, the vendor is assessed the fee. If the purchaser does not pay the tire fee to the vendor, the purchaser is assessed the tire fee [61 Pa. Code § 47.19(b)(2)].

- *Returns and payment of tax*

The tire fee is reported and paid along with the other Public Transportation Assistance Fund taxes and fees. See discussion at ¶725.

• *Exclusions and exemptions*

No exclusions or exemptions from the new tire fee are allowed except the exclusion for governmental entities provided under sales and use tax provisions [72 P.S. § 9301(c)]. See the discussion of exempt governmental entities at ¶705. There is no exclusion for exempt organizations or businesses engaged in manufacturing, processing, farming, dairying, printing, mining, or rendering a public utility service [61 Pa. Code § 47.19(b)(2)].

Thus, only the following transactions are excluded from payment of the tire fee [61 Pa. Code § 47.19(a), (b)]:

(1) Sale of tires not for highway use.

(2) Sale of tires to governmental entities.

(3) Rental or lease of new tires (the lessor is required to pay the tire fee on the purchase).

(4) Sale of used tires (including retreads or recaps).

(5) Sale of tires delivered to the purchaser at a location outside Pennsylvania (subsequent use of the tires within Pennsylvania is not subject to the tire fee).

• *Examples of taxable sales*

The following examples, adapted from 61 Pa. Code § 47.19(b)(4), are examples of taxable sales:

Example 1: Trevor buys an automobile (new or used) with four new tires and one spare tire. His tire fee is $5 on the sale of the five new tires.

Example 2: Tom's Leasing Company buys new replacement tires for its fleet. The purchase of the new replacement tires is subject to the tire fee.

Example 3: A church buys a new replacement tire for a vehicle registered in the name of the church. This purchase is subject to the tire fee.

Example 4: Larry's Trucking Company (LTC) buys tires from a vendor outside Pennsylvania, and the tires are delivered to its place of business in Pennsylvania. LTC must pay the tire fee on this purchase.

Example 5: New Car Dealership (NCD) removes an automobile from its inventory and makes a taxable use of it for sales and use tax purposes. NCD must pay a tire fee directly to the Department.

Example 6: A garage repairs a damaged motor vehicle and in the process replaces a tire on the vehicle. The sale of this tire is subject to the tire fee without regard to whether the cost of the repair is covered by an insurance contract.

• *Examples of nontaxable sales*

The following examples, adapted from 61 Pa. Code § 47.19(b)(5), are examples of sales not subject to the tire fee:

Example 1: New Car Dealership (NCD) purchases tires for a vehicle to be sold. NCD's purchase is not taxable. When NCD sells the vehicle to a purchaser for highway use, the sale is subject to the tire fee.

Example 2: Leslie rents a vehicle with new tires from a leasing company. Leslie does not have to pay a tire fee; the vendor was responsible for payment of the tire fee when it purchased the new tires.

Example 3: Manufacturer purchases new tires for use on forklifts not required to be licensed for highway use. This purchase is not taxable.

Example 4: Trucking Company buys new tires from an out-of-state vendor, and the tires are delivered to Trucking at an out-of-state location. This transaction is not taxable, even if the tires are subsequently used in Pennsylvania.

¶726

Example 5: Retail Tire Dealer (RTD) buys tires from a manufacturer for resale. Because RTD is not purchasing the tires for highway use, the purchase is not taxable. RTD's subsequent sale of the tires to customers for highway use will, however, be subject to the tire fee.

¶727 Motor Vehicle Lease Tax

In addition to the basic sales and use taxes imposed on the lease of motor vehicles, an additional tax of 3% of the total lease price charged is imposed [72 P.S. §9301(d)(1)]. A "motor vehicle" for this purpose is a self-propelled device in, upon, or by which a person or property is or may be transported or drawn upon a public highway except tractors, power shovels, road machinery, agricultural machinery, and vehicles that move upon or are guided by a track or trolley [61 Pa. Code §47.19(c)(1)].

The term "motor vehicle" also does not include trucks in class 4 or higher as defined in 75 Pa.C.S. §1916(a)(1) [72 P.S. §9301(d)(2)]. A "lease" for this purpose is a contract for the use of a motor vehicle for 30 days or more [61 Pa. Code §47.19(c)(1)]. If a lessor fails to collect, report, or remit this fee, the lessor is responsible for the tax. If the lessee does not pay the tax to the lessor, the lessee is responsible for the tax. See ¶704 for an explanation of taxation of rentals and leases under the sales and use tax provisions.

• *Base*

The motor vehicle lease tax is imposed on the total "lease price" charged. "Lease price" means the full consideration paid or delivered (or promised to be paid or delivered) to the lessor for a lease period under a lease agreement (whether in money or otherwise) even though the consideration is separately stated and designated as a payment for down payment, service, maintenance, insurance, repairs, depreciation, excess mileage fees, or similar charges [61 Pa. Code §47.19(c)(1)].

Accelerated payment or buyout purchase price: The lease price also includes an accelerated payment or buyout purchase price whether or not made in connection with the termination of the lease [61 Pa. Code §47.19(c)(1)(i)].

Option purchase price, penalty fees, and damage fees: The lease price does not include the option purchase price, penalty fees for early termination of the lease, damage fees, or similar charges [61 Pa. Code §47.19(c)(1)(ii)].

Sales tax: The lease price does not include sales tax imposed on the lease price [61 Pa. Code §47.19(c)(1)(iii)].

Credits and refunds: Credits or refunds that reduce the lease price also reduce the amount subject to tax even though the credits or refunds are issued after termination of the lease [61 Pa. Code §47.19(c)(1)(iv)].

Separate statement required: If a lessor fails to separately state the lease price of other property included in the sale (*e.g.,* a trailer) from the lease of a motor vehicle, the total lease price is subject to tax [61 Pa. Code §47.19(c)(1)(v)].

Class 4 trucks: Lease payments for the use of trucks in Class 4 or higher (as defined in 75 Pa.C.S. §1916(a)(1)) are not subject to the motor vehicle lease tax [61 Pa. Code §47.19(c)(2)].

• *Collection of tax*

The motor vehicle lease tax is collected by the lessor from the lessee and remitted to the Department of Revenue. If the lessor fails to collect, report, or remit the tax, the lessor is assessed the fee. If the lessee does not pay the tax to the lessor, the lessee is assessed the tax [61 Pa. Code §47.19(c)(2)].

• *Returns and payment of tax*

The motor vehicle lease tax is reported and paid along with the other Public Transportation Assistance Fund taxes and fees. See discussion at ¶725.

• *Exemptions*

Since the motor vehicle lease tax is imposed only on transactions subject to the sales and use tax, a transaction that is exempt for sales and use tax purposes is also exempt for motor vehicle lease tax purposes [72 P.S. §9301(d)]. See ¶514 for an explanation of sales and use tax exemption certificates.

Lease vs. Rental

A lease for purposes of the motor vehicle lease tax is a contract for the use of a motor vehicle for 30 days or more. Payments made subject to a lease contract are subject to tax at the rate of 3%. A rental for purposes of the motor vehicle rental fee (¶728) is a contract for the use of a motor vehicle for less than 30 days. Motor vehicle rentals are subject to a fee of $2 per day or part of a day.

¶728 Motor Vehicle Rental and Carsharing Fees

• *Base and rate*

Motor vehicle rental fee: In addition to the basic sales and use taxes imposed on the rental of motor vehicles, a fee of $2 for each day or part of a day for which the vehicle is rented is imposed [72 P.S. §9301(e)].

See ¶704 for an explanation of taxation of rentals and leases under sales and use tax provisions. Vehicle rentals are also taxable under the Vehicle Rental Tax, explained at ¶730.

Carsharing fee: A fee is imposed on carsharing [72 P.S. §9301(e.1)]. For rentals of:

— less than two hours, the fee is 25 cents;

— two to three hours, the fee is 50 cents;

— more than three but less than four hours, the fee is $1.25; and

— four hours or more, the fee is $2.

The carsharing fee applies to rentals of motor vehicles that are subject to sales tax.

"Carsharing" means a membership-based service that provides an alternative to personal car ownership and:

— does not require a trip-specific written agreement each time a member rents a vehicle;

— does not require an attendant to be present at the beginning or end of a rental;

— offers members access to a dispersed network of shared vehicles 24-hours per day, seven days per week, 365 days per year; and

— allows a vehicle to be rented on a per-minute, per-hour, per-day, or per-trip basis, and at per-mile or per-kilometer rates that typically include fuel, insurance, and maintenance.

• *Motor vehicle*

For purposes of the motor vehicle rental fee, a "motor vehicle" is a self-propelled device in, upon, or by which a person or property is or may be transported or drawn upon a public highway *except* tractors, power shovels, road machinery, agricultural machinery, and vehicles that move upon or are guided by a truck or trolley [61 Pa.

Code § 47.19(d)(1)]. A "rental" is a contract for the use of a motor vehicle for less than 30 days [61 Pa. Code § 47.19(d)(1)]. If a motor vehicle is rented for less than 30 days, and the use of the motor vehicle subsequently extends beyond a 29-day period, the transaction remains a rental and the rental payments continue to be subject to the fee until the rental contract is terminated.

• *Examples of taxable rentals*

The following examples are adapted from 61 Pa. Code § 47.19(d)(4):

Example 1: Suzanne rents an automobile from a rental company for five hours. The rental is subject to a $2 motor vehicle rental fee.

Example 2: Bill rents an automobile from a rental company for one day and returns it to the lessor five hours after the end of the rental period. If Bill is charged the daily rental rate plus an additional charge for the period after the end of the rental period, a rental fee of $4 is due.

Example 3: Phyllis rents an automobile from a rental company under a daily rental contract. The rental is subject to a $2 per day rental fee. Phyllis returns the car at the end of the 15th day and enters into a lease contract. For the first 15 days, Phyllis must pay a rental fee of $2 per day. For the period after the 15th day, she is required to pay a tax of 3% of the lease payment. See "Motor Vehicle Lease Tax," above.

• *Collection of tax*

The motor vehicle rental fee is collected by the lessor from the lessee and remitted to the Department of Revenue. If the vendor fails to collect, report, or remit the fee, the vendor is assessed the fee. If the purchaser does not pay the fee to the vendor, the purchaser is assessed the fee [61 Pa. Code § 47.19(d)(2)].

• *Returns and payment of tax*

The motor vehicle rental fee is reported and paid along with the other Public Transportation Assistance Fund taxes and fees. See discussion at ¶ 725.

• *Exemptions*

Since the motor vehicle rental fee is imposed only on transactions subject to the sales and use tax, a transaction that is exempt for sales and use tax purposes is also exempt for motor vehicle rental fee purposes [72 P.S. § 9301(e)]. See ¶ 514 for an explanation of sales and use tax exemption certificates.

VEHICLE RENTAL TAX (VRT)

¶730 Outline of Tax

The vehicle rental tax (VRT) is imposed on vehicle rental contracts for a period of 29 or fewer consecutive days.

• *Rate of tax*

The tax must be collected, at the time the motor vehicle is rented in Pennsylvania, by the vehicle rental company. The rate is 2% of the purchase price of the rental [72 P.S. § 8602-A]. This tax is in addition to the $2 rental fee imposed under the Public Transportation Assistance Act. See ¶ 725.

For purposes of this tax, a taxable "motor vehicle" is a private passenger motor vehicle designed to transport 15 or fewer passengers or a truck, trailer, or semitrailer used in the transportation of property (other than commercial freight) that is rented without a driver and is part of a fleet of five or more passenger vehicles used for that purpose and owned or leased by the same person or entity. A "vehicle rental company" is any business entity engaged in the business of renting motor vehicles in Pennsylvania with a fleet of five or more rental vehicles [72 P.S. § 8601-A]. Unless otherwise noted, the provisions of Article II of the Tax Reform Code (relating to sales and use taxes) shall apply to the vehicle rental tax [72 P.S. § 8603-A(b)].

• *Exclusions*

If the rental of a motor vehicle is exempt from Pennsylvania sales and use taxes, the rental is also exempt from the vehicle rental tax. A purchaser must support an exemption claim by submitting a completed Pennsylvania exemption certificate setting forth a valid basis for exemption. This may be the same exemption certificate used to claim an exemption from the sales or use tax, but the exemption certificate must clearly indicate that the purchaser is claiming an exemption from the vehicle rental tax. This can be done either by checking the appropriate blocks on the recently revised exemption certificate form or by checking the paragraph labeled "other" on the older form and explaining that an exemption is being claimed from the vehicle rental tax.

• *Taxable rentals*

The following, adapted from 61 Pa. Code § 47.20(c)(2)(i), are examples of rentals subject to the VRT:

> **Example 1:** Austin rents an automobile from a vehicle rental company for 14 days. Due to a death in his family (without entering into a new contract), Austin continues to use the car of a day-by-day basis and eventually returns it on the 36th day. The rental continues to be governed by the rental contract for the entire 36-day period, and the rental payment is subject to the VRT.

> **Example 2:** Barry rents an automobile from a rental company for 10 days. The rental contract provides for an additional charge for excess mileage and a pick-up and drop-off fee. Barry elects to obtain a vehicle damage waiver, a child's car seat, and a car top carrier. Because of the charges for excess mileage, all of the items are included in the rental payment and are subject to the VRT.

> **Example 3:** Connie rents an automobile for seven days from Ronnie, who owns two and leases 28 of the vehicles he rents. Because he has five or more rental vehicles *available for rent*, Ronnie operates a vehicle rental company, and Connie's rental payments are subject to the VRT.

> **Example 4:** Donnie rents a truck to transport a used living room set to Johnnie's hunting camp. Because the furniture does not qualify as commercial freight, the rental payments are subject to the VRT.

• *Nontaxable rentals*

The following, adapted from 61 Pa. Code § 47.20(c)(2)(ii), are examples of rentals not subject to the VRT:

> **Example 1:** Zeb rents a rental vehicle from Donnie for 28 days. Subsequently, Zeb decides to keep the car more than 28 days. He returns the car to Donnie after 28 days, terminates the rental contract, and pays the VRT. Zeb and Donnie enter into a lease agreement whereby Zeb rents the vehicle for two years. The second transaction is a lease agreement, not a rental, and is not subject to the VRT.

> **Example 2:** Yolanda rents a car from a car dealership that has only three vehicles available for rental. Because the dealership has fewer than five cars available for rental, it is not a vehicle rental company and Yolanda's rental payments are not subject to the VRT.

> **Example 3:** X Furniture Company (XFC) rents a truck used exclusively to deliver its own manufactured furniture products to its customers. This furniture qualifies as commercial freight, and the truck rental is not subject to the VRT.

¶731 Reporting and Remittance

The vehicle rental tax is reported and remitted in the same manner as the tax imposed by the Public Transportation Assistance Act, except that, no later than February 15 of each calendar year, each vehicle rental company must file a report with the Department of Revenue on a form prescribed by the Department. The report must include the amount of tax remitted during the previous calendar year and the total amount of motor vehicle licensing and title fees imposed by Pennsylvania under 75 Pa.C.S. (relating to vehicles) on the vehicle rental company's rental vehicles and paid to Pennsylvania by the vehicle rental company in the previous calendar year [72 P.S. § 8603-A(a)].

¶732 Credit Against the Tax

When reconciling the reports and remittances filed during the previous calendar year with the annual report, the Department will allow a credit against the vehicle rental tax equal to the total amount of licensing and title fees imposed by Pennsylvania under 75 Pa.C.S. on the vehicle rental company's rental vehicles and paid to Pennsylvania by the vehicle rental company in the previous calendar year. The Department will refund to the taxpayer the credit verified from the annual report. The amount of the credit cannot exceed the amount of tax collected and remitted by the taxpayer for the calendar year for which the claim is made [72 P.S. § 8603-A(b)].

SALES AND USE TAXES

CHAPTER 8

EXAMINATION, ASSESSMENT, AND APPEAL

¶801 Examination

The Pennsylvania sales and use taxes are self-assessed taxes, but the Department of Revenue can examine sales and use tax returns and impose additional tax if the returns are incorrect. Tax examinations conform with the following rules with respect to verification and audits.

• *Verification of returns, documents, and transactions*

The Department's authorized agents have the power to conduct field examinations (at the location where a taxpayer's records are kept, whether held on the taxpayer's premises or by the taxpayer's agent, representative, employee, accountant, or custodian) for the purpose of examining and verifying books, records, papers, and other documents in order to calculate and assess the sales and use taxes. Taxpayers are required to admit the Department and its authorized agents and to provide them with the necessary means, facilities, and opportunities to examine the records [61 Pa. Code § 35.1(a)(1)].

• *Audits*

When the Department decides to conduct a tax audit, the auditor reviews and verifies the following: (1) the proper charging of tax on taxable transactions; (2) the proper reporting and remittance of tax collected; and (3) the proper payment of tax upon taxable acquisitions [61 Pa. Code § 35.1(a)(2)(ii)].

The auditor may examine periods not barred by statute. The Department may determine the liability based upon a reasonable statistical sample or test audit if records are incomplete or if a complete audit would impose an undue burden on the Department [72 P.S. § 10003.21(b)]. After reviewing and analyzing available records, the nature of the business, the type and frequency of sales, and other pertinent information, the Department will decide whether to examine all the records for the entire audit period or whether to perform a block test audit or a random sample procedure, or some combination of procedures. A block sample is a group of items selected as one unit from a population (*e.g.,* all invoices numbered 100 to 200 or all transactions for the month of May). A random sample is a sample of size "n" selected in a way so that every different sample of "n" elements in the population has an equal probability of being selected. The population is the entire field of entries, documents, or records, from which the sampling is to be made. Procedures to be followed by auditors are specified in the regulations [61 Pa. Code § 35.1(a)(2)(ii)(A—B)].

Border Audit Agreements

Pennsylvania has entered into sales tax border audit agreements with New York, Ohio, and West Virginia. These border audit agreements allow the states to share sales tax audit information and lists of customers who have purchased items but have not paid sales tax to either state. These agreements are designed to reach untaxed sales by merchants on both sides of the borders between these states and are part of a three-pronged program to (1) license firms that should collect sales tax, (2) bill use tax to customers who have not paid it, and (3) educate taxpayers about their use tax responsibilities [*Pennsylvania Tax Update No. 12*, Pennsylvania Department of Revenue, July 1986].

¶802 Procedures and Administration

The Department of Revenue has the responsibility of making sure taxpayers conform to the tax laws and pay the required sales and use taxes. A notice of assessment and demand for payment (setting forth the basis of an assessment) must be mailed to the taxpayer by certified mail [72 P.S. §7230]. With respect to sales and use taxes, this administrative review process is called assessment. See ¶4602 for an explanation of administrative review. If, upon review of any sales/use tax return, the Department determines that the true amount of tax due is greater than the amount of tax shown on the return, it will determine the proper amount of tax. A notice of assessment for the deficiency (the difference between the amount of tax determined by the Department to be due and the amount shown on the return) and the reasons for the assessment will be sent to the taxpayer. The deficiency must be paid within 30 days after the *mailing date* of the assessment notice [72 P.S. §7231(b)]. For assessments issued by the Department of Revenue after December 31, 2007, the notice of assessment must be made by certified mail if the assessment is for $300 or more [72 P.S. § 7230]. A petition for reassessment must be filed with the Board of Appeals within 60 days of the mailing date of the assessment. Petitions can be filed electronically at the Board's website.

• *Estimated assessments*

If a taxpayer fails to file a required return, the Department can make an *estimated assessment* (based on available information) of the amount of tax owed by the taxpayer. The Department will send the taxpayer a notice of assessment for the deficiency, which must be paid within 30 days after the mailing date of the assessment notice [72 P.S. §7231(c)].

• *Penalties*

Additions, penalties, and interest are explained at ¶808.

• *Appeals*

If a taxpayer is not satisfied with an assessment, he/she has the right to petition the Department (*i.e.*, the Board of Appeals) for reassessment [72 P.S. §7232]. See ¶803.

• *Time limitations*

In general, the Department must make all assessments within three years after the later of (1) a return's filing date or (2) the end of the year in which the tax liability arose. The Department can make more than one assessment for a particular tax year in question during this three-year period [72 P.S. §7258].

• *Exceptions*

The exceptions to the three-year limitations period are (1) failure to file a return, (2) filing a false or fraudulent return with the intent to evade the tax, and (3) consent

¶802

by taxpayer to extend the limitation periods. There is no statute of limitations on assessment for failure to file or filing a false or fraudulent return. If a taxpayer consents, in writing, the statute of limitations on assessment may be extended over and over, so long as the last consent is made before the previous extension period expires [72 P.S. § § 7259—7261].

• *Immediate assessment, settlement, or collection to prevent tax avoidance*

The Department of Revenue may make an immediate assessment or settlement of (1) sales and use tax; (2) corporate net income tax; or (3) capital stock/franchise tax and any interest or penalty due if the Department finds that without immediate action the tax, interest, or penalty will be in jeopardy of not being collected because the taxpayer intends to do any of the following without paying the tax, interest, or penalty due [72 P.S. § 10003.14(a)]:

(1) Immediately leave Pennsylvania.

(2) Remove property from Pennsylvania used in activities that are taxable in Pennsylvania.

(3) Discontinue doing business in Pennsylvania.

(4) Do any other act that would prejudice or render ineffective (in whole or in part) proceedings to assess, settle, or collect any tax, interest, or penalty due.

Out-of-State Vendors' Compliance

The provision for immediate assessment discussed above and the expanded definition of "maintaining a place of business" (see ¶507) to include companies sending delivery trucks into Pennsylvania provides increased authority for the Pennsylvania Department of Revenue to ensure the compliance of out-of-state vendors with respect to the collection and remittance of Pennsylvania taxes.

¶803 Reassessment

Any taxpayer who is not satisfied with a Departmental assessment can petition for reassessment to the Board of Appeals of the Department of Revenue [72 P.S. § 7232]. For assessments issued prior to January 1, 2008 notice of an intention to file a petition for reassessment was required to be given to the Department within 30 days of the date the notice of assessment was mailed to the taxpayer, except that the Department for due cause could accept such notice within 90 days of the date the notice of assessment was mailed. The Department then, by registered mail and within 30 days after receiving the notice, supplied the taxpayer with a statement setting forth the basis of assessment. Further, that due date could be extended for up to 120 days. For petitions for reassessments made after December 31, 2007, no notice of intention to file for reassessment is required, and a petition for reassessment must be made within 60 days (90 days, prior to October 30, 2017) after the mailing date of the notice of assessment [72 P.S. § 9702(a)].

¶806 Petition for Refund

Time limitation for filing petition for refund: For a tax collected by the Department of Revenue, a taxpayer who has actually paid tax, interest, or penalty to the Commonwealth or to an agent or licensee of the Commonwealth authorized to collect taxes may petition the Department of Revenue for refund or credit of the tax, interest, or penalty. Except as otherwise provided by state, a petition for refund must be made to the Department within three years of actual payment of the tax, interest, or penalty [72 P.S. § 10003.1(a)]. The three-year statute of limitations begins running when the purchaser pays the tax (not when the vendor remits the tax to the Commonwealth), even if the payment is made in error [*Gray v. Cmwlth.*, 714 A.2d 1124 (Pa.Commw. 1998)].

Time limitation if credit not granted in audit report: The Department of Revenue may grant a refund or credit to a taxpayer for all tax periods covered by a departmental audit. If a credit is not granted by the Department in the audit report, the taxpayer must file a petition for refund for taxes paid with respect to the audit period within six months of the mailing date of the notice of assessment, determination or settlement, or within three years of actual payment of the tax, whichever is later [72 P.S. § 10003.1(b), effective to petitions filed after July 1, 2012].

Time limitation for petition for refund as result of assessment, determination, settlement, or appraisement: In the case of amounts paid is a result of an assessment, determination, settlement, or appraisement, a petition for refund must be filed with the Department of Revenue within six months of the actual payment of the tax [72 P.S. § 10003.1(d)].

Petition for review by Board of Finance and Revenue: A taxpayer may petition the Board of Finance and Revenue to review the decision and order of the Department of Revenue on a petition for refund. The petition for review must be filed with the Board within 90 days of the mailing date of a decision and order of the Department of Revenue upon a petition for refund [72 P.S. § 10003.1(e), effective for petitions filed after July 1, 2012].

Three-Year Rule Shortened in Some Circumstances

The position of the Department of Revenue is that § 10003.1(b) of the Tax Reform Code operates to shorten the general three-year refund provision set forth in § 1003.1(a) [72 P.S. § 1003.1(a),(b)]. According to the Department of Revenue overpayments made during an audit period may only be recovered by filing a petition for refund within six (6) months of the assessment date, even though the overpayments otherwise fall within the three-year refund provision. This position is being challenged on the grounds that the only consequence of failing to request audit period overpayments within six months of the assessment date is that the extended limitations period is lost. For example, what if there is a new case law, clarifying legislation or a change in policy or interpretation that gives rise to new refund claims? Under the Department's interpretation, taxpayers who may have had a recent audit would have their refund claims limited, even though there was no opportunity to have claimed the refund in the audit. Other taxpayers would have the full three-year period to claim refunds.

Late filing: Late filing of refund petitions results in denial of relief. The three-year statute of limitations for filing refund petitions is an absolute condition to the right to obtain relief. See, for example, *Biro v. Cmwlth.*, 707 A.2d 1205 (Pa.Commw. 1998), and *Davis v. Cmwlth.*, 719 A.2d 1121 (Pa.Commw. 1998).

• *Refunds and credits during audit*

The Department of Revenue is required to correct both underpayments and overpayments of tax for the audit period [*McNeil-PPC v. Cmwlth.*, 834 A.2d 515 (Pa. 2003), *rev'g* 802 A.2d 26 (Pa.Commw. 2002)] and *may* grant a refund or credit to a taxpayer for all periods covered by a departmental audit [72 P.S. § 10003.1(b)].

Sales and Use Taxes Considered in Tandem

In the *McNeil-PPC* case, which dealt with overpayments prior to the enactment of 72 P.S. § 10003.1(b), the Department of Revenue asserted that McNeil's Petition for Reassessment operated as a challenge only with respect to *use tax* deficiencies and that the overpaid *sales tax* could not be credited against the *use tax* deficiencies because sales and use taxes are separate taxes. The Pennsylvania Supreme Court, however, disagreed, concluding that the sales and use taxes serve the same purpose and should be treated in tandem in order to ensure that the same rate of tax is paid on a transaction without regard to whether the tax is remitted by the vendor (sales tax) or collected from the consumer (use tax). Thus, an audit cannot focus on sales tax to the exclusion of use tax and cannot focus on use tax to the exclusion of sales tax.

• *Department's response to McNeil-PPC opinion*

In response to the *McNeil-PPC* decision, the Department of Revenue issued *Sales Tax Bulletin 2004-2*, which applies to assessments issued on or after November 19, 2003.

Discovery of overpayment in normal course of audit: If an auditor discovers an overpayment of sales or use tax in the normal course of the examination of a taxpayer's returns and supporting records or a taxpayer discovers an overpayment to a vendor during the audit period under examination and provides sufficient evidence that the tax is not rightfully due the Commonwealth, the auditor *will be permitted* to grant a credit for the overpaid tax [*Sales Tax Bulletin 2004-2*].

Documentation required: In order for the auditor to make a determination that the taxpayer overpaid tax to a vendor, the taxpayer must provide (1) a copy of the source document for the transaction; (2) proof of tax payment; (3) a valid reason for exemption with adequate documentation if the reason requires additional documentation (*e.g.*, predominate use or direct use in manufacturing); and (4) taxpayer's attestation that no credit, memo, tax refund, or any similar reimbursement for tax overpayment was provided to the taxpayer. If insufficient evidence is submitted to the auditor, the auditor may deny the credit [*Sales Tax Bulletin 2004-02*].

Handling of overpayment: The tax payment made to a vendor that is determined to be nontaxable will be either subtracted from the final deficiency or added to any overpayment determined for taxpayer's returns. This credit will not enter into the calculations used in the test audit procedure [*Sales Tax Bulletin 2004-02*].

Does Refusal to Include Test Period Credits Distort Projections?

The refusal to include test period credits in the calculation of a projected deficiency seems to be contrary to the *McNeil-PPC* decision and raises a question of whether the projection would reasonably represent the actual tax liability.

Credit not granted: A notice of assessment will notify the taxpayer of the Department's finding of overpayment, underpayment, or no discrepancy for taxes due in the audit period. If, for any reason, the auditor does not grant credit for a sales or use tax overpayment made by the taxpayer for tax not rightfully due the Commonwealth for *any* time period covered by the audit, the taxpayer must file a petition for refund within six months of the mailing date of the notice of assessment for the audit period as required by 72 P.S. § 10003.1(b) or the taxpayer forfeits the right to claim a refund or credit for any overpayment made during the audit period [*Sales Tax Bulletin 2004-02*].

DOR Says Refund Petition Only Recourse for Denied Credits

The Department of Revenue takes the position in *Sales Tax Bulletin 2004-02* that if an auditor denies a taxpayer's requested credit, the taxpayer does not have the option to contest the denial when it challenges the assessment; the taxpayer's *only* recourse is to file a petition for refund, even if the credit arose during the credit period. Some tax practitioners believe that the Department's position is inconsistent with the refund statute and the *McNeil-PPC* decision. Therefore, in order to protect the right to claim a refund for a sales or use tax overpayment made during the audit period and not credited by the auditor, taxpayers should consider filing a petition for refund of such overpayments.

CAUTION

It is the Department of Revenue's position that all claims for overpayments made within an audit period must be made within six months of the assessment date. Thus, if you discover audit period overpayments six months and one day after the assessment, a refund request will be denied even though the overpayments might fall within the normal three-year refund statute.

Interest on overpayments vs. interest on underpayments: For the interest on refund payments and underpayments see ¶4612. Interest on refund payments does not begin to accrue in taxpayers' favor until 60 days after the petition is filed [72 P.S. §806.1(a)(4)]. Also, since 2004 interest on refunds is paid at the lower rate. If a taxpayer is granted credits against audit deficiencies (as required by *McNeil*), only the net deficiency is subject to interest. If a taxpayer is forced to request refunds, the gross deficiency is assessed interest from the date of underpayment while interest is paid on the refund at a lesser rate for a shorter period of time.

• *Contents of refund petition*

The refund petition must set forth in reasonable detail the grounds upon which the taxpayer claims refund of tax, interest or penalty and must be accompanied by an affidavit affirming that the facts contained in the petition are true and correct. The Department may hold necessary hearings at times and places of its determination; the petitioner will be notified of the times and places [72 P.S. § 7253(a)].

• *Special petitions*

A party to a transaction with respect to which the Department is assessing tax against another person may, within six (6) months after the Department files an assessment against the other person, file a special petition for refund, even if the taxpayer did not file a timely petition pursuant to 72 P.S. § 10003.1. The Department is not required to act on a special petition until there is a final determination of the propriety of the assessment filed against the other party. When a special petition is filed, overpayments by the petitioner will be refunded, but only to the extent of the actual tax paid by the other party to the transaction (without consideration of interest and penalties). The purpose of this section is to avoid duplicate payment of tax where the Department determines that one party to a transaction is subject to tax and another party to the transaction has actually paid the tax [72 P.S. § 7256].

• *Refund of sales attributed to bad debts*

A vendor may file a petition for refund of sales tax paid that is attributed to a bad debt if all of the following apply [72 P.S. § 7247.1(a)]:

(1) The purchaser fails to pay the vendor the total purchase price.

(2) The purchase price is written off, in whole or in part, as a bad debt on the books and records of the vendor or an affiliate of the vendor.

(3) The bad debt has been deducted for federal income tax purposes under IRC § 166.

Assignment of right to petition for refund: A vendor or lender may assign its right to petition for a refund of sales tax attributed to a bad debt to an affiliate [72 P.S. § 7247.1(c)].

Time limitation: The petition must be filed within three years of actual payment of the tax, interest, or penalty. For petitions made after December 31, 2007, the petition must be filed under the provisions of Article XVII of the Tax Reform Code [72 P.S. § 7247.1]. The provisions of Article XVII are discussed at¶ ¶4604 and 4605.

¶806

Caution: Bad Debts

72 P.S. § 7247.1 is the sole authority for claiming a refund or credit of sales tax attributed to bad debts, and it does not authorize any other bad debt deductions. No deduction or credit for bad debt is allowed on any return filed with the Department [72 P.S. § 7247.1(h)].

Bad debts associated with private label credit card accounts: In the case of private label credit card accounts that do not meet the three requirements listed above, a vendor or lender that makes an election pursuant to 72 P.S. § 7247(a.3) is entitled to file a petition for refund of sales tax that the vendor has previously reported and paid to the Department if all of the following conditions are met [72 P.S. § 7247(a.2)]:

(1) No refund was previously allowed with respect to the portion of the account written off as a bad debt.

(2) The account has been found worthless and written off (either in whole or in part) as bad debt on the books and records of the lender or an affiliate of the lender.

(3) The account has been deducted for federal income tax purposes under IRC § 166 by the lender or an affiliate of the lender.

In order to be eligible for a refund under 72 P.S. § 7247(a.2), the lender and the vendor must execute and file with the Department a joint election (signed by both parties) designating which party is entitled to claim the refund. This election cannot be revoked unless a written notice is signed by the party that signed the election being revoked and is filed with the Department [72 P.S. § 7247(a.3)].

Interest: No interest is paid on refunds of sales tax attributed to bad debt [72 P.S. § 7247.1(g)].

Time limitations: The time limitations for filing of refund petitions of 72 P.S. § 10003.1 apply [72 P.S. § 7247.1(a1)].

Caution: To Record Bad Debts Promptly

The three-year refund period begins when the sales tax is paid to the Commonwealth. Much of that period may elapse before a receivable is actually deducted as a bad debt on the federal tax return. Act promptly to record bad debts and to apply for refunds.

Amount limitations: The refund available under 72 P.S. § 7247.1 is limited to the sales tax paid that is attributed to the bad debt, less any discount under 72 P.S. § 7227. Partial payments by the purchaser must be prorated between the original purchase price and the sales tax due on the sale. Payments made any transaction that includes both taxable and nontaxable components must be allocated proportionally between the taxable and nontaxable components [72 P.S. § 7247.1(b)].

Partial payments: Partial payments by the purchaser to the vendor must be prorated between the original purchase price and the sales tax due on the sale [72 P.S. § 7247.1(b)].

Mixed transactions: Payments made to a vendor on any transactions that include both taxable and nontaxable components must be allocated proportionally between the taxable and nontaxable components [72 P.S. § 7247.1(b)].

Recovery of bad debts: If the purchase price that is attributed to a prior bad debt refund is later collected (in whole or in part) by the vendor or lender or an affiliate of the vendor or lender, the entity claiming the refund must remit the proportional tax to the Department with the first return filed after the collection. If the entity is not required to file periodic returns, the entity must remit the proportional tax to the

¶806

Department with another return pursuant to 72 P.S. § 7217(c) [72 P.S. § 7247.1(f)(1)]. Any consideration received for the assignment, sale, or other transfer of a bad debt with respect to which a refund has been granted is deemed to be a collection of a prior bad debt. This does not apply to a transfer to an entity that is part of the same affiliated group as defined by IRC § 1504 [72 P.S. § 7247(a)(f)(2)]. A person that collects (in whole or in part) the purchase price attributed to a prior bad debt refund is required to maintain books, records, and other documentation to allow the Department to determine whether the purchase price attributed to a prior bad debt refund has been collected, including the pertinent facts required by 72 P.S. § 7247.1(e) [72 P.S. § 7247.1(f)(3)]. If it is determined that a prior bad debt has been collected, and the proportional tax has not been properly reported and paid to the Department, the person that claimed the refund on the transaction must report and pay the proportional tax to the Department plus applicable interest and penalty [72 P.S. § 7247.1(f)(4)].

Disallowed items: No refund is allowable for (1) interest; (2) finance charges; or (3) collection expenses [72 P.S. § 7247.1(d)].

Assignment of rights: A vendor may assign its right to refund under 72 P.S. § 7247.1 to an affiliate.

Documentation: Documentation requirements are as follows [72 P.S. § 7247.1(e)]:

(1) Any person claiming a refund under 72 P.S. § 7247.1 must, on request, make available adequate books, records, or other documentation supporting the claimed refund, including the items listed in 72 P.S. § 7247.1(e)(1).

(2) A person claiming a refund under 72 P.S. § 7247.1 may provide alternative forms of documentation acceptable to the Department if appropriate in light of the volume and character of uncollectible accounts, including the items listed in 72 P.S. § 7247.1(e)(2).

Definitions

Terms with respect to refunds associated with bad debts can be found in 72 P.S. § 7247(1)(i).

¶807 Petition for Abatement of Additions and Penalties

When a taxpayer files a petition for reassessment or refund, additions or penalties may be waived or abated (in whole or in part) *if* the petitioner has established that she/he has acted in good faith without negligence and with no intent to defraud. Petitions for abatement can be incorporated into a petition for reassessment or refund or made separately. Rules of procedure for filing and hearing petitions for abatement of additions and penalties are like those for filing petitions for refund (explained at ¶806) [61 Pa. Code § 7.4].

¶808 Additions, Penalties, and Interest

The Tax Reform Code (TRC) imposes additions to tax and penalties. Additions are *not* penalties. The difference is important, because penalties cannot be deducted for federal purposes, while additional taxes can. All penalties, additions, interest, and liabilities imposed must be paid upon notice and demand by the Department and are assessed and collected in the same manner as taxes. Unless otherwise provided, any reference to "tax" includes penalties, additions, interest, and liabilities [72 P.S. § 7267(a)].

• *Late payment of tax*

If any amount of sales and use taxes due are not paid on or before the due date, *interest* is imposed on the unpaid amount. The due date is determined without regard to any extension of time. In the case of tax assessed as a deficiency or as an estimated assessment, the due date is 30 days after notice of such assessment [72 P.S. § 7265]. All taxes due the Commonwealth bear simple interest from the date they become due and payable until paid [72 P.S. § 806]. See ¶ 4612 for an explanation of interest provisions.

• *Late filing*

Failure to file a return on or before the due date (determined with regard to extensions of time for filing) results in an *addition to tax*. The addition to tax is 5% of the tax due if the delay in filing is not more than one month, with an additional 5% for each additional month (or fraction thereof) during which failure to file continues. However, this addition to tax may not exceed 25%, nor will it be less than $2 [72 P.S. § 7266(a)].

• *Underpayment of tax*

If, upon examination by the Department, it is determined that a return shows more tax due or collected than the amount of tax remitted with the return, the Department will issue an assessment for the difference, together with an *addition to tax* of 3% of the difference. This addition to tax must be paid within 10 days *after mailing of notice of assessment* to the taxpayer. If the assessment is not paid within 10 days, an additional 3% of the difference will be added to the tax for each month during which the assessment remains unpaid. The total of all additions under this provision shall not exceed 18% of the difference shown on the assessment [72 P.S. § 7231(a)]. If an assessment is made under this provision, *i.e.*, 72 P.S. § 7231(a), interest is added to the amount of the deficiency from the due date of the return to the date of the assessment notice [72 P.S. § 7266(c)].

• *Understatement of tax*

If a return is filed that understates the true amount of tax due by more than 50%, an *addition to tax* is imposed. The additional tax is the same as the additional tax for late filing (see above) [72 P.S. § 7266(a)].

• *Assessment of deficiency*

If the Department issues a notice of assessment of additional tax, an *addition to tax* equal to 5% of the amount of the deficiency is imposed, and no addition to tax under 72 P.S. § 7231(a) is imposed [72 P.S. § 7266(b)]. Addition to tax under 72 P.S. § 7231(a) is explained above under "Underpayment of tax." See ¶ 802 for an explanation of assessment and deficiency. If the Department makes an assessment of deficiency under this provision, *i.e.*, 72 P.S. § 7231(b), interest is added to the amount of the deficiency from the due date of the return to the date of the notice of assessment [72 P.S. § 7266(c)].

• *Estimated assessments*

If the Department makes an estimated assessment, *interest* is added to the amount of the deficiency from the due date of the return to the date of the assessment notice [72 P.S. § 7266(c)]. Estimated assessments are explained at ¶ 802. Since an estimated assessment is made when a taxpayer fails to file a required return, the taxpayer is also subject to the *addition to tax* for late filing discussed above.

• *Uncollectible checks*

Whenever a check issued in payment of tax (or for any other purpose) is returned to the Department as uncollectible, the Secretary shall charge a fee of 10% of the face amount of the uncollectible check, plus all protest fees, to the person who presented the check. This charge is in addition to interest and penalties otherwise imposed. However, the additions imposed shall not exceed $200 or be less than $10 [72 P.S. § 7266(d)].

¶808

• *Tax evasion*

Willful evasion of the sales/use tax results in a *penalty* equal to 50% of the total amount of the tax evaded. This penalty is in addition to other penalties provided by law. In any proceeding involving fraud or willful evasion of tax, the burden of proof is on the Department of Revenue to prove fraud or willful evasion. This penalty also applies to an improper attempt to receive a refund [72 P.S. § 7267(b)].

Assisting in evasion: A person who willfully assists a taxpayer to evade or defeat the tax is also liable for the 50% *fraud penalty* [72 P.S. § 7267(b)].

• *Fraudulent return*

Filing a fraudulent return is a misdemeanor. A taxpayer convicted of filing a fraudulent return is subject to a fine of up to $2,000 or imprisonment of up to three years, or both [72 P.S. § 7268(a)].

• *Other crimes*

The following acts are among those that are misdemeanors punishable by a fine of up to $1,000 and costs of prosecution or imprisonment of up to one year, or both (in addition to any other penalties that may be imposed) [72 P.S. § 7268(b)]:

(1) Advertising or holding out to the public that the tax will be absorbed, not added to the purchase price, or refunded. However, a person who maintains a place of business outside Pennsylvania may absorb the tax on taxable sales made in the normal course of business at the out-of-state location without being subject to fines and penalties.

(2) Willful failure to collect tax from the purchaser and timely remit it to the Department.

(3) Willful failure or neglect to timely file a return.

(4) Refusal to pay timely any tax, penalty, or interest imposed by law.

(5) Willful failure to preserve records as required.

(6) Refusal to allow the Department to examine books, records, or papers.

(7) Failure to make full disclosure on a return.

(8) Issuance of a fraudulent exemption certificate.

It is not necessary to maintain a place of business in Pennsylvania to be subject to these penalties.

• *Failure to obtain license*

Vendors that conduct business in Pennsylvania for the purpose of selling or leasing taxable services or tangible personal property without a sales tax license are, upon conviction, guilty of a summary offense punishable by a fine of not less than $300 or more than $1,500. If the fine is not paid, the sentence is imprisonment of not less than five days or more than 30 days. This fine or imprisonment is in addition to any other penalties imposed [72 P.S. § 7208(c)].

De Facto Owner Liability

The Court of Common Pleas of Dauphin County has held that a *de facto* owner of a business may be held personally liable for failure to remit sales tax [*Cmwlth. v. Morris*, 48 Pa. D. & C. 3d 568 (1988)]. The fact that the business is in another's name will not exonerate a taxpayer from willful failure to file returns or remit sales tax where the taxpayer is, in fact, a co-owner and responsible person. In the *Morris* case, the defendant signed forms as partner, officer, or other owner and indicated that she was "Secretary" of the business (a service station). There was no evidence that she was an employee. She received no W-2 Statement, and the business card for the service station listed both defendant and her spouse (the individual who was the owner of record).

¶809 Tax Liens

If a taxpayer who owes sales or use tax neglects or refuses to pay after a demand for payment, the amount (including any interest, addition, penalty, and any additional costs that may accrue) becomes a lien in favor of the Commonwealth against the taxpayer's property, both real and personal, except merchandise regularly sold in the course of the taxpayer's business [72 P.S. § 7242(a)].

• *Priority of lien*

Sales and use tax liens have priority over any other obligation, judgment, claim, lien, or estate arising after the filing and docketing of the personal income tax lien and are subordinate only to the following [72 P.S. § 7242(b)].

(1) Mortgages against the realty duly recorded before the tax lien.

(2) Cost of the writ and the judicial sale.

(3) Real estate taxes on the real estate.

(4) Municipal claims against the property.

Comment: Tax Lien Filing

Even though unpaid taxes create a lien against you, the lien is not perfected until a lien against you has been filed by the Department of Revenue with a prothonotary of the Commonwealth Court and the prothonotary has docketed the lien [61 Pa. Code § 119.11(a)(2)]. The Commonwealth cannot take any action against you (*e.g.*, publish the lien in the newspaper, start action to take your property) until the lien is perfected. Make sure you are complying with all requirements to contest the tax in order to prevent perfection of the lien.

NOTE: Tax liens no longer have to be renewed every five years to maintain their priority (see ¶4618).

• *Failure to file bond*

The Department of Revenue may file a lien against any taxpayer who fails to file a required sales tax bond. All funds received upon execution of the judgment on the lien will be refunded to the taxpayer with 3% interest if a final determination is made that the taxpayer does not owe any payment to the Department of Revenue [72 P.S. § 7277(c)].

• *Writ of execution*

The Department of Revenue may issue a writ of execution directly upon a sales and use tax lien without the issuance and prosecution in judgment of a writ of *scire facias,* provided that notice of the filing of the lien is sent by registered mail to the taxpayer's last known post office address at least 10 days before the issuance of any execution of the lien. The lien has no effect on any stock of goods, wares, or merchandise regularly sold or leased in the ordinary course of the taxpayer's business unless and until a writ of execution has been issued and a levy made upon the goods [72 P.S. § 7242(b)].

NOTE: See ¶4618 for more information about tax liens.

PART IV

CORPORATE NET INCOME TAX

CHAPTER 9
TAX RATE, RETURNS, AND PAYMENT

INTRODUCTION

¶901   History and Sources of Authority

• *History of the tax*

The corporate net income tax was first enacted in 1935 [Act of May 16, 1935, P.L. 208] and was a privilege (excise) tax on corporations "doing business" in Pennsylvania. In 1951, the corporation income tax was enacted [Act of August 24, 1951, P.L. 1417]. It applied to corporations that conducted activities in Pennsylvania insufficient to constitute "doing business." It was designed to reach those corporations that were thought to be exempt from the corporate net income tax because of U.S. constitutional restrictions on taxation of interstate commerce. In 1971, the original corporate net income tax and corporation income tax were repealed and reenacted as part of the Tax Reform Code of 1971, effective for years beginning after December 31, 1970 [Tax Reform Code of 1971, Act of March 4, 1971, P.L. 6, Article IV and Article V]. In 1981 (after the U.S. Supreme Court's *Complete Auto Transit* decision), the corporation income tax was repealed, effective for tax years beginning after December 31, 1980. Corporations formerly taxed under the corporation income tax were made subject to the corporate net income tax [Act of December 21, 1981, P.L. 482]. See the discussion of "doing business" in Pennsylvania at ¶913.

• *Sources of authority*

The corporate net income tax is Article IV of the Tax Reform Code, sections 401 through 412. Article IV of the Tax Reform Code has been codified in Title 72 of the Unconsolidated Pennsylvania Statutes as Chapter 5, Article 4, Sections 7401 through 7412, and is cited as such herein (*e.g.*, 72 P.S. §7402). The corporate net income tax regulations are part of Title 61 of the Pennsylvania Code, sections 153.1 through 153.71. The general provision regulations for corporation taxes are found in Title 61 of the Pennsylvania Code, sections 151.1 through 151.24.

NOTE: For a discussion of constitutional restrictions, see ¶1402.

• *Revenue information*

According to Department of Revenue regulation [61 Pa. Code §3.4], informational materials are issued to provide general information that will assist individuals or organizations. Revenue information material is issued for informational purposes only and should not be relied upon or used in tax appeals. Examples of revenue information are the *Pennsylvania Tax Update*, forms, pamphlets, tax bulletins, or information notices provided to taxpayers. Instructions on tax forms and instructional booklets accompanying forms also fall within this category. A corporation tax bulletin falls within the category of revenue information.

¶902 Administration

The Pennsylvania corporate net income tax is administered by the Department of Revenue, Harrisburg, Pennsylvania [72 P.S. §7408].

¶903 Definitions

In order to provide a guide to the important corporate net income tax terms, a glossary is provided in this paragraph for quick reference. All definitions are contained in 72 P.S. §401 unless otherwise indicated. Some definitions specific only to certain situations are defined in context when discussing the situation.

• *Annual year*

The term "annual year" has the same meaning as "taxable year." See below.

• *Business income*

"Business income" means income arising from transactions and activity in the regular course of the taxpayer's trade or business and includes income from tangible and intangible property if the acquisition, the management, or disposition of the property constitutes an integral part of the taxpayer's regular trade or business operations. The term includes all income that is apportionable under the Constitution of the United States [72 P.S. §7401(3)2(a)(1)(A)].

• *Commercial domicile*

"Commercial domicile" means the principal place from which the trade or business of the taxpayer is directed or managed [72 P.S. § 7401(3)2(a)(1)(B)].

• *Compensation*

"Compensation" means wages, salaries, commissions, and any other form of remuneration paid to employees for personal services [72 P.S. § 7401(3)2(a)(1)(C)].

• *Corporation*

See ¶ 910.

• *Department*

The word "Department" means the Pennsylvania Department of Revenue [72 P.S. § 7401(2)].

• *Determination*

The ascertainment of tax liability. The term includes a redetermination [72 P.S. § 7401(7)].

• *Fiscal year*

"Fiscal year" has the same meaning as "taxable year" [72 P.S. § 7401(5)].

• *Internal Revenue Code*

In general, references to the Internal Revenue Code for Pennsylvania corporate net income tax purposes are to the Internal Revenue Code of 1986. Although Pennsylvania does not explicitly incorporate the Internal Revenue Code by reference, in general, amendments to the Internal Revenue Code take effect for Pennsylvania corporate net income tax purposes when they take effect for federal purposes. Therefore, in general, Pennsylvania, for corporate net income tax purposes, follows federal law except where specific adjustments to federal taxable income are required. Required additions to federal taxable income are discussed at ¶ 1002; and required deductions from federal taxable income are discussed at ¶ 1003.

• *Net loss*

A net loss for a taxable year is the negative amount for that taxable year. Net losses are discussed at ¶ 1003 [72 P.S. § 7401(3)4(b)].

• *Nonbusiness income*

All income other than business income [72 P.S. § 7401(3)2(a)(1)(D)].

• *Person*

The word "person" means a natural person, an association, or a corporation. When used to prescribe and impose fines or imprisonment on associations, "person" means the partners or members of the association [72 P.S. § 7401(4)]. When used to prescribe and impose fines or imprisonment to corporations, "person" means the officers of the corporation.

• *Regulated financial institution*

A "regulated financial institution" is an entity subject to tax under Articles VII (Bank and Trust Companies Shares Tax) or XV (Mutual Thrift Institutions Tax) and regulated by the Pennsylvania Department of Banking, the Federal Reserve Board, the Office of the Comptroller of the Currency, the Office of Thrift Supervision, the National Credit Union Administration or the Federal Deposit Insurance Corporation [72 P.S. § 7401(6)].

• *Sales*

"Sales" means all gross receipts of the taxpayer not allocated under the definition of taxable income other than dividends received, interest on United States, State, or political subdivision obligations and gross receipts received from the sale, redemption, maturity, or exchange of securities (except those held by the taxpayer primarily for sale to customers in the ordinary course of trade or business) [72 P.S. §7401(3)2(a)(1)(E)].

• *State*

"State" means any state of the United States, the District of Columbia, the Commonwealth of Puerto Rico, any territory or possession of the United States, and any foreign country or political subdivision thereof [72 P.S. §7401(3)2(a)(1)(F)]. "This state" means the Commonwealth of Pennsylvania or, in the case of application of the definition of taxable income to the apportionment and allocation of income for local tax purposes, the subdivision or local taxing district in which the relevant tax return is filed [72 P.S. §7401(3)2(a)(1)(G)].

• *Tax period*

"Tax period" has the same meaning as "taxable year" [72 P.S. §7401(5)].

• *Tax year*

"Tax year" has the same meaning as "taxable year" [72 P.S. §7401(5)].

• *Taxable in another state*

For purposes of allocation and apportionment of income a taxpayer is "taxable in another state" if in that state the taxpayer is subject to (1) a net income tax, (2) a franchise tax measured by net income, (3) a franchise tax for the privilege of doing business, or (4) a corporate stock tax [72 P.S. §7401(3)2.(a)(3)]. If that state has jurisdiction to subject the taxpayer to a net income tax, the taxpayer is taxable in that state regardless of whether, in fact, that state does or does not.

• *Taxable income*

Taxable income is defined at ¶1001.

• *Taxable year*

"Taxable year" means the taxable year that the corporation, or any consolidated group with which the corporation participates in the filing of consolidated returns, actually uses in reporting taxable income to the Federal Government [72 P.S. §7401(5)].

TAX RATE

¶905 Imposition, Base, and Tax Rate

• *Imposition*

The Pennsylvania corporate net income tax is an excise tax imposed on corporations for exercising (whether in its own name or through any person, association, business trust, corporation, joint venture, limited liability company, limited partnership, partnership, or other entity) any of the following privileges:

(1) Doing business in Pennsylvania. The term "doing business in Pennsylvania" is explained at ¶914.

(2) Carrying on activities in Pennsylvania, including solicitation that is not protected activity under the Interstate Income Act of 1959 (discussed at ¶914).

(3) Having capital or property employed or used in Pennsylvania.

(4) Owning property in Pennsylvania.

Even though the wording of the statute implies that the Pennsylvania corporate net income tax is a franchise or excise tax on the privilege of doing business in the Commonwealth, the Supreme Court of Pennsylvania has held that it is in fact a direct tax on corporate net income [*Commonwealth Securities and Investments, Inc. v. Cmwlth.*, 514 A.2d 1373 (Pa. 1986), *aff'g per curiam*, 488 A.2d 1187 (Pa.Commw. 1985)]. If the sole contact of a corporation with Pennsylvania is the lease of property located in the Commonwealth under a safe harbor lease where title to the property (determined under Pennsylvania law) does not pass to the corporation, the corporation is not subject to taxation in Pennsylvania (because it does not own property in Pennsylvania). However, if the lessor actually takes title (determined under Pennsylvania law) to the property covered by the lease and the property is located in Pennsylvania, the lessor is subject to Pennsylvania corporate taxation [61 Pa. Code § 153.30(d)].

• *Base*

The Pennsylvania corporate net income tax is levied on taxable income. Taxable income for purposes of the corporate net income tax is federal taxable income (amount reported on federal Form 1120, Line 28) with Pennsylvania modifications. (Taxable income is explained at ¶1001.) Corporate taxpayers that transact business outside Pennsylvania and are taxable in another state may allocate nonbusiness income and apportion business income.

• *Rate*

For taxable years beginning January 1, 1995, and each year thereafter, the Pennsylvania corporate net income tax rate is 9.99% [72 P.S. § 7402(b)].

¶906 Accounting Periods and Methods

Corporations have the same taxable period and accounting methods for Pennsylvania corporate net income tax purposes as for federal income tax purposes. However, Pennsylvania does not permit corporations to file consolidated returns [72 P.S. § 7404]. Corporations that file consolidated returns for federal purposes must file separate Pennsylvania returns reflecting only their income and deductions. A corporation filing a consolidated return for federal purposes may, therefore, be entitled to larger contribution deductions for Pennsylvania corporate net income tax purposes than for federal. It is allowed a deduction to which it would have been entitled had it filed a separate return for federal purposes [61 Pa. Code § 153.14(2)].

Consolidated Group

A member of a consolidated group is required only to submit a specially prepared federal Form 1120 (*i.e.*, one that is prepared on a separate basis). A member of a consolidated group is not required to submit a copy of its federal consolidated return.

• *52-53 week year*

A corporation with a 52-53 week year ending on one of the last seven days of December or the first seven days of January is considered a calendar-year taxpayer for Pennsylvania corporate tax purposes [72 P.S. § 7401(3)(1)(k)]. This becomes important in the case of rate changes or other statutory changes.

> **Example 1:** Before the enactment of the statute classifying 52-53 week years ending in the last week of December or first week of January as calendar years, some taxpayers were able to escape a tax rate hike for one year. The Commonwealth Court held that a rate hike applying to calendar year 1969 and fiscal years beginning after 1968 did not apply to taxpayers with fiscal years ending December 28, 1969 and December 26, 1969 [*Allentown Wholesale Grocery Co. v. Cmwlth.*, 291 A.2d 336 (Pa.Commw. 1972); *Eastman Kodak v. Cmwlth.*, 291 A.2d 340 (Pa.Commw. 1972)]. Under current law these taxpayers would be considered calendar-year taxpayers and would be subject to the rate hike. For example, assume that the Pennsylvania legislature passed a rate change applying to

years beginning after 1986 (which it did). A corporation with a fiscal year ending on December 28, 1987 would be considered a calendar-year taxpayer (*i.e.*, tax year beginning on January 1, 1987, not December 29, 1986) and thus subject to the rate change.

Example 2: In 1994 the Legislature amended the definition of "corporation" to include business trusts [Act 48 of 1994 (H.B. 868), § 13]. Eat'n Park Restaurants Business Trust operated on a 52-53 week fiscal year beginning on December 27. Eat'n Park argued that it was not subject to the corporate net income tax for 1995. However, the Department of Revenue asserted that the business trust was a calendar-year taxpayer by virtue of 72 P.S. § 7401. The Commonwealth Court agreed with the Department of Revenue, noting that the statute [72 P.S. § 7401(3)1.(k)] clearly states that a corporation with a 52-53 week year ending on one of the last seven days of December or the first seven days of January is considered a calendar-year taxpayer for Pennsylvania corporate tax purposes [*Eat'n Park Restaurants Business Trust v. Cmwlth*, Pa.Commw. 802 A.2d 276 (Pa.Commw. 2002), *exceptions sustained in part, overruled in part, by* 821 A.2d 160 (Pa.Commw. 2003)].

• *Partnership interests*

When a corporation has an interest in a partnership, joint venture, association, or other unincorporated enterprise (all referred to as "partnership"), the corporate taxpayer and the partnership must maintain their accounting periods as prescribed by IRC § 706. If the partnership keeps its books on a tax year that is different from that of the corporate partner, the corporate partner reports its share of the partnership income and apportionment factors in its tax year in which or with which the partnership year ended [61 Pa. Code § 153.29(f)(1), (2)].

A corporate partner must use the same method of accounting that the partnership uses to determine its distributive share of the partnership income. This is true even if the partnership method of accounting differs from the corporate partner's method of accounting. For example, a cash-basis corporate partner includes in its Pennsylvania corporate net income tax return items that are accrued but unpaid by an accrual basis partnership [61 Pa. Code § 153.29(g)].

TAXABLE AND EXEMPT CORPORATIONS

¶910 "Corporation" Defined

For Pennsylvania corporate net income tax purposes, the term "corporation" means any of the following [72 P.S. § 401(1)]:

(1) A corporation.

(2) A joint-stock association.

(3) A business trust, limited liability company, or other entity that is classified as a corporation for federal income tax purposes.

• *Exclusions from definition of corporation*

The term "corporation" does not include the following:

(1) A business trust that qualifies as a real estate investment trust under IRC § 856 or that is a qualified real estate investment trust subsidiary under IRC § 856(i).

(2) A business trust that qualifies as a regulated investment company under IRC § 851 and that is registered with the United States Securities and Exchange Commission under the Investment Company Act of 1940 or a related business trust that confines its activities in Pennsylvania to the maintenance, administration, and management of intangible investments and activities of regulated investment companies.

(3) A corporation, trust or other entity that is an exempt organization as defined by IRC § 501.

¶910

(4) A corporation, trust or other entity organized as a not-for-profit under the laws of Pennsylvania or the laws of any other state that

(a) Would qualify as an exempt organization under IRC § 501.

(b) Would qualify as a homeowners association as defined by IRC § 528(c).

(c) Is a membership organization subject to the federal limitations on deductions from taxable income under IRC § 277 (but only if no pecuniary gain or profit inures to any member or related entity from the membership organization).

• *Corporations without capital stock*

A corporation that otherwise qualifies as a corporation for Pennsylvania corporate net income purposes will be taxed as a corporation, even if it has no capital stock.

¶911 Taxable Corporations

Any corporation (defined at ¶910) that exercises one of the following privileges (whether in its own name or through any person, association, business trust, corporation, joint venture, limited liability company, limited partnership, partnership, or other entity) is subject to the Pennsylvania corporate net income tax:

(1) Doing business in Pennsylvania [72 P.S. § 7402(a)(1)]. See discussion of "doing business in Pennsylvania" at ¶914.

(2) Carrying on activities in Pennsylvania, including solicitation that is not protected activity under the Interstate Income Act of 1959 [72 P.S. § 7402(a)(2)]. The Interstate Income Act of 1959 is discussed at ¶914.

(3) Having capital or property employed or used in Pennsylvania [72 P.S. § 7402(a)(3)].

(4) Owning property in Pennsylvania [72 P.S. § 7402(a)(4)].

Taxable Activity Required

In order to be a taxable corporation for Pennsylvania corporate net income tax purposes, a corporation must be doing business or carrying on activities in Pennsylvania, employ or use capital in Pennsylvania, or own property in Pennsylvania.

• *Cooperative agricultural associations*

Incorporated cooperative agricultural associations are subject to a tax on dividends in lieu of the corporate net income tax [72 P.S. § 3420-23]. For this purpose a "cooperative agricultural association" is an incorporated association (1) composed of persons engaged in agriculture, (2) instituted for purposes of mutual help, (3) having capital stock, (4) organized under the laws of Pennsylvania, the United States, or any state territory, or foreign country, or dependency, and (5) doing business in Pennsylvania or having capital or property employed or used in Pennsylvania by or in the name of itself or any person, partnership, or association [72 P.S. § 3420-22]. An "association" for this purpose means any cooperative agricultural association as defined in 72 P.S. § 3420-22.

The tax on cooperative agricultural associations is imposed at the rate of 4% of net income [72 P.S. § 3420-23], defined as the sum of the dividends declared and paid on the shares of common and preferred stock during the year [72 P.S. § 3420-22].

The annual reports of cooperative agricultural associations (filed on form RCT-125) are due on or before the 15th of April for calendar-year taxpayers and on or before the 15th day of the 4th month after the close of the fiscal year for fiscal-year taxpayers [72 P.S. § 3420-24].

An association that does not conduct its entire business in Pennsylvania is taxable only on the portion of its net income (*i.e.*, dividends declared and paid during the year) attributable to business transacted in Pennsylvania by multiplying its total net income by a fraction, the numerator of which is its gross receipts received from business transacted in Pennsylvania and the numerator of which is the amount of its gross receipts received from all of its business [72 P.S. § 3420-22].

¶912 Exempt Corporations

The following entities are exempted from the Pennsylvania corporate net income tax:

(1) Real estate investment trusts that qualify under IRC § 856 or qualified real estate investment trust subsidiaries that qualify under IRC § 856(i) [72 P.S. § 7401(1)1].

(2) Regulated investment companies that qualify under IRC § 851 and that are registered with the United States Securities and Exchange Commission under the Investment Company Act or 1940 or related business trusts that confine their activities in Pennsylvania to the maintenance, administration and management of intangible investments and activities or regulated investment companies [72 P.S. § 7401(1)2].

(3) Charitable organizations as defined by IRC § 501 [72 P.S. § 7401(1)3].

(4) Not-for-profit entities that would qualify as one of the following [72 P.S. § 7401(1)4]:

(a) An exempt organization under IRC § 501.

(b) A homeowners association under IRC § 528(c).

(c) A membership organization subject to the federal limitations on deductions from taxable income under IRC § 277 but only if no pecuniary gain or profit inures to any member or related entity from the membership organization.

(d) A nonstock commodity or nonstock stock exchange (applicable retroactively to taxable years beginning after December 31, 1997).

(5) Banks and trust companies subject to the bank and trust companies shares tax [72 P.S. § 7402(c)].

(6) Entities subject to the title insurance companies shares tax [72 P.S. § 7402(c)].

(7) Insurance companies subject to the insurance premiums tax [72 P.S. § 7402(c)].

(8) Mutual thrift institutions subject to the mutual thrift institutions tax [72 P.S. § 7402(c)].

(9) Pennsylvania S corporations. However, Pennsylvania S corporations are subject to the corporate net income tax on their net recognized built-in gain to the extent of and as determined for federal income tax purposes under IRC § 1374(d). For Pennsylvania corporate net income tax purposes, a Pennsylvania S corporation and each qualified subchapter subsidiary are treated as separate corporations [72 P.S. § 7401(p)]. Pennsylvania S corporations are discussed at ¶ 1801—1812.

Effect of Federal Tax Treaties

Unless there is an express exemption from state income taxes, no treaty of the federal government shall be construed to exempt a corporation from the Pennsylvania corporate net income tax or the Pennsylvania capital stock/franchise tax. In the case of a corporation not subject to federal income taxation or reporting, taxable income for purposes of the Pennsylvania corporate net income tax is taxable income that would have been reported to the federal government if the corporation had not been exempted by treaty [72 P.S. § 10003.11].

NOTE: Taxation of pass-through entities (S corporations, partnerships, trusts, and limited liability companies) is discussed in Chapter 18.

• *Cooperative agricultural associations*

Cooperative agricultural associations are subject to a special tax of 4% on net income (as specially defined) in lieu of the corporate net income tax. See discussion at ¶ 911.

¶913 Doing Business in Pennsylvania

A corporation is subject to the Pennsylvania corporate net income tax if it exercises (whether in its own name or through any person, association, business trust, corporation, joint venture, limited liability company, limited partnership, partnership, or other entity) any of the following privileges: (1) doing business in Pennsylvania; (2) carrying on activities in Pennsylvania; (3) having capital or property employed or used in Pennsylvania; or (4) owning property in Pennsylvania [72 P.S. § 7402(a)]. The terms "doing business" and "having capital or property employed or used" have been held to be synonymous [*Cmwlth. v. The Reading and Southwestern Street Railway Co.*, 54 Dauph. 277 (1943)].

P.L. 86-272

The major restriction on the income taxation of corporations engaged in interstate commerce is the Interstate Income Act of 1959 (P.L. 86-272), which prohibits imposition of a state net income tax on foreign corporations whose only activity in the state is mere solicitation. See discussion of P.L. 86-272 at ¶ 914.

The term "doing business" is not defined in the Pennsylvania tax statutes, nor have the courts provided a clear definition, although they have set some guidelines. The power of a state to tax its own residents is not subject to the limitations placed on interstate commerce by federal law. The question of whether a domestic corporation is doing business in Pennsylvania does not depend on how much business it does but whether it does *any* business in Pennsylvania [*Budd Realty Corp.*, 54 Dauph. 387 (1944)]. Thus, the question of whether a corporation is "doing business" in Pennsylvania almost always arises in the context of taxation of a foreign corporation. The best information on what the term means can be obtained by examining the authority on constitutionally permissible state taxation of interstate commerce.

• *State taxation of income from interstate commerce*

The Commerce Clause of the U.S. Constitution prohibits any state taxation that imposes a burden on interstate commerce. At one time it was believed that this clause placed significant restrictions on the ability of states to tax corporations engaged in interstate commerce, particularly those engaged *solely* in interstate commerce. Prior to 1977, the U.S. Supreme Court had ruled that, under the Commerce Clause, it was unconstitutional for a state to levy a tax upon the privilege of carrying on a business that was exclusively interstate in character, no matter how fairly it was apportioned to business done within the state [*Spector Motor Service, Inc. v. O'Connor*, 340 U.S. 602 (1951)]. However, in 1977, the U.S. Supreme Court overturned its decision in *Spector*. In *Complete Auto Transit v. Brady*, 430 U.S. 274 (1977), the Court ruled that a state tax on interstate commerce is not unconstitutional if it meets the following four criteria:

(1) The tax is applied to an activity with a substantial nexus with the taxing state.

(2) The tax is fairly apportioned (see discussion of *Fair apportionment*, below).

(3) The tax does not discriminate against interstate commerce.

(4) The tax is fairly related to the services provided by the state.

• *Substantial nexus*

Consideration of federal restrictions on income taxation of interstate commerce leads to the conclusion that the test of whether a corporation is "doing business" is nexus. A nexus is a connection. There must be a substantial connection between the taxed activity and the taxing state, something beyond mere solicitation. This is often referred to as "solicitation plus," or "doing business." This is a vague definition of "doing business," and, in fact, the determination of whether a corporation is doing business in a state is based on the facts and circumstances of individual cases. In view of the U.S. Supreme Court's requirement in *Complete Auto Transit* that an activity, to be taxable in a state, must have a substantial nexus with the taxing state, the distinction between "doing business" and "carrying on activities" is merely semantic. In either case, a nexus (connection) must exist, and the label of the activity is irrelevant. Examination of Pennsylvania court cases is helpful in locating the parameters of "doing business." Some of these cases are discussed at the end of this paragraph. In *South Dakota v. Wayfair, Inc.,* 138 S. Ct. 2080, 201 L. Ed. 2d 403 (June 21, 2018), the United States Supreme Court ruled that out-of-state online retailers can be required to collect use tax from their customers without the retailers having a physical presence in the state. In so holding, the Supreme Court overturned the physical presence requirement that had been previously established by it in the *Quill* case. The Court explained that the substantial nexus requirement under *Complete Auto Transit* did not necessarily mandate a physical presence. Although *Wayfair* is a sales and use tax case, states will aggressively apply it to other types of state taxes.

• *Fair apportionment*

In order to be fairly apportioned, a tax must be both "internally consistent" and "externally consistent" [see, for example, *Goldberg v. Sweet,* 488 U.S. 252 (1989); *Container Corporation of America v. Franchise Tax Board,* 463 U.S. 159 (1983)].

Internal consistency: A tax is internally consistent if it is structured so that if every taxing jurisdiction were to apply the identical tax on interstate activities, no multiple taxation would result. The internal consistency inquiry, therefore, " . . . focuses on the text of the challenged statute and hypothesizes a situation where other States have passed an identical statute" [*Goldberg v. Sweet,* 488 U.S. 252 (1989)].

External consistency: The external consistency test asks whether the State has taxed only that portion of the revenues from the interstate activity that reasonably reflects the in-state component of the activity being taxed [*Goldberg v. Sweet,* 488 U.S. 252 (1989)]. A tax will fail the external consistency test if the taxpayer demonstrates by clear and cogent evidence that the income attributed to the state either (1) is out of all appropriate proportion to the business transacted by the taxpayer in that state; (2) has led to a grossly distorted result for the taxpayer; (3) is inherently arbitrary; or (4) produces an unreasonable result [*Northwood Construction Co. v. Township of Upper Moreland,* Pa.Sup.Ct., No. 12 M.D. Appeal Docket 2003 (September 2, 2004), *rev'g in part* 802 A.2d 1269 (Pa.Commw. 2002)].

Exercise of corporate objectives: One criterion that has been used to determine whether a corporation is doing business in Pennsylvania is whether the activity conducted in Pennsylvania is within the scope of the corporate charter [*Budd Realty Corp.,* 54 Dauph. 387 (1944); *Cmwlth. v. South Philadelphia Terminal, Inc.,* 75 Dauph. 233, *aff'd,* 171 A.2d 758 (Pa. 1961)]. Under these decisions, mere ownership of property in Pennsylvania does not constitute doing business. In order to be doing business, a corporation must be *exercising corporate objectives.*

¶913

Isolated transactions: Isolated transactions do not constitute doing business [*Cmwlth. v. Wilkes-Barre & H.R. Co.,* 95 A 915 (Pa. 1915)]. For example, a foreign corporation employing agents in the Commonwealth to solicit orders was held not to be doing business, and thus not subject to the capital stock tax, even though it maintained an office for the agents and a bank account in Pennsylvania and occasionally stored raw material temporarily in Pennsylvania [*Cmwlth. v. Johnson & Johnson,* 23 Dauph. 270 (1918)].

Interstate trucking: An interstate trucking company authorized to do business in Pennsylvania was held to be doing business in Pennsylvania when it hauled freight between two points in Pennsylvania [*C.I. Whitten Transfer Co. v. Cmwlth.,* 382 A.2d 1251 (Pa.Commw. 1978)].

No employees or property in Pennsylvania: A Delaware corporation headquartered in Ohio was found to be subject to the Pennsylvania corporate net income tax and the franchise tax on foreign corporations, even though it had neither property nor employees in the Commonwealth. The taxpayer is engaged in interstate motor transportation. It transports property through Pennsylvania (pass-through miles), delivers property to Pennsylvania destinations from outside the state, and picks up property in Pennsylvania for delivery out of state. Since 15% to 20% of the company's revenue miles were logged in Pennsylvania, these activities provide a sufficient nexus to impose the corporate net income tax and the franchise tax on foreign corporations. All of the other criteria of *Complete Auto Transit* were also met [*Erieview Cartage, Inc. v. Cmwlth.,* 654 A.2d 276 (Pa.Commw. 1995)]. For discussion of doing business in Pennsylvania for capital stock/franchise tax purposes, see ¶1310.

RETURNS AND PAYMENT OF TAX

¶914 P.L. 86-272

The major restriction on the taxation of corporations engaged in interstate commerce now is the Interstate Income Act of 1959, P.L. 86-272 [15 U.S.C. § 381]. P.L. 86-272, which prohibits imposition of a state net income tax on foreign corporations whose only activity in the state consists of "mere solicitation." P.L. 86-272 [15 U.S.C. § 381(a)] provides the following:

"No State, or political subdivision thereof, shall have power to impose, for any taxable year ending after September 14, 1959, a net income tax on the income derived within such State by any person from interstate commerce if the only business activities within such State by or on behalf of such person during such taxable year are either, or both, of the following:

(1) The solicitation of orders by such person, or his representative, in such State for sales of tangible personal property, which orders are sent outside the State for approval or rejection, and, if approved, are filled by shipment or delivery from a point outside the State.

(2) The solicitation of orders by such person, or his representative, in such State in the name of or for the benefit of a prospective customer of such person, if orders by such customer to such person to enable such customer to fill orders resulting from such solicitation are orders described in paragraph (1)."

Thus, in order to create a nexus sufficient to make a taxpayer subject to a state income tax, the activities within the state must consist of more than mere solicitation, referred to as "solicitation plus." Solicitation plus will be easier to find given the United States Supreme Court's holding in *South Dakota v. Wayfair, Inc.,* 138 S. Ct. 2080, 201 L. Ed. 2d 403 (June 21, 2018). In *Wayfair,* the Court ruled that out-of-state online retailers can be required to collect use tax from their customers without the retailers having a physical presence in the state. In so holding, the Supreme Court overturned the physical presence requirement that had been previously established by it in the *Quill* case. The Court explained that the substantial nexus requirement under *Com-*

plete Auto Transit did not necessarily mandate a physical presence. Although *Wayfair* is a sales and use tax case, states will aggressively apply it to other types of state taxes.

Other Taxes Differ

Because P.L. 86-272 applies only to taxes that are measured by net income, it is possible that a corporation may be exempt from the corporate net income tax but not exempt from the capital stock/franchise tax or the sales and use tax. See ¶ 507 and ¶ 1310. For example, a taxpayer soliciting orders in Pennsylvania on behalf of its parent corporation was exempt from the Pennsylvania corporate net income tax under P.L. 86-272, but it was subject to the Pennsylvania franchise tax [*Schering-Plough Healthcare Products Sales Corporation v. Cmwlth.*, 802 A.2d 1284 (Pa.Commw. 2002)].

• *Domestic corporations and persons domiciled in or residents of a state*

The provisions of 15 U.S.C. § 381(a) do not apply, within a state, to corporations incorporated under the laws of the state or any individual who, under the laws of the state is domiciled in, or a resident of, the State [15 U.S.C. § 381(b)]. Thus, the protection afforded by P.L. 86-272 does not apply to any corporation incorporated within Pennsylvania or to any person who is a resident of or domiciled in Pennsylvania.

Registration or Qualification to Do Business

A corporation that registers or otherwise qualifies within Pennsylvania does not, by that fact alone, lose its protection under P.L. 86-272. If, however, separate from or ancillary to registration or qualification, the company receives and seeks to use or protect any additional benefit or protection from Pennsylvania through activity not otherwise protected under P.L. 86-272 or *Corporate Tax Bulletin 2004-01*, its protection will be removed [*Corporate Tax Bulletin 2004-01*, § I.G].

• *Sales or solicitation of orders for sales by independent contractors*

A person is not considered to have engaged in business activities within a state merely by reason of (1) sales or solicitation of orders for sales in the state of tangible personal property on behalf of the person by one or more independent contractors or (2) the maintenance of an office in the state by one or more independent contractors whose activities on behalf of the person in the state consist solely of making sales, or soliciting orders for sales, for tangible personal property [15 U.S.C. § 381(c)]. For this purpose, "independent contractor" means a commission agent, broker, or other independent contractor who is engaged in selling, or soliciting orders for the sale of, tangible personal property for more than one principal and who holds himself out as such in the regular course of his business activities [15 U.S.C. § 381(c)(1)].

• *Missionary salesmen*

In 1978 the Pennsylvania Supreme Court considered a case in which a foreign corporation engaged solely in interstate commerce in Pennsylvania sent "missionary representatives" into Pennsylvania to solicit orders [*U.S. Tobacco Co. v. Cmwlth.*, 386 A.2d 471 (Pa. 1978), *cert. den.*, 439 U.S. 880 (1978)]. The sales representatives in the *U.S. Tobacco* case were engaged in the following activities: informing customers of new products, distributing product samples, assisting customers in product display, and taking orders. They could not approve orders or make collections, but they did drive company cars. The court held that these activities constituted mere solicitation insufficient to subject the corporation to income taxation in Pennsylvania.

¶914

- *Taxpayer does not own product for which orders are solicited*

The Pennsylvania Commonwealth Court has held that a taxpayer that limited its activities in Pennsylvania to the solicitation of orders on behalf of its parent company (carried out by representatives and independent contractors) was exempt from the Pennsylvania corporate net income tax under P.L. 86-272 [*Schering-Plough Healthcare Products Sales Corporation v. Cmwlth.*, 805 A.2d 1284 (Pa.Commw. 2002)]. The Department argued that because the taxpayer never took title to the goods sold it did not fall within the protection of P.L. 86-272 and that Congress intended only to protect the actual owner of property sold to an in-state customer. The Court disagreed, stating, "It cannot seriously be argued that a company which limits its activity in a State to solicitation of orders for goods to which it will never take title has a greater nexus to that State than a company taking similar orders for goods it owns someplace else." The Commonwealth has appealed to the Pennsylvania Supreme Court.

Department's Interpretation of Application of P.L. 86-272

The Department of Revenue has issued *Corporate Tax Bulletin 2004-01*, which explains its interpretation of the application of P.L. 86-272 and *de minimis* standards (discussed at ¶914A) to the corporate net income tax and Pennsylvania activities. The discussion below incorporates the provisions of *Corporate Tax Bulletin 2004-01*. The provisions of this bulletin, issued April 13, 2004, are effective immediately and apply to all open cases, tax settlements, and appeals [*Corporate Tax Bulletin 2004-01*, § III.].

- *Solicitation*

P.L. 86-272 does not define the term "solicitation," so the boundaries of the term are not clear. Moreover, different states have arrived at different conclusions with respect to what constitutes "mere solicitation." According to the U.S. Supreme Court, "mere solicitation" includes only those activities that are entirely ancillary to the solicitation of orders [*Wisconsin Department of Revenue v. William Wrigley, Jr., Co.*, 505 U.S. 214 (1992)].

Pennsylvania definition: For Pennsylvania corporate net income purposes, "solicitation" means (1) speech or conduct that explicitly or implicitly invites an order; and (2) activities that neither explicitly nor implicitly invite an order but are entirely ancillary to requests for an order [*Corporate Tax Bulletin 2004-01*, § I.B.].

De minimis exception: The Court, in *Wrigley*, recognized that there is a *de minimis* exception to the "mere solicitation" rule that applies to protect trivial nonimmune activities. *De minimis* standards are discussed at ¶914A.

Loss of P.L. 86-272 Protection

The Department of Revenue takes the position that the conducting of activities not falling within the Pennsylvania definition of solicitation will cause the company to lose its protection from the corporate net income tax afforded by P.L. 86-272 unless the disqualifying activities, taken together, are either *de minimis* (see ¶914A) or otherwise permitted under *Corporate Tax Bulletin 2004-01* [*Corporate Tax Bulletin 2004-01*, § I.B.]. The protection afforded under P.L. 86-272 and *Corporate Tax Bulletin 2004-01* is determined on a tax-year-by-tax-year basis. Thus, if at any time during a tax year a company conducts activities that are not protected under P.L. 86-272 or *Corporate Tax Bulletin 2004-01*, no Pennsylvania sales or income earned by the company attributed to Pennsylvania during any part of that tax year is protected from corporate net income taxation [*Corporate Tax Bulletin 2004-01*, § I.H.].

- *Ancillary activities*

Ancillary activities are those that serve no independent business function for the seller apart from their connection to the solicitation of orders (*e.g.*, recruiting, training, and evaluating sales personnel; use of hotels or homes for sales-related meetings; management involvement in credit disputes; providing a car and stock of free samples to salespersons) [*Corporate Tax Bulletin 2004-01*, §I.B.; see also *Wisconsin Department of Revenue v. William Wrigley, Jr., Co.*, 505 U.S. 214 (1992)]. The U.S. Supreme Court, in *Wrigley*, held that the statutory phrase "solicitation of orders" as used in P.L. 86-272 should not be interpreted narrowly to cover only actual requests for purchases or the actions that are absolutely essential to making those requests, but includes the entire process associated with inviting an order. Thus, providing a car and a stock of free samples to salesmen is part of the "solicitation of orders" because the only reason for providing them is to facilitate purchase requests. On the other hand, said the Court, the phrase should not be interpreted broadly to include all activities that are routinely, or even closely, associated with solicitation or customarily performed by salesmen. Activities that the company would have reason to engage in anyway, but chooses to allocate to its in-state sales force, are not covered by P.L. 86-272 (*e.g.*, employing salesmen to repair or service the company's product).

Promotion activities: Activities that seek to promote sales are not ancillary. P.L. 86-272 only protects ancillary activities that facilitate the request for an order [*Corporate Tax Bulletin 2004-01*, §I.B.].

• *Leasing, renting, licensing*

Only the solicitation to sell tangible personal property is afforded immunity from the Pennsylvania corporate net income tax under P.L. 86-272. Thus, the leasing renting, licensing, and other disposition of tangible personal property are not protected activities under P.L. 86-272 [*Corporate Tax Bulletin 2004-01*, §I.A.].

• *Intangibles*

Since only solicitation is a protected activity under P.L. 86-272, transactions involving intangibles (*e.g.*, franchises, patents, copyrights, trademarks, service marks) are not protected activities under P.L. 86-272 [*Corporate Tax Bulletin 2004-01*, §I.A.].

• *Sale or delivery of services*

The sale or delivery and the solicitation for the sale or delivery of any type of service that is not either (1) ancillary to solicitation or (2) listed as a protected activity under §I.D. of *Corporate Tax Bulletin 2004-01* are not protected activities [*Corporate Tax Bulletin 2004-01*, §I.A.]

• *Consignment sales*

The maintaining of a stock of goods in the state by an independent contractor under consignment or any other type of arrangement with the company (except for purposes of display and solicitation) removes the protection of P.L. 86-272 [*Corporate Tax Bulletin 2004-01*, §I.E.2.].

• *Protection of principal*

Independent contractors may engage in the following limited activities in the state without causing the principal's loss of immunity:

(1) Soliciting sales.

(2) Making sales.

(3) Maintaining an office.

• *Sales representatives representing a single principal*

Sales representatives who represent a single principal are not considered to be independent contractors. Thus, activities conducted by them subject their principal to tax to the same extent as if they were performed by the principal [*Corporate Tax Bulletin 2004-01*, §I.E.3.].

¶914

Independent Contractor Is Not a Representative

Note that, for purposes of P.L. 86-272, the term "representative" does not include an independent contractor [15 U.S.C. § 381(c)(1)].

• *Protected activities*

Under *Corporate Tax Bulletin 2004-01*, the following in-state activities will not cause the loss of protection for otherwise protected sales:

(1) *Advertising:* soliciting orders for sales by any type of advertising [*Corporate Tax Bulletin 2004-01*, § I.D.1.].

(2) *In-state employees or representatives:* soliciting of orders by an in-state resident employee or representative of the company *if* the employee or representative does not maintain or use any office or other place of business in Pennsylvania other than an "in-home" office [*Corporate Tax Bulletin 2004-01*, § I.D.2.]. An "in-home" office is one located in the residence of the employee or representative that (a) is not publicly attributed to the company or to the employee or representative in an employee or representative capacity and (b) is used only for soliciting and receiving orders, for transmitting orders outside Pennsylvania for acceptance or rejection or for any other protected activity [*Corporate Tax Bulletin 2004-01*, § I.C.17.].

(3) *Samples and promotional materials:* carrying samples and promotional materials only for display or distribution without charge or other consideration [*Corporate Tax Bulletin 2004-01*, § I.D.3.].

(4) *Display racks:* furnishing and setting up display racks and advising customers on the display of the company's products without charge or other consideration [*Corporate Tax Bulletin 2004-01*, § I.D.4.].

(5) *Automobiles:* providing automobiles to sales personnel for their use in conducting protected activities [*Corporate Tax Bulletin 2004-01*, § I.D.5.].

(6) *Passing orders and information to home office:* passing orders, inquiries, and complaints to the home office [*Corporate Tax Bulletin 2004-01*, § I.D.6.].

(7) *Missionary sales activities:* the solicitation of indirect customers for the company's goods. For example, a manufacturer's solicitation of retailers to buy the manufacturer's goods from the manufacturer's wholesale customers is protected if such solicitation activities are otherwise immune [*Corporate Tax Bulletin 2004-01*, § I.D.7.].

(8) *Coordinating shipment or delivery:* coordinating shipment or delivery without payment or other consideration and providing information with respect to shipment or delivery either prior or subsequent to the placement of the order [*Corporate Tax Bulletin 2004-01*, § I.D.8.].

(9) *Checking inventories for re-order:* checking of customers' inventories without a charge (for re-order, but not for other purposes such as quality control) [*Corporate Tax Bulletin 2004-01*, § I.D.9.].

(10) *Sample/display rooms:* maintaining a sample or display room for two weeks (14 calendar days) or less at any one location within Pennsylvania during the tax year [*Corporate Tax Bulletin 2004-01*, § I.D.10.].

(11) *Recruiting activities:* recruiting, training, or evaluating sales personnel, including occasionally using homes, hotels, or similar places for meeting with sales personnel [*Corporate Tax Bulletin 2004-01*, § I.D.11.].

(12) *Customer complaints:* mediating direct customer complaints when the purpose is solely to ingratiate the sales personnel with the customer and facilitate requests for orders [*Corporate Tax Bulletin 2004-01*, § I.D.12.].

(13) *Personal property:* owning, leasing, using, or maintaining personal property for use in the employee's or representative's "in-home" office or automobile that is solely limited to the conducting of protected activities. Thus, the use of personal property such as cellular telephones, facsimile machines, duplicating equipment, personal computers, and computer software, that is limited to the carrying on of protected solicitation and entirely ancillary activities does not, by itself, remove the protection of P.L. 86-272 [*Corporate Tax Bulletin 2004-01*, § I.D.13.].

• *Activities not protected*

Under *Corporate Tax Bulletin 2004-01*, the following in-state activities (assuming they are not of a *de minimis* level) will cause otherwise protected sales to lose their protection under P.L. 86-272:

(1) *Repair and maintenance:* making repairs or providing maintenance or service to the property sold or to be sold [*Corporate Tax Bulletin 2004-01*, § I.C.1.].

(2) *Account collection:* collecting accounts (current accounts) whether directly or by third parties, through assignment, or otherwise [*Corporate Tax Bulletin 2004-01*, § I.C.2.].

(3) *Installation:* installation or supervision of installation at or after shipment or delivery [*Corporate Tax Bulletin 2004-01*, § I.C.3.].

(4) *Training for non-solicitation personnel:* conducting training courses, seminars, or lectures for personnel other than personnel involved only in solicitation [*Corporate Tax Bulletin 2004-01*, § I.C.4.].

(5) *Technical assistance:* providing any kind of technical assistance or service (including but not limited to, engineering assistance or design service) when one of the purposes is other than the facilitation of the solicitation of orders [*Corporate Tax Bulletin 2004-01*, § I.C.5.].

(6) *Resolution of customer complaints:* investigating, handling, or otherwise assisting in resolving customer complaints, other than mediating direct complaints when the sole purpose is to ingratiate the sales personnel with the customer [*Corporate Tax Bulletin 2004-01*, § I.C.6.].

(7) *Approving or accepting orders* [*Corporate Tax Bulletin 2004-01*, § I.C.7.].

(8) *Repossessing property* [*Corporate Tax Bulletin 2004-01*, § I.C.8.].

(9) *Securing deposits on sales* [*Corporate Tax Bulletin 2004-01*, § I.C.9.].

(10) *Damaged or returned property:* picking up or replacing damaged or returned property [*Corporate Tax Bulletin 2004-01*, § I.C.10.].

(11) *Non-solicitation personnel activities:* hiring, training, or supervising personnel, other than personnel involved only in solicitation [*Corporate Tax Bulletin 2004-01*, § I.C.11.].

(12) *Agency stock checks:* using agency stock checks or any other instrument or process by which sales are made within Pennsylvania by sales personnel [*Corporate Tax Bulletin 2004-01*, § I.C.12.].

(13) *Sample/display rooms:* maintaining a sample or display room in excess of two weeks (14 calendar days) at any one location within Pennsylvania during the tax year [*Corporate Tax Bulletin 2004-01*, § I.C.13.].

(14) *Sales/exchanges of samples:* carrying samples from which sales, exchanges, or distributions are made in any manner for consideration or other value [*Corporate Tax Bulletin 2004-01*, § I.C.14.].

(15) *In-state facilities:* owning leasing, using, or maintaining any of the following facilities or property in Pennsylvania [*Corporate Tax Bulletin 2004-01*, § I.C.15.]:

¶914

(a) Repair shop.

(b) Parts department.

(c) Any kind of office other than an "in-home" office. See item (17), below.

(d) Warehouse.

(e) Meeting place for directors, officers, or employees.

(f) Stock of goods other than samples for sales personnel or samples that are used entirely ancillary to solicitation.

(g) Telephone answering service publicly attributed to the company or to employees or agents of the company in their representative status.

(h) Mobile stores (*i.e.*, vehicles with drivers who are sales personnel making sales from the vehicles).

(i) Real property or fixtures to real property of any kind.

(16) *Consignment:* Consigning stock of goods or other tangible personal property to any person (including an independent contractor) for sale [*Corporate Tax Bulletin 2004-01,* § I.C.16.].

(17) *Franchising/licensing:* Entering into franchising or licensing agreements; selling or otherwise disposing of franchises and licenses; or selling or otherwise transferring tangible personal property pursuant to franchise or license by franchisor or licensor to franchisee or licensee within Pennsylvania [*Corporate Tax Bulletin 2004-01,* § I.C.18.].

(18) *Nonancillary activities:* Conducting any activity not listed in *Corporate Tax Bulletin 2004-01,* § I.D. that is not entirely ancillary to requests for orders, even if the activity helps to increase purchases [*Corporate Tax Bulletin 2004-01,* § I.C.19.].

(19) *Office/place of business:* maintaining (by any employee or other representative) an in-home office. An "in-home office" is one that is located within the residence of the employee or representative that (a) is not publicly attributed to the company or to the employee or representative of the company in an employee or representative capacity; and (b) the use of which is limited to soliciting and receiving orders from customers, for transmitting orders outside Pennsylvania for acceptance or rejection by the company or for other activities that are protected under P.L. 86-272 or *Corporate Tax Bulletin 2004-01,* § I.D. The maintenance of any office or other place of business in Pennsylvania that does not strictly qualify as an "in-home" office, by itself, causes the loss of protection under *Corporate Tax Bulletin 2004-01* [*Corporate Tax Bulletin 2004-01,* § I.C.17.].

Public Listings, Business Cards, Business Stationery

A telephone listing or other public listing within Pennsylvania for the company or its employee or representative in such capacity, or other indications through advertising or business literature that the company or its employee or representative can be contacted at a specific address within Pennsylvania normally means that the company is maintaining within Pennsylvania an office or place of business attributable to the company or to its employee or representative in a representative capacity. However, the normal distribution and use of business cards and stationery identifying the employee's or representative's name, address, telephone and fax numbers, and affiliation with the company is not, by itself, considered advertising or otherwise publicly attributing an office to the company or its employee or representative [*Corporate Tax Bulletin 2004-01,* § I.C.17.].

¶914A *De Minimis* Standards

According to *Corporate Tax Bulletin 2004-01, de minimis* activities are those that, when taken together, establish only a trivial connection with Pennsylvania. An activity conducted with Pennsylvania on a regular or systematic basis or pursuant to a company policy (whether in writing or not) is normally not considered to be trivial. Whether an activity consists of a trivial or non-trivial connection with Pennsylvania is measured on both a *qualitative* and a *quantitative* basis. If an activity either quantitatively or qualitatively creates a non-trivial connection with Pennsylvania, it is not a *de minimis* activity and exceeds the protection of P.L. 86-272. The fact that an activity only accounts for a relatively small part of the business conducted within Pennsylvania does not, by itself, mean that an activity is a *de minimis* activity protected by P.L. 86-272 [*Corporate Tax Bulletin 2004-01*, § II.A.].

Sales Tax

The *de minimis* standards of *Corporate Tax Bulletin 2004-01* apply *only* to the corporate net income tax and the foreign franchise tax. A company must refer to the applicable statutes and regulations to determine its separate sales and use tax responsibilities [*Corporate Tax Bulletin 2004-01*, § II.A.8.(f)].

No tax return required solely for de minimis *activities:* According to the Department of Revenue, while the activities discussed below are sufficient to subject a person to tax, the Department will not require the filing of a tax return based solely on such *de minimis* activities. However, the taxpayer may be required to document its eligibility for such consideration. The documentation may take the form of a business activities questionnaire, a check-off on a tax return, or a separate form for this purpose [*Corporate Tax Bulletin 2004-01*, § II.A.].

De minimis *standard exceeded in the previous year but not in the current year:* If a company exceeded the *de minimis* standard last year, but is below the standard this year, a return must be filed this year. Companies are required to file a return for years they fall below the *de minimis* standard to document the basis of their claim. However, the Department of Revenue is reviewing whether this requirement can be satisfied by the filing of an affidavit or some alternative documentation [*Corporate Tax Bulletin 2004-01*, § II.A.8.(g)].

• *Time and dollar volume limits*

The following activities are *de minimis* if the total number of calendar days during which any of these activities are conducted in Pennsylvania during the taxable year is no more than seven (7) days and all such activities produce total Pennsylvania sales of $10,000 or less during the taxable year. If the taxable year is less than 12 months, the 12-month period ending with the end of the short taxable year is considered [*Corporation Tax Bulletin 2004-01*, § II.A.1.].

(1) *Installation activities:* installation activities for which a separate charge is made [*Corporation Tax Bulletin 2004-01*, § II.A.1.(a)].

(2) *Repair, maintenance, and service activities* [*Corporation Tax Bulletin 2004-01*, § II.A.1.(b)].

(3) *Technical assistance/service activities:* technical assistance or service activities (including but not limited to engineering assistance or design service) [*Corporation Tax Bulletin 2004-01*, § II.A.1.(c)].

(4) *Training:* the conduct of training courses, seminars, or lectures by the vendor that is incidental to the use of personal property sold by him to persons in the Commonwealth *if* (a) free or for a nominal charge as compared to actual expenses *and* (b) when viewed as a whole, a trivial part of the sale [*Corporation Tax Bulletin 2004-01*, § II.A.1.(d)].

(5) *Shows/flea markets:* attendance at an organized show or "flea market" for the purpose of exhibiting goods and making sales of the exhibited goods [*Corporation Tax Bulletin 2004-01*, § II.A.1.(e)].

Franchise Tax

For franchise tax purposes, solicitation activities in Pennsylvania for seven (7) calendar days or less per year and that produce annual sales in Pennsylvania of $10,000 or less are *de minimis* [*Corporate Tax Bulletin 2004-01*, § II.A.5.]. See discussion of the application of the *de minimis* standard for franchise tax purposes at ¶ 1310.

- *Installation for which no separate charge is made*

Installation activities (including supervision of installation) that are customarily performed by the seller and for which there is no separate charge are generally considered to be *de minimis*. On the other hand, installation activities that customarily would be arranged separately from the purchase of personal property and for which a charge is made are not considered *de minimis*. Note, however, that there is an exception (see above) for installation activities conducted in Pennsylvania during the taxable year for no more than seven (7) days and producing total Pennsylvania sales of $10,000 or less during the taxable year [*Corporation Tax Bulletin 2004-01*, § II.A.2.].

> *Example:* Connecting a clothes dryer to existing venting and electrical outlets is a *de minimis* activity. Installation of electrical outlets or vents into the structure is not *de minimis*.

- *Purchasing activities*

The presence of employees in Pennsylvania solely for the purpose of purchasing goods from vendors located are Pennsylvania is *de minimis* [*Corporation Tax Bulletin 2004-01*, § II.A.3.].

- *Incidental travel in Pennsylvania*

Travel into Pennsylvania that is incidental to a person's principal business is *de minimis* if it is done on an occasional basis [*Corporation Tax Bulletin 2004-01*, § II.A.4.].

> *Example:* A New Jersey contractor travels into Pennsylvania for the purpose of purchasing supplies that it uses in its New Jersey contracting business. The travel in Pennsylvania is *de minimis*.

Trucking Companies

Trucking companies are subject to special *de minimis* standards, discussed below.

- *Personal property incidentally present in Pennsylvania*

The physical presence in Pennsylvania of an out-of-state entity's equipment, tooling, inventory, and employees on a temporary basis for the purpose of having work or services performed by an in-state entity is *de minimis* provided that the activity engaged in is not the pursuit of a market in Pennsylvania, the equipment is not used or held by an affiliated, in-state entity, and the employees have no control over work done in Pennsylvania by the in-state entity [*Corporation Tax Bulletin 2004-01*, § II.A.6.].

- *Commercial printer*

An exclusion from taxation for commercial printers is provided by 72 P.S. § 10003.10. These are *de minimis* activities within the meaning of *Corporation Tax Bulletin 2004-01* [*Corporation Tax Bulletin 2004-01*, § II.A.7.]. The exclusion for commercial printers is discussed at ¶ 720.

¶914A

• *Truck and bus company de minimis activities*

The *de minimis* standard of *Corporation Tax Bulletin 2004-01* applies only to truck and bus companies that meet both of the following criteria [*Corporate Tax Bulletin 2004-01*, § II.B.1.]:

(1) The truck or bus company is a "corporation" as defined in 72 P.S. § 7401(1) or a "foreign entity" as defined in 72 P.S. § 601(a) that is or would be taxed as a truck or bus company under 72 P.S. § 7401(3)2.(b) and that is principally engaged directly in the movement of tangible personal property or persons by motor vehicle or charter bus operations.

(2) The truck or bus company engages solely in interstate commerce in Pennsylvania and does not own or rent any real or personal property in Pennsylvania except for motor vehicles and trailers used in interstate commerce.

All truck and bus companies subject to the Pennsylvania corporate net income are eligible for relief under the Pennsylvania *de minimis* standard [*Corporation Tax Bulletin 2004-01*, § II.B.3.(d)]. Note, however, that relief under the *de minimis* standard for capital stock/franchise tax purposes is available only to truck and bus companies subject to the franchise tax. Companies subject to the Pennsylvania capital stock tax are not eligible for relief under the *de minimis* standard [*Corporation Tax Bulletin 2004-01*, § II.B.3(c)].

See ¶ 1112 for discussion of taxation of truck or bus companies as defined in 72 P.S. § 7401(3)2.(b).

De minimis *activities for truck and bus companies:* A truck or bus company is required to file a corporate net income tax or foreign franchise tax report if its activities during the taxable year exceed *either* of the following standards:

(1) The company travels more than 50,000 loaded miles in Pennsylvania and makes at least one (1) trip with pickups or deliveries in Pennsylvania.

(2) The company has a Pennsylvania apportionment fraction of more than 5% and has more than 12 trips with pickups or deliveries in Pennsylvania. Apportionment fractions for bus and truck companies are discussed at ¶ 1112.

If a taxable year is less than 12 months, the 12-month period ending with the end of the short taxable year is considered [*Corporate Tax Bulletin 2004-01*, § II.B.2.].

Trips through Pennsylvania without pickup or delivery: Trips merely through Pennsylvania without a pickup or delivery are not counted for purposes of the 12-trip limit [*Corporation Tax Bulletin 2004-01*, § II.B.3.(f)].

Company exceeds de minimis *standard:* If a company's activities exceed the *de minimis* standard it is not entitled to exclude the first 50,000 loaded miles or 12 pickups and deliveries from its taxable activity. Exceeding the *de minimis* standard causes all Pennsylvania activity to become reportable [*Corporation Tax Bulletin 2004-01*, § II.B.3.(b)].

Loaded miles: Loaded miles are whenever the vehicle is carrying property for hire. Loaded miles do not include deadhead miles (*i.e.,* miles the vehicle travels empty going to load the property or travels empty between loads or travels empty when returning to home base after unloading the property hauled) [*Corporation Tax Bulletin 2004-01*, § II.B.3.(l)].

Trip with pickups and deliveries: For bus companies, a trip with pickups or deliveries means a trip involving stops in Pennsylvania for the purpose of picking up or discharging passengers or freight or stops related to charter service, touring, sightseeing, excursions and any similar activities. For truck and bus companies, all pickups and deliveries or stops made during the same trip into Pennsylvania count

¶914A

as one trip. A trip may not extend beyond one 24-hour time period; and any travel continuing beyond that period of time is considered another trip [*Corporation Tax Bulletin 2004-01*, § II.B.2.].

> *Example 1:* Truck Company A makes two deliveries and one pickup on the same trip. For purposes of the 12-trip limitation, this is counted as one trip [*Corporate Tax Bulletin 2004-01*, § II.B.3.(a)].

> *Example 2:* Truck Company B picks up property in Philadelphia and delivers it to Pittsburgh. This trip is not protected by the *de minimis* standard. The pickup of property or a passenger at one location in Pennsylvania and delivery of the same property or passenger to another location in Pennsylvania during the same trip constitutes *intrastate* commerce, which does not fall within the protection of the *de minimis* standard.

Incidental stops: Stops that are incidental to the purpose of the trip are not counted. For example, a stop at a restaurant or truck stop for the convenience of its passengers to use the facilities is not considered a "stop" for purposes of the *de minimis* standard [*Corporate Tax Bulletin 2004-01*, § II.B.3.(k)].

De minimis *standard exceeded in the previous year but not in the current year:* If a company exceeded the *de minimis* standard last year, but is below the standard this year, a return must be filed this year. Truck or bus companies are required to document the basis of their claim that they fall below the *de minimis* standard. However, the Department of Revenue is reviewing the form that documentation will take [*Corporate Tax Bulletin 2004-01*, § II.B.3.(g)].

¶915 Annual Reports

Corporations must submit an annual report under oath or affirmation of its president, vice-president, or other principal officer, and of its treasurer or assistant treasurer [72 P.S. § 7403(a)]. Prior to January 1, 2008, this provision did not contain the phrase "or other authorized officers." The report must contain any information required by the Department of Revenue. In practice this requirement is met by filing PA Form RCT-101, with all applicable schedules attached, and a federal Form 1120, prepared on a separate return basis. If a corporation does not file a federal Form 1120, its PA Form RCT-101 must contain the information that would have been required if it had filed a federal return. If the Commonwealth wants additional information, they will write and ask for it. It is important to handle correspondence properly (see ¶4608 for explanation of how to handle correspondence).

A corporation that has an interest in a partnership, joint venture, association, or other unincorporated enterprise (all referred to as "partnership") must file a copy of the partnership's federal Form 1065 and a detailed description of all partnership activity, including a detailed explanation of all business and nonbusiness income [61 Pa. Code § 153.29(h)].

The Department of Revenue does not accept pencil copies of returns; all reports must be either typewritten or printed in ink.

Reproduction of Forms

Authority to reproduce forms must be requested and approved in writing by the Department of Revenue prior to use. To be approved, the reproduction (including computer-produced forms) must be identical to the form provided by the Department. However, the coupons from the Form REV-8571 coupon book cannot be reproduced. The official coupons provided by the Department must be used in all cases. To obtain permission to reproduce forms, write to PA Department of Revenue, Bureau of Corporation Taxes, Annual Report Forms—Reproduction, Dept. 380700, Harrisburg, PA 17128-0700.

- *Skeleton reports—Form RCT-101-I*

A corporation that is qualified to terminate tax reporting but wants to preserve the right to use its name should file Form RCT-101-I (Pennsylvania Corporation Tax Report-Inactive Company) instead of an Out of Existence Affidavit or Withdrawal Affidavit. Corporations filing Form RCT-101-I are still subject to the minimum capital stock/franchise tax of $300.

- *Third-party preparers required to e-file*

Requirement to e-file: For all calendar years following a calendar year in which a third-party preparer prepares 50 or more Pennsylvania corporate net income (CNI) reports, the third-party preparer is required to electronically file (e-file) all CNI reports in the manner prescribed by Department. Once a third-party preparer is subject to this filing mandate, the third-party preparer continues to be subject to the mandate regardless of how many CNI tax reports he or she prepares during a calendar year. A third-party preparer who is subject to this filing mandate must have tax software that is compatible with Department e-filing requirements [Pennsylvania Department of Revenue, *Notice*, 41 Pa.B. 4725, August 27, 2011]. This requirement applies to reports filed for tax years beginning on or after January 1, 2011, during calendar years beginning on or after January 1, 2012.

Third-party preparer defined: For this purpose, a third-party preparer is any natural person, fiduciary, corporation or other entity who or that prepares for remuneration, or who employs one or more persons to prepare for remuneration, any return for a tax administered by the Department or is assigned a Preparer Tax Identification Number (PTIN) by the Internal Revenue Service. None of the following, however, are considered third-party preparers for remuneration: (1) tax return preparers who voluntarily prepare the returns of others for no pecuniary benefit; (2) persons who merely provide mechanical assistance such as typing; (3) regular employees of an employer who prepare returns for other regular employees of the employer or the employer's officers and regular employees; or (4) fiduciaries who prepare returns for the trusts or estates that they serve.

50 report threshold: A third-party preparer must include all Pennsylvania CNI reports that the third-party preparer, or his or her members or employees prepare and submit to the Department. This amount includes all original and amended, resident or non-resident, full-year or part-year reports to the extent that such reports can be e-filed with the Department. If a third-party preparer has multiple business locations, the combined total of all the reports for all locations are included.

Penalty: A third-party preparer who fails to file a CNI report by e-file is subject to a penalty of 1% of the tax due on the improperly filed return up to a maximum of $500, but not less than $10.

Penalty waiver: The Department of Revenue will waive the penalty applicable to a return that is not e-filed in the following situations:

(1) The taxpayer has specifically directed the third-party preparer to file the return pursuant to a different filing method than e-file. The taxpayer's directive must be indicated on the return.

(2) The preparer's tax software does not support e-filing of a required attachment to the return.

(3) The Department of Revenue, at its discretion, may waive the penalties applicable to returns not e-file if the Department of Revenue determines the mandate to e-file constitutes undue hardship of the third-party preparer. The third-party preparer must submit a written request for the waiver (clearly explaining why e-filing causes an undue hardship) for every calendar year. A request for a waiver must be mailed to the Department of Revenue, Bureau of Corporation Taxes, Director's Office, P.O. Box 280700, Harrisburg, Pennsylvania 17128-0700.

• *Due dates*

For tax years beginning on or before December 31, 2015, calendar-year corporations were required to file their annual corporate net income tax reports on or before April 15 following the end of the tax year [72 P.S. § 7403(a)]. A fiscal-year corporation was required file its annual report within 30 days after its federal return was due, or would have been due were one required [72 P.S. § 7403(e)]. In practice, however, this rule was interpreted to mean one month after the federal return was due. Calendar-year DISCs must file annual reports by October 15, and fiscal year DISCs have one month beyond their federal due date. A taxpayer with a 52-53 week year that closes on any of the last seven days in December or the first seven days of January is considered a calendar-year taxpayer with year ending December 31 [72 P.S. § 7403(k)(3)]. Act 84 of 2016 provides, with respect to tax years beginning after December 31, 2015, the deadline to file corporate tax reports is 30 days after the due date of a corporation's federal income tax return.

• *Timely mailing is timely filing*

Timely mailing is considered timely filing. However, the taxpayer must provide adequate proof of timely mailing. The testimony of a taxpayer's manager of state and local taxes that a return was timely mailed was insufficient proof of timely mailing [*Transcontinental Gas Pipe Line Corp. v. Cmwlth.*, 620 A.2d 614 (Pa.Commw. 1993)]. Any report and/or payment postmarked by the U.S. Postal Service on or before the due date is considered to be timely made. Presentation of a receipt indicating that the report or payment was mailed by registered or certified mail on or before the due date is evidence of timely filing and payment [72 P.S. § 7403.1]. Postmarks other than those of the U.S. Postal Service are not acceptable proof of timely filing. If a corporation uses a private mail service and the return does not reach Harrisburg on time, it is not considered to have made a timely filing.

If the last day for filing falls on a Saturday, Sunday, or a legal holiday of the United States or of Pennsylvania, the report or return may be filed on the next regular business day [72 P.S. § 704].

For an explanation of verification of reports and returns, secrecy of returns, and termination of reporting, see ¶ 1320.

• *Section 338 transactions*

Under IRC § 338 a corporation that acquires at least 80% of the stock of another corporation (the target) within a 12-month period may elect or (under certain circumstances) may be treated as having elected to treat the stock purchase as a purchase of assets. Where the target is not includable in a consolidated federal return for a period that includes the acquisition date, the tax liability, if any, resulting from a deemed sale of assets by a target must be reported in the federal return filed for the target's taxable year that ends at the close of the acquisition date. If the target is a member of an affiliated group for the taxable year that includes the acquisition date and the target would be includable in a consolidated federal return by the selling group, the deemed sale of assets is treated as the target's last transaction occurring at the close of the acquisition date in a separate taxable year. The tax liability resulting from the deemed sale is reported by the target in a final, separate deemed sale federal return. 61 Pa. Code § 153.81 sets forth special rules that must be followed by a target subject to Pennsylvania corporate taxation [61 Pa. Code § 153.81(a)].

Reports required: Target corporations must file corporate net income and capital stock/franchise tax reports for periods for which a federal return is required to be filed, including a federal one-day deemed sale return. An election made for federal purposes is binding for Pennsylvania purposes, and a failure to elect for federal purposes is also binding for Pennsylvania purposes [61 Pa. Code § 153.81(b)].

Due date for reports: Pennsylvania reports are due 30 days after the federal return is due, or would be due in the case of a corporation participating in the filing of a consolidated federal return [61 Pa. Code § 153.81(c)]. See also discussion of *"Due dates"* and *"Timely mailing is timely filing,"* above.

Effect of IRC § 338 election on corporate net income tax liability: Taxable income generated as a result of an IRC § 338 election is subject to Pennsylvania corporate net income tax and is treated as business income subject to apportionment, if the taxpayer was entitled to apportionment for the taxable year ending immediately prior to the acquisition date. The income consequences of an IRC § 338 election must be reflected on a separate company basis and not as part of a combined or consolidated report [61 Pa. Code § 153.81(d)(1)]. For a ruling relating to the Department of Revenue's treatment of § 338(h)(10) elections, see Ruling No. CRP-14-001 (April 22, 2014).

Business/Nonbusiness Regulation Invalid in Part

61 Pa. Code § 153.81(d)(1), as written, treats all income generated by an IRC § 338 election as business income, whether as a result of an election under IRC § 338(g) or IRC § 338(h). The Pennsylvania Commonwealth Court, however, has ruled that an election under IRC § 338(h)(10) does not result in business income and that, to the extent 61 Pa. Code § 153.81(d)(1) conflicts with the Pennsylvania Supreme Court's interpretation of the underlying statute in *Laurel Pipe Line,* the regulation is invalid [*Canteen Corporation v. Cmwlth.,* 818 A.2d 594 (Pa.Commw. 2003), *aff'd per curiam,* Pennsylvania Supreme Court, No. 57 MAP 2003 (July 20, 2004)]. See discussion of the *Canteen Corporation* case at ¶ 1104. See also discussion of the *Laurel Pipe Line* case at ¶ 1104.

Effect of IRC § 338 election on capital stock/franchise tax liability: In computing the capital stock value of a target corporation on a deemed sale report, actual net worth as of the close of that day must be used. In computing average net income on a one-day deemed sale report, the average net income for the period ending immediately prior to the acquisition date must be used [61 Pa. Code § 153.81(d)(2)].

Apportionment: Where the effects of an IRC § 338 election are shown on a one-day deemed sale federal return, the apportionment factors or the taxable assets fraction for the period ending immediately prior to the acquisition date must be used [61 Pa. Code § 153.81(e)].

Bulk sales: If only shares of stock are transferred, a deemed sale of assets is not considered a bulk sale. However, if there is also a sale or transfer of assets in addition to the stock transfer, a bulk sale will have occurred if 51% of a stock of goods, wares, or merchandise of any kind, fixtures, machinery, equipment, building, or real estate is sold or transferred [61 Pa. Code § 153.81(f)].

¶916 Payment of Tax

The corporate net income tax must be paid on or before the original due date of the annual report [72 P.S. § 7403(b)]. Estimated tax must be paid under the provisions of 72 P.S. § 10003.2. Form REV-856 is used for payment of any tax due with the return. The amount to be transmitted with the annual report is the amount, if any, that has not been paid through estimated tax payments.

Payment by Electronic Funds Transfer

Payment made by electronic funds transfer (EFT) is discussed at ¶ 4617.

A corporation's tax obligation may also be satisfied by transferring available credits within its corporate account. (See ¶1326 for explanation of transfer of credits.)

• *Collection of tax by Department of Revenue*

The Department of Revenue may collect tax in accordance with the following [72 P.S. §7408.1(b)]]:

(1) Immediately, in the case of any tax that is due by not paid by the due date for payment of the tax.

(2) After 90 days from the mailing date of a notice of assessment, if no petition for reassessment has been filed.

(3) After 90 days from the mailing date of the Department's decision and order disposing of a petition for reassessment, if no petition for review has been filed.

(4) After 30 days from the mailing date of the decision and order of the Board of Finance and Revenue upon a petition for review or from the expiration of the Board's time for acting upon the petition, if no decision has been made.

— Immediately, in all cases of judicial sales, receiverships, assignments, or bankruptcies.

— Immediately, in the case of jeopardy assessments (discussed at ¶1204).

¶917 Extensions of Time

The time for filing corporate net income tax returns may be extended. All requests for extensions of time for filing must be made on or before the due date for the annual report. The Department of Revenue may grant an extension of no more than 60 days unless a federal extension of more than 60 days has been granted, in which case the Department may grant an additional extension of no more than 30 days beyond the federal extension [72 P.S. §7405]. No extensions of time are permitted for payment of tax or for filing estimated tax returns.

• *Automatic extensions*

If the federal income tax authorities grant an extension of time for filing the reports with the federal government, the Pennsylvania Department of Revenue will automatically grant an extension of time for filing the corporate net income tax annual report of 30 days after the termination of the federal extension. However, the amount of tax in such cases is subject to interest from the due date and at the Pennsylvania rate [72 P.S. §7405].

¶918 Estimated Tax

Every corporation subject to the Pennsylvania corporate net income tax must make payments of estimated tax. The estimated corporate net income tax is the estimated amount of corporate net income tax due with the final return.

See ¶4610 for discussion of the estimated tax provisions.

¶919 Amended Returns

Act 84 of 2016 codified procedures for amending corporate tax reports after December 31, 2016. Taxpayers are permitted to file an amended report notifying the Department of a correction to an original report within three years after the due date of the original report. Filing an amended report extends the Department's authority to adjust a taxpayer's tax liability for up to one year after the amended report is filed or three years after the original report is filed, whichever is later. If the Department fails to act on the return within one year, the return is deemed accepted as filed. However, the acceptance of an amended report does not limit the Department's authority to issue an assessment of additional tax within the relevant statute of limitations. Taxpayers may file a petition for review with the Board of Appeals within 90 days of the mailing date of the Department's written notice if they disagree with the Department's action on an amended return.

For years prior to 2017, in a notice, the Pennsylvania Department of Revenue announced that effective January 1, 2006, the Department would only consider for resettlement Amended PA Corporate Tax Reports (Form RCT-101X) received within eighteen (18) months of the date of settlement of the tax report being amended. The amended return must have been on Form RCT-101X; information provided to the Department in any form other than RCT-101X was not considered for resettlement. Amended reports received more than eighteen (18) months from the date of the settlement of the original report would not be considered for resettlement. The Department would not accept amended reports within 90 days after settlement. If a taxpayer sought a resettlement within 90 days of the settlement, the taxpayer was required to file a petition for resettlement with the Board of Appeals. The Department announced that it would pursue revisions to 61 Pa. Code § 153.64, the regulation addressing amended reports, consistent with the notice [*Notice Regarding Amended Corporate Tax Reports*, Pennsylvania Department of Revenue, December 20, 2005].

See ¶ 921 for procedures for filing an amended return in the case of federal changes.

Amended Report Trap

You have 90 days in which to file a petition for resettlement. Don't fall into the "amended report trap" and use this up by filing an amended report. Do as suggested above: File a Petition for Resettlement with an attached amended report in support of your petition.

RECORDS

¶920 Recordkeeping Requirements

Corporations must keep and maintain records with respect to the corporate net income tax for three years after the report is filed. The law states that a corporation must retain such record(s) of business within Pennsylvania for the period covered by the report and other pertinent papers as may be required by the Department of Revenue [72 P.S. § 7409].

¶921 Changes Made by the Federal Government

If the amount of taxable income as reported to the federal government is finally changed or corrected by the IRS or by any other U.S. agency or court, a taxpayer must, within six months (30 days for return filed before January 1, 2013) after the receipt of such final change or correction, make a corrected report, under oath or affirmation, to the Department of Revenue showing the corrected federal taxable income (Form RCT 128-B, "Report of Change"). A Report of Change must be filed whether the federal taxable income is increased, decreased, or remains the same. Petitioners may contest changes that do not affect tax in the current year but may affect liabilities in future years.

Interest on any additional tax starts running on the 31st day. The penalty for failure to file a Report of Change is $5 for every day during which time the corporation is in default, but the Department of Revenue may abate any such penalty in whole or in part [72 P.S. § 7406(a)].

If a report of change is filed after an administrative or judicial appeal has been made, the report of change is considered a part of the original annual report at any later proceeding, and no separate petition for review or appeal from an assessment or resettlement is necessary. After December 31, 2007, this part of the statute also reads " . . . to the extent the identical issues for the taxable year have been raised in the appeal" [72 P.S. § 7406(c)].

• *When federal change is "final"*

A change or correction that *increases* federal taxable income is "final" when a federal Notice and Demand for Payment is issued to the taxpayer. It is "received" by the taxpayer on the date the taxpayer receives the federal Notice and Demand for Payment [61 Pa. Code § 153.54(d)(1)].

A change or correction that *decreases* federal taxable income is "final" when the taxpayer receives a refund or credit and is "received" by a taxpayer on the date it receives the refund or credit [61 Pa. Code § 153.54(d)(2)].

A change or correction that does not increase or decrease a taxpayer's federal tax is "final" when a taxpayer receives a notice from the IRS that its federal return will be adjusted in accordance with the examination report and is "received" by a taxpayer on the date the taxpayer receives notice from the IRS that its federal return will be adjusted in accordance with the examination report [61 Pa. Code § 153.54(d)(3)].

Example 1: Roseanna Corporation is the parent of an affiliate group of corporations that files a consolidated federal income tax return. The IRS made a reallocation of income among the affiliated group pursuant to IRC § 482. Because of a tax credit available to the group, however, the federal tax was unchanged. Nevertheless, Roseanna Corporation, a Pennsylvania corporation, must file a Report of Change with the Pennsylvania Department of Revenue.

Example 2: Rich Corporation timely files a corporate net income tax return in Pennsylvania in conformity with its federal taxable income. The IRS audits Rich Corporation's federal return, which results in an increase in federal taxable income. Rich Corporation does not contest this change. It must file a Report of Change with the Pennsylvania Department of Revenue within 30 days after it receives a Federal Notice and Demand for Payment.

Example 3: Poor Corporation timely files a corporate net income tax return in Pennsylvania in conformity with its federal taxable income. The IRS audits Poor Corporation's federal return, which results in an increase in federal taxable income. Poor Corporation contests this change and files a petition in the U.S. Tax Court, which upholds the action of the IRS. Poor Corporation does not contest the action of the Tax Court. Within 30 days after it receives a Federal Notice and Demand for Payment, Poor Corporation must file a Report of Change with the Pennsylvania Department of Revenue.

Example 4: Stubborn Corporation files a Pennsylvania corporate net income tax return in conformity with its federal taxable income. The IRS audits Stubborn Corporation's federal return, which results in an increase in federal taxable income. Stubborn Corporation contests this change and pursues all administrative and judicial remedies without paying the contested tax. The U.S. Supreme Court finally rules against Stubborn Corporation. Within 30 days after it receives a Federal Notice and Demand for Payment, Stubborn must file a Report of Change with the Pennsylvania Department of Revenue.

Example 5: Ambi Corporation files a Pennsylvania corporate net income tax return in conformity with its federal taxable income. The IRS audits Ambi's federal return. The result is that Ambi's federal taxable income remains the same, but its Pennsylvania taxable income is changed as a result of the federal audit. Ambi must, within 30 days after receiving notification from the IRS of its action, file a Report of Change with the Pennsylvania Department of Revenue.

• *More than one federal change*

If the IRS (or any other agency or U.S. court) changes a corporation's federal taxable income more than one time within a year, that corporation must file a Pennsylvania Report of Change each time [61 Pa. Code § 153.54(e)].

> **Example:** As a result of an IRS audit of its federal income tax return, Deck Corporation's federal taxable income has been increased, and Deck has paid the additional tax. It must also file a Report of Change in Pennsylvania. After Deck has done this, it contests the change in its federal taxable income and receives a refund from the IRS. Since its Pennsylvania taxable income has now decreased because of this later action, Deck must file a second Pennsylvania Report of Change.

• *Amended returns*

Filing an amended report will not satisfy the requirement of filing a Report of Change [61 Pa. Code § 153.54(g)].

Review Options

A corporation must file a Pennsylvania Report of Change if the IRS makes changes to its federal return. However, if a corporation's Pennsylvania taxable income has been decreased, it should take steps to recover the overpaid tax. This can be accomplished by filing either (1) an amended return or (2) a petition for refund. Under prior law, an amended return may be filed any time within one year of settlement or a petition for refund within two years of settlement.

¶921

CORPORATE NET INCOME TAX

CHAPTER 10

TAXABLE INCOME, DEDUCTIONS, AND CREDITS

¶1001 "Taxable Income" Defined

"Taxable income" means federal taxable income before the net operating loss deduction and special deductions (presently Line 28 of Page 1 of federal Form 1120 and often referred to as "Line 28 income"), modified or adjusted by statute or regulation, unless the context clearly indicates otherwise [61 Pa. Code § 153.11(a)] and can be represented by the following formula:

Federal taxable income (before NOL and special deductions)

(+)	Pennsylvania additions
(–)	*Pennsylvania deductions*
=	**Pennsylvania taxable income**

Pennsylvania additions to federal taxable income are discussed at ¶1002; Pennsylvania deductions from federal taxable income are discussed at ¶1003.

• *Consolidated returns not allowed*

All corporations must file separate returns for Pennsylvania corporate net income tax purposes. For affiliated groups of corporations that filed a consolidated return for federal income tax purposes, this means the preparation of a "hypothetical" separate federal return (see also ¶1003).

• *Intracompany transactions/Intangible holding companies*

The Pennsylvania Department of Revenue has expressed concern about transactions involving subsidiaries, particularly Delaware holding companies, when such transactions are less than arm's length. As a result of Act 52 of 2013 and effective for tax years after December 31, 2014, deductions will generally be disallowed for an intangible expense or cost, or an interest expense or cost, paid, accrued or incurred directly or indirectly in connection with transactions with an affiliated entity. This legislation was enacted in an effort to address the state tax planning technique of forming holding companies with a situs in a favorable taxing state such as Delaware to hold intangibles (Delaware, for example, generally exempts income from intangible assets from state income taxation) while at the same time providing tax deductions to related Pennsylvania corporations enabling such corporations subject to the Pennsylvania corporate net income tax to reduce their income tax liability. Intangible expenses are generally royalties, licenses, or fees paid for the acquisition, use, maintenance, management, ownership, sale, exchange, or other disposition of patents, patent applications, trade names, trademarks, service marks, copyrights, mask works or other similar expenses or costs, and interest expense related thereto. Interest expense includes the deduction allowed by under IRC § 163 to the extent such deduction is related to the intangible expense or cost. Information Notice Corporation Taxes 2016-1 issued February 19, 2016 provides guidance regarding the "add-back" provisions of Act 52 of 2013.

A corporate taxpayer that has paid or incurred an intangible expense to an affiliate is allowed a credit against its corporate net income tax if the affiliate is subject to tax in Pennsylvania or any other state or possession of the United States on a tax base that includes the intangible expense it received from the taxpayer. The credit is generally equal to the taxpayer's Pennsylvania apportionment factor multiplied by the affiliate's tax liability (without reduction for any tax credit of the affiliate) with respect to the intangible expense it received from the taxpayer.

An affiliate of the taxpayer generally is a 50 percent or more owner or subsidiary, with attribution rules under IRC § 318 and a component member of a controlled group under IRC § 1563(b). Also, a taxpayer's affiliate includes a person to or from whom there is attribution under IRC § 1563(e). This includes a shareholder of the taxpayer that actually or constructively owns 5 percent or more in value of the taxpayer's stock. An affiliate may be any person – an individual, partnership, limited liability company, estate, or trust as well as another corporation. Intangible expenses paid by the taxpayer to an affiliate may be deducted by the taxpayer if:

• The transaction giving rise to the intangible expense did not have as the principal purpose avoidance of corporate net income tax and was done at arm's-length rates and terms.

• The affiliate is domiciled in a foreign country that has in force a comprehensive income tax treaty with the United States providing for allocation of all categories of income subject to taxation, or withholding of tax on royalties, licenses, fees, and interest for the prevention of double taxation and the sharing of information.

- The affiliate, directly or indirectly, paid, accrued, or incurred a payment to a nonaffiliate, if such amount is equal to or less than the taxpayer's proportional share of the transaction with the nonaffiliate.

• *IRC § 338 elections*

Income of a target corporation resulting from an IRC § 338 election is considered business income subject to apportionment (if the taxpayer was entitled to apportionment for the taxable year ending immediately prior to the acquisition date) and must be reported on a separate (not consolidated) basis [61 Pa. Code § 153.81(d)(1)]. The Pennsylvania Commonwealth Court has held that insofar as the requirements of 61 Pa. Code § 153.81(d)(1) conflict with the Pennsylvania Supreme Court's decision in *Laurel Pipe Line* (see ¶1104), it is invalid. See more detailed discussion at ¶915. Therefore, income resulting from an IRC § 338(h)(10) election is nonbusiness income, not business income [*Canteen Corporation v. Cmwlth.*, 818 A.2d 594 (Pa.Commw. 2003), *aff'd per curiam*, Pennsylvania Supreme Court, No. 57 MAP 2003 (July 20, 2004)].

Canteen Nonbusiness Income Ruling Not Applicable After 1998

It is the policy of the Department of Revenue that the part of the decision in *Canteen Corp. v. Commonwealth* [818 A.2d 594 (Pa. Cmwlth. 2003)] holding that gains or losses from IRC § 338 transactions produce nonbusiness income does not apply to taxable years beginning after December 31, 1998, because of statutory amendments to the definition of "business income." In accordance with 61 Pa. Code § 153.81, taxable income generated as a result of an IRC § 338 election will be treated as business income [*Corporate Statement of Tax Policy 2004-01*, Pennsylvania Department of Revenue, November 9, 2004; 61 Pa. Code § 170.3]. This policy statement is based on 2001 statutory amendments to the definition of "business income."

If only shares of stock are transferred, a deemed sale of assets is not considered a bulk sale [61 Pa. Code § 153.81(f)](see also ¶915, ¶1003, and ¶1004). Since the income from IRC § 338 elections is ordinarily included in federal taxable income, no adjustment is necessary, except for showing any income on the separate return of the target corporation. See ¶1002 for other items that must be added to federal taxable income.

Target Corporation's Sales Factor Includes Certain Proceeds

The part of the *Canteen* decision (discussed above) that held that the fictional sale assets by the target corporation must be recognized by the Commonwealth will be followed. Therefore, the target corporation's sales factor will include, where required by law, the proceeds assigned to each asset that is deemed to have been sold [*Corporate Statement of Tax Policy 2004-01*, Pennsylvania Department of Revenue, November 9, 2004].

• *Regulated investment companies*

The Pennsylvania taxable income of a regulated investment company is taxable income as defined by the Internal Revenue Code [72 P.S. § 7401(3)1(n)].

Allocation and Apportionment

If the entire business of any corporation (except a regulated investment company) is not transacted within Pennsylvania, the taxable income is the portion of taxable income as defined above that is allocated and apportioned to Pennsylvania [72 P.S. § 7401(3)2]. (Allocation and apportionment of income are explained in Chapter 11.)

• *Depreciation*

Since Pennsylvania taxable income is based on federal taxable income before the net operating loss deduction and special deductions, all ordinary deductions allowable for federal purposes will be reflected in Pennsylvania taxable income (including the federal deduction for depreciation under IRC § 168. Depreciation on realty, however, is limited to straight-line depreciation. See discussion of the depreciation additions and subtractions at ¶ 1002 and ¶ 1003.

• *Federal credits*

Federal credits will not be reflected in Pennsylvania taxable income. They are not allowed as a deduction for Pennsylvania corporate net income tax purposes [61 Pa. Code § 153.13]. This means that while a corporation that deducts foreign taxes paid for federal income tax purposes will have this deduction automatically reflected in its Pennsylvania taxable income, a corporation that takes the foreign tax *credit* (instead of deduction) for federal purposes will not automatically have this deduction reflected in its Pennsylvania taxable income and cannot use it to reduce its federal taxable income in arriving at Pennsylvania taxable income [*Cmwlth. v. Westinghouse Electric Corp.*, 386 A.2d 491 (1977), aff'd, 478 Pa. 164, *app. dism'd*, 439 U.S. 805 (1978)]. For an explanation of Pennsylvania treatment of the federal jobs credit, see ¶ 1003.

• *Foreign taxes*

If the foreign tax deducted for federal purposes is a tax on or measured by income, it must be added back to federal taxable income before NOL and special deductions, in which case no deduction is allowed whether the foreign income tax is deducted or taken as a credit. However, if the foreign tax is not a tax on or measured by income, whether it is a deduction or a credit for federal purposes makes a difference.

• *Taxable income of certain automobile clubs*

Effective for taxable years beginning after December 31, 1997, the taxable income of an automobile club is limited to income from the conduct of an insurance business or of a travel agency business [72 P.S. § 10003.13(a)]. For corporate net income purposes, an automobile club is not considered a membership organization subject to federal limitations on deductions from taxable income under IRC § 277.

   NOTE: Similar provisions also apply to the capital stock value of automobile clubs. See ¶ 1306.

¶ 1002 Pennsylvania Additions to Federal Taxable Income

Some items not included in federal taxable income are required to be added in order to arrive at Pennsylvania taxable income. These add-back items are specified in 72 P.S. § 7401(3)1(d).

• *Taxes imposed on or measured by net income*

For corporate net income tax purposes, no deduction is allowed for any taxes imposed on or measured by net income (*e.g.*, state income taxes). To the extent that such taxes have been deducted for federal purposes, they must be added back to federal taxable income *before apportionment* [72 P.S. § 7401(3)1(o)]. This means that this item is subject to apportionment.

In general, income taxes imposed by other states are subject to Pennsylvania corporate net income tax add-back. However, the following states, as of December 2008, do not impose an income tax subject to Pennsylvania corporate net income add-back: (1) Nevada; (2) South Dakota; (3) Texas; (4) Washington; and (5) Wyoming. The Texas franchise tax is subject to add-back if the taxpayer is required to pay the tax based on net earned surplus. The net income portion of the Philadelphia business privilege tax is subject to add-back [*Corporation Tax Bulletin 2008-05*, Pennsylvania Department of Revenue].

• *Taxes not clearly on or measured by net income*

Confusion sometimes exists when taxes are not clearly on or measured by net income (*e.g.*, the Michigan Single Business Tax) or when tax computation is made on an alternative basis of net worth. The position of the Department of Revenue of

Revenue is that the Michigan Single Business tax must be added back to federal taxable income only to the extent that it is actually based upon net income. Only the supplemental gross income tax provision of the Indiana Gross Receipts tax must be added back.

- *Federal environmental tax*

The federal environmental tax is similar to the Pennsylvania corporate net income tax in that both begin with line 28 of the federal Form 1120. The fact that the federal environmental tax is based on federal alternative minimum taxable income (AMTI) instead of federal taxable income does not alter the fact that the tax is imposed on or measured by net income. AMTI, therefore, is merely a different way of calculating net income [*H.J. Heinz Co. v. Cmwlth.*, 678 A.2d 860 (Pa.Commw. 1996)].

- *Tax preference items*

There are no alternative minimum tax provisions in the Pennsylvania corporate net income tax law; and corporate taxpayers are required to add back to federal taxable income preference items specified in 72 P.S. §7401(3)1(d), but only *to the extent the item has not been included in federal taxable income*. These additions are required even if the sum of these items does not exceed the federal amount (*i.e.*, the *total* amount of these preferences must be added back without regard to any federal amount allowed as a deduction). A copy of federal Form 4626 must be attached to the Pennsylvania return even if a Form 4626 was not required to be filed with the federal government.

To the extent not included in federal taxable income, the following preference items must be added back to federal taxable income to arrive at Pennsylvania taxable income [72 P.S. §7401(3)1(d)]:

(1) Excess investment interest.

(2) Accelerated depreciation on real property. See *"Accelerated depreciation on IRC §1250 property"* below.

(3) Accelerated depreciation on personal property subject to a net lease.

(4) Amortization of certified pollution control facilities.

(5) Amortization of railroad rolling stock.

(6) Stock options.

(7) Reserves for losses on bad debts of financial institutions.

(8) Capital gains.

(9) Accelerated cost recovery deduction for 15-year realty, but only to the extent that such preference items are not included in federal taxable income. See *"Accelerated depreciation on IRC §1250 property"* below.

Caution: Add-Back of Tax Preferences

It may not be necessary to add back the entire amount of tax preferences shown on federal form 4626. Only those items specified by Pennsylvania statute must be added back to Line 28 income. See 72 P.S. §7401(c)1(d) for a list of items required to be added back.

- *Accelerated depreciation on IRC §1250 property*

Depreciation on real property for Pennsylvania corporate net income purposes is restricted to straight-line amounts. In any year in which the federal deduction for depreciation on IRC §1250 property exceeds the straight-line amount, the excess over the straight-line amount must be added back to federal taxable income in computing Pennsylvania taxable income [72 P.S. §7401(3)1(d)]. An add-back is also required for accelerated cost recovery deduction for 15-year realty under former IRC

§ 1250(a)(12)(B) to the extent not included in federal taxable income [72 P.S. § 7401(3)1(d)]. See ¶ 1003 for deductions when the federal amount is less than the straight-line amount.

• *Federal bonus depreciation for property placed in service before 9/28/17*

The federal Job Creation and Worker Assistance Act of 2002 (P.L. 107-146) authorized taxpayers to deduct a 30% bonus depreciation for certain qualified assets acquired after September 10, 2001, and before September 11, 2004, for federal income tax purposes [IRC § 168(k)]. The Jobs and Growth Reconciliation Act of 2003 increased the allowable federal bonus depreciation to 50% for property acquired after May 5, 2003, and placed in service before January 1, 2005 (or January 1, 2006, for certain property).

Federal bonus depreciation is not allowed for Pennsylvania corporate net income tax purposes. Taxpayers who claim IRC § 168(k) bonus depreciation must, in arriving at Pennsylvania taxable income, add back the bonus depreciation to federal taxable income in the year claimed. This add-back applies to both the 30% and 50% bonus depreciation. Then, under a formula that approximates federal depreciation deduction without bonus depreciation, taxpayers may subtract an additional amount equal to $3/7$ of the taxpayer's ordinary IRC § 167 deduction.

Recovery of 30% federal bonus depreciation: Over the life of the asset, the full asset cost will be recovered for 30% bonus depreciation, but the timing of the deductions for Pennsylvania corporate net income tax purposes will be different from the timing for federal income tax purposes.

Recovery of 50% federal bonus depreciation: For 50% bonus depreciation, however, the full asset cost will not be recovered. To achieve full recovery of the total amount of 50% bonus depreciation added back, taxpayers are allowed to deduct any remaining unrecovered amount in the last taxable year that the property is depreciated for federal tax purposes (see Example 6, below).

Disallowed bonus depreciation: The federal bonus depreciation deduction for certain qualified property authorized by § 168(k) of the Internal Revenue Code is not allowable in arriving a Pennsylvania taxable income for Pennsylvania corporate net income tax purposes [72 P.S. § 7401(1)]. "Pennsylvania taxable income" is discussed at ¶ 1001.

NOTE: In this *Guidebook,* property that qualifies for bonus depreciation under § 168(k) of the Internal Revenue Code is referred to as "IRC § 168(k) property."

Taxpayers who elect to take federal bonus depreciation under IRC § 168(k) must, therefore, make the following adjustments in arriving at Pennsylvania taxable income (see examples below):

(1) Add to federal taxable income the amount of IRC § 168(k) depreciation taken on the federal income tax return.

(2) Deduct from federal taxable income an additional amount equal to the product of the IRC § 167 depreciation on the qualified property multiplied by $3/7$.

Sale, disposition or fully depreciated IRC § 168(k) property: If bonus depreciation property (*i.e.,* property for which an addition to income on account of federal bonus depreciation has been made) becomes fully depreciated, or is sold or otherwise disposed of during a taxable year, a taxpayer make take an additional deduction to the extent that the bonus depreciation (*i.e.,* depreciation taken under IRC § 168(k)) has not been recovered through the additional deductions provided for by 72 P.S. § 7401(3)1(s)(1).

Decoupling forms: When taxpayers file Pennsylvania corporate tax reports (RCT-101), taxpayers who elected federal bonus depreciation must include Schedule C-3 (Adjustment for Bonus Depreciation) showing the calculation of adjustments and the amount of bonus depreciation to be recovered in subsequent years. If a taxpayer disposes of IRC § 168(k) property or is required to recapture depreciation, the taxpayer must also include Schedule C-4 (Adjustment for Sale of Section 168(k)

¶1002

Property & Recapture of Depreciation on Listed Property). Pennsylvania Form RCT-101XD is to be used by taxpayers filing amended reports for the sole purpose of reporting adjustments for bonus depreciation.

Decoupling examples: The following example illustrates the basic application of the adjustment rules with respect to Pennsylvania's decoupling from federal bonus (IRC § 168(k)) depreciation.

> *Example 1—Basic Example (30% bonus depreciation):* On October 1, 2001, Trevor Tyler Corporation (TT) purchased, at a cost of $100,000, equipment that qualified for IRC § 168(k) bonus depreciation (*i.e.,* IRC § 168(k) property).

Using the MACRS tables for 7-year property placed in service in the fourth quarter (mid-quarter convention), TT's federal depreciation schedule for this asset for 2001 through 2008 is as follows:

Column	(a)	(b)	(c)	(d)	(e)
	-	-	[(a)×(b)]	-	[(c)+(d)]
				Bonus (§168(k))	Total
	Depreciation	Depreciation	§167	Depreciable (30%	Federal
Year	Rate	§167 Basis	Depreciation	of $100,000)	Depreciation
2001	0.0357	$70,000	$2,499	$30,000	$32,499
2002	0.2755	70,000	19,285	-0-	19,285
2003	0.1968	70,000	13,776	-0-	13,776
2004	0.1406	70,000	9,842	-0-	9,842
2005	0.1004	70,000	7,028	-0-	7,028
2006	0.0873	70,000	6,111	-0-	6,111
2007	0.0873	70,000	6,111	-0-	6,111
2008	0.0764	70,000	5,348	-0-	5,348
					$100,000

TT's Pennsylvania depreciation deduction table for years 2001 through 2008 is as follows:

Column	(a)	(b)	(c)	(d)	(e)
	-	-	[(a)–(b)]	[(3/7)×(c)]	[(c)+(d)]
				Additional	Total PA
			Federal		Depreciation
	Total Federal	Bonus (§168(k))	§167	PA	
Year	Depreciation	Depreciation	Depreciation	Depreciation	for the Year
2001	$32,499	$30,000	$2,499	$1,071	$3,570
2002	19,285	-0-	19,285	8,265	27,550
2003	13,776	-0-	13,776	5,904	19,680
2004	9,842	-0-	9,842	4,218	14,060
2005	7,028	-0-	7,028	3,012	10,040
2006	6,111	-0-	6,111	2,619	8,730
2007	6,111	-0-	6,111	2,619	8,730
2008	5,348	-0-	5,348	2,292	7,640
	$100,000				$100,000

Note: Compare columns (a) and (e) in the Pennsylvania schedule. Note that the total amount of depreciation ($100,000) is the same for both federal and Pennsylvania purposes. However, the annual amounts of depreciation (*i.e.,* the timing of the deductions) differ.

> *Example 2—Sale of asset from Example 1 (30% bonus depreciation):* On January 2, 2003, TT sold the equipment (see Example 1) for $50,000. For federal income tax purposes, accumulated depreciation on this asset at the end of 2002 is $51,784 [$32,499 + $19,285]; adjusted basis for determination of gain is $48,216 [$100,000 – $51,784]; and federal gain is $1,784 [$50,000 – $48,216]. For Pennsylvania corporate net income tax purposes, TT has claimed additional deductions under 72 P.S. § 401(r) of $9,336 and is, therefore, entitled to recover an additional $20,664 [$30,000 – $9,336]. This amount is reported as an "Adjustment for Sale" on Schedule B-4. The adjusted basis for sale for Pennsylvania corporate net income tax purposes is $70,000 [$100,000 – ($9,336 + $20,664)]; and Pennsylvania gain on this sale is $20,000 [$50,000 – $30,000].

> *Example 3—Purchase of additional IRC §168(k) property (30% bonus depreciation):* On October 1, 2001, Sydash Corporation purchase IRC § 168(k) property that cost $100,000. Sydash's 2001 federal and Pennsylvania depreciation is the same as that for TT Corporation in Example 1. Assume that on October 1, 2002, without disposing of the

IRC § 168(k) property purchased in 2001, Sydash purchased another $100,000 piece of IRC § 168(k) equipment to be depreciation, like the 2001 equipment, over 7 years using MACRS.

Federal depreciation for 2002 is $51,784 [$32,499 for the 2002 equipment plus $19,285 for the 2001 equipment].

Sydash's 2002 additional Pennsylvania depreciation with respect to IRC § 168(k) property is $9,336 [³/₇ of ($51,784 – $30,000)].

Example 4—Business use falls below 50% (30% bonus depreciation): Assume the same facts as in Example 1, except that in 2003 the business use of the property fell to 40%. TT Corporation would be required to recapture depreciation for federal income tax purposes. It is the policy of the Pennsylvania Department of Revenue that when an asset no longer qualifies as IRC § 168(k) property and the taxpayer is required to recapture depreciation in the calculation of federal income tax, this even is handled like a sale of IRC § 168(k) property. Thus, additional Pennsylvania depreciation of $20,664 would be reported as an "Adjustment for Sale" on Schedule B-3.

Example 5—Depreciable automobiles (30% bonus depreciation): Due to federal limitations on the depreciation of automobiles, it is possible for a taxpayer to recover (for Pennsylvania corporate net income tax purposes) all of the disallowed bonus depreciation before the automobile is fully depreciated. If this occurs, the taxpayer may need to make an adjustment to the additional Pennsylvania depreciation in the year the allowable additional depreciation exceeds the remaining bonus depreciation to be recovered. Assume that on October 1, 2002, Sydash Corporation purchases a luxury automobile that is IRC § 168(k) property and that qualifies for the maximum federal depreciation deduction. Depreciation for 2001 through 2003 is shown in the table below.

	Bonus Depreciation	Regular Federal Depreciation	PA Additional Depreciation
2001	$4,600	$3,060	$1,311
2002		4,900	2,100
2003		2,950	1,264
			$4,676

At the end of 2003, the computed Pennsylvania additional depreciation exceeds the amount of bonus depreciation that can be recovered. The excess must be reported as an adjustment on Pennsylvania Schedule B-3. No further recovery of bonus depreciation can be made in subsequent years, and sale of this asset should not be included on Pennsylvania Schedule B-4 in the year of disposition.

Example 6—50% bonus depreciation: On July 1, 2003, Acacia Corporation purchased equipment with a basis of $100,000. The equipment qualified for the 50% federal bonus depreciation. In 2010 the asset is fully depreciated for federal income tax purposes. The taxpayer, however, will have recovered only $71,429 of the $100,000 cost of the asset for Pennsylvania purposes (see table below). Therefore, in 2010, Acacia will be allowed to deduct the unrecovered asset cost of $28,571 ($100,000 – $71,429), resulting in a total depreciation deduction for Pennsylvania purposes in 2010 of $29,527 ($28,571 + $956 MACRS deduction for 2010).

Year	Depreciable Basis (after (deducting bonus depreciation)	MACRS Percentage For Property Placed In Service In 2003	MACRS Depreciation	Additional PA Depreciation Deduction (3/7 of MACRS)	Total PA Depreciation Deduction (MACRS + Additional)
2003	$50,000	0.1429	$ 7,145	$ 3,062	$10,206
2004	$50,000	0.2449	12,245	5,248	17,493
2005	$50,000	0.1749	8,745	3,748	12,493
2006	$50,000	0.1249	6,245	2,676	8,921
2007	$50,000	0.0893	4,465	1,914	6,379
2008	$50,000	0.0892	4,460	1,911	6,371
2000	$50,000	0.0893	4,465	1,914	6,379
2010	$50,000	0.0446	2,230	956	3,186
Total					$71,429

• *Federal bonus depreciation for property placed in service on or after 9/28/17*

Act 72 of 2018 decoupled the state's corporate net income tax law from the 100 percent bonus depreciation provided in the federal Tax Cuts and Jobs Act of 2017. Act 72 was signed into law by Governor Tom Wolf on June 28, 2018. Administratively, the Department had first stated that a taxpayer was entitled to zero depreciation following the 2017 federal tax changes for qualified property. Corporation Tax Bulletin 2017-02 (December 22, 2017). That Bulletin disallowed all depreciation on assets subject to 100 percent federal bonus depreciation placed in service after Sept. 27, 2017. Following Act 72 (becoming law in June of 2018), however, the Department issued Corporation Tax Bulletin 2018-03, which superseded Bulletin 2017-02, and effectively adopted the Modified Accelerated Cost Recovery System (MACRS) of depreciation as the Department's policy and announced that for property placed in service before September 28, 2017, Corporation Tax Bulletin 2011-01 would continue to apply. Consequently, depreciation for corporate net income tax purposes is thus essentially calculated under the federal MACRS provisions for property acquisitions **on or after** September 28, 2017 pursuant to Act 72. Federal bonus depreciation must continue to be added back to taxable income. See 72 P.S. § 7401(3)1(q). A corporation may deduct any unused bonus depreciation in the tax year in which the corporation sells or disposes of the assets subject to bonus depreciation.

Sale or disposition of IRC § 168(k) property: If bonus depreciation property (*i.e.*, property for which an addition to income on account of federal bonus depreciation has been made) is sold or otherwise disposed of during a taxable year, a taxpayer make take an additional deduction to the extent that the bonus depreciation (*i.e.*, depreciation taken under IRC § 168(k)) has not been recovered through the additional deductions provided for by 72 P.S. § 401(3)1(r). See 72 P.S. § 7401(3)1(s)(2).

• *Employment incentive payments*

Taxpayers who take a credit against the corporate net income tax for employment incentive payments must add back to federal taxable income the amount equal to the credit taken to arrive at Pennsylvania taxable income [§ 491(a), Public Welfare Code (Act of June 13, 1967, P.L. 31)].

If a taxpayer who takes a Pennsylvania employment incentive payment credit (which must be added back) and a federal jobs credit (which may be taken as an additional deduction), the two will tend to offset each other; but they are independent of each other and must be reported separately on the corporate net income tax return. See ¶ 1003 for discussion of the additional deduction for disallowed federal wages.

• *Federal Repatriation Transition Tax*

In Information Notice Corporate Taxes and Personal Income Tax, 2018-1 (issued April 20, 2018), the Department of Revenue announced that the Repatriation Transition Tax (RTT) in the federal Tax Cuts and Jobs Act of 2017 is included in federal taxable income tax for purposes of the Pennsylvania Corporate Net Income Tax, notwithstanding that the RTT is not actually included in line 28 of the Federal Form 1120. The Department explained that 61 Pa. Admin. Code § 153.11 provides for a different interpretation of "taxable income" in certain instances. The Department also determined that the RTT deduction applies for purposes of the corporate net income tax as well as for the dividends received deduction because it is Subpart F income. Although federal law permits the RTT liability to be paid over eight years, the deferral is a federal election that is not available under Pennsylvania law.

¶ 1003 Pennsylvania Deductions from Federal Taxable Income

Corporations may claim deductions from federal taxable income for certain items, discussed below.

Deductions on Separate Returns

Pennsylvania does not permit the filing of consolidated reports by affiliated corporations [72 P.S. § 7404]. Each corporation in an affiliated group must file a separate return as if it had filed a separate federal return. This requires the preparation of a "hypothetical" federal return. Additional deductions may be required in some cases [61 Pa. Code § 153.14]. For example, a corporation filing on a separate basis may be entitled to a larger charitable contribution deduction than the consolidated group if it had a profit and the consolidated group did not. A capital loss of a corporation filing on a separate basis may have been "used" on the federal consolidated return to offset capital gains of other members of the consolidated group, and it would be entitled to an additional deduction for its loss on its Pennsylvania corporate net income tax return.

• *Amortization of certified pollution control facilities*

A taxpayer may take a special deduction for amortization of a certified pollution control facility under IRC § 169 when the rapid amortization period expires. The amount of the deduction for a given tax year is limited to the amount of depreciation that a taxpayer would have been allowed under the depreciation method election under IRC § 167 minus any depreciation taken for a given tax year. The total special deductions for certified pollution control facility amortization may not exceed the amount added to taxable income to be apportioned in prior years [61 Pa. Code § 153.14(4)(i)]. This deduction is not permitted for a tax year when the taxpayer did not have income to be apportioned [61 Pa. Code § 153.14(4)(ii)].

• *Change in ownership under IRC § 381 or IRC § 382*

In the case of a change in ownership by purchase, liquidation, acquisition of stock or reorganization of a corporation under IRC § 381 or 382, the limitations provided in the Internal Revenue Code with respect to net operating losses apply for the purpose of computing the portion of a net loss carryover for Pennsylvania corporate net income tax purposes. When the acquiring corporation or transferor corporation participates in the filing of consolidated federal returns, the entitlement of the acquiring corporation to the Pennsylvania net loss carryover of the acquiring corporation or the transfer corporation is determined as if separate federal returns had been filed prior to the change in ownership [72 P.S. § 7401(3)4(g)]. The applicable limitations provided by 72 P.S. § 7401(3)4(g) include limitations imposed by the IRC solely on account of a change in ownership; and they include (but are not limited to) IRC § 269, IRC § 318 (insofar as it defines the scope of IRC § 382), and IRC § 382. The carryover of net losses is not limited by the federal consolidated return regulations [61 Pa. Code § 153.15(e)].

Carryover of Losses

The Department of Revenue has indicated that it will allow the surviving corporation in a merger to use the net loss carryover deduction of the acquired corporation if the loss would have survived for federal purposes under IRC §§ 381 and 382.

• *Depreciation on IRC § 1250 property*

When accelerated depreciation on IRS § 1250 property falls below the straight-line amount on the federal income tax return, a special deduction for the amount that is less than the straight-line amount is allowed on the Pennsylvania corporate net income tax return. The aggregate adjustment to taxable income to be apportioned for amounts below straight-line may not exceed the aggregate of the amount added to taxable income to be apportioned in previous tax years [61 Pa. Code § 153.14(3)(i)]. This additional deduction is not permitted for a tax year when the taxpayer did not have income to be apportioned [61 Pa. Code § 153.14(3)(iii)].

A taxpayer that depreciated IRC § 1250 property on an accelerated depreciation basis is permitted a special deduction to apportionable taxable income when the property is sold [61 Pa. Code § 153.14(3)(ii)]. This special deduction is not permitted for a tax year when the taxpayer did not have income to be apportioned [61 Pa. Code § 153.14(3)(iii)].

• *IRC § 179 expense*

There is no adjustment to corporate net income for IRC § 179 expense listed in the Pennsylvania statutes. Thus, taxpayers are allowed the same IRC § 179 expense deduction in the calculation of Pennsylvania corporate net income as allowed in the calculation of federal taxable income. Note that this applies only to taxpayers subject to the Pennsylvania corporate net income tax. Income of Pennsylvania S corporations is passed through to individual shareholders and included as part of personal taxable income. Personal income tax treatment of IRC § 179 expense is discussed at ¶ 110.

• *Dividends received*

72 P.S. § 7401(3)1(b) authorizes deductions for dividends received from any other corporation to the extent the dividends are included in federal taxable income. For domestic corporations, the deduction is for 100% of dividends received and included in federal taxable income. For foreign corporations, the amount of the dividends received deduction for dividends included in federal taxable income is as follows [Policy Statement, 61 Pa. Code § 9.12]:

(1) 70% if the dividends are from a less-than-20%-owned foreign corporation.

(2) 80% if the dividends are from a more-than-20%-owned foreign corporation.

(3) 100% if the dividends are from a foreign corporation that meets the "80-percent voting and value test" of § 1504(a)(2) of the Internal Revenue Code of 1986 and would otherwise qualify for a 100% deduction under IRC § 8243(a)(3) if the foreign corporation were a domestic corporation.

The Tax Reform Code implicitly adopts the federal definition of "dividend," so anything that qualifies as a dividend for federal purposes and is included in federal taxable income is a deductible dividend for Pennsylvania purposes. This includes property dividends [*Cmwlth. v. General Refractories, Inc.*, 207 A.2d 833 (Pa. 1965)]. Pro rata distributions to shareholders of cooperatives (commonly called "patronage dividends") were held to be deductible for Pennsylvania purposes [*Murray Corp., Inc. v. Cmwlth.*, 401 A.2d 412 (Pa.Commw. 1979)]. Corporations that include "Subpart F" dividends in federal taxable income may deduct them in the year reported for federal purposes even if they are not actually received in that year [*Cmwlth. v. Emhart Corp.*, 278 A.2d 916 (Pa. 1971)]. However, a corporation that was a partner in a partnership that received corporate dividends was not allowed to deduct its pro rata share of the partnership dividends because the dividends were received by the partnership, not the corporation [*Cmwlth. v. S.W.L. Corp.*, 92 Dauph. 67 (1969)].

• *Foreign dividend gross-up*

Prior to the amendment of 72 P.S. § 7401(3)1(b) to specifically allow the deduction for foreign dividends, wording of the section caused much uncertainty with respect to the proper interpretation of the statute. A literal reading of the statute, combined with the Department's interpretation of the meaning of federal taxable income, could be interpreted to allow only the foreign dividend gross-up under IRC § 78. The Department of Revenue, however, announced that it would follow the U.S. Supreme Court decision in *Kraft General Foods v. Iowa Dept. of Revenue*, 505 U.S. 71 (1992). As of January 1, 1995, there is a statutory basis for the deduction of foreign dividends, as discussed above.

• *Gains on sale of obligations*

Profits, gains or income derived from the sale, exchange or other disposition of government obligations are subject to state or local taxation [72 P.S. § 9901(c)]. If issued prior to February 4, 1994, net gains on the sale of U.S. or Pennsylvania securities are deductible. Under legislation enacted in 1993 [Act of December 3, 1993, No. 68, effective February 1, 1994], gains and losses realized on the disposition of U.S. or Pennsylvania securities acquired on or after February 1, 1994, are taxable [72 P.S. § 9901(c)].

- *Ginnie Maes*

The U.S. Supreme Court has held that "Ginnie Maes" are not exempt from state taxation. The government's obligation as guarantor is secondary and contingent and therefore is not protected by intergovernmental tax immunity [*Rockford Life Insurance Co. v. Illinois*, 482 U.S. 182, 190 (1987)].

- *Interest on U.S. obligations*

Corporations are allowed a deduction from taxable income for any interest income (with certain reductions; see below) from securities issued by the United States or any of its agencies or instrumentalities to the extent included in federal taxable income but exempt from state tax by federal law [72 P.S. § 7401(3)1(b.1)]. The Department of Revenue has issued a Revenue Pronouncement listing obligations it considers federal obligations and obligations it does not consider federal obligations [61 Pa. Code § 9.12].

"Net" U.S. interest deduction: The deduction for U.S. interest must be reduced by the expenses associated with that income [72 P.S. § 7401(3)1(b.1)]. The following items reduce the U.S. interest deduction:

(1) Any interest on indebtedness incurred to carry the securities.

(2) Any expenses incurred in the production of the interest income. "Interest income" for this purpose includes any amount received as a distribution from a regulated investment company (as defined in IRC § 851) to the extent the distribution or dividend is derived from obligations free from state taxation under 72 P.S. § 9901 or from securities issued by the United States or any of its agencies or instrumentalities.

(3) Any other expenses deducted on the federal income tax return that would not have been allowed under IRC § 265 if the interest were exempt from the federal income tax.

NOTE: All exempt income claimed on the corporate net income return must be reduced by any expenses incurred in the production of that income.

- *Money market funds*

The Department of Revenue takes the position that dividends from money market funds that are corporations are deductible but that dividends from money market funds that are trusts are not. However, this is not consistent with the *General Refractories* decision, in which the court held that anything that qualifies as a dividend for federal purposes is a deductible dividend for Pennsylvania purposes. One could argue that, if dividends from money market funds are dividends for federal income tax purposes, they are deductible for Pennsylvania corporate net income tax purposes whether the funds are corporations or trusts.

List as Dividends

To protect your deduction for money market dividends, be sure to list them as dividends on your federal Form 1120. *Do not* list them as interest on your federal return.

- *Interest on repurchase agreements not deductible U.S. interest*

As part of a cash management program, a corporation may invest its cash with a bank or other financial institution overnight and over the weekend in what are commonly referred to as repurchase agreements ("repos"). Quite often this "investment" is secured by U.S. government instruments that the bank has purchased. If the investment is merely secured by the U.S. government instrument (collateralized borrowing) the interest income is not considered to be from a U.S. government instrument. However, if the corporation actually purchases the U.S. security and then resells it to the bank under the "repo" agreement, the interest received is from a U.S. security. The key is the transfer of ownership. The Pennsylvania Department of Revenue has taken the position that interest on repurchase agreements is *not* tax-exempt interest from U.S. obligations; it is taxable interest (*i.e.,* collateralized borrowing). In a case involving a mutual fund, the U.S. Supreme Court ruled that tax on interest on repurchase agreements was not imposed on interest from the obligations themselves. Rather, these transactions were loans, and the interest on these loans was not exempt [*Nebraska Dept. of Revenue v. Loewenstein,* 513 U.S. 123 (1994)]. For more detail, see the discussion of this case at ¶ 209.

• *Manufacturing innovation and reinvestment deduction*

Act 43 of 2017 (H.B. 542) authorized a deduction for taxpayers who make a capital investment in excess of $100 million for the creation of new or refurbished manufacturing capacity within three years of a designated start date. The project must be completed within five years. The Pennsylvania Department of Community and Economic Development will determine the maximum deduction for the taxpayer. The deduction must be equal to 5% of the private capital investment utilized and may be utilized each year for the 5 tax years. The deduction is nontransferable, the taxpayer cannot reduce its liability by more than 50% and any unused portion shall expire at the end of the corresponding tax year.

• *Interest on state obligations*

Interest on obligations of states other than Pennsylvania is not statutorily exempt. It is, however, included in Pennsylvania taxable income because it is not included in federal taxable income before net operating loss and special deductions and it is not a preference item required to be added back under 72 P.S. § 7401(3)1(d). Interest on the obligations of Pennsylvania and its political subdivisions is statutorily excluded from state and local taxation [72 P.S. § 9901].

• *Net operating loss vs. net loss*

Corporations cannot deduct net operating losses allowed by IRC § 172 [72 P.S. § 7401(3)1(m)]. A Pennsylvania net loss deduction, however, is allowed, as provided in 72 P.S. § 7401(3)4(c)(1). Pennsylvania net losses may be carried over as follows:

Taxable Year	Carryover
1990—1993	3 taxable years starting with the 1995 taxable year
1994	1 taxable year
1995—1997	10 taxable years
1998 and thereafter	20 taxable years

For taxable years beginning in 1991—1994, the net loss deduction was suspended, and carryover of net losses from prior years was disallowed. The constitutionality of the suspension of the unused carryovers from 1988, 1989, and 1990 was challenged. In *Surgical Laser Technologies, Inc. v. Cmwlth.,* 626 A.2d 664 (Pa.Commw. 1993), the court denied the Commonwealth's motion to dismiss. *Surgical Laser* alleged a violation of both due process and uniformity, and the court, noting the possibility of such violations, directed the Department of Revenue to file an answer to *Surgical Laser's* petition. However, another panel of the Commonwealth Court ruled that the suspension of unused carryovers was constitutional; it violated neither the uniformity nor due process provisions of the Constitution of Pennsylvania [*Garofolo, Curtiss, Lambert & Maclean, Inc. v. Cmwlth.,* 648 A.2d 1329 (Pa.Commw. 1994)].

"Net loss" defined: For a corporation ineligible to allocate or apportion its income, a Pennsylvania net loss is defined as the negative amount for a taxable year arrived at under 72 P.S. § 7401(3)1. For a corporation eligible to allocate or apportion its income, a Pennsylvania net loss is defined as the negative amount for a taxable year arrived at under 72 P.S. § 7401(3)2. See ¶ 1001 for the definition of taxable income.

Net Loss vs. NOL

Don't confuse the Pennsylvania term "net loss" with federal term "net operating loss." Pennsylvania net loss carryover rules do not apply to capital losses. They apply only to business and nonbusiness losses arising from the operation of a trade or business. Be sure to keep your nonbusiness capital losses separate, because nonbusiness losses retain their nonbusiness character in the year to which they are carried over. Be especially careful about capital losses if you participate in the filing of a federal consolidated tax return. You cannot carry over the consolidated capital losses on your separate Pennsylvania return.

Net loss deduction limitation and carryover: The net loss deduction for taxable years 1999 through 2006 is the lesser of $2,000,000 or the amount of the net losses or losses that may be carried over under 72 P.S. §7401(3)1 or 72 P.S. §7401(3)2 (if applicable). The net loss deduction for taxable years beginning after December 31, 2006, and through December 31, 2009, is the lesser of (1) the greater of 12.5% of taxable income or $3,000,000 or (2) the amount of the net loss or losses that may be carried over under 72 P.S. §7204(3)1 or 72 P.S. §7401(3)2 (if applicable) [72 P.S. §7401(3)4.(c)]. For taxable years beginning after December 31, 2008, the percentage of taxable income eligible for deduction is 15% and 20% for years beginning after December 31, 2009 [Act 48 of 2009 (H.B. 1531)]. The net loss deduction for taxable years beginning after December 31, 2013 is generally the greater of 25% of taxable income or $4,000,000, and the net loss deduction for taxable years beginning after December 31, 2014 is generally the greater of 30% of taxable income or $5,000,000.

The net loss deduction for taxable years beginning after December 31, 2017 is 35% or taxable income and after December 31, 2018 it will be 40% of taxable income if the Department of Revenue publishes a notification that the Pennsylvania Supreme Court has found all or a part of the net loss deduction unconstitutional. [Act 43 of 2017 (H.B. 542)]. *Nextel Communications of Mid-Atlantic, Inc. v. Cmwlth.*, 129 A.3d 1 (Pa.Commw. 2015) held that the limitation on the net loss carryover deduction ($3 million in 2007) violates the Uniformity Clause of the Pennsylvania Constitution. Pa. Const. art. VIII. §1. In *Nextel Communications of Mid-Atlantic, Inc. v. Commonwealth of Pennsylvania*, 171 A.3d 682 (Pa. 2017), the Pennsylvania Supreme Court upheld the Commonwealth Court's decision that a statutory limitation on the net loss carryover deduction violated the Uniformity Clause of the Pennsylvania Constitution and the court determined it was required to sever the $3 million flat deduction from the statute. However, it left in place the percentage based deduction cap. That is, the lower court had ruled that the $3,000,000 limitation was unconstitutional and that the deduction should be unlimited. The Pennsylvania Supreme Court ruled that the $3,000,000 provision was unconstitutional and the only deduction available was 12.5% of the taxpayer's taxable income for the year.

The court's ruling means that taxpayers who had relied on the $3,000,000 provision now find that their losses are actually limited to 12.5% of their taxable income for the year. Most taxpayers have used the $3,000,000 deduction rather than the deduction based on 12.5% of taxable income. Consequently, most taxpayers claimed a net loss deduction in excess of what the *Nextel* decision allows.

In response to *Nextel*, the legislature passed Act 43 of 2017 which amended the net loss (NOL) deduction by removing the $5 million hard NOL cap and increasing the percentage cap to 35% in 2018 and 40% in 2019 and thereafter. The change was to take effect after the Department of Revenue published a notification that all or a part of the net loss deduction has been deemed unconstitutional as a result of a decision by the Pennsylvania Supreme Court. This notice was published on January 27, 2018 by the Secretary of Revenue following the Pennsylvania Supreme Court's denial of reargument. Thus, the Pennsylvania NOL deduction is limited to 35% of taxable income for tax years beginning after December 31, 2017 and to 40% of taxable income for tax years beginning after December 31, 2018. *Nextel's* petition for a writ of certiorari to the U.S. Supreme Court was denied on June 11, 2018 (2018 BL 204767). The Department has announced in Corporation Tax Bulletin 2018-02 (May 10, 2018) that for tax years after 2006 through 2016, it will allow a NOL deduction equal to the greater of the flat dollar net operating loss deduction applicable to any such year and the percentage cap as authorized by statute.

The taxpayer in *RB Alden Corp. v. Cmwlth.*, 142 A.3d 169 (Pa.Commw. 2016) was also allowed to use its net operating losses to offset gain from the disposition of a partnership interest that had been found to generate business income. In *RB Alden Corp. v. Cmwlth.*, 2017 BL 319198 (Pa.Commw. September 12, 2017), the Commonwealth Court denied the Commonwealth's exceptions and reaffirmed its decision that the Pennsylvania cap on the use of corporate and operating losses violated the Uniformity Clause of the Pennsylvania Constitution. The taxpayer's exceptions filed in the same case were denied as moot given the denial of the Commonwealth's exceptions.

Short Years

The Department of Revenue takes the position that a short year counts as a whole year for loss carryforward purposes. This means that the short period returns required in an IRC § 338 election, for example, can use up three years of carryforward in one calendar year or less [*Newbolds Son & Co./Hopper Soliday & Co., Inc. v. Cmwlth.*, 727 A.2d 640 (Pa.Commw. 1999)]. IRC § 338 is discussed at ¶ 915.

Example of computation of Pennsylvania net loss: The carryover amount of a net loss is determined for the loss year after apportionment and applied in the carryforward year to final taxable income after apportionment. The following example illustrates the application of this rule.

Example: Williams Corporation is entitled to allocate and apportion its income and has a three-factor apportionment formula percentage of 25%. It has a loss of $140,000 before allocation and apportionment. Included in the computation of this $140,000 loss, Williams has a nonbusiness loss of $30,000 allocable to New Jersey and nonbusiness income of $10,000 allocable to Pennsylvania. Williams Corporation's Pennsylvania net loss is $20,000, determined as follows:

Taxable Income (Loss)	($140,000)
Less Nonbusiness Loss	($30,000)
Less Nonbusiness Income Allocable to Pennsylvania	$10,000
Apportionable Business Income	($120,000)
Times Apportionment Percentage	(×) 25%
Business Income (Loss)	($30,000)
Add Back Nonbusiness Income Allocable to Pennsylvania	$10,000
Pennsylvania Net Loss	($20,000)

• *Travel and entertainment*

The 50% of travel and entertainment expenditure that is disallowed as a deduction on a federal return is not an allowable deduction for Pennsylvania corporate net income tax purposes.

• *Wages related to federal jobs tax credit*

For federal income tax purposes an employer may claim a tax credit for FICA tax obligations on employees' tips or "targeted jobs" specified in IRC § 51. An employer who takes this credit must reduce this deduction for wages and salaries by the amount of the credit. For Pennsylvania corporate net income tax purposes, a corporation may deduct an additional amount equal to the amount of reduction of the federal wages and salaries deduction due to the exercise of this credit [72 P.S. § 7401(3)1(c), effective January 1, 1998].

Pennsylvania does not have a targeted jobs credit like the federal credit, but it does have a similar credit—the employment incentive credit, discussed at ¶ 127.

Credits Not Deductible

Federal tax credits themselves *cannot* be used as a deduction for Pennsylvania corporate net income tax purposes (*e.g.*, the foreign tax credit or the targeted jobs credit itself).

- *Western hemisphere trade corporations*

Western hemisphere trade corporations are allowed a Pennsylvania deduction in the amount of the deduction permitted under IRC §§ 921 and 922 [61 Pa. Code § 153.14(1)].

¶1004 Credits—General

- *Allowable credits*

Pennsylvania allows the following credits against the corporate net income tax:

(1) Neighborhood assistance tax credit (¶1005).

(2) Employment incentive payment credit (¶1006).

(3) Job creation tax credits (¶1007).

(4) Research and development tax credit (¶1008).

(5) Waste tire recycling equipment investment tax credit (now called the waste tire recycling equipment grant) (See ¶1009).

(6) Coal degasification tax credit (¶1010).

(7) Educational improvement tax credit (¶1011).

(8) Film production credit (¶1012).

(9) Resource enhancement and protection tax credit (¶1016).

(10) First class cities economic development district tax credit (¶1020).

(11) KOZ and KIZ credits. Special credits are available to qualified businesses in Pennsylvania Keystone Opportunity Zones (see ¶1013) and to KIZ companies located in Keystone Innovation Zones (see ¶4623).

(12) Alternative energy production credit (¶1019).

- *Application of Resaleable Restricted Tax Credits*

The Pennsylvania Department of Revenue originally issued Corporate Tax Bulletin 2014-04 on September 30, 2014 in regard to tax credits. More recently, the Department issued Restricted Tax Credit Bulletin 2018-01 which addressed a variety of issues relating to the use and sale of restricted tax credits. The Department explained that a completed tax report must be filed for the period in which the tax credit was approved before the credit may be passed through, carried forward, sold, or assigned. The sale or assignment of a restricted credit will not be approved if the seller has any unpaid state taxes. Consequently, a seller must file all state tax reports and returns and paid all state tax liabilities as of the date the Department is asked to review the seller's records as a part of the process to approve the sale of a credit. Additionally, in order to request a pass-through of a credit, an entity must complete the credit claim form attached to the credit certificate or include a list of the shareholders, members or partners and the amount of the credit to be passed through to each on the business's letterhead, signed by an authorized representative. The Bulletin also explains that buyers of restricted credits must use the credit in the year in which the purchase or assignment is made. Such a credit is prohibited from being carried forward, carried back, refunded, sold or assigned. This Bulletin indicates that it replaces Corporate Tax Bulletin 2014-04.

The saleable restricted tax credits to which the Bulletin applies are as follows:

(1) The Research and Development Tax Credit.

(2) The Film Production Tax Credit.

¶1004

(3) The Neighborhood Assistance Tax Credit.
(4) The Resource Enhancement and Protection Tax Credit.
(5) The Keystone Innovation Zone Tax Credit.
(6) Keystone Special Development Zone Tax Credit.
(7) The Historic Preservation Tax Incentive.
(8) Coal Refuse Energy and Reclamation Tax Credit.
(9) Innovate in Pennsylvania Tax Credit.
(10) Mixed Use Development Tax Credit.

Constitutionality of Credits for Local Investment Questioned

On September 3, 2004, the U.S. Court of Appeals for the Sixth Circuit ruled that an Ohio investment tax credit available to corporate taxpayers for purchases of new manufacturing machinery and equipment discriminated against interstate commerce and was therefore invalid, because the credit was conditioned on the machinery and equipment being installed in Ohio. See *Cuno v. DaimlerChrysler*, 2004 FED App. 0293P (6th Cir.). On appeal the United States Supreme Court vacated the judgment of the Sixth Circuit on the basis that the taxpayers had no standing to challenge the credit [547 U.S. 332 (2006)]. While the decision has no direct application to Pennsylvania, the tax credit involved in that case is similar to the tax credits of Pennsylvania and many other states that condition eligibility for the credit on local investment.

• *Potential Recapture of Tax Credits*

The Pennsylvania Commonwealth Court, in *Vetri Navy Yard, LLC v. Dept. of Community and Economic Dev.*, 189 A.3d 1137 (Pa. Commw. 2018), ruled that the application of the Keystone Opportunity Zone ("KOZ") recapture provisions is not limited to situations where the qualified business physically relocates outside of the KOZ. The taxpayer had constructed and operated a restaurant in the Philadelphia Navy Yard KOZ in 2013 and was granted KOZ benefits. The taxpayer sold the restaurant to a third party on January 30, 2016. Under § 902a of the Keystone Opportunity Improvement Zone Act (Act), when a "qualified business" "relocates" outside a KOZ within a certain period of time, KOZ benefits are subject to recapture. 73 P.S. § 820.902(a). The Commonwealth Court noted that the Act did not define the terms "relocation outside of the zone" but nevertheless determined that the taxpayer's cessation of business through a sale resulted in the equivalent of a relocation outside of the zone - notwithstanding that the purchaser continued to operate a restaurant on the exact same premises. The court's interpretation of the terms "relocation outside of the zone" would logically necessitate a finding that a taxpayer's bankruptcy (another type of cessation of business in a KOZ) would likewise require a recapture of KOZ benefits, thus seemingly making entrepreneurs less likely to attempt development in a blighted area.

¶1005 Neighborhood Assistance Tax Credit

• *Overview*

The Neighborhood Assistance Act (Article XIX-A of the Tax Reform Code) authorizes the Neighborhood Assistance Tax Credit [72 P.S. §§ 8901-A—8906-A]. The credit is available to (1) business firms (defined below) that engage in (or contribute to a neighborhood organization that engages in) the activities of providing neighborhood assistance, comprehensive service projects, job training or education for individuals, community services, or crime prevention in an impoverished area and (2) private companies that make qualified investment to rehabilitate, expand or improve buildings or land located within portions of impoverished areas that have been designated as enterprise zones [72 P.S. § 8904-A]. The total amount of tax credit granted for this purpose may not exceed $36,000,000 in any fiscal year [72 P.S. § 8904-A(c)]. See below for definitions of terms. Of this amount $2,000,000 must be allocated exclusively for pass-through entities. However, if the total amounts allocated to either the group of applicants (exclusive of pass-through entities) or the group of pass-through entity applicants is not approved in any fiscal year, the unused portion becomes available for use by the other group of qualifying taxpayers.

- *Amount of credit*

The amount of the credit normally is 55% of the total amount contributed by a business firm during the taxable year or 25% of qualified investments by a private company in approved programs. However, a tax credit of up to 75% of the total amount contributed by a business firm or up to 35% of the amount of qualified investments by a private company may be allowed for programs whose activities fall within the scope of special program priorities as defined with the approval of the Governor in regulations promulgated by the Secretary of the Department of Community Affairs [72 P.S. § 8905-A]. Further, a tax credit of up to 75% of the total amount contributed during the taxable year by a business firm in comprehensive service projects with five-year commitments and up to 80% of the total amount contributed during the taxable year by a business firm in comprehensive service projects with six-year or longer commitments will be granted. In general the *maximum credit* available to a taxpayer in one year is $500,000 for contributions or investments to fewer than four (4) projects or $1,250,000 for contributions or investments to four (4) or more projects. However, in the case of comprehensive service projects, an additional credit equal to 70% of the qualifying investments made in comprehensive service projects (but not to exceed $350,000 annually) is allowed [72 P.S. § 8905-A]. Taxpayers may carry over any unused credit for five years.

- *Application of credit*

The neighborhood assistance tax credit may be applied against (1) the personal income tax; (2) the corporate net income tax; (3) the capital stock/franchise tax; (4) the bank and trust company shares tax; (5) the title insurance companies shares tax; (6) the insurance premiums tax; and (7) the mutual thrift institutions tax [72 P.S. § 8905-A]. No tax credit is allowable to any bank, bank and trust company, insurance company, national bank, savings association, mutual savings bank or building and loan association for activities that are a part of its normal course of base.

The neighborhood assistance tax credit must be applied against one of the above tax liabilities for the current taxable year as of the date of which the credit was approved before it may be carried over, sold, or assigned [72 P.S. § 8904-A(f)].

- *Carryforwards of credit*

Any credit not used in the period the contribution or investment was made may be carried over for the next five (5) calendar or fiscal years until the full credit has been allowed (but see "pass-through entities" below) [72 P.S. § 8905-A].

- *Carrybacks of credit*

A business firm is not entitled to carry back an unused tax credit [72 P.S. § 8905-A].

- *Refunds of credit*

A business firm is not entitled to obtain a refund of an unused tax credit [72 P.S. § 8905-A].

- *Sale or assignment of credit*

Upon application to and approval by the Department of Community and Economic Development, a taxpayer may sell or assign (in whole or in part) a neighborhood assistance tax credit if no claim for allowance of the credit is filed within one year from the date the credit is granted by the Department of Revenue [72 P.S. § 8904-A(d)].

¶1005

• *Annual proposal required*

In order to receive the credit, a company must submit an annual proposal to the Department and have it approved. The Department of Revenue must notify the taxpayer of approval or disapproval in writing; and, if it approves the proposal, state the maximum credit allowable to the business firm [72 P.S. § 8905-A].

• *Pass-through entities*

If a pass-through entity has any unused neighborhood assistance credit, the entity may elect (in writing) according to the Department's procedures, to transfer all or a portion of the credit to shareholders, members or partners in proportion to the share of the entity's distributive income to which the shareholder, member, or partner is entitled. This is in addition to any neighborhood assistance tax credit to which a shareholder, member, or partner is otherwise entitled. However, a pass-through entity and a shareholder, member, or partner may not claim a credit for the same qualified neighborhood assistance investment or contribution. A transferred credit must be immediately claimed by the shareholder, member, or partner in the taxable year in which the transfer is made; and the shareholder, member, or partner may not carry forward, carryback, obtain a refund of, or sell or assign the credit [72 P.S. § 8907-A].

More NAP Information

More information about credits for Neighborhood Assistance Programs can be obtained by contacting the Department of Community and Economic Development, Office of Community Empowerment & Development, Room 377, Forum Building, Harrisburg, PA 17120; telephone 717-787-4140.

¶1006 Employment Incentive Payment Credit (EIPC)

• *Availability of credit*

The employment incentive payment credit (EIPC) is available to persons or entities that employ an eligible individual and that have a qualified tax liability (see definition below).

No EIPC is available for the following [72 P.S. § 8703-A(b)]:

(1) The employment of a person who displaces any other individual from employment, except persons discharged for cause as certified by the Department of Labor and Industry.

(2) If the taxpayer is an individual, the employment of related individuals within the meaning of IRC § 8152(a).

(3) If the taxpayer is a corporation, the employment of a person closely related to an individual who owns, directly or indirectly, more than 50% of the outstanding stock of the taxpayer.

(4) Wages paid to an individual during the time period for which the employer received job training payments for that individual from the federal government or the Commonwealth.

• *Definition of terms*

For purposes of the EIPC, the following words, terms, and phrases are defined as follows [72 P.S. § 8702-A]:

Eligible individual: Any one of the following:

(1) A person who, at any time within the 12 months preceding the date of hire, received general assistance.

(2) A person who, at any time within the 12 months preceding the date of hire, received temporary assistance to needy families.

¶1006

(3) A person who has a physical or mental disability that is a substantial handicap to employment.

(4) A person who is referred to the employer upon completion of or while receiving rehabilitative services pursuant to an individualized written rehabilitation plan under a State plan for vocational rehabilitation services approved under the Rehabilitation Act of 1973 [P.L. 93-112, 29 U.S.C. §701 *et seq.*] or a program of vocational rehabilitation carried out under Title 1 of the Veterans' Rehabilitation and Education Amendments of 1980 [P.L 96-466, 94 Stat. 2171)].

(5) A person who is referred to the employer upon completion of or while receiving rehabilitative services pursuant to a program of vocational rehabilitation carried out under Title I of the Veterans' Rehabilitation and Education Amendments of 1980.

Employment incentive payment: The employment incentive payment credit.

Pass-through entity: (1) A partnership, limited partnership, limited liability company, business trust, or other unincorporated entity taxable as a partnership for federal income tax purposes or (2) a Pennsylvania S corporation.

Qualified first-year wages: The qualified wages attributable to service rendered by an eligible individual during the one-year period beginning with the day the eligible individual begins work for the employer.

Qualified second-year wages: The qualified wages attributable to service rendered by an eligible individual during the one-year period beginning one year after the eligible individual begins work for the employer.

Qualified tax liability: The liability for (1) the personal income tax, (2) the corporate net income tax, (3) the bank and trust company shares tax, (4) the title insurance companies shares tax, (5) the insurance premiums, or (6) the mutual thrift institutions tax.

Qualified third-year wages: The qualified wages attributable to service rendered by an eligible individual during the one-year period beginning two years after the eligible individual begins work for the employer.

Qualified wages: Wages as defined in IRC §51A(b)(5).

Taxpayer: A person or entity that has a qualified tax liability.

• *Employment of less than one year*

Except in cases where an individual voluntarily leaves the employment of the taxpayer, becomes disabled, or is terminated for cause, no taxpayer is entitled to receive an EIPC if the eligible individual is employed by the taxpayer for less than one year. If the eligible individual leaves voluntarily, becomes disabled, or is terminated for cause in less than one year, the EIPC must be reduced by the proportion of the year not worked [72 P.S. §7803-A(e)].

• *Amount of credit*

ALERT

The amount available for award to each eligible taxpayer has been reduced to 50% of the amounts otherwise available for the fiscal year 2009 – 2010, and to 45% of the amounts otherwise available for 2010 – 2011 [Act 48 of 2009, H.B. 1531].

The employment incentive payment credit is calculated on an annual basis [72 P.S. §8703-A(c)]. The amount of the credit is calculated as the sum of the following three items:

(1) 31% of the first $9,000 of qualified first-year wages.

(2) 20% of the first $9,000 of qualified second-year wages.

(3) 10% of the first $9,000 of qualified third-year wages.

¶1006

Additional credit: A taxpayer eligible to receive an EIPC is eligible to receive an additional credit if (1) the taxpayer provides or pays for day-care services for an eligible individual's children or (2) the taxpayer provides or pays for transportation services that enable an eligible individual to travel to and from work [72 P.S. § 8703-A(c)(2)]. The amount of the additional credit is the expenses incurred by the taxpayer for child-care or transportation services but is limited to $800 per eligible individual during the first year of employment, $600 during the second year of employment, or $400 during the third year of employment.

Deductions from taxable income: In computing a tax liability against which the EIPC may be applied, deductions from taxable income must be reduced by the EIPC [72 P.S. § 8703-A(h)].

• *Limitation and carryover*

The total EIPC cannot exceed 90% of the total taxes paid by the employer against which the credit may be claimed [72 P.S. § 8703-A(f)]. An unused EIPC may be carried over to be used against a qualified tax liability for 10 years [72 P.S. § 8703-A(g)].

• *Sunset*

Employment incentive payments will not be available for employees hired after December 31, 2009, unless reenacted by the General Assembly [72 P.S. § 8706-A].

¶1007 Tax Credit for New Jobs (Formerly Job Creation Tax Credits)

The term "job creation tax credits" refers to the tax credits for which the Department of Revenue has issued certificates under Article XVIII-B ("Tax Credits for New Jobs") of the Tax Reform Code, effective July 1, 2001 [72 P.S. §§ 8801-B—8806-B].

• *Tax credits for new jobs*

A company may apply the job creation tax credit (JCTC) provided for in new Article XVIII-B of the Tax Reform Code to 100% of the company's liability for the following taxes or any combination thereof [72 P.S. § 8804-B(c)]:

(1) Corporate net income tax.

(2) Capital stock/franchise tax.

(3) Capital stock/franchise tax of a shareholder of a Pennsylvania S corporation.

(4) Gross premiums tax on insurance companies.

(5) Gross receipts tax.

(6) Bank and trust company shares tax.

(7) Mutual thrift institution tax.

(8) Title insurance companies shares tax.

(9) Personal income tax.

(10) Personal income tax of a shareholder of a Pennsylvania S corporation.

• *Definition of terms*

Unless the context clearly indicates otherwise, the words and phrases below when used in Article XVIII-B have the following meanings [72 P.S. § 8801-B]:

Base period: The three years preceding the date on which a company may begin creating new jobs that may be eligible for JCTCs.

Department: The Pennsylvania Department of Community and Economic Development (DCED).

Job creation tax credits: Tax credits for which the DCED has issued a job creation tax credit certificate.

¶1007

New job: A full-time job, the average hourly rate (excluding benefits) for which must be at least 150% of the federal minimum wage, created with a Pennsylvania municipality within three years from the start date.

Small business: A company that is engaged in a for-profit enterprise and that employs no more than 100 individuals.

Start date: The date on which a company may begin creating new jobs that may be eligible for JCTCs.

Unemployed individual: An individual who at the time of hiring meets all of the following:

(1) Is hired on or after July 1, 2012.

(2) Certifies by signed affidavit, under penalty of perjury, that the individual has not been employed during the 60-day period ending on the date the individual begins employment.

(3) Is not employed by the company to replace another employee of the company unless the other employee separated from employment voluntarily or for cause.

(4) Will perform duties connected to the new job for at least 52 consecutive weeks.

Year one: A one-year period immediately following the start date.

Year two: A one-year period immediately following the end of year one.

Year three: A one-year period immediately following the end of year two.

- *Eligibility for credit*

In order to be eligible to receive job creation tax credits, a company must demonstrate the following to the Department of Community and Economic Development [72 P.S. § 8802-B]:

(1) The ability to create at least 25 new jobs or to increase its number of employees by at least 20% within three years from the start date (see definition above).

(2) Leadership in the application, development, or deployment of leading technologies.

(3) Financial stability and the project's financial viability.

(4) The intent to maintain operations in Pennsylvania for a period of five years from the date the company submits its tax credit certificate to the Department of Revenue.

- *Application for credit*

In order to receive JCTCs, a company must complete and submit to the Department of Community and Economic Development a JCTC application [72 P.S. § 8803-B(a)].

- *Job creation requirement*

Except for a small business, an applicant must agree to create at least 25 new jobs or to increase the applicant's number of employees by at least 20% within three years of the start date. A small business applicant must agree to increase the applicant's number of employees by at least 10% within three years after the start date [72 P.S. § 8803-B(b)].

- *Commitment letter*

If the DCED approves the company's application, the Department and the applicant must execute a commitment letter [72 P.S. § 8803-B(c)]. After a commitment letter has been signed by both the Commonwealth and the company, the company will receive a job creation tax credit certificate and filing information [72 P.S. §8802-B(d)]. The commitment letter must contain the following information:

(1) A description of the project.

(2) The number of jobs to be created.

(3) The amount of private capital investment in the project.

(4) A statement authorizing the per job credit as a single-year or multiple-year credit.

(5) The maximum JCTC amount that the company may claim.

(6) A signed statement that the company intends to maintain its operation in Pennsylvania for five years from the start date (*i.e.,* the date on which the company may begin creating new jobs eligible for the credit).

(7) Any other information the Department of Community and Economic Development may deem appropriate.

- *Amount and term of credit*

A company may claim a tax credit of $1,000 per new job created or $2,500 per each new job created if the newly created job is filled by a veteran or an unemployed individual, up to the maximum JCTC amount specified in the commitment letter [72 P.S. §8804-B(a)]. A company may claim the approved JCTCs for a one-year, two-year, or three-year period determined by the Department, except that no tax credit may be claimed for more than five years from the date the company first submits a JCTC certificate [72 P.S. §8804-B(d)].

- *Prohibited actions*

The following actions with regard to job creation tax credits are prohibited [72 P.S. §8805-B]:

(1) Approval of jobs that have been created prior to the start date.

(2) Approval for a company that is relocating operations from one municipality in Pennsylvania to another unless (a) special circumstances exist and (b) the municipality that is losing the existing jobs has an opportunity to submit comments prior to action by the Department of Community and Economic Development. If the Department approves the tax credits, the company must commit to preserving the existing employees, and the credit applies only to new jobs.

(3) The assignment, transfer, or use of credits by any other company, except an affiliated entity. Tax credits may be assigned, in whole or in part, to an affiliated entity. "Affiliated entity" for this purpose means an entity that is part of the same "affiliated group" (defined by IRC §504(a)(1)) as the company that is awarded the credit.

- *Penalties*

Failure to maintain operations: A company that fails to substantially maintain existing operations and the operations related to the JCTCs in Pennsylvania for a period of five years from the date of first submission of a JCTC certificate to the Department of Revenue will be required to refund the total amount of credit or credits granted [72 P.S. §8806-B(a)].

Failure to create jobs: A company that fails to create the approved number of new jobs within three years of the start date will be required to refund the total amount of credit or credits [72 P.S. §8806-B(b)].

Waiver of penalties: The Department may waive the penalties for failure to maintain operations or create jobs if it is determined that the failure was due to circumstances beyond the company's control (*e.g.,* natural disasters, unforeseen industry trends, loss of a major supplier or market) [72 P.S. §8806-B(c)].

More JCTC Information

For more information on the JCTC program or to request a program guide and/or JCTC application information, contact the Department of Community and Economic Development, Grants Office, 494 Forum Building, Harrisburg, PA 17120; telephone 717-787-7120.

¶1008 Research and Development Tax Credit

• *Eligibility for credit*

A taxpayer who incurs Pennsylvania qualified research and development expense in a taxable year may apply for a research and development tax credit [72 P.S. §8703-B(a)]. Applications are discussed below. The credit is available to taxpayers subject to the corporate net income tax, the capital stock/franchise tax, and the personal income tax (including a shareholder of a Pennsylvania S corporation entitled to a research and development credit) [72 P.S. § 8702-B].

• *Determination of qualified research and development expenses*

"Pennsylvania qualified research and development expense" means qualified research expense as defined in IRC §41(b) incurred for Pennsylvania qualified research and development [72 P.S. § 8702-B]. "Pennsylvania qualified research and development" means qualified research and development as defined in IRC §41(d) that is conducted in Pennsylvania [72 P.S. § 8702-B].

In prescribing standards for determining which qualified research and development expenses are considered Pennsylvania qualified research and development expenses for purposes of computing the credit provided by this article, the Department may consider the following factors [72 P.S. § 8706-B]:

(1) The location where the services are performed.

(2) The residence or business location of the person or persons performing the service.

(3) The location where qualified R&D supplies are consumed.

(4) Other factors that the Department determines are relevant for the determination.

• *Applications*

Application for qualified expense for a taxable year must be made by September 15 of the following taxable year [72 P.S. § 8703-B(a)]. For example, a taxpayer whose taxable year ends any time in 2004 must submit an application by September 15, 2005. The Department must notify the taxpayer of the amount of credit approved by December 15 of the year in which application is made [72 P.S. § 8703-B(c)].

• *Amount of credit*

If a taxpayer's application is approved, the taxpayer is eligible for a research and development tax credit for the taxable year in the amount of 10% of the excess of the taxpayer's total Pennsylvania qualified research and development expenses for the taxable year over the taxpayer's Pennsylvania base amount [72 P.S. § 8703-B(b)].

20% for Small Businesses

A taxpayer that is a small business and is qualified to receive an R&D credit is entitled to an R&D credit of 20% of the excess of the taxpayer's total Pennsylvania qualified R&D expense for the taxable year over the taxpayer's Pennsylvania base amount [72 P.S. § 8703-B(b)(2)]. A "small business" for this purpose is a for-profit corporation, limited liability company, partnership, or proprietorship with net book value of assets totaling (at the beginning or end of the taxable year for which qualified R&D expense is incurred) less than $5,000,000, as reported on the balance sheet [72 P.S. § 8702-B].

• *Limitation on credit amount*

Until January 1, 2005, the amount of the research and development tax credit that a taxpayer can use against any one qualified tax liability during any year cannot exceed 50% of such qualified tax liability for that taxable year [72 P.S. § 8704-B(a); Act of December 31, 2003, No. 46 (H.B. 200), § § 22 and 33(13)]. For tax years beginning in 2005 and thereafter, the 50% limitation for the use of the tax credit against tax liabilities is eliminated.

• *Carryover of credit*

If a taxpayer cannot use the entire amount of the research and development tax credit for the taxable year in which it is first approved, the excess may be carried over to succeeding taxable years (up to a maximum of 15 years) and used as a credit against the qualified tax liability (see below) of the taxpayer for those taxable years [72 P.S. § 8704-B(a)]. Credits approved by the Department of Revenue in a taxable year must first be applied against the taxpayer's qualified tax liability for the current taxable year as of the date the credit was approved before it can be carried over [72 P.S. § 8704(b)].

Qualified tax liability: "Qualified tax liability" means the liability for the personal income tax, the corporate net income tax, and the capital stock/franchise tax. Personal income taxes imposed on a Pennsylvania S corporation shareholder are included in the qualified tax liability.

• *Carryback and refund of unused credits*

A taxpayer cannot carry back or obtain a refund of an unused research and development tax credit [72 P.S. § 8704-B(c)]. Until January 1, 2003, taxpayers could not assign credits. Effective for credits awarded after December 31, 2002, a taxpayer may sell or assign research and development credits under certain conditions (see *Sale or assignment, of unused credits,* below).

• *Sale or assignment of unused credits*

A taxpayer may, upon application and approval by the Department of Community and Economic Development, sell or assign (in whole or in part) a research and development tax credit granted to the taxpayer. The Department of Community and Economic Development is given authority to establish guidelines for the approval of applications for sale or assignment of unused credits [72 P.S. § 8704-B(d)].

The purchaser or assignee of a portion of a research and development tax credit must immediately claim the credit in the taxable year in which the purchase or assignment occurs. The amount of the research and development credit that a purchaser or assignee may use against any one qualified tax liability cannot exceed 75% of the qualified tax liability for the taxable year. The purchaser or assignee cannot carry over, carry back, assign, or obtain a refund of the research and development tax credit. A purchaser or assignee must notify the Department of Revenue of the seller or assignor of the credit [72 P.S. § 8704-B(e)].

• *S corporation shareholder pass-through (effective through December 31, 2005)*

If a Pennsylvania S corporation does not have an eligible tax liability against which the research and development tax credit may be applied, a shareholder of the S corporation is entitled to a research and development tax credit equal to the credit determined for the S corporation for the taxable year multiplied by the percentage of the S corporation's distributive income to which the shareholder is entitled. This credit is in addition to any research and development tax credit to which a shareholder of a Pennsylvania S corporation is otherwise entitled, but a Pennsylvania S corporation and a shareholder may not claim a credit for the same qualified research and development expense [72 P.S. § 8710-B].

• *Pass-through entities*

If a pass-through entity has any unused research and development tax credit, the entity may elect, in writing, according to the Department's procedures to transfer all or a portion of the credit to shareholders, members, or partners in proportion to the share of the entity's distributive income to which the shareholder, member, or partner is entitled.

Limitation: This credit is in addition to any research and development tax credit to which a shareholder, member, or partner is otherwise entitled. However, a pass-through entity and a shareholder, member, or partner of a pass-through entity may not claim a credit for the same qualified research and development expense.

Immediate application required: A shareholder, member, or partner of a pass-through entity to whom credit is transferred must immediately claim the credit in the taxable year in which the transfer is made. The shareholder, member, or partner may not carry forward, carry back, obtain a refund of, or sell or assign the credit [72 P.S. §8710-B].

• *Limitation on credits*

ALERT

The amount available for award has been reduced to 50% of the amounts otherwise available for the fiscal year 2009 – 2010, and to 45% of the amounts otherwise available for fiscal year 2010 – 2011 [Act 48 of 2009, H.B. 1531; 72 P.S. § 2901-E(c)].

• *Application of Internal Revenue Code*

The provisions of IRC §41 and the regulations promulgated regarding those provisions apply to the Pennsylvania Department of Revenue's interpretation and administration of the Pennsylvania research and development credit. References to the Internal Revenue Code mean the sections of the Internal Revenue Code as existing on any date of interpretation of Article XVII-B of the Pennsylvania Tax Reform Code. If, however, those sections of the Internal Revenue Code referenced in Article XVII-B are repealed or terminated, references to the Internal Revenue Code mean those sections last having full force and effect. If after repeal or termination, the Internal Revenue Code sections are revised or reenacted, references to Internal Revenue Code sections mean those revised or reenacted sections [72 P.S. § 8705-B].

¶1009 Waste Tire Recycling Equipment Grants

Prior to 2000, taxpayers engaged in the business of reducing, reusing, or recycling whole used or waste tires were allowed a credit of 30% of the cost of the waste reduction, reuse, or recycling equipment or infrastructure investments [35 P.S. § 6029.109]. This grant has been replaced by a waste tire remediation grant program under the provisions of the Waste Tire Recycling Act [35 P.S. § 6029.101 et seq.]. Only Commonwealth municipalities are eligible to apply and receive grants from this program.

More Information

For more information, contact the Department of Environmental Protection, Division of Municipal and Residential Waste. 14th Floor, Rachel Carson Building, 400 Market Street, Harrisburg, PA 17101-2301; telephone 717-787-7381; or visit the DEP's Waste Tire Recycling website at http://www.depweb.state.pa.us/landrecwaste/cwp/view.asp?a=1239&Q=463298&landrecwasteNav=.

¶1009

¶1010 Coal Degasification Tax Credit

ALERT
The Coal Degasification Tax Credit was repealed by Act 52 of 2013.

Under the Coal Waste Removal and Ultraclean Fuels Act [72 P.S. § § 8801-A *et seq.*] a developer (defined below) that invests in qualifying property used to produce ultraclean fuels from coal, culm, and silt feedstocks is eligible for a tax credit (referred to as the coal degasification tax credit) equal to 15% of investment costs. In order to claim this credit a developer must enter into a contract with the Commonwealth (see *Contract requirement,* below).

• *Application of credit*

The coal degasification credit can be used to offset (1) sales and use tax; (2) corporate net income tax; and (3) capital stock/franchise tax [72 P.S. § 8803-A(a)].

• *Terms defined*

Terms used in the Coal Waste Removal and Ultraclean Fuels Tax Credit are defined as follows [72 P.S. § 8802-A]:

Department: The Pennsylvania Department of Revenue.

Developer: The owner-operator of a facility (defined below) or the operator of the facility that has sold the facility in new condition to a third party from whom that operator has simultaneously leased back the facility for a minimum period of twelve (12) years.

Facility: All plant and equipment purchased or constructed by or on behalf of the developer that is used within Pennsylvania by the developer to produce one or more qualified fuels.

Internal Revenue Code (IRC): The Internal Revenue Code of 1986 [Public Law 99-514, 26 U.S.C. § 1 *et seq.*].

Qualified fuels: Fuels from non-traditional coal culm and silt feedstocks, as defined in IRC § 29(c).

Qualifying property: Tangible personal property and other forms of tangible property that (1) qualify for investment tax credit treatment and (2) meet *all* of the following requirements:

(a) They are acquired through a purchase [as defined under IRC § 179(d)(2)], or constructed by the developer for its own use.

(b) They are depreciable under IRC § 167.

(c) They have a useful life of equal to or greater than four (4) years.

(d) They are located within Pennsylvania.

(e) They are used by the developer in the production of qualified fuels.

(f) They are acquired by purchase or constructed on or after January 1, 2000, and before January 1, 2013.

(g) They are not the subject of any tax credit otherwise available to the developer under the Tax Reform Code.

Tax credit base: The cost or other basis of qualifying property that is properly transferred to the facility's basis for depreciation for federal income tax purposes between January 1, 2000, and December 31, 2012.

• *Amount of credit*

The coal degasification tax credit is computed as 15% of the tax credit base. The maximum tax credit available is 15% of the capital cost of the facility. Any amount of allowable tax credit not used in the tax year for which it was claimed can be carried forward to succeeding years until the full amount of allowable credit has been used [72 P.S. § 8803-A(b)]. Tax credits allowed, in the aggregate, cannot exceed $18,000,000 during any year [72 P.S. § 8803-A(f)].

• *Transfer of credit*

A developer may, upon notice to the Department of Revenue, sell or assign, in whole or in part, any coal degasification tax credit to one or more taxpayers, if no claim for allowance of such credit has been filed [72 P.S. § 8803-A(c)(1)]. A taxpayer who receives a developer's coal degasification tax credit by purchase or assignment initially claims the credit for the tax year in which purchase or assignment occurs but in no event later than the filing of an income tax return for the year 2012. A taxpayer recipient, by purchase or assignment, of any portion of a developer's coal degasification credit must also notify the Department of the derivative basis of the credit in compliance with specified Departmental procedures [72 P.S. § 8803-A(c)(2)]. Any taxpayer that acquires any portion of a developer's credit for value and without notice by the developer of any irregularity or invalidity will not suffer any disallowance of the credit or the imposition of any adjustment or fraud penalty attributable to conduct by the developer [72 P.S. § 8003-A(c)(3)].

• *Recapture of credit*

If a developer prematurely disposes of any qualifying property in a transaction other than a sale-leaseback transaction and if the Department of Revenue has previously allowed a tax credit on the property to any taxpayer, a portion of credit allowed must be recaptured and added to the developer's tax liability in the year of disposition [72 P.S. § 8803-A(d)]. A premature disposition for this purpose is a disposition that occurs before the expiration of the property's useful life for federal depreciation purposes. The amount of recapture is equal to a fraction the numerator of which is the number of years remaining of the useful life for federal depreciation purposes and the denominator of which is the total number of years over which the property otherwise would have been subject to depreciation by the developer. In computing the recapture percentage, the year of disposition is considered a year of remaining depreciation. The developer is required to notify the Department of any premature dispositions.

• *Contract requirement*

A developer, in order to claim a coal degasification tax credit, must enter into a contract with the Commonwealth that provides as follows [72 P.S. 8804-A]:

(1) The term of the credit shall be twenty-five (25) years, beginning with the first tax year in which the credit is claimed.

(2) The developer shall make periodic payments to the Commonwealth. These payments, in the aggregate, may not exceed $46,800,000 over the term of the contract.

(3) The periodic payments shall be made every five (5) years, and each payment shall be $9,360,000, reduced by any available offsets.

(4) For the first five-year period, the periodic payment may be reduced by an amount equal to the business losses of the developer relating to the facility that are sustained in the first and second years of the contract. The offset, however, may not exceed $3,744,000 for both years. The first periodic payment may also be reduced by allowable offsets (see below), but the offsets may not exceed the required payment ($9,360,000).

(5) For the remaining five-year periods, the periodic payment may be reduced by the amount of allowable offset, up to a maximum amount equal to the periodic payment ($9,360,000). Allowable offsets include *all* of the following:

(a) An amount equal to the corporate net income tax, capital stock/franchise tax, and personal income tax related to the construction, ownership, and operation of the facility.

¶1010

(b) An amount equal to all personal income tax withheld from the developer's employees.

(c) An amount equal to all sales and use tax related to the construction of the facility.

(d) The amount paid by the developer of any new tax enacted by the Commonwealth after July 1, 1999.

¶1011 Educational Improvement and Opportunity Scholarship Tax Credits (EIOSTC)

• *Authorization*

The Department of Revenue may award tax credits to eligible businesses for contributions made to a business firm providing proof of a contribution to a scholarship organization, educational improvement organization, or opportunity scholarship organization [72 P.S. §8705-F(a), (a.1)]. See definitions below. An eligible firm may also receive a credit for contributions to a pre-kindergarten scholarship organization (see below) [72 P.S. §8705-F(c)]. A business firm may receive a tax credit for a contribution under 72 P.S. §8705-F(a) or 72 P.S. §8705-F(c), or both [72 P.S. §8705-F(d)]. The opportunity scholarship organizations must enhance the educational opportunities available to students in Pennsylvania by providing scholarships to eligible students who reside within the attendance boundary of low-achieving schools to attend schools that are not low-achieving schools and that are not a public school within the school district of residents [72 P.S. §8702-F]. Businesses may apply for the alternative credit if the preferred credit is unavailable.

• *Administration*

The EIOSTC program is administered by the Department of Community and Economic Development (DCED). The DCED may transfer unused credits from one program year to another after January 1st of each fiscal year.

• *Eligible business firms*

Firms eligible to apply for credits are businesses authorized to do business in Pennsylvania that are subject to the following taxes (including pass-through entities and pass-through entities owning an interest in a pass-through entity): corporate net income tax, capital/stock franchise tax, bank and trust company shares tax, title insurance companies shares tax, insurance premiums tax, mutual thrift institutions tax, malt beverage tax, as well as the personal income tax for certain pass-through entities [72 P.S. §8702-F]. Partnerships and Pennsylvania S corporations are eligible to receive the credit. A single member LLC has been added to the definition of "pass-through entity" [72 P.S. §8702-F]. A "contribution" for this purpose is a donation of cash, personal property, or services the value of which is the net cost of the donation to the donor or the pro rata hourly wage, including benefits, of the individual performing the services [72 P.S. §8702-F].

• *Amount of credit*

An eligible business firm may receive a tax credit equal to 75% of the business's contribution to a qualifying scholarship organization or a qualifying educational improvement organization, up to a maximum of $750,000 per year [72 P.S. §8705-F(a)]. A business firm providing proof of a contribution may receive a tax credit up to 75% of the total amount contributed to an opportunity scholarship organization, up to a maximum of $750,000 per year [72 P.S. §8705-F(a.1)]. Further limitation is described in 72 P.S. § 8705-F(d) when combining credits.

• *Additional credit amount*

If a business makes a written commitment to provide the qualifying donee entity with the same amount of contribution for two consecutive tax years, it may receive a tax credit equal to 90% of its contribution [72 P.S. §8705-F(b)].

Failure to Fulfill Commitment

If a taxpayer does not fulfill its promise to provide the same amount of contribution for two consecutive tax years, the Department of Revenue will adjust the amount of credit awarded in the first year to 75% of the qualified contribution.

• *Application of EIOSTCs to tax liabilities*

EIOSTCs may be applied against the following taxes [72 P.S. § 8702-F]:

(1) Personal income tax.

(2) Corporate net income tax.

(3) Capital stock/franchise tax.

(4) Bank and trust company shares tax.

(5) Title insurance companies shares tax.

(6) Insurance premiums tax.

(7) Mutual thrift institutions tax.

(8) Malt beverages tax.

• *Limitations*

Total amount: Act 39 of 2018, effective July 1, 2018, increased the aggregate amount of all credits that may be approved for contributions from business firms to scholarship organizations, educational improvement organizations and pre-kindergarten scholarship organizations to $160 million (previously $135 million) per fiscal year. No less than $110 million of that amount must be used to provide tax credits to scholarship organizations. For more information regarding the educational improvement tax credit program, see the Department of Community and Economic Development website at https://dced.pa.gov/download/educational-improvement-tax-credit-program-eitc-guidelines/?wpdmdl=84406.

Activities: No tax credit can be approved for activities that are a part of a business firm's normal course of business [72 P.S. § 8706-F(b)].

Tax liability limit: A tax credit granted for any one taxable year may not exceed the business firm's tax liability [72 P.S. § 8706-F(c)].

Carryovers/carrybacks: A tax credit not used in the tax year in which the contribution was made cannot be carried forward or carried back [72 P.S. § 8706-F(d)].

Refundability or transferability: A credit is generally not refundable or transferable [72 P.S. § 8706-F(d)]. However, a pass-through entity may elect to distribute all or part of the credits to shareholders, members, or partners for use in the year the contribution was made or in the next taxable year [72 P.S. § 8705-F(e)].

• *Scholarship organization*

A scholarship organization for credit purposes is a nonprofit entity that (1) is exempt from federal taxation under IRC § 501(c)(e), and (2) contributes at least 80% of its annual receipts to a scholarship program (*i.e.*, a program to provide tuition to eligible students to attend a school located in Pennsylvania) [72 P.S. § 8702-F]. In order to qualify for an EIOSTC, contributions must be made to scholarship organizations set forth on a list maintained by the Department of Community and Economic Development (DCED).

Pre-kindergarten scholarship organization: A pre-kindergarten scholarship organization is a nonprofit entity that (1) either is exempt from federal taxation under IRC § 501(c)(3) or is operated as a separate segregated fund by a scholarship organization that has qualified under 72 P.S. § 8703-F and (2) contributes at least 80% of its annual cash receipts to a pre-kindergarten scholarship program by expending or otherwise irrevocably encumbering those funds for distribution during the then current fiscal year of the organization or during the next succeeding fiscal year of the organization [72 P.S. § 8703-F].

• *Educational improvement organization*

An educational improvement organization is a nonprofit entity that (1) is exempt from federal taxation under IRC § 501(c)(3), and (2) contributes at least 80% of its annual receipts as grants to a public school, a chartered school as defined in the Public School Code of 1949, or a private school as defined in the Public School Code of 1949 for innovative educational programs [72 P.S. § 8702-F]. A "public school" for this purpose is a public kindergarten, elementary school, or secondary school at which Pennsylvania's compulsory attendance requirements may be met and that meets the applicable requirements of Title VI of the Civil Rights Act of 1964 (P.L. 88-352) as well as career and technical schools. In order to qualify for an EIOSTC, contributions must be made to educational improvement organizations set forth on a list maintained by the Department of Community and Economic Development (DCED).

List of Qualifying Organizations

The current list of scholarship organizations and education improvement organizations can be found on the web site of the DCED at http://www.newpa.com/programDetail.aspx?id=62.

• *Opportunity Scholarship Organization*

An opportunity scholarship organization is a nonprofit entity that meets the following criteria [72 P.S. § 8702-G.1]:

(1) It is exempt from federal taxation under IRC § 501(c).

(2) It contributes at least 80% of its annual cash receipts to a scholarship program. For purposes of this definition, a nonprofit entity "contributes" its annual cash receipts to a scholarship program when it expends or otherwise irrevocably encumbers those funds for distribution during the then current fiscal year of the nonprofit entity or during the next succeeding fiscal year of the nonprofit entity.

In order to qualify, a scholarship organization (i) must submit certain information to the Department of Community and Economic Development (DCED) of Pennsylvania, (ii) must certify annually to the DCED that it is eligible to participate, and (iii) report required information to the DCED by September 1 of each year [72 P.S. § 8703-G.1(a)–(d)].

• *Credit for contributions to pre-kindergarten scholarship organization*

A business firm that makes a contribution to a pre-kindergarten scholarship organization in the taxable year in which the contribution is made may apply for a credit. The credit for this purpose is 100% of the first $10,000 contributed during the taxable year and up to 90% of the remaining amount contributed during the taxable year. This credit cannot exceed $200,000 annually for business firms for contributions made to pre-kindergarten scholarship organizations [72 P.S. § 8705-F(c)]. A business firm may receive a tax credit for a contribution to a scholarship or educational improvement organization or to a pre-kindergarten scholarship organization, or both [72 P.S. § 8705-F(d)].

• *Application and approval*

Scholarship organization or pre-kindergarten scholarship organization: In order to receive a credit for contributions to scholarship or pre-kindergarten scholarship organizations, a business must apply to the DCED. It will receive a credit if the scholarship organization or pre-kindergarten scholarship organization that receives the contribution appears on the list published by the DCED in the *Pennsylvania*

Bulletin [72 P.S. § 8704-F(a)]. The list must also be posted and updated as necessary on the publicly accessible World Wide Web site of the DCED [72 P.S. § 8703-F(f)].

Educational improvement organization: In order to receive a credit for contributions to an educational improvement organization, a business firm must apply to the DCED. The firm will receive a tax credit if the DCED has approved the program provided by the educational improvement organization that receives the contribution [72 P.S. § 8704-F(b)].

Availability of credits: Credits will be made available by the DCED on a first-come, first-served basis within the maximum established for total credits approved [72 P.S. § 8704-F(c)].

Contributions: A contribution by a business firm to a scholarship organization, pre-kindergarten scholarship organization, or educational improvement organization must be made no later than 60 days following the approval of the application [72 P.S. § 8704-F(d)].

CAUTION

This discussion is a general overview for this credit. The requirements for eligibility for this credit are detailed and lengthy. Consult the statute for further information on this credit.

¶1012 Entertainment Production Tax Credit (Formerly Film Production Tax Credit)

The Film Production Tax Credit was renamed the Entertainment Production Tax Credit by Act 84 of 2016. There are three subsections: An expanded Film Production Tax Credit, and two new tax credits, the Concert Rehearsal and Tour Tax Credit and the Video Game Production Tax Credit.

• *Administration of credit*

The Department of Community and Economic Development (DCED) administers the film production credit and is responsible for issuing written guidelines and regulations for the implementation of the film production credit [72 P.S. § 8710-D].

• *Allowance and application of film production credit*

A taxpayer may claim a film production tax credit to be applied against the taxpayer's (1) personal income tax liability (but not personal income tax withheld by an employer); (2) corporate net income tax liability; (3) capital stock/franchise tax liability; (4) bank and trust company shares tax; or (5) insurance premiums tax [72 P.S. §§ 8702-D and 8704-D]. A tax credit approved by the Department of Community and Economic Development (DCED) in a taxable year must first be applied against the taxpayer's qualified tax liability for the current taxable year as of the date of which the credit was approved before the tax credit can be carried over or sold or assigned [72 P.S. § 8705-D(b)]. Effective July 1, 2013, film production companies entitled to the film tax credit must, as a condition of the credit, withhold personal income tax from payments to pass-through entities that represent individual talent. Additionally, taxpayers may begin to earn credits before the first actual day of photography if approved by the Pennsylvania Film Office. The Film Office is authorized to consider any criteria that the applicant submits, so long as the information is designed to ensure maximum employment and benefit within Pennsylvania, in determining whether a project is entitled to the film tax credit. Film tax credits purchased or assigned in 2013 may be carried forward to 2014 and film tax credits purchased or assigned in 2014 may be carried forward to 2015.

No Double Dipping

A taxpayer that has received a film production grant under 12 Pa.C.S. §4106 is not eligible for a film production tax credit.

* Application for film production tax credit

A taxpayer may apply to the DCED for a tax credit. The application must be on the form required by the DCED [72 P.S. §8703-D(a)].

Review and approval: The Department establishes application periods not to exceed 90 days each. All applications received during the application period are reviewed and evaluated by the Department based on the criteria of 72 P.S. §8703-D(b) [72 P.S. §8703-D(b)]. Applications not approved may be reviewed and considered in subsequent application periods. The Department may approve a taxpayer for a tax credit based on its evaluation of the criteria in 72 P.S. §8703-D(b).

Contract: If the DCED approves the taxpayer's application, the Department and the taxpayer must enter into a contract containing (1) an itemized list of production expenses incurred or to be incurred for the film; (2) an itemized list of Pennsylvania production expenses incurred or to be incurred for the film; (3) with respect to a contract entered into prior to completion of production, a commitment by the taxpayer to incur the qualified film production expenses as itemized; (4) the start date; and (5) any other information the Department deems appropriate [72 P.S. §8703(c)].

Certificate: Upon execution of the required contract the DCED will award the taxpayer a film production tax credit an issue the taxpayer a film production tax credit certificate [72 P.S. §8703(d)].

* Limitations

Generally, the aggregate amount of film production tax credits awarded by the DCED to a taxpayer for a film may not exceed 25% of the qualified film production expenses to be incurred. The aggregate amount of film production tax credits awarded in any fiscal year may not exceed $65,000,000 [72 P.S. §8707-D(b)(2)].

* Carryovers

If a taxpayer cannot use the entire amount of the tax credit for the taxable year in which the tax credit is first approved, the excess may be carried over to succeeding taxable years and used as a credit against the qualified tax liability of the taxpayer for those taxable years. Each time the tax credit is carried over to a succeeding taxable year, it must be reduced by the amount that was used as a credit during the immediately preceding taxable year. The credit may be carried over and applied to succeeding taxable years for no more than three (3) taxable years following the first taxable year for which the taxpayer was entitled to claim the credit [72 P.S. §8705-D(a)]. A purchaser or assignee of a film production tax credit in 2011 may carry over the credit for use in the next taxable year [Act 26 of 2011 (S.B. 907A purchaser or assignee may carry forward all or any unused portion of a tax credit purchased or assigned in calendar year 2010 against qualified tax liabilities incurred in taxable years 2011 and 2012 [72 P.S. §8703-D(g)].

* Carrybacks

Taxpayers are not entitled to carry back an unused credit [72 P.S. §8705-D(c)].

* Refunds

Taxpayers are not entitled to obtain a refund of all or any portion of an unused tax credit [72 P.S. §8705-D(c)].

¶1012

• *Sale or assignment of credits*

A taxpayer, upon application to and approval by the DCED, may sell or assign, in whole or in part, a film production tax credit granted to the taxpayer [72 P.S. § 8705-D(e)(1)]. Before an application is approved by the DCED, the Department of Revenue must make a finding that the applicant has filed all required state tax reports and returns for all applicable taxable years and paid any balance of state tax due as determined at settlement, assessment, or determination by the Department of Revenue [72 P.S. § 8705-D(e)(2)].

• *Purchasers and assignees of credits*

A purchaser or assignee of all or a portion of a tax credit must immediately claim the credit in the taxable year in which the purchase or assignment is made. The amount of credit that a purchaser or assignee may use against any one qualified tax liability may not exceed 50% of the qualified tax liability for the taxable year, and the purchaser or assignee may not carry forward, carry back, or obtain a refund of or sell or assign the tax credit. The purchaser or assignee must notify the Department of Revenue of the seller or assignor of the tax credit in compliance with procedures specified by the Department of Revenue [72 P.S. § 8705-D(f)].

• *Penalty*

A taxpayer that claims a tax credit and fails to incur the amount of agreed-upon amount of qualified film productions expenses for a film in that taxable year must repay to the Commonwealth the amount of the film production tax credit claimed for the film [72 P.S. § 8708-D].

• *Pass-through entities*

If a pass-through entity has any unused film production tax credit, it may election in writing, according to procedures established by the Department of Revenue, to transfer all or a portion of the credit to shareholders, members, or partners in proportion to the share of the entity's distributive income to which the shareholder, member, or partner is entitled [72 P.S. § 8709-D(a)]. A pass-through entity and a shareholder, member, or partner may not claim the credit for the same qualified film production expense 72 P.S. § 8709-D(b)]. A shareholder, member, or partner of a pass-through entity to whom a credit is transferred must immediately claim the credit in the taxable year in which the transfer is made and may not carry forward, carry back, obtain of refund of or sell or assign the credit [72 P.S. § 8709-D(c)].

• *Definition of terms [72 P.S. § 8702-D]*

Department: The Department of Community and Economic Development (DCED).

Minimum stage filming requirements: Minimum stage filming requirements depend on the level of Pennsylvania production expense.

(1) Taxpayers with a Pennsylvania production of less than $30,000,000 per production must meet the following stage filming requirements:

(a) Build at least one set at a qualified production facility.

(b) Shoot for a minimum of 10 days at a qualified production facility.

(c) Spend or incur a minimum of $1,500,000 in direct expenditures relating to the use or rental of tangible property or for performance of services provided by a qualified production facility.

(2) Taxpayers with a Pennsylvania production expense of at least $30,000,000 per production must meet the following stage filming requirements:

(a) Build at least two sets at a qualified production facility.

(b) Shoot for a minimum of 15 days at a qualified production facility.

¶1012

(c) Spend or incur a minimum of $5,000,000 in direct expenditures relating to the use or rental of tangible property at or for performance of services provided by a qualified production facility.

Film: A feature film, a television film, a television talk or game show series, a television commercial, or a television pilot or each episode of a television series that is intended as programming for a national audience. The term does not include a production featuring news, current events, weather and mark reports; public programming, sports event, awards show, or other gala event; a production that solicits funds; a production containing obscene material or performances as defined in 18 Pa.C.S. § 5903(b) (relating to obscene and other sexual materials and performances); or a production primarily for private, political, industrial, corporate, or institutional purposes.

Pass-through entity: A partnership as defined in 72 P.S. § 7301(n.0) or a Pennsylvania S corporation as defined in 72 P.S. § 7301(n.1).

Pennsylvania production expense: Production expense incurred in Pennsylvania. See 72 P.S. § 1702-D for a list of activities included in the term "Pennsylvania production expense." In prescribing standards for determining which production expenses are considered Pennsylvania production expenses, the DCED will consider (1) the location where services are performed; (2) the location where supplied are consumed; and (3) other factors the DCED determines are relevant [72 P.S. § 8706-D].

Qualified film production expense: All Pennsylvania production expenses if Pennsylvania production expenses make up at least 60% of the film's total production expenses. The term cannot include more than $15,000,000 in the aggregate of compensation paid to individuals or payment made to entities representing an individual for services provided in the production of the film.

Qualified production facility: A film production facility located within Pennsylvania that contains at least one sound stage with a column-free, unobstructed floor space and meets either of the following criteria:

(1) It has had a minimum of $10,000,000 invested in the film production facility in land or a structure purchased or ground-up, purpose-built new construction or renovation of existing improvement.

(2) It meets at least three of the following criteria:

(a) A sound stage having an industry standard noise criteria rating of 25 or better.

(b) A permanent grid with a minimum point load capacity of no less than 1,000 pounds at a minimum of 25 points.

(c) Built-in power supply available at a minimum of 4,000 amps per sound stage without the need for supplemental generators.

(d) A height from sound stage floor to permanent grid of a minimum of 20 feet.

(e) A sound stage with a sliding or roll-up access door with a minimum height of 14 feet.

(f) A built-in HVAC capacity during shoot days with a minimum of 50 tons of cooling capacity available per sound stage.

(g) Perimeter security that includes a 24-hour, seven days a week security present and use of access control identification badges.

(h) On-site lighting and grip department with an available inventory stored at the film production facility with a minimum cost of investment of $500,000.

(i) A sound stage with contiguous production offices with a minimum of 5,000 square feet per sound stage.

Start date: The first day of principal photography in Pennsylvania.

Taxpayer: A film production company subject to (1) the personal income tax; (2) the corporate net income tax; or (3) the capital stock/franchise tax.

Additional Credit

In addition to the regular film production tax credit, a taxpayer is eligible for a credit in the amount of 5% of the qualified film production expenses incurred by the taxpayer if the taxpayer meets the following requirements: (1) It films a feature film, television film, or television series that is intended as programming for a national audience; and (2) It films in a qualified production facility that meets the minimum stage filming requirements [72 P.S. § 8707-D(b)(1.1)].

• *Video Game Production Tax Credit*

This tax credit is for production expenses incurred by video game production companies. Credits may be awarded for up to 25 percent of qualified expenses in the first four years of production and 10 percent for each year thereafter per taxpayer per fiscal year. The budget allocation is $1 million a year beginning in the 2017-18 fiscal year.

¶1013 Keystone Opportunity Zone (KOZ) Credit and Keystone Opportunity Expansion (KOEZ)

A corporation that is a qualified business (see ¶4622) may claim a credit against the corporate net income tax for tax liability attributable to business activity conducted within a subzone, an expansion subzone, or an improvement subzone. Note that the term "subzone" is used herein to indicate a subzone, an expansion subzone, or an improvement subzone. The tax liability attributable to business activity conducted within a subzone is determined by multiplying the corporation's taxable income attributable to business activity conducted within the subzone by the corporate net income tax rate [73 P.S. § 820.515(b)]. The business activity must be conducted directly by a corporation in the subzone in order for the corporation to claim the tax credit, and no credit may be claimed for activities conducted prior to the designation of the area as a subzone [73 P.S. § 820.515(a)].

Limitation on amount of credit: The credit cannot exceed the corporation's corporate net income tax liability for the tax year [73 P.S. § 820.515(f)].

Attributable tax liability: Tax liability attributable to business activity conducted within a subzone is computed, construed, administered, and enforced in conformity with the corporate net income tax provisions of Article IV of the Tax Reform Code [73 P.S. § 820.515(c)]. If the entire business of the corporation in Pennsylvania is transacted wholly within the subzone, the taxable income attributable to business activity within a subzone is Pennsylvania taxable income as determined under the corporate net income tax provisions [73 P.S. § 820.515(c)(1)]. A corporation, for this purpose, computes its Commonwealth taxable income in conformity with the corporate net income tax statutes with no adjustments or subtractions for subzone taxable income [73 P.S. § 820.515(3)].

Apportionment: If the entire business of the corporation in Pennsylvania is not transacted wholly within the subzone, its taxable income must be apportioned between income attributable to the subzone and income not attributable to the subzone [73 P.S. § 820.515(c)(2)]. For tax years prior to 2008, the income apportioned to activity within the subzone is determined by multiplying the corporation's Pennsylvania taxable income by a fraction, the numerator of which is the property factor plus the payroll factor plus the sales factor and the denominator of which is three. The property factor, payroll factor, and sales factor for this purpose are determined with reference to the total property, payroll, or sales in the subzone and total property, payroll, or sales in Pennsylvania (not the corporation's total property, payroll, or sales if the corporation has business activity outside Pennsylvania) [73 P.S.

§ 820.515(d)]. The sales factor for KOZ tax credit purposes will not necessarily be the same as the sales factor for three-factor apportionment purposes. See *Corporation Tax Bulletin No. 124* for details [73 P.S. § 820.515(e)].

Effective for tax years beginning after 2008, for purposes of the corporate net income tax credit for income attributable to business activity in a KOZ/KOEZ/KOIZ, the income apportionment formula is amended to exclude the sales factor. Income is apportioned to the zone by multiplying Pennsylvania taxable income by a fraction, the numerator of which is the property factory plus the payroll factor, and the denominator of which is two. This apportionment formula also applies to KOZ/KOEZ/KOIZ exemptions from any local taxes that are measured by business gross receipts, gross or net income, or gross or net profits [73 P.S. § 820.515(d)].

Exceptions: Any portion of the taxpayer's taxable income that is attributable to operation of any of the following companies cannot be used to calculate a KOZ tax credit [73 P.S. § 820.515(g)]:

(1) Railroad, truck, bus, or airline companies.

(2) Pipeline or natural gas companies.

(3) Water transportation companies.

(4) Corporations that would qualify as regulated investment companies for corporate net income tax purposes.

(5) Corporations that would qualify as holding companies as defined for capital/stock franchise purposes.

These companies, however, are entitled to a KOZ job creation tax credit, discussed at ¶ 1014.

The KOZ program was expanded by Act 84 of 2016 to include the designation of 12 new Keystone Opportunity Expansion Zones (KOEZ) for up to 10 years effective January 1, 2017 to December 31, 2026. Additionally, designated parcels can be extended up to 10 years for state tax benefits, if the applicant can meet certain job creation and capital investment requirements.

• *Potential Recapture of Tax Credits*

The Pennsylvania Commonwealth Court, in *Vetri Navy Yard, LLC v. Dept. of Community and Economic Dev.*, 189 A.3d 1137 (Pa. Commw.), ruled that the application of the Keystone Opportunity Zone ("KOZ") recapture provisions is not limited to situations where the qualified business physically relocates outside of the KOZ. The taxpayer had constructed and operated a restaurant in the Philadelphia Navy Yard KOZ in 2013 and was granted KOZ benefits. The taxpayer sold the restaurant to a third party on January 30, 2016. Under § 902a of the Keystone Opportunity Improvement Zone Act (Act), when a "qualified business" "relocates" outside a KOZ within a certain period of time, KOZ benefits are subject to recapture. 73 P.S. § 820.902(a). The Commonwealth Court noted that the Act did not define the terms "relocation outside of the zone" but nevertheless determined that the taxpayer's cessation of business through a sale resulted in the equivalent of a relocation outside of the zone - notwithstanding that the purchaser continued to operate a restaurant on the exact same premises. The court's interpretation of the terms "relocation outside of the zone" would logically necessitate a finding that a taxpayer's bankruptcy (another type of cessation of business in a KOZ) would likewise require a recapture of KOZ benefits, thus seemingly making entrepreneurs less likely to attempt development in a blighted area.

¶ 1014 Keystone Opportunity Zone Job Creation Tax Credit

Railroad, truck, bus, or airline companies, pipeline or natural gas companies, and water transportation companies that are subject to special apportionment rules (discussed at ¶ 1112) and are qualified businesses (see ¶ 4622) may apply to the Department of Revenue for a KOZ job creation tax credit. The credit is for all full-time jobs created within a subzone in the taxable year. As used herein, the term "subzone" includes subzones, expansion subzones, and improvement subzones. The job must be held directly with the qualified business in the subzone in order for the qualified business to apply for the tax credit. The Department of Revenue prescribes the form and manner to obtain the credit [73 P.S. § 820.519(a)].

• *Application for and notification of credit*

A qualified business must apply for a KOZ job creation tax credit by January 15 for the previous calendar year [73 P.S. § 820.519(a)]. The Department of Revenue must notify a qualified business of the amount of its KOZ job creation tax credit approved [73 P.S. § 820.519(f)].

• *Application of credit to taxes*

The KOZ job creation tax credit may be applied against the personal income tax, the corporate net income tax, or the capital/stock franchise tax [73 P.S. § 820.519(a)].

• *Determination of credit*

The KOZ job creation tax credit is determined by multiplying the monthly average of all full-time jobs by the allowance shown in the following table [73 P.S. § 820.519(e)]:

Calendar Year	Allowance
2001	$500 per job
2002	750 per job
2003	1,000 per job
2004 through 2018	1,250 per job

• *Limitation on amount of credit*

A KOZ job creation tax credit can only be used to offset a tax liability incurred from subzone activities and cannot exceed 50% of the personal income tax liability, corporate net income tax liability, or capital/stock franchise tax liability of a qualified business or person. The KOZ job creation tax credit may not be carried back or forward to any other year [73 P.S. § 820.519(g)].

• *Apportionment*

The Department of Revenue will apportion a KOZ job creation tax credit for a qualified business that has not operated in a subzone for a full fiscal year [73 P.S. § 820.519(d)].

• *Maximum total credits*

The total amount of KOZ job creation tax credits approved by the Department of Revenue cannot exceed $1,000,000 annually. If the credits exceed $1,000,000, they will be allocated on a pro rata basis [73 P.S. § 820.519(h)].

• *Pass-through entities*

A partner or member of a partnership or association that is a qualified business is entitled to a KOZ job creation tax credit in proportion to the partner's or member's share, whether or not distributed, of the income or gain received by the partnership or association [73 P.S. § 820.519(j)(1)]. A shareholder of a Pennsylvania S corporation that is a qualified business is entitled to a KOZ job creation tax credit in proportion to the shareholder's pro rata share, whether or not distributed, of the income or gain received by the corporation for its taxable year ending within or with the share-holder's taxable year. However, no partnership, association, or Pennsylvania S corporation, or partner, member, or shareholder may claim any other tax benefit, expense, or credit for the same KOZ job creation tax credit [73 P.S. § 820.519(j)(2)].

¶1014

¶1014A Keystone Special Development Zone (KSDZ) Tax Credit

• *Allowance of credit*

For any tax year beginning in 2012 and for a period of up to 10 years during the period beginning July 1, 2012, and ending June 30, 2035, a Keystone special development zone employer may earn a Keystone special development zone tax credit [53 P.S. § 1603-F(e)(1)]. A "Keystone special development zone employer" is a person or entity subject to the following Pennsylvania taxes: (1) personal income tax; (2) corporate net income tax; (3) capital stock/franchise tax; (4) bank and trust companies shares tax; (5) title insurance companies tax; and (6) mutual thrift institutions tax [72 P.S. § 1602-F].

• *Keystone special development zone*

A "Keystone special development zone" is a parcel of real property that meets all of the following [72 P.S. § 1602-F]:

(1) On July 1, 2011, it was within a special industrial area as described in the Land Recycling and Environmental Remediation Standards Act [Act of May 19, 1995 (P.L. 4, No. 2)] for which the Department of Environmental protection has executed a special industrial area consent order and agreement.

(2) On July 1, 2011, it had no permanent vertical structures affixed to it, or (effective July 2, 2012) had a permanent vertical structure affixed to it that has been deteriorated or abandoned for at least 20 years.

(3) It is certified by the Department of Environmental Protection as meeting the previous two (2) requirements.

• *Amount of credit*

The amount of the tax credit a Keystone special development zone employer may earn in any tax year is equal to $2,100 for each full-time equivalent employee in excess of the number of full-time equivalent employees employed prior to January 1, 2012 [72 P.S. 1603-F(c)]. A Keystone special development zone employer must notify the Department of Revenue of its qualification for a Keystone special development zone tax credit by February 1, for tax credits earned during a taxable year ending in the prior calendar year [72 P.S. § 1603-F(a)].

Full-time equivalent employee: The whole number of employees (rounded down) that equals the sum of the following: (1) the total paid hours (including paid time off and family leave) of all of a Keystone special development zone employer's employees classified as nonexempt during the Keystone special development zone employer's tax year divided by 2,000; and (2) a total number arrived at by adding (for each Keystone special development zone employer's employees scheduled to work at least 35 hours per week) the fraction equal to the portion of the year the exempt employee was paid by the Keystone special development zone employer [72 P.S. § 1602-F]. Whether an employee is classified as exempt or nonexempt is determined under the Fair Labor Standards Act of 1938 (52 Stat. 1060, 29 U.S.C. § 201 *et seq.*].

Employee: An "employee" is an individual who (1) is employed in Pennsylvania by a Keystone special development zone employer, or its predecessor hired after June 30, 2011; (2) is employed for at least 35 hours per week by a Keystone special development zone employer; and (3) spends at least 90% of his or her working time for the Keystone special development zone employer at the Keystone special development zone location [72 P.S. § 1602-F].

• *Application of credit*

A Keystone special development zone employer must first use its Keystone special development zone tax credit against its qualified tax liability [53 P.S. § 1603-F(d)]. "Qualified tax liability" for this purpose is any tax owed by a Keystone special development zone employer attributable to a business activity conducted within a Keystone special development zone for a tax year under the following taxes: (1) personal income tax; (2) corporate net income tax; (3) capital stock/franchise tax; (4) bank and trust companies shares tax; (5) title insurance companies tax; and (6) mutual thrift institutions [53 P.S. § 1602-F].

• *Sale or assignment of tax credit*

If the Keystone special development zone employer is entitled to a credit in any year that exceeds its qualified tax liability for that year, upon application to and approval by the Department of Revenue, a Keystone special development zone employer that has been awarded a tax credit may sell or assign, in whole or in part, the tax credit granted to the Keystone special development zone employer. The Application must be on the form required by the Department of Revenue and must include all required information [53 P.S. § 1603-F(d.1)(1)]. The purchaser or assignee of all or a portion of a Keystone special development zone tax credit must claim the credit in the taxable year in which the purchase or assignment is made. The purchaser or assignee of a tax credit may use it against the tax liability of the purchaser or assignee under the following taxes: (1) personal income tax; (2) corporate net income tax; (3) capital stock/franchise tax; (4) bank and trust companies shares tax; (5) title insurance companies tax; and (6) mutual thrift institutions [53 P.S. § 1603-F(d.1)(3)].

• *Use and carryforward*

A Keystone special development zone employer may earn the Keystone special development zone tax credit beginning in any tax year beginning in 2012 and for a period of up to 10 years during the period beginning July 1, 2012, and ending June 30, 2035 [53 P.S. § 1603-F(e)(1)]. A Keystone special development zone employer may carry forward for up to 10 years a Keystone special development zone credit (1) that it is unable to use; or (2) that it does not sell or assign [53 P.S. § 1603-F(e)(2)]. Credits carried forward must be used on a first-in-first-out basis [53 P.S. § 1603-F(e)(3)].

No Double Dipping

In a given year, a Keystone special development zone employer may only earn a Keystone special development zone credit or a credit under the Keystone Opportunity Zone, Keystone Opportunity Expansion Zone and Keystone Opportunity Improvement Zone Act [Act of October 6, 1998 (P.L. 705, No. 92) [53 P.S. § 1603-F(f)]. KOZs are discussed at ¶ 1013. A Keystone special development zone employer may not claim both a Keystone special development zone credit and a credit under Article XVIII-B of the Tax Reform Code (relating to the tax credit for new jobs).

• *Pass-through entities*

If a Keystone special development zone employer is a pass-through entity and has any unused Keystone special development zone credits, it may elect in writing, according to procedures established by the Department of Revenue, to transfer all or a portion of the credit to shareholders, members, or partners in proportion to the share of the entity's distributive income to which the shareholder, member, or partner is entitled [53 P.S. § 1603-F(g)(1)]. Pass-through entities are discussed in Chapter 18.

No Double Dipping

A Keystone special development zone employer that is a pass-through entity and a shareholder, member, or partner of that Keystone special development zone employer may not both claim the Keystone special development zone tax credit for any tax year [53 P.S. § 1603-F(g)(2)].

¶1014A

- *Transfer*

Any tax credit or tax credit carryforward that a Keystone special development zone employer is entitled to use may be transferred to a successor entity of the Keystone special development zone employer [53 P.S. § 1603-F(h)].

- *Penalties*

A company that receives Keystone special development zone tax credits and fails to substantially maintain the operations related to the Keystone special development zone tax credits in Pennsylvania for a period of five years from the date the company first submits a Keystone special development zone tax credit certificate to the Department of Revenue is required to refund to the Commonwealth the total amount of credits granted, with interest and a penalty of 20% of the amount of credits granted. The Department of Revenue may waive the penalties if it is determined that a company's operations were not maintained or the new jobs were not created because of circumstances beyond the company's control (*e.g.*, natural disasters, unforeseen industry trends, loss of a major supplier or market) [53 P.S. § 1603-F(i)].

- *Apportionment*

The Pennsylvania tax liability of an employer is to be apportioned to the Keystone special development zone in accordance with the requirements of 53 P.S. § 1604-F(b)].

¶1015 Organ or Bone Marrow Donor Tax Credit

With the passage of Act No. 193 of 2014 (H.B. 46) the General Assembly amended and reenacted the Organ and Bone Marrow Donor Act, which originally created an organ or bone marrow donor tax credit.

- *Qualification for credit*

The organ or bone marrow donor tax credit is available to a business firm that provides one or more paid leaves of absence to employees for the specific purpose of organ or bone marrow donation [72 P.S. § 8802].

Business firm: A "business firm" for this purpose is an entity authorized to do business in Pennsylvania and subject to the personal income tax, the corporate net income tax, the capital stock/franchise tax, the bank and trust company shares tax, the title insurance company shares tax, the insurance premiums tax, or the mutual thrift institutions tax. The term also includes a natural person as such or as a member of a partnership or a shareholder in a Pennsylvania S corporation as defined in TRC § § 301(n.0) and 301(s.2) and estates and trusts.

Leave of absence period: The "leave of absence period" is the period (not exceeding five working days or the hourly equivalent of five working days per employee) during which a business firm provides a paid leave of absence to the employee for the purpose of organ or bone marrow donation. This period, however, does not include a period during which an employee utilizes any annual leave or sick days that the employee has been given by the employer [72 P.S. § 8802].

- *Application of credit*

A business firm that qualifies for this credit may apply that credit against any of the following taxes [72 P.S. § 8802]:

    (1) Personal income tax.

    (2) Corporate net income tax.

    (3) Capital stock/franchise tax.

    (4) Bank and trust company shares tax.

    (5) Title insurance company shares tax.

    (6) Insurance premiums tax.

    (7) Mutual thrift institutions tax.

Note that this tax cannot be applied against any personal income tax withheld by an employer from an employee [72 P.S. § 8803(A)(2)].

Credit nonrefundable: This credit is a nonrefundable credit [72 P.S. § 8803(C)].

• *Amount of credit*

The bone or organ marrow donor tax credit is equal to the (1) amount of employee compensation paid during the leave of absence period, (2) the cost of temporary replacement help (if any) during the leave of absence period, and any miscellaneous expenses authorized by regulation that are incurred in connection with connection with the leave of absence period.

Pass-through entities: If the employee on paid leave of absence is employed by a pass-through entity, the credit is calculated in proportion to the member's or shareholder's portion of the pass-through entity's income [72 P.S. § 8803(B)(2)].

Estates and trusts: In the case of an estate or trust with income credited to or distributed to a beneficiary, the credit is measured in proportion to the beneficiary's share of income [72 P.S. § 8803(B)(2)].

Apportionment of credit: Credit calculated for a business firm subject to tax in another state must be apportioned by Pennsylvania [72 P.S. § 8803(B)(1)]. The organ or bone marrow tax credit is apportioned to Pennsylvania by multiplying the credit by a fraction, the numerator of which is the total amount paid in Pennsylvania during the tax period by the business firm for compensation and the denominator of which is the total compensation paid everywhere during the tax period.

• *Carryforwards*

Unused credits may be carried over for three taxable years and may not be carried back against preceding taxable years [72 P.S. § 8803(C)].

¶1016 Resource Enhancement and Protection Tax Credit

• *Establishment and grant of credit*

The resource enhancement and protection tax credit program (effective October 13, 2007) is established to encourage private investment in the implementation of best management practices on agricultural operations, the planting of riparian forest buffers, and the remediation of legacy sediment [72 P.S. § 8703-E(a)]. The Department of Revenue is empowered to grant resource enhancement and protection tax credits and must issue, within 60 days of receipt of notice from the State Conservation Commission that a project is complete, a notice of grant of a tax credit to the eligible applicant [72 P.S. § 8708-E(a)]. Before a credit is granted, the Department of Revenue must make a finding that the applicant has filed all required state tax reports and returns for all applicable taxable years and paid any balance of state tax due as determined at settlement or assessment [72 P.S. § 8708-E(2)].

Definition of Terms

Definitions of terms used in this paragraph are found in 72 P.S. § 8702-E.

• *Administration of credit*

The Department of Revenue is responsible for the administration of the resource enhancement and protection tax credit.

• *Application of credit*

A resource enhancement and protection tax credit can be applied against the taxpayer's qualified tax liability for the current taxable year. A "qualified tax credit" is the liability for tax imposed upon an eligible applicant for the following taxes: (1) the personal income tax; (2) the corporate net income tax; (3) the capital stock/

franchise tax; (4) the bank and trust companies shares tax; (5) the title insurance companies shares tax; (6) the insurance premiums tax; or (7) the mutual thrift institutions tax [72 P.S. § 8703-E].

- *General eligibility for credit*

    Projects will be eligible for a tax credit as follows [72 P.S. § 8704-E(a)]:

    (1) Only best management practices completed after October 23, 2007, are eligible.

    (2) An agricultural operation must have in place a current conservation plan, a current agricultural erosion and sediment control plan if engaged in plowing and tilling, and a current nutrient management plan if required, or the development of such plans must be included in a credit application.

    (3) An agricultural operation with an animal concentration area must have implemented best management practices necessary to abate storm water runoff, loss of sediment, loss of nutrients, and runoff of other pollutants from the animal concentration area, or the implementation of such best management practices must be included in a credit application.

    (4) A project must meet the design and construction standards established by the State Conservation Commission. If standards do not exist for a best practice approved by the Commission, the Commission may establish or approve design, construction, and certification standards for a best management practice.

- *Application, review, and authorization by State Conservation Commission*

    Application for credit: An eligible applicant must apply to the Commission for authorization that a project is eligible for a credit. An application will be developed by the Commission [72 P.S. § 8707-E(a)].

    Review and notification: The Commission must, within 60 days of receipt, review each application and notify an applicant whether or not the applicant meets the requirements and is authorized to receive a resource enhancement and protection tax credit [72 P.S. § 8707-E(b)].

    Authorization: The Commission will authorize credits on a first-come, first-served bases and ay not authorize credits that exceed the statutory limitations (see Limitations below) [72 P.S. § 8707-E(c)].

    Completion of project: When an authorized project is completed, an applicant must submit to the Commission a written notice, containing the required information of 72 P.S. § 8707-E(d), that the project is completed [72 P.S. § 8707-E(d)].

    Inspection: Authorized projects may be subject to inspection by the Commission or its designated agent [72 P.S. § 8707-E(f)].

- *75% tax credit*

    A tax credit equal to 75% of the eligible costs of an authorized project will be granted for any of the following [72 P.S. § 8704-E(b)(1)]:

    (1) Development of a voluntary or mandatory nutrient management plan.

    (2) Development of an agricultural erosion and sediment control plan or a conservation plan.

    (3) For an animal concentration area, design and implementation of best management practices necessary to abate storm water runoff, loss of sediment, loss of nutrients, and runoff of other pollutants.

    (4) Design and implementation of best management practices necessary to restrict livestock access to streams if there is established and maintained a riparian forest buffer with a minimum width of 50 feet.

    (5) Establishment of a riparian forest buffer with a minimum width of 50 feet.

• *50% tax credit*

A tax credit equal to 50% of the eligible costs of an authorized project will be granted for any of the following [72 P.S. § 8704-E(b)(2)]:

(1) For an agricultural operation, design and implementation of agricultural best management practices or the installation and use of equipment, provided that the best management practice or equipment is necessary to reduce existing sediment and nutrient pollution to surface waters.

(2) Design and implementation of best management practices necessary to exclude livestock access to streams through fending, stabilized crossings, and improved watering systems, if there is established and maintained a vegetated riparian or riparian forest buffer with a minimum width of 35 feet.

• *25% tax credit*

A tax credit equal to 25% of the eligible costs of an authorized project is will be granted for the remediation of legacy sediment if the legacy sediment is exposed and is discharging or threatens to discharge into surface waters as a result of acute stream bank erosion. The project must meet standards established by the State Conservation Commission as being effective in mitigating or eliminating the harmful effects of legacy sediment [72 P.S. § 8704-E(b)(3)].

• *Limitations*

ALERT

The amount available for award to each eligible taxpayer has been reduced to 50% of the amounts otherwise available for the fiscal year 2009 – 2010, and to 45% of the amounts otherwise available for 2010 – 2011 [Act 48 of 2009, H.B. 1531].

Total amount of credits: The total amount of tax credits authorized by the State Conservation Commission cannot exceed $10,000,000 in any fiscal year [72 P.S. § 8709-E].

Eligible applicants: Except for tax credits granted to a sponsor (see Sponsorship below), an eligible applicant may be granted a maximum of $150,000 in resource enhancement and protection tax credits [72 P.S. § 8703-E(b)(1)]. An eligible applicant may submit an application for a single project or multiple applications for multiple projects within the limits of 72 P.S. § 8703-E [72 P.S. § 8703-E(b)(3)].

Agricultural operations: No more than $150,000 in tax credits may be granted toward projects for an agricultural operation [72 P.S. § 8703-E(b)(2)].

Purchased or assigned credits: There is no limit on the amount of tax credits that may be purchased from or be assigned from an eligible applicant [72 P.S. § 8703-E(b)(4)].

Legacy sediment credits: No credits for legacy sediment will be issued prior to July 1, 2008. Applications for legacy sediment remediation will not be accepted prior to July 1, 2008 [72 P.S. § 8703-E(b)(6)].

Sponsorship: There is no limit on the amount of tax credits granted to a sponsor [72 P.S. § 8703-E(b)(5)]. An eligible applicant may be a sponsor by applying for an authorized tax credit if a written agreement between the eligible applicant and the owner of property on which the project will be completed is submitted to the State Conservation Commission, certifying that the property owner will comply with all of the credit provisions [72 P.S. § 8703-E(e)].

• *Eligible costs of authorized project*

The following are considered eligible costs of a project (including services provided by a conservation district) that qualifies for a tax credit [72 P.S. § 8704-E(c)]:

(1) Project design, engineering, and associated planning.

(2) Project management costs (including contracting, document preparation, and applications).

(3) Project construction or installation.

(4) Equipment, materials, and all other components of eligible projects.

(5) Postconstruction inspections.

(6) Interest payments on loans for project implementation for up to one year prior to the award of the tax credit.

Effect of Public Funding

A tax credit may not be applied to that portion of a project cost for which public funding was received [72 P.S. § 8704-E-(c)(3)].

- *Carryovers of credits*

If an eligible applicant cannot use the entire amount of the credit for the taxable year in which it is first granted, the excess may be carried over to succeeding taxable years and used as a credit against the qualified tax liability of the eligible applicant for those taxable years for a maximum of 15 taxable years following the first taxable year for which the applicant was entitled to the credit. Each time the credit is carried over to a succeeding taxable year, it must be reduced by the amount that was used as a credit during the immediately preceding taxable year [72 P.S. § 8703-E(c)(1)]. Credits must be applied against the taxpayer's qualified tax liability for the current taxable year as of the date of which the credit was granted before it can be carried forward [72 P.S. § 8703-E(c)(2)].

- *Carrybacks and refunds*

Resource enhancement and protection tax credits may not be carried back or refunded [72 P.S. § 8703(c)(3)].

- *Sale or assignment of credit*

Upon application to and approval by the State Conservation Commission, an eligible applicant may sell or assign (in whole or in part) a resource enhancement and protection tax credit if no claim for allowance of the credit is filed within one year from the date the credit is granted by the Department of Revenue [72 P.S. § 8703-E-(d)(1)]. The purchaser or assignee of a portion of a credit must immediately claim the credit in the taxable year in which the purchase or assignment is made. The amount of the credit that a purchaser or assignee may use against a qualified tax liability may not exceed 75% of the qualified tax liability for the taxable year. Purchasers or assignees may not carry over, carry back, obtain a refund of, or sell or assign the tax credit. The purchaser of assignee must notify the Department of Revenue of the seller or assignor of the tax credit [72 P.S. § 8703-E(d)(3)]. Notwithstanding any other provision of law, the Department of Revenue must settle, assess, or determine the tax of a purchaser or assignee within 90 days of the filing of all required final returns or reports [72 P.S. § 8703-E(d)(4)]. Before an application is approved, the Department of Revenue must make a finding that the applicant has filed all required state tax reports and returns for all applicable taxable years and paid any balance of state tax due as determined at settlement, assessment, or determination [72 P.S. § 8703-E-(d)(3)].

- *Pass-through entities*

If a pass-through entity has any unused tax credit, it may elect in writing, to transfer all or a portion of the credit to shareholders, members, or partners in proportion to the share of the entity's distributive income to which the shareholder, member, or partner is entitled [72 P.S. § 8703-E(f)(1)]. The transferred credit is in addition to any resource enhancement and protection tax credit to which the shareholder, member, or partner is otherwise entitled [72 P.S. § 8703-E(f)(2)]. However, a pass-through entity and its shareholders, members, or partners may not claim a tax credit for the same project. A shareholder, member, or partner of a pass-through entity to whom a credit is transferred must immediately claim the credit in the taxable year in which the transfer is made; and the shareholder, member, or partner may not carry forward, carry back, obtain a refund of, or sell or assign the credit [72 P.S. § 8703-E(f)(3)].

• *Project maintenance and life expectancy*

Best management practice: An agricultural operation must maintain a best management practice for the life of the practice as established by the State Conservation Commission [72 P.S. § 8706-E(a)]. If the Commission determines that a best management practice is not maintained for the required period, the owners of the property upon which the project exists must return to the Department of Revenue the amount of the tax credit originally granted [72 P.S. § 8706-E(b)]. There is an exception in the case of sale of the property, cessation of agricultural operation, or other factors. If the recipient of a tax credit provides prior written notification to the State Conservation Commission that the recipient will be unable to maintain a best management practice due to these cases, the Commission may direct the Department of Revenue to prorate the amount of the tax credit that must be returned based on the remaining lifespan of the best management practice in question [72 P.S. § 8706-E(c)].

Riparian forest buffer: A riparian forest buffer must be maintained for a minimum of 15 years [72 P.S. § 8706-E(a)].

¶1017 Credit for Job Creation in a Strategic Development Zone

• *Designation of strategic development area (SDA)*

The Governor is authorized to designate up to four (4) strategic development areas in Pennsylvania [72 P.S. § 9939-C(b)(1)].

• *Authorization of credit*

Effective for taxable years beginning after 2007, a railroad, truck, bus, or airline company, pipeline or natural gas company, or water transportation company that is required to apportion income in accordance with the corporate net income tax may apply for a credit against corporate net income, personal, income, or capital stock/franchise tax for jobs created in a strategic development area (SDA) [72 P.S. § 9939-C(a)].

• *Amount of credit*

The credit amount is determined by multiplying the monthly average of all full-time jobs created within an SDA in a taxable year by an allowance amount established for each calendar year ranging from $500 per job for 2001 to $1,250 per job for 2022 [72 P.S. § 9939-C(e)]. The credit may not exceed 50% of the company's applicable tax liability for the tax year [72 P.S. § 9939-C(b)].

¶1018 Credit for Tax Liability Attributable to Business Activity in Strategic Development Area (SDA)

• *Designation of strategic development area (SDA)*

The Governor is authorized to designate up to four (4) strategic development areas in Pennsylvania [72 P.S. § 9911-C(b)(1)].

• *Authorization and amount of credit*

Effective for taxable years beginning on or after January 1, 2008, a corporation that is a qualified business may claim a credit against the corporate net income tax for tax liability attributable to business activity conducted within the SDA in the taxable year [72 P.S. § 9935-C(a).

• *Limitation on credit*

The credit cannot exceed the corporation's corporate net income tax liability for the tax year [72 P.S. § 9935-C(f)].

¶1019 Alternative Energy Production Tax Credit

ALERT

This tax credit has been suspended by Act 48 of 2009 (H.B. 1531), § 2902-E(e).

• *Authorization of credit*

A taxpayer who develops or constructs an alternative energy production project located in Pennsylvania with a useful life of at least four years may apply for an alternative energy production tax credit [73 P.S. § 1649.703(a)]. This credit is effective for project commencing on or after July 9, 2008 [73 P.S. § 1649.711(2)].

• *"Alternative energy production project defined"*

An "alternative energy production project" is the construction of one of the following [73 P.S. § 1649.102].

(1) A facility that utilizes waste coal, alternative fuels, biomass, solar energy, wind energy, geothermal technologies, clean coal technologies, waste energy technologies as defined in the Alternative Energy Portfolio Standard Act [Act of November 30, 2004 (P.L. 1672, No. 213)] to product or distribute alternative energy.

(2) A facility that manufactures or produces products (including component parts) that provide alternative energy or alternative fuels, improve energy efficiency, or conserve energy.

(3) A facility used for the research and development of technology to provide alternative energy sources or alternative fuels.

(4) A project for the development or enhancement of rail transportation systems that deliver alternative fuels or high efficiency locomotives.

• *Amount of credit*

An eligible taxpayer will receive an alternative energy production tax credit for the taxable year equal to 15% of the total amount of all development, equipment, and construction costs paid for alternative energy production projects, not to exceed $1,000,000 for each taxpayer [73 P.S. § 1649.704(a)].

In calculating the total amount of all development, equipment, and construction costs paid for alternative energy production projects, the taxpayer must deduct the amount of any grant or other subsidy received in relation to the alternative energy production project for which the credit is sought by the taxpayer from a federal, state, or local government entity (including an authority) [73 P.S. § 1649.704(b)].

• *Application of credit*

The credit can be applied against an eligible taxpayer's personal income tax (see ¶ 127), corporate net income tax, or capital stock/franchise tax [73 P.S. § § 1649.702, 704(a)].

• *Carryover*

If the taxpayer cannot use the entire amount of the alternative energy production credit for the taxable year in which the credit is first approved, the excess may be carried over to succeeding taxable years for no more than five years following the first taxable year for which the taxpayer was entitled to claim the credit [73 P.S. § 1649.705(a)].

• *Carryback*

No carryback of any unused alternative energy production tax credit is allowed [73 P.S. §§ 1649.702, 704(c)].

• *Refund*

No refund of any unused alternative energy production tax credit is allowed [73 P.S. §§ 1649.702, 704(c)].

• *Sale or assignment*

Upon application to and approval by the Department of Revenue, a taxpayer may sell or assign (in whole or in part) an alternative energy production project tax credit granted to the taxpayer if no claim for allowance of the credit is filed within one year from the date the credit is approved [73 P.S. §§ 1649.702, 704(d)]. The purchaser or assignee must immediately claim the credit in the taxable year in which the purchase or assignment is made. The amount of the tax credit that a purchaser or assignee may use against any one qualified tax liability (*i.e.*, personal income tax, corporate net income tax, or capital stock/franchise tax) cannot exceed 50% of the tax liability for the taxable year. Purchasers or assignees cannot carry forward, carry back, obtain a refund, or sell or assign the tax credit [73 P.S. § 1649.704(e)].

• *Pass-through entity*

If a pass-through entity has any unused credit, the entity may elect (in writing and according to the Department's procedures) to transfer all or a portion of the credit to shareholders, members, or partners in proportion to the share of the entity's distributed income to which the shareholder, member, or partner is entitled [73 P.S.§ 1649.707(a)]. A pass-through entity for this purpose is a partnership (as defined under 72 P.S. § 301(n.0) or a Pennsylvania S corporation (as defined under 72 P.S. §7301(n) [73 P.S. § 1649.702]. A shareholder, member, or partner of a pass-through entity to whom a credit is transferred must immediately claim the credit in the taxable year in which the transfer is made. Shareholder, members, or partners may not carry forward, carry back, obtain a refund of, or sell or assign the credit [73 P.S. § 1649.707(c)].

¶1020 First Class Cities Economic Development District Act

The First Class Cities Economic Development District Act authorizes tax exemptions, deductions, abatements or credits to persons who own interests in qualified pass through entities and to residents of and qualified businesses located in economic development districts [53 P.S. § 18200.301]. The exemptions, deductions, abatements or credits may not extend beyond December 31, 2018 [53 P.S. § 18200.301(b)]. The Governor may propose the designation of economic development districts within the cities of the first class. All political subdivisions within a proposed district must submit timely applications to the Department of Community and Economic Development to create the district [53 P.S. § 18200.301(d)]. The aggregate amount of property proposed by the Governor for economic development districts may not exceed 85 acres [53 P.S. § 18200.301(e)].

• *Definition of terms*

Business. An association, partnership, Subchapter S corporation, corporation, sole proprietorship, limited liability company or limited liability partnership.

Corporation. A business subject to the tax imposed by Article IV of the act of March 4, 1971 (P.L. 6, No. 2), known as the Tax Reform Code of 1971.

Department. The Department of Community and Economic Development of the Commonwealth.

Deteriorated Property. An area containing industrial or commercial real property which is abandoned, vacant undervalued, underutilized or condemned or which contains economically undesirable land use.

Economic development district. A clearly defined geographic area comprised of deteriorated property located in a city of the first class which has been designated by the Department of Community and Economic Development under section 301(d) as an economic development district.

Political Subdivision. A city of the first class or a school district of the first class.

Qualified business. A business that receives a certificate under section 303 for the taxable year.

Qualified pass-through entity. A partnership, association or qualified business.

Qualified political subdivision. A political subdivision that has real property within its jurisdiction that has been designated by the Department of Community and Economic Development as an economic development district.

Resident. An individual who is domiciled in an economic development district.

• *Qualified businesses*

In order to qualify for the exemptions, deductions, abatement or credits a business must submit a statement to the Department stating that the business owns or leases a property in an economic development district and actively conducts a trade, profession or business on the real property [53 P.S. § 18200.303(a)]. An approved business must obtain an annual renewal of its certification from the Department [53 P.S. § 18200.303(a)]. A qualified business may not claim an exemption, deduction, abatement or credit unless it is in compliance with all state and local tax laws and ordinances [53 P.S. § § 18200.903; 18200.904]. A qualified business is deemed to be in compliance if the business or person has filed a timely administrative or judicial appeal [53 P.S. § 18200.905].

• *Residency*

In order to qualify for an exemption, deduction, abatement or credit as a resident, an individual must be domiciled in and reside in the district for a period of 184 consecutive days during each year [53 P.S. § 18200.304].

• *State tax exemptions*

A qualified business or person who owns an interest in a qualified pass-through entity is entitled to exemptions from sales and use tax, personal income tax and corporate net income tax [53 P.S. § § 18200.511; 18200.512; 18200.513]. For construction contracts performed in a district the sales and use tax exemption is limited to building machinery and equipment [53 P.S. § 18200.511(b)].

• *Local tax exemptions*

A qualified business is entitled to exemptions from business privilege taxes, local sales and use tax and real property tax [53 P.S. § § 18200.711; 18200.712; 18200.713]. For construction contacts performed in a district the local sales and use tax exemption is limited to building machinery and equipment [53 P.S. § 18200.712(b)].

• *Transferability*

An exemption, deduction, abatement or credit is nontransferable and cannot be applied, used or assigned to any other person, business or tax account [53 P.S. § 18200.901].

• *Recapture*

If a qualified business relocates outside the district while the district is designated as an economic development district, the business may be required to refund the exemptions, deductions, abatements or credits [53 P.S. § 18200.902]. If the business relocates within three years from the date of first locating in the district, 75% of all exemptions, deductions, abatements or credits must generally be refunded [53 P.S. § 18200.902(a)(1)]. If the business relocates within four to seven years, 50% of all exemptions, deductions, abatements or credits must generally be refunded [53 P.S.

§ 18200.902(a)(2)]. Recapture does not apply to nonprofit organizations for food distribution [53 P.S. § 18200.902(a)(3)]. The Department may waive recapture under certain circumstances [53 P.S. § 18200.902(b)].

¶ 1021 Resource Manufacturing Tax Credit

CAUTION

This credit is not available until January 1, 2016, and sunsets after December 31, 2043 [Act 85 of 2012 (H.B. 761), § 30(6)].

• *Availability*

The resource manufacturing tax credit is established by new Article XVII-G of the Tax Reform Code (§ 8701-G, et seq.). It may be used against the corporate net income tax, the personal income tax, the capital/stock franchise tax, the bank and trust company shares tax, and the insurance gross premiums tax. It is not available to be used against withheld taxes [72 P.S. § 8702-G]. The tax credit must be applied only after all other statutory tax credits and deductions available to the qualified taxpayer have been used [72 P.S. § 8704-G(c)]. Prior to sale or assignment of a tax credit, a qualified taxpayer must first use the tax credit against the qualified tax liability incurred in the taxable year for which the tax credit was approved [72 P.S. § 8704-G(a)].

A qualified taxpayer that has been granted a resource manufacturing tax credit is ineligible for any other tax credit provided under Act 85 of 2005 (H.B. 761) [72 P.S. § 8704-G)d)].

• *Sunset*

This credit is scheduled to expire December 31, 2043 [72 P.S. § 8710-G].

• *Amount of credit*

The credit is equal to $0.05 per gallon of ethane purchased and used in manufacturing ethylene in Pennsylvania and can be applied against up to 20% of the taxpayer's qualified tax liabilities incurred in the year the credit is approved [72 P.S. §§ 8703-G(a), 8704-G(b)].

• *Qualified taxpayers*

The credit is available to qualified taxpayers. A "qualified taxpayer" is a company that satisfies all of the following [72 P.S. § 8702-G]:

(1) It purchases ethane for use in manufacturing ethylene at a facility in Pennsylvania that has been placed in service on or after July 2, 2012. "Ethane" is a colorless, odorless gaseous alkane, C2H6, that occurs as a constituent of natural gas and is used as the raw material in the manufacturing of ethylene. "Ethylene" is an organic hydrocarbon compound with the formula C2H4 or H2D=CH2 that is derived from natural gas and petroleum.

(2) It has made a capital investment of at least $1,000,000,000 in order to construct the facility and place it into service in Pennsylvania.

(3) It has created at least 2,500 full-time equivalent jobs during the construction phase in order to construct the facility and place it into service in Pennsylvania.

• *Application*

Submission of application: A qualified taxpayer may apply to the Department of Revenue for a tax credit. The application must be submitted to the Department of Revenue by March 1 for the tax credit claimed for ethane purchased and used by the qualified taxpayer during the prior calendar year and must be on the form required by the Department of Revenue [72 P.S. § 8703-G(b)].

¶ 1021

Review and approval: The Department of Revenue will review and approve or disapprove the applications by March 20. Upon approval, the Department will issue a certificate stating the amount of tax credit granted for ethane purchased in the prior calendar year [72 P.S. § 8703-G(c)].

• *Carryover, carryback, and refund*

A resource manufacturing tax credit cannot be carried back, carried forward, or be used to obtain a refund [72 P.S. § 8704-G(d)].

• *Sale or assignment*

Application to sell or assign: If a qualified taxpayer holds a tax credit through the end of the calendar year in which the tax credit was granted, the qualified taxpayer may file an application to sell or assign a tax credit, in whole or in part [72 P.S. § 8706-G(a), (b)].

Purchasers and assignees: The purchaser or assignee must claim the tax credit in the calendar year in which the purchase or assignment is made. The amount of the tax credit that a purchaser or assignee may use against any one qualified tax liability may not exceed 50% of any of the qualified tax liabilities for the taxable year [72 P.S. § 8707-G(a), (b)].

Resale or assignment: A purchaser or assignee may not sell or assign the purchased or assigned tax credit [72 P.S. § 1707-G(c)].

Notification to Department of Revenue: It is the responsibility of the purchaser or assignee to notify the Department of Revenue of the seller or assignor of the tax credit [72 P.S. § 8707-G(d)].

• *Pass-through entities*

Election: If a pass-through entity has an unused tax credit, it may elect in writing, according to procedures established by the Department of Revenue, to transfer all or a portion of the credit to shareholders, members, or partners in proportion to the share to the entity's distributive income to which the shareholders, members, or partners are entitled [72 P.S. § 8708-g(a)].

Limitation: The same unused tax credit of the pass-through entity may not be claimed by both pass-through entity and a shareholder, member, or partner of the pass-through entity [72 P.S. § 8708-G(b)].

Amount: The amount of the tax credit that a transferee of an unused credit of the pass-through entity may use against any one qualified tax liability may not exceed 20% of any qualified tax liabilities for the taxable year [72 P.S. § 8708-G(c)].

Time: A transferee must claim the tax credit in the calendar year in which the transfer is made [72 P.S. § 8708-G(d)].

Sale and assignment: A transferee may not sell or assign the tax credit [72 P.S. § 8708-G(e)].

• *Administration*

Audits and assessments: The Department of Revenue has the following powers [72 P.S. § 8709-G(a)]:

(1) To audit a qualified taxpayer to ascertain the validity of the amount claimed.

(2) To issue an assessment against a qualified taxpayer for an improperly issued tax credit. The procedures, collection, enforcement and appeals of any assessment made are governed by Article II. For discussion of administration and procedure, see Chapters 46 and 47.

Guidelines and regulations: The Department of Revenue is given the authority to develop written guidelines for the implementation of the resource manufacturing tax credit, and that guidelines will remain in effect until the Department promulgates regulations for implementation [72 P.S. § 8709-G(b)].

¶1022 Historic Preservation Incentive Tax Credit

• *Authorization*

The historic preservation incentive tax credit is authorized by Article XVII-H of the Tax Reform Code [72 P.S. §§ 8701-H, et seq.].

• *Administration*

The Department of Community and Economic Development, the Pennsylvania Historical and Museum Commission, and the Department of Revenue will jointly develop written guidelines for the implementation of the tax credit provisions [72 P.S. § 8707-H].

• *Application of the Internal Revenue Code*

The provision of IRC § 47 and the regulations promulgated regarding those provision shall apply the Department of Revenue's interpretation and administration of the historic preservation incentive credit. References to the Internal Revenue Code (Code) shall mean the sections of the Code as existing on any date of interpretation of Article XVII-H, except if those sections of the Code referenced are repealed or terminated, references to the Code thus means those sections last having full force and effect. If, after repeal or termination, the Code sections are revised or reenacted, references to Code section shall mean those revised or reenacted sections [72 P.S. § 8708-H].

• *Application for credit*

A qualified taxpayer may apply to the Department of Community and Economic Development (DCED) for a historic preservation incentive tax credit. The application must be on the form required by the DCED and must include a qualified rehabilitation plan [72 P.S. § 8703-H(a)]. A "qualified rehabilitation plan" is a plan to rehabilitate a qualified historic structure that is approved by the Pennsylvania Historical and Museum Commission as being consistent with the standards for rehabilitation and guidelines for rehabilitation of historic buildings as adopted by the United States Secretary of the Interior [72 P.S. § 8701-H].

Upon approval of an application, the DCED will issue a qualified taxpayer a tax credit certificate. Taxpayers are not entitled to apply for historic preservation incentive tax credit after the seventh (7th) fiscal year following July 7, 2012 [72 P.S. § 8709-H].

• *Qualified taxpayer*

A "qualified taxpayer" is any natural person, corporation, business trust, limited liability company, partnership, limited liability partner, association, or any other form of legal business entity that meets the following criteria [72 P.S. § 8701-H]:

(1) It is subject to one or more of the following taxes (excluding any personal income tax withheld):

(a) Personal income tax.

(b) Corporate net income tax.

(c) Capital stock/franchise tax.

(d) Bank and trust companies shares tax.

(e) Title insurance companies shares tax.

(f) Insurance premiums tax.

(g) Gross receipts tax.

(h) Mutual thrift institutions tax.

(2) It owns a qualified historic structure. A "qualified historic structure" is a commercial building located in Pennsylvania that qualifies as a certified historic structure under IRC § 47(c)(3).

• *Claiming the credit*

Upon presenting a tax credit certificate to the Department of Revenue, the qualified taxpayer may claim a tax credit against the qualified tax liability of the qualified taxpayer [72 P.S. § 8704-H]. A "qualified tax liability" is a tax liability imposed on a taxpayer for one of the following taxes [72 P.S. § 8701-H]:

(1) Personal income tax.

(2) Corporate net income tax.

(3) Capital stock/franchise tax.

(4) Bank and trust companies shares tax.

(5) Title insurance companies shares tax.

(6) Insurance premiums tax.

(7) Gross receipts tax.

(8) Mutual thrift institutions tax.

A tax credit certificate received by the Department of Revenue in a taxable year will be applied first against the qualified taxpayer's qualified tax liability for the current taxable year as of the date on which the credit was issued before the tax can be used as a carryover [72 P.S. § 8705-H(b)].

• *Amount of credit*

In granting tax credit certificates for the historic preservation incentive tax credit, the DCED shall not grant more than $500,000 in tax credit certificates to a single qualified taxpayer in any fiscal year. Total tax credit certificates in any fiscal year cannot exceed $3,000,000 [72 P.S. § 8703-H(b)(5)].

• *Carryovers*

If a qualified taxpayer is unable to use the entire amount of the tax credit for the taxable year in which the tax credit is first approved, the excess may be carried over to succeeding taxable years and used as a credit against the qualified tax liability of the qualified taxpayer for those taxable years. Each time the tax credit is carried over to a succeeding taxable year, it must be reduced by the amount that was used as a credit during the immediately preceding taxable year. The credit may be carried over and applied to succeeding taxable years for not more than seven (7) taxable years following the first taxable year for which the qualified taxpayer was entitled to claim the credit [72 P.S. § 8705-H(a)].

• *No carryback or refund*

A qualified taxpayer may not carry back or obtain a refund of all or any portion of an unused historic preservation incentive tax credit granted to the qualified taxpayer [72 P.S. § 8705-H(c)].

• *Sale or assignment*

A qualified taxpayer, upon application to and approval by the DCED, may sell or assign, in whole or in part, an historic preservation incentive credit [72 P.S. § 8704-(d)(1)].

• *Purchasers and assignees*

The purchaser or assignee of all or a portion of an historic preservation inventive tax credit must immediately claim the credit in the taxable year in which the purchase or assignment is made. The purchaser or assignee may not carry forward, carry back, or obtain a refund of, or sell or assign the credit. The purchaser or assignee must notify the Department of Revenue of the seller or assigner of the tax credit in compliance with procedures specified by the Department of Revenue [72 P.S. § 8704-H(e)].

• *Pass-through entities*

General rule: If a pass-through entity has any unused tax credit, it may elect in writing, according to procedures established by the Department of Revenue, to transfer all or a portion of the credit to shareholders, members, or partners in proportion to the share of the entity's distributive income to which the shareholder, member, or partner is entitled [72 P.S. § 8706-H(a)].

Limitation: A pass-through entity and a shareholder, member, or partner of a pass-through entity may not claim the credit for the same qualified expenditures [72 P.S. § 8706-H(b)]. "Qualified expenditures" are the costs and expenses incurred by a qualified taxpayer in the restoration of a qualified historic structure pursuant to a qualified plan and which are defined as qualified rehabilitation expenditures under IRC § 47(c)(2) [72 P.S. § 8701-H].

Application: A shareholder, member, or partner of a pass-through entity to whom a credit is transferred must immediately claim the credit in the taxable year in which the transfer is made. The shareholder, member or partner may not carry forward, carry back, obtain a refund of, or sell or assign the credit [72 P.S. § 8706-H(c)].

¶1023 Community-Based Services Tax Credit

• *Authorization*

The community-based services tax credit is established and authorized by Article XVII-I of the Tax Reform Code [72 P.S. § 8701-I et seq.].

• *Guidelines*

The DCED, in conjunction with the Department of Revenue and the Department of Public Welfare may establish guidelines as necessary to implement the community-based services tax credit provisions [72 P.S. § 87-7-I].

• *Definitions*

The following words and phrases when used in the community-based services tax credit provisions shall have the meanings given to them in 72 P.S. § 8702-I unless the context clearly indicates otherwise [72 P.S. § 8702-I]:

  — *Business firm:* An entity authorized to do business in Pennsylvania and subject to the following taxes:

    (1) Personal income tax.

    (2) Corporate net income tax.

    (3) Capital stock/franchise tax.

    (4) Bank and trust companies shares tax.

    (5) Insurance premiums tax.

    (6) Mutual thrift institutions tax.

  — *Contribution:* A donation of cash, personal property, or services, the value of which is the net cost of the donation to the donor or the pro rata hourly wage, including benefits, of the donor, or the pro rata hourly wage, including benefits, of the individual performing the services.

  — *Department:* The Pennsylvania Department of Community and Economic Development (DCED).

  — *Individual:* An individual who is eligible for community-based services funded through the Office of Developmental Programs and the Office of Mental Health and Substance Abuse Services of the Department of Public Welfare.

  — *Provider:* A nonprofit entity that meets all of the following:

    (1) It provides community-based services to individuals with intellectual disabilities or mental illness.

    (2) It is exempt from federal taxation under IRC § 501(c)(3).

• *Availability of tax credit*

Application: A business firm may apply to the DCED for a tax credit under 72 P.S. § 1705-I (see "Grant of tax credits") below. A business firm may receive a community-based services tax credit if the provider that receives from the business firm appears on the publication list discussed below [72 P.S. § 8704-I(a)]. However, no credit will be approved for activities that are part of a business firm's normal course of business [72 P.S. § 88706-I(b)].

Availability of tax credit: The credits shall be made available on a first-come-first-served basis within the limitation of 72 P.S. § 8706-I (see "Amount of credits") below [72 P.S. § 8704-I(b)].

Contributions: A contribution by a business firm to a provider must be made no later than 60 days following the approval of the application [72 P.S. § 8704-I(c)].

• *Applying the tax credit*

Eligible taxes: The tax credit certificate issued by the DCED may be used against a tax liability owed by a business firm that provides proof of a contribution to a provider in the taxable year in which the contribution is made. A business may apply the credit against any of the following taxes [72 P.S. § 8705-I(a)]:

(1) Personal income tax (excluding any tax withheld by an employer).

(2) Corporate net income tax.

(3) Capital stock/franchise tax.

(4) Bank and trust companies shares tax.

(5) Insurance premiums tax.

(6) Mutual thrift institutions tax.

• *Amount of tax credits*

Business firm limits: The tax credit shall not exceed 50% of the total amount contributed by a business firm to a provider during the taxable year of the business firm and shall not exceed $100,000 annually per business [72 P.S. § 8705-I(b)]. A tax credit granted for any one taxable year may not exceed the tax liability of a business firm [72 P.S. § 87006-I(c)].

Additional amount: A business firm that contributes to a provider in two or more consecutive years qualifies for a 75% tax credit for the contributions made in the second year and every consecutive year of making a contribution to a provider. However, a business firm is not required to contribute to the same provider every year in order for the business firm to qualify for a credit [72 P.S. § 8705-I(c)].

Total aggregate amount: The total aggregate amount of all tax credits approved shall not exceed $3,000,000 in a fiscal year [72 P.S. § 8706-I(a)].

No carryforward, carryback, refund, or transfer: A tax credit not used in the taxable year the contribution was made may not be carried forward or carried back and is not refundable or transferable [72 P.S. § 8706-I(d)].

• *Information*

Information: In order to qualify for a community-based services tax credit, a provider must submit information to the Pennsylvania Department of Community and Economic Development (DCED) that enables the DCED to confirm that the provider is exempt from taxation under IRC § 501(c)(3) [72 P.S. § 8703-I(b)].

• *Application*

An application submitted to the DCED by the provider must describe the community-based services it provides in individuals on a form provided by the DCED. The DCED will review and approve or disapprove the application and notify the provider that the provider meets the requirements no later than 60 days after the provider has submitted the required application [72 P.S. § 8703-I(c), (d)].

• *Publication of list of qualified providers*

The DCED shall annually publish a list of each provider qualified under this section in the Pennsylvania Bulletin. The list shall be posted and updated as necessary on the publicly accessible Internet website of the DCED [72 P.S. § 8709-I(e)].

• *Restriction on use of contributions*

The contributions received by a provider from a business firm claiming a community-based services tax credit must be used for direct care or services relating to direct care of individuals [72 P.S. § 8703.1-I].

• *Sunset*

A business is not entitled to apply for a tax credit after the seventh fiscal year following July 2, 2012 [72 P.S. § 8708-I].

¶1024 Promoting Employment Across Pennsylvania Act

[This credit was repealed effective December 1, 2016.]

Under the Promoting Employment Across Pennsylvania Act, a qualified business (defined below) is permitted to retain withholding taxes for individuals employed in new jobs [Act 206 of 2012, H.B. 2626, § 302]. Alternatively, a qualified company can also choose to remit 100% of employee withholding tax and receive a rebate equivalent to the amount authorized for individuals employed in new jobs [Act 206 of 2012, H.B. 2626, § 305].

• *Terms Defined*

Terms used in the Promoting Employment Across Pennsylvania Act are defined as follows [Act 206 of 2012, H.B. 2626, § 103]:

County average wage: The average annual wage paid to employees located in the county where the qualified company intends to employ new employees, as reported by the Center for Workforce Information and Analysis.

Department: The Department of Community and Economic Development of the Commonwealth.

Qualified company: A for-profit corporation, partnership or other entity that agrees to create at least 250 new jobs in the state within five years. Provides health insurance coverage to its full-time employees and pays at least 50% of the premium for the health insurance.

• *Qualification*

Qualified companies must be located in the state and create 100 new jobs in the state within two years of entering into an agreement with the department [Act 206 of 2012, H.B. 2626, § 302].

• *Determination of retention period*

Qualified companies will be able to retain 95% of withholding taxes for individuals for one of the following periods [Act 206 of 2012, H.B. 2626, § 302]:

(1) Seven years, if the individuals are compensated at a rate equal to at least 100% of the county average wage.

(2) Eight years, if the individuals are compensated at a rate equal to at least 110% of the county average wage.

(3) Nine years, if the individuals are compensated at a rate equal to at least 120% of the county average wage.

(4) Ten years, if the individuals are compensated at a rate equal to at least 140% of the county average wage.

• *Recapture*

If the company fails to comply with the terms and conditions of the agreement with the department, the company will be required to repay an amount equal to the aggregate withholding taxes retained by the company [Act 206 of 2012, H.B. 2626, § 103].

• *Amount*

The total amount of the benefits retained cannot exceed $5,000,000, and no agreements can be entered into after January 1, 2018 [Act 206 of 2012, H.B. 2626, § 313].

¶1025 City Revitalization and Improvement Zones (CRIZs)

Act 52 of 2013 establishes the CRIZ program designed to promote economic development in cities of the third class. Between July 9, 2013, and December 31, 2016, the Department of Community and Economic Development (DCED) may establish two CRIZs in cities of the third class, allowing for abatement of several Pennsylvania and local taxes within the CRIZ (generally, corporate net income tax, capital stock/franchise tax, bank shares tax and business privilege taxes). CRIZ zones may not overlap locations with other economic development incentive zones or areas. After 2015, DCED may approve two additional CRIZs per year. Pennsylvania cities of the third class must have a population of at least 30,000 based on the most recent federal census. On December 30, 2013, Governor Corbett awarded CRIZ designations to the cities of Bethlehem and Lancaster.

¶1026 Innovate in PA Tax Credit

Act 52 of 2013 enacted the Innovate in PA Tax Credit Program, designed to provide funding for the Ben Franklin Technology Partners, the PA Venture Capital Investment Program, and Life Sciences Greenhouses. Beginning on October 1, 2013, insurance companies may purchase up to $100 million of tax credits from the Department of Community and Economic Development (DCED) to offset insurance premiums taxes. The funds from the purchases of these credits will be used by DCED to support the three venture capital programs. A "qualified taxpayer" eligible to use the credits is an insurance company authorized to do business in Pennsylvania, or a holding company that has at least one insurance company subsidiary authorized to do business in Pennsylvania. The credits may be claimed beginning in 2017 and the total credit applied for all credit claimants in any one tax year may not exceed $20 million. Any unused credits may be carried over to any year prior to the 2026 tax year.

¶1027 Mobile Telecommunications Broadband Investment Tax Credit

Act 52 of 2013 also creates a new tax credit against the corporate net income tax for tax years beginning after December 31, 2013, and before January 1, 2024, (capped at $5 million per year) equal to 5 percent of the cost of investment in qualified broadband equipment located in Pennsylvania. This credit may not be sold or assigned to third parties.

¶1028 Manufacturing and Investment Tax Credit

Act 84 of 2016 enacted a manufacturing and investment tax credit, which applies to taxpayers capable of increasing annual taxable payroll by a minimum of $1 million through the creation of new full-time jobs. The maximum tax credit is 5 percent of the taxpayer's increase in annual taxable payroll and jobs must be maintained for at least five years.

¶1029 Miscellaneous New Credits Under Act 84 of 2016

• Coal Refuse Energy and Reclamation Tax Credit: This tax credit is designed to incentivize eligible facilities that generate electricity in the Commonwealth to use coal refuse for power generation, control acid gasses for emission control and use ash produced by the facility to reclaim mining-affected sites. Credits may be awarded at a rate of $4 per 2,000 pounds of qualified refuse capped at 22.2 percent of the available budget allocation per fiscal year. The allocation is $7.5 million for the 2016-17 fiscal year and $10 million each fiscal year thereafter.

• Waterfront Development Tax Credit: This tax credit is designed to generate funding for waterfront development projects that provide or improve public access to waterfront sites within the Commonwealth. Contributions in the form of cash or personal property may be donated to an approved waterfront organization for up to a 75 percent equivalent tax credit per contributed dollar. The budget allocation is $1.5 million a year beginning in the 2017-18 fiscal year.

• Manufacturing and Investment Tax Credit: This tax credit is designed to support job creation. Eligible taxpayers, capable of increasing annual taxable payroll by a minimum of $1 million through the creation of new full-time jobs can earn a tax credit up to 5 percent of the taxpayer's increase in annual taxable payroll. Jobs must be maintained for at least five years. The budget allocation is $4 million a year beginning in the 2017-18 fiscal year.

• Rural Jobs and Investment Tax Credit: This tax credit is designed to stimulate growth and job creation in rural areas by providing access to capital to rural businesses from businesses supporting rural growth funds. Credit for eligible contributions made by a business firm may be approved for up to a 90 percent equivalent tax credit per contributed dollar. The budget allocation is $1 million a year beginning in the 2017-18 fiscal year, and is not to exceed $4 million for the duration of the program.

• Mixed Use Development Tax Credit: This tax credit is designed to help communities address affordable housing shortages and support business growth. The program allows developers to access funds for construction or rehabilitation projects that enable affordable housing and business in the same structure. Tax credit availability is based on the sale of the credits from the Pennsylvania Housing Finance Agency. The budget allocation is $2 million a year beginning in the 2017-18 fiscal year.

• Malt Beverage Tax Credit: This tax credit is reinstated in the 2017-18 fiscal year with a $5 million a year budget allocation. The credit was formerly effective from January 1, 1974, to December 31, 2008.

• Credit Like—Computer Data Center Equipment Incentive Program: Act 84 of 2016 establishes a data center investment incentive program. Beginning July 1, 2017, an owner, operator, or qualified tenant of a certified data center may apply for a sales or use tax refund related to certain equipment purchased for use in the data center. Applicants must meet capital investment and annual compensation requirements for employees working within the data center. The total refunds of sales and use taxes paid on qualifying purchases may not exceed $5 million in any fiscal year.

¶1030 Concert Rehearsal and Tour Tax Credit

Act 7 of 2017 established a concert rehearsal and tour tax credit in order to attract investment in the Commonwealth by awarding tax credits to tour operators representing musicians for rehearsals and live musical performances within the state. It is anticipated that the credit will provide significant benefits to Allentown's PPL Center and to Lititz in Lancaster County. Concert tours can obtain up to $800,000 in tax credits and the overall budget cap in credits for 2017 is $4 million. The new law offers promoters of big concerts a state tax credit for scheduling an act at a class 2 or class 3 venue. A class 2 venue is any arena or concert facility with at least 6,000 seats that is not in Allegheny or Philadelphia County. A class 3 venue is any of the state colleges outside of Pittsburgh or Philadelphia or any venue in a Neighborhood Improvement Zone. There is currently only one Neighborhood Improvement Zone in Allentown which is the PPL Center. Lititz has constructed concert facilities that are conducive to providing tours with concert rehearsal opportunities. The tax credit is designed to provide more income to entertainers who lose revenue based on the lack of seating capacity in smaller venues. The intent of the credit is to ensure that a performer taking advantage of the tax credit is a significant act. The performer must play at least one date at a venue of at least 14,000 seats in Philadelphia or Allegheny County. Additionally, a performer must spend at least $3 million on tour preparation to be eligible for this credit and is required to spend at least ten (10) days rehearsing in Pennsylvania. These provisions effectively steer the performer to Lititz which has built a niche where many of the world's biggest name performers prepare for their international tours. Many companies that provide services to the live performance industry have set up operations in Lititz and neighboring Warwick Township. Most of the music industry's largest tour sets are built in Lititz. Major performing acts typically spend more than the $3 million minimum in-state investment required by the law to have Lititz's community of concert tour production companies design, build, and test their stage productions in Lititz. The law is effective June 22, 2017.

Governor Wolf signed Act 42 of 2018 which provides that (1) for fiscal year 2018-19 only, the number of tours that may be awarded tax credits for qualified rehearsal and tour expenses is increased to 10 tours and provides that the Department of Community and Economic Development, in consultation with the Department of Revenue, may advance the award of tax credits for qualified rehearsal and tour expenses incurred or to be incurred to a maximum of two additional tours in fiscal year 2018-19; and (2) adds a definition of "entertainment business financial management firm" related to qualified businesses operating in neighborhood improvement zones to enable the contracting authority to identify the responsible party required to fulfill reporting compliance on behalf of a qualified business, for concerts or other performances in a facility in the zone in connection with concert rehearsal and tour credits.

CORPORATE NET INCOME TAX

CHAPTER 11

ALLOCATION AND APPORTIONMENT

¶1101 General

Allocation and apportionment are methods of assigning the income of a corporation among states. Allocation is the assignment in its entirety of nonbusiness income to a state. Apportionment is the division of business income among states. Pennsylvania is an associate member of the Multistate Tax Commission (created by an interstate compact); and Pennsylvania's allocation and apportionment provisions conform to the Commission's Uniform Division of Income for Tax Purposes Act, known as UDITPA [Article IV of the Multistate Tax Compact].

Apportionment of business income before 2013: Prior to 2013, apportionment of business income is done by using a three-factor apportionment formula, which is discussed at ¶1107–¶1110. The constitutionality of Pennsylvania's use of three-factor apportionment has been upheld in numerous cases and is no longer in question. In certain cases, however, special apportionment may be necessary. See ¶1114.

Apportionment of business income after 2012—Single-factor apportionment required: For taxable years beginning after December 31, 2012, all business income is to be apportioned to Pennsylvania by multiplying the income by the sales factor [72 P.S. §7401(a)(9)(A)(iv)].

Allocation vs. Apportionment

Nonbusiness income is *allocated;* business income is *apportioned.*

¶1102 Basic Definitions

The following definitions apply to the Pennsylvania corporate net income tax law. They are contained in 72 P.S. §7401(3)2(a) and are consistent with UDITPA definitions.

¶1102

"Business income" means income arising from transactions in the regular course of trade or business and includes income from tangible and intangible property if either (1) the acquisition, (2) the management, or the disposition of the property constitutes an integral part of the taxpayer's regular trade or business operations. The term "business income" includes all income that is apportionable under the U.S. Constitution.

"Commercial domicile." The principal place from which the taxpayer's trade or business is directed or managed.

"Compensation." Wages, salaries, commissions and any other form of remuneration paid to employees for personal services.

"Nonbusiness income." All income other than business income except income that is apportionable under the Constitution of the United States.

"Sales." All gross receipts of the taxpayer not allocated under this definition (except dividends received, interest on United States, state or political subdivision obligations, and gross receipts from securities transactions other than transactions involving securities held primarily for sale to customers in the ordinary course of trade or business).

"State." Any state of the United States, the District of Columbia, the Commonwealth of Puerto Rico, any territory or possession of the United States, and any foreign country or political subdivision thereof.

"This state." The Commonwealth of Pennsylvania. In the context of application of this definition to allocation and apportion of income for local tax purpose, "this state" refers to the subdivision or local taxing district in which the relevant tax return is filed.

Financial Organizations and Public Utilities

Financial organizations and public utilities (defined in UDITPA) are not subject to the Pennsylvania corporate net income tax. Taxation of financial institutions is discussed in Part VII of this book. Taxes on utilities are discussed in Chapter 24 and Chapter 25.

¶1103 Conditions Precedent to the Use of Allocation and Apportionment

Taxpayers (other than transportation companies) [72 P.S. §7401(3)2(b)]; pipeline and gas companies [72 P.S. §7401(3)2(c)]; and water transportation companies [72 P.S. §7401(3)2(d)] who meet the following two conditions may allocate and apportion income: (1) the taxpayer transacts business both within and outside Pennsylvania, and (2) the taxpayer is taxable in another state. Railroad, truck, bus, or airline companies; pipeline or natural gas companies; and water transportation companies are subject to special allocation and apportionment rules, discussed at ¶1112.

Transacting Business in Another State

• *Definition*

There is no precise definition of what constitutes transacting business outside Pennsylvania. In general, however, a taxpayer is said to be transacting business outside Pennsylvania when its presence outside Pennsylvania is related to its actual business activity. Such presence may be through (but is not limited to) administrative functioning, property ownership, or sales activity [61 Pa. Code §532.21(b)].

According to the Pennsylvania Supreme Court, the test for apportionment is whether or not the corporation's presence outside Pennsylvania is related to its actual business activity. If a corporation owns tangible property outside Pennsylvania for use in conjunction with its business needs, the corporation does not have to be physically conducting operations on or with respect to the property. The operation of a scrap yard by a domestic corporation's lessee on property owned outside Pennsylvania under arrangements benefiting the corporation's business is sufficient to characterize the ownership and leasing of such property as the transaction of business outside the state [*Cmwlth. v. Tube City Iron & Metal Co.*, 248 A.2d 225 (Pa. 1968)].

> **Example 1:** Polo Corporation is engaged in manufacturing farm equipment in Pennsylvania. Polo also owned a manufacturing plant in State W that it leased to Marco Corporation to be used in manufacturing farm equipment. Polo acquired Marco's products and subsidized its operations by advancing money to it. When Marco's lease expired, the manufacturing operations in State W ceased completely. Up to the expiration of the lease, Polo was transacting business outside Pennsylvania. After the expiration of the lease, Polo's ownership of the plant in State W was not related to its actual business activity; and Polo was not, therefore, transacting business outside Pennsylvania.

> **Example 2:** Ross Corporation manufactures spark plugs in Pennsylvania and carries on all its activities in Pennsylvania except that administrative functions and executive policies are performed and established by Ross Corporation's officers located in State O. Since the activities in State O are related to the manufacturing activity in Pennsylvania, Ross Corporation is transacting business outside Pennsylvania.

Taxable in Another State

• *Definition*

A corporation is "taxable in another state" if one of the following applies:

(1) It is subject to one of the following taxes:

(a) A net income tax.

(b) A franchise tax measured by net income.

(c) A franchise tax for the privilege of doing business.

(d) A corporate stock tax.

(2) That state has jurisdiction to subject the taxpayer to a net income tax without regard to whether the state actually imposes such a tax [72 P.S. § 7401(3)2(a)(3)].

Only those specified taxes that are basically revenue-raising are considered in determining whether a taxpayer is subject to one of the taxes. Taxes of the specified types that are regulatory measures are not considered [61 Pa. Code § 153.22(a)].

> **Example:** State A requires that all nonresident corporations that qualify or register in State A pay an annual license fee or tax for the privilege of doing business in that state whether the privilege is exercised or not. The amount paid is determined with reference to the total authorized capital stock of the corporation, with a minimum of $50 and a maximum of $500. Failure to pay the tax bars a corporation from utilizing the state courts for enforcement of its rights. State A also imposes a corporation income tax. A nonresident taxpayer that is qualified in State A and pays the required fee but does not carry on any activities in State A other than utilizing its courts is not "taxable" in State A.

"Subject to." A taxpayer is subject to one of the specified taxes in a particular state within the meaning of 72 P.S. § 7401(3)2(a)(3) if it carries on business activity in that state, that state requires it to file a return, and the taxpayer does in fact file a return in that state. Any taxpayer claiming to be subject to tax in another state may be required to furnish proof that it has filed the required tax report and other necessary information with that state [61 Pa. Code § 153.22(a)].

"Not subject to." A taxpayer is not subject to tax in another state if it voluntarily files returns when not required to do so by that state's laws or if it pays a minimum fee for qualification, organization or privilege of doing business in that state but either (1) does not engage in business activity in that state or (2) actually engages in some business activity in that state, but not activity sufficient for nexus [61 Pa. Code § 153.22(b)].

> *Example:* State A has a corporation franchise tax measured by net income for the privilege of doing business in that state. Turner Corporation files a return in State A (based on its business activity in that state). However, Turner's tax liability is less than the minimum tax in State A. Turner pays the minimum tax. Turner is subject to State A's corporation franchise tax.

"Jurisdiction to tax." A state has "jurisdiction to subject" a taxpayer to a net income tax if the taxpayer's business activity in that state is sufficient to give that state the jurisdiction to impose *at least* a net income tax under the constitution and statutes of the United States. The other state does not have jurisdiction to tax if it is prohibited from imposing the tax by P.L. 86-272 (The Interstate Income Act, explained at ¶914). Whether the state in fact imposes such a tax is irrelevant. The determination of whether another state has "jurisdiction to subject" the taxpayer to a net income tax is made under the same rules that are used to determine whether a taxpayer is subject to the Pennsylvania corporate net income tax [61 Pa. Code § 153.23(a)]. The determination of whether the state has jurisdiction to subject a taxpayer to a net income tax is determined by applying the same rules (see 72 P.S. § 7401) that are applied in determining whether a taxpayer has sufficient activity to be subject to the Pennsylvania corporate net income tax [61 Pa. Code § 153.23(b)].

> *Example 1:* Pin Corporation manufactures pinball machines in Pennsylvania and also has salesmen in State N. These salesmen have the right to and do accept orders in State N. State N has no corporate tax statutes; however, it *does* have "jurisdiction to subject" Pin Corporation to a net income tax because P.L. 86-272 does not prohibit it.

> *Example 2:* Farmer Corporation manufactures farm equipment in Pennsylvania and in a foreign country, both of which impose a net income tax. However, the foreign country exempts corporations that manufacture farm equipment. Nevertheless, the foreign country has jurisdiction to subject Farmer Corporation to a net income tax.

Higher Level of Activity

It has been the experience of the authors that the Department of Revenue may require a higher level of activity in the other state than that described in the Pin Corporation example, above.

• Partnership interests

A corporation that has an interest in a partnership that is transacting taxable business outside Pennsylvania may allocate and apportion its income. Such partnership activity is sufficient to qualify the corporate partner for allocation and apportionment even if the corporate partner itself transacts no business outside Pennsylvania [61 Pa. Code § 153.29(b)(2)]. Conversely, a foreign corporation that owns an interest in a partnership transacting taxable business in Pennsylvania is subject to corporate taxation in Pennsylvania even if it transacts no business on its own in Pennsylvania [61 Pa. Code § 153.29(b)(1)].

Investing in a Partnership

Allocation and apportionment help taxpayers reduce their corporate taxes. If you do not qualify for allocation and apportionment, you should consider the feasibility of investing in a partnership transacting business outside Pennsylvania to qualify for allocation and apportionment. If you have a lot of excess intangibles for capital stock/franchise tax purposes, qualifying for three-factor apportionment, which requires the transaction of business outside Pennsylvania, can be advantageous. Partnership interests can help achieve this goal. See ¶1417.

¶1104 Classification of Income

Corporations that meet the conditions precedent (transacting business outside Pennsylvania and taxable in another state) may allocate and apportion income. The first step in the allocation and apportionment process is to separate net income into two parts: business income and nonbusiness income.

• *Business and nonbusiness income defined*

Prior to amendment in 2001, "business income" included income from tangible and intangible property if the acquisition, management, and disposition of the property constitute integral parts of the taxpayer's regular trade or business operations [72 P.S. § 7401(3)2(a)(1)(A), before amendment by Act 23 of 2001, H.B. 443, § 11]. After amendment "business income" includes income from tangible and intangible property if either the acquisition, the management, or the disposition of the property constitutes an integral part of the taxpayer's regular trade or business operations and includes income which is apportionable under the Constitution of the United States [72 P.S. § 7401(3)2(a)(1)(A), after amendment by Act 23 of 2001 H.B. 443, § 11, emphasis added]. Prior to amendment, "nonbusiness income" meant all income other than business income. After amendment, "nonbusiness income" means all income other than business income but does not include income which is apportionable under the Constitution of the United States [72 P.S. § 7401(3)2(a)(1)(D), emphasis added].

• *Effect of change in nonbusiness definition*

The General Assembly stated that the intent of the amendment of the definitions of business income and nonbusiness income " . . . is to clarify existing law" [Act 23 of 2001, H.B. 334, § 25]. Many tax commentators believe, however, that these amendments are changes to the existing law that effectively eliminate nonbusiness income (and allocation), making all Pennsylvania income apportionable. An apparently minor change in the definition of "business income" could have a profound effect on the classification of income as business or nonbusiness. This "clarification" will probably lead to litigation over the constitutionality of apportioning income.

In *Allied-Signal, Inc. v. Director, Division of Taxation*, 504 U.S. 768 (1992), the U.S. Supreme Court ruled that the state of Idaho could not tax an apportionable part of a gain that arose from a transaction between unrelated corporations. The Court stated that the unitary business principle remains an appropriate device for ascertaining whether a State has unconstitutionally taxed a nondomiciliary corporation.

Multiformity and Unrelated Assets Concepts

The concepts of multiformity (explained at ¶1412) and unrelated assets (explained at ¶1420), which are closely related to the unitary concept, may provide support to multiform or unrelated corporations seeking to have income classified as nonbusiness.

• *Business income*

"Business income" is all income arising from transactions and activity in the regular course of a taxpayer's trade or business and includes income from tangible and intangible property if either (1) the acquisition, (2) the management, *or* (3) the disposition of the property constitutes an integral part of the taxpayer's regular trade or business operations. The term "business income" includes all income that is apportionable under the U.S. Constitution [72 P.S. § 7401(3)2(a)(1)(A)]. Business income is *apportioned* to Pennsylvania by use of a three-factor formula; nonbusiness income is directly *allocated* to a particular state. See ¶1106 for an explanation of apportionment of business income.

¶1104

• *Nonbusiness income*

"Nonbusiness income" is all income other than business income [72 P.S. §7401(3)2(a)(1)(D)]. The most common items of nonbusiness income are (1) rents and royalties from tangible personal property; (2) gains and losses from dispositions of tangible property; (3) interest; and (4) royalties from patents and copyrights. See ¶1105 for discussion of allocation of these items.

The classification of income by labels (*e.g.*, manufacturing income, compensation for services, sales income, interest, dividends, rents, royalties, capital gains, and operating income) is of no aid in determining whether income is business income or nonbusiness income. In practice this means that all income is presumptively business income unless a corporation can prove that it is not.

Inherent in 72 P.S. §7401(3)2(a)(1)(A) are two alternative and independent tests by which to properly classify income as business or nonbusiness: (1) the transactional test and (2) the functional test [*Welded Tube Company of America v. Cmwlth.*, 515 A.2d 988 (Pa.Commw. 1986)].

• *Classification tests*

Transactional test: Income is business income if it arises from transactions and activity in the regular course of a taxpayer's trade or business [72 P.S. §7401(3)2(a)(1)(A)]. This is the transactional test, and the transactional test requires frequency and regularity [*Welded Tube Company of America v. Cmwlth.*, 515 A.2d 988 (Pa.Commw. 1986)].

Functional test: Business income also includes income from tangible and intangible property if the acquisition, management, and disposition of the property constitute integral parts of the taxpayer's regular trade or business operations [72 P.S. §7401(3)2(a)(1)(A)]. This is the functional test; and the functional test does not require frequency and regularity. The key to the functional test, in the case of gain from disposition of an asset, is whether the asset in question produced business income while held by the taxpayer [*Welded Tube Company of America v. Cmwlth.*, 515 A.2d 988 (Pa.Commw. 1986)].

Cases—Business vs. Nonbusiness Income

• *Sale of idle assets*

Laurel Pipe Line: The taxpayer, an Ohio corporation, sold a pipeline and related equipment that had been idle for three years. The taxpayer contended that the gain was nonbusiness income and sought to allocate the gain between Ohio and Pennsylvania on the basis of the mileage located in each state. The Commonwealth Court ruled that the gain was business income. The Pennsylvania Supreme Court, however, reversed the Commonwealth Court decision and held that the income from the sale of the pipeline was not business income because the assets disposed of were not an integral part of the taxpayer's business. Therefore, only the gain on the sale of assets located in Pennsylvania was taxable [*Laurel Pipe Line Co. v. Cmwlth.*, 642 A.2d 472 (Pa. 1994), *rev'g* 615 A.2d 841 (Pa.Commw. 1992)].

Application of Laurel: The Department of Revenue's stated policy with respect to the *Laurel Pipe Line* decisions is that the decision applies only to a liquidation where a separate and distinct aspect of the taxpayer's business ceases and the proceeds are returned to the shareholders. Any disposition of assets for which nonbusiness income is claimed pursuant to a liquidation must have been removed from the relevant apportionment factors prior to the disposition for a period of time consistent with the facts of the individual case. The taxpayer must show by clear and convincing evidence that for that period, the assets were not a part of its regular trade or

¶1104

business operations. Furthermore, the proceeds from such a disposition must be a distribution to shareholders and not used to acquire assets for future use in business operations or to generate income for any future business operations. See Statement of Policy, 61 Pa. Code § 170.1.

- *Sale of unimproved land*

   Ross-Araco: The taxpayer was a general contractor in the construction business. The company owned a 24.5-acre parcel of land located in New Jersey. The company used a building on the fenced 3-acre portion of the parcel for storage of equipment and materials used in its construction business. The remaining 21.5 acres of heavily wooded land purchased concurrently with the 3-acre tract remained unimproved. In 1988, the company sold the 21.5-acre tract and reported the gain from the sale as nonbusiness income allocable to New Jersey. The gain was not business income under the transactional test because the transaction was outside the taxpayer's regular trade or business. The gain was not business income under the functional test because the acquisition, management and disposition of real property were not integral parts of the taxpayer's regular trade or business, and the property did not produce income of any kind during the period of ownership by the taxpayer [*Ross-Araco Corp. v. Cmwlth.*, 674 A.2d 691 (Pa. 1996), *aff'g*, 644 A.2d 235 (Pa.Commw. 1994)].

- *Sale of stock in another corporation*

   Cadbury Schweppes: The taxpayer, Cadbury Schweppes, treated gain from the sale of Dr. Pepper stock as nonbusiness income. The Court denied nonbusiness income treatment for this gain because the taxpayer did not prove that the stock in question did not contribute to its business in Pennsylvania [*Cadbury Schweppes, Inc. v. Cmwlth.*, 734 A.2d 1274 (Pa. 1999), *aff'g per curiam*, 720 A.2d 226 (Pa.Commw. 1998). On December 15, 2015, the Board of Finance and Revenue in the petition of Dollar Tree Stores Inc. permitted the taxpayer to treat its sale of its non-controlling investment in Ollies as nonbusiness income.

- *Sale of partnership interest*

   A Delaware corporation selling a partnership interest wherein the partnership's operations consisted of managing a Philadelphia apartment complex was ruled to give rise to business income. The sale was of a portion of the taxpayer's partnership interest which satisfied the functional test of the business income definition subsequent to the 2001 amendment of 72 P.S. § 7401(3)2(a)(1)(A). [*RB Alden Corp. v. Cmwlth.*, 142 A.3d 169 (Pa.Commw. 2016)]. The Commonwealth Court subsequently denied the Commonwealth's exceptions and reaffirmed its decision that the Pennsylvania cap on the use of corporate net operating losses violated the Uniformity Clause of the Pennsylvania Constitution. The taxpayer's exceptions filed in the same case were denied as moot given the denial of the Commonwealth's exceptions. [*RB Alden Corp. v. Cmwlth.*, 2017 BL 319198 (Pa.Commw. September 12, 2017)].

- *Gain on IRC § 338(h)(10) deemed sale*

   Canteen Corporation: Income resulting from an IRC 338(h)(10) election is nonbusiness income [*Canteen Corporation v. Cmwlth.*, Pa.Commw., No. 856 F.R. 1997 (March 6, 2003), *aff'd per curiam*, Pennsylvania Supreme Court, No. 57 MAP 2001 (July 20, 2004)]. Canteen Corporation had a gain attributable to its parent corporation's sale of stock that the parent elected to treat as an IRC § 338(h)(10) deemed asset sale for federal purposes. For Pennsylvania corporate net income tax purposes, Canteen reported this gain as nonbusiness income, arguing that the gain from the fictional liquidation of assets should be treated the same as the gain from an actual liquidation, which is considered nonbusiness income under the Pennsylvania Supreme Court's holding in *Laurel Pipe Line* (see above). The Commonwealth Court held that " . . . liquidation and distribution, deemed to have occurred as a result of the Section

338(h)(10) election, cannot be recognized by the Commonwealth on the one hand in order to yield a fictitious gain but ignored on the other hand in order to avoid the holding in *Laurel Pipe Line.*" Furthermore, the Court held that insofar as the requirements of 61 Pa. Code § 153.81(d)(1) conflict with the Pennsylvania Supreme Court's decision in *Laurel Pipe Line* (discussed above), the regulation is invalid. See also the discussion of IRC § 338 transactions at ¶ 915.

Osram Sylvania: In an unreported memorandum decision that involved an IRC § 338(h)(10) deemed sale of assets, the Pennsylvania Commonwealth Court has held that a corporate taxpayer's fictitious gain on a transaction subject to an IRC § 338(h)(10) election must be taxed as nonbusiness income [*Osram Sylvania, Inc. v. Cmwlth.*, No. 310 F.R. 1998 (March 6, 2003), Opinion Not Reported]. For a ruling relating to the Department of Revenue's treatment of § 338(h)(10) elections, see Ruling No. CRP-14-001 (April 22, 2014).

• *Sale of timberland*

Glatfelter: Gain on sale of timberland was deemed not to be business income. Glatfelter Pulpwood was a wholly-owned subsidiary of P. H. Glatfelter Corporation, which was engaged in manufacturing paper products. The subsidiary procured pulpwood for its parent corporation by growing and harvesting trees on its own timberland or it purchased pulpwood on the open market. A gain from the sale of a parcel of timberland was found to be business income [*Glatfelter Pulpwood Company v. Cmwlth.*, 61 A.3d 993 (Pa. 2013) *aff'g* 19 A.3d 572].

¶1105 Allocation of Nonbusiness Income

Items of nonbusiness income are directly allocated within and without Pennsylvania according to the rules that follow. See ¶ 1112 for discussion of allocation and apportionment for companies subject to special rules. Allocation and apportionment of income from partnership interests are explained at ¶ 1113.

Reminder

You cannot allocate your nonbusiness income unless (1) you transact business outside Pennsylvania and (2) you are taxable in another state. See ¶ 1103.

Rents and Real Property Royalties

• *Realty*

Net rents and royalties from real property are allocable to the state in which the real property in question is located [72 P.S. § 7401(3)2(a)(5)(A)]. For example, Blue Corporation owns two buildings that it rents—one located in Spokane, Washington, and one located in Pittsburgh, Pennsylvania. The rental income from these buildings is nonbusiness income. The rental income from the building in Spokane is allocable to Washington, and rental income from the building in Pittsburgh is allocable to Pennsylvania.

• *Tangible personalty*

Net rents and royalties from tangible personal property are entirely allocable to Pennsylvania if the taxpayer's commercial domicile is in Pennsylvania and the taxpayer is not organized under the laws of or taxable in the state in which the property is utilized. Otherwise, net rents and royalties from tangible personal property are allocable to Pennsylvania if and *to the extent* that the property is utilized in Pennsylvania [72 P.S. § 7401(3)2(a)(5)(B)].

The extent of utilization of tangible personal property in Pennsylvania is determined by multiplying the rents and royalties by a fraction, the numerator of which is the number of days of physical location of the property in Pennsylvania during the rental or royalty period in the tax year and the denominator of which is the number of days of physical location of the property everywhere during all rental or royalty periods in the tax year. If the physical location of the property during these periods is unknown or unascertainable, the tangible personal property is considered utilized in the state in which the property was located at the time the rental or royalty payer obtained possession [72 P.S. § 7401(3)2(a)(5)(C)].

> *Example:* Crosby Corporation acquired all the assets of Nelson Corporation, including a large piece of earth-moving equipment. Crosby Corporation rented the equipment until it could find a suitable buyer. During tax year 2001, Crosby rented the equipment to Lynn Corporation in New Jersey from July 17 to October 18 and to West Corporation in Pennsylvania from October 20 to December 16. Assume the rental income is nonbusiness income and that net rental income from this piece of equipment is $5,000. The income is allocated as follows:
>
> Income allocable to Pa. = 58/152 × $5,000 = $1,908
>
> Income allocable to N.J. = 94/152 × $5,000 = $3,092

Gains and Losses from Disposition of Property

• *Realty*

Gains and losses from sales or other dispositions of real property are allocable to the state in which the realty is located [72 P.S. § 7401(3)2(a)(6)(A)].

• *Tangible personalty*

Gains and losses from sales or other dispositions of tangible personal property are allocable to Pennsylvania if the property had a situs in Pennsylvania at the time of the sale, or the taxpayer's commercial domicile is in Pennsylvania and the taxpayer is not taxable in the state in which the property had a situs [72 P.S. § 7401(3)2(a)(6)(B)].

• *Intangible personalty*

Gains and losses from sales or other dispositions of intangible personal property are allocable to Pennsylvania if the taxpayer's commercial domicile is in Pennsylvania [72 P.S. § 7401(3)2(a)(6)(C)].

Interest

Interest is allocable to Pennsylvania if the taxpayer's commercial domicile is in Pennsylvania [72 P.S. § 7401(3)2(a)(7)].

Dividends

Dividends are not nonbusiness income subject to allocation for Pennsylvania corporate net income tax purposes. For an explanation of Pennsylvania tax treatment of dividends, see ¶ 1003.

Patent and Copyright Royalties

Royalties from patents and copyrights are allocable to Pennsylvania *if* and *to the extent that* the patent or copyright is utilized by the payer in Pennsylvania, or *if* and *to the extent that* the patent or copyright is utilized by the payer in a state in which the taxpayer is not taxable and the taxpayer's commercial domicile is in Pennsylvania [72 P.S. § 7401(3)2(a)(8)(A)].

A patent is utilized in a state to the extent that it is employed in production, fabrication, manufacturing, or other processing in the state or to the extent that a patented product is produced in the state [72 P.S. § 7401(3)2(a)(8)(B)]. A copyright is utilized in a state to the extent that printing or other publication originates in the state [72 P.S. § 7401(3)2(a)(8)(C)]. If the basis of receipts from patent or copyright royalties does not permit allocation, or if the taxpayer's accounting procedures do not reflect the states in which the patents or copyrights are used, the patent or copyright is considered utilized in the taxpayer's state of commercial domicile.

Allocation Planning Pointers

• *Use of subsidiaries*

Linke Corporation has real estate located in Pennsylvania that it wishes to sell at a substantial gain. Linke can set up a subsidiary, B, in a state with low or no corporate taxes and transfer the property to B Corporation in exchange for its stock. B Corporation in turn sets up its subsidiary, C Corporation, to which it transfers the property in question. Then B Corporation sells the stock of its subsidiary, C. B can then pay the proceeds to the parent, Linke Corporation, and the dividends will not be taxable in Pennsylvania.

Linke can also escape the fate of Screwball Manufacturing Co. (below) by using good planning. Linke has a plant in Illinois that it is going to sell at a $1,000,000 loss. Linke sets up a subsidiary, B Corporation, in Illinois, and then sells the stock of B Corporation at a loss. Linke's loss is then 100% allocated to Pennsylvania. For an explanation of current position of the Department of Revenue with respect to certain intracompany transactions, see ¶ 1001.

• *"Creation" of income or loss*

Taxable income for corporate net income tax purposes is defined by statute as federal taxable income before federal NOL and special deductions (commonly referred to as Line 28 income) plus statutory Pennsylvania additions and less Pennsylvania deductions. However, if Line 28 income is a loss and contains nonbusiness losses and/or income, the resulting Pennsylvania taxable income after Pennsylvania additions and deductions could be greater or smaller than Line 28 income. This is a result of the distinction between business and nonbusiness income losses.

Before the Pennsylvania corporate net income tax law allowed deductions for net losses, the separate classification of business and nonbusiness income/losses did not result in the creation of taxable income. When federal taxable income showed a loss, there was no taxable Pennsylvania income (except in the case of net statutory addbacks, such as accelerated depreciation on Section 1250 property). This was a result of the Department's following the decision in *Cmwlth. v. Columbia Steel and Shafting Co.*, 62 Dauph 298 (1952). However, in 1983, when the first returns involving net loss deductions began to be settled, the Department changed its position. They now maintain that, since net loss carryforwards are allowed, they are no longer constrained by *Columbia Steel and Shafting*.

The following examples illustrate this point.

> *Example 1:* Allen Corporation has a federal loss of $200,000, made up of a $400,000 nonbusiness loss allocable to Ohio and $200,000 of business income from operations 50% apportionable to Pennsylvania. The Department of Revenue takes the position that the $400,000 nonbusiness loss is allocable to Ohio, leaving $100,000 [0.5 × $200,000] of taxable income in Pennsylvania. This "creates" taxable income out of a federal loss.

> *Example 2:* Bailey Corporation has federal income of $250,000 ($600,000 business income 30% apportionable to Pennsylvania and $350,000 nonbusiness loss allocable to Pennsylvania]. Business income apportioned to Pennsylvania is $180,000 [0.3 × $600,000], and the entire $350,000 loss is allocable to Pennsylvania, resulting in a net loss for Pennsylvania corporate income tax purposes of $170,000, which can be carried forward. In this case the Department policy is beneficial to the corporation.

Note: Nonbusiness income can be either advantageous or disadvantageous. For example, if you sell real estate at a gain in another state, that gain is 100% allocated to that state, but if you sell real estate at a gain in Pennsylvania, that gain is 100% allocated to Pennsylvania. However, if a gain of property located in Pennsylvania is business income, it can be apportioned. If a taxpayer's apportionment fraction, for

¶1105

example, is 50%, it will apportion only 50% of a business gain to Pennsylvania. However, if the property is sold in another state at a loss, and the loss is a nonbusiness loss, a taxpayer can use *none* of the loss to offset its Pennsylvania taxable income.

> *Example:* Screwball Manufacturing Co., Inc., sells its plant in Illinois at a $1,000,000 loss. Screwball cannot use any of this loss to offset its Pennsylvania taxable income.

¶1106 Apportionment of Business Income

Business income (except for certain specified corporations) is apportioned to Pennsylvania by using an apportionment fraction.

• *Apportionment before 2013*

Before 2013 all business income was required to be apportioned to Pennsylvania by multiplying the income by a fraction, the numerator of which is the sum of fifteen (15) times the property factor, fifteen (15) times the payroll factor, and seventy (70) times the sales factor, and the denominator of which is one hundred (100) [72 P.S. §7401(3)2.(a)(9)]. For taxable years beginning after December 31, 2008, the weighting of the sales factor is increased to 83% and is further increased to 90% for taxable years beginning after December 31, 2009 [Act 48 of 2009 (H.B. 1531), 72 P.S.§7401(3)2.(a)(9)]. NOTE: See ¶1503 for discussion of apportionment for capital stock/franchise tax purposes.

• *Apportionment after 2012 —Single-factor apportionment*

For taxable years beginning after December 31, 2012, all business income is to be apportioned to Pennsylvania by multiplying the income by the sales factor [72 P.S. §7401(3)2.(a)(9)(A)(v)]. The Department of Revenue issued guidance (Information Notice Corporation Taxes 2014-01) (dated December 12, 2014) with respect to sourcing sales of services under the new market-based sourcing rules. Pursuant to this Information Notice, sales of services should be sourced to Pennsylvania if the services are delivered to a location in the state. The Notice also provides guidelines for specific types of services and service industries, including trade or business services, franchise and service fees, employee services, subscription services, advertising, data processing, internet access, data streaming and storage, information services, computer software, pipeline or natural gas companies, and telecommunications.

• *Special apportionment for satellite television providers*

Act 52 of 2013 provides a special apportionment for satellite television providers effective after December 31, 2013. All business income is apportioned to Pennsylvania by multiplying the income by a fraction based upon the value of equipment owned or rented and located in Pennsylvania in relation to the value of total equipment owned or rented and used by the taxpayer everywhere in generating, processing or transmitting satellite television services irrespective of whether such equipment is affixed to real estate. The values used in the calculation are the costs of the equipment less depreciation per the books and records of the owner.

• *Special allocation*

The following corporations are subject to special allocation formulas: regulated investment companies, transportation companies, pipeline companies, natural gas companies, air freight forwarding companies, and water transportation companies operating on high seas and in inland waters. See ¶1114 for an explanation of special apportionment formulas for these companies. For information on specific procedures for these industries, consult the statutes and regulations.

When You Apportion

You cannot apportion your business income unless (1) you transact business outside Pennsylvania and (2) you are taxable in another state. See ¶1103.

¶1107 Property Factor

CAUTION

2012 is the last year that the property factor is used in apportionment. After 2012, apportionment is done using a single sales factor.

The property factor is a fraction, the numerator of which is the average value of the taxpayer's real and tangible personal property owned or rented and used in Pennsylvania during the tax period and the denominator of which is the average value of all the taxpayer's real and tangible personal property owned or rented and used during the tax period [72 P.S. § 7401(3)2(a)(10)]. A leasehold interest in minerals in place (however designated, described, or characterized by the law of the situs state) is included in the property factor as owned property. Mineral interests that have been severed or extracted are included in the property factor [61 Pa. Code § 153.21(c)(1)]. The property factor does not include the security interest of any corporation as seller or lessor in personal property sold or leased under a conditional sale, bailment lease, chattel mortgage or other contract providing for the retention of a lien or title as security for the sales price of the property [72 P.S. § 7401(3)2(a)(10)].

• *Equitable title*

The Commonwealth Court has held that a taxpayer retained equitable ownership of out-of-state property subject to a financing arrangement interest. The arrangement consisted of a Contract of Lease and Rent and a Contract of Acquisition by Purchase. Under the arrangement, title of the property passed to the municipality in which the property was located, but the taxpayer retained all operating and ownership rights. The taxpayer made "rent" payments in an amount sufficient to service the debt and had an option to purchase the property. The municipality could not sell or assign the property without permission of the taxpayer. The court held that the arrangement in substance was a mortgage agreement under which the taxpayer retained equitable title. Therefore, the property was properly includible in the taxpayer's property factor [*Rockwell International Corp. v. Cmwlth.*, 512 A.2d 1332 (Pa.Commw. 1986)].

Safe Harbor Leases

If title to property covered by a safe harbor lease (as defined in IRC § 168(f)(8)) does not pass to the lessor, the lessee is considered the owner and must include its value in the denominator of the property fraction (and in the numerator if the property is located in Pennsylvania). The lessor cannot then include it in its property fraction. The lessor cannot include down payments or installment payments in its property factor, and the lessor cannot include rental income in its sales [61 Pa. Code § 153.30(e)(1)].

However, if title passes to the lessor, the lessor includes the property in the denominator of its property fraction (and in the numerator if the property is located in Pennsylvania). The lessee then includes the property in its property fraction at eight times its net rental value; and the lessor includes rental income in its sales factor during the time that the purchaser retains title. The lessee includes down payments and installment payments in its sales factor [61 Pa. Code § 153.30(e)(2)].

¶1108 Payroll Factor

CAUTION

2012 is the last year that the payroll factor will be used in apportionment. After 2013 apportionment is done using a single sales factor.

The payroll factor is a fraction, the numerator of which is the total amount paid in Pennsylvania during the tax period by the taxpayer for compensation and the denominator of which is the total compensation paid everywhere during the same period [72 P.S. §7401(3)2(a)(13)]. "Compensation" means wages, salaries, commissions, and any other form of remuneration paid to employees for personal services [72 P.S. §7401(3)2(a)(1)(C)]. An employee for this purpose is an employee of the taxpayer, not the taxpayer's subsidiary or affiliate corporation. In *UPS Worldwide Forwarding, Inc. v. Cmwlth.* [Pa.Commw., Nos. 62 F.R. 2001 (March 1, 2004)], an out-of-state affiliate provided employee services to the taxpayer, and the taxpayer reimbursed the affiliate. The taxpayer stipulated that it had no employees. The Commonwealth Court held that because the taxpayer had no employees, it paid no compensation, and therefore had no payroll factor for corporate net income and capital/stock franchise tax purposes. The Commonwealth Court entered a final order upholding this decision that the taxpayer was required to exclude the payroll factor from the apportionment formula when calculating its Pennsylvania corporate net income tax because it had no employees and paid no compensation [*UPS Worldwide Forwarding, Inc. v. Cmwlth.*, Pa.Commw., Nos. 62 F.R. 2001, 63 F.R 2001, 64 F.R. 2001 & 65 F.R. 2001, *exceptions denied* (December 8, 2004); *appeal denied, Pa. Sup. Ct., Nos. 1-4 MAP 2005*].

American Gas and UPS Worldwide Distinguished

The taxpayer in *UPS Worldwide* relied on the Pennsylvania Supreme Court decision in *Cmwlth. v. American Gas* [42 A.2d 161 (Pa. 1945)], but the Court found significant differences between *American Gas* and *UPS Worldwide*. In *American Gas* the taxpayer had a written agreement with an out-of-state affiliate to provide employee services, for which it reimbursed the affiliate. The Pennsylvania Supreme Court ruled that *American Gas* had compensation. However, the employees at issue in *American Gas* were officers of the taxpayer. In *UPS Worldwide* the taxpayer had no employees, and the Court also found it significant that there was no written agreement between the taxpayer and the out-of-state affiliate.

- *Payroll incurred to produce nonbusiness income*

The law and regulations do not specifically address the issue of whether payroll incurred to produce nonbusiness income is to be used in the payroll factor but seem to imply that all payroll, whether business or nonbusiness, should be included.

- *Compensation paid in Pennsylvania*

Compensation with respect to an individual employee is paid in Pennsylvania if one of the following conditions is met [72 P.S. §7401(3)2(a)(14)]:

(1) The individual's service is performed entirely within Pennsylvania.

(2) The individual's service is performed both within and without Pennsylvania, but the service performed outside Pennsylvania is incidental to his or her service within Pennsylvania.

(3) Some of the service is performed in Pennsylvania and the base of operations is in this state.

(4) Some of the service is performed in Pennsylvania, there is no base of operations, and the individual's service is directed or controlled in Pennsylvania.

(5) The base of operations (or the place from which the service is directed or controlled) is not in any state in which the service is performed, and the individual is a Pennsylvania resident.

Note that if an employee meets one of the criteria above, all of that employee's compensation is considered paid in Pennsylvania. An employee's compensation should not be apportioned between or among states.

• *Effect of method of accounting*

If a taxpayer uses either the cash or accrual method of accounting in reporting to the Internal Revenue Service, the total amount paid to individuals for a tax period is determined upon the basis of the accounting method of the taxpayer [61 Pa. Code § 153.25(b)]. In practice, since many employers have payroll records on the cash basis for unemployment compensation purposes, the Department of Revenue has allowed taxpayers to report on the cash method even if they are for other purposes accrual basis taxpayers.

If the taxpayer reports payroll on the accrual method, all of its properly accrued compensation is considered paid. The Department of Revenue now allows the use of the completed contract method for payroll factor purposes [Corporation Tax Memorandum No. 104].

• *Effect of denial of deduction*

The payroll factor includes all compensation without regard to whether it was deducted in the determination of Pennsylvania taxable income [61 Pa. Code § 153.25(c)]. See also 61 Pa. Code § § 153.12 and 153.14.

¶1109 Sales Factor

The sales factor is a fraction, the numerator of which is total sales in Pennsylvania during the tax year and the denominator of which is total sales everywhere during the tax year [72 P.S. § 7401(3)2.(a)(15)].

• *Exceptions*

By definition, sales include all gross receipts of the taxpayer that are not allocable as nonbusiness income, except the following: (1) dividends received; (2) interest on the obligations of the United States or the Commonwealth of Pennsylvania and its political subdivisions; and (3) gross receipts from the sale, redemption, maturity or exchange of securities not held primarily for sale to customers in the ordinary course of its trade or business [72 P.S. § 7401(3)2.(a)(1)(E)].

• *Sales of tangible personal property*

Sales of tangible personal property are in Pennsylvania if the property is delivered or shipped to a purchaser within Pennsylvania regardless of the f.o.b. point or other conditions of the sale [72 P.S. § 7401(3)2.(a)(16)]. The Pennsylvania Supreme Court has held that the interpretation of this statute employs a destination test rather than a delivery test [*Gilmour Manufacturing Co. v. Cmwlth.*, 822 A.2d 676 (Pa. 2003), *aff'g*, 750 A.2d 948 (Pa.Commw. 2000)]. Act 52 of 2013 clarifies that the rental, lease or licensing of tangible personal property occurs at the location of first possession of the property but the Pennsylvania sale may be reduced if the property is subsequently taken out of state [72 P.S. § 7401(3)2.(a)(16.1)(B)].

Dock sales: Dock sales are excluded from the numerator of the sales fraction when an out-of-state purchaser immediately transfers the products out of state; the statute requires a destination test, not a delivery test for determining inclusion of dock sales in the numerator of the sales fraction [*Gilmour Manufacturing Co. v. Cmwlth.*, 822 A.2d 676 (Pa. 2003), *aff'g*, 750 A.2d 948 (Pa.Commw. 2000)].

Documentation Required

In the wake of the Gilmour decision, the Department of Revenue issued a regulation taking the position that in the absence of sufficient evidence establishing an ultimate destination to an out-of-state location, sales of goods in which delivery is made to the buyer at a Pennsylvania location must be reported as Pennsylvania sales and included in the numerator of the Pennsylvania sales apportionment fraction [61 Pa. § 170.11(b)].

Sufficient documentation [61 Pa. Code § 170.11(c)]:

Documentation sufficient to establish an out-of-state sale includes the following:

(1) Bills of lading of the carrier establishing that the goods were destined for or delivered to an out-of-state location.

(2) Delivery instructions from the purchaser to the carrier establishing that the goods were to be transported out of Pennsylvania.

(3) Warehouse receipts of the purchaser showing that the goods were delivered to an out-of-state location.

(4) Invoices issued by the taxpayer/seller to the purchaser showing an out-of-state delivery address. Note that invoices issued by the taxpayer/seller to the purchaser showing an out-of-state *mailing* address are insufficient to establish an ultimate destination of goods to an out-of-state location.

Insufficient documentation [61 Pa. Code § 170.11(d)]:

Documentation insufficient to establish that the ultimate destination of goods is to an out-of-state location includes the following:

(1) Invoices issued by the taxpayer/seller to the purchaser showing an out-of-state delivery address.

(2) Affidavits or other declarations from the seller, its employees or agents that the ultimate destination of goods was an out-of-state location.

• *Sales other than sales of tangible personal property*

Sales, other than sales of tangible personal property, are in Pennsylvania if they meet either of the following criteria: (1) the income-producing activity is performed in Pennsylvania; or (2) the income-producing activity is performed both within and outside Pennsylvania, but (based on costs of performance) a greater percentage of the income-producing activity is performed in Pennsylvania than in any other state [72 P.S. § 7401(3)2(a)(17)]. Act 52 of 2013 clarifies that the sale, lease, rental, or other use of real property occurs at the location of the real property. A Delaware corporation selling a partnership interest wherein the partnership's operations consisted of managing a Philadelphia apartment complex was ruled to generate an income producing activity in Pennsylvania based on the partnership's Pennsylvania operations regardless of where the sale of the partnership interest may have been negotiated. Moreover, the costs of producing the partnership's income were in Pennsylvania. Again, without regard to where the sale of the interest may have been negotiated. [*RB Alden Corp. v. Cmwlth.*, 142 A.3d 169 (Pa.Commw. 2016)].

• *Sales of services; Special rule*

For tax years beginning after December 31, 2013, gross receipts from the sale of services will be included in the numerator of the sales factor only if the services are delivered to a Pennsylvania location. If the services are delivered to locations both within and outside of Pennsylvania, the value of the Pennsylvania services is included in the numerator of the sales factor. If the location to which the services are delivered cannot be determined, the location generally will be deemed to be the place where the customer ordered the services or, if that cannot be determined, the customer's billing address [72 P.S. § 7401(3)2(a)(16.1)(C)]. The Department of Revenue issued guidance (Information Notice Corporation Taxes 2014-01) (dated December 12, 2014) with respect to sourcing sales of services under the new market-based sourcing rules. Pursuant to this Information Notice, sales of services should be sourced to Pennsylvania if the services are delivered to a location in the state. The Notice also provides guidelines for specific types of services and service industries, including trade or business services, franchise and service fees, employee services, subscription services, advertising, data processing, internet access, data streaming and storage, information services, computer software, pipeline or natural gas companies, and telecommunications.

Sales Factor Definitions

"Delivered." This term refers to the physical transfer of possession of tangible goods to the purchaser. Property is considered to be delivered to a purchaser within Pennsylvania if the shipment terminates in Pennsylvania, even though the purchaser may subsequently transfer the property to another state [61 Pa. Code § 153.26(b)(4)(i)].

"Purchaser." This term includes the ultimate recipient of the property if the taxpayer, at the designation of the purchaser, delivers property in Pennsylvania to the ultimate recipient [61 Pa. Code § 153.26(b)(3)(ii)(A)]. The term "purchaser" also includes a consignee if the taxpayer (consignor) delivers or ships property in Pennsylvania to a consignee who subsequently sells the property [61 Pa. Code § 153.26(b)(3)(ii)(B)].

> *Example 1:* A taxpayer in Pennsylvania sold merchandise to a purchaser in New York and directed the manufacturer of the merchandise in Ohio to ship the merchandise to the purchaser's customer in Pennsylvania, as the customer instructed. This is a Pennsylvania sale.

> *Example 2:* Roy's Ranges, Inc. makes a sale of gas ranges to a purchaser who maintains a central warehouse in Pittsburgh, Pennsylvania. The purchaser reships the sale. All of the ranges shipped to the purchaser's warehouse in Pittsburgh are Pennsylvania sales. If Roy's Ranges is a domestic corporation, this sale is taxable. If Roy's Ranges is a foreign corporation the taxability of the sale depends on whether it is "doing business" in Pennsylvania. See ¶913.

> *Example 3:* A taxpayer produces beer in New York. Taxpayer sells the beer to a distributor located in Pennsylvania. Distributor sends its truck into New York to taxpayer's plant to pick up the beer and bring it back to its business location. Delivery has occurred in New York; this is a New York sale.

> *Example 4:* The taxpayer (consignor), located in Ohio, ships property to a consignee in Philadelphia. Consignee, also a taxpayer, sells and ships the property to New Jersey to its (consignee's) customer. The consignor's sale is in Philadelphia; and the consignee's sale is in New Jersey.

"Shipped." This term refers to the transportation of tangible personal property, including delivery, to the purchaser. When property is being shipped by a taxpayer (consignor) from the state of origin to a consignee in another state and the property is diverted en route and shipped to a purchaser in Pennsylvania, the sale is in Pennsylvania [61 Pa. Code § 153.26(b)(4)(ii)].

¶1110 Examples of Allocation and Apportionment

CAUTION

Tax year 2012 is the last year of three-factor apportionment. Beginning in 2013, taxpayers must use single-factor apportionment, using only a sales factor.

The following examples apply the concepts of allocation and apportionment to specific business situations. Please note the appropriate taxable year.

¶1110

- *General example*

Oberon Corporation is a foreign corporation doing business in Pennsylvania. For the 2010 taxable year, the following information for Oberon Corporation (a calendar-year taxpayer) is available.

Item	Value
Taxable Income	$540,000
Property factor	0.348596
Payroll factor	0.392436
Sales factor	0.446983
2010 tax rate	0.099900

Oberon's apportionment fraction is 0.439201, computed as follows:

$[(5)(0.3458960) + (5)(0.392436) + (90)(0.446983)]/100 = 0.439201$

Oberon's Pennsylvania taxable income is $237,169, computed as follows:

$0.439201 \times \$540,000 = \$237,169$

Oberon's Pennsylvania 2010 corporate net income tax is $23,693 (0.0999 x $237,169).

- *When one of the apportionment factors is nonexistent*

If one of the factors is nonexistent (*i.e.*, both numerator and denominator are zero), the apportionment fraction should be computed by using the remaining factors with the appropriate weights. If two factors are nonexistent, the apportionment fraction is equal to the one existing factor.

Example 1: Missing payroll factor:

For taxable year 2010 the following information for Zero Corporation (a calendar-year taxpayer) is available:

Property factor = $200,000/$500,000 = .0400000

Payroll factor = 0/0 = nonexistent

Sales factor = $1,000,000/$3,000,000 = .0333333

Since Zero has a nonexistent payroll factor, it computes its apportionment fraction by using only the property factor and the sales factor.

Zero has an apportionment fraction of 0.33684, computed as follows:

$[(5)(0.400000) + (90)(0.333333)]/95 = 0.33684$

A factor is nonexistent only if *both* numerator and denominator are zero. If a factor is zero because only the numerator is zero, it should be used.

Example 2: Zero payroll factor:
For taxable year 2010 the following information for Cipher Corporation (a calendar-year taxpayer) is available:

Property factor = $200,000/$500,000 = 0.400000

Payroll factor = 0/$200 = 0

Sales factor = $1,000,000/$3,000,000 = 0.333333

Cipher Corporation does not have a nonexistent payroll factor. The payroll factor does not have a zero denominator. Cipher uses the payroll factor to compute its 2010 apportionment fraction of 0.319999 as follows:

$(0.400000) + (5)(0) + (90)(0.333333)/100 = 0.319999$

Create a Factor

Sometimes it is advantageous to create a factor. Notice the difference between the apportionment fractions for Zero and Cipher, above. Cipher paid only a small amount of employee compensation, but it was enough to keep the payroll factor from being nonexistent; so Cipher's apportionment factor was lower than Zero's, which will result in a lower tax.

• *Single sales factor apportionment, beginning in 2013*

Oberon Corporation is a foreign corporation doing business in Pennsylvania. For the 2010 taxable year, the following information for Oberon Corporation (a calendar-year taxpayer) is available.

Item	Value
Taxable Income	$540,000
Property factor	0.348596
Payroll factor	0.392436
Sales factor	0.446983
2013 tax rate	0.099900

Since the year is 2013, Oberon does not use the property factor or the payroll factor; it uses only the sales factor.

Oberon's apportionment fraction, thus, 0.446983.

Oberon's apportioned income is (0.446983 x $540,000) = $242,925.

Oberon's Pennsylvania 2013 corporate net income tax is $24,268 (0.0999 x $242,925).

¶1111 Part-Year Taxpayers

When a taxpayer has a short period but is engaged in business in Pennsylvania for the entire short period, no special problem is presented. However, when a corporation has operations both within and outside Pennsylvania, and it has not engaged in business in Pennsylvania for an entire period under consideration, special apportionment is necessary. For example, if a foreign corporation that has been doing business in another state for several years begins operations in Pennsylvania in the middle of a tax year, the apportionment factors should be based only on the part of the tax year in which income was earned in Pennsylvania. In such cases the apportionment factors are determined as follows:

Property factor: Numerator is average value of property in Pennsylvania during the period of operation in Pennsylvania, and denominator is total average tangible property for the entire year.

Payroll factor: Numerator is compensation in Pennsylvania during the period of operation in Pennsylvania, and denominator is total compensation everywhere for the entire tax year.

Sales factor: Numerator is Pennsylvania sales for the period of operation in Pennsylvania, and denominator is total sales everywhere for the entire tax year.

> *Example* : Partial Corporation, a calendar-year taxpayer chartered and located entirely in Virginia, began operations in Pennsylvania on August 1, 2008. On August 1, 2008, Partial Corporation purchased tangible property in Pennsylvania at a cost of $100,000. Partial Corporation had tangible property on January 1, 2008, of $500,000 and on December 31, 2008, of $750,000, including the $100,000 located in Pennsylvania. Wages paid in Pennsylvania in 2008 amounted to $35,000, and Partial's total wages in both Virginia and Pennsylvania totaled $3,000,000. Partial's total sales for the year were $5,000,000, of which $450,000 were made in Pennsylvania. Partial Corporation has the following apportionment factors:
>
> Property factor = $100,000 ÷ $625,000 = 0.160000
>
> Payroll factor = $35,000 ÷ $3,000,000 = 0.011667
>
> Sales factor = $450,000 ÷ $5,000,000 = 0.090000

¶1113 Allocation and Apportionment of Income from Partnership Interests

The Pennsylvania corporate net income tax regulations provide that a corporate taxpayer's interest in a partnership is considered a direct interest in the assets of the partnership rather than an intangible asset. Accordingly, the corporate taxpayer's share of partnership payroll, property, and sales are included in or excluded from the payroll, property, and sales factors as provided by regulation [61 Pa. Code § 153.29(a)(1)].

A corporate taxpayer's partnership interest for corporate tax purposes is determined under the partnership agreement and in accordance with the Internal Revenue Code [61 Pa. Code § 153.29(a)(2)]. A corporate partner must determine its distributive share of partnership income using the same method of accounting that the partnership uses in keeping its books. This is true even if the partnership uses a different method of accounting from the one the corporate partner uses on its Pennsylvania corporate return [61 Pa. Code § 153.29(g)]. A corporate partner *and* its partnership must use accounting periods prescribed in IRC § 706. A corporate partner keeping its books on a fiscal year or calendar year that differs from its partnership's tax year, reports its shares of partnership income and apportionment factors in the corporation's tax year in which or with which the partnership year ends [Pa. Code § 153.29(f)]. Beginning January 1, 2014, partnerships must provide any partner classified as a corporation its apportionment factors.

- *Nexus*

If *either* the separate activities of the corporation or the separate activities of its partnership constitute doing business, carrying on activities, having capital or property employed or used, or owning property in Pennsylvania, the corporation is subject to Pennsylvania corporate taxation [61 Pa. Code § 153.29(b)(1)].

- *Allocation and apportionment*

If *either* the separate activities of the corporation or the separate activities of its partnership constitute transacting taxable business outside Pennsylvania, the corporation will be allowed to allocate its nonbusiness income and apportion its business income [61 Pa. Code § 153.29(b)(2)].

Business income means income arising from transactions and activity in the regular course of the *taxpayer's trade or business;* and the taxpayer's (corporate partner's) trade or business *includes* activities performed in partnership. The determination of whether income arose in the regular course of the taxpayer's trade or business is made in accordance with the same rules used for other income. See ¶1104 [61 Pa. Code § 153.29(c)(1)]. Nonbusiness income is all income that is not business income.

> *Example:* Ace Corporation publishes books in Pennsylvania. It owns a 35% interest in Pace Partnership, which sells Ace's books in 10 other states. Ace Corporation has business income of $1,500,000 (not including its distributive share of Pace's income); and Pace Partnership had business income of $1,000,000. Ace Corporation's total business income is $1,850,000 [$1,500,000 + (0.35 × $1,000,000)].

The classification of income by customary labels (*e.g.,* interest, rents, etc.) is of no aid in determining whether distributive partnership income is business or nonbusiness. Such determination is made with reference to the relationship the item of income bears to the trade or business of the corporate partner, *not* to the trade or business of the partnership [61 Pa. Code § 153.29(c)(2)].

¶1113

• *Allocation of partnership nonbusiness income*

A corporate taxpayer first determines its business income and its distributive share of the partnership items that constitute nonbusiness income as defined in 72 P.S. § 7401(3)2(a)(1)—(17). See ¶ 1104. Then it allocates the various items of income directly to specific states pursuant to the provisions of 72 P.S. § 7401(3)2(a)(4)—(8). See ¶ 1105. The taxpayer's distributive share of such nonbusiness income must be reported in the same manner as nonbusiness income derived from its other activities [61 Pa. Code § 153.29(e)].

• *Apportionment of partnership business income*

A corporate partner entitled to apportionment of business income uses the regular three factors (property, payroll, and sales) to compute its apportionment fraction. However, the three factors are subject to special rules that apply only to partnership income [61 Pa. Code § 153.29(d)].

CAUTION

2012 is the last year three-factor apportionment is used. New regulations for use of single-factor apportionment after 2013 have not been issued yet.

Property factor: A corporate partner includes in the numerator and denominator of its property factor a portion of the partnership's tangible property (to the extent of its interest in the partnership), both owned and used and rented and used during the tax year. However, the *value* of such property must be adjusted in the numerator and denominator of its property factor, as follows:

Leased property owned by corporate partner: If the leased property is owned by the corporate partner and leased to the partnership, the corporate partner cannot include it twice (*i.e.*, as both property owned and property rented). It includes only the original cost of the property [61 Pa. Code § 153.29(d)(1)(ii)].

> *Example:* Ace Corporation, which owns 35% of Pace Partnership, may apportion its distributive share of partnership business income. Ace Corporation owns a building (original cost, $150,000) which it leases to Pace Partnership for $20,000 per year. Ace Corporation includes the original cost of the building in its property factor ($150,000) but may not include any amount with respect to the rental.

Leased property owned by partnership: If the leased property is owned by the partnership and leased to the corporate partner, the amount to be included in the corporate partner's property factor is the sum of the following: (1) The value of the property times the taxpayer's partnership interest expressed as a percentage; and (2) The rental value of the property times the interest not held by the taxpayer expressed as a percentage [61 Pa. Code § 153.29(d)(1)(ii)].

> *Example:* Pull Partnership owns a building (original cost, $200,000) which it rents to its corporate partner, Tough Corporation, for $36,000 per year. Tough Corporation has a 30% interest in Pull Partnership. Tough Corporation will include $261,600 in its property factor with respect to this building, computed as follows:

0.30 × $200,000	$ 60,000
[(8 × $36,000) × 0.70]	201,600
Total	**$261,600**

Payroll factor: The partnership's payroll is included in the denominator of the corporate partner's payroll factor to the extent of the corporate partner's partnership interest. Any of the partnership payroll included in the denominator that is attributable to Pennsylvania must also be included in the numerator [61 Pa. Code § 153.29(d)(2)(ii)].

Example: Ace Corporation, which owns 35% of Pace Partnership, can apportion its business income from Pace Partnership. Ace Corporation, using regular rules, has a total payroll of $2,000,000 (not including any payroll attributable to Pace Partnership), and Pace Partnership has payroll of $900,000. The denominator of Ace Corporation's payroll factor is $2,315,000 ($2,000,000 + 0.35 × $900,000).

Pace Partnership paid compensation in Pennsylvania in the amount of $100,000. Ace's share of Pace's Pennsylvania payroll is $35,000. This must be included in the numerator of its payroll factor.

Sales factor: A partnership's sales giving rise to business income are included in the denominator of the sales factor of a corporate partner to the extent of the corporate partner's partnership interest [61 Pa. Code § 153.29(d)(3)]. Any sales included in the denominator that are attributable to Pennsylvania must also be included in the numerator of the corporation's sales factor.

Intercompany sales must be eliminated from both numerator and denominator, as follows:

(1) Corporate sales to the partnership are eliminated to the extent of the corporation's partnership interest.

(2) Partnership sales to the corporation are eliminated in an amount not to exceed the corporation's partnership interest in all partnership sales.

(3) Sales made by either corporate partner or partnership to nonpartners must be included in the corporate partner's sales factor in an amount equal to its interest in the partnership, notwithstanding any intercompany eliminations described in (1) and (2), above.

Example 1: Ace Corporation, which has a 35% interest in Pace Partnership, had sales of $30,000,000 for the calendar year, $465,000 of which were to Pace Partnership. Pace Partnership, also a calendar-year taxpayer, had sales of $16,000,000, none of which were to any of its partners. The denominator of Ace Corporation's sales factor is $35,437,250, computed as follows:

Total sales by Ace	$30,000,000
Add Ace's interest in Pace's sales (0.35 × $16,000,000)	5,600,000
Subtract Ace's interest in its sales to Pace (0.35 × $465,000)	(162,750)
Total	**$35,437,250**

Example 2: Lorna Corporation has a 45% interest in Wood Partnership. Lorna Corporation had sales of $17,000,000 during the year, none of which were made to Wood Partnership. Wood Partnership, also a calendar-year taxpayer, had sales of $3,500,000, $2,000,000 of which were to Lorna Corporation. Wood made no other sales to corporate partners. The denominator of Lorna Corporation's sales factor is $17,000,000 computed as follows:

Total sales by Lorna	$17,000,000
Add Lorna's interest in Wood's sales (0.45 × $3,500,000)	1,575,000
Subtract Wood Partnership's sales to Lorna ($2,000,000), but not to exceed Lorna's interest in Wood's total sales (0.45 × $3,500,000)	(1,575,000)
Total	**$17,000,000**

- *Sale of partnership interest*

A Delaware corporation selling a partnership interest wherein the partnership's operations consisted of managing a Philadelphia apartment complex was ruled to give rise to business income. The sale was of a portion of the taxpayer's partnership interest which satisfied the functional test of the business income definition subsequent to the 2001 amendment of 72 P.S. §7401(3)2(a)(1)(A). [*RB Alden Corp. v. Cmwlth.*, 142 A.3d 169 (Pa.Commw. 2016)].

• *Multiformity and unrelated assets*

If a corporation has a partnership interest in a partnership engaged in a business that is different from the business of the corporation, the principle of multiformity (explained at ¶1412) should apply. The principle of unrelated assets (explained at ¶1420) should also apply if the circumstances warrant. For example, if a corporation engaged in the manufacture of steel in Pennsylvania acquires an interest in a partnership engaged in raising tobacco in North Carolina, the principle of multiformity should apply, so that the income from the partnership is not taxable in Pennsylvania under the principle of multiformity.

¶1114 Other Methods of Allocation and Apportionment

In special cases, extrastatutory methods of allocation and apportionment may be appropriate. The most common extrastatutory allocation methods are (1) multiformity (explained at ¶1412) and (2) unrelated assets (explained at ¶1420). However (at least in theory), other extrastatutory methods are available.

• *"Subparagraph 18"*

The law provides the following:

If the allocation and apportionment provisions of this definition do not fairly represent the extent of the taxpayer's business activity in this State, the taxpayer may petition the Secretary of Revenue or the Secretary of Revenue may require, in respect to all or any part of the taxpayer's business activity: (1) separate accounting; (2) the exclusion of any one or more of the factors; (3) the inclusion of one or more additional factors that will fairly represent the taxpayer's business activity in this State; or (4) the employment of any other method to effectuate an equitable allocation and apportionment of the taxpayer's income. In determining the fairness of any allocation or apportionment, the Secretary of Revenue may consider the taxpayer's previous reporting and its consistency with the relief requested [72 P.S. §7401(3)2(a)(18)].

This provision is commonly referred to as "Subparagraph 18." Either a taxpayer or the Commonwealth can invoke the powers of Subparagraph 18. In order to receive relief under Subparagraph 18, a taxpayer must be able to show that the normal statutory provisions for allocation and apportionment do not achieve results that fairly represent a taxpayer's value or income attributable to Pennsylvania. In practice, the use of this provision has been used by the Commonwealth to attempt to invoke the throw-out rule.

• *Throw-out rule*

In the past, the Department of Revenue has invoked the use of the throw-out rule (*i.e.*, eliminating from the denominator of the sales factor the sales of tangible personal property delivered or shipped to customers in a state(s) in which the taxpayer conducts no taxable business activity). However, this use of the throw-out rule has been held to be invalid [*Paris Mfg. Co., Inc. v. Cmwlth.*, 476 A.2d 890 (Pa. 1984)]. As a result, the Department has amended its regulations [61 Pa. Code §§153.26 and 153.43]to reflect this ruling. 61 Pa. Code §153.43, referring to the sales factor, has been amended to state that the Commonwealth may use Subparagraph 18 (explained above) on a case-to-case basis to effectuate an equitable apportionment if the apportionment's provisions do not fairly represent the extent of the taxpayer's business activity in the Commonwealth.

¶1114

- *"Section 482" reallocation method*

The Department of Revenue has indicated concern about the use of intercompany transactions to avoid Pennsylvania corporate net income tax. Typically, these transactions involve transactions between profitable domestic subsidiaries and their foreign subsidiaries. These "suspect" transactions include royalties and management fees paid by domestic corporations and their foreign subsidiaries and intracompany sales between domestic corporations and their foreign subsidiaries. In an effort to prevent such avoidance, the Department of Revenue has begun to assert the § 482 power (so-called after similar powers available to the IRS under § 482 of the Internal Revenue Code) to reallocate income and deduction items among affiliated corporations when the purpose of the transactions is to avoid Pennsylvania corporate net income tax. There is no statutory basis for the assertion of such powers.

- *Multiformity and unrelated assets*

The concepts of multiformity and unrelated assets are explained in detail at ¶ 1412 and ¶ 1420. The principles are the same for both capital stock/franchise tax and for corporate net income tax purposes.

If a corporation is a multiform business, engaging in a separate business outside Pennsylvania, the income from the unrelated business is excluded from the tax base for Pennsylvania corporate net income tax purposes. Likewise, if a corporation, even though it is a unitary (as opposed to multiform) business, owns assets that are unrelated to the exercise of its franchise in Pennsylvania, the income from such assets would be excluded from the tax base. This means that the net income from the unrelated activity (multiformity) or unrelated assets would be excluded from the income to be allocated or apportioned to Pennsylvania and the property, payroll, and sales related to the unrelated activity or assets would be excluded from the apportionment factors. However, if the business is found to be a unitary business, the principles of unitary apportionment apply.

- *Unitary apportionment*

The issue of unitary apportionment is one of the most controversial issues in state taxation. States that seek unitary apportionment usually are trying to include the income of subsidiaries of a parent corporation in the income of the parent for apportionment purposes. In general, if there is a unity of ownership, operation, and management within the affiliated group or if the business activities within a taxing state depend on or contribute to a corporation's activities in another state, a taxing state that seeks unitary apportionment asserts that a business is unitary. The unitary approach ordinarily results in the collection of more revenue on the part of the state seeking unitary apportionment. However, the states are not uniform in their application of the unitary concept. Some aggressively seek to classify corporations as unitary on a worldwide basis; others may be just as aggressive but seek to include in the income of the parent only the income of U.S. subsidiaries.

Worldwide Unitary Apportionment for Multinationals

California has asserted the right to use worldwide combined reporting to determine the corporate taxes owed by multinational corporations. Under its worldwide combined reporting method, California taxed an apportioned portion of the worldwide income of a foreign multinational corporate group. The U.S. Supreme Court found this method of unitary apportionment to be constitutional, ruling that it did not violate the Foreign Commerce Clause, the Commerce Clause, or the Due Process Clause of the U.S. Constitution. The Court also rejected the contention that worldwide unitary apportionment exposed foreign multinationals to constitutionally forbidden multiple taxation [*Barclays Bank PLC v. Franchise Tax Board*, 512 U.S. 298 (1995)].

In several cases involving the issue of unitary apportionment, the U.S. Supreme Court has developed guidelines to the determination of a unitary business that apply to all states: functional integration, centralization of management, and economies of scale. See, for example, *ASARCO, Inc. v. Idaho State Tax Commission*, 485 U.S. 307 (1982) and *F.W. Woolworth Co. v. Taxation and Revenue Dept. of New Mexico*, 458 U.S. 354 (1982). In a 1992 case [*Allied-Signal, Inc. v. Director, Division of Taxation*, 504 U.S. 768], the state of New Jersey sought to include in the apportionable corporate net income tax base of a foreign multi-state corporation the capital gain on the sale of a minority stock interest in a second foreign corporation. New Jersey's contention was that if a corporation does any business in New Jersey, all of its income is apportionable to New Jersey. The Supreme Court found that this position is not consistent with the Due Process and Commerce Clauses of the U.S. Constitution, which require nexus between a state and that which it seeks to tax. In this case the two companies involved were unrelated business enterprises with no common activities (*i.e.,* no economies of scale); and they did not have centralized management (*i.e.,* each corporation had a separate management). However, the Court said that not being part of the same unitary business does not automatically preclude apportionment in all cases, a gain from a capital transaction must serve an operational function rather than an investment function in order to be included in the income tax base apportionable to a state.

In *Container Corp. of America v. Franchise Tax Board, State of California*, 463 U.S. 159 (1983), the U.S. Supreme Court held that it is up to the states to make the factual determination of whether a business is unitary or not. As a result, a corporation may find that it is considered to be a unitary business in one state but not in another.

Pennsylvania does not seek to apply unitary apportionment with respect to subsidiaries. For example, if X Corporation is subject to tax in Pennsylvania and has subsidiaries in other states, Pennsylvania does not seek to include the income of the subsidiaries in the income of the parent. The issue of multiform versus unitary business in Pennsylvania is restricted to the consideration of one corporation and is not extended to the consideration of groups of affiliated corporations. Thus, when the term unitary taxation is used within the context of Pennsylvania corporate taxation, it does not mean the same thing that it does when used within the context of, for example, California corporation taxation. When a unitary business has been found for purposes of Pennsylvania taxation, the corporation in question was carrying on activities outside the Commonwealth of Pennsylvania. If a subsidiary is, the outcome is different. As the term "unitary taxation" is ordinarily used in state tax literature (*i.e.,* including in the income of the parent the income of unitary subsidiaries), Pennsylvania is not a unitary state.

CORPORATE NET INCOME TAX

CHAPTER 12

PROCEDURES, ENFORCEMENT, ASSESSMENT, AND REVIEW

¶1201 General

The Pennsylvania corporate net income tax is administered and enforced by the Department of Revenue. It is authorized to prescribe, adopt, promulgate, and enforce rules and regulations with respect to the administration and enforcement of the corporate net income tax [72 P.S. § 7408(a)]. It can examine taxpayer records and investigate the character of any corporation's business to verify the accuracy of reports or, in the absence of a return, to determine whether one should have been filed [72 P.S. § 7408(b)]. After December 31, 2007, this process is called assessment and is no longer mandatory (i.e., not all returns will be assessed). The provisions with respect to assessment are discussed at ¶1204. Taxpayers not satisfied with assessments may petition for reassessment (discussed at ¶4604).

¶1202 Communication Function

The communication function refers to the process of supplying information to the Department of Revenue in the form of returns, schedules, attachments to returns, letters, documents—any information that the Department might need in any matter. The importance of the communication function cannot be overstressed. See ¶4608 for explanation of the communication function.

¶1203 Settlement and Resettlement

CAUTION! Old Law

This paragraph refers to the settlement and resettlement of taxes for which a notice of settlement was issued prior to January 1, 2008. New procedures applicable to assessments issued after December 31, 2007, are discussed at ¶1204.

The procedures discussed in this paragraph govern any proceeding, prosecution, action, suit, or appeal involving settlements of tax liability by the Department of Revenue prior to January 1, 2008, and any resettlement resulting from such proceeding, prosecution, suit, or appeal until final resolution by withdrawal, reassessment, redetermination, or resettlement by the Department of Revenue or an administrative board or a decision by a court of competent jurisdiction [Act 119 of 2006 (S.B. 993), § 33(2)].

The Department of Revenue of Revenue reviews every corporate income tax report and "settles" the tax by either accepting it as filed or making adjustments, subject to audit and approval by the Department of the Auditor General [72 P.S. § 7407(a)]. No settlement (except in cases where Revenue and Auditor General disagree and the settlement is made by the Board of Finance and Revenue) is valid without the written approval of the Department of the Auditor General [72 P.S. § 802(g)].

The Secretary of Revenue, after consultation with the Auditor General, has the power to develop and implement procedures for the settlement of taxes employing (among other means) automatic data processing, statistical analysis, computer analysis, mechanical handling and issuance of settlement documents (including documents without original signatures) [72 P.S. § 7407(a)].

• *Procedure after settlement*

After the Department of Revenue makes a settlement, it is sent to the Department of the Auditor General [72 P.S. § 802(a)]. Within 60 days after receipt of the settlement, the Auditor General will either accept the Department's settlement or request "new marking," which means that it goes back to Revenue for modification [72 P.S. § 802(b)]. If the Departments of Revenue and Auditor General cannot agree within four months after original submission to the Auditor General's Department, the matter goes to the Board of Finance and Revenue for settlement [72 P.S. § 802(e)], but this is an unusual occurrence. If this happens, however, the Board of Finance and Revenue must reach a decision within three months after the case is submitted to it. Failure to reach a decision within that period is an automatic validation of the Department of Revenue's settlement [72 P.S. § 802(f)].

Once approved by the Auditor General, a settlement is "processed out," and the tax debit or credit is recorded in the taxpayer's account. The Department of Revenue must send to the taxpayer a copy of the settlement promptly after the date of settlement [72 P.S. § 7407(c)]. The form of the settlement notice depends on the action taken by the Department [61 Pa. Code § 153.62]. If the tax settlement computations differ from the tax computations submitted by the taxpayer, the settlement notice will be a photocopy of the Settlement Sheet, which is on the back of the corporate tax report. If the return is accepted as filed, the settlement notice will be a photocopy of the settlement [61 Pa. Code § 153.62(c)].

• *Documents taxpayer receives*

The taxpayer will receive, along with the settlement notice, an account review and the Department's worksheets if adjustments are made. The account review shows the balance in each tax account for each year, but it does not show all the transactions that took place. The taxpayer's ledger, however, does show all the transactions for a particular tax for a particular year and can be used to determine whether or not any mistakes have been made in the account. It is a good idea to write the Department and ask for a copy of both your open and your closed ledger. An open ledger is one that pertains to an open year, and a closed ledger is one that pertains to a year that has been zeroed out (*i.e.,* there are no open debits or credits for that year).

• *Time limitation*

The statute requires that the Department of Revenue settle (subject to audit and approval by the Department of the Auditor General) the corporate net income tax and that settlement must "so far as possible," be made so that notice thereof may reach the taxpayer within 18 months after the tax report was required to be made [72 P.S. § 7407(a)]. Otherwise, it must be accepted as filed. The Department has one year, not 18 months, to settle the income tax reports of co-operative agricultural associations [Act of May 23, 1945, P.L. 893, § 6]. Corporate regulations, however, provide that settlement is to be made so that notice may be mailed to the taxpayer within 18 months after the report was required to be made [61 Pa. Code § 153.61(a)]. There is a potential conflict between regulation and statute with respect to whether notice must be mailed to or received by the taxpayer within the statutory 18-month period.

• *Time limitation in the case of extensions*

Regulations provide that if a taxpayer requests an extension of time for its federal return, settlement will be made, so far as possible, so that notice may reach the taxpayer within 18 months after the taxpayer files its Pennsylvania return. If a Pennsylvania extension (but not a federal extension) is requested, settlement will be made so that notice may be mailed to the taxpayer within 18 months after the taxpayer files the return [61 Pa. Code § 153.61(b)]. Since the statute [72 P.S. § 7407] requires notice to reach the taxpayer within 18 months of the due date (not the filing date), there is also potential for conflict here. Regulations also provide that in the case of reports filed after the original due date, settlement will be made so that notice may be mailed to the taxpayer within 18 months of the filing date [61 Pa. Code § 153.61(c)].

• *Settlements beyond 18-month period*

The phrase "so far as possible" does, in some cases, allow the Department of Revenue more than 18 months to settle a return, but only if there is a valid reason. The Pennsylvania Supreme Court has held that the only general basis for excusing a late settlement is when the taxpayer does something to delay timely action [*Cmwlth. v. Safe Harbor Water Power Corp.*, 328 A.2d 833 (Pa. 1974), *aff'g*, 305 A.2d 394 (Pa.Commw. 1973)]. In *Safe Harbor*, the court found the Department's delay in settlement to be unjustified. See also *Cmwlth. v. Fruehauf Trailer Co.*, 71 Dauph 7 (1957); *Cmwlth. v. Dresser Industries*, 75 Dauph 111 (1960); *Cmwlth. v. Andale Co.*, 75 Dauph 250 (1960); *Cmwlth. v. Lehval Industries, Inc.*, 75 Dauph 254 (1960); *Cmwlth. v. Pennsylvania Manufacturers Association Casualty Insurance Co.*, 76 Dauph 275, 78 Dauph 28, *modified on other grounds*, 410 Pa.207, 188 A.2d 729 (Pa. 1933).

Caution: Raising Issues During Administrative Review

If a taxpayer wants to raise the issue of timeliness of settlement, it must be done during administrative review or not at all. New issues (including the issue of timeliness) cannot be raised in court proceedings [*Cmwlth. v. Sherwin Equipment, Inc.*, 89 Dauph 330 (1968)].

• *Estimated settlement in case of failure to file a return*

If the officers of any corporation neglect or refuse to file a corporate net income tax return within the time prescribed by statute (including extensions), the Department of Revenue can make estimated settlements against taxpayers and collect the tax. Taxpayers cannot appeal or petition for review of estimated settlements. However, the taxpayer may petition the Department of Revenue for permission to file its return. If permission is denied, the taxpayer may then appeal or petition for review of this denial. If a return is filed, the Commonwealth will cancel the estimated settlement and make a settlement based upon the filed return or report [72 P.S. § 804].

Removing Estimates

It is the authors' experience that estimated settlements can be removed by filing the return for the reporting period for which the estimated settlement pertains without petitioning the Department of Revenue for the right to file such return.

• *Estimated settlement in case of incomplete report*

If, while reviewing a Pennsylvania Corporate Tax Report, the Taxing Officer determines additional information is required, the Taxing Officer will continue to initiate correspondence requesting this information. If the taxpayer fails to respond to this correspondence, the acting taken by the Taxing Officer will be dependent upon the nature of the missing information, as follows:

(1) *Inability to calculate capital stock value, Pennsylvania taxable income, or taxable indebtedness:* If, as a result of the missing information, the Taxing Officer is unable to calculate a capital stock value, Pennsylvania taxable income, or taxable indebtedness, the report will be removed from the corporate tax ledger as an incomplete report, and the Taxing Officer will impose estimates on the tax types involved. The following are examples of this type of missing information: (a) a copy of the federal income tax return; (b) balance sheet (separate company and/ or consolidated); (c) income statement; and (d) history of earnings. Once the information is received, the report will be posted as received on that date. The Taxing Officer will then complete the settlement, and the estimate will be stricken. The Department cites 72 P.S. § 7403 as authority for this position [*Pennsylvania Tax Update No. 103*, Pennsylvania Department of Revenue, January/February 2003].

(2) *Inability to verify a component of taxable capital stock value, Pennsylvania taxable income, or taxable indebtedness:* If, as a result of the missing information the Taxing Officer is unable to verify one of the components used in the calculation of taxable capital stock value, Pennsylvania taxable income, or taxable indebtedness, the Taxing Officer will initiate the settlement, making all adjustments in favor of the Commonwealth. The following are examples of this type of missing information: (a) apportionment information; (b) details of increases to retained earnings reported on federal Schedule M-2; and (c) a schedule of taxes expensed on the federal income tax return.

Importance of the Communication Function

The communication function refers to the process of supplying information to the Department of Revenue. This function is discussed at ¶1202 and ¶4608. A taxpayer can avoid unfavorable situations, such as having all doubts resolved in favor of the Commonwealth, by supplying information to the Department of Revenue as completely and expeditiously as possible.

• *Special settlements*

In cases of dissolution, merger or consolidation, withdrawal from Pennsylvania by a foreign corporation, or bulk sales (discussed at ¶4621), corporations must get a Corporate Clearance Certificate [61 Pa. Code § 151.4]. A Corporate Clearance Certificate is a certificate issued by the Department of Revenue evidencing the payment of all taxes and charges as required by law [61 Pa. Code § 151.4(a)]. Corporate clearance certificates are discussed at ¶4614.

The Department has special internal units of its Compliance Division to facilitate settlement of these special settlements and issuance of Corporate Clearance Certificates. If, later, a full-year return is filed (*e.g.,* in the case of bulk sales), the Department then settles on the basis of the filed return and "strikes off" the estimated settlement.

• *Immediate assessment, settlement, or collection to prevent tax avoidance*

The Department of Revenue may make an immediate assessment or settlement of (1) sales and use tax; (2) corporate net income tax; or (3) capital stock/franchise tax and any interest or penalty due if the Department finds that without immediate action the tax, interest, or penalty due will be in jeopardy of not being collected because the taxpayer intends to do any of the following without paying the tax, interest, or penalty due [72 P.S. § 10003.14(a)]:

(1) Immediately leave Pennsylvania.

¶1203

(2) Remove property from Pennsylvania used in activities that are taxable in Pennsylvania.

(3) Discontinue doing business in Pennsylvania.

(4) Do any other act that would prejudice or render ineffective (in whole or in part) proceedings to assess, settle, or collect any tax, interest, or penalty due.

Immediate assessment is discussed in more detail at ¶4603.

• *Resettlement by the Department*

Resettlement is a procedure available to both the taxpayer and the Commonwealth.

If the Department of Revenue becomes dissatisfied with a settlement within three years after the date of the original settlement, or if, at any time, a taxpayer's federal taxable income is changed by the IRS or by a U.S. court or agency, the Department can make a resettlement of the tax due, based on facts contained in the report or any information it may possess or obtain [72 P.S. §7407(b)). The "date of any settlement" for resettlements initiated by the Department means the date approved by the Auditor General as shown on the bottom of the settlement sheet [72 P.S. §1(a)]. The term "at any time" with respect to resettlements in the case of federal changes means just what it says. *Any time* the federal government makes a change that necessitates the filing of a report of change, the Department of Revenue can resettle the year in question *even if more than 18 months have gone by.* This has the effect of making the Pennsylvania statute of limitations for resettlement in this particular circumstance the same as the federal period. See ¶921 for explanation of Pennsylvania Report of Change when federal changes are made.

Multiple Resettlements

Regulations provide that the Department of Revenue can resettle any settled tax that has been appealed to the Board of Finance and Revenue if the Board has not yet acted upon the taxpayer's petition or if the resettlement of the Department is consistent with the action taken by the Board of Finance and Revenue [61 Pa. Code §153.63(b)]. This means that you can be at risk of resettlement for more than one year, as indicated above, if you have appealed to the Board of Finance and Revenue. Also, note that §1105 of the Fiscal Code authorizes the Department of Revenue to initiate a resettlement of a prior resettlement within two years. It is not clear whether or not this gives the Department the authority to resettle over and over.

• *Resettlement requested by taxpayer*

A taxpayer might want a resettlement in order to (1) correct a clerical error on the return or settlement or (2) seek relief from an unfavorable settlement. A taxpayer also has the right to petition for resettlement to seek relief from imposition of interest and penalties. These are explained below.

If, after settlement, a taxpayer discovers that there is a clerical error on a return, the taxpayer can file an amended report. The Department of Revenue, however, treats this as a resettlement, which means that the taxpayer no longer has the right to file a petition for resettlement with the Board of Appeals [61 Pa. Code §153.64(c), (d)]. However, the right of appeal to the Board of Finance and Revenue for review of the resettlement remains. This means that if a taxpayer has both a clerical error and another issue (*e.g.,* business vs. nonbusiness income), it cannot get relief from the clerical error and preserve its right to petition for resettlement. See ¶919 for explanation of amended returns.

¶1203

• *Filing the petition*

A petition for resettlement can be used when a taxpayer disagrees with the Department's original settlement, and it must be filed within 90 days after the mailing date of a settlement notice and is filed with the Department that made the settlement [72 P.S. § 1102]. A taxpayer shall be deemed to have timely filed a petition for resettlement if the letter transmitting the petition is received by the Department of Revenue or is postmarked by the U.S. Postal Service on or prior to the final day on which the petition is required to be filed [72 P.S. § 10006]. Petitions are accepted on the first business day after a Saturday, Sunday, or holiday if the 90th day falls on such a day.

File Petition on Time

A taxpayer is not protected simply because a petition was mailed to the Board of Appeals in Harrisburg in time to get there. It must physically arrive there on time to be timely filed. If a petition is not received on time, it will be denied by the Board of Appeals on jurisdictional grounds (*i.e.*, they do not have jurisdiction to act on it). A taxpayer who wants to avoid the risk of late filing should file the petition by hand with any Department of Revenue Office in Pennsylvania. Take two copies of the petition to the Department of Revenue Office and have them both date stamped at the office. Leave one (the one that is being filed) and retain the other as proof of timely filing. It is considered received by the Board on that date, regardless of when it reaches Harrisburg.

• *Petition contents*

A corporate petition for resettlement must fully state the reasons that the petitioner believes entitles it to resettlement [72 P.S. § 1102]. Petitions for resettlement must contain the following information:

(1) The business name and address of the corporation.

(2) The name and address of authorized representative.

(3) The box number appearing on certified copy of settlement.

(4) The year involved.

(5) The amount of tax settlement.

(6) The amount petitioner claims is correct.

(7) The mailing date of settlement notice.

(8) A photocopy of settlement.

(9) A concise statement of each item to which exception is taken with detailed explanation of pertinent reasons for disagreement.

(10) Whether or not a hearing is desired.

The petition must be signed, under oath, by a corporate officer authorized to so sign [Instructions for filing resettlement petition].

Form REV-65 BA

This is a petition for resettlement and/or other requested relief. This form, which provides space for all the required information, should be used to file for relief.

• *Letter of authority*

If a taxpayer is to be represented by an attorney, accountant, or other person, the name of the representative must appear on the petition. In addition, the Department of Revenue requires the filing of a letter on the taxpayer's letterhead stationery (called a "letter of authority"), executed by an official of the taxpayer, authorizing the tax

¶1203

practitioner to represent the taxpayer if (1) the name of the tax practitioner does not appear on the corporate tax report as its corporate tax representative or (2) the name of the tax practitioner who presents the petition for filing does not appear either on the corporate tax report named in the petition or within the body of the petition signed by an official of the taxpayer [61 Pa. Code § 151.3].

Payment of Additional Tax

Taxpayers are not required to pay the additional tax imposed by departmental settlement until all administrative remedies (*i.e.*, up through appeal to the Board of Finance and Revenue) have been exhausted. However, interest continues to accrue. See ¶ 4612 for explanation of interest period.

- *Action of the Board*

The Fiscal Code (72 P.S. § 1102) provides that it is the duty of the Department of Revenue to dispose of a petition for resettlement within six months of the filing date unless the resolution of one of its issues will be governed by litigation then pending before any court of competent jurisdiction. If the issue is being litigated, the taxpayer must request, and the Department may grant, deferment of consideration of the petition until the final judgment that affects the issue has been handed down [72 P.S. § 1102]. However, the Commonwealth Court has held that the requirement of § 1102 of the Fiscal Code that the Department (*i.e.*, the Board of Appeals) act within six months is not mandatory but merely directory and refused to rule in favor of a petitioner who sought to have an adverse ruling dismissed because the Board of Appeals took 10 months to dispose of his petition for resettlement [*Beneficial Finance Consumer Discount Co. v. Cmwlth.*, 548 A.2d 1334 (Pa.Commw. 1988)]. See ¶ 4604 for further explanation of the Board of Appeals.

- *Hearings*

After the Board receives a petition, it notifies the petitioner of its hearing date. The Board of Appeals holds hearings in Harrisburg, and Philadelphia. A taxpayer can request the hearing location it wants, and the request is usually granted unless it involves a legal issue. If the issue is complex, the hearing is in Harrisburg. Taxpayers or taxpayers' representatives (*e.g.*, attorney or accountant) may present oral arguments at the hearing.

Well-Drawn Petitions Advisable

Normally, hearings are conducted in a very informal manner and the Commonwealth does not have to maintain records of the proceedings. This means that, even though a taxpayer may present oral arguments, there is no substitute for a well-reasoned, well-drawn petition, with all arguments embodied in the body of the petition.

- *Intradepartmental handling*

After a petition for resettlement is received, a Department of Revenue representative prepares a brief for the hearing officer. The briefer may or may not be the hearing officer but usually is not. Nevertheless, the hearing officer will have learned the facts and issues in the petition before the hearing. All hearings involving corporate taxation matters are attended by at least one representative from the Department of Revenue and the Department of the Auditor General.

Remember the Communication Function

The reason a taxpayer petitions for resettlement is to get relief from taxes the taxpayer feels are not owed to the Commonwealth. Therefore, a taxpayer should do everything possible to ensure the relief sought. Make sure the hearing officer understands the arguments presented. Stay alert to the need to provide additional information. If the hearing officer goes back to Harrisburg without adequate information and asks for more, send it *promptly*. Since the hearing officer is familiar with the facts and issue of a taxpayer's case, the taxpayer does not need to belabor those points. It is critical, however, to provide any additional information the hearing officer may need.

- *Action on petition*

If a petition for resettlement is denied, the taxpayer receives a notice of the denial from the Board. Again, the critical date is the mailing date of the notice. If a petition is accepted, the taxpayer gets a notice of resettlement that indicates the relief granted. A taxpayer may be denied any relief or be granted a total (*i.e.*, petition accepted in full) or partial resettlement (*i.e.*, only part of the petition accepted). In either case, the taxpayer has 90 days from the mailing date of the notice from the Board of Appeals to file a petition for review with the Board of Finance and Revenue in Harrisburg [72 P.S. § 1103].

¶1204 Assessments

CAUTION! *Current Law*

Act 119 of 2006 (S.B. 993) introduced a new system of assessment and reassessment for corporate net income tax. Prior to January 1, 2008, the corporate taxes were "settled." They are now "assessed." Under prior law, all corporate returns were settled. Under the new law corporate taxes are assessed, and assessment is not mandatory, which means that not all returns will be assessed. The old law applies to settlements issued prior to January 1, 2008. Assessments issued after December 31, 2007, are governed by the new provisions [Act 119 of 2006 (S.B. 993), § 33.1]. Assessments are now governed by the provisions of § § 7407.1 through 7407.5. Reassessments are now governed by the provisions of Article XXVII of the Tax Reform Code and are discussed at ¶ 4604.

If the Department of Revenue determines that unpaid or unreported tax is due, the Department will issue an assessment under 72 P.S. § § 7407.1-7407.5. Such as assessment is not subject to the settlement procedure in the Fiscal Code [72 P.S. § 7407.1(a)].

- *Notice of assessment*

A notice and assessment and demand for payment, setting forth the basis of the assessment, will be mailed by to the taxpayer. If the assessment is for $300 or more, it will be sent via certified mail. The assessment is due upon receipt of the notice of assessment. Payment of the assessment is without prejudice to the right of the taxpayer to file a petition for reassessment in the manner prescribed by Article XXVII (discussed at ¶ 4604) [72 P.S. § 7407.1(b)].

- *Estimated assessment*

If a taxpayer fails to file a report, the Department of Revenue may issue an estimated assessment, based upon the records and information available or that may come into the Department's possession. If prior to the filing of a report the Department estimates that additional unpaid or unreported tax is due, the Department may issue additional assessments [72 P.S. § 7407.1(c)].

Notice: A notice of estimated assessment and demand for payment will be mailed by certified mail to the taxpayer. The assessment is due upon receipt of the notice of assessment. Payment of the estimated assessment does not eliminate the taxpayer's obligation to file a report [72 P.S. § 7407.1(d)].

Removal of estimated assessment: The Department will remove an estimated assessment within 90 days of the filing of a report and other information required to determine the tax due the Commonwealth. The Department may then issue an assessment. Any tax due the Commonwealth that is included in an estimated assessment retains its lien priority as of the date of the estimated settlement to the extent such amount is included with an assessment issued upon the review of the filed report [72 P.S. § 7407.1(f)]. A taxpayer has no right to appeal a notice of estimated assessment except as provided in 72 P.S. § 7407.1(f) [72 P.S. § 7407.1(e)].

• *Limitations on assessments*

In general, tax may be assessed within three (3) years after the date the report is filed [72 P.S. § 7407.3(a)]. A report that is filed before the last day prescribed for filing is deemed to have been filed on the last day [72 P.S. § 7407.3(f)].

Failure to file a report: Tax may be assessed at any time if the taxpayer fails to file a required report [72 P.S. § 7407.3(b)].

Filing of a fraudulent return: Tax may be assessed at any time if the taxpayer files a false or fraudulent return with intent to evade tax [72 P.S. § 7407.4(c)].

Department's dissatisfaction with its determination: if at any time within the specified time limitations, the Department is not satisfied with its determination of the taxpayer's liability, it may strike all, or any part of, a previously issued assessment or may issue additional assessments of tax [72 P.S. § 7407.3(d)].

Recovery of refunds or credits: The Department may file an assessment to recover any part or all of a refund or credit that was erroneously made or allowed within the later of (1) three (3) years of the granting of a refund or credit or (2) within the period in which an assessment could have been filed by the Department with respect to the taxable period for which the refund was granted [72 P.S. § 7407.3(e)].

• *Extension of limitation period*

If, before the limitation period has expired, a taxpayer has consented in writing to the extension of the period, the amount of tax due may be assessed at any time within the extended period. The extended period may be further extended by subsequent consents in writing made before the expiration of the extended period [72 P.S. § 7204.4].

• *Audit by auditor general and determination of tax*

The Department of the Auditor General has the power to do all of the following [72 P.S. § 7407.5(a)]:

(1) Audit and approve all determinations by the Department of Revenue of tax liability as reported by the taxpayer, including determinations resulting from a field audit, prior to the issuance by the Department of Revenue of a determination of the taxpayer's account.

(2) Review any tax report filed with the Department of Revenue, determine the amount of tax liability for the tax period covered by the report, and issue to the Department of Revenue for concurrence a determination of tax liability for the tax period.

1. Audit the procedures implemented by the Department of Revenue for the determination of tax liability or the issuance of an assessment, refund or credit, or other action taken by the Department of Revenue with regard to tax liability.

Concurrence of departments: upon the concurrence of the Department of Revenue and the Department of the Auditor General on the determination of tax liability, the Department will issue an assessment, a refund or a credit under § 1108 of the Fiscal Code) or take other appropriate action.

Failure of departments to concur: If the Department of Revenue and the Depart of the Auditor General fail to agree on a determination, the matter will be submitted to the Board of Finance and Revenue for decision. If the Board fails to reach a decision within three(3) months, the determination of the Department of Revenue automatically becomes valid [72 P.S. § 7407.5(c)].

¶1205 Jeopardy Assessments

If the Department of Revenue believes that the assessment or the collection of unpaid or unreported tax will be jeopardized in whole or in part by delay, it will issue a jeopardy assessment [72 P.S. § 7407.2(a)].

CAUTION! *Current Law*

The jeopardy assessment provisions discussed in this paragraph apply to assessments by the Department after December 31, 2007 [Act 119 of 2006 (S.B. 993), § 33(1)].

• *Termination of reporting period*

If the Department of Revenue believes that a tax liability is in jeopardy for any reason (e.g., taxpayer's leaving the Commonwealth, removing property from the Commonwealth, hiding, concealing property) unless action is brought without delay, the Department will declare the current tax period of the taxpayer immediately terminated. The Department will then issue a jeopardy assessment for the tax period declared terminated and for all prior tax periods, whether or not the time otherwise allowed by law for filing a report or paying the tax has expired [72 P.S. § 7407.2(b)].

• *Notice of jeopardy assessment*

A notice of jeopardy assessment and demand for payment must be mailed by certified mail to the taxpayer. The notice of jeopardy assessment must include the amount of the bond or other security required to stay collection of the assessment [72 P.S. § 7407.2(c)].

• *Collection of jeopardy assessment*

A jeopardy assessment is immediately due upon receipt of the notice of jeopardy assessment. Payment of the jeopardy assessment does not eliminate the taxpayer's obligation to file a report. If prior to the filing of a report the Department estimates that additional unpaid tax is due, it may issue additional jeopardy assessments or estimated assessments pursuant to 72 P.S. § 7407.1 (discussed above) [72 P.S. § 7407.2(d)].

A jeopardy assessment is immediately due and payable, and proceedings for collection may begin at once. The following apply:

(1) The collection of any part or all of a jeopardy assessment may be stayed, at any time before the assessment becomes final, by filing with the Department a bond or other security in amounts deemed necessary by the Department but not exceeding 120% of the tax for which the stay is desired [72 P.S. § 7407.2(e)(1)].

(2) Upon the filing of bond or other security the collection of the assessment amount covered by the bond or other security will be stayed. The taxpayer has the right to waive the stay at any time in respect of any part or all of the amount covered by the bond or other security. If the taxpayer waives any part of the amount covered by the bond or other security, the bond or other security will be proportionately reduced upon payment of the amount waived. If any portion of the jeopardy assessment is abated, the bond or other security will be proportionately reduced at the request of the taxpayer [72 P.S. § 7407.2(e)(2)].

• *Petition for reassessment of jeopardy assessment*

A taxpayer may prevent a jeopardy assessment from becoming final by filing a petition for reassessment with the Department of Revenue within 30 days after the mailing date of the notice of jeopardy assessment [72 P.S. § 7407.2(f)(1)].

CAUTION! Sole Method of Relief

Any determination made pursuant to a petition for reassessment of a jeopardy assessment is final and conclusive upon exhaustion of the appeal rights provided in 72 P.S. § 7407.2 and cannot be reviewed in any other proceeding [72 P.S. § 7407.2(g)]. Note that provisions for petition for reassessment of a jeopardy assessment are not included in the reassessment provisions of Article XXVII (discussed at ¶ 4604). Petitions for reassessment of jeopardy assessments are governed solely by 72 P.S. § 7407.2.

Issues to be addressed: The issues to be addressed in the review of the petition for reassessment of a jeopardy assessment include the following [72 P.S. § 7407.2(f)(1)]:

(1) Whether the making of the jeopardy assessment is reasonable under the circumstances.

(2) Whether the amount assessed as a result of the jeopardy assessment is appropriate under the circumstances.

Action of petition: The Department of Revenue must issue a decision and order disposing of a petition for reassessment of a jeopardy assessment within 60 days after the receipt of the petition. Notice of the Department's decision and order disposing of the petition will be mailed to the petitioner [72 P.S. § 7407.2(f)(2)].

Burden of proof: In an action involving the issue of whether the making of a jeopardy assessment is reasonable under the circumstances, the burden of proof is upon the Department of Revenue. In an action involving the issue of whether an amount assessed as a result of jeopardy assessment is appropriate under the circumstances, the burden of proof is upon the taxpayer [72 P.S. § 7407.2(h)].

Relief: If it is determined that the making of the jeopardy assessment is unreasonable or that the amount assessed is inappropriate, the assessment may be abated, the assessment may be redetermined in whole or in part, or the Department or the taxpayer may be directed to take other actions that may be appropriate [72 P.S. § 7407.2(f)(4)].

• *Judicial review*

A taxpayer may file a petition for review of the Department's decision and order in Commonwealth Court within 30 days after the following [72 P.S. § 7407.2(f)(3)]:

(1) The mailing date of the Department's notice of decision and order on a petition for reassessment of a jeopardy assessment.

(2) If the petition is not disposed of by the Department within 60 days after receipt, the 60th day following the date the petition was received by the Department.

¶ 1206 Petition for Review

• *Review by Board of Finance and Revenue*

In cases where a petition was filed with the Board of Appeals on or before December 29, 2017, an appeal to the Board of Finance and Revenue may be made by either the taxpayer or the Department of Revenue within 90 days after the mailing date of the decision of the Board of Appeals. In cases where a petition was filed with the Board of Appeals after December 29, 2017, an appeal to the Board of Finance and Revenue may be made within 60 days after the mailing date of the decision of the Board of Appeals. Petitions for review and procedures of the Board of Finance and Revenue are explained in detail at ¶ 4605.

• *Judicial review*

Either the taxpayer or the Commonwealth may, within 30 days, appeal the decision the Board of Finance and Revenue makes with respect to a petition for review or refund [210 Pa. Code Rule 1571]. For further explanation of the judicial review process, see ¶ 4607.

¶1207 Petition for Refund

A uniform three-year refund period for all taxes collected by the Department of Revenue took effect January 1, 1998 [72 P.S. § 10003.1]. However, in the case of an amount paid as a result of an assessment, determination, settlement, or appraisement, a petition for refund must be filed within six months of the mailing date of the notice of assessment, determination, settlement, or appraisement [72 P.S. § 10003.1(d)]. All petitions for refund, except Liquid Fuels Tax refunds (see ¶ 2602) are filed with the Department of Revenue (Board of Appeals). Filing for a refund does not affect the abatement of interest, additions, or penalties. [72 P.S. § 7253(b)]. An amended return does not constitute a petition for refund. *Quest Diagnostics Venture, LLC v. Commonwealth*, 2015 WL 3561310. In *Mission Funding Alpha v. Cmwlth.*, 173 A.3d 748 (Pa. 2017) the Pennsylvania Supreme Court ruled that in the case of a taxpayer who had paid its tax on the April 15 due date, but later filed its tax report in September, the three-year refund period began on the date on which the tax was required to be paid, not the date on which the tax report was filed. The taxpayer had made installment payments of tax during the year and paid the balance of its tax liability on April 15. The relevant refund statute required that a refund petition be filed within three years of actual payment of the tax, interest or penalty. 72 P.S. § 10003.1(a). The Court held that the actual payment of the tax means the date on which a payment is made with respect to a particular liability. Since the statute required payment on April 15th, that date began the refund period, notwithstanding that the report filed later stated the taxpayer's calculation of its liability. The taxpayer argued that until the report was filed, there was no tax amount due to the Department. Consequently, any payment on April 15th could not be considered to have been an actual payment of tax but instead was merely a deposit. The court rejected that argument (and the Commonwealth Court's reasoning) on the grounds that the statute by its terms required payment of tax liability on April 15th, and charged interest if the payment was late. Thus, statutory liability was imposed on April 15th.

¶1208 Additions, Penalties, and Interest

Pennsylvania imposes both penalties and additions to tax. An addition to tax is not a penalty. The distinction is important, because penalties cannot be deducted for federal purposes but additional taxes can. The following explanation indicates whether the "penalties" are penalties or addition.

• *Failure to file a report*

If the officers of a corporation neglect or refuse to file a timely corporate net income tax report, an *addition* (which does not bear interest) to the tax determined to be due is made, the amount of which is determined as follows [72 P.S. § 7403(d)]: 10% of the first $1,000 of tax; 5% of the next $4,000; and 1% of the amount over $5,000. For years beginning after December 31, 2013, the penalty for failure to file, or for a knowingly false report, is $500 plus 1% of any tax due over $25,000.

Federal/Commonwealth Difference

The Pennsylvania addition to tax will be assessed even if the tax has been timely paid.

• *Penalty*

In addition, the Fiscal Code (FC) provides for a $500 *penalty* for neglecting or refusing to file reports within 30 days of demand by the Department of Revenue [72 P.S. § 1703].

• *False report*

Knowingly filing a false return (on the part of the officers of a corporation) results in an *addition* to tax. This addition is equal to the addition for failure to file. See ¶ 4613 for explanation of petition for remission of penalties.

• *Failure to file a Report of Change*

The penalty for failure to timely file a Report of Change when a federal correction results in an increase in taxable income is $5 for every day of default, but the Department of Revenue may abate such penalty in whole or in part [72 P.S. § 7406(a)]. The Report of Change is explained at ¶ 921.

• *Underpayment of tentative tax*

There is an *addition* to tax for underpayment of tentative tax. This addition is 10% of the underpayment and bears interest from the date the annual or any installment payment of tentative tax was due [72 P.S. § 10003(e)].

• *Criminal penalties under Tax Reform Code*

The corporate net income tax law also provides for criminal penalties in addition to other penalties:

(1) Any person who fails to retain, as required, corporate net income tax records, is (upon conviction) guilty of a misdemeanor and subject to fine (up to $1,000) and prosecution costs or imprisonment (up to six months) or both [72 P.S. § 7410(a)].

(2) A person who willfully makes a false and fraudulent return of taxable income is (upon conviction) guilty of willful and corrupt perjury and subject to the punishment provided by law [72 P.S. § 7410(b)].

(3) A person who willfully fails, neglects, or refuses to file a report or pay tax or who refuses to permit Departmental examination of corporate records is (upon conviction) guilty of a misdemeanor and is subject to fine (up to $1,000) and costs of prosecution, or imprisonment (up to six months), or both [72 P.S. § 7410(c)].

• *Criminal penalties under the Fiscal Code*

The Fiscal Code also provides for criminal penalties for certain tax violations:

(1) *Intentional failure of corporate officers to make reports:* If the officer(s) of a corporation intentionally neglect or refuse to file reports as required by law, for any two successive tax years, they are (upon conviction) guilty of a misdemeanor and subject to fine ($500), or imprisonment (up to one year), or both [72 P.S. § 1704].

(2) *Repeated, unexcused default:* If the officer(s) of a corporation neglect or refuse to file reports for three successive years, unless excused from so doing by the Department of Revenue, the Department must report that fact to the Governor, who may (by proclamation) revoke its charter (in the case of a domestic corporation) or declare a forfeiture of its right to do business in Pennsylvania (in the case of a foreign corporation) [72 P.S. § 1704].

¶1209 Settled and Unsettled Credits

Old Law

This paragraph discusses credits within the framework of settled taxes. After December 31, 2007, there are no longer any settled taxes. The corporate taxes are no longer settled; they are now assessed (see ¶1204). This paragraph refers to settlements that were made prior to January 1, 2008.

The following is a discussion of settled and unsettled credits as they refer to settled taxes (*e.g.*, corporate net income tax, capital stock/franchise tax, corporate loans tax). In this sense, a credit refers to an overpayment that results in a "credit balance" in the corporate taxpayer's tax account. For explanation of credits against the tax itself (*e.g.*, research and development credit, coal degasification credit).

• *Definitions*

An "assignment" is the sale or exchange of a settled credit by a taxpayer (assignor) to another taxpayer (assignee) to be applied to an assignee's tax debit. A "settled credit" is a surplus that has been determined to be an overpayment upon settlement by the Department. A "transfer" is the movement within a taxpayer's account against a tax debit of the same taxpayer. An "unsettled credit" is a surplus resulting from an apparent overpayment as a result of either tentative or regular tax payment prior to settlement. A "tax debit" includes tax principal, penalty and interest. "Conditional statutory credits" are those subject to special conditions. They may be used subject to the special conditions or limitations. An example is the Neighborhood Assistance Tax Credit (see ¶1005) [61 Pa. Code § 151.21].

• *Order of credits*

In the absence of instructions by the taxpayer to the contrary or any law or regulation to the contrary, tax credits are applied to the penalties, legal costs, interest, and tax principal, in that order, of each tax debit in the taxpayer's account, in the chronological order in which the tax debits arose [61 Pa. Code § 151.24]. A tax debit includes tax principal, penalty, and interest [61 Pa. Code § 151.21].

Compare to Taxpayers' Bill of Rights

Note that this order of credits differs from the order of application of payments established by the Taxpayers' Bill of Rights. See ¶4606.

• *Transfer, assignment, and refund of unsettled credits*

Unsettled credits are available for transfer to corporation tax debits within the taxpayer's account when the corporate tax report is received by the Department of Revenue. If all tax obligations have been paid, unsettled credits may be used to pay a tax or other Commonwealth claim, may be refunded, or may be assigned to another person. A transfer of an unsettled credit is not prohibited by the possibility of a subsequent resettlement or account adjustment of a clerical mathematical error by the Department [61 Pa. Code § 151.22(a)].

• *Transfer, assignment, and refund of settled credits*

Except as otherwise provided by law or regulations, any settled corporation tax credits may be transferred in payment of any other tax(es) paid or payable into the General Fund. Credits of other taxes payable into the General Fund may also be used to satisfy corporation tax liabilities [61 Pa. Code § 151.22(b)(1)]. A settled credit may not be assigned to another corporation unless the taxpayer's outstanding tax credits are offset by sufficient credits to satisfy the debits and other obligations due the Commonwealth by the taxpayer [61 Pa. Code § 151.22(b)(2)]. A taxpayer may receive a refund of a settled credit if outstanding tax debits are offset by sufficient credits to satisfy the debits and other Commonwealth obligations have been paid [61 Pa. Code § 151.22(b)(3)]. A settled credit that is the subject of a Petition for Cash Refund cannot be transferred to taxes other than corporation taxes and cannot be assigned to another corporation while the proceedings are pending [61 Pa. Code § 151.22(b)(4)].

• *Taxes paid or payable into the General Fund*

These include personal income taxes, cigarette and beverage taxes, sales and use taxes, inheritance taxes, corporate net income taxes, and capital stock/franchise taxes. For applicability to other taxes, see 61 Pa. Code § 151.22(b)(1).

• *Procedure for transfer by the taxpayer*

A taxpayer may direct the Department of Revenue to transfer its credits (settled or unsettled) to present or anticipated debits by submitting a letter (signed by an authorized representative of the corporation) with the following information: type, year, and amount of credit to be transferred and the debit or debits to which it is to be applied.

• *Procedure for transfer by the Department*

The Department of Revenue may transfer credits (settled or unsettled) within the taxpayer's account. The Department will make the transfer and send the taxpayer a statement of specifically how the credits were applied. The taxpayer may object to the proposed transfer within 30 days of receipt of the statement. If the Department determines that the objection is proper, the transfer will be reversed [61 Pa. Code § 151.22(c)(2)].

• *Procedure for assignment*

To assign a credit (settled or unsettled) to another taxpayer (whether or not a subsidiary corporation), a taxpayer assignor must submit an Assignment of Tax Credit Form signed by an authorized representative to the Department. This application is deemed to authorize the Department to review the assignor's account, transfer any credits necessary, and make other determinations necessary to compute assignor's current available settled or unsettled balance. The Department then will apply the credit assigned (but not to exceed the available balance) in accordance with assignee's instructions, or, in the absence of instructions, in the manner provided by law and regulations (see "Order of credits," above), and will confirm the assignment in writing to both parties [61 Pa. Code § 151.22(c)(3)].

• *Procedure for refund*

To obtain a refund of a credit (settled or unsettled) the taxpayer must submit to the Department a letter (signed by an authorized representative) identifying the refunds requested and containing the following statements: (1) that the taxpayer has no obligations due to the Commonwealth and (2) that the taxpayer is deemed to authorize the Department to review the taxpayer's account, make necessary credit transfers, or make any determination necessary to compute the taxpayer's current available settled and unsettled credit balance [61 Pa. Code § 151.22(c)(4)].

• *Effective date of payment resulting from application of credit*

A tax credit applied in payment of a tax debit is credited as of the postmark date of the payment from which the credit originated [61 Pa. Code § 151.23].

¶1209

PART V

CAPITAL STOCK TAX, FRANCHISE TAX, AND CORPORATE LOANS TAX

>>> NOTE: Chapters 13—16 explain the capital stock and franchise taxes. Chapter 17 explains the corporate loans tax.

In This Part

CHAPTER 13

VALUATION, TAX RATE, AND TAXABLE AND EXEMPT CORPORATIONS

Introduction

¶1301	History, Sources of Authority, and Topics of Interest
¶1302	Administration
¶1303	Definitions

Base and Tax Rate

¶1305	Imposition, Base, and Rates
¶1306	Capital Stock Value
¶1307	Average Net Income
¶1308	Net Worth

Taxable and Exempt Corporations

¶1310	Corporations Subject to Tax
¶1311	Corporations Exempt from Tax

Accounting

¶1315	Accounting Periods and Methods

Reports

¶1320	Annual Reports
¶1321	Estimated Tax Payments

Payment—Extensions

¶1325	Payment of Tax
¶1326	Transfer of Credits
¶1327	Extensions of Time
¶1328	Recordkeeping Requirements
¶1329	Credits Against the Tax

INTRODUCTION

Caution: There is No Capital Stock/Franchise Tax for tax years beginning after 12/31/15

Unless extended, the capital stock/foreign franchise tax will end on December 31, 2015.

¶1301 History, Sources of Authority, and Topics of Interest

• *History of the capital stock tax*

Pennsylvania's first capital stock tax was passed in 1840 [Act of June 11, 1840, P.L. 612]. It imposed a tax on the capital stock of domestic corporations that paid dividends. Corporations paying no dividends were not taxed. In 1868, the capital stock tax was extended to foreign corporations [Act of May 1, 1868, P.L. 108]. In 1879, the tax was codified, and the present capital stock tax began to take shape [Act of June 7, 1879, P.L. 112]. In 1891, the dividend feature of the tax was abandoned (*i.e.*, it was levied whether or not a corporation paid dividends) [Act of June 8, 1891, P.L. 229].

By this time, the capital stock tax was almost in its present form. However, it applied to both domestic and foreign corporations. This created problems. The courts have repeatedly held that the capital stock tax is a property tax. See, for example, *Cmwlth. v. Standard Oil Co.*, 101 Pa. 119 (1882)]. In *Standard Oil*, the court ruled that Pennsylvania could impose a property tax on a foreign corporation only insofar as it brings the property in state in the transaction of its business. Since the situs of intangible property regardless of its physical location is in a taxpayer's domiciliary state, the result was that many foreign corporations conducting a large portion of their business in Pennsylvania paid little or no capital stock tax simply by owning little or no tangible property there. In 1935, the General Assembly solved this problem. The capital stock tax was applied only to domestic corporations, while a franchise tax was imposed on foreign corporations [Act of May 16, 1935, No. 86, P.L. 184].

• *History of the franchise tax*

The franchise tax on foreign corporations is not a property tax. It is a tax on the value of the franchise or right to do business in Pennsylvania. See, for example, *Cmwlth. v. Quaker Oats Co.*, 38 A.2d 325 (Pa. 1944), and *Cmwlth. v. Columbia Gas & Electric Corp.*, 8 A.2d 404 (Pa. 1939). The franchise tax continued to be based on the value of the capital stock of foreign corporations, but since it is not a property tax, previously unreachable assets could be included in the tax base. The franchise tax law also provided a three-factor apportionment formula for foreign corporations instead of the domestic corporations' one-factor apportionment formula.

• *Sources of authority*

The capital stock and franchise tax provisions are part of the Tax Reform Code of 1971, as amended [72 P.S. §§ 7101—10003.9]. Certain administrative provisions pertaining to these taxes are part of the Fiscal Code [Act of April 9, 1929, P.L. 343; 72 P.S. § 1 *et seq.*], and regulations pertaining to these taxes are found in Title 61 of the Pennsylvania Code. See ¶ 101 for an example of a citation to the regulations. The capital stock and franchise tax laws incorporate, by reference, the provisions of the corporate net income tax with respect to the following: reports and payment of tax, administration and enforcement, settlement and resettlement, recordkeeping, and penalties. These provisions are found in Parts III, IV, V, VI, and VII of Article IV of the Tax Reform Code. The Tax Reform Code also provides for the use of the corporate net income three-factor apportionment factor, with modifications, in the computation of capital stock/franchise tax liabilities [72 P.S. § 7602(a), (b)].

• *Minimum tax*

A capital stock/franchise minimum tax in the amount of $300 was imposed for tax years 1991 through 1998. Effective January 1, 1999, the minimum tax was decreased to $200. For tax years beginning on or after January 1, 2000, the minimum tax has been eliminated.

• *Phaseout of the capital stock/franchise tax*

The capital stock/franchise tax rate was originally scheduled to decline year by year until the tax was phased out at the end of 2008. Since then, the phaseout of the tax has been delayed until 2016 and the decrease in the tax rate over the period of the phaseout has also been adjusted. See ¶1305 for discussion of the capital stock/ franchise tax rates and phaseout.

• *Apportionment formulas*

Another problem that existed with respect to the capital stock tax was that domestic corporations that conducted very little business in Pennsylvania but owned a lot of intangible assets paid a capital stock tax that was very large compared to their Pennsylvania business activity. In 1967, the General Assembly amended the capital stock tax to give domestic corporations the ability to elect the three-factor apportionment formula used by foreign corporations [Act of October 19, 1967, P.L. 446]. This led to the question of whether foreign corporations could also elect the one-factor apportionment formula statutorily available only to domestic corporations. In 1982, the Pennsylvania Supreme Court said yes [*Gilbert Associates, Inc. v. Cmwlth.*, 447 A.2d 944 (Pa. 1982)]. In 1983, amending legislation gave foreign corporations the opportunity to elect the one-factor formula [Act of December 23, 1983, No. 90].

In 1971, the capital stock and franchise taxes were rewritten and became Article VI of the Tax Reform Code of 1971 [Act of March 4, 1971, P.L. 6, No. 2, Article VI]. The current capital stock and franchise taxes are governed by the provisions of this act, as amended.

• *Manufacturing exemption*

On November 30, 2001, the Pennsylvania Supreme Court ruled that the franchise tax is not a compensatory tax and that the manufacturing exemption is therefore unconstitutional because it violates the Commerce Clause. The Court further ruled that the unconstitutional manufacturing exemption provision is severable and directed the Commonwealth to provide a retrospective remedy consistent with its opinion [*PPG Industries, Inc.*, 709 A.2d 261 (Pa. 2001)]. See ¶1601.

In December 1999, new legislation was enacted that, for taxable years beginning after December 31, 1998, and before January 1, 2001, excluded property and payroll from the numerators of the property and payroll factors if they relate to manufacturing with respect to whether the production operations occur in Pennsylvania or in other states [Act 63-1999].

In May 2000, the General Assembly enacted legislation that repealed the sunset legislation of Act 63, restructured the manufacturing exemption, and changed the formula for the manufacturing exemption for taxable years beginning after December 31, 1999 [Act 23-2000]. This exclusion was later made permanent [§7, S.B. 2, 2000 Session].

¶1302 Administration

The capital stock and franchise taxes are administered by the Department of Revenue, Harrisburg, Pennsylvania [72 P.S. §7602]. The Bureau of Tax and Revenue Audits of the Department of the Auditor General reviews and approves all settlements and resettlements.

• *Appeals*

The Board of Appeals of the Department of Revenue hears taxpayers' petitions for resettlement. A taxpayer who is not satisfied with the decision of the Board may petition the Board of Finance and Revenue to review the Board of Appeals' decision. Appeals from the Board of Finance and Revenue are made to the Commonwealth Court of Pennsylvania. Appeals of decisions of the Commonwealth Court may be made to the Pennsylvania Supreme Court.

• *Procedures, enforcement, and penalties*

Parts III, IV, V, VI, and VII of Article IV (corporate net income laws) are incorporated by reference into Article VI (capital stock/franchise laws) in so far as they are applicable to the capital stock/franchise tax [72 P.S. § 7603].

Note that Part I of Article IV (Definitions) and Part II of Article IV (Imposition of Tax) are not incorporated by reference.

• *Immediate assessment, settlement, or collection to prevent tax avoidance*

The Department of Revenue may make an immediate assessment or settlement of (1) sales and use tax; (2) corporate net income tax; or (3) capital stock/franchise tax and any interest or penalty due if the Department finds that without immediate action the tax, interest, or penalty due will be in jeopardy of not being collected because the taxpayer intends to do any of the following without paying the tax, interest, or penalty due [72 P.S. § 10003.14(a)]:

(a) Immediately leave Pennsylvania.

(b) Remove property from Pennsylvania used in activities that are taxable in Pennsylvania.

(c) Discontinue doing business in Pennsylvania.

(d) Do any other act that would prejudice or render ineffective (in whole or in part) proceedings to assess, settle, or collect any tax, interest, or penalty due.

Immediate assessment is discussed in more detail at ¶ 4603.

• *Communication function*

The communication function (the process of supplying information to the Department of Revenue) is a critical function. It cannot be overstressed. The communication function is explained at ¶ 4608.

• *Petition for refund*

The petition for refund for capital stock/franchise tax purposes is the same as that for corporate net income tax purposes.

¶1303 Definitions

In order to provide a guide to important capital stock/franchise tax terms, a glossary is provided in this paragraph for quick reference. All definitions are contained in 72 P.S. § 601 unless otherwise indicated. Some definitions specific only to certain situations are defined in context when discussing the situation.

• *Average net income*

"Average net income" means the sum of the net income or loss for each of the current and immediately preceding four years, divided by five. See ¶ 1307 for discussion of "average net income."

• *Capital stock*

"Capital stock" means the capital stock, certificates, memberships, and all other interests in a domestic or foreign entity.

¶1303

- *Capital stock value*

  "Capital stock value" means the amount computed pursuant to the statutory formula prescribed by 72 P.S. § 7601(a). This formula is discussed at ¶ 1306.

- *Corporation*

  The word "corporation" includes the following entities [72 P.S. § 7601(a)]:

  (1) A corporation.

  (2) A joint-stock association.

  (3) A business trust.

  (4) A limited liability company. This clause excludes a restricted professional company that is subject to 15 Pa.C.S. Ch. 89, Subch. L (relating to restricted professional companies).

  (5) Any entity that, for federal income tax purposes, is classified as a corporation.

  (6) A captive REIT (*i.e.*, a business trust that is a real estate investment trust as defined in IRC § 856 more than 50% of the voting power or value of the beneficial interests or shares of which are owned (directly or indirectly) by a single corporation that is not (a) a real estate investment trust as defined in IRC § 856; (b) a qualified real estate investment trust subsidiary under IRC § 856(i); (c) a regulated financial institution as defined by 72 P.S. § 7401(6); or (d) formed as a holding company, subsidiary or affiliate of a regulated financial institution prior to December 1, 2003).

  (7) A captive QRS (*i.e.*, a business trust that is a qualified real estate investment trust subsidiary under IRC § 856(i) owned, directly or indirectly, by a real estate investment trust as defined in IRC § 856 more than 50% of the voting power or value of the beneficial interest or shares of which are owned or controlled (directly or indirectly) by a single corporation that is not (a) a real estate investment trust as defined in IRC § 856; (b) a qualified real estate investment trust subsidiary under IRC § 856(i); (c) a regulated financial institution as defined by 72 P.S. § 7401(6); or (d) formed as a holding company, subsidiary or affiliate of a regulated financial institution prior to December 1, 2003.

  Not a corporation: The term "corporation" for Pennsylvania capital stock/ franchise purposes does not include any of the following [72 P.S. § 7601(b)]:

  (1) A business trust (a) that qualifies as a real estate investment trust under IRC § 856 or (b) that is a qualified real estate investment trust subsidiary under IRC § 856(i).

  (2) A business trust (a) that qualifies as a regulated investment company under IRC § 851 and (b) that is registered with the United States Securities and Exchange Commission under 15 U.S.C. § 80a-1 or a related business trust that confines its activities in Pennsylvania to the maintenance, administration, and management of intangible investments and activities of regulated investment companies.

  (3) A corporation, trust, or other entity that is an exempt organization under IRC § 501.

  (4) A corporation, trust, or other entity that is organized as a not-for-profit under the laws of Pennsylvania or any other that (a) would qualify as an exempt organization under IRC § 501; (b) would qualify as a homeowners association as defined by IRC § 528(c); (c) is a membership organization subject to the federal limitations on deductions from taxable income under IRC § 277 (but only if no pecuniary gain or profit inures to any member or related entity from the membership organization); or (d) a nonstock commodity or a nonstock stock exchange (applicable retroactively to taxable years beginning after December 31, 1997).

¶ 1303

Corporation Tax Bulletin 2007-01

A Limited Liability Company or a Business Trust that is owned by an exempt IRC § 501 organization may be exempt from the tax even though it has not separately obtained federal tax exempt status. To qualify as a not-for-profit entity the Articles of Organization, Trust Agreement, or By-Laws must specifically state that the Limited Liability Company or Business Trust is organized as a not-for-profit entity and limit the activity of the entity to those of a not-for-profit or tax exempt organization. A copy of the Articles of Organization or Trust Agreement and a copy of the By-Laws must be provided to the Bureau of Corporation Taxes.

---

(5) A cooperative agricultural association subject to 15 Pa.C.S. Ch. 75.

(6) A business trust if the trust is all of the following: (a) created or managed by an entity that is subject to the bank and trust companies shares tax or the mutual thrift institutions tax; (b) created and managed for the purpose of facilitating the securitization of intangible assets; and (c) classified as a partnership for federal income tax purposes.

• *Department*

"Department" means the Pennsylvania Department of Revenue.

• *Domestic entity*

A "domestic entity" is any corporation organized under the laws of Pennsylvania.

• *Foreign entity*

A "foreign entity" is any corporation organized by or under the laws of any jurisdiction other than Pennsylvania that exercises (whether in its own name or through any individual, association, business trust, corporation, joint venture, limited liability company, limited partnership, partnership, or other entity) any of the following privileges:

(1) Doing business in Pennsylvania.

(2) Carrying on activities in Pennsylvania, including solicitation.

(3) Having capital or property employed or used in Pennsylvania.

(4) Owning property in Pennsylvania.

• *Holding company*

A corporation is a "holding company" if (1) at least 90% of its gross income for the taxable year is derived from dividends, interest, gains from the sale, exchange, or other disposition of stock or securities and the rendition of management and administrative services to subsidiary corporations; and (2) at least 60% of the actual value of the total assets consists of stock securities or indebtedness of subsidiary corporations.

• *Net worth*

The "net worth" of an entity is the sum of its issued and outstanding capital stock, surplus, and undivided profits as per books set forth for the close of such tax year on the income tax return filed by the entity with the federal government, or if no such return is made, as would have been set forth had such return been made. If this results in a value of net worth that is greater than twice or less than one-half of the net worth that would have been calculated as of the first day of the current year, net worth for the current year is the average of beginning net worth and ending net worth. Net worth is discussed in more detail at ¶ 1308.

¶ 1303

● *Processing*

"Processing" means engaging in specified activities as a business enterprise. See ¶ 1603 for discussion of "processing."

● *Research and development (R&D)*

The term "research and development" means the activities relating to the discovery of new and the refinement of known substances, products, processes, theories and ideas, but not including activities directed primarily to the accumulation or analysis of commercial, financial, or mercantile data.

● *Student loan assets*

The term "student loan assets" includes the following assets:

(1) Student loan notes.

(2) Federal, state, or private subsidies or guarantees of student loans.

(3) Instruments that represent a guarantee of debt, certificates, or other securities issued by an entity created for the securitization of student loans, or by a trustee on its behalf.

(4) Contract rights to acquire or dispose of student loans and interest rate swap agreements related to student loans.

(5) Interests in or debt obligations of other student loan securitization trusts or entities.

(6) Cash or cash equivalents representing reserve funds or payments on or with respect to student loan notes, the securities issued by an entity created for the securitization of student loans or the other student loan related assets. Solely for purposes of this definition, "cash or cash equivalents" shall include direct obligations of the U.S. Treasury Department; obligations of federal agencies, which obligations represent the full faith and credit of the United States; investment grade debt obligations or commercial paper; deposit accounts; federal funds and banker's acceptances; prefunded municipal obligations; money market instruments; and money market funds.

● *Subsidiary corporation*

A corporation is a "subsidiary" corporation if a majority of its total issued and outstanding shares of voting stock are owned by the taxpayer corporation directly or through one or more intervening subsidiary corporations.

BASE AND TAX RATE

¶1305 Imposition, Base, and Rates

The Pennsylvania capital stock tax is a *property* tax imposed on the capital stock value of domestic corporations [72 P.S. § 7602]. The Pennsylvania franchise tax is a *privilege* tax imposed on the capital stock value of foreign corporations doing business, carrying on activities, or employing or using capital or property in Pennsylvania [72 P.S. § 7601(a)]. Corporations subject to tax are discussed in ¶ 1310, and exempt corporations are discussed at ¶ 1311. Holding companies and regulated investment companies are subject to special rules. See ¶ 1505. Shares of stock in corporations that are subject to the capital stock/franchise tax are not subject to the personal property tax.

● *Imposition of capital stock/franchise tax*

A company subject to the capital stock/franchise tax must (1) determine the total value of its capital stock (called "valuation") (discussed in this chapter); (2) determine its taxable assets (called "allocation") (see Chapter 14); (3) determine the taxable portion of its total capital stock value (called "apportionment") (see Chapter 15); and (4) apply the applicable mill rate to its taxable capital stock value (rates discussed below).

- *Tax rates*

The capital stock/franchise tax is imposed on the capital stock value (see below of a corporation. The capital stock/franchise tax rates for years beginning in 1971 and thereafter are as follows [72 P.S. § 7602(h)]:

Taxable Year	Regular Rate	Surtax	Total Rat
1/1/05 — 12/31/05	5.99 mills	0	5.99 mill
1/1/06 — 12/31/06	4.89 mills	0	4.89 mill
1/1/07 — 12/31/07	3.89 mills	0	3.89 mill
1/1/08 — 12/31/08	2.89 mills	0	2.89 mill
1/1/09 — 12/31/09	1.89 mills	0	2.89 mill
1/1/10 — 12/31/10	0.89 mills	0	2.89 mill
1/1/11 — 12/31/11	2.89 mills	0	2.89 mill
1/1/12 — 12/31/12	1.89 mills	0	1.89 mill
1/1/13 — 12/31/13	0.89 mills	0	0.89 mill
1/1/14 — 12/31/14	0.67 mills	0	0.67 mill
1/1/15 — 12/31/15	0.45 mills	0	0.45 mill

Phaseout Modified

The capital stock/franchise tax was originally planned to be completely phased out at the end of 2008 through a series of rate reductions. The phaseout is continued but at a slower rate, and the end of the phase-out period has been extended to December 31, 2015 [72 P.S. § 7607].

- *Minimum tax*

For tax years beginning on or after January 1, 2000, the capital stock/franchise minimum tax has been eliminated.

Computation of Tax for Short Taxable Years

- *Proration*

If a corporation files a return for a short taxable year (doing business in Pennsylvania for less than one year), the tax due is prorated on the basis of (1 proration of tax on a per day basis or (2) proration of the property factor, depending on the circumstances (the payroll or sales factors may not be prorated) [61 Pa. Code § 155.28(b)]. This applies to both first-year and last-year companies. The tax due can be prorated only when all three factors are derived 100% from the Commonwealth The proration of the property factor involves an adjustment to the numerator of the property factor (*i.e.,* the average value of property in Pennsylvania). The denominator (*i.e.,* the average value of property everywhere) is not adjusted. See Chapter 15 for an explanation of property factors and apportionment. See below for a discussion o capital stock value.

Short Tax Year Example Computations

The examples below (which are based on examples in Pennsylvania Regulation § 155.28(b), 61 Pa. Code § 155.28(b)) count the first day of operation (*e.g.,* July 1, September 1) as a day of operation in the computations. Also, fractions are converted to decimal fractions and carried to six decimal places, as required by the instructions to the corporate tax forms.

- *First-year companies*

The method of proration of tax for first year of a company's operation in Pennsylvania depends on the relationship between the time of doing business in Pennsylvania and the time of doing business outside Pennsylvania.

Doing business less than a year in Pennsylvania, more than a year outside: The tax on a company doing business inside Pennsylvania for less than one year, but outside Pennsylvania for more than one year, is prorated on the basis of the property factor, unless all three factors are 100% Commonwealth (then the tax due is prorated). The property factor is prorated by adjusting the numerator (*i.e.*, property in Pennsylvania) by the ratio of the number of days of operation in Pennsylvania to the number of days in the year.

Caution: New Apportionment Formula

When considering the examples below, one should keep in mind that under the new apportionment formula, the property or payroll factors will not include any property or payroll attributable to manufacturing, processing, research or development activities (whether within or without of Pennsylvania).

Example 1: TJB Corporation is a calendar-year North Carolina corporation that has been in existence for more than one year but that has been subject to the Pennsylvania franchise tax for less than one year (90 days) during 2001. The average value of its property in Pennsylvania is $80,000, and the average value of its property everywhere is $150,000. The numerator of the property factor is $19,726 ($80,000 × 90/365 days). The tax would not be otherwise prorated.

Example 2: If all three apportionment factors (property, sales, and payroll) of TJB Corporation (see Example 1, above) were 100% Commonwealth, the tax due, and not the property factor, would be prorated on the basis of days of doing business in Pennsylvania (*i.e.*, the tax due would be multiplied by 90/365).

Doing business in and out of Pennsylvania for less than one year: If a corporation has been doing business outside Pennsylvania for the same period that it has been doing business in Pennsylvania (and that period is less than one year), the tax due is prorated on the basis of days doing business during the year.

Example: If TJB Corporation (see above) were incorporated on July 1 but did not conduct business anywhere until August 1 (when it began doing business in both North Carolina and Pennsylvania), the property factor would not be prorated; the tax would be prorated on the basis of days of operation during the year (153/365).

Doing business less than one year both in and outside of Pennsylvania, but for less time in Pennsylvania than outside Pennsylvania: If a corporation has been doing business outside Pennsylvania for less than one year but has been subject to Pennsylvania taxation for a shorter time than it has done business outside Pennsylvania, both the property factor and the tax due are prorated *unless* all Pennsylvania factors are 100%, in which case the tax due is prorated on the basis of days of operation *in* Pennsylvania. The numerator of the property factor is prorated on the basis of days of operation in Pennsylvania and then the tax due is prorated on the basis of days of operation everywhere.

Example 1: Stephens Corporation (a calendar-year corporation) began doing business outside Pennsylvania on July 1, 2001, and became subject to the Pennsylvania franchise tax on September 1, 2001. The average value of its property in Pennsylvania is $180,000, and the average value of property everywhere is $1,000,000. The numerator of the property factor is $60,164 ($180,000 × 122/365 days). The tax due (using the prorated property factor) would be prorated on the basis of total days in operation both inside and outside of Pennsylvania ((Tax due) × (184/365)).

Example 2: If Stephens Corporation (above) incorporated on July 1 but did not transact business anywhere until September 1, the numerator of the property tax would not be prorated. The tax due would be prorated for the Commonwealth period only (September 1—December 31), a period of 122 days (*i.e.*, multiply the tax due by 122/365).

Example 3: If Stephens Corporation (above) reported 100% Commonwealth factors, the numerator of the property factor would not be prorated and the tax due would be prorated by multiplying the tax due by the Commonwealth fraction (122/365).

• *Last-year companies*

A corporation that ceases doing business everywhere prorates its tax due on a per-day basis. A corporation that ceases doing business in Pennsylvania but continues operations elsewhere prorates the numerator of its property factor.

¶1306 Capital Stock Value

• *Fixed computation formula*

Pennsylvania uses a statutory formula for the computation of capital stock value. This fixed formula replaces the former, more subjective valuation method in place prior to 1984. If a taxpayer's computations are accurate, the valuation determined under the fixed formula will not be challenged. See ¶1204 for an explanation of resettlement. The doctrines of multiformity (see ¶1412) and unrelated assets (see ¶1420) continue to be available to taxpayers under the fixed formula. The statutory formula is as follows:

> [T]he product of one-half times the sum of the average net income [defined below] capitalized at the rate of nine and one-half percent plus seventy-five percent of net worth [defined below], from which product shall be subtracted one hundred sixty thousand dollars ($160,000), the algebraic equivalent of which is: (0.5 × (average net income ÷ 0.095) + ((0.75)(net worth))) – $160,000 [72 P.S. § 7601(a)].

> *Example:* Harrison Corporation (a domestic corporation) has an average net income of $114,000 and a net worth of $1,500,000. Its 2010 capital stock value is $1,037,500, computed as follows: (0.5 × (($114,000 ÷ 0.095) + (0.75 × 1,500,000))) – $160,000 = $1,002,500.

• *Certain automobile clubs*

Effective for taxable years beginning after December 31, 1997, the capital stock value of an automobile club is limited to the value attributed to the conduct of an insurance business or of a travel agency business [72 P.S. § 10003.13(b)]. See below for definitions of these terms. For capital stock/franchise tax purposes, an automobile club is not considered a membership organization subject to federal limitations on deductions from taxable income under IRC § 277.

Note: Similar provisions also apply to the taxable income of automobile clubs. See ¶1001.

Definition of terms: "Automobile club" is a nonprofit corporation, trust, or other entity whose membership is open to the general public and that provides services and conducts activities on behalf of its members [72 P.S. § 10003.13(d)]. These services include (1) motor vehicle registration, title transfer and license application, and renewal services, (2) motor vehicle travel assistance (*e.g.*, road maps, trip itineraries, tour guides, emergency roadside assistance), (3) promotion of the development and provision of safe and convenient motor vehicle travel conditions, services, and facilities, (4) promotion of the construction, maintenance, and use of efficient, adequate, and safe highway systems, and (5) education of motorists and the traveling public in the principles of traffic and motor vehicle safety and related matters.

"Insurance business" is the conduct of the business of insurance by the automobile club, or a subsidiary or affiliate thereof, in the capacity of an insurance company, association, or exchange, insurance agency or brokerage as these terms are defined in The Insurance Department Act of 1921 [Act of May 17, 1921 (P.L. 780, No. 285)].

"Travel agency business" is the arrangement, in exchange for a fee, commission, or salary, of vacation or travel packages or services, sightseeing tours, travel reservations or accommodations, tickets for domestic or foreign travel by air, rail, ship, bus, or other mode of transportation, or hotel or other accommodations.

¶1306

- *Circularity problem with fixed formula*

This fixed formula creates problems in computation because the capital stock tax, which is a function of capital stock value, is deductible for federal income tax purposes and is, therefore, a component of both net income and net worth. This leads to a circular reference (*i.e.,* capital stock value is defined in terms of itself). Theoretically, you must use simultaneous equations to compute the value accurately. However, in practice, most taxpayers accrue (*i.e.,* estimate) the capital stock tax to use for this purpose and then adjust the next year's accrual for any over-or under-accrual of the current year.

- *IRC § 338 transactions*

In computing the capital stock value of a target corporation on a deemed sale report, actual net worth as of the close of that day is used. In computing average net income on a one-day deemed sale report, the average net income for the period ending immediately prior to the acquisition date is used [61 Pa. Code § 153.81(d)(2)]. See ¶ 1307 for treatment of average net income in § 338 transactions.

- *Settled capital stock value*

Technically, these taxes are self-assessed (*i.e.,* a company values its own capital stock and files annual reports based on its valuation). However, *every* capital stock/ franchise tax return is settled by the Department of Revenue. A settlement is in essence a desk audit performed at the Department of Revenue and reviewed at the Auditor General's office. However, a settlement does not preclude a field audit, which can be conducted before, after, or during the settlement process. The Department notifies the taxpayer of its settlement decision, indicating that the return is accepted as filed or that the Department has revised computations and adjusted the amount of tax due. If you are not satisfied with your settlement, you can petition for a resettlement. For more details, see Chapter 46 on "Procedures, Protests, and Appeals."

Allocation (Chapter 14) and apportionment (Chapter 15) and the issue of what constitutes doing business in Pennsylvania (see ¶ 1310) are common sources of adjustments at settlement. The Department checks the fixed formula for such things as accuracy of computation and correctness of the net worth figure (*e.g.,* use consolidated net worth where appropriate). The accuracy of the earnings figure is also checked.

Settlement Process Discontinued

The settlement process has been discontinued as of January 1, 2008. See ¶ 4603 for assessment procedures.

¶1307 Average Net Income

- *Generally*

Average net income is the sum of the net income or loss for the current and each of the immediately preceding four years divided by five. Net income or loss is the book income shown on the corporation's federal return (or what would have been shown had it filed a federal return). Net income or loss is computed on an unconsolidated basis, without regard to how the corporation is treated for federal income tax purposes. The net income or loss of an investee corporation is not included in a corporation's net income, whether or not accounted for under the equity method of accounting (see also "Subsidiary Dividends," below). Federal taxable income is adjusted by adding back dividends received from investee corporations (including those from investments accounted for under the equity method of accounting). In computing average net income, losses are entered as computed, but in no case can average net income be less than zero [61 Pa. Code § 155.26(b); 72 P.S. § 7601].

Example 1: Saunders Corporation, a calendar-year domestic corporation, has been in business for 20 years and had net income per books (as shown on its federal return) as follows:

Year	Net Income
2006	$100,000
2005	178,000
2004	190,000
2003	300,000
2002	278,000
Five-year Total	$1,046,000

Example 2: Martin Corporation, a calendar-year domestic corporation, has been in business for 20 years and had net income per books (as shown on its federal return) as follows:

Year	Net Income
2006	$2,000
2005	(5,000)
2004	(15,000)
2003	8,000
2002	5,000
Five-year Total	($5,000)

Martin's average net income for 2004 is zero, since its average net income (an average loss of $1,000) is below zero.

Pennsylvania S Corporations

Assumption of shareholders' tax liabilities: A Pennsylvania S corporation cannot assume the tax liability of its shareholders and then deduct that amount as an expense for its calculation of average net income for capital stock purposes [*Scott Electric Co. v. Cmwlth.*, 692 A.2d 289 (Pa.Commw. 1997)].

Hypothetical federal taxes: The Pennsylvania Supreme Court has held that S corporations are not entitled to a deduction for hypothetical federal taxes for capital stock/franchise tax purposes [*Tool Sales & Service Co. Inc. v. Cmwlth.; Tom Mistick & Sons Inc. v. Cmwlth.*, 637 A.2d 607 (Pa. 1993), cert. den., 513 U.S. 822 (1994)].

- *Earnings included*

All earnings within the last five years must be included in the computation of average net income, without regard to when Pennsylvania activity began. There may be more than five tax periods in the last five years, due to a short period. The beginning of the oldest tax period used in computation of average net income, however, may not go back more than five full years.

Example 1: Williams Electrical Corporation was incorporated in New Jersey in 1975. On January 1, 2001, Williams began doing business in Pennsylvania and became subject to the Pennsylvania franchise tax. Williams must include its 1997—2000 book income as well as its 2001 book income for purposes of computing its 1999 average net worth.

Example 2: Bowen & Rust (B & R), a domestic publishing corporation, filed on a fiscal-year basis until September 30, 1996, when it changed its filing to a calendar-year basis. For 1996, the company filed a short-period return for the period October 1, 1996, through December 31, 1996. In its computation of 2000 average net income, B & R included income from the calendar years 1997 through 2000, and the short period October 1, 1996, through December 1, 1996. The fiscal year ending September 30, 1996, could not be included because it would have extended the computation period beyond five years. The denominator of the fraction used to compute average net income was 4.252, not five (5). See also the example at "Existence period less than five years," below.

¶1307

- *Distributions of limited liability companies*

A limited liability company that is not taxable as a corporation may reduce net income or loss by the amount of distributions made to any member who satisfies the material participation requirements of IRC § 469. Distributions made to a member within 30 days of the end of a given year may be treated as having been made in the preceding year and not in the year in which actually made [72 P.S. § 7601(a)]. In the case of a limited liability company or business trust that for federal income tax purposes is a disregarded entity of a natural person, the net income or loss of the limited liability company or business trust for any given year must be reduced by the amount of distributions made by the limited liability company or business trust to a natural person.

Single-member LLCs: The statute is silent with respect to whether single-member LLCs can reduce net income or loss for distributions made to materially participating members for capital stock/franchise tax purposes. However, it is the position of the Department of Revenue that single-member limited liability companies (SMLLCs) treated as disregarded entities for federal tax purposes can reduce book income by distributions made to the sole member for capital stock/franchise tax purposes *if the single member is a natural person.*

- *IRC § 338 transactions*

In computing average net income on a one-day deemed sale report, the average net income for the period ending immediately prior to the acquisition date is no longer used [61 Pa. Code § 153.81(d)(2)].

Policy Change

The Department of Revenue has announced that it will not include in book income the gains of an S corporation or other corporate entities created by exercising an IRC § 338(h)(10) election (relating to elective recognition of gain or loss by target corporation, together with nonrecognition of gain or loss on stock sold by selling consolidated group). Because this is a policy change, the Department will administratively resettle any report that was settled within the three-year statutory period. The appropriate documentation should be forwarded to Bureau of Corporation Taxes, Taxing Division, 6th Floor, Strawberry Square, Harrisburg, PA 17128 [*Pennsylvania Tax Update No. 93,* Pennsylvania Department of Revenue, May/June/July 2001].

- *Dividends from investee*

The Pennsylvania Supreme Court held that the Department of Revenue was correct in adding dividends from investments to income per books to arrive at average net income for purposes of the capital stock/franchise tax [*Philadelphia Suburban Corp. v. Cmwlth.,* 635 A.2d 116 (Pa. 1993), *rev'g* 601 A.2d 893 (Pa.Commw. 1992)]. The Department's position was held to be consistent with the explicit language of the statute and the regulation [61 Pa. Code § 155.26(b)]that required the addition of dividends from investments to book income was found to be valid to the extent it adjusts the income per books of a taxpayer. This controversy arose when the fixed formula replaced the older subjective valuation method for valuation of capital stock. Under the older method, taxpayers had a choice between the cost method and the equity method when determining the value of capital stock. After the passage of the fixed formula, the Department insisted that the cost method was the only acceptable method and that, therefore, dividends from investments must be added to income per books. The Pennsylvania Supreme Court upheld the Department's position. Dividends paid to a corporate taxpayer must be included in the calculation of average net income for capital stock/franchise tax purposes.

¶ 1307

- *Subsidiary dividends—the Unisys case*

Commonwealth Court decision: Unisys Corporation computed and calculated its franchise tax liability on an unconsolidated basis. In computing its tax base, contrary to statute, the company utilized the separate company basis and did not include subsidiary dividends in its income. This was done to be consistent with the calculation of the three-factor apportionment fractions, which were required by statute. The Department of Revenue increased the company's franchise tax by using consolidated income and net worth on settlement but did not adjust the separate apportionment fractions reported by the company. The Department of Revenue increased the amount of Unisys's reported net worth to include the value of its investments in subsidiaries and increased the amount reported as average net income by adding the amount of dividends Unisys received from subsidiaries and investee corporations. The company argued that the method used by the Department of Revenue imposed tax on more than the company's operations in Pennsylvania. The Court held that the tax was "unfair" but stopped short of stating that the method amounted to a constitutional violation. The Court concluded that the strict statutory formulation resulted in a disparity of tax due large enough to require some form of Subparagraph 18 relief and remanded the case to the Department of Revenue to determine a fair and equitable result, suggesting that one solution would be to use consolidated factors [*Unisys Corporation v. Cmwlth.*, 726 A.2d 1096 (Pa.Commw. 1999)]. See ¶1114 for explanation of Subparagraph 18.

Pennsylvania Supreme Court decision: The Pennsylvania Supreme Court reversed the Commonwealth Court decision and upheld the settlement made by the Department of Revenue. The Court ruled that the taxpayer failed to prove that the settlement made by the Department of Revenue violated the Due Process Clauses of the U.S. Constitution or the Pennsylvania fair apportionment statute. The Pennsylvania Supreme Court noted that Pennsylvania's scheme for taxation of foreign business franchises may be less than ideal, but in Unisys's case the level of disparity was not sufficient to require relief in the computation of its apportionment fractions [*Unisys Corporation v. Cmwlth.*, 812 A.2d 448 (Pa. 2002), *rev'g*, 726 A.2d 1096 (Pa.Commw. 1999).

- *Existence period less than five years*

If a taxpayer has not been in existence for a period of five calendar years, average net income is the average net income for the number of years that the taxpayer has been in existence. A taxpayer in existence for a part of a year is considered to have been in existence for that year based on the number of days the taxpayer was in existence during that year. This requirement that average net income be computed by using the actual number of days in a partial year has been upheld by the Commonwealth Court in *Doyle Equipment Co. v. Cmwlth.*, 542 A.2d 644 (Pa.Commw. 1988), and *Consolidated Rail Corporation v. Cmwlth.*, 379 A.2d 303 (Pa.Commw. 1996), *aff'd*, 691 A.2d 456 (Pa. 1997).

> *Example:* Angela Fabrics Corporation was incorporated October 1, 1996, and reports on a calendar-year basis. Its net income for the period August 1 through December 31, 1998 (153 days) was $20,000. Its net income for 1997 was $70,000 and for 1998, $90,000. Average net income for 1998 is $88,835 ($200,000 ÷ 2 92/366). Note that 1996 was a leap year. Note also that if Angela Fabrics uses a decimal equivalent with three decimal places, as the Commonwealth did in *Consolidated Rail*, above, its average net income would be $88,849 ($200,000 ÷ 2.251).

- *Existence period more than five years*

In *Consolidated Rail Corporation v. Cmwlth.* (see above), the taxpayers contended that the word "year" means "taxable year" if the corporation has been in existence more than five years. According to the taxpayer's interpretation, a taxpayer who has been in existence more than five years may use five (5) in the denominator, even if

¶1307

the last "year" is a short taxable year. The Commonwealth Court disagreed, and its decision was upheld by the Pennsylvania Supreme Court.

> *Example:* Ashley's Country Music Corporation (a domestic corporation incorporated in 1990) filed on a calendar-year basis until December 1996. In 1996 it changed its filing period to a fiscal year ending June 30 and filed a short-period report for January 1 through June 30, 1996. In computing its average net income for the period ending June 30, 2000, the company would include its January 1 through June 30, 1996, net income or loss as well as its July 1, 1996, through June 30, 1997, net income or loss and divide the result by 4 181/365. Note that the short period January 1 through June 20, 1994, counts as one of the five years in the calculation, but only for 181 days.

- *Pre-incorporation income*

Average net income does not include net income or loss incurred prior to incorporation (*e.g.,* net income of a partnership prior to incorporation). Net income or loss of a predecessor corporation cannot be attributed to a successor corporation (except in the case of a mere change in identity, form, or place of organization). Net income or loss can be adjusted in the event of a change in corporate structure. However, if the change is a result of a tax evasion motive, average net income will be determined on the basis of the substance of the transaction [61 Pa. Code § 155.26(f)].

Business trusts: The incomes of business trusts for periods in which they were exempt from the capital stock/franchise tax do not have to be included as book income for purposes of computing average net income for taxable years after the business trusts become subject to the capital stock/franchise tax. See the explanation at ¶1830.

- *Mergers, consolidations, and reincorporations*

The following examples, adapted from regulations, illustrate the application of the pre-incorporation rules with respect to mergers, consolidations, and reincorporations [61 Pa. Code § 155.26(f)]:

> *Example 1:* Effective December 31, 2000, Allred Corporation merged into Bennett Corporation. The net income or losses for the two corporations are as follows:

Year	Allred Corp.	Bennett Corp.
2000	$60,000	$150,000
2001	10,000	100,000
2002	(100,000)	80,000
2003	(100,000)	60,000
2004	—	100,000
Total		$490,000

> The average net income for 2004 for Bennett Corporation (which survived the merger) is $98,000 ($490,000 ÷ 5), determined without regard to net income or loss of Allred Corporation prior to the merger.

> *Example 2:* Effective December 31, 2004, Allred Corporation and Bennett Corporation consolidate to form new Craig Corporation. Allred and Bennett have been in existence for five years prior to the consolidation. Craig Corporation's average net income is determined for 2005 based only on the corporation's net income or loss for 2005, and no recognition is given to the net income or loss of either Allred Corporation or Bennett Corporation prior to the consolidation.

> *Example 3:* Effective December 31, 2004, Allred Corporation (formerly incorporated in State Y) incorporates in State X. The average net income for 2005 is computed taking into account net income or loss for 2005, as well as net income or loss for the four years prior to January 1, 2005.

- *Extraordinary or nonrecurring items*

Net income cannot be adjusted for nonrecurring or extraordinary items [61 Pa. Code § 155.26(h)]. A common error is to include a gain incurred in an IRC § 337 liquidation. This gain must be recognized for computation of taxable income but not for purposes of computation of average net income.

¶1307

• *Income from discharge of indebtedness*

A taxpayer restructured its debt, and, over a four-year period, more than $38,000,000 in debt was forgiven. The taxpayer was insolvent both before and after the forgiveness of the debt. The Commonwealth included the discharge of indebtedness in book income at settlement. The Commonwealth Court panel held that, because the company was insolvent after the debt forgiveness, there was no income from the discharge of indebtedness [*Shawnee Development v. Cmwlth.*, 764 A.2d 659 (Pa.Commw. 2000)]. The Court, noting that the term "income per books" was not defined by Pennsylvania statute, looked to federal income tax rules governing debt forgiveness to reach its conclusion. The Commonwealth appealed this decision. Exceptions were filed, and the full Court reversed the panel decision [*Shawnee Development, Inc. v. Cmwlth.*, 799 A.2d 882 (Pa.Commw. 2002), *rev'g* 764 A.2d 659 (Pa.Commw. 2000)]. The Court stated that regulations enforcing the Tax Reform Code will not be disregarded unless they are clearly inconsistent with the Code and that Shawnee's assertion that its stock was of no value because it was insolvent was insufficient to meet its heavy burden to establish that 61 Pa. Code § 155.26(h) is clearly erroneous or its at least equally heavy burden of showing that application of 72 P.S. § 7601(a) works an unconstitutional confiscation of its property. This decision was affirmed by the Pennsylvania Supreme Court [*Shawnee Development, Inc. v. Cmwlth*, 819 A.2d 528 (Pa. 2003), *aff'g*, 799 A.2d 822 (Pa.Commw. 2002)].

• *Cessation of operations*

A corporation that totally ceases operations, abandoning the business for which it was incorporated and divesting itself of assets, is considered to have ceased to exist for purposes of computing average net income. If it recommences business activities, it is considered to have come into existence on the date it resumes activities (unless the cessation is due to a tax evasion motive). Corporations planning significant reductions in operations, as well as liquidating corporations, should be aware of the effects these "tail earnings" may have on subsequent years' tax liability and plan accordingly [61 Pa. Code § 155.26(i), (j)].

Tail Earnings

It is important to remember the possible effect of tail earnings if you reactivate your company. While you are in an inactive status, your net income is considered to be zero, but you must include earnings from any active period within the past five years if you reactive your company. For example, consider a calendar-year company that becomes inactive on December 31, 1999, and remains inactive until January 1, 2003, at which time it resumes operations. Its net income for the inactive years (2000, 2001, 2002) is zero, but it must include the tail earnings from 1998 (as well as its earnings from 1999) in the numerator in the computation of average net income. One way to avoid this trap is to liquidate your old corporation, form a new corporation or a Pennsylvania business trust (see ¶ 912), and transfer the old name to the new corporation. This also has the advantage of preserving the corporate name.

• *Planning for inactive companies*

A corporation that wants to terminate its responsibility to file annual reports but does not want to dissolve formally (domestic corporation) or withdraw from business (foreign corporation) may terminate the filing responsibility by filing Form REV-238 (Out of Existence/Withdrawal Affidavit). Out-of-state corporations soliciting business in Pennsylvania are subject to tax and should file this document only upon ceasing activity in Pennsylvania.

¶1307

Corporation Using Pennsylvania Charter in Other States

A Pennsylvania corporation that utilizes its Pennsylvania charter to conduct business in another state should not file a REV-278.

Corporate name: The filing of this Affidavit does not affect the status of the Certificate of Incorporation (domestic corporation) or Authority (foreign corporation) but does permit the Department of State to relinquish the use of the corporation's present name to another corporation. The advantage of not filing Form REV-238 is that the corporation will not lose the right to its corporate name.

No operations and no assets: In order to qualify as an inactive corporation under 61 Pa. Code § 155.26(i) the corporation must have no operations and cannot own any assets. Even ownership of $1 in a bank or one stick of furniture will cause a corporation to be considered active. If immediate distribution of all assets is not feasible in the case of a liquidation, use of a liquidating trust to hold assets should be considered. Alternatively, if a liquidating trust is not feasible, a corporation should consider holding nothing except exempt assets, so that its asset fraction will be zero.

Taxpayer Allowed to Prorate Tax Liability

Taxpayer (a Delaware holding company) ceased doing business in Pennsylvania and filed a withdrawal affidavit with the Department of Revenue. The taxpayer computed its franchise tax liability using single-factor apportionment, then reduced this amount by prorating it on a daily basis. The Commonwealth Court held that the use of single-factor apportionment did not preclude the pro-rating of tax liability computed using single-factor apportionment [*Wilmington Trust Corp. v. Cmwlth.,* 854 A.2d 644 (Pa. Commw. 2004); aff'd per curiam, No. 56 MAP 2005 (Pa., April 20, 2006)].

¶1308 Net Worth

• *Computation of net worth*

Net worth is the sum of the entity's issued and outstanding capital stock, surplus and undivided profits as per books set forth for the close of such tax year on the income tax return filed by the entity with the federal government (or, if no federal return is made, would have been made if a federal return had been made). In the case of any entity that has investments in other corporations, the net worth is the consolidated net worth of such entity computed in accordance with generally accepted accounting principles. Net worth shall in no case be less than zero [72 P.S. § 7601(a)]. See Chapter 18 for discussion of the net worth of limited liability companies and business trusts.

Net worth does not include the cost of treasury stock, but it does include the amount of a contingent liability or surplus reserve not recorded as a liability or reduction of assets in the books. However, use of a contingent liability or surplus reserve disclosed in a parenthetical comment or footnote cannot be used to increase or decrease net worth [61 Pa. Code § 155.27(d), (f)].

Value of Investment in Subsidiaries

Unisys Corporation computed and calculated its franchise tax liability on an unconsolidated basis. In computing its tax base, contrary to statute, the company utilized the separate company basis and did not include subsidiary dividends in its income. This was done to be consistent with the calculation of the three-factor apportionment fractions, which was *required by statute.* The Department of Revenue increased the company's franchise tax by using consolidated income and net worth on settlement but did not adjust the separate apportionment fractions reported by the company. The Department of Revenue increased the amount of Unisys's reported net worth to include the value of its investments in subsidiaries and increased the amount reported as average net income by adding the amount of dividends Unisys received from subsidiaries and investee corporations. The company argued that the method used by the Department of Revenue imposed tax on more than the company's operations in Pennsylvania.

Commonwealth Court: The Court held that the tax was "unfair" but stopped short of stating that the method amounted to a constitutional violation. The Court concluded that the strict statutory formulation resulted in a disparity of tax due large enough to require some form of Subparagraph 18 relief and remanded the case to the Department of Revenue to determine a fair and equitable result, suggesting that one solution would be to use consolidated factors [*Unisys Corporation v. Cmwlth.*, Pa.Commw., 726 A.2d 109 (Pa.Commw. 1999)].

Pennsylvania Supreme Court: The Pennsylvania Supreme Court, however, disagreed with the Commonwealth Court. Noting that a taxpayer alleging Commerce and Due Process Clause violations bears a substantial burden to demonstrate by clear and cogent evidence that the state is taxing income earned outside its jurisdiction, which Unisys failed to bear, the Pennsylvania Supreme Court reversed the Commonwealth Court and remanded the case for reinstatement of the original settlement [812 A.2d 448 (Pa. 2002), *rev'g*, 726 A.2d 109 (Pa.Commw. 1999)]. See ¶1114 for explanation of Subparagraph 18.

If the end-of-the-year net worth is greater than twice or less than one-half of the beginning-of-the year net worth (computed as above), the net worth for the current tax year is the average of these two amounts [72 P.S. § 7601(1)].

Example 1: Landry Corporation was incorporated in Pennsylvania on September 1, 2002, and on January 1, 2003, Landry Corporation had a net worth of zero. Landry's net worth on December 31, 2003, was $2,000,000. Landry's average net worth for purposes of computation of its 2003 capital stock value is $1,000,000 ($2,000,000 ÷ 2).

Example 2: Susan's Interiors, Inc. (SII), has been subject to the Pennsylvania capital stock tax since 1975. On January 1, 2003, SII had a net worth of $300,000; on December 31, 2003, SII's net worth was $775,000. Since the end-of-year net worth is more than twice the beginning-of-the-year net worth, SII will use an average net worth of $375,500 to compute its 2003 capital stock value.

Example 3: The Carnie Company, a calendar-year New Hampshire corporation, liquidated its business on June 30, 2003. Its net worth on its final report, therefore, was zero. Its net worth at the beginning of the year was $832,000. For purposes of computing its 2003 capital stock value, Carnie will use an average net worth of $416,000.

- *Negative net worth*

72 P.S. § 7601 provides that in no case shall net worth be less than zero. The Department of Revenue has interpreted the provision that net worth can never be less than zero to mean that if either beginning net worth or ending net worth is negative, a zero must be substituted for the negative figure in computing average net worth, even if the average net worth using the actual figures is not negative (*i.e.*, the positive figure is larger than the negative figure). See the instructions to Form RCT-101. This position has been challenged by several taxpayers. For example, see *I.S.C. Group, Inc. v. Cmwlth.*, 320 F&R 1991.

- *Book value of stock in another corporation*

In the case of a taxpayer that has investments in the common stock of another corporation, net worth is the consolidated net worth of the taxpayer computed in accordance with generally accepted accounting principles. Book value for investments in stock of other corporations includes original cost plus the investor's share of the investee's earnings or losses. For this purpose, investments in other corporations means investments that are accounted for using the equity method of accounting or that are consolidated under generally accepted accounting principles [61 Pa. Code § 155.27(b)].

¶1308

• *Changes in capital structure*

Changes in capital structure (*e.g.*, contribution of capital, purchases of treasury stock, liquidating distributions) are not prorated [61 Pa. Code § 155.27(g)].

> **Example 1:** A calendar-year taxpayer with net worth of $700,000 on January 1 and $1,000,000 on December 31 (due to issuance of common stock on July 1) uses a net worth of $1,000,000 to compute capital stock value.

> **Example 2:** Comity Concepts, a calendar-year corporation, discontinued business operations during 2004. On January 1, 2004, the taxpayer had a net worth of $500,000 and total assets of $4,500,000. The net worth to be used in the computation of 2004 capital stock value is zero.

TAXABLE AND EXEMPT CORPORATIONS

¶1310 Corporations Subject to Tax

All domestic corporations (unless specifically exempt) are subject to the Pennsylvania capital stock tax. All foreign corporations *doing business in Pennsylvania* (unless specifically exempt) are subject to the Pennsylvania franchise tax [72 P.S. § 7601]. See ¶1303 for the definition of "corporation" for Pennsylvania capital stock/franchise tax purposes. See ¶1311 for a discussion of exempt corporations.

Interests in Unincorporated Entities

A corporation's interest in an entity that is not a corporation is considered a direct ownership interest in the assets of the entity rather than an intangible interest [72 P.S. § 7602.6]. Therefore, out-of-state corporations that have a presence in Pennsylvania through an interest in a pass-through entity are subject to Pennsylvania corporation taxes, and apportionment fractions flow through from unincorporated entities to corporate partners. Taxation of pass-through entities is discussed in Chapter 18.

Note, however, that this rule does not apply to real estate investment trusts as described in 72 P.S. § 7601(a)(b)(1) or regulated investment companies as described in 72 P.S. § 7601(a)(b)(2) [72 P.S. § 7602.6].

• *Exclusions from definition of corporation*

The term "corporation" for Pennsylvania capital stock/franchise tax purposes does not include any of the following [72 P.S. § 7601]:

(1) Business trusts that qualify as real estate investment trusts under IRC § 856 or that are qualified real estate investment trust subsidiaries under IRC § 856(i).

(2) Business trusts that qualify as regulated investment companies under IRC § 851 and that are registered with the United States Securities and Exchange Commission under the Investment Company Act of 1940 [15 U.S.C. § 80a-1 *et seq.*] or related business trusts that confine their activities in Pennsylvania to the maintenance, administration, and management of intangible investments and activities of regulated invest companies.

(3) Corporations, trusts, or other entities that are exempt organizations as defined by IRC § 501.

(4) Corporations, trusts, or other entities organized as not-for-profit organizations under Pennsylvania law or the laws of any other state that (a) would qualify as exempt organizations under IRC § 501; (b) would qualify as homeowners associations under IRC § 523(c); or (c) are membership organizations subject to the federal limitations on deductions from taxable income under IRC § 277 (but only if no pecuniary gain or profit inures to any member or related entity from the membership organization).

Corporation Tax Bulletin 2007-01

A Limited Liability Company or a Business Trust that is owned by an exempt IRC § 501 organization may be exempt from the tax even though it has not separately obtained federal tax exempt status. To qualify as a not-for-profit entity the Articles of Organization, Trust Agreement, or By-Laws must specifically state that the Limited Liability Company or Business Trust is organized as a not-for-profit entity and limit the activity of the entity to those of a not-for-profit or tax exempt organization. A copy of the Articles of Organization or Trust Agreement and a copy of the By-Laws must be provided to the Bureau of Corporation Taxes.

(5) Cooperative agricultural associations subject to 15 Pa.C.S. Ch. 75 (relating to cooperative agricultural associations).

(6) Business trusts if they are all of the following: (a) created and managed by an entity that is subject to the bank and trust companies shares tax; (b) created and managed for the purpose of facilitating the securitization of intangible assets; and (c) classified as a partnership or a disregarded entity for federal income tax purposes.

- *"Doing business" in Pennsylvania*

The term "doing business" has no statutory definition. The issue of what constitutes doing business within a state is part of the question of the constitutionality of state taxation of interstate commerce. The U.S. Supreme Court has held that it is constitutional for a state to levy a tax on the privilege of doing business in a state if (1) there is sufficient nexus with the state to justify the tax, (2) the tax does not discriminate against interstate commerce, (3) the tax is fairly apportioned, and (4) the tax is fairly related to the services provided by the state [*Complete Auto Transit, Inc. v. Brady*, 430 U.S. 274 (1977)]. The terms "doing business in" and "having capital or property employed or used in" have been held to be synonymous [*Cmwlth. v. American Sugar Refining Co.*, 53 Dauph 219 (1942)].

Income Tax and Franchise Tax Difference

P.L. 86-272 [15 U.S.C. § 381] places restrictions on the imposition of a state income tax that do not apply to franchise taxes. Mere solicitation is not enough to establish nexus for corporate net income tax purposes. See ¶¶ 913, 914, and 914A.

Employees or ownership of property in Pennsylvania not necessary to establish nexus: A Delaware corporation headquartered in Ohio was found to be subject to the Pennsylvania corporate net income and the franchise tax on foreign corporations, even though it had neither property nor employees in the Commonwealth. The taxpayer is engaged in interstate motor transportation. It transports property through Pennsylvania (pass-through miles), delivers property to Pennsylvania destinations from outside the state, and picks up property in Pennsylvania for delivery out of state. Since 15% to 20% of the company's revenue miles were logged in Pennsylvania, these activities provide a sufficient nexus to impose the corporate net income tax and franchise tax on foreign corporations. All of the other criteria of *Complete Auto Transit* were also met [*Erieview Cartage, Inc. v. Cmwlth.*, 654 A.2d 276 (Pa.Commw. 1995)]. For discussion of doing business in Pennsylvania for corporate net income tax purposes, see ¶ 913.

Isolated transactions do not constitute "doing business": The Pennsylvania Supreme Court has held that isolated transactions do not constitute "doing business" for tax purposes [*Cmwlth. v. Wilkes-Barre and Hazelton Railroad Co.*, 95 A 915 (Pa. 1915)]. However, the Pennsylvania Supreme Court has also ruled that active presence in the Commonwealth is all that is needed to establish nexus for franchise tax purposes and that mere solicitation by the taxpayer is enough to establish the requisite presence

[*Clairol, Inc. v. Cmwlth.*, 518 A.2d 1165 (Pa. 1986), *rev'g*, 478 A.2d 282 (Pa.Commw. 1995)]. In the *Clairol* case, the company sent "missionary" salesmen into the Commonwealth to solicit business for the company. This decision broadens the reach of the franchise tax and overrules (without citation or discussion) a long line of cases cited in *Peoples Gas System, Inc. v. Cmwlth.*, 314 A.2d 36 (Pa.Commw. 1974).

"Not Subject to" Tax Report

If your foreign corporation is conducting activities in Pennsylvania that you believe are insufficient to establish nexus and make you subject to the Pennsylvania franchise tax, you should still file annual reports with the Department of Revenue, indicating on your reports that you are "not subject" to the franchise tax. The filing of such a return starts the running of the statute of limitations, so that if you are later found to be subject to the franchise tax, the Department can go back no more than the statutory period to settle or resettle your taxes. See ¶1203 and ¶1204. If you have never filed a return, the statute of limitations has never started running, and the Department can then go back to your first year of doing business to settle and resettle your tax.

• *De minimis activities*

Even though mere solicitation is sufficient to subject a taxpayer to the Pennsylvania franchise tax, the Department of Revenue takes the position that, for franchise tax purposes, solicitation activities in Pennsylvania for seven (7) calendar days or less per year that produce annual sales in Pennsylvania of $10,000 or less are *de minimis* [*Corporate Tax Bulletin 2004-01*, § II.A.5.]. Thus, a franchise taxpayer ordinarily will not be required to file a Pennsylvania franchise tax return for such *de minimis* activities but may be required to document its eligibility for such consideration [*Corporate Tax Bulletin 2004-01*, § II.A.]. *Corporate Tax Bulletin 2004-01* is discussed in more detail at ¶914A. The following examples, adapted from *Corporate Tax Bulletin 2004-01*, § II.A.8. illustrate application of the *de minimis* standard to the Pennsylvania franchise tax.

Example 1: Company A, an Ohio corporation, is a calendar-year taxpayer. It exhibits at a Pennsylvania trade show for eight (8) days during the taxable year. It makes no sales at the trade show and has no other Pennsylvania contacts during the taxable year. However, it has $9,000 of Pennsylvania sales during the taxable year. Company A has exceeded the seven-day limitation and must file a Pennsylvania franchise tax report for the taxable year.

Example 2: Company B, a West Virginia corporation, is a calendar-year taxpayer. It exhibits at a Pennsylvania trade show for three days during the taxable year but makes no sales at the trade show. Company B also solicits sales in Pennsylvania for five days during the taxable year and has $8,000 of Pennsylvania sales for the taxable year. Exhibiting at a trade show is solicitation. Therefore, the trade show days must be included in determining the total number of days upon which solicitation activities occurred. Since Company B engaged in solicitation activities on eight days during the taxable year, the seven-day limitation is exceeded and Company B must file a Pennsylvania franchise tax report for the taxable year.

Example 3: Company B, a Virginia corporation, is a calendar-year taxpayer. It exhibits at a Pennsylvania trade show for three days during the taxable year but makes no sales at the show. During the taxable year Company B has $15,000 of Pennsylvania sales. Company C has exceeded the $10,000 limit and must file a Pennsylvania franchise tax report for the taxable year.

Example 4: Company D, a New Jersey corporation, is a calendar-year taxpayer. It exhibits and sells for three days at a Pennsylvania trade show during the taxable year and makes trade show sales of $4,000. Company D also solicits sales in Pennsylvania for three days during the taxable year, producing additional sales of $7,000. Including trade show sales, Company D's total Pennsylvania sales for the taxable year are $11,000. There are six solicitation days for Company C during the taxable year, which does not exceed the seven-day limit. However, since trade show sales and other sales must be added together to determine total Pennsylvania sales for the taxable year, which amount to $11,000. Company D has exceeded the $10,000 limitation. Since exceeding either limit alone requires the filing of a franchise tax report, Company C must file a Pennsylvania franchise tax report for the taxable year.

Example 5: Company E, a New York corporation, is a calendar-year taxpayer. During the taxable year Company E exhibits at a Pennsylvania trade show for five days, making $5,000 in sales. Company E had no other Pennsylvania sales for the taxable year. Company E does not have a Pennsylvania franchise tax return for the taxable year because a company that exhibits at a Pennsylvania trade show but does not exceed either the seven-day limitation or the $10,000 limitation is not required to file a Pennsylvania franchise tax report. However, based on information received by the Department of Revenue, an entity may be requested to complete a Business Activities Questionnaire (BAQ) to assist in the determination of appropriate tax report filing requirements [*Corporate Tax Bulletin 2004-01,* §II.A.8.(e)].

¶1311 Corporations Exempt from Tax

The following entities are not subject to the Pennsylvania capital stock/franchise tax:

(1) Real estate investment trusts that qualify under IRC §856 or qualified real estate investment trust subsidiaries that qualify under IRC §856(i) or related business trusts that confine their activities in Pennsylvania to the maintenance, administration, and management of intangible investments and activities of real estate investments trusts or qualified real estate investment trust subsidiaries. A business trust that is a qualified real estate investment trust subsidiary under IRC §856(i) is treated as part of the real estate investment trust that owns all of its stock [72 P.S. §7601(b)(1)].

(2) Regulated investment companies that qualify under IRC §856 and that are registered with the United States Securities and Exchange Commission under the Investment Company Act or 1940 or related business trusts that confine their activities in Pennsylvania to the maintenance, administration and management of intangible investments and activities or regulated investment companies [72 P.S. §7601(b)(2)].

(3) Charitable organizations as defined by IRC §501, including any not-for-profit organization organized under the laws of Pennsylvania or any other state that would qualify as an exempt organization as defined by IRC §501 [72 P.S. §7601(b)(3)].

(4) Not-for-profit entities that would qualify as exempt organizations under IRC §501 [72 P.S. §7601(b)(4)(i)].

(5) Not-for-profit entities that qualify as a homeowners association as defined by IRC §528(c) [72 P.S. §7601(b)(4)(ii)].

(6) Not-for-profit entities that are membership organizations subject to the federal limitations on deduction from taxable income under IRC §277 (relating to certain deductions incurred in transactions with members), but only if no pecuniary gain or profit inures to any member or related entity from the membership organization [72 P.S. §7601(b)(4)(iii)].

(7) Cooperative agricultural associations subject to 15 Pa.C.S. Ch. 75 [72 P.S. §7601(b)(5)].

(8) Business trusts that meet all of the following criteria [72 P.S. §7601(b)(6)]:

(a) Created or managed by an entity that is subject to the tax imposed by Article VII (Bank and Trust Companies Shares Tax) or Article XV (Mutual Thrift Institutions Tax) of the Tax Reform Code or that is an affiliate of the entity that shares at least 80% common ownership.

(b) Created and managed for the purpose of facilitating the securitization of intangible assets.

(c) Classified as a partnership or a disregarded entity for federal income tax purposes.

(9) Banks and trust companies taxable under Article VII of the Tax Reform Code [72 P.S. § 7602(i)].

(10) Title insurance companies taxable under Article VIII of the Tax Reform Code [72 P.S. § 7602(i)].

(11) Insurance companies taxable under Article IX of the Tax Reform Code [72 P.S. § 7602(i)].

(12) Mutual thrift institutions taxable under Article XV of the Tax Reform Code [72 P.S. § 7602(i)].

Pennsylvania S Corporations

Pennsylvania S corporations are not subject to the corporate net income tax, but they are subject to the capital/stock franchise tax.

(13) Business trusts. Domestic or foreign business trusts, provided:

(a) The trust is created or managed by an entity subject to the bank and trust companies tax or the mutual thrift institutions tax.

(b) The trust is created and managed for the purpose of facilitating the securitization of intangible assets.

(c) The trust is classified as a partnership or a disregarded entity for federal income tax purposes.

Effect of Federal Tax Treaties

Unless there is an express exemption from state income taxes, no treaty of the federal government shall be construed to exempt a corporation from the Pennsylvania corporate net income tax or the Pennsylvania capital stock/franchise tax. In the case of a corporation not subject to federal income taxation or reporting, taxable income for purposes of the Pennsylvania corporate net income tax is taxable income that would have been reported to the federal government it the corporation had not been exempted by treaty [72 P.S. § 10003.11].

- **Family farm corporation exemption**

A corporation (domestic or foreign) that qualifies as a family farm corporation is exempt from the capital stock/franchise tax if it is actually engaged in the business of agriculture. A family farm corporation for this purpose is a Pennsylvania corporation that devotes at least 75% of its assets to agriculture and at least 75% of the stock of which is owned by members of the same family [72 P.S. § 7602.2(b)(1)].

Leased assets: Effective January 1, 1998, assets devoted to the business of agriculture include leased assets, to members of the same family, that are directly and principally used for agricultural purposes [72 P.S. § 7602.2(b)(3)].

Members of the same family: Members of the same family for purposes of this exemption means an individual, such individual's brothers and sisters, the brothers and sisters of such individual's parents and grandparents, the ancestors and lineal descendants of any of the foregoing and a spouse of any of the foregoing. Individuals related by the half blood or by legal adoption shall be treated as if they were related by the whole blood [72 P.S. § 7602.2(b)(2)].

Business of agriculture: The business of agriculture means commercially cultivating the ground to produce products in fields or in large quantities (*e.g.,* soil preparation, planting of seeds, raising and harvesting of crops, beekeeping, rearing, etc., of livestock]. The business of agriculture also includes aquaculture (*i.e.*, raising of fish and other aquatic animals for direct commercial use as a food or food product) [61 Pa. Code § 155.2(a)(1)]. Raising flowers and plants in greenhouses also qualifies as agriculture for purposes of the family farm exemption [*Reiniger Brothers, Inc. v. Cmwlth.*, 522 A.2d 187 (Pa.Commw. 1987)].

No Exemption If Owners of Assets Not Engaged in Farming

A corporation that leases its property to others for farming does not qualify for the family farm exemption because the owners themselves are not the ones actually engaged in farming [*Peters Orchard Co. v. Cmwlth.*, 496 A.2d 1313 (Pa.Commw. 1985)]. The Commonwealth Court has also held that a corporation that contracted with farmers to produce hybrid farm seed was not entitled to the exemption because the owners themselves were not actually engaged in farming [*Hoffman Seed, Inc. v. Cmwlth.*, 497 A.2d 668 (Pa.Commw. 1985)].

ACCOUNTING

¶1315 Accounting Periods and Methods

Companies have the same tax year (calendar or fiscal) and the same accounting method for Pennsylvania capital stock and franchise tax purposes as for federal income tax purposes [72 P.S. §§ 7401(5), 7601(b),].

The capital stock/franchise provision governing taxable year specifically provides that the taxable year for capital stock/franchise tax purposes is the same as that for corporate net income tax purposes, as defined in 72 P.S. § 7401(5) [72 P.S. § 7601(b)].

52-53 week year: Section 401 of the Tax Reform Code [72 P.S. § 7401] is in Part I of Article IV, which is not incorporated by into the capital stock/franchise tax provisions. The capital stock/franchise tax definition of taxable year incorporates 72 P.S. § 7401(5), but not 72 P.S. § 7401(3)(1)(k), which provides that taxpayers with a fiscal year ending during the last seven days of December or the first seven days of January is considered a calendar-year taxpayer. Thus, a taxpayer with a year fiscal year ending December 26 is not a calendar-year taxpayer for capital stock/franchise tax purposes [*Eat'n Park Restaurants Business Trust v. Cmwlth.*, 802 A.2d 1280 (Pa.Commw. 2002)].

• *Short periods*

If a corporation is required to file a corporate tax report for a short taxable year, the tax imposed must be prorated on a daily basis. This is accomplished by multiplying the tax liability by a fraction equal to the number of days in the taxable year divided by three hundred sixty-five days [72 P.S. § 7602(g)].

> *Example:* In 2004, Kay Corporation, a calendar-year taxpayer, changed to a fiscal year ending September 30. Kay's 2004 total capital stock value is $500,000. Kay Corporation must file a return for the short period beginning January 1, 2004, and ending September 30, 2004. Kay Corporation has a 2004 capital stock value of $500,000 and a 2004 single-factor apportionment fraction of 0.890368. The 2004 capital stock tax rate is 6.99 mills (.00699). The short period from January 1, 2004, through September 30, 2004, is 274 days (2004 is a leap year). Kay has a taxable capital stock value for the short period of $445,184 (0.890368 x $500,000), and its capital stock tax for the short period is $2,329.61 (274/366 x 0.00699 x $445,184).

Other short periods: Short-period reports should also be filed in the following situations: sale or transfer of more than half the corporation's assets during the year; bankruptcy or receivership; organization of a new corporation; liquidation, merger, consolidation, or dissolution of a domestic corporation; and dissolution or withdrawal from Pennsylvania in the case of a foreign corporation.

Sales Tax

In the case of the sale of over half of its assets, a corporation may have sales and use tax consequences as well.

New corporation with a short first year: In the case of a new domestic corporation with a short first year, the short taxable year begins on the date of incorporation. In the case of a new foreign corporation with a short first year, the short taxable year begins on the earlier of the date it obtained a Certificate of Authority or the date it first transacted business in Pennsylvania. Tax due for a short taxable year resulting from the commencement of business activities within Pennsylvania during the taxable year is prorated either (1) on the basis of proration of tax or (2) proration of the property factor. The sales factor may not be prorated [61 Pa. Code § 155.28(b)(1)]. The following rules apply:

(1) In the case of a corporation that has done business outside Pennsylvania for more than 1 year but has been subject to Pennsylvania taxation for less than 1 year, the numerator of the property factor is prorated. The tax due is prorated only where all three factors are 100% Commonwealth. See examples at 61 Pa. Code § 155.28(b)(1)(i).

(2) In the case of a corporation that has been doing business outside Pennsylvania for the same period that it has been subject to Pennsylvania taxation, which is less than 1 year, the property factor is not prorated, but the tax due is prorated based on the portion of the year during which the corporation did business in and out of Pennsylvania [61 Pa. Code § 155.28(b)(1)(ii)].

(3) In the case of a corporation that has done business outside of Pennsylvania for a period of less than 1 year and has been subject to Pennsylvania taxation for a shorter period than it has done business outside Pennsylvania, the property factor is prorated unless it reports 100% Commonwealth factors, in which case the tax due (not the numerator of the property factor) would be prorated. The tax due would be prorated for the period of operation everywhere. See examples at 61 Pa. Code § 155.28(b)(1)(iii).

Last-year companies: In the case of a corporation that ceases business activities everywhere, tax due is prorated on a per-day basis. See example at 61 Pa. Code § 155.28(b)(2)(i). In the case of a corporation that withdraws from Pennsylvania but continues to do business elsewhere, the numerator of the property factor is prorated. See example at 61 Pa. Code § 155.28(b)(2)(ii).

- *IRC § 338 elections*

In the case of an acquisition for which an election under IRC § 338 is made, the Department of Revenue requires reports for all federal periods, including a federal one-day deemed sale return. Federal elections are binding for Pennsylvania purposes, as is a failure to elect [61 Pa. Code § 153.81(b)].

Legal Status Changes

It is good practice to file for the short period when your legal status changes (*e.g.,* bankruptcy, receivership, bulk sale of assets, sales of shares of stock) to avoid estimated settlements. An estimated settlement is one that is based on estimated figures and is made when a taxpayer fails to file a report. Taxpayers must file short-period returns in the case of bulk sales, sales of real estate, and auction sales. However, the Department of Revenue will sometimes make estimated settlements in other situations.

REPORTS

¶1320 Annual Reports

The law requires corporations subject to the capital stock or franchise tax to file reports annually on Department of Revenue forms [72 P.S. §7601(b)]. In practice this requirement is met by filing PA Form RCT-101, with all applicable schedules attached, and a federal Form 1120, prepared on a separate return basis. Pennsylvania does not allow the filing of consolidated returns. If the Commonwealth wants additional information, they will write and ask for it.

• *Forms*

The report is submitted on Form RCT-101 (Pennsylvania Corporate Tax Report), which is also used to report for corporate net income tax and corporate loans tax purposes. A copy of federal Form 1120 must be attached to the Form RCT-101.

Electronic Filing

The Department of Revenue may now allow the electronic filing of any tax return or document [72 P.S. § 10008].

The Department of Revenue will not accept pencil copies of returns. All reports must be either typewritten, written in ink, or photocopied. Forms may be reproduced, but authority to reproduce corporate forms must be requested and approved in writing by the Department prior to use. To be approved, the reproduction (including computer-generated forms) must be identical to the form provided by the Department of Revenue. Coupons from the Form REV-8571 coupon book cannot be reproduced under any circumstances: Official coupons provided by the Department must be used.

• *Due dates*

The capital stock and franchise tax provisions incorporate, by reference, the provisions of the corporate net income tax law regarding reports and payment of tax [72 P.S. §7603]. The statutory deadline for filing is April 15 for calendar-year taxpayers [72 P.S. §7403(a)]and 105 days after the end of the tax year for fiscal-year taxpayers [72 P.S. §702]. However, in practice this is interpreted to mean one month after the federal return is due or would be due if one were required.

The first taxable period for domestic corporations begins with the date of incorporation, and returns must be filed for the first period and all periods thereafter, even though no business activity is conducted during the tax year. The first taxable period for foreign corporations begins with the earlier of the date of the issuance of the Certificate of Authority or the date of the commencement of activities in the Commonwealth. A Certificate of Authority is a document certifying that a corporation has registered to do business in Pennsylvania. Once a corporation is granted a Certificate of Authority, it is assigned a Box Number and placed on the mailing list to receive the appropriate forms. A Box Number is a taxpayer identification number.

What If You Conduct No Business

So long as a corporation is a registered corporation it must file a corporate tax return, even if no business is conducted, and it must file Form RCT 101-I (referred to as a skeleton report). A corporation with any activity, real property, or other assets, or any income is not considered inactive.

Timely mailing: Any report and/or payment postmarked by the U.S. Postal Service on or before the due date is considered to be timely made. Presentation of a receipt indicating that the report or payment was mailed by registered or certified

¶1320

mail on or before the due date is evidence of timely filing and payment [72 P.S. § 7403.1]. If the last day of the tax year falls on a Saturday, Sunday, or a legal holiday, the report or return may be filed on the next regular business day [72 P.S. § 704].

Postmarks

Only postmarks and receipts of the U.S. Postal Service are evidence of timely filing. If you use a private postal service and your report or payment does not reach the Department of Revenue in time, you are out of luck, even if you can present proof that you delivered the report or payment to the service on or before your due date.

• *Verification of reports and returns*

Every tax report or return filed with the Department of Revenue must be verified by affirmation. In the case of any such report or return made or filed by a corporation or association, such affirmation must be made by one officer of the corporation or association or, if the association does not have any officers, by one of its members [72 P.S. § 703].

• *Amended returns*

Amended corporate reports are discussed at ¶ 919. Amended capital stock/ franchise tax returns to reflect changes in net book income or net worth are not required as a result of (1) changes in taxable income based on filing an amended federal Form 1120X or (2) changes in taxable income as a result of a federal audit. Adjustments to net book income and net worth are recognized in the same period that the change in the balance sheet regarding federal income tax is recognized. Taxpayers that do not agree with this position may file petitions of appeal at the applicable level [*Pennsylvania Tax Update No. 44*, Pennsylvania Department of Revenue, May/June 1993]. Note, however, that amended corporate net income tax returns (Form RCT-101X) or reports of change in corporate net income tax (Form RCT-128C) must be filed to reflect the changes in taxable income.

• *Secrecy of returns*

All information gained by the Department of Revenue as a result of returns, investigations, or verifications required by law is confidential, except for official purposes, and it is a misdemeanor to divulge such information [72 P.S. § 7408(b)].

• *Termination of reporting*

If a corporation wishes to stop filing annual reports but does not want to formally dissolve or withdraw, it may end its filing responsibility by submitting the required information and documentation [61 Pa. Code § 151.11(a)].

Skeleton Report

A corporation that is qualified to terminate reporting but wants to preserve the right to use its name can submit a skeleton report in lieu of an Out of Existence Affidavit or a Withdrawal Affidavit. See ¶ 915.

Effect of termination of reporting: After the Department of Revenue receives and accepts the required documentation, the name of the corporation is removed from the active tax rolls of the Department and the corporation no longer has to file annual reports. However, a corporation that files a Withdrawal Affidavit or an Out of Existence Affidavit may lose the right to use its name [61 Pa. Code § 151.11(b)]. If a corporation would like to keep the right to use its name, it should not submit a Withdrawal Affidavit or Out of Existence Affidavit. Instead, it should submit a Skeleton Report and Skeleton Affidavit annually on its due date for reporting. A Skeleton Report is simply a report form filed with only the identification and affirmation sections completed. All Skeleton Reports are settled at a minimum tax [61 Pa. Code § 151.12(a), (b), (c)].

¶1321 Estimated Tax Payments

Corporations subject to the capital stock/franchise tax must make quarterly payments of estimated capital stock/franchise tax [72 P.S. § 10003.2(a)(ii)]. See ¶4610 for discussion of estimated tax payments.

PAYMENT—EXTENSIONS

¶1325 Payment of Tax

Payment of estimated tax must accompany the estimated tax report. The balance of the tax due has to be paid by the original due date of the final return [72 P.S. § 707]. See ¶1320 for due dates.

Payment by Electronic Funds Transfer

Payment by electronic funds transfer (EFT)is discussed at ¶4617.

¶1326 Transfer of Credits

A corporation's tax obligation may be satisfied by transferring available credits within its corporate account.

• *Definitions*

The following definitions are used in the explanation of the transfer and assignment of credits [61 Pa. Code § 151.21]:

"Application." Used by the Department of a credit to pay a tax debit.

"Assignment." The sale or exchange of a settled credit by a taxpayer (the assignor) to another taxpayer (the assignee) for application by the assignee to a tax debit in the assignee's account.

"Conditional statutory credit." Those statutory credits that are subject to special conditions set forth by the statute establishing those credits. Such credits may be utilized in the manner set forth by regulation, *subject* to the special conditions or limitations set forth by the statute that creates them. An example is the neighborhood assistance tax credit (explained at ¶1005).

"Settled credit." A surplus that has been determined to be an overpayment upon settlement by the Department of the annual tax report to which it relates.

"Tax debit." Includes tax principal, penalty, and interest.

"Transfer." The movement by the Department of a credit within the account of a taxpayer against a tax debit of the same taxpayer.

"Unsettled credit." A surplus resulting from an apparent overpayment of a tax with which a payment is made, either as a result of a tentative tax payment or of a regular payment, prior to settlement of the annual report to which it relates.

• *Procedure for use of credits*

Use of unsettled credits: Unsettled credits are available for transfer to corporation tax debits within the taxpayer's account as soon as the final report is received by the Department of Revenue. If obligations due the Commonwealth have been paid, unsettled credits may be used to pay a tax or other claim due the Commonwealth, may be refunded, or may be assigned to another person. The possibility of a later resettlement or account adjustment to correct a clerical or mathematical error does not block the transfer of an unsettled credit [61 Pa. Code § 151.22(a)].

Use of settled credits: Settled corporate tax credits may be transferred in payment of any other tax or taxes paid or payable into the General Fund (except as otherwise provided by law or regulation), and credits of other taxes paid into the General Fund may be transferred in payment of corporate taxes. Taxes payable into the General Fund include personal income taxes, cigarette and beverage taxes, sales and use taxes, inheritance taxes, and corporation taxes. Settled corporate tax credits can also be interchanged with tax credits from special funds, such as the Unemployment Compensation Fund or the Motor Vehicle Fund. A settled credit can be assigned to another corporation or refunded to the taxpayer if outstanding tax debits reflected in the account are sufficient to satisfy the debits and other obligations due the Commonwealth have been paid. A settled credit that is the subject of a petition for cash refund cannot be transferred to other taxes or assigned to other corporations while proceedings for refund are pending [61 Pa. Code § 151.22(b)].

• *Procedure for transfer and assignment*

Transfer by corporation: To transfer credits (settled or unsettled) to its present or anticipated debits, a corporation must submit a letter, signed by an authorized representative, setting forth the type, year, and amount of the credit to be transferred and the debit to which it is to be applied [61 Pa. Code § 151.22(c)(1)].

Transfer by Department: The Department may transfer credits (settled or unsettled) of the taxpayer within its account. The Department will first make the transfer and then send the taxpayer a statement of how the credits have been applied. The taxpayer may object to the proposed transfer within 30 days of receipt of the statement. If the Department agrees with the taxpayer's objection, the transfer will be reversed [61 Pa. Code § 151.22(c)(2)].

Assignment: To assign a tax credit to another taxpayer (whether or not a subsidiary corporation), the assignor must complete and submit to the Department an Assignment of Tax Credit form signed by an authorized representative of the assignor corporation. This application is considered authorization for the Department to review the assignor's account, transfer credits, and make other determinations necessary to compute the assignor's current available credit balance. The Department will then assign the credit in accordance with assignee's instructions. In the absence of instructions, the assignment will be made in accordance with 61 Pa. Code § 151.24 (relating to order of application, discussed below). The Department will then confirm the assignment in writing to both parties [61 Pa. Code § 151.22(c)(3)].

Refund: To obtain a refund, a taxpayer must submit to the Department a letter signed by an authorized representative of the taxpayer. The letter must specify which credits are requested to be refunded and must include a statement that the taxpayer has no obligations due the Commonwealth. A refund request is considered authority for the Department to review the taxpayer's account, transfer credits, and make other determinations necessary to bring the taxpayer's account up to date. The Department will then refund the credit in accordance with the taxpayer's instructions [61 Pa. Code § 151.22(c)(4)].

• *Order of application of credits*

Unless the taxpayer directs otherwise, tax credits are applied to debits in chronological order. Within each account the credits are assigned to items in the following order: (1) penalties; (2) legal costs; (3) interest; and (4) tax principal [61 Pa. Code § 151.24].

• *Effective date of credit*

Tax credits that are applied in payment of a tax debit are credited as of the postmark date of the payment from which the credit originated [61 Pa. Code § 151.23].

¶1326

¶1327 Extensions of Time

The time for filing capital stock or franchise returns may be extended [72 P.S. §7601(b)]. All requests for extensions of time for filing must be made on or before the due date for the annual report. Extensions are allowed for not more than 60 days. If a federal extension of more than 60 days is granted, the Department of Revenue may grant an additional extension of not more than 30 days after the termination of the federal extension. The amount of tax due, however, is subject to interest from the due date [72 P.S. §7405].

¶1328 Recordkeeping Requirements

Corporations must keep and maintain records with respect to the capital stock or franchise tax for three years after the report is filed. The law states that a corporation must keep such record(s) of business within Pennsylvania for the period covered by the report and other pertinent papers as may be required by the Department of Revenue [72 P.S. §7409].

¶1329 Credits Against the Tax

The following tax credits may be claimed by taxpayers subject to the capital stock/franchise tax:

(1) Neighborhood assistance tax credit. See ¶1005.

(2) Research and development tax credit. See ¶1008.

(3) Job creation tax credit (JCTC). See ¶1007.

(4) Waste tire recycling equipment investment grants (replacing former waste tire recycling equipment investment tax credit). See ¶1009.

(5) Coal degasification tax credit (Coal Waste Removal and Ultraclean Fuels Credit [72 P.S. §8801-A *et seq.*]. See ¶1010.

(6) Educational improvement tax credit (EITC). See ¶1011.

(7) Film production tax credit (repealed and replaced with film production grant). See ¶1012.

(8) Organ or bone marrow donor tax credit. See ¶1015.

(9) Resource enhancement and protection tax credit. See ¶1016.

(10) Credit for job creation in strategic development area. See ¶1017.

(11) Credit for capital employed in strategic development area (discussed below).

(12) Keystone special development zone tax credit. See ¶1014A.

(13) Resource manufacturing tax credit. See ¶1021.

(14) Educational opportunity scholarship tax credit. See ¶1022.

(15) Historic preservation incentive tax credit. See ¶1023.

(16) Community-based services tax credit. See ¶1024.

Credit for job capital employed in strategic development area (SDA): The Governor is authorized to designate up to four (4) strategic development areas in Pennsylvania [72 P.S. §9911-C(b)(1)]. Effective for taxable years beginning on or after January 1, 2008, qualified businesses may claim a credit against the capital stock/franchise tax for tax liability attributable to the capital employed within the SDA in the taxable year [72 P.S. §9936-C(a)]. The amount of the credit is computed by multiplying the corporation's taxable value attributable to the capital employed within the SDA by the capital stock/franchise rate [72 P.S. §9936-C(c)]. If the entire business of the corporation is not wholly transacted within the SDA, the taxable value must be apportioned [72 P.S. §9936-C(a)(2)].

KOZs and KIZs

Special credits are available to qualified businesses in Pennsylvania Keystone Opportunity Zones (discussed below) and to KIZ companies located in Keystone Innovation Zones (see ¶ 4623).

* Keystone opportunity zone (KOZ) credit

A corporation that is a qualified business (see ¶ 4622) may claim a credit against the capital/stock franchise tax for tax liability attributable to capital employed within a subzone, an expansion subzone, or an improvement subzone. Note that the term "subzone" is used herein to indicate a subzone, an expansion subzone, or an improvement subzone. The tax liability attributable to capital employed within a subzone is determined by multiplying the corporation's taxable value attributable to capital employed within the subzone by the capital stock/franchise tax rate [73 P.S. § 820.516(b)]. The business activity must be conducted directly by a corporation in the subzone in order for the corporation to claim the tax credit, and no credit may be claimed for capital employed prior to the designation of the area as a subzone [73 P.S. § 820.516(a)].

Limitation on amount of credit: The credit cannot exceed the corporation's capital/stock franchise tax liability for the tax year [73 P.S. § 820.516(e)].

Tax liability: The corporation's tax liability attributable to capital employed within a subzone is determined by multiplying the corporation's taxable value attributable to capital employed within the subzone by the rate of the capital/stock franchise tax. Pennsylvania taxable value must be computed in conformity with Article VI (relating to the capital/stock franchise tax) of the Tax Reform Code with no adjustments or subtractions for the capital employed in the subzone [73 P.S. § 820.516(b)].

Determination of attributable tax liability: If the entire business of the corporation in Pennsylvania is transacted wholly within a subzone, the taxable value attributable to the capital employed within a subzone consists of the Pennsylvania taxable value as determined under the capital/stock franchise statutes [73 P.S. § 820.516(c)(1)]. If the entire business of the corporation in Pennsylvania is not wholly transacted within a subzone, the taxable value of a corporation in a subzone is determined upon the portion of the Pennsylvania taxable value attributable to the capital employed within the subzone by using the apportionment factors set forth in 73 P.S. § 820.515(d) [73 P.S. § 820.516(c)(2)]. These apportionment factors are discussed at ¶ 1013.

Exceptions: Any portion of a taxpayer's tax liability that is attributable to the capital employed in the operation of one of the following companies cannot be used to calculate a KOZ credit:

(1) Railroad, truck, bus, or airline companies.

(2) Pipeline or natural gas companies.

(3) Water transportation companies.

(4) Entities that would qualify as regulated investment companies for corporate net income tax purposes.

(5) Entities that would qualify as holding companies as defined for capital/stock franchise purposes.

These companies, however, are entitled to a KOZ job creation tax credit, discussed at ¶ 1014.

CAPITAL STOCK TAX, FRANCHISE TAX, AND CORPORATE LOANS TAX

CHAPTER 14

ALLOCATION AND EXEMPT ASSETS

GENERAL

Caution: There is No Capital Stock/Franchise Tax for tax years beginning after 12/31/15

¶1401 Allocation and Apportionment

A company subject to the capital stock/franchise tax must (1) determine the total value of its capital stock (called "valuation") (¶ 1306), (2) determine its taxable assets (called "allocation") (this Chapter), (3) determine the taxable portion of its total capital stock value (called "apportionment") (Chapter 15), and (4) apply the applicable rate to its taxable capital stock value (see ¶ 1305 for table of applicable rates).

• *Reasons for allocation and apportionment*

Allocation and apportionment are necessary to ensure that states do not (1) violate federal laws or public policy, (2) tax assets outside their jurisdiction, or (3) subject taxpayers to unwarranted double taxation.

• *Definition of terms*

"Allocation" refers to the assignment of items of nonbusiness income to a particular state [61 Pa. Code § 153.24(a)(2)]. "Apportionment" refers to the division of business income between or among states by using a formula containing apportionment factors [61 Pa. Code § 153.24(a)(3)]. These definitions are found in the corporate net income tax regulations. Neither the statute nor the regulations applicable to the capital stock/franchise tax provide a definition of allocation and apportionment. However, the Tax Reform Code provides that the taxable value of the capital stock of a foreign corporation is to be determined by using the relevant apportionment factors set forth in the corporate net income tax provisions [72 P.S. § 7602(b)]. Thus, apportionment, within the context of the capital stock/franchise tax, means the division of total capital stock value into taxable and nontaxable portions.

"Allocation" *has no technical meaning* within the context of the capital stock/franchise tax. Commentators in this area often use the terms "allocation" and "apportionment" interchangeably. At times the term "allocation" is used to refer to the process of determining the taxable portion of property, payroll, and sales for three-factor apportionment. The term "allocation" is also often used to refer to the process of classifying assets as taxable or exempt, particularly when a corporation has assets that are used in both exempt and nonexempt activities (mixed assets), when a corporation's structure is multiform, or when a corporation owns assets that are unrelated to its business in Pennsylvania.

Meaning of "allocation": The term "allocation" (for capital stock/franchise tax purposes) refers to classification of assets as taxable or exempt (whether exempt by their very nature or exempt by situs or use) and to the classification of payroll and sales as taxable or exempt (within the context of three-factor apportionment). However, most of the problems with respect to allocation are encountered in the allocation of assets. Apportionment refers to the process of determining the portion of the capital stock value that is taxable. See Chapter 15 for an explanation of apportionment.

Different Meanings in Different Taxes

The term "allocation" has a specific meaning within the framework of the corporate net income tax. "Allocation" refers to the assignment of items of nonbusiness income to a particular state. The use of the term "allocation" to refer to the classification of assets as taxable or exempt is specific to this text and specific to the capital stock/franchise tax. Don't confuse the valuation and allocation processes. In determining the total value of capital stock (valuation), do not exclude any of your assets. The exemptions for nontaxable assets are in the form of subtractions from total assets in the numerator of the apportionment fraction and not by deducting the value of the exemption from the actual value of the capital stock [*Cmwlth. v. After Six, Inc.,* 413 A.2d 1017 (Pa.Commw. 1980)], aff'd, 489 Pa. 69 (Pa. 1980) Note, also, that for valuation purposes, value is actual value as of the end of the year, while for apportionment purposes value is average actual value at the end of the tax year.

¶1402 Allocation in General

The Department of Revenue takes the position that foreign corporations must use the same exemption rules that domestic corporations do. This means that the rules for exempting assets, sales, and payroll are the same for both domestic and foreign corporations. The rules for exempting assets, however, differ between single-factor apportionment and three-factor apportionment. Determination of actual value of tangible assets is also different for three-factor apportionment. Consideration of exempt assets within the framework of three-factor apportionment does not take intangible assets into consideration. This simplifies the allocation process. The only assets that are exempt in three-factor apportionment are tangible property with a

¶1402

situs outside Pennsylvania and tangible property used exclusively in manufacturing within Pennsylvania. Thus, the manufacturing exemption is important in three-factor apportionment, as it is in single-factor apportionment.

"Allocation" *is the process between valuation and apportionment.* It is used to determine which assets are included in the numerator of apportionment fractions. This process in terms of single-factor apportionment is depicted in the following chart. The chart below shows the classification process for a single asset and explains whether the value of the asset in question is taxable (included in the numerator of the apportionment fraction) or exempt (excluded from the numerator of the apportionment fraction). Note that in the cases of multiformity and unrelated assets, the value of the asset is excluded entirely from the tax base.

• *Scope*

The remainder of this chapter provides detailed explanations of exempt assets. However, three situations warrant special mention here: (1) multiformity; (2) unrelated assets; and (3) allocation of mixed assets.

"Multiformity" exists when a corporation is engaged in two distinct, separable businesses. For example, a corporation may be engaged in the manufacture of clothing and the manufacture of shoes and operate the two segments as independent businesses. (Multiformity is explained in detail at ¶1412.) According to the concept of multiformity, if one of these activities is conducted entirely outside of Pennsylvania, the value of the corporation's capital stock employed in the out-of-state activity should be excluded from the tax base for purposes of the franchise tax. This means that the average actual value of these assets will be excluded from the total capital stock value as well as from both the numerator and the denominator of the apportionment fractions.

The "unrelated assets" concept arises when a unitary (as opposed to multiform) business owns assets that are unrelated to the business it conducts in Pennsylvania. (The concept of unrelated assets is explained in detail at ¶1420.) According to the concept of unrelated assets, assets that are unrelated to the exercise of a corporation's franchise in Pennsylvania should be excluded from the tax base for purposes of the franchise tax. This means that the average actual value of these assets is excluded from the total capital stock value as well as from both the numerator and the denominator of the apportionment fractions.

A "mixed asset" is one that is used in both exempt and nonexempt activities. For example, assets used in manufacturing, processing, and research and development in Pennsylvania are exempt, but assets used in other activities, such as retailing or the offering of personal services, are not.

"Manufacturing" Defined

The term "manufacturing" is commonly used to encompass all three exempt activities—manufacturing, processing, and research and development—and is used in that way in this guidebook. When you see the term "manufacturing," interpret it to mean "manufacturing, processing, or research and development" unless the context specifically implies otherwise.

Some firms are engaged in both manufacturing (exempt) and nonmanufacturing (nonexempt) activities and use some assets in both (*e.g.,* storing both resale and manufacturing inventories in the same warehouse). In such cases, that part of the value of the asset used in the exempt activity is excluded from the numerator of the apportionment factor, while that part of the value of the asset that is not used in the exempt activity is not excluded. Allocation of mixed assets affects only the numerator of the apportionment fraction. The process of determining what part of the value of a mixed asset can be excluded is referred to here as allocation of a mixed asset. See ¶ 1418 for an explanation of allocation of mixed assets.

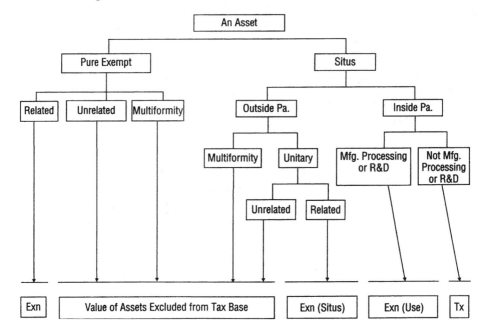

• *Exemption of assets*

Assets are exempt for three basic reasons: (1) constitutional restrictions, (2) statutory provisions, and (3) considerations of public policy.

• *Constitutional restrictions*

The primary constitutional restrictions, within the context of the capital stock/ franchise tax, are the following:

    (1) *Due Process Clause of the U.S. Constitution* [U.S. Constitution, Amendment 14, § 1]. This clause prohibits the taking of property without due process of law. Within the context of the capital stock/franchise tax it deals primarily with whether or not a state has given anything in return for the taxes it has taken. An example of property exempt by the Due Process Clause is property with a situs outside the Commonwealth.

    (2) *Equal Protection Clause of the U.S. Constitution* [U.S. Constitution, Amendment 14, § 1]. This clause prohibits discrimination, particularly in the context of taxation of interstate commerce.

    (3) *Commerce Clause of the U.S. Constitution* [U.S. Constitution, Article I, § 8, Cl. 3]. This clause (in conjunction with the Interstate Income Act) [15 U.S.C.A. § 381] places restrictions on the taxation of corporations engaged in interstate commerce. Basically, it prohibits discriminatory taxation of interstate commerce. See the explanation at ¶ 911.

    (4) *Federal immunity from state taxation.* The U.S. Constitution prohibits state taxation of the federal government [*M'Culloch v. Maryland,* 17 U.S. 316 (1819)]. This has the effect of exempting national bank shares and obligations of the federal government, federal agencies, and federal territories.

¶1402

(5) *Uniformity Clause of the Pennsylvania Constitution* [Pennsylvania Constitution, Article VIII, §I]. This clause prohibits discrimination among the same class of subjects of taxation and works to prevent discrimination much like the Equal Protection Clause of the U.S. Constitution.

(6) *Double taxation.* Technically, this is not a constitutional restriction because the Pennsylvania Constitution does not prohibit double taxation. However, it is often referred to as a constitutional restriction. The policy of Pennsylvania has consistently been to avoid double taxation. The Pennsylvania Supreme Court has repeatedly stated that double taxation will never be imposed in the absence of a clear expression of legislative intent. This operates to exempt shares of stock of other corporations subject to the capital stock tax. Nevertheless, taxation of more than 100% of a company's income is not expressly forbidden [*Penske Realty, Inc. v. Cmwlth.*, Pa.Commw., Nos. 73 F.R. 1995, 74 F.R. 1995 (July 27, 1998)].

Constitutional Protections

It is easy, in the process of trying to conform to the statutory provisions of tax laws, to forget (or consider unimportant) the large constitutional issues. However, this can be an expensive oversight. Tax planning requires familiarity not only with statutory and administrative requirements but also the underlying political and constitutional issues. You should not overlook the protections afforded by the federal and Commonwealth Constitutions.

• *Statutory exemptions*

The following assets are exempt by statute: (1) assets employed in manufacturing within Pennsylvania (see ¶1415); (2) pollution control devices (see ¶1419); (3) obligations of the Commonwealth of Pennsylvania and its political subdivisions (see ¶1405); and (4) stock of majority-owned foreign corporations (see ¶1405).

• *Public policy exemptions*

In a real sense, the exemptions to avoid double taxation are public policy exemptions. Also exempt as a matter of public policy are shares of stock in certain cooperative associations (see ¶1405).

• *Categories of exempt assets*

Although the technical basis for exemption of assets is constitutional, statutory, or public policy, in practice it is useful to use another framework for asset classification. Analysis of the rules for exemption of assets reveals three categories of exempt assets: (1) "pure" exempt assets (*i.e.*, those that are exempt regardless of situs or use, such as U.S. government obligations), (2) assets exempt by situs (*e.g*, tangible property located outside Pennsylvania), and (3) assets exempt by use (*e.g.*, assets used in manufacturing within Pennsylvania). The remainder of this chapter provides detailed explanations of assets that fall into these three categories.

"PURE" EXEMPT ASSETS

¶1405 Assets Exempt Regardless of Situs or Use

"Pure" exempt assets are assets that are exempt regardless of situs or use and are available to manufacturing and nonmanufacturing corporations alike. Since all of these assets are intangible assets, they are available for exemption only if a corporation uses single-factor apportionment. This has been expressly held in the case of stock of domestic corporations and majority-owned foreign corporations [*Cmwlth. v. After Six, Inc.*, 413 A.2d 1017 (Pa.Commw. 1980), *aff'd*, 489 Pa. 69 (Pa. 1980)].

¶1405

• *Attribution of ownership*

The statute is silent about the rules for attribution of ownership from subsidiary to parent. In one case [*Cmwlth. v. Union Collieries Co.*, 59 Dauph 220 (1948), *aff'd*, 93 A.2d 460 (1953)], the facts show that a parent corporation (Bessemer) owned 96.66% of its subsidiary (Union Collieries), and Union Collieries owned 33.19% of a third corporation (Consolidation Coal). The parent, Bessemer, also owned 17.02% of Consolidation Coal. If only the parent's pro rata share of Union Collieries's ownership of Consolidation Coal were attributed to Bessemer, Bessemer would fail to have more than 50% of Consolidation Coal, either directly or indirectly [(0.9666 x 0.3319) + 0.1702 = 0.4910]. However, Bessemer was given credit for all of its subsidiary's ownership and thus majority ownership [17.02% + 33.19% = 50.21%]. However, the parent's ownership was not an issue in this case, and the court later, in considering the same case, refused to determine the meaning of the clause "shall own, either directly or through subsidiary or sub-subsidiary corporations . . . ." [*Cmwlth. v. Union Collieries Co.*, 93 A.2d 460 (Pa. 1953)].

No "upstream" attribution of ownership: What the *Union Collieries* case does illustrate, however, is that ownership cannot be attributed "upstream." Union Collieries could not claim ownership of Consolidation Coal through its parent. Ownership can be attributed to a parent through subsidiaries but not to subsidiaries through parents.

• *"Pure" exempt assets*

The following assets are "pure" exempt assets:

(1) *Obligations of the federal government, federal agencies, and U.S. territories:* Examples of federal agencies are the FDIC and the Federal Intermediate Credit Bank. These are exempt because of federal immunity from state taxation.

(2) *Commonwealth and local obligations:* Obligations of the Commonwealth of Pennsylvania, any public authority, commission, board or other agency created by the Commonwealth, any political subdivision of the Commonwealth or any public authority created by the Commonwealth are exempt by statute [Act of August 31, 1971, P.L. 395, § 2].

Pass-Through Exemption

The Department of Revenue will allow a pass-through exemption in computing the exempt single-asset fraction for capital stock/franchise tax purposes. The exemption will apply to all applicable settlements and resettlements and must be claimed by the taxpayer by completing page 1 of the insert sheet, Form RCT-106. The exemption applies to investments in mutual funds and/or regulated investment companies that invest in Pennsylvania and/or U.S. government securities that would be exempt assets if directly owned by the taxpayer. The investment in the mutual fund and/or regulated investment company is granted an exemption for the same percentage as the deduction allowed from taxable income, on a pass-through basis, for purposes of the corporate net income tax [*Pennsylvania Tax Update No. 75*, Pennsylvania Department of Revenue, May/June 1998].

---

(3) *Stock of a majority-owned foreign corporation:* If a corporation owns, either directly or through subsidiary or sub-subsidiary corporations, over 50% of the outstanding shares of voting stock of a foreign corporation, such stock is exempt [72 P.S. § 1895].

Example: If Corporation A (a domestic corporation) owns 100% of Corporation B (a domestic corporation) and 10% of Corporation C, and Corporation B owns 45% of Corporation C (a foreign corporation), Corporation A may exclude both the B stock and the C stock because it owns 100% of Corporation B directly and 55% of Corporation C (10% directly and 45% indirectly). This would be true even if Corporation B were a foreign corporation. On the other hand, Corporation B cannot exclude its C stock, since it does not own more than 50% itself or through subsidiaries.

(4) *Stock of domestic corporations and domestic financial institutions:* Stock of domestic corporations subject to the capital stock tax or of financial institutions subject to the shares tax (*e.g.*, banks and trust companies) is exempt to prevent double taxation. See Chapter 16 (which contains an explanation of companies subject to the financial institutions shares tax).

Use Single-Factor Apportionment

You can exclude the value of stock in domestic corporations and majority-owned foreign corporations *only if you use single-factor apportionment.*

---

(5) *Foreign corporation holdings in domestic corporation:* It has been held that a foreign corporation subject to the franchise tax is not entitled to the exemption for holdings in domestic corporations [*Cmwlth. v. Monessen Amusement Co.*, 42 A.2d 158 (Pa. 1945)]. However, this was before the decision in *Gilbert Associates, Inc. v. Cmwlth.*, 447 A.2d 944 (1982), and *Quality Market Inc. v. Cmwlth.*, 514 A.2d 228 (Pa.Commw. 1986), *aff'd per curiam*, 526 A.2d 357 (Pa. 1987), *cert. den.*, U.S. Supreme Court (October 19, 1987). Now, a foreign corporation using single-factor apportionment must use the same rules that apply to domestic corporations. See ¶1501. This means that foreign corporations electing single-factor apportionment may now exclude holdings in domestic corporations.

(6) *Stock of nonprofit corporations:* These are exempt as a matter of public policy.

(7) *Stock of credit unions:* These are exempt as a matter of public policy.

(8) *Stock and obligations of cooperative agricultural associations and agricultural credit unions:* These are exempt as a matter of public policy.

(9) *National bank shares:* These are exempt because of federal immunity from state taxation.

(10) *Imports and exports:* The Import-Export Clause of the U.S. Constitution restricts state taxation of imports and exports [U.S. Constitution, Article 1, § 10]. Until 1976 the rule was that imports were exempt so long as they were in their original package (see, *e.g.*, *Brown v. Maryland*, 25 U.S. 419 (1827)). However, in 1976, the United States Supreme Court overruled the original package doctrine [*Michelin Tire Corp. v. Wages*, 423 U.S. 276 (1976)]. In *Michelin*, the U.S. Supreme Court held that the Import-Export Clause prohibited duties on imports but did not prohibit nondiscriminatory ad valorem taxes (*e.g.*, capital stock taxes) on goods that were no longer in transit. If imported goods are no longer in transit or have been put to the use for which they were imported, they are no longer exempt as imports. Exemption must then be based on situs or use. The question with respect to exports is whether they have physically begun movement to a scheduled foreign destination (see, *e.g.*, *Department of Revenue (Washington) v. Association of Washington Stevedoring Cos.*, 435 U.S. 734 (1978)).

(11) *Student loan assets:* Student loan assets owned or held by an entity created for the securitization of student loans are excluded from the capital stock tax base by 72 P.S. § 7602(a) and 72 P.S. § 7602(b). Student loan assets include the following:

(a) Student loan notes.

(b) Federal, state or private subsidies or guarantees of student loans.

(c) Instruments that represent a guarantee of debt, certificates or other securities issued by an entity created for the securitization of student loans, or by a trustee on its behalf.

(d) Contract rights to acquire or dispose of student loans and interest rate swap agreements related to student loans.

(e) Interests or debt obligations of other student loan securitization trusts or entities.

(f) Cash or cash equivalents representing reserve funds or payments on or with respect to student loan notes, the securities issued by an entity created for the securitization of student loans or the other student loan related assets. Solely for this purpose cash or cash equivalents include the following:

(i) Direct obligations of the U.S. Department of the Treasury.

(ii) Obligations of federal agencies that represent the full faith and credit of the United States.

(iii) Investment grade debt obligations or commercial paper.

(iv) Deposit accounts.

(v) Federal funds and banker's acceptances.

(vi) Prefunded municipal obligations.

(vii) Money market instruments and money market funds.

ASSETS EXEMPT BECAUSE OF SITUS

¶1410 Tangible Assets Located Outside Pennsylvania

Tangible assets located outside of Pennsylvania are excluded from the numerator of the single-factor apportionment fraction and from the numerator of the tangible property factor in three-factor apportionment.

• *Movable tangible property*

In the case of real estate, determination of location (*i.e.,* taxable situs) is relatively simple. However, in the case of movable tangible property, determination of taxable situs may be more difficult. If movable tangible property (*e.g.,* office equipment, trucks, machinery) is used exclusively in out-of-state operations, it is exempt. However, if tangible property is moved in and out of the Commonwealth during a taxable period, an allocation must be made [*Delaware, Lackawanna and Western R.R. Co. v. Pennsylvania,* 198 U.S. 341 (1905)]. These assets are mixed assets (*i.e.,* partially exempt and partially taxable). The value of these assets must be allocated on the basis of some logical criterion. See ¶1418 for an explanation of allocation of mixed assets.

• *Interstate commerce corporations*

The problem of determining taxable situs of tangible property is primarily one of corporations engaged in interstate commerce (*e.g.,* utility companies, railroads, motor carriers, marine transportation companies). A commonly used method of allocating these mixed assets is by the use of revenue miles. Revenue miles are explained at ¶1112.

¶1411 Intangible Assets with an Out-of-State Situs

In general, intangible assets have a taxable situs in the domiciliary state of the owner. In the case of corporations the domiciliary state is the state of incorporation. However, if intangible assets have acquired a "business situs" in Pennsylvania (*i.e.,* they are used in a trade or business in Pennsylvania), they are subject to tax in Pennsylvania, even if they are owned by a foreign corporation. On the other hand, all

¶1410

the intangible assets of a domestic corporation are subject to tax in the Commonwealth, even if they have acquired a "business situs" in another state [*Cmwlth. v. Universal Trades, Inc.*, 141 A.2d 204 (Pa. 1958), *app. dism'd*, 358 U.S. 129 (1959), *reh'g den.*, 358 U.S. 938 (1959)].

• *No exclusion from numerator*

One issue with respect to the taxable situs of intangibles is in regard to whether or not foreign corporations can exclude the value of their out-of-state intangibles from the numerator of the single-factor apportionment formula. The Commonwealth takes the position that they cannot. See the explanation at ¶ 1501.

A much more important question with respect to intangible assets within the framework of the capital stock/franchise tax is the issue of the exemption of intangibles used in manufacturing. This is explained at ¶ 1417.

¶1412 Multiformity

If a corporation's business is multiform and one or more of the unrelated enterprises is carried on totally outside Pennsylvania, the doctrine of multiformity provides that the value of the out-of-state enterprise(s) is to be excluded: (1) from the total capital stock value, (2) from the numerator of the apportionment fractions, and (3) from the denominator of the apportionment fractions. In other words, the value of the out-of-state enterprise(s) is completely eliminated from the tax base. This is different from the usual rule that assets are exempt only from the numerator of the apportionment fractions. Multiformity applies to both tangible and intangible assets.

Unitary Apportionment

If a business is found not to be multiform it is unitary. The issue of unitary apportionment is controversial and is more often encountered within the context of the corporate net income tax (although it does apply to capital stock taxation). For a more complete discussion of unitary apportionment, see ¶ 1114. In all of the cases discussed below, the corporation in question was itself carrying on activities outside the Commonwealth of Pennsylvania. If a subsidiary had been involved, the outcome might have been different. For example, if the corporations in the cases below had subsidiaries carrying on the out-of-state activities (instead of themselves engaging in the out-of-state activities), Pennsylvania would not have included the income of the out-of-state subsidiary in the income of the parent. As the term "unitary taxation" is ordinarily used in state tax literature, Pennsylvania is not a unitary state.

• *Definition of "multiformity"*

The Dauphin County Court (predecessor of the Commonwealth Court) has provided a succinct and widely quoted definition of multiformity: "Multiformity in business activity exists where two separate and segregated enterprises are not related to each other and are conducted as separate and independent units, and the corporation derives benefits from each independent unit that are not related to the operation of the other units." [*Cmwlth. v. The L.D. Caulk Co.*, 69 Dauph 289 (1956)].

The concept of multiformity within the framework of the franchise tax was first applied in 1939 [*Cmwlth. v. Columbia Gas and Electric Corp.*, 8 A.2d 404 (Pa. 1939)]. Columbia Gas and Electric Corporation was a Delaware company authorized to produce oil, gas, and electricity and to hold real estate in Pennsylvania. However, the largest part of its activities consisted of acting as a holding company, and it was not authorized to act as a holding company in Pennsylvania. The Pennsylvania Supreme Court held that the capital stock value associated with the holding company business must be excluded from the total taxable capital stock value because it bore no relation to the exercise of the corporation's franchise in Pennsylvania. The concept of multiformity as stated by the Pennsylvania Supreme Court requires that property outside the Commonwealth be taken into consideration only if it is an organic or functional part of the business done in the Commonwealth.

• *Later cases*

In later cases, the Pennsylvania Supreme Court dealt with two cases in which the taxpayers tried to show multiform business operations by separating the company into functional areas [*Cmwlth. v. Ford Motor Company*, 38 A.2d 329 (Pa. 1944), *app. dism'd*, 324 U.S. 890 (1945); *Cmwlth. v. Quaker Oats Co.*, 38 A.2d 325 (1944)]. For example, in the *Ford Motor* case the taxpayer contended that its business comprised four distinct corporate functions: (1) the purchase and production of raw materials, (2) the manufacture of steel, glass, cement, paint, etc., (3) the assembly of finished automobiles, and (4) the sale and servicing of the finished automotive products. Ford Motor further asserted that it conducted only the latter two functions in Pennsylvania. The U.S. Supreme Court found Ford Motor's reasoning to be fallacious and refused to find multiformity for Ford Motor and later for Quaker Oats, which made the same kind of argument. A Delaware corporation selling a partnership interest wherein the partnership's operations consisted of managing a Philadelphia apartment complex was denied multiform treatment. The taxpayer's interest in the partnership was found to be integrally related to its business activities in Pennsylvania. [*RB Alden Corp. v. Cmwlth.*, ___ A.3d ___ (Pa.Commw. 2016)].

• *General rules for multiformity*

In 1970 the Pennsylvania Supreme Court laid down some general rules of guidance in the areas of multiformity and reiterated its position that functional division was not multiformity [*Cmwlth. v. ACF Industries, Inc.*, 271 A.2d 273 (Pa. 1970)]. In the *ACF* decision the Pennsylvania Supreme Court stated that multiform or unrelated assets cases deal with an apportionment dependent on factual considerations unique to each case but that some consistent principles are clear and listed them as follows:

(1) If a multistate business enterprise is conducted in such a way that one, some or all of its business activities operated outside Pennsylvania are independent of and do not contribute to the business operations within Pennsylvania, the factors attributable to the outside activity may be excluded.

(2) In applying the principle of multiformity to a particular case, the focus is upon the relationship between the Pennsylvania activity and the non-Pennsylvania activity, not the common relationship between these activities and the central corporate structure. Only if the impact of the central corporate structure on the operating activities is so pervasive as to negate any claim that they function independently is multiformity denied.

(3) The manufacturing, wholesaling and retailing (or manufacturing and selling) activities of a single entity are not fit subjects for division and partial exclusions. However, a truly divisionalized business, conducting disparate activities with each division internally integrated with respect to manufacturing and selling, may well be in a position to make a valid claim for exclusion.

• *Two divisions manufacturing same products*

Most multiformity cases have involved companies engaged in two distinct kinds of businesses, such as the following:

(1) A rental business in Pennsylvania and a sand and gravel business outside Pennsylvania [*Cmwlth. v. Morewood Realty Corp.*, 327 A.2d 328 (Pa. 1974)].

(2) Rental or real estate in Pennsylvania and general securities investment business outside Pennsylvania [*Cmwlth. v. Kirby Estates, Inc.*, 246 A.2d 120 (Pa. 1968)].

¶1412

(3) Mining of coal in Pennsylvania and a tugboat business outside of Pennsylvania [*Cmwlth. v. Baker-Whitely Coal Co.*, 60 Dauph 434 (1950), *exceptions dism'd*, 62 Dauph 207 (1950)].

However, in a 1974 case, the Commonwealth Court found multiformity in the case of a corporation with two divisions—one in Pennsylvania and one in Ohio—both of which manufactured clay products [*Logan Clay Products Co. v. Cmwlth.*, 315 A.2d 346 (Pa.Commw. 1974)]. The Commonwealth Court, in *Logan Clay Products*, emphasized the fact that each division was operated independently, the products they made were not interchangeable, and the Ohio Division activities neither enhanced nor diminished the firm's business activities in Pennsylvania.

• *Not all firms will benefit from multiform treatment*

Ordinarily multiform treatment is advantageous to firms whose out-of-state business has a capital stock value far in excess of the capital stock value of the in-state business. See ¶ 1504 for an example of multiform apportionment.

Overall Planning Is Important

The doctrine of multiformity also applies to the corporate net income tax. If you are subject to both the franchise tax and the corporate net income tax, you must consider your overall tax liability, not just your franchise tax liability alone. Apportionment under multiformity may or may not reduce your franchise tax, but it may increase your corporate net income tax; it may increase your franchise tax, but reduce your corporate net income tax; or it may increase or reduce both taxes at the same time. You should evaluate your situation very carefully before deciding to invoke the doctrine of multiformity.

• *Filing as multiform business optional*

Apparently, a taxpayer cannot be forced to file as a multiform business if it does not elect to do so. This was the ruling of the Pennsylvania Supreme Court in *Cmwlth. v. American Telephone and Telegraph Co.*, 115 A.2d 373 (Pa. 1955).

• *How to claim multiformity*

In order to claim multiformity, taxpayers simply file a franchise tax return computing their total capital stock value and their apportionment fraction or fractions on a multiform basis, but they should be sure to document their claims.

Caution: Unitary Filing May Become Unavailable

Taxpayers should be aware that they may not be able to return to filing on a unitary basis after they have filed on a multiform basis. It is the position of the Department of Revenue that Subparagraph 18 (72 P.S. §7401(3)2(a)(18)) of the Tax Reform Code (explained at ¶1114) gives it the authority to require taxpayers to continue filing on a multiform basis, even if filing on a unitary basis should become advantageous in the future.

ASSETS EXEMPT BECAUSE OF USE

¶1415 Assets Used in Manufacturing, Processing, and Research and Development

A corporation (except one that enjoys and exercises the right of eminent domain; *i.e.*, the right to appropriate or condemn private property for authorized purposes) that is organized for manufacturing, processing, research or development purposes may exclude from the numerator of its apportionment fraction the value of assets that are "invested in and actually and exclusively employed in carrying on manufacturing, processing, research or development within the state . . . ." [72 P.S. § 7602(a)] This exemption applies to both tangible and intangible property.

• *Exemption basis*

The exemption for assets (tangible or intangible) used in manufacturing, processing, or research and development is available only for assets used in manufacturing *in Pennsylvania.*

Classification of Activities as Exempt or Nonexempt

A table of classification of activities as exempt as determined by statute or case law is provided at ¶ 1605. Consult this table for the classification of specific activities.

The manufacturing exemption also applies to both single-factor and three-factor apportionment. However, the valuation rules for the property factor in three-factor apportionment differ from those used in single-factor apportionment. (See ¶ 1107 for an explanation of the property factor.)

• *Major exemption issues*

The major difficulties in consideration of exemption of assets devoted to manufacturing are (1) whether the activity to which they are devoted is manufacturing and (2) what portion of the asset is exclusively devoted to manufacturing. The definition of what constitutes manufacturing is discussed in Chapter 16.

The second problem is that of mixed assets—assets that are used in both exempt and nonexempt activities. For example, if a corporation is engaged in both manufacturing and dealing in goods for resale, part of a manufacturing corporation's administrative office is devoted to manufacturing and part is devoted to the resale business. The question is the proportion that is devoted to each part. The answer lies in finding a logical basis for allocation. (Allocation of mixed assets is explained at ¶ 1418.)

¶ 1416 Exempt Manufacturing Tangibles

Tangible property includes cash on hand, supplies, inventories, land, buildings, machinery, equipment, motor vehicles, and other property capable of perception by the physical senses. For single-factor apportionment, tangible property includes only property owned by the taxpayer. This means that the taxpayer must hold beneficial title. In the case of leasehold improvements, the lessee has beneficial title if the lease is for a period of 99 years or longer or if the lessee has the right to remove the improvements when the lease expires. Retention of title solely as a security interest does not constitute ownership. Liens are not tangible property. However, property need not be in the physical possession of the taxpayer to be owned by the taxpayer. For example, if a taxpayer sends goods out on consignment, and retains title to them, the taxpayer owns these goods. A taxpayer's property held in a warehouse (for which the taxpayer holds a warehouse receipt) is owned by the taxpayer. Ownership of property in transit also depends upon who holds title. (For three-factor apportionment purposes, tangible property also includes tangible rented property; see ¶ 1107.)

• *Cash on hand*

Since a corporation needs cash to engage in manufacturing, the amount of cash on hand is ordinarily considered working capital used in manufacturing. (See the detailed explanation of cash at ¶ 1417.)

• *Inventories*

Like cash, inventories are ordinarily considered working capital assets. Raw materials to be used in manufacturing, manufacturing work in progress, finished manufactured goods, and supplies are exempt. However, in the case of raw materials and supplies, some caution is advised. The Department of Revenue takes the position that no exemption is allowable for raw materials and supplies in excess of an amount necessary for one year's manufacturing activity *in Pennsylvania*. See also *Cmwlth. v. Custer City Chemical Co.*, 16 Dauph 46 (1913), and *Cmwlth. v. New York & Pennsylvania Co.*, 435 U.S. 734 (1978).

• *Plant, property, and equipment*

The manufacturing exemption applies to such assets as office buildings, delivery equipment, vehicles for use of officers and employees, and administrative facilities, as well as plants, land, and equipment used in manufacturing. Remember, tangible assets located outside Pennsylvania are exempt because of situs, not use.

• *Leased property*

Property owned by a taxpayer and leased to another person who uses the property in manufacturing is entitled to the manufacturing exemption for those assets if the lessor is organized for manufacturing purposes [Act of July 11, 1901, § 1]. However, for three-factor apportionment purposes the receipts from leased assets are includable in the numerator of the sales factor. See the explanation of the sales factor at ¶ 1109.

¶1417 Exempt Manufacturing Intangibles

Like tangible assets used in manufacturing, intangible assets used in manufacturing (in Pennsylvania) are exempt. However, often a taxpayer corporation owns more intangibles than necessary for working capital (excess intangibles). Excess intangibles require allocation. (See the explanation of allocation of mixed assets at ¶ 1418).

• *Cash*

Cash is necessary in carrying on any business and, therefore, is ordinarily considered working capital (*i.e.,* used in the activity in which a corporation engages). Funds in demand deposits (*e.g.,* checking account) are considered working capital and thus exempt. For interest-bearing accounts, the Department of Revenue uses the minimum cash balance method for determining the amount of exempt cash. Under this method the lowest daily balance is not exempt. The Commonwealth Court has upheld the Department's use of this method in an unreported decision [*Audio General, Inc. v. Cmwlth.*, No. 63 F&R 1989 (November 26, 1991)]. See also *Fizzano Brothers, Inc. v. Cmwlth.*, 645 A.2d 431 (Pa.Commw. 1994), *aff'd,* 664 A.2d 1308 (Pa. 1995), where the minimum cash balance of a money market account was held to be not exempt. If a corporation has excess cash, it might consider investing in "pure" exempt assets (*e.g.,* U.S. Treasury bills) or in other exempt assets, such as raw materials, to avoid the taxability of excess cash. Note, however, that excessive stockpiling of raw materials may lead to taxability. See ¶ 1416. Note that the Department of Revenue reserves the right to utilize an alternative method of determining the taxable portion of cash when it determines that balances are being manipulated for the purpose of tax avoidance [*Corporate Tax Bulletin 2008-04*, December 1, 2008].

Review Options

If a company has been refused an exemption for a minimum cash balance in an interest-bearing account, it should review its appeal options (*e.g.,* refund, resettlement). The policy of the Department of Revenue has routinely been to allow exemption of the minimum cash balance in an interest-bearing account.

• *Receivables and advances*

Accounts and notes receivable from customers ordinarily are considered working capital and, thus, exempt. However, receivables from and advances to persons other than customers usually are not exempt. For example, it has been held that advances to, and accounts receivable from, a wholly owned subsidiary are not assets used in manufacturing, even though the subsidiary itself uses the funds advanced in manufacturing [*Cmwlth. v. Prudential Industries, Inc.*, 80 Dauph 381 (1963)]. It has also been held that advances made by a subsidiary to its parent are not manufacturing assets, even though the parent used the funds in manufacturing [*Chrysel Corp. v. Cmwlth.*, 295 A.2d 624 (Pa.Commw. 1972)]. Advances to officers and employees ordinarily are not exempt; however, see the explanation of prepaid expenses below.

• *Prepaid expenses*

If the property or service acquired with a prepayment is connected with manufacturing (*e.g.*, supplies, inventory, rent, insurance), the prepayment is an exempt asset. If an advance has been made to a person who is to render services to the corporation (*e.g.*, plant repairs), it should be considered a prepaid expense. Advances made to officers and employees for exempt expenditures (*e.g.*, salaries, travel expenses), therefore, are exempt. However, care should be taken to substantiate thoroughly advances to noncustomers, since advances to noncustomers are highly suspect.

• *Cash surrender value of life insurance policies*

Life insurance cash surrender values are not exempt assets [*Cmwlth. v. Steel Heddle Manufacturing Co.*, 41 Dauph 315 (1935)]. However, if a corporation has pledged the life insurance policies as collateral to get manufacturing capital to be used in Pennsylvania, the cash value is considered employed in manufacturing in Pennsylvania and is, thus, exempt.

• *Securities*

Some stocks and bonds are "pure" exempt assets. See ¶1405. These are exempt without regard to manufacturing. Other securities are taxable unless they can be shown to be part of a manufacturing corporation's working capital. For example, if certain marketable securities are held as temporary income-producing investments of cash needed for business operation (as in the case of a seasonal business), they are exempt. See the explanation of reserves (below).

Securities pledged as collateral: Securities pledged as collateral to obtain manufacturing working capital (to be used in manufacturing in Pennsylvania) are considered to be invested in, and used in, manufacturing. However, it is the position of the Department of Revenue that, if the value of the collateral exceeds the amount borrowed, only that value of the capital to the extent of the amount of the loan is exempt. This issue has not yet been decided in the courts.

• *Reserves and sinking funds*

If assets are held in reserve to meet some purpose, whether or not the assets are exempt depends upon the purpose for which they are retained. However, in practice it is very difficult to sustain the position that funds invested in stocks, bonds, certificates of deposit, etc., are used in manufacturing. In order to be exempt, assets must be used in manufacturing *during the taxable year* in question.

This point was made in a case in which a taxpayer invested $700,000 in certificates of deposit. The investment was made in 1975, and later the funds were used to pay for an expansion of its physical plant, the purchase of new printing presses, and payment of federal income taxes. The Commonwealth Court held that it did not matter how the funds were used after the certificates matured. The important fact was that the certificates of deposit were not used *during the taxable year* for any purpose directly related to its manufacturing business. They were not used to maintain a day-to-day cash flow essential for conducting business but instead were invested for a set period of time for the purpose of earning interest [*Fry Communications, Inc. v. Cmwlth.*, 433 A.2d 601 (Pa.Commw. 1981)]. In this case, the funds were not expressly set aside for future expansion. However, it would not have mattered. Funds *expressly* set aside for future manufacturing expansion are not exempt [*Cmwlth. v. Nagle Engine and Boiler Works*, 23 Dauph 235 (1920)].

In an earlier case a taxpayer had purchased shares of stock to finance its self-insured employee pension fund. The Commonwealth Court held that the stock had been withdrawn from the manufacturing process and was, therefore, not exempt [*Cmwlth. v. Bachman Brothers, Inc.*, 87 Dauph 311 (1968)]. In another case a taxpayer acquired shares of stock to settle a claim for damages that had been brought against it, but the claimant refused to accept the shares. The taxpayer held the stock for several years, hoping to avoid a loss on the sale of the shares. The Commonwealth Court held that this stock was not used in manufacturing [*Cmwlth. v. McClintic-Marshall Construction Co.*, 25 Dauph 210 (1922)].

• *Sinking fund*

When a corporation sets up a sinking fund to retire some of its bonds, the bonds acquired through the sinking fund are extinguished debt, not assets, and reduce the corresponding liability account. However, if the assets in the sinking fund exceed the cost of retiring the debt, such funds are not exempt. Likewise, if a corporation acquires its own indebtedness without the use of a sinking fund, the acquired bonds are not assets; they are extinguished debt and reduce the corresponding liability account.

• *Treasury stock*

Treasury stock is *not* an asset. It is a contra-equity account and should be used as an offset against stockholder equity.

• *Patents and copyrights*

Patents and copyrights are not "pure" exempt assets. However, if they relate to goods that a taxpayer manufactures, they are exempt manufacturing intangibles.

• *Minimizing excess intangibles*

A corporation may minimize its "excess intangibles" problem by qualifying for three-factor apportionment, in which intangible assets are not used. A corporation can do this by establishing taxable business activity on its own in another state, becoming a member of a partnership conducting taxable business activity outside Pennsylvania, or forming a new corporation in another state to handle corporate investments. The excess intangibles would be transferred to the new corporation. The stock of a majority-owned subsidiary is a "pure" exempt asset in the hands of the parent, and the subsidiary can pass the earnings up to the parent in the form of dividends without the parent's incurring Pennsylvania corporate net income tax liability. See the explanation of sales factor at ¶1109 and the explanation of corporate partnership interest at ¶906.

¶1418 Allocation of Mixed Assets

Allocation of mixed assets is necessary in many situations (*e.g.*, rolling stock used in and outside Pennsylvania; excess intangibles; assets used in both manufacturing and nonmanufacturing activities). The allocation process divides the value of the asset into taxable and exempt portions.

• *Methods*

The method of allocating mixed assets must yield logical results under the facts and circumstances of individual cases. There is no one method to be used in all situations. A commonly used method of allocating mixed assets is to use sales as the basis for allocation of mixed assets. Other methods include square footage (*e.g.*, a warehouse); specific identification (*e.g.*, two computers used exclusively in billing related to the manufacturing activity and two other computers used exclusively in billing related to the nonmanufacturing activity); number of invoices (*e.g.*, one computer used for billing for both exempt and nonexempt activities); number of employees (*e.g.*, two of five warehouse employees handling only manufacturing inventory).

¶1419 Pollution Control Devices

The law provides that equipment, machinery, facilities, and other tangible property employed or utilized *within Pennsylvania* for water and air pollution control or abatement devices that are being employed or utilized for the benefit of the general public are exempt for capital stock/franchise tax purposes [72 P.S. § 7602.1].

Corporations using single-factor apportionment use average net book value to determine the amount excluded from the numerator of the asset fraction (apportionment fraction), and corporations using three-factor apportionment should exclude the original cost from the numerator of the property factor. Corporations claiming the exemption for pollution control devices should submit with their Form RCT-106 a schedule providing a description, the location, and the value of the pollution control device. This is done annually. In addition, a taxpayer must submit with the *first* claim for exemption for a new device a copy of the certification issued by the Pennsylvania Department of Environmental Resources.

Tax Practice Advice

In practice, pollution control devices are sometimes taken as a manufacturing exemption rather than as an exemption under the special provisions. However, if you are a nonmanufacturing corporation, the only way you can get the exemption for pollution control devices is under the special statutory provisions for exemption of such assets.

The Department of Revenue has the power, through publication in the *Pennsylvania Bulletin*, to prescribe the manner and method by which this exemption shall be granted and claimed [72 P.S. § 7602.1].

¶1420 Unrelated Assets

The concept of unrelated assets is similar and related to the concept of multiformity. However, the two concepts are not identical. The concept of unrelated assets is used to answer the same questions that the concept of multiformity does: (1) what is the value of the corporate franchise being exercised in Pennsylvania and (2) have all elements of value bearing no relation to the exercise of the privilege of doing business in Pennsylvania been eliminated from the value of the franchise? [*Cmwlth. v. Kirby Estates, Inc.*, 246 A.2d 120 (Pa. 1968)]. However, the concept of unrelated assets operates to exclude assets from the franchise tax base, *even though a corporation may be engaged in a unitary business.* For example, in *Cmwlth. v. The Mundy Corporation*, 30 A.2d 878 (Pa. 1943), the Pennsylvania Supreme Court dealt with a case in which the taxpayer, a Delaware corporation, was authorized to conduct a general real estate business in Pennsylvania. Mundy owned a large amount of securities held for investment. The court held that the securities, even though kept in Pennsylvania, had no function in the conduct of Mundy's real estate business and were not working capital, so Pennsylvania could not tax them. The concept of unrelated assets applies to both tangible and intangible assets.

The classic unrelated assets case is *Cmwlth. v. ACF Industries, Inc.*, 271 A.2d 273 Pa. 1970). In this case the taxpayer, a New Jersey corporation, conducted the same kinds of activities both inside and outside Pennsylvania and conceded that its business enterprise was unitary. The assets involved were shares of stock in another corporation purchased with the intention of acquiring assets or effecting a merger. After 16 months, ACF decided not to pursue acquisition of assets or a merger and sold the stock in question. In the *ACF* decision, the court emphasized that the issue was not whether assets were used for general business purposes but whether the assets were used in any way that was related to or contributed to the taxpayer's business in Pennsylvania. Because the court found no relationship between the stock and the exercise of ACF's franchise in Pennsylvania, the court held that the value of the stock must be excluded from its apportionment fractions for the years in question.

• *Exclusion from franchise tax base*

If assets are unrelated assets, within the meaning of this doctrine, the value of these assets is excluded from (1) the total capital stock value, (2) the numerator of the apportionment fraction, and (3) the denominator of the apportionment fraction. Just as in the case of multiformity, these assets are completely removed from the franchise tax base.

¶1421 Scope of Multiformity and Unrelated Assets

So far the concepts of multiformity and unrelated assets have been applied only to foreign corporations. The Department of Revenue has taken the position that these concepts cannot be invoked by domestic corporations.

The corporate net income tax law, however, provides the following:

If the allocation and apportionment provisions of this definition do not fairly represent the extent of the taxpayer's business activity in this State, the taxpayer may petition the Secretary of Revenue for, or the Secretary of Revenue may require, in respect to all or any part of the taxpayer's business activity: (A) separate accounting; (B) the exclusion of any one or more of the factors; (C) the inclusion of one or more additional factors that will fairly represent the taxpayer's business activity in this State; or (D) the employment of any other method to effectuate an equitable allocation and apportionment of the taxpayer's income [72 P.S. § 7401(3)2(a)(18)].

This provision is commonly referred to as "Subparagraph (18)." Either a taxpayer or the Commonwealth can invoke the powers of Subparagraph (18). In order to receive relief under Subparagraph (18), a taxpayer must be able to show that the normal statutory provisions for allocation and apportionment do not achieve results that fairly represent a taxpayer's value or income attributable to Pennsylvania. See ¶1114 for explanation of Subparagraph (18) (also called Subsection (18)).

The Commonwealth Court has ruled that Subparagraph (18) relief applies to the capital stock/franchise tax [*Unisys Corporation v. Cmwlth.*, 726 A.2d 109 (Pa.Commw. 1999). Unisys Corporation did not include as income dividends it received from subsidiaries or other investee corporations. The Department of Revenue increased the amount of Unisys's reported net worth to include the value of its investments in subsidiaries and increased the amount reported as average net income by adding the amount of dividends Unisys received from subsidiaries and investee corporations. The Commonwealth Court concluded that the strict statutory formulation resulted in a disparity of tax due large enough to require some form of Subparagraph (18) relief. The Pennsylvania Supreme Court, however, disagreed with the Commonwealth Court. Noting that a taxpayer alleging Commerce and Due Process Clause violations bears a substantial burden to demonstrate by clear and cogent evidence that the state is taxing income earned outside its jurisdiction, which Unisys failed to bear, the Pennsylvania Supreme Court reversed the Commonwealth Court and remanded the case for reinstatement of the original settlement [812 A.2d 448 (Pa. 2002), *rev'g*, 726 A.2d 109 (Pa.Commw. 1999)].

The concepts of multiformity and unrelated assets can apply equally to the corporate net income tax and the franchise tax. Whether the franchise tax and/or the corporate net income tax are involved, the principles are the same [*Cmwlth. v. ACF Industries, Inc.*, 271 A.2d 273 (Pa. 1970)]. If it is true that this section applies to the capital stock/franchise tax, it should provide a vehicle for domestic corporations to claim the benefits of multiformity and unrelated assets (explained earlier).

• *Concepts apply to foreign corporations*

Whether or not the section quoted above applies to the capital stock/franchise tax, multiformity and unrelated assets are well-established judicial concepts available to foreign corporations.

EXEMPT PAYROLL AND SALES

¶1425 Exempt Payroll

The law provides that the payroll factor used in three-factor apportionment shall not include any payroll attributable to manufacturing, processing, research or development activities anywhere [72 P.S. §7602(b)]. (The payroll factor is explained in detail at ¶1108.) Under prior law, only payroll attributable to manufacturing, processing, research or development activities *in Pennsylvania* were exempt (see ¶1301).

As in the case of allocation of mixed assets, allocation of payroll must be based on some logical criterion. See the explanation at ¶1418. Careful recordkeeping is needed to ensure the highest supportable allocation. Be sure to include thorough documentation of payroll allocation with your return. See ¶1113 for an explanation of allocation of partnership payroll.

¶1426 Exempt Sales

No Pennsylvania-source sales are exempt. All sales that are sourced to Pennsylvania (including those attributable to manufacturing, processing, research or development activities) are taxable [72 P.S. §76029b)(1)(ii)]. See ¶1109 and ¶1503 for further discussion of the sales factor.

CAPITAL STOCK TAX, FRANCHISE TAX, AND CORPORATE LOANS TAX

CHAPTER 15

APPORTIONMENT

¶1501	Apportionment in General
¶1502	Single-Factor Apportionment
¶1503	Three-Factor Apportionment
¶1504	Apportionment Under Multiformity
¶1505	Special Rules

Caution: There is No Capital Stock/Franchise Tax for tax years beginning after 12/31/15

¶1501 Apportionment in General

Apportionment refers to the process of determining how much of a corporation's capital stock value is subject to the capital stock/franchise tax. This is done by first determining the company's capital stock value (see ¶1306) and then applying one of two formulas—the single-factor apportionment formula (see ¶1502) or the three-factor apportionment formula (see ¶1503). The factors used to apportion total capital stock value are fractions, the numerators and denominators of which are expressed at *average actual value.*

• *Average actual value*

The term "actual value" technically means cash value, but in practice book value is used for all assets [61 Pa. Code § 155.10(b)(2)].

Subsidiaries

If a subsidiary is subject to the Pennsylvania capital stock/franchise tax, the parent should use its pro rata share of the subsidiary's *total* book value, not its pro rata share of the taxable value of its capital stock. For example, if Corporation P owns 100% of a subsidiary that has a book value of $2,000,000 and an apportionment fraction of 60%, Corporation P should report its stock at a value of $2,000,000, *not* $1,200,000.

"Average value" normally means the simple average of the beginning and ending values. However, the Department of Revenue may require the monthly or daily averaging of book values of real and tangible and intangible personal property owned by the taxpayer if more frequent averaging is reasonably required to reflect the value of the property or if substantial property is acquired or disposed of during the taxable year [61 Pa. Code § 155.10(e)]. See ¶1502 for an explanation of the direct buildup method (using simple averaging).

Domestic corporations may use either single-factor apportionment or three-factor apportionment if they meet the requirements for three-factor apportionment. See ¶1503.

The normal method of apportionment for foreign corporations is three-factor apportionment, but foreign corporations can elect to use single-factor apportionment. If a foreign corporation elects to use single-factor apportionment, it will be treated as if it were a domestic corporation for the purpose of determining which of its assets are exempt from taxation and for the purpose of determining the proportion of the value of its capital stock that is subject to taxation [61 Pa. Code § 155.10(a)(2)]. This means that foreign corporations must include intangibles in their apportionment factors just like domestic corporations, ignoring the long-standing rule that the situs of intangibles is the domiciliary state of the taxpayer. This requirement was challenged in *Quality Market, Inc. v. Cmwlth.*, 514 A.2d 228 (1986); *aff'd per curiam*, 526 A.2d 357 (1987), and held to be constitutional. The case was appealed to the U.S. Supreme Court (Dkt. No. 87-314), which denied certiorari for want of a substantial federal question (October 19, 1987).

¶1502 Single-Factor Apportionment

The Pennsylvania capital stock tax law provides the following:

> Whenever any corporation, joint-stock association, limited partnership, or company subject to tax upon its capital stock, imposed by and under the laws of this Commonwealth, owns assets that are exempted or relieved from the capital stock tax under the laws of this Commonwealth, the proportion of the capital stock exempted or relieved from the capital stock tax by reason of the ownership of such assets shall be the proportion that the value of such assets bears to the value of the total assets owned by such corporation, joint-stock association, limited partnership, or company [72 P.S. § 1896].

Pass-Through Exemption

Investments in mutual funds or regulated investment companies that have investments in Pennsylvania or U.S. government securities that would be exempt assets if owned directly by a taxpayer are granted a pass-through exemption (equal to the percentage of the deduction allowed from taxable income for purposes of the corporate net income tax) in computing the exempt single-asset fraction for Pennsylvania capital stock/franchise tax. This exemption applies to all settlements and resettlements and must be claimed by completing page 1 of the insert sheet Form RCT-106 [*Pennsylvania Tax Update No. 75*, Pennsylvania Department of Revenue, May/June 1998].

• *Single-factor apportionment formula*

The single-factor apportionment formula is a fraction that can be written out in general terms as follows:

> Single-factor apportionment formula = Average Actual Value of Taxable Assets/Average Actual Value of Total Assets

This factor is applied to the total value of the capital stock to arrive at the taxable capital stock value:

> (Single-factor apportionment factor) × (Total value of capital stock) = Taxable capital stock value.

The capital stock or franchise tax (using single-factor apportionment) is computed by applying the statutory rate to the taxable value of the capital stock. For rates see ¶1305.

> *Example:* For 2004 Verry Corporation has a total capital stock value of $5,000,000 and a single-factor apportionment fraction of 0.758963. Verry Corporation's taxable capital stock value is $3,794,815 (0.758963 × $5,000,000); and its capital stock tax for 2004 is $26,525.76 (0.00699 × $3,794,815).

• *Determination of numerator*

The numerator of the single-factor apportionment fraction is determined by the direct buildup method.

Direct buildup method: The Department of Revenue requires all corporations to use the direct buildup method of determining the numerator of the single-factor apportionment formula. This is done by determining the total actual value of *taxable* assets at the start of the year and at the end of the year, adding them, and dividing the sum by two (2). Average value in this case is simple average value for both numerator and denominator.

Values of exempt assets: When a taxpayer uses the direct buildup method to determine the numerator of the apportionment factor, the values of all exempt assets (tangible or intangible) are based on simple averages.

Decimals

Pennsylvania corporate tax forms indicate that decimals in apportionment fractions should be carried out six (6) places.

• *Disposition of exempt intangibles*

If a corporation sells a substantial amount of intangible assets during a tax year, the Department of Revenue will permit daily averaging to be employed in arriving at the asset fraction.

• *Corporations engaged solely in manufacturing in Pennsylvania*

If a corporation is engaged in manufacturing, processing, or research and development in Pennsylvania, it can exclude from the apportionment factor numerator the value of assets used exclusively in manufacturing in Pennsylvania. See Chapter 16 for an explanation of manufacturing, processing, and research and development.

¶1503 Three-Factor Apportionment

In order to be eligible to use three-factor apportionment, a taxpayer must have taxable activity in another state. For purposes of apportionment a taxpayer is taxable in another state if "in that state he is subject to a net income tax, a franchise tax measured by net income, a franchise tax for the privilege of doing business, or a corporate stock tax, or that state has jurisdiction to subject the taxpayer to a net income tax regardless of whether, in fact, the state does or does not" [72 P.S. § 7401(3)2(a)(3)]. See ¶1103 for a complete explanation of what "taxable in another state" means.

• *Taxability in another state*

The rule that taxability in another state is a condition that must be satisfied in order to use three-factor apportionment applies to both domestic and foreign corporations. The Pennsylvania Supreme Court ruled that domestic corporations must be taxable in another state in order to use three-factor apportionment in *Cmwlth. v. Greenville Steel Car Co.*, 366 A.2d 569 (Pa. 1976). The Pennsylvania Department of Revenue has taken the position that the requirement of taxability in another state also applies to foreign corporations. This position is consistent with the Pennsylvania Supreme Court's conclusion in *Greenville Steel* that taxability in another state is a condition precedent to the use of the three-factor apportionment formula.

Foreign Corporations

The Pennsylvania Commonwealth Court (citing the *Greenville* decision) held that a Pennsylvania corporation taxable only in Pennsylvania could not use three-factor apportionment, even for the purpose of availing itself of the manufacturing exemption provided for in three-factor apportionment [*Electro-Space Fabricators, Inc. v. Cmwlth.*, 514

A.2d 260 (Pa.Commw. 1986)]. However, whether or not a foreign corporation can use three-factor apportionment if it is not taxable in another state has not been established.

- *No triple-weighting of sales factor*

There is no triple-weighting of the sales factor for capital stock/franchise tax purposes as there is for corporate net income tax purposes. Effective for taxable years beginning after December 31, 1998, the sales factor for corporate net income tax purposes must be multiplied by three. However, a new corporate net income tax apportionment formula goes into effect for tax years beginning after 2006. See ¶ 1106.

- *The three-factor apportionment fraction*

The three-factor apportionment fraction is an arithmetic average of three other fractions:

    (1) The property factor.

    (2) The payroll factor.

    (3) The sales factor.

- *Important differences between net income tax and capital stock/franchise tax*

The computation of three-factor apportionment for corporate net income tax purposes and capital stock/franchise tax purposes is essentially the same. However, there are some important differences, as follows:

    (1) There is no manufacturing exemption for tangible property and payroll attributable to manufacturing, processing, or research and development for corporate net income purposes, while there is one for capital stock/franchise tax purposes. Prior to January 1, 1999, there was a manufacturing exemption for sales attributable to manufacturing, processing, or research and development for capital stock/franchise tax purposes. See ¶ 1426.

    (2) The value of tangible property included in the numerator of the property factor is net book value for capital stock/franchise tax purposes, but it is original cost for corporate net income tax purposes.

    (3) The Department of Revenue takes the position that dividends must be included in the numerator if the sales factor for capital stock/franchise tax purposes, although they are exempt for corporate net income tax purposes. In some situations, however, the strict application of this department rule may need to be modified in the interest of fairness.

Strict Application May Need to Be Modified

In special cases, extrastatutory methods of allocation and apportionment may be appropriate. The most common extrastatutory allocation methods are (1) multiformity (explained at ¶ 1412) and (2) unrelated assets (explained at ¶ 1420). However (at least in theory), other extrastatutory methods are available. See explanation at ¶ 1114.

- *Intangible property*

Intangible property is not included in any of the three apportionment fractions in three-factor apportionment. However, intangible property is considered in arriving at the total value of capital stock to which the apportionment factor is applied.

¶1504 Apportionment Under Multiformity

Multiformity is explained at ¶ 1412.

- *Firms benefiting from multiformity*

Ordinarily, multiform treatment is advantageous to firms whose out-of-state business has a capital stock value far in excess of the capital stock value of the in-state business. Apparently, a taxpayer cannot be made to file as a multiform business if it does not elect to do so. This was the ruling of the Pennsylvania Supreme Court in *Cmwlth. v. American Telephone and Telegraph Co.*, 115 A.2d 373 (Pa. 1955).

• *Unrelated assets*

Apportionment in the case of unrelated assets would be like multiform apportionment. The doctrine of unrelated assets is explained at ¶ 1420.

Overall Tax Planning Is Important

The doctrine of multiformity also applies to the corporate net income tax. This is explained at ¶ 1114. If you are subject to both the franchise tax and the corporate net income tax, you must consider your overall tax liability, not just your franchise tax liability. Multiform apportionment may or may not reduce your franchise tax. It may reduce your franchise tax but increase your corporate net income tax; it may increase your franchise tax but reduce your corporate net income tax; it may increase or reduce both taxes at the same time. It is impossible to offer any rules for multiformity use that apply in all cases. You should evaluate your situation very carefully before deciding to invoke the doctrine of multiformity. Also note that, once you are reporting on a multiform basis, you may not be able to go back to reporting on a unitary basis. See explanation at ¶ 1412.

¶ 1505 Special Rules

Some situations, in addition to multiformity and unrelated assets, require apportionment formulas that differ from the general formulas.

• *Holding companies*

Holding companies subject to the capital stock/franchise tax follow the same rules for valuation of their capital stock and computation of their capital stock/franchise tax liability that other corporations follow. See ¶ 1305 for a discussion of capital stock/franchise tax rates and capital stock value. However, holding companies may elect, in lieu of the standard apportionment formula, a special apportionment formula that is applied to its total capital stock value [72 P.S. § 7602(e)]. If a holding company elects this special formula, it computes its capital stock/franchise tax liability by applying the current rate to 10% of its total capital stock value.

For this purpose, a holding company is any corporation that meets the following tests: (1) at least 90% of its gross income for the taxable year is derived from dividends, interest, gains from the sale, exchange or other disposition of stock or securities, and the rendition of management and administrative services to subsidiary corporations; *and* (2) at least 60% of its actual value of total assets consists of stock, securities, or indebtedness of subsidiary corporations [72 P.S. § 7602(e)]. In *Systems & Computer Technology Corporation v. Commonwealth*, 41 A.3d 961 (Pa. Cmwlth. 2012) taxpayer met the asset test for a holding company and was, therefore, eligible to compute its franchise tax liability utilizing the 10% holding company apportionment method because the goodwill on its balance sheet was attributable to the corporation's subsidiaries.

> *Example 1 (three-factor apportionment):* Kay Corporation is a holding company for Pennsylvania capital stock tax purposes. In 2004 Kay Corporation has a total capital stock value of $3,000,000 and a three-factor apportionment factor of 0.335829. Kay Corporation's 2004 capital stock liability is $7,042 [(0.335829 x $3,000,000) x 0.00699].

> *Example 2 (single-factor apportionment):* Assume the same facts as in Example 1 except that Kay Corporation uses single-apportionment and has a single-factor apportionment factor of 0.389013. Using single-factor apportionment, Kay Corporation's 2004 capital stock tax liability is $8,158 [(0.389013 x $3,000,000) x 0.00699].

> *Example 3 (special apportionment):* If Kay Corporation elects special apportionment as a holding company, its 2004 capital stock tax liability will be only $2,097 [(0.10 x $3,000,000) x 0.00699].

¶ 1505

Create a Holding Company

As the above example illustrates, a taxpayer may sometimes benefit if it is a holding company. A taxpayer may want to consider reorganizing its corporate group so as to qualify one or more of the group's companies as a holding company to minimize its capital stock/franchise tax. However, beware of federal personal holding company rules.

• *Regulated investment companies*

A regulated investment company is any corporation (domestic or foreign) that meets the following four criteria:

(1) It is registered to do business in Pennsylvania.

(2) It maintains an office in Pennsylvania.

(3) It has filed a timely federal election to be taxed as a regulated investment company.

(4) It qualifies as a regulated investment company for federal purposes.

The capital stock/franchise tax is computed in four steps:

(1) Divide the net asset value by 1,000,000.

(2) Multiply the result of step one by $75 and round to the nearest $75.

(3) Multiply the company's apportioned undistributed personal income tax income by the current personal income tax rate.

(4) Add (2) and (3) to arrive at tax liability.

Net asset value is determined by adding together the monthly net asset values as of the last day of each month during a taxable period and dividing by the number of months involved. Personal income tax income is income determined under § 303 of the Tax Reform Code [72 P.S. § 7602(f)].

• *Industries with special apportionment rules*

Railroad, truck, bus or airline companies, pipeline companies, natural gas companies, and water transportation companies operating on the high seas and on inland waters are subject to special apportionment rules. See the explanation at ¶ 1112.

CAPITAL STOCK TAX, FRANCHISE TAX, AND CORPORATE

LOANS TAX

CHAPTER 16

EXEMPTION FOR MANUFACTURING, PROCESSING, AND RESEARCH AND DEVELOPMENT

¶ 1601	Requirements for Exemption
¶ 1602	What Is Manufacturing?
¶ 1603	What Is Processing?
¶ 1604	What Is Research and Development?
¶ 1605	Classification of Activities as Exempt or Nonexempt

> *Caution: There is No Capital Stock/Franchise Tax for tax years beginning after 12/31/15*

¶1601 Requirements for Exemption

• *Manufacturing exemption remedy*

The remedy adopted by the Commonwealth is to impose the tax without the exemption for tax years beginning on or before January 1, 1999 [*Pennsylvania Tax Update No. 98*, Pennsylvania Department of Revenue, March/April 2002]. On or after July 1, 2002, the Department of Revenue will settle all cases for taxpayers who have pending appeals for tax years beginning prior to January 1, 1999, that present manufacturing exemption claims, assessing additional tax in the amount that would have been due without the invalid manufacturing exemption. However, taxpayers who withdrew their appeals, or amended their appeals to remove manufacturing exemption claims before July 1, 2002, will not be settled additional tax. The Department of Revenue will also settle tax without the manufacturing exemption against taxpayers who (on or after July 1, 2002) take appeals for tax years beginning prior to 1999 that raise manufacturing exemption claims.

Taxpayers with unsettled tax years beginning prior to 1999 will have their tax settled, the amount of tax due to be determined without the invalid manufacturing exemption. These taxpayers, however, will be offered a pre-appeal compromise in which the Commonwealth, in return for a waiver of any manufacturing exemption issues, will offer a credit equal to the tax that would have been saved if the manufacturing exemption had been valid.

Taxpayers with settled tax years beginning prior to January 1, 1999, who have not taken appeals presenting a manufacturing exemption issue are not affected by this remedy unless they take the appeals.

Inquiries about this remedy should be directed to the Department's Office of Chief Counsel (717) 787-1382. Information about this remedy can also be found at the Department's web site at www.revenue.state.pa.us.

• *"Manufacturing exemption" defined*

The law imposing the capital stock tax provides the following:

[T]he provisions of this section shall not apply to taxation of the capital stock of entities organized for manufacturing, processing, research or development purposes, which are invested in and actually and exclusively employed in carrying on manufacturing, processing, research or development within the state, except such companies as enjoy and exercise the right of eminent domain [72 P.S. § 7602(a)].

This is called the manufacturing exemption. The term "manufacturing exemption" is used to refer to the exemption for all three activities—manufacturing processing, and research and development. Manufacturing is explained at ¶ 1602, processing at ¶ 1603; and research and development at ¶ 1604. The manufacturing exemption is available to both domestic and foreign corporations.

Derivative Manufacturing Exemption Not Available for Capital Stock Tax Purposes

For sales and use tax purposes, the Commonwealth Court has held that a taxpayer that conducts testing on products that are still within its client's production cycle qualifies for the manufacturing exemption. See ¶ 710. However, the Pennsylvania Supreme Court has interpreted the manufacturing exemption to the capital stock tax differently from the manufacturing exemption to the sales and use tax. A taxpayer that conducts testing on products that are still within its client's production cycle does not qualify for the capital stock tax manufacturing exemption. Therefore, it is possible for the taxpayer to qualify for the sales and use tax manufacturing exemption but not qualify for the capital stock tax manufacturing exemption for the same activity [*Lancaster Laboratories, Inc. v. Cmwlth.*, 631 A.2d 739 (Pa.Commw. 1993)].

• *Conditions for exemption*

The law provides two conditions to qualify for the manufacturing exemption (1 the corporation must be organized for the purpose of manufacturing, processing, or research and development, and (2) the capital must be invested in and actually and exclusively used in manufacturing, processing, or research and development.

Scope of Explanation

The terms "processing" and "research and development" are statutorily defined; the term "manufacturing" is not. Thus, almost all of the case law principles have developed within the framework of the manufacturing exemption. However, the principles are the same in terms of purpose of organization and capital invested and used in the exempt purposes; therefore, the following explanation applies to processing and research and development as well as manufacturing, even though the case law principles are stated in terms of manufacturing.

The manufacturing exemption for corporations was first allowed in 1885. Since then it has been repealed and reinstated twice. However, the principles involved have changed very little, and the judicial decisions under prior law that are cited in this *Guidebook* still apply.

• *Organization purpose*

In order to claim the manufacturing exemption, a corporation must be organized for the purpose of manufacturing, processing, or research and development. The courts will look to the charter of a corporation to determine its purpose. It is the main purpose for which the corporation is organized that is controlling:

In order to exempt corporations from the payment of capital stock tax it must appear from their charters that they were organized as manufacturing corporations, and this conclusion must be reached, not by implication, but directly from the language used. It is the main purpose expressed, and not an ancillary one, which determines whether or not a corporation is within the exemption [*Cmwlth. v. Paul W. Bounds Co.*, 173 A. 633 (Pa. 1934)].

¶1601

A corporation *organized* for manufacturing purposes meets this condition, even though its certificate of authority for doing business in Pennsylvania does not state that it is entitled to engage in manufacturing in Pennsylvania [*Cmwlth. v. E.W. Twitchell, Inc.*, 80 Dauph 267 (1963)].

• *Wording of charter not controlling*

The mere presence of the words "manufacturing," "processing," or "research and development" in a corporation's charter, however, is not sufficient. For example, in one case a corporation was chartered for the purpose of "manufacturing steam." The Pennsylvania Supreme Court held that one does not "manufacture" steam; therefore, the corporation was not entitled to the exemption for manufacturing [*Cmwlth. v. Arrott Steam-Power Mills Co.*, 22 A. 243 (Pa. 1891)]. In a later case, a corporation chartered, among other things, for the purpose of "manufacturing buildings" was found not to be organized for manufacturing purposes. The court held that the term "manufacture of buildings" was an anomaly [*Cmwlth. v. Wark Co.*, 151 A. 786 (Pa. 1930)].

• *Words do not have to appear in charter*

On the other hand, it is not necessary that the words "manufacturing," "processing," or "research and development" appear in the charter. For example, a corporate charter might define a business that is in fact manufacturing without mentioning the word "manufacture" [*Cmwlth. v. Bornot, Inc.*, 34 Dauph 178 (1931)]. In one case a taxpayer was chartered, among other things, for the purpose of "photo finishing." The court held that, although the corporation's charter did not specifically mention "manufacturing," the charter purpose of "photo finishing" encompassed activities held to be manufacturing. Therefore, the taxpayer was organized for manufacturing purposes [*Cmwlth. v. Perfect Photo, Inc.*, 371 A.2d 580 (Pa.Commw. 1977)].

Charter Too Restrictive

If a charter is too restrictive, the corporation may not qualify for the manufacturing exemption. When organizing to do business in Pennsylvania, it is a good idea for a corporation to have an "omnibus" charter that authorizes "any legal act" that a corporation may do in the Commonwealth. If the charter is too restrictive and it does not appear in the eyes of the Commonwealth to authorize the corporation to engage in manufacturing, processing, or research and development, it will be denied the benefits of the manufacturing exemption, even though it is actually engaged in exempt activities.

• *Capital invested in manufacturing in Pennsylvania*

A corporation engaged in manufacturing does not lose its exemption if it carries on nonexempt activities as well. However, the capital invested in the nonexempt activity is not exempt. See, *e.g., Fry Communications, Inc. v. Cmwlth.*, 433 A.2d 601 (Pa.Commw. 1981); *Cmwlth. v. Juniata Coke Co.*, 27 A. 373 (Pa. 1893); *Cmwlth. v. Interstate Amiesite Corp.*, 194 A.2d 191 (Pa. 1963); *Cmwlth. v. National Oil Co., Ltd.*, 157 Pa. 516 (Pa. 1893); *Cmwlth. v. Savage Fire Brick Co.*, 27 A. 274 (Pa. 1893)]. See ¶1416 for a discussion of exempt manufacturing tangibles and ¶1417 for a discussion of exempt manufacturing intangibles.

• *Presumption*

If a corporation is engaged solely in exempt activities, there is a presumption that its assets are used in the exempt activity [*Cmwlth. v. Dilworth, Porter & Co.*, 88 A. 933 (Pa. 1913)]. However, if a manufacturing corporation has assets not needed in its manufacturing operations, it may not claim an exemption for assets in excess of the amount that is reasonably necessary in carrying on its business [*Cmwlth. v. Curtis Publishing Co.*, 85 A. 360 (Pa. 1912); *Cmwlth. v. Nagle Engine & Boiler Works*, 23 Dauph 235 (1920)].

Out-of-State Manufacturing

Manufacturing carried on outside Pennsylvania is an exempt activity because of situs.

• *Capital actually and exclusively employed in manufacturing, processing, research and development*

If a corporation is organized for an exempt purpose but does not engage in its exempt purpose, exemption is not allowed. For example, in the *Paul W. Bounds* case (mentioned above), the court stated that if a corporation organized for manufacturing purposes does not in fact engage in manufacturing, it cannot claim the manufacturing exemption. Furthermore, the exempt activity must be a significant activity and not just an activity incidental to a nonexempt activity. For example, one taxpayer engaged in laundering (a nonexempt activity) was denied an exemption for capital invested in manufacturing soaps and dyes because the manufacturing activity was merely incidental to its nonexempt activity. Its principal business determined its right to exemption [*Cmwlth. v. Keystone Laundry Co.*, 52 A. 326 (Pa. 1902); *Cmwlth. v. Bornot*, 34 Dauph 178 (1931)].

• *Engagement in exempt activity*

A corporation is not considered to be engaged in an exempt activity unless it conducts such activity itself (except in the case of assets leased to others who use them in an exempt activity (see below). For example, a foreign corporation whose wholly owned Pennsylvania subsidiary engaged in manufacturing within Pennsylvania was not allowed the manufacturing exemption because it did not engage in manufacturing. It simply supplied its manufacturing subsidiary with raw materials [*Cmwlth. v. Weldon Pajamas, Inc.*, 248 A.2d 204 (Pa. 1968)]. Another corporation that purchased raw materials and then subcontracted the manufacturing activity was denied the manufacturing exemption [*Cmwlth. v. Williamsport Rail Co.*, 95 A. 795 (1915), *aff'g*, 18 Dauph. 189 (1915)].

• *Nonmanufacturing periods*

Even if a corporation's capital is invested in manufacturing assets, it may not claim the manufacturing exemption for any taxable period in which it carries on no manufacturing activities [*Cmwlth. v. Altoona Foundry and Machine Co.*, 18 Dauph 569 (1915)]. This is true even if the corporation intends to use the assets in future manufacturing activities [*Cmwlth. v. Custer City Chemical Co.*, 16 Dauph 46 (1913); *Cmwlth. v. Nagle Engine & Boiler Works*, 23 Dauph 235 (1920); *Fry Communications, Inc. v. Cmwlth.*, 433 A.2d 601 (Pa.Commw. 1981)]. The exemption is not available for any taxable period in which no manufacturing was conducted if the reason for lack of activity is liquidation [*Cmwlth. v. Excelsior Brick & Stone Co.*, 81 A. 933 (Pa. 1911)]. However, if a liquidating corporation has conducted manufacturing activities for a part of the year, the exemption is available for the portion of the year it conducted business. A corporation in the process of constructing manufacturing facilities may claim an exemption for such assets if the Department of Revenue is satisfied that the assets will be engaged in an exempt activity.

• *Property leased to persons engaged in manufacturing, processing, or research and development within Pennsylvania*

With respect to assets leased to others, the law provides the following:

"No corporation or limited partnership association organized for manufacturing purposes, whose manufacturing plant or plants, in whole or in part, are or may be leased to another corporation, limited partnership, individual or individuals, shall, by reason of

¶1601

such leasing, be deprived of the exemption from taxation upon its capital stock or any part thereof, to which under existing laws it would be entitled if such lease had not been made" [Act of July 11, 1901, P.L. 668, § 1].

• *Application to processing or research and development*

This statute has not been amended to include property leased to lessees who are engaged in processing or research and development, but the Department of Revenue takes the position that it applies to processing and research and development as well as to manufacturing. This means that a corporation *organized for exempt purposes* is entitled to an exemption for property leased to parties that use the assets for exempt purposes. The exemption for leased property used in manufacturing by the lessees is available to lessors even if the lessors themselves are not engaged in manufacturing [*Cmwlth. v. Jeca Corp.*, 81 Dauph 36 (1963); *Chrysel Corp. v. Cmwlth.*, 295 A.2d 624 (Pa.Commw. 1972)].

• *"Manufacturing plant"*

The term "manufacturing plant" is not defined in the statute, nor has it been defined judicially. The ordinary meaning of the word "plant" is the land, buildings, machinery, and other equipment used in carrying on a trade or business, and, in the absence of legislative intent to impose another meaning, this is the meaning that should be used:

> [W]ords in a legislative enactment are to be taken in their ordinary and general sense; and unless the act sufficiently explains or qualifies the terms so as to necessitate an interpretation out of the current and popular signification, they must be deemed to have been used by the legislature in the former sense [*Cmwlth. v. Wark Co.*, 151 A. 786 (Pa. 1930)].

In any event, the courts have held that the exemption for "plant" leased to manufacturers does not extend to income from leased property or to payroll of a nonmanufacturing lessor [*J.L. Mott Corp. v. Cmwlth.*, 345 A.2d 650 (Pa. 1975), *aff'g*, 316 A.2d 921 (Pa.Commw. 1974)].

¶1602 What Is Manufacturing?

Since the statute does not provide a definition of manufacturing, the courts have been called upon repeatedly to decide what is and what is not manufacturing. They have repeatedly held that the term is to be given its ordinary meaning (*i.e.*, its meaning in the popular understanding of language; see, *e.g.*, *Cmwlth. v. Paul W. Bounds Co.*, 173 A. 633 (Pa. 1934); *Cmwlth. v. Wark Co.*, 151 A. 786 (Pa. 1930)). One succinct definition of "manufacturing" is the following:

> The word "manufacturing," when employed in a statute or other taxing measure without further definition, consists in the application of labor and skill to material whereby the original article is changed into a new, different and useful article [*Morrisville Scrap Processing Co., Inc., Tax Appeal*, 307 A.2d 905 (1973); *aff'd* without opinion 453 Pa. 610 (1973)].

• *Judicial definition*

The classic judicial definition of "manufacturing" is the following:

> It is making. To make in the mechanical sense does not signify to create out of nothing; for that surpasses all human power. It does not often mean the production of a new article out of materials entirely raw. It generally consists in giving new shapes, new qualities, or new combinations to matter which has already gone through some other artificial process [*Norris Brothers v. Cmwlth.*, 27 Pa. 494 (Pa. 1856)].

Other courts have provided insight into the definition of manufacturing. Manufacturing comprises the following elements:

(1) The application of labor, skill, art or science.

(2) Changes or modifications in existing materials, effected by processes popularly regarded as manufacturing.

(3) Evolution of new forms, qualities, properties, combinations or adaptability to certain uses.

(4) The production of a different material with a new use, capable of, or adapted to, the satisfaction of some want or desire of man [*Cmwlth. v. Harrisburg Gas Co.,* 50 Dauph 383 (1941)]. In order to satisfy the definition, the manufactured articles must be sold as articles of commerce [*Cmwlth. v. McCrady-Rodgers Co.,* 174 A. 395 (Pa. 1934)]. "If there is merely a superficial change in the original materials, without any substantial and well signalized transformation in form, qualities and adaptability in use, it is not a new article or new production" [*Cmwlth. v. Berlo Vending Co.,* 202 A.2d 94 (Pa. 1964)]. The concept of a new and different article evolving at the final stage is essential to the conclusion that manufacturing has occurred [*Cmwlth. v. Perfect Photo, Inc.,* 371 A.2d 580 (Pa.Commw. 1977)].

Permanency Not Required

In *Cmwlth. v. American Ice Co.,* 178 A.2d 768 (Pa. 1962), the court said that "the new shape that we find in a manufactured article must be a permanently new shape." However, in *Ski Roundtop, Inc., v. Cmwlth.,* 553 A.2d 928 (Pa. 1989), the Pennsylvania Supreme Court rejected the notion that manufactured products must be permanent and held that snowmaking was manufacturing.

• *Activities needed to produce and sell a product*

The statute explicitly says that "the object of this proviso [is] to relieve from State taxation only so much of the capital stock as is invested purely in the manufacturing, processing, research or development plant *and business."* (emphasis added) [72 P.S. §7602(a)].

The term "manufacturing" thus encompasses not only the direct manufacturing process but all activities necessary to produce and sell a product. For example, capital invested in administrative buildings, working capital, and capital used to sell manufactured products are exempt.

Case Law

In order to understand the scope and nature of the manufacturing exemption, one *must* read the court cases in this area. To make or defend a claim for the manufacturing exemption, one must understand the case law and structure the description of the manufacturing activity so that the manufacturing exemption is not lost simply because of failure to describe a corporation's activity properly. A properly constructed description should clearly show that all the conditions to qualify for the manufacturing exemption as set out in both statute *and* case law have been met.

• *Specially classified activities*

See ¶1605 for a list of certain activities that are classified as exempt or nonexempt. Some of the activities are classified as exempt by statute, but most of them have been classified by judicial decision. However, a few activities need explanation beyond classification as exempt and nonexempt, and they are explained more fully here.

• *Natural resources*

Any activity that consists of appropriating an article that is furnished by nature is not manufacturing [*Cmwlth. v. National Oil Co., Ltd.,* 157 Pa. 516 (Pa. 1893)]. Thus,

¶1602

mining is not manufacturing; producers of crude oil or natural gas are not manufacturers; and corporations engaged in quarrying are not engaged in manufacturing.

Manufacturing corporations that own property from which they get their own raw material (e.g., timber, oil, coal) are not engaged in manufacturing with respect to the process of raw material production. For example, an oil refinery that owned its own oil-producing property was held taxable on the portion of its capital invested in crude oil production and transportation [*Cmwlth. v. National Oil Co., Ltd.*, 157 Pa. 516 (Pa. 1893)]; a manufacturing company that owned timber land from which it obtained its raw material was not entitled to an exemption for the capital invested in the timber land [*Cmwlth. v. Custer City Chemical Co.*, 16 Dauph 46 (1913)]; and a company engaged in manufacturing fire brick and other clay products was not entitled to an exemption on the portion of its capital invested in clay mining [*Cmwlth. v. Savage Fire Brick Co.*, 157 Pa. 512 (Pa. 1893)]. Once such natural materials have become raw material inventory, they become exempt. However, see ¶1416 for an explanation of excess inventory.

• *Quarrying*

Quarrying has consistently been held not to be manufacturing when it consists of quarrying the material and merely crushing or cutting it. In one case, a taxpayer engaged in quarrying large blocks of slate from which it produced assorted articles (e.g., blackboards, lintels, hearths, household utensils, mantels, and tabletops) was held to be engaged in manufacturing, but a taxpayer engaged in quarrying silica rock that it crushed and used to produce colored sand (by the addition of colored clay) was held not to be engaged in manufacturing [*Cmwlth. v. The Welsh Mountain Mining & Kaolin Manufacturing Co.*, 108 A. 722 (Pa. 1919)].

• *Construction and paving*

Construction of such things as bridges and buildings is not manufacturing [*Cmwlth. v. Wark Co.*, 151 A. 786 (Pa. 1930)]. However, when a corporation manufactures the components of the structure it erects, it is engaged in manufacturing [*Cmwlth. v. Pittsburgh Bridge Co.*, 27 A. 4 (Pa. 1893); *Cmwlth. v. Keystone Bridge Co.*, 27 A. 1 (Pa. 1893)]. Paving is not manufacturing, but production of asphalt for use in a corporation's paving operation is [*Cmwlth. v. Interstate Amiesite Corp.*, 194 A.2d 191 (Pa. 1963)]. In such cases a corporation's activities must be separated into exempt and nonexempt activities. The corporation is not entitled to exemption for capital invested in nonmanufacturing activities.

• *Corporations engaged primarily in nonmanufacturing*

It has been held that if a corporation is engaged primarily in nonmanufacturing, it is not entitled to exemption because it also engages in manufacturing activities unless the capital for which the exemption is sought is actually engaged in manufacturing and the article manufactured is sold as an article of commerce [*Cmwlth. v. McCrady-Rodgers Co.*, 174 A. 395 (Pa. 1934)].

Claim Two Exemptions

When making or defending a claim for the manufacturing exemption, a claim under the processing exemption should also be made, if possible. Some activities fall within the description of both activities. Then, even if the manufacturing exemption is denied, the benefits of the processing exemption might still be allowed.

¶1603 What Is Processing?

The term "processing" means, and is limited to, the following business activities [72 P.S. § 7601(a)]:

— *Alcohol or alcoholic liquors:* The blending, rectification or production by distillation or otherwise of alcohol or alcoholic liquors, except the distillation of alcohol from by-products of wine making for the sole purpose of fortifying wines.

— *Animal or poultry feed:* The preparation of animal feed or poultry feed for sale.

— *Coffee:* The cleaning and roasting and the blending, grinding or packaging for sale of coffee from green coffee beans or the production of coffee extract.

— *Computer programs or software:* The development or substantial modification of computer programs or software for sale to unrelated persons for their direct and independent use.

— *Fibers, yarns, and fabrics:* The scouring, carbonizing, cording, combing, throwing, twisting or winding of natural or synthetic fibers, or the spinning, bleaching, dyeing, printing or finishing of yarns or fabrics, when such activities are performed prior to sale to the ultimate consumer.

— *Flour or meal:* The milling for sale of flour or meal from grains.

— *Fruits and vegetables:* The processing of fruits or vegetables by cleaning, cutting, coring, peeling or chopping and treating to preserve, sterilize or purify and substantially extend the useful shelf life of the vegetables, when the person engaged in such activity packages such property in sealed containers for wholesale distribution.

— *Honey, fruits, vegetables, mushrooms, fish, seafood, meats, or poultry:* The filtering or heating of honey, the cooking or freezing of fruits, vegetables, mushrooms, fish, seafood, meats or poultry, when the person engaged in such business packages such property in sealed containers for wholesale distribution. This provision overrules the *Stewart Honeybee* decision [579 A.2d 872 (Pa. 1990)].

— *Lubricating oils:* The processing of used lubricating oils.

— *Metals:* The blanking, shearing, leveling, slitting or burning of metals for sale to or use by a manufacturer or processor.

— *Metals and plastics:* The electroplating, galvanizing, enameling, anodizing, coloring, finishing, impregnating or heat treating of metals or plastics for sale or for use in the process of manufacturing.

— *Metals, ferrous and nonferrous:* The rolling, drawing or extruding of ferrous and nonferrous metals.

— *Metals, ornamental or structural:* The fabrication for sale of ornamental or structural metal or metal stairs, staircases, gratings, fire escapes or railings (not including fabrication work done at the construction site).

— *Mining and quarrying:* The refining, blasting, exploring, mining, and quarrying for or otherwise extracting limestone, sand, gravel, or slag from the earth or from waste or stock piles or from pits or banks, and the cleaning, crushing, grinding, pulverizing, sizing, or screening of limestone, sand, gravel, or slag, including blast furnace slag.

— *Nonalcoholic beverages:* The production, processing and bottling of nonalcoholic beverages for wholesale distribution.

— *Publishing and broadcasting:* The publishing of books, newspapers, magazines or other periodicals, printing and broadcasting radio and television programs by licensed commercial or educational stations. The Commonwealth Court has held that cable television systems are entitled to the processing exemption because they operate within the definition of broadcasting [*Suburban Cable TV Co., Inc. v. Cmwlth.*, 570 A.2d 601 (Pa.Commw. 1990)]. The court rejected the Department's argument that the broadcasting exemption is available only to those stations licensed by the Federal Communications Commission, not to those licensed by local authorities.

— *Recycling:* The salvaging, recycling or reclaiming of used materials to be recycled into a manufacturing process.

— *Sawmill or planing mill:* The operation of a sawmill or planing mill for the production of lumber or lumber products for sale. The saw mill or planing mill operation begins with the unloading, by the operator of the saw mill or planing mill, of logs, timber, pulpwood or other forms of wood material to be used in the mill.

— *Slaughtering and dressing of animals:* The slaughtering and dressing of animals for meat to be sold or to be used in preparing meat products for sale, and the preparation of meat products, including lard, tallow, grease, cooking and inedible oils for wholesale distribution.

— *Tobacco:* The aging, stripping, conditioning, crushing and blending of tobacco leaves for use as cigar filler or as components of smokeless tobacco products for sale to manufacturers of tobacco products.

Some of these processes were formerly considered manufacturing. For example, dyeing and finishing woolen and cotton goods and yarn was held to be manufacturing [*Cmwlth. v. G.W. Littlewood and Sons,* 19 Dauph 201 (1916)], as was the printing and publishing of books and periodicals [*Cmwlth. v. J.B. Lippincott Co.,* 7 Dauph 193 (1904)].

• *Not exempt as processing, but as manufacturing*

Some processes not exempted by this statute may be considered manufacturing. For example, in one case involving a producer of skim milk powder and buttermilk powder, the taxpayer was found to be engaged in manufacturing, not processing [*Kirks Milk Products, Inc. v. Cmwlth.,* 427 A.2d 688 (Pa.Commw. 1981)].

• *Not exempt as manufacturing, but as processing*

Some processes that formerly failed to qualify as manufacturing are now covered by the processing exemption. For example, the operation of a sawmill was held to be nonmanufacturing, but sawmill operation is now covered by the processing exemption [*Cmwlth. v. Hardes Lumber Corp.,* 77 Dauph. 359 (1961)]. The pasteurizing of milk has been held to be nonmanufacturing but is now covered by the processing exemption [*Reick-McJunkin Dairy Co. v. Pittsburgh School District,* 66 A.2d 295 (Pa. 1949)].

• *"Processing" definition is precise*

Unlike manufacturing, processing has a precise statutory meaning. Even if an activity falls within the popular meaning of "processing," it is not an exempt processing activity unless it is described in the statute [*Cmwlth. v. Rudd-Melikian, Inc.,* 86 Dauph 275 (1966)]. For example, in one case a taxpayer was engaged in cutting, screening, granulating, magnetizing and floating to separate nonferrous metals from wire. This was held to be neither manufacturing nor processing. The taxpayer failed to qualify for the processing exemption because it was not engaged in rolling, drawing, or extrusion of nonferrous metals [*Eastern Diversified Metals Corp. v. Cmwlth.,* 297 A.2d 167 (1972); *aff'd per curiam,* 306 A.2d 300 (Pa. 1973)]. One taxpayer engaged in producing coffee and tea concentrates and roll tapes of ground coffee was denied the processing exemption because its product was not a beverage and it was not involved in cooking or freezing fruits or vegetables [*Cmwlth. v. Rudd-Melikian, Inc.,* 86 Dauph 275 (1966)].

¶1604   What Is Research and Development?

Research and development is statutorily defined as follows:

"Research and development" shall mean activities relating to the discovery of new and the refinement of known substances, products, processes, theories and ideas, but shall not include activities directed primarily to the accumulation or analysis of commercial, financial or mercantile data [72 P.S. § 7601(a)].

A taxpayer who receives samples from its customers and tests the samples for the presence of various elements, compounds, or pollutants has been held not to be engaged in research and development within the meaning of the statute [*Lancaster Laboratories, Inc. v. Cmwlth.*, 631 A.2d 739 (Pa.Commw. 1993)].

¶1605   Classification of Activities as Exempt or Nonexempt

The following table provides the classification of certain activities as exempt or nonexempt as determined by statute or case law. This list is not intended to be exhaustive but to furnish guidelines to the user with respect to certain activities that are statutorily exempt or have been held to be exempt.

Product or Activity	Exempt	Basis for Exemption	Authority
Alcohol, denatured (for industrial use only)	Yes	Statute	Act of July 22, 1913, P.L. 914
Alcoholic beverages: Blending, rectification or production by distillation or otherwise of alcohol or alcoholic liquors (except the distillation of alcohol from by-products of wine-making for the sole purpose of fortifying wine)	Yes	Processing	72 P.S. § 7601
Animal feed	Yes	Processing	72 P.S. § 7601
Asphalt products (but not paving)	Yes	Mfg.	*Cmwlth. v. Filbert Paving & Construction Co.*, 229 Pa. 231 (1910); *Cmwlth. v. Interstate Amiesite Corp.*, 194 A.2d 191 (Pa. 1963)
Beverages, nonalcoholic: The production, processing and bottling of nonalcoholic beverages for wholesale distribution	Yes	Processing	72 P.S. § 7601
Brick and tile	Yes	Mfg.	*Cmwlth. v. Excelsior Brick and Stone Co.*, 1 Dauph. 96 (1893) (note); *Cmwlth. v. Savage Fire Brick Co.*, 157 Pa. 512 (Pa. 1893)
Bridge building: If taxpayer manufactures components	Yes	Mfg.	*Cmwlth. v. Keystone Bridge Co.*, 27 A. 4 (Pa. 1893); *Cmwlth. v. Pittsburgh Bridge Co.*, 156 Pa. 507 (Pa. 1893); *Cmwlth. v. Wark Co.*, 151 A.2d 786 (Pa. 1930)
If taxpayer does not manufacture components	No	-	*Cmwlth. v. Wark Co.*, 151 A.2d 786 (Pa. 1930)
Broadcasting: Broadcasting radio and television programs by licensed commercial or educational stations	Yes	Processing	72 P.S. § 7601
Cabinet making	Yes	Mfg.	*Norris Brothers v. Cmwlth.*, 27 Pa. 494 (1856) (dictum)
Cable: Underground and aerial cable for transmission of electricity	Yes	Mfg.	*Cmwlth. v. Standard Underground Cable Co.*, 17 Dauph. 281 (1914)
Cable television broadcasting	Yes	Processing	*Suburban Cable TV Co. v. Cmwlth.*, 570 A.2d 601 (Pa.Commw. 1990)

¶1604

Product or Activity	Exempt	Basis for Exemption	Authority
Candy	Yes	Mfg.	*Cmwlth. v. Croft & Allen Co.,* 5 Dauph. 86 (1902)
Cement floors (also see "Concrete")	Yes	Mfg.	*Cmwlth. v. Filbert Paving & Construction Co.,* 229 Pa. 231 (1910)
Clothing:			
Construction of garments	Yes	Mfg.	*Appeal of Maransky Co., Inc.,* Philadelphia Tax Review Board (1969)
Embroidering logos on	No	-	*Kimberton Company v. Cmwlth.,* 520 A.2d 904 (1987)
Coffee:			
Production, processing, and bottling of nonalcoholic beverages for wholesale distribution	Yes	Processing	72 P.S. §7601
Decaffeination of coffee	No	-	*General Goods Corp. v. City & School District of Pittsburgh,* 383 Pa. 244 (1955)
Cleaning coffee beans	No	-	*Cmwlth. v. Lowry-Rodgers Co.,* 279 Pa. 361 (1924)
Grinding, roasting, and blending coffee	No	-	*Cmwlth. v. Glendora Products Co.,* 297 Pa. 305 (1929)
Production of coffee concentrates and coffee tapes	No	-	*Cmwlth. v. Rudd-Melikian, Inc.,* 86 Dauph. 275 (1966)
Coke:			
Production of coke from coal	Yes	Mfg.	*Cmwlth. v. Hecla Coke Co.,* 1 Dauph. 96 (1892) (note); *Cmwlth. v. Juniata Coke Co.,* 157 Pa. 507 (1893)
Cold storage	No	-	*Cmwlth. v. The Industrial Cold Storage and Warehouse Co.,* 18 Dauph. 143 (1915)
Computers:			
Development or substantial modification of computer programs or software	Yes	Processing	72 P.S. §7601
Concrete (see "Cement"):			
Structural	Yes	Mfg.	*Cmwlth. v. Filbert Paving & Construction Co.,* 229 Pa. 231 (1910)
Ready-mixed	Yes	Mfg.	*Cmwlth. v. McCrady-Rogers Co.,* 174 A.2d 395 (Pa. 1934)
For sale to others	Yes	Mfg.	*Cmwlth. v. H.J. Williams Co., Inc.,* 78 Dauph. 377 (1962)
For taxpayer's own use	No	-	*Cmwlth. v. H.J. Williams Co., Inc.,* 78 Dauph. 377 (1962)
Construction:			
Building (Taxpayer does not manufacture components.)	No	-	*Cmwlth. v. Wark Co.,* 151 A.2d 786 (Pa. 1930) (see "Bridge building")
Roads (Taxpayer does not manufacture components.)	No	-	*Cmwlth. v. H.J. Williams Co., Inc.,* 78 Dauph. 377 (1962)
Dairy products:			
The production, processing and bottling of nonalcoholic beverages for wholesale distribution	Yes	Processing	72 P.S. §7601
Skim milk powder, buttermilk powder	Yes	Mfg.	*Kirks Milk Products, Inc. v. Cmwlth.,* 427 A.2d 688 (Pa.Commw. 1981)
Sour cream	Yes	Mfg.	*Reick-McJunkin Dairy Co. v. Pittsburgh School District,* 66 A.2d 295 (Pa. 1949)
Butter, cottage cheese, ice cream	Yes	Mfg.	*Reick-McJunkin Dairy Co. v. Pittsburgh School District,* 66 A.2d 295 (Pa. 1949)
Dyes:			
For taxpayer's own use	No	-	*Cmwlth. v. Keystone Laundry Co.,* 203 Pa. 289 (Pa. 1902)

Product or Activity	Exempt	Basis for Exemption	Authority
For sale to others	Yes	Mfg.	*Cmwlth. v. A. Colburn Co.,* 1 Dauph. 96 (1892) (note)
Electrical appliances	Yes	Mfg.	*Cmwlth. v. Westinghouse Electric & Manufacturing Co.,* 151 Pa. 265 (1892)
Electricity, production of	No	-	*The Potomac Edison Co. v. Cmwlth.,* 411 A.2d 1287 (1980), *aff'd* 421 A.2d 214 (1980), app. to U.S. Supreme Court dism'd (1981)
Engineering	No	-	*Cmwlth. v. Boon & Sample, Inc.,* 35 Dauph. 404 (1932)
Felt (also see "Hair")	Yes	Mfg.	*Cmwlth. v. Densten Felt & Hair Co.,* 304 Pa. 536 (1931)
Film processing: Making prints, slides, and movie film from negatives	Yes	Mfg.	*Cmwlth. v. Perfect Photo, Inc.,* 371 A.2d 580 (Pa. 1977)
Making photographs from plates	No	-	*Cmwlth. v. Trinity Court Studios,* 39 Dauph. 244 (1934)
Flavoring extract	Yes	Mfg.	*Cmwlth. v. J. Frank & Sons, Inc.,* 46 Dauph. 51 (1936)
Flour (also see "Meal"): The milling for sales of flour or meal from grains	Yes	Processing	72 P.S. § 7601
Food processing: The cooking or freezing of fruits, vegetables, mushrooms, fish, seafood, meats or poultry, when the person engaged in such business packages such property in sealed containers for wholesale	Yes	Processing	72 P.S. § 7601
Slaughtering and dressing of animals for meat to be sold or to be used in preparing meat products for sale; and the preparation of meat products, including lard, tallow, grease, cooking and inedible oils for wholesale distribution	Yes	Processing	72 P.S. § 7601
Production, processing, and bottling of nonalcoholic beverages for wholesale distribution	Yes	Processing	72 P.S. § 7601
Fruit, preserving	Yes	Mfg.	*Cmwlth. v. Ritter Conserve Co.,* 1 Dauph. 97 (1896) (note)
Furniture	Yes	Mfg.	*Cmwlth. v. American Ice Co.,* 178 A.2d 768 (1962)
Gas: Converting coke oven gas to gas for public use	Yes	Mfg.	*Cmwlth. v. The Harrisburg Gas Co.,* 50 Dauph. 383 (1941)
Producing gas from coal	Yes	Mfg.	*Cmwlth. v. Northern Electric Light & Power Co.,* 145 Pa. 105 (1891)
Producing illuminating gas	Yes	Mfg.	*Emerson v. Cmwlth.,* 108 Pa. 111
Producing artificial gas	Yes	Mfg.	*Cmwlth. v. Allegheny Gas Co.,* Dkt. 691 (1939)
Hair: Washing and cleaning hair from tanneries to be used in production of felt	No	-	*Cmwlth. v. Densten Felt & Hair Co.,* 304 Pa. 536 (1931)

¶1605

Product or Activity	Exempt	Basis for Exemption	Authority
Heating:			
Installing heating, plumbing, and ventilating systems	No	-	*Cmwlth. v. J. Frank Boyer Plumbing and Heating Co.,* 23 Dauph. 296 (1920); *Cmwlth. v. Harry F. Murphy Co., Inc.,* 24 Dauph. 314 (1921)
Hides (also see "Leather"):			
Cleaning and preserving (pickling) sheep skins without tanning	No	-	*Cmwlth. v. Pittsburgh Wool Co.,* 36 Dauph. 257 (1933)
Honey:			
Transforming raw honey into honey fit for human consumption under federal standards	Yes	Processing	72 P.S. § 7601
Laundry	No	-	*Cmwlth. v. Keystone Laundry Co.,* 203 Pa. 289, 52 A. 326 (Pa. 1902); *Cmwlth. v. Barnes Brothers Co.,* 5 Dauph. 75 (1902)
Leather (also see "Hides"):			
Tanning	Yes	Mfg.	*Cmwlth. v. Elk Tanning Co.,* 1 Dauph. 96 (1896) (note)
Cutting tanned leather into pieces for customers	No	-	*Cmwlth. v. Cover,* 215 Pa. 556 (1906)
Lighting fixtures:			
Lamps, gas fixtures, electric fixtures	Yes	Mfg.	*Cmwlth. v. Thackara Manufacturing Co.,* 156 Pa. 510 (1893)
Lumber:			
The operation of a saw mill or planing mill for the production of lumber or lumber products for sale	Yes	Processing	72 P.S. § 7601
Kiln drying pre-cut lumber	No		*Cmwlth. v. Babcock Lumber Co.,* 272 A.2d 522 (1971)
Manufacture of wooden components for bridges	Yes	Mfg.	*Cmwlth. v. Keystone Bridge Co.,* 27 A. 4 (Pa. 1893)
Machinery and equipment:			
Gas-producers (machines for making artificial gas from bituminous coal) and gas furnaces on customer's site	Yes	Mfg.	*Cmwlth. v. William Swindell & Brothers Co.,* 22 Dauph. 184 (1919)
Engines, boilers, foundry castings, machines	Yes	Mfg.	*Cmwlth. v. Nagle Engine and Boiler Works,* 23 Dauph. 235 (1920)
Railway cars	Yes	Mfg.	*Cmwlth. v. American Car and Foundry Co.,* 203 Pa. 302 (1902)
Locomotive engines	Yes	Mfg.	*Norris Brothers v. Cmwlth.,* 27 Pa. 494 (1856)
Meal (also see "Flour"):			
The milling for sale of flour or meal from grains	Yes	Processing	72 P.S. § 7601
Meat and meat products:			
The slaughtering and dressing of animals for meat to be sold or to be used in preparing meat products for sale; and the preparation of meat products, including lard, tallow, grease, cooking and in edible oils for wholesale distribution	Yes	Processing	72 P.S. § 7601
Metal and metal products:			
The salvaging, recycling or reclaiming used materials to be recycled into a manufacturing process	Yes	Processing	72 P.S. § 7601
The rolling, drawing or extruding of ferrous and nonferrous metals	Yes	Processing	
The electroplating, galvanizing, enameling, anodizing, coloring, finishing, impregnating or heat treating of metals or plastics for sale or in the process of manufacturing	Yes	Processing	72 P.S. § 7601

Product or Activity	Exempt	Basis for Exemption	Authority
The fabrication for sale of ornamental or structural metal or metal stairs, staircases, gratings, fire escapes or railings (not including fabrication work done at the construction site)	Yes	Processing	72 P.S. § 7601
The blanking, shearing, leveling, slitting, or burning of metals for sale to or use by a manufacturer or processor	Yes	Mfg.	72 P.S. § 7601
Converting iron into steel	Yes	Mfg.	*Cmwlth. v. Lackawanna Iron & Coal Co.,* 129 Pa. 346 (1889); *Cmwlth. v. Midvale Steel Co.,* 1 Dauph. 97 (1886)
Production of pig-metal from iron ore	Yes	Mfg.	*Cmwlth. v. Dunbar Furnace Co.,* 1 Dauph. 97 (1892) (note)
Processing scrap metal by scrap metal dealers	Yes	Mfg.	*Cmwlth. v. Eastern Diversified Metals Corp.,* 297 A.2d 167 (Pa.Commw. 1972), *aff'd per curiam,* 306 A.2d 300 (Pa. 1973); *Cmwlth. v. Morrisville Scrap Processing, Corp., Inc.,* 6 Pa.Commw. 604 (1972), *aff'd* 307 A.2d 905 (1973); *Cmwlth. v. Deitch Co.,* 295 A.2d 824 (1972)
Recovery of nonferrous metals from scrap wire	No	-	*Cmwlth. v. Eastern Diversified Metals Corp.,* 297 A.2d 167 (1972), *aff'd per curiam,* 306 A.2d Pa.Commw. 300 (Pa. 1973)
Metal parts for bridges, roofs, and girders	Yes	Mfg.	*Cmwlth. v. Keystone Bridge, Co.,* 27 A. 4 (Pa. 1893); *Cmwlth. v. Pittsburgh Bridge Co.,* 156 Pa. 507 (Pa. 1893)
Straightening, cutting, and bending wire for concrete construction	No	-	*Cmwlth. v. Taylor-Davis, Inc.,* 37 Dauph. 391 (1933)
Manufacturing wire mats	Yes	Mfg.	*Cmwlth. v. Taylor-Davis, Inc.,* 37 Dauph. 391 (1933)
Shearing, cutting, twisting, bending, and welding metal rods and bars for use in concrete construction	No	-	*Cmwlth. v. Taylor-Davis, Inc.,* 37 Dauph. 391 (1933)
Cutting and threading nuts and bolts for use in concrete construction	No	-	*Cmwlth. v. Taylor-Davis, Inc.,* 37 Dauph. 391 (1933)
Art metal work	Yes	Mfg.	*Cmwlth. v. Thackara Manufacturing Co.,* 156 Pa. 510 (1893)
Metal analysis	No	-	*Westmoreland Mechanical Testing & Research, Inc.,* Board of Finance and Revenue, Docket No. 25214 (1994)
Mining	No	-	*Cmwlth. v. Lackawanna Iron & Coal Co.,* 129 Pa. 346 (1889); *Cmwlth. v. The Welsh Mountain Mining & Kaolin Manufacturing Co.,* 265 Pa. 380 (Pa. 1919); *Cmwlth. v. Savage Fire Brick Co.,* 157 Pa. 512 (Pa. 1893); *Cmwlth. v. Juniata Coke Co.,* 157 Pa. 507 (Pa. 1893)
Molasses: Straining, heating, and blending	No	-	*Cmwlth. v. P. Duff & Sons, Inc.,* 36 Dauph. 1 (1933)
Mustard: Preparation of mustard from whole mustard seed	Yes	Mfg.	*Cmwlth. v. A. Colburn Co.,* 1 Dauph. 96 (1892) (note)
Oil: Refining of crude oil into other products	Yes	Mfg.	*Cmwlth. v. National Oil Co., Ltd.,* 157 Pa. 516 (1893); *Cmwlth. v. Chester Oil Co.,* 1 Dauph. 95 (1896) (note); *Cmwlth. v. Atlantic Refining Co.,* 7 Dauph. 189 (1904); *Atlantic Refining Co.,* 398 Pa. 30 (1959)
Processing used lubricating oils	Yes	Processing	72 P.S. § 7601
Production and transportation of oil	No	-	*Cmwlth. v. National Oil Co., Ltd.,* 157 Pa. 516 (1893)

Product or Activity	Exempt	Basis for Exemption	Authority
Paper products:			
Stationery	Yes	Mfg.	*Cmwlth. v. J.B. Lippincott Co.*, 7 Dauph. 193 (1904)
Sealing tape	Yes	Mfg.	*Cmwlth. v. Peerless Paper Specialty, Inc.*, 25 A.2d 323 (1942)
Envelopes, paper cups, fly paper, blank books	Yes	Mfg.	*Cmwlth. v. William Mann Co.*, 150 Pa. 64 (1892)
Paving	No	-	*Cmwlth. v. Interstate Amiesite Corp.*, 94 A.2d 191 (Pa. 1963); *Cmwlth. v. H.J. Williams Co.*, 78 Dauph. 377 (1962)
Peanut butter	Yes	Mfg.	*Cmwlth. v. P. Duff & Sons, Inc.*, 36 Dauph. 1 (1933)
Plastics:			
The electroplating, galvanizing, enameling, anodizing, coloring, finishing, impregnating or heat treating of metals or plastic for sale or in the process of manufacturing	Yes	Processing	72 P.S. §7601
Plumbing:			
Installing heating, plumbing, and ventilating systems	No	-	*Cmwlth. v. Harry F. Murphy Co., Inc.*, 4 Dauph. 314 (1921); *Cmwlth. v. J. Frank Boyer Plumbing and Heating Co.*, 23 Dauph. 296 (1920)
Popcorn	No	-	*Cmwlth. v. Berlo Vending Co.*, 202 A.2d 94 (1964)
Potato chips	Yes	Mfg.	*Cmwlth. v. Snyder's Bakery*, 35 A.2d 260 (1944)
Printing:			
The publishing of books, newspapers, magazines or other periodicals; printing and broadcasting radio and television programs by licensed commercial or educational stations	Yes	Processing	72 P.S. §7601
Publication of a daily racing paper	Yes	Processing	*Cmwlth. v. The Armstrong Daily, Inc.*, 90 Dauph. 199 (1968)
Quarrying	No	-	*Cmwlth. v. The John T. Dyer Quarry Co.*, 250 Pa. 589 (1915); *Cmwlth. v. Lackawanna Iron & Coal Co.*, 129 Pa. 346 (1889)
Radio (see "Broadcasting")			
Raw materials:			
Production of raw materials for taxpayer's manufacturing process	No	-	*Cmwlth. v. National Oil Co., Ltd.*, 157 Pa. 516 (1893); *Cmwlth. v. Savage Fire Brick Co.*, 157 Pa. 512 (Pa. 1893); *Cmwlth. v. Juniata Coke Co.*, 157 Pa. 507 (Pa. 1893)
Recycling:			
The salvaging, recycling or reclaiming used materials to be recycled into a manufacturing process	Yes	Processing	72 P.S. §7601
Research and development:			
Activities relating to the discovery of new and the refinement of known substances, products, processes, theories and ideas, but does not include activities directed primarily to the accumulation or analysis of commercial, financial, or mercantile data	Yes	R & D	72 P.S. §7601

Product or Activity	Exempt	Basis for Exemption	Authority
Rock (see "Stone")			
Sand:			
Crushing rock to make sand	No	-	*Cmwlth. v. Elmwood Sand Co.,* 21 Dauph. 114 (1918)
Crushing rock and adding clay to make colored sand	No	-	*Cmwlth. v. The Welsh Mountain Mining & Kaolin Manufacturing Co.,* 265 Pa. 380 (Pa. 1919)
Shipbuilding:			
Building engines and other components	Yes	Mfg.	*Cmwlth. v. William Cramp & Sons Ship & Engine Building Co.,* 1 Dauph. 95 (1893) (note); *Cmwlth. v. Delaware River Iron Ship Building and Engine Works,* 2 Dauph. 232 (1889); *Cmwlth. v. Philadelphia Ship Repair Co.,* 21 Dauph. 44 (1918)
Ship repairs (by company that manufactures the parts)	Yes	Mfg.	*Cmwlth. v. Philadelphia Ship Repair Co.,* 21 Dauph. 44 (1918)
Wharves and docks necessary for shipbuilding	Yes	Mfg.	*Cmwlth. v. Philadelphia Ship Repair Co.,* 21 Dauph. 44 (1918)
Shoemaking	Yes	Mfg.	*Norris Brothers v. Cmwlth.,* 27 Pa. 494 (1856) (dictum)
Slate:			
Quarrying large blocks of slate, finishing them, and making articles (*e.g.,* roof slates, school slates, blackboards, kitchen and dairy utensils, mantels, table tops)	Yes	Mfg.	*Cmwlth. v. East Bangor Consolidated Slate Co.,* 1 Dauph. 96 (1887) (note)
Snow making	Yes	Mfg.	*Ski Roundtop, Inc., v. Cmwlth.,* 553 A.2d 928 (Pa. 1989); *rev'g* 527 A.2d 699 (1987)
Soap:			
Making soap for taxpayer's own use in laundry	No	-	*Cmwlth. v. Keystone Laundry Co.,* 203 Pa. 289 (Pa. 1902)
Spices:			
Conversion of whole spices into salable products	Yes	Mfg.	*Cmwlth. v. A. Colburn Co.,* 1 Dauph. 96 (1892) (note)
Steam:			
Production of steam for sale to customers	No	-	*Cmwlth. v. Arrott Steam-Power Mills Co.,* 22 A. 243 (Pa. 1891)
Stone:			
Crushed stone for sale to customers	No	-	*Cmwlth. v. The John T. Dyer Quarry Co.,* 250 Pa. 589 (1915)
Crushing limestone for railroad ballast	No	-	*Cmwlth. v. Bellefonte Lime Co.,* 18 Dauph. 139 (1915)
Splitting, shaping, and dressing rough stone for exterior and interior walls of buildings	No	-	*Cmwlth. v. Paul W. Bounds Co.,* 316 Pa. 29 (1934)
Designing, selling, and erecting cemetery monuments	Yes	Mfg.	*Horigan v. City of Pittsburgh,* 178 Pa. 558 (1955)
Tea and tea bags	No	-	*Cmwlth. v. Tetley Tea Co.,* 220 A.2d 832 (1966)
Television (see "Broadcasting")			
Textiles:			
The scouring, carbonizing, cording, combing, throwing, twisting or winding of natural or synthetic fibers, or the spinning, bleaching, dyeing, printing or finishing of yarns or fabrics, when such activities are performed prior to sale to the ultimate consumer	Yes	Processing	72 P.S. § 7601
Tile (see "Brick")			

Product or Activity	Exempt	Basis for Exemption	Authority
Tobacco:			
Aging, stripping, conditioning, crushing, and blending of tobacco leaves for use as cigar filler or as components of smokeless tobacco products for sale to manufacturers of tobacco products (effective July 1, 1997)	Yes	Processing	72 P.S. § 7601
Preparing leaf tobacco for chewing and smoking by stripping the stems from the leaves and cutting up the leaves by machinery into different sizes	Yes	Mfg.	*Cmwlth. v. Clark & Snover Co.*, 1 Dauph. 95 (1893) (note)
Curing, stripping, and baling tobacco	No	-	*Cmwlth. v. Clark & Snover Co.*, 1 Dauph. 95 (1893) (note)
Vegetables:			
Processing for wholesale distribution	Yes	Processing	72 P.S. § 7601
Ventilating systems:			
Installing heating, plumbing, and ventilating systems	No	-	*Cmwlth. v. J. Frank Boyer Plumbing and Heating Co.*, 23 Dauph. 296 (1920)
Warehousing	No	-	*Cmwlth. v. The Industrial Cold Storage and Warehouse Co.*, 18 Dauph. 143 (1915)
Water distilling	No	-	*Cmwlth. v. Sunbeam Water Co.*, 284 Pa. 180 (1925)
Well drilling	No	-	*Cmwlth. v. Thomas B. Harper Co.*, 24 Dauph. 25 (1921)
Wire:			
Straightening, cutting, and bending for concrete construction	No	-	*Cmwlth. v. Taylor-Davis, Inc.*, 37 Dauph. 391 (1933)
Making wire mats for concrete construction	Yes	Mfg.	*Cmwlth. v. Taylor-Davis, Inc.*, 37 Dauph. 391 (1933)
Wood products:			
Wooden components for bridge construction	Yes	Mfg.	*Cmwlth. v. Keystone Bridge Co.*, 27 A. 4 (Pa. 1893)

CAPITAL STOCK TAX, FRANCHISE TAX, AND CORPORATE LOANS TAX

CHAPTER 17
CORPORATE LOANS TAX

¶1701 Overview

[The Corporate Loans Tax was repealed by Act 71 of 2013 effective for tax years beginning after December 31, 2013]

The Pennsylvania corporate loans tax was first imposed in 1844 [Act of April 29, 1844, P.L. 486]. Until 1913, Pennsylvania collected both the corporate loans tax and the personal property tax. In 1913, the two laws were separated by the Act of June 17, 1913, P.L. 507. The Commonwealth still collected the corporate loans tax for tax years ending before January 1, 2014, but the personal property tax is now a county tax. The corporate loans tax was imposed by the Act of June 22, 1935, P.L. 414 and is codified in 72 P.S. § 3250-10 *et seq.*

Personal Property Tax Interaction

Obligations subject to the corporate loans tax are *not* subject to the personal property tax. On the other hand, obligations that are exempt from the corporate loans tax may be subject to the personal property tax in the hands of a taxable holder. The corporate loans tax takes precedence.

It is important to remember that the personal property tax is based on fair market value, while the corporate loans tax is based on nominal value. See ¶ 1704 for an explanation of nominal value.

• *Administration*

The corporate loans tax is administered by the Pennsylvania Department of Revenue.

• *Sources of authority*

The corporate loans tax falls under the provisions of 72 P.S. § 3250-10 *et seq.* Current provisions with respect to assessment, withholding, and payment are found in the Act of May 18, 1937, P.L. 633 (replacing the provisions of the Act of June 30, 1885, P.L. 193), and the current provision exempting municipal loans was added by 72 P.S. § 3250-10.

¶1702 Imposition

For tax years beginning before January 1, 2014, the Pennsylvania corporate loans tax is imposed on indebtedness owed to Pennsylvania residents by Pennsylvania corporations and foreign corporations doing business in Pennsylvania [72 P.S. §3250-10]. The tax is imposed on "All scrip, bonds, certificates, and evidences of indebtedness issued, and all scrip, bonds, certificates, and evidences of indebtedness assumed, or on which interest shall be paid by any and every private corporation, incorporated or created under the laws of this Commonwealth, or the laws of any other state or of the United States and doing business in this Commonwealth and having a resident corporate treasurer therein, except first class or nonprofit corporations . . . ."

Requirement of Resident Treasurer

The corporate loans tax is imposed on indebtedness owed to Pennsylvania residents by Pennsylvania corporations and foreign corporations doing business in Pennsylvania. A foreign corporation is required to withhold the corporate loans tax only if it has a treasurer who performs his or her duties in Pennsylvania. Thus, a foreign corporation that elects a corporate treasurer who officially resides and performs his or her duties outside Pennsylvania is not required to withhold the Pennsylvania corporate loans tax on indebtedness owed to residents of Pennsylvania [*Pennsylvania Corporate Tax Ruling No. CRP-00-007*, September 22, 2000].

¶1703 Withholding

• *Imposition of tax*

At various times in the history of the Pennsylvania corporate loans tax the person on whom the tax was imposed has changed. At times it was imposed on the corporation (the debtor); at other times, on the holder of the debt (the creditor). The corporate loans tax in its current form is imposed on the creditor and withheld by the debtor corporation.

Private Corporation

The term "private corporation" in this context means a corporation in the private sector and does not refer to whether the corporation is closely held or publicly traded. Incorporated municipalities are nonprivate corporations.

The tax is imposed on *resident individuals* who hold the debt, but the corporations who issue, assume or pay interest on the debt must withhold and remit the tax to the Commonwealth [72 P.S. § 3250-10]. Technically, the corporate treasurer is responsible for the withholding and remittance of tax to Pennsylvania. However, since a corporation is liable in the event of default by its treasurer, the corporation is responsible for the tax.

Federal Deduction

The Pennsylvania corporate loans tax is not a tax on corporations. It is a tax on resident holders of corporate obligations. See, for example, *Sharon Herald Co. v. Granger*, 97 F.Supp. 295 (D.C. Pa. 1951), *aff'd*, 195 F.2d 890 (3rd Cir. 1952); *Cmwlth. v. Rittenhouse Square Corp.*, 62 Dauph 49 (1952) *exceptions overruled*, 62 Dauph 285 (1952). Therefore, when a corporation pays the corporate loans tax for its creditors, it is not deductible for federal income tax purposes unless it is a tax-free covenant bond (*i.e.*, the corporation is legally liable for the tax). To ensure federal deductibility, you should be certain that all the documents pertaining to the loan indicate that your corporation is liable for the tax.

• *Withholding*

Corporations must withhold tax when interest is paid and remit the tax to Pennsylvania annually.

Interest Paid

The law imposes the corporate loans tax only on interest paid, not on interest due. If you do not pay interest, do not withhold the tax.

There is, however, an exception to this rule in the case of a corporation that assumes a debt and/or interest payments on a debt.

Example: A New Jersey corporation whose treasurer is a resident of New Jersey merges into a Pennsylvania corporation, and the Pennsylvania corporation assumes the New Jersey corporation's debt. The Pennsylvania corporation must notify any Pennsylvania resident holders of the New Jersey corporation's debt (within 10 days and in writing) of the assumption.

In addition, a corporation assuming debt must notify the creditors before October 1 of every subsequent year. If a corporation assumes debt and/or interest before October 1 and gives the required notice, the corporation is not liable for withholding the corporate loans tax for the remainder of the year of assumption. If the corporation assumes debt and/or interest on or after October 1 and gives the required notice, the corporation is not liable for withholding the corporate loans tax for the remainder of the year of assumption and the following year. For the period after the assumption of the debt and/or interest in which the corporation need not withhold the corporate loans tax, the holder remains subject to the personal property tax [72 P.S. § 3250-10].

Notice of Assumption

If you fail to give the required notice to your taxable creditors, you are subject to penalties. Failure to notify holders of assumption within 10 days causes you to be liable for the loans tax for the entire period for which you pay interest. If you fail to give notice before October 1 of any subsequent year, you must pay the tax for the following year and cannot deduct it from interest paid. In other words, you become liable for the tax, must pay the tax, and can't deduct it for federal income tax purposes. The holder, however, is still not subject to the personal property tax because the obligation is subject to the loans tax.

The term "doing business in Pennsylvania" means carrying out corporate purposes and exercising corporate franchise within Pennsylvania. The location of the corporation's property, although an important factor, does not, in and of itself, determine the location of the business operations (*i.e.,* a corporation can have no assets in Pennsylvania but still be doing business in Pennsylvania). Isolated transactions and acts incidental to business do not constitute "doing business" [*Cmwlth. v. Jessup & Moore Paper Co.,* 31 Dauph 273 (1928)]. For more details on what constitutes "doing business" in Pennsylvania, see ¶ 913.

The "residency" of a corporate treasurer for purposes of the Pennsylvania corporate loans tax is not necessarily "residency" for other purposes. A corporate officer's official domicile is where their official duties are performed. If a corporate treasurer, for example, lives in New Jersey but performs corporate duties in Pennsylvania, that treasurer is a "resident" treasurer for purposes of the corporate loans tax [*Cmwlth. v. Sun Oil Co.,* 143 A 495 (Pa. 1928)]. If a corporate officer comparable to a treasurer (*e.g.,* an assistant treasurer) performs duties in Pennsylvania, the indebtedness of the corporation may be subject to the corporate loans tax. See, for example, *Cmwlth. v. Welsbach Co.,* in which a foreign corporation doing business in Pennsylvania and having no resident treasurer had to withhold corporate loans tax on interest paid to resident holders because the interest on the bonds in question was paid by the assistant treasurer, who both resided and performed his official duties in Pennsylvania [*Cmwlth. v. Welsbach Co.*, 16 Dauph 130 (1913)].

¶1704 Base and Rate

The Corporate Loans Tax was repealed by Act 71 of 2013 effective for tax years beginning after December 31, 2013. For years in which the tax was in effect, the corporate loans tax rate was 4 mills (0.004) per dollar of "nominal value" of taxable indebtedness of a corporation. The nominal value of a corporation's indebtedness is the amount of interest paid divided by the stated interest rate on the indebtedness; this is the par value of the debt [72 P.S. § 3250-10].

> *Example:* A corporation, during the tax year, paid $1,000,000 in interest to resident holders of its debentures. The interest rate on the debentures is 10%. The nominal value of the debt is $10,000,000 ($1,000,000 ÷ 0.10), and the amount of loans tax the corporation must withhold is $40,000 ($10,000,000 × 0.004).

Watch Interest Period

> Do not withhold a full year's tax if interest is not paid for a full year. For instance, in the example above, if interest is paid for only six months, the amount of tax to be withheld is only $20,000 [($500,000 ÷ .10) × .004].

It is the position of the Department of Revenue that if corporations pay more than the stated interest rate, corporate loans tax is due on the full amount of interest paid. On the other hand, the law defines nominal value as par value; therefore, if a holder accepts less than the stated rate in full payment of any interest, tax is due on the face value of the obligations.

For example, if a corporation has one year's interest in arrears on a $1,000,000 loan at 12% interest and negotiates with the creditor to accept $100,000 in full payment of the year's interest in arrears, corporate loans tax is due on the full face amount of the obligation.

In general, taxable indebtedness includes notes, mortgages, debentures, bonds, trust certificates, and interest-bearing accounts (but see ¶1706). Specific types of indebtedness held to be taxable include the following (if they are interest-bearing): open book accounts (*e.g.*, accounts payable); articles of agreement; car or equipment trust certificates; notes discounted by a private banker; and customer deposits.

Debt Liability Not Controlling

> Corporations must withhold the corporate loans tax on taxable indebtedness for which they are not legally liable if they pay the interest. Payment of interest, not liability for the debt, is the factor that determines liability for withholding of the corporate loans tax.

Although corporations need not withhold tax unless interest is paid, the rate of tax to be paid depends on the year the interest accrues, not the year paid, if the two years are different. Since the corporate loans tax rate has been 4 mills since 1944, this is important only in the event of future rate changes.

Interest Paid in Kind

> Interest is ordinarily paid in cash. However, it is possible for interest to be paid in the form of property other than cash. For example, it is the position of the Department of Revenue that, in the case of a recapitalization that involves the retirement of debt (*e.g.*, the issuing of preferred stock for bonds), any accrued interest is satisfied by the

payment of preferred stock and the corporate loans tax becomes due. The Department has been successful in imposing the corporate loans tax in such a situation. If you are considering such a recapitalization, you should consider the corporate loans tax consequences carefully.

¶1705 Exemptions

Like most taxes, the Pennsylvania corporate loans tax has exemptions: (1) some indebtedness is exempt, (2) some corporations are exempt from withholding the loans tax (*i.e.,* the holders of these securities pay no loans tax), and (3) some holders of obligations of non-exempt corporations are exempt (*i.e.,* where the corporation normally must withhold the corporate loans tax, it need not for these holders).

The following are exempt from the corporate loans tax:

(1) Bank notes or notes discounted or negotiated by any bank or banking institution, savings institution or trust company. This exemption applies only to notes discounted by incorporated banks. Promissory notes discounted by private bankers are taxable [*Cmwlth. v. Stephano Bros.,* 55 Dauph 424 (1943)].

(2) Interest-bearing accounts in any bank, banking institution, savings institution, employees' thrift or savings association (whether operated by employees or the employer, or trust company).

(3) Any scrip, bonds, certificates or evidences of indebtedness held in any trust forming part of a stock, bonus, pension or profit-sharing plan of an employer for the exclusive benefit of employees, or their beneficiaries, which trust under the latest ruling of the Commissioner of Internal Revenue is exempted from federal income tax.

(4) Any personal property held under the provisions of a plan established by or for an individual or individuals for retirement purposes, if such plan meets the requirements for exemptions from federal income tax of income earned on investments held under its provisions.

(5) Building and loan associations or savings institutions having no capital stock, and if at any time either now or hereafter, any persons, individuals, or bodies corporate have agreed or shall hereafter agree to issue his, their or its securities, bonds or other evidences of indebtedness, clear of and free from the tax or any part thereof, provided for in paying sick or death benefits, or either or both, from funds received from voluntary contributions or assessments, upon members of such associations, societies, or unions.

(6) Corporations, limited partnerships, and joint-stock associations, liable to tax on capital stock for state purposes, are not required to pay corporate loans tax on the mortgages, bonds, and other securities owned by them in their own right.

Obligations Held by Fiduciaries

The law is not clear with respect to the status of obligations held by fiduciaries (taxable or exempt). The commonly accepted interpretation is that the status depends on who holds title to the property. Thus, the taxability of the obligations differs, depending on whether the property is held by a trustee (taxability depends on residence of title-holding trustee) or by an agent without title (taxability depends on residence of beneficiary). See ¶1706 for a detailed explanation of the status of indebtedness held by fiduciaries.

Tax-Free Covenant Bonds

If Pennsylvania savings institutions with no capital stock hold tax-free covenant bonds, they are taxable under the corporate loans tax on such bonds. Tax-free covenant bonds are bonds issued with an agreement (by the issuer) to pay any or all of the taxes levied against the holders of the bonds.

• *Diligence in locating*

Formerly, there was a statutory presumption that unknown holders of taxable indebtedness were resident individuals. This presumption has been eliminated. Now, corporations need not withhold the loans tax for unknown owners if they exercise reasonable diligence in trying to locate the holders. For the judicial interpretation of reasonable diligence, see *Cmwlth. v. Safe Harbor Water Power Corporation*, 43 Dauph 415 (1937), in which the court held that the treasurer or corporation was not held to a standard so high as to require the expenditure of more money to locate holders than the commission to be earned.

¶1706 Indebtedness Held by Fiduciaries

The law provides that personal property held for a nonresident decedent is exempt. This rule applies whether the fiduciary is a resident or a nonresident. Indebtedness held for a resident decedent is taxable, regardless of the residency of the fiduciary [72 P.S. § 3250-10].

Taxability of indebtedness held by an agent depends on the residency of the individual who owns the property. The corporate loans tax is imposed only on *resident* individuals [72 P.S. § 3250-10].

If obligations are held for an exempt beneficiary, they are not taxable regardless of the residency of the trustee. Indebtedness held by a nonresident trustee is exempt, regardless of the residency of the beneficiary. Indebtedness held by a resident trustee for a resident beneficiary is taxable. Indebtedness held by a resident trustee for a nonresident beneficiary may be taxable or exempt, depending on how the property was acquired [72 P.S. § 3250-10]. If it was acquired with property or money received from a nonresident grantor, it is exempt. If it was acquired with property or money received from a resident grantor, it is taxable.

Resident Beneficiaries

If you are a resident beneficiary of a nonresident trust, you are liable for the personal property tax on your equitable interest in the trust, even though the trustee is not liable for the corporate loans tax.

• *Indebtedness held by guardians*

In accordance with the general rules in the statute, obligations held by a resident guardian for a resident owner are clearly taxable. Obligations held by a nonresident guardian for a nonresident owner are clearly exempt [Act of June 22, 1935, P.L. 414, § 17]. However, the law is silent with respect to obligations held by nonresident guardians for resident owners and by resident guardians for nonresident owners.

¶1707 Returns and Payment of Tax

The Corporate Loans Tax was repealed by Act 71 of 2013 effective for tax years beginning after December 31, 2013. For tax years beginning before January 1, 2014, the resident treasurer of every corporation, except those exempt from withholding

¶1706

the corporate loans tax, must submit an annual report to the Department of Revenue on or before April 15 of the taxable year [72 P.S. § 708]. The corporate loans report is submitted simultaneously with the capital stock tax and corporate net income tax [Form RCT-101].

Payment by Electronic Funds Transfer

Payment of tax made by electronic funds transfer (EFT) is discussed at ¶ 4617.

No tentative reports are required for corporate loans tax purposes.

¶ 1708 Extensions of Time

A corporation may receive an extension of time for filing the annual report. However, there is no extension of time in which to remit the loans tax withheld; it must be paid by the due date for the original report.

Details on requests for extensions of time are at ¶ 1327.

¶ 1709 Treasurer's Commission

The law provides that if a corporate treasurer withholds and remits the tax on a timely basis, the treasurer is entitled to a commission, computed as follows: 5% of the first $1,000; 1% of the second $1,000; and 0.5% of all amounts over $2,000 [72 P.S. § 216].

¶ 1710 Procedure and Enforcement

The corporate treasurer acts as the collecting agent for the Commonwealth [72 P.S. § 606]. The rules for penalties for noncompliance, assessment, settlement, resettlement, review, appeal, and refunds are governed by the general provisions of the Fiscal Code (FC).

PART VI

PASS-THROUGH ENTITIES

CHAPTER 18

PASS-THROUGH ENTITIES

INTRODUCTION

¶1801 General

"Pass-through entities" are entities that do not pay tax on the income earned, received, or realized in each Pennsylvania income class but pass through the classified income, allowable losses, and credits to the shareholders and partners [*Instruc-*

¶1801

tions, Form PA-20S/PA-65]. The shareholders and partners then report the classified income and losses on their individual Pennsylvania income tax returns. Most pass-through entities are (1) S corporations (discussed at ¶¶1802—1812); (2) partnerships (discussed at ¶1815—1818); (3) limited liability partnerships (discussed at ¶1819); or (4) limited liability companies (discussed at ¶1820—1824). Also included in this chapter are Pennsylvania Business Trusts (discussed at ¶1830) and restricted professional companies (discussed at ¶1831).

• *Pass-Through Business Office*

The Department of Revenue's Pass Through Business Office was created through a joint effort by the Revenue Department Bureaus of Individual Taxes, Information Systems, Fiscal Management, and the Office of Chief Counsel. It contains an examination unit and an analytical unit. The examination unit ensures that information on individual returns and schedules is filed according to Department rules and regulations. The analytical unit conducts specialized and highly detailed financial and tax accounting analyses of complex pass through business organizations. This unit also documents ownership interests in multi-tiered business structures, classification of (taxable) personal income at the entity and individual levels and the allocation of income inside and outside Pennsylvania.

• *Entity level assessments*

Under Act 52 of 2013, for tax years beginning after December 31, 2013, the tax treatment of partnership items and S corporation items is determined at the partnership or S corporation level. If certain partnerships underreport their income by more than $1 million in any tax year, the partnership may be liable for the tax (but not interest, penalties, or additions) on the underreported income, without regard to the partners' actual tax liability. The partnership must provide each partner a Pennsylvania K-1 reporting the partner's share of the underreported income within 90 days of the assessment becoming final. Each partner is allowed a credit for the partner's share of the tax assessed against and paid by the partnership. All reassessments at the partnership level are binding on the partners, and any appeals relating to any alleged underreporting are to be taken only by the partnership. A partnership is covered by these rules if it has partners that are only natural persons and elects to have the partnership level assessment procedure apply, the partnership has 11 or more partners that are natural persons, or the partnership has at least one partner that is an entity or trust. A publicly traded partnership is not subject to these rules.

Similar rules apply to Pennsylvania S corporations that have 11 or more shareholders or that elect to have the S corporation level assessment procedure apply. That is, as is the case with partnerships described above, S corporation shareholders receive a credit for their share of the tax paid by the S corporation. Assessments that are made at the S corporation level are binding on the shareholders. Finally, any appeals must be taken by the S corporation, itself.

• *Owner lists*

Beginning January 1, 2014, every partnership, S corporation, estate and trust must maintain a list of its owners or beneficiaries. Failure to do so will cause the entity and its officers or responsible partners to be liable for tax, penalty and interest with respect to the entity.

• *Interests in unincorporated entities*

In general, a corporation's interest in an entity that is not a corporation is considered a direct ownership interest in the assets of the entity rather than an intangible interest [72 P.S. §7402.2]. Thus, out-of-state corporations that have a presence in Pennsylvania through an interest in a pass-through entity are subject to Pennsylvania corporation taxes, and apportionment fractions flow through from unincorporated entities to corporate partners. The general rule with respect to unincorporated entities does not apply to a corporation's interest in an entity described in 72 P.S. § 7401(1)1 or 72 P.S. § 7401(1)2 (see ¶ 912) other than the following:

(1) *A captive REIT:* A captive REIT is a business trust that is a real estate investment trust as defined in IRC § 856 more than 50% of the voting power or value of the beneficial interest or shares of which are owned or controlled (directly or indirectly) by a single corporation that is not (a) a real estate investment trust as defined in IRC § 856 [72 P.S. § 7402.2(b)(1)(i)]; (b) a qualified real estate investment trust subsidiary under IRC § 856(i) [72 P.S. § 7402.2(b)(1)(ii)]; (c) a regulated financial institution [72 P.S. § 7402.2(b)(1)(iii)]; or (d) formed as a holding company, subsidiary or affiliate of a regulated financial institution prior to December 1, 2003 [72 P.S. § 7402.2(b)(1)(iv)]. A corporation that owns an interest in a business trust that is a captive REIT is considered to own a direct ownership interest in the assets of the REIT.

(2) *A captive QRS:* A captive QRS is a business trust that is a qualified real estate investment trust subsidiary under IRC § 856(i) owned (directly or indirectly) by a real estate investment trust as defined in IRC § 856 more than 50% of the voting power or value of the beneficial interests or shares of which are owned or controlled (directly or indirectly) by a single corporation that is not (a) a real estate investment trust as defined in IRC § 856 [72 P.S. § 7402.2(b)(2)(i)]; (b) a qualified real estate investment trust subsidiary under IRC § 856(i) [72 P.S. § 7402.2(b)(2)(ii)]; (c) a regulated financial institution [72 P.S. § 7402.2(b)(2)(ii)]; or (d) formed as a holding company, subsidiary or affiliate of a regulated financial institution prior to December 1, 2003 [72 P.S. § 7402.2(b)(2)(iv)]. A corporation that owns an interest in a business trust that is a captive QRS is considered to own a direct ownership interest in the assets of the QRS.

Net income per books of corporate member: The Department of Revenue takes the position that the net income per books of a corporate member of a limited liability company (LLC) excludes the pass-through income or loss from the LLC and includes distributions from the LLC. In making those adjustments the corporate member must provide the following information:

(1) A schedule showing these adjustments and the reason for the adjustments.

(2) For investments in LLCs filing as partnerships for federal income tax purposes, a copy of the K-1 issued by the LLC showing the reconciliation of the member's capital account.

(3) For investments in LLCs that are disregarded for federal income tax purposes, beginning and ending balance sheets and a reconciliation of the member's capital account for each LLC.

(4) For corporate taxpayers who are removing the income from the LLC but are not including 100% of the distribution from the LLC because due to the income was not included in the net income per books in a prior year, a schedule showing the income and distributions for prior years.

Failure to Provide Information

If the corporation member does not provide this information, the Department of Revenue will assume that all income from the LLC was distributed in the year it was reported in net income per books on the federal return (Letter from Deputy Secretary for Tax Policy, March 30, 2004).

S CORPORATIONS

¶1802 Pennsylvania S Corporations

A Pennsylvania S corporation is a small corporation that does not have a valid election under 72 P.S. §7307 in effect. A small corporation is any corporation that has a valid election in effect under subchapter S of Chapter 1 of the Internal Revenue Code of 1986, as amended to January 1, 2005 [72 P.S. §7301(s.2)]. A qualified Subchapter S subsidiary owned by a Pennsylvania S corporation is treated as a Pennsylvania S corporation without regard to whether an election under 72 P.S. §7307 has been made with respect to the subsidiary [72 P.S. §7301(n.1)]. A qualified subchapter S subsidiary is a corporation (domestic or foreign) that for federal income tax purposes is treated as a qualified Subchapter S subsidiary as defined in IRC §1361(b)(3)(b), as amended to January 1, 2005 [72 P.S. §7301(o.3)]. See ¶1803 for discussion of 72 P.S. §7307 elections.

The shareholders of a Pennsylvania S corporation are subject to the Pennsylvania personal income tax on their pro rata share of the Pennsylvania S corporation's income or loss [72 P.S. §7207.9(a)]. The taxable year for a Pennsylvania S corporation is the same as for federal purposes [72 P.S. §7307.7].

S Corporations Remain Liable for Other Corporate Taxes

Pennsylvania S corporation status applies only to the corporate net income tax, but it has personal income tax implications for the shareholders. See ¶212 for an explanation of taxation of shareholders. A Pennsylvania S corporation remains subject to other Pennsylvania corporate taxes (e.g., capital stock/franchise tax, corporate loans tax) and must file a Form RCT-101 for capital stock/franchise tax and corporate loans tax purposes, but it does not have to complete Schedule C of the Form RCT-101.

¶1803 Electing Not To Be a Pennsylvania S Corporation

Act 67 of 2006 amended the Tax Reform Code of 1971 by eliminating the requirement for federal Subchapter S corporations to file the *Pennsylvania "S" Corporation Election and Shareholders' Consent (REV-1640)* in order to be granted Pennsylvania S corporation status. Effective for tax years beginning after December 31, 2005, any corporation with a valid federal Subchapter S corporation election will automatically be a Pennsylvania S corporation unless it elects not to be a Pennsylvania S corporation [72 P.S. §7307].

Exception

A qualified Subchapter S subsidiary owned by a Pennsylvania S corporation is treated as a Pennsylvania S corporation whether or not an election has been made with respect to the such subsidiary.

Opting Out: Any federal Subchapter S corporation that does not desire to be a Pennsylvania S corporation must file an *Election Not To Be Taxed As A Pennsylvania "S" Corporation (REV-976)*. For corporations required to file a Pennsylvania RCT-101, this election must be filed on or before the due date (or extended due date) of the report for the **first** tax period in which the election is to be in effect. For corporations not required to file a Pennsylvania RCT-101 (*i.e.*, does not do business in Pennsylvania and is not registered to do business in Pennsylvania), the due date for filing this election is 30 days **after** the due date or extended due date of the federal return. These corporations must check the box indicating **"Corporation is not subject to PA Corporate Taxes; election is for PA Resident Shareholder purposes only."**

¶1802

The *REV-976* must be signed by 100% of the shareholders of the S corporation on the date of election and send via **Certified Mail** to

PA Department of Revenue
Bureau of Corporation Taxes
PA "S" Unit
PO Box 280705
Harrisburg, PA 17128-0705

Once made, this election cannot be revoked for five years. Any federal Subchapter S corporation not making this election will be considered a Pennsylvania S corporation, and each resident shareholder will be subject to the Pennsylvania personal income tax on his or her pro rata share of the S corporation income, whether distributed or not. Each nonresident shareholder is subject to tax on the shareholder's personal income from sources within Pennsylvania [*Corporation Tax Bulletin 2008-01*, issued January 11, 2008, Pennsylvania Department of Revenue].

Transitional Election

All federal S corporations are automatically considered Pennsylvania S corporations unless they make separate elections *not* to be taxed as a Pennsylvania S corporation. Thus, "new" Pennsylvania S corporations may not have previously tracked the Pennsylvania accumulated adjustment account (AAA) and Pennsylvania earnings and profits (E&P). Because it may be difficult for these S corporations to obtain the necessary information to compute the initial PA E&P, they may elect to use their federal AAA as the functional equivalent of the PA E&P For more details on this transitional election, see *Notice to New Pennsylvania S Corporations About Pennsylvania Personal Income Tax Record-Keeping Requirements for Informational Reporting of Distributions to Shareholders*, Pennsylvania Department of Revenue, available at *http://www.revenue.state.pa.us/revenue/ CWP/view.asp?A=180&QUESTION_ID=270588*.

• *Qualified Subchapter S subsidiaries*

For Pennsylvania personal income tax purposes a qualified Subchapter S subsidiary (QSSS) is a corporation (foreign or domestic) that is treated as a qualified Subchapter S subsidiary under § 1361 of the Internal Revenue Code of 1986, as amended to January 1, 2005 [72 P.S. § 7301(o.3)]. For purposes of determining whether a corporation qualifies as a small corporation [72 P.S. § 7301(s.2)]:

(1) A QSSS owned by a Pennsylvania S corporation is not treated as a separate corporation.

(2) All gross receipts and passive investment income of a QSSS are treated as earned by the parent corporation.

(3) All inter-corporate payments or distributions between the parent corporation and any QSSS owned by it are eliminated.

For corporate net income tax purposes and for capital stock/franchise tax purposes, each Pennsylvania S corporation and each QSSS are treated as separate corporations [72 P.S. § 7401(2)(p); 72 P.S. § 7602.4]. For personal income tax purposes, however, a QSSS owned by a Pennsylvania S corporation is not treated as a separate corporation, and all assets, liabilities and items of income, deduction and credit of each QSSS are treated as assets, liabilities and items of income, deduction and credit of the parent Pennsylvania S corporation [72 P.S. § 7307.9(e)].

S Corporations and Employee Stock Option Plans (ESOPs)

The federal Small Business Job Protection Act included some changes affecting S corporations. Beginning in 1998, tax-qualified retirement plans may be shareholders in an S corporation. Each ESOP is treated as a single shareholder. This allows S corporations to set up Esops. An ESOP set up by an S corporation will not enjoy all of the tax advantages of an ESOP sponsored by a C corporation, but the tax advantages for some S corporations could be substantial. Because an ESOP is exempt from taxes, the income allocated to it escapes immediate taxation. Taxpayers should consult advisers about the potential benefits of setting up an ESOP.

¶1804 Form and Method of Opting Out of Pennsylvania S Corporation Status

An opt-out election under 72 P.S. § 7307 may be made for any taxable year at any time during the preceding taxable year or at any time on or before the due date or extended due date of the small corporation's corporate net income tax return [72 P.S. § 7307.1(b)]. The law requires that elections to opt out of Pennsylvania S corporation status must be made in the manner prescribed by the Pennsylvania Department of Revenue [72 P.S. § 7307.1(a)].

CAUTION: Foreign Corporations with No Nexus

The Department of Revenue takes the position that corporation that is not a domestic corporation and does not have nexus with Pennsylvania must nevertheless opt out of Pennsylvania S status. Otherwise, the corporation will be treated as a Pennsylvania S corporation and resident shareholders will be required to include the income on their returns.

¶1805 Termination of Pennsylvania S Corporation Status

If a corporation ceases to be a small corporation, the corporation's status as a Pennsylvania S corporation terminates, effective on the date on which the corporation ceases to be a small corporation [72 P.S. § 7307.4]. The portion of the termination year of a Pennsylvania S corporation ending before the first day for which the termination is effective is treated as a short taxable year for which the corporation is a Pennsylvania S corporation [72 P.S. § 7307.5(a)]. The portion of the termination year beginning on the first day for which the termination is effective is treated as a short taxable year for purposes of the corporate net income tax [72 P.S. § 7307.5(b)]. The allocation of income and expense items to be taken into consideration in each short year is made in accordance with regulations issued by the Department of Revenue [72 P.S. § 7307.5(c)].

¶1806 Revocation of Opt-Out Election

An opt-out election may be revoked if shareholders holding more than one-half of the shares of stock of the corporation on the day on which the revocation is made consent to the election. The corporation and any successor corporation is not eligible to revoke an election for any taxable year prior to its fifth taxable year that begins after the first taxable year for which an election is effective, unless the corporation becomes a qualified Subchapter S subsidiary [72 P.S. § 7307.3(a)]. Revocation is effective on the first day of the taxable year if made on or before the fifteenth day of the third month thereof. If the revocation is made after the fifteenth day of the third month, it is effective for the following taxable year [72 P.S. § 7307.3(b)].

¶1807 Income of a Pennsylvania S Corporation

In general, the income of a Pennsylvania S corporation reported on an information return is computed in the same manner as the Pennsylvania taxable income of an individual. The Pennsylvania S corporation, like an individual, may deduct allowable costs and expenses attributable to income from the operation of a business, profession

¶1804

or farm or disposition of property or rents and royalties. See Chapter 2 for details. The income reported by a Pennsylvania S corporation is taxable to its shareholders whether distributed or not.

Differences in Federal/Commonwealth Rules

As a result of 1992 and 1993 federal income tax legislation and judicial decisions, the Department of Revenue has revised the rules for certain deductions of sole proprietorships, partnerships, and S corporations for personal income purposes [*Pennsylvania Tax Update No. 50*, Pennsylvania Department of Revenue, May/June 1994]. See the discussion at ¶213.

• *Deductions of C corporation years*

Any deduction (except a net loss deduction) that was disallowed when a corporation was a C corporation (subject to the corporate net income tax) is allowed in a year in which the corporation is a Pennsylvania S corporation to the same extent and in the same manner that would have been allowed if the Pennsylvania S corporation had remained a C corporation [72 P.S. § 7307.8(e)]. A net loss incurred in a C corporation year cannot be used in a Pennsylvania S corporation year. See ¶1003. The Pennsylvania Supreme Court has held that S corporations are not entitled to a deduction for hypothetical federal taxes for capital stock/franchise tax purposes [*Tool Sales & Service Co. Inc. v. Cmwlth.; Tom Mistick & Sons Inc. v. Cmwlth.*, 637 A.2d 607 (1993), *cert. den.*, 513 U.S. 822 (1994)]. See ¶1307 for a discussion of average net income.

No Pennsylvania At-Risk Rules

Pennsylvania does not have at-risk rules like those of IRC § 465 that restrict deductibility of pass-through losses.

Average Net Income for Capital Stock/Franchise Tax

A Pennsylvania S corporation cannot assume the tax liability of its shareholders and then deduct that amount as an expense for its calculation of average net income for capital stock purposes [*Scott Electric Co. v. Cmwlth.*, 692 A.2d 289 (Pa.Commw. 1997)].

¶1808 Taxation of Shareholders

Each shareholder of a Pennsylvania S corporation takes into account (on his or her personal income tax return) his or her pro rata share of the income or loss in each applicable class of income received by a Pennsylvania S corporation for its taxable year ending within or with the shareholder's taxable year. A shareholder's pro rata share of any item for a taxable year is the sum of the amounts determined with respect to the shareholder by assigning an equal portion of all items to each day of the taxable year and then dividing that portion pro rata among the shares outstanding on that day. The character of any item included in a shareholder's pro rata share is determined as if the item were realized directly by the shareholder from the source from which it was realized by the corporation or incurred in the same manner as incurred by the corporation [72 P.S. § 7307.9]. Nonresidents are taxed only on their portion of the Pennsylvania S corporation's Pennsylvania-source income.

• *Limitations on pass-through of losses to shareholders*

The aggregate amount of losses taken into account by a shareholder of a Pennsylvania S corporation cannot exceed the sum of (1) the adjusted basis of the shareholder's stock in the Pennsylvania S corporation (determined after basis adjustments under 72 P.S. § 7307.11) for the taxable year and (2) the shareholder's adjusted basis of the Pennsylvania S corporation's indebtedness (after adjustments required by 72 P.S. § 7307.11). No carryover of losses by Pennsylvania S corporation shareholders is allowed [72 P.S. § 7307.10].

• *Adjustments to basis of stock*

The basis of the stock of shareholders in a Pennsylvania S corporation is increased by their pro rata shares of the Pennsylvania S corporation's income (including nontaxable income) and decreased by their pro rata shares of the Pennsylvania S corporation's losses (to the extent that the losses reduced taxable income). Basis is also decreased by any corporate distributions not included in the income of shareholders. Stock basis, however, cannot be reduced below zero. When a shareholder's stock basis has been reduced to zero, excess losses may then reduce the shareholder's basis in any indebtedness of the Pennsylvania S corporation to the shareholder (but also not below zero). If basis in indebtedness is reduced, the indebtedness basis must be restored before the shareholder can increase his or her stock basis [72 P.S. § 7307.11]. The denial of carryover of losses by Pennsylvania S corporation shareholders has been held to be constitutional [*DelGaizo v. Cmwlth.*, 558 F.R. 2008 (October 18, 2010].

• *Distributions*

Property distributions by a Pennsylvania S corporation that has no accumulated earnings and profits are not included in shareholder income to the extent that they do not exceed adjusted stock basis. Distributions in excess of basis are treated as gains from the sale, exchange or other disposition of property. Property distributions by a Pennsylvania S corporation that has accumulated earnings and profits are treated in the same manner as distributions by a Pennsylvania S corporation without earnings and profits to the extent of the corporation's accumulated adjustment account. Distributions in excess of the accumulated adjustment account are treated as dividends to the extent of accumulated earnings and profits. Distributions in excess of earnings and profits are treated in the same manner as distributions from a Pennsylvania S corporation without accumulated earnings and profits. In the case of a non-pro rata distribution of property, the adjustment is limited to an amount that bears the same ratio to the balance in the account as the number of shares sold, exchanged or otherwise disposed of bears to the number of shares in the corporation outstanding immediately before such sale, exchange or disposition [72 P.S. § 7207.12]. See also the discussion at ¶ 212.

• *Accumulated adjustment account*

"Accumulated adjustment account" means an account of a Pennsylvania S corporation that is cumulatively adjusted for the most recent continuous period during which the corporation has been a Pennsylvania S corporation by increasing the account for corporate income and decreasing the account for corporate losses and property distributions that were not included in shareholder income. No adjustment, however, is allowed for any income or loss not in any of the classes of income enumerated in 72 P.S. § 7303 or for any non-deductible expense [72 P.S. § 7307.12(c)].

¶ 1809 Returns of a Pennsylvania S Corporation

Pennsylvania S corporations must file an information return (Form PA-20S) on or before the fifteenth day of the fourth month following the close of the corporation's tax year. The Pennsylvania S corporation's capital stock/franchise tax return (Form RCT-101) is also due on or before the fifteenth day of the fourth month following the close of the Pennsylvania S corporation's tax year. A Pennsylvania S corporation is not required to complete Section C of the Form RCT-101. The U.S. Postal Service postmark date on the envelope is proof of timely filing.

A corporation that has elected federal S corporation status but has not elected Pennsylvania S corporation status must file Form RCT-101 (including completion of Section C). A copy of the corporation's federal Form 1120S must be attached to the Pennsylvania Form RCT-101. A schedule reflecting adjustments to Line 21 of federal Form 1120S for the pass-through items on Schedule K must be attached. These adjustments should produce Pennsylvania taxable income similar to that for a C corporation.

Other Required Forms

Some Pennsylvania S corporations may have to complete and file other forms. Questions regarding Pennsylvania S taxation may be referred to Pennsylvania Department of Revenue, Bureau of Corporation Taxes, 7th Floor, Strawberry Square, Harrisburg, PA 17126; telephone 717-783-6035.

¶1810 Withholding Requirements

If a Pennsylvania S corporation has Pennsylvania-source income for any taxable year and any part of it is allocable to a nonresident shareholder, partner or member, the entity must pay a withholding tax at the time and in the manner prescribed by the Department of Revenue. All withholding tax must be paid over on or before the fifteenth day of the fourth month following the end of the tax year [72 P.S. § 7324(a)]. This requirement does not apply to any publicly traded partnership, as defined under IRC § 7704, with equity securities registered with the Securities and Exchange Commission under § 12 of the Securities Exchange Act of 1934 [72 P.S. § 7324(b)].

If a Pennsylvania S corporation fails to timely pay withholding tax as required but later pays the tax, it is not relieved of the liability for any penalty, interest or addition as a result of failure to properly withhold tax [72 P.S. § 7324.3].

Nonresident shareholders and partners are entitled to credits for their share of the withholding tax paid by the pass-through entity for the year in which, or with which, the entity's taxable year (for which the tax was withheld) ends. This credit is also available to holders of beneficial interests in pass-through entities [72 P.S. § 7324.2].

If any amount of tax required to be withheld by a Pennsylvania S corporation is not paid on or before the due date, an addition of 5% of the underpayment for each month or fraction thereof past the due date is imposed until the tax is paid. The total additions cannot exceed 50% of the amount of the tax [72 P.S. § 7352(j)].

¶1811 Information Returns

Any person who makes payments to a taxpayer of more than $10 from a pension or profit-sharing plan for any reason other than death, disability, or retirement must file (on or before February 28 of each year for distributions of the preceding year) an information return if the distribution to the taxpayer exceeds the taxpayer's contributions [61 Pa. Code § 117.18]. A separate return must be made for each person. "Person" means individuals, employers, associations, fiduciaries, partnerships, corporations or other entities, and estates and trusts—whether resident or nonresident, singular or plural [61 Pa. Code § 101.1].

Information returns must be made in a way that substantially conforms to IRS Form 1099R. If approval is obtained from the Department of Revenue, magnetic tapes or computer printouts in lieu of copies of Form 1099R may be used [61 Pa. Code § 117.18].

¶1812 Credits

Job creation tax credit: The job creation tax credit may be claimed against the capital stock/franchise tax of a shareholder of the company if the company is a Pennsylvania S corporation and against the personal income tax of shareholders of a Pennsylvania S corporation. This credit is explained at ¶1007.

Organ or bone marrow donor tax credit: The organ or bone marrow donor tax credit may be claimed by members or shareholders of pass-through entities. This credit is discussed at ¶1015.

PARTNERSHIPS

¶1815 Pennsylvania Partnerships

A partnership is a domestic or foreign general partnership, joint venture, limited partnership, limited liability company, business trust or other unincorporated entity that for federal income tax purposes is classified as a partnership [72 P.S. § 7301(n.0)].

• *General taxability of partners and members*

Partners must report their shares of the net income of a partnership for its taxable year ending within or with the taxable year of the partners. A partner's share of the net income of a partnership includes his or her share of any guaranteed payments received from the partnership. A partner's share of partnership income is reported as (1) net profits from the operation of a business, profession, or other activity, (2) net gains or income from disposition of property, (3) net gains or income derived from or in the form of rents, royalties, patents, and copyrights, (4) dividends, (5) interest, (6) gambling or lottery winnings, or net gains or income derived through estates and trusts, depending upon which class within which it falls [61 Pa. Code § 107.1]. There are only seven classes of income for a partnership because compensation is reported at the individual level and is a deduction for a business. The eight classes of Pennsylvania taxable income are discussed at ¶201.

• *Taxability of resident and nonresident partners and members*

The share of a partner of the net income of a partnership is his or her share of the net income whether or not distributed [61 Pa. Code § 107.2(a)]. Partners who are Pennsylvania residents must report their entire shares of the partnership's net income regardless of where the income was earned [61 Pa. Code § 107.2(b)]. Partners who are not Pennsylvania residents report only partnership income from sources within Pennsylvania [61 Pa. Code § 107.2(c)].

• *Classification of partnerships for tax purposes*

Partnerships may choose how they are classified for federal tax purposes by filing federal Form 8832 (Entity Classification Election). In general, a partnership can choose to be classified as either an association taxable as a corporation or a partnership. The partnership's entity classification for Pennsylvania tax purposes will be the same as the federal classification.

• *Partnership not a taxable entity*

A partnership is not subject to the Pennsylvania personal income tax; instead, partners are subject to tax on their individual shares of partnership income at the individual level. Partnerships, however, are required to file information returns for the partnership taxable year. See ¶906 for more information on corporate partners.

¶1812

Withholding for Nonfiling Corporate Partners

Entities that are classified as partnerships for federal income tax purposes must withhold and remit corporate net income tax from nonfiling corporate partners. See discussion at ¶1816.

• *Partnership withholding*

The withholding rules for partnerships are the same as those for Pennsylvania S corporations. See ¶1810.

• *Partnership allocation and apportionment*

Allocation and apportionment of income from partnership interests are discussed at ¶1113. Beginning January 1, 2014, partnerships must provide any partner classified as a corporation its apportionment factors.

¶1816 Partnership Returns

Filing a return is required for partnerships engaged in a trade or business within Pennsylvania or having Pennsylvania-source income, whether or not their principal place of business is in Pennsylvania and whether or not all of their members are nonresidents [61 Pa. Code § 117.17]. If a Commonwealth resident is a partner in a partnership with no Pennsylvania-source income, she or he must file a return, that states specifically the items of partnership gross income and allowable deductions, the names and addresses of all resident partners, and the amount of the distributive shares of income, gain, loss, deduction, or credit allocable to each resident partner [61 Pa. Code § 117.17(c)]. See ¶1811 for a discussion of information returns.

• *Due date*

A calendar-year partnership must file its return on or before April 15 of the year following the close of the taxable year. A fiscal-year partnership must file its return on or before the fifteenth day of the fourth month following the close of the taxable fiscal year. If the due date falls on a Saturday, Sunday or holiday, the return is due no later than midnight on the first business day following. The U.S. Postal Service postmark date on the envelope is proof of timely filing. A partnership may use a 52-53 week year if it keeps its books on that basis.

• *Extension of time to file*

If a partnership has a federal extension for filing its federal Form 1065, the Department of Revenue will grant the same extension for filing its Form PA-65. A partnership may also request an extension of time to file by submitting Form REV-276 ("Application of Extension of Time to File"). It must be received by the Department in sufficient time for the Department of Revenue to review it and make a determination to grant the extension. Payment of tax withheld from nonresident partners must be made with the extension request; there is no extension for paying withheld taxes. An extension of time for filing a Form PA-65 does not automatically grant an extension of time for the partners' individual returns; each partner must request his or her own extension.

• *Group returns for nonresident partners*

Pennsylvania allows the filing of group tax returns for qualifying nonresident partners. A qualifying nonresident partner is one who (1) is a calendar-year taxpayer, (2) is a domiciliary of another state or country for the entire calendar year, (3) maintains no permanent place of abode in Pennsylvania during the calendar year, (4) has no other Pennsylvania source of taxable income, and (5) has elected to join in the group return. The group return should be filed by the partnership on Form PA-40NRC. The return must show the partnership identifying information, the combined profit/loss sharing percentage, the combined ownership of capital, the combined Pennsylvania-source taxable income, and the combined available Employment Incentive Payment credit. The group return must also have a statement showing the estimated taxes paid on behalf of the nonresident partners and the combined tax due or overpaid. The balance of tax due, if any, must be paid with the group return. A copy of federal Form 1065 must also be filed with the group return. The partnership is required to maintain and make available for inspection or audit a complete list of all electing nonresident partners and a certification that each qualifying partner has elected to join the group filing. Form PA-65 is used for this purpose.

• *Returns for nonfiling corporate partners*

Requirement of return: A partnership must file a return for the taxable year of its net nonfiling corporate partners' shares of income and deductions if it engages (whether in its own name or through any person, association, business trust, corporation, joint venture, limited liability company, limited partnership, partnership, or other entity) in any of the following activities [72 P.S. § 7403.2(a)]:

(1) Doing business in Pennsylvania.

(2) Carrying on activities in Pennsylvania, including solicitation that is not protected activity under Public Law 86-272. Public Law 86-272 is discussed at ¶ 914.

(3) Having capital or property employed or used in Pennsylvania.

(4) Owning property in Pennsylvania.

The return must be filed in a form prescribed by the Department, and payment must be made on or before the 15th day of the 4th month following the end of the taxable year [72 P.S. § 7403.2(d)].

Definitions: The following definitions, when used with respect to 72 P.S. § 7403.2, have the following meanings, unless the context clearly indicates a different meaning [72 P.S. § 7403.2(e)]:

(1) *Net nonfiling corporate partners' shares of income and deductions:* That portion of the income, less the deductions (1) reported on Schedule K of the Federal Form 1065 filed with the federal government for the taxable year; and (2) allocated on federal Schedule K-1 to nonfiling corporate partners. If the entire business of the partnership is not transacted in Pennsylvania, the amount computed under this definition must be apportioned to Pennsylvania as provided in 72 P.S. § 401(3)2 as if the partnership were a corporation subject to the corporate net income tax.

(2) *Nonfiling corporate partner:* A partner that (1) is a corporation as defined in 72 P.S. § 401 and (2) has not filed a tax report and paid the tax required by 72 P.S. § 7402 and 72 P.S. § 7403 for the previous taxable year.

(3) *Partner:* An owner of an interest in the partnership, in whatever manner that owner and ownership interest are designated.

(4) *Partnership:* An entity classified as a partnership for federal income tax purposes. The term includes (1) a partnership, limited partnership, limited liability partnership, limited liability company, and (2) any syndicate-group, pool, joint venture, business trust, association, or other unincorporated organization, through or by which a business, financial operation, or venture is carried on. The term does not include an entity that is (1) listed on a United States national stock exchange or (2) described in 72 P.S. § 401(1)1 or 2.

Amount to be withheld: A partnership required to file a return for its net nonfiling partners must withhold and remit to the Department a tax on behalf of its nonfiling corporate partners in an amount equal to its net nonfiling corporate partners' shares of income and deductions as reported to the federal government multiplied by the tax rate applicable to the taxable year being reported [72 P.S. § 7403.2(b)].

Amount withheld credited to partner: Any amount withheld and paid to the Department of Revenue on behalf of a nonfiling corporate partner is considered a tax payment by that partner and credited to its account as if it were directly paid by the partner [72 P.S. § 7403.2(b)].

Underpayments: If tax required to be withheld and paid is not paid on or before the date prescribed, a penalty of 5% of the underpayment for each month or fraction of a month from the due date to the date paid will be added to the tax and paid to the Department. For purposes of computing the penalty for any month, the underpayment is reduced by any part of the tax that is paid by the beginning of that month. The total additions to tax cannot exceed 50% of the amount of the tax [72 P.S. § 7403.2(c)].

• *Other forms*

A partnership return (Form PA-65) must be filed if required; filing only a copy of the federal Form 1065 is insufficient. Partnerships must provide each of their resident partners with a Form PA Schedule RK-1 and each of their nonresident partners with a Form PA Schedule NRK-1. Copies of these should be attached to the Form PA-65. The Department of Revenue does not require the reconciliation of partners' capital accounts. The partnership, however, is responsible for maintaining capital account records. For more detail, consult the instructions to Form PA-65. Beginning January 1, 2014, a copy of the partnership's federal information return must be filed with the Department of Revenue.

¶ 1817 Partnership Income

The net income of a partnership is determined and reported on the basis of accepted accounting principles and practices after provision for all costs and expenses incurred in the conduct of the business. Deductions are not allowed for expenses not related to the production of income, nor are taxes based on income allowed as a deduction [61 Pa. Code § 107.3]. Because compensation is reported at the individual level and is a deduction for a business, there are only seven classes of income for a partnership. A partnership cannot carry forward or back any gains or losses from the sale or disposition of property or offset income or gain in one class of income with a loss in another class.

Federal/Commonwealth Difference in Taxable Income

It is possible for the taxable income of a partnership, estate, or trust to be different for Pennsylvania personal income tax purposes than it is for federal income tax purposes because Pennsylvania does not have an all-encompassing concept of income like that found in IRC § 61. (For an explanation of classes of income, see Chapter 2.) For example, for Pennsylvania personal income tax purposes, sole proprietorships, partnerships, and Pennsylvania S corporations can claim charitable contributions as a business expense in the determination of net business income if the contributions are made publicly and from the entity's checking account. Under these circumstances, charitable contributions are considered an expense of the business entity rather than an itemized deduction of the shareholders.

• *Classification of income*

Classification or characterization of income from a partnership is made at the partnership level [72 P.S. § 7301.1]. A partnership determines each partner's share of income (loss) as if the partner realized it directly from the same source and in the same manner that the partnership realized it. Each partner receives a Form RK-1 (resident partner) or a Form NRK-1 (nonresident partner) that shows the amount of partnership income that falls into each class of income.

Guaranteed payments: In the case of guaranteed payments to partners, the partnership is responsible for informing the partners of the classification of the income from which guaranteed payments are made. The guaranteed payment is identified as the class of income from which the payments were made. Whether or not the partner can offset any loss against the guaranteed payment depends upon whether the guaranteed payment and the loss are from the same class of income. Losses from one class cannot be used to offset gains in other classes.

Interest and dividends: In general, Pennsylvania does not tax dividends and interest received by nonresidents. Only if the income-producing property is used in a trade or business in Pennsylvania is the interest or dividend considered Pennsylvania-source income. In the case of interest or dividends received by a partnership, the ordinary interest or dividends not received in the operation of a business are not taxable to nonresident partners. In fact, there are no lines on Schedule NRK-1 to report ordinary dividends and interest.

Federal/Commonwealth Difference

Pennsylvania does not follow federal rules for taxation of guaranteed payments. For Pennsylvania personal income tax purposes, if a guaranteed payment is paid for services or for the use of capital, it is classified as follows:

　　(1) A withdrawal proportionately from the capital of all partners.

　　(2) A gain from the disposition of the recipient's partnership interest and a loss from the disposition of the other partners' partnership interests, to the extent derived from the capital of the other partners.

　　(3) A return of capital by the recipient to the extent derived from the recipient's own capital.

- *Not all partnership income is business income*

Income from the operation of a business is classified as net profits. A partnership that is not engaged in a business has some other form of income for Pennsylvania personal income tax purposes. A law partnership formed another partnership to hold ownership in a building that was then rented, primarily to the law partnership. The Commonwealth Court held that the rental partnership was not engaged in a business because it did not render goods and services to others in the marketplace and that the income from the rental partnership was therefore rental income, not net profits from a business. In this case, the rental partnership realized a loss. Since loss from one class cannot be used to offset income of another class, the partnership was not allowed to offset the business income from the law partnership with the loss from the rental partnership. The taxpayer argued that the law partnership and the rental partnership were a single entity. The court rejected this argument. The law partnership had such a close relationship with the rental partnership that the rental partnership did not operate in the marketplace. Thus, they could not offset the income of the law partnership with losses of the rental partnership [*Wettach v. Cmwlth.*, 620 A.2d 730 (Pa.Commw. 1993), *aff'd per curiam*, 677 A.2d 831 (Pa. 1995)]. Corporations that invest in partnerships should be careful about the passive-income rule for Pennsylvania S corporation purposes. Passive income received from a partnership could result in termination of the corporate partner's Pennsylvania S corporation status.

Partnership Contributions to Partner's Retirement Plan

Contributions by a partnership to the retirement plans of its partners are not deductible as a business expense for purposes of computing partnership net income and are not excludable from compensation for purposes of the Pennsylvania personal income tax [*Smith v. Cmwlth.*, 684 A.2d 647 (Pa.Commw. 1996)].

¶1818 Basis of Partnership Interest

The general rules for determination of a partner's basis in a partnership are as follows:

(1) The basis of a partner's interest in a partnership is the amount of cash paid by the partner and/or the adjusted basis of property contributed by the partner to the partnership.

(2) If a partner contributes property subject to indebtedness or if the partnership assumes a partner's indebtedness, the contributing partner must reduce his or her basis by the amount of the indebtedness assumed by the other partners. The partners assuming indebtedness must increase their basis.

(3) If a partner's interest is for rendering services, his or her basis is equal to the income for those services. The partnership recognizes that income when the partner performs the services and the partnership removes any restrictions on withdrawal or disposition of the income.

(4) The basis of a partnership interest acquired by inheritance is the fair market value of the interest as of the date of death.

(5) The basis of a partnership interest acquired by gift is the donor's basis.

(6) In certain cases when it is impractical to apply the general rules, a partner's adjusted basis is determined by reference to the partner's share of the adjusted basis of partnership property that would be distributed upon termination of the partnership (*e.g.*, inadequate records exist to determine basis under the general rules).

No Negative Basis

The adjusted basis of a partnership can never be less than zero.

• *Adjustments to basis*

The original basis of a partnership interest is increased by further contributions to the partnership and by the partner's distributive share of partnership taxable income and tax-exempt income. The original basis is decreased by distributions (*e.g.*, withdrawals), distributive shares of partnership losses, and nondeductible partnership expenditures that are not capital expenditures (*e.g.*, contribution to partner's retirement plan, premiums on partner's life and health insurance). In computing adjusted basis of a partnership interest the partnership takes into account all distributions to a partner before any losses. In general, a partner's basis is increased for an increase in his or her share of partnership liability and decreased for a decrease in his or her share of partnership liability. If the decrease in liabilities exceeds basis, the partner has a gain.

NOTE: For more details regarding determination of partnership basis, see the instructions for Form PA-65.

¶1819 Limited Liability Partnerships

A limited liability partnership (LLP) is a general or limited partnership that elects to register as a limited liability partnership with the Pennsylvania Department of State. Foreign partnerships may also elect LLP status. A partnership desiring to register as a Pennsylvania LLP must file a statement of registration with the Department of State setting forth all the information required by 15 Pa.C.S. §8201. LLP status can be elected without any change in partnership form or agreement. LLP status confers limited liability for torts but does not offer financial protection. General partners remain liable for other debts just as in a regular partnership. Election of LLP status does not change the taxation of an existing partnership that is taxed as a partnership.

• *Limitation on liability of partners*

In general, a partner in a registered LLP is not individually liable directly or indirectly, whether by way of indemnification, contribution or otherwise, for debts and obligations of, or chargeable to, the partnership that arise from any negligent or wrongful acts or misconduct committed by another partner or other representative of the partnership [15 Pa.C.S. § 8204]. The limitation on liability, however, does not apply if the LLP fails to carry the liability insurance required by 15 Pa.C.S. § 8206.

• *Annual registration and fee*

Limited liability partnerships are required to file annual certificates of registration for any year in which they are registered to do business in Pennsylvania on December 31. The annual certificate of registration is due on or before April 15 of the following year. The certificate of annual registration must be signed by a general partner. An annual registration fee is paid when filing a certificate of annual registration. A schedule of fees and payments is available at the Corporation Bureau's web site [http://www.dos.state.pa.us/corps/cwp].

• *Withholding requirements*

The withholding requirements for LLPs are the same as for Pennsylvania S corporations. See ¶ 1810.

LIMITED LIABILITY COMPANIES

¶1820 Pennsylvania Limited Liability Companies (LLCs)

A Pennsylvania limited liability company is an association that is a limited liability company organized and existing under Chapter 89 of Title 15 of the Pennsylvania Consolidated Statutes [15 Pa.C.S. § 8903]. An "association" is a corporation, a partnership, a limited liability company, a business trust, or two or more persons associated in a common enterprise or undertaking. The term does not include a testamentary trust or an *inter vivos* trust as defined in 20 Pa.C.S. § 711(3) (relating to mandatory exercise of jurisdiction through orphans' court division in general) [15 Pa.C.S. § 102]. A foreign limited liability company is an association organized under the laws of any jurisdiction other than Pennsylvania [15 Pa.C.S. § 8903].

For purposes of Pennsylvania taxation, a domestic or foreign limited liability company that is not a domestic or qualified foreign restricted professional company is deemed to be a corporation, and each member is deemed to be a shareholder of a corporation. Such a company may elect to be treated as a Pennsylvania S corporation if the company satisfies the conditions for electing that status [15 Pa.C.S. § 8925]. See ¶ 1831 for a discussion of restricted professional companies. Limited liability companies must file a corporate tax report [Form RCT-101].

¶1821 Formation of LLCs

One or more persons may organize a limited liability company under the provisions of the Limited Liability Company Law of 1994 by filing a certificate of organization with the Pennsylvania Department of State. The person or persons do not have to be members of the company at the time of organization or at any time thereafter [15 Pa.C.S. § 8912].

¶1820

• *Certificate of organization*

The certificate of organization must be signed by all organizers and contain the information required by 15 Pa.C.S. § 8913. The LLC is organized when the certificate is filed with the Department of State or at a later effective date if so specified in the certificate of organization [15 Pa.C.S. § 8914].

¶ 1822 Liability of Members and Managers of LLCs

In general, neither the members nor the managers of a LLC are liable, solely by reason of being a member or manager, under an order of a court or in any other manner for a debt, obligation or liability of the company of any kind or for the acts or omissions of any other member, manager, agent or employee of the company [15 Pa.C.S. § 8922(a)]. However, the certificate of organization may provide that some or all of the members shall be liable for some or all of the debts, obligations, and liabilities of the company to the extent and under the circumstances provided in the certificate [15 Pa.C.S. § 8922(e)].

Professional liability, however, is not affected by the LLC provisions [15 Pa.C.S. § 8922(b)]. Members and managers of a LLC have no greater immunity than that available to the officers, shareholders, employees or agents of a professional corporation. Thus, members and managers of LLCs remain personally and fully liable and accountable for any negligent or wrongful acts or misconduct committed by them or by any person under their direct supervision and control while rendering professional services on behalf of the company [15 Pa.C.S. § 2925(b)].

¶ 1823 Taxation of LLCs

Pennsylvania taxation of limited liability companies is consistent with the federal treatment. Prior to January 1, 1998, a limited liability company that was not a restricted professional company was taxable as a corporation in Pennsylvania. Effective January 1, 1997, for federal tax purposes LLCs may choose how they are classified for federal tax purposes by filing federal Form 8832 ("Entity Classification Election"). In general, a business entity with at least two members can choose to be classified as either an association taxable as a corporation or a partnership, and a business entity with a single member can choose to be either classified as an association taxable as a corporation or disregarded as an entity separate from its owner. LLCs existing before January 1, 1997, and having an established federal tax classification do not need to make an election unless they choose to change their tax classification. The entity classification for Pennsylvania purposes is the same as the federal classification.

• *LLC taxed as corporation*

Limited liability companies that are taxable as corporations for federal income tax purposes are taxable as corporations for Pennsylvania corporate net income tax and capital stock/franchise tax purposes. Limited liability companies may elect Pennsylvania S corporation status if they qualify [72 P.S. § 7401, effective January 1, 1998].

• *LLC taxed as partnership*

Limited liability companies that are partnerships for federal income tax purposes are taxed as partnerships for Pennsylvania purposes (*i.e.*, under the personal income tax provisions) but are still subject to the capital stock/franchise tax so long as the capital stock/franchise tax is in effect (except restricted professional corporations) [72 P.S. § 7601, effective January 1, 1998].

• *Distributions to partners that reduce net income or loss*

A limited liability company taxable as a partnership may reduce net income or loss by the amount of distributions made to any member who satisfies the material participation requirements of §469 of the Internal Revenue Code of 1986. Distributions made to a member within 30 days of the end of a given year may be treated as having been made in the preceding year and not in the year in which actually made [72 P.S. §7601(a)].

Distributions of SMLLCs

The statute is silent with respect to whether single-member LLCs can reduce net income or loss for distributions made to materially participating members for capital stock/franchise tax purposes. However, it is the position of the Department of Revenue that single-member limited liability companies (SMLLCs) treated as disregarded entities for federal tax purposes can reduce book income by distributions made to the sole member for capital stock/franchise tax purposes if the single member is a natural person.

• *LLC taxed as proprietorship for federal purposes*

A single member limited liability company (SMLLC) that does not elect to be taxed as a corporation for federal tax purposes will be treated as a proprietorship for federal income tax purposes. The Department of Revenue has not yet issued any guidance on the Pennsylvania treatment of these entities. The Department has indicated, however, that a single member limited liability company (SMLLC) is a separate entity for sales and use tax purposes and must register with the state independently of the member/owner. An SMLLC taxed as a proprietorship for federal tax purposes is still subject to the Pennsylvania capital stock/franchise tax.

• *Returns*

If a company is not required to file a federal income tax return, the Pennsylvania corporate net income tax and capital stock/franchise taxes are computed as if a federal return had been filed.

In the case of limited liability companies and business trusts taxable as partnerships for federal income tax purposes, net income or loss for any given year (for capital stock/franchise tax purposes) is reduced by the amount of distributions made by the LLC or business trust to any member who is deemed to materially participate in the activities of the LLC or business trust for purposes of IRC §469. For this purpose, distributions that are made to a member of a limited liability company or business trust within thirty (30) days of the end of a given year may be treated as having been made in the preceding year, and not in the year in which such distribution is actually made [72 P.S. §7601]. See ¶1307 for a discussion of average net income.

• *Withholding requirements*

The withholding requirements for LLCs are the same as for Pennsylvania S corporations. See ¶1810.

¶1824 Business and Management of LLCs

In general, a limited liability company has the legal capacity of natural persons to act [15 Pa.C.S. §8921(a)]. This rule, however, is not intended to authorize any entity to do anything prohibited by any regulatory law [15 Pa.C.S. §103; 15 Pa.C.S. §8931(a)]. An LLC must file a certificate of organization with the Pennsylvania Department of State. See 15 Pa.C.S. §§8912—8915 for rules with respect to certificates of organization.

Subject to the limitations and restrictions imposed by statute or contained in its certificate of organization, a LLC may carry on any business that a partnership without limited partners may carry on and has the power to perform any act a partnership may perform [15 Pa.C.S. §8921(b)].

Unless otherwise provided in the certificate of organization, in any case not provided for in the Limited Liability Companies Act (Chapter 89 of Pennsylvania Consolidated Statutes), the following rules apply:

— If the certificate of organization does not contain a statement to the effect that the LLC is to be managed by managers, the provisions relating to general partnership govern, and the members are deemed to be general partners for LLC purposes [15 Pa.C.S. § 8904(a)(1)].

— If the certificate of organization provides that the company is to be managed by managers, the provision relating to limited partnerships govern; the managers will have the authority of general partners, and the members will be deemed to be limited partners for LLC purposes.

BUSINESS TRUSTS AND RESTRICTED PROFESSIONAL COMPANIES

¶1830 Pennsylvania Business Trusts

For Pennsylvania tax purposes, a business trust is a trust subject to Chapter 95 of Title 15 of the Pennsylvania Consolidated Statutes [15 Pa.C.S. § 102]. A Pennsylvania business trust is taxable for Pennsylvania purposes. The Pennsylvania taxation of business trusts is consistent with the federal treatment.

Check-the-Box Regulations

Business trusts may choose how they are classified for federal tax purposes by filing federal Form 8832 ("Entity Classification Election"). In general, a business entity with at least two members can choose to be classified as either an association taxable as a corporation or a partnership; and a business entity with a single member can choose to be either classified as an association taxable as a corporation or disregarded as an entity separate from its owner. Business trusts existing before January 1, 1997, and having an established federal tax classification do not need to make an election unless they choose to change their tax classification.

The entity classification for Pennsylvania purposes is the same as the federal classification.

• *Taxation*

A business trust taxable as a corporation for federal purposes is taxed as a corporation for Pennsylvania corporate net income and capital stock/franchise tax purposes, and a business trust taxable as a partnership for federal purposes is taxed as a partnership for Pennsylvania purposes, effective January 1, 1998. Business trusts taxable as partnerships, however, are subject to the capital stock/franchise tax [72 P.S. § 7601, effective January 1, 1998].

Business trusts that are taxed as corporations must elect a federal S Corporation status in order to be considered an S corporation for Pennsylvania purposes.

It is possible that a foreign corporation that owns a Pennsylvania business trust with federal partnership attributes may have nexus with Pennsylvania due to that ownership.

• *Distributions that reduce income or loss*

A business trust taxable as a partnership may reduce net income or loss by the amount of distributions made to any member who satisfies the material participation requirements of § 469 of the Internal Revenue Code of 1986. Distributions made to a member within 30 days of the end of a given year may be treated as having been made in the preceding year and not in the year in which actually made [72 P.S. § 7601(a)].

¶1830

• *Withholding requirements*

Withholding requirements for business trusts are the same as for Pennsylvania S corporations. See ¶ 1810.

• *Pre-incorporation income*

The position of the Department of Revenue has been that earnings of a business trust for periods when the business trust was not subject to the capital stock/ franchise tax (because it was an exempt entity) had to be included in book income for purposes of computing average net income after the trust becomes taxable as a corporation. The Board of Finance and Revenue, however, is not requiring taxpayers to include pre-incorporation book income in average net income for the periods the trust was an exempt entity.

¶1831 Restricted Professional Companies

Restricted professional companies (RPCs) are governed by the provisions of 15 Pa.C.S. § § 8995—8998. The major advantage for Pennsylvania tax purposes of a restricted professional company is its pass-through attribute (*i.e.*, taxation at only one level). The major nontax advantage of a restricted professional company is limited liability.

A "domestic restricted professional company" is a limited liability company that renders one or more restricted professional services. A "qualified foreign restricted professional company" is a qualified foreign limited liability company (*i.e.*, one registered under Subchapter J to do business in Pennsylvania). The restricted services are chiropractic, dentistry, law, medicine and surgery, optometry, osteopathic medicine and surgery, podiatric medicine, public accounting, psychology or veterinary medicine [15 Pa.C.S. § 8903].

• *Taxation of RPCs*

In general, a restricted professional company is taxed as a partnership for Pennsylvania tax purposes [15 Pa.C.S. § 8997(a)]. An exception applies to certain domestic or qualified foreign restricted professional companies [15 Pa.C.S. § 8997(b)].

• *Annual registration*

Restricted professional companies (domestic or foreign) are required to file annual certificates of registration for any year in which they are registered to do business in Pennsylvania on December 31. The annual certificate of registration is due on or before April 15 of the following year. The certificate of annual registration must include a statement by the company as to whether it is engaged in any business other than the practice of the services for which it was specifically organized [15 Pa.C.S. § § 8998(a), 8996(a)]. A restricted professional company may own property necessary to render its professional services and invest its funds in real estate, securities, or other types of investments [15 Pa.C.S. § 8996(a)(1)] and be a partner, shareholder, member or other owner of a partnership, corporation, LLC, or other association rendering restricted services [15 Pa.C.S. § 8996(a)].

• *Annual registration fee*

An annual registration fee is paid when filing a certificate of annual registration. A schedule of fees and payments is available at the Corporation Bureau's web site [http://www.dos.state.pa.us/corps/cwp].

• *Withholding requirements*

The withholding requirements for RPCs are the same as for Pennsylvania S corporations. See ¶ 1810.

¶1831

PART VII

TAXES ON FINANCIAL INSTITUTIONS

CHAPTER 19
BANK AND TRUST COMPANIES SHARES TAX

¶1901 History of Tax

Pennsylvania has taxed bank shares since 1866 [Act of February 23, 1866, P.L. 82]. When the Tax Reform Code was enacted in 1971 [Act of March 4, 1971], the bank shares tax was included as Article VII. The tax was imposed for the privilege of doing business in or having capital or property employed or used in Pennsylvania and was imposed on the statutory "actual value" of bank shares, including the value of the shares represented by holdings of U.S. obligations [72 P.S. §7701, before amendment by the Act of December 1, 1983, P.L. 288].

In 1983, the U.S. Supreme Court ruled that federal law exempts United States obligations from all forms of taxation (with exceptions only for nondiscriminatory franchise taxes or other nonproperty taxes and estate or inheritance taxes) that require United States obligations or the interest on them to be considered, directly or indirectly, in the computation of the tax [*American Bank & Trust Co. v. Dallas County*, 463 U.S. 855 (1983)]. In accordance with this decision, the Pennsylvania Supreme Court ruled that the inclusion of the value of U.S. obligations in the computation of the bank shares tax required by 72 P.S. §7701 was unconstitutional [*Dale National Bank v. Cmwlth.*, 465 A.2d 965 (Pa. 1983)]. The Pennsylvania General Assembly then amended §701 of the Tax Reform Code to remove the value of United States obligations from the tax base [Article VII, Act of December 1, 1983, P.L. 288]. The new bank shares tax became effective for tax years beginning in or after 1984.

In an effort to minimize the cash outflow necessary to refund taxes paid under the unconstitutional provisions of the bank shares tax, the General Assembly also imposed a one-time single excise tax equal to the refunds that would be due as a result of the *Dale National Bank* case. The single excise tax was found to be unconstitutional [*First National Bank of Fredericksburg v. Cmwlth.*, 553 A.2d 937 (Pa. 1989)]. The Commonwealth responded to this decision by imposing a retroactive tax at a rate of 10.77 percent of a bank's capital for the calendar year 1989 and creating a New Bank Tax Credit Law that provided a tax credit for banks that had not paid bank shares tax on U.S. obligations (those chartered after January 1, 1979). The one-time rate of 10.77 percent has survived constitutional challenges in the Commonwealth Court [*Fidelity Bank, N.A. v. Cmwlth.*, 645 A.2d 452 (Pa.Commw. 1994); *Royal Bank of Pennsylvania v. Cmwlth.*, 705 A.2d 515 (Pa.Commw. 1998)]. The tax credit for new banks, however, was held to be unconstitutional [*Fidelity Bank, N.A. v. Cmwlth.*, 645 A.2d 452 (Pa.Commw. 1994)].

In 1995, the bank shares tax was made applicable to trust companies. The tax, however, is still commonly referred to as the bank shares tax. As a result of Act 52 of 2013, the tax is imposed on institutions that are "doing business" in Pennsylvania.

¶1902 Outline of Tax

The Pennsylvania bank shares tax is a property tax imposed on banks and trust companies, referred to as "institutions" in §701 of the Tax Reform Code. See definition of taxable "institutions" at ¶1905. The tax is imposed on the "value" of the total shares of capital stock subscribed for or issued as of the preceding January 1. See ¶1906 for explanation of value. Institutions may pay the tax with their own funds or from taxes collected from shareholders [72 P.S. §7701]. The tax, however, is not imposed on the shareholders. Thus, imposition of the tax on foreign banks does not violate the Due Process Clause of the U.S. Constitution. See *Allfirst Bank v. Cmwlth.*, Nos. 82 & 83 MAP 2006 (Pa. 2007), *aff'g* Pa.Commw. Nos. 619 F.R. 2003, 620 F.R. 2003, March 27, 2006. Prior to January 1, 1995, the bank shares tax applied only to banks having capital stock and incorporated by or under any law of Pennsylvania or the United States and located in Pennsylvania.

Valuation of Shares After the Allfirst Decision

On October 17, 2007, the Pennsylvania Supreme Court held that the bank shares tax is levied against the financial institution rather than its shareholders (see above). Pursuant to this decision, the Pennsylvania Department of Revenue issued a bulletin that provides that there is no basis for an exemption from bank shares tax based upon the *identity* of the shareholder. Accordingly, financial institutions are no longer permitted to reduce the taxable amount of shares by the value attributed to shares held by charitable, religious or educational institutions, effective for the calculation of the bank shares tax for January 1, 2008, and thereafter [*Corporation Tax Bulletin 2007-02*, issued November 28, 2007, Pennsylvania Department of Revenue].

• *Exemption from other taxes*

Banks and trust companies are specifically exempt by statute from the capital stock/franchise tax [72 P.S. §7602(i)], the corporate net income tax [72 P.S. §7402(c)], and the personal property tax [Act of July 17, 1913, P.L. 507, §1]. There are no statutory provisions that authorize local jurisdictions to impose taxes on banks and trust companies.

• *Act 52 changes to be reviewed*

Act 52 of 2013 directs the Department of Revenue, working together with the Secretary of Banking and Securities and representatives from the banking industry, to prepare a report within 18 months of July 9, 2013, analyzing the changes to the bank shares tax and proposing changes to the revised bank shares tax (including the rate and apportionment formula) to ensure that Pennsylvania generates a reasonable amount of revenue under the revised taxing structure but remains competitive with other states.

¶1902

¶1903 Sources of Authority

The bank shares tax is governed by the provisions of Article VII of the Tax Reform Code [72 P.S. §§ 7701—7706].

¶1904 Administration

The bank shares tax is administered by the Pennsylvania Department of Revenue, Harrisburg, Pennsylvania. The procedure, enforcement, and penalty provisions of the corporate net income tax are incorporated by reference [72 P.S. § 7702]. These provisions are explained in Chapter 12.

¶1905 Taxable Institutions

The bank shares tax is imposed on "institutions" [72 P.S. § 7701]. Up until January 1, 2014, "institutions" for purposes of the bank shares tax were defined as follows [72 P.S. § 7701.5]:

(1) Banks operating as such and having capital stock that are incorporated under any law of Pennsylvania, the United States, or any other jurisdiction and that are located within Pennsylvania.

(2) Trust companies having capital stock that are located within Pennsylvania.

(3) Companies organized and operating as bank and trust companies or as trust companies having capital stock that are located in Pennsylvania, whether the institution is incorporated under Pennsylvania law, U.S. law, or any law of any jurisdiction.

Effective January 1, 2014, the term "institutions" is defined as follows [72 P.S. § 7701.5]:

(1) Banks operating as such and having capital stock that are incorporated under any law of Pennsylvania, the United States, or any other jurisdiction and that are located within Pennsylvania.

(2) Trust companies having capital stock that are located within Pennsylvania.

(3) Companies organized and operating as bank and trust companies or as trust companies having capital stock that are located in Pennsylvania, whether the institution is incorporated under Pennsylvania law, U.S. law, or any law of any jurisdiction.

(4) A corporation organized under 12 U.S.C. Ch. 6 (relating to the organization of corporations to engage in foreign banking).

(5) An agency or branch of a foreign depository as defined in 12 U.S.C. § 3101.

• *Doing business*

Effective January 1, 2014, an institution will be considered to be doing business in Pennsylvania and therefore subject to the bank shares tax if it generates $100,000 or more of gross receipts that are apportionable to Pennsylvania (however, for years beginning after December 31, 2016, Act 84 of 2016 eliminates the $100,000 gross receipts threshold) and satisfies any of the following conditions:

(1) The institution has an office or branch in Pennsylvania;

(2) One or more employees, representatives, independent contractors, or agents conduct business activities on its behalf in Pennsylvania;

(3) Any person, directly or indirectly, solicits business on the institution's behalf in Pennsylvania through person-to-person contact, mail, telephone, or

electronic means, or advertising that is produced, published, or distributed in Pennsylvania;

(4) The institution owns, leases, or uses real or personal property located in Pennsylvania;

(5) The institution holds a security interest, mortgage, or lien on real or personal property located in Pennsylvania; or

(6) Any basis exists under Pennsylvania law or the U.S. Constitution to apportion the institution's receipts to Pennsylvania.

An institution is not be considered to be doing business in Pennsylvania merely because the bank uses independent professionals to perform services in Pennsylvania if such services are not significantly associated with creating a market in Pennsylvania, or the institution uses financial intermediaries in Pennsylvania to process or transfer checks, credit card receivables, commercial paper, or other similar items.

• *Exemptions*

Otherwise taxable companies whose shares are owned by another company subject to the bank shares tax (except for shares necessary to qualify directors) are not subject to the bank shares tax [72 P.S. § 7701.5].

Other Taxes on Financial Institutions

Pennsylvania also imposes a tax on private bankers (see ¶ 3305) and on credit unions (see ¶ 3306).

¶ 1906   Rate and Base

• *Rate*

The bank shares tax was levied at the rate of 1.25% per dollar of taxable amount of capital stock shares for calendar years beginning before January 1, 2014. Effective January 1, 2017, the bank shares tax rate is levied at the rate of 0.95% [72 P.S. § 7701].

• *Base—Taxable amount*

Effective for calendar years beginning on and after January 1, 2014, the taxable amount of capital stock shares is ascertained by book value of total bank equity capital determined by the Reports of Condition at the end of the preceding calendar year. There is no longer in use the six-year moving average formula in determining the value of equity capital. Additionally, the prior three-factor apportionment percentage (payroll, deposits, and receipts) used for apportionment is replaced by a single receipts factor based on receipts from Pennsylvania customers [72 P.S. § 7701.4(1)].

In the case of institutions that do not file Reports of Condition, book values are determined by generally accepted accounting principles as of the end of the preceding year.

• *Share value*

A deduction for the value of the United States obligations shall be provided from the taxable amount of shares in an amount equal to the same percentage of total bank equity capital as the book value of obligations of the United States bears to the book value of the total assets, except that for the value of shares reported on tax returns due on March 15, 2008, and thereafter, any goodwill recorded as a result of the use of purchase accounting for an acquisition or combination as described in this section and occurring after June 30, 2001, may be subtracted from the book value of total equity capital and disregarded in determining the deduction provided for obligations of the United States [72 P.S. § 7701.1(b)]. Act 84 of 2016 changes the bank shares tax

¶ 1906

base by clarifying that the goodwill deduction applies to both the bank shares tax base and the deduction for U.S. obligations. Act 84 provides for a deduction from the bank shares tax base for goodwill arising from the use of purchase accounting for an acquisition or combination occurring after June 30, 2001.

Exclusion for U.S. obligations: A deduction from the total value of shares is allowed for U.S. obligations. This deduction is determined by applying a percentage to the base (total value) determined by dividing the book value of U.S. obligations by the total book value of shares [72 P.S. § 7701.1(b)].

Exempt shares: Shares held by charitable, religious, or educational institutions are held to be exempt by the Department of Revenue. The value of these exempt shares may be subtracted in computing the taxable amount of shares. Student loans guaranteed by the Pennsylvania Higher Education Assistance Agency are exempt [*Corporation Tax Bulletin F-81,* Department of Revenue, January 1976].

Edge Act: Set forth by the Federal Reserve in 2006, Regulation K requires banks' foreign subsidiaries, as well as other foreign investments, be held through a special type of entity known as an "Edge Act corporation" (see 12 U.S.C. Section 611). An Edge Act corporation acts as a holding company for the bank's foreign investments and conducts other permitted overseas activities, directly or indirectly. Act 84 of 2016 allows a phased-in exemption from the tax base for subsidiaries formed under the federal Edge Act to conduct international business effective January 1, 2018. The exclusion will be gradually phased in, starting with a 20 percent exclusion for calendar years beginning January 1, 2018, and increasing 20 percent each calendar year through the calendar year beginning January 1, 2022, at which time taxpayers will be allowed a 100 percent exclusion.

¶1907 Apportionment

An institution that is subject in another state to a tax based on or measured by net worth, gross receipts, net income, or other similar base of taxation (or that could be subject to such a tax whether or not it is actually imposed) is entitled to apportion its taxable amount of shares [72 P.S. § 7701.4]. For calendar years beginning before January 1, 2014, the apportionment fraction specified by statute was a three-factor apportionment fraction, the numerator of which was the sum of the payroll factor, the receipts factor, and the deposits factor, and the denominator of which was three. If one of the factors was inapplicable, the denominator was two; if two of the factors were inapplicable, the denominator was one [72 P.S. § 7701.4(1)]. For calendar years beginning on or after January 1, 2014, the apportionment factor is based solely on the receipts factor [72 P.S. § 7701.4(1)(ii)].

• *Receipts factor*

The receipts factor is generally a fraction, the numerator of which is total receipts located in Pennsylvania and the denominator of which is total receipts located in all states. For calendar years beginning before January 1, 2014, receipts for this purpose did not include principal repayment on loans or credit, travel and entertainment cards. Receipts from sale or disposition of intangible and tangible property include only the net gain from the disposition. See 72 P.S. § 7701.4(3)(i)—(viii) for more detail. For calendar years beginning on or after January 1, 2014, the receipts factors is based upon fifteen different types allocation schemes, depending upon the specific type of receipt at issue. The bank shares tax apportionment rules allow banks to apportion receipts from investments and trading using either Method 1 (the fraction of other receipts that are sourced to Pennsylvania) or Method 2 (the fraction of investment and trading assets that are in Pennsylvania). On April 14, 2014, the Department of Revenue issued Information Notice 2014-1 related to the receipts factor apportionment provisions of 72 P.S. § 7701.4(3)(xiii) which purportedly requires certain institutions to use Method 2 to apportion receipts. This notice was followed up by the issuance of Information Notice 2015-01, dated February 17, 2015, asserting essentially the same position. Act 84 of 2016 reverses the published position of the Department and makes clear that all banks—even those with receipts from both investment and trading assets—may elect to use Method 1. In computing Pennsylvania receipts from investment and trading activities under Method 1 however, a taxpayer will now be required to multiply the total amount of receipts from investment and trading assets and activities times a fraction the numerator of which is the total amount of all other receipts attributable to the Commonwealth and the denominator of which is the total amount of all other receipts. Under prior law, only receipts from trading assets and activities were multiplied by the fraction. A taxpayer must make an irrevocable election to use amended Method 1 or Method 2 with the filing of the January 1, 2017 tax report. A taxpayer that had previously availed itself of Method 1, as previously enacted, may have an obligation to file an amended report, as this change is retroactive to January 1, 2014. Act 84 of 2016 clarifies that the goodwill deduction applies to the bank shares tax base and changes the definition of "total receipts" used in an institution's apportionment denominator to include all receipts reported on the bank's call sheet (it is not necessary to calculate this factor on a separate company basis). Effective for the calendar years beginning January 1, 2017, Act 84 also changes the apportionment methodology from a "separate company" receipts apportionment to a "consolidated" receipts apportionment. The bank's total receipts reported in the denominator of a bank's receipts factor shall no longer be based on the receipts as reported, or that would have been reported, on a separate company federal return. The receipts factor must include all income amounts reported on the income statement of the institution's consolidated Reports of Condition or, if no quarterly Reports of Condition are filed, on a consolidated income statement prepared under generally accepted accounting principles.

¶1908 Credits

Institutions subject to the bank shares tax can take the following credits:

(1) Educational improvement and opportunity scholarship tax credit (discussed at ¶1011).

(2) Employment incentive payment credit (discussed at ¶1006).

(3) Job creation tax credit (discussed at ¶1007).

(4) Neighborhood assistance tax credit (discussed at ¶1005).

(5) Organ or bone marrow donor tax credit (discussed at ¶1015).

(6) Resource enhancement and protection tax credit (discussed at ¶1016).

(7) Keystone special development zone tax credit (discussed at ¶1014A).

(8) Film production credit (discussed at ¶1012).

(9) Resource manufacturing tax credit (discussed at ¶1021).

(10) Historic preservation incentive tax credit (discussed at ¶1023).

(11) Community-based services tax credit (discussed at ¶1024).

KOZs and KIZs

Qualified businesses in a KOZ may claim a credit against the bank and trust company shares tax. See discussion below. Purchasers/assignees of KIZ tax credits may qualify for a KIZ tax credit (see ¶4623).

• *Keystone opportunity zone (KOZ) tax credit*

An institution that is a qualified business (see ¶4622) may claim a credit against bank and trust company shares tax or mutual thrift institutions tax for tax liability attributable to business activity conducted within a subzone, an expansion subzone, or an improvement subzone. Note that the term "subzone" is used herein to indicate a subzone, an expansion subzone, or an improvement subzone. The business activity must be conducted directly by an institution in the subzone, and no credit may be claimed for business conducted prior to the designation of the area as a subzone [73 P.S. § 820.517(a)].

Tax liability: The institution's tax liability attributable to business activity conducted within a subzone is determined by multiplying the taxable amount of its shares or net income that is attributable to business activity conducted within the subzone for the taxable year [73 P.S. § 820.517(b)].

Attributable tax liability: The taxable shares or the income of an institution that is a qualified business must be apportioned to the subzone by multiplying the Pennsylvania taxable shares or income by a fraction, the numerator of which is the payroll factor plus the receipts factor plus the deposits factor and the denominator of which is three [73 P.S. § 820.517(c)]. These factors are defined in 73 P.S. § 820.517(c).

Limitation on the amount of credit: The allowable KOZ credit cannot exceed 50% of the taxpayer's bank and trust company shares tax or mutual thrift institutions tax [73 P.S. § 820.517(d)].

¶1909 Reports and Payment of Tax

Institutions must file bank shares tax reports (on Form RCT-132) on or before March 15 of each calendar year. The bank shares tax is filed annually, but it does not cover a year's operations. It is a tax based on the value of shares on a given day— January 1 preceding the filing date. Payment of the entire amount of tax due must accompany the annual report [72 P.S. § 7701].

For calendar years beginning January 1, 1971, through January 1, 1991, taxpayers were required to pay at least 80% of the tax due when the annual report was filed and the remaining tax when the next year's report was filed.

Payment by Electronic Funds Transfer

Payment by electronic funds transfer(EFT)is discussed at ¶4617.

Tentative reports are not required for bank shares tax purposes.

Extensions of time to file may be granted. The corporate net income tax provisions govern. (See ¶917.)

¶1910 Penalties, Interest, Enforcement, Refund, and Review

With the exception of extensions of time to file, the bank shares tax provisions incorporate, by reference, the corporate net income tax provisions with respect to reports and payment of tax, administrative review, enforcement, interest, and penalties [72 P.S. § 7702(a)]. Corporate net income tax review provisions are also followed [72 P.S. § 7702]. Assessment provisions are discussed at ¶1204. Reassessment and refund provisions are discussed at ¶4604. If a taxpayer makes an application by the last day for filing and in a form prescribed by the Department, the Department may grant an extension of not more than six (6) months for filing the annual report [72 P.S. § 7702(b)].

TAXES ON FINANCIAL INSTITUTIONS

CHAPTER 20

MUTUAL THRIFT INSTITUTIONS TAX

¶2001 Imposition of Tax

The mutual thrift institutions tax is imposed on the net taxable income received or accrued by a mutual thrift institution (defined at ¶2003) from all sources during the preceding year. Before the 1987 tax year, the tax base was net earnings or income. The tax was nominally an excise tax for the privilege of doing business in the Commonwealth [72 P.S. §8502]. However, based on the "practical operation and effect" of the tax measure, the Pennsylvania Supreme Court held that the Mutual Thrift Institutions Tax was a direct tax imposed on net income, the Commonwealth unsuccessfully argued that the tax was an indirect franchise tax on the privilege of doing business in Pennsylvania. Therefore, since the income derived from Commonwealth obligations is specifically exempt from state and local tax, the interest earned by a mutual thrift institution on Pennsylvania securities held for investment was not subject to the tax on mutual thrift institutions [*First Federal Savings & Loan Assn. of Philadelphia, v. Cmwlth.,* 528 A.2d 942 (1987)].

• *Exemption from other taxes*

Mutual thrift institutions are exempt from all other corporate Pennsylvania taxes and from all local taxes except taxes on real estate or real estate transfers [72 P.S. §8502(e)].

¶2002 Sources of Authority; Administration

The tax on taxable net income of mutual thrift institutions is imposed by Article XV of the Tax Reform Code [72 P.S. §§8501—8505]. Before 72 P.S. §§8501 *et seq.,* the tax was governed by the Act of June 22, 1964, P.L. 16. The 1983 Act repealed the old mutual thrift institutions earnings tax and added Article XV, the provisions of which apply to 1983 and later tax years. As a response to the *First Federal Savings and Loan Association of Philadelphia* case (see ¶2001), amendments were made to Article XV by 1988 Act, No. 106.

The tax is administered by the Pennsylvania Department of Revenue, Harrisburg, Pennsylvania.

¶2003 Taxable Institutions

The tax is imposed on mutual thrift institutions. These include every savings bank without capital stock, every building and loan association, every savings and loan association, and every savings institution having capital stock whether the institution is incorporated by or under any Commonwealth or U.S. law, or under the law of any other jurisdiction and is located within the Commonwealth [72 P.S. § 8501].

¶2004 Rate and Base

The tax is levied upon taxable net income received or accrued from all sources at the rate of 11.5% for 1992 and later calendar years and for fiscal years starting in 1992 and years thereafter [72 P.S. § 8502(a)].

• *Determination of net income/loss*

Net income or net loss must be determined per in accordance with generally accepted accounting principles [72 P.S. § 8502(a)], with the following exceptions:

(1) Net income/loss must be determined on a separate company unconsolidated basis, using cost instead of equity accounting for investments in a subsidiary [72 P.S. § 8502(c)(1)].

(2) The accounting method may be on a cash, accrual, or combined cash and accrual basis, depending on the method used to keep the books [72 P.S. § 8502(c)(2)].

(3) In the case of a business combination entered into after December 31, 1986 that is treated as a reorganization for purposes of IRC § 368 (or a similar successor provision) and accounted for under the purchase method, net income/loss must be determined as though the acquisition had been accounted for as a pooling of interests [72 P.S. § 8502(c)(3)].

(4) Net income/loss does not include amounts credited or paid as interest to holders of accounts or depositors or as dividends to shareholders (except that no deduction is permitted for dividends paid by an institution having capital stock to its stockholders with regard to their stock) [72 P.S. § 8502(c)(4)].

(5) Net income/loss does not include income or loss derived from (i) obligations of the United States that are exempt by federal law from state and local taxation or (ii) obligations of the Commonwealth that are, by Pennsylvania law, exempt from Commonwealth taxation. For this purpose United States obligations are those falling within the scope of 31 U.S.C. § 3124; and Commonwealth obligations are obligations of the Commonwealth, any public authority, commission, board, or other agency created by the Commonwealth, any political subdivision of the Commonwealth or any public authority created by political subdivisions that are, by Pennsylvania law, exempt from Commonwealth taxation [72 P.S. § 8502(c)(5)]. Interest received from a demand deposit with the Federal Home Loan Bank is not excludable. The *Smith* test [*Smith v. Davis*, 323 U.S. 111 (1944)] requires a binding promise to pay a specified sum at a specified date. The payment on a demand deposit account is neither fixed nor certain and is not authorized under the borrowing power of the FHLB. See *Roxborough Manayunk Federal Savings and Loan Association v. Cmwlth.*, 687 A.2d 1202 (1997).

(6) No deduction is allowed for interest expense that is allocable to tax-exempt income derived from United States and Commonwealth obligations. The portion of an institution's interest expense that is allocable to tax-exempt income is an amount that bears the same ratio to total interest expense as the institution's tax-exempt interest income bears to the institution's total interest income. An institution's interest expense does include amounts credited or paid as interest to holders of accounts or depositors or as dividends to shareholders (except dividends paid by an institution having capital stock to its shareholders with regard to their stock) [72 P.S. § 8502(c)(6)].

• *Taxable year*

The taxable year of an institution is the taxable year that it (or any consolidated group with which it participates in the filing of a consolidated return) actually uses in reporting taxable income for federal income tax purposes. Within the context of the mutual thrift institutions tax the terms "year," "annual year," "fiscal year," "annual or fiscal year," "tax year," and "tax period" have the same meaning as an institution's "taxable year" [72 P.S. § 8501].

• *Taxable net income*

"Taxable net income" is the net income of an institution after apportionment and after any deduction for a net loss carryover [72 P.S. § 8501]. A net loss carryover deduction (discussed below) is allowed in the determination of taxable net income [72 P.S. § 8502(d)(1)].

• *Net loss carryover deduction*

A net loss carryover deduction is allowed in determining taxable net income. For any taxable year, the net loss carryover deduction is the sum of any net losses for the preceding three taxable years, beginning with the earliest year, to the extent that the net loss has not previously been allowed as a deduction in a prior taxable year [72 P.S. § 8502(d)(2)].

A net loss for a preceding taxable year is an amount determined as a negative amount for the year in accordance with the rules for determination of net income/loss (discussed above), after any apportionment applicable to the preceding year [72 P.S. § 8502(d)].

• *Change in ownership*

If ownership is changed, by purchase, liquidation, acquisition of stock or reorganization in accordance with IRC § 381 or § 382, certain limitations provided in the Internal Revenue Code with respect to net operating losses apply when computing the allowable portion of a recognized net loss carryover for mutual thrift institutions tax purposes. These limitations include all those limitations imposed solely on account of a change in ownership, including but not limited to IRC §§ 269, 318, 381 and 382. Carryover of tax losses is not limited by the federal consolidated return regulations or IRC § 338, providing for the deemed termination of corporate existence upon the making of certain elections for federal income tax purposes. When any acquiring institution or a transferor institution participated in the filing of consolidated federal income tax returns, the entitlement of the acquiring institution to the Pennsylvania net loss carryover of the acquiring or transferor institution is determined as if separated federal returns had been filed prior to the change in ownership [72 P.S. § 8502(e.1)].

¶2005 Apportionment

An institution may apportion its net income (or net loss) if it is subject to tax in another state that is based on or measured by net worth, gross receipts, net income, or some similar base of taxation or if it could be so taxed whether or not such a tax has been enacted. Income or loss is apportioned in accordance with a fraction, the numerator being the sum of the payroll, receipts, and deposits factors and the denominator of which is three [72 P.S. § 8502.1(a), (b)].

• *Payroll factor*

The payroll factor is a fraction, the numerator being total wages paid in Pennsylvania and the denominator being total wages paid in all states. Wages are paid in a state if paid to an employee having a regular presence there [72 P.S. § 8502.1(c)].

• *Receipts factor*

The receipts factor is a fraction, the numerator being total receipts located in Pennsylvania and the denominator being total receipts located in all states. Receipts do not include principal repayments on loans or credit, or travel and entertainment cards. Receipts from the sale or disposition of intangible and tangible property include only the net gain therefrom. The law goes into detail as to how to determine the location of receipts [72 P.S. § 8502.1(d)].

• *Deposits factor*

The deposits factor is a fraction, the numerator being the average value of deposits located in Pennsylvania during the tax year and the denominator being the average value of total deposits during the tax year. The average value of deposits is to be computed quarterly. The law details how to determine the location of deposits [72 P.S. § 8502.1(e)].

¶2006 Reports and Payment of Tax

Annual reports of calendar-year mutual thrift institutions must be filed (on Form RCT-143) with the Department of Revenue on or before April 15 following the end of the tax year [72 P.S. § 8502(a)]. Mutual thrift institutions subject to tax that fail to file an annual report cannot initiate actions in Pennsylvania courts until the report is filed. Failure to file does not affect the validity of contracts or acts of the institutions and cannot stop an institution from defending an action in Pennsylvania courts [72 P.S. § 8502.4].

Payment by Electronic Funds Transfer

Payment made by electronic funds transfer (EFT) is discussed at ¶4617.

Fiscal-year institutions must file reports within 105 days after the close of their fiscal years [72 P.S. § 8502(b)]. A timely mailed return is considered timely filed if it bears a postmark dated on or before the due date [72 P.S. § 8504]. The Department of Revenue may grant extensions for filing (up to 60 days) upon application. The Department may further extend the filing time to not more than 30 days after the end of any federal extension [72 P.S. § 704].

• *No extension of time to pay is allowed*

Payment must be made on or before the original due date of the return without regard to extensions [72 P.S. § 704].

• *Payment of estimated tax*

Payments of estimated tax must be made in equal installments on or before the 15th day of the third, sixth, ninth, and twelfth months of the taxable year. The remaining portion, if any, must be paid on or before the due date for the final return without regard to extensions [72 P.S. § 10003.2(c)(3)]. Procedures regarding underpayments of estimated tax are the same as those explained at ¶918.

¶2007 Credits

Mutual thrift institutions can take the following credits:

    (1) Employment incentive payment credit (discussed at ¶1006).

    (2) Job creation tax credit (discussed at ¶1007).

    (3) Neighborhood assistance tax credit (discussed at ¶1005).

    (4) Organ or bone marrow donor tax credit (discussed at¶1015).

    (5) Resource enhancement and protection tax credit (discussed at ¶1016).

    (6) Keystone special development zone tax credit (discussed at ¶1014A).

(7) Resource manufacturing tax credit (discussed at ¶1021).

(8) Educational improvement and opportunity scholarship tax credit (discussed at ¶1011).

(9) Historic preservation incentive tax credit (discussed at ¶1022).

(10) Community-based services tax credit (discussed at ¶1023).

KOZs and KIZs

Qualified businesses in a KOZ may claim a credit against the mutual thrift institutions tax. Purchasers/assignees of KIZ tax credits may qualify for a KIZ tax credit against its mutual thrift institutions tax (see ¶4623).

• *Amount of credit*

For each state in which the institution is taxable, the credit is the lesser of (1) the actual tax paid to the state or (2) the total mutual thrift institutions tax due without regard to apportionment multiplied by a fraction, the numerator being the amount of the institution's income (or other applicable basis of taxation) subject to tax by such state, and the denominator being the institution's entire net income (or other basis of taxation) to which a system of apportionment or allocation is applied by the state. If a state does not allocate or apportion, the numerator is the institution's income (or other applicable base of taxation) that would be subject to taxation in such state if the apportionment fraction were computed per the mutual thrift institutions tax.

If the election to take the credit is exercised, the credit is in lieu of any other apportionment to which the institution would otherwise be entitled [72 P.S. § 8502.2].

¶2008 Assessment, Reassessment, and Penalties

Except for a separate provision for extensions of time to file, the assessment, reassessment, penalties, and interest provision of the corporate net income are incorporated by reference into Article XV (mutual thrift institutions tax) insofar as they are applicable [72 P.S. § 8503(a)]. Assessment is discussed at ¶1204, and reassessment is discussed at ¶4604.

Extension of time: The Department may grant an extension of time of up to six (6) months for filing the annual mutual thrift institutions tax return [72 P.S. § 8503(b), effective for taxable years beginning after December 31, 2000].

Failure to file: Any institution that neglects or refuses to make any report required by Article XV (Mutual Thrift Institutions Tax) is liable for a $5,000 penalty [72 P.S. § 8502(f)].

Prior Law

Under prior law this administrative review process was called settlement (discussed at ¶1203). After December 31, 2007, the administrative review process is called assessment. The administrative review process is discussed in Chapter 12.

¶2008

TAXES ON FINANCIAL INSTITUTIONS

CHAPTER 21
TITLE INSURANCE COMPANIES SHARES TAX

¶2101 Outline of Tax

The shares tax on title insurance companies is imposed on the "value" (explained at ¶2105) of the full number of shares of capital stock subscribed for or issued as of January 1 preceding the filing date (explained at ¶2107).

• *Exemption from other taxes*

Title insurance companies must withhold corporate loans tax (see ¶1703) but are exempt from the capital stock/franchise tax [72 P.S. §7602(i)]and the corporate net income tax [72 P.S. §402(c)]. These companies may pay the tax with their own funds or from taxes collected from shareholders [72 P.S. §7801]. In practice, however, title insurance companies file reports and pay the tax themselves. Companies that pay the shares tax are exempt from all other Pennsylvania taxation on the portion of their capital stock, surplus, profits, and deposits that is not invested in real estate [72 P.S. §7801(b)].

¶2102 Sources of Authority

The title insurance companies shares act is imposed by Article VIII of the Tax Reform Code [72 P.S. §§7801—7806].

¶2103 Administration

The shares tax on title insurance companies is administered by the Pennsylvania Department of Revenue, Harrisburg, Pennsylvania. The procedure, enforcement, and penalty provisions of the corporate net income tax are incorporated by reference [72 P.S. §7802]. See Chapter 12.

¶2104 Taxable Companies

The title insurance companies shares tax is imposed on companies incorporated for the insurance of owners of real estate, mortgages, and others interested in real estate from loss by reason of defective titles, liens, and encumbrances (commonly known as title insurance companies) [72 P.S. §7801(a)].

• *Exemption*

If all of the shares of capital stock of a title insurance company (other than shares necessary to qualify directors) are owned by a company that is itself subject to a Pennsylvania shares tax, the title insurance company is exempt from the title insurance companies shares tax [72 P.S. §7801(b)].

¶2105 Rate and Base

• *Rate*

The title insurance companies shares tax is levied at the rate of 1.25% per dollar of taxable amount of capital stock shares [72 P.S. § 7801].

• *Taxable amount*

The taxable amount of shares is ascertained by adding together the value of shares, as defined below, for the current and preceding five years and dividing the resulting sum by six. If a company has not been in existence for six years, the taxable amount of shares will be ascertained by adding together the values for the number of years the company has been in existence and dividing the resulting sum by such number of years [72 P.S. § 7801.1].

• *Share value*

The value of shares each year is ascertained by adding together the book value of capital stock paid in, the book value of surplus, the book value of undivided profits, and the book value of unearned premium reserve and dividing by the number of shares subscribed for or issued, with a deduction from this total of an amount equal to the same percentage of the total as the book value of obligations of the United States bears to the book value of the total assets. For this purpose book values and the deduction for U.S. obligations for each year are determined by the Reports of Condition made in each calendar quarter in the preceding calendar year (*i.e.,* the average of the quarterly values) in accordance with the requirements of the Board of Governors of the Federal Reserve System, the Comptroller of the Currency, the Federal Deposit Insurance Corporation, or other applicable regulatory authority. If a company does not file Reports of Condition, book values are determined by generally accepted accounting principles as of the end of each calendar quarter in the preceding calendar year. U.S. obligations are those within the scope of 31 U.S.C. § 3124 [72 P.S. § 7801.1]. For any year in which a company does not file four quarterly Reports of Condition, the book values and deductions for U.S. obligations shall be determined by adding together the book values and deductions for U.S. obligations from each quarterly Reports of Condition filed for such year and dividing the resulting sums by the number of such Reports of Condition. A partial year is treated as a full year.

• *Ownership restructuring*

Change of identity, form, or place of organization of one company is treated as if a single company had been in existence prior to as well as after such change. The combining of two or more companies into one is treated as if the companies had been a single company in existence prior to as well as after the combination, and the book value and deductions for U.S. obligations from the Reports of Condition shall be combined [72 P.S. § 7801.1(c)].

¶2106 Credits

Title insurance companies can take the following credits:

(1) Employment incentive payment credit (discussed at ¶1006).

(2) Job creation tax credit (discussed at ¶1007).

(3) Neighborhood assistance tax credit (discussed at ¶1005).

(4) Organ or bone marrow donor tax credit (discussed at ¶1015).

(5) Keystone special development zone tax credit (discussed at ¶1014A).

(6) Resource manufacturing tax credit (discussed at ¶1021).

(7) Educational improvement and opportunity scholarship tax credit (discussed at ¶1011).

(8) Historic preservation incentive tax credit (discussed at ¶1022).

¶2107 Shares Tax Reports

Title insurance companies must file shares tax reports on or before March 15 of each calendar year [72 P.S. §7801].

• *Filing*

The report is filed annually, but it does not cover a year's operations. Like the bank shares tax, it is a tax based on the value of shares on a given day—January 1 preceding the filing date [72 P.S. §7801]. Payment of the entire amount of tax due must accompany the annual report [72 P.S. §7801]. For calendar years beginning January 1, 1971, through January 1, 1991, taxpayers were required to pay at least 80% of the tax due when the annual report was filed and the remaining tax when the next year's report was filed.

Payment by Electronic Funds Transfer

Payment by electronic funds transfer (EFT) is discussed at ¶4617.

¶2108 Reports, Payment, Review, Enforcement, Interest, and Penalties

The title insurance companies tax provisions incorporate, by reference, the corporate net income tax provisions regarding reports and payment, review, enforcement, interest, and penalties [72 P.S. §7802]except that §1104.1 of the Fiscal Code is the exclusive method by which an appeal from the assessment of the title insurance companies shares tax may be made [72 P.S. §9702(b)]. Assessment provisions are discussed at ¶1204. Reassessment provisions are discussed at ¶4604.

PART VIII

TAXES ON INSURANCE COMPANIES

CHAPTER 22

GROSS PREMIUMS TAX ON INSURANCE COMPANIES

¶2201 Scope of Chapter

The major Pennsylvania tax on insurance companies is the gross premiums tax [72 P.S. § 7901 *et seq.*]. This chapter contains an explanation of the gross premiums tax. In addition to the gross premiums tax, Pennsylvania levies the following taxes on insurance companies: (1) tax on marine insurance underwriting profits; (2) insurance premiums tax on insurance with unauthorized companies; (3) reinsurance premiums tax on insurance with unauthorized companies; (4) retaliatory tax on foreign insurance companies; and (5) surplus lines. These taxes are explained in Chapter 23.

¶2202 Administration and Fees

• *Administration*

All of the insurance taxes are administered by the Pennsylvania Department of Revenue in Harrisburg, Pennsylvania, but the Insurance Commissioner is authorized to enforce collection of the retaliatory tax on foreign companies. The Insurance Commissioner also charges and collects fees with respect to insurance companies [Act of April 9, 1929, P.L. 177, Art. VI-A, § 612-A].

• *Fees*

The Insurance Commissioner charges and collects various insurance fees. A list of the fees and current charges is contained in § 612-A of the Administrative Code of 1929 [71 P.S. § 51 *et seq.*].

¶ 2203 Definitions

In order to provide a guide to the important insurance premiums tax terms, a glossary is provided in this paragraph for quick reference. All definitions are contained in 72 P.S. § 7901, unless otherwise indicated. Some definitions specific only to certain situations are defined in context when discussing the situation.

• *Assessment*

"Assessment" means an assessment imposed by the guaranty association pursuant to § 1808 of The Insurance Company Law of 1921 [Act of May 17, 1921 (P.L. 682, No. 284)].

• *Assessment base*

"Assessment base" means the amount of net direct written premiums used by the guaranty association to calculate a member insurer's assessment on an account under § 1808 of The Insurance Company Law of 1921 [Act of May 17, 1921 (P.L. 682, No. 284)].

• *Gross premiums*

"Gross premiums" means premiums, premium deposits or assessments received by any insurance company, whether received in money or in the form of notes, credits, or any other substitutes for money, and whether collected in Pennsylvania or elsewhere. See ¶ 2204 for a more detailed discussion of inclusions and exemptions from the gross premiums tax base.

• *Guaranty association*

"Guaranty association" means the Pennsylvania property and casualty insurance guaranty association created pursuant to § 1803 of The Insurance Company Law of 1921 [Act of May 17, 1921 (P.L. 682, No. 284)].

• *Insurance company*

"Insurance company" means every insurance company, association, or exchange, incorporated or organized by or under the laws of Pennsylvania, the United States, territories, dependencies, other states, or foreign governments, and engaged in transacting insurance business of any kind or classification within this Commonwealth, except purely mutual beneficial associations whose funds for the benefit of members and families or heirs are made up entirely of the weekly, monthly, quarterly, semiannual, or annual contributions to their members and the accumulated interest thereon and corporations organized under the Nonprofit Hospital Plan Act [Act of June 21, 1937 (P.L. 1948)]and the Nonprofit Medical, Osteopathic, Dental and Podiatry Service Corporation Act [Act of June 27, 1939 (P.L. 1125)].

• *Member insurer*

"Member insurer" means an insurance company, association, or exchange that is required to participate in the guaranty association pursuant to Article XVIII of The Insurance Company Law of 1921 [Act of May 17, 1921 (P.L. 682, No. 284)].

• *Net direct written premiums*

"Net direct written premiums" has the meaning assigned to it in § 1802 of The Insurance Company Law of 1921 [Act May 17, 1921 (P.L. 682, No. 284)].

¶2204 Imposition, Base, and Rate

• *Rate*

The gross premiums tax on insurance companies is imposed on insurance companies that transact business in Pennsylvania and is levied at the rate of 2% of gross premiums received from business done in Pennsylvania during each calendar year [72 P.S. §7902(a)]. Premiums are considered received from business done in Pennsylvania if the risk is located in Pennsylvania (*i.e.*, if the object of the insurance coverage is located in Pennsylvania).

• *Exemption from other taxes*

Insurance companies subject to the gross premiums tax are exempt from the corporate net income tax [72 P.S. §7402(c)] and the capital stock/franchise tax [72 P.S. §602(i)].

• *Gross premiums*

"Gross premiums" means premiums, premium deposits, or assessments received by any insurance company from business done in Pennsylvania (regardless of form of payment or place of collection) [72 P.S. §7901(2)]. See above for explanation of "business done in Pennsylvania."

• *Items not gross premiums*

Gross premiums do not include the following items [72 P.S. §7901]:

(1) Amounts returned on policies canceled or not taken.

(2) Premiums received for reinsurance.

(3) In the case of mutual insurance companies, associations, exchanges, and stock companies with participating features, that portion of the advanced premiums, premium deposits, or assessments returned in cash or credited to members or policyholders, whether as dividends, earnings, savings, or return deposits, upon the expiration or termination of their contacts.

(4) Notes or other obligations received by mutual insurance companies to secure contingent premium liabilities to the extent that no assessment has been made and collected against the notes or obligations.

• *Credits*

Insurance companies are entitled to three credits against the gross premiums tax. *All* insurance [Act of April 8, 1982, P.L. 231, §23] companies subject to the premiums tax may take the employment incentive payment tax credit and the job creation tax credit. Insurance companies (except foreign fire or casualty insurance companies) may take the Neighborhood Assistance Credit [Act of November 29, 1967, P.L. 636, §5]. The tax credit for contributions to the mortgage emergency assistance fund was also available to use against the insurance tax, but this credit was repealed effective February 21, 1999. These credits are explained at ¶1004.

¶2205 Taxable Corporations

The term "insurance company" means every insurance company, association, or exchange, incorporated or organized by or under the laws of Pennsylvania, the United States, territories, dependencies, other states, or foreign governments, and engaged in transacting insurance business of any kind or classification within Pennsylvania, except for specifically exempted companies [72 P.S. §7901(1)]. Exempt corporations are explained at ¶2206. This statute is broad enough to include almost all insurance companies, domestic or foreign, that transact business in Pennsylvania, including *foreign* title insurance companies. Domestic title insurance companies are subject to a tax on their shares instead of gross premiums (see ¶2206).

¶2206 Exempt Corporations

The following insurance companies are exempt, by statute, from the insurance gross premiums tax [72 P.S. § 7901(1)]:

(1) Title insurance companies subject to the title insurance companies shares tax (explained in Chapter 21).

(2) Purely mutual beneficial associations whose funds for the benefit of members and families or heirs are made up entirely of the contributions from their members and the accumulated interest on them.

(3) Corporations organized under the Nonprofit Hospital Plan Act [Act of June 21, 1937, P.L. 1948].

(4) Corporations organized under the Nonprofit Medical, Osteopathic, Dental and Podiatry Service Corporation Act [Act of June 27, 1939, P.L. 1125].

¶2207 Reports and Payment of Tax

The gross premiums tax statute incorporates, by reference, the procedure, enforcement, and penalty provisions of the corporate net income tax law [72 P.S. § 7904]. These are explained in Chapter 12.

• *Forms*

Every insurance company must file a gross premiums report on a form prescribed by the Department of Revenue [72 P.S. § 7903]. The prescribed form depends on the kind of insurance company.

• *Time of filing and payment*

All insurance gross premiums tax reports are filed on a calendar-year basis. The reports are due on or before April 15 following the end of the calendar year [72 P.S. § 7903]. Timely mailing is considered timely filing (see ¶915). However, the taxpayer must supply adequate proof of timely mailing. The testimony of a taxpayer's manager of state and local taxes that a return was timely mailed was insufficient proof of timely mailing See *Transcontinental Gas Pipe Line Corp. v. Cmwlth.*, 620 A.2d 614Ca Commw.1993). Payment is due with the reports [72 P.S. § 7903].

Payment by Electronic Funds Transfer

Payment by electronic funds transfer (EFT)is discussed at ¶4617.

• *Recordkeeping requirements*

Recordkeeping requirements are controlled by the corporate net income tax provisions, which are explained at ¶920.

¶2208 Estimated Tax

Insurance companies subject to the gross premiums tax must make payments of estimated tax [72 P.S. § 10003.2(c)(4)]. The estimated insurance premiums tax is the amount that the company estimates as the amount of tax due with its final return. Prior to January 1, 1998, insurance companies were required to pay tentative tax in an amount equal to the current tax rate applied to 90% of the prior year's tax base.

Payment of the estimated insurance premiums tax must be made in a single installment on or before the fifteenth day of March of the taxable year. The remaining portion, if any, must be paid on or before the due date for the final return without regard to any extension of time [72 P.S. § 10003.2(c)(4)].

Procedures regarding underpayments of estimated tax are the same as those explained at ¶918.

¶2206

¶2209 Extensions of Time

The Department of Revenue may, if a taxpayer applies for an extension, grant an extension of time to file annual reports, but the extension cannot exceed 60 days [72 P.S. § 7405]. There is, however, *no* extension time for the filing of a tentative report.

¶2210 Administrative and Judicial Review

The gross premiums tax on insurance companies is a settled tax. The gross premiums tax law incorporates, by reference, the settlement and resettlement provisions of the corporate net income tax law [72 P.S. § 7904] explained at ¶1204. The Department of Revenue has generally three years in which to settle the gross premiums tax on insurance companies. The judicial review process (as opposed to the administrative review process) is the same for all taxes and is explained at ¶4607. See ¶4602 for a general discussion of the administrative review process.

¶2211 Interest and Penalties

The gross premiums tax law incorporates, by reference, the interest and penalty provisions of the corporate net income tax law [72 P.S. § 7904]. These are explained at ¶1208.

¶2212 Credit for Assessments Paid to the Pennsylvania Property and Casualty Insurance Guaranty Association

A member insurer that has paid assessments to the Pennsylvania Property and Casualty Insurance Guaranty Association is entitled to a credit equal to the amount by which the assessment paid to the association exceeds one percent (1%) of the member insurer's "assessment base" as calculated for the preceding calendar year [72 P.S. § 7902.1]. For assessments paid prior to January 1, 1999, the assessment was based on "net direct written premiums" instead of the "assessment base." See ¶2203 for definitions of terms.

• *Application and timing of the credit*

Except for retaliatory taxes, this credit applies to the insurance gross premiums insurance in equal portions for each of the five calendar years following payment of the assessment. If a member insurer ceases doing business, all unused credit may be applied against its premium tax liability for the year it ceases doing business. Member insurers, however, are not entitled to refunds of unused credits [72 P.S. § 7902.1(a)].

• *Refunds*

A member insurer that acquires any sums (whether by refund or by receipt of an offset that may be used against an assessment and that have been used to calculate this credit) from the Guaranty Association will either (1) reduce the amount of unused credit or (2) be remitted to the Commonwealth, as the Department of Revenue may require. The Guaranty Association must notify the Department and the insurance commissioner that such sums have been acquired by a member insurer [72 P.S. § 7902.1(b)].

Premium adjustment: This credit is not permitted to the extent that a member insurer's rates and premiums have been adjusted as permitted by § 1810 of The Insurance Company Law of 1921 (Act of May 17, 1921 (P.L. 682, No. 284)), [72 P.S. § 7901.2(c)].

Firefighters and police officers: The credit cannot be used to reduce amounts that would otherwise be payable for firemen's relief pension or retirement purposes or for police pension, retirement, or disability purposes. By June 30 of each fiscal year, the Department will transfer an amount equal to the total amount of this credit allowed to foreign fire and casualty insurance companies from the General Fund to the Municipal Pension Aid Fund and the Fire Insurance Tax Fund, as appropriate [72 P.S. §7902.1(d)].

¶2213 Credit for Assessments Paid to the Pennsylvania Life and Health Insurance Guaranty Association

A member insurer may offset against its Pennsylvania premium tax liability a proportionate part of its assessment to the extent of 20% of the amount of the assessment (as defined in 40 P.S. §991.1707) for each of the five calendar years following the year in which the assessment was paid [40 P.S. §991.1711(a)]. The proportionate part of an assessment that may be offset against a member company's Pennsylvania premium tax liability is determined according to a fraction the denominator of which is the total premiums received by the company during the calendar year immediately preceding the year in which the assessment is paid and the numerator of which is that portion of the premiums received during the immediately preceding calendar year on account of policies of life or health and accident insurance in which the premium rates are guaranteed during the continuance of the respective policies without a right exercisable by the company to increase premium rates [40 P.S. §991.1711(b)]. See details at 40 P.S. §991.1701 *et seq.*

On April 24, 2018 the Department issued Corporation Tax Bulletin 2018-01 Credits Against the Gross Premiums Tax Liability Under the Provisions of the Pennsylvania Life and Health Insurance Guaranty Association Act of 1992. In this Bulletin, the Department explained the proper method to calculate the Pennsylvania insurance premiums tax credit available to insurance companies. Key to the availability of a credit is the manner in which the credit is permitted to be claimed. The Department explained how to calculate the proportionate part of an assessment which may be claimed as a credit for each type of assessment. Critical to the calculation of the credit is the amount of guaranteed premiums that an insurance company receives. Guaranteed premiums are those premiums in which the premium rates are guaranteed during the continuance of a policy without a right exercisable by the company to increase the premium rate. 40 P.S. §991.1711(b). The Department did not provide any advice, however, in regard to when it will consider premiums to be guaranteed premiums. It is this area that is generating significant litigation in Pennsylvania. The Department's historic position is that premiums related to group accident and health insurance policies are not to be included in the numerator of the proportionate part calculation.

¶2214 Strategic Development Area Job Tax Credit

Effective for tax years beginning on or after January 1, 2008, a qualified insurance company may apply to the Department of Revenue for a job tax credit for all full-time jobs within a strategic development area (SDA) [72 P.S. §9938-C(a)]. The amount of the credit is determined by multiplying the monthly average of all full-time jobs by an allowance amount established for each calendar year ranging from $500 per job for 2001 to $1,250 per job for 2022 [72 P.S. §9938-C(e)]. The credit may not exceed 50% of the insurance company's premiums tax liability for the tax year [72 P.S. §9938-C(g)]. An insurance company must apply for the credit by January 15 for the previous calendar year [72 P.S. §9938-C(c)].

¶2215 Other Credits Against the Tax

The following credits may also be taken against the gross premiums tax on insurance companies:

(1) Educational improvement tax credit (discussed at ¶1011).

(2) Employment incentive payment tax credit (discussed at ¶1006).

(3) Job creation tax credit (discussed at ¶1007).

(4) Neighborhood assistance tax credit (discussed at ¶1005).

(5) Organ or bone marrow donor tax credit (¶1015).

(6) Resource enhancement and tax protection credit (¶1016).

(7) Film production tax credit (¶1012).

(8) Resource manufacturing tax credit (¶1021).

(9) Historic preservation incentive tax credit (¶1022).

(10) Innovate in PA Tax Credit (¶1026).

KOZ Tax Credits

Qualified businesses in a KOZ may claim a credit against the insurance gross premiums tax company shares tax. See discussion below.

- **Keystone opportunity zone (KOZ) tax credit**

An insurance company that is a qualified business (see ¶4622) may apply to the Department of Revenue for a job tax credit against the insurance gross premiums tax for all full-time jobs within a subzone, an expansion subzone, or an improvement subzone in the taxable year. Note that the term "subzone" is used herein to indicate a subzone, an expansion subzone, or an improvement subzone. The jobs must be held directly with an insurance company in the subzone in order for the insurance company to apply for a KOZ job tax credit. Note that the term "KOZ job tax credit" as used herein includes a KOZ job tax credit, a KOEZ job tax credit, or a KOIZ tax credit.

Relocation: An insurance company that relocates from a location in a political subdivision in Pennsylvania that is not in a subzone to a location in a subzone may not apply for an existing job that is transferred, discontinued, or lost in Pennsylvania that is attributable to relocation [73 P.S. § 820.518(b)(1)]. An insurance company that has relocated from a location in a political subdivision in Pennsylvania that is not in a subzone to a location in a subzone may apply for a KOZ job tax credit for a new full-time job that is created in the subzone. A new full-time job is created with an insurance company if the average monthly employment for that insurance company has increased from the prior 12-month calendar year in the subzone [73 P.S. § 820.518(b)(2)].

Application: An insurance company must apply for a credit by January 15 for the previous calendar year [73 P.S. § 820.518(c)].

Notification of credit: By March 15, the Department of Revenue must notify an insurance company of the amount of the insurance company's tax credit approved [73 P.S. § 820.518(f)].

Apportionment: The Department of Revenue will apportion a KOZ job tax credit for an insurance company that is a qualified business that has not operated in a subzone for a full fiscal year [73 P.S. § 820.518(d)].

Determination of credit: The KOZ job tax credit is determined by multiplying the monthly average of all full-time jobs by the allowance shown in the following table [73 P.S. § 820.518(e)]:

Calendar Year	Allowance
2001	$500 per job
2002	$750 per job
2003	$1,000 per job
2004 through 2018	$1,250 per job

Limitation on amount of credit: The KOZ job tax credit allowed cannot exceed 50% of the company's insurance premiums tax liability for the tax year. An insurance company may not carry back or forward any KOZ job tax credit [73 P.S. § 820.518(g)].

Limit on total amount of credits: The total amount of KOZ job tax credits for insurance companies cannot exceed $1,000,000 annually. If the credits exceed $1,000,000 in a given year, the credits will be allocated on a pro rata basis [73 P.S. § 820.518(h)].

Partnership arrangements: The KOZ job tax credit for insurance companies may be allocated to an insurance company that is a partner in a partnership that is also a qualified business in proportion to the full-time jobs within a subzone that are provided to the partner by the partnership. However, the partnership and a partner of that partnership may not claim any other tax benefit, expense, or credit for the same subzone job tax credit [73 P.S. § 820.518(j)].

Relief from retaliatory tax: The KOZ job credit taken by an insurance company is not included in determining liability for retaliatory taxes (discussed at ¶ 2205) [73 P.S. § 820.518(k)].

Hold-harmless clause: The KOZ job tax credits do not reduce the amounts that would otherwise be payable for firemen's relief pension or retirement purposes or for police pension retirement or disability purposes. The Department of Revenue must transfer by June 30 of each fiscal year an amount equal to the KOZ job tax credits taken by foreign fire and casualty insurance companies from the General Fund to the Municipal Pension Aid Fund and the Fire Insurance Tax Fund, as appropriate [73 P.S. § 820.518(l)].

• *Innovate in PA tax credit*

The Innovate in PA Tax Credit Program is designed to provide funding for the Ben Franklin Technology Partners, the PA Venture Capital Investment Program, and Life Sciences Greenhouses. Beginning on October 1, 2013, insurance companies may purchase up to $100 million of tax credits from the Department of Community and Economic Development (DCED) to offset insurance premiums taxes. The funds from the purchases of these credits will be used by DCED to support the three venture capital programs. A "qualified taxpayer" eligible to use the credits is an insurance company authorized to do business in Pennsylvania, or a holding company that has at least one insurance company subsidiary authorized to do business in Pennsylvania. The credits may be claimed beginning in 2017 and the total credit applied for all credit claimants in any one tax year may not exceed $20 million. Any unused credits may be carried over to any year prior to the 2026 tax year.

TAXES ON INSURANCE COMPANIES

CHAPTER 23
MISCELLANEOUS INSURANCE TAXES

¶2301 Scope of Chapter

Pennsylvania has several miscellaneous insurance taxes, which are briefly explained here. For details of these taxes, refer to the statutes cited.

¶2302 Marine Insurance Tax

Marine insurance companies licensed to do business in Pennsylvania are subject to a tax on their underwriting profits in lieu of the gross premiums tax. This tax is levied at the rate of 5% of the portion of their underwriting profits attributable to transacting business in Pennsylvania. The tax must be reported and paid to the Department of Revenue on or before June 1 annually. This tax is imposed by 72 P.S. § 2281 *et seq.*

¶2303 Insurance Premiums Tax on Insurance with Unauthorized Companies

This tax is imposed on the insured, not the insurance company. Insured persons or entities (individuals, corporations, co-partnerships, or associations) that enter into contracts of insurance or reinsurance with a foreign insurance company not registered or entitled to do business in Pennsylvania are subject to tax on the insurance premiums. Insured persons or entities entering into the such contracts must deduct (at the time of making such contracts and at the time of making any periodical payment) from all premiums a per centum thereof. The per centum is equal to the rate imposed on the premiums of foreign insurance companies that are registered and entitled to do business in Pennsylvania, currently 2%. The tax must be deducted from each premium payment and remitted to the State Treasury. This tax applies only to life insurance and annuities. This tax is imposed by 72 P.S. § 2265 *et seq.*, as amended by the Act of January 24, 1966.

¶2304 Reinsurance Premiums Tax on Insurance with Unauthorized Companies

Insurance companies authorized to do business in Pennsylvania are subject to a tax on their gross premiums of reinsurance when the reinsurance is with companies that are not authorized to do business in Pennsylvania. These companies may take a credit for the reserves of each ceded risk to the extent reinsured. However, unless an unlicensed reinsurer is qualified to accept reinsurance from Pennsylvania insurers, no credit is allowed as an admitted asset or as a reduction of liability relative to risks ceded by such licensed insurers. Qualified reinsurers are those meeting the conditions for reinsurers specified by the Commissioner, at his discretion, and included on a list of qualified reinsurers published by the Commissioner. Reinsurance agreements between or among affiliates covering all or substantially all of one or more lines of insurance of an affiliated domestic or foreign stock or mutual insurance company, association, or exchange are exempt *if* the amount of net written premium retained and the amount of the reinsurance and retrocession assumed by any affiliate participating agreement shall not be unreasonably large in relationship to its policyholders' surplus. Control for this purpose exists if any person (directly or indirectly) owns, controls, holds with power to vote, or holds shares representing 80% or more of the voting power of any other person. This tax is imposed by the Act of May 17, 1921, P.L. 682, No. 284.

¶2305 Retaliatory Taxes

The retaliatory taxes are imposed by The Insurance Department Act of 1921 [40 P.S. §22 *et seq.*] and are imposed on foreign insurance companies and agents when the insurance tax imposed by their state or country is greater than the insurance taxes imposed on them by Pennsylvania. Even though the retaliatory tax is referred to as a "tax," it is not technically a tax, but is more properly a business license fee or charge, the purpose of which is to encourage equal treatment of domestic and foreign insurance companies and to break down interstate barriers [*Cmwlth. v. Fireman's Fund Insurance Co.*, 87 A.2d 255 (1952)]. The retaliatory tax is the difference between the Pennsylvania insurance tax and the amount a Pennsylvania insurance company would have to pay in its state or country. The retaliatory tax is a settled tax (*i.e.*, it is subject to the review process called settlement).

Tax Applies to Insurance Companies, Not Insurance Business

A California insurance company that collected annuity considerations in Pennsylvania was held to be subject to the retaliatory tax, even though annuities are not insurance, because the Pennsylvania retaliatory tax applies to insurance companies, not the insurance business [*Executive Life Insurance Co. v. Cmwlth.*, 606 A.2d 1282 (Pa.Commw. 1992)].

Review procedures: For a discussion of the review process (*i.e.*, settlement, assessment, appraisement, or determination), see ¶4602. The statute is silent on the question of the time limit for settlement by the Commonwealth. However, the Commonwealth Court has held that the appropriate time limit is that which allows the Department of Revenue to settle the gross premiums tax on insurance companies and the retaliatory tax at the same time—18 months [*The Guardian Life Insurance Co. of America v. Cmwlth.*, 611 A.2d 797 (Pa.Commw. 1992)]. See ¶2211.

Tax Applies on a Company-by-Company Basis Not a State-by-State Basis

In *United Services Automobile Association v. Cmwlth.*, 618 A.2d 1155 (Pa.Commw. 1992), the Department of Revenue undertook a state-by-state analysis in order to determine whether a Texas-based insurance company was subject to Pennsylvania's retaliatory insurance tax. Texas imposes a gross premiums tax that is variable and dependent upon the amount of money an insurer has invested in Texas investments. A state-by-state analysis indicated that the insurer, United Services, was subject to Pennsylvania's retaliatory tax. However, the court held that the language of the applicable statute (40 P.S. §49 *et seq.*) required a company-by-company analysis. Such analysis indicated that a Pennsylvania insurer holding Texas investments equal to the Pennsylvania investments held by the taxpayer would be assessed a Texas gross premiums tax of only 1.2%. Therefore, the taxpayer was not subject to the Pennsylvania retaliatory insurance tax.

¶2306 Surplus Lines Insurance

A surplus lines tax at the rate of 3% is imposed on all premiums charged for insurance that is placed with either an eligible surplus lines insurer, other than a risk retention group, or other nonadmitted insurer. The tax is based on the gross premiums charged less any return premiums and is in addition to the full amount of the gross premium charged by the insurer for the insurance. The tax on any unearned portion of the premium must be returned to the insured. Surplus lines insurance is insurance placed through a surplus lines licensee with a nonadmitted insurer, other than reinsurance, wet marine and transportation insurance, independently procured insurance, life and health insurance and annuities, and coverage obtained from risk retention groups under the Risk Retention Amendments of 1986. The tax is levied on the insured person, but it is collected by the insurance agents. The agent must file a report with the Department of Revenue and pay the tax on or before January 31 annually. This tax formerly was imposed by the Act of January 24, 1966, P.L. 1509. However, this act was repealed and the surplus lines tax provisions were recodified as part of the Act of May 17, 1921, P.L. 682, No. 284, and amended to include references to the risk retention provisions.

Recent Legislation

Senate Bills 1096 and 1097 amend statutes to allow the Commonwealth to collect tax on 100% of the premium when Pennsylvania is the home state of the insured. The legislation provides that no state other than the home state of the insured may require premium taxes on nonadmitted insurance. The bills also change the taxation for multistate surplus lines policies and independently procured insurance placed after June 30, 2011, from an allocation method, taxing only that risk that is in the Commonwealth, to a gross premiums method, taxing the entire premium, regardless of where the risk is located [S.B. 1096 and S.B. 1097, Laws 2011, effective July 1, 2011].

• *Risk retention*

The Act of May 17, 1921, P.L. 682, No. 284, has been amended to regulate the formation and operation of risk retention groups and purchasing groups in Pennsylvania. Each risk retention group is liable for payment of premium taxes and taxes of premiums of direct business for risks resident or located within Pennsylvania. A risk retention group is subject to tax on the same basis as a foreign admitted insurer, pursuant to 72 P.S. § 7902.

Licensed agents, brokers, or surplus lines agents with Pennsylvania licenses must report to the Department of Revenue the premiums for direct business for risks resident or located within Pennsylvania that such licensees have placed with or on behalf of a risk retention group not registered in Pennsylvania.

Premiums paid by purchasing groups for coverage obtained from admitted insurers and risk retention groups doing business in Pennsylvania are taxed on the same basis as premiums paid to admitted insurers under 72 P.S. § 7902, currently 2%. Premiums paid for coverage obtained from a nonadmitted insurer are taxed at the rate applicable to premiums paid to surplus lines insurers, currently 3%. To the extent that the purchasing group or its members pay premiums for coverage of risks resident or located in Pennsylvania to admitted insurers or risk retention groups doing business in Pennsylvania, the insurer or risk retention group receiving the premiums is responsible for remitting the tax to the Department of Revenue. To the extent that the purchasing group or its members pay premiums for coverage of risks resident or located in Pennsylvania to a non-admitted insurer, the surplus lines agent who places the business shall collect and remit the taxes for premiums. To the extent a surplus lines agent does not effect coverage, the purchasing group must collect and remit the tax for the coverage of risks resident or located in Pennsylvania. To the extent the purchasing group does not remit the tax, the purchasing group shall inform each member of the responsibility for individual remittance of the tax.

KIZs

Purchasers/assignees of KIZ tax credits may qualify for a KIZ tax credit against the title insurance companies shares tax (see ¶4623).

• *Credits against tax*

The educational improvement and opportunity scholarship tax credit (discussed at ¶1011) is available to be used against the surplus lines tax.

PART IX

TAXES ON PUBLIC UTILITIES

CHAPTER 24

GROSS RECEIPTS TAX

¶2401	Scope of Chapter; Sources of Authority; Administration
¶2402	Taxable and Exempt Companies
¶2403	Tax Rate and Base
¶2404	Credits Against the Tax
¶2405	Reports and Payment of Tax
¶2405A	Method of Accounting
¶2406	Estimated Tax
¶2407	Public Utility Exemption
¶2408	Municipal Utilities
¶2409	Procedures, Enforcement, and Penalties

¶2401 Scope of Chapter; Sources of Authority; Administration

This chapter explains the gross receipts tax. The public utility realty tax (PURTA) is discussed in Chapter 25.

The gross receipts tax is imposed by Article XI of the Tax Reform Code and is administered by the Department of Revenue in Harrisburg, Pennsylvania. Gross receipts regulations are contained in Chapter 160 of Title 61 of the Pennsylvania Code.

¶2402 Taxable and Exempt Companies

• *Taxable companies—general rule*

All of the following entities that (1) are incorporated or organized by or under any law of Pennsylvania, any other state, the United States, or any foreign government and (2) do business in Pennsylvania are subject to the Pennsylvania gross receipts tax on taxable receipts (see below) [72 P.S. § 8101(a)]:

(a) Pipeline companies.

(b) Conduit companies.

(c) Steamboat companies.

(d) Canal companies.

(e) Slack water navigation companies.

(f) Transportation companies.

(g) All companies, associations, joint-stock associations, or limited partnerships (i) incorporated or organized by or under any law of Pennsylvania or (ii) organized or incorporated by any other state or by the United States or any foreign government if they are doing business in Pennsylvania.

(h) All copartnerships, person or persons owning, operating, or leasing to or from another corporation, company, association, joint-stock association, limited partnership, copartnership, person or persons any pipeline, conduit, steamboat, canal, slack water navigation, or other device for the transportation of freight, passengers, baggage, or oil (except motor vehicles and railroads).

(i) Limited partnerships, associations, joint-stock associations, corporations, or companies engaged in the transportation of freight or oil within Pennsylvania.

(j) All telephone companies, telegraph companies, and providers of mobile telecommunications service (i) incorporated or organized by or under any law of Pennsylvania or (ii) organized or incorporated by any other state or by the United States or any foreign government if they are doing business in Pennsylvania.

(k) Limited partnerships, associations, joint-stock associations, copartnerships, person, or persons engaged in telephone business, telegraph business, or providing mobile telecommunications services in Pennsylvania.

Statutory Terms Identify Taxpayers by Function, Not Regulation

In *Solar Turbines Inc. v. Cmwlth.*, [816 A.2d 362 (Pa.Commw. 2003), *aff'd per curiam*, Pa.Sup.Ct., Nos. 18 & 19 MAP 2004, November 23, 2005], the Commonwealth Court, relying on *Hanley and Bird v. Commonwealth*, 590 A.2d 1382 (Pa.Commw., 1991), concluded that the statutory terms imposing the gross receipts tax identified taxpayers by the function they perform, without regard to whether they are regulated as a public utility. The *Solar* case involved a company engaged in the production of electricity; the *Hanley and Bird* case involved a company engaged in the production and sale of natural gas, which was taxable in 1991. Note, however, that gas companies are no longer subject to the gross receipts tax.

• *Taxable receipts*

Taxable entities are subject to the gross receipts tax on each dollar of its gross receipts. Act 52 of 2018 revised the Pennsylvania gross receipts tax to clarify that sales of telephones, modems, tablets and related accessories, including cases, charges, holsters, clips, screen protectors and such are not subject to the gross receipts tax in regard to telephone and mobile telecommunications companies. The Pennsylvania Department of Revenue then issued guidance regarding the receipts from telecommunications businesses that are subject to utility gross receipts tax under Article XI of the Tax Reform Code (72 P.S. § 8101). Corporation Tax Bulletin 2018-04 (dated August 20, 2018) provides a general discussion of the application of the gross receipts tax and the clarifications of the tax as provided by the Pennsylvania Supreme Court in *Verizon Pennsylvania, Inc. v. Cmwlth*, 127 A.3d 745 (Pa. 2015). The Bulletin also provides a sampling of sales of services and equipment that give rise to taxable receipts, and a detailed list of authorized deductions. See discussion of gross receipts in ¶ 2403.

International Telephone Messages

Unless exempted by law, gross receipts with respect to telephone messages transmitted in interstate commerce that either originate or terminate with Pennsylvania and for which the charges are billed to a service address in Pennsylvania are taxable for gross receipts tax purposes even if the messages end or begin in a foreign country or political subdivision thereof. For gross receipts tax purposes, the phrase "transmitted in interstate commerce" means between Pennsylvania and any other state of the United States or possess of the United States, and any foreign country or political subdivision thereof. See *Corporation Tax Bulletin 2005-01*.

• *Electric light, water power, and hydroelectric utilities*

The following utilities are also subject to the gross receipts tax [72 P.S. § 8101(b)]:

(1) Electric light companies, water power companies, and hydroelectric companies (a) incorporated or organized by or under any law of Pennsylvania or (b) organized or incorporated by any other state or the United States or any foreign government if they are doing business in Pennsylvania; and

(2) Limited partnerships, associations, joint-stock associations, copartnerships, person, or persons engaged in electric light and power business, water power business, and hydroelectric business in Pennsylvania.

In *American Electric Power Service Corp. v. Cmwlth.*, 184 A.3d 1031 (Pa. Commw. 2018), the Commonwealth Court *en banc* affirmed the decision of a panel of the court which had considered the effects of the Electricity Generation Customer Choice and Competition Act ("EGCCA"). In 1996, the EGCCA was signed into law and allowed consumers to purchase electricity from any supplier and have that electricity delivered by the local utility in the purchasing customer's area. Companies like American Electric Power ("AEP") were, thus, permitted to make sales of electricity in Pennsylvania even though they were not registered as public utilities. AEP sold electricity on a wholesale basis to the Letterkenny Industrial Development Authority ("LIDA"). LIDA was formed in 1997 under the Pennsylvania Economic Development Financing Law when the Letterkenny Army Depot was closed by Franklin County. AEP first argued that it was not subject to the gross receipts tax because it was not a public utility and was not subject to the jurisdiction of the Pennsylvania Public Utility Commission. In the alternative, AEP argued that it was entitled to the resale exemption for the sales for resale to LIDA.

The Commonwealth Court determined that the licensure of a seller of electricity from the Pennsylvania Public Utility Commission was not determinative as to whether a business was engaged in the electric light business and, therefore, subject to the gross receipts tax relying on *Hanley & Byrd v. Cmwlth*, 590 A.2d 1382 (Pa. Commw. 1991). *Hanley & Bird* determined that the function a taxpayer performs, rather that PUC jurisdiction, gives rise to application of the tax. The taxpayer was an electric distribution company because the EGCCA provides that the phrase "engaged in electric light and power business" used in the gross receipts tax includes the direct or indirect engaging in business for the purpose of establishing or maintaining a market in the sales of electric energy. The Commonwealth Court also found that the resale exemption was not applicable. LIDA was found to be a political instrumentality of the Commonwealth. Thus, it was not a private corporation and not subject to the gross receipts tax itself. Because LIDA was not subject to the tax, the resale exemption could not be applicable to AEP.

Taxpayer (Solar), a wholly owned subsidiary of Caterpillar, Inc. (Caterpillar), was a worldwide designer and manufacturer of gas turbine engines. Solar also operated an electricity generation project in York County (its only electricity generation project) that provided Caterpillar with electricity for its York County plant. The electricity generated by Solar was sold to Caterpillar at cost. Solar contended that § 1101(b) of the Tax Reform Code [72 P.S. § 8101(b)] applied only to public utilities and that, since it was not a public utility, it was not subject to the gross receipts tax. The Commonwealth Court, however, concluded that § 1101(b) of the Tax Reform Code [72 P.S. § 8101(b)]is unambiguous and by its plain language expressly imposes the tax upon *all entities* that are "engaged in electric light and power business" and receive revenue from "the sale of electric energy." Because all such entities (including private electricity producers) are subject to the tax, Solar's alternative arguments that it was exempt because its sales of electricity represented only a *de minimis* portion of its business operation and/or because it made no profit on its sale of electricity to its parent company were also rejected by the Court [*Solar Turbines Inc. v. Cmwlth.*, 816 A.2d 362 (Pa.Commw. 2003)].

• *Managed care organizations*

Effective October 1, 2009, managed care organizations doing business in Pennsylvania are subject to the gross receipts tax on receipts from a Medicaid managed care contract with the Department of Public Welfare. The tax also applies to a Medicaid managed care organization, as defined in §1903(m)(1)(A) of the Social Security Act [42 U.S.C. § 1396b(m)(1)(A]; to a county Medicaid managed care organization; and to a permitted assignee of a Medicaid managed care contract. [72 P.S. §8101 (b.1)].

• *Exempt companies*

Motor vehicle carriers: Motor vehicle carriers are exempt from the gross receipts tax. Prior to 1998, motor vehicle carriers were subject to a separate gross receipts tax, but the motor vehicle carriers gross receipts tax was repealed in 1998.

Railroads: Railroads have been specifically exempt from the gross receipts tax since 1995.

Internet access: Gross receipts derived from the sale of access to the Internet made to the ultimate consumer are exempt from the gross receipts tax.

• *Taxable transactions of other utilities*

Motor vehicles carriers, railroads, and sales of internet access companies are the only companies specifically exempt from the gross receipts tax [72 P.S. §8101(a)]. However, certain *transactions* of other utilities are excluded from the tax base. These are explained at ¶2403.

Payphone Service Providers

Gross receipts of a payphone service provider derived from providing payphone service through payphone service provider access lines (dialtone lines) are not subject to the Gross Receipts Tax ("GRT") imposed by 72 P.S. §§8101-8103. However, a payphone service provider that also engages in business as an interexchange reseller (as defined in 52 Pa. Code §§63.112 and 63.113) and acquires interexchange telephone service capacity to sell telecommunications services to retail consumers is subject to the gross receipts tax on the gross receipts derived from its interexchange reseller operations.

Gross receipts of LECs, CLECs and any other similar providers from the provision of pay telephone lines to payphone service providers are not eligible for the resale exemption [*Corporation Tax Bulletin 2005-02*, Pennsylvania Department of Revenue, October 11, 2005].

This bulletin implements a global settlement agreement of litigation entered into by the Office of Attorney General. The policy stated in this bulletin will be changed only if the Office of Attorney General determines that the agreement is in conflict with subsequent changes in case or statutory law.

¶2403 Tax Rate and Base

• *Tax rate*

General rate: Except for electric light companies, water power companies, and hydroelectric companies, the gross receipts tax is levied at the rate of 50 mills (a tax of 45 mills with a surtax equal to five mills) on each dollar of the gross receipts [72 P.S. §8101(a)].

Electric light, water power, and hydroelectric companies: The tax basic rate on electric light companies, water power companies, and hydroelectric companies is 44 mills per dollar of gross receipts [72 P.S. §8101(b)]. Prior to January 1, 2002, the Secretary of Revenue, however, was required to adjust the basic rate and publish the revenue neutral reconciliation (RNR) rate in the *Pennsylvania Bulletin* by October 1 of each year. The RNR rate for 2000 was 0.006, making the combined rate 0.050, rather than 0.044. The RNR rate for 2001 was negative (-0.001), making the combined rate 0.043, rather than 0.044. The rate for utilities other than electric distribution companies and electric generation suppliers, however, remained at 0.050. The 2002 RNR rate was 0.015 and was made permanent for periods beginning January 1, 2003 and thereafter. [72 P.S. § 8101.2]

• *Managed care organizations*

Effective October 1, 2009, managed care organizations are subject to tax at the rate of 59 mills on receipts from a Medicaid managed care contract with the Department of Public Welfare.

• *Revenue neutral reconciliation*

When the restructuring of the electric industry was implemented, the Pennsylvania General Assembly, expressing its intention not to cause a shift in proportional tax obligations among customer classes or individual electric distribution companies, established the revenue replacement mechanism known as "revenue neutral reconciliation" (RNR) to adjust the base rate on sales of electric energy [66 Pa.C.S. § 2810(a)]. The RNR is imposed on the gross receipts of the following:

(1) Electric distribution companies and electric generation suppliers [66 Pa.C.S. § 2810(b)1].

(2) Municipality-owned or municipality-operated public utilities or public utility service furnished by any municipality. Gross receipts are exempt from the tax to the extent that gross receipts are derived from sales of electric energy inside the limits of the municipality owning or operating the public utility or furnishing the public utility service [66 Pa.C.S. § 2810(b)2].

(3) Electric cooperatives owning or operating a public utility or furnishing a public utility service. Gross receipts are exempt to the extent that they are derived from sales for resale or sales of electric energy within the limits of the cooperatives' service territories [66 Pa.C.S. § 2810(b)3].

Electric Generation Suppliers

Electric generation suppliers are excluded from the definition of "public utility" in the Pennsylvania Public Utility Code [66 Pa.C.S. §§ 101 *et seq.*] except for the limited purposes described in § 2809 (relating to regulatory expense assessments) and § 2810 (relating to revenue neutral reconciliation) of the Public Utility Code [66 Pa.C.S. § 102(2)(vi)]. See *PPL Energyplus, LLC v. Cmwlth.*, Pa.Commw., No. 525 M.D. 2002, June 6, 2002.

Gross receipts for RNR purposes: For purposes of the RNR the term "gross receipts" means the gross receipts from the retail sales of electric energy as defined in 72 P.S. § 8101(b) [66 Pa.C.S. § 2810(n)].

Negative RNR rates: If the RNR rate is negative, a credit equal to the negative tax rate multiplied by the taxable gross receipts for that tax year is allowed against the taxpayer's liability for any tax imposed for that year under 72 P.S. § 8101(b) or (f) [66 Pa.C.S. § 2810(c)5]. The RNR rate for 2001 was –0.001. Therefore, a taxpayer's effective combined rate for the year was 0.043 rather than 0.044. Note, however, that the 2002 rate of 0.015 is now permanent [72 P.S. § 8101.2].

The tax base (gross receipts) depends on the form of company, as explained below. In any case where the works of a company are operated by another company, the gross receipts tax is apportioned between the lessor and the lessee according to the terms of their respective leases or agreements. Pennsylvania looks first to the operator of the works for payment [72 P.S. § 8101(e)].

¶2403

• *Tax base—"gross receipts" defined*

Generally: Except for electric light companies, water power companies, and hydroelectric companies, the gross receipts tax is imposed upon each dollar of the gross receipts of the corporation, company or association, limited partnership, joint-stock association, copartnership, person or persons, received from the following [72 P.S. §8101(a)]:

(1) Passengers, baggage, oil, and freight transported wholly within Pennsylvania. The Dauphin County Court (predecessor of the Commonwealth Court) has held that the transportation of U.S. mail is exempt [*Cmwlth. v. Lehigh Valley Railroad Co.*, 4 Dauph 174 (1901)].

(2) Telegraph or telephone messages transmitted wholly within Pennsylvania and telegraph or telephone messages transmitted in interstate commerce if (a) the messages originate or terminate in Pennsylvania and (b) the charges for the messages are billed to a service address in Pennsylvania, except gross receipts derived from the following:

(i) The sales of access to the Internet, as set forth in the Pennsylvania sales and use tax statutes (Article II of the Tax Reform Code), made to the ultimate consumer.

(ii) The sales for resale to persons, partnerships, associations, corporations, or political subdivisions subject to the gross receipts tax imposed upon gross receipts derived from such resale of telecommunications services, including the following:

(a) Telecommunications exchange access to interconnect with a local exchange carrier's network.

(b) Network elements on an unbundled basis.

(c) Sales of telecommunications services to interconnect with providers of mobile telecommunications services.

Note: For discussion of allowable credit against the tax, see ¶2404.

(3) Mobile telecommunications services sourced to Pennsylvania based on the place of primary use standard set forth in the Mobile Telecommunications Sourcing Act (4 U.S.C. §117), except gross receipts derived from the following:

(a) The sales of access to the Internet (as set forth in the sales and use tax statutes), made to the ultimate consumer.

(b) The sales for resale to persons, partnerships, associations, corporations, or political subdivisions subject to the gross receipts tax on gross receipts derived from the resale of mobile telecommunications services, including sales of mobile telecommunications services to interconnect with providers of telecommunications services.

Note: For discussion of allowable credit against the tax, see ¶2404. The Department has issued a Corporate Tax Bulletin regarding the payment of gross receipts taxes by mobile telecommunications companies. Corporation Tax Bulletin 123—February 1, 2004, updated November 26, 2013. See also Corporation Tax Bulletin 2018-04 (dated August 20, 2018) which provides a general discussion of the application of the gross receipts tax in regard to telephone and mobile telecommunications providers and clarifications of the tax in light of *Verizon Pennsylvania, Inc. v. Cmwlth*, 127 A.3d 745 (Pa. 2015). The Bulletin also provides a sampling of sales of services and equipment that give rise to taxable receipts, and a detailed list of authorized deductions.

¶2403

Electric light, water power, and hydroelectric companies: The gross receipts tax on electric utility companies, water power companies, and hydroelectric companies is imposed on each dollar of the gross receipts received from the following [72 P.S. §8101(b)]:

(1) Sales of electric energy within Pennsylvania, except gross receipts derived from the sales for resale of electric energy to persons, partnerships, associations, corporations or political subdivisions subject to the tax imposed by this subsection upon gross receipts derived from such resale.

(2) Sales of electric energy produced in Pennsylvania and made outside of Pennsylvania in a state that has taken action since December 21, 1977, which results in higher costs for electric energy produced in that state and sold in Pennsylvania unless the action that was taken after December 21, 1977, is rescinded according to the required formula.

- *Itemization of gross receipts tax*

Interexchange telecommunications carriers may surcharge and disclose as a separate line item on a customer's bill all gross receipts taxes imposed on interexchange telecommunications carriers services performed wholly within Pennsylvania [72 P.S. §8101(i)(1)].

- *Telephone operators*

Taxable gross receipts will include receipts from the provision of private telephone lines and directory assistance charges, but not receipts from non-recurring service charges such as telephone line installation, moving telephone lines and repairs of telephone lines. *Verizon Pennsylvania, Inc. v. Commonwealth,* 72 A.3d 799 (Pa.Cmwlth. 2013).

- *Natural gas companies*

The sale of natural gas is not subject to the gross receipts tax [§7, Act 21 of 1999].

- *Electric light, water power, and hydroelectric companies*

These companies pay tax on gross receipts from sales of energy in Pennsylvania except those specifically exempt (see below) [72 P.S. §8101(b)(1)]. Sales of electric energy produced in Pennsylvania and sold outside Pennsylvania in any state that has taken action that results in higher costs for electric energy produced in that state and sold in Pennsylvania, unless that action has been rescinded, are subject to the tax. Out-of-state sales of electric energy in such states are apportioned to Pennsylvania by multiplying gross receipts from such states by a fraction, the numerator of which is the producer's operating and maintenance expenses in Pennsylvania and depreciation attributable to property in Pennsylvania and the denominator of which is the producer's total operating and maintenance expenses and depreciation [72 P.S. §8101(b)(2)]. These are the only out-of-state sales that are taxable; all others are exempt. Electric cooperative corporations that provide generation electric service at retail to persons outside their service territory are subject to the gross receipts tax to the extent of sales outside their service territory (effective January 1, 1997) [15 Pa.C.S. §7406(c)(2)].

Late Payments

Gross receipts from late payment charges imposed by Pennsylvania Power & Light Co. on customers who had failed to pay their electric bills in a timely manner were properly included in the gross receipts tax base pursuant to 72 P.S. §8101(b) [*Pennsylvania Power & Light Co. v. Cmwlth.,* 668 A.2d 620 (Pa.Commw. 1995)].

Exempt energy sales: The following gross receipts from the sale of electricity are exempt:

(1) Sales for resale of electric energy to persons, partnerships, associations, corporations, or political subdivisions that are also subject to tax on gross receipts on the sale of electricity [72 P.S. § 8101(b)(1)].

(2) Sales of electric energy produced in Pennsylvania and made outside of Pennsylvania in a state that has taken action since December 21, 1977, which result in higher costs for electric energy produced in that state and sold in Pennsylvania but has rescinded that action according to the statutory formula [72 P.S. § 8101(b)(2)].

(3) Certain receipts of nuclear generating facilities, as follows:

(a) The net increase in gross receipts resulting from recovery from customers of the costs of purchasing additional energy required by physical or legal inability to operate a nuclear generating facility as a result of an accident or natural disaster causing material damage and causing a facility and/or another facility located immediately adjacent to be removed from the rate base for a period exceeding 25 months. The net increase will be determined by the Public Utility Commission upon request by the Department of Revenue [72 P.S. § 8101(g)(1)].

(b) Recovery from customers of costs incurred in connection with the cleanup and decontamination of a nuclear generating facility that has experienced a major accident or natural disaster resulting in removal from the electric light company's rate base [72 P.S. § 8101(g)(2)].

(c) Recovery from customers of costs for amortization of investments in a nuclear generating facility whose removal from the rate base of an electric light company has been proved by the Public Utility Commission on account of a major accident or natural disaster [72 P.S. § 8101(g)(3)].

¶2404 Credits Against the Tax

Eligible companies may claim the job creation tax credit. This credit is explained at ¶1007.

• *Telegraph or telephone companies or providers of mobile telecommunications services*

Telegraph or telephone companies or providers of mobile telecommunications services that pay a gross receipts tax to another state on messages or services that are subject to the Pennsylvania gross receipts tax are entitled to a credit against the Pennsylvania gross receipts tax. This credit, however, cannot exceed the amount of the Pennsylvania gross receipts tax on these messages or services [72 P.S. § 8101(a.1)].

• *Resource manufacturing tax credit*

Eligible companies may claim the resource manufacturing tax credit, discussed at ¶1021.

• *Historic preservation incentive tax credit*

This credit is discussed at ¶1022.

¶2405 Reports and Payment of Tax

Gross receipts tax annual reports (prepared on a calendar-year basis) must be filed on or before March 15 of each year following the end of the tax year. The tax is due with the return [72 P.S. § 8101(c)]. The time for filing annual reports may be extended, but there are no extensions for the filing of tentative reports or reports of estimated tax [72 P.S. § 8101(c)].

¶2404

Credit

A credit against the sales and use tax on telecommunications services paid by a call center may be granted to the call center for gross receipts tax paid by a telephone company on the receipts derived from the sale of incoming and outgoing interstate telecommunications services to the call center. See discussion of call center at ¶ 513.

¶2405A Method of Accounting

Effective for tax years beginning on or after January 1, 2011, taxpayers subject to the gross receipts tax must file their Pennsylvania gross receipts tax report using the same method of accounting used by the taxpayer to file their reports with the Federal Energy Regulatory Commission (FERC) or the Federal Communications Commission (FCC). Taxpayers who have no regulatory requirement to the FERC or the FCC must file their Pennsylvania gross receipts tax using the same method of accounting used by the taxpayer to file their reports with the Pennsylvania Public Utility Commission (PUC). Taxpayers who have no regulatory reporting requirement to the FERC, the FCC, or the PUC must file their Pennsylvania gross receipts tax report using the same method of accounting used to file their Federal income tax reports with the United States Internal Revenue Service [Pennsylvania Department of Revenue, *Corporation Tax Bulletin 2011-02*, July 20, 2011].

• *Bulletin requires change in accounting method*

If *Corporation Tax Bulletin 2011-02* requires the taxpayer to change the accounting method for reporting Pennsylvania gross receipts tax, the following rules apply for the transition year:

(1) If the taxpayer is changing from the cash method to the accrual method, the taxpayer must include all receipts previously accrued that have not been previously reported on its Pennsylvania gross receipts tax reports.

(2) If the taxpayer is changing from the accrual method to the cash method, the taxpayer must reduce its receipts that that amount equal to the receipts previously accrued but not received until the transition year.

AUTHORS' COMMENT

There is no provision to abate or waive underpayment penalties that could result from the change.

¶2406 Estimated Tax

All taxpayers subject to the gross receipts tax must make payments of estimated gross receipts tax during their taxable year [72 P.S. § 10003.2(a)(5)]. Payment of the estimated gross receipts tax must be made in a single installment on or before the 15th day of March of the taxable year. The remaining portion of the gross receipts tax due, if any, must be paid by the due date of the annual report without reference to any extension of time for filing [72 P.S. § 10003.2(c)(5)].

• *Underpayment of estimated tax*

Procedures for underpayment of estimated tax are the same as those explained in ¶918.

• *Estimated tax payments of mobile telecommunications services*

For purposes of the estimated tax requirements, the "safe harbor base year" tax amount for providers of mobile telecommunications services is the amount that would have been required to be paid by the taxpayer if the taxpayer had been subject to the gross receipts tax [72 P.S. § 8101(c.1)].

Penalty for substantial underpayment of initial estimated gross receipts tax: If the amount of estimated gross receipts tax paid by a provider of mobile telecommunications services in the first year it is required to pay estimated tax is underpaid, a penalty is imposed in the amount of 5% of the underpayment per month for the period of the underpayment (up to a maximum of 25% of the underpayment) [72 P.S. § 8101(k)].

¶2407 Public Utility Exemption

The law provides that the term "sale at retail" shall not include the rendition of services or the transfer of tangible personal property (including, but not limited to, machinery and equipment and parts thereof), and supplies to be used or consumed by the purchaser *directly* in the producing, delivering, or rendering of a public utility service or in constructing, reconstructing, remodeling, repairing, or maintaining facilities that are *directly used* in producing, delivering, or rendering a public utility service [72 P.S. § 7201(k)(8)(c)]. The public utility exemption is explained at ¶713.

¶2408 Municipal Utilities

The gross receipts tax on utilities applies to municipalities. Gross receipts derived from (1) municipality-owned public utilities; (2) municipality-operated public utilities; and (3) municipality-furnished public utility services are taxable, except that gross receipts are exempt to the extent derived from business done inside the limits of a municipality owning or operating a public utility or furnishing public utility [72 P.S. § 8101(f)].

¶2409 Procedures, Enforcement, and Penalties

The gross receipts tax provisions incorporate, by reference, the settlement, enforcement, interest, and penalty provisions of the corporate net income tax law [72 P.S. § 7904]. These are explained in Chapter 12.

TAXES ON UTILITIES

CHAPTER 25
PUBLIC UTILITY REALTY TAX (PURTA)

¶2501 Overview

The public utility realty tax (PURTA) is imposed on the taxable value of a public utility's utility realty for the taxable year (see ¶2502 for definition of these terms). PURTA was first imposed by the Act of March 10, 1970, P.L. 168. This original act was repealed in 1970 [Act of July 4, 1970, P.L. 60], and the PURTA provisions (revised) were reenacted as Article XI-A [72 P.S. § 8101-A *et seq.*], which is the current statutory authority for the tax. The Commonwealth imposes PURTA in lieu of local real estate taxes and distributes the local realty tax equivalent (see ¶2503) to local taxing authorities. Payment of, or any exemption from, the public utility realty tax and the prescribed distribution to local taxing authorities is in lieu of local taxes upon utility realty, as contemplated by Article VIII, § 4, of the Constitution of Pennsylvania [72 P.S. § 8104-A(a)].

Public utilities are subject to both the gross receipts tax (discussed in Chapter 24) and PURTA. The Pennsylvania Supreme Court has held that the imposition of a gross receipts tax on utility companies does not preclude imposition of PURTA—a separate tax on realty in lieu of local property taxes [*American Telephone and Telegraph Co.*, 337 A.2d 844 (1975)].

¶2502 Base

The base for the computation of PURTA is the taxable value of a public utility's utility realty for the taxable year [72 P.S. § 8102-A(c)].

• *Public utility defined*

A public utility (which is not limited to corporations) is any person, partnership, association, corporation, or other entity furnishing public utility service under the jurisdiction of the Pennsylvania Public Utility Commission or the corresponding regulatory agency of any other state or of the United States on December 31 of the taxable year and any electric cooperative corporation authority furnishing public utility service on December 31 of the taxable year [72 P.S. § 8101-A(2)]. Nonprofit electric cooperative corporations that provide electricity only to their members are not subject to PURTA [*Adams Electric Cooperative, Inc. v. Cmwlth.*, Docket No. 54 F.R. 2000 (July 16, 2004), *aff'd*, Pa.Sup.Ct., No. 213 MAP 2004 (November 23, 2005)].

Exemptions: The following entities are specifically exempt from the definition of public utility [72 P.S. § 8101-A(2)]:

(1) Any public utility furnishing public utility sewage services.

(2) A municipality or municipality authority furnishing public utility services [72 P.S. § 8101-A(2)].

¶2502

Equitable Owner of Railroad Property Not a Public Utility

Consolidated Coal Company (Consol) owned various coal properties in Greene County. Consol was a client of Monongahela Railway Company (Monongahela), a common carrier. Consol acquired property between Monongahela's main line and its proposed coal mine in Richhill Township for a railroad right-of-way and agreed with Mononga-hela that the property would be titled in Monongahela's name. PURTA's exclusion of railway right-of-way property only applies to "utility realty." Therefore, the Commonwealth Court held that, since equitable title was held by Consol (not a public utility), the property was not exempt as a railway right-of-way [*Consolidated Coal Co. v. Board of Assessment Appeals of Greene County*, 617 A.2d 858 (Pa.Commw. 1992)].

• *Utility realty defined*

"Utility realty" means land, together with the following [72 P.S. § 8101-A(3)]:

(1) Buildings.

(2) Towers.

(3) Smokestacks.

(4) Dams.

(5) Dikes.

(6) Canals.

(7) Cooling towers.

(8) Storage tanks.

(9) Reactor structures.

(10) Pump houses.

(11) Supporting foundations.

(12) Enclosing structures.

(13) Supporting structures.

(14) Containment structures.

(15) Reactor containment outer shells.

(16) Reactor containment vessels.

(17) Turbine buildings.

(18) Recovery tanks.

(19) Solid waste area enclosures.

(20) Primary auxiliary buildings.

(21) Containment auxiliary safeguard structures.

(22) Fuel buildings.

(23) Decontamination buildings.

(24) All other structures and enclosures that are physically affixed to the land, no matter how such structures and enclosures are designated and without regard to their classification for local real estate taxation purposes.

(25) Land and improvements to land that meet the following requirements:

(a) They are located in Pennsylvania at the end of the taxable year.

(b) They are indispensable to the generation of electricity.

(c) They are owned by a public utility or its affiliate either directly or through a subsidiary.

¶2502

(d) They are used, or in the course of development and construction for used, in whole or in part, in the furnishing (including producing, storing, distributing, or transporting) of public utility service.

(e) They are not subject to local real estate taxation under any law in effect on April 23, 1968.

Exempt property: The following specified properties are exempt from PURTA [72 P.S. § 8101-A(3)];

(1) Easements or similar interests.

(2) Certain railroad property, as follows:

(a) Railroad beds or rails.

(b) Land owned or used by a railroad as a right-of-way for a rail line, including superstructures on the land. This subclause does not include stations, buildings, warehouses, shops, engine houses, plants or miscellaneous structures, or the appurtenant land.

(3) Pole, transmission tower, pipe, rail, or other lines (whether or not attached to the land or to any structure or enclosure that is physically affixed to the land.

Taxability Determined Solely by Statutory Definition

The term "utility realty" is specifically defined, and it is the express intent of the General Assembly that the question of whether or not property is subject to PURTA be determined solely by the application of the term "utility realty" as defined in the Tax Reform Code [72 P.S. § 8108-A(2)].

• *Scope of exemption*

A railroad public utility was denied a real estate tax exemption for a parcel of property that was used for moving vehicles to and from a temporary storage location. The railroad, as such, could operate its business without the subject property and, therefore, was not a necessary part of the railroad's operations. *CSX Transportation, Inc. v. Delaware County Board of Assessment Appeals*, 104 A.3d 612 (2014).

In *Lehigh Valley Rail Mgmt. LLC v. County of Northampton*, 178 A.3d 950 (Pa. Commw 2018), the Commonwealth Court remanded an appeal to the trial court to identify the portions of an 85 acre tract that were subject to the Public Utility Realty Tax Act Tax ("PURTA Tax"). PURTA subjects Pennsylvania utility real property to the PURTA tax instead of the local real property tax. PURTA exempts certain items from its reach as taxable property. Any exempted property does not then become part of the formula for the distribution of PURTA taxes to localities. The 85 acres at issue were used by the taxpayer generally for intermodal facilities. Intermodal facilities enable the railroad to move rail-ready containers from a train to a truck, a truck to a train, or between trains. The court ruled that such facilities are indeed taxable for PURTA purposes because such facilities are part of the real estate necessary for the operation of the railroad on a 24-hour basis. However, certain portions of the 85 acres were used for a driveway, parking lot and an office trailer. The court directed the lower court to identify and quantify the acreage that was devoted to such purposes, and to eliminate those portions from the PURTA exemption.

• *Taxable value defined*

"State taxable value" means current market value calculated by adjusting the assessed value for county real estate tax purposes for the common level ratio of assessed values to market values of the county as established by the State Tax Equalization Board after July of the taxable year. Common level ratios are discussed at ¶3507. While an assessment appeal is pending, "state taxable value" means the amount that the public utility has stipulated or alleged as the current market value for the current year [72 P.S. § 8101-A(4)].

Assessed value determined locally: Elected and appointed assessors of real property are required to assess, value, and enroll all utility realty in the same manner prescribed for the assessment, valuation, and enrollment of real estate. However, assessors must enroll utility realty separately from the other real estate of a public utility, affiliate, or subsidiary [72 P.S. § 8105-A(a)].

¶ 2503 Rate

PURTA is imposed on the state taxable value of utility realty at a variable rate determined annually by the Secretary of Revenue. In addition to the basic variable rate, an additional tax rate (see below) is applied to the tax base for transfer to the Public Transportation Assistance Fund [72 P.S. § 8112-A; Act 46 of 2003 (H.B. 200), § 33(12.1)]. A public utility surcharge is also applied if PURTA refunds exceed $5,000,000 (see ¶ 2504).

• *Millage rate*

PURTA is imposed at a variable rate. The Department of Revenue sets the rate annually in order to raise an amount of revenue equal to the distribution of the realty tax equivalent (RTE) to the local taxing authorities. The Department must calculate the millage rate for the taxable year on or before August 1 of the taxable year and notify the public utilities of the rate and the state taxable value of its utility realty [72 P.S. § 8102-A].

Realty tax equivalent: "Realty tax equivalent" is the total amount of real estate taxes that a local taxing authority could have imposed on utility realty for its fiscal year beginning in the taxable year but for the imposition of PURTA. Unless otherwise provided, the "realty tax equivalent" is the real estate property tax rate multiplied by the assessed valuation of utility realty [72 P.S. § 8101-A(6)].

• *Additional rate*

An additional 7.6 mills is levied on state taxable value for deposit into the Public Transportation Assistance Fund [72 P.S. § 8112-A].

¶ 2504 PURTA Gross Receipts Surcharge

If PURTA refunds exceed $5 million in a fiscal year, an annual surcharge may be imposed on utilities gross receipts (except gross receipts from providing mobile telecommunications services and telegraph or telephone messages transmitted in interstate commerce) [72 P.S. § 8111-A].

• *Surcharge reports*

If a surcharge is imposed for a calendar year, utilities subject to the surcharge must file a report (RCT-127) by March 15 of the calendar year [72 P.S. § 8111-A(e)]. Report requirements for the PURTA gross receipts surcharge are consistent with the requirements for filing of the gross receipts tax. See ¶ 2405.

• *Rate*

The surcharge rate is the total reduction in liabilities reported to the Department of Revenue divided by the total amount of taxable gross receipts reported to the Department for the prior calendar year. The Department determines the rate and must publish it in the form of a notice in the *Pennsylvania Bulletin* by October 1 of each year [72 P.S. § 8111-A(d)]. The PURTA surcharge rate is determined by the Secretary of Revenue, and the Secretary is required under 72 P.S. § 8111-A(d) to publish the surcharge rate in the form of a notice in the *Pennsylvania Bulletin* by October 1 [72 P.S. § 1111-1(d)]. The PURTA surcharge rate for tax years 2012-2019 is zero mills [44 Pa.B. 5741].

¶ 2503

Surcharge Conditional

Note that the PURTA gross receipts surcharge is conditional; it will be imposed only if the reduction of PURTA liabilities for a prior fiscal year exceeds $5,000,000.

• *Estimated payments of surcharge*

A taxpayer subject to the public utility realty surcharge must make payments of estimated public utility realty surcharge during its taxable year [72 P.S. § 10003.2(a)(6)]. "Estimated public utility realty surcharge" means the amount that the taxpayer estimated as the amount of public utility realty surcharge for the taxable year [72 P.S. § 10003.2(b)(4.5)]. Payment of the estimated public utility realty surcharge must be made in a single installment on or before March 15 of the taxable year. The remaining portion of the public utility realty surcharge due (if any) must be paid on the date the report is required to be filed without reference to any extension of time for filing the report [72 P.S. § 10003.2(c)(6)].

¶2505 Reports and Payment of Tax

A tentative payment and the utility realty report are due on May 1 of the taxable year [72 P.S. § 8102-A(c)]. A final payment is due on September 15 of the taxable year. A payment of PURTA tentative tax must include a report of the amount and manner of computation of the state taxable value of all utility realty and adjustments for the immediate preceding year; and the report must be in the manner prescribed by the Department under oath or affirmation of the owner or responsible officer of the public utility [72 P.S. § 8102-A(f)].

• *Tentative tax*

The PURTA tentative tax, which is due on or before May 1 of the taxable year, is lesser of the following:

    (1) The tax for the second preceding year.

    (2) An amount computed under the law applicable to the taxable year and the estimated state taxable value of the utility's utility realty for the taxable year at the rate applicable to the second preceding taxable year.

Amount of Tentative Tax

In no case can the tentative tax be less than 90% of the final amount of tax due.

• *Filing extensions*

The law makes no provisions for extension of time for filing PURTA returns but seems to imply that the Department of Revenue may grant extensions [72 P.S. § 8102-A(e)]. The current policy of the Department of Revenue is to grant 60-day extensions if requested.

¶2506 Administration, Enforcement, Interest, and Penalties

• *Administration*

The Public Utilities Realty Tax (commonly called PURTA) is administered by the Pennsylvania Department of Revenue [72 P.S. § 8103-A(a)]. PURTA regulations are contained in Chapter 159 of Title 61 of the Pennsylvania Code. PURTA is in addition to the gross receipts tax on public utilities [72 P.S. § 8108-A(a)].

• *Enforcement*

The Department of Revenue makes all inquiries, determinations, and assessments of tax, interest, additions, and penalties necessary to enforce the public utility realty tax. The provisions of 72 P.S. §§ 7337—7345 apply to the assessment and collection of the public utility realty tax. A public utility cannot raise a defense or objection in a proceeding that could have been presented as part of an administrative or judicial remedy under 72 P.S. § 8105-A or § 8109-A. The amount of any tax or penalty imposed under PURTA will be assessed within three (3) years after the close of the taxable year or within one year of a final determination resulting from the public utility's appeal under 72 P.S. § 8105-A.

• *Interest and penalties*

If the tax is not paid by the due date, or within any extension granted by the Department of Revenue, the unpaid tax bears interest at a prescribed rate (see ¶ 4612). In addition, the taxpayer incurs a penalty of 5% of the amount of the tax. The penalty may be waived or abated, in whole or in part, by the Department unless the public utility has acted in bad faith, negligently, or with intent to defraud. If tentative tax is not paid by the due date, the unpaid tentative tax bears interest for the period of underpayment, but not beyond September 15 of the year following the close of the taxable year [72 P.S. § 8102-A(e)].

¶ 2507 Refunds and Rebates

If the Department of Revenue determines that the amount of tax due from a public utility is less than the amount paid by the public utility (and the public utility is satisfied with the amount due), the excess will be credited to the public utility's account.

PURTA credit: If for a taxable year the total amount of tax collected exceeds the amount determined by the Department, the Department will compute the ratio (to four decimal places) that the amount of the excess bears to the total state taxable value of all utility realty and notify the reporting public utility of the ratio, and the State Treasurer will rebate the excess to the public utility as a credit to its account in an amount equal to the product of the ratio and the state taxable value of its utility realty. For interest purposes, any amount rebated is deemed to have been overpaid 75 days following the date of notice [72 P.S. § 8104-A(d)].

PART X

LIQUID FUELS TAXES

CHAPTER 26
LIQUID FUELS TAXES

¶2601	Scope of Chapter, Source of Authority, Definitions, and Administration
¶2602	Liquid Fuels and Fuels Tax
¶2603	Alternative Fuels Tax
¶2604	Oil Company Franchise Tax
¶2605	Motor Carriers Road Tax/IFTA

¶2601 Scope of Chapter, Source of Authority, Definitions, and Administration

There are four taxes pertaining to the use or purchase of motor fuels in Pennsylvania: (1) the liquid fuels and fuels tax; (2) the alternative fuels tax; (3) the oil company franchise tax; and (4) the motor carriers/IFTA tax. These taxes are known collectively as the "liquid fuels taxes." This chapter provides an overview of these four taxes.

Liquid Fuels vs. Fuels

The term "liquid fuels" does not have the same meaning as the term "fuels." See definitions below.

• *Source of authority—The Vehicle Code*

The enabling legislation for the four taxes discussed in this chapter is the Vehicle Code. Pennsylvania's Vehicle Code is Title 75 of the Pennsylvania Consolidated Statutes.

(1) *Liquid fuels and fuels tax:* Enabling legislation for this tax is Chapter 90 of the Vehicle Code. See ¶2602 for explanation of this tax.

(2) *Alternative fuels tax:* Enabling legislation for this tax is Chapter 90 of the Vehicle Code. See ¶2603 for explanation of this tax.

(3) *Oil company franchise tax:* Enabling legislation for this tax is Chapter 95 of the Vehicle Code. See ¶2604 for explanation of this tax.

(4) *Motor carriers road tax/IFTA:* Enabling legislation for this tax is Chapter 21 and Chapter 96 of the Vehicle Code. See ¶2605 for explanation of this tax.

• *Definition of terms*

Unless indicated otherwise by the context, the following words and phrases apply to all of the provisions of the Liquid Fuels and Fuels Tax Act [75 Pa.C.S. § 9002]:

Alternative fuels: Natural gas, compressed natural gas (CNG), liquid propane gas and liquified petroleum gas (LPG), alcohols, gasoline-alcohol mixtures containing at least 85% alcohol by volume, hydrogen, hythane, electricity, and any other fuel used to propel motor vehicles on the public highways that is not taxable as "fuels" or "liquid fuels."

¶2601

Alternative fuel dealer-user: Any person who delivers or places alternative fuels into the fuel supply tank or other device of a vehicle for use on the public highways.

Association: Any form of unincorporated enterprise owned by two or more persons (*e.g.,* partnership, limited partnership).

Average wholesale price: The average wholesale price per gallon of all taxable liquid fuels and fuels, excluding the federal excise tax and all liquid fuels taxes, as determined by the Department of Revenue for the 12-month period ending on the September 30 immediately prior to January 1 of the year for which the rate is to be set. The "average wholesale price" can never be less than 90¢ per gallon or more than $1.25 per gallon.

Cents per gallon equivalent basis: The average wholesale price per gallon multiplied by the decimal equivalent of any tax imposed by 75 Pa.C.S. § 9502 (*i.e.,* the oil company franchise tax), the product of which is rounded to the next highest tenth of a cent per gallon. The rate of tax is determined by the Department of Revenue on an annual basis beginning every January 1 and is published as a notice in the Pennsylvania Bulletin no later than the preceding December 15. If the oil company franchise tax rate changes, the Department of Revenue will predetermine the rate of tax as of the effective date of the change and give notice as soon as possible.

Corporation: A corporation or joint stock association organized under the laws of Pennsylvania, the United States, or any other state, territory, or foreign country or dependency.

Dealer: Any person engaged in the retail sale of liquid fuels or fuels.

Department: The Pennsylvania Department of Revenue.

Diesel fuel: Any liquid (other than liquid fuels) that is suitable for use as a fuel in a diesel-powered highway vehicle. The term "diesel fuel" includes kerosene.

Distributor: Any person that:

(1) Produces, refines, prepares, blends, distills, manufactures, or compounds liquid fuel or fuels in Pennsylvania for the person's use or for sale and delivery in Pennsylvania.

(2) Imports or causes to be imported from any other state or territory of the United States, or from a foreign country, liquid fuels or fuels for the person's use in Pennsylvania or for sale and delivery in and after reaching Pennsylvania, other than in the original package, receptacle, or container.

(3) Imports or causes to be imported from any other state or territory of the United States liquid fuels or fuels for the person's use in Pennsylvania or for sale and delivery in Pennsylvania after they have come to rest or storage in the other state or territory, whether or not in the original package, receptacle, or container.

(4) Purchases or receives liquid fuels or fuels in the original package, receptacle, or container in Pennsylvania for the person's use or for sale and delivery in Pennsylvania from any person who has imported them from a foreign country.

(5) Purchases or receives liquid fuels or fuels in the original package, receptacle, or container in Pennsylvania for the person's use in Pennsylvania or for sale and delivery in Pennsylvania from any person who has imported them from any other state or territory of the United States, if the liquid fuels or fuels have not, prior to purchase or receipt, come to rest or storage in Pennsylvania.

(6) Receives and uses or distributes liquid fuels or fuels in Pennsylvania on which the tax provided for by Chapter 90 of Title 75 of the Pennsylvania Consolidated States has not been previously paid.

¶2601

(7) Owns or operates aircraft, aircraft engines, or facilities for delivery of liquid fuels to aircraft or aircraft engines and elects, with the permission of the Secretary of Revenue, to qualify and obtain a permit as a distributor.

(8) Exports liquid fuels or fuels other than in the fuel supply tanks of motor vehicles.

Dyed diesel fuel: Any liquid (other than liquid fuels) that is suitable for use as a fuel in a diesel-powered highway vehicle and that is dyed pursuant to federal regulations issued under IRC § 4082 or that is a dyed fuel for purposes of IRC § 6715.

Export: Accountable liquid fuels or fuels delivered out of state by or for the seller constitutes an export by the seller. Accountable liquid fuels or fuels delivered out of state by or for the purchaser constitutes an export by the purchaser.

Fuels: Includes diesel fuel and all combustible gases and liquids used for the generation of power in aircraft or aircraft engines, or used in an internal combustion engine for the generation of power to propel vehicles on the public highways. The term does not include liquid fuels or dyed diesel fuels.

Gallon-equivalent basis: The amount of any alternative fuel as determined by the Department of Revenue to contain 114,500 btus. The rate of tax on the amount of each alternative fuel is the current liquid fuels tax and oil company franchise tax applicable to one gallon of gasoline.

Highway: Every way or place open to the use of the public, as a matter of right, for purposes of vehicular travel.

Import: Accountable liquid fuels or fuels delivered into Pennsylvania from out of state by or for the seller constitutes an import by the seller. Accountable liquid fuels or fuels delivered into Pennsylvania from out-of-state by or for the purchaser constitutes an import by the purchaser.

Liquid fuels: All products derived from petroleum, natural gas, coal, coal tar, vegetable ferments, and other oils. The term includes gasoline, naphtha, benzol, benzine, or alcohols, either alone or when blended or compounded, that are practically and commercially suitable for use in internal combustion engines for the generation of power or that are prepared, advertised, offered for sale or sold for sale for that purpose. The term does not include kerosene, fuel oil, gas oil, diesel fuel, tractor fuel by whatever trade name or technical name known having an initial boiling point of not less than 200 degrees Fahrenheit and of which not more than 95% has been recovered at 464 degrees Fahrenheit (ASTM Method D-86), liquefied gases that would not exist as liquids at a temperature of 60 degrees Fahrenheit and pressure of 14.7 pounds per square inch absolute, or naphthas and benzols and solvents sold for use for industrial purposes.

Magistrate: An officer of the minor judiciary, including a district judge.

Mass transportation systems: Persons subject to the jurisdiction of the Pennsylvania Public Utility Commission and municipality authorities that transport persons on schedule over fixed routes and derive 90% of their intrastate scheduled revenue from scheduled operations within the county in which they have their principal place of business or within contiguous counties.

Permit: A liquid fuels permit or a fuels permit.

Person: Every natural person, association, or corporation. Whenever used in any provision prescribing and imposing a fine or imprisonment, the term "person" includes partners or members of associations and officers of corporations.

Sale; sale and delivery: Includes invoicing or billing of liquid fuels or fuels free of tax as provided in 75 Pa.C.S. § 9005 (relating to taxpayer) from one distributor to another regardless of whether the purchasing distributor is an accommodation party for purposes of taking title or takes actual physical possession of the liquid fuels or fuels.

Secretary: The Secretary of Revenue of the Commonwealth of Pennsylvania.

Vehicle Code: Title 75 of the Pennsylvania Consolidated Statutes.

- *Administration*

The liquid fuels and fuels taxes are administered by the Department of Revenue, which has the authority to examine records, determine and redetermine taxes, and impose penalties and interest [75 Pa.C.S. §§ 9007 and 9008].

Payment by Electronic Funds Transfer

All four of the liquid fuels taxes are subject to the requirement to make payments by electronic fund transfer (EFT). See ¶ 4617.

¶ 2602   Liquid Fuels and Fuels Tax

Act 2013-89 Repeal

The Liquid Fuels and Fuels Tax was repealed on November 25, 2013 by Act 2013-89; however, liquid fuels and fuels (and their respective definitions) will remain subject to tax under the Oil Company Franchise Tax discussed below.

- *Imposition*

The liquid fuels and fuels tax was imposed on all liquid fuels and fuels used or sold and delivered by distributors in Pennsylvania [75 Pa.C.S. § 9004(a)] prior to 2014. The tax was imposed on the ultimate consumer, but the distributor was liable for collecting and remitting the tax [75 Pa.C.S. § 2004(g)]. The definitional terms remain effective for the other Pennsylvania taxes on fuel-related products.

- *Permit required*

A distributor may not engage in the use or sale and delivery of liquid fuels in Pennsylvania without a liquid fuels permit or engage in the use or sale and delivery of fuels within Pennsylvania without a fuels permit. For details on liquid fuels and fuels permits, see 75 Pa.C.S. § 9003.

Surety bond required: A permit will not be granted until a surety bond is filed, which is payable to the Commonwealth in an amount fixed by the Department of Revenue of at least $2,500 [75 Pa.C.S. § 2003(d)]. For more details on surety bonds, see 75 Pa.C.S. § 9003(d), (d.1), and (e).

Renewal of permits: Permits may be renewed annually, before June 1, by making an application to the Department of Revenue. Permit renewals will not be made until a new surety bond is filed [75 Pa.C.S. § 9003(f)].

- *Base*

"Liquid fuels" primarily include gasoline but also include products derived from petroleum, natural gas, coal, coal tar, vegetable ferments, and other oils [75 Pa.C.S. § 9002]. "Fuels" include diesel fuel and all other special fuels except dyed diesel fuel, liquid fuels, and alternative fuels [75 Pa.C.S. § 9002]. See "Definition of terms" in ¶ 2601 for complete definitions of "liquid fuels" and "fuels." Aviation gasoline and jet fuel are also taxed under the liquid fuels and fuels tax (see below), but they are imposed at a separate rate.

- *Exempt fuels and entities*

The following fuels are not taxable:

(1) Kerosene, fuel oil, gas oil, diesel fuels, and tractor fuel are specifically exempt from the definition of "liquid fuels" [75 Pa.C.S. § 9002]. See "Definition of terms" at ¶ 2601.

(2) Liquid fuels, fuels, or alternative fuels used or sold and delivered that are not within the taxing power of Pennsylvania under the Commerce Clause of the United States Constitution are exempt [75 Pa.C.S. § 9004(e)2.].

(3) Liquid fuels, fuels, and alternative fuels used as fuel in aircraft or aircraft engines are exempt from the liquid fuels and fuels tax, the oil company franchise tax, and the alternative fuels tax but are subject to the aviation gasoline tax [75 Pa.C.S. § 9004(e)3.].

(4) Liquid fuels, fuels, and alternative fuels delivered to the following entities are exempt:

(a) The federal government (on presentation to the Department of Revenue of an authorized federal government exemption certificate or other satisfactory evidence) [75 Pa.C.S. § 9004(e)1.].

(b) The Commonwealth of Pennsylvania [75 Pa.C.S. § 9004(e)4.].

(c) A political subdivision of the Commonwealth of Pennsylvania [75 Pa.C.S. § 9004(e)4.].

(d) A volunteer fire company [75 Pa.C.S. § 9004(e)4.].

(e) A volunteer ambulance service [75 Pa.C.S. § 9004(e)4.].

(f) A volunteer rescue squad [75 Pa.C.S. § 9004(e)4.].

(g) A second class county port authority [75 Pa.C.S. § 9004(e)4.].

(h) A nonpublic school not operated for profit that presents satisfactory evidence to the Department of Revenue [75 Pa.C.S. § 9004(e)4.].

- *Rates*

Liquid fuels and fuels tax rate: The liquid fuels and fuels tax was imposed at a permanent rate of 12¢ per gallon or fractional part thereof [75 Pa.C.S. § 9004(a)]. In addition to the permanent rate of 12¢, an oil company franchise tax (OFT) is imposed and collected on all gallons of liquid fuels and fuels on a cents-per-gallon equivalent basis [75 Pa.C.S. § 9004(b)]. The oil company franchise tax is discussed at ¶ 2604.

Aviation gasoline tax rate: In lieu of the liquid fuels and fuels tax, a separate rate is imposed and assessed upon (1) aviation gasoline and (2) all other liquid fuels used or sold and delivered by distributors within Pennsylvania for use as fuel in propeller-driven piston engine aircraft or aircraft engines [75 Pa.C.S. § 9004(c)(1)]. Consequently, these taxes survived the repeal of the liquid fuels tax and fuels tax. The aviation gasoline rate consists of the per gallon tax imposed by 75 Pa.C.S. § 9004(c)(1) and the per gallon additional tax imposed by Pa.C.S. § 6121(b). As limited by 74 Pa.C.S. § 6121(b), the combined rate of these two component taxes may never exceed 6¢ per gallon or be less than 3¢ per gallon [36 Pa.B. 7511]. The aviation gasoline rate for each succeeding calendar year is announced in the Pennsylvania Bulletin in December. The 2018 rate was $0.057 cents per gallon for aviation gasoline.

Jet fuels tax rate: In lieu of the liquid fuels and fuels tax, a separate rate is imposed on jet fuels used or sold and delivered by distributors within Pennsylvania for use as fuel in turbine-propeller jets, turbojets, and jet-driven aircraft, and aircraft engines [75 Pa.C.S. § 9004(c)(2)]. The rate for each succeeding calendar year is announced in the Pennsylvania Bulletin in December. The 2018 rate was $0.018 cents per gallon for jet fuel.

- *Oil company franchise tax (OFT) rate*

See ¶ 2604.

• *Reports and payment of tax*

On or before the 20th day of each month, distributors must file a report with the Department, under oath or affirmation, of the liquid fuels and fuels used or delivered within Pennsylvania during the preceding month. Payment of tax is due with the return. A distributor having more than one place of business in Pennsylvania must combine, in each report, the use or delivery of liquid fuels and fuels at all places of business [75 Pa.C.S. § 9006(a)].

• *Discounts*

If the distributor's report is filed and the tax paid on time, the distributor is entitled to a discount [75 Pa.C.S. § 9006(b)]. The amount of the discount is determined by the amount of the tax on liquid fuels and fuels (but not on the amount of the oil company franchise tax), as follows:

Amount of tax	Amount of discount
$50,000 or less	2.0%
More than $50,000 but not more than $75,000	1.5%
More than $75,000 but not more than $100,000	1.0%
More than $100,000	0.5%

Example: Alpha Motor Company had a total liquid fuels and fuels tax for the month of July of $110,000. This amount does not include any amount applicable to the oil company franchise tax. Alpha's allowable discount for July is $1,675 [2% of $50,000 + 1.5% of $25,000 + 1% of $25,000 + 0.5% of $10,000].

Online Reporting and Payment of Tax

The Secretary of Revenue has announced that registered distributors of liquid fuels now are able to file and pay their monthly Liquid Fuels and Fuels Taxes online with the Electronic Tax Information and Data Exchange System (e-TIDES). The site is available on the PA PowerPort site at www.state.pa.us. Liquid fuel distributors registered with e-TIDES can now log receipts and disbursements daily, as well as compile their monthly reports and schedules. After a filer's data are submitted, a filer will receive notification that its return has been sent. Distributors who are not registered with the e-TIDES program can obtain an electronic signature and register as a filer. The e-TIDES program is discussed in more detail at ¶ 4620. See also the discussion of the Electronic Funds Transfer (EFT) program at ¶ 4617.

• *Allowable losses*

The Department of Revenue will allow for handling and storage losses of liquid fuels and fuels that are satisfactorily substantiated [75 Pa.C.S. § 9004(h)]. For a case providing the Department with discretion to determine allowable losses, see *Miller v. Commonwealth*, 88 A.3d 304 (2014).

• *Sales to exempt entities*

A taxpayer was a distributor of petroleum products making sales at wholesale and retail. Taxpayer recorded diesel fuel sales to the Uniontown School District as non-taxable. However, these sales were not received by or billed to the school district. Instead, the sales were made to bus operators that contracted with the school district to provide busing for students. Because the taxpayer could not show that the sales were actually sold to and delivered to the school district, the tax exemption was denied. *Miller v. Commonwealth*, 88 A.3d 304 (2014). This case will also be applicable to the Oil Company Franchise Tax.

• *Refunds*

In general, refunds of liquid fuels taxes are administered by the Department of Revenue pursuant to the provisions of 72 P.S. § 10003.1 [75 Pa.C.S. § 9017(a)]. How ever, reimbursements and refunds of liquid fuels and fuels taxes on the following are administered by the Board of Finance and Revenue [75 Pa.C.S. § 9017(a.1)]:

(1) Farm tractors (any nonlicensed tractor or licensed tractors used off the highway for agricultural purposes relating to actual production of farm products) [75 Pa.C.S. § 9017(b)(1)].

(2) Volunteer fire rescue and ambulance services [75 Pa.C.S. § 9017(b)(2)].

(3) Motorboats and watercraft used on Commonwealth waters, including waterways bordering on Pennsylvania [75 Pa.C.S. § 9017(c)(1)].

(4) Aircraft and aircraft engines (propeller-driven, jet, or turbojet-propelled). Refunds for aircraft and aircraft engines are made for tax imposed in excess of 1.5¢ per gallon [75 Pa.C.S. § 9017(c)].

Forms: Refund claims for taxes paid with respect to these items must be made using a form furnished by the Board of Finance and Revenue (accompanied by receipts indicating that the liquid fuels tax has been paid or that the excess liquid fuels tax was paid) and must include all information required by Board regulations as well as the following [75 Pa.C.S. § 9017(f)]:

(1) Name and address of claimant.

(2) Description of the farm machinery, aircraft or aircraft engine in which the liquid fuels have been used.

(3) Purposes for which the machinery, aircraft or aircraft engine has been used.

(4) Size of the firm and part in cultivation on which liquid fuels have been used.

All claims submitted to the Board of Finance and Revenue must contain statements that:

(1) The liquid fuels for which reimbursement is claimed have been used only for purposes for which reimbursements are permitted.

(2) Records of the amounts of fuel used have been kept.

(3) No part of the claim has been paid except as stated.

Claimants must also assert that the claim and accompanying receipts are true and correct to the best of their knowledge [75 Pa.C.S. § 9017(f)].

Refund claims due date: Refund claims must be made annually on or before September 30 for the preceding year ending on June 30. Records of purchases of liquid fuels and use in each tractor or powered machinery, aircraft or aircraft engine must be kept for two years. A filing fee of $1.50 is deducted from every claim for reimbursement granted [75 Pa.C.S. § 9017(f)].

Truck refrigeration units: Taxpayers may claim reimbursement for tax paid on undyed diesel fuel used in truck refrigeration units on any purchase that is not more than 75 gallons per purchase and is delivered into a fuel tank designed to supply only an internal combustion engine mounted on a registered vehicle used exclusively for truck refrigeration. Claims for reimbursement must be filed within 60 days following the end of the quarter for which reimbursement is being claimed [75 Pa.C.S. § 9017(e.1)(3)]. See 75 Pa.C.S. § 9017(e.1) for details.

Agricultural power takeoff: Taxpayers may claim reimbursement for the full amount of tax paid if the person uses or buys liquid fuels or fuels and consumes them for delivery or to unload at a farm feed, feed products, lime or limestone products for agricultural use from a vehicle by means of a power takeoff, provided all requirements are met. See 75 Pa.C.S. § 9017(e.2) for details.

¶2603 Alternative Fuels Tax

• *Imposition*

An alternative fuels tax is imposed on alternative fuels used to propel vehicles on the public highways [75 Pa.C.S. § 9004(d)(1)]. The term "alternative fuels" means natural gas, compressed natural gas (CNG), liquified natural gas (LNG), liquid propane gas and liquified petroleum gas (LPG), alcohols, gasoline-alcohol mixtures containing at least 85% alcohol by volume, hydrogen, hythane, electricity and any other fuel not taxable as liquid fuels or fuels [75 Pa.C.S. § 9002]. CNG must be converted from cubic feet or pounds to gallons. See the instructions for the alternative fuels tax report [DMF-77].

• *Rate*

The rate of tax applicable to each alternative fuel is computed by the Department on a gallon equivalent basis and published as necessary by notice in the Pennsylvania Bulletin. "Gallon-equivalent basis" is the amount of any alternative fuel determined by the Department to contain 114,500 BTUs.

The 2018 calendar year tax rates on alternative fuels were as follows:

Alternative Fuel	Tax Rate Per Gallon of Alternative Fuel
Ethanol	$0.384
Methanol	$0.289
Propane/LPG	$0.425
E-85	$0.413
M-85	$0.332
Compressed Natural Gas	$0.576/GGE
Liquified Natural Gas	$0.648/DGE
Electricity	$0.0172/KWH

• *Reports and payment of tax*

Reports and payments are due on or before the 20th day of each month for fuel sold or used in the preceding month. The Pennsylvania Motor Fuels Tax Report must be filed electronically starting with the September 2016 report, due October 20, 2016. The Department of Revenue may permit dealer-users to report the tax due for reporting periods greater than one month, up to an annual basis, provided the tax is prepaid on an estimated basis. The tax is required to be paid by alternative fuel dealer-users rather than by distributors [75 Pa.C.S. § 9004(d)(2)]. An "alternative fuel dealer-user" is any person who delivers or places alternative fuels into the fuel supply tank or other device of a vehicle for use on the public highways [75 Pa.C.S. § 9002].

Extended reporting periods: The Department of Revenue may permit alternative fuel dealer-users to report the tax due for reporting periods greater than one month up to an annual basis if the tax is prepaid on the estimated amount of alternative fuel to be used in the extended period [75 Pa.C.S. § 9004(d)(2)].

Licensing and bonding: The licensing and bonding requirements for the alternative fuels tax are applicable to alternative fuel dealer-users instead of distributors [75 Pa.C.S. § 2003(d)(2)]. See ¶2602 for overview of permits and bonds.

¶2604 Oil Company Franchise Tax

• *Imposition*

An oil company franchise tax is imposed on liquid fuels and fuels used or sold and delivered by distributors within Pennsylvania [75 Pa.C.S. § 9004(b)]. The term "liquid fuels and fuels" for this purpose has the same meaning as for the liquid fuels tax (discussed at ¶2602). The oil company franchise tax automatically preempts any similar tax on the privilege of processing or refining petroleum products imposed by any political subdivision of this Commonwealth except local, personal, or real property tax of general application or to any tax imposed by the Commonwealth [75 Pa.C.S. § 9502].

- *Exempt entities and sales*

Exempt entities: Entities exempt from the liquid fuels and fuels tax are also exempt from the oil company franchise tax [75 Pa.C.S. § 9004(e)(4)].

First sales: Certain first sales are exempt. First sales are sales to a wholesale or retail dealer, consumer, or direct use in Pennsylvania of petroleum products occurring immediately after importation or production [61 Pa. Code § 351.5(a)]. First sales of petroleum products not actually used on the public highways to propel motor vehicles do not generate petroleum revenue, provided the sales are documented as required by 61 Pa. Code § 351.5(d). However, products for which the actual use is unknown are presumed to be taxable until it has been ascertained that the product will be used off-highway [61 Pa. Code § 351.5(c)]. See Information Notice Sales and Use Taxes 2014-01 - Pennsylvania Sales Tax Documentation Requirements for Sales of Fuel Oil, Kerosene, Natural Gas, and Propane issued January 24, 2014 which provides guidance for when fuel is sold for off-road use and may be exempt from fuel taxes; however, such sales become subject to sales tax unless a sales tax exemption applies. This Notice provides that residential sales should be supported by a valid, properly executed exemption certificate or equivalent documentation to support the exemption and that certain small sales are presumed exempt.

Exempt first sales: First sales to the following purchasers are exempt [61 Pa. Code § 351.5(b)]:

(1) United States Government.

(2) Commonwealth of Pennsylvania and its political subdivisions.

(3) Nonprofit elementary and secondary schools as defined in 61 Pa. Code § 315.2 (relating filing requirements).

(4) Volunteer rescue squads, volunteer fire companies, and volunteer ambulance associations.

(5) Second Class County Port Authorities.

Electric cooperatives: Fuel purchases for vehicles operated by electric cooperatives are exempt from tax [15 Pa.C.S. § 7333].

First sales to other oil companies: First sales to another oil company that has an oil franchise tax account number and agrees to report and pay the oil company franchise tax when it subsequently sells or uses the products do not generate revenue, provided all such sales are documented as required by 61 Pa. Code § 351.6. Therefore, the selling oil company is relieved of the obligation to pay the applicable tax on such first sales to other oil companies [61 Pa. Code § 351.6].

- *Rate*

The oil company franchise tax for 2018 was imposed on liquid fuels and fuels (on a cents-per-gallon equivalent basis) at the rate of 192.5 mills for liquid fuels and 247.5 mills for fuels [75 Pa.C.S. § 9502(a); 75 Pa.C.S. § 9004(b)]. "Cents-per-gallon equivalent basis" is the average wholesale price per gallon multiplied by the decimal equivalent of any tax imposed by 75 Pa.C.S. § 9502 (relating to imposition of tax, rounded to the next highest tenth of a cent per gallon). The Department of Revenue determines the rate on an annual basis beginning every January 1 and publishes it as a notice in the *Pennsylvania Bulletin* no later than the preceding December 15. In the event of a change in the rate of tax imposed by section 9502, the Department shall redetermine the rate of tax as of the effective date of such change and give notice as soon as possible [75 Pa.C.S. § 9002]. On a cents-per-gallon equivalent basis, the 2018 rate for liquid fuels (such as gasoline and gasohol) was $0.576 cents per gallon and $0.741 cents per gallon for fuels (such as undyed diesel and undyed kerosene).

• *Reports and payment of tax*

The oil company franchise tax is collected at the same time as the liquid fuels and fuels tax. See ¶2602 for details on reporting and paying tax.

¶2605 Motor Carriers Road Tax/IFTA

• *Imposition*

The motor carriers road tax (actually a fuel tax) is imposed on motor carriers engaged in operations on Pennsylvania highways and is in addition to other motor carrier taxes [75 Pa.C.S. § 9603]. As a result of the Pennsylvania Supreme Court's decision in *Senex Explosives, Inc. v. Commonwealth*, 91 A.3d 101 (Pa. 2014), the Department of Revenue issued Motor and Alternative Fuels Taxes Tax Bulletin 2015-02 (March 9, 2015). This bulletin provides for certain types of vehicles to be exempt from reporting and paying the motor carriers road tax.

• *Definitions*

Highway: A "highway" is the Pennsylvania Turnpike and every way or place, of whatever nature, open to the use of the public as a matter of right for purposes of vehicular travel. The term does not include a roadway or driveway upon grounds owned by private persons, colleges, universities or other institutions [75 Pa.C.S. § 9602].

Motor carrier: A "motor carrier" is any person who operates or causes to be operated any qualified motor vehicle on any highway in Pennsylvania [75 Pa.C.S. § 9602].

Motor fuel: The term "motor fuel" includes "fuels," "liquid fuels," and "alternative fuels." See definitions at ¶2601.

Operations: The term "operations" includes operations of all qualified motor vehicles, whether loaded or empty, whether operated singly or in combination with trailers or semitrailers, whether for compensation or not for compensation, and whether owned by or leased to the motor carrier who operates them or causes them to be operated [75 Pa.C.S. § 9602].

Qualified motor vehicle: A "qualified motor vehicle" is a vehicle (other than a recreational vehicle) that is used, designed, or maintained for transportation of persons or property and (1) has two axles and a gross weight or registered gross weight exceeding 26,000 pounds; (2) has three or more axles regardless of weight; and (3) is used in combination, when the gross weight or registered gross weight of the combination exceeds 26,000 pounds. If there is no registered gross weight, the gross vehicle weight rating (GVWR) or gross combination weight rating (GCWR) of the motor vehicle shall be used [75 Pa.C.S. § 2604; 75 Pa.C.S. § 2101.1]. Drilling rigs are not qualified motor vehicles even if they are mistakenly identified as such with an IFTA decal. *Senex Explosives, Inc. v. Cmwlth.*, 58 A.3d 131 (Pa.Commw. 2012).

Recreational vehicle: A "recreational vehicle" is a vehicle such as a motor home, pickup truck with attached camper and bus when used *exclusively* for personal pleasure by individuals. In order to qualify as a recreational vehicle, the vehicle cannot be used in connection with any business endeavor [75 Pa.C.S. § 9602].

• *International Fuel Tax Agreement (IFTA)*

Pennsylvania is a signatory to the International Fuel Tax Agreement (IFTA), which makes it possible for motor carriers to file a single road tax return in its home (base) state. This single return covers travel in all states that are members of IFTA.

• *Motorbus credit for motor fuel tax payment*

The motorbus road tax has been repealed, but the motorbus credit or reimbursement has been retained for fuel used by motorbuses (except school buses) that have a seating capacity of 20 or more passengers (excluding the driver) and qualify as "motor vehicles" under the Motor Carriers Road Tax Act (see above). A bus company may apply for reimbursement of 55 mills of the tax on fuels paid directly or indirectly on fuel consumed in its operations of motorbuses within Pennsylvania. The application must be submitted on or before the last day of the month immediately following the close of each quarter [75 Pa.C.S. § 9805].

• *Rate and base*

Motor carriers pay a road tax equivalent to the rate per gallon currently in effect on Pennsylvania liquid fuels, fuels or other alternative fuels (see ¶ 2604) and is calculated on the amount of fuel used in operations on Pennsylvania highways [75 Pa.C.S. § 9603(a)]. In the absence of adequate records or other evidence satisfactory to the Department of Revenue showing the miles per gallon of gas consumed, a qualified motor vehicle is deemed to have consumed one gallon of motor fuel for each four miles operated [75 Pa.C.S. § 9609]. In an unreported opinion, the Pennsylvania Commonwealth Court upheld the Department's right to use the statutory estimate of four miles per gallon in the absence of adequate records to prove actual mileage of six miles per gallon [*Terry Reddinger, Inc. v. Cmwlth.*, Pa.Commw., No. 198 F.R. 1996 (April 5, 2001), opinion not reported].

The motor carriers road tax is in addition to any taxes of whatever character imposed on them by any other statute [75 Pa.C.S. § 9603(a)]. The tax is computed by multiplying the total motor fuel used everywhere times a fraction, the numerator of which is the total number of miles traveled on Pennsylvania highways and the denominator of which is the total number of miles traveled everywhere [75 Pa.C.S. § 9607].

• *Credit for motor fuel tax payment*

Motor carriers may take a credit equal to Pennsylvania taxes paid on all gasoline or other motor fuel purchased in Pennsylvania for use in their operations anywhere. If the allowable credit is more than a carrier's motor carrier road tax liability, the Department will, upon application, allow the excess as a credit against taxes that would otherwise be due for any of the six succeeding quarters [75 Pa.C.S. § 9604]. Credits will be denied for failure to maintain proper records. *R & Express v. Cmwlth.*, 65 A.3d 900 (Pa. 2013) *aff'g per curiam*, 37 A.3d 46 (2012).

• *Refunds*

Refunds of the motor carriers road tax must comply with the uniform refund requirements discussed in ¶ 4611.

• *Reports and payment of tax*

Motor carriers road tax reports are due quarterly on or before the last day of April, July, October and January of every year for the quarter ending the last day of the preceding month. The Department may by regulation permit motor carriers whose estimated annual liability under this chapter is $250 or less to file on an annual basis [75 Pa.C.S. § 9608]. The tax due must be paid at the time of filing the report [75 Pa.C.S. § 9605].

• *Identification markers*

In general, it is unlawful to operate or cause to be operated in Pennsylvania any qualified motor vehicle unless the vehicle bears a Pennsylvania identification marker or a valid and unrevoked IFTA identification marker issued by another IFTA jurisdiction [75 Pa.C.S. § 2102(d)]. The Secretary of Revenue, however, may by regulation exempt clearly identifiable vehicles. It is also unlawful to operate or cause to be operated in Pennsylvania any qualified motor vehicle unless the vehicle carries either the IFTA license or Pennsylvania road tax registration card [75 Pa.C.S. § 2102(e)]. In general, qualified motor vehicles subject to IFTA are issued identification markers (decals) and an IFTA license, and qualified motor vehicles not subject to IFTA are issued identification markers and a road tax registration card. Identification markers are required to be permanently affixed on the exterior portion of both sides of the cab of the qualified motor vehicle in accordance with the directions on the reverse side of the marker [75 Pa.C.S. § 2102(a)].

- *Temporary marker permits*

For a period not to exceed 30 days with respect to any one motor carrier, the Secretary of Revenue by letter or telegram may authorize the operation of a qualified motor vehicle or vehicles without the identification markers required when *both* of the following criteria are met: (1) enforcement of requirement of identification marker would cause undue delay and hardship in the operation of the motor vehicle; and (2) the motor carrier is registered and/or licensed for the motor carriers road tax with the Department of Revenue or has filed an application. The fee for temporary permits is $5 per qualified motor vehicle [75 Pa.C.S. § 2102(d)(2)].

- *Trip permits*

In lieu of filing returns and paying the motor carriers road tax with respect to a particular qualified motor vehicle, taxpayers may obtain from the Department of Revenue a trip permit that authorizes the carrier to operate the qualified motor vehicle for a period of five consecutive days, specified by the Department of Revenue. The fee for a trip permit is $50 per qualified motor vehicle [75 Pa.C.S. § 2102(d)(3)].

PART XI

DOING BUSINESS IN PENNSYLVANIA

CHAPTER 27
DOING BUSINESS IN PENNSYLVANIA

¶2701 Scope of Chapter and Sources of Authority

This chapter discusses the annual fees and taxes required of a corporation doing business in Pennsylvania (both domestic and foreign) and the procedures and fees associated with the initial incorporation of a business in Pennsylvania. Requirements such as classes of stock and stated capital are beyond the scope of this chapter. The rules governing incorporation and fees are contained in Title 15 of Pennsylvania Consolidated Statutes.

Two nontax fees are discussed: (1) registration with the Department of Revenue and (2) reports of abandoned and unclaimed property. Registration requirements are governed by provisions of the Fiscal Code (FC). Abandoned and unclaimed property provisions are contained in Title XIII.1 of the Fiscal Code.

• *Specific taxes*

For licenses, fees, certificates, etc., with respect to specific taxes, consult the part on the specific tax.

¶2702 Formation of a Corporation

The following discussion provides the basic procedures and requirements necessary for formation of a corporation in Pennsylvania.

• *Business Corporation Law of 1988*

The Business Corporation Law of 1988 [Act of December 21, 1988, P.L. 1444, No. 177] governs the formation of corporations for profit in Pennsylvania [Pennsylvania Consolidated Statutes, Title 15, Subpart B]. This act should be consulted for detailed requirements. The Business Corporation Law of 1988 replaces the former Business Corporation Law of 1933 [Act of May 5, 1933, P.L. 364].

• *Incorporation*

In order to incorporate in Pennsylvania, articles of incorporation containing the required information must be prepared. The articles of incorporation must be filed

¶2702

with the Department of State, and the corporation must advertise by officially publishing a notice of intention to file or of the filing of articles of incorporation. The notice may appear prior to or after the day the articles of incorporation are filed with the Department of State and shall set forth briefly the name of the proposed corporation and a statement that the corporation is to be or has been incorporated under the provisions of the Business Corporation Law of 1988. The corporate existence begins upon the later of the filing of the articles of incorporation with the Department of State or the effective date specified in the articles of incorporation. The filing of articles of incorporation (or recording in the office of the recorder of deeds under former law) is conclusive evidence of the fact that the corporation has been incorporated [15 Pa.C.S. §§ 1307—1309].

• *Fees*

The Department of State is authorized by law to receive fees for services performed, as specified by Subchapter C of the Business Corporation Law of 1988 [15 Pa.C.S. § 105(a)] or any other applicable provisions of law. Any other department, board, commission, or officer of Pennsylvania is also entitled to receive such fees as may be lawfully charged for services performed as required by Title 15 of the Business Corporation Law of 1988 or similar services [15 Pa.C.S. § 105(b)].

• *Registered office*

Every business corporation (domestic or foreign) must maintain continuously in Pennsylvania a registered office that may be, but need not be, the same as its place of business [15 Pa.C.S. § 1507].

• *Domestication of foreign corporations*

Any qualified foreign business corporation may become a domestic business corporation by filing articles of domestication with the Department of State. The articles of domestication upon filing become the articles of the domesticated foreign corporation, and the formerly foreign corporation becomes, and continues to be, a domestic business corporation [15 Pa.C.S. § 4161]. A domesticated corporation has all the powers and privileges of a domestic business corporation and is subject to all the duties and limitations granted and imposed upon domestic business corporations. The property, franchises, debts, liens, estates, taxes, penalties, and public accounts due the Commonwealth shall continue to be vested in and imposed upon the corporation to the same extent as if it were the successor by merger of the domesticating corporation with and into a domestic business corporation under Subchapter C of Chapter 19 (relating to merger, consolidation, share exchanges, and sale of assets). The shares of the domesticated corporation shall be unaffected by the domestication except to the extent, if any, they are reclassified in the articles of domestication [15 Pa.C.S. § 4162].

¶2703 Domestic Corporation Costs

The following explanation discusses the initial taxes and fees and the annual taxes related to operating a domestic corporation in Pennsylvania.

• *Initial taxes and fees*

The current fee schedule for domestic corporations can be found at the Department of State's web site at http://www.dos.state.pa.us/corps/cwp/view.asp?a=1093&Q=431161&corpsNavDLTEST=.

• *Annual taxes*

Pennsylvania imposes the following taxes on domestic corporations:

    (1) A capital stock tax.

    (2) A corporate net income tax.

Capital stock tax: The Pennsylvania capital stock tax is imposed on the capital stock value (see ¶1306). See the rate schedule at ¶1305. This tax ended as of 12/31/15.

Corporate net income tax: The Pennsylvania corporate net income tax is imposed on the net income of domestic corporations. Rate is discussed at ¶905. The corporate net income tax is explained in chapters 9—12.

¶2704 Foreign Corporation Costs

The following explanation discusses the initial costs and annual taxes related to operating a foreign corporation in Pennsylvania.

• *Initial costs*

The current fee schedule for foreign corporations can be found at the Department of State's web site at http://www.dos.state.pa.us/corps/cwp/view.asp?a=1093&Q=431161&corpsNavDLTEST=.

• *Annual taxes*

Pennsylvania imposes the following taxes on foreign corporations:

(1) A franchise tax.

(2) A corporate net income tax.

Franchise tax: The Pennsylvania franchise stock tax is imposed on the capital stock value. The franchise stock tax is explained (along with the capital stock tax for domestic corporations) at ¶¶1301—1605.

Corporate net income tax: The Pennsylvania corporate net income tax is imposed on the net income of foreign corporations. The corporate net income tax is explained at ¶¶901—1209.

¶2705 Partnerships and Limited Liability Companies

The following is an explanation of the initial costs and annual taxes related to operating a partnership or limited liability company in Pennsylvania.

• *Initial costs*

The current fee schedule for partnerships and limited liability companies can be found at the Department of State's web site at http://www.dos.state.pa.us/corps/cwp/view.asp?a=1093&Q=431161&corpsNavDLTEST=.

• *Annual taxes*

Partnerships, in general, are not taxable as separate entities. The partners pay Pennsylvania personal income tax on their share of the partnership's earnings. A partnership, however, may elect to be taxed as an association. See ¶¶1815—1819 for a discussion of the taxation of partnerships.

The Pennsylvania taxation of *limited liability companies* is consistent with the federal treatment. See ¶¶1820—1824 for a specific discussion of the taxation of limited liability companies.

¶2706 Business Trusts

The following is an explanation of the initial costs and annual taxes related to operating a business trust in Pennsylvania.

• *Initial costs*

The Corporation Bureau of the Department of State charges the following fees for *business trusts* [Act 47 of 2003 (H.B. 172), §7]:

(1) Deed of trust or other initial instrument for a business trust_$125.

(2) Each ancillary transaction_$70.

• *Annual taxes*

The Pennsylvania taxation of business trusts is consistent with the federal treatment. See ¶1830 for a discussion of the taxation of Pennsylvania business trusts.

¶2707 Registration Reports

Every limited partnership, bank, joint-stock association, association, insurance company, corporation (except domestic and foreign business corporations and non-profit corporations), or company whatsoever, formed, erected, incorporated, or organized under any Pennsylvania law or under the laws of another state and doing business in Pennsylvania must register with the Department of Revenue before going into operation [72 P.S. §§730 and 1722].

• *Address changes*

Address changes must be reported to the Department of Revenue immediately, and change in officers must be reported annually.

• *Penalty*

Any company required to register with the Department of Revenue that neglects or refuses to do so is subject to a penalty of $500, collected on an account settled by the Department in the same manner as taxes on capital stock are settled and collected.

Enterprise Registration (PA-100)

Enterprises are also required to register for certain taxes and services administered by the PA Department of Revenue and the PA Department of Labor & Industry. Pennsylvania Form PA-100 is used for this purpose. Enterprise registration is discussed at ¶4619.

¶2708 Reports of Abandoned and Unclaimed Property

All abandoned and unclaimed property and property without a rightful or lawful owner is subject to the custody and control of the Commonwealth of Pennsylvania if it meets the following criteria [72 P.S. §1301.2]:

(1) It is tangible and physically located in Pennsylvania.

(2) It is intangible and is one of the following:

(a) The last known address of the owner (as shown by the records of the holder) is within Pennsylvania.

(b) The last known address of the owner (as shown by the records of the holder) is in a jurisdiction that has no laws providing for the escheat or custodial taking of such property and the domicile of the holder is in Pennsylvania.

(c) No address of the owner appears on the records of the holder and the domicile of the holder is in Pennsylvania (last known address in the case of travelers check or money order presumed to be in state of last known address of owner).

¶2707

(d) No address of the owner appears on the records of the holder and the domicile of the holder is not in Pennsylvania, but it is proved that the last known address of the owner is in Pennsylvania.

Owner of Unclaimed Property Not Entitled to Interest

If unclaimed property is sold by the Treasury Department, the original owner is entitled to a return of the amount actually received by the State Treasurer upon the sale of the property [72 P.S. § 1301.17(d)]. Thus, the original owner is not entitled to receive any interest on the proceeds that may be received by the Treasury Department [*Smolow v. Hafer*, Pa.Commw., No. 208 M.D. 2004 (February 9, 2005)].

• *Property presumed abandoned and unclaimed*

Property (see definition below) is presumed abandoned and unclaimed when no transactions or communication with respect to the property has occurred within a stated period of time (the dormancy period), generally five (5) years in Pennsylvania. In the explanation below the term "has not been claimed" means also that no communication (oral or written) with the owner has occurred during the statutory period. Examples of abandoned and unclaimed property are inactive bank accounts, unclaimed securities, unused gift certificates, abandoned safe deposit boxes, retirement benefits, jewelry, rare coins, and stamps. Act 126 of 2014 shortened the holding period from five years to three years for various types of property held by certain financial institutions, insurers, utilities, business associations, fiduciaries, and courts or public officers.

• *Property defined*

The term "property" includes all real and personal property (tangible or intangible), all legal and equitable interests in property, together with any income, accretions, or profits from the interests, and all other rights to property, subject to legal demands on them. The term "property" does not include property deemed lost at common law [72 P.S. § 1301.1].

• *Reports*

Persons who hold abandoned or unclaimed property during the preceding year must file a report with the State Treasurer [72 P.S. § 1301.11]. The report must be verified and include the following information:

(1) Except with respect to travelers checks and money orders, the name (if known) and last known address (if any) of each person appearing from the records of the holder to be the owner of any property worth $50 or more.

(2) The nature and identifying number (if any) or description of the property the amount appearing from the records to be due. Items with a value under $50 each may be reported in the aggregate.

(3) The date when the property became payable, demandable, returnable, or the date upon which the property was declared or found to be without a rightful or lawful owner, and the date of the last transaction with the owner with respect to the property.

(4) Other information consistent with law that the State Treasurer prescribed by regulations as necessary for administration.

Holders Must File

A person or entity in possession of unclaimed property is commonly referred to as a "holder." A holder is a person obligated to hold for the account of or deliver or pay to the owner property and includes any person in possession of unclaimed and abandoned property [72 P.S. § 1301.1]. Holders include, but are not limited to, financial institutions, insurance companies, corporations, associations, and sole proprietorships. It is the responsibility of holders to file reports of unclaimed and abandoned property in their possession [72 P.S. § 1301.11(a)].

Due date: The report is due on or before April 15 of the year following the year in which the property first became subject to custody and control of the Commonwealth. Upon written request by a person required to file a report, the State Treasurer may postpone the reporting date for a period not to exceed six (6) months [72 P.S. § 1301.11(d)].

• *Payment or delivery of abandoned and unclaimed property*

Every person holding property subject to the custody and control of the Commonwealth must, after complying with the reporting requirements of 72 P.S. 1301.11, and on or before April 15 of the year following the year in which the property first became subject to custody and control of the Commonwealth, pay or deliver to the State Treasurer all property subject to custody and control of the Commonwealth unless the owner establishes right to receive the property to the satisfaction of the holder or it appears for some other reason that the property is not then subject to custody and control of the Commonwealth. If the holder does not pay or deliver the property because it appears the Commonwealth is not entitled to it, the holder must, in lieu of delivery or payment, file a verified written explanation of the proof of claim or reason the property is not subject to the Commonwealth's control [72 P.S. § 1301.13(a)]. After a holder pays or delivers property to the State Treasurer, the holder is relieved of all liability with respect to the safekeeping of the property [72 P.S. § 1301.14].

• *Administration and enforcement*

The Department of Revenue can examine records of persons holding abandoned and unclaimed property [72 P.S. § 1301.23(a)]. If a holder has not maintained records or has not maintained records sufficient for examination, the State Treasurer may apply sampling and estimation procedures to determine a holder's liability [72 P.S. § 1301.23(b); 61 Pa. Code § 651.8]. If a person refuses to report or deliver property, the Commonwealth can initiate court action to enforce it.

• *Finder registration*

Effective January 6, 2015, an individual who is not an attorney is prohibited from engaging in activities related to locating and recovering abandoned or unclaimed property for a fee unless they register with the State Treasurer, maintain certain records and file reports related to such transactions. Finders violating the certification requirements are subject to civil and criminal penalties.

• *Interest*

A holder that fails to report or deliver property is liable for interest at the rate of 12% per annum from the time the report should have been filed and computed on the value of the property not reported or delivered [72 P.S. § 1301.24(b)].

• *Penalties*

Consult the statute for penalties. Among the punishable violations are failure to file a report and failure to pay or deliver property as required.

¶2708

PART XII

UNEMPLOYMENT COMPENSATION INSURANCE TAX

CHAPTER 28

UNEMPLOYMENT COMPENSATION INSURANCE TAX

¶2801 Unemployment Insurance

Pennsylvania unemployment insurance tax is governed under the provisions of the Act of Dec. 5, 1936, Special Session 2, P.L. 2897, No. 1, Unemployment Compensation Law. Comprehensive coverage of unemployment insurance is provided in Wolters Kluwer, CCH Unemployment/Social Security Reporter. For more information go to CCHGroup.com or contact an account representative at 888-CCH-REPS (888-224-7377).

PART XIII

INHERITANCE AND ESTATE TAX

CHAPTER 29

INTRODUCTION, TRANSFERS SUBJECT TO TAX, RATES OF TAX

¶2901 History, Sources of Authority, and Administration

Pennsylvania was the first state to adopt an inheritance tax. It was first imposed in 1826 as a tax on inheritances received by collateral relatives (*i.e.,* those not in direct line of descent). The Pennsylvania inheritance tax has been amended several times since first enacted and now applies to inheritances received by direct relatives (*i.e.,* spouse and lineal heirs) and strangers in blood (*i.e.,* nonrelatives). The inheritance tax was a tax on the succession of property, not a property tax. See, for example, *Estate of Beck,* 414 A.2d 65 (1980).

In 1961 the inheritance tax was recodified and titled "Inheritance and Estate Tax Act of 1961." The Pennsylvania estate tax, imposed by the 1961 act, was a "pick-up" tax that was imposed to pick up the difference between the maximum federal credit for state inheritance taxes and the amount of state inheritance taxes due.

In 1982, the 1961 Act was repealed and the Inheritance and Estate Tax Act of 1982 was enacted, which was applicable to estates of decedents dying on or after December 13, 1982.

In 1991, the Inheritance and Estate Tax Act of 1982 (Chapter 17, Title 72 of the Pennsylvania Consolidated Statutes) was repealed; and the inheritance and estate tax provisions were recodified as Article XXI of the Tax Reform Code of 1971 [Act of August 4, 1991, No. 22, §36]. The substance of the inheritance and estate tax

¶2901

provisions was not changed; the inheritance and estate tax provisions were merely made part of the Tax Reform Code instead of being legislation separate from the Tax Reform Code.

- *Sources of authority*

The Pennsylvania inheritance and estate tax is governed by the provisions of Article XXI of the Tax Reform Code [72 P.S. § 9101 *et seq.*]. The addition of Article XXI to the Tax Reform Code applies to the estates of decedents dying on or after the effective date of the bill and to *inter vivos* transfers made by decedents dying on or after October 3, 1991, regardless of the date of transfer [Act of August 4, 1991, No. 22, § 43(2)]. The current provisions may be cited as the "Inheritance and Estate Tax Act" [72 P.S. § 9101].

Caution: Which Inheritance and Estate Tax Act?

One must be careful to specify which Inheritance and Estate Tax Act is being cited. Both the repealed Inheritance and Estate Act of 1961 and the repealed Inheritance and Estate Act of 1982 were also cited as the "Inheritance and Estate Tax Act."

- *Administration*

The inheritance and estate tax is administered by the Department of Revenue, which has the power to adopt and enforce rules and regulations [72 P.S. § 9103(a)]. The Department has complete supervision of making appraisements, allowance of deductions, and assessment of tax [72 P.S. § 9103(b)]. The county registers of wills are the local representatives of the Department in the administration of the tax. In the event a register of wills fails to perform satisfactorily in the administration of the tax, the Department of Revenue has all the powers vested in the register to administer the tax [72 P.S. § 9103(c)].

Repeal of Federal Estate Tax Decoupling

In order to prevent the loss of state tax revenue because of the passage of the federal Economic Growth and Tax Relief Reconciliation Act of 2001 (EGTRRA, P.L. 107-16), Act 89 of 2002 decoupled the Pennsylvania estate tax from current federal law, basing the Pennsylvania estate tax on federal law as amended to June 1, 2001. However, Act 46 of 2003 provided for the repeal federal decoupling, effective for decedents who die after June 30, 2002 [Act of December 23, 2003 (H.B. 200), § 24]. The Pennsylvania estate tax now continues to be based on federal law.

¶2902 Definitions

The following words, terms, and phrases when used within the context of the Pennsylvania inheritance tax have the meanings ascribed to them by 72 P.S. § 9102.

Adverse interest: A substantial beneficial interest in the property transferred that might be adversely affected by the exercise or nonexercise of the power or right reserved or possessed by the transferor.

Business of agriculture: This term (for decedents dying after June 30, 2012) includes the leasing to members of the same family or the leasing to a corporation or association owned by members of the same family of property that is directly and principally used for agricultural purpose. However, the "business of agriculture" does *not* include the following:

      (1) Recreational activities (*e.g.,* hunting, fishing, camping, skiing, show competition, racing).

(2) The raising, breeding, or training of game animals or game birds, fish, cats, dogs or pets, or animals intended for use in sporting or recreational activities.

(3) Fur farming.

(4) Stockyards and slaughterhouse operations.

(5) Manufacturing or processing operations of any kind.

Children: Includes (1) natural children whether or not they have been adopted by others, (2) adopted children, and (3) stepchildren.

Clerk: The clerk of the orphans' court division of the court of common pleas having jurisdiction.

Court: The orphans' court division of the court of common pleas of (1) the county in which the decedent resided at the time of his or her death; (2) the county in which letters, if any, are granted if the decedent was not a Pennsylvania resident; (3) Dauphin County in all other cases.

Date of death: The date of actual death. In the case of a presumed decedent, the "date of death" is the date found by the final decree to be the date of the absentee's presumed death. For the purpose of determining interest and discount, "date of death" means the date upon which the court enters its final decree of presumptive death.

Death taxes: Includes inheritance, succession, transfer and estate taxes, and any other taxes levied against the estate of a decedent by reason of his or her death.

Decedent or transferor: Any person by or from whom a transfer is made. The term includes any testator, intestate, grantor, settler, bargainor, vendor, assignor, donor, joint tenant and insured.

Department: The Pennsylvania Department of Revenue.

Estate: See Property or estate.

Exemption income: All moneys or property including, without limitation, interest, gains or income derived from obligation that are statutorily free from state or local taxation under any other federal state or state laws, received of whatever nature and from whatever source derived.

Financial institution: A bank, a national banking association, a bank and trust company, a trust company, a savings and loan association, a building and loan association, a mutual savings bank, a credit union, a savings bank, and a company that rents safe deposit boxes.

Future interest: Includes a successive life interest and a successive interest for a term certain.

Lineal descendants: (1) All children of the natural parents and their descendants, whether or not they have been adopted by others, (2) adopted descendants and their descendants and (3) stepdescendants.

Members of the same family: Any individual, such individual's brothers and sisters, the brothers and sisters of such individual's parents and grandparents, the ancestors and lineal descendants of any of the foregoing, a spouse of any of the foregoing, and the estate of any of the foregoing. Individuals related by the half blood or legal adoption are treated as if they were related by the whole blood.

Notice: Written notice.

Presumed decedent: A person found to be presumptively dead under the provisions of 20 Pa.C.S., Ch 57 or, if not a Pennsylvania resident, under the laws of his or her domicile.

Property or estate: Includes the following:

(1) All real property and all tangible property of a resident decedent or transferor having its situs in Pennsylvania.

(2) All intangible personal property of a resident decedent or transferor.

(3) All real property and all tangible personal property of a resident decedent having its situs outside Pennsylvania, that the decedent had contracted to sell, provided the jurisdiction in which the property has its situs does not subject it to death tax.

(4) All real property and all tangible personal property of a nonresident decedent or transferor having its situs in Pennsylvania, including property held in trust.

(5) A liquor license issued by the Commonwealth of Pennsylvania.

Register: The register of wills having jurisdiction to grant letters testamentary or of administration in the estate of the decedent or transferor.

Secretary: The Secretary of Revenue of Pennsylvania.

Sibling: An individual who has at least one parent in common with the decedent, whether by blood or by adoption.

Territory: Includes the District of Columbia and all possessions of the United States.

Transfer: Includes the passage of ownership of property, or interest in property or income from property, in possession or enjoyment (present or future) in trust or otherwise.

Transfer of property for the sole use: A transfer to or for the use of a transferee if, during the transferee's lifetime, the transferee is entitled to all income and principal distributions from the property and no person (including the transferee) possessed a power of appointment over the property.

Transferee: Any person to whom a transfer is made. The term includes any legatee, devisee, heir, next of kin, grantee, beneficiary, vendee, assignee, donee, surviving joint tenant, and insurance beneficiary.

Transferor: See Decedent or transferor.

Value: The price at which property would be sold by a willing seller (not compelled to sell) to a willing buyer (not compelled to buy), both of whom have reasonable knowledge of the relevant facts. In determining the value of property, no reduction can be made on account of income, excise or other taxes that may become payable subsequent to the valuation date by the transferee or out of the property. "Value" as to land in agricultural use, agricultural reserve, or forest reserve means the value that the land has for its particular use according to the standards provided in 72 P.S. § 9122.

¶2903 Imposition and Base

• *Imposition*

The inheritance tax is a transfer tax imposed on taxable transfers of property (explained at ¶2905) at a flat rate (see ¶2904). Because the inheritance tax is not a property tax, it can be imposed on the transfer of property that would be exempt from property taxation. See *Orr v. Gilman*, 183 U.S. 278 (1902). The inheritance tax is imposed on the value of the property (less allowable deductions) in the estate (the base).

¶2903

• *Property or estate of a resident decedent*

If the decedent was a resident of Pennsylvania, the inheritance tax is computed on the value of the property (wherever situated) in excess of allowable deductions at the rates in effect at the time of the decedent's death [72 P.S. §9116(b)(1)]. See definition of "property or estate" at ¶2902. Note that the property or estate of a resident decedent includes all intangible property (*e.g.*, stocks, bonds, bank accounts, loans receivable) regardless of where it is located at the time of the decedent's death.

• *Property or estate of a nonresident decedent*

If the decedent was not a resident of Pennsylvania, the tax is computed on the value of real property and tangible personal property having a situs in Pennsylvania that is in excess of unpaid property taxes assessed on the property and any indebtedness for which it is liened, mortgaged, or pledged [72 P.S. §9116(b)(2)]. See definition of property or estate at ¶2902. Note that the property or estate of a nonresident decedent includes only real property and tangible personal property located in Pennsylvania.

• *Disclaimers*

When any person entitled to a distributive share of an estate (whether under an *inter vivos* trust, a will, or the intestate law) renounces the right to receive it (and therefore receives no consideration) or exercises the elective rights of a surviving spouse under 20 Pa.C.S., Ch. 22 (receiving no consideration other than the interest in assets passing to her/him as the electing spouse), the tax is computed as though the persons who benefit by the renunciation (disclaimer) or election were originally designated to be the distributees (conditioned upon an adjudication or decree of distribution expressly confirming distribution to them). The disclaimer must be made within nine months of the death of the decedent. In the case of a surviving spouse taking his/her elective share of an estate, the disclaimer must be made within the time for election (plus any extension) under 20 Pa.C.S. §2210(b). Notice of the filing of the account and its call for audit or confirmation must include notice of the renunciation or election to the Department of Revenue. When an unconditional vesting of a future interest does not occur at the decedent's death, the renunciation may be made within three months after the occurrence of the event or contingency that resolves the vesting of the interest [72 P.S. §9116(c)]. If the rate of tax that will be applicable when a future interest vests cannot be established with certainty, the Department (after consideration of relevant actuarial factors, valuations, and other relevant circumstances) may enter into an agreement with the person responsible for payment to establish a specified amount of tax. If this specified amount is paid within 60 days after the agreement, it will constitute full payment of all tax otherwise due on the transfer [72 P.S. §9116(e)]. Estate's unliquidated survival claim was not a "future interest" of decedent's children at the time of decedent's death, such that the children could delay their renunciation of their distributive share of decedent's estate beyond nine months after decedent's death. The children's eventual renunciation being untimely, the Department of Revenue's preliminary objection to the portion of the appraisement that assessed inheritance tax on decedent's surviving children's intestate share of decedent's estate was sustained. [*In re Estate of O'Connor*, 140 A.3d 77 (Pa. Commw. Ct. 2016)]

• *Compromise of a dispute*

In the case of a compromise of a dispute regarding rights and interests of transferees that is made in good faith, the tax is computed as if the persons receiving the property were originally entitled to it (conditioned upon an adjudication or decree of distribution expressly confirming distribution to them). Notice of the filing of the account and of its call for audit or confirmation must include notice to the Department of Revenue [72 P.S. §9116(d)].

¶2903

- *Property subject to power of appointment*

Property subject to a power of appointment (whether or not the power is exercised and notwithstanding any blending of the property with the property of the donee) is taxed only as part of the estate of the donor [72 P.S. § 9116(f)].

- *Decedent or transferor*

A decedent or a transferor is any person by or from whom a transfer is made and includes any testator, intestate, grantor, settler, bargainor, vendor, assignor, donor, joint tenant, and insured [72 P.S. § 9102].

¶2904 Rate

The inheritance tax is a tax on the right of succession or privilege of receiving property from a decedent; it is imposed on taxable transfers of property (explained at ¶2905) at a flat rate.

The rate of the inheritance tax depends on the relationship of the beneficiary to the decedent [72 P.S. § 9116(a)]. There are four rate categories. The categories and rates that apply to dates of death on or after July 1, 2000, are shown in the table below.

Category	Rate	Explanation
Spousal	0%	Applies to the wife or husband of the decedent at the date of death. Common-law spouses are recognized if the common-law marriage can be documented. Inheritance Tax Bulletin 2015-01 provides that legally recognized same-sex marriages will be provided the same benefits as a statutory husband and wife.
Lineal	4.5%	Applies to grandparents, parents, children, spouse or widow(er) of a child and lineal descendants. "Children" for this purpose means (i) natural children (even if adopted by others); (ii) adopted descents and their descendants; and (iii) step-descendants.
Sibling	12%	Applies to siblings who are (i) brothers or half-brothers; (ii) sisters or half-sisters; and (iii) persons having at least one parent in common with the decedent (either by blood or by adoption). Prior to July 1, 2000, transfers to siblings were taxed at a rate of 15%.
Collateral	15%	Applies to all beneficiaries other than spouses, lineal descendants, and siblings

- *Transfers to spouses with right of survivorship*

When property passes to or for the use of a wife *and* husband with right of survivorship, one of whom is taxable at a lower rate than the other (*i.e.*, one is a lineal descendant and one is a nonlineal descendant), the property is taxed at the lower rate [72 P.S. § 9116(a)(3)]. For example, if property passes from a decedent to a grandchild (a lineal descendant) and the grandchild's spouse (a nonlineal descendant) with right of survivorship, the property is taxed at 4.5% (formerly, 6%).

- *Poverty exemption for spouses*

The poverty exemption for spouses explained at ¶2908 has been repealed for estates of decedents dying on or after January 1, 1995.

¶2905 Taxable Transfers

All transfers of property by will, by the intestate laws of Pennsylvania, or (in the case of a transfer from a nonresident) by the laws of succession of another jurisdiction are subject to the inheritance and estate tax. The transfer of a person determined by decree of a court of competent jurisdiction to a presumed decedent is taxable [72 P.S. § 9102]. A presumed decedent is a person found to be presumptively dead under the provisions of 20 Pa.C.S., Ch. 57 or (if the presumed decent is a nonresident of Pennsylvania) under the laws of his/her domicile [72 P.S. § 9102].

¶2904

Partial Transfers

When the decedent retained or reserved an interest or power with respect to only a part of the property transferred (causing the property to be subject to tax), the amount of the taxable transfer is only the value of that portion of the transferred property that is subject to the retained or reserved interest or power [72 P.S. § 9107(c)(2)]. This provision does not apply to gifts made in contemplation of death. See below.

● *Inter vivos transfers*

The following *inter vivos* transfers are taxable to the extent that they are made without valuable and adequate consideration in money or money's worth at the time of transfer [72 P.S. § 9107(c)(1)].

(1) *Transfer made in contemplation of death:* A transfer made within one year of decedent's death *if,* at the time of the transfer, the aggregate value of the transfer (with respect to each transferee) was more than $3,000 during any calendar year (called a gift in contemplation of death) [72 P.S. § 107(c)(3)].

(2) *Reversionary interest:* A transfer that takes effect in possession or enjoyment at or after the decedent's death and under which the transferor (decedent) retained a reversionary interest in the property worth more than 5% of the value of the property immediately before the decedent's death. The term "reversionary interest" includes a possibility that the transferred property may return to the transferor or the estate, or may be subject to a power of disposition by transferor. The term does not include a possibility that the income alone from the property may return to the transferor or become subject to a power of disposition by the transferor [72 P.S. § 107(c)(4)].

(3) *Reservation of life estate:* A transfer under which the transferor expressly or impliedly reserves for life or any period that does not in fact end before the transferor's death, the possession or enjoyment of, or the right to the income from, the property transferred, or the right, either alone or in conjunction with someone else not having an adverse interest, to designate the persons who shall possess or enjoy the property transferred or the income from the transferred property [72 P.S. § 107(c)(5)].

(4) *Payments from transferee:* A transfer under which the transferee promises to make payments to, or for the benefit of, the transferor during the remainder of the transferor's life [72 P.S. § 107(c)(6)].

(5) *Power to amend, alter, or revoke:* A transfer under which the transferor has at the time of death, either alone or in conjunction with anyone not having an adverse interest, a power to alter, amend, or revoke the beneficiary's interest. If at any time during the year before decedent's death, he/she relinquishes the power to amend, alter, or revoke, the transfer is treated as a gift in contemplation of death (see first item above) and is taxable if its value exceeds $3,000 per beneficiary [72 P.S. § 9107(c)(7)].

● *Joint tenancy*

When property is held in joint tenancy or deposited in a financial institution in the names of two or more persons with the right of survivorship, the decedent's portion of the jointly held property is subject to tax. The decedent's portion is determined by dividing the value of the whole property by the number of joint tenants in existence immediately preceding the deceased joint tenant's death [72 P.S. § 9108(a)]. This provision does not apply to property passing by right of survivorship to a spouse, unless the transfer occurred within one year of the decedent's death and exceeded $3,000 [72 P.S. § 9108(b)]. In the case of any joint tenancy created within one year of the decedent's death, the entire value of the property in the joint tenancy is taxable as part of the estate of the person who created the co-ownership to the extent that the transfer exceeds $3,000 [72 P.S. § 9108(c)]. Inheritance Tax Bulletin 2015-01 provides that legally recognized same sex marriages will be provided the same benefits as a statutory husband and wife and that financial institutions shall treat joint accounts titled in the names of individuals in a same-sex marriage as accounts held by "husband" and "wife."

Deductions are explained in Chapter 31.

¶ 2906 Exempt Transfers

The following transfers of property are exempt from Pennsylvania inheritance taxation [72 P.S. § 9111]:

• *Adjusted service certificates and bonds*

Adjusted service certificates issued under the Act of Congress of May 19, 1924, and adjusted service bonds issued under the Act of Congress of January 27, 1936, are exempt [72 P.S. § 9111(j)].

• *Advancements*

Transfers made as advancement of, or on account of, an intestate share or in satisfaction or partial satisfaction of a gift by will are exempt unless the gift was made within a year of death and gifts to the transferee exceeded $3,000 during that calendar year [72 P.S. § 9111(i)].

• *Agricultural commodities and other agricultural items*

A transfer of an agricultural commodity, agricultural conservation easement, agricultural reserve, agricultural-use property or a forest reserve (as those terms are defined in 72 P.S. § 9122(a) to lineal descendants or siblings is exempt from inheritance tax [72 P.S. § 9111(s.1)]. For additional information, see Informational Notice Inheritance Tax 2012-01 issued September 6, 2012.

• *Agriculture, business of*

A transfer of real estate devoted to the business of agriculture between members of the same family, provided that after the transfer the real estate continues to be devoted to the business of agriculture for a period of seven years beyond the transferor's date of death and the real estate derives a yearly gross income of at least $2,000 [72 P.S. § 9111(s)]. See 72 P.S. § 9111(s)(1, 2, 3) for further requirements (effective for decedents dying after June 30, 2012). However, if the real estate does is not devoted to the business of agriculture for at least seven years, it is taxable in the amount that would have been paid for nonexempt transfers, plus interest. For additional information, see Informational Notice Inheritance Tax 2012-01 issued September 6, 2012.

• *Charitable and fraternal organizations*

Transfers to or for the use of the following organizations are exempt from the Pennsylvania inheritance tax:

(1) Any corporation, unincorporated association, or society organized and operated exclusively for religious, charitable, scientific, literary, or educational purposes (including the encouragement of art and the prevention of cruelty to children or animals) if no part of the net earnings of the organization inures to the benefit of any private stockholder or individual and no substantial part of the activities of the organization is carrying on propaganda or otherwise attempting to influence legislation [72 P.S. § 9111(c)(1)].

(2) Any trustee or trustees, or any fraternal society, order, or association operating under the lodge system but only if the property transferred is to be used exclusively for religious, charitable, scientific, literary, or educational pur-

poses (or for the prevention of cruelty to children or animals) and no substantial part of the organization's activities is carrying on propaganda or otherwise attempting to influence legislation [72 P.S. § 9111(c)(2)].

(3) Any veterans' organization incorporated by act of Congress (or its departments or local chapters or posts) if no part of its net earnings inures to the benefit of any private shareholder or individual [72 P.S. § 9111(c)(3)].

• *Commonwealth as statutory heir*

Property awarded to Pennsylvania as statutory heir, by or without escheat (other than as custodian for a known distributee), is exempt from inheritance tax. If the Commonwealth later distributes the property, the inheritance tax is deducted at the applicable rate without interest before distribution [72 P.S. § 9111(l)].

• *Governmental units*

Transfers to or for the use of the United States, the Commonwealth of Pennsylvania, or any political subdivision of Pennsylvania are exempt from the inheritance tax [72 P.S. § 9111(b)].

• *Intangibles of nonresidents*

Intangible personal property held by, for, or for the benefit of a decedent who was a nonresident at time of death is exempt [72 P.S. § 9111(h)].

• *Inter vivos transfers to exempt donees*

Inter vivos transfers to governmental bodies and charities are exempt [72 P.S. § 9111(g)].

• *Life insurance*

Proceeds of life insurance on the decedent's life are exempt, including refunds of unearned premiums for the current policy period and post mortem dividends [72 P.S. § 9111(d)]. Life insurance proceeds are exempt even if paid under a pension, stock bonus, profit-sharing, Keogh, or other retirement plan [72 P.S. § 9111(r)].

• *Nominal ownership*

Property held in the name of a decedent who had no beneficial interest in the property is exempt [72 P.S. § 9111(n)].

• *Pennsylvania lottery winnings*

The proceeds of a Pennsylvania lottery prize, including a Powerball prize, are not subject to the Pennsylvania inheritance tax. Pennsylvania inheritance tax is not imposed on the present value of unpaid future installments of a decedent's Pennsylvania lottery prize. However, property purchased with lottery winnings is subject to inheritance tax; inheritance tax is imposed on a decedent's, transfer of real property or personal property (tangible or intangible) that was purchased or funded with proceeds from the decedent's Pennsylvania lottery winnings [*Pennsylvania Tax Update No. 100*, Pennsylvania Department of Revenue, August 2002].

• *Powers of appointment*

Property subject to a power of appointment, whether or not exercised and notwithstanding any blending of such property with property of the donee, is exempt from inheritance tax in the estate of the donee of the power of appointment [72 P.S. § 9111(k)].

General Power of Appointment Trusts

Unlike IRC § 2041, the Pennsylvania inheritance tax does not apply to the grantee (holder) of a general power of appointment over transferred property. Pennsylvania only taxes the grantor of the power at the time the interest is created. Thus, a husband could grant his spouse a general power of appointment over an irrevocable inter vivos trust, as well as a life income interest (with remainder to children at spouse's death), which property would only be taxed once at the husband's death. The tax imposed at the husband's death would also be less than the tax that would be due on an outright transfer, as life interests are valued actuarially. As the holder of the power, the wife is not subject to the state inheritance tax, even though she will have the ability to consume the trust funds during her lifetime provided she survives the decedent by nine months. See also ¶ 2908.

- *Proceeds obtained by estates of Vietnam veterans*

Pay and allowances determined by the United States to be due a member of its armed forces for service in Vietnam after August 5, 1964, for the period between the date declared by it as the beginning of the decedent's missing in action status to the date determined by it to be the date of death are exempt.

- *Railroad retirement burial benefits*

Lump-sum burial benefits from the U.S. Railroad Retirement Board are exempt (whether or not payable to the decedent's estate) [72 P.S. § 9111(q)].

- *Retirement benefits*

Payments under pension, stock bonus, profit-sharing, and other retirement plans are exempt. These include (but are not limited to) Keoghs, IRAs, and individual retirement bonds to distributees designated by the decedent or designated in accordance with the terms of the plan, to the extent that the decedent did not, before death, have the right (including proprietary rights at termination of employment) to possess, enjoy, assign, or anticipate the payment made. However, even if the decedent possessed any of these rights, these payments are exempt from Pennsylvania inheritance tax to the same extent that they are exempt from the federal estate tax under the provisions of the Internal Revenue Code of 1986, as amended, any supplement to the Code, or any similar provision in effect from time to time for federal estate tax purposes. A payment that would otherwise be exempt for federal purposes if it had not been made in a lump sum or other nonexempt form of payment is still exempt for Pennsylvania inheritance and estate tax purposes [72 P.S. § 9111(r)].

- *Spouses*

For decedents dying on or after January 1, 1995, transfers to or for the use of a spouse are exempt from inheritance tax. Property owned by spouses with right of survivorship is exempt unless the ownership was created within one year of decedent's death, in which case the property is entirely taxable in the estate of the spouse who created the co-ownership to the extent that the value of the property exceeds $3,000 [72 P.S. § 9111(m)].

- *Qualified family owned businesses*

Effective for estates of decedents who die on or after July 1, 2013, Act 52 excludes from inheritance tax the transfer of qualified family-owned businesses between members of the same family. Exempt transfers include:

— The transfer of a business operated as a sole proprietorship if, at the time of the decedent's death, the net book value of the assets is less than $5 million, and the business has fewer than 50 full-time equivalent employees.

— The transfer of an interest in a business entity if, at the time of the decedent's death, (i) the net book value of the assets is less than $5 million, (ii) the business has fewer than 50 full-time equivalent employees, (iii) the business is wholly owned by the decedent or the members of the decedent's family, (iv) the entity is engaged in a trade or business other than managing investments or income-producing assets, and (v) the entity has been in existence for at least five years as of the time of the decedent's death.

To be eligible for the exemption, a qualified transferee of the decedent must continue to own the business for seven years following the decedent's death. Failure to do so results in the imposition of the inheritance tax that would have been paid,

¶ 2906

plus interest accrued from the date of the decedent's death. To enforce this provision, the each qualified transferee must annually certify that he or she is continuing to operate the business and is required to notify the Department of Revenue of any subsequent transfer. An owner's failure to annually certify results in the loss of the exemption. The tax becomes due on the date of a transfer that causes the transferee to fail to operate the business as required by Act 52 [72 P.S. § 9111(t)]. Act 84 of 2016 broadens the exemption for family farms and family businesses, allowing for farms and businesses that are transferred "to or for the benefit of" a member of the same family to be exempt from the taxable estate. This language extends the family farm and business exclusions to transfers to trusts for the benefit of members of the same family. This amendment also added relatives of a decedent's spouse to the definition of "members of the same family." The farm provision is effective retroactive to dates of death after December 31, 2012, while the business provision is retroactive to dates of death after June 30, 2013.

• *Veterans*

The lump-sum death payment from the Social Security Administration or Veterans Administration or any county veterans' death benefit or other similar death benefit, whether or not paid to the decedent's estate, is exempt from inheritance tax [72 P.S. § 9111(p)].

• *War risk insurance*

Proceeds of any Federal War Risk Insurance, National Service Life Insurance, or similar governmental insurance are exempt from inheritance tax, including refunds of unearned premiums for the current policy period and post- mortem dividends [72 P.S. § 9111(e)].

• *Worthless obligations*

Obligations owing to the decedent that are worthless immediately before death are exempt, even if collectible from the obligor's distributive share of the estate [72 P.S. § 9111(o)].

¶2907 "Pick-Up" Estate Tax

The estate tax is a "pick-up" tax in the sense that it is imposed in the event that a federal estate tax is payable and the Pennsylvania inheritance tax is less than the federal maximum credit for state death taxes allowable under the Internal Revenue Code [72 P.S. § 9117(a)]. Thus, the Pennsylvania estate tax is designed to "pick up" the difference between the Commonwealth inheritance tax and the maximum federal credit for state taxes.

Repeal of Federal Estate Tax Decoupling

In order to prevent the loss of state tax revenue because of the passage of the federal Economic Growth and Tax Relief Reconciliation Act of 2001 (EGTRRA, P.L. 107-16), Act 89 of 2002 decoupled the Pennsylvania estate tax from current federal law, basing the Pennsylvania estate tax on federal law as amended to June 1, 2001. However, Act 46 of 2003 provided for the repeal of federal decoupling, effective for decedents who die after June 30, 2002 [Act of December 23, 2003 (H.B. 200), § 24]. The Pennsylvania estate tax now continues to be based on federal law.

• *Resident decedents*

The "pick-up" tax is imposed when federal estate tax is payable on the transfer of the taxable estate of a decedent who is a resident of Pennsylvania and the inheritance tax actually paid to the Commonwealth (disregarding interest or the amount of any discount allowed under 72 P.S. § 9142 (explained at ¶ 3112)) is less than the maximum federal credit allowable under IRC § 2011. If the inheritance tax for state death taxes paid to the Commonwealth is less than the maximum allowable federal credit, the "pick-up" tax is the excess of the maximum allowable federal credit over the Commonwealth inheritance tax [72 P.S. § 9117(a)].

• *Credit for resident decedents with property in another state*

If a resident decedent owned or had an interest in real or tangible personal property having a situs in another state, the Pennsylvania inheritance tax is reduced by the greater of the following: (1) the amount of death taxes actually paid to the other state, *excluding* any death tax expressly imposed to receive the benefit of the federal credit for state death taxes [72 P.S. § 9117(a)(1)]; or (2) an amount computed by multiplying the maximum federal credit for state death taxes by a fraction, the numerator of which is the value of the real and tangible personal property included in the decedent's gross estate for federal estate tax purposes that has a situs in the other state and the denominator of which is the decedent's gross estate for federal estate tax purposes [72 P.S. § 9117(a)(2)].

• *Nonresident decedents*

A "pick-up" tax is also imposed in the event that a federal estate tax is payable on the transfer of the taxable estate of a decedent who was not a resident of Pennsylvania at the time of death but who owned or had an interest in real or tangible personal property having a situs in Pennsylvania. The tax is computed by (1) multiplying the maximum federal credit for state death taxes by a fraction, the numerator of which is the value of the real and tangible personal property included in the decedent's gross estate for federal estate tax purposes that has a situs in Pennsylvania and the denominator of which is the decedent's gross estate for federal estate tax purposes and (2) deducting from that amount the inheritance tax actually paid to the Commonwealth (disregarding interest or the amount of any discount allowed under 72 P.S. § 9142 (explained at ¶ 3112)) [72 P.S. § 9117(b)].

• *Credit for estate tax paid*

When an inheritance tax is imposed after an estate tax has been paid, the estate tax paid is allowed as a credit against the inheritance tax [72 P.S. § 9117(c)].

• *Returns and payment of tax*

The person required to make the inheritance tax return is initially liable for payment of the estate tax [72 P.S. § 9145(a)]. The personal representative of a decedent or (if there is no personal representative) any other fiduciary charged by law with the duty of filing a federal estate tax return must (within one month of the filing or receipt of the return) file with the register a copy of the decedent's federal estate tax return. If the decedent was a nonresident, the filing is made with the register who issued letters, if any, in Pennsylvania (otherwise with the Department of Revenue). The assessment of estate tax is made by the register or the Department of Revenue within three (3) months after the filing of the required documents. If the required documents are not filed, the assessment is made within an additional period as the court, upon application of any party in interest, fixes [72 P.S. § 9145(b)].

¶ 2907

• *Due date and payment of tax*

The estate tax is due at the date of decedent's death. It does not, however, become delinquent until nine (9) months after the decedent's death. Any estate tax resulting from a final change in the federal return or of the tax due does not become until one (1) month after the person(s) liable for payment have received final notice of the increase of the federal estate tax [72 P.S. § 9145(c)].

Payment: If the decedent was a Pennsylvania resident, the estate tax is paid to the register; if the decedent was not a Pennsylvania resident, the estate tax is paid to the register who issued letters, if any, in Pennsylvania. Otherwise, it is paid to the Department of Revenue [72 P.S. § 9145(g)].

No discount: No discount is allowed in paying the estate tax [72 P.S. § 9145(d)].

• *Interest on unpaid tax*

If the inheritance tax is not paid before the date it becomes delinquent, interest on the unpaid tax shall be charged after the date of delinquency at the rate established under the Fiscal Code (see ¶ 4612) [72 P.S. § 9145(e)]. When payment of inheritance tax is not made because of litigation or other unavoidable cause of delay and the property on which the tax has been calculated has remained in the hands of a fiduciary and has not produced a net income equal to rate of interest provided in this section annually, interest for such period shall be calculated at the rate of the net income produced by the property. Any payment on delinquent inheritance tax shall be applied first to any interest due on the tax at the date of payment and then, if there is any balance, to the tax itself [72 P.S. § 9143].

¶2908 Spousal Poverty Exemption

[This provision was repealed by Act 52 of 2013 effective immediately.] The General Assembly, in recognition of the powers contained in § 2(b)(11) of Article VIII of the Pennsylvania Constitution, has established a poverty exemption (in the Act of August 4, 1991, No. 22, § 36) for transfers of property to or for the use of surviving spouses who qualify under the provisions of 72 P.S. § 9117 [72 P.S. § 9112]. The poverty exemption for inheritance and estate tax purposes is treated as a credit [72 P.S. § 9112(d)].

Spousal Poverty Exemption Expired in 1995

The spousal poverty exemption does not apply to estates of decedents dying on or after January 1, 1995 [72 P.S. § 9112(g)]or to *inter vivos* transfers made by decedents dying on or after January 1, 1995, without regard to the date of the transfer.

• *Eligibility requirements*

A claim for an inheritance tax poverty exemption will be allowed if the following three requirements are met [72 P.S. § 9112(c)]:

(1) The transferee is the spouse of the decedent at the date of decedent's death.

(2) The value of the decedent's estate does not exceed $200,000 after reduction for actual liabilities of the decedent as evidenced by a written agreement.

(3) The average of the joint exemption income of the decedent and the transferee for the three taxable years immediately preceding the date of the decedent's death does not exceed $40,000. Exemption income means all moneys or property (including, without limitation, interest, gains or income derived

from obligations exempt from state or location taxation under any other federal or state laws) received of whatever nature and from whatever source derived [72 P.S. §9102(a)].

• *Credit against the inheritance tax*

An eligible spouse is entitled to the benefit of the following exemptions as a credit against the inheritance and estate tax [72 P.S. §9112(d)]:

(1) For decedents dying on or after January 1, 1992, and before January 1, 1993, the credit is the lesser of (a) 2% of the taxable value of the property transferred to or for the use of the surviving spouse or (b) 2% of $100,000 of the taxable value of the property transferred to or for the use of the surviving spouse.

(2) For decedents dying on or after January 1, 1993, and before January 1, 1994, the credit is the lesser of (a) 4% of the taxable value of the property transferred to or for the use of the surviving spouse or (b) 4% of $100,000 of the taxable value of the property transferred to or for the use of the surviving spouse.

(3) For decedents dying on or after January 1, 1994, the credit is the lesser of (a) 6% of the taxable value of the property transferred to or for the use of the surviving spouse or (b) 6% of $100,000 of the taxable value of the property transferred to or for the use of the surviving spouse.

Maximum Credit

The amount of the credit computed under the poverty exemption provisions is limited to the amount of the tax imposed [72 P.S. §9112(f)].

• *Nonresident decedents*

For qualifying nonresident decedents, the poverty exemption credit bears the same ratio as that of the decedent's estate in Pennsylvania bears to the decedent's total estate without regard to situs [72 P.S. §9112(d)].

• *Filing and payment requirements*

Filing and payment requirements are explained along with the inheritance tax requirements in Chapter 31.

¶2909 Trusts and Similar Arrangements for Spouses

In the case of a transfer of property for the sole use of surviving spouse of the decedent (transferor) during the surviving spouse's lifetime, all succeeding interests that follow the interest of the surviving spouse are not taxable as transfers by the transferor but are deemed to be transfers subject to tax by the surviving spouse of the property held in the trust or similar arrangement at the death of the surviving spouse. The succeeding interests are valued at the death of the surviving spouse and taxed at the tax rates applicable to dispositions by the surviving spouse. Any exemption from tax based on the kind or location of property is based upon the kind or location of property held in the trust or similar arrangement at the surviving spouse's death [72 P.S. §9113].

Transfer for the Sole Use

The definition of "a transfer of property for the sole use" has been amended to mean "a transfer to or for the use of a transferee if, during the transferee's lifetime, the transferee is entitled to all income and principal distributions from the property and no person, including the transferee, possesses an inter vivos power of appointment over the property" [72 P.S. §9102]. This change in definition prevents the avoidance of inheritance tax through the creation of trusts over which a transferee or some other person has an inter vivos power of appointment over the property.

In the absence of a contrary intent appearing in the instrument creating the trust or similar arrangement and in the absence of a contrary direction by the surviving spouse, the inheritance tax (including interest) due at the death of a surviving spouse with respect to a trust or similar arrangement under 72 P.S. §9113 is to be paid out of the principal of the trust or similar arrangement. The payment must be made by the trustee or other fiduciary in possession of the property. If the payment is not made by the trustee or fiduciary, the payment must be made by the transferee of such principal [72 P.S. §9144(e.1)].

NOTE: These provisions are applicable to the estates of decedents dying on or after January 1, 1995, and to the *inter vivos* transfers made by decedents dying on or after January 1, 1995, without regard to the date of the transfer.

INHERITANCE AND ESTATE TAX

CHAPTER 30
VALUATION OF ESTATE

¶ 3001	Valuation of Property
¶ 3002	Special Valuation for Farmland

¶ 3001 Valuation of Property

In general, property subject to the inheritance and estate tax is valued at its fair market value on the date of decedent's death. If a federal estate tax return is filed, the Commonwealth normally accepts the federal values. In the case of an *inter vivos* transfer not made in trust, property is valued at the date of decedent's death. When an *inter vivos* transfer was made to a trust, the property to be valued is that comprising the portion of the trust that exists at the transferor's death and that is traceable from property subject to the inheritance and estate tax [72 P.S. § 9121(a)]. See ¶ 2905 for explanation of taxable transfers. Certain special valuation situations are explained below.

• *Real estate valuation suspensions for inheritance tax*

The department recently established the time period during which it will allow a real estate valuation suspension for inheritance tax calculation purposes. To ensure all such suspensions are handled uniformly, suspensions will now be allowed for up to 15 months after a decedent's date of death. Previously, the department did not specify a timeframe during which a suspended valuation would be accepted. Pennsylvania's inheritance tax law provides that the value of property upon which inheritance tax is imposed is the value at the date of the decedent's death. The value of real estate often is difficult to establish, absent a sale between unrelated parties (also known as an arms-length sale). The department therefore has allowed the personal representative of an estate, upon filing an otherwise complete REV-1500 Inheritance Tax Return, to request that the tax calculation on the real estate be suspended until the value of the property is determined at the time of sale. Effective immediately, the department will allow an estate to suspend the valuation on the original and timely filed inheritance tax return for up to 15 months. The 15-month period includes the nine months after which the inheritance tax return becomes delinquent, plus the additional six-month filing extension. When the property is sold after the inheritance tax return is timely filed and the suspension requested, the estate should then report the arms-length sales price on a supplemental inheritance tax return. If the real property is not sold within 15 months of the date of death, an estate will have to report an alternate means of establishing the value, including a professional appraisal or the common level ratio value. A personal representative also may choose to report a value of real property on a timely filed inheritance tax return and pay the inheritance tax due on its transfer. If the estate then, at a point within 15 months from the decedent's date of death, sells the property at an arms-length sale for a lesser value, it may, on a timely filed petition, request a refund of any overpaid tax [Pennsylvania Tax Update No. 158, October/November 2011, Pennsylvania Department of Revenue].

• *Stocks and bonds*

Market value is determined by taking the mean of the highest and lowest quoted selling prices on the date of death. If death occurs on a weekend, the valuation of any stock listed on the New York or American Stock Exchange is the average of the mean between the high and low for Friday and the mean between the high and low on the Monday after death. If death occurs on a holiday, the valuation is the average of the mean of the high and the low on the day preceding the holiday and the mean between the high and low of the succeeding market day. If there were no sales on the valuation date, but there were sales on dates within a reasonable period before and after the valuation date, the value is determined by taking a weighted average of the means between the highest and lowest sales on the nearest date before and after the valuation date. The average is weighted inversely by the respective numbers of trading days between the selling dates and the valuation date. In cases of over-the-counter stocks, use the mean between the bid and asked [Instructions for Form REV-1500].

• *Life interest*

The value of a life interest is determined in accordance with federal estate tax regulations until the Department of Revenue promulgates rules and regulations to the contrary [72 P.S. § 9121(b)].

• *Interest for term certain*

Until the Department of Revenue promulgates rules and regulations to the contrary, the value of an interest for a term certain must be determined under federal estate tax regulations [72 P.S. § 9121(c)].

• *Annuity or life estate terminated within nine months of decedent's death*

If an annuity or a life estate is terminated by the death of the annuitant or life tenant or by the happening of a contingency within nine months after the decedent's death, its value is the value, at date of the decedent's death, of the amount of the annuity or income actually paid or payable to the annuitant or life tenant during the period he/she was entitled to the annuity or were in possession of the estate. If an appraisement of an annuity or life estate is filed before termination of the annuity or life estate, the appraisement and any assessment based on it will be revised upon request by any party in interest (including the Commonwealth and the personal representative) insofar as the appraisement and assessment relate to the valuation of the terminated annuity or life estate. This can be done without following the procedures for protest, notice, and appeal. See ¶ 3204 for explanation of these procedures [72 P.S. § 9121(d)].

• *Future interest*

The value of a future interest must be determined in accordance with federal estate tax regulations until the Department of Revenue promulgates rules and regulations to the contrary [72 P.S. § 9121(e)].

• *Property subject to option or agreement*

When property is subject, during decedent's lifetime and at time of death, to a binding option or agreement to sell, its appraised value cannot exceed the price established by the option or agreement if the option or agreement is a bona fide arrangement and not a device to transfer the property for less than full and adequate consideration. If the option or agreement is not exercised, the property's appraised value is not limited to the established price. However, it cannot exceed the value of the property on the date of decedent's death. If tax has been assessed on the basis of an established price and the option or agreement is not exercised or is exercised at an amount greater than the established price, the fiduciary or transferee must file a supplemental return reporting the facts [72 P.S. § 9121(f)].

• *Awards received in reparation*

Property or income received by a decedent's estate for the seizure, theft, requisition, or involuntary conversion of property or income of victims of Nazi persecution

¶3001

have a value of zero at the decedent transferor's death, if the decedent died on or before the date of award or settlement [61 Pa. Code § 94.2].

• *Mineral Rights and Natural Gas Interests*

All mineral and natural gas rights shall be reported on *Inheritance Tax Schedule (REV-1508)* as Cash, Bank Deposits and Misc. Personal Property at the taxable values [*Inheritance Tax Bulletin 2012-01*, Pennsylvania Department of Revenue, July 10, 2012]:

(a) (1) *Mineral rights:* The taxable value of mineral rights is determined using the same methodology used to value any real property or tangible personal property interest. Taxable value is most clearly established by determining the actual monetary worth of the interest determined by either a *bona fide* sale or, if the transfer is for no or nominal consideration, computed value (based on the common-level ratio applies to the assessed value of the mineral right). In the event that there is no sale and no computed value, the taxable value is the interest's actual monetary worth. The term "actual value" technically means cash value, but in practice book value is used for all assets.

(2) *Natural gas rights:* The taxable value of natural gas rights shall be determined using the same methodology used to value any real property or tangible personal property interest. Taxable value is most clearly established by determining the actual monetary worth of the interest determined by a *bona fide* sale. If there is no *bona fide* sale, natural gas rights can be determined from a credible appraisal. A computed value using assessed value cannot be accomplished because natural gas rights do not have assessed values. Absent a *bona fide* sale, an appraisal, or other credible evidence to the contrary, the value shall be determined as follows:

Leased and producing properties: An estate shall value natural gas rights at an amount equal to any amounts receive that were attributable to actual production of the natural gas interest, at issue during the 12 months *prior* to the decedent's date of death, multiplied by two.

(b) Leased, non-producing properties (including unconventional natural gas wells as defined by 58 Pa.C.S. § 2301), interests shall be reported at a value of zero unless, at the time of death, the properties were part of a *contractual arrangement* whereby the properties generated fixed future payments, in which case the natural gas rights shall be calculated by reducing the fixed future payments to present value as of the decedent's date of death using established Internal Revenue Service actuarial tables as found in *IRS Publication 1457 Actuarial Values* Table B, Section 3 Annuity, Income, and Remainder Interests For a Term Certain.

(c) For non-leased, non-producing properties, interests shall be reported at a value of zero.

¶3002 Special Valuation for Farmland

Farmland is eligible for special valuation (*i.e.*, the value it has for its particular use). Farmland for this purpose is land or an interest in land that is owned by a decedent and devoted to agricultural use, agricultural reserve, or forest reserve and that meets the necessary conditions explained below [72 P.S. § 9122(b)(1)].

Agricultural Conservation Easements

The transfer of land or an interest in land that is part of an agricultural conservation easement is 50% of the value of the easement for inheritance tax purposes [72 P.S. § 9211(3)]. An "agricultural conservation easement" is as defined in § 3 of the Act of June 30, 1981 (P.L. 128, No. 43), known as the "Agricultural Area Security Law" [72 P.S. § 9211(a)].

• *Agricultural use*

Agricultural use means use for the purpose of producing an agricultural commodity. An agricultural commodity is any plant or animal product (including Christmas trees produced in Pennsylvania for commercial purposes). Land devoted to and meeting the requirements and qualifications for payments or other compensation pursuant to a soil conservation program under an agreement with an agency of the federal government is considered to be used for agricultural use [72 P.S. §9122(a)].

Necessary conditions: The land must have been devoted to agricultural use for the three years preceding the death of the decedent; must be at least 10 contiguous acres in area or have an anticipated yearly gross income derived from agricultural use of $2,000; and must be the entire contiguous area of the owner used for agricultural use purposes [72 P.S. §9122(b)(1)(i), (iv)].

• *Agricultural reserve*

Agricultural reserves are noncommercial open-space lands (1) used for outdoor recreation or enjoyment of scenery or nature and (2) open to the public without charge on a nondiscriminatory basis [72 P.S. §9122(a)].

Necessary conditions: The land must be at least 10 contiguous acres in area and the entire contiguous area of the owner must be used for agricultural reserve [72 P.S. §9122(b)(1)(ii), (iv)].

• *Forest reserve*

A forest reserve is land (10 acres or more) stocked by forest trees of any size and capable of producing timber or other wood products [72 P.S. §9122(a)].

Necessary conditions: The land must be at least 10 contiguous acres in area and the entire contiguous area of the owner must be used for forest reserve purposes [72 P.S. §9122(b)(1)(iii), (iv)].

• *Valuation factors*

In determining the value of farmland under special valuation rules, consideration must be given to available evidence of the land's capability for its particular use as derived from the soil survey at the Pennsylvania State University, the National Cooperative Soil Survey, the United States Census of Agricultural Categories of land use classes, and other evidence of the capability of the land devoted to such use. In addition, if the land is assessed under the provisions of the Pennsylvania Farmland and Forest Land Assessment Act of 1974, consideration must be given to the valuation determined by the local county assessor [72 P.S. §9122(b)(2)].

• *Abandonment of special use*

If land valued for inheritance tax purposes for a special use is applied to a use other than agricultural use, agricultural reserve, or forest reserve or is removed from the category of land preferentially valued (for any reason except condemnation) within seven years of the decedent's death, the owner of the land is liable for the tax savings achieved through special use valuation. The tax due upon removal from agricultural use is an amount equal to the difference, if any, between the taxes paid or payable on the basis of the special valuation and the taxes that would have been paid or payable on the market value at time of a decedent's death, plus interest from date of death to the change of use. Interest is explained at ¶4612. The tax is due on the date of change of use and becomes a lien upon the property in favor of the Commonwealth. Owners of land must notify the register of wills in the county or counties in which the land is located of any change or proposed change in land use. Failure to make notification is a misdemeanor of the third degree [72 P.S. §9122(c)].

¶3002

• *Separation, split-off, or transfer*

The split-off of a part of land that has been valued as farmland for a use other than agricultural use, agricultural reserve, or forest reserve within the seven years following the decedent's death subjects the split-off land and the entire parcel from which it was split to inheritance tax at the higher valuation, except in certain cases:

(1) The special valuation is not lost if the split-off occurs because of condemnation [72 P.S. § 9122(d)(1)].

(2) An owner may, without invalidating the special valuation, split off a maximum of two acres per year of farmland if it is used only for (a) residential purposes, (b) agricultural use, agricultural reserve, or forest reserve purposes, or (c) construction of a residential dwelling to be occupied by the person to whom the land is transferred. However, the total amount of land that can be split off for these purposes cannot exceed the lesser of 10 acres or 10% of the entire tract of farmland [72 P.S. § 9122(d)(2)].

"Split-off" means a division (by conveyance or other action of the owner) of farmland into two or more tracts of land, the use of which on one or more tracts does not meet the requirements of § 3 of the Act of December 19, 1974 (P.L. 973, No. 319), known as the "Pennsylvania Farmland and Forest Land Assessment Act of 1974" [72 P.S. § 9122(a)].

An owner may separate farmland within seven years of decedent's death without jeopardizing its special valuation unless a subsequent abandonment of preferential use occurs within seven years of the separation [72 P.S. § 9122(d)(3)]. Separation means the division (by conveyance or other action of the owner) of farmland into two or more tracts of land that continue to be farmland, if all tracts separated meet the requirements of § 3 of the Act of December 19, 1974 (P.L. 973, No. 319), known as the "Pennsylvania Farmland and Forest Land Assessment Act of 1974" [72 P.S. § 9122(a)]. When farmland is separated among beneficiaries and one beneficiary changes the use within seven years of the decedent's death, only the tract held by the beneficiary who changes the use loses its special valuation [72 P.S. § 9122(d)(4)].

INHERITANCE AND ESTATE TAX

CHAPTER 31
DEDUCTIONS, DETERMINATION, AND PAYMENT OF TAX

GENERAL

¶3101 Scope of Chapter

This chapter explains the allowable deductions from the gross estate for inheritance tax purposes and the procedure for filing returns and paying the tax.

DEDUCTIONS

¶3105 General

Only those deductions specifically allowable under the statute can be claimed. Allowable deductions may be taken regardless of whether or not assets included in the decedent's taxable estate are used to pay the deductible items. Deductions are allowed to transferees only to the extent they actually paid the deductible items and either the transferees were legally obligated to pay the deductible items or the estate subject to administration by a personal representative is insufficient to pay the deductible items [72 P.S. § 9126].

¶3106 Expenses

The expenses discussed below are deductible [72 P.S. § 9127].

• *Administration expenses*

All reasonable expenses of administering the decedent's estate and the assets in decedent's taxable estate are deductible.

• *Bequest to fiduciary or attorney in lieu of fees*

A transfer to an executor, trustee, or attorney in lieu of compensation for services is deductible to the extent it does not exceed reasonable compensation for the services to be performed.

• *Family exemption*

A family exemption of $3,500 ($2,000 prior to January 31, 1995) may be deducted from the value of the property transferred [72 P.S. § 9127(3)]. The family exemption is a right given to specific individuals to retain or claim certain types of a decedent's property as provided in 20 Pa.C.S. § 3121. The spouse of any decedent dying domiciled in Pennsylvania may retain or claim as an exemption either real or personal property or both, not theretofore sold by the personal representative. Property specifically devised or bequeathed by the decedent, or otherwise specifically disposed of by the decedent, may not be so retained or claimed if other assets are available for the exemption. If there is no surviving spouse, the exemption may be claimed by children who are members of the same household as the decedent; if there are no such children, the exemption may be claimed by parent(s) of the decedent who are members of the same household as the decedent [20 Pa.C.S. § 3121].

• *Funeral and burial expenses*

Reasonable and customary funeral expenses, including the cost of a family burial lot or other resting place, are deductible. Also deductible are reasonable and customary expenses for the purchase and erection of a monument, gravestone, or marker on decedent's burial lot or final resting place.

• *Burial trusts or contracts*

Bequests or devises in trust, or funds placed in trust after decedent's death, or funds paid under a contract after decedent's death (in reasonable amounts) to be applied to the care and preservation of the family burial lot or other final resting place, in which decedent is buried or the remains of the decedent repose and the structure on the burial lot or other final resting place, are deductible.

• *Bequests for religious services*

Reasonable bequests for the performance or celebration of religious rites, rituals, services, or ceremonies because of decedent's death are deductible.

• *Taxes*

Deductible taxes are discussed at ¶ 3107.

• *Debts of the decedent*

Deductible debts are discussed at ¶ 3108.

¶3107 Taxes

The taxes discussed below are deductible [72 P.S. § 9128].

• *Property taxes*

A deduction is allowed for taxes imposed against decedent or any property in decedent's gross taxable estate that were owed before decedent's death. If the decedent wasn't personally liable for the taxes, the deduction is limited to the value of the property against which the taxes are imposed.

• *State and foreign death taxes*

The federal estate tax is not deductible, but death taxes (disregarding interest and penalty) paid to other states and U.S. territories and to taxing jurisdictions outside the United States and its territories are deductible if (1) the transfer is taxable in Pennsylvania or, (2) the taxes had to be paid to bring the assets into Pennsylvania or to transfer them to the new owner.

¶3108 Liabilities

The general rule is that all of the decedent's liabilities are deductible [72 P.S. § 9129].

¶3107

- *Debts*

Debts based on a contract or agreement are deductible only if they are bona fide and based on an adequate and full consideration.

- *Secured loans*

Secured loans are deductible whether or not the security is part of the gross taxable estate, except in the case of certain security located outside Pennsylvania. See ¶3109.

- *Joint obligation*

Decedent's liability (net of all collectible contribution) on a joint obligation is deductible whether or not payment is secured by property that passes to another under the right of survivorship. Debt secured by property located outside of Pennsylvania is not deductible.

- *Support contract*

Indebtedness arising from a contract for decedent's support is deductible.

- *Legacy in discharge of decedent's obligation*

Decedent's debts are deductible even if they are discharged by testamentary gift.

- *Outlawed debt*

Debt that is unenforceable because of a statute of limitations is deductible if the estate pays it.

- *Pledge to exempt transferee*

A pledge to an exempt transferee is deductible if the estate pays it, even if it is not legally enforceable.

- *Liability for tort or as accommodation party*

Liabilities arising from decedent's tort or status as an accommodation endorser, guarantor, or surety are deductible unless it can be reasonably anticipated that decedent's estate will be exonerated or reimbursed by others primarily liable or subject to contribution.

- *Obligations of surviving spouse*

Any item that would be deductible if the decedent were unmarried is deductible even if the surviving spouse is legally liable for and financially able to pay the item.

- *Medical expenses*

Decedent's medical expenses are not deductible if the estate will be exonerated or reimbursed from other sources.

¶3109 Disallowed Deductions

The following deductions are specifically disallowed by statute [72 P.S. §9130]:

(1) Claims of former or surviving spouse, or others, with respect to an agreement with the decedent if they arise in consideration of relinquishment or promised relinquishment of marital or support rights.

(2) Litigation expenses of beneficiaries.

(3) Indebtedness secured by real or tangible personal property with a situs outside of Pennsylvania (except to the extent the indebtedness is more than the value of the property).

RETURNS AND PAYMENT OF TAX

¶3110 Who Must File Returns

The personal representative of the decedent's estate must file an inheritance tax return. A transferee of property must file a return only if the property is not included in the return of the personal representative. The inclusion of property in a return does not constitute an admission that its transfer is taxable. A personal representative or transferee required to file a return must promptly file a supplemental return if additional assets and transfers come to his/her knowledge after the filing of the original return [72 P.S. §9136].

¶3111 Time and Place of Filing Returns

Inheritance tax returns must be filed (on forms prescribed by the Department of Revenue) within nine months after decedent's death. At any time before expiration of the nine-month period, the Department may grant an extension of time for filing a return for an additional six months [72 P.S. §9136(d), (e)].

Returns for a resident decedent must be filed with the register of wills having jurisdiction to grant letters testamentary or of administration in decedent's estate. This is the register in the decedent's domiciliary county. Returns for nonresident decedents must be filed with the register who issued letters, if any, in Pennsylvania. If no Pennsylvania register issued letters, returns for nonresident decedents must be filed with the Department of Revenue [72 P.S. §9136(f)].

• *Estate tax*

The personal representative of every decedent or, if there is no personal representative, any other fiduciary that would be chargeable by law with the duty of filing a federal estate tax return, must (within 1 month of the filing or receipt of the return) file with the register or, if the decedent was a nonresident, with the register who issues letters if any, in Pennsylvania or otherwise with the Department of Revenue, a copy of the federal estate tax return, and of any communication from the federal government making any final change in the return or of the tax due. The assessment of estate tax must be made by the register or Department within three (3) months after the filing of the required documents. If the required filings are not made, the assessment must be made within such additional period as the court, upon application of any party in interest, including the personal representative shall fix [72 P.S. §9145(b)].

¶3112 Payment of Tax

The inheritance tax is due at the date of decedent's death and becomes delinquent nine months after decedent's death. If it is paid within three months after decedent's death, a 5% discount is allowed [72 P.S. §9142]. The Department of Revenue may, for reasonable cause, extend the time for payment of any part of the inheritance tax. The Department has discretionary authority to impose a bond not in excess of double the estate tax due upon granting an extension of payment or in other circumstances where the bond is considered necessary to protect the Commonwealth's interest. However, if the trustee or one of the trustees is a bank and trust company or a trust company organized in Pennsylvania or a national banking association with principal office in Pennsylvania, no bond is required. Any required bond is filed with the register of wills [72 P.S. §9150].

If the inheritance tax is not paid before the date it becomes delinquent, interest on the unpaid tax is charged under Fiscal Code (FC) provisions (explained at ¶4612). If delay in payment is due to litigation or other unavoidable cause of delay and the property has remained in the hands of a fiduciary and has not produced income

¶3110

equal to the rate of interest provided by law, interest is calculated at the rate of net income produced by the property. Any payment of delinquent inheritance tax is applied first to interest due on the date of payment and then to the tax itself [72 P.S. § 9143].

In the absence of contrary intent appearing in a will or *inter vivos* trust, the inheritance tax (including interest) is paid out of the residuary estate or trust. The tax on transfers for limited periods is paid out of the principal of the property. However, the ultimate liability for the tax is upon the transferee [72 P.S. § 9144]. The personal representative of an estate is responsible for deducting tax from property or collecting it from transferees, and cannot be compelled to transfer property to transferees without withholding or collecting the tax. If a transferee refuses to pay the tax, the personal representative, under direction of the court, may sell the property subject to the tax [72 P.S. § 9146].

Inheritance tax due on certain small business interests may be paid in quarterly installments over a period of several years. The quarterly payments may be spread over five years [72 P.S. § 9154].

• *Estate tax*

The estate tax is due on the decedent's death and becomes delinquent nine months after decedent's death. Additional estate tax caused by a final change in decedent's federal return becomes delinquent one month after the person(s) liable to pay the tax receive final notice of the increase in federal estate tax. There are no discounts for early payment of the estate tax. Interest provisions for the estate tax are the same as those for the inheritance tax [72 P.S. § 9145].

INHERITANCE AND ESTATE TAX

CHAPTER 32
ADMINISTRATION AND REVIEW

¶3201 Appraisement

Appraisement is a review procedure unique to the inheritance tax. See ¶4602 for explanation of other review procedures. Appraisement, like the other departmental review procedures, is a kind of "desk audit." A departmental representative reviews and verifies the return.

The Department of Revenue is responsible for appraisement of taxable property. The appraisement, unless suspended until audit, must be made within six months after the inheritance tax return is filed or within an additional period fixed by the court, upon application of any party in interest [72 P.S. §9137].

¶3202 Review of Deductions

The official with whom the return is filed (see ¶3111) determines the allowance or disallowance of deductions. This determination, unless suspended until audit, must be made within six months after the claim for allowance is filed or within an additional period fixed by the court. However, a fiduciary may request at the audit that the determination and allowance be made by the court. If requested, the court may determine and allow as deductions all properly deductible credits claimed or allowed at the audit without requiring the filing of a separate claim, fix the amount of tax, and decree payment of the tax. The court cannot allow deductions totaling more than $100 unless the Commonwealth is represented at the audit by counsel or there is proof that the register has had at least 30 days' notice of the claim [72 P.S. §9138].

¶3203 Assessment Procedures

After appraisement and determination of deductions have been made, the official with whom the return is required to be filed will assess the tax due. The assessment, unless suspended until audit, must be made within one month after the later of the filing of the appraisement or determination of deductions or within an additional period fixed by the court [72 P.S. §9139]. The Department of Revenue must give (or cause to be given) notice of the filing of the appraisement, the determination of the deductions, and the amount of the tax assessed to the personal representative and any transferee who filed a return, or to their attorneys [72 P.S. §9140].

¶3204 Protest, Notice, and Appeal

Any party in interest, including the Commonwealth and the personal representative, may appeal the appraisement, determination of deductions, assessment of tax, or any other inheritance or estate tax matter within 60 days after receipt of notice of the action. Taxpayers have the following three options to effect an appeal [72 P.S. §9186(a)]:

(1) Filing a written protest with the Department of Revenue (sending a copy to the Office of the Attorney General).

(2) Giving the register written notification that they elect to have the correctness of the action determined at the audit of the account of the personal representative.

(3) Filing an appeal to the court to have the correctness of the action determined at the audit of the account of the personal representative or at a time fixed by the court.

The protest, notification, or appeal must specify all objections to the action. When the protest, notification, or appeal is filed by the Commonwealth, a copy must be sent to the personal representative and to all other persons who filed a return.

If a notification or appeal has been filed from an assessment with respect to a future interest, contending that the rate of tax that will be applicable when the future interest vests cannot be determined with certainty, the court, after considering relevant evidence, determines what portion of the transfer is to be taxed and the rate of tax applicable [72 P.S. §9186(b)].

Whenever any appeal or protest is brought with respect to special valuation of farmland (explained at ¶3002), the forum designated by the Department to hear the appeal or protest must include at least two farmers and the Secretary of Agriculture [72 P.S. §9186(c)].

Bonds are not required of parties in interest who file protest, notification, or appeals from appraisements, deduction determinations, assessments of tax, or other matters relating to the tax, or from a departmental decision following a protest or who petition for removal of the record to the court [72 P.S. §9187].

• *Appeal and removal to the court*

Any party in interest not satisfied with the departmental decision on a protest can appeal to the Court of Common Pleas, orphan's court division, in the county in which the decedent resided at death, within 60 days after receipt of notice of the entry of the Department of Revenue's decision. If the Department has not rendered a decision within 30 days after the protest was filed, the court may, upon petition of any party in interest, direct the Department to transmit the entire record to the court. When appeal is taken from the departmental decision or the court directs transmission of the record to the court, the court either proceeds to a determination of the issues or suspends determination until the audit of the account of the personal representative [72 P.S. §9188(a)].

¶3205 Domiciliary Compromises

When both Pennsylvania and another state claim a decedent as a resident, the Department of Revenue may, with the approval of the Attorney General, enter into a compromise with the other taxing authority and the decedent's personal representative that a certain sum will be accepted by each state in satisfaction of the tax [72 P.S. §9157].

¶3206 Refunds

Petitions for refund of the inheritance tax are filed with the Department of Revenue [72 P.S. §9181(e)]. Refund petitions formerly were made to the Board of Finance and Revenue. Applications for refunds must be made within three years (two years prior to January 1, 1998) after the later of several enumerated events. See 72 P.S. §9181(d).

¶3207 Safe Deposit Boxes

Persons who have actual knowledge of the death of a decedent must give notice to the Department of Revenue before entering a safe deposit box of a decedent except in the following cases [72 P.S. §§9191—9793]:

(1) Entry in the presence of an authorized official (*i.e.*, bank employee, representative of the Department of Revenue), who makes a record of the contents of the box.

(2) Entry under court order.

(3) Entry, with departmental authorization, by a firm whose business requires access to the box's contents.

(4) Entry to remove will and cemetery deed where representative is accompanied by a bank employee.

There is provision for entry under other conditions if proper notice is sent to the Department using some form of return-receipt-requested mail [72 P.S. §§9102 and 9193]. See also 61 Pa. Code §§93.31—93.73.

¶3208 Penalties

The penalty for willful failure to file a required return or report is 25% of the tax ultimately found to be due or $1,000 (whichever is less) [72 P.S. §9153(a)]. Willful filing of a false return is a misdemeanor of the third degree [72 P.S. §9153(c)].

Any financial institution that fails to notify the Department of Revenue, as required, within 10 days after knowledge of the death of a decedent who has funds deposited or invested with the institution is liable for a penalty of $100 [72 P.S. §9153(b)].

Any bank employee of a financial institution or any other person who, having actual knowledge of the death of a decedent, enters or permits entry into a safe deposit box of a decedent without proper authorization commits a misdemeanor of the third degree. Disclosure of confidential information obtained from the contents of a safe deposit box is also a misdemeanor of the third degree [72 P.S. §9196].

PART XIV

OTHER COMMONWEALTH TAXES

CHAPTER 33

OTHER COMMONWEALTH TAXES

¶3301 Scope of Chapter

This chapter provides a brief explanation of several Pennsylvania taxes not covered in other Parts. The explanation is not complete and relevant statutes should be consulted for detail.

¶3302 Malt Beverage Tax

• *Administration*

The Pennsylvania Liquor Control Board administers and issues alcoholic beverage licenses and permits (*e.g.*, malt beverage licenses, wholesale and retail liquor control licenses, manufacturer's permits). The malt beverage tax is administered by the Department of Revenue through the Bureau of Cigarette and Beverage Taxes. Both the Liquor Control Board and the Department of Revenue may promulgate necessary regulations for the administration of the alcoholic beverage tax laws. Pennsylvania also levies a tax on all liquors sold by the Liquor Control Board. This tax is not discussed in this *Guidebook*.

• *Imposition*

The malt beverage tax is levied on malt or brewed beverages (1) manufactured and sold for use in Pennsylvania or (2) manufactured outside Pennsylvania but sold for importation and use in Pennsylvania. The enabling legislation for this tax is Article XX of the Tax Reform Code (P.L 6, No. 2), as amended. The tax is borne by the consumer, but manufacturers, distributors, and importers must collect and remit the tax to the Commonwealth. The term "malt or brewed beverages" includes alcoholic beverages (*e.g.*, beer, lager beer, ale, porter or similar fermented malt liquor) containing 0.5% or more of alcohol, by whatever name the liquors may be called.

• *Rates of tax*

The malt beverage tax rates have remained unchanged since 1947. The tax rates per original container or standard fraction of container are as follows [61 Pa. Code §74.12(a)]:

Standard Fraction	Malt Beverage Tax Rate
1 Barrel	$2.48
1/2 Barrel	1.24
50 Liter	1.06
12 Gallon	0.96
1/4 Barrel	0.62
1/6 Barrel	0.42
1/8 Barrel	0.32
160 Ounce	0.10
40 Ounce	0.03
25 Ounce	0.02
4 Liter	0.09
1 Gallon	0.08
2 Liter	0.05
1 Quart	0.02
1 Pint	0.01
1/2 Pint	0.0066

In all cases, the tax imposed upon a half-pint of eight fluid ounces or fraction thereof, the tax shall be $ 0.0066 [61 Pa. Code § 74.12].

• *Returns and payment of tax*

Manufacturers and importers of malt or brewed beverages must file returns on or before the 15th day of the month following the month in which the beverages are first sold or used in Pennsylvania. An exception is made for malt or brewed beverages sold to public service licensees. Public service licensees must file reports and pay the tax on all malt or brewed beverages they sell in Pennsylvania [Act of May 5, 1933, P.L. 284, § 4]. Payment of tax is due with the return [61 Pa. Code § 74.51(c)].

• *Malt beverage tax credit*

Manufacturers of malt or brewed beverages are entitled to a malt beverage tax credit if their annual production of malt or brewed beverages does not exceed 1,500,000 barrels [72 P.S. § 9010(b)]. The tax credit cannot be greater than the amount of qualifying capital expenditures made by the taxpayer and certified by the Secretary of Revenue [72 P.S. § 9010(b)]. The term "qualifying capital expenditures" means the amounts paid by a taxpayer for items of plant, machinery, or equipment for use by the taxpayer within Pennsylvania in the manufacture and sale of malt or brewed beverages during the effective tax credit period. However, the total amount of qualifying capital expenditures made by a taxpayer within a single year cannot exceed $200,000 [72 P.S. § 9010(b)].

Effective tax credit period: The effective period for the malt beverage emergency tax credit period began January 1, 1974, and was scheduled to end December 31, 1998. The credit has been extended to December 31, 2008 [72 P.S. § 9010]. No credit will be allowed against any tax due for any taxable period ending after December 31, 2008 [72 P.S. § 9010].

Reports: Taxpayers desiring to claim a malt beverage tax credit must, within one (1) year of the date of the original purchase of qualifying capital expenditures, report annually to the Secretary the nature, amounts, and dates of qualifying capital expenditures made by the taxpayer and other information that might be required [72 P.S. § 9010(c)].

Carryforward: Any unused credit in a calendar year may be carried forward for three (3) calendar years [72 P.S. § 9010(e)]. Unused credits may not be carried back.

Payment by Electronic Funds Transfer

Payment by electronic funds transfer (EFT)is discussed at ¶ 4617.

• *Review*

If a taxpayer fails to pay any tax imposed, the Department of Revenue is authorized and empowered to make an assessment of additional tax [72 P.S. § 9005(a)]. Promptly after the date of assessment, the Department must send a copy of any assessment, including the basis of assessment, to the taxpayer. Within 90 days after the mailing date of the assessment, the taxpayer may file a petition for reassessment. The Department must dispose of any reassessment within six (6) months after the date of assessment to dispose of any petition for reassessment [72 P.S. § 9005(b)]. Within 90 days (60 days prior to January 1, 2008) after the mailing date of notice of the action taken on any petition for reassessment, the taxpayer may petition the Board of Finance and Revenue to review the Department's action [72 P.S. § 9005(c)].

¶3303 Cigarette and Tobacco Related Products Tax

• *Administration and review*

The cigarette tax is administered by the Department of Revenue. Penalties are provided for various infractions of the cigarette tax statutes. Administrative review of all Department actions taken is provided by the Board of Appeals [72 P.S. § 8207-A(a)]. If a tobacco product manufacturer wants to begin selling cigarettes in Pennsylvania, it should contact the Tobacco Enforcement Section of the Attorney General's office at (717) 783-1794.

• *Stamping agency, retailer, wholesaler, and dealer defined*

Stamping agency: A "cigarette stamping agency" is any person who is licensed as such by the Department of Revenue for the purpose of affixing cigarette tax stamps to packages of cigarettes and transmitting the property tax to the Commonwealth, and who maintains separate warehousing facilities for the purpose of receiving and distributing cigarettes and conducting their business, who have received commitments from at least two (2) cigarette manufacturers whose aggregate market share is at least 40% of the Commonwealth cigarette market and purchases cigarettes directly from cigarette manufacturers [72 P.S. § 8201].

Retailer: A "retailer" is any of the following:

(1) Any person who, in the usual course of business, purchases or receives cigarettes from any source whatsoever for the purpose of sale to the ultimate consumer.

(2) Any person who, in the usual course of business, owns, leases, or otherwise operates one or more vending machines for the purpose of sale of cigarettes to the ultimate consumer.

(3) Any person who buys, sells, transfers, or deals in cigarettes for profits and is not licensed as a cigarette stamping agency or wholesaler.

Wholesaler: Any of the following:

(1) Any person that meets all of the following:

(i) In the usual course of business, purchases cigarettes from a cigarette stamping agent or other wholesaler and receives, stores, sells and distributes within Pennsylvania at least 75% of the cigarettes purchased by him or her to retail dealers or wholesale dealers or any combination who buys the cigarettes from him or her for the purpose of resale to the ultimate consumer.

(ii) Maintains an established place of business for the receiving, storage and distribution of cigarettes.

(2) Any person that meets all of the following:

(i) Is engaged in the business of distributing cigarettes through vending machines to the ultimate consumer by means of placing the cigarette vending machines, owned or leased by him, in various outlets within this Commonwealth.

(ii) Pays to the owner or lessee of the premises a commission or rental for the use of the premises.

(iii) Operates at least ten vending machines.

(iv) Meets all the other requirements for licensing of wholesalers under Article II-A of the act of April 9, 1929 (P.L. 343, No. 176), known as "The Fiscal Code", including maintaining an established place of business for the receiving, storage and distribution of cigarettes.

(3) Any person, including a franchisee, that meets all of the following:

(i) Owns and operates no fewer than three (five prior to September 1, 2012) retail outlets in this Commonwealth, having 100% common ownership.

(ii) Purchases cigarettes from a cigarette stamping agency or another wholesaler for resale to the ultimate consumer.

(iii) Maintains complete and accurate records of all purchases and sales in his or her main office and also in the retail outlet.

Dealer: A "dealer" is any cigarette stamping agency, wholesaler, or retailer as defined above [72 P.S. § 8201].

• *Base*

The cigarette tax is an excise tax imposed on the sale or possession of cigarettes within Pennsylvania [72 P.S. § 8206]. The cigarette tax is levied upon the sale of cigarettes to any person (as defined in 72 P.S. § 8201) and to the Commonwealth of Pennsylvania or any other state, or any department, board, commission, authority or agency thereof [72 P.S. § 8207]. The cigarette tax is not a sales tax and cannot be deducted from gross volume of business for purposes of a local mercantile tax [*Blair Candy Company, Inc. v. Altoona Area School District*, 613 A.2d 159 (Pa.Commw. 1992)].

Don't Confuse Cigarette Tax and Sales Tax

The tax collected when cigarettes are sold at retail is a sales and use tax and should not be confused with the cigarette tax, which is a separate tax that is paid by cigarette stamping agencies and wholesale dealers. The cigarette tax is included in the cost of cigarettes sold at retail. Sales tax collected on the sale at retail of cigarettes is handled like any other taxable item. The Pennsylvania sales and use tax is explained in Part III of this *Guidebook*.

"Cigarette" defined: A "cigarette" means any roll for smoking made wholly or in part of tobacco, without regard to size or shape or any flavoring, adulterated and mixed with any other ingredient, the wrapper or cover of which is made of paper or any other substance or material, except tobacco, and does not include cigars [61 Pa. Code § 71.4]. Effective November 1, 2009, "little cigars" are added to the definition of cigarette. A little cigar is any roll for smoking that weighs not more than four pounds per thousand, where the wrapper or cover is made of natural leaf tobacco or of any substance containing tobacco [72 P.S. § 8201].

• *Tobacco Related Products*

Act 84 of 2016 imposes a new .55-cents-per-ounce tax on tobacco products such as smokeless, pipe, and roll-your-own cigarette tobacco (excluding cigars and cigarettes) and also imposes a new tax on electronic cigarettes, including vapor producing devices, and e-liquids in an amount equal to 40% of the purchase price charged to retailers. The tax on e-cigarettes, chewing tobacco, snuff and pipe tobacco is effective at 12:01 AM on October 1, 2016. The tax on roll-your-own tobacco is effective 60 days after the Office of the Attorney General publishes a bulletin that they have reached an agreement with the participating manufacturers under a master settlement agreement.

¶3303

In *East Coast Vapor, LLC. v. Pa. Dept. of Rev.*, 189 A.3d 504 (Pa. Commw. 2018), the Commonwealth Court ruled that e-cigarette devices and the e-liquids used in such devices are not subject to the Tobacco Products Tax Act ("TPTA"). The TPTA imposes a 40% tax on tobacco products, which includes electronic cigarettes, or e-cigarettes. As an initial matter, the court rejected the Department's argument that the case should be dismissed because the taxpayer had failed to exhaust its administrative remedies. Instead, the court found that the taxpayer had raised a substantial constitutional challenge to the TPTA which could not have been decided by an administrative agency. The court's preliminary finding was that there was a rational basis for including e-cigarette devices and e-liquid in the definition of tobacco products under the TPTA because the General Assembly was concerned that young people who started using e-cigarettes would become addicted to nicotine and turn to cigarettes. However, the plain language of the TPTA did not support authorizing the Department to tax separately packaged component parts of an e-cigarette that may be considered "integral" to, or an "integral component" of, an e-cigarette. The plain language of 72 P.S. §8201-A defined "tobacco products" to include "electronic cigarettes." Electronic cigarettes were further defined as an electronic oral device, such as one composed of a heating element and battery or electronic circuit, or both, which provides a vapor of nicotine or any other substance, the use or inhalation of which simulates smoking. The statutory language did not, however, extend the reach of the tax to items that were "integral" pieces of an e-cigarette or to its "component parts."

In light of the decision in *East Coast Vapor, LLC*, in an unreported decision, the Commonwealth Court granted a request for a declaration that integral component parts were not subject to tax under the TPTA. The court noted that it would serve no useful purpose to dismiss the taxpayers' petition and require them to exhaust their administrative remedies when the issue had been decided in *East Coast Vapor*. Consequently, the court issued summary judgment stating that the Department's interpretation of the TPTA to include separately packaged component parts of an e-cigarette as taxable was unsupported by the plain language of the TPTA. *Kingdom Vapor and Smoke 4 Less, LLC v. Pa Dept. of Revenue*, (Pa. Dkt. 697 M.D. 2016, unreported June 22, 2018) (2018 WL 3078891).

Following *East Coast Vapor* and *Kingdom Vapor*, the Department of Revenue issued guidance on the application of tobacco products tax as it relates to electronic cigarettes and components of electronic cigarettes. Pennsylvania Tobacco Products Tax Bulletin 2018-01, issued July 20, 2018 and amended August 15, 2018. In this Bulletin, the Department advises that electronic cigarettes, any liquid or substance placed in or sold for use in the electronic cigarette (regardless of whether the liquid or substance contains nicotine), and any component not sold separately from the electronic cigarettes, are subject to the tobacco products tax. Components such as, but not limited to, coils, batteries, and reservoirs, are not subject to the tax if sold separately. The Department finds that the tobacco products tax should not be collected on separately packaged components from and after June 22, 2018.

• *Rate*

The cigarette tax is imposed on a per-cigarette basis. Effective August 1, 2016, the rate is $0.13 cents per cigarette, or $2.60 per pack of cigarettes [Act 84 of 2016 (H.B. 1189)]. (The result in Philadelphia specifically is that a pack of cigarettes will carry a $4.60 tax per pack.) The rate of tax on roll-your-own, chewing tobacco and pipe tobacco is $0.55 per ounce. For tobacco products other than e-cigarettes that weigh less than 1.2 ounces per container the tax shall be not less than $0.66 per package of these tobacco products. For example, if the retailer purchases 100 ounces of tobacco in two-ounce packages the tax due would be $55. If the same quantity is purchased in one-ounce packages, the tax due would be $66. The Pennsylvania sales and use tax also applies to the foregoing sales.

All Sales Presumed Taxable

All sales are presumed to be taxable, and the burden of proving the right to an exemption is on the person claiming the exemption [72 P.S. § 8209(b)].

Only one sale taxable: Only one sale of cigarettes (whether of individual cigarettes, packages, cartons, or cases) is taxable and used in computing the amount of tax cigarette tax [72 P.S. § 8208]. The tax is paid by the use of tax stamps affixed by dealers (*i.e.*, any cigarette stamping agency, wholesaler, or retailer. Cigarette stamps or meters can be obtained from the Bureau of Cigarette and Beverage Taxes.

• *Returns and payment of tax*

Dealers: Licensed dealers must file a report at the times and in the form prescribed by the Department of Revenue [72 P.S. § 215-A].

Cigarette stamping agents: Licensed cigarette stamping agents must establish a fiscal or calendar monthly reporting period and file a cigarette tax report covering the preceding month on or before the 20th day following the end of each fiscal or calendar month [61 Pa. Code 71.9(a)]. Cigarette stamping agencies who violate this filing requirement are subject to fines [61 Pa. Code 71.9(b)]. A "cigarette stamping agency" is any person licensed for the purpose of affixing cigarette tax stamps to packages of cigarettes and transmitting the proper tax to the Commonwealth and who (1) maintains separate warehousing facilities for the purpose of receiving and distributing cigarettes and conducting business; (2) has received commitments from at least two cigarette manufacturers whose aggregate market share is at least 40% of the Commonwealth cigarette market; and (3) purchases cigarettes directly from cigarette manufacturers [72 P.S. § 8201].

Payment on a deferred basis: The Department may, by regulation, permit a cigarette stamping agency to pay for purchases on a deferred basis, upon the filing of a surety bond. Effective January 7, 2004, in lieu of a surety bond, the Department must accept other forms of security (*e.g.*, a line of credit) if the Department deems it sufficient [72 P.S. § 8215(e)].

Unstamped cigarettes: Effective January 7, 2010, any person selling unstamped cigarettes to retailers and any person purchasing unstamped cigarettes on which the tax was not paid must file a report with the Department of Revenue. The report is due on the 20th of each month and must report the amount of tax due for the prior month on unstamped cigarettes [72 P.S. § 8216.1].

• *Floor tax on inventory of vendors/dealers*

The cigarette floor tax is a tax on cigarettes that have been previously taxed and that have not been sold to the ultimate consumers [72 P.S. § 8206.1]. Anyone who possesses cigarettes for commercial distribution in Pennsylvania is required to pay the floor tax. This includes all dealers (*i.e.*, retailers, wholesalers, and cigarette stamping agencies). The floor tax return and payment of tax due are required to be submitted to the Department of Revenue within 90 days of the effective date of the law. Dealers who fail to adhere to reporting and payment requirements are subject to fines and penalties. The Department of Revenue may also suspend or revoke a cigarette dealer's license for failure to file and pay the cigarette tax [72 P.S. § 8206.1(b), (c)]. A floor tax also applies to Other Tobacco Products under Act 84 of 2016.

• *Licensing*

Anyone who sells, transfers, or delivers cigarettes within Pennsylvania must first obtain a property license [72 P.S. § 8203-A (a)], and all cigarette licenses must be conspicuously displayed at the place for which issued [72 P.S. § 8208-A(b)]. Cigarette tax licensees will need a separate "Other Tobacco Products" license if such vendor sells other tobacco products described above.

¶3303

Annual licenses: License applicants must complete and file an application with the Department of Revenue. The application must be in prescribed form, contain prescribed information, and set forth truthfully and accurately the information desired by the Department of Revenue. If the application is approved, the Department of Revenue licenses the dealer for a period of one year; the license may be renewed annually thereafter [72 P.S. §8203-A(b)]. For licensing requirements for cigarette stamping agents, wholesalers, and retailers see 72 P.S. §§8204-A, 8205-A, and 8206-A.

License fees: At the time of applying for a license, an applicant must pay a license fee. The fee for a cigarette stamping agency license is $1,000; for a wholesale cigarette dealer's license, $500; a retail cigarette dealer's license, $25; and for a vending machine license, $25 [72 P.S. §8208-A(a)].

Cigars: No cigarette license is required for the sale of cigars, except for "little cigars" [72 P.S. §8202-A].

• *Presumptive minimum costs*

It is illegal for any dealer, with intent to injure competitors, destroy or substantially lessen competition, or avoid payment of the tax, to advertise, offer to sell, or sell cigarettes at less than the cost to the cigarette dealer [72 P.S. §217-A]. Cigarette stamping agents, wholesalers, and retailers are prohibited from selling cigarettes at a price lower than their respective presumptive minimum costs unless the dealer applies for and receives approval for selling at a lower price. Cigarette dealers desiring to prove a cost different from the Department's presumptive costs must follow the procedures provided under 61 Pa. Code, Chapter 76 (relating to unfair sales of cigarettes). Certain combinations sales and inducements (see 61 Pa. Code 76.2) and promotional sales plans (see 61 Pa. Code 76.3) are prohibited.

The Department of Revenue (under the authority of 72 P.S. §227-A) determines presumptive minimum costs and publishes them in the *Pennsylvania Bulletin.*

Other packaging and brands: Cigarette dealers who either sell cigarettes under a different packaging setup (*i.e.,* eight packs per carton) or sell cigarettes that do not qualify as premium or generic brands (*i.e.,* subgeneric, foreign or specialty cigarettes) as previously described are prohibited from selling cigarettes at a price lower than the cost of the stamping agent, cost of the wholesaler, or cost of the retailer, respectively, as further defined and explained in 61 Pa. Code Part I, Subpart B, Article III (relating to cigarette and beverage taxes) [34 Pa.B. 6046].

More than one license: If a person holds more than one license, the presumptive minimum price includes all presumptive costs of doing business if the product is sold at retail [72 P.S. §8202-A].

• *Commission on sales*

A cigarette stamping agent is entitled to a commission for the agent's services and expenses in affixing cigarette tax stamps [72 P.S. §8216]. Effective November 1, 2009, the commission is equal to 0.87% (0.0087) of the total value of Pennsylvania cigarette tax stamps purchased by the agent to be used in the stamping of packages of cigarettes for sale within Pennsylvania [72 P.S. §8216]. The prior rate was 0.98% (0.0098). Stamping agents may deduct the commission from the amount owed for the stamps purchased. This commission does not apply to purchases of stamps in an amount less than $100 [72 P.S. §8216].

• *Exempt sales*

The following sales are exempt: (1) sales not taxable under the Constitution or statutes of the United States [72 P.S. §8209(a)]; (2) sales to recognized veterans organizations buying cigarettes for free distribution to veteran patients in federal, state, and state-aided hospitals [72 P.S. § 8209(a)(1)]; (3) sales to voluntary unincorporated organizations or military forces operating under the jurisdiction of the U.S. Secretary of Defense [72 P.S. § 8209(a)(2)]; and (4) sales to patients by retailers located in V.A. hospitals [72 P.S. § 8209(a)(3)].

Payment by Electronic Funds Transfer

Payment by electronic funds transfer (EFT) is discussed at ¶ 4617.

- *Sample packs*

The receipt, distribution, and payment of tax on sample packs of cigarettes issued for free distribution are administered by the Department of Revenue [72 P.S. § 8217(a)]. However, the bringing into Pennsylvania by a manufacturer of sample packs of cigarettes that contain not five (5) or fewer cigarettes and that are delivered and distributed only through licensed dealers or the manufacturers or their sales representative cannot be prohibited [72 P.S. § 8217(b)].

- *Refunds*

The refund procedures with respect to the cigarette tax are governed by provisions for filing petitions with the Board of Finance and Revenue. See ¶ 4605 for explanation of these provisions.

- *Property rights, confiscation, and forfeiture*

No property rights exist in the following:

(1) Any vending machine in which unstamped cigarettes are found or any vehicle containing 2,000 or more unstamped cigarettes or containing more than 200 unstamped cigarettes if the owner has been previously convicted of the illegal sale, possession, or transportation of unstamped cigarettes in this or any other jurisdiction [72 P.S. § 8285(a)].

(2) Any packages of cigarettes that have been taken from any person who has been found in possession of unstamped cigarettes [72 P.S. § 8285(c)]. (See also 72 P.S. § 8273.)

(3) Any cigarettes sold or offered for sale by any person without a proper license [72 P.S. § 8285(c)].

(4) Any cigarettes sold or offered for sale by any person not possessing proper documentation showing legal purchase of said cigarettes [72 P.S. § 8285(c)].

(5) Any machinery, equipment, fixtures, stenciling device, stamp, stamping device, or other paraphernalia designed or used to counterfeit Pennsylvania cigarette tax stamps [72 P.S. § 8285(d)].

(6) Any packages of cigarettes confiscated in connection with the operation of any counterfeiting or other scheme designed to evade the payment of proper Pennsylvania cigarette tax [72 P.S. § 8285(d)].

The Department is responsible for disposing of forfeited cigarettes by sale or destruction pursuant to regulations promulgated by the Secretary of Revenue [72 P.S. § 8278(e)]. The proceedings for the forfeiture of any cigarette vending machine or motor vehicle in which unstamped cigarettes are in rem (*i.e.*, proceeding against the property without reference to the persons involved). The Commonwealth is the plaintiff, and the property is the defendant [72 P.S. § 8285(f)].

- *Health care provider retention account*

A health care provider retention account is a special general-fund account. Eighteen and fifty-two hundredths percent (18.52%) of the proceeds of the cigarette tax imposed must be deposited in the account. Funds in the account are subject to an annual appropriation and shall be administered as provided by law [72 P.S. § 8211, effective January 7, 2004].

¶ 3303

Compliance with State Statutes Required

A tobacco manufacturer's cigarettes cannot be sold in Pennsylvania unless the manufacturer complies with two acts: (1) the Tobacco Settlement Agreement Act (TSAA) and (2) the Tobacco Product Manufacturer Directory Act (TPMDA). These are discussed below.

- *Tobacco Settlement Agreement Act (TSAA)*

Under the Tobacco Settlement Agreement Act [35 P.S. §§ 5671–5675], tobacco product manufacturers that sell cigarettes to consumers in Pennsylvania must do one of the following:

(1) Become a participating manufacturer and generally perform their financial obligations under the Master Settlement Agreement [35 P.S. § 5674(a)(1)].

(2) For nonparticipating manufacturers, place required amounts into a qualified escrow fund [35 P.S. § 5674(a)(2)].

Licensed cigarette stamping agencies must file Schedule DAS-95 for cigarette sales in Pennsylvania of nonparticipating manufacturer (NPM) brands. Schedule DAS-95 is due the 20th of each month and should be attached to a cigarette stamping agent's monthly reports.

- *Tobacco Product Manufacturer Directory Act (TPMDA)*

Overview: The Tobacco Product Manufacturer Directory Act (TPMDA) requires manufacturers to certify that they are in compliance with the Tobacco Settlement Agreement Act (TSAA) and directs the Attorney General to publish a directory of cigarette manufacturers that are in compliance. The Directory contains a list of approved brands that may be sold within Pennsylvania.

Certification: A tobacco product manufacturer whose cigarettes are sold in Pennsylvania must execute and deliver to the Attorney General a certification under penalty of perjury that, as of the date of the certification, the tobacco product manufacturer is either a participating manufacturer or is in full compliance with the TSAA and the TPMDA. In the cases of a nonparticipating manufacturer, the certification must include a statement that (1) it is registered to do business in Pennsylvania or has appointed a resident agent for service of process and provided notice of the registration or appointment under TPMDA 305 and (2) it has established and continuously maintains a qualified escrow fund and has executed a qualified escrow agreement approved by the Attorney General [TPMDA 303]. Certification forms and instructions are available at http://www.attorneygeneral.gov/consumers.aspx?id=272.

Directory: The Attorney General is required to develop and publish (on the Attorney General's Office web site) a directory of all tobacco product manufacturers and their brand families that have provided current and accurate certification that they are in compliance with the TSAA and the TPMDA [TPMDA 301(a)]. The Tobacco Product Directory is available at http://www.attorneygeneral.gov/consumers.aspx?id=272. Tobacco manufacturers and brand families can be added to the directory at any time and removed from the list within 21 days of notice [TPMDA 301].

Prohibition

A cigarette brand is not included in the Attorney General's Directory, it may not be stamped or sold within Pennsylvania [TPMDA § 302]. Cigarette stamping agents that violate this prohibition may have their licenses revoked or suspended. The Department of Revenue may also assess a civil penalty not to exceed 500% of the retail value of the cigarettes sold [TPMDA § 307(a)]. Cigarettes that are sold, offered for sale, or possessed for sale in violation of the TPMDA are contraband and subject to seizure [TPMDA § 307(b)].

Reports: A cigarette stamping agent must submit to the Department of Revenue, no later than 20 days following the end of each month, a report documenting the quantity, brand, and style of tobacco product sold. These reports must also contain any additional information that may be required by the Department of Revenue or the Attorney General [TPMDA 306(b), (e)].

Recordkeeping requirements: Cigarette stamping agents must maintain and make available to the Department of Revenue and the Attorney General all invoices and documentation of sales of all nonparticipating manufacturer cigarettes and any other information relied upon to make monthly reports for a period of five years [TPMDA 306(a)].

¶3304 Realty Transfer Tax

The realty transfer tax provisions are contained in Article XI-C of the Tax Reform Code [72 P.S. § 8101-C *et seq.*]. The realty transfer tax is a documentary stamp tax on the value of any interest in real estate transferred by deed. The tax is payable by any person who makes, executes, delivers, accepts, or presents for recording any taxable document [72 P.S. § 8102-C]. The United States, the Commonwealth, or any of their instrumentalities, agencies or political subdivisions are exempt from payment of the realty transfer tax [72 P.S. § 8101-C.2].

• *Rate and base*

The realty transfer tax is imposed at the rate of 1% of the value of the real estate transferred [72 P.S. § 8102-C].

"Value" can be established by one of the following four methods [72 P.S. § 8101-C]:

(1) In the case of any bona fide sale of real estate at arm's length for actual monetary worth, the amount of the actual consideration therefor, paid or to be paid, including liens or other encumbrances thereon existing before the transfer and not removed thereby, whether or not the underlying indebtedness is assumed, and ground rents, or a commensurate part thereof where such liens or other encumbrances and ground rents also encumber or are charged against other real estate. If the documents set forth a nominal consideration, the "value" thereof is determined from the price set forth in or actual consideration for the contract of sale.

(2) In the case of a gift, sale by execution upon a judgment or upon the foreclosure of a mortgage by a judicial officer, transactions without consideration or for consideration less than the actual monetary worth of the real estate, a taxable lease, an occupancy agreement, a leasehold or possessory interest, any exchange of properties, or the real estate of an acquired company, the actual monetary worth of the real estate determined by adjusting the assessed value of the real estate for local real estate tax purposes for the common level ratio of assessed values to market values of the taxing district as established by the State Tax Equalization Board, or a commensurate part of the assessment where the assessment includes other real estate.

(3) In the case of an easement or other interest in real estate the value of which is not determinable under (1) or (2), above, the actual monetary worth of such interest.

(4) The actual consideration for or actual monetary worth of any executory agreement for the construction of buildings, structures or other permanent improvements to real estate between the grantor and other persons existing before the transfer and not removed thereby or between the grantor, the agent or principal of the grantor or a related corporation, association, or partnership and the grantee existing before or effective with the transfer.

• *Real estate valuation factors*

Real estate valuation factors for Pennsylvania realty transfer tax purposes, which are published in the *Pennsylvania Bulletin*, are the mathematical reciprocals of the actual common level ratio and are based on sales data compiled by the State Tax Equalization Board. For factors applicable for documents accepted from July 1, 2006, to June 30, 2007, see 36 Pa.B. 6174. The date of acceptance of a document is rebuttably presumed to be its date of execution (*i.e.*, the date specified in the body of the document as the date of the instrument) [61 Pa. Code § 91.102].

• *Statement of value required to claim exemption*

In order to claim exemptions from the realty transfer tax, the true, full and complete value of the transfer must be shown on the statement of value (Form REV-183). For leases of coal, oil, natural gas, or minerals, the statement of value may be limited to an explanation of the reason the document is not subject to the realty transfer tax.

• *Taxable documents*

A taxable document for purposes of the realty transfer tax is any deed, instrument or writing that conveys, transfers, demises, vests, confirms or evidences any transfer or demise of title to real estate [72 P.S. § 8101-C]. It includes a declaration or acquisition required to be presented for recording under 72 P.S. § 8102-C.5.

• *Division and transfer of interests in oil and natural gas*

Documents that effectuate or evidence the transfer of mineral rights are taxable for Pennsylvania realty transfer tax purposes. Taxable documents are those that transfer interests in a mineral rights estate itself. Documents that transfer personal property rights associated with the mineral rights estate are not taxable (*e.g.*, the assignment of the right to receive income from an oil or gas lease, such as a royalty payments). However, because the reservation of a royalty creates an interest in real estate, if the royalty itself (*i.e.*, reservation by the lessor of an interest to the oil and gas production) is conveyed, the document of conveyance is subject to realty transfer tax. For details see *Realty Transfer Tax Bulletin 2011-XX* (Department of Revenue, January 2011).

• *Exempt documents*

The following documents are specifically exempt from the realty transfer tax [72 P.S. § 8101-C]:

(1) Wills.

(2) Deeds of trust or other instruments of like character given as security for a debt and deeds of release thereof to the debtor.

(3) Land contracts whereby the legal title does not pass to the grantee until the total consideration specified in the contract has been paid or any cancellation thereof unless the consideration is payable over a period of time exceeding 30 years.

(4) Instruments that solely grant, vest or confirm a public utility easement.

• *Exempt conveyances*

Certain transfers of real estate or interests in real estate are exempt from the realty transfer tax. Only those transactions and parties specifically exempt by law or by judicial decision are exempt. Exemptions are strictly construed, and it is the responsibility of interested parties to qualify for any alleged exemption. The following transfers are specifically exempt by 72 P.S. § 8102-C.3:

(1) A transfer to the Commonwealth, or to any of its instrumentalities, agencies or political subdivisions, by gift, dedication or deed in lieu of condemnation or deed of confirmation in connection with condemnation proceedings, or a reconveyance by the condemning body of the property condemned to the

owner of record at the time of condemnation which reconveyance may include property line adjustments, provided said reconveyance is made within one year from the date of condemnation.

(2) A document that the Commonwealth is prohibited from taxing under the Constitution or statutes of the United States.

(3) A conveyance to a municipality, township, school district or county pursuant to acquisition by the municipality, township, school district or county of a tax delinquent property at sheriff sale or tax claim bureau sale.

(4) A transfer for no or nominal actual consideration that corrects or confirms a transfer previously recorded, but which does not extend or limit existing record legal title or interest.

(5) A transfer of division in kind for no or nominal actual consideration of property passed by testate or intestate succession and held by co-tenants; however, if any of the parties take shares greater in value than their undivided interest, tax is due on the excess.

(6) A transfer between the following:

(a) Husband and wife (See Realty Transfer Tax Bulletin 2015-01 wherein husband and wife is deemed to mean spouses so that legally married persons of the same sex are included thereby giving effect to *Whitewood v. Wolf*, 992 F. Supp. 2d 410 (M.D. Pa. 2014)).

(b) Persons who were previously husband and wife who have since been divorced, provided the property or interest therein subject to such transfer was acquired by the husband and wife or husband or wife prior to the granting of the final decree in divorce.

(c) Parent and child or the spouse of such child.

(d) A stepparent and a stepchild or the spouse of the stepchild (effective retroactively to documents made, executed, delivered, accepted or presented for recording on or after July 1, 2010).

(e) Brother or sister or spouse of a brother or sister.

(f) A grandparent and grandchild or the spouse of such grandchild, except that a subsequent transfer by the grantee within one year shall be subject to tax as if the grantor were making such transfer.

(7) A transfer for no or nominal actual consideration of property passing by testate or intestate succession from a personal representative of a decedent to the decedent's devisee or heir.

(8) A transfer for no or nominal actual consideration to a trustee of an ordinary trust where the transfer of the same property would be exempt if the transfer was made directly from the grantor to all of the possible beneficiaries that are entitled to receive the property or proceeds from the sale of the property under the trust, whether or not such beneficiaries are contingent or specifically named. A trust clause that identifies the contingent beneficiaries by reference to the heirs of the trust settlor as determined by the laws of the intestate succession does not disqualify a transfer from the exclusion provided by this clause. No such exemption will be granted unless the recorder of deeds is presented with a copy of the trust instrument that clearly identifies the grantor and all possible beneficiaries. An "ordinary trust" is any trust (other than a business trust or a living trust) that takes effect during the lifetime of the settlor and for which the trustees of the trust take title to property primarily for the purpose of protecting, managing or conserving it until distribution to the named beneficiaries of the trust. An ordinary trust does not include a trust that has an objective to carry on business and divide gains nor does it either expressly or impliedly have any of the following features: (a) the treatment of beneficiaries as associates; (b) the treatment of the interests in the trust as personal property; (c) the free transfera-

¶3304

bility of beneficial interests in the trust; (d) centralized management by the trustee or the beneficiaries; or (e) continuity of life [72 P.S. § 8101-C].

(9) A transfer for no or nominal actual consideration to a trustee of a living trust from the settlor of the living trust. No such exemption will be granted unless the recorder of deed is presented with a copy of the living trust instrument. See definition of "ordinary trust," above. A "living trust" is any trust (other than a business trust) intended as a will substitute by the settlor that becomes effective during the lifetime of the settlor, but from which trust distributions cannot be made to any beneficiaries other than the settlor prior to the death of the settlor [72 P.S. § 8101-C].

(10) A transfer for no or nominal actual consideration from a trustee of an ordinary trust to a specifically named beneficiary that is entitled to receive the property under the recorded trust instrument or to a contingent beneficiary where the transfer of the same property would be exempt if the transfer was made by the grantor of the property into the trust to that beneficiary. However, any transfer of real estate from a living trust during the settlor's lifetime shall be considered for the purposes of this article as if such transfer were made directly from the settlor to the grantee. See definition of "ordinary trust," above.

(11) A transfer for no or nominal actual consideration from a trustee of a living trust after the death of the settlor of the trust or from a trustee of a trust created pursuant to the will of a decedent to a beneficiary to whom the property is devised or bequeathed. See definition of "living trust," above.

(12) A transfer for no or nominal actual consideration from the trustee of a living trust to the settlor of the living trust if such property was originally conveyed to the trustee by the settlor. See definition of "living trust," above.

(13) A transfer for no or nominal actual consideration from a trustee to a successor trustee.

(14) A transfer (a) for no or nominal actual consideration between a principal and an agent or straw party or (b) from or to an agent or straw party where, if the agent or straw party were his principal, no tax would be imposed under this article. Where the document by which title is acquired by a grantee or statement of value fails to set forth that the property was acquired by the grantee from, or for the benefit of, his principal, there is a rebuttable presumption that the property is the property of the grantee in his individual capacity if the grantee claims an exemption from taxation under this clause.

(15) A transfer made pursuant to the statutory merger or consolidation of a corporation or statutory division of a nonprofit corporation, except where the department reasonably determines that the primary intent for such merger, consolidation or division is avoidance of the tax imposed by this article.

(16) A transfer from a corporation or association of real estate held of record in the name of the corporation or association where the grantee owns stock of the corporation or an interest in the association in the same proportion as his interest in or ownership of the real estate being conveyed and where the stock of the corporation or the interest in the association has been held by the grantee for more than two years.

(17) A transfer from a nonprofit industrial development agency or authority to a grantee of property conveyed by the grantee to that agency or authority as security for a debt of the grantee or a transfer to a nonprofit industrial development agency or authority.

(18) A transfer from a nonprofit industrial development agency or authority to a grantee purchasing directly from it, but only if (a) the grantee directly uses the real estate for the primary purpose of manufacturing, fabricating, compounding, processing, publishing, research and development, transportation,

energy conversion, energy production, pollution control, warehousing or agriculture, and (b) the agency or authority has the full ownership interest in the real estate transferred.

(19) A transfer by a mortgagor to the holder of a bona fide mortgage in default in lieu of a foreclosure or a transfer pursuant to a judicial sale in which the successful bidder is the bona fide holder of a mortgage, unless the holder assigns the bid to another person.

(20) Any transfer between religious organizations or other bodies or persons holding title for a religious organization if the real estate is not being or has not been used by such transferor for commercial purposes.

(21) A transfer to a conservancy that possesses a tax-exempt status pursuant to IRC § 501(c)(3) and that has as its primary purpose preservation of land for historic, recreational, scenic, agricultural or open-space opportunities; or a transfer from such a conservancy to the United States, the Commonwealth or to any of their instrumentalities, agencies or political subdivisions; or any transfer from such a conservancy where the real estate is encumbered by a perpetual agricultural conservation easement as defined by the Act of June 30, 1981 (P.L. 128, No. 43), known as the "Agricultural Area Security Law," and such conservancy has owned the real estate for at least two years immediately prior to the transfer.

(22) A transfer of real estate devoted to the business of agriculture to a family farm business by a member of the same family that directly owns at least 75% of each class of the stock thereof or the interests in that family farm business or a family farm business, which family directly owns at least 75% of each class of stock thereof or the interests in that family farm business. The business of agriculture includes the leasing, to members of the same family, of property that is directly and principally used for agricultural purposes [72 P.S. § 8101-C].

CAUTION

Any reference in any law or in this *Guidebook* to the former definition of "family farm corporation" or "family farm partnership" in 72 P.S. § 8101-C shall be deemed to be references to "family farm business" under 72 P.S. § 8101-C [Act 85 of 2012 (H.B. 761), § 27].

(23) A transfer between members of the same family of an ownership interest in a real estate company, family farm corporation or family farm partnership which owns real estate.

(24) A transaction wherein the tax due is one dollar ($1) or less.

(25) Leases for the production or extraction of coal, oil, natural gas or minerals and assignments thereof.

(26) A transfer for no or nominal consideration from the Commonwealth (or its instrumentalities) to a volunteer emergency medical services agency, volunteer fire company or volunteer rescue company or between two or more volunteer emergency medical services agencies, volunteer fire companies or volunteer rescue companies.

Conveyance Between Sole Limited Partner and Partnership

A conveyance between a partner and a partnership is taxable. Thus, a conveyance from an individual to a limited partnership was subject to the Pennsylvania realty transfer tax even though the individual was the sole limited partner. The taxpayer argued that the deed was not a document that conveyed an interest in real estate to someone other than himself, but the Court ruled that the partner, an individual, is different from the limited partnership [*Penn Towers Associates, LP v. Cmwlth.*, Pa.Commw., No. 225 F.R. 2003 (January 25, 2004)].

¶3304

Effective September 12, 2016, Act 84 of 2016 exempts transfers of certain conservation and preservation easements from the realty transfer tax as well as transfers of real estate to or from a land bank. Also effective September 12, 2016, Act 175 of 2016 retroactively included veterans' organizations which have a valid tax exemption under Section 501(c)(19) of the Internal Revenue Code of 1986 as exempt from the Pennsylvania Realty Transfer Tax. Act 175 applies to transfers made after September 12, 2016 and the period for obtaining refunds of overpaid taxes was extended. Act 175 amended Act 84 of 2016.

• *Reporting and payment of tax*

Every document, when lodged with or presented to any recorder of deeds for recording, must show the true, full, and complete value or be accompanied by an affidavit executed by a responsible person showing the true, full, and complete value [72 P.S. § 8109-C]. This is accomplished by filing with the Recorder of Deeds Form REV-183, Realty Transfer Tax Statement of Value. A Statement of Value is not required if the transfer is wholly exempt from tax based on family relationship or public utility easement.

The tax is paid at the time the document is presented for recording, within 30 days of acceptance of such document, or within 30 days of becoming an acquired company, whichever is earliest [72 P.S. § 8102-C]; and payment is evidenced by the affixing of documentary stamps to documents.

Responsibility for payment of the realty transfer tax is the joint and several legal duty of the parties to the transaction. This duty may be discharged by the parties as they agree but without prejudice to the rights of the Commonwealth against the parties [61 Pa. Code § 91.111(b)].

Payment by Electronic Funds Transfer

Payment by electronic funds transfer (EFT) is discussed at ¶ 4617.

• *Assessment and notice of tax*

If a taxpayer fails to pay realty transfer tax, the Pennsylvania Department of Revenue is authorized to make an assessment of additional tax and interest due by the taxpayer [72 P.S. § 8111-C]. An assessment of tax must be made within three years after the date of the recording of the document, subject to the following (applicable to any document made, executed, delivered, accepted, or presented on or after October 5, 2005):

(1) *Underpayment of at least 25%:* If the taxpayer underpays the correct amount of the tax by 25% or more, the tax may be assessed at any time within six years after the date the document is recorded.

(2) *Fraud or disregard of rules and regulations:* If any part of an underpayment of tax is due to fraud or an undisclosed, intentional disregard of rules and regulations, the full amount of the tax may be assessed at any time.

Notice of assessment: Promptly after the date of assessment, the Department must send by certified mail a copy of the assessment, including the basis of the assessment, to the person against whom it was made [72 P.S. § 8111-C(b). Any taxpayer against whom an assessment is made may petition the Department for a reassessment pursuant to Article XXVII (discussed at ¶ 4604) [72 P.S. § 8111-(c)]. This provision is effective for assessments issued after December 31, 2007.

Important Issues

• *Computed value*

A mortgage holder rendered the successful bid at a foreclosure sale and then transferred the right to the successful bid to Hilltop Properties for $1.2 million. Hilltop paid transfer tax in the amount of $12,000, representing 1% of the amount paid for the assignment. Subsequently, the Department of Revenue issued a notice of determination that valued the taxable transfer at $3,353,790, the computed value of the realty and determined that the tax due upon recordation of the deed was $33,537. Hilltop contested this determination. The Pennsylvania Commonwealth Court, however, held that the taxable value was "computed value" as required by 61 Pa. Code § 91.135. "Computed value" for this purpose is determined by multiplying the assessed value of the realty for local real estate tax purposes by the common level ratio factor of the taxing district [61 Pa. Code § 91.131]. The object of the transaction is the conveyance of the property, not the sale of assignment rights. The Department's determination of tax was correct [*Hilltop Properties Associates Limited Partnership v. Cmwlth.*, 768 A.2d 1189 (Pa.Commw. 2001)].

• *Terms of trust agreements may subject property to realty transfer tax*

Under the provisions of the realty transfer tax, a transfer into an ordinary trust is exempt if the grantor of property can transfer real estate directly to *all* of the possible beneficiaries (contingent or specifically named). Often the terms of a trust utilize another realty tax exclusion—the familial exemption [72 P.S. § 8102-C.3(6)]. A transfer of realty by the grantor to any of the family members mentioned in 72 P.S. § 8102-C.3(6) is an exempt conveyance.

However, inclusion of an "Armageddon" or intestacy clause may cause transfer of realty into the trust to be subject to the realty transfer tax. This type of clause provides for all contingencies that might occur, and the result could be the transfer of trust property to individuals who do not qualify under the familial exemption (*e.g.*, aunts, uncles, nieces, nephews). Because all possible intestate heirs do not qualify under the familiar exemption, a transfer into a trust that includes them as beneficiaries is subject to the realty transfer tax.

The Department of Revenue has determined that the inclusion of a provision with the following features will protect the exemption for a transfer into a trust:

    (1) The trust will terminate if there are no surviving lineal descendants.

    (2) The remaining trust assets must be distributed through the estate of the trustor either in accordance with his/her will or in accordance with the intestacy law of the jurisdiction in which the trustor resides.

Inclusion of such a provision preserves the familial exemption because the heirs are not considered to receive property as beneficiaries under the trust agreement but as heirs to the grantor's estate [*Pennsylvania Tax Update No. 52*, Pennsylvania Department of Revenue, September/October 1994].

• *Cash transfer to third party*

In a case involving a trust that was created for the benefit of spouses, the total value of assets transferred to the trust was $520,000, of which nearly thirty-three percent consisted of securities and other personalty. The trust agreement provided for a transfer of $5,000 to Planned Parenthood after the death of the spouses. Planned Parenthood executed a disclaimer and renunciation of the bequest pursuant to 20 Pa.C.S. § 6205(a) three months prior to the date the deed transferring the real property was recorded. The disclaimer made the transfer of real property to the trust exempt from realty transfer tax [*Leigh v. Cmwlth.*, 541 A.2d 187 (Pa. 1995)]. The Pennsylvania Supreme Court did not consider the question of whether, in the absence of the disclaimer, the transfer would have been subject to tax. The Commonwealth Court had ruled that the gift to Planned Parenthood was a bequest of personalty and not a devise of real estate, with the real estate and the remainder of the personalty going to immediate family members so that the gift did not render the trust taxable [*Leigh v. Cmwlth.*, 648 A.2d 1346 (Pa.Commw. 1994)].

• *Property purchased by exercise of inherited option*

A daughter exercised an option (granted in her father's will) to buy property owned by the decedent and claimed exemption from the realty transfer tax as a direct transfer between family members. 72 P.S. § 8102-C.3 provides that the realty transfer tax shall not be imposed upon "[a] transfer for no or nominal actual consideration of

¶ 3304

property passing by testate or intestate succession from a personal representative of a decedent to the decedent's devisee or heir." The Commonwealth Court, however, held that the estate of the beneficiary's father was not, in fact, the same person as the beneficiary's father. She acquired the property from the estate, not the decedent. Therefore, the purchase of the property pursuant to an option acquired through her father's estate was subject to the realty transfer tax [*Meridian Trust Co. v. Cmwlth.*, 613 A.2d 654 (Pa.Commw. 1992)].

• *Transfer of real property to irrevocable living trust*

A couple transferred title to their house and farm to an irrevocable trust and did not pay realty transfer tax, claiming it was a transfer to a living trust. The Department of Revenue disagreed. The Commonwealth Court agreed with the taxpayer, concluding that to be excluded from the realty transfer tax, a living trust need not be a revocable trust so long as it functions as a will substitute [*Miller v. Cmwlth.*, 992 A.2d 950 (Pa.Commw. 2010, *aff'd* 757 F.R. 2007, March 29, 2011)].

• *Unrelated contingent beneficiary subjects transfer to tax*

The transferor to a revocable trust was sole beneficiary during her lifetime. The trust document provided that if her children predeceased her, the principal was to be distributed to her grandchildren; if her children predeceased her without issue, the transferor's brother and a friend were to share the principal. The Commonwealth Court ruled that the transfer was subject to the realty transfer tax because the friend is not an exempt beneficiary within the meaning of 72 P.S. §8102-C.3(8): "a transfer for no or nominal actual consideration to a trustee of an ordinary trust where the transfer of the same property would be exempt if the transfer was made directly from the grantor to all of the possible beneficiaries that are entitled to receive the property or proceeds from the sale of the property under the trust, whether or not such beneficiaries are contingent or specifically named" [*Holmes v. Cmwlth.*, 618 A.2d 1160 (Pa.Commw. 1992)].

Holmes argued that the transfer of the realty was exempt because she is the sole beneficiary of the trust during her lifetime. The court, however, ruled that the plain language of 72 P.S. §8102-C.3(8) requires examination of ". . . all of the possible beneficiaries, whether or not such beneficiaries are contingent or specifically named." If all possible beneficiaries are in an exempt category (in this case, intra-family), no realty transfer tax is due. Holmes's inclusion of a friend, however, as a contingent beneficiary took this transfer out of the exempt status.

• *Value of assignment contracts*

Taxpayers entered into an agreement of sale to sell a tract of land for $610,000. Subsequently, the buyer and other parties entered into a string of assignments involving the land. The taxpayers eventually conveyed the land to the assignee at the time for $657,828. The assignee had paid $3,200,000 for its rights to purchase the property. The taxpayers paid realty transfer tax of $6,578.38 on the transfer of the land, based on a value of $657,828. The Supreme Court of Pennsylvania upheld the taxpayers' contention that the amounts paid for the assignments were not to be included in the value of the transfer for purposes of the realty transfer tax [*Allebach v. Cmwlth.*, 683 A.2d 625 (Pa. 1996) Pa.Commw.].

The Department of Revenue asserted that the true value of the land was $3,200,000, basing its position on the fourth method above (the actual consideration for the executory agreement paid by the assignee). The Board of Appeals and the Board of Finance and Revenue agreed with the Department. However, the Commonwealth Court (affirmed by the Pennsylvania Supreme Court), found in favor of the taxpayers. First, said the court, the fourth method applies specifically to executory agreements for the *construction of buildings, etc.* Second, the taxpayers were not parties to any of the assignment contracts.

¶3304

• *Value of lease assignment*

A taxpayer in 1984 contracted for the construction of a medical office building on property owned by the hospital. The hospital, in order to finance the building, leased the land to a county industrial development authority. The development authority then entered into an installment sale agreement with the taxpayer, in which the taxpayer would purchase the leasehold in exchange for payments sufficient to meet the authority's obligation under the not. At the same time, the authority assigned its interest in the installment sale agreement to a bank, the proceeds going to finance the office building, which was completed in May 1986. In 1989, the parties restructured the financing arrangement. The installment sale agreement was terminated and the authority assigned its interest in the lease to the taxpayer, which obtained its own financing from a bank. On April 13, 1989, when the lease assignment was recorded, the taxpayer filed a statement of value and paid realty transfer tax based on the appraised value of the land alone. The court held that the taxpayer must pay realty transfer on the value of both the land and the building because taxpayer did not acquire property interests in the building until after the lease assignment [*East Norriton Medical Associates Ltd. v. Cmwlth.*, 650 A.2d 1169 (Pa.Commw. 1994)].

• *Lease terms of less than 30 years but with renewal terms*

In *Saturday Family LP v. Cmwlth.*, 148 A.3d 931 (Pa.Commw. 2016) the court examined the terms of a ground lease between the taxpayer and a tenant. The lease provided for an initial term of 29 years and 11 months and the tenant had options to renew for up to six periods of five years each for fair market value rent as determined by the parties at the time of the extension based on rents of similar parcels in Westmoreland County. If the parties were unable to agree as to the fair market value rent at the time of the extension, then the rent was to be based upon an appraisal. The court ruled that the extensions should not be included in the lease term for realty transfer tax purposes. Accordingly, given that the ground lease was for a term of less than 30 years, the lease was not subject to Pennsylvania Realty Transfer Tax. The Commonwealth Court denied the exceptions filed by the Commonwealth in *Saturday Family LP v. Cmwlth.*, 2017 BL 282922 (Pa.Commw. August 14, 2017).

• *Transfer between principal and agent*

A parent corporation (Armco) in December of 1987 transferred assets of one of its divisions (for no or nominal actual consideration within the meaning of 72 P.S. § 8102-C.3(11)) to its wholly owned subsidiary (AAMC), paying a realty transfer tax of $204,635.32. In June 1988, Armco filed for refund of the realty transfer tax paid on this transfer, asserting it was a transfer from parent to subsidiary and that the parent and subsidiary had a principal/agent relationship within the meaning of 72 P.S. § 8102-C.3(11). Armco, however, did not claim an exclusion from the realty transfer tax at the time of transfer. Furthermore, Armco failed to show that it retained a beneficial interest in the property as required by regulation [61 Pa. Code § 91.153(b)(1)]. The court held that Armco acted in its individual capacity, not in its capacity as agent for AAMC. The transfer was, therefore, taxable [*Armco, Inc. v. Cmwlth.*, 654 A.2d 1191 (Pa.Commw. 1993)].

• *Conversion from general partnership to limited partnership*

Exton Plaza Associates was a general partnership (with two equal partners) that acquired title to a shopping center, its only asset. In order to obtain financing, Exton Plaza Associates converted itself into a limited partnership that was owned 49.5% by each former general partner and 1% by a limited liability company, which became the general partner of the limited partnership. The limited liability company was also owned by the former general partners. The Commonwealth Court held that the principals' property rights in the shopping center remained essentially unchanged, the execution of the deed transferring the shopping center merely memorializing the conversion from general to limited partnership. A "document" within the meaning of the statute conveys an interest in real estate to someone other than the grantor. The

¶3304

deed in this case did not effect a transfer of a beneficial interest in the partnership to someone other than the grantor. Therefore, the realty transfer tax did not apply because the deed was not a "document" within the meaning of the statute [*Exton Plaza Associates v. Cmwlth.*, 763 A.2d 521 (Pa.Commw. 2000)].

- *Transfer from individuals to wholly owned partnership*

Taxpayers who owned property as tenants in the entirety transferred the property to a limited partnership in which they owned 100% of the interest. The Commonwealth Court held that the transfer was subject to the realty transfer tax because the transfer was to someone other than the grantors. The grantors, as individuals, are not the same entity as their partnership. The Court distinguished its findings in this case from its findings in *Exton Plaza* (see above), noting that these taxpayers, as grantors, were individuals, and not a business partnership wishing to change its business form under Pennsylvania law [Pa.Commw., No. 493 F.R. 2002 (May 11, 2004)]. See, also, *Kline v. Commonwealth of Pennsylvania*, Pa.Commw., No. 124 F.R. 2005, May 19, 2006.

- *Division and transfer of oil and natural gas interests*

The Pennsylvania Department of Revenue (DOR) has issued a notice regarding the property, realty transfer, and personal income tax treatment associated with the division and transfer of interests related to oil and natural gas. The realty transfer tax implications are addressed relative to transfer of mineral rights, easements, public utility easement exclusion, oil and gas lease exemptions, and assignment of oil or gas leases. [*Informational Notice 2012-04*, Pennsylvania Department of Revenue, October 10, 2012].

- *Real estate company 89-11 transactions*

Act 52 of 2013 expanded the application of the realty transfer tax in the context of "real estate company" transactions. A real estate company is an entity of which 90 percent or more is owned by 35 or fewer persons and that is primarily engaged in the business of holding, selling, or leasing real estate that derives 60 percent or more of its annual gross receipts from the ownership or disposition of real estate, or holds real estate, the value of which comprises 90 percent or more of its tangible assets. Upon a change of 90 percent of the ownership of a real estate company in a three-year period, the real estate company owes realty transfer tax on its Pennsylvania real estate. It was commonplace to transfer 89% of the ownership interests to a purchaser and wait three years to transfer the remaining 11% in an effort to avoid triggering application of the Pennsylvania realty transfer tax.

Effective January 1, 2014, several changes in the law attempt to restrict the use of 89-11 transactions. A legally binding option or commitment will be counted as a transfer for purposes of determining whether 90 percent or more of the ownership interests in an entity has been transferred so as to trigger application of the state realty transfer tax, irrespective of whether the option may expire unexercised. Also, a corporation or association will be deemed to be a real estate company if it holds a 90 percent or greater ownership interest in a corporation or association that itself meets the definition of a real estate company (similar to the case of Philadelphia's real estate transfer tax). In determining whether a corporation or association is a real estate company, real estate held everywhere will be counted for purposes of the determination, whereas previously only Pennsylvania real estate was considered.

- *Applicability of federal exemptions*

Congress exempted the Federal National Mortgage Association ("Fannie Mae") and the Federal Home Loan Mortgage Corporation ("Freddie Mac") from state and local taxes "except that any real property of [either Fannie Mae or Freddie Mac] shall be subject to State, territorial, county, municipal, or local taxation to the same extent as other real property is taxed." 12 U.S.C. §§1723a(c)(2) and §1452(e). The Third

Circuit has held that these entities were exempt from the state and local realty transfer taxes. *Delaware County et al. v. Federal Housing Finance Agency et al.*, 747 F.3d 215 (2014).

¶3305 Tax on Private Bankers

The tax on private bankers authorized to do business in Pennsylvania is imposed by the Act of May 16, 1861 [72 P.S. § 2221].

• *Return, base, and rate*

Private bankers in Pennsylvania must, on or before February 15, annually, make a written return (Form RCT-131), under oath or affirmation, to the Department of Revenue. The return must show the full amount of gross receipts from commissions, discounts, abatements, allowances, and all other receipts arising from business during the calendar year. The tax is 1% of total gross receipts. Payment accompanies the report. This tax has little current application because the conduct of a private banking business in Pennsylvania is restricted, by the Pennsylvania Banking Code of 1933, to those private banks authorized to do business on July 3, 1933.

Payment by Electronic Funds Transfer

Payment by electronic funds transfer (EFT) is discussed at ¶4617.

¶3306 Tax on Credit Unions

The provisions governing credit unions are found in the Act of September 20, 1961 [Act of September 20, 1961, P.L. 1548].

Credit unions are under the supervision of the Pennsylvania Department of Banking [Act of September 20, 1961, P.L. 1548, §7]. For tax purposes they are considered savings institutions, and none of their assets are subject to taxation except real estate [Act of September 20, 1961, P.L. 1548; § 31].

• *Reports and assessments*

Credit unions must report to the Department of Banking at least once a year and are examined at least once a year by the Department. Supplementary reports and examinations may be required from time to time. The cost of examinations is paid by the credit union. A credit union must also pay annually its proportionate share of the overhead expenses of the Department of Banking. Failure to file reports when due, unless excused for cause, results in a charge of $5 for each day of delinquency [Act of September 20, 1961, P.L. 1548, §7]. For payment by electronic funds transfer see ¶4617.

• *Action upon violations*

If the Department finds that a credit union is violating these provisions, is conducting business in an unsafe manner, is in an unsafe and unsound condition to transact business, or is insolvent, the Department may take possession of its business and property and keep possession until the unsatisfactory conditions are remedied or its affairs are liquidated. The Department may also take similar action if any report is not filed within a period of 15 days after it is due [Act of September 20, 1961, P.L. 1548, §7].

• *Appeal*

Any person aggrieved by the Department's action in taking possession of a credit union may appeal to the Commonwealth Court [Act of September 20, 1961, P.L. 1548, §7].

¶3307 Slot Machine Tax

As part of the Pennsylvania Race Horse Development and Gaming Act [Act 71 of 2004 (H.B. 2330), effective July 5, 2004], the Pennsylvania General Assembly authorized the issuance of licenses to operate slot machines and imposed a slot machine tax on slot machine revenue. The state will allow a maximum of 61,000 slot machines at 14 venues, which include race tracks, non-track locations, and resort hotels.

Reference and Citation

The Pennsylvania Race Horse Development and Gaming Act is referred to as Act 71 in this *Guidebook*. All citations in this paragraph are to Act 71 of 2004 unless otherwise specified.

• *Administration*

A Gaming Control Board established under the authority of Act 71 has jurisdiction over most of the responsibilities and the oversight of gaming [§ 1202]. The Department of Revenue, however, is responsible for implementing and administratively managing a Central Control System (CCS) that controls and links all operational slot machines to one central computer system [§ 1103]. The Department of Revenue is also responsible for the accurate accounting and collection of the many different earmarked revenues due the Commonwealth from slots operations.

• *Imposition of slot machine tax*

The Department of Revenue must determine and each slot machine licensee must pay a daily tax of 34% and a local share assessment of 4% of its daily gross terminal revenue from the slot machines in operation at its facility into the state gaming fund [§ 1403(b)]. "Gross terminal revenue" is the total of wagers received by a slot machine minus the total of (1) payouts to those who play the slot machines and (2) cash paid to purchase annuities to fund prizes [§ 1103]. The state gaming fund is a fund established within the state treasury [§ 1403(a)].

In *Mount Airy #1, LLC v. DOR*, 154 A.3d 268 (2016), a casino brought an action against the Commonwealth seeking a declaration that the municipal portion of the local share assessment levied on gross slot machine revenue under the Race Horse Development and Gaming Act (Gaming Act) violated the Uniformity Clause of the Pennsylvania Constitution because it imposed grossly unequal local share assessments upon similarly situated slot machine licensees. Under the Gaming Act, slot machine licensees are subject to a 34% tax on all gross terminal revenue ("GTR"). Slot machine licensees also must pay a local share assessment, which the Commonwealth collects and distributes to the casino's host municipality and/or county. For most casinos, the local share assessment consists of two distinct parts: the county local share assessment and the municipal local share assessment. A casino located *outside* of Philadelphia County must pay both (a) an annual county local share assessment of 2% of its GTR and (b) a municipal local share assessment of either 2% of its GTR or a lump sum of $10 million, whichever is greater. Therefore, a non-Philadelphia casino with GTR at or below $500 million will always pay a $10 million municipal local share assessment, and a non-Philadelphia casino with GTR above $500 million will always pay more than $10 million. Mount Airy asserted that the municipal local share assessment violated the Uniformity Clause because non-Philadelphia casinos are divided into two categories (i.e., those with GTR above $500 million and those with GTR below $500 million, which are taxed differently.) Two casinos located outside of Philadelphia would pay differing local share assessments. If one casino's GTR were $100 million, it would pay a lump sum $10 million municipal local share assessment. A casino with GTR of $600 million would pay a $12 million municipal local share assessment (2% of its GTR). The Pennsylvania Supreme Court found that the Gaming Act violated the Uniformity Clause because it effectively created a variable-rate tax. One rate for non-Philadelphia casinos with GTR below $500 million and another for non-Philadelphia casinos with GTR greater than $500 million. The Uniformity Clause prohibits the Pennsylvania General Assembly from imposing disparate tax rates upon income that exceeds a particular threshold.

In *Chester Downs and Marina LLC v. Pa. Dept. of Rev.*, __ A.3d __, (Pa. July 18, 2018), the Pennsylvania Supreme Court dismissed a request for a refund of a taxpayer's local share assessment levied on gross slot machine revenue under the Gaming Act because no retroactive relief was available for taxes paid prior to the Court's decision in *Mount Airy #1, LLC v. Pa. Dept. of Rev.* (cited above). In regard to any claims for a refund of taxes paid after the *Mount Airy #1* decision, the Court lacked original jurisdiction to entertain those claims. The taxpayer apparently petitioned the Supreme Court seeking a refund of the local share assessment taxes under the court's exclusive jurisdiction to hear constitutional challenges to the Gaming Act. See 4 Pa. C.S. § 1904. The Court's decision in *Mount Airy #1* held that the local share assessment imposed under the Gaming Act was a non-uniform tax prohibited under the Uniformity Clause of the Pennsylvania Constitution and severed the local share assessment provision from the Gaming Act. The *Chester Downs* ruling prohibited a refund in the case at bar because Supreme Court decisions invaliding a state tax statute are effective as of the date of the decision, and cannot be applied retroactively.

• *Property tax relief fund*

Section 1409 of Act 71 establishes in the state treasury a special fund to be known as the Property Tax Relief Fund, which receives money from the state gaming fund and any other money from any source designated for deposit in the Property Tax Relief Fund [§ 1409(a)]. Money in the Property Tax Relief Fund must be used for local property and wage tax relief [§ 1409(b)]. Under the provisions of the Homeowner Tax Relief Act, money from the property tax relief fund is used to fund gaming allocations for homestead and farmstead exclusions. The Homeowner Tax Relief Act is discussed at ¶ 3514.

¶3308 Gaming Table Tax

Effective January 7, 2010, a Pennsylvania gaming table tax is imposed. Each certificate holder must pay daily 14% of its gross table game revenue for the first two years after the beginning of table game operations at its licensed facility and 12% thereafter. Act 84 of 2016 imposes an additional 2% tax on the daily gross table game revenue thus, 12% becomes 14% effective August 1, 2016 which is set to expire on June 30, 2019. In addition, the certificate holder must pay daily 34% of its gross table game revenue from each table game played on a fully automated gaming table. The certificate holder must also pay a weekly 2% local share assessment. Category 1 or Category 2 slot machine licensees who submit a petition for a table game operation certificate prior to June 1, 2010, must pay a nonrefundable authorization fee of $16.5 million. After June 1, 2010, the fee is $24.75 million. For Category 3 slot machine licensees, those fees are $7.5 million prior to June 1, 2010, and $11.25 million thereafter. For Category 1 or Category 2 slot machine licenses issued after June 1, 2010, the fees are $16.5 million and $7.5 million, respectively.

¶3309 Hospital Assessment Fee

Imposition: A fee, known as a quality care assessment is imposed on Pennsylvania hospitals [Article VIII-G, Public Welfare Code (Act of June 13, 1967 (P.L. 31) effective July 9, 2010, and applicable retroactively to July 1, 2010]. A "hospital" is a facility licensed under P.A. Code Pt. IV, Subpt. B (relating to general and special hospitals). Act 40 of 2018, effective 07/01/2018, extends the Quality Care Assessment until June 30, 2023, and provides new assessment rates for fiscal years from 2018 through 2023. For fiscal years starting on or after July 1, 2018, the assessment percentage is calculated using the covered hospital's net inpatient revenue and net outpatient revenue. [62 Pa. Stat. Ann. § 804-G(a).]

Rate: For fiscal years 2015-2016, 2016-2017 and 2017-2018, each covered hospital pays this fee at an adjusted amount equal to 3.71% of net inpatient revenue. [62 Pa. Stat. Ann. § 803-G(b)(3).] For fiscal year 2018-2019, the rate of the assessment equals 2.98% of the net inpatient revenue of each covered hospital and 1.55% of the net outpatient revenue of each covered hospital. For fiscal years 2019-2020, 2020-2021,

2021-2022 and 2022-2023, the rate of the assessment equals 3.32% of the net inpatient revenue of each covered hospital and 1.73% of the net outpatient revenue of each covered hospital.

Net inpatient revenue: "Net inpatient revenue" is gross charges for facilities for inpatient services less any deducted amounts for bad debt expense, charity care expense, and contractual allowances as reported on the Medicare cost report for federal fiscal year 2008 or to the Pennsylvania Health Care Cost Containment Council for federal fiscal year 2008, if the Medicare cost report is not available, and validated by the Public Welfare Department. The definition of "net inpatient revenue" is amended to include gross charges for facilities for inpatient services less any deducted amounts for bad debt expense, charity care expense and contractual allowances as reported on forms specified by the Department of Health and Human Services and (a) as identified in the hospital's records for the state fiscal year commencing July 1, 2014, or such later state fiscal year, as may be specified by the department for use in determining an annual assessment amount owed on or after July 1, 2018, or (b) as identified in the hospital's records for the most recent state fiscal year, or part thereof, if amounts are not available under clause (a). Additional amendments allow the Secretary of Health and Human Services to adjust the assessment percentage for all or part of the fiscal year for inpatient or outpatient services, or both; expand or clarify provisions for calculating and rebasing assessments for fiscal years after 2016; and set limitations for fiscal years 2018 through 2023.

Net outpatient revenue: "Net outpatient revenue" is defined as gross charges for facilities for outpatient services less any deducted amounts for bad debt expense, charity care expense and contractual allowances as reported on forms specified by the Department of Health and Human Services and (1) as identified in the hospital's records for the state fiscal year commencing July 1, 2014, or a later state fiscal year, as may be specified by the Department for use in determining an annual assessment amount owed on or after July 1, 2018, or (2) as identified in the hospital's records for the most recent state fiscal year, or part thereof, if amounts are not available under clause (1).

Exempt hospitals: The fee does not apply to an exempt hospital. An "exempt hospital" is any of the following:

(1) A federal Veterans' Affairs hospital.

(2) A hospital that provides care, including inpatient hospital services, to all patients free of charge.

(3) A private psychiatric hospital.

(4) A State-owned psychiatric hospital.

(5) A critical assess hospital.

(6) A long-term acute care hospital.

Payment of the assessment is to be made in four quarterly installments, which are due on or before the first day of the second month of the quarter, or 30 days from the date of the notice of the quarterly assessment amount, whichever is later. [62 Pa. Stat. Ann. §804-G(b).]The Secretary of Public Welfare may adjust the assessment percentage provided the Secretary gives public notice of the proposed assessment by Publication in the Pennsylvania Bulletin and a 30 period for public comment. [62 Pa. Stat. Ann. §803-G(c).] A new hospital that begins operation as a covered hospital during a fiscal year in which an assessment is in effect is not subject to assessment during such year. For the following fiscal year, the assessment is calculated using the net inpatient revenue from the fiscal year in which the covered hospital began operation or became a covered hospital provided the covered hospital began operation or became a covered hospital prior to July 1, 2018. If the new hospital began operation or became a covered hospital on or after July 1, 2018, the assessment is calculated the net inpatient revenue and net outpatient revenue from the fiscal year in which the covered hospital began operation. For fiscal years following the first full fiscal year, but ending prior to July 1, 2018, the assessment is calculated using the net inpatient revenue from the prior fiscal year. For fiscal years following the first full fiscal year starting on or after July 1, 2018, the assessment is calculated using the net inpatient and net outpatient revenue from the prior fiscal year.

The quality care assessment is set to expire on June 30, 2023.

¶3310 Covered Device Recycling Fee

• *Registration and fee*

A manufacturer of new covered devices offered for sale in Pennsylvania must register with the Department of Environmental Protection (DEP) by January 30, 2011, and pay a registration fee of $5,000 [Act No. 108 (H.B. 708), § 304(1)]. A new covered device is one manufactured after January 22, 2011 [Act No. 108 (H.B. 708), § 102].

• *Covered device—In general*

A covered device is (i) a covered computer device and (ii) covered television device marketed and intended for use by a consumer. The term does not include the following [Act No. 108 (H.B. 708), § 102; effective January 22, 2011]:

(1) A device that is a part of a motor vehicle or any component part of a motor vehicle assembled by or for a vehicle manufacturer or franchised dealer, including replacement parts for use in a motor vehicle.

(2) A device that is functionally or physically a part of or connected to or integrated within equipment or a system designed and intended for use in an industrial, governmental, commercial, research and development, or medical setting, including, but not limited to, diagnostic, monitoring, control or medical products as defined under the Federal Food, Drug, and Cosmetic Act (52 Stat. 1040, 21 U.S.C. § 301 et seq.), or equipment used for security, sensing, monitoring, antiterrorism, emergency services purposes or equipment designed and intended primarily for use by professional users.

(3) A device that is contained within a clothes washer, clothes dryer, refrigerator, refrigerator and freezer, microwave oven, conventional oven or range, dishwasher, room air conditioner, dehumidifier, air purifier, or exercise equipment.

(4) Any of the following:

(i) Telephone of any type, including a mobile phone.

(ii) Personal digital assistant.

(iii) Global positioning system devices.

• *Covered computer device*

The term "covered computer device" means a desktop or notebook computer or computer monitor or peripheral, marketed and intended for use by a consumer. The term does not include a covered television device [Act No. 108 (H.B. 708), § 102].

• *Covered television device*

The term "covered device" means an electronic device that contains a tuner that locks on to a selected carrier frequency and is capable of receiving and displaying television or video programming via broadcast, cable or satellite, including, without limitation, any direct view or projection television with a viewable screen of four inches or larger whose display technology is based on cathode ray tube, plasma, liquid crystal, digital light processing, liquid crystal on silicon, silicon crystal reflective display, light emitting diode or similar technology marketed and intended for use by a consumer primarily for personal purposes. The term does not include a covered computer device or a mobile phone [Act No. 108 (H.B. 708), § 102].

• *Fees for collection or recycling of covered devices*

No manufacturer or retailer may charge a fee or cost to a consumer for the collection, transportation, or recycling of a covered device, unless a financial incentive of equal or greater value is provided to the consumer. The financial incentive may be in the form of a coupon or rebate [Act No. 108 (H.B. 708), § 504].

• *Annual renewal*

A registered manufacturer must submit an annual renewal of its registration to the Department of Environmental Protection and pay to the DEP a registration fee of $5,000 by January 1 of each program year. The registration and each annual renewal must include a list of all brands the manufacturer is using on its covered devices regardless of whether the manufacturer owns or licenses the brand, and shall be effective upon receipt by the department [Act No. 108 (H.B. 708), § 304(3)].

• *Environmentally sound management requirements*

General rule: Covered devices collected through any program in Pennsylvania (whether by a manufacturer, retailer, for-profit or not-for-profit corporation, or unit of government) must be recycled in a manner that is in compliance with all applicable Federal, State and local laws, regulations, and ordinances and may not be exported for disposal in a manner that poses a significant risk to the public health or the environment [Act No. 108 (H.B. 708), § 505(a).

Performance requirement: All entities must, at a minimum, demonstrate to the satisfaction of the Department of Environmental Protection that the facility to be used to recycle covered devices has achieved and maintained third-party accredited certification from one of the following [Act No. 108 (H.B. 708), § 505(b)]:

(1) The Responsible Recycling (R2) Practice Standard.

(2) The E-Stewards Standard.

(3) An internationally accredited third-party environmental management standard for the safe and responsible handling of covered devices.

Information required: All entities must provide information about their certification and its standing to the Department of Environmental Protection, along with any other relevant requirements that may be mandated by federal or State law [Act No. 108 (H.B. 708), § 505(b)].

• *Departmental website*

For more information see the DEP's website at http://www.portal.state.pa.us/portal/server.pt/community/household/14079/electronics_management_program/589592.

• *Disposal ban*

Two years after the effective date (January 22, 2011) of this legislation, no person may place in a municipal solid waste a covered device or any of its components, excluding any nonhazardous residuals produced during recycling in any solid waste disposal facility [Act No. 108 (H.B. 708), § 506(a)].

• *Penalties*

Failure to label, register, or pay fee: Any manufacturer who fails to label its new covered devices with a brand, as required by § 303 of this Act, who fails to register with the Department of Environmental Protection and pay a registration fee, as required by section 304(a), may be assessed a penalty of up to $10,000 for the first violation and up to $25,000 for the second and each subsequent violation in addition to paying for any fees, payments and penalties required by or imposed pursuant to this Act [Act No. 108, H.B. 708), § 506(b)(1)].

Violation of other provision: Except for failure to label, register, or pay, any person (including a retailer) who violates any requirement of this act may be assessed a penalty of up to $1,000 for the first violation and up to $2,000 for the second and each subsequent violation, in addition to paying for any fees, payments and penalties required by or imposed pursuant to this Act [Act No. 108, H.B. 708), § 506(b)(2)].

• *Regulations*

The Environmental Quality Board may adopt rules and regulations as shall be necessary for the purpose of administering this Act. The regulations shall be promulgated in accordance with the act of June 25, 1982 (P.L. 633, No. 181), known as the Regulatory Review Act [Act No. 108 (H.B. 708), § 508].

¶3311 Pari-mutuel Wagering Tax

On February 23, 2016, Governor Tom Wolf signed into law House Bill 941, now Act 7 of 2016, which repeals Article XVI-B of the Tax Reform Code as well as the Race Horse Industry Reform Act. Effective February 23, 2016, a licensed racing entity that conducts horse race meetings or a secondary pari-mutuel organization shall pay tax to the Department of Revenue at the following rates: 1.5 percent of the amount wagered each racing day on win, place or show wagers and 2.5 percent of the amount wagered on multiple and exotic pools, including an exacta, daily double, quinella and trifecta wagers. Previously, Act 52 of 2013 established a 10 percent tax on advance deposit account wagering through any non-licensed corporation on a horse race or harness horse race made over the telephone or online over the internet where the wagers were placed from locations in the Commonwealth, including wagers made by an advance deposit account wagering system in which the wagers are included in common pool wagering through a pari-mutuel system.

¶3312 Medical Marijuana Tax

Act 16 of 2016 signed into law on April 17, 2016 establishes a program for the medical use of marijuana and imposes a gross receipts tax of 5 percent on receipts from the sale of medical marijuana by a grower/processor to a dispensary to be paid by the grower/processor. The sale of medical marijuana is not subject to sales tax.

PART XV

LOCAL TAXES

CHAPTER 34

GENERAL PRINCIPLES OF LOCAL TAXATION

¶3401 Classification of Political Subdivisions

Cities, counties, townships, and school districts of Pennsylvania are divided into classes according to population. The taxing powers of districts often vary according to classification.

• *Classification of cities*

Cities are divided into four classes [53 P.S. § 101]:

(1) *First Class Cities:* Those containing a population of 1,000,000 or over. Philadelphia is the only First Class City.

(2) *Second Class Cities:* Those containing a population of 250,000 and under 1,000,000. Pittsburgh is the only Second Class City.

(3) *Second Class A Cities:* Those containing a population of 80,000 and under 250,000 and that by ordinance elect to be a city of the second class A.

(4) *Third Class Cities:* Those containing a population under 250,000 and that have not elected to become a city of the second class A.

• *Classification of counties*

Counties are divided into nine classes:

(1) *First Class Counties:* Those having a population of 1,500,000 inhabitants and over [16 P.S. § 210(1). Philadelphia County is the only First Class County.

(2) *Second Class Counties:* Those having a population of 800,000 and more but fewer than 1,500,000 inhabitants [16 P.S. § 210(2)]. Allegheny is the only Second Class County.

(3) *Second Class A Counties:* Those having a population of 500,000 and more but fewer than 800,000 inhabitants [16 P.S. § 210(2.1))].

(4) *Third Class Counties:* Those having a population of 210,000 and more but fewer than 500,000 inhabitants [16 P.S. § 210(3)].

(5) *Fourth Class Counties:* Those having a population of 145,000 and more but fewer than 210,000 inhabitants [16 P.S. § 210(4)].

(6) *Fifth Class Counties:* Those having a population of 95,000 and more but fewer than 145,000 inhabitants [16 P.S. § 210(5)].

(7) *Sixth Class Counties:* Those having a population of 45,000 and more but fewer than 95,000 inhabitants and those having a population of 35,000 and more but fewer than 45,000 inhabitants that by ordinance or resolution of the Board of County Commissioners elect to be a county of the sixth class [16 P.S. § 210(6)].

(8) *Seventh Class Counties:* Those having a population of 20,000 and more but fewer than 45,000 inhabitants and those having a population of 35,000 and more but fewer than 45,000 inhabitants that have not elected to be a county of the sixth class [16 P.S. § 210(7)].

(9) *Eighth Class Counties:* Those having a population of fewer than 20,000 inhabitants [16 P.S. § 210(8)].

• *Classification of townships*

Townships are divided into two classes—townships of the first class and townships of the second class [53 P.S. § 65201]:

(1) *First Class Townships:* Those townships having a population of at least 300 inhabitants to the square mile (a) that have fully organized and elected their officers and are functioning as townships of the first class or (b) that may hereafter be created townships of the first class in the manner provided by the laws relating to townships of the first class.

(2) *Second Class Townships:* All townships not townships of the first class are townships of the second class. A change from one class to the other shall hereafter be made only as provided by this act, or the laws relating to townships of the first class.

• *Classification of school districts*

School districts are divided into five classes [24 P.S. § 2-202]:

(1) *First Class School Districts:* Those having a population of 1,000,000 or more inhabitants. The Philadelphia School District is the only First Class School District.

(2) *First Class A School Districts:* Those having a population of 250,000 or more but fewer than 1,000,000 inhabitants. The Pittsburgh School District is the only First Class A school district.

(3) *Second Class School Districts:* Those having a population of 30,000 or more but fewer than 250,000 inhabitants.

(4) *Third Class School Districts:* Those having a population of 5,000 or more but fewer than 30,000 inhabitants.

(5) *Fourth Class School Districts:* Those having a population of fewer than 5,000 inhabitants.

¶3402 Enabling Legislation

The power of local jurisdictions to tax is limited to the powers granted by the Commonwealth. The existing taxing powers of local jurisdictions are granted by various acts referred to as enabling legislation. There are two general enabling acts: (1) The Sterling Act [Act of August 5, 1932, Sp. Sess., P.L. 45] and (2) The Local Tax Enabling Act (LTEA) [Act of December 31, 1965, P.L. 1257, No. 511; 53 P.S. § 6924.101 *et seq.*]. These acts are discussed at ¶3601.

¶3402

The Sterling Act applies to the city of Philadelphia, and the LTEA applies to other classes of political subdivisions except counties and the Philadelphia and Pittsburgh school districts.

There is separate legislation authorizing the county personal property tax. The personal property tax of the school districts of Philadelphia (not currently levied) and Pittsburgh is established by the school code, and the Pittsburgh personal property tax is authorized by a provision of the Local Tax Enabling Act (Act 511). In general, school districts have the authority to levy taxes under § 507 of the Public School Code of 1949 [24 P.S. § 1-101 *et seq.*]. See below, however, for the discussion of the special case of the Philadelphia School District. The real property tax is governed by the General County Assessment Law [72 P.S. § 5020-101 *et seq.*]. There are various other codes of law that apply to political subdivisions. These are explained in each specific tax.

* *The Sterling Act*

The Sterling Act grants broad taxing powers to the city of Philadelphia. It can tax any person, transaction, occupation, privilege, subject, and personal property within its city limits as it sees fit. The only limitation on Philadelphia's taxing power is that it cannot tax anything that is subject to a state tax or license fee [Act of August 5, 1932, Sp. Sess., P.L. 45]. The Sterling Act places no limits on the rates of tax that Philadelphia may impose, but the Tax Reform Code limits the rate on earned income of nonresidents [72 P.S. § 7359(b)].

Business privilege tax: Philadelphia is given an explicit authority to collect a business privilege tax. Section 4 of The First Class City Business Reform Act [Act of May 30, 1984, P.L. 345, No. 69] provides that "[n]otwithstanding a contrary provision of law of the Commonwealth, including, but not limited to, the act of March 4, 1971 (P.L. 6, No. 2), known as the Tax Reform Code of 1971, and unless otherwise exempted or excluded from the payment of tax by an ordinance of the city council of a city of the first class taking advantage of this authorization to tax, every person engaging in any business in a city of the first class, beginning with the tax year 1985, and annually thereafter, shall pay an annual tax at the rate or rates specified by the city council of the city of the first class." Thus, a beer distributor, despite Commonwealth regulation of the industry, was not exempt from the Philadelphia business privilege tax. Legislative intent was clear, and the Commonwealth's pervasive regulation of the industry did not preempt the enabling legislation [*City of Philadelphia v. Clement & Muller, Inc.; City of Philadelphia v. Garabet, Ltd.*, 715 A.2d 397 (Pa. 1998), *aff'g* 659 A.2d 596 (Pa.Commw. 1995)].

Philadelphia school district: The Commonwealth granted the city of Philadelphia, not the School District, the authority to levy, assess, and collect taxes under the authority of the Sterling Act. The School District itself is *not* empowered to levy taxes. In general, school districts have the authority to levy taxes under § 507 of the Public School Code of 1949, 24 P.S. §§ 2201 *et seq.*, as amended. However, the Philadelphia School District is not authorized to levy taxes, because members are appointed by the mayor of Philadelphia and the Legislature may not delegate the power to tax to appointed officials [*Danson v. Casey*, 399 A.2d 360 (Pa. 1979); Philadelphia Home Rule Charter, 351 Pa. Code § 12.12-201]. Therefore, taxation by the school district of distributors of alcoholic beverages is pre-empted by the Commonwealth regulation and taxation even if the tax is imposed for the benefit of the school district. See discussion of the *Wissinoming* case below.

Use and occupancy tax: A school distinct use and occupancy tax on distributors of malt beverages was preempted by the Liquor Code and the taxes on alcoholic beverages imposed by the Commonwealth because the privilege of operating a malt and brewed beverages distributorship is granted by the Commonwealth. The legislature has adopted a scheme of regulation over the entire alcoholic beverages industry

¶3402

that is so pervasive that it has preempted the field [*Wissinoming Bottling Co. v. School District of Philadelphia*, 654 A.2d 208 (Pa.Commw. 1995)]. See also *City of Philadelphia and School District of Philadelphia v. Tax Review Board of the City of Philadelphia and Shott, t/a Thrifty Scott Beverage*, 713 A.2d 718 (Pa.Commw. 1998)].

• *Local Tax Enabling Act [53 P.S. § 6924.101 et seq.]*

The taxing powers granted by the Local Tax Enabling Act (Act 511) to other political subdivisions are not as broad as those granted to Philadelphia by the Sterling Act. The Act grants express powers to levy certain taxes at certain rates. Because the Act does not, however, contain specific definitions of the taxes it authorizes (except for the earned income tax), most definitions have developed through local tax ordinances and judicial decisions. See specific local taxes in Parts XVI and XVIII.

The local jurisdictions under the authority of the LTEA are as follows:

(1) Cities of the second class.

(2) Cities of the second class A.

(3) Cities of the third class.

(4) Boroughs.

(5) Towns.

(6) Townships of the first class.

(7) Townships of the second class.

(8) School districts of the second class.

(9) School districts of the third class.

(10) School districts of the fourth class, in all cases including independent school districts.

Right-to-Know Act vs. Confidentiality

A newspaper requested that the Scranton Single Tax Office make available copies of the delinquent tax lists for business entities that had not paid their wage, business privilege, or mercantile taxes. When the Tax Office denied the request because no such lists existed, the newspaper filed a complaint asserting that the release of those lists was mandated by the Right-to-Know Act [65 P.S. § § 66.1—66.4], under which citizens have the right to examine, inspect, and duplicate the public records of public agencies. The Commonwealth Court disagreed, pointing out that nothing in the Act requires an agency to compile information from public records. If the records are, indeed, public, then it is up to those seeking to examine them to go through each record and gather the information [*Scranton Times v. The Scranton Single Tax Office*, 736 A.2d 711 (Pa.Commw. 1999)]. Furthermore, the information sought by the newspaper concerned taxes levied by the Local Tax Enabling Act (LTEA) and, under the LTEA, no information gathered from these tax records can be divulged [53 P.S. § 6913(V)(f)]. Not only is the tax information confidential, but the LTEA makes it a crime to divulge tax information [53 P.S. § 6913(IX)(b)]. See also *Juniata Valley School District v. Wargo*, 797 A.2d 428 (Pa.Commw. 2002), in which a taxpayer was refused a request for a list of names of other taxpayers who paid local earned income tax in a Pennsylvania school district. This case is discussed in more detail at ¶ 3607.

• *County Code*

In general, taxation in counties of the third to eighth classes is controlled by the County Code [16 P.S. § 1770 *et seq.*].

• *Second-Class County Code*

The provisions of the Second Class County Code apply to counties of the second class and counties of the second class A [16 P.S. § 3102].

• *Third-Class City Code*

Enabling legislation for third class cities (*i.e.*, all cities except Philadelphia, Pittsburgh, and Scranton) is found in the Third Class City Code [53 P.S. § 36801 *et seq.*].

• *First-Class Township Code*

Taxation in first-class townships (*i.e.*, those with a population of at least 300 inhabitants per square mile) is controlled by the First-Class Township Code [53 P.S. § 55201 *et seq.*].

• *Borough Code*

The Borough Code [53 P.S. § 45102 *et seq.*]contains enabling legislation for all other cities, boroughs, and towns.

• *Home rule charter laws*

The Pennsylvania Constitution grants municipalities the right and power to frame and adopt home rule charters [Art. IX, § 2]. Adoption, amendment or repeal of a home rule charter must be made by referendum. The General Assembly provides the procedure by which a home rule charter may be framed and its adoption, amendment or repeal presented to these electors.

The enabling legislation under which most home rule counties in Pennsylvania have adopted their home rule charters is the Home Rule Charter and Optional Plans Law [Act 62 of 1972; 53 P.S. § 2901 *et seq.*]. The home rule charter laws of second class counties (*e.g.*, Allegheny County) are established under special enabling legislation—the Second Class County Charter Law [Article XXXI-C of the Second Class County Act, enacted by Act 12 of 1997 (H.B. 329), § 3]. A municipality that has adopted a home rule charter may exercise any powers and perform any function not denied by the Pennsylvania Constitution, statute, or its home rule charter [53 Pa.C.S. § 2961]. There are no limits on tax rates imposed on residents of home rule municipalities. However, nonresidents may not be taxed at rates exceeding those that would be applicable if the municipality did not have a home rule charter law [53 Pa.C.S. § 2962(b)].

• *Home rule charters*

Municipalities have the right and power to frame and adopt home rule charters by referendum. A municipality that has a home rule charter may exercise any power or perform any function not denied by the Constitution of the Commonwealth of Pennsylvania, by its home rule charter, or by the General Assembly of Pennsylvania [Pennsylvania Constitution, Article IX, § 2]. These grants of municipal power are to be liberally construed in favor of the municipality [Home Rule Charter and Optional Plans Law, Act of April 13, 1972, P.L. 184, Article III, § 301]. Among the powers granted to a home rule municipality is the authority to impose local taxes on any subject of taxation granted by the General Assembly to municipalities of the class to which it would belong without a home rule charter; and the taxes can be imposed at any rate determined by the governing body. A home rule municipality, however, cannot levy a rate of tax on nonresidents that is greater than the rate permitted in the absence of a home rule charter [Home Rule Charter and Optional Plans Law, Act of April 13, 1972, P.L. 184, Article III, § 302(a.1)]. Home rule municipalities are limited in subjects of taxation to those expressly provided by acts of the General Assembly that are applicable in all parts of Pennsylvania or to all municipalities or to a class or classes of municipalities [Home Rule Charter and Optional Plans Law, Act of April 13, 1972, P.L. 184, Article III, § 302(d)].

¶3402

¶3403 Limitations on Local Taxing Powers

The power of the Commonwealth of Pennsylvania and its local jurisdictions to tax its subjects is restricted by the Constitution of the United States and the Constitution of the Commonwealth. The power of local jurisdictions to tax their subjects is also limited by enabling legislation. In addition, there are general restrictions that apply to all local jurisdictions. These restrictions are discussed below.

• *Constitutional restrictions*

The primary (but not only; see, *e.g.,* the explanation of the doctrine of governmental immunity discussed below) constitutional restrictions on the power of local jurisdictions to tax their subjects are as follows:

(1) *Due Process Clause of the U.S. Constitution* [U.S. Constitution, Amendment 14, §1]. This clause prohibits the taking of property without due process of law. An example of property exempt by the Due Process Clause is property with a situs outside the taxing jurisdiction.

(2) *Equal Protection Clause of the U.S. Constitution* [U.S. Constitution, Amendment 14, §1]. This clause prohibits discrimination among subjects of taxation, particularly in the context of taxation of interstate commerce.

(3) *Uniformity Clause of the Pennsylvania Constitution* [Pennsylvania Constitution, Article VIII, §I]. This clause prohibits discrimination among the same class of subjects of taxation and works to prevent discrimination much like the Equal Protection Clause.

(4) *Commerce Clause of the U.S. Constitution* [U.S. Constitution, Article I, §8, Cl. 3]. This clause (in conjunction with the Interstate Income Act, 15 U.S.C.A. §381) places restrictions on the taxation of corporations engaged in interstate commerce. Basically, it prohibits discriminatory taxation of interstate commerce.

(5) *Double taxation.* Technically, this is not a constitutional restriction because the Pennsylvania Constitution does not prohibit double taxation. However, it is often referred to as a constitutional restriction. The policy of Pennsylvania has consistently been to avoid double taxation.

• *Preemption doctrine*

A local jurisdiction cannot levy a tax on anything the Commonwealth taxes [Act of August 5, 1932, Sp. Sess., P.L. 45, §1; Act of December 31, 1965, P.L. 1257, §3]. Under this restriction against local taxes (referred to as the preemption doctrine), if the Commonwealth imposes a levy on a subject already taxed by a local jurisdiction, the local tax becomes invalid at the end of the fiscal year in which the Commonwealth law is passed. See also the discussion of limitations on subjects of taxation imposed by the Local Tax Enabling Act (below).

> *Example 1:* A local business privilege tax that was imposed on a private, for-profit nursing home was not preempted by a license fee imposed by the Commonwealth. The license fee and the business privilege tax were different bases of taxation. Nor did the Commonwealth regulation of the nursing home industry rise to a level that required preemption of local taxes [*Rose View Manor, Inc. v. City of Williamsport and Williamsport Area School District,* 630 A.2d 474 (Pa.Commw. 1993)].

> *Example 2:* A school district use and occupancy tax on distributors of malt beverages was preempted by the Liquor Code and the taxes on alcoholic beverages imposed by the Commonwealth because the privilege of operating a malt and brewed beverages distributorship is granted by the Commonwealth. The legislature adopted a scheme of regulation over the entire alcoholic beverages industry that was so pervasive that it preempted the field [*Wissinoming Bottling Co. v. School District of Philadelphia,* 654 A.2d 208 (Pa.Commw. 1995)].

> *Example 3:* Taxpayer (Baltimore Life Insurance Co.) was an insurance company doing business in Pennsylvania that was subject to Pennsylvania's gross premiums tax. The

Township (Spring Garden) enacted an ordinance that imposed a business privilege tax of 1.5 mills on the gross receipts of every person engaged in business in the Township. Taxpayer alleged that this business privilege tax (measured by their gross insurance premiums) duplicated the Commonwealth's gross receipts tax. The Commonwealth Court agreed that the Township's business privilege tax imposed a tax on the same subject as the Commonwealth's gross premiums tax and was, thus, preempted by §2(1) of the Local Tax Enabling Act [*Baltimore Life Insurance Co. v. Spring Township*, 699 A.2d 847 (Pa.Commw. 1997)].

• *Sovereign immunity*

A local jurisdiction cannot tax real estate owned by the Commonwealth unless it points to a statute clearly authorizing it to do so [*Pennsylvania State Employees' Retirement System*, 6 A.2d 870, 872 (1939)]. The prohibition against taxing real estate owned by the Commonwealth (called sovereign immunity) applies to all real estate owned by the Commonwealth or any instrumentality of the Commonwealth, whether or not it is used for a public purpose.

• *Tax immunity*

Tax immunity extends to real estate owned by a state agency or instrumentality, whether or not the real estate is used for a public purpose. The concept of tax immunity is separate and distinct from sovereign immunity.

PSU Not an Instrumentality of the Commonwealth

The Pennsylvania Supreme Court has ruled that Pennsylvania State University is not an instrumentality of the Commonwealth [*Pennsylvania State University v. Derry Township School District*, 731 A.2d 1272 (Pa. 1999)].

NOTE: The taxable years in question were 1993, 1994, 1995. This decision, therefore, was not affected by the enactment in 1997 of the Institutions of Purely Public Charity Act, 10 P.S. §§371—385, which addresses exemptions from real estate tax for state-related universities. The Institutions of Purely Public Charity Act is discussed at ¶3505.

• *Governmental immunity*

The prohibition against taxing public property used for a public purpose (called governmental immunity) applies to property owned by local jurisdictions. This immunity, however, does not extend to property owned by a local jurisdiction that is not used for a public purpose [*West View Borough Municipal Authority Appeal*, 113 A.2d 307 (Pa. 1955)].

> *Example 1:* An unincorporated association of municipalities operating a sanitary landfill was held to be exempt from a township's business privilege tax because the municipalities conducted activities on public property for public purposes. This immunity extended to property acquired or used for an authorized purpose and was not restricted to the minimum amount needed for that purpose [*Township of West Mahanoy v. North Schuylkill Landfill Association*, 569 A.2d 1005 (Pa.Commw. 1990)].

> *Example 2:* The fact that the authority holds the property in a corporate name does not automatically defeat the property's immune status. A local authority held land in a corporate name; but no interest was held by any other party except that prior stockholders retained the right to repurchase the property if the authority failed in successful operation of a landfill [*Delaware County Solid Waste Authority v. Berks County Board of Assessment Appeals and Boyertown Area School District*, 626 A.2d 528 (Pa. 1992)].

NOTE: Some recent developments in the area of governmental immunity (*i.e.*, public property used for public purposes) are also discussed at ¶3504A below.

Community colleges: The Commonwealth Court has ruled that community colleges are local agencies rather than instrumentalities of the Commonwealth and are, therefore, entitled to governmental immunity from local taxation but not sovereign immunity. This means that real estate owned by community colleges is exempt from local taxation only to the extent it is used for public purposes. This is in contrast to state-owned and state-related universities, which have been held to be instrumentalities of the Commonwealth, entitled to immunity from local taxation [*Bucks County Community College v. Bucks County Board of Assessment Appeals*, 608 A.2d 622 (Pa.Commw. 1992)].

Land annexed to a school: School district land that is annexed to and adjoins other district lands that include the site of a school is exempt as public property used for public purposes. The school district is not required to demonstrate that all of the land annexed to the school district is in use for school purposes [*Wellsboro Area School District v. Tioga County Board of Assessment and Revision of Taxes*, 651 A.2d 592 (Pa.Commw. 1994)].

Open spaces acquired by a municipality but used by sellers: A township purchased a 157-acre tract from the owners of the property to fulfill the township's goal of preserving open spaces through acquisition of farmland and other underdeveloped areas. However, the township did not purchase the tract in fee simple. The owners transferred the tract to the township subject to a life estate plus 21 years in certain members of their family. The family (sellers) retained the right to use their land for agricultural and recreational purposes. In 1988, the township established a system of eight-foot-wide trails along the perimeter of the property. Members of the public were only permitted on the trails; they could not enter upon the rest of the land. The fact that the public can view agricultural uses from a perimeter trail was not considered a sufficient public use to warrant an exemption from taxation. Furthermore, sellers continued to use the property for farming, as they had in the past. Therefore, the property was not exempt from property taxation. The court affirmed the trial court's opinion with respect to its determination that the property was not exempt and remanded the case for redetermination of market value [*In re Appeal of Township of Middletown*, 654 A.2d 195 (Pa.Commw. 1995)].

Property purchased for sewage treatment plant: Property purchased by a township for use as a sewage treatment plant was exempt from Pennsylvania real property tax because the land was put to a public use. The Pennsylvania Supreme Court has held that a taxing authority has the burden of proving tax liability for property owned by a governmental body, and the county board of assessment failed in that burden of proof [*Granville Township v. Board of Assessment Appeals of Mifflin County*, Pa.Commw., No. 1942 C.D. 2005, June 5, 2006].

Property rented to commercial tenants: The Southeastern Pennsylvania Transportation Authority (SEPTA) purchased property to use as its administrative headquarters and leased part of the property to commercial tenants. According to the Commonwealth Court, SEPTA is an instrumentality of the Commonwealth and immune from taxation as long as it acts in accordance with the powers granted to it. The rented portion of the property, however, was not related to its public purpose of operating a transportation system and was not, therefore, exempt from taxation [*Southeastern Pennsylvania Transportation Authority v. Board of Revision of Taxes, City and School District of Philadelphia*, 777 A.2d 1234 (Pa.Commw. 2001)].

Land owned by a municipality and leased to a county: Real estate owned by a municipality and leased to the county government solely for use as a hearing room and offices of a district justice was found to be public property used for a public purpose [*Wesleyville Borough and McKean Borough v. Erie County Board of Assessment Appeals and McKean Borough, Intervenor*, 676 A.2d 298 (Pa.Commw. 1996)].

Land owned by Port Authority: The Commonwealth Court held that property owned by the Erie-Western Pennsylvania Port Authority and leased to a partnership that operated two private marinas was not immune from taxation in *Bay Harbor Marina Limited Partnership v. Erie County Board*, 177 A.3d 406 (Pa. Commw. 2018). The

¶3403

Port Authority was formed pursuant to the Third Class City Port Authority Act. The court first held that the lessee of the property had standing to appeal an assessment of the property and that the Port Authority was a proper party to the proceedings. In regard to the substantive legal issues, the court affirmed that significant portions of the property was not immune from taxation. Because the Port Authority was a public body, the property was immune unless it could be shown that it was not used for the Port Authority's authorized purposes. The burden was on the taxing authority to prove that the use was not as authorized. The court easily found that the Port Authority's authorized purpose was to operate port facilities. The operation of private marinas did not fall within that purpose. Nevertheless, some portions of the property were open to the public and the court remanded the matter for a determination of the extent to which there was a public use of the property.

Land owned by Transit Authority: In an unreported decision, the Commonwealth Court held that property owned by a transit authority and used as part of a public transit facility was immune from real property taxation. *In re Appeal of City of Lancaster ex rel. Property of Red Rose Transit Authority*, No. 665 C.D. 2017 (Pa. Commw. Jan. 3, 2018). The Transit Authority was a municipal authority formed under the Municipality Authorities Act of 1945. The parcel involved in the litigation was used by the Transit Authority for various purposes, such as a waiting area for passengers, a parking garage, bus bays, and a roadway for bus entry and exit. The parcel was used as a part of the Transit Authority's Queen Street Transit Center. The decision found that the property was immune from local real property taxation as governmental property. Because the property was used for a public purpose that was within the authorized purpose of the Transit Authority, the property could not be subject to local real property taxes.

- *Limitations on subjects of taxation*

The Sterling Act places almost no limitations on the taxing powers of Philadelphia. The Local Tax Enabling Act (LTEA) limits the maximum tax rates a local jurisdiction can levy and prohibits local taxation of certain subjects. See the discussion of subjects of taxation prohibited by the LTEA below.

- *Limitations on rates*

The Local Tax Enabling Act limits local rates of taxation. The applicable statutes should always be checked to determine current rates of local taxes. Rate limitations are inapplicable to taxes imposed on residents of home rule municipalities.

- *Limitations on specific taxes*

Admissions to automobile racing: No political subdivision can levy a tax rate on admissions to automobile racing facilities with a seating capacity of over 25,000 and a continuous race area of one mile or more in excess of the per centum rate collected as of January 1, 2002. The tax base upon which the tax is levied cannot exceed 40% of the cost of admission to an automobile racing facility [72 P.S. § 5020-203.2].

Admissions to ski facilities: No political subdivision can levy, assess, or collect a tax on admissions to ski facilities after December 1, 2002 [72 P.S. § 5020-201.3].

- *Taxation by more than one subdivision*

If two coterminous political subdivisions (except for Pittsburgh) impose a tax on the same person, privilege, subject, business, or transaction at the same time, they must split the maximum rate equally between them, unless they agree on a nonequal split. The combined rates of tax by coterminous jurisdictions cannot exceed the maximum allowable rate. This limitation does not apply to Pittsburgh because the Pittsburgh School District does not fall under the provisions of the LTEA. Pittsburgh can levy at the maximum rate without regard to what rate the Pittsburgh School District levies [53 P.S. § 6924.311].

Business Privilege Tax vs. Mercantile License Tax

The Commonwealth Court has held that two political subdivisions were not required to split the maximum rate of business privilege taxes. Two local taxing jurisdictions were allowed to impose the maximum rate. The maximum rate was required to be split in the case of a mercantile tax but not in the case of business privilege taxes on service providers [*Carpenter and Carpenter v. City of Johnstown and Greater Johnstown School District*, 605 A.2d 456 (Pa.Commw. 1992)].

Boundary determinations—Counties of the second and third class: No county of the second class may impose or collect any tax on any subject or property of an individual who has paid taxes on that subject or property to a county of the third class prior to a legally recognized boundary determination [72 P.S. § 4755].

Merger of political subdivisions: When a political subdivision that currently levies, assesses, or collects a mercantile or business privilege tax merges with one or more political subdivisions to form a new political subdivision on or after August 1, 2008, the new political subdivisions may levy that mercantile or business privilege tax but not at a rate greater than the rate necessary to generate the same revenues generated in the last fiscal year that the merging political subdivision generated in the last fiscal year that the merging political subdivision generated before the merger. If the merging political subdivision had previously shared the rate of taxation with another political subdivision, the nonmerging political subdivision that had shared the rate is capped at the rate it was previously levying [53 P.S. § 6924.311(2)].

¶3404 Local Taxpayers Bill of Rights

The Local Taxpayers Bill of Rights Act [53 Pa.C.S. § 8421 *et seq.*] establishes legal rights of taxpayers and requires local taxing authorities to adopt rules and regulations with respect to procedures and appeals. With the exception of the provisions concerning interest on overpayments, the provisions of the Local Taxpayers Bill of Rights do not apply to real property taxes. The Local Taxpayers Bill of Rights applies to all local jurisdictions.

• *Eligible taxes*

Any of the following (including interest and penalty provided by law) when levied by a political subdivision is an eligible tax [53 Pa.C.S. § 8422]:

(1) Any tax authorized by the Local Tax Enabling Act.

(2) Any per capita tax levied under any act.

(3) Any occupation, occupation assessment, or occupation privilege tax levied under any act.

(4) Any income tax levied under any act.

(5) Any tax measured by gross receipts levied under any act.

(6) Any tax on a privilege levied under any act.

(7) Any tax on amusements or admissions levied under any act.

(8) Any tax on earned income and net profits.

Disclosure Requirements

• *Simple language*

The Local Taxpayers Bill of Rights requires political subdivisions to disclose, in simple and nontechnical terms, the following:

¶3404

(1) The rights of a taxpayer and the obligation of the local taxing authority during an audit or an administrative review of the taxpayer's books or records [53 Pa.C.S. § 8423(a)(1)].

(2) The administrative and judicial procedures by which a taxpayer may appeal or seek review of any adverse decision of the local taxing authority [53 Pa.C.S. § 8423(a)(2)].

(3) The procedure for filing and processing refund claims and taxpayer complaints [53 Pa.C.S. § 8423(a)(3)].

(4) The enforcement procedure [53 Pa.C.S. § 8423(a)(4)].

Notice required: Local taxing authorities must notify any taxpayer contacted regarding an assessment, audit, determination, review, or collection of an eligible tax of the availability of the required disclosure statements (see above), and they must make copies of the statements available to taxpayers upon request (free of charge to the taxpayer, including mailing costs) [53 Pa.C.S. § 8423(b)]. The notification must be stated as follows:

> You are entitled to receive a written explanation of your rights with regard to the audit, appeal, enforcement, refund, and collection of local taxes by calling (name of local taxing authority) at (telephone number) during the hours of (hours of operation).

Taxpayer Rights

• *Response time*

Taxpayers have at least 30 calendar days to respond to requests for information by a local taxing authority. The local taxing authority must notify the taxpayer of the procedures to obtain an extension in its initial request and cannot take any lawful action against a taxpayer for the tax year in question until the expiration of the applicable response period, including extensions [53 Pa.C.S. § 8424(a)(1)].

• *Refunds*

A taxpayer who has paid an eligible tax to a local taxing authority may file a written request with the authority for refund or credit of the eligible tax within the later of (1) three years of the due date for filing the report as extended or (2) one year after actual payment of the eligible tax [53 Pa.C.S. § 8425(a)]. For this purpose, a tax return filed by the taxpayer with the local taxing authority showing an overpayment of tax shall be deemed to be a written request for a cash refund unless otherwise indicated on the tax return [53 Pa.C.S. § 8425(a)(1)]. For amounts paid as a result of a notice asserting or informing a taxpayer of an underpayment, a written refund request must be filed within one year of the date of the payment (which is the later of the date paid or the date deemed to have been overpaid) [53 Pa.C.S. § 8425(b)].

Decisions on petitions: Decisions on petitions submitted under the Local Taxpayers Bill of Rights Act must be issued within 60 days of the date a complete and accurate petition is received. Failure to act within 60 days will result in the petition being deemed approved [53 Pa.C.S. § 8433]. In an unreported decision, the Commonwealth Court found that the failure of a township tax collector to issue decisions to taxpayers within 60 days resulted in the deemed approval of their claims [*Briggs v. East Goshen Township*, Pa.Commw., Nos. 1754 C.D. 2002, 1755 C.D. 2002, 1756 C.D. 2002, and 1757 C.D. 2002 (May 14, 2003)].

• *Interest*

All overpayments of tax due a local taxing authority (including taxes on real property) bear simple interest from the date of overpayment until the date of resolution [53 Pa.C.S. § 8426(a)]. Taxpayers are entitled to interest on overpayments at the same rate as the Commonwealth is required to pay [53 Pa.C.S. § 8426(b)]. See

¶4612 for discussion of interest. No interest is allowed if an overpayment is refunded or applied against any other tax, interest, or penalty due the local taxing authority within 75 days after the last date prescribed for filing the report of the tax liability or within 75 days after the date the return or report of the liability due is filed, whichever is later [53 Pa.C.S. §8426(c)(1)]. Overpayments of interest or penalty do not bear interest [53 Pa.C.S. §8426(c)(2)].

- *Underpayment notification*

A local taxing authority must provide the taxpayer with written notification of the basis for any underpayment determined to exist [53 Pa.C.S. §8427]. The notification must contain the following information:

(1) The tax period(s) for which understatement is asserted [53 Pa.C.S. §8427(1)].

(2) Amount of underpayment detailed by the tax period [53 Pa.C.S. §8427(2)].

(3) Legal basis of the determination of underpayment [53 Pa.C.S. §8427(3)].

(4) Itemization of revisions made that resulted in a determination of underpayment [53 Pa.C.S. §8427(4)].

Taxing bodies are permitted (but not required) to abate all or part of the interest on any underpaid taxes in the event of error by the taxing jurisdiction [53 Pa.C.S. §8428].

- *Installment payments*

Political subdivisions may enter into written agreements for installment payment of taxes in certain instances [53 Pa.C.S. §8436]. Consult the statutes for more detail.

- *Reliance on mistaken written advice*

When a taxpayer relies on mistaken written advice by a taxing body, the abatement of penalties or excess interest is required [53 Pa.C.S. §8428(b)].

- *Appeals boards*

The Local Taxpayers Bill of Rights requires the appointment of local tax appeals boards by all political subdivisions [53 Pa.C.S. §8430]. Petitions for reassessment must be filed with this local board within 90 days of the assessment in question. The mail box rules apply. The local board hears petitions for refund. If the local board of appeals does not render a decision within 60 days of the filing of a complete and accurate petition, the petition will be deemed to be approved [53 Pa.C.S. §8433].

Caution: 30-Day Appeal Period

The Local Taxpayers Bill of Rights requires an "appeal" from any adverse decision to the court vested with jurisdiction of local tax appeals. This has been interpreted to mean that an appeal must be filed within thirty (30) days of an adverse decision [42 Pa.C.S. §5571(b)].

¶3405 Local Tax Reform

Taxpayers' Local Control Act (Act 50)

The Taxpayers' Local Control Act was passed as part of what is commonly referred to as Act 50 [Act of May 5, 1998, No. 50 (S.B. 669)] and is codified in 53

Pa.C.S. § § 8707—8717. The Act gives school districts the power to impose a tax on the earned income and net profits of resident individuals. The provisions of Act 50 do not apply to Philadelphia. Some provisions of the Taxpayers' Local Control Act apply only to school districts, some only to municipalities, and some generally to all political subdivisions. These provisions of Act 50 (except for the homestead exemption) are discussed below. The homestead exemption provisions (applicable to all jurisdictions) are discussed at ¶3406. Act 50 also provides for deferral of increases in property taxes for qualified senior citizens. These provisions are discussed at ¶3513.

• *School districts*

The provisions of the Taxpayers' Local Control Act applicable to school districts are designed to shift school districts' reliance on property taxes to taxes on earned income and net profits (but not on stocks and bonds). The Act allows school districts to exempt a portion of a homeowners' property value from taxation and to impose an earned income tax instead [53 Pa.C.S. § 8701(a)]. This so-called homestead exemption is explained in more detail at ¶3406. Earned income and net profits for this purpose are defined in the Local Tax Enabling Act [53 P.S. § 6913]. Act 50 also allows school districts to get rid of "nuisance" taxes (*e.g.,* occupational taxes, per capita taxes). If a school board has not placed a referendum question on the earned income tax option on a ballot within two years of the effective date of the legislation, voters can force the issue by circulating a petition. The law does not apply to the Philadelphia School District.

Front-end referendum: The taxing powers established in the Act are optional for school districts. School boards are permitted (but not required) to appoint a local tax study commission to recommend changes in a district's tax structure. The commission would make a public nonbinding recommendation to the school board within 90 days of its appointment. In order to implement a new system, voters must give their consent at the municipal election prior to the fiscal year in which the new system would be initiated (referred to as a front-end referendum). A ballot question is required to provide statutorily specified information.

Implementation: If voters give their approval in a referendum, a school district may implement a new earned income/net profits tax at the rate specified in the ballot question (*i.e.,* 1.0%; 1.25%; or 1.5%) [53 Pa.C.S. § 8711].

Prohibited taxes: School districts that adopt a new earned income/net profits tax can retain amusement, realty transfer, and business privilege/mercantile taxes but must repeal the following taxes [53 Pa.C.S. § 8701(b)]:

(1) Occupation taxes.

(2) Occupational privilege taxes.

(3) Per capita taxes.

(4) The earned income and net profits tax levied under the Local Tax Enabling Act.

(5) An earned income tax under the First Class A School District Earned Income Tax Act [Act of August 24, 1962 (P.L. 1135, No. 508) or under § 652.1(a)(2) of the Public School Code of 1949 [24 P.S. § 6-652.1(a)(2)].

(6) Any tax under § 652.1(a)(4) of the Public School Code of 1949 [72 P.S. § 1-101 *et seq.*] except as it pertains to real estate transfer taxes.

(7) Any other tax authorized or permitted under the Local Tax Enabling Act, except for taxes permitted under 53 Pa.C.S. § 8402(b), (c), (d), (e), and (f) (*i.e.,* real estate transfer taxes, amusement and admissions taxes, mercantile taxes, sign or sign privilege taxes, and motor vehicle transfer taxes).

Regardless of whether a school district implements a new tax system, Act 50 also imposes certain limitations on existing taxing powers. Amusement or admissions taxes levied as of June 30, 1997, may continue to be levied, provided there is no increase in the rate or the amount collected. School districts not imposing the tax prior to June 30, 1997, are prohibited from levying such taxes. Similarly, school districts that levied sign privilege or motor vehicle transfer taxes prior to January 1, 1998, may continue to collect them, but after that date, other school districts are not permitted to impose those taxes.

Tax offsets: For the fiscal year of implementation of a newly imposed income tax or for the fiscal year of implementation of an increase in the rate of an existing earned income and net profits tax, all earned income and net profits tax revenue received by a school districts must be used in the following manner [53 Pa.C.S. § 8717]:

First, to replace all prohibited "nuisance" taxes previously levied by the district.

Second, to provide an increase in budgeted revenues over the preceding fiscal year, as specified in the ballot question in the front-end referendum.

Third, to reduce property taxes in the following order:

(a) By means of a homestead property exclusion pursuant to 53 Pa.C.S. § 8583. See discussion of the Homestead Property Exclusion Program Act at ¶ 3504 and ¶ 3406.

(b) By means of a reduction in the millage rate after the limit on the homestead property exclusion has been reached under 53 Pa.C.S. § 8586.

Back-end referendum: If a school board adopts a new tax system, it may not raise property tax rates in the future without the approval of the school district's voters (referred to as a back-end referendum). This back-end referendum must be held during the primary election immediately preceding the fiscal year in which the taxes are proposed to be increased. If the voters reject the higher millage rate, the school board is limited to the rate already in effect.

No voter approval, however, is required for a property tax rate increase that causes total local revenues to rise by less than the percentage increase in the Statewide Average Weekly Wage (calculated by the Department of Labor and Industry) for the preceding year. That figure is intended to reflect the typical growth in personal earnings. Act 50 permits other exceptions to the general requirement that future increases in property taxes previously reduced by the earned income tax be subject to voter approval. See Act 50 for details.

Initiative process: Act 50 also permits voters to initiate efforts to implement the new tax system if a school board has not placed the referendum question on the ballot within two years of the effective date of the legislation.

The initiative process is begun by the circulation of a petition. A petition signed by the equivalent of 2% of the number of voters in the most recent election for governor would compel the school board to appoint a local tax study commission that would be organized in the manner described above. If the commission recommends the imposition of an earned income/net profits tax and the school board fails to place the recommendation on the ballot, another petition may be circulated. A second petition signed by the equivalent of 5% of the voters in the last gubernatorial election and filed at least 90 days prior to the next municipal election would cause the question to be placed on the ballot. If approved by a majority of voters, the new tax system would be implemented.

Philadelphia Wage Tax Credit

Act 50 provides for a credit against Philadelphia's wage tax paid by nonresidents of the city. This credit, however, is available only if the resident's local government adopts the local tax reform provisions of Act 50. See also ¶ 127.

¶3405

• *Municipalities*

The key provisions applicable to municipalities impose limitations to existing municipal taxing powers. If an overlapping school district adopts a new taxing structure (as passed under Act 50), the municipal tax will be capped at shared rates established by an existing agreement of the Local Tax Enabling Act for taxes on earned income or net profits. The provisions of Act 50 do not apply to Philadelphia.

Amusement or admissions tax: Any municipality that levied an amusement or admissions tax under the Local Tax Enabling Act prior to January 1, 1998, may continue to levy that tax at the greater of the existing rate or 5%. Any municipality that did not levy an amusement or admissions tax prior to January 1, 1998, may impose such a tax, but the maximum allowable rate is 5%.

Sign privilege or motor vehicle transfer tax: Municipalities that levied a sign privilege taxes or motor vehicle transfer taxes prior to January 1, 1998, may continue to collect them; other municipalities are not permitted to impose them after that date.

Act 130 (Optional Occupation Tax Elimination)

This act allows local jurisdictions to replace the occupation tax with an income tax. The following provides an overview of the act. For details, consult the statute.

• *Definitions [53 P.S. § 6924.402]*

Earned income tax: A tax on earned income and net profits levied under Act 130 or the repealed Act 24.

Income tax: An earned income tax or a personal income tax imposed under Act 130.

Occupation tax: A tax based upon an assessed valuation of a particular trade, occupation, or profession. The term includes a tax imposed on a flat rate on all trades, occupations, or professions. The term does not include a tax upon persons employed in a taxing district, commonly known as an occupational privilege tax.

Personal income tax: A tax on classes of income enumerated under the Tax Reform Code by 72 P.S. § 7303.

Political subdivision: Any city, borough, incorporated town, township, or school district.

• *Imposition*

A political subdivision that levies an occupation tax may replace the revenues provided by the occupation tax by increasing the rate of the income tax as provided in Act 130 [53 P.S. § 6924.403]. This act applies to political subdivisions that levy an occupation tax as of October 15, 2008 [53 P.S. § 6924.408]. A municipality may not impose a personal income tax under this act. The authority to levy, assess, or collect a personal income tax only applies to a school district in which a board of school directors sought to impose a personal income tax under the repealed Act 24 (Taxpayer Relief Act), and the referendum was approved by the electorate [53 P.S. § 6924.409].

• *Occupation tax prohibited*

For the first fiscal year beginning after approval of the required referendum to impose an income tax and each fiscal year thereafter a political subdivision is prohibited from leving, assessing, or collecting an occupation tax [53 P.S. § 6924.405].

• *Initial maximum rates*

The initial maximum rates of tax are governed by the provisions of 53 P.S. § 6924.404.

¶3405

• *Increasing maximum rates—referendum required*

A political subdivision may increase the maximum rate of the income tax only by obtaining the approval of the electorate of the affected political subdivision in a public referendum at the general or municipal election preceding the fiscal year when the maximum rate of the income tax will be increased [53 P.S. § 6924.407].

¶3406 Homestead and Farmstead Exclusions

Enabling legislation: Homestead and farmstead exclusions are permitted under the authority of the Homestead Property Exclusions Program Act [53 Pa.C.S. § 8581 *et seq.*]. A governing body of a political subdivision may provide for a tax exclusion for homestead and farmstead property. A "governing body" for this purpose is a city council, borough council, incorporated town council, board of township commissioners, board of township supervisors, a governing council of a home rule municipality or optional plan municipality, a similar governing council of any similar general purpose unit of government that may be created by statute, or a board of school directors of a school district [53 Pa.C.S. § 8422].

Homestead property: "Homestead property" is a homestead for which an application has been submitted and approved under 53 Pa.C.S. § 8584 [53 Pa.C.S. § 8401]. Application under 53 Pa.C.S. § 8584 is discussed below. A "homestead" is a dwelling (including the parcel of land on which the dwelling is located and the other improvements located on the parcel) primarily used as the domicile of an owner who is a natural person. A dwelling for this purpose includes a condominium as defined in 68 Pa.C.S. § 3103 or a portion of a dwelling used as the domicile of an owner who is a natural person. If the land on which a dwelling is located is not owned by a person who owns the dwelling, the land does not qualify for exclusion [53 Pa.C.S. § 8401].

Farmstead property: A governing body that provides an exclusion for homestead property must also provide an exclusion for farmstead property in an amount not to exceed the exclusion for homestead property [53 Pa.C.S. § 8585(b)]. The exclusion for farmstead property is in addition to any exclusion for homestead property for which the farm dwelling may qualify. Thus, a farmer may qualify for both a homestead exclusion and a farmstead exclusion. "Farmstead property" is a farmstead for which an application has been submitted and approved under 53 Pa.C.S. § 8584 [53 Pa.C.S. § 8582]. Application under 53 Pa.C.S. § 8584 is discussed below. A "farmstead" is all buildings and structures on a farm of at least ten (10) contiguous acres in area that are not otherwise exempt from real property taxation or qualified for any other abatement or exclusion and that are used primarily for one of the following purposes [53 Pa.C.S. § 8582]:

(1) To produce or store any farm produce produced on the farm for commercial agricultural production purposes.

(2) To house or confine any animal raised or maintained on the farm for commercial agricultural production purposes.

(3) To store any agricultural supply to be used on the farm in commercial agricultural production.

(4) To store any machinery or equipment used on the farm in commercial agricultural production.

Owner: An "owner" includes any of the following [53 Pa.C.S. § 8401]:

(1) A joint tenant or tenant in common.

(2) A person who is purchasing real property under a contract.

(3) A partial owner.

(4) A person who owns real property as a result of being a beneficiary of a will or trust or as a result of intestate succession.

(5) A person who owns or is purchasing a dwelling on leased land.

(6) A person holding a life lease in real property previously sold or transferred to another.

(7) A person in possession under a life estate.

(8) A grantor who has placed the real property in a revocable trust.

(9) A member of a cooperative as defined in 68 Pa.C.S. § 4103 (relating to definitions).

(10) A unit owner of a condominium as defined in 68 Pa.C.S. § 3103 (relating to definitions).

(11) A partner or a shareholder of a family farm business as the terms are defined in 72 P.S. § 8101-C.

Limited to Farms Used as Domiciles

The term "farmstead" applies only to farms used as the domicile of an owner [53 Pa.C.S. § 8582].

Limits on exclusion: A political subdivision cannot authorize an exclusion for homestead property in excess of the amount that is one-half of the median assessed value of homestead property in the political subdivision [53 Pa.C.S. § 8586(a)(1)]. If a political subdivision is located in more than one county, the median assessed value of homestead property for the entire political subdivision is determined after dividing the assessed value of each homestead property by the common level ratio of the county in which the homestead property is located [53 Pa.C.S. § 8586(a)(2)].

• *Application under 53 Pa.C.S. § 8584*

In order to have property approved as homestead or farmstead property, the owner(s) must file an application (on the proper form) with the assessor, who determines the qualification of all or a part of a parcel of real property as homestead or farmstead property [53 Pa.C.S. § 8584(a)]. Initial applications are due on or before March 1 of each year. The governing body of a county may adopt a schedule for review or reapplication for previously approved property [53 Pa.C.S. § 8584(b)].

Change of use: If property approved as homestead or farmstead property no longer qualifies as homestead or farmstead property, the property owner must notify the assessor within 45 days of the date the property no longer qualifies. Failure to provide such note is treated as the filing of a false application [53 Pa.C.S. § 8584(j)(1)].

Duties of assessors: Assessors must provide sufficient public notice of the availability of applications and all filing deadlines at least 75 days before the filing deadline [53 Pa.C.S. § 8584(c)]. Assessors must provide written notice of denial to property owners whose applications are denied, in whole or in part. The written notice must be provided by first class mail no later than 120 days after the filing deadline and must include all reasons for denial. Failure of an assessor to provide such notice is deemed to be approval of the application [53 Pa.C.S. § 8584(d)]. Assessors may select (randomly or otherwise) filed applications to review for false or fraudulent information [53 Pa.C.S. § 8584(g)].

Appeals: Decisions of assessors may be appealed to the local board of tax appeals established by the political subdivision pursuant to 53 Pa.C.S. § 8430. Such appeals are limited to whether the application meets the requirements for application and timely filing or whether the parcel for which appeal is made meets the definition of "farmstead property" or "homestead property" [53 Pa.C.S. § 8584(e)]. Appeals with respect to the assessed value of the property are made before application of the homestead or farmstead property exclusion [53 Pa.C.S. § 8584(f)].

¶ 3406

Penalties: Persons who file applications that are false as to any material matter are subject to the following provisions:

(1) They must pay any taxes that would have been due but for the false application plus simple interest computed at the established rate (discussed at ¶4612) [53 Pa.C.S. §8584(h)(1)].

(2) They must pay a penalty equal to 10% of the unpaid taxes computed in (1) [53 Pa.C.S. §8584(h)(2)].

(3) Upon conviction of filing a false application they knew to be fraudulent, they are guilty of a misdemeanor of the third degree and subject to a fine of no more than $2,500 [53 Pa.C.S. §8584(h)(3)].

¶3407 Municipal Tax Liens

Municipal tax liens are governed by the provisions of the Municipal Claim and Tax Lien Law [53 P.S. §7101 *et seq.*]. "Municipality" for this purpose means any county, city, borough, incorporated town, township, school district, or a body politic and corporate entity created as a Municipal Authority pursuant to law and any assignees thereof [53 P.S. §7101]. Commonwealth tax liens are discussed at ¶4618.

• *Tax claim bureaus*

The tax claim bureaus of Pennsylvania counties may adopt and use the procedures set forth in the Municipal Claim and Tax Lien Law in addition to the procedures set forth in the Real Estate Tax Sale Law [53 P.S. §7193.5]. The Real Estate Tax Sale Law provisions are contained in 72 P.S. §5860.101 *et seq.*].

• *Taxes are first lien*

All taxes imposed and assessed by municipalities are a first lien on real property (but subordinate to the lien of taxes imposed by the Commonwealth) [53 P.S. §7102]. Commonwealth tax liens are discussed at ¶4618. "Taxes" for this purpose means any county, city, borough, incorporated town, township, school, bridge, road, or poor taxes, together with and including all penalties, interest, costs, charges, expenses, and fees, including reasonable attorney fees [53 P.S. §7101].

• *Attorney fees*

Attorney fees may be imposed upon all taxes, tax claims, tax liens, municipal claims, municipal liens, writs of scire facias, judgments, or executions filed on or after December 19, 1990 [53 P.S. §7106(d)]. This provision was added by §2 of the Act of August 14, 2003, No. 20 (S.B. 442).

¶3408 Local Income Tax Collection

In 2008, the General Assembly passed legislation (Act 32 of 2008 (S.B. 1063)) that amended the Local Tax Enabling Act (LTEA) to consolidate the collection of local income taxes at the county-wide level, effective January 1, 2012. There are 69 Tax Collection Districts ("TCD"). Allegheny County is divided into four TCD's and the remaining districts are generally congruent with county lines. Philadelphia County is not included. Act 32 provides for uniform withholding, remittance and distribution of local income tax. The term "local income tax" is used so that these provisions will apply to earned income tax collection systems as well as any personal income tax collection systems that might be established in the future. Employer withholding provisions are also amended.

• *Withholding*

Employers will be required to withhold the entire local tax owed by each employee, and to remit those taxes to the tax collector for the TCD where the employer is located. The phrase "entire tax owed by an employee" includes the tax levied by the school district and municipality where an employee is domiciled, and

¶3407

any nonresident tax levied by the municipality where an employee works. Employers will be required to withhold the higher of the resident rate or the non-resident rate. That term also includes any local personal income tax that either has been or may be enacted.

* *Mobile employees*

Where does a mobile employee "work"? To date, no official guidance has been provided. This will be an issue when the mobile employee works in a jurisdiction that has a higher non-resident rate than the employee's residence.

* *Remittance*

Employers will be subject to the same basic quarterly remittance requirement as currently exists under Act 511, 30 days after the end of each quarter. Remittance will be made to the tax collector for the TCD where the employer is located.

* *Optional remittance*

Act 32 permits employers with workplaces in more than one county to remit local taxes for all their employees to one TCD collector. If employers elect this option, they must remit monthly and electronically.

* *Distribution*

Act 32 requires uniform distribution, based on quarterly detail. The Act requires that prior to April 1, 2013, tax collectors must distribute taxes within the later of (1) 60 days of receipt of the quarterly employer remittance or (2) the remittance deadline. After April 1, 2013, the time between receipt by the tax collector and distribution is reduced to 30 days. A Tax Collection Committee ("TCC") may require its collector to distribute more frequently or negotiate with other districts for more frequent distribution. Under the optional remittance provision that applies to employers with locations in more than one TCD, taxes for jurisdictions outside the district where the taxes are remitted must be distributed within thirty (30) days.

* *Effective date*

Most of the provisions of Act 32 are not effective until January 1, 2012. However, some of the provisions are effective as of July 2, 2008. These changes are noted within the discussion of earned income taxes in Chapter 36.

* *LTEA renumbered*

Act 32 also provides for the renumbering of the provisions of the LTEA. The provisions of the LTEA, formerly numbered 53 P.S. § 6901 *et seq.*, are numbered 53 P.S. § 6924.101 *et seq.*, effective July 2, 2008.

* *More information*

The Department of Community and Economic Development ("DCED") is charged with promulgating regulations, as well as prescribing standardized forms. More information is available at www.newpa.com.

¶3409 Financial Recovery School Districts

* *Authorization*

Pennsylvania has amended the Public School Code [24 P.S. § 1-101 et seq.] to establish financial recovery school districts [Act No. 141 of 2012 (H.B. 1307), effective July 12, 2012].

A "financial recovery school district" is a school district of the First Class A, Second Class, Third Class, or Fourth Class declared by the Secretary of Education to be in financial recovery.

A financial recovery school district can increase property tax levies in such amounts and at such times as is recommended by the chief recovery officer of the district, subject to the Act of June 27, 2006 (1st Sp. Sess. P.L. 1872, No. 1), known as the Taxpayer Relief Act.

More Information

For details with respect to financial recovery school districts, consult Act No. 141 of 2012 (H.B. 1307).

LOCAL TAXES

CHAPTER 35

TAXATION OF PROPERTY

¶ 3550	Personal Property Assessments
¶ 3551	Estimated Assessments
¶ 3552	Petitions for Reassessment
¶ 3553	Petitions for Review
¶ 3554	Claim for Refund
¶ 3555	Statute of Limitations: Assessments and Reassessments
¶ 3556	Failure to File Return—Penalties

REAL PROPERTY TAXES

¶ 3501 Overview

Prior to January 1, 2011, assessment of real property taxes in local jurisdictions in Pennsylvania was governed, in general, by the General County Assessment Law. Each class of county was subject to special assessment tax laws. However, on October 27, 2010, the Governor signed into law the Consolidated County Assessment Law [Act 93 (S.B. 918), effective January 1, 2011)]. These new provisions are located in new Chapter 88 of Title 53 of the Pennsylvania Consolidated Statutes [53 Pa.C.S. §§ 8801 *et seq.*].

The Consolidated County Assessment Law (Act 93) provides for the consolidation of Pennsylvania county assessment procedures for local property taxation for the following:

(1) Counties of the second class A, third, fourth, fifth, sixth, seventh, and eighth classes of the Commonwealth [53 Pa.C.S. § 8801(b)(i)].

(2) Cities in counties to which Act 93 applies that elect to become subject to the Act [53 Pa.C.S. §§ 8801(b)(1)(ii); 8867(a)].

Two Assessment Laws

In general, Act 93 does not apply to first and second class counties. However, the following provisions of Act 93 do apply to counties of the first and second counties [53 Pa.C.S. § 8801(b)(2)]:

(1) Section 8811(b)(5), relating to exemption of wind turbine generators or related wind energy appliances and equipment.

(2) Section 8842(b)(2), relating to valuation of real property used for the purpose of wind energy generation for assessment purposes.

The Consolidated County Assessment Act specifically provides that it does not repeal or modify the General County Assessment law as it applies to counties of the first and second classes [53 Pa.C.S. § 8803(3)]. Thus, after the passage of Act 93 we have one assessment law for first and second class counties (General County Assessment Law) and another for all other classes of counties (Consolidated County Assessment Law). In this chapter, both assessment laws are discussed.

• *Continuations of former law under the Consolidated County Assessment Law*

Most, but not all, of the former provisions stay the same. Act 93 specifically provides that the Consolidated County Assessment Law is a continuation of the following provisions, even though they are repealed by the act [Act 93 (S.B. 918), § 7]:

(1) Third Class County Assessment Board Law [Act of June 26, 1931 [P.L. 1379, No. 348; 72 P.S. § 5342 *et seq.*].

(2) Fourth to Eighth Class and Selective County Assessment Law [Act of May 21, 2943 (P.L. 571, No. 254); 72 P.S. § 5453.101 *et seq.*].

(3) Sections 1770.3 (related to appointment of auxiliary board of assessment appeals) and 1770.9 (related to assessment of signs and sign structures) of the County Code [Act of August 9, 1955 (P.L. 323, No. 130); 16 P.S. § 1770 et seq.].

Other Laws Not Affected by the Consolidated County Assessment Law

The Consolidated County Assessment does not repeal or modify the following:

(1) The personal property tax [53 Pa.C.S. § 8803(1)].

(2) Any law relating to cities, boroughs, towns, townships, school districts and poor districts [53 Pa.C.S. § 8801(2)].

• *Repeals under the Consolidated County Assessment Law*

Certain former provisions are repealed, as follows:

(1) The Third Class County Assessment Board Law [Act of June 26, 1931 [P.L. 1379, No. 348; 72 P.S. § 5342 et seq.] is repealed absolutely [Act 93 (S.B. 918), § 6(1)(i)].

(2) The Fourth to Eighth Class and Selective County Assessment Law [Act of May 21, 2943 (P.L. 571, No. 254); 72 P.S. § 5453.101 et seq.] is repealed absolutely [Act 93 (S.B. 918), § 6(1)(ii)].

(3) Sections 1770.3 (related to appointment of auxiliary board of assessment appeals) and 1770.9 (related to assessment of signs and sign structures) of the County Code [Act of August 9, 1955 (P.L. 323, No. 130); 16 P.S. § 1770 et seq.] are repealed absolutely [Act 93 (S.B. 918), § 6(1)(iii)].

(4) The General County Assessment Law [Act of May 22, 1933 (P.L. 858, No. 155); 72 P.S. § 5020-101 et seq.] is repealed insofar as it relates to second class A, third, fourth, fifth, sixth, seventh, and eighth class counties [Act 93 (S.B. 918), § 6(2)].

(5) All other acts and parts of acts are repealed insofar as they are inconsistent with the Consolidated County Assessment Law [Act 93 (S.B. 918) § 6(3)].

Grandfather Clause

The following provisions of Act 93 do not affect an agreement or agreed to assessment practice actively in place in a county on January 28, 2007 [Act 93 (S.B. 918) § 5]:

(1) Section 8801(b)(2), relating to applicability of the act to first and second class counties.

(2) Section 8811(b)(5), relating to exemption of wind energy property.

(3) Section 8842(b)(2), relating to valuation of wind energy property.

• *Real property assessment laws*

The real property tax laws after January 1, 2011, are as follows:

(1) Consolidated County Assessment Law [53 Pa.C.S. § 8801 et seq.], applicable to (a) counties of the second class A, third, fourth, fifth, sixth, seventh, and eighth classes of the Commonwealth [53 Pa.C.S. § 8801(b)(i)] and (b) cities in counties to which Act 93 applies that elect to become subject to the Act [53 Pa.C.S. §§ 8801(b)(ii); 8867(a)].

(2) General County Assessment Law [72 P.S. § 5020-101 et seq.], applicable to first and second class counties.

(3) First Class County Assessment Law [72 P.S. § 5341.1 et seq.].

(4) Second Class County Assessment Law [72 P.S. § 5452.1 et seq.].

(5) Third Class City Code [53 P.S. § 37501 et seq.].

¶3501

¶3502 Outline of Tax

The Commonwealth does not impose a general tax on realty. The only realty tax levied by the Commonwealth is the Public Utility Realty Tax Act (discussed in Chapter 25), [72 P.S. §8101-A]. General realty taxes are imposed by counties, cities, boroughs, towns, townships, and school districts. Counties, cities, townships, and school districts are divided into classes for tax purposes. See ¶3401 for classification of political subdivisions.

The administration of local real property taxes is handled by local jurisdictions. Appeals from local assessment decisions are made to the courts (¶3511).

The explanation of the real property tax in this Guidebook is a general explanation of the tax. Detailed explanations of specific local taxes are beyond the scope of this Guidebook.

The Commonwealth Court, in *In Re Appeal of Springfield Hospital, ex rel. Prospect Crozer, LLC*, 179 A.3d 632 (Pa. Commw. 2018), held that the assets of a charitable hospital became taxable upon the date of a sale of the property in Delaware County, Pennsylvania to a for-profit entity, not on the first day of the forthcoming tax year. The court noted that, under the general common law rule, a change in the tax exempt status of an entity takes effect on the first day of the coming tax year, not on the day of the change. However, amendments to the General County Assessment Law (GCAL) in 1978 changed this general rule in many counties to provide for an immediate change in the tax exempt status of the property. The court determined, however, that GCAL was not applicable to a second class county and found that the tax assessment day rule remains applicable for Delaware County which is a second class county. Therefore, a change in tax status of a taxpayer becomes effective on the first day of the next year, not on the date of the change. The majority nonetheless held that the effective date of the transfer of the nonprofit hospital's assets on July 1st to a for-profit entity was the applicable date on which the property became subject to real estate tax, not January 1 of the coming tax year due to the existence of a PILOT agreement in effect with respect to the subject realty. The court held that a judicial order enforcing a PILOT agreement modified what would otherwise be the tax assessment day rule.

¶3503 Taxable Property Under the General County Assessment Law

All real estate (unless specifically exempt) is taxable. The law does not define real property. The general understanding of the term is that real estate is land and anything permanently attached to land. The General County Assessment Law specifically states that real estate includes such items as houses, land, house trailers permanently attached to land, ground rents, parking lots, factories, ferries, wharves, and structures that enclose and protect machinery and equipment. The Pennsylvania Supreme Court has held that coal or other minerals beneath the surface are "land" and thus subject to property taxation [*Lillibridge v. Lackawanna Coal Company*, 22 A. 1035 (Pa. 1891)]. See also, *Coolspring Stone Supply, Inc. v. Fayette County*, Pa.Commw., No. 128 C.D. 2005 (May 25, 2005), where the Commonwealth Court held that subsurface limestone is subject to Pennsylvania real estate taxation. In addition, the law states that "all other real estate not exempt by law from taxation" is subject to the real property tax [72 P.S. §5020-201(a)]. Property is taxable under the General County Assessment Law unless a special assessment law has provisions to the contrary.

• *Cell phone towers*

A cellular/wireless communications tower was held to be real estate subject to Pennsylvania property tax. The tower could be easily removed, but it was attached to a large concrete base that could not be easily removed. Following the reasoning in

Sheetz (see below), the Court held that the tower is real property. The Court also found the requisite intention to leave the towers in place [*Shenandoah Mobile Company v. Dauphin County Board of Assessment Appeals*, Pa.Commw. No. 1299 C.D. 2004 (February 1, 2005)].

• *Condominiums*

Taxation of condominiums created after October 29, 1980, is governed by the Uniform Condominium Act, Act of July 2, 1980, P.L. 286 [68 Pa.C.S. § 3201 *et seq.*]. In general, each unit with its common element interest is a separate parcel of real estate [68 Pa.C.S. § 3105(a)]. Condominiums created before October 30, 1980, are governed by the provisions of the Act of July 3, 1963, P.L. 196.

• *Estates, rights, and interest in air space*

Estates, rights, and interest in air space, whether or not contiguous to the surface of the ground, is real estate that is subject to separate assessment if separately owned [Act of August 14, 1963, P.L. 871, § 3].

• *Leased tax-exempt property*

A school district imposed a 10% tax on the privilege of leasing real estate that is listed on the assessment rolls as exempt from the payment of real estate tax, excluding property used for residential dwelling purposes. A city that owned property within the school district and affected parties challenged the validity of the tax on the grounds that the school district had no authority to tax leasing activity on tax-exempt property and that the tax violated the Uniformity Clause of the Pennsylvania Constitution and the Equal Protection Clause of the U.S. Constitution. The Commonwealth Court disagreed, holding that the tax was not a disguised property tax but a transaction tax, which is permissible. The fact that the tax applied only to leases of tax-exempt property and not all other property leases was a reasonable use of classification of subjects because a very large portion (42%) of the property in the school district was tax-exempt, which made the school district's job of raising sufficient revenue a "formidable one" [*City of Harrisburg v. The School District of the City of Harrisburg*, 675 A.2d 758 (Pa.Commw. 1996), rev'd on other grounds, 710 A.2d 49 (Pa. 1998)].

• *Oil and gas interests*

Oil and gas interests are not taxable property because they do not fall within the meaning of the term "lands" under the General County Assessment Law [*Independent Oil and Gas Association of Pennsylvania v. Fayette County Board of Assessment Appeals*, 814 A.2d 180 (Pa. 2005), *rev'g* 780 A.2d 795 (Pa.Commw. 2002)].

• *Division and transfer of oil and natural gas interests*

The Pennsylvania Department of Revenue (DOR) has issued a notice regarding the property, realty transfer, and personal income tax treatment associated with the division and transfer of interests related to oil and natural gas. For property tax purposes, the DOR discusses the types of estates, oil and gas leases, and real estate versus personal property relative to an oil or gas lease. [*Informational Notice 2012-04*, Pennsylvania Department of Revenue, October 10, 2012].

• *Personal property used in connection with real estate*

Three classes of personal property used in connection with real estate: In *Clayton v. Lienhard*, 167 A. 321 (Pa. 1933), the Pennsylvania Supreme Court stated that personal property used in connection with real estate falls into the following three classes: (1) those that are not permanently attached to the realty (and thus remain personalty); (2) those that are attached to the realty and that can only be removed with material injury to the realty or to the attached personalty (and thus remain realty); or (3) those that are attached to the realty but are removable without substantial injury to either personalty or realty and either become part of the realty or remain personal depending upon the intention of the parties. In *Pedersen v. Monroe County Board of Assessment Appeals*, 84 A.3d 402 (2014), a storage shed was not taxable real estate since it was not permanently attached to the land.

Gas pump canopies: A taxpayer (Sheetz) owned and operated convenience stores in Pennsylvania. Sheetz contended that the canopies used to protect the gas pumps were not real property subject to taxation because the canopies were removable without substantial damage to the canopies or the realty. The Court found that while a canopy can be removed with little damage to the real property (requiring only removal of the concrete and bolts), significant effort is required to dissemble it, and it would leave the poured concrete foundations in place. Thus, according to the Court, the canopies were substantially affixed to the land. Furthermore, the Commonwealth Court held that the intention of the parties when they attached the property was of paramount importance and that just because canopies can be and have been removed does not mean that the intention of the parties was not to make them permanent. The court found that the intention of Sheetz was to leave the canopies in place as long as the property was operated as a convenience store. As such, they are a part of the realty and are taxable as real estate [*In re Sheetz, Inc.*, 657 A.2d 1011 (Pa.Commw. 1995), *app. den.* 666 A.2d 1060 (1995)].

• *Tax on improvements in mobile home park*

Real property taxes on garages and decks located in a mobile home community should be assessed to the landowner and not the individual mobile homeowners, regardless of the ownership of the improvements. *Douglass Village Residents Group v. Berks County Board of Assessment Appeals*, 84 A.3d 407 (2014).

• *Planned communities*

Statutory authority: Assessment and taxation of planned communities are governed by the provisions of the Uniform Planned Community Act, Act of 1996, No. 180, P.L. 206 [68 Pa.C.S. § 5101 *et seq.*].

Definition: A "planned community" is real estate with respect to which a person, by virtue of ownership of an interest in any portion of the real estate, is or may become obligated by covenant, easement or agreement imposed on the owner's interest to pay any amount for real property taxes, insurance, maintenance, repair, improvement, management, administration or regulation of any part of the real estate other than the portion or interest owned solely by the person. For purposes of this definition, "ownership" includes holding a leasehold interest of more than 20 years, including renewal options, in real estate. The term includes nonresidential campground communities [68 Pa.C.S. § 5103].

Cooperatives and Condominiums Not Planned Communities
Institution of Purely Public Charity

Cooperatives and condominiums are not planned communities, but a condominium or cooperative may be a part of a planned community [63 Pa.C.S. § 5103].

Separate assessment and taxation: Individual units are separately taxed and assessed, and the value of an individual unit includes the value of that unit's appurtenant interest in the common facilities (excluding convertible or withdrawable real estate) [68 Pa.C.S. § 5105(b)].

Common facilities: Since the value of common facilities is included in the value of the units in the planned community, common facilities are exempt from separate taxation and assessment. "Common facilities" include any real estate within a planned community that is owned by or leased to the association; a unit is not a common facility [68 Pa.C.S. § 5103].

¶3503

Properties Owned But Not Occupied by Association Are Common Facilities

A restaurant and a real estate office located in a planned community were owned by the community homeowners' association but were leased and operated by private business entities. The Court noted that the definition of "common facilities" does not list "occupancy" of the real estate as one of the required elements. The statute requires only that the real estate be (1) within the planned community and (2) owned by or leased to the association, to be considered common facilities [68 Pa.C.S. 5103]. Furthermore, associations are authorized to grant easement, leases, licenses and concessions through or over the common facilities [68 Pa.C.S. § 5302(a)(9)]. Therefore, the two buildings were "common facilities" exempt from separate taxation and assessment under 68 Pa.C.S. § 5105(b) [*Saw Creek Estates Community Association v. Pike County*, No. 29 MAP 2003 (Pa. 2005), *aff'g* 808 A.2d 322 (Pa.Commw. 2002)].

¶3503A Taxable Property Under Consolidated County Assessment Law

The Consolidated County Assessment Law states that, unless specifically exempt, all subjects and property made taxable by the laws of Pennsylvania for county, city, borough, town, township, and school district purposes shall be valued and assessed at the annual rate including the following [53 Pa.C.S. § 8811(a)]:

(1) Real estate, namely the following:

(a) Houses.

(b) House trailers and mobile homes permanently attached to land or connected with water, gas, electric, or sewage facilities.

(c) Buildings permanently attached to land or connected with water, gas, electric, or sewage facilities.

(d) Lands, lots of ground and ground rents, trailer parks, and parking lots.

(e) Mills and manufactories of all kinds, furnaces, forges, bloomeries, distilleries, sugar houses, malt houses, breweries, tan yards, fisheries, ferries, and wharves.

(f) All office buildings.

(g) That portion of a steel, lead, aluminum or like melting and continuous casting structure that encloses or provides shelter or protection from the elements for the various machinery, tools, appliances, equipment, materials, or products involved in the mill, mine, manufactory, or industrial process.

(h) Telecommunication towers that have become affixed to land.

(2) All other things now taxable by the laws of Pennsylvania for taxing districts.

¶3504 Constitutionally Exempt Property

Exemptions from real estate taxation are granted by the Pennsylvania Constitution and by specific statutes. The Constitutional exemptions are discussed in this paragraph.

• *Places of regularly stated worship service*

This exemption applies to property used for regularly stated worship service [Pennsylvania Constitution, Article VIII, § 2(i)]. In *Mullen v. Commissioners of Erie County*, 85 Pa. 288 (1877), the Court stated that they must be places of stated worship.

¶3504

It has been held that the word "stated" means fixed, established, occurring at regular times, as stated hours of business. So, "stated" means at certain times, not occasionally [*Mullen v. Commissioners of Erie County*, 85 Pa. 288 (Pa. 1877)].

Place of Regularly Stated Worship Service vs. Institution of Purely Public Charity

There is a distinction between "actual places of regularly stated religious worship" and "institutions of purely public charity" that has been consistently recognized by Pennsylvania courts. In the case of the latter, all property actually and regularly used for the purpose of the institution is subject to the exemption, whereas the more restricted exemption status afforded to the former has not been extended beyond ingress and egress, and light and air [*Appeal of Laymen's Weekend Retreat League of Philadelphia*, 343 A.2d 714 (Pa.Commw. 1975) (relying on *Second Church of Christ Scientist of Philadelphia v. City of Philadelphia*, 157 A.2d 54 (1959))]. Where there is a conflict between a specific constitutional provision that is applicable to a particular case and certain general provisions that, but for such conflict, might apply, the specific provision will prevail [*Walsh v. Tate*, 444 Pa. 229, 234; 282 A.2d 284, 287 (1971)]. Thus, the second floor of a parish house did not qualify for exemption as an institution of purely public charity because allowing the more liberal public charity provision would give greater effect to a general constitutional provision than to a specific constitutional provision (*i.e.*, the exemption for places of regularly stated religious worship) [*St. Aloysius R.C. Church v. Fayette County Board of Assessment Appeals*, Pa.Commw., No. 1414 C.D. 2003 (May 11, 2004)]. See, also, *In re: Appeal of Order of St. Paul The First Hermit from the County of Bucks Board of Assessment Appeals*, Pa.Commw., No. 1778 C.D. 2004 (April 22, 2005)].

• *Burial places*

This exemption applies to actual burial places when the property is used or held by a person or organization deriving no private or corporate profit therefrom and no substantial part of whose activity consists of selling personal property in connection therewith [Pennsylvania Constitution Article VIII, § 2(ii)].

• *Public property used for public purposes*

This exemption applies to that portion of public property that is actually and regularly used for public purposes [Pennsylvania Constitution, Article VIII, § 2(iii)]. In *Reading Housing Authority v. Board of Assessment Appeals of Berks County*, 103 A.3d 869 (2014), the Commonwealth Court ruled that an apartment building owned by the authority housing a mix of 20% low income and 80% market rate tenants was immune from tax.

• *Property owned and occupied by certain veterans' organizations*

This exemption applies to the portion of the property owned and occupied by any branch, post, or camp of honorably discharged servicemen or servicewomen that is actually and regularly used for benevolent, charitable, or patriotic purposes [Pennsylvania Constitution, Article VIII, § 2(iv)].

• *Institutions of purely public charity*

This exemption applies only to that portion of real property that is actually and regularly used for the purposes of the institution [Pennsylvania Constitution, Article VIII, § 2(v)].

• *Residences of disabled veterans*

The Pennsylvania Constitution requires that residences owned and occupied by war veterans who are blind, paraplegic, double or quadruple amputees, or 100% disabled and certified as needy by the State Veterans' Commission be exempt [Pennsylvania Constitution, Article VIII, § 3(c)].

¶3504

• *Public utility property*

The Pennsylvania Constitution specifically permits local taxation of public utility property. However, it also provides that payment of the gross receipts tax or other special levies to the Commonwealth would preempt direct local taxation of realty used or useful in furnishing public utility services [Pennsylvania Constitution, Article VIII, §4]. The Pennsylvania Supreme Court ruled that PURTA (see ¶2501) was a special Commonwealth levy that exempted utilities from local real estate taxation [*American Telephone and Telegraph Co.*, 337 A.2d 844 (1975)]. This restriction does not, however, apply to Philadelphia and Pittsburgh taxation of railroad property.

• *Homestead exemption*

An amendment to Article VIII of the Pennsylvania Constitution, approved by the voters in 1997, authorized local taxing authorities to exclude from taxation an amount based on the assessed value of homestead property (referred to as the homestead exemption) [Pennsylvania Constitution, Article VIII, §2(b)(vi)]. The homestead exemption cannot exceed one-half of the median assessed value of all homestead property within a local taxing jurisdiction; and a local taxing authority may not increase the millage rate of its tax on real property to pay for these exclusions. The law authorizing local tax jurisdictions to implement homestead exemptions [53 Pa.C.S. §8581 *et seq.*] is discussed at ¶3405 and ¶3406.

¶3504A Statutorily Exempt Property

• *General county assessment law exemptions*

The General County Assessment Law [72 P.S. §5020-101 *et seq.*] provides specific exemptions from county, city, township, road, poor, and school taxes [72 P.S. §5020-204]. The following property is specifically exempt from real estate taxes in first and second class counties:

(1) *Places of worship:* Churches, meeting houses, or other places of regularly stated religious worship (including annexed ground necessary for the occupancy and enjoyment of the property) [72 P.S. §5020-204(a)(1)].

(2) *Burial places:* Actual places of burial, including burial grounds, mausoleums, vaults, crypts, and structures intended to hold or contain bodies) not held or used for private profit and no substantial part of whose activity consists of selling personal property in connection with the burial places [72 P.S. §5020-204(a)(2)].

(3) *Institutions maintained by public or private charity:* Hospitals, universities, colleges, seminaries, academies, associations and institutions of learning, benevolence, or charity (including fire and rescue stations) founded, endowed, and maintained by public or private charity, provided all of their revenue is used for no other purpose than to support charitable goals (including annexed ground necessary for the occupancy and enjoyment of the property). However, a public charity need not be fully maintained by charitable contributions to be deemed to be maintained by charity [*Mt. Macrina Manor, Inc. v. Fayette County Board of Assessment Appeals*, 683 A.2d 935 (Pa.Commw. 1996)]. In order to qualify as a charity under this provision, the organization must be a "purely public charity" (see ¶3505 for a discussion of "purely public charity") [72 P.S. §5020-204(a)(3)].

(4) *Schoolhouses:* Schoolhouses belonging to any county, borough, or school district (including annexed ground necessary for the occupancy and enjoyment of the property). Note that there is no exemption for municipal improvements abutting land owned by a school district other than a school district of the first class or first class A or school districts of the second, third, or fourth class that is coterminous with a city, borough, town, or township, except that any school

district of the second, third, or fourth class coterminous with a city, borough, town, or township may agree to pay all or part of any such assessment charges [72 P.S. § 5020-204(a)(4)].

(5) *Courthouses, jails, and poorhouses* (including annexed ground necessary for the occupancy and enjoyment of the property) [72 P.S. § 5020-204(a)(5)].

(6) *Public parks:* Public parks owned and held by trustees for the benefit of the public and used for amusements, recreation, sports, and other public purposes without profit (including annexed ground necessary for the occupancy and enjoyment of the property) [72 P.S. § 5020-204(a)(6)].

(7) *Public property used for public purposes* (including annexed ground necessary for the occupancy and enjoyment of the property): This exemption does not apply to property otherwise taxable that is owned or held by an agency of the U.S. government. Note, also, that this provision does not exempt from taxation any privilege, act, or transaction conducted on public property that persons or entities that would be taxable if conducted on nonpublic property [72 P.S. § 5020-204(a)(7)]. See discussion of public property used for public purposes below.

(8) *Veterans' organizations:* Property owned, occupied, and used by any branch, post, or camp of honorably discharged servicemen or servicewomen that is actually and regularly used for benevolent, charitable, or patriotic purposes [72 P.S. § 5020-204(a)(8)].

(9) *Institutions of purely public charity:* Property owned and used by institutions of purely public charity, used and occupied partly by the owners and partly by other institutions of purely public charity, and necessary for the occupancy and enjoyment of the charitable institutions using the property. See ¶ 3505 for a discussion of purely public charities [72 P.S. § 5020-204(a)(9)].

(10) *Playground maintained by public or private charity:* Playgrounds founded, endowed, and maintained by public or private charity, which apply their revenue to the support and repair of the property and to increase the efficiency and facilities of the property (and for no other purpose), and owned, leased, possessed, or controlled by public school boards or properly organized and duly constituted playground associations, and approved and accepted by the board of commissions (or board of revision of taxes) of the county in which the playgrounds are located [72 P.S. § 5020-204(a)(10)].

(11) *Libraries:* Free, public, nonsectarian libraries (including the land on which they stand and that is immediately and necessarily appurtenant to the libraries). The fact that some portion(s) of the library building or lands appurtenance may be yielding rentals to the corporation or association managing the library does not remove the exemption, if the net receipts of the managing corporation or association are used solely for the purpose of maintaining the library [72 P.S. § 5020-204(a)(11)].

(12) *Museums, art galleries, and concert music halls:* Property (including annexed ground necessary for the occupancy and enjoyment of the property) that is provided and maintained by public or private charity, used exclusively for public museums, art galleries, or concert music halls and not used for private or corporate profit (so long as public use continues). In the case of concert music halls used partly for exempt purposes and partly for nonexempt purposes, that part used for nonexempt purposes (measured either in area or in time, whichever is less) is subject to real estate taxation [72 P.S. § 5020-204(a)(12)].

(13) *Fire and rescue stations:* All fire and rescue stations that are founded, endowed, and maintained by public or private charity (including annexed ground necessary for the occupancy and enjoyment of the property) and social

¶3504A

halls and grounds owned and occupied by fire and rescue stations that are used on a regular basis for activities that contribute to the support of the stations if the net receipts from the activities are used solely for the charitable purpose of the fire and rescue stations [72 P.S. § 5020-204(a)(13)].

(14) *Machinery, tools, appliances, and other equipment:* Machinery, tools, appliances, and other equipment contained in any mill, mine, manufactury, or industrial establishment are not considered or included as part of the real estate in determining the value of the facility [72 P.S. § 5020-201(a)]. The Pennsylvania Supreme Court has held that in order for property to be excluded from real estate taxation under the Fourth through Eighth Class County Assessment Law, the property must meet two requirements: (a) It must constitute machinery, tools, appliances, or other equipment; and (b) it must be contained in a mill, mine, manufactory, or industrial establishment as required by 72 P.S. § 5354.201. Thus, dry kilns used to dry lumber are excluded from assessment for real property taxation purposes [*BFC Hardwoods, Inc. v. Crawford County Board of Assessment Appeals*, 771 A.2d 759 (Pa. 2001)]. The Commonwealth Court has held that oil storage tanks that are an integral and direct part of the refining process are excluded from real estate taxation under this provision [*Gulf Oil v. Delaware County Board of Assessment*, 489 A.2d 321 (Pa.Commw. 1985)].

(15) *Farm structures:* The following are not included in determining the value of real estate used predominantly as a farm: (a) silos used predominantly for processing or storage of animal feed incidental to operation of the farm on which they are located, (b) free-standing detachable grain bins or corn cribs used exclusively for processing or storage of animal feed incidental to operation of the farm on which they are located, and (c) structures and containments (above- or below-ground) used predominantly for processing and storage of animal waste and composting facilities incidental to operation of the farm on which they are located [72 P.S. § 5020-201(a)].

(16) *Amusement park rides:* Amusement park rides are not assessed or taxed as real estate regardless of whether they have become affixed to the real estate [72 P.S. § 5020-201(a)].

(17) *Public property used for public purposes:* The exemption of property used for public purposes is permitted by the Pennsylvania Constitution (see discussion of governmental immunity at ¶3403). The General County Assessment Law exempts "all other property used for public purposes, with the ground thereto annexed and necessary for the occupancy and enjoyment . . . " [72 P.S. § 5020-101]. However, this does not include otherwise taxable property owned or held by a U.S. government agency, nor does it include any privilege, act or transaction conducted upon public property, persons, or entities that would be taxable if conducted upon nonpublic property without regard to the purpose of the activity, nor even if the activity is conducted as agent for or lessee of any public property.

(a) *Land annexed to school:* School district land that is annexed to and adjoins other district lands that include the site of a school is exempt as public property used for public purposes. The school district is not required to demonstrate that all of the land annexed to the school is in use for school purposes [*Wellsboro Area School District v. Tioga County Board of Assessment and Revision of Taxes*, 651 A.2d 592 (Pa.Commw. 1994)].

(b) *Open spaces acquired by a municipality but used by sellers:* A township purchased a 157-acre tract from the owners of the property to fulfill the township's goal of preserving open spaces through acquisition of farmland and other underdeveloped areas. However, the township did not purchase the tract in fee simple. The owners transferred the tract to the township subject to a life estate, plus 21 years, in certain members of the family. The family (sellers) retained the right to use their land for agricultural and recreational purposes. In 1988, the township established a system of eight-foot-wide trails along the perimeter of the property. Members of the public were only permitted on the trails; they could not enter upon the rest of the land. The fact that the public can view agricultural uses from a perimeter trail was not considered a sufficient public use to warrant an exemption from taxation. Furthermore, sellers continued to use the property for farming as they had in the past. Therefore, the property was not exempt from taxation [*In re Appeal of Township of Middletown*, 654 A.2d 195 (Pa.Commw. 1995)].

Wind Energy Generation Property

Wind turbine generators or related wind energy appliances and equipment, including towers and tower foundations are specifically exempt from tax under the Consolidated County Assessment Tax [53 Pa.C.S. §§ 8801(b)(2), 8811(b)(5)]. Wind energy generation property is valued under 53 Pa.C.S. § 8842.

• *Exemptions under the consolidated county assessment law (Act 93)*

Exemptions specific to Act 93: The following are exceptions to 53 Pa.C.S. § 8811(a), *i.e.,* not included in the definition of taxable property for purposes of Act 93:

(1) Machinery, tools, appliances, and other equipment contained in any mill, mine, manufactory, or industrial establishment [53 Pa.C.S. § 8811(b)(2)].

(2) Silos used predominantly for processing or storage of animal feed incidental to operation of the farm on which it is located, freestanding detachable grain bins or corn cribs used exclusively for processing or storage of animal feed incidental to the operation of the farm on which it is located, and inground and aboveground structures and containments used predominantly for processing and storage of animal waste and composting facilities incidental to operation of the farm on which the structures and containments are located [53 Pa.C.S. § 8811(b)(2)].

(3) Amusement park rides (whether or not affixed to land) [53 Pa.C.S. § 8811(b)(3)].

(4) Signs and sign structures (whether or not affixed to the real estate [53 Pa.C.S. § 8811(b)(4)].

(5) Real property used for the purpose of wind energy generation [53 Pa.C.S. § 8811(b)(5)].

Applicability of Exemptions

While the list immediately above enumerates exceptions to taxable property under Act 93 only (*i.e.,* in all counties other than those of the first or second classes), the following property appears to be exempt from real estate taxation in all jurisdictions.

General exemptions: The following property is exempt from all county, borough, town, township, road, poor, county institution district and school real estate taxes [Pa.C.S. § 8812(a)]:

(1) Places of regularly stated religious worship (along with the ground annexed necessary for their occupancy and use) [53 Pa.C.S. § 8812(a)(1)].

(2) Burial places [53 Pa.C.S. § 8812(a)(2)].

(3) Hospitals, universities, colleges, seminaries, academies, associations and institutions of learning (including fire and rescue stations) endowed and maintained by public or private charity as long as all of the following apply [53 Pa.C.S. § 8812(a)(3)]:

¶3504A

(a) All revenue derived by the entity is applied to support the entity and to increase efficiency and facilities of the entity, repair the necessary increase of grounds and buildings of the entity and for no other purpose.

(b) The property of purely public charities is necessary to and actually used for the principal purposes of the institution and not used in such a manner as to compete with commercial enterprise.

(4) Property of a charitable organization that provides residential housing services and for which it receives subsidies for at least 95% of the residential housing units from a low-income federal housing program [53 Pa.C.S. § 8812(a)(4)].

(5) School buildings belonging to any municipality or school district [53 Pa.C.S. § 8812(a)(5)].

(6) Courthouses and jails [53 Pa.C.S. § 8812(a)(6)].

(7) Public parks owned and held by trustees for the benefit of the public and used for amusements, recreation, sports, and other public purposes without profit [53 Pa.C.S. § 8812(a)(7)].

(8) Public property used for public purposes [53 Pa.C.S. § 8812(a)(8)].

(9) Real property used for limited access highways and maintained by public funds [53 Pa.C.S. § 8812(a)(9)].

(10) Real and personal property owned, occupied, and used by any branch, post, or camp of honorably discharged servicemen or servicewomen and actually and regularly used for benevolent, charitable, or patriotic purposes [53 Pa.C.S. § 8812(a)(10)].

(11) Real property owned by one or more institutions of purely public charity, used and occupied partly by the owner or owners and partly by other institutions of purely public charity and necessary for the occupancy and use of the institutions using it [53 Pa.C.S. § 8812(a)(11)]. Purely public charities are discussed at ¶ 3505.

(12) Playgrounds founded, endowed, or maintained by public or private charity that apply revenue to support and repair of the playground and to increase the efficiency and facilities thereof and for no other purpose [53 Pa.C.S. § 8812(a)(12)]. This includes school playgrounds.

(13) Buildings owned and occupied by free public nonsectarian libraries [53 Pa.C.S. § 8812(a)(13)]

(14) Property provided and maintained by public or private charity and used exclusively for public libraries, museums, or art galleries and not used for private or corporate property [53 Pa.C.S. § 8812(a)(14)].

(15) Fire and rescue stations [53 Pa.C.S. § 8812(a)(15)].

Institutions of Purely Public Charity Act

The Institutions of Purely Public Act remain in full effect under the Consolidated County Assessment Law. Each provision of the Consolidated County Assessment Law is to be read in para materia with the Institutions of Purely Public Charity Act [Act of November 26, 1997, P.L. 55, referred to as Act 55], discussed at ¶ 3505 [53 Pa.C.S. § 8812(c)].

Temporary tax exemption for residential construction: New single and multiple dwellings constructed to residential purposes and improvements to existing unoccupied dwellings or improvements to existing structures for purposes of conversion to dwellings shall be valued or assessed for purposes of real property taxes until occupied, conveyed to a bona fide purchaser, or 30 months from the first day of the month after which the building permit was issued. If no building permit or other

¶3504A

notification of improvement was required, the building is exempt for 30 months from the date construction commenced [53 Pa.C.S. § 8813].

• *Exemptions under the Local Economic Revitalization Tax Assistance Act*

The Local Economic Revitalization Tax Assistance Act (LERTA) [72 P.S. §§ 4722—4728] authorizes local taxing authorities to exempt new construction in deteriorated areas of economically depressed communities and improvements to certain deteriorated property [72 P.S. § 4723]. An exemption from local real property taxes authorized by the LERTA is upon the property and does not terminate upon the sale or exchange of the property [72 P.S. § 4726(c)].

A "deteriorated property" for this purpose is (1) any industrial, commercial, or other business property owned by an individual, association, or corporation and (2) located in a deteriorating area, provided it is not subject to an order to be vacated, condemned, or demolished for noncompliance with laws, ordinance, or regulations. The term "local taxing authority" includes counties, cities, boroughs, incorporated towns, townships, institution districts, or school districts having authority to levy real property taxes [72 P.S. § 4724]. The designation of "deteriorated areas" is made by local taxing authorities; and areas so designated must meet the criteria set forth in 72 P.S. § 4725(a)].

Amount of exemption: Local taxing authorities may provide for tax exemption (1) on the assessment attributable to the actual cost of new construction or improvements or (2) up to any maximum cost uniformly established by the municipal governing body (*i.e.,* a city, borough, incorporated town, or township) [72 P.S. § 4726(a)].

Exemption Discretionary

The statutory language of LERTA states that local taxing authorities "may" grant exemptions but does not require them to do so. A school district refused to grant a taxpayer an exemption. The taxpayer argued that the denial of exemption violated LERTA because the township in which the school district was located had already designated a deteriorated area that included the taxpayer's property and that the school district (which had no LERTA designation of its own) was, therefore, required to pass its own LERTA resolution. The Commonwealth Court disagreed, pointing out the discretionary nature of LERTA exemptions. The Court also held that the taxpayer was not denied due process because the school district refused its exemption request without a due process hearing and adjudication, pointing out that the LERTA statute does not create a right to a hearing and adjudication before a taxing body where that taxing body has not adopted a LERTA designation [*Jennison Family L.P. v. Montour School District*, 802 A.2d 1257 (Pa.Commw. 2002)].

Limitations: Whether based upon actual cost or a maximum cost, the actual amount of taxes exempted must be in accordance with the schedule of taxes exempted established by a local taxing authority subject to the following limitations [72 P.S. § 4726(b)]:

    (1) The length of the schedule of taxes exempted cannot exceed ten (10) years.

    (2) The schedule of taxes exempted must stipulate the portion of new construction or improvements to be exempted each year.

    (3) The exemption from taxes is limited to (a) the additional assessment valuation attributable to the actual costs of new construction or improvements to deteriorated property or (b) not in excess of the maximum cost per unit established by a municipal governing body.

Application for exemption: A person who desires a tax exemption under the provisions of the LERTA must submit a written request for exemption to each local

¶3504A

taxing authority granting an exemption on a form provided by the local taxing authority. The written request must be submitted at the time a building permit is secured. If no building permit or other notification of new construction or improvement is required, the written request for exemption must be submitted at the time construction commences [72 P.S. § 4727(a)].

Effect of amendments: The cost of new construction or improvements to be exempted and the schedule of taxes exempted existing at the time of a taxpayer's initial request for exemption is applicable to that request; and subsequent amendment to the ordinance, if any, does not apply to requests initiated prior to their adoption [72 P.S. § 4727(b)].

Appeals: Appeals from the reassessment and the amounts eligible for the exemption may be taken by the taxpayer or the local taxing authorities as provided by law [72 P.S. § 4727(a)]. Note that this provision allows appeals from reassessment and the amounts eligible for exemption, which is clearly conditioned upon someone seeking relief under ordinances already in place. See *Jennison Family L.P. v. Montour School District*, 802 A.2d 1257 (Pa.Commw. 2002).

• *Improvement of Deteriorating Real Property or Areas Tax Exemption Act*

The Improvement of Deteriorating Real Property or Areas Tax Exemption Act authorizes local taxing authorities to exempt the assessed valuation of improvements to deteriorated residential property within deteriorated neighborhoods [72 P.S. § 4711-102]. The provisions of this act are codified in 72 P.S. §§ 4711-101—4711-305.

Assessment of other properties: If a deteriorated property is granted tax exemption for an improvement, the improvement cannot, during the exemption period, be considered as a factor in assessing other properties [72 P.S. § 4711-204].

Two or more jurisdictions: Two or more local taxing authorities may join together for the purpose of determining the boundaries of a deteriorated neighborhood, and they must cooperate fully with each other for implementation [72 P.S. § 4711-202(b)].

Exemption schedules: Taxing authorities may design exemption schedules, which may be up to 10 years in duration. Exemption schedule options are specified in 72 P.S. § 4711-203(a). This exemption is limited to the additional assessment valuation attributable to the actual costs of improvements to deteriorated property [72 P.S. § 4711-203(b)].

Exemption requests: Requests for exemption must be submitted on forms provided by the taxing authority at the time the owner secures a building permit or (if no building permit is required) at the time construction commences. A copy of the exemption request must be forwarded to the board of assessment of taxes or other appropriate assessment agency. After the improvement is completed, the assessment agency must make a separate assessment, calculate the amounts of the assessment eligible for tax exemption, and notify the taxpayer and taxing authorities of the reassessment and amounts eligible for exemption. Appeals from the reassessment and the amounts eligible for exemption may be taken by the taxpayer or the local taxing authorities as provided by law [72 P.S. § 4711-205].

• *Homestead Property Exclusion Program Act [53 Pa.C.S. § 8581 et seq.]*

A governing body of a political subdivision may exclude from taxation a fixed dollar amount of the assessed value of each homestead or farmstead property in the political subdivision that does not exceed the limits on the exclusion [53 Pa.C.S. § 8583(a); § 8585(b)]. However, the governing body of the political subdivision cannot increase the millage rate of its real property tax to pay for homestead property and farmstead property exclusions [53 Pa.C.S. § 8586(b)]. A "governing body" for this purpose is a city council, borough council, incorporated town council, board of township commissioners, board of township supervisors, a governing council of a home rule municipality or optional plan municipality, a similar governing council of any similar general purpose unit of government that may be created by statute, or a board of school directors of a school district [53 Pa.C.S. § 8422]. See ¶ 3406for discussion of the provisions of the Homestead Property Exclusion Program Act.

• *Veterans' organizations*

Any branch, post, or camp of honorably discharged servicemen or servicewomen (or an affiliated organization) is exempt from any real property taxes for that portion of the real property that is actually and regularly used for benevolent, charitable, or patriotic purposes [51 Pa.C.S. § 9303(a)(2)]. An affiliated organization for this purpose is one defined as an affiliated organization in § 461.a(b) of the Liquor Code [72 P.S. § 372]. Note, however, that the purchase of alcoholic beverages is not exempt. There is also a sales and use tax exemption for veterans' organizations. See ¶ 705.

• *Property in keystone opportunity zones (KOZs)*

Each qualified political subdivision must by ordinance or resolution abate 100% of the real property taxation on the assessed valuation of deteriorated property in an area designated as a KOZ subzone, expansion subzone, or improvement subzone [73 P.S. § 820.702]. See ¶ 4622 for discussion of KOZs.

Calculations for education subsidy for school districts: In determining the market value of real property in each school district, the State Tax Equalization Board must exclude any increase in value above the base value prior to the effect of the abatement of local taxes to the extent and during the period of time that the real estate tax revenues attributable to the increased value are not available to the school district for general school district purposes [73 P.S. § 820.702(f)].

• *Certain donated property*

A local taxing district (including a municipal authority or a school district) accept the donation of property that is subject to a claim for property taxes [72 P.S. § 5860.303(b)]. A donation of property that meets all of the requirements of 72 P.S. § 5860.303 relieves the owner of all liens against the property possessed by the local taxing district accepting the donation and all other local tax liens recorded prior to the date of donation. For purposes of 72 P.S. § 5860.303, "claims for taxes" includes all penalties, interest, and fees assessed against the property [72 P.S. § 5860.303(e)].

¶ 3505 Purely Public Charities

The origin of the charitable exemption under the General County Assessment Law (see ¶ 3504) is Article VIII, 2(a)(v) of the Pennsylvania Constitution, which authorizes the General Assembly to provide by law for the exemption from taxation of "[i]nstitutions of purely public charity, but in the case of any real property tax exemptions only that portion of real property of such institution which is actually and regularly used for the purposes of the institution." The benchmark case, *Hospital Utilization Project (HUP)*, 487 A.2d 1306 (Pa. 1985), set forth five criteria for identifying purely public charities that meet the constitutional requirements.

Prior to the passage of The Institutions of Purely Public Charities Act [10 P.S. § 372 et seq. and 72 P.S. § 5020 et seq.], there was no statutory definition of the term "purely public charity." The Institutions of Purely Public Charities Act provided a statutory definition of the term "purely public charity." Now there are two sets of criteria—the constitutional criteria set forth in *HUP* and the statutory criteria set forth in the Institutions of Purely Public Charity Act.

• *HUP criteria*

In *HUP*, the Pennsylvania Supreme Court stated that an entity qualifies as a purely public charity if it possesses the following five (5) characteristics:

(1) It advances a charitable purpose.

(2) It donates or renders gratuitously a substantial portion of its services.

(3) It benefits a substantial and indefinite class of persons who are legitimate subjects of charity.

(4) It relieves the government of some of its burden.

(5) It operates entirely free from private profit motive.

Institutions of Purely Public Charity Act

• *General*

According to the Institutions of Purely Public Charity Act, an institution of purely public charity is an institution that meets the five criteria of §5 of the Institutions of Purely Public Charity Act (referred to below as Act 55). The five statutory criteria, which essentially codify the five criteria of *HUP,* are as follows:

(1) Charitable purpose.

(2) Freedom from private profit motive.

(3) Community service.

(4) Charity to persons.

(5) Government service.

Entities Must Satisfy Both Constitutional and Statutory Criteria

An entity seeking a statutory exemption for taxation must first establish that it is a "purely public charity" under Article VIII, §2, of the Pennsylvania Constitution before the question of whether that entity meets the qualifications of a statutory exemption can be reached. See, for example, *G.D.L. Plaza Corp. v. Council Rock Sch. Dist.,* 526 A.2d 1173, 1175 (Pa. 1987) and *Community Options, Inc. v. Allegheny County Board of Property Assessment, Appeals and Review,* 813 A.2d 680 (Pa. 2002). The Pennsylvania Supreme Court set forth a five-prong test for determining whether an entity qualifies as a "purely public charity" under the Pennsylvania Constitution in *Hospital Utilization Project,* 487 A.2d 1306 (Pa. 1985). The *HUP* criteria are discussed below. If an entity satisfies the constitutional requirements, it must then comply with the provisions of the Institutions of Purely Public Charity Act [Act of November 26, 1997, P.L. 55, referred to as Act 55]. The provisions of the Institutions of Purely Public Charity Act are discussed below.

Statutory Criteria for Qualification as a Purely Public Charity

• *Criterion 1—Charitable purpose*

The institution must advance a charitable purpose [10 P.S. §375(b)]. This criterion is satisfied if the institution is organized and operated primarily to fulfill any one or a combination of the following purposes:

(1) Relief of poverty.

(2) Advancement and provision of education (including postsecondary education).

(3) Advancement of religion.

(4) Prevention and treatment of disease or injury (including mental retardation and mental disorders).

(5) Government or municipal purposes.

• *Criterion 2—Freedom from private profit motive*

The institution must operate entirely free from private profit motive [10 P.S. §375(c)]. Regardless of whether the institution's revenues exceed its expenses, this criterion is satisfied if the institution meets all of the following:

(1) Neither the institution's net earnings nor donations received inure to the benefit of private shareholders or other individuals as interpreted under § 501(c)(3) of the Internal Revenue Code.

(2) The institution applies or reserves all revenue (including contributions) in excess of expenses to further its charitable purpose or to fund other institutions of purely public charity.

(3) Compensation (including benefits) of directors, officers, or employees is not based (primarily) upon the financial performance of the institution.

(4) The governing body has adopted as part of its articles of incorporation or, if unincorporated, other governing legal documents a provision that expressly prohibits the use of any surplus funds for private inurement to any person in the event of a sale or dissolution of the institution.

Provision in Articles of Incorporation

To establish that it operates entirely free from private profit motive, an institution must meet all four parts of the statutory criterion. A taxing jurisdiction contended that a taxpayer (RHA) did not have the required provision in its articles of incorporation. According to the Commonwealth Court, taxpayers are not required to have the specific words of the Act in its articles of incorporation. Rather, it is sufficient if the institution's articles of incorporation contain provisions that have the required effect. RHA's articles of incorporations contained provisions that satisfied the requirement [*In re RHA Pennsylvania Nursing Homes v. Cmwlth.*, 747 A.2d 1257 (Pa.Commw. 2000)].

• *Criterion 3—Community service*

The institution must donate or render gratuitously a substantial portion of its services [10 P.S. § 375(d)]. This criterion is satisfied if the institution benefits the community by actually providing any one of the following:

(1) Goods or services to *all* who seek them without regard to their ability to pay for what they receive if *all* of the following apply:

(a) The institution has a written policy to this effect.

(b) The institution has published this policy in a reasonable manner.

(c) The institution provides uncompensated goods or services at least equal to 75% of its net operating income but not less than 3% of its total operating expenses.

(2) Goods or services for a fee, based on the individual's ability to pay, if *all* the following apply:

(a) The institution can demonstrate that it has implemented a written policy and a written schedule of fees based on individual or family income. This requirement is met if the institution consistently applies a formula.

(b) At least 20% of the individuals receiving goods or services pay no fee (or a fee that is lower than the cost of goods or services provided).

(c) At least 10% of the individuals receiving goods or services receive a discount of at least 10% of the cost of goods or services provided to them.

(d) No individual receiving goods or services pays a fee equal to or greater than the cost of the goods or services.

(3) Wholly gratuitous goods or services equal to at least 5% of those individuals receiving similar goods or services.

(4) Financial assistance or uncompensated goods or services equal to at least 20% of those individuals receiving similar goods or services if at least 10% of the individuals either paid no fees or fees that were 90% or less than the cost

of goods or services provided after consideration of any financial assistance provided to them by the institution.

(5) Uncompensated goods or services that (in the aggregate) are equal to at least 5% of the institution's costs of providing goods or services.

(6) Goods or services at no fee or reduced fees to government agencies or individuals eligible for government programs.

Check the Statute

Provisions with respect to community service are extensive and complicated and should be consulted for more details.

- *Criterion 4—Charity to persons*

The institution must benefit a substantial and indefinite class of persons who are unable to provide themselves with what the institution provides for them (*i.e,* legitimate subjects of charity) [10 P.S. §375(e)]. This criterion is satisfied if an institution is one of the following:

(1) Primarily engaged in fundraising on behalf of or making grants to qualifying entities and there is an actual contribution of a substantial portion of the funds raised to the qualifying entities. Qualifying entities for this purpose include institutions of purely public charity, an entity similarly recognized by another state or foreign jurisdiction, a qualifying religious organization, or a government agency.

(2) Operating exclusively on a voluntary basis to provide emergency health and safety service to the community.

(3) Providing funds and support exclusively to volunteer institutions that provide emergency health and safety services to the community.

Exceptions: An institution cannot not meet the above criterion if it is not qualified under §501(c)(3) of the Internal Revenue Code and it is qualified under IRC §501(c)(4), (5), (6), (7), (8), or (9) as any of the following:

(1) An association of employees limited in membership to employees of a designated person(s).

(2) A labor organization.

(3) An agricultural or horticultural organization.

(4) A business league.

(5) A chamber of commerce.

(6) A real estate board.

(7) A board of trade.

(8) A professional sports league.

(9) A club organized for pleasure or recreation.

(10) A fraternal beneficiary society, order, or association.

In an unreported decision of a panel of the Commonwealth Court, in *Helping Enjoying and Loving People, v. Del. County Bd. of Assessment Appeals,* Pa. Commw. Dkt. No. 558 C.D. 2017, (July 9, 2018) a nonprofit corporation that owned a community center and provided a variety of services, including free coats, free food, free computer classes and free computers, failed to qualify for a property tax exemption because the nonprofit did not meet the criteria for being a purely public charity under *Hospital Utilization Project v. Cmwlth.,* 487 A.2d 1306 (Pa. 1985). The taxpayer established that it advanced a charitable purpose; donated or gratuitously rendered a substantial portion of its services; and that it operated entirely free from a profit motive (3 of the 5 HUP tests), but failed to demonstrate that it (i) benefited a substantial and indefinite class of persons who are legitimate subjects of charity (the third prong of the HUP test), or (ii) relieved the government of some of its burden (the fourth prong of the HUP test). In regard to the third prong of the HUP test addressed by the Commonwealth Court in *Helping Enjoying and Loving People*, the court looked to its prior decision in *Appeal of Sewickley Valley YMCA*, 774 A.2d 1 (Pa. Commw. 2001) holding that in order to meet the third prong of the HUP test an entity must show that it makes a bona fide effort to service those persons who are unable to afford the usual fee or for whom the fee is outside of their financial reach. The taxpayer provided no evidence whatsoever regarding whether the recipients of goods and services under its various programs were unable to pay. Therefore, the court could not find that the taxpayer benefited a substantial and indefinite class of persons who are legitimate subjects of charity and denied the taxpayer an exemption from real estate taxes.

- *Criterion 5—Government service*

The institution must relieve the government of some of its burden. This criterion is satisfied if the institution meets any one of the following:

(1) It provides a service to the public that the government would otherwise be required to fund or provide.

(2) It provides services that are either the responsibility of the government by law or historically have been assumed, offered, or funded by the government.

(3) It receives regular payments for services rendered under a government program and the payments are less than its full costs as determined by generally accepted accounting principles.

(4) It provides a service to the public that reduces (directly or indirectly) dependence on government programs, or relieves or lessens the burden borne by government for the advancement of social, moral, educational, or physical objectives.

(5) It advances or promotes religion and is owned and operated by a corporation or other entity as a religious ministry (and it otherwise satisfies the criteria for purely public charities).

(6) It has a voluntary agreement under §7 of Act 55 (10 P.S. §377). See discussion below.

Other Provisions of the Institutions of Purely Public Charity Act

- *Compliance*

Institutions of purely public charity must comply with both the provisions of Act 55 and the provisions of the sales and use tax imposed by Article II of the Tax Reform Code [10 P.S. §382].

- *Founded, endowed, and maintained by public or private charity*

An institution that meets these five criteria shall be considered to be founded, endowed, and maintained by public or private charity. Prior to the passage of Act 55, the requirement of being founded, endowed, and maintained by public or private charity was a requirement in addition to the requirement of meeting the five criteria [*The Couriers-Susquehanna, Inc. v. County of Dauphin*, 693 A.2d 626 (Pa.Commw. 1997)].

- *Application for exemption*

The application and evaluation process complies with the provisions of the Institutions of Purely Public Charity Act. All applicants applying for exemption status under 72 P.S. §7201(10) are required to complete the revised Form REV-72 (replacing Form PA-100, which was formerly accepted for exemption application) as

¶3505

well as supplying all necessary supporting documentation [*Pennsylvania Tax Update No. 73*, Pennsylvania Department of Revenue, January/February 1998]. Questions about tax exemption issues should be directed to the Department of Revenue's Sales Tax Exemption Unit at 717-782-5473 or 717-722-6922.

• *Annual reports*

Institutions of purely public charity that do not register with the Department of State under the Solicitation of Funds for Charitable Purposes Act [Act of December 19, 1990, P.L. 1200, No. 202] must file an annual report (including institutions exempted from registration under §6 of the Solicitation of Funds for Charitable Purposes Act). The report is due within 135 days after the close of the institution's fiscal year (unless an extension is granted). Institutions that receive contributions of less than $25,000 per year and that also have program service revenue of no more than $5,000,000, and religious institutions, are exempt from the reporting requirements. See ¶705 for more detail about annual reports.

• *Rebuttable presumption of exemption*

Institutions of purely public charity that possess a valid exemption from the sales and use tax (see ¶705) are entitled to assert a rebuttable presumption that they meet the statutory criteria. Such a presumption may only be asserted with regard to a challenge made by a political subdivision with which that institution has a voluntary agreement in effect (see below), and only if its exemption under 72 P.S. §7204(1) is granted or renewed on or after November 26, 1997 [10 P.S. §385(c)]. If an institution asserts a presumption under this provision, the challenging political subdivision bears the burden, by a preponderance of the evidence, of proving that the institution does not comply with the statutory requirements. An institution that has annual program service revenue less than $10,000,000 is automatically entitled to assert the presumption if it holds a valid exemption under 72 P.S. §7204(10). An institution that has annual program service revenue equal to or exceeding $10,000,000 is entitled to assert the presumption only if it possesses a valid exemption under 72 P.S. §7204(10) and has a voluntary agreement (see below) with a political subdivision in which it conducts substantial business operations. See §6 of the Institutions of Purely Public Charity Act. The threshold amount of $10,000,000 is increased (beginning July 1, 1997, and every year thereafter) by 1% [10 P.S. §376(a)(5)].

• *Waiver of confidentiality*

When an institution asserts a rebuttable presumption (see above), it is deemed to have waived any right to confidentiality with regard to all records in the possession of the Department relating to the application for exemption. These records become public records that the Department must furnish to any person upon request. A political subdivision challenging a presumption may request from the institution all relevant financial statements, records and documents used to obtain the sales and use tax exemption. Failure by that institution to supply or, at its option, to permit inspection of relevant information in its possession within 30 days, surrenders the right to assert the presumption with respect to that challenge [72 P.S. §7006(d)].

• *Voluntary agreement*

A political subdivision may execute an agreement with an institution that owns real property within the political subdivision to make voluntary contributions to the local jurisdiction to compensate a local jurisdiction for the loss of property tax revenue due to its exemption as a purely public charity. Charitable organizations may (with the agreement of the local jurisdiction) establish a public service foundation for the purpose of receiving contributions from purely public charities. Upon agreement, the foundation will make distributions or grants to participating political subdivisions. A political subdivision that receives a distribution or grant from a public service foundation cannot assess or seek a separate contribution for services from institutions participating in the foundation. Existing agreements are not disturbed by the law [10 P.S. § 377].

• *Additional credit for voluntary agreements*

An institution that has entered into a voluntary agreement is entitled to an additional credit for purposes of computing the community service criterion (see Criterion 3, above) [Act 55, § (c)]. The additional credits for voluntary agreements are allowed as follows:

(1) If the reasonable value of the institution's contribution is equal to or less than 0.15% of its program service revenue, the institution may credit the entire contribution at 150% of its value.

(2) If the reasonable value of the institution's contribution is greater than 0.15% but less than 0.25% of its program service revenue, the institution may credit the entire contribution at 250% of its value.

(3) If the reasonable value of the institution's contribution is equal to or greater than 0.25% of its program service revenue, the institution may credit the entire contribution at 350% of its value.

• *Unfair competition with small businesses*

It is the policy of Act 55 that institutions of purely public charity do not use their tax-exempt status to compete unfairly with small businesses [10 P.S. § 378(a)]. An institution of purely public charity may not fund, capitalize, guarantee the indebtedness of lease obligations of, or subsidize a commercial business that is unrelated to its charitable purpose as stated in its charter or governing legal documents [10 P.S. § 378(a)]. A small business is any self-employed individual, sole proprietorship, firm, corporation, partnership, association, or other entity that (1) has fewer than 101 full-time employees and (2) is subject to income taxation under the Tax Reform Code of Pennsylvania [10 P.S. § 373].

Exceptions: Institutions are not in violation of this prohibition if any of the following apply:

(1) The commercial business is intended only for the use of its employees, staff, alumni, faculty, members, students, clients, volunteers, patients or residents. This does not include those whose only relationship with the institution is the receipt of products or services of the commercial business.

(2) The commercial business results in sales to the general public that are incidental or periodic rather than permanent and ongoing.

(3) The institution engages in a new commercial business upon formal request to do so by the Commonwealth or a political subdivision.

(4) The institution engages in or supports a commercial business in existence prior to the effective date of this prohibition and does not substantially expand the scope of the commercial business. Any injunction issued against such an institution is limited to restraining any substantial expansion of the scope of the commercial business that is initiated after the effective date of this prohibition. The unfair competition prohibition became effective 120 days after the enactment of Act 55 on November 26, 1997.

Mandatory arbitration: The Department of State will establish a system of mandatory arbitration to receive all complaints from aggrieved small business relating to an institution of purely public charity's alleged unfair competition. Upon receipt of a complaint, the Department will direct how the complaint is to be resolved. For details see 10 P.S. § 378(i). Either party may initiate a de novo appeal from the arbitrator's decision in the court of common pleas of the judicial district in

¶3505

which the arbitration took place within 30 days of the arbitrator's decision. [Act 55, § 8(i)(9)]. The remedies set forth in § 8(i) of Act 55 are the exclusive remedies available to an aggrieved small business [10 P.S. § 378(i)(14)].

• *State-related universities*

All real property owned by state-related universities (or owned by the Commonwealth and used by a state-related university) is and shall be deemed public property for purposes of the Constitution of Pennsylvania and Commonwealth tax laws and shall be exempt from all state and local taxation when actually and regularly used for public purposes [Act 55, § 4(b); 10 P.S. § 374(b)]. See the discussion of the *Pennsylvania State University* case at ¶ 3403 under Tax Immunity for treatment of state-related universities prior to passage of the Purely Public Charities Act.

• *Residential housing*

A charitable organization providing residential housing services in which the charitable nonprofit organization receives subsidies for at least 95% of the residential housing units from a low-income federal housing program shall remain a "purely public charity" with tax-exempt status, provided that any surplus from such assistance or subsidy is monitored by the appropriate governmental agency and is used solely to advance common charitable purposes within the charitable organization [72 P.S. § 7204(a)(3)]. The Institutions of Purely Public Charity Act did not repeal this provision.

• *Lobbying and campaigning*

An institution of public charity may conduct activities intended to influence legislation, provided that no substantial part of its activities consists of (1) carrying on propaganda (except as otherwise provided in IRC § 501(h)) or (2) participating in or intervening in (including the publishing or distributing of statements) any political campaign on behalf of, or in opposition to, any candidate for public office (as interpreted under IRC § 501(h)) [10 P.S. § 375(i)].

• *Civil penalty*

In addition to any penalties authorized by the Tax Reform Code, the Department of Revenue may impose an administrative penalty not to exceed $500 for any willful and knowing violation of Act 55. This penalty does not apply to any violation of the unfair competition provisions of § 8 of Act 55 [10 P.S. § 383].

• *Parcel review*

A political subdivision may make a determination whether a parcel of property or a portion of a parcel of property is being used to advance the charitable purposes of an institution and make an assessment of the taxability based on the use of the parcel. A political subdivision may file challenges or make determinations as to whether a particular parcel of property is being used to advance the charitable purposes of an institution of purely public charity [10 P.S. § 375(h)].

Caution

Some of the cases discussed below were decided prior to the passage of the Institutions of Purely Public Charity Act (Act 55) and do not address the issue of whether the entity meets the requirements of Act 55. Entities must meet first the constitutional requirements set out in *Hospital Utilization Project* and then the statutory requirements of the Institutions of Purely Public Charity Act. See, for example, *G.D.L. Plaza Corp. v. Council Rock Sch. Dist.*, 526 A.2d 1173 (Pa. 1987) and *Community Options, Inc. v. Allegheny County Board of Property Assessment, Appeals and Review*, 813 A.2d 680 (Pa. 2002).

¶3505

Cases—Qualify as Purely Public Charities

• *Arboretum*

Longwood Gardens is a large, world-renowned garden in Chester County. It was held to be a purely public charity [*Unionville-Chadds Ford School District v. Chester County Board of Assessment Appeals and Longwood Gardens, Inc.*, 719 A.2d 397 (Pa. 1998), *aff'g* 692 A.2d 1136 (Pa.Commw. 1997)]. The main issue in this case was whether Longwood benefited a substantial and indefinite class of persons who are legitimate subjects of charity. The school district contended that legitimate subjects of charity consist only of the poor, the infirm, and the needy. The courts did not agree. There is no requirement that all benefits bestowed by a purely public charity go only to the financially needy; a purely public charity can provide members of the general public with resources that would not otherwise be within their financial reach.

• *Care facility for members of religious order*

A nonprofit corporation that maintained a personal care service facility for members of its religious order and for qualified members of the public met the criteria for a total exemption from Pennsylvania property taxes as a purely public charity. The county taxing authority had adjusted the status of the property from completely tax exempt to partially tax exempt once the corporation began admitting members of the public to the facility. The county reasoned that services provided to public residents were taxable because the residents were required to pledge assets to cover the costs of residency. However, the Court ruled that the corporation still qualified as an institution of purely public charity and was therefore still entitled to a full tax exemption [*Missionary Sisters of the Most Sacred Heart of Jesus, Inc. v. Berks County Board of Assessment Appeals*, Pa.Commw., No. 1286 C.D. 2005, December 14, 2005].

• *Church property*

Job center: A job center to assist displaced workers that was owned by St. Mary Magdalen Church and the Diocese of Pittsburgh satisfied all of the requirements of the Institutions of Purely Public Charity Act. Therefore, the job center was a purely public charity even though 95% of the building was leased to for-profit and nonprofit entities whose missions involved helping the unemployed and generating new businesses for the local economy [*Borough of Homestead v. St. Mary Magdalen Church*, 798 A.2d 823 (Pa.Commw. 2002)].

• *Colleges and universities*

Staff housing: A college provided residences to certain employees. One residence was provided to the vice-president for alumni development and alumni relations, and he was required, as a condition of his employment, to live in the house and use it to encourage a personal and informal relationship with college donors. The residence, in fact, was used for such functions as meetings, picnics, receptions, and dinners for donors and potential donors. The Commonwealth Court found that the use of the residence furthered the general purpose of the college and was, therefore, exempt [*In re Swarthmore College*, 643 A.2d 1152 (Pa.Commw. 1994)].

In another case, Swarthmore College provided residences to college maintenance personnel who had to agree to be on constant call to respond to emergencies and nighttime calls. The Commonwealth Court held that having personnel available at all times to handle emergencies was an actual and regular use of the property for the purposes of the college and was reasonably necessary to the occupancy and enjoyment of the college. Therefore, the residences were exempt [*In re Swarthmore College (508 Field House Lane)*, 645 A.2d 470 (Pa.Commw. 1994)].

College property: Washington and Jefferson College (W&J), a private liberal arts college, was found to be a purely public charity because it satisfied the five-prong test

¶3505

of *Hospital Utilization* [*City of Washington v. Washington & Jefferson College*, 704 A.2d 120 (Pa. 1997), *aff'g* 666 A.2d 352 (Pa.Commw. 1995)].

• *Hospitals*

The following hospitals that satisfied all the criteria of *HUP* were held to be purely public charities:

(1) *Carbon-Schuylkill Community Hospital, Inc. t/a Miners Memorial Medical Center v. Schuylkill County Board of Assessment Appeals*, Pa.Commw., No. 1969 C.D. 2000 (July 9, 2001), opinion not reported.

(2) *In re Appeal of Community General Hospital from a Decision of the Board of Assessment Appeals of Berks County*, 708 A.2d 124 (Pa.Commw. 1998).

(3) *Lehighton Area School District v. Carbon County Board of Assessment and Gnaden Huetten Memorial Hospital*, 708 A.2d 1297 (Pa.Commw. 1998), *app. den.*, 732 A.2d 1211 (Pa. 1998).

(4) *Lewistown Hospital v. Mifflin County Board of Assessment Appeals*, 706 A.2d 1269 (Pa.Commw. 1998).

(5) *Saint Joseph Hospital v. Berks County Board of Assessment Appeals*, 709 A.2d 928 (Pa.Commw. 1998).

(6) *Wilson Area School District v. Easton Hospital*, 747 A.2d 877 (Pa. 2000), *aff'g* 708 A.2d 835 (Pa.Commw. 1998).

• *Legal education*

The American Law Institute (ALI) is a nonprofit corporation organized under the law of the District of Columbia with its principal place of business in Philadelphia. ALI's charitable purposes are education and legal reform. The Board of Finance and Revenue denied renewal of ALI's sales and use tax exemption as an institution of purely public charity, arguing that ALI was not entitled to the exemption because its purpose is to provide educational services, that it does not benefit an indefinite number of persons but, rather, a large, definite class of beneficiaries, and that its primary beneficiaries are attorneys, who are not the legitimate subjects of charity. On appeal, the Commonwealth Court disagreed, holding that continuing legal education for attorneys helps ensure that attorneys are able to discharge their duties to the public, thus benefiting a substantial and indefinite class of persons who are legitimate subjects of charity. ALI, therefore, qualified as a purely public charity [*American Law Institute v. Cmwlth.*, 890 A.2d 436 (Pa.Commw. 2006); aff'd per curiam, 901 A.2d 1030 (Pa. 2006)].

• *Nursing homes*

Margaret Seneca Place: A nursing home qualified as a purely public charity even though it accepted Medicaid payments to help defray the cost of caring for patients. The nursing home was established by a hospital organization to care for the indigent elderly. The Commonwealth Court had held that the nursing home did not qualify as a purely public charity because all of the residents are either self-paying or are paid for by Medicare or Medicaid and that the home intended to make a profit (even though it had never made a profit). The Commonwealth Court opinion was reversed by the Pennsylvania Supreme Court, which ruled that the nursing home met all five prongs of the *Hospital Utilization* case. Accepting Medicaid on behalf of indigent patients did not negate the fact that much of the nursing home's care was rendered gratuitously [*St. Margaret Seneca Place v. Board of Assessment Appeals and Review, et al.*, 640 A.2d 380 (Pa. 1994), *rev'g* 604 A.2d 1119 (Pa.Commw. 1992)].

RHA: A taxing district asserted that a taxpayer, an operator of a nursing, home did not (1) donate or gratuitously render a substantial portion of its services or (2) operate entirely free form private profit motive, as required by the Institutions of Purely Public Charities Act. The other three purely public charity criteria were not in question. The Commonwealth Court held that the taxpayer met both of the contested criteria in the enabling legislation [*In re RHA Pennsylvania Nursing Homes v. Cmwlth.*, 747 A.2d 1257 (Pa.Commw. 2000)].

Lutheran Home: The taxing authority and taxpayer stipulated that Lutheran Home is an institution of purely public charity within the meaning of the Institutions of Purely Public Charity Act, but they could not agree that the portion of the Home known as Luther Ridge met the Act's criteria. Luther Ridge admitted only residents who had enough assets to pay for its services for a reasonable period of time. However, the home had a non-eviction policy that essentially provided that the costs of meeting residents' most basic needs will be furnished free of charge they run out of funds. Schuylkill County denied a property tax exemption because, it said, Luther Ridge did not advance a charitable purpose or relieve the government of some of its burden. The Court, however, found that the non-eviction policy advanced the Home's charitable purpose and relieved the government of some of its burden by providing free services to residents who had no funds and by providing Ministries programs to the community [*The Lutheran Home at Topton, Pennsylvania v. Schuylkill County Board of Assessment Appeals*, Pa.Commw., No. 989 C.D. 2000 (May 23, 2001)].

Hahn Home: Hahn Home was held to advance a charitable purpose by providing a home and financial support to its residents (elderly women) even though it required the residents to turn over all their assets to the Home. The residents' contributions were insufficient to pay all of their future living, medical, and nursing home expenses and continue to have quality of life [*Hahn Home v. York County Board of Assessment Appeals*, 778 A.2d 755 (Pa.Commw. 2001)].

Albright Care Services: Albright Care Services owned and operated two licensed continuing care facilities in Pennsylvania. The facilities provided a continuum of care for residents including independent living facilities, assisted living/personal care facilities, and a skilled nursing facility. The Commonwealth Court, in an unreported decision, found Albright to be an institution of purely public charity entitled to an exemption from real estate taxes. *Albright Care Services v. Union County Board of Assessment*, 2014 WL 316588 (Jan. 29, 2014).

• *Property under construction*

Property may be exempt even though it is still under construction or renovation and not actually occupied by the charitable institution [*Senior Citizen Health Care Council of Erie County, Pennsylvania, Inc. v. Board of Tax Assessment Appeals of Erie County*, 678 A.2d 430 (Pa.Commw. 1996)].

• *Rehabilitation center*

An alcohol and drug rehabilitation center was held to be a purely public charity [*Gateway Rehabilitation Center, Inc.*, 710 A.2d 1239 (Pa.Commw. 1998)].

• *Residential housing services*

Any charitable organization providing residential housing services in which the charitable nonprofit organization receives subsidies for at least 95% of the residential housing units from a low-income federal housing program will remain a purely public charity if any surplus from any assistance or subsidy is monitored by the appropriate governmental agency and is used solely to advance common charitable purposes within the organization [72 P.S. § 7204(a)(3)].

• *Schools*

The Hill School is a private school for boys providing college preparatory courses. The Pottstown School District, where the Hill School is located, challenged the tax-exempt status of land owned by the Hill School. The parties agreed that the School met all the necessary legal criteria necessary to qualify as a purely public charity except that of benefitting a substantial and indefinite class of persons. The

¶3505

School District argued that not accepting female students violated this criterion. The Court disagreed: "A charity may restrict its admission to a class of humanity, and still be public." The test was whether the school excluded students based on a voluntary association or an involuntary characteristic. Thus, the Hill School met the requirement to benefit a substantial and indefinite class of people and qualified as a "purely public charity" for Pennsylvania real property tax purposes [*Pottstown School District v. Hill School*, 786 A.2d 312 (Pa.Commw. 2001)]. In *Friends of Pa. Leadership Charter Sch. v. Chester Cnty. Bd. of Assessment Appeals*, 627 Pa. 446, 101 A.3d 66 (2014), a charter school exemption could not be applied retroactively.

• *Senior citizens' home*

   Center Presbyterian: A nonprofit corporation that operated an apartment building for low-income elderly or disabled persons satisfied the requirements as a purely public charity [*Center Presbyterian Housing, Inc.*, Pa.Commw., No. 2838 C.D. 2002 (August 6, 2003), opinion not reported].

   Grace Center: A three-judge panel of the Commonwealth Court has ruled that a non-profit community living home that rented apartments to senior citizens satisfied all constitutional and statutory requirements as a purely public charity [*Grace Center Community Living Corp. v. Indiana County*, 796 A.2d 1008 (Pa.Commw. 2002)].

• *Theater*

   Nonprofit theater was uncompensated for more than 5% of its goods and services and was found to relieve the government of a burden for purposes of the HUP test. [*Pocono Cmty. Theater v. Monroe Cty Bd. of Assessment*, 142 A.3d 110 (Pa.Commw. Ct. 2016)]

• *YMCA*

   The Borough of Sewickley challenged the exemption of YMCA property. The Commonwealth Court held that the YMCA was entitled to a Pennsylvania real property tax exemption on the portion of its property that was open to both members and nonmembers because it qualified as a purely public charity under both the *HUP* criteria and the criteria of Act 55. It was not, however, entitled to an exemption on the portion of its property that was open only to members or on the portion of its property that was leased to a rehabilitation center [*Sewickley Valley YMCA v. Borough of Sewickley*, 774 A.2d 1 (Pa.Commw. 2001)].

Cases—Do Not Qualify as Purely Public Charities

• *Charitable and religious nonprofit corporation*

   A charitable and religious community was held not to be a purely public charity because the president of the corporation and his wife exercised "reality of control" over the organization and because the organization did not operate free from a private profit motive (*e.g.*, the value of the goods and services provided to the president and his family exceeded the total value of all goods and services provided to the needy in 2003) [*St. Joseph's House v. Chester County Board of Assessment Appeals*, Pa.Commw., No. 1645 C.D. 2004 (February 28, 2005)].

• *Church*

   The Court of Common Pleas held that the property owned by the Catholic Church (a purely public charity) and rented to a pro-life organization (also a purely public charity) was exempt from real estate taxation [*Appeal of Archdiocese of Philadelphia*, 617 A.2d 821 (1992); *appeal withdrawn* 624 A.2d 112 (1993)]. However, this decision was reversed by the Commonwealth Court [*Appeal of the Archdiocese of Philadelphia*, Pa.Commw., No. 1269 C.D. 1991 (June 15, 1992)]. The Commonwealth Court ruled that the property was not exempt because (1) the Church received rental income from the property and (2) the Church did not use and occupy the property.

• *Hospitals*

Hospital not free of profit motive: A hospital, following a corporate reorganization, no longer met the five-prong test of *Hospitalization Utilization* [*School District of City of Erie and County of Erie v. Hamot Medical Center of the City of Erie and Erie County Board of Assessment Appeals*, 602 A.2d 407 (Pa.Commw. 1992)]. The hospital in this case was required, as condition of its licensure, to provide emergency room treatment to patients who could not afford it. It aggressively pursued patients who did not pay bills; and, in the opinion of the court, demonstrated that it did not service primarily those who cannot afford the usual fee, causing it to fail the second prong of the *Hospital Utilization* test. In addition, the hospital in *Hamot* also failed the third, fourth, and fifth prongs of the *Hospital Utilization* test. In the *Hamot* case, the court clearly indicated that the five-prong test of *Hospital Utilization* was the appropriate test to use to test for status as a public charity under the real property laws [*Trustees of the University of Pennsylvania*, 649 A.2d 154 (Pa.Commw. 1994)].

Excessive compensation: A hospital that did not operate free of a profit motive was held not to be a purely public charity. Executive compensation was excessive, and the hospital diverted substantial funds to a nonprofit corporation that exercised supervision over hospital finances [*Pinnacle Health Hospitals (Harrisburg Hospital), Pinnacle Health Hospitals (Polyclinic Medical Center) v. Dauphin County Board of Assessments*, 708 A.2d 1284 (Pa.Commw. 1988)].

• *Independent living component of retirement community*

Taxpayer operated as a licensed continuing care retirement community. Located on its property was a 59-bed skilled nursing home, a 53-bed assisted living compound, and 93 apartments that functioned as the independent living component of the retirement community. The skilled nursing home and the assisted living compound were exempted from property tax. However, the Commonwealth Court held that the independent living component was not entitled to exemption because there was no evidence that the taxpayer donated a substantial portion of its services to residents living in the independent living apartments; therefore, the independent living component did not meet the definition of a purely public charity [*Alliance Home of Carlisle v. Board of Assessment Appeals*, Pa.Commw., No. 595 C.D. 2002 (June 15, 2004)]. See, also, *Appeal of Lutheran Social Services*, 539 A.2d 895 (Pa.Commw. 1988) and *Appeal of Bethlen Home*, 557 A.2d 828 (Pa.Commw. 1989).

• *Medical clinic*

A medical clinic (Guthrie) did not qualify as a purely public charity because it did not carry its burden of showing that it operated entirely free from private profit motive. Guthrie claimed that physician compensation was not based on its financial performance, but physician compensation was based on each physician's "productivity." In addition, Guthrie offered a profit sharing plan and could give discretionary bonuses to employees. The Court ruled that each physician's compensation was based on the revenue that the physician produced for the clinic [*Guthrie Clinic, Ltd. V. Sullivan County Board of Assessment Appeals* (Pa.Commw., No. 1099 C.D. 2005, April 25, 2006].

• *YMCA*

Property used primarily by members: The city of Pittsburgh and Allegheny County challenged the exempt status of a new building of the downtown YMCA. The position of the city and county was that the facility existed primarily to serve dues-paying members rather than the general public and failed to satisfy several of the criteria of *Hospital Utilization* [*City of Pittsburgh v. Board of Property Assessment*, 564 A.2d 1026 (Pa.Commw. 1989)].

Leased property and property used only by members: The Borough of Sewickley challenged the exemption of YMCA property. The Commonwealth Court held that

¶3505

the YMCA was entitled to a Pennsylvania real property tax exemption on the portion of its property that was open to both members and nonmembers because it qualified as a purely public charity under both the *HUP* criteria and the criteria of Act 55. It was not, however, entitled to an exemption on the portion of its property that was open only to members or on the portion of its property that was leased to a rehabilitation center [*Sewickley Valley YMCA v. Borough of Sewickley*, 774 A.2d 1 (Pa.Commw. 2001)].

• *Personal care home*

A nonprofit corporation that operated a personal care home was denied status as a purely public charity because it charged an average monthly rental of $1,400. Residents signed an agreement that stated the home could terminate the agreement in the event that no funds were available, and the home had never accepted a client who could not afford to pay the monthly rental fee [*In re Appeal of Capital Extended Care from Dauphin County Board of Assessment Appeals*, 609 A.2d 896 (Pa.Commw. 1992)].

• *Nursing home/Group home*

A long term/skilled care nursing home was denied an exemption because it was not founded, endowed, and maintained by a public or private charity. It was created by a gospel singing group known as The Couriers, not a public or private charity [*The Couriers-Susquehanna, Inc. v. County of Dauphin*, 693 A.2d 626 (Pa.Commw. 1997)]. The operator of a group home for intellectually disabled persons was denied purely public charity status because it failed to demonstrate that it donated or gratuitously rendered a substantial portion of its services. *ARC Human Services, Inc. v. Clearfield County Assessment Office*, 2015 WL 4179786 (2015).

• *Summer camp*

The court found that three nonprofit corporations that conducted summer camps to educate children in the Jewish religion were not purely public charities because they did not prove that their activities relieved the government of some of its burden [*Associated YM-YWHA of Greater New York/Camp Poyntelle v. County of Wayne*, 613 A.2d 125 (Pa.Commw. 1992)]. Even though the corporations provided food and medical services to campers, the camps received government subsidies of food, milk, and dry goods. The corporations' claim that they were making the campers morally responsible citizens was an indirect benefit that did not support a charitable exemption. However, the court concluded that the buildings in which religious services were held (and five acres surrounding each building) were exempt under the religious exemption.

Standard-setting body for graduate medical education: An institution whose primary purpose is to provide standards for graduate medical education in internal medicine throughout the United States is not a purely public charity because the internists are the beneficiaries of the organization's activities. The sole purpose of the organization's activities is to give the internists additional credentials needed to practice medicine in their chosen area, not to provide medical care to segments of society, who are legitimate objects of charity [*Board of Tax Revision of the City of Philadelphia v. American Board of Internal Medicine*, 623 A.2d 418 (Pa.Commw. 1993)].

• *Colleges and universities*

Commercial building on land owned by University: A retail/office building was built on land owned by the University of Pennsylvania by a for-profit partnership, in which the University was one of the partners. The land was leased to the partnership for 99 years. Since the partnership, not the University, was the owner of the building, the University was not entitled to a property tax exemption. The University was not entitled to a partial exemption based on its ownership share in the partnership because the partnership was not purely a public charity. The University's share of partnership profits was taxable as an interest in a for-profit business. Furthermore, the University was not entitled to an exemption for the land because it was leased to a commercial enterprise [*The Trustees of the University of Pennsylvania*, 649 A.2d 154 (Pa.Commw. 1994)].

• *County-funded youth services organization*

One of the requirements for classification as a purely public charity is that the organization relieves the government of some of its burden. Community Services Foundation, Inc., was a not-for-profit corporation that provides residential, educational, and counseling services to troubled youth. It was tax-exempt for federal tax purposes. However, it was not, according to the court, a purely public charity for Pennsylvania property tax purposes because it relied primarily upon funds provided by the county and thus did not relieve the government of some of its burden [*Community Services Foundation, Inc. v. Bucks County Board of Assessment and Revision of Taxes*, 672 A.2d 373 (1996), *app. den.*, 687 A.2d 379 (Pa.Commw. 1996)].

Supreme Court Rejects Analysis in Community Service

The Pennsylvania Supreme Court has rejected the Commonwealth Court's analysis in Community Service's Foundation as inconsistent with the *Hospital Utilization Project* test as a matter of law [*Community Options, Inc. v. Allegheny County Board of Property Assessment, Appeals, and Review*, 747 A.2d 877 (Pa. 2000)]. In *Community Options* (discussed below), the Supreme Court held that the *Hospital Utilization Project* test does not require a specific threshold of private funding and ruled that an organization that received most of its funds from government sources was entitled to an exemption.

• *Public housing*

Public housing for elderly and handicapped maintained by a not-for-profit corporation: Organizations that have mutual benefit functions primarily for members are not exempt, even though they may perform some work that is charitable in nature. See *G.D.L. Plaza Corp. v. Council Rock School District*, 526 A.2d 1173 (Pa. 1987), in which it was held that a nonprofit corporation operating a housing project for elderly and handicapped persons was not a purely public charity because a federal subsidy eliminated the financial risk so that the project was not maintained by public or private charity as required by statute.

• *Rehabilitation center*

Nonprofit rehabilitation center: A nonprofit rehabilitation center in Neshannock Township School District was held to be ineligible for a Pennsylvania real property tax exemption because it competed with for-profit rehabilitation centers [*Jameson Care Center, Inc. v. County of Lawrence*, 753 A.2d 902 (Pa.Commw. 2000)].

• *Retirement community*

A continuing care retirement community was not exempt from real estate tax as a purely public charity because it did not satisfy the constitutional five-prong test established by the Pennsylvania Supreme Court in *Hospital Utilization Project* (HUP test). Rather than advancing a charitable purpose benefitting the general public, the community catered to well-qualified seniors who could afford substantial entrance fees, monthly fees, and other fees. See *Re: Appeal of Dunwoody Village*, Pa.Commw., No. 1311 C.D. 2011, July 9, 2012.

• *Services for mentally disabled*

Community Options, Inc., a not-for-profit corporation that provided housing and related services to the mentally disabled, was entitled to a Pennsylvania real property tax exemption because it satisfied the requirements of a purely public charity under the Pennsylvania Constitution and the Institutions of Purely Public Charity Act [*Community Options, Inc. v. Board of Property Assessment, Appeals and*

¶3505

Review and Borough of Churchill, 813 A.2d 680 (Pa. 2002), *rev'g* 764 A.2d 645 (Pa.Commw. 2000)]. The Commonwealth Court had concluded that the taxpayer did not relieve the government of some of its burden because most of its funds came from government sources. Relieving the government of some of its burden is one of the criteria set forth in *Hospitalization Utilization Project (HUP) v. Cmwlth.*, 487 A.2d 1306 (Pa. 1985). Therefore, the Commonwealth Court concluded that the taxpayer was not entitled to an exemption. However, the Supreme Court held that the *Hospital Utilization Project* test does not require a specific threshold of private funding. According to the Pennsylvania Supreme Court, the Commonwealth has a statutory duty to provide care for individuals diagnosed with mental retardation and would bear the full burden of providing facilities and services to care for these individuals if it were not for institutions such as the taxpayer. Furthermore, the taxpayer performed some services without government funding and provided services that the government could not provide without acquiring facilities and incurring costs much greater than the fees it paid the taxpayer. Therefore, the taxpayer relieved the government of some of its burden and was entitled to an exemption.

¶3506 Rates

Rates vary among local jurisdictions. Consult the statutes for current rates.

Preferential Rates for Farmland

A borough may levy separate and different rates of taxation for municipal purposes on all real estate classified as nonfarmland (exclusive of building) and on all real estate classified as either buildings on land or farmland [§ 1302.1, of the Borough Code (Act of February 1, 1966, P.L. 1656)]. A higher rate may be levied on real estate classified as nonfarmland than on real estate classified as either buildings on land or farmland if the respective rates on nonfarmland and on buildings or farmland do not constitute a greater levy in the aggregate than that resulting from the maximum rate allowed by law on all real estate. The rates must be uniform as to all real estate within the classification. For this purpose, farmland includes any tract of land actively devoted to agricultural use, including (but not limited to) the commercial production of "crops, livestock, and livestock products" as defined in § 3 of the Agricultural Area Security Law [Act of June 30, 1981 (P.L. 128)].

Consult statutes for current rates.

• *Adjustment of rate after county-wide reassessment or change of predetermined ratio*

Except in counties of the first and second class, after any county makes a county-wide revaluation of real property at values based upon an established predetermined ratio or after any county changes its established predetermined ratio; such county must reduce each tax rate levied by the taxing district, if necessary, the first time it levies its real estate taxes on that revised assessment or valuation for the properties contained in the duplicate for that rate for the preceding year so that the total amount it levies on duplicate properties under the revised assessment is equal to the total amount it levied on duplicate properties the preceding year. Each tax rate must be fixed at a figure that will accomplish this purpose [53 Pa.C.S. § 8823(b)]. Two laws enacted on November 4, 2016, and effective January 3, 2017 (one for Allegheny County (Class 2) and one for county classes 2A-8), clarify provisions that require the readjustment of rates of tax on real property following a countywide reassessment. Each statute requires that a tax levied on an assessment roll must be made revenue neutral after a countywide reassessment. This provision clarifies that multiple tax rates cannot be adjusted differently so long as total revenue neutrality was the final outcome. The new measures require that tax rates previously set by referendum also must be adjusted in a revenue neutral manner, notwithstanding the fact that the rate was established by referendum. However, subsequent changes in the rate of those referendum taxes must be made according to the procedure established in the enabling act.

Increased rate by separate and specific vote: After establishing a tax rate under 53 Pa.C.S. § 8823(b), explained above, a political subdivision may, by a separate and specific vote, establish a final tax rate for the first year it levies its real estate taxes on a revised assessment [53 Pa.C.S. § 8823(c)]. However, each tax rate fixed by a separate and specific vote must be fixed at a figure that limits the total amount of taxes levied for that year against the real properties contained in the duplicate for the preceding year to not more than 10% greater than the total amount it levied on the duplicate properties for the preceding year.

New buildings, structures, and improvements: For the purpose of determining the total amount of taxes to be levied for the first year that a political subdivision levies its real estate taxes on a revised assessment or valuation, the amount levied on newly constructed buildings or structures or on increased valuations based on new improvements made to existing houses need not be considered [53 Pa.C.S. § 8823(d)].

Judicial exception: Notwithstanding the provisions limiting an increase in tax rate after a revised assessment or valuation, a political subdivision, with the approval of the Court of Common Pleas (upon showing good cause) may increase its tax rate [53 Pa.C.S. § 8823(e)].

Limitations on changes to certain rates: Notwithstanding 53 Pa.C.S. § 8823(c) or (e), the rate of any tax that was established by referendum and adjusted as provided in subsection (b) shall be subject to any subsequent increase, decrease, or elimination only as provided otherwise by law [53 Pa.C.S. § 8823(f)].

• *Special rule for fourth through eighth class counties*

Establishing initial rate: After any county has established and completed, for the entire county, the permanent system of records consisting of tax maps, property record cards, and property owner's index as required by law and has made its first county assessment of real property or subsequently makes a county-wide revision of assessment of real property under that system and at values based upon an established predetermined ratio or when a county changes its established predetermined ratio, each political subdivision must first reduce its real property tax rate to ensure that the total amount levied equals the amount levied the previous year, notwithstanding the increased valuations of such properties under the revised assessment. The tax rate must be fixed at a figure that will accomplish this purpose [72 P.S. § 5354.602(b)(1)].

Establishing final rate: After establishing an initial rate, a political subdivision may, but a separate and specific vote, establish a final tax rate for the first year it levies its real estate taxes on a revised assessment or valuation. This tax rate must be fixed at a figure that limits the total amount of taxes levied for that year against the real properties contained in the duplicate for the preceding year to not more than 110% in the case of a school district, and in the case of any other taxing district, not more than 105% of the total amount it levied on such properties the preceding year, notwithstanding the increased valuations of such properties under the new assessment system [72 P.S. § 5453.602(b)(2)]. For the purpose of determining the total amount of taxes to be levied for the first year, the amount to be levied on newly constructed buildings or structures or on increased valuations based on new improvements made to existing houses need not be considered [72 P.S. § 5453.602(b)(3)].

¶3507 Assessment and Valuation for First and Second Class Counties (General County Assessment Law)

Effective January 1, 2011, the new Consolidated County Assessment Law [Act 93 of 2010 (S.B. 218); 53 Pa.C.S. §§ 8801 *et seq.*], which is applicable to counties of Second Class A through Eighth, was passed. The Consolidated County Assessment Law replaced the General County Assessment with respect to all counties except those of the first and second class. See discussion at ¶3501.

A board is established in each county to supervise and revise assessments and hear appeals. This board is known by different names, usually the Board of Revision of Taxes (Philadelphia) or the Board of Assessment Appeals. Boards of assessment appeals examine reassessments and raise and lower assessments to ensure uniformity. There is no state supervision of local taxation. Taxpayers may appeal local decisions to the Court of Common Pleas (see ¶ 3511).

• *Valuation by assessors*

The law requires assessors to value property "according to the actual value thereof, and at such rates and prices for which the same would separately bona fide sell" [72 P.S. § 5020-402(a)]. The price at which any property may actually have been sold is a factor to be considered in the determination of actual value but is not controlling. In arriving at the actual price of real property, the impact of applicable rent restrictions, affordability requirements, or any other related restrictions prescribed by any federal or State programs must be considered [72 P.S. § 5020-402(c)(1)]. Federal or state income tax credits with respect to property are not considered real property or income attributable to real property [72 P.S. § 5020-402(c)(3)]. Assessment of property is the responsibility of local county assessors. Assessment is done annually. In practice, however, assessors set value at market value and then assign a tax value at a certain percentage of market (the ratio of assessed value to actual value (called the common level ratio). Common level ratios for all counties are published by the Pennsylvania State Tax Equalization Board on their web site at http://www.steb.state.pa.us/Default.asp. The common level ratio factors are published in the Pennsylvania Bulletin. See 35 Pa.B. 3365 for the 2004 common level ratio factors.

Preferential Assessment

Land devoted to agricultural use, agricultural reserve, and/or forest reserve use is subject to special assessment. See ¶ 3508A.

It is generally acknowledged that once an evaluation has been established for a taxable property, the valuation cannot be changed unless it is the result of a county-wide reassessment [*Radecke v. York County Board of Assessment Appeals*, 798 A.2d 265 (Pa.Commw. 2002)]. However, valuation that is not part of a county-wide reassessment can be changed under the following conditions [72 P.S. § 5453.602a]:

(1) When a parcel of land is divided and conveyed away in smaller parcels.

(2) When the economy of the county or any portion has depreciated or appreciated to such extent that real estate values generally in that area are affected.

(3) When improvements made to real property or existing improvements are removed or destroyed.

• *Methods of valuation*

There are three methods of valuation (*i.e.*, determining fair market value): (1) the cost approach; (2) the comparable sales approach; and (3) the income approach. These three methods, specified in § 402 of the General County Assessment Law, must be considered in conjunction with one another [72 P.S. § 5020-402].

(1) *Cost approach*: The cost approach considers the reproduction or replacement cost, as applicable, less depreciation and all forms of obsolescence [72 P.S. § 5020-402]. The cost approach is useful for valuing specialty property or newly developed property when the other approaches may not yield realistic results.

¶3507

However, when applying the cost approach to valuation, the value of the property for a specific use and the value of that use to the owner are not relevant [*In re PP&L, Inc.*, 838 A.2d 1 (Pa.Commw. 2003)]. Thus, it was proper to determine obsolescence factors in the valuation of a power plant by considering the site as one in general use [*Allegheny Energy Supply Company, LLC v. Greene County Board of Assessment Appeals*, Pa.Commw., No. 261 C.D. 2004 (February 23, 2005)].

(2) *Comparable sales approach*: The comparable sales approach involves the comparison of property to prices at which comparable properties have recently been sold. Most residential property is valued by using the comparable sales approach.

(3) *Income approach*: The income method of valuation involves the determination of the present value of the income from the property at an appropriate rate of return. This method is often used for residential and commercial rental properties.

Value-in-Use Approach

"Value-in-use" or "use value" is an approach that uses the specific income of a specific user of a property to value property. This approach is not permissible as a reflection of fair market value in any tax assessment case, regardless of which of the three approaches (see above) is used. Thus, an income approach valuation that relied on revenue generated by the number of turns of a turnstile as patrons entered an entertainment property was an improper method of valuation [*Hershey Entertainment and Resorts Co. v. Dauphin County Board of Assessment Appeals*, Pa.Commw., No. 1617 C.D. 2004 (May 18, 2005, *petition for appeal denied*, Pa.Sup.Ct., No. 522 MAL 2005, December 30, 2005)]. See also, *F & M Schaeffer Brewing Co. v. Lehigh County Board of Appeals*, 610 A.2d 1 (Pa. 1992), where a cost approach valuation that depended on the number of barrels of beer produced by a beer producer was held not permissible.

• *Spot reassessments*

A "spot reassessment" is the reassessment of a property or properties that is not conducted as part of a county-wide revised reassessment and that creates, sustains, or increases disproportionality among properties' assessed values [72 P.S. § 5342.1]. Spot reassessments are prohibited [72 P.S. § 4348.1]. A county's reassessment of an electric generating station after the expiration of the station's 10-year status as a Keystone Opportunity Zone property was an illegal spot assessment. *Duke Energy Fayette II, LLC v. Fayette County Board of Assessment Appeals*, No. 1406 C.D. 2014 (May 28, 2015). *Valley Forge Towers Apartments N, LP v. Upper Merion Area School District*, 163 A.3d 962 (2017), involved a declaratory judgment action filed by a group of apartment owners seeking to establish that the Upper Merion Area School District's practice of exclusively targeting high value, commercial properties selected by its tax consultant violated the Uniformity Clause of the Pennsylvania Constitution by effectively asserting that the school district was undertaking spot assessments in their property tax appeals. The Consolidated County Assessment Law, 53 Pa.C.S.A. § 8801, et seq. allows taxing jurisdictions (defined to include counties, municipalities and school districts) to place at issue and seek an increase in the assessment of any real property within their respective jurisdictions after certification of the assessment by the applicable county's chief assessor. The Consolidated County Assessment Law expressly excludes a real estate tax assessment appeal, whether filed by either a taxpayer or a taxing jurisdiction, from being classified as a spot assessment. Nevertheless, the Pennsylvania Supreme Court found that the Upper Merion School District's practice effectively represented spot assessments. The court found that under the Uniformity Clause all real property within any taxing jurisdiction is a single class and, therefore, taxing jurisdictions are not permitted to treat different real property subclassifications within their jurisdictions in a disparate manner. The court held that a Uniformity

¶3507

Clause violation is presented if the taxing jurisdiction intentionally or systematically subjects only commercial property within its jurisdiction to a reverse tax assessment appeal. The court also held that a taxpayer injured by such conduct was not limited to raising the constitutional violation as a defense to a property tax appeal. To the contrary, a taxpayer may affirmatively bring an action to curb the unlawful conduct of the taxing jurisdiction.

Improvement vs. interior renovation: A Montgomery County taxpayer owned a commercial property that was converted from a women's apparel shop to a brokerage office. The interior renovations included removal of dressing rooms, storage rooms, counters, carpeting, lighting, shelving and hanging fixtures, plus rewiring and installation of partition walls to create three offices at a cost of about $58,000. No changes were made to the outside of the building. Alerted by the taxpayer's building permit, the Monroe County Tax Assessor raised the assessment value from $136,200 to $176,148. The issue in this case was whether the renovations constituted an "improvement." If the renovations constituted an "improvement," the change in the valuation would be allowed under 72 P.S. §5453.602.1; if the renovations did not constitute an "improvement," the change in valuation would be an illegal spot reassessment. The Court concluded that the conversion from apparel store to brokerage office did not constitute an "improvement" within the meaning of the statute. Therefore, the reassessment was an illegal spot reassessment [*Groner v. Monroe County Board of Assessment Appeals*, 803 A.2d 1270 (Pa. 2002)].

• *Common-level ratios*

"Common-level ratio" means the ratio of assessed value to current market value used generally in the county as last determined by the State Tax Equalization Board. The common-level ratios established by the State Tax Equalization Board are published annually in *The Pennsylvania Bulletin*. The common-level ratios for different jurisdictions are not the same. Consult appropriate authorities for the common-level ratios for different years and counties. Common level ratios are also published on the web site of the Department of Community and Economic Development (DCED) at http://www.inventpa.com.

• *State Tax Equalization Board*

The State Tax Equalization Board was established by the General Assembly pursuant to the State Tax Equalization Board Law [Act of June 24, 1947 (P.L. 1046, No. 477)]. The State Tax Equalization Board is responsible for determining annually the aggregate market value of real estate in local jurisdictions and for establishing common level ratios for Pennsylvania counties. More information about the Board can be obtained at its web site located at [www.steb.state.pa.us/Default.asp].

Cases—Assessment and Valuation

Expert witness testimony: An expert witness's valuation of property need not be accepted in its entirety, even if it is unrebutted [*Green v. Schuylkill County Board of Assessment Appeals*, 772 A.2d 419 (Pa. 2001)]. In *Green*, the Pennsylvania Supreme Court upheld the action of the Commonwealth Court in its decision that the value of the taxpayer's property fell between the official valuation and the valuation of the taxpayer's expert witness. The Supreme Court held that a trial court may determine the value of property if its determination is based on its findings of evidence of record and its court's authority as a fact finder, so long as the court based its findings on the evidence of record and its reasoning is clearly stated.

Income approach to valuation: Taxpayer (V.V.P.) operates a tennis, racquetball, and squash facility. V.V.P.'s expert provided an appraisal of the fair market value of the property, relying primarily on the income approach (using actual business income and expense figures). The taxing district asserted that this approach resulted in a value to the current owners. However, the court stated that the income approach is the most appropriate method for appraisal of investment property (such as the tennis club) because such a property is valued by a purchaser for its ability to produce income. The taxpayer's expert explained that the property was severely limited as investment property and was currently being managed at maximum possible efficiency. Therefore, stated the court, the use of the income approach was reasonable and logical, given the circumstances surrounding this property [*In re Appeal of V.V.P. Partnership*, 647 A.2d 990 (Pa.Commw. 1994)].

Self-imposed restrictions did not affect valuation: A nonprofit housing cooperative imposed restrictions on the sale of units and voluntarily priced units at a rate far below that of comparable real estate in northeast Philadelphia. Fair market value is measured by the price that a willing, but not obligated, purchaser would pay to a willing, but not obligated, seller, taking into consideration all uses to which the property is adapted and might, in reason be applied [*Brooks Building Tax Assessment Case*, 137 A.2d 273 (Pa. 1958)]. Self-imposed restrictions on selling price are not like legally mandated restrictions that cannot be controlled by the buyer and seller. The actual price paid, also, was not indicative of the true market value of the property. The Philadelphia taxing authorities were justified in ignoring both the self-imposed restrictions and the actual selling price in valuation of the property for purposes of taxing real property [*Pennypack Woods Home Ownership Association v. Board of Revision of Taxes and City of Philadelphia and School District of Philadelphia*, 639 A.2d 1302 (Pa.Commw. 1994)].

Informal system of preferential treatment for active farms unconstitutional: For many years Susquehanna County had assessed actively farmed land at a lower rate than land not actively farmed. However, the Commonwealth Court held that this informal system of assessment violated the uniformity clause of the Pennsylvania Constitution because it resulted in nearly identical parcels of real estate being assessed at different rates merely because one parcel was actively farmed and the other was not. Both the Pennsylvania Farmland and Forest Land Assessment Act of 1974 and the Act of January 13, 1965, P.L. 1292, authorize counties to give preferential tax treatment to farmland pursuant to procedures set forth in the statutes. However, Susquehanna's informal system of preferential treatment did not conform to the procedures specified by these acts, and the county had no legal authority to adopt a system of preferential treatment not authorized by the statutes [*In re Appeal of Sidorek*, Pa.Commw., Nos. 1016 & 1094 C.D. 1992 (February 12, 1993)]. Preferential assessment is discussed at ¶3508A.

Ground water and soil contamination may lower property value: The Board of Assessment of Jefferson County did not consider environmental contamination in determining the value of a taxpayer's property that had been contaminated with chemicals. The Commonwealth Court held that the Board erred in doing so and remanded the case to the trial court to determine whether the Board's valuation of the property was excessive in light of the ground water and soil contamination. If the trial court concludes that the assessment is excessive, it must determine the fair market value of the property in its contaminated condition [*In re B.P. Oil Co., Inc. v. Board of Assessment Appeals of Jefferson County*, 633 A.2d 1241 (Pa.Commw. 1993)].

Valuation as an average of contending parties not an abuse of court's discretion: However, arbitrary averaging of common level ratio is not acceptable. The Pennsylvania Supreme Court held that setting the fair market value of property by splitting the difference between valuations when presented with conflicting testimony by equally credible witnesses was appropriate. However, splitting the difference between contentions of the contending experts was arbitrary. The Uniformity Clause of the Pennsylvania Constitution requires that the same common level ratio must be applied equally and uniformly to all real estate within a taxing authority's jurisdiction. The case was remanded to the trial court for resolution of the common level ratio issue [*Westinghouse Electric Co. v. Board of Property Assessment, Appeals and Review of Allegheny County,* 652 A.2d 1306 (Pa. 1995, *aff'g* 587 A.2d 820 (Pa.Commw. 1991)].

Reassessments must meet requirements of the "equalization objective": [Third Class County Assessment Act, 72 P.S. §5348(d)]: The objective of §7(d) is to reach an assessment that will accomplish equalization with other similar properties within the taxing district, of the Third Class County Assessment Law, as well as satisfy the Uniformity Clause of the Pennsylvania Constitution. Dauphin County conducted a county-wide reassessment in 1973. In 1983, the county determined that 90% of the properties were underassessed but that another county-wide reassessment was not economically feasible. Instead, the county attempted substantial revision of assessment in the city of Harrisburg using a ratio reassessment program. In 1984, using the ratio program, every property in the Shipoke area of Harrisburg was reassessed; it was the only area where the revised assessments were implemented. In 1985, the county implemented a county-wide reassessment after determining that the current assessment system had become increasingly unequal. In 1987—1988, the county focused on reassessing allegedly remodeled or rehabilitated property in the city of Harrisburg. The rehabilitated properties were assessed by first establishing the current market value in the year of the inspection (1987 or 1988), but unrehabilitated properties were still assessed under a base year system utilizing 1973 market value. These reassessments were found to violate both the Uniformity Clause of the Pennsylvania Constitution and the equalization objective of 72 P.S. §5348(d). The courts found that the reassessments were done in an arbitrary and careless manner and aggravated the lack of uniformity throughout Dauphin County [*City of Harrisburg v. Dauphin County Board of Assessment Appeals,* 677 A.2d 350 (Pa.Commw. 1996), *app. den.,* 693 A.2d (Pa. 1997) Pa.Commw.].

Levies on real estate taxes on county-wide reassessment cannot be implemented until the county-wide reassessment is 100% complete: Except in counties of the first class, no political subdivision can levy real estate taxes on a county-wide revised assessment of real property until the reassessment has been completed for the entire county [General County Assessment Law, Act of May 22, 1988, P.L. 853, §402(a)]. See *City of Harrisburg v. Dauphin County Board of Assessment Appeals,* discussed above. Philadelphia County is the only first class county. See discussion of classification of cities and counties at ¶3401.

¶3508 Assessment and Valuation for Second Class A through Eighth Class Counties (Consolidated County Assessment Law)

Assessments in counties of the second class A through the eighth class are governed by the provisions of 53 Pa.C.S. §8801 *et seq.* (The Consolidated County Assessment Law, effective January 1, 2011]. The Consolidated County Assessment Law replaces the Third Class Counties Assessments Act [72 P.S. §5342 *et seq.*]. See discussion at ¶¶3501 and 3502.

Caution: Act Should Also Be Consulted

This paragraph is an overview of the Consolidated County Assessment Law. It is not a complete explanation of assessment procedures in counties of second class A through eighth class counties. For details, consult the Act.

• *Valuation of property*

The county assessment office shall assess real property at a value based upon an established predetermined ratio that may not exceed 100% of actual value. The ratio is established and determined by the board of county commissioners may utilize the current market value or it may adopt a base-year market value. The base year is the year upon which real property market values are based for the most recent county-wide revision of assessment of real property or other prior year upon which the market value of all real property of the county is based for assessment purposes. Real property market values shall be equalized within the county and any changes by the board shall be expressed in terms of base-year values [53 Pa.C.S. § 8842(a)].

• *Actual value—General rule*

The following general rules apply in the determination of actual value:

(1) In arriving at actual value, the price at which any property may actually have been sold, either in the base year or in the current taxable year, is considered but is not controlling [53 Pa.C.S. § 8842(b)(1)(i)].

(2) The selling price is subject to revision by increase or decrease to accomplish equalization with other similar property within the county [53 Pa.C.S. § 8842(b)(1)(ii)].

(3) In arriving at the actual value, the following methods must be considered in conjunction with one another [53 Pa.C.S. § 8842(b)(1)(iii)]:

(a) Cost approach (*i.e.*, reproduction or replacement, as applicable, less depreciation and all forms of obsolescence.

(b) Comparable sales approach.

(c) Income approach.

• *Actual value—Wind energy generation property*

The valuation of real property used for the purpose of wind energy generation for assessment purposes must be arrived at by utilizing the capitalization approach to value. The valuation is determined by the capitalized value of the land lease agreements, supplemented by the sales comparison data approach as deemed necessary by the county assessor [53 Pa.C.S. § 8842(b)(2)].

• *Valuation—Catastrophic losses*

Persons who have suffered catastrophic losses to their property have the right to appeal before the board within the remainder of the county fiscal year in which the loss occurred, whichever period is longer. The duty of the board is to reassess the property to reflect the loss in value from the date of the property to the end of the taxable year. Any property improvements made subsequent to the catastrophic loss in the same year is not added to the assessment for the remainder of that year but is added for the following year [53 Pa.C.S. § 8815(a)]. The adjustments in assessment due to a catastrophe can be reflected in the form of a credit for the succeeding tax year or in the form of a refund if the property owner applies for a refund [53 Pa.C.S. § 8815(b)].

• *Changes in assessed valuation*

Assessors may change the assessed valuation on real property when a parcel of land is subdivided into smaller parcels or when improvements are made to real property or existing improvements are removed from real property or are destroyed [53 Pa.C.S. § 8817(a)].

• *Spot reassessments*

Spot reassessments are prohibited [53 Pa.C.S. § 8843]. *Valley Forge Towers Apartments N, LP v. Upper Merion Area School District*, 163 A.3d 962 (2017), involved a declaratory judgment action filed by a group of apartment owners seeking to establish that the Upper Merion Area School District's practice of exclusively targeting high value, commercial properties selected by its tax consultant violated the Uniformity Clause of the Pennsylvania Constitution by effectively asserting that the school district was undertaking spot assessments in their property tax appeals. The Consolidated County Assessment Law, 53 Pa.C.S.A. § 8801, et seq. allows taxing jurisdictions (defined to include counties, municipalities and school districts) to place at issue and seek an increase in the assessment of any real property within their respective jurisdictions after certification of the assessment by the applicable county's chief assessor. The Consolidated County Assessment Law expressly excludes a real estate tax assessment appeal, whether filed by either a taxpayer or a taxing jurisdiction, from being classified as a spot assessment. Nevertheless, the Pennsylvania Supreme Court found that the Upper Merion School District's practice effectively represented spot assessments. The court found that under the Uniformity Clause all real property within any taxing jurisdiction is a single class and, therefore, taxing jurisdictions are not permitted to treat different real property subclassifications within their jurisdictions in a disparate manner. The court held that a Uniformity Clause violation is presented if the taxing jurisdiction intentionally or systematically subjects only commercial property within its jurisdiction to a reverse tax assessment appeal. The court also held that a taxpayer injured by such conduct was not limited to raising the constitutional violation as a defense to a property tax appeal. To the contrary, a taxpayer may affirmatively bring an action to curb the unlawful conduct of the taxing jurisdiction.

¶ 3508A Preferential Assessment for Land Devoted to Agricultural Use, Agricultural Reserve, and/or Forest Reserve

• *In general*

Land devoted to agricultural use, agricultural reserve, and/or forest reserve (as defined in 72 P.S. § 5490.2) is subject to preferential assessment under the provisions of the Pennsylvania Farmland and Forestland Assessment Act of 1974 [72 P.S. § 5490.1 *et seq.*].

• *Agricultural use*

Agricultural use means use for the purpose of producing an agricultural commodity or is devoted to and meets the requirements and qualifications for payments or other compensation pursuant to a soil conservation program under an agreement with an agency of the federal government [72 P.S. § 5490.2]. The term includes the following:

(1) Any farmstead land on the tract.

(2) A woodlot.

(3) Any land that is rented to another person and used for the purpose of producing an agricultural commodity.

(4) Effective December 26, 2010, any land devoted to the development and operation of an alternative energy system, if a majority of the energy annually general is utilized on the tract.

• *Agricultural reserve*

Agricultural reserve means noncommercial open space lands used for outdoor recreation or the enjoyment of scenic or natural beauty and open to the public for such use, without charge or fee, on a nondiscriminatory bases. Effective December 26, 2010, the term includes any land devoted to the development and operation of an alternative energy system if a majority of the energy annually generated is utilized on the tract [72 P.S. § 5490.2].

• *Forest reserve*

Land, ten acres or more, stocked by forest trees of any size and capable of producing timber or other wood products. Effective December 26, 2010, the term includes any land devoted to the development and operation of an alternative energy system [72 P.S. § 5490.2].

• *Alternative energy system*

An alternative energy system is a facility or energy system that utilizes a Tier I energy source to generate alternative energy, including a facility or system that generates alternative energy for utilization onsite or for delivery of the energy generated to an energy distribution company or to an energy transmission system operated by a regional transmission organization. A Tier I energy source is one that is defined in § 2 of the Act of November 30, 2004 (P.L. 1672, No. 213), known as the "Alternative Energy Portfolio Standards Act." Alternative energy means electricity, heat, or other usable form of energy generated from a Tier I energy source [72 P.S. § 5490.2].

Retention of Land Use Category

With respect to the development of an alternative energy system that continues to meet the definition of agricultural use, agricultural reserve, or forest reserve, the land devoted to that development and operation retains the same land use category for preferential assessment as was approved for the land before the devotion took place [72 P.S. § 5490.5(b.1), effective December 26, 2010].

• *Eligibility for preferential assessment*

For general property tax purposes, the value of land that is presently devoted to agricultural use, agricultural reserve, and/or forest reserve shall, on application and approval of the owners for enrollment in the preferential assessment program (see discussion below), be the value the land has for its particular land use category, not its fair market value (*i.e.*, its "best and highest value"), if the following conditions are also met [72 P.S. § 5490.3(a)]:

(1) *Land presently devoted to agricultural use* must meet the following criteria [72 P.S. § 5490.3(a)(1)]:

(a) It was devoted to agricultural use for the preceding three years.

(b) It is not less than 10 contiguous acres in area (including the farmstead land) or has an anticipated annual gross income of at least $2,000.

(2) *Land presently devoted to agricultural reserve* must be not less than 10 contiguous acres in area (including the farmstead land) [72 P.S. § 5490.3(a)(2)].

(3) *Land presently devoted to forest reserve* must be not less than 10 contiguous acres in areas (including the farmstead land) [72 P.S. § 5490.3(a)(3)].

• *Enrollment in for preferential assessment*

A landowner may enroll one tract or more than one contiguous tract for enrollment if the total area to be enrolled meets the minimum requirements for eligibility. A landowner may not enroll less than the entire contiguous portion of land described in the deed applicable to a tract for which clean and green enrollment is sought. A tract of land that is used for agricultural use, agricultural reserve, or forest reserve purposes that does not meet the minimum eligibility requirements may be enrolled for preferential assessment if it is contiguous to a tract or tracts that have been previously enrolled by the landowner for preferential assessment [72 P.S. § 5490.3(a.1)].

• *Application for preferential assessment*

The county board for assessment appeals has the responsibility to accept and process applications for enrollment in the clean and green program. A complete and accurate application will be accepted by a county board or a county assessor if the property qualifies for preferential assessment (see above) [72 P.S. § 5490.4]. The deadline for applications is June 1 of the year immediately preceding the tax year for which preferential assessment is sought. Once enrolled, a homeowner does not have

¶3508A

to reapply for enrollment. However, landowners are required to notify their county tax assessment office of any changes to the status of their enrolled land. One application may include more than one land use category.

• *Separation of land covered by the preferential use assessment*

A "separation" is a division, by conveyance or other action of the owner, of lands enrolled qualifying for preferential assessment into two or more tracts of land [72 P.S. § 5490.2]. When a separation occurs, all tracts formed by the separation continue to receive preferential assessment, unless a subsequent abandonment of preferential use occurs within seven years of separation. If abandonment of the preferential use occurs within seven years of separation, the person changing the use is subject to liability for roll-back taxes (discussed below) [72 P.S. § 5490.6(a.2)].

• *Split-off of land covered by the preferential use assessment*

A "split-off" is a division, by conveyance or other action of the owner, of preferentially assessed lands devoted to agricultural use, agricultural reserve, or forest reserve into two or more tracts of land, one of which does not qualify for preferential assessment [72 P.S. § 5490.2]. The split-off of a part of land preferentially assessed land subjects the split-off land and the entire tract from which it was split off to roll-back taxes (discussed below). The landowner who conducts the split-off is liable for payment of roll-back taxes. [72 P.S. § 5490.6(a.1)(1)].

Split-off of small tracts: In the case of a split-off of a small tract that meets the requirements of 72 P.S. § 5490.6(a.1)(1), the landowner who conducts the split-off is liable for payment of roll-back taxes only with respect to the split-off portion of land. If the owner of the split-off tract subsequently changes the use of that land to an ineligible use, the owner of the original tract that continues to be eligible for preferential assessment is not liable for any roll-back taxes triggered as a result [72 P.S. § 5490.6(a.1(2)].

Condemnations: No roll-back taxes are due if a split-off occurs through a condemnation [72 P.S. § 5490.6(a.1)(2.1)].

• *Roll-back taxes due when special-use abandoned*

General rule: The general rule is that if special use of part of a tract of special-use land is abandoned within seven years of separation from the entire tract, the person changing the use is subject to liability for roll-back taxes at the rate of 6% per year on the entire tract of special-use land (not just the separated part) [72 P.S. § 5490.6]. See, for example, *Feick v. Berks County Board of Assessment Appeals and Antietam School District*, 720 A.2d 504 (Pa.Commw. 1998), in which the court ruled that the transfer of a tract of preferentially assessed forest reserve must satisfy the 10-acre requirement of the Pennsylvania Farmland and Forest Land Assessment Act irrespective of the status of the property contiguous to the tract. The taxpayer in *Feick*, who owned a 56.879-acre tract of preferentially assessed land, conveyed a 53.6-acre tract of the land (which continued to be eligible for preferential assessment), retaining 3.279 acres. Because the retained tract did not meet the eligibility requirements for preferential assessment (*i.e.*, it was less than 10 acres), the owner was subjected to roll-back taxes on all tracts.

Due date: Roll-back taxes become due on the change of use or on the date a well site restoration report is filed with the county assessor or any other termination of preferential use [72 P.S. § 5490.8(b)].

• *Roll-back taxes a lien upon property*

Unpaid roll-back taxes are a lien upon the property collectible in the manner provided by law for collection of delinquent taxes. Roll-back taxes become due on the date of the abandonment of the special use by the person causing the change in use [72 P.S. § 5490.8(b)]. Property is subject to lien even though the owners are not liable for taxes. See *Ertel v. Lycoming County Board of Assessment Appeals*, Pa.Commw., No. 1190 C.D. 2004 (March 2, 2005), *opinion not reported*, where couple who purchased property after it had been split-off were not liable for the roll-back taxes penalty arising from the split-off. However, the unpaid taxes triggered the attachment of a lien on the property, and the couple's challenge to the authority of the County tax assessor to calculate the amount of rollback taxes and to file a lien was unsuccessful.

Special circumstances: Taxing bodies of the taxing district in which special-use land is granted preferential assessment are not required to accept the roll-back taxes (and the accrued interest due and payable) if special use is abandoned for the purpose of granting or donating the special-use land to one of the following entities [72 P.S. § 5490.8(b)]:

(1) A school district.

(2) A municipality.

(3) A county.

(4) A volunteer fire department.

(5) A volunteer ambulance service.

(6) A not-for-profit corporation tax exempt under IRC § 501(c)(3) that, prior to accepting ownership of the land, enters into an agreement with the municipality in which the land is located that guarantees that the land will be used exclusively for recreational purposes, all of which will be available to the general public free of charge.

(7) A religious organization for construction or regular use as a church, synagogue, or other place or worship (including meeting, parking, and housing facilities and other facilities that further the religious purposes of the organization.

Exception for cemeteries: No roll-back taxes are due if special-use land is transferred to a not-for-profit corporation for use as a cemetery and at least 10 acres of land remain special-use property after removal [72 P.S. § 5490.8(e)(1)].

• *Exception for easement or right-of-way*

No roll-back taxes are due if special-use land, or an easement or a right-of-way in that land, is conveyed to a nonprofit corporation if the subject land meets the following requirements [72 P.S. § 5490.8(e)(1)]:

(1) It does not exceed 20 feet in width.

(2) It is used as a trail for nonmotorized passive recreational use.

(3) It is available without charge to the public.

(4) At least 10 acres of land remain in preferential assessment after conveyance.

• *Land devoted to or used for exploration for and removal of gas and oil*

Land subject to preferential assessment: Land subject to preferential assessment may be leased or otherwise devoted to the exploration for and removal of gas and oil, including the extraction of coal bed methane, and the development of appurtenant facilities, including new roads and bridges, pipelines, and other buildings or structures related to exploration for and removal of gas and oil and the extraction of coal bed methane [72 P.S. § 5490.6(c.1)(1), effective December 26, 2010]. No roll-back tax shall be imposed upon a landowner for activities related to the exploration for or removal of oil or gas, including the exploration for or removal of oil or gas, including the extraction of coal bed methane, conducted by parties other than the landowner that hold the rights to conduct such activities pursuant to an instrument, conveyance, or other vesting of the rights if the transfer of the rights occurred (1) before the land was enrolled for preferential assessment and (2) before December 26, 2010 [72 P.S. § 5490.6(c.2)(4), effective December 26, 2010].

¶3508A

Portions of land subject to preferential assessment: Portions of land subject to preferential assessment may be used for exploration for and removal of gas and oil, including the extraction of coal bed methane, and the development of appurtenant facilities, including new roads and bridges, pipelines, and other buildings or structures related to those activities [72 P.S. § 5490.6(c.1)(2), effective December 26, 2010]. Roll-back taxes are imposed upon those portions of land actually used for exploration for and removal of gas and oil, including the extraction of coal bed methane, and the development of appurtenant facilities, excluding land devoted to subsurface transmission or gathering lines, which is not subject to roll-back tax. The portion of land subject to roll-back tax is the restored well site and land that is incapable of being immediately used for agricultural use, agricultural reserve, or forest reserve activities, as measured from the well site restoration report approved by the Department of Environmental Protection as required by 25 Pa. Code 78.65 (relating to site restoration) or its subsequent version [72 P.S. § 5490.6(c.1)(4)].

Temporary leases: The owner of property subject to preference assessment may temporarily lease a portion of the land for pipe storage yards. However, roll-back taxes are imposed on those portions of land subject to preferential assessment that are temporarily leased or otherwise devoted for pipe storage yards; and the fair market value of those portions of land must be adjusted accordingly. Imposition of roll-back taxes of portion temporarily leased or devoted for pipe storage yards does not invalidate the preferential assessment of land that is not so leased or devoted. The lease may not exceed two years and cannot be extended or renewed. Following the exploration of the lease, the land must be restored to the original use that qualified it for preferential assessment [72 P.S. § 5490.6(c.3)].

• *Land leased or devoted to noncoal surface mining (effective July 7, 2011)*

The owner of property subject to preferential assessment may lease or otherwise devote land subject to preferential assessment to small noncoal surface mining [72 P.S. § 5490.6(c.4)(1)]. Rollback taxes shall be imposed upon those portions of land leased or otherwise devoted to small noncoal surface mining and the fair market value of those portions of the land shall be adjusted accordingly. Roll-back taxes on those portions of the land does not invalidate the preferential assessment of the land that is not leased or devoted to small noncoal surface mining, which continues to be eligible for preferential assessment if it continues to meet the requirements [72 P.S. § 5490.6(c.4)(1)]. Only one small noncoal surface mining permit may be active at any one time on land subject to a single application for preferential assessment [72 P.S. § 5490.6(c.4)(1)].

Subsequent Changes Activate Roll-Back Taxes

Any acquisition or subsequent resale or change in use of any of the removed land conveyed under 72 P.S. § 5490.8(e)(1) for use other than as a cemetery or as a trail will subject the nonprofit corporation to payment of roll-back taxes and interest due on the entire tract of land removed.

¶3509 Returns and Payment of Tax

Due dates for payment of real property taxes vary from jurisdiction to jurisdiction. Local dates should be checked. Local jurisdictions may allow installment payment of taxes (but no more than four installments) and discounts are allowed for prompt payment.

Real estate property tax returns are required in only one instance—acquisition of unseated lands. The term "unseated land" refers to privately-owned land in which no one has taken an interest that would indicate personal responsibility for taxes. If a person acquires unseated lands, he/she must file a statement with the county commissioners or board of assessment or revisions within one year of acquisition. This report must contain the required title information [General County Assessment

Law, Act of May 22, 1933, P.L. 853, Art. IV, §409]. Unseated land is assessed like other property unless someone fails to file the required report. Failure to file causes the assessment of the unseated land to be four times what it would otherwise be.

¶3509A Residential Visitability Design Tax Credit

• *Authorization of credit*

A residential visitability design tax credit is available for eligible property owners who renovate or build a new dwelling that contains design features that enhance the usability of the dwelling for persons with significant mobility impairment and that minimize the cost of full accessibility modifications, if necessary, at a later date [Act No. 132 of 2006 (S.B. 1158), §4(b)].

• *Amount of credit*

The amount of the credit is determined by the local taxing authority that levies tax on the property and cannot exceed the lesser of (1) $2,500 or (2) the total amount of the increased amount of property taxes owed during the first five years from the time the tax credit is approved [Act No. 132 of 2006 (S.B. 1158), §4(c)].

Temporary Storm Abatement and Refund Authorization

Pennsylvania political subdivisions that impose real property taxes may abate those taxes for the year 2011 on property that was damaged or destroyed by Hurricane Irene or Tropical Storm Lee. In addition, taxing authorities may, for a limited period, exempt from real property taxation the assessed valuation of reconstruction or repairs made to properties damaged or destroyed by those storms. For more details see Act No. 2012-71 (H.B. 1913).

¶3510 Collection of Tax

Usually, the owner of property is responsible for payment of real estate taxes. However, in some cases the authorities may look to someone else for payment (*e.g.,* tenants). There are various provisions for enforcement of collection, the most common of which are tax liens against property and sale of property to satisfy the taxes. Tax sales are discussed in this paragraph. Municipal tax liens are discussed at ¶3407, and Commonwealth tax liens are discussed at ¶4618.

• *Sources of authority*

Enabling legislation for the collection of property taxes in third to eighth class counties is the Local Tax Collection Law [72 P.S. §5511.1 *et seq.*]. The Local Tax Collection Law is applicable to all jurisdictions in Pennsylvania except for (1) first, second, and second class A cities (*i.e.,* Philadelphia, Pittsburgh, and Scranton) and (2) first and second class counties (*i.e.,* Philadelphia and Allegheny).

• *Tax collectors*

The terms "tax collector" or "elected tax collector" include all persons duly elected or appointed to collect property taxes [72 P.S. §5511.2].

Joint Collection

If a vacancy exists in the office of tax collector in a taxing district, the governing body of the taxing district may, by ordinance or resolution, enter into an agreement with the governing body of an adjoining or conveniently located taxing district for the joint collection of taxes under this act. Two or more taxing districts may enter into a joint collection agreement [72 P.S. §5511.4.2(a)].

• *Tax notices*

Tax notices (*i.e.,* bills) are sent to taxpayers by tax collectors. Under the Local Tax Collection Law (which applies to all counties except Philadelphia and Allegheny) tax collectors are required to send tax bills to all taxpayers on the tax duplicate within 30 days of receipt of the tax duplicate unless the taxing district extends the time. A tax notice, however, must be sent to taxpayers no later than the first day of July following receipt of the tax duplicate or no later than 15 days after delivery of the duplicate if the tax duplicate is delivered after June 16 [72 P.S. § 5511.6]. A "duplicate" is a listing of the valuation of persons and property within a taxing district taxable for the applicable year and may include a computerized billing register of annual taxes [72 P.S. § 5511.2].

Municipalities with home rule charters: Municipalities that have adopted a home rule charter may establish a different date for the sending of tax notices [72 P.S. § 5511.6].

No Notice Does Not Mean No Tax

Failure to receive notice does not relieve taxpayers from the payment of any taxes imposed by any taxing district. Taxpayers who do not receive notice are charged with their taxes as though they had received notice [72 P.S. § 5511.7].

• *Discounts*

The discount and penalty rates are established by the taxing district. However, taxpayers are entitled to a discount of at least 2% if their taxes are paid within two months after the date of the tax notice. This provision applies to cities of the second class A [72 P.S. § 5511.10(a)].

• *Penalties*

Taxpayers who fail to pay their taxes for four months after the date of the tax notice will be charged a penalty of up to 10%, which will be added to the taxes by the tax collector and collected by the tax collector. This provision applies to cities of the second class A [72 P.S. § 5511.10(a)].

Special Notice for Elderly

If a taxpayer has not paid real estate taxes within four months after the date of the tax notice, and the tax collector has reason to believe that the taxpayer is at least 60 years old, the tax collector must send a special notice in large print (eighteen point or larger) to the taxpayer. Failure to receive such special notice, however, does not relieve a taxpayer from the payment of tax [72 P.S. § 5511.10(b)].

• *Tax Claim Bureau*

Unless provision is made for alternative collective of taxes (see below), a tax claim bureau is created in each county in the office of the county commissioners [72 P.S. § 5860.201]. The county bureaus (or the alternative collection mechanisms) are responsible for the collection and distribution of taxes [72 P.S. § 5860.204].

• *Alternative collection of taxes*

In lieu of creating a bureau, counties are authorized to provide (by ordinance) for the appointment and compensation of agents, clerks, collectors, and other assistants and employees responsible for the collection and distribution of property taxes. These personnel may come from the private or public sector (*e.g.*, existing departments).

Any alternative collection method is subject to all of the notices, time frames, fees, and protections for property owners provided by law. Two or more counties may enter into a joint agreement to provide for the alternative collection of taxes [72 P.S. § 5860.201.1].

In *Lehighton Area School Dist. v. Carbon County Tax Claim Bur.*, 187 A.3d 280 (Pa Commw. 2018), the Commonwealth Court found that the trial court erred in holding that school districts that hired a private entity to collect delinquent property taxes was not entitled to second priority status in the distribution of proceeds from the sale of properties for delinquent property taxes. The Tax Claim Bureau sold the properties at a judicial sale. The Bureau then filed petitions for confirmation of the sales and prepared schedules for distribution of the sales proceeds. The school districts were not included on the distribution schedule. When the school districts filed a protest, the Bureau argued (and the trial court agreed) that by hiring a private party to collect delinquent property taxes on behalf of the school districts (as permitted under the Tax Liens Act), the school districts had opted out of the Bureau's collection services under the Tax Sale Law; thereby causing any sale proceeds due to the districts to no longer be considered "taxes" entitled to treatment as second priority claims under the Tax Sale Law. The Commonwealth Court disagreed with the Bureau and trial court, ruling that both the Tax Liens Act and the Tax Sale Law establish that all taxes levied on property by any taxing district are considered a first lien on the property, subordinate only to tax liens imposed by the Commonwealth. The court determined that the Tax Liens Act and Tax Sale Law are not mutually exclusive, but instead their provisions are designed to operate in conjunction with one another. Thus, when possible, the courts should give effect to the provisions of both.

• *Tax sale defined*

A tax sale is any sale at which a property is sold because the owner is delinquent in paying taxes. When a property owner is delinquent in the payment of taxes due, an upset sale is scheduled. If the upset price is not bid at an upset sale, a judicial sale may be scheduled. The requirements with respect to tax sales are contained in the "Real Estate Tax Sale Law" [72 P.S. § 5860.101 *et seq.*]. The notice requirements for tax sales apply to both upset sales and judicial sales [*Appeal of Richard Popkin*, Pa.Commw., No. 1669 C.D. 1999 (July 2, 2002)].

Upset price not bid: In cases where the upset price is not bid at a tax sale, the sale continues (but not beyond the end of the calendar year) without further advertising. At any time during or after the continuance, the county tax claim bureau may file a petition in the court of common pleas of the county to sell the property in a judicial sale pursuant to 72 P.S. §§ 5860.612 and 5860.612.1. If the taxing district gives written direction, the bureau must immediately file a petition for judicial sale [72 P.S. § 5860.10].

• *Notice requirements for tax sales*

Three types of notice are required for a valid tax sale: (1) publication; (2) certified mail; and (3) posting [72 P.S. § 5860.602]. The published notice, the mail notice, and the posted notice must state that the sale of any property may, at the option of the Bureau, be stayed if the property owner or any lien creditor of the owner on or before the actual sale enters into an agreement with the Bureau to pay the sales in installments [72 P.S. § 5860.602(f)]. Costs of advertising and notice is added as part of the costs of sale proceedings and must be paid by the owner the same as other costs [72 P.S. § 5860.602(i)].

Judicial Sales—Service of Rule Required

In a judicial sale, actual notice of sale is inadequate. In the case of a judicial sale, a property owner must receive service of the rule to show cause by personal service or registered mail, not just actual notice of the sale [72 P.S. § 5860.611]. A judicial sale of property for nonpayment of tax was held to be invalid because the property owner was not notified by personal service or registered mail, even though the taxpayer had actual notice of the sale. Actual notice is insufficient because service of the rule to show cause under 72 P.S. §5860.611 is the only opportunity for interested parties to appear and contest the validity of the judicial sale. [*Montgomery County Tax Claim Bureau v. Mermelstein Family Trust*, 836 A.2d 1010 (Pa.Commw. 2003)].

If the property of any corporation, limited partnership, or joint-stock association is advertised for sale, the Bureau must give notice to the Department of Revenue at least thirty (30) days prior to the date of the sale 72 P.S. §5860.602(h). Such notice must be by certified mail on a form provided by the Department of Revenue and must set for (1) the name and address of the Bureau; (2) the date of the sale; (3) the name and address of each corporation, limited partnership, or joint-stock association whose property is scheduled for sale; and (4) the total number of corporations, limited partnerships, and joint-stock associations are scheduled for sale. Upon receipt of the notice and at least seven (7) days prior to the date of sale the Department of Revenue will mail to the Bureau, by certified mail, a proof of claim for payment of Commonwealth taxes that are accorded priority by §1401 of the Fiscal Code [72 P.S. §1401]. The Bureau must include in the upset sale price of the property the amount of Commonwealth taxes set forth on the proof of claim received from the Department of Revenue. If the Bureau complies with the required notice provisions and the Department of Revenue fails to timely mail the required proof of claim to the Bureau, the lien upon the property is forever discharged and divested, notwithstanding any other provision of law to the contrary. However, if the Bureau does not receive a reply from the Department of Revenue prior to the scheduled date of sale, the Bureau has a duty to contact the Department to determine if the Department mailed a reply. The Bureau may then opt to reschedule the sale if circumstances warrant.

Publication: At least thirty (30) days prior to any scheduled sale the county Tax Claim Bureau must give notice of the sale not less than once in two (2) newspapers of general circulation in the county, if so many are published therein, and once in the legal journal, if any, designated by the court for the publication of legal notices. Notices of sale must set forth (1) the purposes of the sale; (2) the time of the sale; (3) the place of the sale; (4) the terms of the sale, including the approximate upset price; and (5) descriptions of the properties to be sold and the name of the owner [72 P.S. §5860.602(a)].

Certified mail: At least thirty (30) days before the date of the sale, the Bureau must give notice by United States certified mail, restricted, delivery, return receipt requested, postage prepaid, to each owner. If return receipt is not received from each owner, then at least ten (10) days prior to the date of sale, similar notice must be given to each owner who failed to acknowledge the first notice by United States first-class mail, proof of mailing, at the owner's last known post office address by virtue of the knowledge and information possessed by the Bureau, by the tax collector for the taxing district making the return, and by the county office responsible for assessments and revisions of taxes. The Bureau has a duty to determine the past post office address known to the collector and county assessment office [72 P.S. §5860.602(e)(1), (2)].

Posting: At least ten (10) days prior to the sale, notice of the sale must be posted on the property to be sold [72 P.S. §5860.602(e)(3)]. All notices (except newspaper and legal journal notices) must contain the statutory warning set out in 72 P.S. §5860.602(g) conspicuously placed on the notice and set in at least 10-point type in a box [72 P.S. §5860.602(g)].

• *Removal of property from sale and agreements to stay sale*

Removal from sale: Owners or lien creditors of owners may (at the option of the Bureau) prior to the actual sales cause the property to be removed from the sale by payment in full of taxes than have become absolute and of all charges and interest due on the time of payment [72 P.S. §5860.603].

Stay of sale: Owners or lien creditors of owners may (at the option of the Bureau) prior to the actual sale enter into a written agreement with the Bureau to stay the sale of the property by paying 25% of the amount due on all tax claims and judgments filed or entered against the property and the interest and costs on the taxes returned to date and agreeing to pay the balance in nor more than three (3) installments within one (1) year of the date of the agreement. So long as the taxpayer fully complies with the agreement, the property sale covered by the agreement will be stayed. In a taxpayer defaults on his or her agreement with the Bureau, the property will be put up for sale at the next scheduled upset or at a special upset sale, either of which is to be held at least ninety (90) days after default. The Bureau cannot, within three (3) years of a default, enter into a new installment agreement with any party to an installment agreement who has defaulted [72 P.S. § 5860.603].

Oral Agreements Not Valid

An agreement to a stay of sale *must* be in writing as required by 72 P.S. § 5860.603; oral agreements are not valid [*Appeal of Sky Bank*, 829 A.2d 797 (Pa.Commw. 2003)]. A bank alleged that a county solicitor orally agreed to continue a sale, and no written agreement to stay the sale was executed. When the property was sold as scheduled, with no stay of sale, the bank contended the sale was invalid. The Commonwealth Court, however, said that an oral agreement is ineffective to stay the sale because 72 P.S. § 5860.603 requires an agreement to a stay of sale to be *in writing*. Therefore, the sale was valid.

• *Repurchase by owner*

An owner has no right to purchase his or her own property at a judicial sale, a private sale, or from the Bureau's repository for unsold property [72 P.S. § 5860.618(a)]; and this prohibition cannot be defeated by a change in name or business status [72 P.S. § 5860.618(b)].

For the purpose of 72 P.S. § 5860.618, "owner" means any individual, partner, shareholder, trust, partnership, limited partnership, corporation, or any other business association or any trust, partnership, limited partnership, corporation or any other business association that has any individual as part of the business association who had any ownership interest or rights in the property [72 P.S. § 5860.618(c)].

• *Extension for elderly*

County commissioners may enact legislation to grant a three-month extension of time for payment of property tax on residential real estate owned and occupies solely by a person 65 years of age or older or owned and occupied jointly by persons, all of whom are 65 years of age or older if the taxpayers meet certain income limitations [72 P.S. § 5860.504(a), (b)].

If an elderly homeowner wants to continue to reside in his or her residence and cannot afford to pay the tax, the tax sale may be deferred until title of the property is transferred or the elderly owner is no longer the sole occupant of the property [72 P.S. § 5860.504(b)(2)].

• *Hardship extension*

In the case of hardship, where extenuating circumstances beyond the taxpayer's control have caused a tax claim to arise and there is a reasonable probability that the taxpayer will be able to pay the tax if granted an extension, counties may extend the period for payment of delinquent taxes for twelve (12) additional months [72 P.S. § 5860.503.1(a)]. "Extenuating circumstances" for this purpose include serious illness and/or injury and prolonged unemployment [72 P.S. § 4860.503.1(d)]. A hardship extension will be extended only to one (1) owner-occupied property per taxpayer [72 P.S. § 5860.503.1(e)].

¶3510

Payment after extension: Payment of the amount due must be made in at least four (4) separate payments, spaced at least thirty (30) days apart, with a required initial payment of not more than 25% of the total indebtedness. However, the county commissioners may, in their discretion, in special hardship cases, establish payment schedules specifically suited to the capabilities of the taxpayer [72 P.S. § 5860.503.1(b)].

Burden of proving posting on Bureau: Because posting of a notice of sale is required under § 602(e)(3) of the Fiscal Code and the Court chose to credit the testimony of one of the owners that no posting had been made, the Bureau failed to meet its burden of proof. Therefore, the sale was void [*Leroy and Loretta Funk v. County of York, et al.*, 803 A.2d 878 (Pa.Commw. 2002), opinion not reported].

Reasonable effort to locate owners: On September 29, 2000, the Schuylkill County Tax Claim Bureau (Bureau) offered for sale fractional interests of certain property as a result of nonpayment of taxes for tax years 1994-1998. The owners of one fractional interest objected to the sale of their parcel because they were not provided notice as required by law. The taxing Bureau is required to exercise reasonable efforts to discover the whereabouts of owners and notify them. In this case the Bureau conducted a title search in order to determine the names of owners but was unable to determine the owners of 2% of the property. This effort was in excess of what is required, even though not all owners received notification. Thus, the notice requirements were met [*Appeal of Spotts*, 798 A.2d 845 (Pa.Commw. 2002)]. In *McElvenny v. Bucks County Tax Claim Bureau*, 804 A.2d 719 (Pa.Commw. 2002), the Commonwealth Court held a Pennsylvania real property tax sale to be invalid because the county tax claim Bureau did not make a reasonable effort to notify the taxpayer. The Bureau had received notification of the taxpayer's change of address but did not update its records, sending the notice to the taxpayer at the taxpayer's previous address.

• *Judicial developments*

Installment agreement option: In 1989, taxpayers (because of financial difficulties) entered into a stay of sale agreement with Erie County for payment of back taxes. The taxpayers complied with the provisions of this agreement until 1991, when they again (because of financial difficulties) fell behind in their payments. On July 2, 1991, the Bureau notified the taxpayers that their property would be sold for delinquent taxes at a tax sale in September. On July 17, 1991, in response to the notice, the taxpayers mailed a check for $500 to the Bureau, which the Bureau accepted and applied to their back taxes. The Bureau mailed them a receipt acknowledging payment on which a handwritten notation stated that they had to pay the remainder of the taxes due ($148.29) by September 26, 1991, in order to avoid having the property sale advertised in the paper. However, the taxpayers were not informed in the receipt acknowledgment that in making a payment in excess of 25% of the back taxes due, they were qualified to enter into an installment agreement to pay the remainder. The property subsequently was sold. The taxpayers appealed, but the Court of Common Pleas of Erie County affirmed the Bureau's action. The Commonwealth Court disagreed with the decision of the trial court. Because the Bureau retained the payment in excess of 25% of the taxes owed, the Commonwealth Court held, the Bureau had an affirmative duty to inform the taxpayers of the option to enter into an installment agreement. The opinion of the trial court was reversed [*Sotack v. Roach and the Tax Claim Bureau of Erie County*, 639 A2d 1291 (Pa.Commw. 1994)].

Notice to owners: Taxpayers (spouses) were sent notice by certified mail and the husband received written notice by first-class mail after he failed to respond to attempts to notify him of the pending sale of taxpayers' property. The wife argued that the sale was not valid because she did not receive notice of the sale by first-class mail at least 10 days before the date of the sale as required by § 5860.602(e) of the Real Estate Tax Sale Law [Act of July 7, 1947, P.L. 1368, as amended, 72 P.S. § § 5860.101— 5860.803]. The Commonwealth Court ruled that, since the evidence clearly demonstrated that the wife was personally served with the notice of the sale of the property, the sale was valid [*In re Tax Sales by the Tax Claim Bureau*, 651 A.2d 1157 (Pa.Commw. 1994)].

Tax collector's office not an "agency" for public access purposes: Under Pennsylvania's Right-to-Know Act [65 P.S. § § 66.1—66.4], citizens have the right to examine, inspect, and duplicate the public records of public agencies. Current Status, Inc., a New Jersey corporation registered to do business in Pennsylvania, sought access to the records of the Tax Collector of Upper Merion Township. The Court, however, denied Current Status access to the records, ruling that the Tax Collector is not an "agency" as defined by the Right-to-Know Act [*Current Status, Inc. v. Hykel*, 778 A.2d 781 (Pa.Commw. 2001), *app. den.*, 790 A.2d 1019 (Pa. 2001)].

¶3511 Revision and Appeal

Local tax assessors place an assessment value on property, and the boards of revision of the various local jurisdictions may revise assessments upward or downward to insure uniformity of taxation throughout the jurisdiction. Any taxpayer who disagrees with a property tax assessment can appeal the decision of a board of revision to the Court of Common Pleas of the county in which the property is located within 60 days of the action of the board. After May 26, 1988, appeals to the Courts of Common Pleas are referred by the courts to boards of arbitrators (judicial arbitration) or to boards of viewers [General County Assessment Law, Act of May 22, 1933, P.L. 853, Art. V. § 518.1]. In Allegheny County, assessment appeal is made to the county court. Municipalities can also appeal tax assessments. Appeals from the Court of Common Pleas are taken to the Superior Court or Supreme Court.

Taxpayer Relied on County Board's Deadline Extension

A taxpayer was assessed property tax in January 1996. The statutory deadline to file appeals was the last day of February 1996. On February 13, 1996, the Allegheny County Board of Property Assessment, Appeals and Review issued an order extending the deadline to April 1. Taxpayer subsequently filed an assessment appeal on March 27, 1996. The Pittsburgh school district sought to quash the appeal on the grounds that the appeals were not timely filed. The Pennsylvania Supreme Court held that it was reasonable for the taxpayer to rely on the County Board's order and allowed the appeal to be reinstated [*Union Electric Corporation v. Board of Property, Assessment, Appeals & Review of Allegheny County*, 746 A.2d 581 (Pa. 2001)].

¶3512 Senior Citizens' Property Tax and Rent Rebate Program

Repeal

With the passage of the Taxpayer Relief Act (discussed at ¶3515), the Senior Citizens Rebate and Assistance Act is repealed and reenacted (with changes) as Chapter 13 of the Taxpayer Relief Act, effective June 27, 2006 [Act No. 1 of Special Session of 2005 (H.B. 39), § 5005(3)]. The discussion below is of the new Senior Citizens Property Tax And Rent Rebate Program (PTRR) of Chapter 13 of the Taxpayer Relief Act, unless otherwise indicated.

Except as otherwise provided in Chapter 13 of the Taxpayer Relief Act, all activities initiated under the former Senior Citizens Rebate and Assistance Act continue and remain in full force and effect and may be completed under Chapter 13. Orders, regulations, rules and decisions that were made under the former Senior Citizens Rebate and Assistance Act and that are in effect as of June 27, 2006 remain in full force and effect until revoked, vacated, or modified under Chapter 13.

The property tax and rent rebate program is governed by the provisions of the Senior Citizens Property Tax and Rebate Assistance provisions of the Taxpayer Relief Act [§ 1301 et seq.]]. The discussion below is an outline of the basic provisions of the property tax and rent rebate program. For details consult the statutes and other authorities.

• *Amount of property tax rebate*

The total amount of property tax rebate consists of a base amount and a supplemental amount.

Base amount: The base amount of property tax rebate available to eligible individuals for calendar year 2006 and thereafter is determined in accordance with the following schedule [Taxpayer Relief Act, § 1304(a)(2)(ii)]:

Household Income	Amount of Real Property Taxes Allowed as Rebate
$0 - $ 8,000	$650
8,005 - 15,000	500
15,001 - 18,000	300
18,001 - 35,000	250

Through December 31, 2016, the term "income" is redefined so that anyone who is otherwise eligible for the rebate will remain eligible if the household income limit is exceeded due solely to a Social Security cost-of-living adjustment (COLA). (Act 156 (H.B. 1067), Laws 2014)

Supplemental amount: A supplemental amount for an eligible claimant with a household income of $30,000 or less is determined under § 1304(a)(2)(ii) of the Tax Relief Act.

Maximum rebate: The maximum amount of property tax rebate in lieu of property taxes payable cannot exceed the lesser of (1) the amount shown in the table above or (2) the amount of real property taxes actually paid [Taxpayer Relief Act, § 1304(b)(2)].

Veterans' disability payments: On November 2, 2016, Governor Wolf signed into law Act 117 of 2016 (House Bill 683) that removed veterans' disability payments from the definition of income that is used to determine an individual's eligibility for the property tax rent rebate program and thereby helps disabled veterans qualify for property tax rebates. Veterans' disability payments include compensation approved by and received from the federal Veterans Administration as a result of an illness or injury that is directly connected to active military service, as well as compensation under several state programs.

Civil service employees: Act 42 of 2018 that provides that, effective for claim year 2018 and thereafter, retired federal civil service employees receiving benefit payments from the Civil Service Retirement System (CSRS) who did not have to contribute to Social Security for that equivalent period of employment will be able to exclude 50% of the average annual Social Security benefit amount from their property tax rent rebate income on claim forms reporting their eligibility income for Property Tax and Rent Rebate purposes by amending the definition of income.

• *Amount of rent rebate*

The amount of rent rebate in lieu of property taxes for rent due and payable for during calendar year 2006 and thereafter is determined in accordance with the following table [Taxpayer Relief Act, § 1304((a)(3)]:

Household Income	Amount of Rent Allowed as Rebate
$0 - $ 8,000	$650
8,005 - 15,000	500

Maximum rebate: The maximum amount of rent rebate in lieu of property taxes payable cannot exceed the lesser of (1) the amount shown in the table above or (2) the amount of rent actually paid [Taxpayer Relief Act, § 1304(b)(2)].

* *Eligible claimants*

An eligible claimant is a person who files a claim for property tax rebate or rent rebate in lieu of property taxes and meets one of the following criteria [Taxpayer Relief Act, § 1303]:

(1) Taxpayer or taxpayer's spouse (if a member of the household) was at least 65 years of age during a calendar year in which real property taxes or rent were due and payable.

(2) Taxpayer was a widow(er) and was at least 50 years of age during a calendar year or part thereof in which real property taxes or rent were due and payable.

(3) Taxpayer was a permanently disable person 18 years of age or older during a calendar year or part thereof in which the real property taxes or rent were due and payable.

Beginning with tax claim year 2013, the Pennsylvania Department of Revenue will pay property tax and rent rebate claims filed on behalf of claimants who lived at least one day during a claim year and met all other eligibility criteria. Such claims can be filed by spouses, personal representatives, or estates on behalf of the deceased claimants. Claims on behalf of deceased claimants are subject to the December 31, 2014. (*Revenue Department Expands Property Tax/Rent Rebate Program*, Pennsylvania Department of Revenue, September 8, 2014)

¶3513 Senior Citizens' Tax Deferrals

Under the provisions of Act 50, enacted April 30, 1998 (Taxpayers' Local Control Act), persons whose income meets the eligibility requirements for the Senior Citizens' Property Tax or Rent Rebate Program are permitted to defer increases in property taxes levied on their homesteads. Applications (which provide information about income, property ownership and insurance coverage) must be submitted to school districts and other political subdivisions. Once an application is approved, taxpayers may defer increases in property taxes on homestead property above the level imposed in the year prior to participation in the program. The annual deferral is equal to the increase in property taxes on homestead property. Deferrals are not permitted if the amount of deferred taxes and other unsatisfied liens on the property (along with outstanding principal on all mortgages) exceeds 85% of the homestead's market value. The deferred taxes may be paid in whole or in part at any time. If the deferred taxes are not paid by the claimant or his/her spouse during their lifetimes (or while they own the property) they must be paid when the homestead is sold to a third party or when title passes to the claimant's heirs.

¶3514 Homeowner Tax Relief Act (Act 72)

Act 72 Repealed

With the passage of the Taxpayer Relief Act (discussed at ¶3515), Act 72 (Homeowner Tax Relief Act) is repealed, effective June 27, 2006 [Act No. 1 of Special Session of 2005 (H.B. 39), § 5005(4)]. However, unless otherwise provided in Chapter 1, 3, 5, or 7 of the Taxpayer Relief Act, actions, orders, regulations, rules, designations, and decisions that were made by the Department of Education or by a school district under the former Homeowner Tax Relief Act and that have been completed or are in effect on June 27, 2006 shall continue and remain in full force and effect for the purposes of Chapters 1, 3, 5, and 7 to the extent that such actions, orders, regulations, rules, designations, and decisions apply to the 2006-2007 fiscal year unless revoked, vacated, or modified by the Taxpayer Relief Act, the Department of Education, or the school district pursuant to Chapter 1, 3, 5, and 7 [Act No. 1 of Special Session of 2005 (H.B. 39), § 5006(b)].

• *Summary of Act 72*

Act 72 allowed school districts to reduce residential property taxes up to the maximum permitted by the homestead provision in the Pennsylvania Constitution, established a formula for the distribution of state property tax relief funds, allowed for electoral participation in tax burden decisions, mandated state reimbursement for nonresident Philadelphia wage tax deductions and prescribed how Philadelphia must reduce its wage tax. School districts would reduce residential property taxes through (1) the enactment of a 0.1% increase in the earned income and net profits tax; (2) state funds from a tax on gaming; and (3) the enact of an additional earned income tax for purposes of residential property tax relief or the enactment of a personal income tax for the purposes of residential property tax relief and to replace the currently imposed earned income tax.

¶3515 Taxpayer Relief Act

• *Overview*

The Taxpayer Relief Act [Act No. 1 of Special Session of 2005 (H.B. 39)] expands the Property Tax and Rent Rebate Program, provides property tax reductions in 2007 if local voters approve increases in school district earned income taxes or authorize the school district to levy a personal income, and makes backend referendum spending controls mandatory for school districts, allows additional referenda to authorize further property tax reductions beginning in 2009, prohibits school districts that opted in to Act 72 of 2004 from levying the 0.1% earned income tax, and repeals Act 72. The following discussion of the Taxpayer Relief Act is based on the Conference Committee Report on Special Session House Bill 39.

• *Expansion of Property Tax and Rent Rebate Program (PTRR)*

Program expansion: The expansion will increase the number of eligible claimants from the current level of 338,946 claimants to a new level of 761, 018 claimants. The amount of payments will increase by $200 million, more than doubling the size of the current program. The expansion payments will be made in 2007 for taxes paid in 2006.

Income eligibility limits: The income eligibility requirements for homeowners will be increased to $35,000. The current limit is $15,000. For renters, the income eligibility requirements will remain at $15,000. However, the amount of payments to renters will increase.

Base payment schedule: The PTRR payment schedule will be streamlined to provide the following payments, based on an eligible claimant's income:

Eligible Claimants Income	Homeowners	Renters
$0-$8,000	$650	$650
$8,000-$15,000	$500	$500
$15,001-$18,000	$300	$0
$18,001-$35,000	$250	$0
Over $35,000	$0	$0

Gaming and lottery funds: $200 million from gaming license fees will be used to offset the cost of the expansion of the PTRR program. Fiscal year 2009-2010 gaming revenues will be used to offset the cost of the expansion of the PTRR program. Any Lottery Fund monies used to pay for all or part of the cost of the PTRR expansion in fiscal year 2007-2008 and fiscal year 2008-2009 will be repaid with gaming funds within five years.

Annual report: The Department of Revenue will be required to provide the General Assembly with an annual report of the PTRR program, including claimants and payments by school district, county, and income level.

• *Primary election referendum—2007*

Property tax reductions authorized by referendum: In the 2007 primary election, each school district will propose a referendum question asking voters to authorize an increase in the earned income tax or authorize a personal income tax in order to provide property tax reductions through the homestead and farmstead exclusion (discussed at ¶3406). School districts may only levy a personal income tax after state regulators governing local collections have been approved.

Minimum property tax reduction: The referendum question must propose to increase the earned income tax rate or levy a personal income tax to provide a property tax reduction of at least 50% of the maximum homestead and farmstead exclusion. However, a school district will not be required to propose to increase the rate by more than the equivalent of a 1.0% increase in the earned income tax.

Local tax study commission: Prior to a school district proposing a referendum question to authorize an increase in the local income tax, the school district will appoint a local tax study commission to make a recommendation.

• *Mandatory backend referendum/spending controls—beginning 2006*

School districts that opted-in to Act 72: School districts that opted-in to Act 72 will be governed by backend referendum requirements, beginning in 2006.

School districts that did not opt-in to Act 72: For 2006 only school districts that did not opt-in to Act 72 will be prohibited from increasing their tax rates above the annual inflationary percentage and will not be able to place referendum questions before the voters to approve further increases. The deadlines for these school districts to submit preliminary budgets to the Department of Education and to apply for backend referendum exceptions will be extended to May and June. These school districts may petition a court of common pleas for an additional tax increase if the school district proves that it cannot otherwise balance its budget. Beginning in 2007, these school districts will be governed by the same backend referendum require-ments that apply to school districts that opted-in to Act 72.

Backend referendum exceptions: The backend referendum exception for school construction will be expanded to provide an exception for school construction indebtedness incurred before the effective date of the new act by a school district that did not opt-in to Act 72 and the exceptions for special education increases and the Public School Employees Retirement System (PSERS) cost increases will be expanded to include cost increases above the index.

Expanded backend referendum exceptions: School districts that opted-in to Act 72 will qualify for any expanded backend referendum exceptions.

Resolution to forego preliminary budget process: Beginning in 2007, school districts may adopt a resolution stating that they will not increase their tax rates above the annual inflationary percentage. If they adopt such a resolution, they will not be required to complete early preliminary budgets.

• *Prohibit school districts from levying 0.1% earned income tax (EIT)*

Act 72 requirement: School districts that opted-in to Act 72 were required to adopt resolutions authorizing a 0.1% EIT to be levied in the year in which gaming revenues were available for property tax reductions.

Levy of tax prohibited: The 111 school districts that adopted such resolutions will be prohibited from levying the 0.1% EIT.

¶3515

• *Additional referenda—municipal election years*

Additional property tax reductions authorized by referendum: Beginning with the municipal election of 2009, each school district, except Philadelphia, may propose a referendum question asking voters to authorize and increase in the earned income tax or personal income tax.

• *Gaming revenues add relief unless a district opts-out*

Participation: School districts will receive property tax reduction payments from gaming revenues.

Opt-out program: When gaming revenues are available for property tax reduction payments, a school district may adopt a resolution to opt-out of gaming revenues. Voters may reverse the school district's decision to opt-out by approving a referendum question at the next general or municipal election.

• *Property tax reduction payments and reserve fund*

Property tax reduction formula: The Act 72 formula will be used to distribute gaming revenues for property tax reduction payments. It distributes funds based on a school district's tax capacity, tax effort, and tax burden.

Initial distribution amount: The amount of gaming revenues required for an initial property tax reduction payment will be set at $400 million. Under Act 72, it was set at $500 million.

Property tax reserve fund: The amount required to be deposited in the Property Tax Reserve Fund will be set at 25% of the amount of property tax reduction payments for that year up to a maximum of $150 million. Under Act 72, it was set at $400 million.

• *Property tax installment payments*

Installment payment option: Beginning in 2007, all school districts, except Philadelphia and Pittsburgh, will be required to offer homestead and farmstead property owners the option to pay their property taxes in installments. School districts will be required to notify homestead and farmstead property owners of this option as part of their property tax bills. A taxpayer who elects this option and who is delinquent by more than ten days on two or more installment payments will be ineligible for the installment option in the following year.

• *Repeal of Act 72*

Act 72 of 2004 is repealed.

PERSONAL PROPERTY TAX

¶3516 History and Sources of Authority of Personal Property Tax

The personal property tax in Pennsylvania was first levied in 1831 by the Act of March 25, 1831, P.L. 206. Until 1913, Pennsylvania collected both the corporate loans tax and the personal property tax and paid part of the property taxes collected to the counties. In 1913, the personal property tax was made a tax of the counties and cities coextensive with counties (Philadelphia). The city of Pittsburgh, the Pittsburgh School District, and the Philadelphia School District are also authorized to levy a personal property tax. However, the Philadelphia School District in 1968 dropped the personal property tax in order to levy a tax on unearned income (income generated from securities). The city of Philadelphia discontinued imposing and collecting its personal property tax for tax years 1997 and thereafter (as well as suspending personal property tax imposed under the authority of the Sterling Act [53 P.S. § 15971 *et seq.*). In 1978, commissioners of counties of the second through the eighth classes

¶3516

and the councils of cities and counties of the first class (Philadelphia) were given the authority to decide whether or not to impose a personal property tax [72 P.S. § 4821.1]. Before this time, the tax was not optional.

• *Constitutionality questioned—Annenberg case*

Relying on the U.S. Supreme Court decision in *Fulton Corp. v. Faulkner*, 516 U.S. 325 (1996), the Pennsylvania Supreme Court, on April 7, 1998, ruled that Pennsylvania's personal property tax statute facially discriminates against interstate commerce. At issue was a provision that exempts the stock of corporations that are subject to the Pennsylvania capital stock/franchise tax, thus taxing only the stock of corporations that have no nexus with Pennsylvania. The tax, according to the court, could withstand the taxpayer's challenge only if it was found to be a legitimate compensatory tax [*Annenberg v. Cmwlth. (Annenberg I)*, 757 A.2d 333 (Pa. 1998)]. The Pennsylvania Supreme Court remanded the case to the Montgomery County Court of Common Pleas for a determination of (1) whether the Pennsylvania personal property tax is a "compensatory tax" as defined by *Fulton Corp. v. Faulkner*, 516 U.S. 325 (1996), and (2) what would be the appropriate remedy if it is determined that the tax is not a valid "compensatory tax," but is unconstitutionally violative of the Commerce Clause of the U.S. Constitution.

On October 7, 1998, Judge Smyth of the Court of Common Pleas of Montgomery County published an *Interim Report* to the Pennsylvania Supreme Court [Montgomery, CP No. 98-08615, Pennsylvania Supreme Court Nos. 003 and 004 Miscellaneous Docket 1997]. The report concluded that the tax was not compensatory, but that the provision that excluded stock issued by domestic corporations and foreign corporations doing business in Pennsylvania could be severed from the statute, leaving the counties the authority to tax all corporate stock in the hands of Pennsylvania residents. The report concluded that counties could do this prospectively, retaining funds already collected. On June 1, 2000, the Pennsylvania Supreme Court issued its decision, holding that the stock clause is not a compensatory tax and is, therefore, unconstitutional [*Annenberg v. Cmwlth. (Annenberg II)*, 757 A2d 338 (Pa. 2000), *cert. den.*, 531 U.S. 959 (2000)].

Tax Still Valid But Not Imposed

The Pennsylvania Supreme Court decided that the unconstitutional stock clause is severable from the tax. This means that the personal property tax is valid, and only the invalid stock clause (*i.e.*, the exemption for stock in companies subject to the Pennsylvania capital stock/franchise taxes) is invalid. The court left it to the counties to provide a restrospective remedy consistent with the court's opinion. No local jurisdictions currently impose the personal property tax.

• *Refund remedies*

Following the Supreme Court's decision in *"Annenberg II,"* several local jurisdictions in Pennsylvania issued remedies to comply with the Court's decision. Most counties basically followed the remedy established by Montgomery County, where the Annenberg suit was filed (see below). See ¶ 4006 for the remedy implemented by Philadelphia.

• *Montgomery County remedy*

The Board of Assessment Appeals of Montgomery informed taxpayers (in a letter dated January 26, 2001) that they had no reasonable alternative but to tax previously exempt stock for each of the individual years 1993, 1994, 1995, and 1996. However, the County was aware that collecting the tax would be expensive and that some taxpayers had expressed an intention to challenge the County's right to tax previously exempt tax. Taxpayers were informed that they could sign a Mutual Release that would terminate all taxpayer claims against the County (*i.e.*, the taxpayer

¶3516

would seek no refund) and all County claims against the taxpayer (*i.e.*, the County would not tax previously exempt assets for the years 1993—1996). Taxpayers who did not respond by February 15, 2001, were taxed for the amounts of tax the County determined the taxpayers to owe for the years 1993 through 1996, inclusive (including previously exempt stock in the tax base) [*Letter to Taxpayers*, Montgomery County Board of Assessment Appeals]. See ¶4006 for discussion of the Philadelphia remedy.

As anticipated by the County, a taxpayer suit was filed in an attempt to block the agreement. The presiding judge, however, rejected the taxpayers' effort to block the agreement, stating that the County has the lawful authority to settle claims and enter into the proposed Mutual Release agreements [*Annenberg v. Montgomery County Board of Commissioner and Board of Assessment Appeals*, Court of Common Pleas, Montgomery County, Pennsylvania, Case #01-03713 (August 31, 2001)]. Taxpayers should be on the alert for an appeal by the Annenbergs.

• *Sources of Authority*

The personal property tax in Pennsylvania is governed by the provisions of the Act of June 17, 1913, as amended [72 P.S. § 5871]. In general, only counties may levy a personal property tax. There are four exceptions: the cities of Philadelphia and Pittsburgh, and the Philadelphia School District and the Pittsburgh School District. The Philadelphia School District does not, however, currently impose a personal property tax, imposing instead a tax on unearned income (*i.e.*, dividends and interest).

The city of Philadelphia (as a city coextensive with a county) is authorized to impose a personal property tax by the same act that authorizes counties to do so [72 P.S. § 5871]. The city of Pittsburgh (as a second class city) is authorized by The Local Tax Enabling Act to impose a personal property tax [Act of December 31, 1965, P.L. 1257, § 2(6)] and the Pittsburgh School District levies a personal property tax under the authorization of P.L. 733 [Act of June 20, 1947, P.L. 733, § 2]. The Philadelphia School District has the authority, under the Act of May 23, 1949, to impose a personal property tax, but cannot impose a personal property tax if it levies a tax on nonbusiness income from personal property [Act of May 23, 1949, P.L. 1676, § 2].

The collection of the personal property tax is governed by The Local Tax Collection Law [72 P.S. § 5511.1 *et seq.*], except in the cities of Philadelphia, Pittsburgh, and Scranton, and in Allegheny County. Scranton, however, is subject to the penalty, discount, and installment provisions of the Act [Local Tax Collection Law, § 3].

¶3517 Outline of Tax

The personal property tax in Pennsylvania is a tax on intangible personal property. The largest class of taxable intangibles is corporate stocks and bonds. Tangible property is not taxed under the provisions of the personal property tax. The personal property tax is not a tax on all intangible personal property but only on "personal property of the classes hereinafter enumerated . . ." [72 P.S. § 4821]. See ¶3527 for an explanation of taxable property. If personal property is owned that does not fall within any of the classes enumerated, personal property tax on the property need not be paid.

Intangible personal property that is subject to the corporate loans tax cannot be made subject to the county personal property tax (see ¶1701). It does not matter whether or not the corporate loans tax has been withheld and/or remitted to Pennsylvania.

Exemptions from the personal property tax fall into two classes: (1) exempt holders (¶3526) and (2) exempt property (¶3528).

¶3518 Administration

Pennsylvania law authorizes local authorities to adopt and enforce rules and regulations for the administration, enforcement, and collection of the personal property tax [72 P.S. § 4844.3(a)]. Local authorities can examine the books, papers, and records of any resident in order to verify and assess the tax [72 P.S. § 4844.2(b)].

• *Philadelphia*

The Board of Revision of Taxes is responsible for the administration of the county, city, and school district taxes in Philadelphia. This Board appoints assessors of property (both real and personal), revises assessments, and hears appeals. Philadelphia no longer imposes a personal property tax. See ¶4006. [72 P.S. §§5452.3—5452.14].

• *Allegheny County*

The personal property tax in Allegheny County is administered by the Board of Property Assessment, Appeals and Review. This board appoints assessors, revises assessments, and hears appeals [72 P.S. §§5452.3—5452.4]. The County Treasurer collects the tax [72 P.S. §5527]. Allegheny County no longer imposes a personal property tax; it was replaced by the Allegheny County sales tax (discussed in Chapter 45).

• *Pittsburgh*

The Pittsburgh personal property tax is also administered by the Allegheny County Board of Property Assessment, Appeals and Review, but the city treasurer collects the tax and enforces collections [Pittsburgh Code of Ordinances, Title 2, Art. IX, Ch. 261, §261.07(b)].

• *Second-class A and third-class counties*

A special Board of Assessment Appeals administers the tax in second class A and third class counties [72 P.S. §5344]. See ¶3401 for an explanation of classes of counties and cities in Pennsylvania.

¶3520 Imposition of Personal Property Tax

The personal property tax is imposed on "each dollar of the value . . . " of certain intangible personal property held by any resident of Pennsylvania [72 P.S. §4821]. "Resident" for this purpose has the following meaning:

> [A]ny person, persons, copartnership, or unincorporated association or company, resident, located, or liable to taxation within this Commonwealth, or by any joint-stock company or association, limited partnership, bank or corporation whatsoever, formed, erected or incorporated by, under or in pursuance of any law of this Commonwealth or of the United States, or of any other state or government, and liable to taxation within this Commonwealth [72 P.S. §4821].

For an explanation of taxable and exempt persons, see ¶3525 and ¶3526. For an explanation of taxable and exempt property, see ¶3527 and ¶3528.

Effective January 1, 1995, the Allegheny County and Pittsburgh personal property tax was replaced by the Allegheny County sales and use tax. See ¶4501.

¶3521 Personal Property Tax Base and Rates

The base for the computation of the personal property tax is the total value of taxable property. In general, property is assessed at actual value, which is the price that the property would bring in a bona fide sale (the fair market value). However, some counties assess property at less than full fair market value (see ¶3535). Al-

¶3518

though the actual selling price may be considered in placing a value on the property, it is not controlling [Act of May 22, 1933, P.L. 853, Art. IV, § 402]. See ¶ 3535 for an explanation of the valuation of intangible personal property.

• *Rates*

The rate of the personal property tax is 4 mills (0.004) on each dollar of assessed value [72 P.S. § 4821]. Residents of Pittsburgh pay 12 mills (0.012) because they are subject to a 4-mill Allegheny County tax, a 4-mill Pittsburgh School District tax [Pittsburgh School District Resolution] and a 4-mill Pittsburgh City tax [Pittsburgh City Code of Ordinances, Title 2, Art. IX, Ch. 261, § 261.02].

¶3525 Who Is Subject to the Personal Property Tax

The personal property tax is imposed on certain personal property (1) held by any resident (explained at ¶ 3520), whether "owned, held, or possessed by such resident in his, her, their, or its own right, or as active trustee, agent, attorney-in-fact, or in any other capacity" [72 P.S. § 4821], or (2) owned, held, or possessed "by any resident as trustee, agent, or attorney-in-fact, jointly with one or more trustees, agents, or attorneys-in-fact, domiciled in another state, where such personal property is held and managed in this Commonwealth" [72 P.S. § 4821]. All residents are taxable unless specifically exempt.

¶3526 Exempt Persons

Exempt owners and holders of personal property for personal property tax purposes fall into the following general categories: (1) nonresidents [72 P.S. § 4821]; (2) persons holding property received from and held for the benefit of nonresidents [72 P.S. § 4821]; (3) executors of a nonresident decedent's estate [72 P.S. § 4821]; (4) persons holding property in trust for a religious, charitable, or educational organization [72 P.S. § 4821]; (5) certain exempt organizations (*e.g.*, mutual insurance companies, labor unions, and beneficial societies) [72 P.S. § 4821]; (6) companies liable for gross premiums or shares taxes and companies subject to Pennsylvania capital stock or franchise tax [72 P.S. § 4821]; and (7) instrumentalities of the federal government.

In general, exempt holders of personal property for personal property tax purposes are the same as for corporate loans tax purposes. See ¶ 1705 for a detailed explanation of exempt holders.

¶3527 What Personal Property Is Taxable

The following intangibles are subject to the Pennsylvania personal property tax [72 P.S. § 4821]:

(1) All mortgages (whether or not at interest).

(2) All monies owing by solvent debtors (whether by promissory note, penal or single bill, bond, or judgment).

(3) All articles of agreement and accounts bearing interest (except those of banks).

(4) All public loans, except those issued by Pennsylvania, political subdivisions of Pennsylvania, and the United States.

(5) All loans issued by any corporation, association, company, or limited partnership (including car-trust certificates and loans secured by bonds or any other evidence of indebtedness).

Double Tax

The corporate loans tax takes precedence over the personal property tax if you pay the corporate loans tax on evidences of corporate indebtedness. In that case, do not pay the personal property tax on the same property.

---

(6) All shares of stock in any bank, corporation, association, company, or limited partnership except those of corporations subject to or expressly exempt from bank shares or gross premiums, or liable to or relieved from capital stock and franchise taxes.

(7) Equitable interests in out-of-state property held by exempt trustees for residents (see ¶ 3535).

(8) Shares of stock in regulated investment companies.

Interests in Limited Partnerships

The Commonwealth Court held that interests in limited partnerships formed under the Uniform Limited Partnerships Act are *not* personal property subject to the Intangible Personal Property Tax [*Provident National Bank v. Board of Assessment Appeals*, 565 A.2d 508 (Pa.Commw. 1989)].

¶3528 Exempt Property

The following property is exempt from the intangible personal property tax [72 P.S. § 4821]:

(1) Shares of stock in any bank, bank and trust company, national banking association, savings institution, corporation, or limited partnership liable to a tax on its shares or a gross premiums tax, or liable to or relieved from the Pennsylvania capital stock or franchise tax.

Tax Payment

It is not necessary that a company that is subject to the shares or capital stock-franchise tax actually pay such tax in order for the shares to be exempt from the personal property tax. For example, you may own stock in a company that is subject to the Pennsylvania franchise tax but which does not actually pay any franchise tax because it employs capital in manufacturing in Pennsylvania. The shares of such a company are not subject to the personal property tax even though exempt from the franchise tax. The fact that the company is subject to the franchise tax provisions is enough to exempt its shares from the personal property tax [*Dupuy v. Johns*, 104 A 565 (Pa. 1918); *Arrott's Estate*, 185 A. 697 (Pa. 1936)].

---

(2) Bank notes, or notes discounted or negotiated by any bank or banking institution, savings institution, or trust company.

(3) Loans, shares of stock, or other securities, held by bankers or brokers solely for trading purposes.

(4) Accounts or debit balances owing by customers of bankers or brokers in the usual course of business.

(5) Interest-bearing accounts in any bank or banking institution, savings institution, employees' thrift or savings association (whether operated by employees, employer, or trust company).

(6) Personal property held in the commercial department and owned in its own right by a banking institution, savings institution, or trust company.

(7) Personal property held in liquidation by a receiver, trustee, or other fiduciary.

(8) Personal property formerly held by a banking institution in its own right, but which it has assigned to one or more trustees for liquidation and payment to creditors and stockholders.

(9) Proceeds of life insurance policies held in whole or in part by the insurers.

(10) Principal value of annuities.

(11) Personal property held in any trust that forms part of a stock bonus, pension or profit-sharing plan of an employer for the exclusive benefit of employees or their beneficiaries *if* such trust is exempt from federal income tax.

(12) Personal property held under the provisions of a plan established by or for an individual or individuals for retirement purposes *if* such plan is exempt from federal income tax.

(13) Evidences of indebtedness subject to the corporate loans tax.

(14) Property acquired from nonresidents and held for the benefit of nonresidents (including foreign corporations).

(15) Personal property held for the use, benefit, or advantage of any resident who in each of the 10 preceding calendar years has given or contributed all of his net income to any corporation organized or operated exclusively for religious, charitable, scientific, literary, or educational purposes.

¶3530 Situs of Intangible Personal Property

The general rule is that the situs of intangible personalty for tax purposes is the domicile of the owner of the property. See *Appeal of Sauer*, 74 A.2d 700 (Pa.Super. 1950).

• *Estates of decedents*

Property in the estate of a resident decedent is taxable in the decedent's county of residence at the time of death.

• *Property held in trust*

When property is held in trust by a resident fiduciary for a resident beneficiary, the property is taxable in the county in which the fiduciary resides, regardless of the beneficiary's county of residence. On the other hand, property held by a nonresident fiduciary is taxable in a resident beneficiary's county of residence. When property is held in trust by two or more resident fiduciaries, each fiduciary is responsible (in his/her county of residence) for the tax on his/her proportionate share of the tax (based on the number of fiduciaries). This means that if the fiduciaries live in different counties, the tax is apportioned among two or more counties [72 P.S. § 4841]. When property is held jointly by both resident and nonresident fiduciaries, the trustees are taxable in Pennsylvania only if the property is held and managed in Pennsylvania. In such cases, the property is taxable entirely in the county in which the trust is domiciled. See *Appeal of Biddle*, 135 A.2d 915 (Pa. 1957).

¶3535 Valuation and Listing of Personal Property

In general, the personal property tax is imposed on the fair market value of the taxable property. However, some counties assess property at less than full fair market value. Personal property must be assessed at full value in Philadelphia County and in counties of classes 4 through 8. In Allegheny County and counties of classes 2d-A and 3 property may be assessed at less than fair market value but must be uniform within the district.

- *Securities*

The fair market value of securities is the selling price on the last day before assessment date. For unlisted or untraded stock, the value is the average of bid and asked prices. If these are not available, usual factors, such as actual sales and earnings, are used to value the security.

- *"Blockage theory"*

The Pennsylvania Supreme Court has ruled out the use of the "blockage theory" except in cases where a sale is shown to be necessary or probable. See *Appeal of McNeil,* 257 A.2d 835 (1969), in which the Pennsylvania Supreme Court ruled that taxpayers who owned large blocks of stock of a corporation had to pay personal property tax on the full market price of the stock instead of a discounted value under the "blockage theory," which holds that a sale of a large block of stock at one time would depress the price of the stock.

- *Equitable interests*

If the title of property is held by a nonresident trustee for the benefit of a resident beneficiary, the resident beneficiary cannot be taxed on the property itself. The resident beneficiary is taxable on the value of equitable interests in out-of-state property even if the trust property is held and managed in another state.

Situs Controls

A resident of Pennsylvania cannot escape the personal property tax simply by housing property outside Pennsylvania. As long as you hold title to intangible property and reside in Pennsylvania, the situs of the intangible property is Pennsylvania. Therefore, having a person hold property for you outside Pennsylvania as an agent without title will not remove the situs of the intangible property from Pennsylvania. However, if a nonresident trustee, agent, or attorney-in-fact holds title to property for your benefit, you do not own the property and the situs of the property is outside Pennsylvania. Thus, the nonresident fiduciary cannot be taxed on the property. You can, nevertheless, be taxed on the value of your equitable interest in the trust property if you are entitled to receive some income from the trust.

The value of the equitable interest in personal property subject to tax is measured by ascertaining the value of the personal property in which the resident has the sole equitable interest, or in case of divided equitable interests, by ascertaining the part of the value of the whole that represents the equitable interest of the taxpayer [72 P.S. § 4821]. If the resident beneficiary is entitled only to income, either for life or a specified number of years, and has no interest in the property itself, the value of the equitable interest will ordinarily be less than the full value of the underlying assets.

- *Regulated investment company shares*

The value of taxable shares of stock issued by any regulated investment company is found by multiplying the total current value of the company's shares by a fraction, the numerator of which is the total value of personal property owned by the company that would be taxable if owned by a Pennsylvania resident, and the denominator of which is the total value of all personal property owned by the company [72 P.S. § 4821].

¶3536 Assessment Date

The assessment date (listing day) of personal property is set by the appropriate board of revision of taxes or county commissioners. This date must be between January 1 and January 15, inclusive, and specified on returns furnished to the taxpayers. If a valuation date is not set or if the date does not appear on the forms, the date for listing property is January 1 [72 P.S. § 4843.2]. Taxpayers are responsible for tax on property held or owned by them on the assessment date.

¶3536

Trust Beneficiaries

You must pay tax on property you own on the listing day even though you do not own it for the entire year. If you dispose of property after a listing day, the liability for the tax is transferred as of the next listing day.

If you are a resident of Pennsylvania and are the beneficiary of a trust, the property of which is held by a resident fiduciary, the fiduciary, and not you, is liable for the personal property tax. However, if the fiduciary moves out of the state still holding title to the property, the fiduciary is no longer responsible for the tax as of the next valuation date. Since the situs of the property has been removed from Pennsylvania, you are not responsible for tax on the property itself. However, on the next listing date, you become responsible for tax on the value of your equitable interest in the trust property.

¶3540 Personal Property Return Forms

Taxpayers use forms prescribed, prepared and furnished by the board of revision of taxes or the county commissioners to make personal property tax returns [72 P.S. §4843]. The board of revision of taxes or the county commissioners must furnish blank forms to the assessors of the local taxing districts and the assessors must furnish copies to taxpayers within their districts [72 P.S. §4841]. The responsibility of assessors to "furnish a copy" of the return to each taxpayer has been held to mean merely that they must make copies *available* to taxpayers, not that they must personally deliver a copy to each taxpayer [*City of Philadelphia v. Kolb*, 30 D. & C. 229 (1937)].

• *Data on returns*

The law requires that taxpayers must indicate on the returns the aggregate actual value of each part of the different classes of taxable property they hold or own and any other relevant information required by the local taxing authority [72 P.S. §4843]. However, the law does not specify the form of the return so each local district prepares its own form. This means that the forms differ among counties.

¶3541 Certification of Personal Property Returns

Every taxpayer must certify that his or her personal property tax return is "full, true, and correct to the best of his or her knowledge and belief," and failure to do so is a misdemeanor punishable by a fine not exceeding $500 or a term of imprisonment not exceeding two years, or both [72 P.S. §4841].

Individuals must certify their own returns. A member must certify the return of a copartnership, unincorporated association, or joint-stock association or company. The president, chairman, or treasurer must certify the return of a limited partnership or corporation. [72 P.S. §4843].

¶3542 Due Dates for Personal Property Returns and Payment

The due date for both filing a return and payment of tax is set by the board of revision of taxes or the county commissioners [72 P.S. §4843]. The return date is usually, but not always, February 15. Local taxing officers verify the returns received, compute the tax, and bill the taxpayers. The tax notice sent to the taxpayer must designate the place and time of tax payment, the time during which an abatement or discount will be allowed, when full amount of tax will be collected, and when a penalty will be added [Local Tax Collection Law, §6].

• *Tax notices*

The law states that tax collectors must send tax notices within 30 days after receiving tax duplicates from the taxing district but not later than July 1 [Local Tax Collection Law, §6]. Therefore, there are no uniform payment dates. Except in Philadelphia and Allegheny County (see ¶3546), taxes become delinquent (and thus subject to penalties) four months after the date of the tax notice [Local Tax Collection Law, § 10]. The date of the tax notice is the date the tax notice is mailed to the taxpayer and not the date stated in the tax notice [*Appeal from Aliquippa Auditors' Report,* 24 Beaver 142 (1963)].

¶3543 Place of Filing

Personal property tax returns must be sent to the board of revision of taxes or the county commissioners in a taxpayer's county of residence [72 P.S. § 4843].

¶3545 Discounts and Delinquencies

Philadelphia allows a 1% discount on all personal property taxes paid up to and including the last day of February or within 20 days of the date of the tax notice. No discount is allowed for taxes paid during March, April, or May. Taxes become delinquent on June 1 [Philadelphia Code § 19-1101].

In Pittsburgh, taxes are due and payable on May 1. Taxes paid during May, June, and July get a 2% discount. The face amount is due in August. Taxes become delinquent on September 1 [Pittsburgh City Code of Ordinances, Title 2, Art. IX, Ch. 261, § 261.07].

Allegheny County allows a 2% discount on taxes paid by July 31. Taxes become delinquent after August 31 [Instructions to County of Allegheny 1988 Personal Property Tax Return].

In all other counties, a discount of at least 2% is allowed if payment is made within two months of the date of the tax notice. Taxes become delinquent if not paid within four months of the tax notice date [Local Tax Collection Law, § 10].

¶3546 Penalties and Interest

A 10% penalty is imposed if taxes are not paid within four months of the date of the tax bill [Local Tax Collection Law, § 10] and interest at the rate of 6% per year is charged from the date the tax becomes delinquent [72 P.S. § 4881]. Consult local statutes for different discount rules for the local jurisdictions in and within Philadelphia County and Allegheny County.

¶3550 Personal Property Assessments

The personal property tax is assessed annually [72 P.S. § 4821]. The appropriate county officials (see ¶3518) prepare printed blanks and send them to the assessors in their jurisdictions, who deliver them to the taxpayers [72 P.S. § 4841]. Taxpayers indicate the value of their taxable personal property on their personal property tax returns. If the valuation shown on the return is found to be too low, the board of revision of taxes or the county commissioners must raise the valuation and notify the taxpayer of the increase and that the increase can be appealed at the same time and in the same way as the original assessment [Act of June 17, 1913, P.L. 507, § 12]. However, if the return valuation is found by the court to be correct, the taxpayer's assessment is the return amount, and county officials need not notify the taxpayer of the amount of her or his personal property assessment and of the time and place for appeal [*Appeal of Courlaender's Estate,* 18 A.2d 494 (Pa.Super. 1941)].

¶3551 Estimated Assessments

If a taxpayer fails to report all taxable property, files a false, incomplete, incorrect, or inaccurate return, or fails to file a return, the board of tax revision or county commissioners must make an assessment against the taxpayer for the amount of tax that they believe the taxpayer owes. They must notify the taxpayer, by mail, of the estimated assessment and the day fixed for appeals [72 P.S. § 4844].

¶3543

• *Taxpayer's recourse—Penalty for false return*

A taxpayer who is not satisfied with an estimated assessment may, on or before the day fixed for appeals from assessments, give the board or commissioners their reasons for failing to file the return or include all property in the return. If the board or commissioners are satisfied with the taxpayer's excuse, they may permit the taxpayer to substitute his or her own return for the estimated return.

However, when a false return has been filed, the board or commissioners cannot relieve the taxpayer from the payment of the 12% penalty for filing false returns. The estimated return is final unless the taxpayer submits a true and correct return showing a higher valuation than the estimated valuation, in which case both the tax and the penalty will be based on the taxpayer's higher valuation [72 P.S. § 4844].

¶3552 Petitions for Reassessment

A taxpayer may petition the county taxing authorities for reassessment [72 P.S. § 4844.1]. Notice of intention to file such a petition, or to appear before the taxing authorities, must be made to the board of revision of taxes or the county commissioners within 30 days after notice of assessment. The taxing authorities must inform all taxpayers who give such notice of the time and place of the hearings.

Petitions for reassessment must set forth specifically and in detail the reasons the assessment is claimed to be erroneous or unlawful and must be accompanied by a sworn affidavit certifying the correctness of the facts contained in the petition. A taxpayer may, in lieu of filing a petition for reassessment, appear at the hearing and present an oral petition under oath [72 P.S. § 4844.1].

¶3553 Petitions for Review

Taxpayers who are not satisfied with the action taken by the board of revision of taxes or the county commissioners on a petition for reassessment have 60 days after notification of action to appeal to the Court of Common Pleas in the county in which they reside [72 P.S. § 4844.1]. In such appeals taxpayers must specify all objections to the assessment. Any objections not specified in the appeal will not be considered by the court. In Allegheny County, in cases in which the amount of tax involved does not exceed $2,500, appeals are made to the County Court of Allegheny County instead of to the Court of Common Pleas. Decisions of the Court of Common Pleas may be appealed to the Pennsylvania Superior Court or the Pennsylvania Supreme Court.

¶3554 Claim for Refund

When a taxpayer has paid taxes of any sort to which the political subdivision is not legally entitled, the proper authorities of the political subdivision must refund such taxes. A taxpayer seeking a refund of taxes paid must file a written claim for refund with the political subdivision involved within two years of payment of the tax [72 P.S. § 5566(b)]. Philadelphia and Allegheny counties have special refund rules.

Taxpayers cannot resort to a claim of refund in the manner specified above if they have or have had available a specific remedy by way of review, appeal, refund or otherwise, for the recovery of the tax under any other statute, ordinance or resolution, unless the claim for refund is for the recovery of taxes paid under a provision subsequently held by a court of competent jurisdiction, to be unconstitutional or erroneously interpreted [72 P.S. § 5566(b)].

• *Assumpsit action*

If a refund claim is refused, the taxpayer may bring suit for recovery of the tax by instituting an action *in assumpsit* in the Court of Common Pleas [72 P.S. § 5566(c)].

¶3555 Statute of Limitations: Assessments and Reassessments

Boards of tax revision or county commissioners may make estimated assessments or reassessments at any time within five years after returns are made or should have been made. These assessments may be made even if the taxpayer has filed a return and paid tax and even if the board of revision of taxes or the county commissioners have made previous assessments against the taxpayers involved [72 P.S. § 4844].

• *Limitations on assessments*

The taxing authorities cannot go back more than five years to make an assessment because the failure to file a return is the action that starts the running of the statute of limitations. Taxes do not become delinquent until assessed, so taxes that should have been paid in years when a taxpayer files no return do not become delinquent until the taxing authorities make an assessment of the taxes due.

¶3556 Failure to File Return—Penalties

The penalty for failure to file a return, for omission of taxable property from a return, or for filing a false, incomplete, incorrect, or inaccurate return is 12%. In such cases the taxpayers receive no credit for any penalty formerly assessed and paid [72 P.S. § 4844].

For penalty for late payment of personal property taxes, see ¶3546.

PART XVI

LOCAL TAXES IN JURISDICTIONS OTHER THAN PITTSBURGH AND PHILADELPHIA

CHAPTER 36

LOCAL TAXES

GENERAL

¶3601 Local Power to Tax

• *Sterling Act (Act 511)*

Philadelphia derives its taxing power from the Sterling Act (see ¶3402).

• *Local Tax Enabling Act (LTEA)*

ALERT

The LTEA provisions have been renumbered as of July 2, 2008 [Act 32 of 2008 (S.B. 1063)].

Most other local jurisdictions (including Pittsburgh) derive their primary taxing authority from other enabling legislation, primarily the Local Tax Enabling Act (LTEA) [53 P.S. § 6924.101 *et seq.*]. The Local Tax Enabling Act gives broad taxing powers to local jurisdictions. There is separate legislation authorizing the county personal property tax. In general, school districts have the authority to levy taxes under § 507 of the Public School Code of 1949 [24 P.S. § 1-101 *et seq.*]. There are various other codes of law that apply to political subdivisions. These are discussed with the specific local taxes. Municipalities that adopt home rule charters are also subject to the home rule charter statutes (discussed at ¶3402). For a more detailed discussion of the LTEA, see ¶3402.

• *Other enabling legislation*

Enabling legislation can also be found in the County Code, the Second Class County Code, the Third Class City Code, the First Class Township Code, and the Borough Code. See ¶3402 for more detail.

¶3602 Prohibited Subjects of Local Taxation

Not all limitations on local taxing powers are provided by the LTEA [53 P.S. § 6924.101 *et seq.*], but the major limitations are found in the LTEA. The LTEA specifically forbids local taxation of the following subjects of taxation:

(1) Certain realty transfers specified by 53 P.S. § 6924.301.1(f)(1).

(2) The gross receipts from utility service of any person or company whose rates and services are fixed and regulated by the Pennsylvania Public Utility Commission or on any public utility services rendered by any such person or company or on any privilege or transaction involving the rendering of any such public utility service [53 P.S. § 6924.301.1(f)(2)].

(3) The privilege of employing tangible property that is now or hereafter becomes subject to a State tax (except for admission to places of amusement or on sales or other transfers of title or possession of property) [53 P.S. § 6924.301.1(f)(3)]. This is a codification of the preemption doctrine discussed at ¶3402.

(4) Manufactured goods or articles (or the by-products of manufacture) produced in the taxing jurisdiction. Note that in the wake of the *PPG* decision the long-term status of the manufacturing exemption is uncertain [53 P.S. § 6924.301.1(f)(4)]. See ¶1601 for further discussion of the manufacturing exemption; see also ¶1301 for discussion of the *PPG* decision [*PPG Industries, Inc. v. Cmwlth.*, 790 A.2d 216 (Pa. 2001)]. Note also that local authorities may impose taxes on the occupation, occupational privilege, per capita, and earned income or net profits of natural persons engaged in manufacturing activities whether doing business as an individual proprietorship or as members of partnerships or other association [53 P.S. § 6924.301.1(f)(4)].

(5) Minerals, timber, natural resources and farm products produced in the taxing jurisdiction (including the production, preparation, or processing of these products) [53 P.S. § 6924.301.1(f)(4)].

(6) Salaries, wages, commissions, compensation, and earned income of nonresidents of the political subdivisions (applicable only to school districts of the second, third, and fourth classes) [53 P.S. § 6924.301.1(f)(5)].

¶3602

(7) Personal property owned by persons, associations, and corporations specifically exempted by law from taxation under the county personal property tax law (not applicable to cities of the second class) [53 P.S. § 6924.301.1(f)(6)].

(8) Membership in or membership dues, fees, or assessment of charitable, religious, beneficial, or nonprofit organizations (including but not limited to sportsmen's, recreational, golf, and tennis clubs, girl and boy scout troops and councils) [53 P.S. § 6924.301.1(f)(7)].

(9) Mobile homes or house trailers subject to a real property tax unless the same tax is imposed on other real property in the political subdivision [53 P.S. § 6924.301.1(f)(8)].

(10) The privilege of engaging in an occupation by a political subdivision that is not the taxpayer's place of employment [53 P.S. § 6924.301.1(f)(9)].

(11) Admissions to motion picture theatres (not applicable to cities of the second class) [53 P.S. § 6924.301.1(f)(10)].

(12) Construction of or improvement to residential dwellings or application for building permits for residential dwellings [53 P.S. § 6924.301.1(f)(11)].

(13) Certain mercantile or business privilege receipts [53 P.S. § 6924.301.1(f)(12)].

(14) Membership in or admission to places to engage in activities, the predominant purpose or nature of which is exercise, fitness, health maintenance, improvement or rehabilitation, health or nutrition education, or weight control [53 P.S. § 6924.301.1(f)(13)].

• *Constitutional restrictions*

The power of the Commonwealth and its local jurisdictions to tax its subjects is also restricted by the Constitution of the United States and the Constitution of the Commonwealth. These restrictions are discussed at ¶ 3403.

• *Local Taxpayers Bill of Rights*

For a discussion of restrictions on local powers of taxation imposed by the Local Taxpayers Bill of Rights, see ¶ 3404.

Keystone Opportunity Zone Limitations

Local governments with Pennsylvania Keystone Opportunity Zones (KOZs), Keystone Opportunity Expansion Zones (KOEZs), or Keystone Opportunity Improvement Zones (KOIZs) cannot impose the following taxes in a KOZ/KOEZ/KOIZ: (1) earned income/net profits tax; (2) business gross receipts tax; (3) realty use and occupancy tax; (4) business privilege and mercantile taxes; (5) local property tax; and (6) local sales and use taxes. Keystone opportunity zones are discussed at ¶ 4622.

SPECIFIC LOCAL TAXES

¶3605 Amusement and Admissions Taxes

The Local Tax Enabling Act (LTEA) permits imposition of a tax on admissions to places of amusement, athletic events, and the like, at the maximum rate of 10% [53 P.S. § 6924.311(6)]. Local jurisdictions cannot impose a tax on admissions to motion picture theaters (except Pittsburgh; see ¶ 4304) or on exercise, fitness, and health clubs [53 P.S. § 6924.301.1(10), (13)].

School Districts

School districts imposing an amusement or admissions tax prior to July 1, 1997, may continue to impose and collect the tax. School districts that did not impose such a tax as of June 30, 1997, may not now impose one [53 P.S. § 8402].

- *Ski facilities*

Admissions to ski facilities may be taxed at the maximum rate of 10%, but the tax base upon which the tax shall be levied cannot exceed 40% of the cost of the lift ticket, which must include all costs of admissions to the facility [53 P.S. § 6924.311(9)].

- *Golf courses*

Admissions to golf courses may be taxed at the maximum rate of 10%, but the tax base upon which the tax shall be levied cannot exceed 40% of the cost of the greens fee, which must include all costs of admissions to the facility [53 P.S. § 6924.311(10)].

Miniature golf course: In 1990, Derry Township adopted an amusement tax under the authority of the LTEA. San Van, Inc. (San Van) operates a miniature golf course in the township and the township imposed the 10% amusement tax on the miniature golf course. Conventional golf courses are not subject to the amusement tax. San Van contended that the tax on a miniature golf course violated § 53 P.S. § 6924.311(10) of the LTEA, which provides that the tax base upon which the amusement tax can be levied cannot exceed 40% of the green fees. The Commonwealth Court, however, ruled that a miniature golf course was not a golf course within the meaning of the LTEA. San Van also contended that the discrimination between miniature and conventional golf courses was an unconstitutional violation of the Uniformity Clause of the Pennsylvania Constitution, which requires that all taxes must be uniform upon the same class of subjects, because conventional golf courses and miniature golf courses are in the same class of amusements. The court, however, ruled that the township's distinction between conventional golf courses and miniature golf courses was not unreasonable or unconstitutional [*San Van, Inc. v. School District of Derry Township*, 635 A.2d 254 (Pa.Commw. 1993), *app. den.*, 644 A.2d 740 (Pa. 1994)].

Golf course on public property: Allegheny County owns and operates two golf courses located in South Park, a second class township subject to the LTEA (see above). South Park attempted to collect a 10% amusement tax from the patrons of the county golf courses. Allegheny County contended that the township did not have a clear right to impose and collect the amusement tax on the golf course patrons and blocked collection of the tax. South Park sought a preliminary injunction to prevent the county's interference with the collection of the tax. The court ruled that the township had a clear right to impose and collect the tax on the golf course patrons, and the fact that the golf courses were located on public property and operated by county employees did not exempt the golf courses from the township's amusement tax. The court granted the injunction because South Park had sustained its burden of proof that it had a clear right to relief that was immediate and would suffer irreparable harm in the absence of the injunction [*Township of South Park v. County of Allegheny*, 641 A.2d 20 (Pa.Commw. 1994), *app. den.*, 663 A.2d 697 (Pa. 1995)].

Nonprofit golf club: All recreational membership dues and fees paid to nonprofit organizations, regardless of their purpose, are exempt from taxation. Exempting membership fees to nonprofit golf clubs while taxing fees charged by for-profit golf courses does not violate the Equal Protection Clause of the U.S. Constitution or the Uniformity Clause of the Pennsylvania Constitution [*Conley Motor Inns v. The Township of Penn*, 728 A.2d 1012 (Pa.Commw. 1999), *app. den.*, 745 A.2d 1225 (Pa. 1999)].

- *Bowling alleys*

Effective December 4, 2004, admissions to bowling alleys or bowling lanes may not be taxed [53 P.S. § 6924.301.1(f)(16)].

- *Selective enforcement of taxes unconstitutional*

A school district strictly enforced its amusement tax provisions against one taxpayer (Music Fair) but compromised claims against other taxpayers. Representatives of the district told Music Fair that compromise was not possible because the rate must remain uniform for all taxpayers, but secretly settled claims for liabilities for

¶3605

other taxpayers. This, according to the court, amounted to systematic unequal enforcement of the statute, which violated both the Due Process Clause of the U.S. Constitution and the Uniformity Clause of the Pennsylvania Constitution [*Tredyffrin-Easttown School District v. Valley Forge Music Fair, Inc.*, 627 A.2d 814 (Pa.Commw. 1993)].

¶3606 Business Privilege Taxes

Under the authority of the LTEA local jurisdictions may impose a business privilege tax (BPT) on taxpayers' gross receipts.

• *BPT on gross receipts prohibited*

The imposition of a business privilege tax on gross receipts after November 30, 1988 is prohibited [72 P.S. § 4750.533]. However, the Commonwealth Court has held that a flat tax is not prohibited [*Smith and McMaster, P.C. v. Newton Borough*, 669 A.2d 452 (Pa.Commw. 1995)]. In 2009 the Warrington Township Board of Supervisors enacted an ordinance imposing a $2,600 flat tax for 2008 on all businesses in the township with gross receipts in excess of $1,000,000. A group of taxpayers challenged the ordinance, claiming that it violates the prohibition of business privilege taxes in 72 P.S. § 4750.533. The Commonwealth Court upheld the Bucks County Court of Common Pleas decision the ordinance did not violate 72 P.S. § 4750.533 because it is a flat tax, albeit one with an exemption for businesses with gross receipts of $1,000,000 or less, not a tax on gross receipts [*Shelly Funeral Home, Inc., et al. v. Warrington Twp, et al.*, Pa.Commw., No. 769 C.D. 2009 (December 31, 2009), Opinion Not Reported]. This decision has been appealed to the Pennsylvania Supreme Court.

• *KOZ tax benefits*

If a political subdivision has enacted a business privilege tax (BPT) that is imposed within the boundaries of a subzone, it must provide an exemption, deduction, abatement, or credit from the BPT for a person or qualified business (see ¶4622) exercising the privilege of engaging in a business or profession within a subzone. See discussion of KOZs at ¶4622.

• *Uniformity*

The Uniformity Clause of the Pennsylvania Constitution prohibits discrimination among subjects of taxation, requiring that "[a]ll taxes shall be uniform upon the same class of subjects, within the territorial limits of the authority levying the tax . . . ." [Pennsylvania Constitution, Article VIII, § I].

Class of taxation may consist of only one member: For a period of three (3) years the Mount Carmel Area School District imposed a 10% tax on the rental income derived from leases on unimproved land. There were several owners of unimproved land in the School District subject to this tax, but only one taxpayer, Susquehanna Coal Company, leased its unimproved land. The Commonwealth Court held that the fact that only one member of a class is liable for a tax because only that member engaged in a taxable activity, or even because it is the sole member of its class does not, in and of itself, invalidate a tax, as long as the legislating body exercises good faith and does not make arbitrary and unjust distinctions [*Susquehanna Coal Company v. Mount Carmel Area School District*, 798 A.2d 321 (Pa.Commw. 2002)].

Higher tax rate on services than on sales: A BPT imposed by the city of Allentown that levied a higher tax rate on services than it did on wholesale or retail sales did not violate the Uniformity Clause of the Pennsylvania Constitution. Allentown's differential rate of tax for wholesale, retail, and service businesses was permissible because each class was a separate and distinct classification allowing for a different tax rate within each of those classes [*City of Allentown v. MSG Associates, Inc.*, 747 A.2d 1275 (Pa.Commw. 2000), *app. dism'd* 772 A.2d 413 (Pa. 2001)].

Blanket deduction for broker commissions: A city ordinance that provided a blanket deduction on all commissions paid by a listing real estate broker to another real estate broker, no matter what the arrangement is between the brokers, was found to violate the requirement of uniformity because no constitutionally valid distinction exists between brokers and other taxpayers that pay for work performed [*City of Allentown v. MSG Associates, Inc.*, 747 A.2d 1275 (Pa.Commw. 2000), *app. dism'd*, 772 A.2d 413 (Pa. 2001)].

• *Fair apportionment*

The Pennsylvania Supreme Court has ruled that a Pennsylvania township's business privilege tax (BPT) on 100% of the gross receipts of a taxpayer that had its principal offices in the township but performed a substantial amount of work outside of the township violated the Commerce Clause of the U.S. Constitution because the tax was not fairly apportioned [*Northwood Construction Co. v. Township of Upper Moreland*, Pa.Sup.Ct., No. 12 M.D. Appeal Docket 2003 (September 2, 2004), *rev'g in part* 802 A.2d 1269 (Pa.Commw. 2002)]. See discussion of *"Fair apportionment"* at ¶913. The township argued that its exclusionary provision that excluded from taxable receipts any receipts on which a taxpayer had already paid a BPT from tax to another political subdivision removed the risk of multiple taxation. The Court agreed that the township's exclusionary rule provided internal consistency but ruled that it ignored external consistency. Avoiding the risk of multiple taxation does not mean that apportionment is not required. The township's BPT plainly taxed more than the revenue attributable to in-state activities and was, therefore, unconstitutional.

In *Upper Moreland Township v. 7-Eleven, Inc.*, 160 A.3d 921 (Pa.Commw. 2017), the Commonwealth Court found that Upper Moreland Township's business privilege tax violated the U.S. Constitution because it violated a four-part test laid out by the U.S. Supreme Court in *Complete Auto Transit Inc. v. Brady*. Upper Moreland Township was home to a 7-Eleven regional office that oversaw stores in Pennsylvania and New England generally. The township's business privilege tax was assessed at a rate of 3.5 mills on taxable gross receipts. The township calculated taxable gross receipts where multi-state offices were present by combining (1) all receipts from within Pennsylvania; and (2) receipts from outside of Pennsylvania multiplied by an apportionment factor. The tax assessment essentially subjected 100% of the franchise fees paid by franchise stores in Pennsylvania to tax without any reduction or consideration of how interstate commerce may have assisted the generation of those receipts. The court found that the Pennsylvania 7-Eleven franchise fee receipts were the result of interstate activity that required apportionment. In finding that the franchise fees paid by stores in Pennsylvania should be apportioned, the court did not require 7-Eleven to prove the amount of the fees that resulted from interstate commerce as an affirmative matter of proof.

• *Coterminous jurisdictions*

Coterminous jurisdictions are not required to split the maximum rate of business privilege taxes [*Carpenter and Carpenter v. City of Johnstown and Greater Johnstown School District*, 605 A.2d 456 (Pa.Commw. 1992), *app. den.*, 613 A.2d 1210 (Pa. 1992); *Airpark International I v. Cmwlth.*, 677 A.2d 399 (Pa.Commw. 1996), *aff'd per curiam* 735 A.2d 656 (Pa. 1999)].

• *Management fees*

Taxpayer provided management services to a group of affiliated corporations. The Court held that the management fees received from the affiliated corporations were subject to business privilege tax [Applied Tech Products Corp. v. Radnor Township, 882 A.2d 1035 (Pa.Commw. 2005)].

• *Situs of services—base of operations*

Because a company with a place of business in one taxing jurisdiction may provide services to customers in many other jurisdictions, determining where the services are taxable is often difficult. The following cases address the issue of the situs of services.

¶3606

Office in city, activities outside city (Gilberti): The Pennsylvania Supreme Court has ruled that having a place of business within a city gives a taxpayer a base of operations from which to manage, direct, and control business activities occurring both inside and outside the city limits, thus rendering gross receipts of the business, including income derived from services outside the city, subject to the city's business privilege tax [*Gilberti v. City of Pittsburgh*, 511 A.2d 1321 (Pa. 1986), *rev'g* 493 A.2d 137 (1985)].

No office in township (QED): A township (Lower Merion) was not permitted to impose a business privilege tax on a taxpayer (QED) that had no base of operations in the township. QED, a residential building improvement contractor, subcontracted all phases of its remodeling work and did not own or operate a truck or other construction equipment. QED had its only office in Radnor Township and, according to the Commonwealth Court, was not doing business in Lower Merion Township within the meaning of the statute [*Township of Lower Merion v. QED, Inc.*, 738 A.2d 1066 (Pa.Commw. 1999), *app. den.*, 775 A.2d 811 (Pa. 2001)]. The *QED* case supplements the *Gilberti* decision (discussed above) by establishing that a local business privilege tax cannot be imposed in the absence of an office (base of operations) within the local jurisdiction. *Gilberti* established that a taxpayer with an office within a city was subject to the city's business privilege tax, even though it had substantial transactions outside the city.

Temporary on-site trailers: A company (Rendina) that was engaged in a construction project in Harrisburg and maintained a job trailer to use as an office at the construction site was held subject to Harrisburg's business privilege tax [*Rendina, Inc. v. City of Harrisburg*, No. 130 MAP 2005 (Pa. 2007), *rev'g* 859 A.2d 888 (Pa.Commw. 2004)]. The company's general office was located in Lancaster County, not in Harrisburg. The trailer was not used to solicit business, conduct meetings, store supplies, or perform office work other than communications limited to performance on the project. All general management, accounting, estimating, and other administrative functions were completed at Rendina's principal place of business (Lancaster). Rendina's superintendent on the project did not receive mail at the trailer or use the trailer for project-related meetings. Rendina contended that it did not have a "place of business" in Harrisburg, even though the project lasted three years. The city of Harrisburg responded that Rendina maintained a field office in the city that provided it with a base of operations from which to manage, direct, and control its business activities necessary to complete the project. The Commonwealth Court ruled that it was clear that the job site trailer was not a "place of business" (*i.e.*, a base of operations from which Rendina could manage, direct, and control business activities occurring both inside and outside city limits within the meaning of *Gilberti*, discussed above). Thus, Rendina was not subject to Harrisburg's business privilege tax (BPT). However, the Pennsylvania Supreme Court concluded that Rendina's work in Harrisburg in connection with the construction of the project was subject to taxation under Harrisburg's business privilege tax regardless of whether the job site trailer was used as a "base of operations" as that term was utilized in *Gilberti* (see above) or whether the three-year construction project can be viewed as constituting a single, "lengthy transaction."

Rendina Dilemma

For BPT purposes, the base-of-operations rule provides that a taxpayer must maintain a permanent base of operations in a jurisdiction in order to be subject to its BPT. For many years the base-of-operations rule has served as a bright-line test for determining whether a taxpayer is subject to the BPT in a taxing jurisdiction. However, in reversing the Commonwealth Court's *Rendina* decision, the Pennsylvania Supreme Court effectively eliminated the base-of-operations rule by ruling that it was not necessary that the taxpayer maintain a permanent base of operations in Harrisburg in order to be subject to its BPT.

This creates a problem for taxpayers who do business in multiple jurisdictions. The jurisdiction in which it maintains its permanent base of operations may impose a tax on the taxpayer's entire business activities, while another jurisdiction may tax receipts attributable to operations in its jurisdiction. This would result in double taxation unless some reasonable apportionment rules are applied or the law is changed.

H.B. 1513 was signed into law on May 6, 2014 effective for tax years beginning on or after January 1, 2014 and is also known as Act 42 of 2014. This legislation limits the authority of local taxing authorities to impose business privilege taxes. A taxpayer will be subject to tax if it conducts transactions for more than 14 days within the jurisdictional limits of the taxing authority within a taxable year or if the taxpayer maintains a "base of operations" in the locality. Base of operations is defined as an actual, physical and permanent place of business from which a taxpayer manages, directs and controls its business activities at that location. Act 42 also reduces the potential for double taxation by providing that any gross receipts subject to tax through a base of operations may not include any receipts subject to tax measured by conducting transactions for fifteen or more days within the tax year.

Temporary on-site trailers (Valvano): A taxpayer (Valvano) maintained its only permanent place of business outside Scranton (in Dickson City) but maintained on-site construction trailers inside Scranton. The Commonwealth Court has ruled that on-site construction trailers are not permanent offices that would allow a local jurisdiction to impose a business privilege tax (BPT) on the taxpayer' construction activities within the city of Scranton [*Scranton v. R.V. Valvano Construction Co.,* Pa.Commw., No. 763 C.D. 2004 (November 5, 2004), *aff'g Scranton v. R.V. Construction Co., Inc.,* Lackawanna County Court of Common Pleas (2002)].

Warehouse outside borough: The taxpayer operated a retail store in the borough of Bridgeville, where all of its business was managed, controlled, and directed. The taxpayer also maintained a warehouse in Cecil Township that was associated with one of its lines of business. The taxpayer argued that the Cecil Township location was a base of operations and that Bridgeville was not entitled to tax the gross receipts from that line of business. The Commonwealth Court concluded that the company was subject to the borough's business privilege tax because the warehouse was not a base of operations because it was not used to solicit business, conduct meetings, store supplies other than inventory, or perform office work other than that related to the single line of business [*Rusmur Floors, Inc. v. Borough of Bridgeville,* No. 983 C.D. 2005 (Pa.Commw. 2005, *opinion not reported*)].

Wording of local ordinance (J&K Trash Removal): A local ordinance of the City of Chester provided for a business privilege tax on (BPT) the gross volume of business "transacted within the territorial limits of the City [Chester]." Thus, a taxpayer (a trash removal service) was not subject to the city's BPT on gross receipts from business transactions outside the city limits because the city ordinance imposed territorial limitations on its BPT [*J & K Trash Removal, Inc. v. City of Chester,* 842 A.2d 981 (Pa.Commw. 2004)]. In *Gilberti v. City of Pittsburgh,* 511 A.2d 1231 (Pa. 1986) the Pennsylvania Supreme Court ruled that a taxing body has the authority to levy a BPT on the gross receipts from business transactions outside the territorial limits of the taxing jurisdiction. However, in *Gilberti,* the city ordinance imposing the BPT did not contain territorial limitations like those in *J&K Trash Removal.*

Comment

The issue of whether a business privilege tax requires a base of operations has been litigated only within the context of the Local Tax Enabling Act. Whether or not the result would be the same under another enabling act (*e.g.,* the Sterling Act, which applies to Philadelphia) is an issue that has not been resolved by the courts.

¶3606

• *Clarification provided by Act 2014-42*

In May of 2014, Act 42 of 2014 amended LTEA to provide that a business privilege tax can be applied where a taxpayer is "conducting transactions in the jurisdiction" for fifteen or more calendar days within the calendar year, or maintains a "base of operations" in the jurisdiction. Base of operations is defined to be a physical and permanent place of business that manages, directs and controls its business activities at that location. Act 42 also attempts to limit the possibility of double taxation of the same gross receipts by providing that the gross receipts subject to the business privilege tax in a taxing jurisdiction (as a result of having a base of operations in such jurisdiction) shall not include any receipts that were subject to tax as a result of the same taxpayer being subject to tax elsewhere as a result of conducting transactions in another jurisdiction for fifteen or more days.

• *Construction of residential dwellings*

Cheltenham Township imposes a business privilege tax measured by gross receipts. Taxpayer, a developer engaged in the business of constructing residential dwellings, contended that it was not subject to the business privilege tax because of a statute that prohibited imposition by local jurisdictions of a tax on the construction of or improvement to residential dwellings (53 P.S. § 6924.301.1(f)(11)). However, the Commonwealth Court (in an unreported memorandum decision) ruled that the taxpayer was subject to the business privilege tax because the tax was imposed on the privilege of doing business, not on the construction of or improvement to residential dwellings. The taxpayer, therefore, was found to be subject to the township's business privilege tax [*Cheltenham Township v. Breyer Associates*, Pa.Commw., Nos. 2750 & 3061 C.D. 1993 (August 10, 1994), opinion not reported]. See, also, *John Deklewa & Sons, Inc. v. Township of Collier*, Pa.Commw., No. 2319 C.D. 2004 (May 20, 2005), *opinion not reported*, where taxpayer was not subject to tax from business transactions outside the township's limits because the township's ordinance provided for a tax on each and every dollar of gross volume of business transacted *within the territorial limits of the Township.*

NOTE: Memorandum opinions designated "opinion not reported" may not be cited in a brief, an argument, or an opinion.

• *Providing commercial leasehold space*

In *Reaman v. Allentown Power Center, L.P.*, 74 A.3d 371 (2013), the Commonwealth Court found that the provision of commercial office space represented the provision of personal services under the relevant local business privilege tax. But see *Fish v. Township of Lower Merion*, 100 A.3d 746 (2014) where the imposition of the township's business privilege tax to a taxpayer's gross receipts from leasing violated the statutory exclusion under LTEA for leases and lease transactions.

• *Preemption—movie theater admissions*

The Local Tax Enabling Act (LTEA) provides that local jurisdictions do not have the authority to impose a tax on admissions to motion picture theaters [53 P.S. § 6924.301.1(f)(10)]. Cheltenham Cinema, relying on the LTEA, refused to pay a township's business privilege tax (BPT). The Pennsylvania Supreme Court, however, held that the township's BPT did not tax the same subject matter that is excluded from taxation under the LTEA. The LTEA prohibits the imposition of a tax directly on movie theater admission sales, while the township's BPT is imposed on the *privilege to do business*, measured by gross volume and determined by gross receipts. Thus, a township may impose a tax on the privilege of doing business in the township, even if the taxpayer is a motion picture theater [*Cheltenham Township v. Cheltenham Cinema, Inc.*, 697 A.2d 258 (Pa. 1997), *aff'g* 661 A.2d 23 (Pa.Commw. 1995)].

• *Business privilege tax vs. transaction tax*

The Interboro School District imposed a 6% tax on commercial parking fees. A taxpayer challenged the tax as invalid because it violated the prohibition against local business privilege taxes of the Local Tax Reform Act [72 P.S. § 4750.533]. A Commonwealth Court found that the tax was a transaction tax permitted by the Local Tax Enabling Act [53 P.S. § 6924.301.1], and not a business privilege tax that would be prohibited by the Local Tax Reform Act. According to the court, a business privilege tax is a tax imposed on all gross receipts from *all business activities*, while the district's tax is a transaction tax that is imposed on the receipts from *designated transactions*. The fact that all of a taxpayer's gross receipts may come from the designated taxable transaction is immaterial. The Commonwealth Court's decision was affirmed by the Pennsylvania Supreme Court [*Airpark International I*, 677 A.2d 388 (Pa.Commw. 1996), *aff'd per curiam*, 735 A.2d 656 (Pa. 1999)].

• *Business privilege tax vs. mercantile license tax*

A pharmacy's gross receipts derived from the preparation and dispensing of prescription drugs and devices were not subject to a borough's business privilege tax because they were gross receipts from the sales of goods subject to the borough's mercantile tax, and the borough's business privilege ordinance specifically excluded gross receipts subject to the mercantile tax [*Hegner Pharmacy Service Inc. v. Borough of Beaver*, 786 A.2d 1030 (Pa.Commw. 2001)].

• *Prohibition Against Taxing Leases*

On December 21, 2015, the Supreme Court of Pennsylvania held that the exception in 53 P.S. § 6924.301.1(f)(1) of the Local Tax Enabling Act, which prohibits the taxation of leases and lease transactions, does not preclude a municipality from applying its business privilege tax to businesses whose income is derived solely from leasing real property. [*Fish, Hrabrick and Briskin v. Township of Lower Merion*, 128 A.3d 764 (Pa. 2015).]

• *Rendering Public Utility Service*

In *S&H Transport, Inc. v City of York*, 140 A.3d 1 (Pa. 2016), the Pennsylvania Supreme Court found that a transportation broker was not involved in the rendering of any public utility service so as to be exempt from the city's business privilege tax under LTEA because the taxpayer was merely brokering freight transportation services between its customers and common carriers. 140 A.3d 1 (Pa. 2016)

¶3607 Earned Income/Net Profits Tax Authorized by the LTEA

The earned income tax is the only tax authorized by the Local Tax Enabling Act that is also defined by that Act [53 P.S. § 6913]. All of the provisions of 53 P.S. § 6913 are included in, or construed to be a part of, each tax levied and assessed on earned income by any political subdivision. The earned income tax is imposed on earned income received and net profits earned in each taxable year of the taxpayer.

Act 18 of 2018, effective July 3, 2018, amended provisions of the Local Tax Enabling Act, 53 P.S. § 6924.101 et seq., relating to local earned income tax. The amendments generally (i) add definitions for "contingent fee audit" and "private collection agency;" (ii) update the definition of "nonresident," "nonresident tax," and "taxpayer;" (iii) prohibit second class cities from using contingent fee audits by private collection agencies as part of an effort to collect payroll taxes; (iv) provide that an individual who does not meet the domicile requirements for purposes of determining and paying tax under the Tax Reform Code will be deemed not to meet the domicile requirements for purposes of local earned income tax; and (v) provide that for purposes of collecting earned income taxes (and for crediting purposes), the terms "earned income" and "net profits" will include all taxes on earned income or net profits whether authorized by the Local Tax Enabling Act or any other Pennsylvania law, unless the law specifically provides otherwise. This act also allows taxpayers who have paid pay earned income tax to avoid penalties for late payment provided that the taxpayer has made timely estimated tax payments (in four equal instalments) that at least equal the taxpayer's previous year's tax liability, or amount to 90% of the current year's tax liability (less withholding).

• *Exemption*

A local taxing authority may, by ordinance or resolution, exempt any person from an earned income tax, or any portion thereof, whose total income from all sources is less than twelve thousand dollars ($12,000) per annum and may adopt regulations for the processing of claims for exemptions [LTEA, 53 P.S. § 6924.301.1]. Consult the local tax statute for an allowable exemption, if any, under this provision of the LTEA.

• *Rate limitation*

The earned income tax may be levied at a rate not to exceed 1% [LTEA, § 8]. If two political subdivisions both impose an earned income tax on the same subjects, they may divide the rates between them. They may divide the rate unequally, as they agree. An exception to this rule is made for cities of the second class (*i.e.*, Pittsburgh). Pittsburgh may impose an earned income tax at a maximum rate of 1% even though a school district levies an earned income tax on the same person at the maximum rate of 1% [LTEA, § 8]. Since neither jurisdiction can impose a rate greater than 1%, the maximum combined rate is 2%. A "distressed school district" is permitted to levy an additional tax at a rate sufficient to liquidate the indebtedness of the district. A distressed school district may, therefore, levy an earned income tax at a rate greater than 1% [24 P.S. § 6-694].

• *Withholding requirements*

Local earned income tax, in general, is subject to withholding requirements. See local statutes for withholding details.

Local tax withholding of Commonwealth employees: The Commonwealth of Pennsylvania must collect and remit, on a quarterly basis, local earned income tax withheld from Commonwealth employees that reside or work in a local jurisdiction that imposes a tax on earned income [Administrative Code of 1929, § 224 (71 P.S. § 84)].

• *"Earned income" defined*

Earned income means "compensation" (income as determined for personal income tax purposes under 72 P.S. § 7303) and personal income tax regulations (discussed at ¶ 202), Act 32 of 2008 was intended to streamline the collection of the local earned income tax. However, it also expanded the scope of earned income. Effective for earned income tax collected after December 31, 2015, active duty military pay is exempted. Employee business expenses that are deductible for Pennsylvania personal income tax purposes (discussed at ¶ 203) are allowable deductions for earned income tax purposes. The amount of any housing allowance provided to a member of the clergy is not taxable as earned income [53 P.S. § 6913.I]. Act 32 of 2008 (H.B. 1063) provides that military pay will be taxable in the same manner as for personal income tax [53 P.S. § 6924.501].

What Is the Status of the O'Reilly Case?

In *O'Reilly v. Fox Chapel Area School District*, 555 A.2d 1288 (Pa. 1988), the Pennsylvania Supreme Court held that, for local earned income tax purposes, business losses could be used to offset earned income. Until July 2, 2008, the definition of earned income for local purposes was the same as the definition of compensation for Pennsylvania personal income tax purposes found in 72 P.S. § 7303, under which losses in one class (*e.g.*, net profits) cannot be used to offset income in another class (*e.g.*, compensation). Tax gatherers nonetheless continued to allow the O'Reilly offset. Effective January 1, 2012, the term "earned income" does not include offsets for business losses [53 P.S. § 6924.501, effective January 1, 2012]. This definitely overrules *O'Reilly*. What is not clear is whether *O'Reilly* is overruled effective July 2, 2008, or January 1, 2012

Employee business expenses: Employee business expenses are allowable deductions as determined under Article III of the Tax Reform Code [53 P.S. § 6913.I].

Clergy housing allowances: The amount of any housing allowance provided to a member of the clergy is not taxable as earned income [53 P.S. § 6913].

Right-to-Know Act vs. Confidentiality

A school district taxpayer made a formal written request for a list of the names and addresses of persons who paid earned income tax to the school district. The school district asserted that disclosure of the requested information is statutorily forbidden under The Local Tax Enabling Act [53 P.S. § 6913] and the Local Taxpayers Bill of Rights Act [53 Pa.C.S. § 8437]. The Court agreed with the school district.

The Right-to-Know Act [65 P.S. §§ 66.1—66.4] provides that public records must be open for public inspection and examination and gives citizens of Pennsylvania the right to take extracts and/or make copies, photographs, and/or photostats of public record. However, the Right-to-Know Act also provides that information gained by the officers, their agents, or by any other officials or agents of the taxing district, as a result of any declarations, returns, investigations, hearings or verifications required or authorized by the ordinance or resolution, is confidential and can be divulged only for official purposes, in accordance with a proper judicial order, or as otherwise provided by law. Furthermore, the Local Taxpayers Bill of Rights Act provides that any information gained by a local taxing authority as a result of any audit, return, report, investigation, hearing, or verification is confidential tax information and forbids local taxing authorities to divulge such information except for official purposes or as provided by law [53 Pa. P.S. § 8437]. The Pennsylvania Commonwealth Court held that the identity of the taxpayer falls within the category of confidential information obtained from tax declarations and returns, the release of which is expressly forbidden by both the Local Tax Enabling Act and the Local Taxpayers Bill of Rights [*Juniata Valley School District v. Wargo,* 797 A.2d 428 (Pa.Commw. 2002)].

* *"Net profits" defined*

"Net profits" means the net income from the operation of a business, profession, or other activity (except corporations) determined under 72 P.S. § 7303 and regulations in 61 Pa. Code Pt. I, Subpt. B, Art. V (relating to personal income tax). The term does not include income that is not paid for services provided and that is in the nature of earnings from an investment [53 P.S. § 6913].

Farming: For taxpayers engaged in the business, profession or activity of farming, net profits does not include:

(1) Any interest earnings generated from any monetary accounts or investment instruments of the farming business.

(2) Any gain on the sale of farm machinery.

(3) Any gain on the sale of livestock held 12 months or more for draft, breeding or dairy purposes.

(4) Any gain on the sale of other capital assets of the farm.

S corporation net profits: The law excludes net profits of corporations from the definition of net profits [53 P.S. § 6913]. Therefore, the net profits of Pennsylvania S corporations are still not subject to local net profits taxes. See *Scott v. Hempfield Area School District and Hempfield Township,* 643 A.2d 1140 (Pa.Commw. 1994), where the Court concluded that net profits passing through to a sole shareholder in an S corporation constituted investment income rather than earned income and thus were not subject to the local net profits tax.

What Is the Status of the Aronson Case?

Under the definition of net profits for local net profits tax purposes prior to February 16, 2003, losses in one business (*e.g.,* a real estate business) could not be used to offset net profits in another business (*e.g.,* a law practice). See *Aronson v. City of Pittsburgh,* 485 A.2d 890 (Pa.Commw. 1985). The new definition of net profits for local net profits tax purposes, however, is the same as the definition of net profits for personal income tax purposes under 72 P.S. § 7303. Under the personal income tax provisions, a taxpayer can use a loss from one business to offset gain from another business if both gain and loss qualify as "net income from the operation of a business." There is some uncertainty about the status of the *Aronson* case. Given the facts of *Aronson* and the new definition of net profits for local net profits tax purposes, would the court reach the same conclusion? Act 32 of 2008 (H.B. 1063), which overruled the O'Reilly, offset was silent on the status of Aronson.

Investment income: The term "net profits" does not include income that is not paid for services provided and that is in the nature of earnings from an investment [53 P.S. § 6913.I].

Farming income: For taxpayers engaged in farming, the term "net profits" does not include the following [53 P.S. § 6913.I]:

(1) Interest earnings generated from monetary accounts or investment instruments of the farming business.

(2) Gain on the sale of farm machinery.

(3) Gain on the sale of livestock held 12 months or more for draft, breeding, or dairy purposes.

(4) Gain on the sale of other capital assets of the farm.

Definitions Applicable to All Earned Income/Net Profits Taxes

This definition of earned income and net profits is included in or construed to be a part of any earned income or net profits tax levied and assessed under the authority of the LTEA by any political subdivision and cannot be altered or changed by any political subdivision [53 P.S. § 6913].

• *Indispensable parties*

Montella: A taxpayer's lawsuit alleging that a private debt collector hired by two Pennsylvania townships to collect local earned income taxes on retirement benefits in violation of the Local Tax Enabling Act and local earned income ordinances was properly dismissed because the taxpayer failed to join the townships, which were indispensable and necessary parties. The townships were vicariously liable for the actions of the debt collector and would be bound by any court judgments. Furthermore, the taxpayer's action sought injunctive and declaratory relief, and, therefore, a meaningful remedy could not be fashioned if the townships were not included [*Montella v. Berkheimer Associates et al.*, 690 A.2d 802 (Pa.Commw. 1997)].

• *S corporation profits*

The Hempfield Area School District and Hempfield Township levied their earned income tax on the sole shareholder of an S corporation with respect to both the shareholder's salary from the corporation and the net profits of the corporation. The LTEA authorizes municipal governing bodies to impose a tax on earned income, which is defined as compensation for services rendered. The Commonwealth Court held that the net profits of the corporation did not represent compensation for services rendered because the taxpayer received a salary from the corporation for the services he performed. The fact that the taxpayer is the sole shareholder and plays an active role in his corporation does not automatically make all income from the corporation (whether classified as salary or corporate net profits) earned income. The net profits of the corporation are characterized as realized income, which is investment income, not earned income. Because these net profits of the S corporation are not earned income they are not subject to the school district and township earned income tax [*Scott v. Hempfield Area School District and Hempfield Township*, 643 A.2d 1140 (Pa.Commw. 1994)].

• *Investment income*

Taxpayer (Pugliese) participated in his employer's corporate incentive compensation plan, which administers compensation awards to designated employees based on merit and performance. Recipients may elect to accept awards entirely in cash or choose to defer half to be invested in the employer's convertible debentures. In 1984 and 1985 Pugliese elected to defer $317,600 of his awards and accepted this amount in convertible debentures. In 1990, Pugliese received a total distribution of $760,798.88, which represented the deferred amount plus appreciation and interest of $443,198.88. Pugliese reported only $317,600 of this as earned income and compensation. However, his employer reported the entire amount on Pugliese's W-2. The taxing jurisdiction (Township) required that he report the entire amount, consistent with his W-2. The Court of Common Pleas ruled in Pugliese's favor, and the Township appealed to the Commonwealth Court. The court ruled that the Local Tax Enabling Act authorized a local jurisdiction to impose a tax on earned income. However, the court said that the interest and appreciation were investment income, not compensation. Therefore, the Township asserted an improper expansion of the definition of earned income by requiring the amount of earned income to be consistent with the amount reported on Pugliese's W-2. Since investment income is not taxable by local jurisdictions, Pugliese was required to pay earned income tax only on the deferred $317,600 [*Pugliese v. Township of Upper St. Clair*, 660 A.2d 155 (Pa.Commw. 1995)].

• *Employee stock options*

The Pennsylvania Supreme Court has ruled that the value of stock options received by an employee from a company's nonqualified stock option plan resulted in earned income for purposes of the local earned income tax [*Marchlen v. The Township of Mt. Lebanon*, 746 A.2d 566 (2000), *rev'g Marchlen v. The Township of Mt. Lebanon*, 707 A.2d 631 (1998)]. Thus, the difference between the price paid by the employee and the market price of the underlying stock when the options are exercised constitutes taxable earned income. Because the value of the stock is speculative at the time options are granted, the spread is not taxable until the options are exercised. Pursuant to its decision to reverse *Marchlen*, the Pennsylvania Supreme Court also reversed the Commonwealth Court decision in *Newbrey* [*Newbrey v. Township and School District of Upper St. Clair*, 750 A.2d 304 (Pa. 2000), *rev'g* 710 A.2d 96 (Pa.Commw. 1998)].

The Pennsylvania Commonwealth Court, however, has held that nonqualified stock options granted to the chief executive officer of a company located within Whitpain Township, Pennsylvania, but exercised after the taxpayer had retired and moved to another state, were not subject to the Township's earned income tax. The taxable income from the stock options was received when those options were exercised by the taxpayer and could be taxed upon a readily ascertainable value. Because the taxpayer neither lived nor worked in the Township at that time, it had no authority to tax such income [*In Re Appeal of Whitpain Township Board of Supervisors*, Pa.Commw., No. 2059 C.D. 2006 (February 13, 2008)].

KOZ Tax Benefits

If a political subdivision has imposed an earned income and net profits tax, it must provide an exemption, deduction, abatement, or credit from the earned income received by a resident of a KOZ subzone, expansion subzone, or improvement subzone or the net profits of a qualified business attributable to business activity conducted within a subzone, an expansion subzone, or an improvement subzone. See discussion of KOZs at ¶4622.

¶3608 Earned Income/Net Profits Tax Authorized by Other Enabling Legislation

• *Earned income/net profits tax authorized by the Taxpayers Local Control Act*

The Taxpayers' Local Control Act was passed as part of what is commonly referred to as Act 50 [Act of May 5, 1998, No. 50 (S.B. 669)]. The Act gives school districts the power to impose a tax on the earned income and net profits of resident individuals. Under the provisions of Act 50, school districts are authorized to impose a tax on the earned income and net profits of resident individuals of the school district at a rate of 1.0%, 1.25%, or 1.5% [53 Pa.C.S. §8711]. A school district that imposes an Act 50 earned income/net profits tax may exempt any person whose total income from all sources is less than $7,500 [53 Pa.C.S. §8714] Act 50 is discussed in more detail at ¶3504.

Issues Related to Change of Definitions

Since Act 50 incorporated the definitions of earned income and net profits from the LTEA, the same issues relating to the *Aronson* and *O'Reilly* cases (discussed at ¶3607) arise within the context of Act 50 earned income/net profits tax.

A school district that imposes an earned income/net profits tax under Act 50 cannot impose an earned income/net profits tax under the LTEA (discussed at ¶3607). Residents of school districts that impose an earned income/net profits tax under Act 50 who are also subject to Philadelphia's earned income/net profits tax may claim a credit against their state personal income tax (see ¶127).

NOTE: A chart of current local earned income taxes (listed alphabetically by county and jurisdiction) can be found in the CCH PENNSYLVANIA STATE TAX REPORTS at ¶229-101.

¶3609 Mercantile License Taxes

The Local Tax Enabling Act authorizes the imposition of a mercantile license tax on business volume at the following maximum rates [53 P.S. §6924.311]:

(1) *Wholesalers:* One mill on each dollar of business volume by wholesale dealers in goods, wares, and merchandise.

(2) *Retailers:* One and one-half mills on each dollar of business volume by retail dealers in goods, wares, and merchandise.

(3) *Restaurants:* One and one-half mills on each dollar of business volume by proprietors of restaurants or other places where food, drink, and refreshments are served.

Rate Limitation

In cities of the second class (*i.e.*, Pittsburgh), mercantile license tax rates may not exceed one mill on wholesale dealers and two mills on retail dealers and restaurant proprietors [LTEA, §8].

For wholesalers and retailers, sales of items taken as trade-in are not taxable except to the extent the selling price exceeds the amount allowed as trade-in.

After November 30, 1988, no political subdivision can impose a new business mercantile license. Any political subdivision that had a mercantile license tax on or before November 30, 1988, may continue to impose it [Local Tax Reform Act of December 13, 1988, P.L. 1121, §533]. Consult local statutes to determine whether a mercantile license tax is still in effect.

Keystone Opportunity Zone (KOZ) Tax Benefits

Qualified persons and businesses in KOZs are entitled to relief from mercantile license taxes. See discussion of KOZs at ¶4622.

¶3610 Per Capita Taxes

The Local Tax Enabling Act authorizes the local imposition of a per capita or head tax at the maximum rate of $10. A local taxing authority may, by ordinance or resolution, exempt any person whose total income from all sources is less than ten thousand dollars ($10,000) per year from the per capita or similar head tax and may adopt regulations for the processing of claims for exemptions [53 P.S. § 6924.301.1].

A school district of the second, third, or fourth class may levy a per capita tax of not less than $1 or more than $5. A school district may exempt (in whole or in part) any person whose total income from all sources is less than $5,000 [24 P.S. § 6-679].

¶3611 Occupation Taxes

The following is a discussion of local occupation and occupation privilege taxes in jurisdictions other than Pittsburgh and Philadelphia. See ¶3625 for a discussion of cases related to local occupation taxes.

• *Occupation taxes (flat rate)*

A local jurisdiction may impose a flat rate occupation tax (not using a millage or percentage as a basis) at a maximum rate of $10 [53 P.S. § 6924.311(7)].

• *Occupation taxes (millage rate)*

Municipalities and school districts may levy a flat-rate occupation tax (see above) or a millage-rate occupation tax (often referred to as an occupation assessment tax) based on the assessed value of occupations. Unlike the flat-rate occupation tax, there is no limit on the millage rate when an occupation tax is levied on the assessed value of the occupation. This has sometimes resulted in extremely high occupation tax rates.

Occupation Tax vs. Occupational Privilege Tax

In practice, the occupational privilege tax is often referred to as an occupation tax. The occupational privilege tax, however, is a tax on the privilege of engaging in an occupation while the occupation tax (flat-rate or millage-rate) is a tax on occupations themselves. The millage-rate version of the occupation tax, based on the assessed value of occupations, has its roots in seventeenth-and eighteenth-century England, when occupations were often viewed as a form of property that could be taxed. Thus, the occupation tax can be viewed broadly as a tax on property, while the occupational privilege tax is a tax on privilege, not property. This distinction is important.

• *Occupational privilege taxes (flat rate)*

Until January 1, 2005, a local jurisdiction could impose an occupational privilege tax at a maximum rate of $10. A local taxing authority may, by ordinance or resolution, exempt any person whose total income from all sources is less than twelve thousand dollars ($12,000) per year from the occupational privilege tax and may adopt regulations for the processing of claims for exemptions [LTEA, 53 P.S. § 6924.301.1]. An occupational privilege tax may be levied, assessed, and collected only by the political subdivision of the taxpayer's place of employment [LTEA, 53 P.S. § 6924.301.1(f)(9)].

Beginning January 1, 2005, the occupational privilege tax is replaced by the local services tax, discussed at ¶3618. Any occupational privilege tax enacted by a political subdivision prior to December 1, 2004, continues in full force and effect (without reenactment) as if it had been levied, assessed, or collected as an LST Tax [Act 222 of

2004 (H.B. 197), § 6]. Any reference in any act or law to an occupational privilege tax means the local services tax (formerly called the emergency and municipal services tax).

Existing Occupational Privilege Taxes Treated As LST

Municipalities do not have to amend their existing occupational privilege taxes unless they wish to enact a higher LST rate under Act 222 [Act 222 of 2004, § 6]. Section 6 of Act 222 provides that existing municipal ordinances adopting occupational privilege taxes will continue to be in full for and effect, without reenactment, as if they had been levied, assessed, or collected as an LST under § 2(9) of Act 222. All references in any ordinance or resolution to a tax on the privilege of engaging in an occupation are deemed to be a reference to an LST for purposes of Act 222 [Act 222 of 2004, § 6].

• *Statute of limitations*

In 1989 and 1990, the Tyrone Area School District filed actions against taxpayers for collection of delinquent occupation taxes dating as far back as 1970. The taxpayers filed an answer and a new matter asserting that the collection was barred by the three-year statute of limitations provided by § 13(VII)(b) of the LTEA (see above). The court, however, ruled that § 13 of the LTEA applied only to earned income taxes. Thus, the school district was not time barred from collecting delinquent occupation taxes by the three-year statute of limitations against collecting earned income tax [*Tyrone Area School District v. Delbaggio*, 638 A.2d 416 (Pa.Commw. 1994)].

¶3612 Property Taxes

Real property taxes are discussed beginning at ¶3501 and personal property taxes are discussed beginning at ¶3516.

¶3613 Realty Transfer Taxes

The following political subdivisions may impose a tax upon the transfer of real property or an interest in real property within their subdivision limits [72 P.S. § 8101-D]:

    (1) Cities of the second class.

    (2) Cities of the second class A.

    (3) Cities of the third class.

    (4) Boroughs.

    (5) Incorporated towns.

    (6) Townships of the first class.

    (7) Townships of the second class.

    (8) School districts of the first class A.

    (9) School districts of the second class.

    (10) School districts of the third class.

    (11) School districts of the fourth class.

Local realty transfer taxes can be imposed regardless of where the instruments making the transfers are made, executed or delivered, or where the actual settlements on the transfer take place, to the extent that the transactions are subject to the Commonwealth realty transfer tax imposed by Article XI-C of the Tax Reform Code. In addition, qualifying political subdivisions may impose a local real estate transfer tax upon additional classes or types of transactions if the tax is imposed by the subdivision under the Local Tax Enabling Act prior to July 2, 1986 [72 P.S. § 8101-D].

• *Rate Limitations*

Local realty transfer taxes are subject to the rate limitations imposed by §5, §8, and §17 of the Local Tax Enabling Act and are administered, collected, and enforced under the Local Tax Enabling Act [72 P.S. §8102-D].

Caution

The following discussion includes amendments that are applicable to documents made, executed, delivered, accepted, or presented for recording on or after October 5, 2005 [Act 40 of 2005 (H.B. 176) §24(5)].

• *Determination and notice of tax*

A local jurisdiction may authorize the Pennsylvania Department of Revenue to collect delinquent local realty transfer taxes [72 P.S. §8109-D]. If the correct amount of the tax is not paid by the last date prescribed for timely payment as provided for in 72 P.S. §8102-C (see ¶3304), the Department of Revenue may determine the tax, interest and penalty as provided for in 72 P.S. §8109-D and collect and enforce the tax, interest, and penalty in the same manner as provided for in the Commonwealth realty transfer tax provisions (discussed at ¶3304) [72 P.S. §8102-D]. The local realty transfer tax, interest, and penalty that the Department of Revenue collects will be remitted to the appropriate recorder of deeds [72 P.S. §8105-D]. 72 P.S. §8109-D provides the following:

(1) If a taxpayer underpays the correct amount of a local realty transfer tax by 25% or more, the tax may be assessed at any time within six years after the date on which the document was recorded.

(2) If any part of an underpayment of tax is due to fraud or an undisclosed, intentional disregard of rules and regulations, the full amount of the tax may be assessed at any time.

Any local realty transfer that determined by the Department of Revenue to be due that remains unpaid after demand for payment, and all penalties and interest thereon, are a lien in favor of the affected political subdivision upon the property, both real and personal, of the person but only after the lien has been entered and docketed of record by the prothonotary of the county where the property is situated [72 P.S. §8110-D(a)].

• *Refunds*

Whenever the amount due upon determination, redetermination, or review is less than the amount paid, the political subdivision must refund the difference [72 P.S. §8111-D(a)]. If there has been no determination of unpaid tax, a taxpayer must make an application for refund to the political subdivision in the manner prescribed by statute [72 P.S. §8111-D(b)].

• *Regulations*

The regulations promulgated under the Commonwealth realty transfer tax are applicable to the local realty transfer taxes [72 P.S. §8103-D(a)].

• *Documentary stamps*

The payment of local realty transfer tax must be evidenced by the affixing of a documentary stamp or stamps to every document by the person making, executing, delivering, or presenting the document for recording; and the stamps must be affixed in a way that their removal will require the continued application of steam or water. The person using or affixing the stamps must write, stamp, or cause to be written or stamped thereon the initials of the person's name and the date upon which the stamps are affixed or used so that the stamps cannot be used again. The Department of Revenue, however, may prescribe another method of cancellation if it deems to expedient [72 P.S. §8104-D].

¶3613

• *Collection agent*

The recorder of deeds is the collection agent for any political subdivision that levies a local realty transfer tax. The recorder of deeds is responsible for remitting tax, interest, and penalty collected to the appropriate political subdivision [72 P.S. § 8105-D].

• *Proceeds of judicial sale*

The local realty transfer tax must be fully paid and has priority out of the proceeds of any judicial sale of real estate before any other obligation, claim lien, judgment, estate, or costs of the sale and of the writ upon which the sale is made [72 P.S. § 8107-D].

• *Civil penalties*

If any part of any underpayment of a local realty transfer tax is due to fraud, an amount equal to 50% of the underpayment will be added to the tax [72 P.S. § 8112-D(a)]. In the case of failure to record a required declaration, unless it is shown that the failure is due to reasonable cause, 5% of the amount of tax will be added to the tax if the failure is not for more than one month, with an additional 5% for each additional month or fraction thereof during which the failure continues, not to exceed 50% in the aggregate [72 P.S. § 8112-D(b)].

• *Unlawful acts and penalty*

The statute provides penalties for specified unlawful acts (*e.g.*, failure to comply with required rules and regulations, fraudulent removal of documentary stamp) [72 P.S. § 8113-D].

¶3614 Sales Taxes

The City of Philadelphia and Allegheny County are authorized to impose a 1% sales, use, and occupancy tax on the sale at retail of tangible personal property. Effective October 8, 2009, through June 30, 2014, the City of Philadelphia is authorized to impose sales and use tax at a rate of 2%. For an explanation of the Allegheny County sales tax, see Chapter 45. For explanation of the Philadelphia sales tax, see ¶ 4008.

• *Situs of local sales tax on mobile telecommunications service*

The situs of the sales of mobile telecommunications services that are deemed to be provided to a customer by a home service provider under the provisions of the Mobile Telecommunications Sourcing Act is the customer's place of primary use regardless of where the mobile telecommunications services originate, terminate, or pass through [72 P.S. § 7203-A]. See ¶ 721 for more information.

• *Leases*

For purposes of local sales taxes, the lease of a motor vehicle, trailer, semitrailer, or mobile home (as defined in 75 Pa.C.S., relating to vehicles), or of a motorboat, aircraft, or other similar tangible personal property, required under either federal or state laws to be registered or licensed, is deemed to have been completed or used at the address of the lessee. In the case of a lease, the lessee must pay the tax to the lessor. In the case of a rental of these items, the rental is deemed to be consummated at the retailer's place of business, and the renter must pay the tax due to the retailer. These rules apply to any sales tax imposed only under the Second Class County Code and the Pennsylvania Intergovernmental Cooperation Authority Act for Cities of the First Class. For this purpose a "lease" is a contract for the use of personal property for a period of 30 days or more; a "rental" is a contract for the use of tangible personal property for a period of less than 30 days.

¶3615 Municipal Video Programming Tax

The duly constituted authorities of municipalities of Pennsylvania are authorized to impose a video programming tax [Video Programming Municipal Tax Authorization Act (72 P.S. § 6171 *et seq.*)] on the gross receipts from sales by any person (unless they are otherwise subject to federally authorized or permitted local fees or taxes on gross receipts from cable television service or video programming services in the municipality) to subscribers within Pennsylvania of (1) video programming by any means of transmission (other than wireless or direct-to-home satellite transmission) and (2) access to video programming by any means of transmission (other than wireless or direct-to-home satellite transmission).

Gross receipts subject to the video programming municipal tax are not subject to the gross receipts tax or to any local tax or fee on the provision of video programming or access to video programming to subscribers in the municipality. However, persons subject to this tax remain subject to local *business privilege* taxes.

• *Rate*

The rate of tax is the franchise fee rate imposed by local cable ordinance or (if no local cable ordinance exists) the rate agreed upon by the local cable television operator and the municipality. However, the rate cannot exceed 5%. The tax rate is imposed on the gross receipts of the taxable person. Any person subject to this tax may elect to pass through to subscribers the tax as a separate itemized line charge.

• *Tax credits*

Two credits against this tax are allowed:

(1) A credit equal in amount to any similar tax on gross receipts (other than a general sales or use tax or corporate income tax) paid to another state or government entity.

(2) A credit equal in amount to fees on gross receipts paid under any franchise or similar fee authorized or permitted by federal, state, or local law, imposed by municipal ordinance, or agreed upon between the person and the municipality.

The tax must be paid quarterly on or before April 30, July 31, October 31, and January 31. Quarterly payments are calculated based on the gross receipts of the three months prior to the month of payment.

¶3616 Hotel Room Rental Tax

A hotel room rental tax is an excise tax on the consideration received from the rental of rooms to transients. A "transient" for this purpose is an individual who obtains accommodation in a hotel by means of registering at the facility for the temporary occupancy of a room for the personal use of the individual by paying a fee to the operator. The hotel room rental tax is collected by the operator from the patron of the room or rooms and paid over to the county as required. Because rates vary among jurisdictions, consult local statutes. See below for specific judicial decisions involving the local hotel room rental tax.

Amendment and Repeal

The hotel room rental tax provisions were amended by Act No. 12 of 2005 (H.B. 157) in order to effectuate the addition of 16 P.S. § 1770.8, the Act of June 22, 2000 (P.L. 203, No. 28), known as the Hotel Room Rental Tax Act [16 P.S. § 13212 *et seq.*], was repealed effective July 5, 2005 [Act No. 12 of 2005 (H.B. 157), § 7].

• *Enabling legislation and administration*

The county hotel room rental taxes are imposed under the authority of The County Code [16 P.S. § 1770.2 *et seq.*]. The county commissioners are authorized to impose requirements for keeping of records, filing of tax returns, time and manner of

¶3615

collection and payment of tax, and imposition of penalties and interest for failure to comply with ordinances [16 P.S. § 1770.2(b)]. County treasurers have the duty to collect the tax and deposit the tax revenues in a special fund established for that purpose [16 P.S. § 1770.2(c)].

Hotel Occupancy Regulations Do Not Apply

The hotel room rental tax and the hotel occupancy tax are different taxes—authorized by different enabling legislation and administered by different authorities. The Department of Revenue has issued a policy statement that states that Chapter 38 of the Department's regulations applies only to the hotel occupancy tax and has no application to taxes imposed by county governments under separate statutory authority (*e.g.,* hotel room rental tax). Therefore, 61 Pa. Code § 38.2(f) applies only to the hotel occupancy tax and cannot properly be cited as a basis for a county government to impose a hotel room rental tax upon a Commonwealth official or employee staying overnight in a hotel in the course of performing official Commonwealth business [61 Pa. Code § 38a.1(d)(2)]. The hotel occupancy tax is discussed at ¶ 724.

• *Counties with recognized tourist promotion agencies*

The county commissioners of any county that has a recognized tourist promotion agency designated to act within the county may impose an excise tax not to exceed 3% of the consideration received on room rentals to transients [The County Code, 16 P.S. § 1770.2]. The following counties qualify to impose the tax:

(1) Third class counties having a population under the 1990 Federal Decennial Census of more than 337,000 residents, but fewer than 341,000 residents.

(2) Third class counties having a population under the 1990 Federal Decennial Census of more than 374,000 residents, but fewer than 380,000 residents.

(3) Third class counties having a population under the 1990 Federal Decennial Census of more than 415,000 residents, but fewer than 500,000 residents.

(4) Fourth class counties having a population under the 1990 Federal Decennial Census of more than 159,000 residents, but fewer than 175,000 residents.

(5) Fifth class counties having a population under the 1990 Federal Decennial Census of more than 123,000 residents.

(6) Fifth class counties having a population under the 1990 Federal Decennial Census of more than 117,000 residents, but fewer than 121,050 residents.

(7) Sixth class counties having a population under the 1990 Federal Decennial Census of more than 87,000 residents.

Note: Classification of counties is discussed at ¶ 3401. Counties that qualify under this statue may impose a tax rate of up to 3% on hotel room rentals. Because rates vary among the statutes, consult specific local statutes for the applicable rate.

• *Third-class counties*

The county commissioners of any county of the third class having a population under the 1990 Federal Decennial Census in excess of 237,000 residents, but fewer than 240,000 residents, may impose a hotel tax not to exceed 5% of the consideration of rental of rooms to transients [16 P.S. § 1770.5].

• *Third-class counties with second class cities*

The county commissioners of any third class county having a second class A city located therein may impose a hotel tax not to exceed 4% of the consideration received by each operator of a hotel within the county from each transaction of renting a room or rooms to transients [16 P.S. § 1770.4(a)].

¶ 3616

• *Third through eighth class counties*

The county commissioners of any county of the third class through the eighth class that does not have the authority to levy a hotel occupancy or room rental tax may impose an excise tax not to exceed 3% on the consideration received by each operator of a hotel from each transaction of renting a room or rooms to accommodate transients [16 P.S. § 1770.6(a)].

Certain sixth class counties: The county commissioners of any sixth class county having a population under the 1990 Federal Decennial Census in excess of 78,250 residents, but fewer than 79,000 residents, may impose a hotel tax not to exceed 3% of the consideration received by each operator of a hotel within the county from each transaction of renting a room or rooms to transients [16 P.S. § 1770.7(a)].

• *Certain third class counties*

A county that is, on June 22, 2000, a county of the third class having a population under the 1990 Federal Decennial Census in excess of 290,000 residents but fewer than 295,000 residents or a county of the third class having a population under the 1990 Federal Decennial Census in excess of 245,000 residents but fewer than 250,000 residents may, by ordinance, impose a hotel room rental tax of 4% on the consideration received by each operator of a hotel within the county from each transaction of renting a room or rooms to accommodate temporary residents. The tax must be collected by the operator from the patron of the room and remitted to the county where the hotel is located [16 P.S. § 1770.8(a), (b), (c); effective September 3, 2005]. A "temporary resident" for this purpose is any person who has occupied or has the right to occupy, a room or rooms in a hotel as a patron or otherwise for a period of time not in excess of 30 consecutive days. A person who has occupied or has the right to occupy a room or rooms in a hotel as a patron or otherwise for a period in excess of 30 consecutive days is a "permanent resident." In order to qualify as a "room," a space must have at least one bed or other sleeping accommodations provided [16 P.S. § 1770.8(e)].

• *Convention center tax (repealed)*

Counties of the third class: Counties of the third class in which a convention center is located are authorized to impose a hotel room rental tax not to exceed 5% [16 P.S. § 2399.23].

Philadelphia: The city council of the city in which the Pennsylvania Convention Center Authority locates its convention center (*i.e.,* Philadelphia) is authorized to impose or continue to impose a hotel room rental tax on hotels within the city at a rate not to exceed 6% [64 Pa.C.S. §§ 6001, 6025].

• *Tourism and marketing tax*

The council of a city in which a convention center is located is authorized to impose an excise tax on the consideration received by each operator of a hotel within the city from each transaction of renting a room or rooms to accommodate transients at a rate not to exceed 1%. This is in addition to the state hotel room rental tax and the convention center tax [Act of December 21, 1998, No. 174 (H.B. 2858), § 10].

• *Berks County—Convention Center*

A convention center in Berks County that was designed for use for sporting events qualified as a "convention center" for purposes of the 5% "convention center" tax because the facility was also to be used for such events as consumer shows and trade shows. The Berks County tax, therefore, was not unconstitutional [*John M. Eways II and Park Road Inn, Inc. v. Board of Commissioners of Berks County,* 717 A.2d 8 (Pa.Commw. 1998), *app. den.,* 634 A.2d 396 (Pa. 1998)].

• *Lancaster County—Convention center*

A Lancaster County ordinance provided that 80% of the revenues from the hotel room rental tax were to be used to fund development, construction, and operation of a convention center in downtown Lancaster, and the remaining 20% was to be used by the Pennsylvania Dutch Convention and Visitors Bureau to promote tourism in Lancaster County. A privately financed and privately owned hotel was to be built adjoining the convention center. Furthermore, the convention center would not be built without the hotel and vice versa. A group of Lancaster County hoteliers argued that the hotel room rental violated their due process and equal protection rights because they were being forced to fund a competing business. The Pennsylvania Supreme Court, however, held that they failed to prove that the burdens of the tax outweighed the benefits to them; the tax was not unconstitutional [*Bold Corporation v. County of Lancaster*, 801 A.2d 469 (Pa. 2002)].

• *Luzerne County—Convention center*

A county's 5% hotel room rental tax, which was authorized by the legislature in order to fund the construction of the county's convention center, was constitutional. Under the "rational basis test," the enabling legislation could be construed as having been enacted on the basis of reasonable distinctions between counties that had a convention center and counties that did not have a convention center. A classification for tax purposes does not violate the Equal Protection clause of the U.S. Constitution if, as with the statute at issue, it is based upon some legitimate distinction between the classes and provides a non-arbitrary, reasonable and just basis for the different treatment [*Wilkes-Barre Inn v. Luzerne County*, 696 A.2d 1141 (Pa. 1997)].

KOZ Considerations

If a political subdivision has enacted a tax on the occupancy or use of real property pursuant to certain enabling legislation, it must provide exemption, deduction, abatement, or credit from the imposition and operation of local tax ordinance resolution for the use or occupancy tax [73 P.S. § 820.703(b)]. See discussion at ¶ 3608.

¶3617 Vehicle Rental Tax

Counties of the first class are authorized to impose an excise tax on the rental of a motor vehicle in that county. If the county is coterminous with a city of the first class, imposition of the tax in that county, if any, shall be by that city. The tax may be imposed on any person renting a motor vehicle at a rate of up to 2% of the purchase price of the motor vehicle. The situs of the rental of the vehicle is the place where the renter takes possession of the rental vehicle [The County Code, 16 P.S. § 2398].

¶3618 Local Services Tax (formerly called the Emergency and Municipal Services Tax)

• *Enabling legislation*

Act 222 of 2004 (H.B. 197) amended the Local Tax Enabling Act to authorize municipalities and school districts (except the Pittsburgh School District) to impose an LST tax (formerly called the Emergency and Municipal Services Tax (EMST)) [53 P.S. § 6924.301.1(f)(1); Act 222, § 8]. The LST replaces the occupational privilege tax, discussed at ¶ 3611. Any occupational privilege tax enacted by a political subdivision prior to December 1, 2004, continues in full force and effect (without reenactment) as if it had been levied, assessed, or collected as an LST [Act 222 of 2004 (H.B. 197), § 6]. Any reference in any act or law to an occupational privilege tax means the emergency and municipal services tax [53 P.S. § 22.1]. The LST may be imposed in all jurisdictions under the authority of the Local Tax Enabling Act (except the Pittsburgh School District). The Pittsburgh LST (formerly called the EMST) is discussed at ¶ 4302.

Law Change

Beginning in 2008, the name of this tax is changed to the "local services tax." Any reference to the emergency and municipal services tax (EMST) in this handbook should be understood to mean the local services tax (LST).

• *Rate*

Municipalities are authorized to levy an LST of at least $10, but no more than $52 [53 P.S. §§ 6924.301.1(f)(9), 6924.311(8)] less the amount of the school district tax, if any. No person is required to pay more than $52 in any calendar year as an LST without regard to the number of political subdivisions within which the person may be employed in a given calendar year [53 P.S. § 6924.301.1(f)(9)].

List of Rates in DCED Register

Employers are usually notified of new tax rates and policies by the taxing district or their tax collectors. Employers can also find the most recently filed LST rates in the *Register* on the web site of the Department of Community and Economic Development (DCED) at http://www.newpa.com/default.aspx?id=134.

Limit on school tax rates: In the case of duplication of LSTs by both a school district (other than a school district of the First Class A) and another taxing body, the school district's share of the tax shall not exceed the amount of an occupational privilege tax collected by the school district as of December 1, 2004 [53 P.S. § 6924.311]. In the case where a school district did not levy an occupational privilege tax on December 1, 2004, the school district may impose a future levy not to exceed five dollars ($5).

• *Withholding*

Withholding required: All employers with work sites within a taxing jurisdiction are required by law to deduct the LST from their employees at the site of employment if the tax is listed in the LST Register of the Department of Community and Economic Development. If the municipality and/or school district's tax rates are not listed in the Register, employers are not required to withhold taxes levied under the Local Tax Enabling Act from employee wages but may do so voluntarily [http://www.newpa.com/default.aspx?id=135].

Withholding rate: Employers should withhold the LST rate based on the most recent information available from the taxing jurisdiction and/or in the Tax Register (see above).

Frequency of withholding: Employers may not be required to withhold the LST from any one employee more than one time in any calendar year. However, local taxing jurisdictions may permit employers to withhold the LST in installments. Many taxing jurisdictions require the employers to withhold the LST as soon as possible in the calendar year (during the first quarter) and remit all withheld taxes by April 30. This is generally the same procedure that has been used for the administrations of the occupational privilege tax. For employees hired in subsequent quarters who have not already paid the tax, municipalities can require the employer to withhold the tax during that quarter and remit the tax 30 days after the end of the quarter. Note, however, that withholding policies vary among local taxing jurisdictions, so employers should check with their local taxing jurisdictions for guidance on withholding policies.

Employee move to jurisdiction with higher rate: If an employee moves to a municipality where the rate is higher than the rate at the former jurisdiction, the employer should withhold the difference.

¶3618

Example: Edward worked in Municipality A, which levies a $10 LST, until June 10, when he started employment at a new job in Pittsburgh, which levies a $52 LST. Edward's new employer in Pittsburgh should withhold the $42 difference between the two rates.

• *Exemptions*

Low-income exemption: Until 2008, local taxing authorities could (but were not required to) exempt any person whose total annual income from all sources is less than $12,000 from the LST (as well as earned income, per capita, and occupation taxes) [53 P.S. § 6924.301.1]. Local jurisdictions could provide for no exemption or an exemption in any amount so long as the exemption did not exceed $12,000. Beginning in 2008, each political subdivision levying the local services tax at a rate exceeding $10 must, and each political subdivision levying the local services tax at a rate of $10 may (by ordinance or resolution) exempt any person from the local services tax whose total earned income and net profits from all sources within the political subdivision is less than $12,000 for the calendar year in which the tax is levied [53 P.S. § 6924.301.1(d)].

War-time services exemption: Any person who services in any war or armed conflict in which the United States was engaged and is honorably discharged or released under honorable circumstances from active service is exempt if, as a result of military service, the person is blind, paraplegic, or a double or quadruple amputee or has a service-connected disability declared by the United States Veterans' Administration or its successor to be 100% disabled [53 P.S. § 6924.301.1(c)(1)(i)].

Active duty exemption: Any person who services as a member of a reserve component of the armed forces who is called to active duty at any time during the taxable year is exempt [53 P.S. § 6924.301.1(c)(1)(ii)].

• *Situs of tax*

The situs of the LST is the place of employment. If a person is engaged in more than one occupation, or an occupation that requires working in more than one political subdivision during the calendar year, the priority of claim to collect the tax is in the following order [53 P.S. § 6924.301.1(f)(9)]:

(1) The political subdivision in which a person maintains a principal office or is principally employed.

(2) The political subdivision in which the person resides and works (if the tax is levied by that political subdivision).

(3) The political subdivision in which a person is employed and which imposes the tax nearest in miles to the person's home.

The place of employment is determined as of the day the taxpayer first becomes subject to the tax during the calendar year.

• *Restricted uses*

Any municipality that imposes an LST may use the funds only for the following purposes [53 P.S. § 6924.308(a)]:

(1) Police, fire and/or emergency services.

(2) Road construction and/or maintenance.

(3) Reduction of property taxes.

This provision does not apply to school districts [53 P.S. § 6924.308(b)].

¶3619 Allegheny County Sales Tax

Allegheny County is authorized to impose a 1% sales, use, and occupancy tax on the sale at retail of tangible personal property within the county [Article XXXI-B of the Second Class County Code]. For an explanation of the tax, see ¶4501.

¶3620 Allegheny County Alcoholic Beverage Tax

On December 4, 2007, Allegheny County enacted a 10% tax (effective January 1, 2008) on alcoholic beverages [Ordinance No. 54-07-OR/3548-07]. Effective January 1, 2009, Allegheny County Council reduced the rate from 10% to 7%. All sales of alcoholic beverages, including mixed drinks, wine, and beer (opened or unopened), are taxable transactions http://www.alleghenycounty.us/treasure/alcoholtax.aspx.

The Allegheny County alcoholic beverage tax regulations can be found at http://www.alleghenycounty.us/treasure/alcoholtax.pdf.

¶3621 County Unconventional Gas Well Fee Law

CAUTION

Two provisions of this law authorizing county fees on unconventional gas wells have been declared unconstitutional by the Pennsylvania Commonwealth Court [*Robinson Township v. Commonwealth of Pennsylvania*, Cmwlth. Ct., No. 284 M.D. 2012, July 26, 2012].

A requirement under the law that municipal zoning ordinances be amended to include oil and gas operations in all zoning districts violated substantive due process rights under the U.S. and Pennsylvania Constitutions on three different bases. Specifically, the provision did not protect the interests of neighboring property owners from harm, altered the character of neighborhoods, and made irrational classifications. The classifications were "irrational" because the provision required municipalities to allow drilling operations and impoundments, gas compressor stations, storage and use of explosives in all zoning districts, and applied industrial criteria to restrictions on height of structures, screening and fencing, lighting, and noise.

Another provision of the law violated Pennsylvania's nondelegation doctrine, under which legislation must contain adequate standards that will guide and restrain the exercise of delegated administrative functions. In this case, the law gave the DEP discretion when it administered mandatory waivers from water body and wetland setbacks for wells. However, according to the court, the provision gave the DEP insufficient guidance to permit it to waive setbacks, and instead gave the agency the power to make legislative policy judgments otherwise reserved to the General Assembly.

Eight other claims were dismissed.

• *Authorization*

The governing body of a county that has a spud unconventional gas well located within its borders may elect whether to impose a fee on unconventional gas wells that have been spud in the county [58 P.S. § 2302(a)]. "Spud" means the actual start of drilling of an unconventional oil well [53 P.S. § 2301]. Pennsylvania counties must have adopted an ordinance to impose the fee, and each county must have notified the Public Utility Committee and given public notice that it intended to do so [58 P.S. § 2302(a.1)]. Counties that did not adopt a fee ordinance are prohibited from receiving funds from the fees collected [58 P.S. § 2302(a.3)].

• *Unconventional oil well defined*

An "unconventional oil well" is a bore hole drilled or being drilled for the purpose of or to be used for the production of natural gas from an unconventional formation [58 P.S. § 2301]. An "unconventional formation" is a geological shale formation existing below the base of the Elk Sandstone or its geologic equivalent stratigraphic interval where natural gas generally cannot be produced at economic flow rates or in economic volumes except by vertical or horizontal well bores stimulated by hydraulic fracture treatments or by using multilateral well bores or other techniques to expose more of the formation to the well bore [53 P.S. § 2301].

¶3620

• *Fee amounts in the year actual drilling is started*

The fee amounts in the year actual drilling is started are as follows [58 P.S. § 2302(b)(1)]:

Average Annual Price of Natural Gas	Fee
Not more than $2.25	$40,000
More than $2.25, but less than $3.00	$45,000
More than $2.99, but less than $5.00	$50,000
More than $4.99, but less than $6.00	$55,000
More than $5.99	$60,000

Average annual price of natural gas: The "average annual price of natural gas" is the arithmetic mean of the New York Mercantile Exchange (NYMEX) settled price for the near-month contract, as reported by the Wall Street Journal for the last trading day of each month of a calendar year for the 12-month period ending December 31 [58 P.S. § 2301].

• *Fee amounts in the years subsequent to the year actual drilling is started*

Similar schedules in which the fees decrease in amount apply for wells in existence for subsequent years. See 58 P.S. § 2302.

• *Due dates*

For wells drilled before 2012, the first fee is due on September 1, 2012. After 2012, the fee is due annually on April 1 [58 P.S. § 2303].

• *Drilling permits*

Prior to issuing a permit to drill an unconventional gas well in Pennsylvania, the department shall determine whether the producer has paid all fees owed for an existing unconventional gas well. The department shall not issue a permit to drill an unconventional gas well until all unconventional gas well fees owed that are not in dispute have been paid to the commission [58 P.S. § 2305(a), (b)].

• *Penalties*

Failure to make a timely payment: If a producer fails to make timely payment of the fee, there shall be added to the amount of the fee due a penalty of 5% of the amount of the fee if failure to file a timely payment is for not more than one month, with an additional 5% penalty for each additional month, or fraction of a month, during which the failure continues, not to exceed 25% in the aggregate [58 P.S. § 2308(b)].

Violation of the unconventional gas well fee law: In addition to any other proceeding authorized by law, the commission may assess a civil penalty not to exceed $2,500 per violation upon a producer for the violation of the unconventional gas well fee law. In determining the amount of the penalty, the commission shall consider the wilfulness of the violation and other relevant factors. Each violation for each separate day and each violation of the fee law shall constitute a separate offense [58 P.S. § 2310(a), (b)].

• *Expiration of the unconventional gas well fee law*

The fee will expire if Pennsylvania adopts a severance tax on unconventional gas wells. The fee will expire on the date that notice of the severance tax is published in the *Pennsylvania Bulletin* [58 P.S. § 2318].

SPECIAL TOPICS

¶3624 Manufacturing Exemption

The Local Tax Enabling Act prohibits local taxation of manufactured products, by-products of manufacture, or processing of by-products of manufacture [53 P.S. § 6924.301.1]. Because the statute does not define "manufacturing," the courts must do so, and they will often look to other tax statutes for help in defining the term. It is

¶3624

helpful to refer to the discussion of manufacturing at ¶1602. Some cases involving local taxes pertaining to manufacturing are discussed below.

• *Manufacturing*

Cardboard recycling: Taxpayer (Mar-Pat Co., Inc.) purchased odd lots and odd pieces of poor quality cardboard from cardboard manufacturers and then scored, stamped, cut and folded those pieces to make products (*e.g.,* shirt boards, collar supports, ribbon reel covers, hosiery packaging inserts). Those items were sold to manufacturers of shirts, blouses, hosiery and other products to be used in packaging. Because Mar-Pat does not start and end with the same product (*i.e.,* it created new articles from scrap cardboard), it was engaged in manufacturing for purposes of the LTEA and was entitled to an exemption from the Allentown business privilege tax [*Mar-Pat Co., Inc. v. The City of Allentown,* 687 A.2d 1198 (Pa.Commw. 1997), *app. den.,* 694 A.2d 624 (Pa. 1997)].

Doughnut maker: A doughnut maker qualified for a manufacturing exemption from a city of Scranton business privilege and mercantile tax even though it was supplied with a premixed blend used to make the doughnuts. The taxpayer met the test of manufacturing because the processes it used to convert the premixed blend into doughnuts resulted in a final product substantially different from the raw material [*City of Scranton v. Krispy Kreme Donuts,* Court of Common Pleas, Lackawanna County, No. 90-CIV-760 (September 25, 1990); *aff'd per curiam,* 595 A.2d 1329 (Pa. 1992)].

Catalog and brochure production: A company engaged in commercial printing produced catalogs, brochures, reports, carbon forms, and programs. Production included design, layout, typography, making printing plates, and printing onto paper, which was then folded, cut, and/or bound. This production process, according to the Commonwealth Court, constituted manufacturing for purposes of a local business privilege tax [*A+ Printing, Inc. v. City of Altoona,* 778 A.2d 769 (Pa.Commw. 2001)].

Bookbinder: The Pennsylvania Supreme Court has ruled that the business of commercial bookbinding is manufacturing for purposes of a Pittsburgh business privilege tax [*Binder v. Pittsburgh,* 475 A.2d 1820 (Pa. 1984)].

• *Not manufacturing*

Meat processing and packing: A wholesale meat processor and packer was held not to be engaged in manufacturing [*Allied Foods, Inc. v. The School District of Scranton and the City of Scranton,* 654 A.2d 273 (Pa.Commw. 1995)].

Photocopying: Taxpayer was engaged in the business of photocopying and document binding services. The Commonwealth Court held that these activities created no more than a superficial change in the original materials and was, therefore, not manufacturing for purposes of the Pittsburgh business privilege tax [*Ikon Office Solutions, Inc. v. City of Pittsburgh,* 771 A.2d 870 (Pa.Commw. 2001)].

Printing designs on ready-made clothing: A taxpayer engaged in the business of printing designs and wording on ready-made clothing (*e.g.,* T-shirts, sweat shirts, underwear) and then selling that merchandise to retailers was denied a manufacturing exemption from a local school district's mercantile tax [*Ohiopyle Prints v. Uniontown Area School District,* 662 A.2d 672 (Pa.Commw. 1995), *app. den.,* 675 A.2d 1254 (Pa. 1996)].

Chemical treatment of fabric: Taxpayer, a corporation engaged in the business of treating unfinished cloth, was held not to be entitled to the manufacturing exemption under the LTEA because the chemical treatment of fabric did not result in something new or different from that which the taxpayer received. Therefore, the taxpayer was subject to Allentown's business privilege tax [*HAB Industries, Inc. v. City of Allentown,* 649 A.2d 198 (Pa.Commw. 1994)].

¶3624

Steel annealing and galvanizing: Taxpayer (Metaltech) purchased rolls of steel that were uncoated "full-hard" steel coils. The steel was uncoiled, cleaned, and passed through a furnace (annealing) and molten zinc pot (galvanizing). The Commonwealth Court held that Metaltech did not qualify for a manufacturing or processing exemption from the Pittsburgh business privilege tax [*Metaltech v. City of Pittsburgh,* 623 A.2d 401 (Pa.Commw. 1993)].

¶3625 Financially Distressed Municipalities

• *Background*

The Municipalities Financial Recovery Act (Act of July 10, P.L. 246, as amended, 53 P.S. §§ 11701.101—11701.501) empowers The Department of Community Affairs to declare certain municipalities as financially distressed and provides for the restructuring of debt of such municipalities. After a determination of financial distress is made, a coordinator is appointed by the Secretary of the Department to prepare and implement a financial recovery plan addressing the municipality's financial problems. After a municipality has adopted an approved plan, it may petition the court of common pleas of the county in which it is located to increase its rates of taxation for earned income, real property, or both, beyond maximum rates provided by law [53 P.S. § 11701.128 (b)].

• *Scranton*

On January 10, 1992, the city of Scranton was declared a distressed municipality. On June 17, 1993, the city filed a petition with the Court of Common Pleas seeking to raise its nonresident earned income tax from 1.0% to 1.6%. The petition was required because the increase would exceed the limit of 1.0% for the earned income tax on nonresidents provided by the LTEA and the Home Rule Charter Act. The Court of Common Pleas of Lackawanna County denied the city's petition because the tax would be largely used to finance services of Scranton residents and the city failed to establish that the increase was necessary to meet the city's budget. However, the Commonwealth Court reversed the decision of the Court of Common Pleas. The Recovery Act specifically authorizes distressed cities to raise rates beyond the statutory maximum rates, and nonresident earned income taxes are not exempt from this legislative grant of authority, the Commonwealth Court found. The Court of Common Pleas was incorrect when it ruled that taxes could not be increased on nonresidents when an option for increasing revenues from residents exists. Furthermore, the increase in the nonresident rate was not unconstitutional because the city's financial recovery will bestow a great benefit on its commuters, more so than on "other citizens" of Pennsylvania [*In re The City of Scranton Request for Approval of Enactment and Levying of an Increase in the Earned Income Tax for Nonresidents of the City of Scranton,* 638 A.2d 379 (Pa.Commw. 1994)].

• *Clairton*

In January 1988, the Department of Community Affairs declared Clairton to be a financially distressed municipality and appointed the Pennsylvania Economy League, Western District, to coordinate and develop a recovery plan for the City. In February of 1996, the City petitioned the Common Pleas Court of Allegheny County for approval to set its earned income tax rates for calendar year 1996 at levels above the statutory maximum rate of 1%, and the city's petition was granted. Although the proposed rates were reduced from those approved by the trial court in preceding years, court approval is required each year where the rate proposed exceeds the rate allowed by law. Taxpayers appealed the trial court's decision, arguing that the existence of 1995 year-end fund balances, particularly a balance of $446,399 in the City's general fund, precluded a finding of an actual deficit for 1996. The Commonwealth Court disagreed, noting that a policy that requires a distressed municipality to operate without emergency financial reserves is one that effectively guarantees that the financial distress of the municipality will continue. In this case, the surplus in the city's general fund was necessary for operations for the first four months of the calendar year when the city received very little income tax revenue. Thus, the existence of a year-end surplus did not preclude Clairton from imposing additional taxes [*In re Petition of the City of Clairton*, 704 A.2d 1383 (Pa. 1997)].

¶3626 Preemption Doctrine

• *Security industry regulation*

The Commonwealth's regulation of the securities industry did not preempt that industry from local taxation. Although the regulation was extensive, the intent of the regulation was to protect the investing public, which related primarily to the ethical conduct of broker-dealers rather than the taxation of securities transactions. The license fees imposed by the Commonwealth were not an extensive system of taxation, even though the receipts from the fees exceeded the expenditures of the Pennsylvania Securities Commission. The local taxing jurisdiction, therefore, could impose a mercantile license tax on securities dealers [*City of Philadelphia v. Tax Review Board to the use of Janney Montgomery Scott*, 601 A.2d 875 (Pa.Commw. 1992), *app. den.*, 612 A.2d 486 (Pa. 1992)]. See ¶3403 for a discussion of the preemption doctrine.

¶3627 Service Fees

The city of Washington imposed service fees for police and fire services on Washington & Jefferson College, a tax-exempt entity. The Court of Common Pleas of Washington County held that the imposition of these fees was in fact an unlawful assessment of taxes being used for the purpose of raising additional revenue. Since neither the Third Class City Code nor the Local Tax Enabling Act authorized the imposition of such a tax, the underlying ordinance was found to be invalid as an unlawful exercise of the municipality's authority [*City of Washington v. Washington & Jefferson College*, Court of Common Pleas, Dauphin County, No. 94-4148 (June 15, 1995)]. Limitations on local taxing powers are discussed at ¶3403.

PART XVII

PHILADELPHIA CITY AND SCHOOL DISTRICT TAXES

CHAPTER 37
PHILADELPHIA TAXES IN GENERAL

¶3701 Scope of Chapter

This chapter provides an overview of the tax system of Philadelphia and the Philadelphia School District and the general provisions governing Philadelphia taxes.

• *Philadelphia Keystone Opportunity Zone (KOZ)*

Philadelphia's KOZ ordinance provides for the exemption, abatement, or credit of specified taxes (*i.e.*, real estate tax, realty use and occupancy tax, business income and receipts tax (formerly business privilege tax), net profits tax, city sales and use tax, wage tax, within the geographical area designated as the Philadelphia KOZ [Philadelphia Code § 19-3203]. See ¶ 4622 for more information about KOZs.

¶3702 Sources of Authority—City of Philadelphia

The City of Philadelphia receives its authority to impose or levy taxes through legislative acts of the Commonwealth (discussed below).

Philadelphia derives its taxing power through several specific legislative enactments. The Act of August 9, 1963, P.L. 640, gives the Philadelphia City Council the power to authorize the Philadelphia Board of Public Education to tax anything the city could tax. However, it specifically provides that the school district can impose wages or income taxes only on residents of the school district. Neither jurisdiction, under the Sterling Act, can tax anything that is subject to a Commonwealth tax. Unlike Act 511 (the enabling legislation for most Pennsylvania political subdivisions), the Sterling Act, which applies only to Philadelphia, does not limit the rates of tax that Philadelphia can impose.

• *The Sterling Act (Act of August 5, 1932, P.L.45) [53 P.S. § 15971 et seq.]*

The Sterling Act grants broad taxing powers to the city of Philadelphia. It can tax any person, transaction, occupation, privilege, subject, and personal property within its city limits as it sees fit. The only limitation on Philadelphia's taxing power is that it cannot tax anything that is subject to a state tax or license fee [53 P.S. § 15971(a)]. The Sterling Act places no limits on the rates of tax that Philadelphia may impose, but the Tax Reform Code limits the rate on earned income of nonresidents [72 P.S. § 7359(b)].

• *The First Class City Business Tax Reform Act (Act of May 30, 1984, P.L. 345) [53 P.S. § 16181 et seq.]*

This act grants Philadelphia the authority to impose a business income and receipts tax (formerly the business privilege tax). Since the city cannot impose both the mercantile license tax and the business income and receipts tax [53 P.S. § 16193], the Philadelphia mercantile license tax (authorized by the Public School Code of 1949) has not been imposed since 1985.

• *The General County Assessment Law (Act of May 22, 1933, P.L. 853) [72 P.S. § 5020-1 et seq.]*

This act authorizes the city (county) to impose a tax on real property located within its boundaries.

• *The Pennsylvania Convention Center Authority Act [64 Pa.C.S. § 6001 et seq.]*

The city council of the city in which the Pennsylvania Convention Center Authority locates its convention center (*i.e.,* Philadelphia) is authorized to impose or continue to impose a hotel room rental tax on hotels within the city at a rate not to exceed 6% [64 Pa.C.S. § § 6001, 6025].

   NOTE: The original Pennsylvania Convention Center Authority Act (Act of June 27, 1986, P.L. 124), codified at 53 Pa.C.S. § 5901 *et seq.,* was repealed and most of its provisions have been moved to 64 Pa.C.S. § 6001 et seq. [Act 3 of 2004 (H.B. 1733), § § 1, 2].

• *The Pennsylvania Intergovernmental Cooperation Authority Act for Cities of the First Class (Act of June 5, 1991, P.L. 9) [53 P.S. § 12720.101 et seq.]*

This act gave the city of Philadelphia authority to establish an authority with a dedicated funding stream. The funding stream is a tax on wages and net profits at the rate of 1.5%. The Pennsylvania Intergovernmental Cooperation Authority (PICA) tax is combined with the city wage and net profits tax imposed by Philadelphia Code § 19-1400 *et seq.* and is imposed only on residents of the city. This act also authorizes the imposition of sales and use tax and a hotel occupancy tax. The revenues from these taxes are collected by the authority for its use in administering the bond debt of the city of Philadelphia [Philadelphia Code, § 19-2800].

• *Act of June 25, 1999, P.L. 25 (S.B. 366) [16 P.S. § 2398]*

This act authorizes the imposition of a motor vehicle license tax.

• *Community and Economic Improvement Act (Act 174 of 1998, P.L. 1307, H.B. 2858)*

This act authorizes the cities in which a convention center is located to impose a tourism and marketing tax in addition to the hotel room rental tax. The tourism and marketing tax must be used for tourist promotion activities.

¶3702

¶3703 Sources of Authority—Philadelphia School District

The taxing power of the Philadelphia School District is granted by several specific legislative enactments, the most important of which are discussed below. See also ¶3402 for a discussion of local tax enabling legislation and ¶3403 for a discussion on the limitations of local taxing powers.

• *Little Sterling Act (Act of August 9, 1963, P.L. 640) [53 P.S. §16101 et seq.]*

The "Little Sterling Act" gives the Philadelphia City Council the power to authorize the Philadelphia Board of Public Education to tax anything the city could tax. However, it specifically provides that the school district can impose wages or income taxes only on residents of the school district. Neither the city nor the county, under the Sterling Act, can tax anything that is subject to a Commonwealth tax.

• *The General County Assessment Law (Act of May 22, 1933, P.L. 853) [72 P.S. §5020-1 et seq.]*

This act authorizes the city (county) to impose a tax on real property located within its boundaries.

• *Public School Code (Act of March 10, 1949) [24 P.S. §1-101 et seq.]*

The Public School Code authorizes the board of directors of a school district of the first class coterminous with a city of the first class (Philadelphia) to levy and collect taxes in order to establish, enlarge, equip, furnish, operate, and maintain its schools or to pay school indebtedness [24 P.S. §5-507].

• *First Class School District Liquor Sales Tax Act of 1971 (Act of June 10, 1971, P.L. 154) [53 P.S. §16131 et seq.]*

This act authorizes the Philadelphia City Council to impose a tax on the retail sale of liquor and malt or brewed beverages on behalf of the Philadelphia School District.

GENERAL PROVISIONS

¶3705 Recordkeeping Requirements

Records and copies of tax returns for city and school district taxes must be kept for six years. Taxpayers must produce records upon request by the Department of Revenue to allow examination of records for verification of return data [Philadelphia Code §19-506(1)].

¶3706 Payment Date

If a due date for payment of any city tax falls on a day when the agency collecting the tax is not open for a full business day, the Department of Collections can postpone the due date until the following business day [Philadelphia Code §19-503].

• *Extensions*

The Revenue Department can, upon proper cause shown, grant an extension of not over 60 days for the filing of any tax return. Application for extension must be made on or before the statutory due date for payment. If a taxpayer gets a federal extension of over 60 days, the Department can grant an additional extension until the end of the federal extension period. Interest and penalties are due on the tax from the original due date. In order for the extension to be granted, the taxpayer must file a tentative return and pay 100% of the tax estimated to be due on or before the statutory due date for filing the return [Philadelphia Code §19-504].

¶3707 Electronic Filing

• *ROAD (Returns On A Disk) Program*

Philadelphia business tax returns can be filed electronically by using "ROAD." Details can be found at http://www.phila.gov/revenue/ Electronic_Filing.html#ROAD.

• *Electronic payment*

All tax payments can be made electronically via the Electronic Funds Transfer program. Details can be found at http://www.phila.gov/revenue/ Electronic_Filing.html#Elec%20Pay.

The Philadelphia Department of Revenue has adopted regulations regarding the electronic filing and payment of general taxes as well as specific requirements for various taxes. Effective January 1, 2011, any taxpayer that remits an average of $20,000 or more per month will be required to file the tax return and remit the attending tax payment electronically through electronic funds transfer. The monthly threshold will be calculated using the monthly average from the immediate prior calendar year's filings. Taxpayers who do not comply will be subject to a penalty. Taxpayers who submit returns for parking tax, vehicle rental tax, and liquor sales tax must comply with the general electronic filing requirements [General Tax Regulation § 203, Income Tax Regulation § 304, Tobacco and Tobacco-Related Products Tax Regulation § 103, Liquor Sales Tax Regulation § 302, Parking Tax Regulation § 304, Vehicle Rental Tax Regulation § 303, Philadelphia Department of Revenue, effective January 1, 2011].

¶3708 Audit, Assessment, and Request for Ruling

The Department of Revenue's policy is to audit selected returns. The taxpayer gets a notice of audit that generally asks for the taxpayer's books and records for a six-year period. The taxpayer should call the number listed on the notice to set up a mutually convenient appointment.

• *Appeal*

If the audit and assessment process fails to resolve the issues, an appeal may be made to the Tax Review Board. See ¶3711.

• *Document preparation*

Whenever the Law Department prepares a document (*i.e.*, contract, bond, deed, instrument, lease, license, easement, any other agreement, any amendment to a document), the City Solicitor is authorized to impose a fee for the service rendered on the person contracting or otherwise party to the document with the City, provided that the City Solicitor need not charge any fee when, in the City Solicitor's judgment, circumstances justify a waiver of the fee [Philadelphia Code, § 17-701]. For the current document preparation fee schedule, see Philadelphia Code § 17-102.

• *Rulings*

A request for a ruling is used to try to resolve issues before the audit process. If a return is under examination, the Department will not issue a ruling. However, if a return is already filed, a ruling can be requested (as long as the return is not already under examination). Normally, however, a request for a ruling would be made before the return is filed. A request for a ruling should be filed with the Technical Staff. It can be done on either a "name" or a "no-name" basis (*i.e.*, the taxpayer does not have to be identified in the request for ruling). There is no specified form, but all relevant facts and authority should be cited. Ordinarily, the request is made in the form of a letter.

• *Private tax opinions*

The Philadelphia Law Department is authorized to issue a "private tax opinion" in response to a taxpayer's request. A private tax opinion is the written opinion of the Department issued in response to a taxpayer's request about his/her liability under the tax laws with respect to a particular transaction described in the taxpayer's request [Philadelphia Code § 17-703(1)]. The request must comply with procedures prescribed by the City Solicitor, who may, but is not obligated to, issue a private tax opinion [Philadelphia Code § 17-703(2)]. A private tax opinion is valid only with respect to the taxpayer who requested the opinion; it may not be used or cited as precedent; and no taxpayer can rely on a private tax opinion issued to another taxpayer [Philadelphia Code § 17-703(3)].

Whenever the Law Department issues a private tax opinion at the request of a private party, the City Solicitor is authorized to impose a fee on the person requesting the opinion, and the fee must be paid at the time a request for a private tax opinion is made [Philadelphia Code § 17-703(4)]. The amount of the fee is determined in accordance with the schedule promulgated pursuant to Philadelphia Code § 17-703(b).

Withdrawal of requests: The City Solicitor may, from time to time, by regulation, revise the schedule of fees set forth in Philadelphia Code § 17-703(4); and the City Solicitor's schedule of fees need not follow the classification scheme of Philadelphia Code § 17-703(4). However, revised fees cannot exceed the Law Department's cost of issuing private tax opinions [Philadelphia Code § 17-703(5)]. When preparing requests for private tax opinions, taxpayers should check sources carefully to see whether the City Solicitor has issued a revised schedule.

A taxpayer may withdraw a request for a private tax opinion at any time before the opinion has been issued, but withdrawing the request does not entitle the taxpayer to a refund unless more than 120 days have elapsed since the Law Department received a properly filed request. The fee is also nonrefundable once a private tax opinion has been issued, regardless of the conclusion of the opinion with respect to the tax liability of the taxpayer who requested the opinion [72 P.S. § 17-703(6)].

¶3709 Interest, Penalties, and Costs

The law provides for interest and penalties on unpaid taxes [Philadelphia Code § 19-509]. Consult the ordinances for current rates of interest and penalties. If the city brings suit to recover tax, the person liable for the tax is also liable for the costs of collection in addition to interest and penalties on underpayment. Certain violations are punishable by fine and/or imprisonment. Consult the statute.

¶3710 Suit to Recover Taxes

Any suit brought by the city to recover taxes (except real estate and personal property taxes and general business taxes) must be begun within six years after a return or report was filed. There is, however, no statute of limitation on suit to recover taxes if no return was filed, a fraudulent return was filed, or a taxpayer has failed to remit taxes withheld as agent or trustee for the city or school district [Philadelphia Code § 19-510].

¶3711 Tax Review Board

The Tax Review Board is the body to which taxpayers appeal decisions of the Department of Revenue. Taxpayers who disagree with any decisions or determinations for unpaid taxes, interest, and penalties can file a petition for review with the Board within 60 days after the mailing date of notice of decision or determination. The petition must state the reasons upon which the petitioner relied and contain a certification that all facts in it are true [Philadelphia Code §§ 19-1701—§ 1702]. All petitions for self-assessed taxes should be sent to the Philadelphia Tax Review Board, Philadelphia, Pennsylvania. The filing of a petition for review does not stop the accrual of interest, but it does toll the statute of limitations for assessment until final determination is made [Philadelphia Code § 19-601(3)].

• *Decisions*

The Board must list all matters coming before it and hear them within a reasonable time after filing. A decision or action of the Tax Review Board can be appealed to any court of competent jurisdiction within 30 days after the mailing date of notice of that decision or action to the petitioner or her/his attorney. Decisions of the Board concerning compromises and waiver of interest or penalty are final and not subject to further review by any court.

• *Failure to exhaust administrative remedies*

Taxpayers who fail to exhaust administrative remedies may not later raise issues that could and should have been raised in the administrative process. See *Joseph Krug v. City of Philadelphia*, 620 A.2d 46 (Pa.Commw. 1993).

¶3712 Petitions for Refund

If the Department of Revenue determines that any tax has been paid under mistake of law or fact or under an invalid law, it can grant refunds [Philadelphia Code § 19-1703]. Petitions for refund for city and school district taxes must be made within three years from the date of payment. A petition for refund must state the reasons upon which petitioner relies and include a certification that the facts in it are true.

• *Procedure*

The Department of Revenue must dispose of a petition for refund within a reasonable time and notify the petitioner in writing of its decision. Unless the refund arises because of any overpayment resulting from duplication of payments or mathematical error in computation or other mechanical error (*e.g.,* typographical error) or is less than $1,000, a refund decision of the Department must be reviewed by the Tax Review Board. If the Board disapproves or modifies any refund granted by the Department, it must grant both petitioner and the Department a hearing.

• *Appeals*

Any Departmental decision denying a refund (in whole or in part) can be appealed to the Tax Review Board within 90 days of the mailing date of notice of the decision. Decisions of the Tax Review Board can be appealed to any court of competent jurisdiction within 30 days after notice of decision is given.

¶3713 Petitions for Compromise

A taxpayer may file a petition for compromise with the Department of Revenue, stating why he/she believes a compromise would be in the best interest of the city or school district. The Department must, within a reasonable time, consider the petition and notify petitioner in writing of its decision. The Department's decision becomes final only after it has been reviewed, approved, and/or modified by the Tax Review Board [Philadelphia Code § 19-1704].

¶3714 Petitions for Waiver of Penalties and Interest

Taxpayers may petition the Tax Review Board for waiver of interest and penalties. If the Board decides that the petitioner acted in good faith, without negligence or intent to defraud, it may abate the interest and penalties in whole or in part. Filing of a petition for review is considered a request for waiver of interest and penalties, even if it is not specifically stated. The Board must rule upon the waiver of interest and penalties with its ruling upon the petition for review. If the Board fails to abate interest or penalties, it is considered to be a denial of abatement. These decisions cannot be appealed [Philadelphia Code § § 19-1705—19-1706].

¶3712

PHILADELPHIA CITY AND SCHOOL DISTRICT TAXES

CHAPTER 38

PHILADELPHIA CITY WAGE AND NET PROFITS TAX

¶3801 Sources of Authority

Philadelphia levies a tax on wages and net profits under the authority of the Sterling Act (explained at ¶3402), the Pennsylvania Intergovernmental Cooperation Authority Act. The city statutes imposing the wage and net profits tax are contained in Chapters 19-1500 and 19-2800 of the Philadelphia Code. The Philadelphia Department of Revenue has issued regulations governing the city wage and net profits tax. Administration, interest, penalties, and review are controlled by the general provisions explained in Chapter 37.

PICA Tax on Wages & Net Profits

The tax imposed by Philadelphia Code §2801 *et seq.* (Pennsylvania Intergovernmental Cooperation Authority Tax on Wages and Net Profits) is combined with the wage and net profits tax imposed by Philadelphia Code §19-1501 *et seq.* (Wage and Net Profits Tax). The term "wage and net profits tax" is used to refer to the combination of these two taxes. Note that the PICA tax is imposed only on Philadelphia residents. For taxable years beginning on or after January 1, 2012, the PICA tax shall not apply to any net profits from any activity described in Philadelphia Code §19-2601 (relating to certain investment companies and investment company managers [Philadelphia Code §19-2803(5)].

¶3802 Imposition of Tax

Wage tax: The Philadelphia wage tax (also called the earnings tax) is imposed on salaries, wages, commissions, and other compensation [Philadelphia Code §§19-1502 and 19-2803]. All compensation of residents, wherever earned, is taxable, but nonresidents are taxed only on compensation and net profits earned in Philadelphia.

Net profits tax: The net profits tax is imposed on the net profits earned in any business, profession, or enterprise carried on by any person as owner or proprietor, either individually or in association with other person(s) [Philadelphia Code §§19-1502 and 19-2803].

Corporations

Corporations (including corporate partners in a partnership) are not subject to the net profits tax. They are, however, subject to the business income and receipts tax. The business income and receipts tax is discussed in Chapter 39. Philadelphia follows the federal tax treatment for LLCs. Thus, if an LLC elects to be treated as a corporation, it is not subject to the net profits tax. If, however, it elects to be treated as a partnership or disregarded entity, it is subject to the net profits tax.

- *Tax imposed on earned income*

The Philadelphia wage and net profits tax is imposed on earned income only; passive income is not taxable under this statute. If property is purposefully acquired and used for business purposes, the income from the business is earned income, not passive income. See, for example, *Kurtz v. City of Philadelphia*, 718 A.2d 916 (Pa.Commw. 1998), *app. den.*, 732 A.2d 616 (Pa. 1998). It is the position of the City of Philadelphia Department of Revenue that the rental of property, in most cases, constitutes the operation of a business.

- *Business located outside of Philadelphia*

A taxpayer whose principal place of business is located outside Philadelphia must remit city wage tax for employees who perform duties within Philadelphia. See *In re Christopher J. Rohner*, Philadelphia Tax Review Board, Opinion No. 94k, Docket No. 40-930310-2 (October 11, 1994) and City of Philadelphia Income Tax Regulations § 201.

¶3803 Rate

For the 2018 tax year, the Philadelphia tax on wages and net profits is imposed on residents at the rate of 3.8809% and on nonresidents at the rate of 3.4567%.

The differential between the rate for residents and nonresidents was upheld as constitutional by the Supreme Court of Pennsylvania because of the disparity in political representation and use of city-supported services [*Leonard v. Thornburgh*, 489 A.2d 1349 (Pa. 1985)].

- *Withholding rate*

The Philadelphia city wage tax should be withheld and remitted at the rate in effect on the date of the paycheck.

- *Credit against tax*

Sixty percent of the city business income and receipts tax (formerly the business privilege tax) based on net income is allowed to be taken as credit against net profits tax [Philadelphia Code § 19-1506]. This credit must be calculated without regard to any reduction in tax with respect to the credit for contributions to community development corporations [Philadelphia Code § 19-1506(1)(a)]. The credit for contributions to community development corporations is discussed at ¶ 3910.

¶3804 Base

Taxable compensation includes all salaries, wages, commissions, bonuses, incentive payments, fees, and tips that may accrue or be received by an individual for services rendered, whether directly or through an agent and whether in cash or property [Philadelphia Code § 19-1501(8)]. Net profits include the net gain from the operation of a business, profession, or enterprise, after deduction for all allowable costs and expenses [Philadelphia Code § 19-1501(4)]. Taxpayers cannot use net business losses to offset compensation income, and net losses cannot be carried forward or back to any other year.

¶3803

• *Exempt compensation*

Taxable compensation does *not* include the following:

(1) Periodical payments for sick or disability benefits and those 1501(10)(a)].

(2) Retirement pay, or pensions paid to persons retired from service after reaching a specific age or after a stated period of employment [Philadelphia Code § 19-501(10)(b)].

(3) Any wages or compensation paid to any person for active service in the Army, Navy or Air Force of the United States, or to a member of the National Guard for active federal duty [Philadelphia Code § 19-1501(10)(c)].

(4) Any bonus or additional compensation paid by the United States, the Commonwealth of Pennsylvania, or any other state for such service Philadelphia Code § 19-1501(10)(d).

(5) Any statutory per diem compensation paid any witness or juror, or member of the District Election Board Philadelphia Code § 19-1501(10)(e].

(6) Stock options with no readily ascertainable fair market value on the date the option is granted are exempt. However, stock options that have a readily ascertainable fair market value on the date the option is granted are considered compensation and must be included in the taxable wage base [Philadelphia Code § 19-1501(10)(f)].

Regulations

See Philadelphia Income Tax Regulations, § 104 for more detail on exclusions from taxable income.

Covenant Not to Compete

The taxpayer withdrew from an architectural firm and received payments for his interest in a partnership and his agreement not to compete as an architect for a period of three years. The covenant not to compete is taxable as earned income because refraining from engaging in competition is equivalent to personal services. Amounts received for the covenant not to compete, therefore, are taxable as compensation for services rendered [*Rauch v. Tax Review Board of the City of Philadelphia and the City of Philadelphia*, 708 A.2d 142 (Pa.Commw. 1998)].

• *Taxable net profits*

The concept of net profits is essentially an earned income concept. Only earned income is subject to the net profits tax. See, *e.g., Sharps v. Revenue Commissioner*, 10 D&C 2d 450 (1957). Investment income is taxable if the taxpayer is engaged in an investment business. The key to taxability is whether or not a taxpayer is engaged in a trade or business as opposed to a passive investment holding.

Net profits include, but are not limited to, income from the following activities [Philadelphia Income Tax Regulations § 220(b)]:

(1) *Income from rentals and/or sale of real estate.* Net profits do not include rental if the property meets all of the following criteria: (a) it is the principal residence of the owner; (b) it is totally residential; and (c) it comprises three or fewer units. If the property is located outside Philadelphia, the income from it is taxable to the extent of the interest of Philadelphia residents in the income. If the property is located within Philadelphia, the residence of the income beneficiaries is immaterial. The full amount of "the gain, loss, or profit" from the sale of real

estate is taxable without regard to length of time of ownership [*Samuel Rappaport Limited Partnership v. Tax Review Board of the City of Philadelphia*, 682 A.2d 862 (Pa.Commw. 1996)].

(2) Commissions or fees received by a fiduciary if (a) the fiduciary is regularly engaged in a business or profession as a fiduciary or engaged in a business or profession commonly regarded as incidental or collateral to business as a fiduciary (*e.g.*, attorneys or real estate agents); (b) commissions or fees represent a substantial portion of the income of the fiduciary; or (c) the administration of the trust requires a substantial portion of the fiduciary's available time.

(3) Royalties.

(4) Income from a profession.

¶3805 Computation of Taxable Wages

• *Deductible employee business expenses*

Employees can deduct employee business expenses they pay if the expenses meet the following criteria:

(1) They are directly connected with and incurred in the actual performance of their duties or services in or attributable to Philadelphia.

(2) They are ordinary, necessary, and reasonable. See *In re: Jesse Biddle*, No. 36WMREFZZ9598, September 12, 2014 wherein the Tax Review Board allowed a baseball player to deduct agent's fees and management fees as unreimbursed employee expenses.

(3) They are deductible in computation of AGI for federal income tax purposes.

(4) They are in excess of reimbursement.

• *Nondeductible employee business expenses*

The following employee business expenses are not deductible:

(1) Those incurred while commuting to and from work.

(2) Educational expenses.

(3) The cost and upkeep of wearing apparel.

(4) The cost and repair to tools.

(5) Union dues.

(6) Association dues.

(7) Subscription payments.

(8) Pension plan payments.

The wages of a nonresident whose entire compensation is earned in Philadelphia are entirely taxable. Nonresidents who work full time in Philadelphia cannot exclude compensation for days paid but not required to work (*e.g.*, vacation, weekends, holidays). The wages of a nonresident employee who performs services both within and outside Philadelphia must be allocated or apportioned to determine the amount of wages subject to the city wage tax.

¶3806 Computation of Net Profits

The net profit of a business, profession, or other activity is computed by subtracting cost of goods sold and all ordinary and necessary business expenses from gross receipts [Philadelphia Income Tax Regulations, § 223]. A taxpayer uses the same method for computation of net profits for Philadelphia purposes as for federal purposes.

¶3805

• *Gross receipts*

These include (but are not limited to) receipts from sales of merchandise, goods, wares, chattels, notes, securities, choses-in-action, services (except as an employee), and commissions (except as an employee).

"Gross profit" is the difference between gross receipts and cost of goods sold.

"Business deductions" are the ordinary and necessary expenses actually incurred in the operation of the business. The following are examples of allowable business deductions:

(1) *Salaries and wages paid.* Withdrawals by the owner or proprietor of a business are not allowable expenses.

(2) *Rent for property actually used in the business.* If a proprietor owns the building in which business is conducted, rent cannot be claimed as a deduction.

(3) *Interest on business indebtedness.* Mortgage interest is allowable if the proprietor owns the building.

(4) Taxes directly connected with business operation or property (*e.g.*, unemployment compensation payments, employer's share of Social Security payments, real estate tax if proprietor owns the building). The following taxes are not deductible: taxes based on income (federal, state, or local); gift, estate, or inheritance taxes; and taxes for local benefits or improvements to property that increase the property's value.

(5) Casualty losses (if they are thoroughly substantiated).

(6) Business bad debts for accrual-basis taxpayers.

(7) *Depreciation.* If different from the amount reported to the IRS, the taxpayer must clearly report the difference and the reasons for it; federal cost recovery (including ACRS and MACRS) can be used.

(8) Repairs.

• *Certain investment companies*

For taxable years beginning on or after January 1, 2012, the BIRT tax shall not apply to any net profits from certain activities of certain investment companies and investment company managers [Philadelphia Code § 19-1502(2)(e)]. These entities and activities are described in Philadelphia Code § 19-2601(7).

• *Investment companies managers*

Effective for tax year 2012 and thereafter, the activities of the general partners or managing members of investment companies registered under the Investment Company Act of 1940 are exempt from the BIRT and the NPT to the extent that their compensation is measured by or based on the financial performance of the entities they manage. The activities of the investment entities were previously exempted from the BIRT and the NPT [Bill No. 120007].

¶3807 Returns and Payment of Tax

An employee must file a return if the employer is not required to withhold city wage tax. Every person engaged in any business, profession or other activity in Philadelphia must file a net profits return. Taxpayers must use the method of accounting (*e.g.*, cash, accrual, installment, completed contract) and tax period (calendar year, fiscal year) they use for federal purposes. If a taxpayer has more than one business location, the combined net profits of all locations must be shown on one return, accompanied by a schedule showing the computation of the net profits of the individual locations [Philadelphia Code § 19-1503]. Payment of the wage tax is ordinarily made through withholding by employers, and payment of the net profits tax is ordinarily made by means of payments of estimated tax.

• *Net profits tax returns*

Calendar-year taxpayers must file returns on or before April 15, and fiscal-year taxpayers must file returns within 105 days from the end of the fiscal year [Philadelphia Code § 19-1503(1)]. A return must be filed even if a loss is incurred. If no return is filed, non-filer penalties will be imposed.

• *Information returns*

Anyone engaged in business in Philadelphia who pays $600 or more in a tax year to another person (except corporations) in the form of commission, fees, compensation, rents, and royalties on which city wage tax was not withheld must file an information return on or before February 28 following the year paid. The information return must show: (1) name and address of payer; (2) name and address of recipient; and (3) amount of payment [Income Tax Regulations, § 303(b)(2)].

• *Wage tax returns*

Employees who receive taxable compensation from which wage tax was not withheld by the employer must file quarterly returns on or before the last day of April, July, and October, and on February 15, reporting and paying the tax due [Philadelphia Code §§ 19-1503(2) and 19-2800].

• *Extensions of time*

Extensions of time for filing and paying the city wage and net profits tax are governed by the general provisions explained at ¶ 3706.

• *Personal liability of corporate officers*

The officers of a corporation that in the course of its operations collects taxes as an agent for a city and fails to remit them to the city may be personally liable for the payment of the unremitted taxes if they had the responsibility or control over the collection and remitting of the taxes [*Brown v. Cmwlth.*, 670 A.2d 1222 (Pa.Commw. 1996)]. See ¶ 604 for further discussion of *Brown*. Whether a particular corporate officer had such responsibility or control is a question of fact [*City of Philadelphia v. Hertler*, 539 A.2d 268 (Pa.Commw. 1988)]. The president of a corporation who applied for his corporation's business license and signed the corporation's annual wage tax reconciliation forms was found to have the requisite responsibility or control and was held personally liable for the payment of the corporation's unremitted Philadelphia city wage tax [*City of Philadelphia v. Petherbridge*, 781 A.2d 263 (Pa.Commw. 2001)].

¶3808 Withholding

Employers in Philadelphia who employ one or more persons on a salary, wage, commission, or other compensation basis must deduct, at the time compensation is paid, the Philadelphia wage tax from the compensation and remit the withheld tax as required [Philadelphia Code § 19-1504(1)]. Returns and payment of tax are discussed at ¶ 3807. The tax must be deducted by the employer from (1) all compensation paid to nonresident employees for activities in the city of Philadelphia and (2) from salaries paid to employees who are residents of Philadelphia, regardless of the place where the services are rendered [Income Tax Regulations, § 401].

No Reciprocal Tax Agreements

The City of Philadelphia has no reciprocal tax agreement with any other state or with any political subdivision of another state.

• *"Employee" defined*

In general, the key element in the definition of employee is the amount of direction and control exercised by the employer over the employee's work.

Students Employed by an Independent Contractor

Taxpayer (Battistone) was an independent contractor in the business of soliciting magazine sales. He hired students to sell magazines for him through telephone and in-person solicitation and paid them on a commission basis. He provided training for the students and had the power to fire students who did not perform adequately. Battistone received all commissions for the magazine sales and from them paid the students. The Philadelphia Tax Review Board held that Battistone exerted sufficient direction and control over the students to qualify them as employees for withholding purposes. See *In re Frank Battistone*, Philadelphia Tax Review Board, Docket No. 40-911002, Opinion No. 95-B (March 1, 1995).

Withholding reports must be made on forms furnished by the Department, and the tax due must be remitted with the return [Philadelphia Code § 19-1504(1)]. Withholding for domestic servants is optional [Regulations, § 406].

• *Deposit of tax*

Employers who withhold an aggregate amount of tax over $50 but less than $250 during one calendar month (except March, June, September, and December) must, within 25 days after the last day of the month, deposit the tax with the Department of Revenue (or designated bank) and file with the deposit a return on forms furnished by the Department. When these employers file quarterly returns, they attach validated receipts for monthly deposits and remit any tax still owed (if any).

Employers who withhold more than $250 during one calendar month must deposit the withheld tax with the Department within three banking days after each payroll period deduction date but not more frequently than once in a seven-day period. At the time of deposit all employers must file a depository form furnished by the Department [Philadelphia Code § 19-1504(3)].

• *Reconciliation statement*

Employers who withhold city wage tax must file an annual reconciliation statement with the city in which they reconcile taxes remitted to the city with taxes withheld from employees. Employers who fail to withhold tax from employees are personally liable for the tax, but the Department can collect it from the employee if it cannot be collected from the employer [Philadelphia Code § 19-1504(1)(c)]. Consult the current statute for penalties for late payment or underpayment of withheld taxes.

• *Employees of employers not required to withhold*

Persons who are subject to the Philadelphia city wage tax and who work for employers who are not required to withhold the Philadelphia city wage tax (*e.g.,* Philadelphia residents employed outside Pennsylvania who receive compensation on which tax is not withheld) must register for an Earnings Tax Account. A taxpayer can establish an Earnings Tax Account by calling the Business/Earnings Tax Unit of the Philadelphia Department of Revenue at 215-686-6600 or visiting the Municipal Services Building, Public Concourse Level, 1401 John F. Kennedy Boulevard.

¶3809 Estimated Net Profits Tax

Everyone with taxable net profits must file estimated tax returns and pay estimated tax for the current tax year. The estimated tax is the amount of tax due for the preceding tax year after giving effect to the tax credit explained at ¶3803 [Philadelphia Code § 19-1505(2)].

• *Returns and payment*

Estimated tax returns and payment of estimated tax for calendar year taxpayers are due in two installments. One-fourth of estimated tax is due on or before April 15 and another one-fourth is due on or before June 15. Fiscal-year taxpayers report and pay one-half of the estimated tax in two equal installments of one-fourth within three months and five and one-half months after the beginning of the tax year.

• *Credit*

If a taxpayer's final tax due is less than the amount of estimated tax paid, the excess is applied as a credit against the estimated tax for the following tax year. This is the only credit allowed for wage and net profits purposes. If the excess estimated payments are more than the estimated tax for the following year, the excess is refunded.

• *Exempt from estimated tax*

The following persons are not required to file and pay estimated tax: (1) new taxpayers (*i.e.*, those not in business the prior year), (2) taxpayers with net profits tax liability for the preceding year of no more than $100, or (3) persons who terminated business activity before the due date of the net profits tax return for the preceding tax year.

¶3810 Homeowner Tax Relief Act (Act 72)

Act 72 Repealed

With the passage of the Taxpayer Relief Act (discussed at ¶3515), Act 72 (Homeowner Tax Relief Act) is repealed, effective June 27, 2006 [Act No. 1 of Special Session of 2005 (H.B. 39), §5005(4)]. However, unless otherwise provided in Chapter 1, 3, 5, or 7 of the Taxpayer Relief Act, actions, orders, regulations, rules, designations, and decisions that were made by the Department of Education or by a school district under the former Homeowner Tax Relief Act and that have been completed or are in effect on June 27, 2006 shall continue and remain in full force and effect for the purposes of Chapters 1, 3, 5, and 7 to the extent that such actions, orders, regulations, rules, designations, and decisions apply to the 2006-2007 fiscal year unless revoked, vacated, or modified by the Taxpayer Relief Act, the Department of Education, or the school district pursuant to Chapter 1, 3, 5, and 7 [Act No. 1 of Special Session of 2005 (H.B. 39), §5006(b)].

• *Overview*

The Homeowner Tax Relief Act [Act 72 of 2004 (S.B. 100), effective September 3, 2004] is a free-standing act that allows school districts (except Philadelphia) to reduce taxes for the purpose of funding homestead and farmstead exclusions (discussed at ¶3406). In all school districts except Philadelphia homestead and farmstead exclusions are funded by state gaming allocations and imposition of earned income and net profits taxes (EIT) or personal income taxes (PIT). Act 72 as it relates to school districts other than Philadelphia is discussed at ¶3514. In Philadelphia, the state funding for tax relief will be used to reduce the city wage and net profits tax instead of property taxes.

• *Opting into Act 72*

In order to qualify for a state gaming allocation, Philadelphia would have to reduce the rate of wage and net profits tax on residents and nonresidents levied under the authority of the Sterling Act. See ¶3801. State gaming allocations to Philadelphia must be used to reduce its wage and net profits tax rate [§703(a)]. Opting into Act 72 would mandate a schedule of future wage tax reductions that could be deviated from only under limited circumstances, generally by a supermajority vote of city council and with the approval of the Pennsylvania Intergovernmental Cooperation Authority [§703(b), (c)].

• *Rate reductions*

The city must calculate the amount of the tax rate reductions so that, when combined with any reduction in the rate of the school district income tax (discussed at ¶4016), they equal the amount of gaming allocations paid to the city [§703(b)]. Allocation of wage tax reduction between residents and nonresidents would be based on a formula. Provision is first made for resident wage tax reduction, and the amount of nonresident wage tax reduction (if any) is made from any of the allocation to Philadelphia left over after providing for resident rate reduction [§505(c)].

• *Senior citizen property tax rebate*

Any Philadelphia resident who is eligible to receive a property tax rebate pursuant to The Senior Citizens Property Tax and Rebate Assistance Program is eligible to receive an additional property tax rebate equal to 50% of the amount the individual is eligible to receive under The Senior Citizens Property Tax and Rebate Assistance Program [§704(a)(1)]. The Senior Citizens Property Tax and Rebate Assistance Program is discussed at ¶3512. The additional senior citizen property tax rebate cannot exceed the difference between the property tax paid by the eligible resident and the rebate received by the eligible resident under the Senior Citizens Property Tax and Rebate Assistance Program for the same year [§704(a)(2)].

By June 30 of the year in which a gaming allocation will be made, the state treasurer must transfer from the property tax relief fund to the state lottery fund an amount sufficient to fund the additional senior citizen property tax rebate. All revenue transferred to the state lottery fund must be distributed in accordance with the provisions of the Senior Citizens Property Tax and Rebate Assistance Program [§704(b)].

Only Philadelphia residents who pay property tax are entitled to an additional property tax rebate under Act 72. The additional rebate provisions do not apply to Philadelphia residents who are entitled to receive a rent rebate in lieu of property taxes under the Senior Citizens Property Tax and Rebate Assistance Program [§704(c)].

¶3811 Philadelphia Keystone Zone Credits

Taxpayers with business activity in a Philadelphia Keystone Opportunity Zone (KOZ), Keystone Opportunity Expansion Zone (KOEZ), or Keystone Opportunity Improvement Zone (KOIZ) may claim a credit against the Philadelphia net profits tax. In order to qualify for the credit, a person or business must own or lease real property in the zone from which a trade, business, or profession is actively conducted. The credit is based on an apportionment formula consisting of the ration of property, payroll, and receipts within the zone to property, payroll, and receipts outside the zone. For explanation of KOZ, KOEZ, or KOIZ see ¶4622.

Credit certification must be received from the Pennsylvania Department of Community and Economic Development (DCED) and must be renewed annually. A copy of the certification approval letter and zone credit worksheets must accompany the net profits tax returns.

For more information see https://beta.phila.gov/services/payments-assistance-taxes/tax-credits/keystone-opportunity-zone-tax-credit/.

PHILADELPHIA CITY AND SCHOOL DISTRICT TAXES

CHAPTER 39

BUSINESS INCOME AND RECEIPTS TAX (BIRT)
(formerly PHILADELPHIA BUSINESS INCOME AND RECEIPTS TAX)

¶3901 History and Sources of Authority

The Philadelphia Business Income and Receipts Tax (formerly Business Privilege Tax) is a privilege tax imposed under the authority of the First Class City Tax Reform Act [53 P.S. § 16181 *et seq.*]. This enabling legislation permits the city to impose either the business privilege tax or the mercantile license tax (authorized by the Sterling Act).

The business privilege tax provisions are found in the Philadelphia Code § 19-2601 *et seq.* Regulations have been issued by the city [Philadelphia BIRT Regulations § 101 *et seq.*].

¶3902 Administration

The Philadelphia business income and receipts tax (BIRT) is administered by the Philadelphia Department of Revenue. Recordkeeping, collection, penalties, interest, refund, review and appeal are controlled by the general provisions explained in Chapter 37 [Philadelphia Code § § 19-2607—19-2608].

¶3903 Commercial Activity Licenses (formerly Business Privilege Licenses)

Prior to engaging in business in the City of Philadelphia, persons desiring to engage in or continue to engage in any business within the City must procure a commercial activity license from the Department of Licenses and Inspections. A taxpayer who does business in the City must procure a commercial activity license even if he or she does not maintain a place of business in the City [Philadelphia Code § 19-2602(1)]. Two types of commercial activity licenses are issued:

(1) Permanent licenses [Philadelphia Code § 19-2602(2)(a)].

(2) Annual licenses [Philadelphia Code § 19-2604(2)(b)].

Termination of Commercial Activity License Fees

Effective January 1, 2014, there will be no fee for the issuance of a commercial activity license. Previously, a permanent license was subject to a $300 fee, and an annual license was subject to a $50 fee [Philadelphia Code § 19-2602(2)(b)].

¶3904 Imposition of Tax

No more than an "active presence" is required to constitute "doing business" in Philadelphia [Philadelphia BIRT Regulations, § 103(b)]. Note, however that the term "business" does not include any hobby or other not-for-profit activity. Thus, the Philadelphia business income and receipts tax (formerly business privilege tax) is imposed annually upon any person having an active presence in Philadelphia [Philadelphia Code § 19-2603(3)]. See "*Active presence defined*," below. A "person" for this purpose is any individual, partnership, limited partnership, association, corporation, estate or trust. Whenever used in any provision imposing a penalty, the term "person" as applied to associations means the partners or members, and as applied to corporations the term means the officers thereof. If a single-member limited liability company (LLC) is a disregarded entity for federal income tax purposes, its entity status will also be disregarded for purposes of the Philadelphia business income and receipts tax; the net income of a single-member LLC is reported by its owner. The BIRT is a completely separate tax from the Net Profits Tax. Consequently, it is possible to be subject to both the BIRT and the Net Profits Tax.

The city business income and receipts tax (BIRT) is levied on a combination of gross receipts and net income [Philadelphia Code § 19-2601]. Whether taxpayers are subject to the full BIRT or only to the gross receipts portion depends on the level and nature of the taxpayer's activity within Philadelphia. A taxpayer is subject to the gross receipts portion of the BIRT when it has sufficient contact with Philadelphia to be taxed without violating the United States Constitution. A taxpayer is subject to the net income portion of the BIRT when it has sufficient contact with Philadelphia to be taxed without violating the United States Constitution and Public Law 86-272. Anyone subject to the Philadelphia business income and receipts tax whose activity within Philadelphia does not exceed solicitation is not subject to the net income portion of the tax [Philadelphia Code § 19-2603(4)]. See ¶914 for discussion of the Interstate Income Act of 1959 [P.L. 86-272, 15 U.S.C.A. § 31], the source of the Philadelphia (and Commonwealth) standard of nexus called "solicitation plus."

• *Exemptions*

Bookbinders: Receipts attributable to the *bona fide* delivery of goods, wares, or merchandise by persons engaged in bookbinding to a location regularly maintained by the other party to the transaction outside the limits of the city, and not for the purpose of evading or avoiding payment of tax, are exempt from the Philadelphia business income and receipts tax (formerly business privilege tax). "Bookbinding" means any business categorized as tradebinding (NAIC 323121) under the North American Industry Classification System, 2002 codes established by the Office of Management and Budget, Executive Office of the President [Philadelphia City Ordinance no. 060014, Philadelphia City Council, June 8, 2006].

Certain investment companies: For taxable years beginning on or after January 1, 2012, the BIRT tax shall not apply to any net profits from certain activities of certain

¶3904

investment companies and investment company managers [Philadelphia Code § 19-1502(2)(e)]. These entities and activities are described in Philadelphia Code § 19-2601(7).

- *Investment companies managers*

Investment companies' managers: Effective for tax year 2012 and after, the activities of the general partners or managing members of investment companies registered under the Investment Company Act of 1940 are exempt from the BIRT and the NPT to the extent that their compensation is measured by or based on the financial performance of the entities they manage. The activities of the investment entities were previously exempted from the BIRT and the NPT.

Business Located Outside of Philadelphia

A taxpayer whose principal place of business is located outside Philadelphia is responsible for the business income and receipts tax for business transacted in Philadelphia. See *In re Christopher J. Rohner*, Philadelphia Tax Review Board, Opinion No. 94k, Docket No. 40-930310-2 (October 11, 1994), and City of Philadelphia Income Tax Regulations § 103(a).

- *Period used in computation of tax*

In general, a taxpayer determines taxable receipts and net income using the net income for the "tax measurement year" ending in the tax year [Philadelphia Code § 19-2609(1)]. A "tax measurement year" is the fiscal or calendar year by which the person engaging in business keeps its books and records for federal tax purposes [Philadelphia Code § 19-2601].

Certain new businesses: A taxpayer that does not have a tax measurement year ending in the tax year must file a return stating that no tax is due for the tax year [Philadelphia Code § 19-2609(2)].

Terminating businesses: The period used to file the final tax year return of a terminated business depends on whether a person has a calendar or fiscal tax measurement year and, in the case of a person with a fiscal tax measurement year, on whether or not a person starts engaging in business within Philadelphia prior to tax year 2002 [Philadelphia BIRT Regulations § 203(d)]. As noted immediately above, certain new businesses with a fiscal tax measurement year are required to file their first tax year returns stating that there is no tax due. This results in the postponement of payment of taxes for some months until termination of business activity within Philadelphia occurs. For this reason, the months used in filing such businesses', final tax year returns will be more than the number of months in business in their final tax years. Every person terminating business activity within Philadelphia during a tax year falls into only one of the following categories for the purpose of filing its final tax year return:

(1) All calendar-year taxpayers regardless of starting date.

(a) If the fiscal year ends prior to the termination date within the tax year, the person must file its final tax year return based on the combined net income and combined taxable receipts of the fiscal tax measurement year ending in the tax year and the short period ending on the termination date, divided by the total number of days in the combined periods, and multiplied by the number of days in business during the final privilege year. Any capital gain or loss reported in either one of the periods shall be taken out of the calculation and added back to or subtracted from the tax base.

(b) If termination occurs within a tax year prior to the end of the fiscal tax measurement year ending in that tax year, the person must file its final year tax return based on the net income and the taxable receipts of the short fiscal year ending on the date of termination, divided by the number of days

¶3904

in business within Philadelphia during the short fiscal year, and multiplied by the total number of days in business during the final privilege year. Any capital gain or loss reported in the short fiscal year shall be taken out of the calculation and added back to or subtracted from the tax base.

(2) Fiscal-year taxpayers starting business within Philadelphia prior to 2002.

(a) If the fiscal year ends prior to the termination date within the tax year, the person must file its final tax year return based on the combined net income and combined taxable receipts of the fiscal tax measurement year ending in the tax year and the short period ending on the termination date, divided by the total number of days in the combined periods, and multiplied by the number of days in business during the final privilege year. Any capital gain or loss reported in either one of the periods shall be taken out of the calculation and added back to or subtracted from the tax base.

(b) If termination occurs within a tax year prior to the end of the fiscal tax measurement year ending in that tax year, the person must file its final year tax return based on the net income and the taxable receipts of the short fiscal year ending on the date of termination, divided by the number of days in business within Philadelphia during the short fiscal year, and multiplied by the total number of days in business during the final privilege year. Any capital gain or loss reported in the short fiscal year shall be taken out of the calculation and added back to or subtracted from the tax base.

(3) Fiscal-year taxpayers starting business within Philadelphia after 2002.

(a) If the fiscal year ends prior to the termination date within the tax year, the person must file its final tax year return based on the combined net income and the combined taxable receipts of the fiscal tax measurement year ending in the tax year and the short period ending on the termination date.

(b) If termination occurs within a tax year prior to the end of the fiscal tax measurement year ending in the tax year, the person must file its final year tax return based on the short fiscal year ending on the termination date.

Changes in tax measurement year: A taxpayer that changes its tax measurement year may have multiple tax measurement years within a tax year and must pay the tax for all periods in business [Philadelphia Code § 19-2609(4)]. See Philadelphia BIRT Regulations § 203(f) for details.

• *"Business" defined*

The word "business" for purposes of the Philadelphia business income and receipts tax is defined as carrying on or exercising for gain or profit within the city, any trade, business (including financial business), profession, vocation or commercial activity, including the partial or complete liquidation or sale of business assets, or making sales to persons within the city [Philadelphia Code § 19-2601]. A real estate investment company and its related real estate management company were held to be engaged in business in Philadelphia with respect to gains on sales of properties [*Samuel Rappaport Limited Partnership v. Tax Review Board of the City of Philadelphia*, 682 A.2d 862 (Pa.Commw. 1996)].

• *Excluded businesses*

The definition of "business" does not include the following businesses; thus, they are exempt for Philadelphia business income and receipts tax purposes [Philadelphia Code § 19-2601]:

(1) Any business conducted by a nonprofit corporation or association organized for religious, charitable, or educational purposes other than a commer-

cial activity that does not directly serve and is not directly connected with the entity's exempt purpose.

(2) Any political subdivision, or any authority created and organized under the laws of Pennsylvania.

(3) Any credit union chartered under laws of Pennsylvania.

(4) The specific business conducted by any public utility regulated by the Pennsylvania Public Utility Commission or the Interstate Commerce Commission.

(5) The business of any insurance company, association or exchange, or any fraternal, benefit or beneficial society of any other state (if the other state imposes retaliatory taxes on similar Pennsylvania organizations doing business in that state). The operation of a commercial realty business is not the business of an insurance company [*Principal Life Insurance Company v. City of Philadelphia*, Pa.Commw., No. 1391 C.D. 2003 (December 22, 2003)]. Thus, an insurance company that owned and operated commercial properties was subject to the Philadelphia BIRT and would be subject to the BIRT even if a retaliatory tax were triggered.

(6) Employment for a wage or salary.

(7) The business of loading or discharging cargo to or from vessels conducted on piers, wharves or marine terminal facilities in the Port of Philadelphia and business activities related thereto (*e.g.,* furnishing dockage, wharfage, truck and/or railroad car loading and unloading and storage of cargo that is to be loaded or has been discharged from vessels at a pier, wharf or marine terminal facility in the Port of Philadelphia) [Philadelphia Code § 19-2601].

- *"Active presence" defined*

Any person having an active presence in Philadelphia is subject to the Philadelphia BIRT. Any activity within Philadelphia by a person (including, but not limited to, solicitation through one or more employees, agents, or independent contractors) that makes it possible to create, realize, or continue contractual relationships between the person and customers located in Philadelphia is sufficient to establish an active presence. Physical presence (maintenance of office or property) in Philadelphia is not required to establish an active presence [Philadelphia Code § 19-2603(3)].

- *Partnerships*

The Philadelphia business income and receipts tax is imposed on businesses, not on individuals (*i.e.,* at the entity level). A limited partnership was not allowed to exclude the income of an out-of-state partnership from its taxable receipts [*Nine Penn Center Associates v. Tax Review Board of the City of Philadelphia*, 692 A.2d 246 (Pa.Commw. 1997). The statute is imposed on every "person" doing business in the city.

Securities Industry Regulation Does Not Bar Imposition

Commonwealth regulation of the securities industry does not preempt that industry from local taxation. Even though the regulation is extensive, the intent of the regulation is to protect the investing public and relates primarily to the ethical conduct of broker-dealers rather than taxation of securities transactions. The system of license fees imposed by the Commonwealth is not an extensive system of taxation, even though the receipts from the fees exceed the expenditures of the Pennsylvania Securities Commission. The local taxing jurisdiction, therefore, can impose a mercantile license tax on securities dealers [*City of Philadelphia v. Tax Review Board to the Use of Janney Montgomery Scott*, 601 A.2d 875 (1992), *app. den.,* 612 A.2d 486 (1992)]. Similarly, Commonwealth regulation of the liquor industry does not preclude imposition of a local business income and receipts tax. Philadelphia's business income and receipts tax is intended to raise revenue, not to regulate the liquor industry [*City of Philadelphia v. Clement & Muller, Inc.*, 715 A.2d 397 (Pa. 1998), *aff'g* 659 A.2d 596 (Pa.Commw. 1995) (see below)]. See also ¶3402.

- *Tax applies to manufacturers in first class cities (i.e., Philadelphia)*

Insinger Machine Company, a manufacturer of kitchen equipment located in Philadelphia, contended that it was not subject to the Philadelphia business income and receipts tax because it is unconstitutional to levy the tax on manufacturers. The city of Pittsburgh is specifically prohibited under the provisions of the LTEA (see above) from taxing goods and articles manufactured with the city's limits. However, there is no prohibition against taxing a manufacturer in a first class city (Philadelphia) under the Tax Reform Code. The Philadelphia business income and receipts tax satisfied the four prongs of the *Complete Auto Transit* test. Therefore, the Philadelphia business income and receipts tax was properly applied to manufacturers [*Insinger Machine Company v. Philadelphia Tax Review Board*, 645 A.2d 365 (Pa.Commw. 1994), *app. den.*, 657 A.2d 494 (Pa. 1995)]. See ¶913 for explanation of the *Complete Auto Transit* case.

- *Preemption*

A local jurisdiction cannot levy a tax on anything the Commonwealth taxes [Act of August 5, 1932, Sp. Sess., P.L. 45, §1; Act of December 31, 1965, P.L. 1257, §3]. This concept is referred to as the preemption doctrine (explained at ¶3403), and it has been an important issue and a subject of considerable litigation in the context of local taxation. Preemption cases relevant to the Philadelphia business privilege tax are discussed below.

Beer distributors: In a case involving the Business Income and Receipts and the Mercantile Tax of Harrisburg, the Pennsylvania Supreme Court ruled that existence of comprehensive regulatory schemes in the liquor industry preempts local taxation of beer distributors [*Commonwealth v. Wilsbach Distributors, Inc.*, 513 Pa. 215 (Pa. 1986)]. Relying on *Wilsbach*, beer distributors (Clement & Muller, Inc.) filed petitions for refund appeals and petitions for review of the business income and receipts tax with the Philadelphia Tax Review Board [*City of Philadelphia v. Clement & Muller, Inc.*, 715 A.2d 397 (Pa. 1998), *aff'g* 659 A.2d 596 (Pa.Commw. 1995)]. The court noted that the enabling legislation for Philadelphia's business income and receipts tax [The First Class City Business Reform Act, Act of May 30, 1984, P.L. 345, No. 69] granted Philadelphia a broader authority than the authority granted to Harrisburg under its enabling legislation (The Local Tax Enabling Act), expressly stating that the Philadelphia business privilege tax was to be imposed notwithstanding a contrary provision of law of the Commonwealth. Therefore, legislative intent was not in question, and Commonwealth's pervasive regulation of the industry did not preempt the enabling tax legislation; and the taxpayers were subject to the Philadelphia business income and receipts tax.

¶3905 Base and Rates of Tax

- *Imposition*

The Philadelphia business income and receipts tax is imposed on persons engaging in any business in Philadelphia [Philadelphia Code §2603(1)(1)] or having an active presence in Philadelphia [Philadelphia Code §19-2603(3)]. See *"Active presence defined"* at ¶3904. The gross receipts portion of the Philadelphia business income and receipts tax is not limited by P.L. 86-272 [Philadelphia Code §2603(2)]. The net income portion of the tax, however, is not imposed on any person whose activity within Philadelphia does not exceed solicitation [Philadelphia Code §2603(4)]. P.L. 86-272 and "solicitation" are discussed at ¶914.

¶3905

• *Base*

The base for the computation of the Philadelphia income and receipts privilege tax is a combination of taxable gross receipts and net income [Philadelphia Code, §§ 19-2601, 19-2604, 19-2605]. See ¶ 3906 for discussion of gross receipts and 3907 for discussion of methods of accounting for net income.

City/Federal Difference

Deductions for federal tax purposes cannot be used as deductions for Philadelphia business income and receipts tax purposes unless they are specifically exempted by code or regulations. The fact that a taxpayer received special consideration for federal tax purposes is irrelevant to a determination of the taxpayer's Philadelphia business income and receipts tax obligation [*City of Philadelphia v. Arsenal Associates*, 798 A.2d 876 (Pa.Commw. 2002); *opinion not reported*].

Definition of "agency" in determination of "receipts": The Commonwealth Court has held that, when determining whether a taxpayer could exclude tenant payments from its receipts for Philadelphia business income and receipts tax purposes, the trial court should have applied the definition of "agency" contained in the city's business income and receipts tax regulations, not the definition contained in the Second Restatement of Agency [*Arsenal Associates v. City of Philadelphia*, Pa.Commw., No. 601 C.D. 2001 (May 1, 2002); *opinion not reported*]. The case was remanded to the trial court to apply the appropriate legal standard consistent with the Commonwealth Court's decision.

Fees paid to subcontractors: The Philadelphia Tax Review Board has held that fees received by a firm from its clients for work performed by subcontractors must be included in its gross receipts for Philadelphia business income and receipts tax purposes, even when 100% of those fees are passed through to the subconsultants [*In re Wallace, Roberts, and Todd, Philadelphia Tax Review Board*, Nos. 36BPMERZZ9785 and 36NPMERZZ9883 (April 4, 2002)].

Apportionment of gross receipts attributable to work of subcontractors: The taxpayer is not entitled to apportion its gross receipts when the work performed by subcontractors, who are not employees of the taxpayer, is not entirely located within Philadelphia [*In re Wallace, Roberts, and Todd, Philadelphia Tax Review Board*, Nos. 36BPMERZZ9785 and 36NPMERZZ9883 (April 4, 2002)].

• *Rates*

Businesses (except regulated industries) pay an annual tax on each dollar of annual receipts plus an annual tax on net income [Philadelphia Code § 19-2604(1)]. The rates for taxable years since 2008 are as follows:

Year(s)	Receipts Rate in Mills	Net Income Rate %
2014	1.415 mills	6.43%
2015	1.415 mills	6.41%
2016	1.415 mills	6.39%
2017	1.415 mills	6.35%
2018	1.415 mills	6.30%
2019	1.415 mills	6.25%
2020	1.415 mills	6.20%
2021	1.415 mills	6.15%
2022	1.415 mills	6.10%
2023 and thereafter	1.415 mills	6.00%

Regulated industries: A regulated industry pays only an annual tax on each dollar of annual receipts at the general rate and in an amount not to exceed the percentage of net income computed at the general rate (currently 6.5%) [Philadelphia Code § 2604(1)]. A "regulated industry" is one that is subject to (1) the bank and trust company shares tax, (2) the title insurance companies shares tax, (3) the insurance premiums tax, (4) the mutual thrift institutions tax, or (5) a public utility operating under the laws, rules, and regulations administered by the Pennsylvania Public Utility Commission, all or a portion of the activities of which is to furnish or supply service or services at the rates specified in its tariffs [Philadelphia Code § 19-2601].

Securities brokers/dealers: Sellers of securities are subject to the tax at the general rates discussed above. The tax, however, may not be less than (1) 4.6 mills on taxable receipts computed without deduction for commissions effected for persons resident and having their principal place of business outside Philadelphia plus (2) the lesser of (a) 2.3 mills of taxable receipts or (b) 2.3% of net income, both computed without deduction for commissions effected for persons resident and having their principal place of business outside Philadelphia [Philadelphia Code § 19-2604(2)].

New Business

Beginning with tax year 2012 and for the first two years it qualifies as a new business, a business will be subject to the BIRT (formerly BPT) at a rate of 0%. For definition of "new business" and further details see Philadelphia Code Chapter 19-3800.

- *Alternative receipts tax computation*

An optional alternative tax computation is provided for manufacturers (other than a regulated industry), wholesalers (other than a regulated industry), and retailers (other than a regulated industry) [Philadelphia Code, § 19-2604(3)].

Manufacturers: A manufacturer (other than a regulated industry) may compute the gross receipts tax on manufacturing sales at the an alternative rate multiplied by receipts from manufacturing sales after deducting the applicable cost of goods sold computed under the rules of the Internal Revenue Code. A "manufacturer" is a person whose business is the sale of goods, commodities, wares, or merchandise of its own manufacture, growth, or production [Philadelphia Code § 19-2601]. This definition mirrors the language employed in Commonwealth tax statutes. See also *City of Philadelphia, Dept. of Revenue v. Tax Review Board of the City of Philadelphia to the Use of Sawin Systems, Inc.,* 628 A.2d 1220 (Pa.Commw. 1993).

Wholesalers: A wholesaler (other than a regulated industry) may compute the gross receipts tax on wholesale sales at an alternative rate multiplied by receipts from wholesale sales after deducting the applicable cost of goods and the applicable cost of labor. A "wholesaler" is a person whose business is the sale of goods, commodities, wares, or merchandise to dealers or vendors of those goods, commodities, wares, or merchandise [Philadelphia Code § 19-2601].

Retailers: A retailer (other than a regulated industry) may compute the gross receipts tax on retail sales at an alternative rate multiplied by receipts from retail sales after deduction of the applicable cost of goods and the applicable cost of labor. A "retailer" is a person whose business is the sale of goods, commodities, wares or merchandise to persons who are not dealers or vendors of those goods, commodities, wares, or merchandise [Philadelphia Code § 19-2601].

No Special Treatment for REITs

There are no special provisions for REITs. Dividends paid to shareholders must be included in net income for Philadelphia business income and receipts tax purposes [*In re New Plan Realty,* Philadelphia Tax Review Board, Docket No. 40-900112-2, Opinion No. 95-C (April 4, 1995), *appeal quashed,* 675 A.2d 802 (Pa.Commw. 1996)].

¶3906 Gross Receipts

The term "receipts" for Philadelphia BIRT purposes includes cash, credits, property of any kind or nature, received from conducting any business or by reason of any sale made, including resales of goods, wares or merchandise taken by a dealer as a trade-in or as part payment for other goods, wares, or merchandise or services rendered or commercial or business transactions, without deduction for any expenses (*e.g.*, cost of goods sold, materials used, service, or interest) [Philadelphia Code § 19-2601. Alternative receipts tax computations are available to certain taxpayers; these are discussed at ¶ 3905.

New Exclusion from Receipts

The BIRT definitions have been amended to provide a new exclusion from "receipts." The excluded amount is $100,000 for tax year 2016 and thereafter [Philadelphia Code § 19-2601].

Insurance business: In determining receipts from the business of insurance, taxable receipts are those from premiums received from risks within Philadelphia without deduction for any expenses. However, dividends that are in the nature of an adjustment of the premiums charged and premiums received for reinsurance are not taxable. Receipts of a person engaged in the insurance business also include receipts from rental real estate situated in Philadelphia but do not include interest, dividends, and capital gains. Nothing in this definition precludes the taxation of other non-premium business receipts of persons engaged in the insurance business.

Federal New Market Tax Credit Program

Interest or fees received on loans made under the federal New Market Tax Credit Program do not constitute "receipts" for purposes of the Philadelphia business privileges tax [Bill No. 110373, City of Philadelphia, effective beginning with tax year 2011].

- *Exclusions*

For a list of items excluded from gross receipts, see Philadelphia Code § 19-2601 and Philadelphia BIRT Regulations § 302.

- *Receipts from rental or license of tangible personal property*

Persons doing business in Philadelphia who own, lease, or license tangible person property that is leased or licensed to others are required to report the gross receipts from rental or license of such property according to the following rules [Philadelphia BIRT Regulations § 303]:

(1) If the original situs of the property is within the limits of the city of Philadelphia, the receipts from tangible personal property leased or licensed to others are wholly taxable if the property is delivered to lessees or licensees within Pennsylvania but are excludable if the property is delivered to lessees outside of Pennsylvania.

(2) If the original situs of the property is outside Philadelphia, the receipts from tangible personal property leased or licensed to others are wholly taxable if the property is delivered to a lessee within Philadelphia but are excludable if the property is delivered to lessees outside Philadelphia.

Original situs: "Original situs" means the point at which the property is warehoused when not leased to others and to which point the property is returned upon termination of the lease. If there is no such established point, the "original situs" is the taxpayer's principal office [Philadelphia BPT Regulations § 303(3)].

Conditional sales: The above rules do not apply to conditional sales of tangible personal property [Philadelphia BIRT Regulations § 303(4)].

- *Sales of tangible personal property*

All receipts from the sale of goods, commodities, wares, and merchandise must be included in taxable gross receipts, except for any receipts attributable to sales involving the bona fide delivery of goods, commodities, wares, or merchandise to a location regularly maintained by the customer or customer's agent outside of Philadelphia, if not for the purpose of evading the tax [Philadelphia BIRT Regulations § 304(1)].

Bona fide delivery to location outside Philadelphia: Receipts excludable by virtue of a bona fide delivery to a location outside Philadelphia are governed by the following rules:

(1) If a delivery occurs in Philadelphia, the receipts are taxable, unless both the purchaser and seller are located outside Philadelphia and the delivery is made to the purchaser's customer inside Philadelphia, in which case the seller's receipts are not taxable [Philadelphia BIRT Regulations § 304(2)(a)].If a customer from outside Philadelphia has a common carrier take possession of goods inside Philadelphia for delivery to the customer outside the city, the receipts are taxable [*Style Setter Fashion, Inc.*, Philadelphia Tax Review Board, No. 36BPMERZZ9319, October 24, 2005].

(2) If a delivery occurs outside Philadelphia to a location regularly maintained by the purchaser or the purchaser's agent, the receipts are not taxable [Philadelphia BIRT Regulations § 304(2)(b)].

(3) If a delivery occurs outside Philadelphia to the purchaser's customer, or at a location not regularly maintained by the purchaser or the purchaser's agent, the delivery is deemed to be in Philadelphia and the receipts are taxable unless the purchaser is located outside of Philadelphia, in which case the receipts are not taxable [Philadelphia BIRT Regulations § 304(2)(c)].

Delivery by carrier: Delivery to a common carrier destined for a location constitutes delivery to that location regardless of which party to the transaction selects or pays the common carrier and regardless of whether the goods are sold "f.o.b. shipping point" or "f.o.b. destination point" [Philadelphia BIRT Regulations § 304(3)(a)]. Delivery to a contract carrier, under contract to the seller, destined for a location, constitutes delivery to that location. Delivery to a contract carrier under contract to anyone other than the seller constitutes delivery at the location where physical possession is transferred, including the location at which the property is placed on the vehicle or carrier [Philadelphia BIRT Regulations § 304(3)(b)].

¶3907 Net Income

Net income for Philadelphia BIRT purposes can be computed by either of two methods, at the option of the taxpayer [Philadelphia Code § 19-2601]. Once made, this election is irrevocable. The method that a taxpayer uses to compute its net income for BPT purposes on its first BPT return is the method that must be used in all consecutive succeeding years [Philadelphia BPT Regulations § 401(1)].

• *Method I*

Method I net income is the net gain from the operation of a business, after provision for all allowable deductions. The allowable deductions are the costs and expenses actually incurred in the conduct of the business, either actual or incurred in accordance with the accounting system used [Philadelphia Code § 19-2601]. No deductions are allowed for taxes based on income or fines and penalties. Method I net income is income as allocated and apportioned and after adjustment for the distributive share of net income or loss received by one partner from a partnership where the receiving partner's ownership of capital at the end of the year is at least 20% of the distributing partnership [Philadelphia BIRT Regulations § 403]. See ¶ 3908 for discussion of allocation and apportionment for Philadelphia BIRT purposes. The rules and regulations applicable for determining net income under Method I are the ones imposed for purposes of the net profits tax in Chapter 19-1500 of The Philadelphia Code [Philadelphia BIRT Regulations §403]. The Philadelphia wage and net profits tax is discussed in Chapter 38 of this *Guidebook.*

Federal bonus depreciation: Taxpayers reporting net income under Method I must use the depreciation method(s) consistent with the elected accounting system. The Philadelphia Department of Revenue announced changes to the treatment of bonus depreciation as applied to Business Income and Receipts Tax (BIRT) and Net Profits Tax (NPT) on July 31, 2018. The Tax Cuts and Jobs Act of 2017 (TCJA) modified federal tax law to allow businesses to immediately deduct the cost of various assets placed in service between September 28, 2017 and December 31, 2022, but the Commonwealth of Pennsylvania decoupled from the federal changes. By law, the City of Philadelphia is required to follow the Commonwealth's treatment of bonus depreciation, so Philadelphia announced that it is also decoupled from changes made by the TCJA. Pennsylvania Act 72 became law in June of 2018 and requires taxpayers to add back any federal bonus depreciation taken. Pennsylvania and Philadelphia taxpayers are permitted to take normal depreciation as determined under IRC §167. See Advisory Notice - Bonus Depreciation Policy Update - July 31, 2018.

New Receipts Exclusion Added to Method One

Taxpayers' first current option for net income is amended to reflect the new receipts exclusion. Specifically, the "net income" option for net gain from the operation of a business after provision for all allowable costs and expenses actually incurred, with restrictions is now subject to a deduction for the pro rata portion of net income attributable to the new exclusion for taxable receipts [Philadelphia Code §19-2601. The new exclusion for taxable receipts is discussed at ¶3906].

• *Method II*

Method II net income is the taxable income from any business activity as returned to and ascertained by the federal government before the exclusion for dividends received and net operating loss and subject to the following adjustments [Philadelphia Code §19-2601]:

(1) *Corporate dividend, interest, and royalty income:* A deduction is allowed for the following (to the extent included in federal taxable income) [Philadelphia Code §19-2601]:

(a) Dividends, interest, and royalties received by one corporation from (i) a corporation of the same affiliated group or (ii) a corporation of which the receiving corporation owns at least 20% of the voting power of all classes of stock and at least 20% of each class of nonvoting stock.

(b) Receipts by a corporation that is a member of an affiliated group from other members of the same affiliated group.

(2) *Public utility receipts:* A deduction is allowed for receipts from the specific business conducted by any public utility operating under the laws, rules, and regulations administered by the Pennsylvania Public Utility Commission or conducted by a business subject to the jurisdiction of the Interstate Commerce Commission of furnishing or supplying service or services at the rates specified in its tariffs.

(3) *Port of Philadelphia:* A deduction is allowed for receipts from the business of load or discharging cargo to or from vessels conducted on piers, wharves, or marine terminal facilities in the port of Philadelphia and from business activities related to loading or unloading (*e.g.,* furnishing dockage, wharfage, truck and/or railroad car loading and unloading, cargo storage).

(4) *Government obligations:* A deduction *and* an increase are required for government obligations, as follows:

(a) A deduction is allowed for income received from all obligations of the United States (*e.g.*, stock, bonds, Treasury notes).

(b) Net income must be *increased* for interest expense attributable to obligations of U.S. government or any of its political subdivisions that is exempt from income tax under the laws of the United States or the Commonwealth of Pennsylvania. The increase, however, shall not exceed the deduction allowed in (a).

(5) *Securities dealers:* A deduction is allowed for net income of persons registered under the Pennsylvania Securities Act of 1972 other than the net income attributable to commissions and similar charges on account of transactions effected for persons residing or having their principal place of business within Philadelphia.

(6) *Federal bonus depreciation:* The Philadelphia Department of Revenue announced changes to the treatment of bonus depreciation as applied to Business Income and Receipts Tax (BIRT) and Net Profits Tax (NPT) on July 31, 2018. The Tax Cuts and Jobs Act of 2017 (TCJA) modified federal tax law to allow businesses to immediately deduct the cost of various assets placed in service between September 28, 2017 and December 31, 2022, but the Commonwealth of Pennsylvania decoupled from the federal changes. By law, the City of Philadelphia is required to follow the Commonwealth's treatment of bonus depreciation, so Philadelphia announced that it is also decoupled from changes made by the TCJA. Pennsylvania Act 72 became law in June of 2018 and requires taxpayers to add back any federal bonus depreciation taken. Pennsylvania and Philadelphia taxpayers are permitted to take normal depreciation as determined under IRC § 167. See Advisory Notice - Bonus Depreciation Policy Update - July 31, 2018. Depreciation under the Commonwealth's position is discussed at ¶ 1002.

• *Consolidated returns*

Taxpayers are not allowed to file consolidated or combined tax returns for Philadelphia BPT purposes. In the case of a corporation participating in the filing of a consolidated corporate return for federal income tax purposes, net income for Philadelphia BPT purposes means the income from any business activity that would have been returned to and ascertained by the federal government [Philadelphia Code § 19-2601].

¶3908 Allocation and Apportionment

The following is a brief discussion of allocation and apportionment based on receipts and net income.

• *Gross receipts base*

Taxable receipts from business done in the city must be segregated from receipts from sources outside the city. It is only when taxable receipts are incapable of segregation that the collector will require or set rules for allocation and apportionment [Philadelphia Code § 19-2601].

Keep Records to Support Segregation of Services

A company that picked up trash from private customers in Philadelphia and disposed of it at sites in New Jersey was allowed to segregate the part of the fees paid for out-of-city services and was taxed only the portion of the fees allocable to activities in Philadelphia. In this case the company was required to pay tax only on 35% of its fees. The company was able to present as evidence agreements that showed the division of its service into three components (pickup, transportation to disposal site, disposal at the site) and the breakdown of its fee for each component [*City of Philadelphia, Department of Revenue v. Tax Review Board to the Use of Ace Dump Truck Service and Ace Service Corporation*, 631 A.2d 1072 (Pa.Commw. 1993)].

- *Net income base*

The collector shall establish rules and methods of apportionment and allocation and evaluation so that only that part of net income (or net operating loss) that is properly attributable to the doing of business in the city is taxed [Philadelphia Code § 19-2601].

Income from Broadcast Rights

The Commonwealth Court held that income received by a National Football League (NFL) team from a television network for the exclusive right to broadcast football games was allocable to Philadelphia for Philadelphia business income and receipts tax purposes because it was royalty income and Philadelphia was the team's commercial domicile. Playing games outside of Philadelphia does not amount to having a place of business outside of Philadelphia for purposes of the business income and receipts tax. The Pennsylvania Supreme Court, however, disagreed with the Commonwealth Court's conclusion that the city could properly tax 100% of the Football Club's media receipts when calculating the Football Club's BIRT liability. The Supreme Court agreed with that portion of the Commonwealth Court's decision holding that the Football Club's media receipts were subject to assessment under the gross receipts component of the BIRT as copyright royalties but disagreed with that portion of the decision holding that the Commerce Clause does not require apportionment of the media receipts. The Supreme Court reversed and remanded the matter to the Court of Common Pleas of Philadelphia County to apportion the receipts in a manner consistent with the Supreme Court's decision [*Philadelphia Eagles Football Club, Inc. v. City of Philadelphia*, 823 A.2d 108 (Pa. 2003), rev'g 758 A.2d 236 (Pa.Commw. 2000)].

- *Single sales factor apportionment tax credit*

Definition: Single sales factor apportionment tax liability is a business's liability for the net income portion of the business income and receipts tax if the business's taxable income was apportioned based solely on the ration of taxable receipts of the business from within the City of Philadelphia to the total receipts of the business [Philadelphia Code § 19-2604(12)(a)].

Allowance of credit: Starting in tax year 2013, businesses shall be eligible to receive a non-refundable single sales factor apportionment tax credit against the business income and receipts tax. Any unused tax credits may not be carried forward [Philadelphia Code § 19-2604(12)(b)(i)].

Calculation of credit: The single sales factor apportionment tax credit shall be calculated under the provisions of Philadelphia Code § 19-2604(12)(b)(ii).

- *Market-based sourcing for software company sales*

A regulation with an effective date of December 6, 2013 provides that software companies should source receipts from the sale of products and services to the location where the recipient received the benefit of the products and services.

¶3909 Returns and Payment of Tax

Every person engaged in business is required to file a business income and receipts tax (BIRT) return for each tax year in business and pay any tax balance due for that tax year on or before the 15th day of April of the year following each tax year [Philadelphia Code § 19-2606]. A return must be filed even if a loss is incurred. If no return is filed, non-filer penalties will be imposed. A tax year for Philadelphia BIRT purposes is a calendar year [Philadelphia Code § 19-2601]. A person who commences engaging in business within Philadelphia in any tax year and whose first fiscal year in business within Philadelphia does not end in that tax year must file a return stating that no tax is due for the tax year [Philadelphia BIRT Regulations § 203(c)].

Estimated tax: In addition to any tax balance due, a mandatory estimated tax payment(s) equal to 100% of the actual tax due for the current tax year must be paid. Estimated tax payments are to be made at such times and on such forms as provided by the Philadelphia Department of Revenue. Failure to make the required estimated payment on the due date subjects a taxpayer to interest, penalties, and costs as provided in Philadelphia Code § 19-509. Any overpayment of the current year tax will be applied first to the payment of an estimated tax for the tax year that follows or to other taxes due. Any remaining balance, if any, will be applied to future BIRT years unless the taxpayer requests a refund of the amount. An extension to file the current year tax return will not relieve the taxpayer from the obligation to pay an amount equal to 100% of the current year's tax due as an estimated tax for the following tax year on the due date. A person may petition the Department of Revenue for permission to pay less than 100% of the current year tax liability as a mandatory estimated tax for the tax year following the current tax year. The petition must provide an explanation as to why the estimate should be less than 100%. Acceptable reasons may be unusual, unique, or nonrecurring transaction(s) that caused an unusually high current year tax liability or may result in unusually low tax liability in the year following the current tax year. The petition must be filed, using a form provided by the Department, on or before the 20th day of March of the year following the current tax year. A petitioner may presume approval of the petition if the Department does not communicate its disapproval by April 10 of the year following the current tax year. Interest and penalty will be imposed, and will not be waived, if the payment is found to be lower than the following year's actual tax liability [Philadelphia BIRT Regulations § 202].

Estimated BIRT payments for any given tax year shall be calculated without taking into account reductions in tax rates or changes to apportionment formulas required by Bill No. 110554 for such tax year [Philadelphia Code § 19-2610].

Temporary, seasonal, or itinerant business: Each person engaged in a temporary, seasonal, or itinerant business is required to file a tax return for each tax year within thirty (30) days of the day completing each business during any tax year [Philadelphia BIRT Regulations § 202(E)]. A temporary, seasonal, or itinerant business is any business that is conducted for a total of less than 30 consecutive or intermittent days in any one tax year. The net income of a temporary, seasonal, or itinerant business that is reportable for the tax year is the net income for that portion of the tax year in which the business was actually conducted [Philadelphia BIRT Regulations § 203(a)(2)].

• *Inactive Businesses*

Persons who maintain a business income and receipts license but do not actively engage in business must file a return indicating a lack of business. Failure to file may result in the imposition of court costs.

• *Payment*

Payment of the business income and receipts tax must be made separately from the filing of the tax returns. Payment by electronic funds transfer (ACH Debits and Credits) is acceptable. Taxpayers may register for the EFT program by calling the Electronic Filing Unit at 215-686-6519 or visiting the Philadelphia Department of Revenue web site at www.phila.gov/revenue.

¶3909

¶3910 Credit for Contributions to Community Development Corporations and Nonprofit Intermediaries

A tax credit against the business income and receipts tax liability is available to businesses that sponsor a Qualifying Community Development Corporation (QCDC) or a nonprofit intermediary by contributing $100,000 per year in cash over a ten-year period to the QCDC [Philadelphia Code § 19-2604(6)(a)(1)]. A QCDC is one that undertakes economic development activities within Philadelphia [Philadelphia Code § 19-2604(6)(a)(.1)]. A qualifying nonprofit intermediary is a nonprofit organization with an established record of providing financial, technical, policy, or related assistance to community development corporations undertaking neighborhood economic development activities within Philadelphia [Philadelphia Code § 19-2604(a)(.2)]. See also Philadelphia BIRT Regulations § 501. No credit is available for contributions made to a QCDC other than contributions made pursuant with a contribution agreement with the city of Philadelphia [Philadelphia Code § 19-2604(6)(a)(c)].

• *Amount of credit*

Effective in 2015, a business is eligible for a tax credit of $100,000 per year against its Philadelphia business income and receipts tax liability for each year in which it makes the required cash contributions [Philadelphia Code § 19-2604(6)(1)(b)]. The change to $100,000 in the credit amount does not apply to any business that has executed a contribution agreement with the city prior to that date. However, if such an agreement is terminated before the end of its term, the new limit would apply to any business that executes a new agreement for the years remaining in the terminated agreement.

• *Application for credit*

The Revenue Department will provide application forms for businesses that wish to apply for the CDC credit, and it will enter into agreements with up to 42 applicants on a "first come, first-served" basis, including up to three Nonprofit Intermediaries. The Revenue Department will, when necessary, randomly choose among applicants that apply on the same date [Philadelphia Code § 19-2604(6)(d)]. Two businesses can partner to sponsor a qualifying organization. Under such circumstances, both businesses will be parties to a contribution agreement with the City. The $100,000 annual tax credit is divided between the two businesses in proportion to each business's contribution, as specified in the contribution agreement.

• *Termination of contribution agreement*

A business may terminate its contribution agreement with the city at any time. A business that terminates its contribution agreement will not lose any tax credits it has taken for contributions made under the contribution agreement, but it will not be eligible to apply for any future CDC tax credits [Philadelphia Code § 19-2604(6)(e)].

A new business may apply for the CDC credits remaining on a terminating business's contribution agreement, but the credit will be limited to the number of years that were remaining on the terminating business's contribution agreement. Furthermore, the new business must enter into a contribution agreement with the city under which it agrees to make contributions of $100,000 per year to the *same* QCDC that was the recipient under the terminating business's contribution agreement and for the number of years that remained under that agreement [Philadelphia Code § 19-2604(e)].

• *Administrative requirements*

Full compliance required: In order to claim or receive a QCDC credit, an applicant must be in full compliance with all Philadelphia tax laws, ordinances, and regulations [Philadelphia BIRT Regulations § 501(e)(1)].

Inadequate annual contribution: If an applicant makes an annual payment of less than $100,000 to a QCDC, the applicant must petition the Revenue Commissioner to be reinstated in the program [Philadelphia BIRT Regulations § 501(e)(2)].

Annual reports: Every person engaged in business is required to file a return on or before April 15 of the year following each tax year it is in business [Philadelphia Code § 19-2606(1)]. All returns must be filed on forms furnished by the Department of Revenue, and the person making the return must certify the correctness of the return [Philadelphia Code § 19-2606(2)].

¶3911 Job Creation Tax Credit

A regulation governing the Philadelphia job creation tax credit has been issued [Philadelphia BIRT Regulations § 502].

• *Allowance and term of credit*

Eligible taxpayers who agree to create at least 25 new jobs or to increase their number of employees by at least 20% within five (5) years of the "start date" (*i.e.,* the date on which a business may begin creating new jobs that may be eligible for job creation tax credits) may be allowed a job creation tax credit [Philadelphia Code § 19-2604(7)]. An eligible business may claim the job creation tax credit for a period not to exceed five (5) years from the date the business first submits a Job Creation Tax Credit Certificate to the Department of Revenue [Philadelphia Code § 19-1604(d)(4)]. This credit can be applied only against the Philadelphia business income and receipts tax [Philadelphia Code § 19-2604(7)(d)(3)].

• *Amount of credit*

A business may claim a tax credit of $5,000 per new job created or $5,000 per new job created in the case of new employment opportunities for ex-offenders, up to the maximum job creation amount specified in the commitment letter An "ex-offender" is a person who was previously convicted of a felony or who was incarcerated for any conviction, or who is currently on probation or parole for any conviction [Philadelphia Code § 19-2406(d)(1)]. See discussion of *"Commitment letter"* below. A "new job" for this purpose is a full-time job paying an average hourly rate (excluding benefits) that is at least 150% of the federal minimum wage and that is created within the city and county of Philadelphia within five (5) years from the start date [Philadelphia Code § 19-2604(7)(a)(3)].

• *Job Creation Tax Certificate*

After a commitment letter has been signed by both the city of Philadelphia and the business and the city determines that new jobs have been created pursuant to that commitment, the business will receive a Job Creation Tax Certificate reflecting the number of jobs created and filing information [Philadelphia Code § 19-1604(c)(40)].

• *Applications for credit*

A business must complete and submit to the Revenue Department a Job Creation Tax Credit Application in which it agrees to create at least 25 new jobs or to increase its number of employees by at least 20% within five (5) years of the start date. If the Revenue Department approves the company's application, the Department and the Company must execute a commitment letter [Philadelphia Code § 19-2604(c)].

• *Commitment letter*

A "commitment letter" is an agreement executed between the Department of Revenue and the taxpayer that contains the following information: (1) a description of the project; (2) the number of new jobs to be created; (3) the amount of private capital investment in the project; (4) the maximum job creation tax credit amount that

¶3911

may be claimed by the taxpayer; (5) a signed statement that the taxpayer intends to maintain its operation in Philadelphia for five (5) years from the start date; and (6) any other information deemed appropriate by the Department of Revenue [Philadelphia Code § 19-2604(7)(c)(3)].

• *Prohibited actions*

The following actions are prohibited with respect to Job Creation Tax Credits [Philadelphia Code § 19-2604(e)(1)]:

(1) Approval of jobs created prior to the start date.

(2) Assignment, transfer, or use of credits by any other company.

(3) Approval for a company that is relocating operations from one Philadelphia.

• *Penalties*

Failure to maintain operations: A business that receives job creation tax credits and fails to substantially maintain existing operations and its operations related to the credit in Philadelphia for at least five (5) years from the date the business first submits a Job Creation Tax Credit Certificate to the Department of Revenue must refund the total amount of credit(s) it has been granted [Philadelphia Code § 19-2604(7)(f)(1)].

Failure to create jobs: A business receiving job creation tax credits that fails to create the approved number of new jobs within five (5) years of the start date must refund the total amount of credit(s) granted [Philadelphia Code § 19-1604(7)(f)(2)].

Waiver of penalties: The Department of Revenue may waive these penalties if it determined that failure to maintain operations or to create jobs was due to circumstances beyond the business's control (*e.g.*, natural disasters, acts of terrorism, unforeseen industry trends, or loss of major supplier or market) [Philadelphia Code § 19-2604(7)(f)(3)].

¶3912 Green Roof Tax Credit

Philadelphia has enacted a credit against its business income and receipts tax for construction of a "green roof" [Philadelphia Code § 19-1604]. A "green roof" is defined as "an addition to a roof that supports living vegetation and includes a synthetic, high quality waterproof membrane, drainage layer, soil layer and light weight medium plants" [Philadelphia Code § 19-2604(8)(a)(1)].

• *Application*

A business seeking a green roof tax credit must file an application with the Philadelphia Department of Revenue, in the form and manner prescribed by the Revenue Department [Philadelphia Code § 19-2604(8)(b)].

• *Commitment letter*

If the application is approved, the applicant must execute a commitment letter with the Revenue Department containing all information required by the Revenue Department [Philadelphia Code § 19-2604(8)(c)].

• *Granting of credit*

After an applicant has certified that it has completed in green roof in accordance with the plans set forth in the commitment, the applicant may claim a tax credit of 50% (prior to 2015 the percentage was 25%) of all costs actually incurred to construct the green roof, up to a maximum of $100,000 per year. The credit is applied against the applicant's total business privilege tax liability for the tax year during which the applicant certifies completion of the green roof. Any unused credits may be carried forward until fully used [Philadelphia Code § 19-2604(8)(d)(1)]. A business may receive one set of green roof credits per building, but may receive green roof tax credits for each building it owns [Philadelphia Code § 19-2604(8)(d)(2)]. In the event that the aggregate amount of tax credits to which all businesses are entitled in any tax year would exceed $1 million, the amount of the tax credit awarded to any business will be computed by: (1) obtaining a reduction factor by dividing $1 million by the aggregate amount of all tax credits sought in the year; and (2) multiplying the amount of the tax credit to which a business is entitled by the reduction factor.

- *Repayment of tax credits*

A business that has received green roof tax credits must repay those tax credits to the City if it fails to maintain the green roof in accordance with the provisions of the commitment letter. The Revenue Department may waive a repayment if it determines the green roof was because of a natural disaster or other act of God, an act of terrorism, or similar circumstances beyond the control of the business [Philadelphia Code § 19-2604(8)(e)].

¶3913 Philadelphia Keystone Zone Credits

Taxpayers with business activity in a Philadelphia Keystone Opportunity Zone (KOZ), Keystone Opportunity Expansion Zone (KOEZ), or Keystone Opportunity Improvement Zone (KOIZ) may claim a credit against the Philadelphia business income and receipts tax. In order to qualify for the credit, a person or business must own or lease real property in the zone from which a trade, business, or profession is actively conducted. The credit is based on an apportionment formula consisting of the ration of property, payroll, and receipts within the zone to property, payroll, and receipts outside the zone. For explanation of KOZ, KOEZ, or KOIZ see ¶4622.

Credit certification must be received from the Pennsylvania Department of Community and Economic Development (DCED) and must be renewed annually. A copy of the certification approval letter and zone credit worksheets must accompany the business income and receipts tax returns. For more information see http://www.philakoz.org/faq.html.

¶3914 Sustainable Business Credit

A sustainable business is eligible for a credit of $4,000 [Bill No. 0901119-A, Laws 2010, effective December 16, 2009]. Unused tax credits may not be carried forward. For tax years 2012 through 2016, no more than 25 applicants were allowed to participate in this credit program. For tax years 2017 and 2018, up to 50 applicants will be allowed to participate. For tax years 2019 through 2022, the number of applicants is increased to 75. All applicants will be certified as eligible on a "first-come, first-served" basis. For tax years 2016 through 2022, an eligible business shall receive a tax credit against the applicant's total Business Income and Receipts Tax liability (i.e. both gross receipts and net income bases).

- *Sustainable business*

A sustainable business is one that meets the standards of a B Lab certified B corporation (referred to as a "B Lab company), that were in effect on November 15, 2009 (or as may be in effect on a later date pursuant to regulations promulgated by the Office of Sustainability). The Mayor's Office of Sustainability can be found at http://www.phila.gov/green/.

- *Regulations*

The Office of Sustainability will detail regulations with respect to how a business must demonstrate that it qualified as a sustainable business. Once certified a business remains eligible for the credit each year the credit is available. However, the business may be required to submit documentation each year that it continues to be a sustainable business.

¶3915 Credit for Hiring Veterans

Philadelphia has enacted a credit for employment of returning veterans of the Armed Forces [Philadelphia Code § 19-2604(13), effective June 27, 2012]. The credit is available for each qualifying employee who has been employed by the business for more than six months.

• *Amount of credit*

The business will receive a credit of $5,000 for a full-time position, multiplied by the percentage of the tax year that the veteran was employed by the business or $2,500 for a part-time position, multiplied by the percentage of the tax year that the veteran was employed by the business. The credit is available for a total of 36 months of employment, and the total amount of credit a business may receive for a full-time employee over all tax years is $15,000 and the maximum for a part-time employee is $7,500.

• *"Veteran" defined*

A "veteran" is an individual who meets all of the following requirements:

(1) The veteran has received an honorable discharge from any branch of the United States Armed Forces, including the national guard forces and reserves.

(2) The veteran has served a minimum of six months in active full-time duty within ten years prior to their hiring.

(3) The veteran has met the qualifications under the Vow to Hire Heroes Act of 2011 as part of the federal Work Opportunity Tax Credit (WOTC).

• *Qualifying Employee*

A "qualifying employee" is a veteran who meets all of the following three requirements:

(1) The veteran is employed by a business in a position where he or she earns wages that are subject to the wage and net profits tax.

(2) The veteran receives compensation that is either (a) equivalent to those wages and benefits including sick leave, holiday and vacation absences, and tuition benefits afforded regular employees in comparable positions as part of the employer's regular payroll process or (b) if a comparable position does not exist, at an average hourly rate (excluding benefits) of at least 150% of the federal minimum wage and the employment package includes the same benefits as are provided to other full time employees.

(3) The veteran is hired between July 1, 2012, and June 30, 2020, inclusive.

A "qualifying full-time employee" is a qualifying employee who is employed by a business for at least 37 hours per week. A "qualifying part-time employee" is a qualifying employee who is employed by a business for at least 20 hours per week but fewer than 37 hours per week.

• *Application for credit*

In order to receive a credit, a business must file an application in the form and manner prescribed by the Department that includes the location of employment and proof that the individual to be hired is a veteran as defined under Philadelphia Code § 19-2604.

¶3916 Jump Start Philly Program

Jump Start Philly is a program for entrepreneurs and new businesses in Philadelphia. A business in its first two years of operation may be exempt from paying the Business Income and Receipts Tax, and does not have to pay for a variety of licenses and registrations. These businesses are still required to apply for applicable licenses, but eligible new businesses pay no fee. To qualify for this exemption, a business must meet certain requirements. For more information, see https://business.phila.gov/what-is-jump-start-philly/.

PHILADELPHIA CITY AND SCHOOL DISTRICT TAXES

CHAPTER 40
OTHER PHILADELPHIA CITY & SCHOOL DISTRICT TAXES

OTHER CITY TAXES

¶4001 Realty Transfer Tax

The Philadelphia realty transfer tax is imposed on every person who transfers ownership of realty situated within Philadelphia or who makes, executes, delivers, accepts or presents for recording any document, or a person on whose behalf any document is made, executed, delivered, accepted, or presented for recording or who accepts ownership of realty located in Philadelphia [Philadelphia Code §§ 19-1401—19-1417]. Unless specifically exempt under § 19-1405, transfers between associations or corporations and their members, partners, shareholders, or stockholders are fully taxable. For purposes of the Philadelphia realty transfer tax, corporations and associations are entities separate from their members, partners, stockholders, or shareholders [Philadelphia Code § 19-1406].

The Philadelphia realty transfer tax is imposed at the rate of 3.278% of the value of the real estate represented by the document [Philadelphia Code § 19-1403]. In addition to the city realty transfer tax, the Commonwealth imposes a 1% realty transfer tax (see ¶3304), making a combined rate of 4.278%.

¶4001

- *"Value" defined*

"Value" for Philadelphia realty transfer tax purposes means the value computed by using one of the methods provided for by Philadelphia Code § 19-1402(14). These methods are discussed at ¶ 3304. In cases where a transfer is pursuant to a gift or other transactions without consideration, Philadelphia ordiances provide that the value shall never be less than the readily ascertainable market value of the property for which the real estate is exchanged. Philadelphia Code § 19-1402(14)(b).

Transfer by Deed in Lieu of Foreclosure

The Commonwealth Court found that the actual monetary value of a transfer of property by deed in lieu of foreclosure was the proper basis for computing the Philadelphia realty transfer tax [*Kennedy Boulevard Associates v. Tax Review Board, 751 A.2d 719 (Pa.Commw. 2000)*].

- *"Document" defined*

A "document" is any deed, instrument, or writing (including a certificate of transfer) that conveys, transfers, demises, vests, confirms, or evidences any transfer or demise of title to real estate located in Philadelphia presented for recording. "Title to real estate" is (1) any interest in real estate that endures for a period of time, the termination of which is not fixed or ascertained by a specific number of years, including without limitation, an estate in fee simple, life estate, or perpetual leasehold or (2) any interest in real estate enduring for a fixed period of years but which, either by reason of the length of the term or the grant of a right to extend the term by renewal or otherwise, consists of a group of rights approximating those of an estate in fee simple, life estate, or perpetual leasehold, including without limitation, any leasehold interest or possessory interest under a lease or occupancy agreement for a term of 30 years or more or a leasehold interest or possessory interest in real estate in which the lessee has equity. In determining the term of a lease, it shall be presumed that a right or option to renew or extend a lease will be exercised if the rental charge to the lessee is fixed or if a method for calculating the rental charge is established [Philadelphia Code § 19-1402(12)].

- *Exempt persons*

The United States, the Commonwealth of Pennsylvania, or any of their instrumentalities, agencies or political subdivisions are exempt from payment of the Philadelphia realty transfer tax. However, the exemption of governmental bodies does not relieve any other party to a transaction from liability for the tax [Philadelphia Code § 19-1404].

Mortgage Holder's Exemption Lost in Merger

The Commonwealth Court has held that the exemption from Philadelphia realty transfer tax for transfers of property to the original holder of a mortgage does not apply where the original mortgage holder is party to a merger in which it is not the surviving entity [*Provident Mutual Life insurance Company v. Tax Review Board, 750 A.2d 942 (Pa.Commw. 2000)*].

- *Exempt transactions*

The list of transactions exempt under the provisions of Philadelphia Code § 19-1405 is extensive, but it generally follows those listed for the Commonwealth realty transfer tax, discussed at ¶ 3304. In general, the transfer of real estate between family members is exempt (*e.g.*, a transfer between spouses, children of the same parent, and lineal ascendants/descendants). See Philadelphia ordinances and regulations for exceptions.

¶4001

In 1998 the Philadelphia realty transfer tax provisions were amended to include "life partners" (a special status available to same-sex couples) in the definition of "marital status." In 2018, the transfer tax exemption for transfers between husband and wife was changed to "spouses."

- *Statement of value*

Every document presented for recording must contain the true, full, and complete value of the property transferred and be accompanied by a statement of value executed by a responsible person connected with the transaction showing his or her connection and setting forth the true, full and complete value of the property or the reason, if any, why the document is not subject to the city realty transfer tax. This requirement does not apply to real estate transfers that are exempt based on family relationship [Philadelphia Code § 1409].

- *Documents presented for affixation of stamps*

Documents presented for affixation of stamps must be accompanied by a certified copy of the document and a statement of value as defined above [Philadelphia Code § 1409].

- *Payment of tax*

The tax is payable at the earlier of (1) the time the document is presented for recording with the city (2) or within 30 days of the date when a company becomes an acquired real estate company or family farm business. Payment is evidenced by the affixing of an official stamp or writing by the recorder stating the date of payment, amount of tax, and signature of the collecting agent [Philadelphia Code § 19-1403]. Documents should be filed with the Records Department, Room 154, Philadelphia City Hall.

Payment of tax is evidenced by affixing a documentary stamp or stamps to every document by the person making, executing, issuing, or delivering the document. Stamps must be affixed in such a way that their removal requires the continued application of steam or water; and the person using or affixing stamps must cause them to be cancelled in such a way that they may not be used again either (1) by writing or stamping or by causing to be written or stamped thereon the initials of his or her name and the date the stamps were affixed or used or (2) by complying with any other method of cancellation prescribed by the Department Philadelphia Code § 19-1413].

- *Acquired real estate company*

The conversion of a real estate company to an "acquired real estate company" is subject to realty transfer tax. A real estate company is an "acquired real estate company" upon a change in the ownership interest in the company, however effected, if the change (1) does not affect the continuity of the company and (2) of itself or together with prior changes has the effect of transferring, directly or indirectly, 75% or more of the total ownership interest in the company within a period of six (6) years. A transfer is considered to have occurred within a period of six (6) years of another transfer or transfers if a legally binding commitment to execute that transfer was made within that period. The tax is based on the monetary value of the Company's Philadelphia real estate which is presumed to be the actual consideration paid for the company measured by the value of the cumulative percentage of change [Philadelphia Code § 19-1407(1)].

A "real estate company" is, in general, a corporation or association that is primarily engaged in the business of holding, selling, or leasing real estate, 90% or more of the ownership in which is held by 35 or fewer persons and which (1) derives 60% or more of its annual gross receipts from the ownership or disposition of real estate or (2) holds real estate, the value of which comprises 50% or more of the value of its entire tangible asset holdings, exclusive of tangible assets that are freely transferable and actively traded on an established market [Philadelphia Code § 19-1402(11)(a)]. A corporation or association that holds, directly or indirectly, as 90% or more of the value of its assets, an interest in a real estate company is also a "real estate company" [Philadelphia Code § 19-1402(11)(b)].

• *Credits against the tax*

There are credits available for certain transfers of real estate:

(1) If a licensed real estate broker transfers residential property that was transferred to the broker within the preceding year as consideration for the purchase of other residential property, the broker is entitled to a credit for the amount of the tax paid at the time of transfer to the broker toward the amount of tax due upon the transfer [Philadelphia Code § 19-1408(1)].

(2) If a builder transfers residential property that was transferred to the builder within the preceding year as consideration for the purchase of new, previously unoccupied resident property, the builder is entitled to a credit for the amount of the tax paid at the time of the transfer to the builder toward the amount of tax due upon the transfer [Philadelphia Code § 19-1408(2)].

(3) Where there is a transfer of real estate that is demised (*i.e.*, transferred for years or life, but not beyond that), a credit for the amount of tax paid at the time of the demise is given to the grantor toward the tax due upon the transfer [Philadelphia Code § 19-1408(3)].

(4) Where there is a conveyance by deed of real estate that was previously sold under a land contract by the grantor, a credit for the amount of tax paid at the time of the sale is given to the grantor toward tax due upon the deed [Philadelphia Code § 19-1408(4)].

If the tax due upon a transfer is greater than the available credit, the difference must be paid. If the available credit is greater than the amount of tax due, no refund or carryover credit is allowable [Philadelphia Code § 19-1408(5)].

More information: More information about the Philadelphia realty transfer tax can be obtained by contacting the Compliance Development Section of the Philadelphia Department of Revenue, Municipal Services Building, Room 440, 1401 John F. Kennedy Boulevard or by calling 215-686-6614.

¶4002 Amusement Tax

• *Base*

The city amusement tax is an admissions tax imposed on the fee or privilege of attending or engaging in any amusement [Philadelphia Code §§ 19-601—19-604]. The term amusement includes almost every kind of entertainment. Except for bona fide employees of a producer, municipal or state officers on official business, or totally blind persons admitted free or at reduced rates, the Philadelphia amusement tax, when an established price is charged to other persons, is computed on the established price charged to other persons of the same class for the same or similar accommodations [Philadelphia Code § 19-601(2)]. In the case of persons having the permanent use of boxes or seats or leases for the use of boxes or seats, the amusement tax is computed on the established price for which a similar box or seat is sold for each performance or exhibition at which the box or seat is used or reserved by or for the lessee or holder [Philadelphia Code § 19-603(2)].

• *Rate*

The amusement tax is imposed at the rate of 5% of the established price (admissions) for city fiscal year starting July 1, 1994 and subsequent years.

• *"Established price" defined*

The "established price" (or admission) for amusement is the regular monetary charge of any character (including donations, contributions, dues, or membership fee, periodical or otherwise), fixed and exacted, or in any manner received by producers from the public, or a limited or selected number thereof, directly or indirectly, for the privilege to attend or engage in any amusement [Philadelphia Code § 19-601].

Special Definition for Social Clubs and Fraternal Organizations

When amusement is conducted at a social club or fraternal organization that also furnishes entertainment for which a separate charge is made, the "established price" is the higher of (1) 50% of the gross receipts or (2) 10% of the dues.

- **"Amusement" defined**

The term "amusement" includes any theatrical or operatic performance, concerts, motion picture shows, vaudeville, circuses, carnivals, side shows, exhibitions, shows, displays, dancing, all forms of entertainment at fair grounds, amusement parks, and athletic contests including wrestling matches, boxing and sparring exhibitions, baseball, football, and basketball games, golfing, tennis, hockey, archery and shooting where a charge, donation, contribution, or monetary charge of any character is made for admission. The term does not apply to persons participating in any athletic game or contest or to the exceptions specified in § 19-601 (see below) [Philadelphia Code § 19-601(1)(a)]. In an unreported decision, the amusement tax could not be applied to lap dances or other charges following admission to a place of business. *City of Philadelphia v. Tax Review Board,* 2014 STT 163-4 (Tax Analysts); 2014 STT 138-28 (Tax Analysts).

- **Basic requirements for determining exemptions**

The fact that an institution, society, or organization is not organized or operated for profit is not sufficient, by itself, to afford a basis for exemption. The institution, society, or organization must also meet the following requirements [Philadelphia Amusement Tax Regulations § 18(I)]:

(1) The proceeds of the amusement must inure exclusively to the benefit of the enumerated institutions, societies, or organizations. If any part of the net earnings of the enumerated institutions, organizations, or societies inure to the benefit of any private individuals or persons, no exemption can be granted [Philadelphia Code § 19-601(2)(b); Philadelphia Amusement Tax Regulations § 18(II)(h)].

(2) Such institutions, societies, or organizations must have a bona fide existence and possess adequate facilities for carrying out their purposes.

- **Types of exemptions**

The term "amusement" does not apply to the following:

(1) *Television broadcasts*: Reception and exhibition of television broadcasts where no admission charge (direct or indirect) is made [Philadelphia Code § 19-601(2)(a)].

(2) *Entertainment:* Any form of entertainment (regardless of the nature) if the proceeds of the entertainment (after payment of reasonable expenses) inure exclusively to one of the following [Philadelphia Code § 19-601(2)(b)(.1)]; Philadelphia Amusement Tax Regulations § 18(II)(a)]:

(a) *Religious Institutions, Societies or Organizations:* The term "religious" connotes a gathering for the purpose of divine worship. Churches, synagogues, tabernacles, chapels, convents, monasteries and cathedrals are such institutions. Societies for the propagation of a particular faith are an example of a religious society or organization as are certain religious orders [Philadelphia Code § 19-601(2)(b)(.1); Philadelphia Amusement Tax Regulations § 18(II)(a)].

(b) *Educational Institutions, Societies or Organizations:* The term "educational" connotes the teaching or imparting of knowledge. The institution, society, or organization must offer instruction of a general nature in its particular field to its students, not limited to technical advice or merely providing an answer to particular questions. Elementary and high schools, colleges, seminaries, and music conservatories are examples of such educational institutions. Societies and organizations offering courses in various subjects are within the exemption. Societies or clubs organized within a school for social or athletic purposes are not exempt. Societies organized for the purpose of advancement of a particular interest or group are not deemed educational [Philadelphia Code § 19-601(2)(b)(.1); Philadelphia Amusement Tax Regulations § 18(II)(b)].

(c) *Charitable Organizations:* A charitable institution, society or organization must meet two tests, as follows:

(i) Whatever it does for others must be done free of charge or at least so nearly free of charge as to make the charges nominal or negligible.

(ii) Those to whom it renders help or services are those who are unable to provide themselves with what the institution provides for them, that is, they are legitimate objects of charity.

Where an institution, society, or organization engages in a number of activities, some of which may not be considered charitable, exemption may be granted only if the proceeds of the entertainment insure solely to the benefit of the charitable activities of the organization [Philadelphia Code § 19-601(2)(b)(.1); Philadelphia Amusement Tax Regulations § 18(II)(c)].

(d) *Societies for the Prevention of Cruelty to Children or Animals:* The basic requirements for determining exemptions (see above) must be met [Philadelphia Code § 19-601(2)(b)(.1); Philadelphia Amusement Tax Regulations § 18(II)(d)].

(e) *Societies or Organizations Conducted for the Sole Purpose of Maintaining Symphony Orchestras, Opera Performances and Artistic Presentations:* Such societies or organizations, in addition to meeting the basic requirements for determining exemptions (see above), must show that they receive substantial support from voluntary contributions apart from funds derived from entertainment [Philadelphia Code § 19-601(2)(b)(.1). Philadelphia Amusement Tax Regulations § 18(II)(e)];

(f) *Societies or Organizations Conducted or Maintained for the Purpose of Improving any Municipal Corporation:* Such societies or organizations, in addition to meeting the basic requirements for determining exemptions (see above), must show that the purpose of such society is for the betterment of the Municipal Corporation itself [Philadelphia Code § 19-601(2)(b): Philadelphia Amusement Tax Regulations § 18(II)(f)].

(g) *Societies or Organizations for the Purpose of Maintaining a Cooperative or Community Center, Moving Picture Theatre or Swimming Pool:* Such societies or organizations must, in addition to meeting the basic requirements for determining exemptions (see above), show actual maintenance of an existing center, moving picture or swimming pool, which is open to all residents of the particular community in which the facility is located [Philadelphia Code § 19-601(2)(b)(.1); Philadelphia Amusement Tax Regulations § 18(II)(g)].

(h) *Athletic Games or Contests, Wrestling Matches, etc.:* Athletic games or contests between universities or colleges are specifically excepted from the exemptions granted. No such exemption is made as to athletic contests between other types of educational institutions. Wrestling matches, boxing, sparring or other pugilistic matches are not exempt regardless of the type of institution, society, or organization to which the proceeds thereof may inure [Philadelphia Code § 19-601(2)(b)(.1); Philadelphia Amusement Tax Regulations § 18(II)(i)].

(3) *Organizations or Persons in the Military or Naval Forces of the United States:* The exemption applies to entertainments, the proceeds of which inure to the benefit of organizations or persons in the military or naval forces of the United States. Such organization must have official status as being a part of the military or naval forces of the United States. Organizations even though composed solely of members of the armed forces, but not authorized by Act of Congress or Presidential Proclamation are not exempt. Entertainments for the benefit of persons in the military or naval service must be for a group or class of such persons, not for a single individual [Philadelphia Code § 19-601(2)(b)(.2); Philadelphia Amusement Tax Regulations § 18(III)(a)].

(4) *National Guard Organizations, Reserve Officers Associations, or Organizations, Posts, or Organizations of War Veterans, or Auxiliary Units or Societies of Such Posts or Organizations:* Such organizations, associations, units, or societies must, in addition to meeting the basic requirements for determining exemptions (see above), show official recognition of their status by the organization of which they are alleged to be a part or with which they claim affiliation. Such association must be organized within the Commonwealth of Pennsylvania and no part of their funds may inure to the benefit of any private shareholder or person [Philadelphia Code § 19-601(2)(b)(.2); Philadelphia Amusement Tax Regulations § 18(III)(b)].

(5) *Organizations or Associations for the Purpose of Benefiting Members, or the Dependents of, or Heirs of, Members of Police, or Paid or Volunteer Fire Departments*: Such organizations or associations must in addition to meeting the basic requirements for determining exemptions (see above), be actively functioning. The funds of such association must be devoted to rendering benefits to members of police or fire departments, their dependents, or heirs. The Departments of which they are members must have received official recognition as such by the political subdivision of the Commonwealth of Pennsylvania in which such Department serves [Philadelphia Code § 19-601(2)(b)(.3); Philadelphia Amusement Tax Regulations § 18(IV)].

• *Collection of tax*

The tax is imposed on the person purchasing amusement, but the collection of the tax is the responsibility of producers. A "producer" is any person conducting any place of amusement where the general public, or a limited or select number of the general public, may, upon payment of an established price, attend or engage in any amusement [Philadelphia Code § 19-601(1)(d)]. If the tax collected by a producer is less than the amount of amusement tax imposed, the producer must collect an additional sum to reach the full amount of imposed tax at or before the time of holding or conducting the amusement [Philadelphia Code § 19-603(3)]. If licenses are obtained for conducting temporary amusements by persons who are not the owners, lessees, or custodians of the place of amusement, the tax must be paid by the owner, lessee, or custodian of the place of amusement if the producer does not pay the tax. If an owner, lessee, or custodian of a place of amusement permits a temporary amusement for which a license has not been procured, the owner, lessee, or custodian must pay the tax if the producer does not [Philadelphia Code § 19-604(2)].

• *Producers' licenses*

Producers must get an amusement license for each place of amusement [Philadelphia Code § 19-602]. A "place of amusement" is any place, indoors or outdoors, within Philadelphia, where the general public, or a limited or selected number thereof, may, upon payment of an established price, attend taxable amusements [Philadelphia Code § 19-601(1)(c)]. The amusement license fee is $25 per year for each permanent place of amusement or $25 per year ($5 per day prior to January 13, 2010) for each temporary place of amusement.

• *Returns and payment of tax*

Producers must file reports on official forms by the 15th day of each month following the month in which taxes are collected for permanent places of amusement. Reports for temporary places of amusement must be made within five (5) days after the performance [Philadelphia Code § 19-604(6)(a)]. The tax is due with the report.

¶4003 Mechanical Amusement Device Tax

Every person who uses or permits the use for profit of any mechanical amusement device must pay an annual tax of $100 per mechanical amusement device [Philadelphia Code § 19-903]. A "mechanical amusement device" is any machine or device for amusement or entertainment that is operated by the insertion of coins or tokens (*e.g.*, jukeboxes, pinball machines, video games). However, any machine or device that is operated by a sound reproduction licensee pursuant to § 9-303(3) is exempt from this tax.

• *Registration*

A device must be registered with the Philadelphia Department of Revenue before it can be used. An application for a license must describe it and give its serial number.

• *Payment of tax*

The tax is due on or before January 1 of each year. At the time the tax is paid, the Department issues a label, disc, or tag for the year for which the tax has been paid. The label, disc, or tag must be attached to the mechanical amusement device for which it is issued.

Prior Restraint of Free Speech?

Taxpayers operated mechanical amusement devices (specifically, devices that exhibit film, video, or live presentations of an adult nature) and were subject to the Philadelphia mechanical amusement devices tax. Taxpayers asserted that the tax acted as an unconstitutional prior restraint on their First Amendment rights of free speech. The Pennsylvania Commonwealth Court, however, found that the tax did not act as a prior restraint on the First Amendment rights of the taxpayers. The tax, according to the Court, was a revenue-raising provision that applied to all mechanical amusement devices regardless of the content of the entertainment. The tax in no way prohibited speech prior to publication, and it involved no censorship, no prohibition, and no discretion with respect to which devices were registered and which devices were denied registration [*Brighton Management Service, Inc. v. City of Philadelphia, Tax Review Board*, 669 A.2d 757 (Pa.Commw. 1995), *app. den.*, 679 A.2d 230 (Pa. 1996)].

¶4004 City Parking Tax

The Philadelphia city parking tax is imposed on every person who parks or stores a motor vehicle in any parking facility in Philadelphia [Philadelphia Code § 19-1202(1)(a)]. A "parking facility" is any outdoor or indoor area where more than three motor vehicles may be parked or stored for a consideration except common elements or limited common elements of a condominium that are used for parking exclusively by one or more unit owners or tenants of unit owners who are residents of that condominium [Philadelphia Code § 19-1201(2)].

• *Base and rate*

The tax is levied at the rate of 22.5% of the gross receipts from parking or storage of motor vehicles. Persons who violate the provisions of the city parking tax may have their licenses or permits revoked, suspended, or cancelled [Philadelphia Code § 19-1206].

¶4003

• *Collection of tax*

The tax is imposed on the person who parks or stores a vehicle, but parking lot operators are responsible for collecting the tax and remitting it to the Philadelphia Department of Revenue [Philadelphia Code § 1202(a), (c)].

Tax Does Not Have to Be Collected by All Users

A hotel that provided valet parking had an agreement with a nearby garage for the use of 90 spaces in the garage for a fee but did not operate the facility. The hotel, therefore, was not responsible for collecting and remitting the Philadelphia parking tax [*City of Philadelphia v. OLS Hotel Partners, L.P.*, 781 A.2d 268 (Pa.Commw. 2001).

Parking lot operators must keep accurate books and records to which the Department has full access at all times [Philadelphia Code § 1204(1)]. These records must include the following information: (1) a daily return sheet showing the number of cars parked or stored on an hourly, daily, weekly, or monthly basis, gross receipts, and the actual tax due; and (2) copies of all claim checks issued in connection with all transactions for each parking facility. All books, records, daily record sheets and claim check stubs must be retained for a period of six (6) years subsequent to the year of the transaction [Philadelphia Code § 19-1205(3)].

• *Returns and payment of tax*

The tax is imposed on the person who parks or stores a vehicle, but parking lot operators must collect the tax and file returns with and remit the tax to the Philadelphia Department of Revenue [Philadelphia Code § 1202(a)(c)]. Parking lot operators must file returns at times set by the Commissioner of Revenue by regulation. Returns must contain the following information: (1) gross receipts from all transactions; (2) total number of cars parked during the preceding calendar month; (3) the amount of tax due; and (4) any other pertinent information that may be required by the Department by regulation or otherwise. Payment of tax must accompany returns [Philadelphia Code § 19-1203]. Taxpayers can obtain more information on the parking tax by contacting the Parking Tax Unit of the Department of Revenue, Municipal Services Building, Room 530, 1401 John F. Kennedy Boulevard, or by calling 215-686-2670.

¶4005 Hotel Room Rental Tax

The hotel room rental tax is imposed at the rate of 8.5% on the consideration received by operators of Philadelphia hotels from transactions of renting rooms to transients (*i.e.,* temporary occupants).

NOTE: The Philadelphia hotel room rental tax is separate from the city hotel occupancy tax (discussed at ¶4009), which is imposed in conjunction with the Commonwealth hotel occupancy tax.

• *"Hotel" defined*

The word "hotel" means a hotel, motel, inn, guesthouse, or other building located in Philadelphia that holds itself out by any means (*e.g.,* advertising, license, registration with an innkeeper's group) as being available to provide overnight lodging or use of facility space for consideration to persons seeking temporary accommodation; any place that advertises to the public at large or any segment thereof that it will provide beds, sanitary facilities, or other space for a temporary period to members of the public at large or any place recognized as a hostelry. However, portions of a hotel devoted to persons who have established permanent residence are not included in the definition of "hotel" [Philadelphia Code § 19-2401(5)]. "Temporary" means a period of time not exceeding thirty (30) consecutive days [Philadelphia Code § 19-2401(12)]. A "transient" is an individual who registers at a hotel for temporary occupancy [Philadelphia Code § 19-2401(15)].

- *"Consideration" defined*

    "Consideration" means receipts, fees, charges, rentals, leases, cash, credits, property of any kind or nature, or other payment received by operators in exchange for or in consideration of the use or occupancy by a transient of a room or rooms in a hotel for any temporary period [Philadelphia Code § 19-2401(2)].

- *Collection of tax*

    Although the Philadelphia hotel room rental tax is imposed on hotel patrons, hotel operators are responsible for collecting the tax from patrons and remitting the tax to the Commonwealth [Philadelphia Code § 19-2402(a)].

- *Returns and payment of tax*

    Hotel room rental tax returns are due on the 15th day of the month following the month when the rooms were rented. The Monthly Hotel Tax Coupon Book is available to simplify tax payments. Payment is due with the return. More information on the Philadelphia hotel room rental tax can be obtained by calling 215-686-2670.

¶4006 Personal Property Tax

Philadelphia imposed a personal property tax based on the value of certain intangible person property (*e.g.*, stocks, bonds) until December 31, 1996. The tax was imposed at the rate of 4 mills and was administered by the Board of Revision of Taxes. After the first *Annenberg* decision, the city of Philadelphia discontinued imposing and collecting its personal property tax for tax years 1997 and thereafter (as well as suspending personal property tax imposed under the authority of the Sterling Act) [Act of August 5, 1932, Sp. Sess., P.L. 45]. The *Annenberg* decision is discussed at ¶3515. In *Annenberg II* [757 A.2d 338 (2000)] the Pennsylvania Supreme Court ruled that the counties must provide a retroactive remedy consistent with the Court's decision that the exclusion from the personal property tax of stock held in companies subject to the capital stock and franchise taxes is unconstitutional.

¶4007 Real Estate Nonutilization Tax

Philadelphia imposes a real estate nonutilization tax on the privilege of utilizing property as a vacant lot or abandoned property [Philadelphia Code § 19-2503].

- *Base and rates*

    The tax is levied on the assessed value of the property most recently returned by the Board of Revision of Taxes. The tax rate for abandoned property is 5% of the assessed value, and the rate for vacant lots is 10% of the assessed value [Philadelphia Code § 2504(2)].

- *"Vacant lot" and "abandoned property" defined*

    A "vacant lot" is any property that is unimproved or contains no building that are in compliance with the safety provisions of the Philadelphia Code and has a lien for demolition of any structures by the Department of Licenses and Inspections [Philadelphia Code § 19-2502(5)(a)].

    "Abandoned property" includes any property that is not classified as a "vacant lot" and that meets one of the following criteria:

    (1) It has remained continuously unoccupied during the privilege year (*i.e.*, a calendar year) and for the prior four calendar years. Property is "continuously unoccupied" if it is listed during the entire privilege year as vacant or is designated by the Department of Licenses and Inspections as vacant during both the privilege year and the year immediately preceding the privilege year.

    (2) It has been licensed as vacant for the entire privilege year in accordance with the provisions of Ch. 4-200, § PM-102.4 of Title 4 of the Philadelphia Code.

    (3) In the case of property containing one or more buildings used in whole or in part for one or more dwelling units immediately prior to becoming vacant,

the property has been under continuous designation as a public nuisance pursuant to Ch. 4-200, § PM-307.0 of Title 4 of the Code during the privilege year and for the year immediately preceding the privilege year.

(4) In the case of property containing one or more buildings none of which was used in whole or in part for one or dwelling units immediately prior to the time it became vacant, the property has been under continuous citation for violation of the safety and health provisions of the Philadelphia Code during the privilege year and for the year immediately preceding the privilege year.

(5) In the case of land not containing any building, the land has been continuously under citation for violating Ch. 4-200, § PM-102.4 or Ch. 4-200, § PM-302.0 of Title 4 of the Philadelphia Code during the privilege year.

• *Returns and payment of tax*

Returns must be filed, accompanied by payment, on or before April 15 of the year after the year of imposition. Use forms furnished by the Revenue Department [Philadelphia Code § 19-2505].

¶4008 Sales and Use Tax

Prior to October 8, 2009, Philadelphia imposed a 1% sales tax on the sale at retail of tangible personal property or services [Philadelphia Code § 19-2701(1)] and a 1% use tax on the use within Philadelphia of tangible personal property and services purchased at retail [Philadelphia Code § 19-2701(2)]. The sales and use tax rate was increased from 1% to 2% for the period October 8, 2009, through June 30, 2014. Beginning July 1, 2014, the 2% sales tax was made permanent. Philadelphia also imposes a 1.21% hotel occupancy tax (discussed at ¶4009).

These taxes are administered by the Pennsylvania Department of Revenue. The rules for reporting, collection and enforcement are the same as those that apply to the Commonwealth sales and use tax, discussed in Chapters 5—8.

• *City sales tax*

The Philadelphia sales tax is governed by the provisions of The Pennsylvania Intergovernmental Cooperation Authority Act [53 P.S. §§ 12720.501—12720.509]. The local tax is imposed in addition to the Commonwealth tax (discussed in Chapters 5—8) if a sale is deemed to have occurred in a taxable county. There are no transactions subject only to the local tax [61 Pa. Code § 60.16(a)(11)]. A "taxable county" for this purpose is (1) the city of Philadelphia or (2) a county that has adopted the local tax [61 Pa. Code § 60.16(a)(13)].

The city sales tax is imposed on each separate sale at retail within Philadelphia of tangible personal property or services, as defined in Article II of the Tax Reform Code [53 P.S. § 12720.503(a)]. Taxable property and services are discussed at ¶702 and ¶703, respectively. The vendor is responsible for collecting the sales tax from the purchaser of taxable goods and services and remitting the tax to the Department of Revenue [Philadelphia Code § 19-2701(1)]; and the owner or operator is responsible for collecting the hotel occupancy tax from the occupant. The tax base for this tax (with respect to goods and services) is the same as the Pennsylvania sales tax, but the situs rules for the city sales tax (discussed below) differ from the Commonwealth sales tax.

• *City use tax*

The Philadelphia use tax is governed by the provisions of The Pennsylvania Intergovernmental Cooperation Authority Act [53 P.S. §§ 12720.501—12720.509]. The local tax is imposed in addition to the Commonwealth tax (discussed in Chapters 5—8) if a sale is deemed to have occurred in a taxable county. There are no transactions subject only to the local tax [61 Pa. Code § 60.16(a)(11)]. A "taxable county" for this purpose is (1) the city of Philadelphia or (2) a county that has adopted the local tax [61 Pa. Code § 60.16(a)(13)].

The user of taxable goods and services for which no city sales tax has been paid is responsible for paying the city use tax [Philadelphia Code § 19-2701(2)].

• *Situs for retail sales*

A local sales tax is imposed at the point of sale (*i.e.*, the place where the sale is consummated) [61 Pa. Code § 60.16(a)(11)]. A sale at retail is deemed to be consummated at the retailer's place of business unless the tangible personal property sold is delivered by the retailer or an agent of the retailer (1) to a destination outside Pennsylvania; (2) to a common carrier for delivery to a destination outside Pennsylvania; or (3) to the United States mail for delivery to a destination outside Pennsylvania. If a retailer has more than one place of business in Pennsylvania that participates in the sale, the sale is deemed to be consummated at the retailer's place of business where the initial order for the tangible personal property is taken, even though the order must be forwarded elsewhere for acceptance, approval of credit, ship, or billing. A sale by a retailer's employee is deemed to be consummated at the place of business where the employee works [53 P.S. § 12720.504(a)].

• *Situs for vehicle, aircraft, and motorcraft sales*

A sale or use of motor vehicles, trailers, mobile homes, boats or aircraft that are required to be registered or licensed under federal or Pennsylvania laws is deemed to be consummated at the address of the purchaser [53 P.S. § 12720.504(b)]. This means that nonresidents can purchase these types of items in Philadelphia without paying the city's sales tax on them. The purchaser or user is responsible for the payment of tax due directly to the Department of Transportation when application for the issuance of a certificate is made. If licensing by the Department of Transportation is not required or obtained, the purchaser or user is responsible for payment of the tax directly to the Philadelphia Department of Revenue.

• *Situs for sales of utility services*

A sale or use of utility service is deemed to occur at the service address in Philadelphia. Utility services for this purpose include steam, natural and manufactured gas, electricity, and telephone and telegraph service. The "service address" is the address where (1) the telephone equipment is located and to which the telephone number is assigned; (2) where the telegraph originates; or (3) where the meter registering the services is located, without regard to where the services are rendered [53 P.S. § 12720-504(c)].

• *Situs for road construction materials*

For purposes of Philadelphia's sales and use tax, the sale or use of road construction material (including recycled asphalt, recycled concrete, asphalt, concrete, and road aggregates) is deemed to have been consummated at the location of its final destination, which is determined by reference to delivery or shipping documents [72 P.S. § 7202-A, effective July 1, 2001]. Prior to July 1, 2001, the sale was deemed to occur at the retailer's place of business, unless the material was delivered to an out-of-state destination.

• *Sources of information*

For more information about the Philadelphia sales and use tax, consult the statutes and regulations [53 P.S. § § 12720.501—12720.509; 61 Pa. Code § 60.16] or call the Commonwealth of Pennsylvania at 717-787-6229.

¶4009 Hotel Occupancy Tax

The city hotel occupancy tax is imposed at the rate of 1% of the charge for occupancy of a room or rooms in a hotel in Philadelphia. Hotel operators are responsible for collecting the tax from occupants and remitting it to the Commonwealth [Philadelphia Code § 19-2701(3)]. The local hotel occupancy tax is in addition to the Commonwealth hotel occupancy tax (discussed at ¶724) if a sale is deemed to have occurred in a taxable county. There are no transactions subject only to the local

¶4009

tax [61 Pa. Code § 60.16(a)(11)]. A "taxable county" for this purpose is (1) the city of Philadelphia or (2) a county that has adopted the local tax [61 Pa. Code § 60.16(a)(13)].

The city hotel occupancy tax is governed by the provisions of The Pennsylvania Intergovernmental Cooperation Authority Act [53 P.S. § § 12720.501—12720.509] and is administered by the Pennsylvania Department of Revenue. The rules for reporting, collection and enforcement are the same as those that apply to the Commonwealth sales and use tax (discussed in Chapters 5—8). For more information, consult the statutes and regulations [61 Pa. Code § 60.16].

NOTE: This tax is part of the Commonwealth sales and use tax provisions; there are no local hotel occupancy taxes without corresponding Commonwealth hotel occupancy taxes. The Philadelphia hotel room rental tax (discussed at ¶ 4005) is a separate tax imposed by the City of Philadelphia.

¶4010 Real Estate Tax

Beginning with tax year 2016, the real property tax rate is .6317% (City) and .7681% (School District) for a 1.3998% total tax rate of the assessed value of taxable real property returned by the Board of Revision of Taxes in the year immediately preceding the stated year and a homestead exemption of $40,000. However, notwithstanding the tax rate set forth in Philadelphia Code § 19-1301 or any other law to the contrary, the tax levied on any real property shall not be greater than 104% of the prior years, tax levy, provided that the property is owned by the same person who owned the property at the time of the prior year's tax levy [Philadelphia Code § 19-1306(1)]. The school district also imposes a real estate tax (see ¶ 4019).

• *Payment of tax*

Real estate tax bills are normally sent out annually in the middle of December of the year prior to the tax year. Payment is due on or before March 31 of the tax year [Philadelphia Code § 19-1303(2)]. Taxpayers who pay the tax on or before February 28 receive a 1% discount [Philadelphia Code § 19-1303(1)]. Payments made after March 31 are subject to additions to tax ranging from 1½% for payments made in April to 13½% for payments made in December [Philadelphia Code § 19-1301(3)]. Provision is made for installment payment of tax for low-income households [Philadelphia Code § 19-1305].

Credit for National Guard and Reservists

Effective beginning with tax year 2007, a credit against Philadelphia real estate taxes is provided for members of the National Guard or a reserve component of the Armed Forces of the United States who are called to duty outside the Commonwealth. The credit applies only to property that is the principal residence of a taxpayer called to active duty. The credit equals the amount of tax due on the property, multiplied by a fraction equal to the number of days served on active duty divided by the number of days in the base year. If the individual called to active duty owns the property as a tenant in common, the credit amount is reduced by multiplying that amount by the individual's fractional share of ownership of the property. There is no reduction of the credit amount if the individual owns the property as a joint tenant or as a tenant by the entireties [Philadelphia Bill No. 050740].

• *Deferrals of real estate tax [Philadelphia Code § 19-1307]*

The Philadelphia Department of Revenue is authorized to grant deferrals (partial or whole) of increases in real estate taxes imposed by the city or school district of Philadelphia to eligible property owners. Eligibility for a deferral may be granted for any increase (or portion thereof) that is greater than 15% in any given year. The following factors are considered in granting deferrals: (1) household income; (2) reasonable household expenses (*e.g.*, housing, food, transportation, education, health care, debt service payments, overall tax burden); and (3) available liquid assets. Interest at the rate of 6% is assessed on the total deferred amount due, and the deferral is effective until the property is sold. However, a property owner may satisfy the debt consisting of the deferred amount and the accumulated interest at any time prior to the sale of the property.

• *Board of Revision of Taxes*

In Philadelphia the Board of Revision of Taxes is responsible for supervising and revising assessments and hearing appeals. The Philadelphia Board of Revision of Taxes is also responsible for numbering all buildings, houses, condominiums, or other structures located in Philadelphia and providing owners or occupants of all buildings, houses, structures, or condominium units located in Philadelphia with a written notice of the correct number of the building, house, structure, or condominium units [Philadelphia Code § 19-1304].

¶4011 Vehicle Rental Tax (VRT)

Under the authority of The County Code [16 P.S. § 2398], Philadelphia imposes a vehicle rental tax (VRT) at the rate of 2% of the purchase price. A taxable rental occurs whenever a renter takes possession of a rental vehicle in Philadelphia [Philadelphia Code § 19-3301(4)]. The "purchase price" is the full consideration paid or delivered or promised to be paid to the vehicle rental company for the vehicle rental, including (but not limited to) charges for vehicle use, excess mileage, pick up or drop off, vehicle damage waiver, insurance child car seat, car top carrier, and cellular phone. Charge for state and local taxes, however, are not included in the purchase price [Philadelphia Code § 19-3301(4)].

• *"Rental vehicle" and "vehicle rental company" defined*

A "rental vehicle" is a (1) private passenger motor vehicle designed to transport 15 or fewer passengers or (2) truck, trailer, or semitrailer used in the transportation of property (other than commercial freight) that is rented without a driver, is part of a fleet of five (5) or more rental vehicles that are used for that purpose and owned or leased by the same person or entity, and is rented for a period of 29 or fewer consecutive days. A "vehicle rental company" is any business entity engaged in the business of renting motor vehicles in the Commonwealth of Pennsylvania [Philadelphia Code § 19-3301].

• *Collection of tax*

Vehicle rental companies are responsible for collecting the tax at the time a rental vehicle is rented and remitting the tax to the City. A vehicle rental company that fails to collect the tax is liable for payment of the tax, including penalties and interest as provided in Philadelphia Code, Ch. 19-500, § 19-509 [Philadelphia Code § 19-3302(2)].

• *Returns and payment of tax*

On or before the 15th day of the month a vehicle rental company must file a return for the preceding month. Payment must accompany returns. The return must show the amount of consideration received for the transactions for the return period, the amount of tax due, and any other information the Department may require. Failure to pay the tax when it is due subjects the company to penalties and interest as provided in Philadelphia Code, Ch. 19-500, § 19-509. The first return for a new company is due on the 15th day of the month subsequent to the month in which business began [Philadelphia Code § 19-3304].

• *Recordkeeping*

Vehicle rental companies must maintain records, available to the Department upon request, that include the number of rental transactions on a daily or weekly basis, the rate(s) charged for each rental the consideration received from all transactions during the month for which each return is made, and any other information the Department may require [Philadelphia Code § 19-3304].

¶4012 Water/Sewer Fees

Homeowners and owners of commercial or industrial properties in Philadelphia must pay water/sewer fees. The Water Department sets the rates and maintains the water/sewer system; and the Philadelphia Department of Revenue reads meters, bills customers, and collects the water/sewer fees [Philadelphia Home Rule Charter, §6-201]. Senior citizens who meet the income criteria may be eligible for a Senior Citizen Water Discount. More information about water/sewer fees can be obtained by calling the Water Revenue Bureau at 215-686-6880 or visiting the Customer Service Office in the Municipal Services Building, Public Concourse Level, 1401 John F. Kennedy Boulevard. A booklet that explains the regulations governing Customer Service can be obtained from the Philadelphia Department of Revenue.

¶4013 Tobacco Tax

• *Imposition*

A tax is imposed on the privilege of selling at retail any tobacco and tobacco-related (unless it is specifically excluded) including, but not limited to, sales from vending machines [Philadelphia Code, §19-3602(1)].

• *Exclusion*

The tobacco tax shall not be imposed on the privilege of making any retail sale involving the bona fide delivery of tobacco or tobacco-related products to a location regularly maintained by the other party to the transaction outside the limits of Philadelphia, and not for the purpose of evading or avoiding payment of the tax or any portion thereof [Philadelphia Code, §19-3602(2)]. This tax also does not apply to cigarettes and little cigars which are instead subject to the Commonwealth's cigarette tax. This tax is collected and remitted to the Department of Revenue in the same manner as the state cigarette tax.

• *Definitions*

Cigarette: Any roll for smoking made wholly or in part of tobacco, the wrapper or cover of which is made of any substance or material other than tobacco regardless of the size or shape of the roll and regardless of whether or not the tobacco is flavored, adulterated, or mixed with any other ingredient. The term cigarette does not include cigars, little cigars, or cigarillos [Philadelphia Code, §19-3601(1)].

Little cigars: Any roll for smoking that weighs not more than four pounds per thousand, where the wrapper of cover is made of natural leaf tobacco or of any substance containing tobacco [Philadelphia Code, §19-3601(2)].

Smokeless tobacco: A product containing finely cut, ground, powdered, blended, or leaf tobacco made primarily for individual consumption that is intended to be placed in the oral or nasal cavity and not intended to be smoked. The term includes chewing tobacco, dipping tobacco, and snuff [Philadelphia Code, §19-3601(3)].

Tobacco and tobacco-related product: A product containing tobacco for smoking or other consumption, including any cigar, smokeless tobacco, pipe tobacco, or other loose tobacco, but not including a cigarette or a little cigar, and rolling papers [Philadelphia Code, §19-3601(4)].

Rolling papers: Any product consisting of sheets, rolls, or leaves of paper or tobacco that are sold for use as the wrapper or cover for any roll for smoking [Philadelphia Code, §19-3601(5)].

• *Rates*

The tobacco tax is imposed at the following rates:

(1) For any tobacco and tobacco-related product that consists of individual items rolled for smoking, including, but not limited to, cigars — $0.036 per item [Philadelphia Code, §19-3602(1)(a)].

(2) For all other tobacco and tobacco-related products — $0.36 per ounce [Philadelphia Code, § 19-3602(1)(b)].

(3) For rolling papers — $0.36 per pack [Philadelphia Code, § 19-3602(1)(c)].

• *Payment of tax*

A return and payment of the tobacco tax must be submitted annually, or on such other schedule as the Philadelphia Revenue Department determines by regulation and in such form as the Department provides [Philadelphia Code § 19-3603].

• *Local Option Cigarette Tax*

Act 131 of 2014 authorizes a $2-per-pack cigarette tax on all cigarettes and little cigars sold in Philadelphia in order to supplement public school funding in the city. This equates to a Philadelphia School District $0.10 cents per cigarette tax. Act 84 of 2016 increased the Pennsylvania cigarette tax to $0.13 cents per cigarette causing the tax on a pack of 20 cigarettes in Philadelphia to be $4.60.

¶4014 Philadelphia Sweetened Beverage Tax

In June of 2016, a tax was enacted to be imposed sugary drinks and diet sodas. The tax is levied on the wholesale distribution of sweetened beverages when they come into the city and is assessed based on volume - $0.015 cents per ounce. On July 8, 2018 the Pennsylvania Supreme Court upheld the Philadelphia beverage tax in *Williams, et al. v. City of Philadelphia*, 188 A.3d 421 (Pa. 2018). The Philadelphia beverage tax applies broadly to sugar-sweetened beverages and is a tax paid by a registered distributor. The tax is imposed on the distribution of sugar-sweetened beverages on a per ounce basis and legal liability to pay the tax is on the distributor. The Pennsylvania Supreme Court found that the tax was authorized under the Sterling Act and was not duplicative of any other tax as contended by the plaintiffs. The subject matter of the tax, the non-retail distribution of sugar-sweetened beverages for sale at retail in the city, and the measure of the tax, per ounce of sugar-sweetened beverage, are distinct from the sales tax imposed under the Sterling Act upon the retail sale of the sugar-sweetened beverage to the ultimate purchaser. The Court declined to determine whether duplicative taxation was present through an examination of where the economic incidence of the tax fell.

PHILADELPHIA SCHOOL DISTRICT TAXES

¶4015 General Taxing Powers of Local School Boards

The authority of the Philadelphia School District to impose taxes is granted by various acts passed by the Pennsylvania General Assembly. The major sources of authority are discussed below.

• *The Little Sterling Act (Act of August 9, 1963, P.L. 640) [53 P.S. § 16101 et seq.]*

The Little Sterling Act grants the Philadelphia School District the right to impose a tax on any transaction the city can tax under the Sterling Act except for taxes on wages or net income of nonresidents [53 P.S. § 16101(a)]. The school district income tax and the school district realty use and occupancy tax have been imposed under the authority of the Little Sterling Act.

• *Act of May 23, 1949, P.L. 1699*

This act gives the Philadelphia School District the authority to impose a general business tax. However, this tax has not been imposed since 1984 when it was repealed in order to impose a business income and receipts tax (formerly business privilege tax).

• *General County Assessment Law (Act of May 22, 1933, P.L. 853) [72 P.S. § 5020-1 et seq.]*

The General County Assessment Act gives the city (county) the authority to impose a tax on real property located within its boundaries.

• *First Class School District Liquor Sales Tax (Act of June 10, 1971, P.L. 153) [53 P.S. §16131 et seq.]*

This act gives the Philadelphia City Council the authority to impose a tax on the retail sale of wine, liquor, or malt and brewed beverages on behalf of the Philadelphia School District.

• *Public School Code of 1949 (Act of March 10, 1949, P.L. 30) [24 P.S. §1-101 et seq.]*

Some taxing authority of the Philadelphia School District derives from parts of the Public School Code.

¶4016 School District Income Tax

The Philadelphia School District income tax is a tax on investment net income and is imposed by provisions of the Philadelphia Code [Philadelphia Code § 19-1804]. It is imposed only on natural individuals who are residents of the School District.

• *Administration*

Administration of the tax is handled by city authorities. The statute provides that the Commissioner of School Revenue is the "collector" of the school district income tax. The Bureau of School Revenue is part of the City Department of Revenue; so, in practice, the "collector" is the city Revenue Commissioner. Regulations governing the school district income tax have been promulgated.

• *Imposition*

The Philadelphia School District income tax is a tax on *investment* net income and is imposed by provisions of the Philadelphia Code [Philadelphia Code § 19-1804]. It is imposed only on natural individuals who were or are residents of the school district. Persons who were or are residents of the school district for less than a full tax year are liable for tax on the net income received or credited to them during their period of residence [Philadelphia Code § 19-1804(2)(b)].

Persons subject to tax: The list of taxpayers includes (but is not limited to) the following residents of the School District [School Income Tax Regulations § 101]:

(1) Individuals.

(2) Individual limited partners of partnerships that are not themselves subject to the city wages and net profits tax. These individuals are taxable on their pro rata share of the partnership's taxable income.

(3) Members of unincorporated associations with respect to the taxable income of the association received by or credited to the member.

(4) Beneficiaries of trusts and estates as to current or accumulated taxable income paid to them.

(5) Individuals treated as substantial owners of trusts and estates.

• *Base*

In general, the Philadelphia school district income tax is imposed on the net income from the ownership, lease, sale or other disposition of real property and tangible and intangible personal property, including the net income tax paid to any beneficiary of a trust or estate and the income of any trust or estate of which such person is the substantial owner [Philadelphia Code § 19-1804(2)]. See also *"Items included in taxable income,"* below. For a given fiscal year, the base is income received during the corresponding tax year (*i.e.,* calendar year) as set forth in the table below. For example, the tax for fiscal year 2019 is imposed on income received during calendar year 2018.

Net income: Net income (*i.e.,* taxable income) is determined after deduction of all allocable and reasonable costs and expenses paid in the production of income [Philadelphia Code § 19-1804(1)(c)]. See also *"Deductible costs and expenses,"* below.

• *Exclusions*

The following income items are excluded from the Philadelphia School District income tax:

(1) All interest on public loans issued by Pennsylvania or the United States, and public loans and obligations of any county, city, borough, town, township, school district, and incorporated district of Pennsylvania, and bonds and obligations of bodies corporate and public of Pennsylvania known as municipal authorities [Philadelphia Code § 19-1804(3)(a)].

(2) Interest and dividends received or credited on savings deposits and savings certificates issued by any private bank, building and loan association, savings and loan association, credit union, savings bank, bank and trust company, or trust company [Philadelphia Code § 19-1804(3)(b)].

(3) Gains realized upon the sale, exchange or other disposition of tangible or intangible personal property or of real estate that has been owned by the resident for a period of more than six months prior to the disposition [Philadelphia Code § 19-1804(3)(c)].

(4) Income that is subject to the Philadelphia City Net Profits Tax or Wage Tax [Philadelphia Code § 19-1804(3)(d)].

(5) Old age, retirement and pension payments [Philadelphia Code § 19-1804(3)(e)].

(6) Sick pay and disability benefits [Philadelphia Code § 19-1804(3)(f)].

(7) Benefits arising under the Workmen's Compensation Act and Unemployment Compensation Act [Philadelphia Code § 19-1804(3)(g)].

(8) Active military service pay [Philadelphia Code § 19-1804(3)(h)].

(9) Bonuses paid by any governmental unit for active military service [Philadelphia Code § 19-1804(3)(i)].

(10) Death benefits [Philadelphia Code § 19-1804(3)(j)].

(11) Proceeds from insurance policies [Philadelphia Code § 19-1804(3)(k)].

(12) Gifts and bequests [Philadelphia Code § 19-1804(3)(l)].

(13) Compensatory damages arising from any claim or cause of action [Philadelphia Code § 19-1804(3)(m)].

• *Rate*

The Philadelphia School District income tax is imposed at the following rate(s) [Philadelphia Code § 19-1804(2)(a)]:

For Fiscal Year	On Net Income Received or Credited During Calendar Year(s)	Rate
2005	2004	4.4625%
2006	2005	4.3310%
2007 and thereafter	The calendar year prior to the fiscal year.	Same as Philadelphia resident wage and net profits tax rate (see ¶ 3803) for the tax year prior to the school district's fiscal year.

Rates in excess of statutory maximum: In the event the rate of tax is determined to exceed any limitation imposed by statute, the tax will be imposed at the maximum permissible rate [Philadelphia Code § 19-1804(2)(a)].

• *Items included in taxable income (net income)*

The income items received by any resident (directly or through an agent) whether in cash or property are included in taxable income. Losses in one class of income cannot be used to offset income in another class (*e.g.,* a loss from the short-term sale of property cannot be used to offset dividend income) [School District Income Tax Regulations § 203]. Taxable income includes, but is not limited to, the following items:

¶4016

(1) *Dividends* (except those discussed in § 206 of the School District Income Tax Regulations). All dividends taxable for Pennsylvania personal income tax purposes (discussed at ¶ 208) are taxable for school district income tax purposes. Any "distribution other than a dividend" declared by an S corporation is taxable regardless of whether the distribution was made to the shareholder. Effective beginning in 2015, however, income will not be treated as received or credited from an S corporation until it is actually distributed. (Philadelphia Bill No. 140884). For more details, see § 203(a) of the School District Income Tax Regulations.

(2) *Interest.* All interest received or credited (except interest specifically exempt under § 206 of the School District Income Tax Regulations) is taxable [School District Income Tax Regulations § 203(b)].

(3) *Rentals.* All gross income (net of reasonable operating costs and expenses) from the ownership of property (real or personal) regardless of the situs of the property. Note, however, that rental income subject to the Philadelphia City tax on net profits is not taxable for school district income tax purposes. For more details, see § 203(c) of the School District Income Tax Regulations.

(4) *Gains from the disposition of property.* Taxable gains are those from the sale, exchange, or other disposition of property (real or personal) that has been owned by the taxpayer for a period not exceeding six months before the date of the disposition. For more details, see § 203(d) of the School District Income Tax Regulations. Note that losses can be offset against gains from disposition of property but cannot be offset against any other class of income [School District Income Tax Regulations § 204(b)]. For example, Alice sold stock in Z Corporation at a gain of $1,500 and stock in X Corporation at a loss of $1,000. Alice may offset her $1,500 loss on Z stock to the extent of $1,000. However, Alice may not offset any of her loss on property disposition against any other class of income (*e.g.,* interest, dividends).

(5) *Royalties.* Income received as a royalty from a patent or copyright, to the extent not subject to the net profits tax, must be included in taxable income [School District Income Tax Regulations § 203(e)].

(6) *Punitive damages.* Punitive damages received as a result of a violation of a contractual agreement or through an action of the law are taxable [School District Income Tax Regulations § 203(f)].

(7) *Prizes and awards.* Prizes and awards (including net gambling gains but *excluding* net gains from the Pennsylvania Lottery) are taxable [School District Income Tax Regulations § 203(g)].

(8) *Annuity policies.* Income received by an annuitant under an insurance policy is included in taxable income unless payable from an employment contract as part of a retirement or pension plan. In computing tax due, the formula used in determining federal tax on annuity income is acceptable [School District Income Tax Regulations § 203(h)].

(9) *Limited partnership income.* The pro rata share of taxable income of limited partners not otherwise subject to the net profits tax is includable in taxable income. Income and losses within this class may be offset. This class of income is considered distributed when credited to the partner as reflected on the partnership's schedules and forms [School District Income Tax Regulations § 203(i)].

Net Income from Securities Margin Account Interest

The Philadelphia School District income tax is a tax on net income. In a case involving the school district income tax [*Ash v. Tax Review Board of the City of Philadelphia; the City of Philadelphia; and the School District of Philadelphia,* Pa.Commw., No. 1370 C.D. 1993 (June 20, 1994), *opinion not reported*], the Philadelphia Department of Revenue argued that the margin account interest expense of procuring a particular security cannot be used to offset dividend payments of other margin account securities. The taxpayer, on the other hand, argued that the net income from all securities means total income from all securities held minus total expenses of holding the securities, including total interest expense. The court held that the position of the Philadelphia Department of Revenue was incorrect; the taxpayer's reasonable position prevailed. The case was remanded for recomputation of the amount of school income tax that should be properly assessed against the taxpayer.

- *Deductible costs and expenses*

All allocable and reasonable costs and expenses incurred in the production of income are allowed as deductions from gross income. However, taxes based on income (*e.g.,* this tax, the Philadelphia wage and net profits tax, federal income tax, foreign income taxes) are not deductible. Expenses directly incurred in the production of taxable income are deductible from gross income if they are reasonable and were paid solely for the production of such income [School District Income Tax Regulations § 204(a)]. Examples of deductible expenses are personal property tax paid on property subject to this tax, the cost of a safety deposit box, the fee for preparation of the school income tax return, and margin interest (not to exceed the yield of the security). For part-year taxpayers (i.e., taxpayers who were residents for only part of the year), both income and deduction items must be allocated according to the portion of the year they resided in Philadelphia.

- *Returns and payment of tax*

Who must file a return: The following persons must file Philadelphia School District income tax returns [School District Income Tax Regulations § 301]:

(1) Persons who receive income from the ownership, sale, lease, or other disposition of real property or personal property (tangible or intangible).

(2) Persons who receive or are credited with income as beneficiary of an estate or trust.

(3) Persons who are deemed to be the substantial owner of an estate or trust and receive or are credited with income from the estate or trust.

Where to file: School district income tax returns are filed with the Department of Revenue of the City of Philadelphia [School District Income Tax Regulations § 302(a)].

Joint returns: If spouses receive taxable income from property owned individually or as a beneficiary of an estate or trust and/or from property owned by them as tenants by the entireties, they may elect to file a joint return. However, if a combined return is filed, the tax liability of the spouses must be the same as would result from the filing of individual returns. For example, losses from property owned separately by either spouse may not offset income received or credited to the other [School District Income Tax Regulations § 302(b)].

Due date: The Philadelphia School District tax is due and payable by April 15 of the fiscal year for which the tax is imposed [Philadelphia Code § 19-1804(4)]. The return covers the calendar year preceding the due date of the return [School District Income Tax Regulations § 303]. Persons who keep their books and file federal returns on a fiscal-year basis are *not* allowed to file a Philadelphia School District return on a fiscal-year basis [School District Income Tax Regulations § 303].

Payment of tax: Tax due must be paid at the time a return is filed [School District Income Tax Regulations § 304].

Information returns: Trust or estate fiduciaries must file annual information returns on or before March 31, showing the name, address, and social security number of any resident beneficiaries, and the amount of income distributed or credited to them during the preceding year [School District Income Tax Regulations § 302(d)].

- *Penalties and interest*

The law provides for interest and penalties on unpaid taxes [Philadelphia Code § 19-509]. Consult the ordinances for current rates of interest and penalties. If the city

¶4016

brings suit to recover tax, the person liable for the tax is also liable for the costs of collection, in addition to interest and penalties on any underpayment. Certain violations are punishable by fine and/or imprisonment. Consult the statute.

• *Taxpayer remedies*

Appeals from the assessing authority are made to the Philadelphia Tax Review Board.

Abatements and compromises: Appeals covering the abatement or waiver of interest or penalty, or of a compromise of the tax due, may be filed with the Philadelphia Tax Review Board within 60 days after the date of mailing of the notice of assessment to the taxpayer or his or her representative. There is no appeal from Tax Review Board decisions regarding abatements and compromises [School District Income Tax Regulations § 801].

Assessments and refunds: If the Tax Review Board denies any petition for review of an assessment, or a petition for refund, an appeal from the denial may be made to the Court of Common Pleas within 30 days after the date of the mailing of the notice of the decision by the Tax Review Board [School District Income Tax Regulations § 802].

¶4017 School District Realty Use and Occupancy Tax

• *Enabling legislation*

In general, school districts have the authority to levy taxes under § 507 of the Public School Code of 1949, Act of March 10, 1949, P.L. 30, as amended [24 P.S. § 1-101 *et seq.*]. However, the Philadelphia School District is not authorized to levy taxes because its members are appointed by the mayor of Philadelphia and the legislature may not delegate the power to tax to appointed officials [*Danson v. Casey*, 399 A.2d 360 (Pa. 1979); *Philadelphia Home Rule Charter*, 351 Pa. Code § 12.12-201]. The Philadelphia school district realty use and occupancy tax is imposed by ordinance of the Philadelphia City Council [Philadelphia Code § 19-1806]. It must be renewed annually by the City Council, which has done so every year since the tax was first imposed. Philadelphia use and occupancy regulations have been issued [Philadelphia Use and Occupancy Tax Regulations § 101 *et seq.*].

• *Administration*

The tax is administered by the School Revenue Commissioner of Philadelphia, which, in practice, is the City Revenue Commissioner.

• *Imposition*

The school district realty use and occupancy tax is imposed on the use or occupancy of real estate within the Philadelphia school district for the purpose of carrying on any business, trade, occupation, profession, vocation, or any other commercial or industrial activity [Philadelphia Code § 19-1806(2)]. The tax is imposed on the user or occupier of real estate but is collected monthly from tenants by landlords and their rental agents.

When landlord relieved of liability: If a landlord or rental agent for the landlord fails to collect tax from a user or occupier, the landlord or agent is liable for payment of the tax due. However, if the landlord or agent required to collect the tax provides the Commissioner, concurrently with the timely filing of a tax return for the period for which the tax is due, in writing, all required information (*e.g.*, name, address, amount of tax due), the landlord is excused from liability for the tenant's unpaid taxes [Philadelphia Code § 19-2806(5)(b)]. For more information, see the Philadelphia School District Realty Use and Occupancy Tax Regulations.

Burden Shifted to Landlord

Taxpayer leased property to a tax-exempt entity—a non-profit theater. The lease agreement provided that the theater must pay any taxes that might be due. However, the landlord failed to make a timely filing of a tax return and supporting information to establish that its tenant was entitled to an exemption from the school district business use and occupancy tax. The burden of liability for the tax shifted from tenant to landlord when the landlord failed to file the required tax return (Form UO-3) with supporting documentation to identify its tenant and establish its entitlement to exemption from tax [*In re New York Cafe Theater, Dexacon Corporation, and Harold Wolfe,* Philadelphia Tax Review Board, Opinion No. 94-L, Docket No. 45-102093-2 (November 8, 1994)].

Self-storage facilities: The self-storage industry operates under the Self-Service Storage Facility Act [73 P.S. §§ 1901—1917]. Under this statute, a self-storage facility is defined as, "Any real property designed and used for the purpose of renting or leasing individual storage space to occupants who are to have access to such space for the purpose of storing and removing personal property. No occupant shall use a self-storage facility for residential purposes" [73 P.S. § 1902]. The owners, not the customers, are users of self-storage facilities; and the owners, not the customers, are subject to the Philadelphia realty use and occupancy tax [*In re Northeast Oxford Enterprises, L.P.,* Philadelphia Tax Review Board, Nos. 36UOREFZZ9875, 36UOREFZZ9930, & 36UOREFZZ9877 (February 11, 2002); *In re Shurgard Self Storage Centers, Inc.,* Philadelphia Tax Review Board, Nos. 36UOREFZZ9874 & 36UOREFZZ9928 (February 11, 2002)].

Service, utility, and common areas: Service, utility, and common areas are excluded from the determination of the square feet available for use or occupancy, provided they are under the landlord's control. For more details, see § 103 of the School District Use and Occupancy Regulations.

• *Exclusions*

The school district is not authorized to levy a tax on the use and occupancy of the following:

(1) The use or occupancy of real estate as the dwelling or principal place of residence of the user or occupier or its use or occupancy is subject to tax by the Commonwealth [Philadelphia Code § 19-1806(3)(a)].

(2) Any person exempt from real estate taxes in the city of Philadelphia [Philadelphia Code § 19-1806(3)(b)].

(3) The use or occupancy of facilities used in or occupied by those engaged in port-related activities [Philadelphia Code § 19-1806(3)(c)]. "Port-related activities" include loading or discharging cargo to or from vessels conducted on piers, wharves, or marine terminal facilities in the port of Philadelphia and related activities (*e.g.,* dockage, wharfage, truck and/or railroad car loading and unloading, storage or cargo that is to be loaded or has been discharged from vessels at a pier, wharf or marine terminal facility in the Port of Philadelphia) [Philadelphia Code § 19-1806(1)(d)].

• *Base and rate*

The school district realty use and occupancy tax is measured by the assessed value of the real estate, effective July 1, 2013, is imposed at a rate of 1.21% per $100 of the assessed value of the real estate as most recently returned by the Board of Revision of Taxes with a $165,300 exemption amount from the assessed value for each property actually used for the purpose of doing business (translating into an annual tax exemption of $2,000).

¶4017

• *Computation of tax*

The tax for each occupant is based on the tax rate multiplied by the assessed value. Previously the tax was computed separately, based on square feet occupied, and was prorated according to the number of days of actual use or occupancy during the business year (360 days) [Philadelphia Code § 19-1806(4)(b)].

(Square feet occupied or used)/(Total sq. ft. available for use or occupancy)	×	Assessed Value	×	Rate of Taxation per $100	×	(Days of Actual Use or Occupancy)/(Total sq. ft. available for use or occupancy)

• *Returns and payment of tax*

Tax is collected and returns are filed by owners of property and remitted to the Department of Revenue. Returns must be filed monthly, quarterly, semi-annually, or annually, as required by regulation [Philadelphia Code §19-2806(5)(a)]. The frequency of filing depends on the total assessed value of the property, as shown in the table below [Philadelphia School District Realty Use and Occupancy Tax Regulations §504(a)].

Assessed Value	Filing Period
Less than $6,000	Annual
At least $6,000 but less than $12,000	Semiannual
At least $12,000 but less than $36,000	Quarterly
$36,000 or more	Monthly

Due date: Returns are due on or before the 25th day of the last month in the filing period [Philadelphia School District Realty Use and Occupancy Tax Regulations §503].

> *Example 1:* Roger is required to file monthly use and occupancy returns. His return for July must be filed on or before July 25.

> *Example 2:* Samantha is required to file quarterly use and occupancy returns. Her return for the third quarter is due on or before September 25.

> *Example 3:* Thomas is required to file semi-annual use and occupancy returns. His returns for the year are due on or before June 25 (for the first period) and December 25 (for the second period).

> *Example 4:* Uma is required to file annual use and occupancy returns. Her return for 2013 is due on or before December 15, 2013.

• *Discount*

Any person who collects the tax from users or occupiers and who remits the tax, due by the 25th day of the month, is entitled to deduct a discount of 1% as compensation for the expense of collecting and remitting the tax and as consideration for prompt payment [Philadelphia Code §19-2806(5)(c)].

• *Preemption*

A local jurisdiction cannot levy a tax on anything the Commonwealth taxes [Act of August 5, 1932, Sp. Sess., P.L. 45, §1; Act of December 31, 1965, P.L. 1257, §3]. This concept is referred to as the preemption doctrine (explained at ¶3403), and it has been an important issue and a subject of considerable litigation in the context of local taxation. Preemption cases relevant to the use and occupancy tax are discussed below.

Alcoholic beverage distributor: Philadelphia's taxation of distributors of alcoholic beverages is preempted by Commonwealth regulation and taxation, even if the tax is imposed for the benefit of the school district. In the case of Philadelphia, the school district itself is not authorized to levy taxes because its members are appointed (see discussion above) [*Wissinoming Bottling Co. v. School District of Philadelphia*, 654 A.2d 208 (1995)]. See also the discussion of the *Wissinoming* case at ¶3402.

Title insurance companies: The Pennsylvania Supreme Court has held that local taxation of an industry is preempted by Commonwealth regulation only where relevant laws clearly disclose the intention on the part of the Legislature to exclusively occupy the industry [*Allegheny Valley Bank of Pittsburgh*, 412 A.2d 1366 (Pa.

1980)]. Upon reviewing the legislative history of the relevant statutes, the Court could not ascertain a legislative intent to exempt title insurance companies from local taxation. Thus, the Philadelphia School District's imposition of realty use and occupancy tax on a title insurance was not prohibited [*Industrial Valley Title Insurance Co.,* 661 A.2d 497 (Pa.Commw. 1996)]. The Commonwealth Court, citing the Pennsylvania Supreme Court decision in *City of Pittsburgh v. Allegheny Valley Bank of Pittsburgh,* 412 A.2d 1366 (Pa. 1978), held that Commonwealth regulation of the insurance industry did not preempt local taxation of title insurance companies [*Industrial Valley Title Insurance Co.,* 661 A.2d 497 (Pa.Commw. 1995)]. According to the Court, local taxation of an industry is preempted only where relevant laws clearly indicate a legislative intent to exclusively occupy the industry. The Court also held that the statutes regulating title insurance companies did not reflect a legislative intent to exempt title insurance companies from local taxation.

Beer distributor: The existence of comprehensive regulatory schemes in the liquor industry preempts local taxation of beer distributors [*Commonwealth v. Wilsbach Distributors, Inc.,* 513 Pa. 215 (Pa. 1986)]. Although the *Wilsbach* case involved the Harrisburg business privilege and mercantile tax, it is the controlling case with respect to the issue of local taxation of beer distributors. In a later case, the Commonwealth Court, citing *Wilsbach,* ruled that the Philadelphia use and occupancy tax on a beer distributor was also preempted because of extensive Commonwealth regulation of the liquor industry [*Wissinoming Bottling Co. v. School District of Philadelphia,* 654 A.2d 208 (Pa.Commw. 1995)]. The Commonwealth Court later upheld its *Wissinoming* decision in *City of Philadelphia and School District of Philadelphia v. Tax Review Board of the City of Philadelphia and Anna M. Shott t/a Thrifty Scott Beverage,* 713 A.2d 718 (Pa.Commw. 1998).

Mutual insurance company: A mutual life insurance company (Provident) with its principal place of business in Philadelphia rented property in Philadelphia and paid the Philadelphia School District's use and occupancy tax with respect to the leased property. Provident, which is also subject to a number of taxes and fees payable to the Commonwealth, filed a petition for refund of the local use and occupancy tax but lost administrative appeals. Provident then appealed to the Commonwealth Court, contending that the preemption doctrine (explained at ¶3403) prevented local taxation of an industry extensively regulated by the Commonwealth. Furthermore, Provident contended, the local tax duplicates Commonwealth taxation of its activity. The Commonwealth Court held that the preemption doctrine did not prevent local taxation of Provident. With respect to the duplication issue, the court pointed out that the Commonwealth tax on insurance premiums is imposed on companies for the privilege of transacting business in Pennsylvania and is measured by gross premiums, whereas the local tax is imposed on the privilege of using and occupying real estate located in the district and used for commercial purposes and is measured by the assessed value of the real estate used and occupied by the business. Therefore, there is no duplication of taxes or fees [*Provident Mutual Life Insurance Co. of Philadelphia v. Tax Review Board of the City of Philadelphia,* 658 A.2d 500 (Pa.Commw. 1995)].

¶4018 School District Liquor Sales Tax

The Board of Education of the School District of Philadelphia is authorized to impose a tax for general public school purposes upon sales at retail during the tax year in the school district of liquor and malt and brewed beverages that are sold or dispensed by any hotel, restaurant, or club, or other person licensed by the Commonwealth of Pennsylvania to sell or dispense liquor or malt or brewed beverages [Philadelphia Code § 19-1805(2)]. Sales by Pennsylvania liquor stores and malt beverage distributors are not subject to the liquor sales tax. A "person" for this purpose is an individual, limited partnership, partnership, association, or corporation. When used in a clause prescribing or imposing a fine or imprisonment or both, the term "person" means individuals who, under the bylaws of the clubs, have jurisdiction over the possession and sale of liquor at the club [Philadelphia Code § 19-1805(a)(c)].

The "tax year" is the fiscal year of the school district beginning July 1 of any calendar year and ending June 30 of the following calendar year [Philadelphia Code § 19-1805(1)(e)]. The tax is administered and enforced by the Revenue Commissioner [Philadelphia Code § 19-1805(5)(a)].

School District Across-the-Bar Tax Valid

Taxpayer challenged the validity of the Philadelphia School District liquor sales tax (often referred to as the "across-the-bar" tax) on the grounds that the tax was not renewed annually. The Commonwealth Court ruled that the across-the-bar tax is a valid and enforceable ordinance granting the School Board *continuing authority* to levy the tax. The authority does not need to be renewed by vote of City Council on an annual basis [*Licensed Beverage Association of Philadelphia v. Board of Education of the School District of Philadelphia and the City of Philadelphia Law Department*, 680 A.2d 1198 (Pa.Commw. 1996)].

• *Base and rate*

The tax is imposed at the rate of 10% of the sale price on the sale at retail of alcoholic beverages. A sale for this purpose is a transfer at retail for consideration in any manner or by any means whatsoever of liquor and malt and brewed beverages. However, a sale for this purpose does not include any transaction that is subject to tax by the Commonwealth under the Tax Reform Code of 1971 [Philadelphia Code § 19-1805(1)(d)].

• *Collection of the tax*

Vendors must collect the tax from the purchaser at the time of the sale and remit the tax to the Revenue Commissioner. Vendors who fail to collect the proper amount of tax are liable for the full amount of the tax that should have been collected and are subject to any other remedies at law or in equity [Philadelphia Code § 19-1805(3)(a), (b)]. A "vendor" for this purpose is any person maintaining a place of business in the School District of Philadelphia and licensed by the Commonwealth to sell or dispense liquor or malt and brewed beverages [Philadelphia Code § 19-1805(1)(f)]. However, an employee who in the ordinary scope of employment renders service in exchange for wages or salaries is not a vendor. The term "person" includes any individual, limited partnership, partnership, association or corporation.

• *Reports and payment of the tax*

Vendors must file monthly tax reports within 25 days after the last day of any month for which the return is filed. Payment must accompany the reports. Forms for the return are provided by the Commissioner; but the failure to procure or receive forms does not excuse a vendor from making a return and paying the taxes collected [Philadelphia Code § 19-1805(4)]. The Department of Revenue issues a Monthly Retail Liquor Sales Tax Coupon Book to simplify tax payments. Call the Liquor Sales Tax Unit at 215-686-6600 for further information. An annual reconciliation of liquor tax is mailed separately and is due by February 28 of the following tax year.

• *Reviews and appeal*

The methods and procedure for review and appeals is the same as those governing reviews and appeals with respect to other local taxes [Philadelphia Code § 19-1805(6)].

• *Penalties and enforcement*

The following are in addition to any other remedy provided by law or equity:

(1) A vendor who willfully fails or refuses to appear in person with his/her records or to permit inspect of records when required to do so, or who willfully falsifies his/her return, or who willfully fails or refuses to file a return and remit taxes is liable for a fine of $300 or imprisonment for not more than 90 days or both [Philadelphia Code § 19-1805(7)(a)].

(2) A vendor who fails to make timely payment of taxes collected is liable for a penalty of 1% per month or fraction thereof on the tax from the time the tax becomes due and interest at the rate of 0.5% per month or fraction thereof. Penalties and interest are paid to the School District of Philadelphia [Philadelphia Code § 19-1805(7)(b)].

(3) The statute of limitations for recovery of unpaid taxes (together with penalties and interest) is the later of six (6) years after a return was due or has been filed. However, this limitation does not apply if the vendor has failed to file a report or if the vendor has filed a fraudulent return (which includes a substantial understatement of sales) [Philadelphia Code § 19-1805(7)(c)].

¶4019 School District Real Estate Tax

The Board of Education is authorized by the Philadelphia City Council to impose an annual tax for school district purposes on real estate within the City of Philadelphia [Philadelphia Code § 19-1801(1)]. Consult the statutes for current rates. For explanation of local real property taxation, see Part XV, beginning at ¶3401.

• *Administration and enforcement*

Except where otherwise provided by law, the Philadelphia school district real estate tax is levied, assessed, and collected in accordance with all provisions, restrictions, rights of notice, appeals, interest, penalties, and such other matters as are applicable to City taxes [Philadelphia Code § 19-1802]. The City real estate tax is discussed at ¶4010. General administration and enforcement provisions are discussed at ¶3705—3714.

¶4020 Philadelphia Cigarette Tax

• *Local Option Cigarette Tax*

Act 131 of 2014 authorizes a $2-per-pack cigarette tax on all cigarettes and little cigars sold in Philadelphia in order to supplement public school funding in the city. This equates to a Philadelphia School District $0.10 cents per cigarette tax. Act 84 of 2016 increased the Pennsylvania cigarette tax to $0.13 cents per cigarette causing the tax on a pack of 20 cigarettes in Philadelphia to be $4.60.

PART XVIII

PITTSBURGH CITY AND SCHOOL DISTRICT TAXES

In This Part

CHAPTER 41
PITTSBURGH TAXES IN GENERAL

¶4101   Scope of Chapter
¶4102   Sources of Authority
¶4103   Administration
¶4104   General Provisions

¶4101 Scope of Chapter

This chapter provides an overview of the tax system of Pittsburgh and the Pittsburgh School District.

¶4102 Sources of Authority

Pittsburgh derives its taxing power from the Local Tax Enabling Act (LTEA), also referred to as Act 511 [53 P.S. § 6924.101 *et seq.*]. The Pittsburgh School District derives its taxing power from the Public School Code [24 P.S. § § 1-101 *et seq.*]. Because the city and the school district are governed by different enabling legislation, the city of Pittsburgh is not required to split the maximum allowable rates of taxation with the School District as required by Act 511 when two local taxing jurisdictions impose the same tax on the same person. Pittsburgh also has local tax ordinances and regulations that apply to city taxes. These should be consulted for details.

• *Restrictions on taxation of broker/dealers*

Pittsburgh has no power to impose, levy, or collect (1) a business income and receipts tax; (2) a mercantile license tax; or (3) any tax on or measured by gross receipts of any regulated financial services institution [53 P.S. § 25942(b)]. A "regulated financial services institution" is an entity that is registered as a broker/dealer under the Securities Exchange Act of 1934 [48 Stat. 881, 15 U.S.C. § 78a *et seq.*] or the Pennsylvania Securities Act of 1972 [Act of December 5, 1972 (P.L. 1280, No. 284)]. This prohibition also applies to an entity affiliated with a broker/dealer to the extent that the entity provides investment fund-related management or administrative services.

¶4103 Administration

The City Treasurer administers and enforces tax provisions in Pittsburgh and is empowered to prescribe, adopt, promulgate, and enforce rules and regulations [Pittsburgh Code § 201.04]. The City Treasurer is charged with the duty to collect and receive taxes, fines, and penalties and to keep a record showing inter alia, the date, amount type of tax paid, and method of payment [Pittsburgh Code § 201.02]. The City Treasurer or agents designated by him or her can examine taxpayer's records to verify the accuracy of returns and amounts of tax due [Pittsburgh Code § 201.05]. The City Treasurer is also authorized to make refunds [Pittsburgh Code § § 203.02, 203.03, 203.04]. The City Treasurer serves as collector of delinquent taxes and is authorized to conduct sales for delinquent taxes on property as provided by statute [Pittsburgh Code § 205.01]. The City Treasurer may sue to compel production of any documents required for audit [Pittsburgh Code § 211.01].

¶4104 General Provisions

This paragraph contains a discussion of provisions of general application to Pittsburgh City and School District taxes. Provisions that apply to a specific tax are discussed along with the specific tax.

• *Payment of tax*

Payment of tax must be made at the time returns are filed [Pittsburgh Code § 203.01]. It is the taxpayers' responsibility to file returns and pay tax when due. Failure to receive or obtain the necessary filing forms does not excuse taxpayers from filing requirements nor exonerate them from penalties. [Pittsburgh Code § 209.05]. The City Treasurer may sue for the recovery of any taxes due [Pittsburgh Code § 211.01].

No Extensions of Time

There is no provision for extension of time for the payment of taxes of Pittsburgh and Pittsburgh School District, and no extensions are ever granted. Taxpayers who do not pay taxes on time are subject to penalties and interest.

• *Refunds*

Claims for refunds must be made within two years from the date of any payment identified as a possible overpayment or duplicate payment [Pittsburgh Code § 203.04]. The City Treasurer is authorized to make refunds of taxes or other charges to which the City is not legally entitled if (1) a certified written claim for the refund is submitted to him or her within two years after the date of payment of the sum involved and (2) the sum is verified [Pittsburgh Code § 203.02]. The refund procedure afforded by Pittsburgh Code § 203.02 if not applicable until all other refund remedies have been exhausted, unless the claim is for recovery of payments made under a provision subsequently held by final judgment of a court of competent jurisdiction to be unconstitutional, invalid, or erroneously interpreted [Pittsburgh Code § 203.03].

• *Penalties and interest*

If for any reason a tax is not paid when due, interest at the rate of 12% per annum on the amount of unpaid tax and an additional penalty of 0.5% of the amount of the unpaid tax for each month or fraction thereof during which the tax remains paid are imposed unless the statute under which a particular tax is imposed provides for a different rate of interest and penalty. Once due and owing, interest and penalty become part of the tax. A taxpayer's good paid belief that no tax is due is no defense to the imposition of penalty. When suit is brought for the recovery of any tax, the person bringing suit is liable for any costs of collection and for any interest and penalty imposed [Pittsburgh Code § 209.04].

¶4103

- *Violations and fines*

The City of Pittsburgh imposes a fine of $500 and costs for any of the following violations [Pittsburgh Code § § 209.02, 209.03]:

(1) Failure, neglect, or refusal to make any required declaration or return.

(2) Failure, neglect, or refusal (as an employer) to remit the tax collected from employees.

(3) Refusal to permit examination of records by the Treasurer or his or her designee.

(4) Filing an incomplete, false, or fraudulent return or attempt to do anything to avoid full disclosure of the amount of his or her net profits or earnings to avoid full payment of any tax.

(5) Divulging information that is confidential under the provisions of Pittsburgh Code § 201.06.

A taxpayer who defaults in payment of fines may be imprisoned for not more than 50 days. The fines imposed under Pittsburgh Code § 209.03 are in addition to any other penalty imposed. Each and every day in violation constitutes a separate offence.

- *Limitation on assessment*

No assessment of tax can be made more than five (5) years after that date on which it should have been paid except where a fraudulent return or no return has been filed [Pittsburgh Code § 211.03].

- *Limitation on time to sue for recovery of tax*

Any suit brought to recover tax must be begun within three (3) years after the later of: (1) the date the tax was due or (2) the date the declaration or return was filed [Pittsburgh Code § 211.02]. This limitation, however, does not prevent the institution of a suit for the collection of any tax due or determined to be due in the following cases:

(1) Where no required declaration or return was filed, there is no limitation.

(2) Where a fraudulent evasion of taxes has occurred, there is not limitation.

(3) Where there is substantial understatement of tax liability of 25% or more not due to fraud, suit must begin within six (6) years.

(4) Where a person has withheld or collected tax and has failed to remit the amount withheld or collected to the City Treasurer, there is no limitation.

(5) Where a person has willfully failed or omitted to withhold or collect any tax required to be withheld or collection, there is no limitation.

PITTSBURGH CITY AND SCHOOL DISTRICT TAXES

CHAPTER 42
PITTSBURGH CITY EARNED INCOME & NET PROFITS TAX

GENERAL

¶4201 Sources of Authority

Pittsburgh levies an earned income tax and net profits tax under the authority of Act 511 [Local Tax Enabling Act, 53 P.S. § 6924.301.1 *et seq.*] and Chapters 245 and 246 of the Pittsburgh Code of City Ordinances.

¶4202 Imposition of Tax

The Pittsburgh tax on earned income is imposed on the salaries, wages, commissions, and other compensation earned by both residents and nonresidents of Pittsburgh for work done or services performed or rendered in Pittsburgh [Pittsburgh Code of City Ordinances, Title 2, Article VII, Ch. 245, § 245.02]. Nonresidents subject to an earned income tax in the jurisdiction in which they are domiciled are exempt. The net profits tax is imposed on the net profits of any business, profession or enterprise conducted in Pittsburgh on residents or nonresidents as owner or proprietor, either individually or in association with some other person or persons [Pittsburgh Code of City Ordinances, Title 2, Article VII, Ch. 245, § 245.02].

• *Nonresident*

A "nonresident" is a person, partnership, association, or other entity domiciled outside the taxing district [53 P.S. § 6913]. A "domicile" is the place where one lives and has his/her permanent home and to which she/he has the intention of returning whenever absent. In the case of businesses, or associations, the domicile is the place considered the center of business affairs and the place where functions are discharged.

• *Earned income*

"Earned income" means "compensation" as defined by 72 P.S. § 7303 (discussed at ¶ 202). Employee business expenses that are deductible for Pennsylvania personal income tax purposes are allowable deductions for earned income tax purposes. The amount of any housing allowance provided to a member of the clergy is not taxable as earned income [53 P.S. § 6913].

¶4202

• *Taxable compensation*

The Pittsburgh earned income tax regulations provide that the following are taxable compensation: salaries, wages, commissions, drawing accounts, bonuses, incentive payments, tips, fees, benefits accruing by virtue of employment (*e.g.,* vacation, holiday, and separation pay); taxes assumed by the employer; fellowships, grants, and stipends that require full-time services (unless the payment is solely for the advancement of the education of the grantee and no primary and material benefit accrues to the grantor). Vacation, holiday, and separation pay are fully taxable if an individual is employed entirely in Pittsburgh and prorated if an employee works only part of the time in Pittsburgh [Pittsburgh Regulations].

• *Net profits*

"Net profits" means the net income from the operation of a business, profession, or other activity, except corporations, determined under 72 P.S. §7303 and the Pennsylvania personal income tax regulations. Net profits are discussed at ¶205.

For taxpayers engaged in the business, profession, or activity of farming, the term "net profits" does not include any of the following [53 P.S. §6913]:

(1) Interest earned on monetary accounts or investment instruments of the farming business.

(2) Gain on the sale of farm machinery.

(3) Gain on the sale of livestock held at least 12 months for draft, breeding, or dairy purposes.

(4) Gain on the sale of other capital assets of the farm.

According to Pittsburgh regulations, net profits include rental income from the operation of a real estate business, gain from the sale of property in a real estate business, royalties, and professional income. If a person performs services both as an employee and as an independent professional, the two types of income are taxed separately. For example, if a physician is employed at a salary at a hospital and also maintains a private office, the salary is taxed as earned income and the income from the private practice is taxed as net profits. If the private practice results in a loss for a tax period, it cannot be used to offset the salary to determine taxable income [Pittsburgh Regulations].

¶4203 Rate

The Pittsburgh earned income and net profit taxes are imposed at the rate of 1% on residents and nonresidents [Pittsburgh Code §245.02]. The school district earned income and net profit taxes (see ¶4402) are imposed at the rate of 2% on residents only.

COMPUTATION OF TAXABLE INCOME

¶4205 Exemptions, Exclusions, and Deductions

Corporations are specifically exempt from the net profits tax [53 P.S. §6913]. Nonresidents are exempt from the earned income tax to the extent they are subject to an earned income tax in their places of residence. This is true even if they work full-time in Pittsburgh. If their places of residence impose an earned income tax at a rate less than 1%, they are subject to the Pittsburgh earned income tax at a rate equal to the difference between 1% and their local rate [Pittsburgh Regulations]. Any person who is beyond the legal power of the city to tax because of statutory or constitutional restrictions is exempt. Institutions, organizations, trusts and foundations operated for public, religious, educational, or charitable purposes, and nonprofit institutions or organizations are exempt [Pittsburgh Code of City Ordinances, Title 2, Article VII, Ch. 246, §246.09].

¶4203

Certain items of income are excluded from the definition of taxable compensation. These are explained at ¶4202.

• *Deduction of expenses*

There are no specifically authorized deductions for the net profits tax. Act 511 states that the net income from the operation of a business, profession, or other *activity*, after deduction of all costs and expenses (except taxes on income), is taxable [53 P.S. §6913; 72 P.S. §7303(a)(2)]. Investment income is excluded from the net profits tax. Pittsburgh regulations provide that ordinarily no deduction will be allowed for expenses that are not deductible for federal income tax purposes. Net losses cannot be carried over to any other year [Pittsburgh Regulations].

Consult current regulations and form instructions for deductibility of unreimbursed employee business expenses.

RETURNS AND PAYMENT OF TAX

¶4210 Forms and Dates

All persons subject to the Pittsburgh earned income tax or net profits tax must file returns annually on or before April 15 for the preceding year. Payment of any tax due (after credit for withholding and estimated payments) must accompany the return. Returns are made on forms prescribed by the city. No extensions of time are allowed for filing returns [53 P.S. §6913; 72 P.S. §7303(a)(2)], Pittsburgh Code of City Ordinances, Title 2, Article VII, Ch. 245, §245.03].

Ordinarily, taxpayers report on a calendar-year basis. However, the City Treasurer is authorized to establish different filing, reporting, and payment dates for taxpayers with fiscal years. Net profits can be reported either on a cash or accrual basis in accordance with the accounting system used. Records to support returns must be kept and maintained for a period of six years [Pittsburgh Regulations].

¶4211 Withholding

Every employer having an office, factory, workshop, branch, warehouse, or other place of business in Pittsburgh who employs at least one person, other than domestic servants, for a salary, wage, commission, or other compensation must register name, address, and any other required information with the City Treasurer within 15 days after becoming an employer and withhold the Pittsburgh earned income tax for all employees. Failure to withhold for employees does not relieve an employer from responsibility for the tax. Willful or negligent failure to make deductions makes the employer liable for payment of taxes that should have been deducted [Pittsburgh Code of City Ordinances, Title 2, Article VII, Ch. 245, §245.04].

• *Withholding returns*

On or before April 30, July 31, October 31, and January 31 (succeeding year), employers must file withholding returns and remit taxes collected to the Treasurer. Employers who withhold, or expect to withhold, an aggregate of $200 per month in earned income taxes, must remit the withheld taxes to the Treasurer, together with a depository form supplied by the Treasurer, on or before the 15th day of February, March, May, June, August, September, November, and December. Depository payments are then taken as a credit on the quarterly returns. Failure to remit withheld taxes on or before the due date results in a penalty of 5% per month or fraction of a month on the underpayment from the due date to date of payment (up to a maximum of 50%) [Pittsburgh Code of City Ordinances, Title 2, Article VII, Ch. 245, §245.04].

Employers must file annual returns and employee returns on or before February 28 of the succeeding year on prescribed forms. Annual returns must show the total amount of salaries, wages, commission, and other compensation paid, the total amount of tax deduction, and the total amount of tax paid to the Treasurer during the preceding calendar year. Employee returns (one for each employee employed for any part of the calendar year) must give name, address, social security number, amount of compensation, amount of tax deducted, amount of tax paid to the Treasurer on the employee's account, and any other information. Employers must furnish two copies of the individual return to each employee. Employee annual returns can be a federal W-2, city W-2, or a listing, as long as it contains all the required information [Pittsburgh Regulations].

¶4212 Estimated Tax Payments

Taxpayers who make or expect to make net profits must file a declaration of estimated net profits on or before April 15 of the current year on a form prescribed by the Treasurer, based on a "good faith" estimate of the current year's income [Pittsburgh Code of City Ordinances, Title 2, Article VII, Chs. 245 and 246, §245.03]. A "good faith" estimate is one which is at least 75% of the amount of tax reported on the final return for the current tax year or the full amount of income reported and paid on the preceding year's return.

Estimated tax due must be paid in installments on April 15, June 15, September 15, and January 15 (following year). Taxpayers who anticipate profits after any one of the four installment dates must file a declaration and pay an installment on the next installment date. For example, a taxpayer who first expects to make a net profit on July 15 must file a declaration on September 15 and make payments on September 15 and January 15. A taxpayer may elect, in lieu of a fourth payment, to file an annual return on or before January 31.

Taxpayers may file adjusted declarations if they anticipate additional net profits or discover that they have made an overestimate. If additional profits are anticipated to be 25% or more of the reported estimate, adjusted declarations are required. Adjusted declarations in the case of overestimates (*i.e.,* profits will be less than originally estimated) are optional [Pittsburgh Regulations].

PITTSBURGH CITY AND SCHOOL DISTRICT TAXES

CHAPTER 43
OTHER PITTSBURGH CITY TAXES

¶4301   Recent Developments

• *Occupational privilege tax*

Effective for the 2005 tax year, the City of Pittsburgh will no longer levy and collect the occupational privilege tax. The occupation tax has been replaced with the Local Services Tax (LST). See ¶4302 for discussion of the Pittsburgh EMST.

• *Mercantile license tax*

Effective for the 2005 tax year, the City and School District of Pittsburgh will no longer levy and collect the mercantile license tax. The tax and license fee for prior years will still be collected [*Bulletin*, City of Pittsburgh, Department of Finance *http://www.city.pittsburgh.pa.us/finance/assets/05_bulletin-tax_changes.pdf*].

¶4302   Local Services Tax (LST)

Law Change

Beginning in 2008, the name of this tax was changed to the "local services tax". Any reference to the emergency and municipal services tax (EMST) in this handbook should be understood to mean the local services tax.

• *Imposition*

Act 222 of 2004 (H.B. 197) amended the Local Tax Enabling Act to authorize municipalities and school districts (except the Pittsburgh School District) to impose an Emergency and Municipal Services Tax (EMST) beginning on or after January 1, 2005 [Act 222, §8]. Beginning in 2008, the Emergency and Municipal Services Tax has been renamed the Local Services Tax (LST). Jurisdictions under the authority of the Local Tax Enabling Act are discussed at ¶3402. The general LST provisions are discussed at ¶3618. The city of Pittsburgh LST provisions are found in Title II, Article VII, Chapter 252 of the Pittsburgh City Code. The regulations issued pursuant to this statute can be found at *http://www.city.pittsburgh.pa.us/finance/assets/forms/2005_EM-1_tax_regs.pdf*.

• *Rate and base*

The LST (which replaces the occupational privilege tax) is imposed at the rate of $52 per year on the privilege of engaging in an occupation [Pittsburgh Code,

§ 252.02(a)]. Any person that has total income from all sources that is less than $12,000 is subject to the tax at a reduced rate of $10 [Pittsburgh Code, § 252.02(b)]. Effective for the 2005 tax year, the City of Pittsburgh will no longer levy and collect an occupational privilege tax. No person is required to pay more than $52 LST in any calendar year irrespective of the number of political subdivisions within which the person may be employed within a given calendar year. In the case of a dispute, a tax receipt (EM-2) of the taxing authority for that calendar year declaring that the taxpayer has made proof payment constitutes *prima facie* evidence of payment to all other political subdivisions [LST Regulations, § 201].

• *Situs*

The situs of the LST is the place of employment [53 P.S. § 6924.301(f)(9)]. For purposes of the Pittsburgh LST, "place of employment" means the actual location where the individual works. It is not the headquarters of the employer where payroll checks are prepared *Frequently Asked Questions: Local Services Tax (LST) http://www.city.pittsburgh.pa.us/finance/forms/2008/2008_ LST_FAQ.pdf.*

More than one occupation or work location: If a person is engaged in more than one occupation or an occupation that requires working in more than one political subdivision during the calendar year, the priority of claim to collect the LST is in the following order:

(1) The political subdivision in which a person maintains a principal office or is principally employed.

(2) The political subdivision in which the person resides and works, if the LST is levied by the political subdivision.

(3) The political subdivision in which a person is employed and which imposes the tax nearest in miles to the person's home.

The place of employment is determined as of the day the taxpayer first becomes subject to the tax during the calendar year.

• *Low-income exclusion*

The LST provisions provide an exclusion for lower income individuals of $12,000. If an employee earns less than $12,000 from all sources, the employee will be entitled to a refund of $42 from the City after the employee has provided adequate proof of earnings for the entire year. The employer will still be required to withhold $52, and it will be the responsibility of employees to file the refund request and supply their W-2s and federal tax return [*Bulletin*, City of Pittsburgh, Department of Finance *http://www.city.pittsburgh.pa.us/finance/assets/05_bulletin-tax_changes.pdf.*].

• *Refunds*

No person is required to pay more than $52 in any calendar year even if the person is employed in more than one municipality.

• *Reports and payment of tax*

The Pittsburgh $52 LST will be collected as a payroll deduction from all employees who work in the City of Pittsburgh and will be reported and paid monthly (unlike the occupation tax, which was reported quarterly).

Examples

Examples of the application of the Pittsburgh LST tax can be found at *http://www.city.pittsburgh.pa.us/finance/assets/forms/2008/2008_LST_faq.pdf.*

¶4302

¶4303 Business Privilege Tax

Repealed

The Pittsburgh business privilege tax has been eliminated for 2010 and forward. No business privilege tax return was due on April 15, 2010; the last business privilege tax was due in 2009 [*Tax Bulletin for 2010*, Pittsburgh Department of Finance].

¶4304 Amusement Tax

Pittsburgh imposes an amusement tax for the privilege of attending or engaging in any amusement [City Code, Title 2, Chapter 241]. The tax is imposed on the patrons, but the producers of the entertainment are responsible for collection of the tax and filing returns. The Pittsburgh amusement tax is administered by the Pittsburgh City Treasurer.

• *Limitations*

The Local Tax Enabling Act (LTEA) imposes some restrictions on Pittsburgh's authority to impose an amusement tax:

(1) *Exercise, fitness, and health clubs:* Local authorities do not have the authority to impose an amusement tax on membership, membership dues, fees or assessments, contributions or monetary charges of any character paid by the general public (or a limited or selected number thereof) for the use of facilities the predominant purpose or nature of which is exercise, fitness, health maintenance, improvement or rehabilitation, health or nutrition education, or weight control [53 P.S. § 6924.301.1(f)(13)].

(2) *Ski facilities:* The rate on admission to ski facilities cannot exceed 10%, and the tax base upon which the tax is levied cannot exceed 40% of the cost of the lift ticket, which includes all costs of admissions to the ski facility [53 P.S. § 6924.311(9)].

(3) *Golf courses:* The rate on admission to golf courses cannot exceed 10%, and the tax base upon which the tax is levied cannot exceed 40% of the greens fee, which includes all costs of admissions to the golf course [53 P.S. § 6924.311(10)].

(4) *Bowling alleys:* The rate on admission to bowling alleys or bowling lanes cannot exceed 10%; and the tax base upon which the tax is levied cannot exceed 40% of the admission charge [53 P.S. § 6924.311(11)].

• *Definitions*

Amusement: All manner and forms of entertainment (*e.g.,* sports events, circuses, movies, recreational activities such as tennis, golf, and swimming) except those private annual affairs sponsored by nonprofit organizations for members and their guests at which the admission charges equal or approximate expenses [Pittsburgh Code § 241.01(a)].

Established price: Regular monetary charge of any character (including donations and contributions) fixed and exacted or in any manner received (directly or indirectly) by producers from the general public (or a limited or selected number thereof) for the privilege of attending or engaging in any entertainment or amusement [Pittsburgh Code § 241.01(b)]. The established price for certain specified situations is as follows:

(1) *Charge included in price of food, service, or merchandise:* If entertainment or amusement is conducted at any place (*e.g.,* roof garden, night club, cabaret) where the charge is wholly or in part included in the price paid for refreshments,

service, or merchandise, the amount subject to the amusement tax is deemed to be 10% of the amount paid for refreshments, service, or merchandise [Pittsburgh Code § 241.01(b)(1)].

(2) *Social clubs and fraternal organizations:* When amusement is conducted at a social club or fraternal organization that also furnishes entertainment for which a separate charge is not made, the established price is 50% of the gross receipts [Pittsburgh Code § 241.01(b)(2)].

(3) *Benefits for charitable organizations:* Where admission is obtained to any amusement (a) solely or partly by a contribution or donation; (b) there is no fixed price for such amusement; and (c) not less than 75% of the proceeds of the amusement inure exclusively to the benefit of a charitable organization, the established price is 25% of the total donation, contribution and other monetary charge [Pittsburgh Code § 241.01(b)(3)].

(4) *Amusements sponsored by charitable organizations:* Where a fixed price has been established for the general public for an amusement sponsored by a charitable organization, the fixed price is the established price for purposes of the amusement tax without regard to the requirement that not less than 75% of the proceeds inure exclusively to the benefit of a charitable organization [Pittsburgh Code § 241.01(b)(3)].

Patron: Anyone participating in the privilege of engaging in an amusement [Pittsburgh Code § 241.01(c)].

Place of amusement: Any place (indoors or outdoors) within Pittsburgh where the general public (or a limited or selected number thereof) may, upon payment of an established price, attend or engage in any amusement [Pittsburgh Code § 241.01(d)].

Producer: Any person conducting a place of amusement where the general public or a limited or selected number thereof, may, upon the payment of an established price, attend or engage in any amusement [Pittsburgh Code § 241.01(e)].

• *Permit required*

Producers cannot begin or continue to conduct any form of amusement at any place of amuse (permanent or temporary) or any itinerant form of amusement within Pittsburgh without an amusement permit [Pittsburgh Code § 241.02]. Applications for permits and payment of fees are made to the Treasurer [Pittsburgh Code § 241.03(a)]. Permits are not assignable, are valid only for the persons in whose names they are issued, and must at all times be conspicuously displayed at the places for which they are issues [Pittsburgh Code § 241.03(b)]. Failure to comply with any of the amusement tax provisions may result in the suspension or revocation of permits [Pittsburgh Code § 241.03(c)].

• *Rate of tax*

The Pittsburgh amusement tax is currently imposed at the rate of 5% upon the fee charged as the established price for the privilege of attending or engaging in any amusement [Pittsburgh Code § 241.04(1)]. The total ticket price includes the amusement tax; the tax due is computed by multiplying the established price by 0.04762 [Instructions, Pittsburgh Form AT 2015].

Box seats: The tax on permanent boxes or seats is computed on the price or rental charged for the boxes or seats [Pittsburgh Code § 241.04(c)].

• *Free admissions and reduced admission rates*

If persons are admitted free to any place of amusement where other persons are charged an established price, the tax (to be paid by the person admitted) on the free admission must be computed on the established price charged to other patrons for the same or similar accommodations. If persons are admitted at a reduced rate, the tax is computed on the reduced rate. However, children under the age of 12, disabled veterans, and members of the armed services when on active duty and in uniform are not required to pay tax when admitted free of charge [Pittsburgh Code § 241.04(b)].

• *Collection, reports, and payment of tax*

Producers are responsible for collecting amusement tax and remitting the tax collected to the City. Amusement tax reports must be filed on or before the 15th day of the month following the billing period for permanent types of amusement [Pittsburgh Code § 241.05(d)]. Producers of temporary or itinerant types of amusement (*i.e.,* an amusement that is conducted in the City for a period of time not exceeding 30 days) must file reports promptly after each performance [Pittsburgh Code § 241.05(e)]. If an operator fails to collect tax from a patron, the operator is liable for tax upon the full consideration received from the patron [Pittsburgh Code § 253.02(c)].

• *Penalty and interest*

A producer who neglects or refuses to make any report and payment must pay a penalty of 5% of the amount of the tax for each month (or fraction thereof) during which the tax remains unpaid together with interest at the statutory rate authorized in Chapter 209 [Pittsburgh Code § 241.05(a)].

¶4305 Realty Transfer Tax

The Pittsburgh realty transfer tax is imposed on transfers of interests in real property located within Pittsburgh [Pittsburgh Code of City Ordinances, Title 2, Article VII, Chs. 255 and 256]. It is where the property is located, not where the document is made, that determines taxability. The Pittsburgh realty transfer tax is imposed on the person who accepts delivery of any document (the grantee). The City Treasurer is responsible for administration of this tax. The tax is imposed at the rate of 2% of the document's value. An additional tax of 1% is imposed by the Pittsburgh School District (see ¶ 4405).

The statute provides for penalties for noncompliance. Consult the statute for details. There are no specific provisions for refunds, but see ¶ 4611. The Pittsburgh realty transfer law is similar to the Commonwealth realty transfer law, which is explained at ¶ 3304.

¶4306 Property Tax

Pittsburgh levies a property tax at the rate of 8.0600 mills on each dollar of assessed valuation. For a detailed explanation of the local real property taxes, see Chapter 35.

¶4307 Parking Tax

Pittsburgh imposes a parking tax upon each parking transaction by a patron of a nonresidential parking place [Pittsburgh Code § 253.02(1)]. Although the tax is imposed on parking patrons, it is the responsibility of parking operators to collect and remit the tax [Pittsburgh Code § 253.05]. The Pittsburgh parking tax is administered by the Pittsburgh City Treasurer.

• *Definitions*

Consideration: The payment or compensation of any nature received by an operator from a patron from a transaction involving the parking or storing of a motor vehicle by the patron. "Consideration," however, does not include the parking tax imposed on a transaction [Pittsburgh Code § 253.01(h)].

Nonresidential parking place (parking place): The term "nonresidential parking place" includes any place within Pittsburgh (whether wholly or partially enclosed or open) at which vehicles are parked or stored for any period of time in return for a consideration and any parking area or garage operated exclusively by an owner or lessee of a hotel, an apartment hotel, tourist court, or trailer park to the extent that the parking area or garage is provided to guests or tenants of the hotel, tourist court, or trailer park for an additional consideration [Pittsburgh Code § 253.01(b)]. The term "nonresidential parking place" does not, however, include areas or garages leased to residents in connection with, and as an accessory to, the occupancy of a dwelling unit in Pittsburgh [Pittsburgh Code § 253.01(b)(1)].

Operator: Any person who conducts the operation of a parking place or receives consideration for the parking or storage of motor vehicles at parking places, including (but not limited to) any governmental body, governmental subdivision, municipal corporation, public authority nonprofit corporation, or any person operating as an agent of one of these entities [Pittsburgh Code § 253.01(f)].

Patron: Any natural person who drives a vehicle into a parking place for the purpose of parking or storing the vehicle for any length of time or any natural person who has a vehicle in his or her custody taken by a parking valet to be parked or stored at a nonresidential parking place [Pittsburgh Code § 253.01(a)].

Resident: Any natural person who occupies a dwelling unit within Pittsburgh for a period of more than 30 consecutive days [Pittsburgh Code § 253.01(c)].

Transaction: The activity involved in the parking or storing of a motor vehicle at a nonresidential parking place for a consideration [Pittsburgh Code § 253.01(g)].

• *Rate, returns, and payment of tax*

The Pittsburgh parking tax is imposed on parking patrons at a percentage of the consideration paid for the transaction and is collected from patrons by operators, who must remit the tax to the City. The 37.5% rate of tax may be changed for any tax year by legislative actions of the mayor and City Council. Therefore, it is advisable to check § 253.02 of the Pittsburgh Code to determine the effective rate for the current tax year [Pittsburgh Parking Tax Regulations, § 201]. Operators must file parking tax returns with the City Treasurer on or before the 15th day of each month for the preceding month's collections. Payment of tax must accompany the return [Pittsburgh Code § 253.05].

Missing tickets: Whenever tickets or stubs issued during the preceding month are missing or unaccounted for at the time the parking tax return is filed, the operator must report the number missing and remit a fee equal to the maximum daily rate for the missing tickets [Pittsburgh Code § 253.05].

• *Registration and annual license*

Operators who begin or intend to begin operation of a nonresidential parking place must register with the City Treasurer before commencing business [Pittsburgh Code § 253.03(a)]. Operators of parking places must also obtain (before beginning operations) an annual license for each parking place from the Superintendent of the Bureau of Building Inspection. Licenses are not transferable between one operator and another or between one parking place and another; and they must be returned to the Superintendent of the Bureau of Building Inspection by any operator who ceases to operate a parking place.

• *Recordkeeping requirements*

Retention period: Parking place operators must retain all books, records, daily record sheets, and ticket stubs for a period of five (5) years subsequent to the year of the transaction, and this requirements applies to all cases unless advance written permission to destroy the records has been obtained from the City Treasurer [Pittsburgh Code § 253.04(a)(1)].

Tickets: Operators must issue tickets to all patrons, in numerical sequence without interruption [Pittsburgh Code § 253.04(b)]. Electro-mechanical devices that meet the requirements of §253.04(b)(1)(A) or 253.04(b)(1)(B) of the Pittsburgh Code and meet the specifications of the License Officer may be used to issue tickets. At least five (5) days prior to using tickets, operators must certify in writing to the Treasurer (1) the beginning and ending serial numbers; (2) the location of the nonresidential parking place at which they will be used; (3) the location at which they may be inspected by the Treasurer; and (4) and any other identifying information required by the Treasurer [Pittsburgh Code §253.04(b)(2)]. It is unlawful for any operator to use tickets for which the required information has not been delivered to the Treasurer at least five (5) days prior to use [Pittsburgh Code §253.04(b)(3)].

• *Penalties*

If an operator neglects, refuses, or fails to file or pay, a penalty of 5% of the amount of tax is added for every month or fraction of a month that the tax remains unpaid, but the penalty cannot exceed 50% [Pittsburgh Code §253.06]. In addition, operators who violate any parking tax provisions is subject to a penalty of $1,000 for the first occurrence, $2,000 for the second occurrence, and $3,000 for the third and all subsequent occurrences [Pittsburgh Code §253.07].

¶4308 Institution and Service Privilege Tax

• *Imposition and rate*

An institution and service privilege tax is imposed at the rate of six mills on the gross annual receipts of persons engaging in any institutional or nonprofit service in Pittsburgh [Pittsburgh Code § 247.02].

• *"Institution" defined*

An "institution" is any organization, foundation, corporation, or unincorporated association operating under a nonprofit charter or organized as a nonprofit entity by the Commonwealth, including (but not limited to) hospitals, nursing homes, colleges, universities, schools other than elementary and secondary schools, cemeteries, veterans organizations, and all other organizations that provide service to the general public [Pittsburgh Code §247.01(c)]. The term "institution" does not include any political subdivision, any agency of government (federal Commonwealth, or local), any elementary or secondary school within Pittsburgh, or a truly public charity in respect to transactions directly related to its principal charitable purpose.

Exemption: Pittsburgh provides for a $20,000 exemption from the ISP tax [Pittsburgh City Ordinance #6 of 1996].

• *Computation of tax*

Persons who have been in business at least one full year prior to the beginning of a taxable year compute their annual receipts upon the actual receipts received during the preceding calendar year. Persons who have been in business for less than one full year prior to the beginning of a taxable year compute their tax upon the actual gross receipts generated during the first month service is rendered multiplied by twelve (12). Persons who begin service subsequent to the beginning of a taxable year compute their tax upon the gross receipts generated by the service during the first month of the service multiplied by the number of months or fraction thereof remaining in the taxable year [Pittsburgh Code §247.03].

• *Gross receipts*

"Gross receipts" include cash, credits, property of any kind received in or allocable to Pittsburgh for any transaction or service rendered, including payments from insurance or other third-party payments for the cost of service [Pittsburgh Code §247.01(d)]. Gross receipts, however, do not include receipts subject to the mercantile license tax, business privilege tax, earned income tax, or any taxes collected as an agent for any government, membership dues and fees, contributions unrelated to individual services, or assessments that fall equally upon all members. Any activity conducted by a beneficial, charitable, religious, political or educational nonprofit corporation, foundation, or unincorporated association, the receipts of which inure in their entirely to the entity are excluded from the institution and service privilege tax if the activity is sponsored and conducted solely and completely by and for that entity by unpaid volunteers [Pittsburgh Code § 247.01(d)(2)].

¶4309 Payroll Tax

• *Enabling legislation*

The Pittsburgh payroll tax is authorized by 53 P.S. § 6924.303. The Pittsburgh provisions are found in Title II, Article VII, Chapter 258, of the Pittsburgh City Code. The Pittsburgh payroll tax regulations can be found at http://www.city.pittsburgh.pa.us/finance/assets/forms/2006/2006_et-1_payroll_tax_regs.pdf.

• *Imposition, base, and rate*

The city of Pittsburgh levies a payroll tax (which is separate and distinct from the earned income tax) on employers. The payroll tax is levied at the rate of 0.55% (0.0055) on payroll amounts generated as a result of an employer conducting business activity within Pittsburgh [Pittsburgh Code § 258.02]. The payroll tax is not imposed on the salary expense of workers who perform services outside Pittsburgh. See Examples 2 and 3 below.

Other Entities

The Pittsburgh payroll tax is also imposed on the net earnings distribution of sole proprietors, individuals, partnerships, associations, joint ventures, or other entities that work, provide service or makes sales within the city of Pittsburgh [Pittsburgh Payroll Tax Regulations, § 102].

For this purpose the term "employer" means any person conducting business activity within Pittsburgh, except for a government entity, and the phrase "payroll expense or amount" means all compensation earned by an employee or by a self-employed individual [Pittsburgh Code § 258.01].

No Reduction of Compensation or Benefits

The law states that an employer cannot offset the amount of payroll tax paid by reducing compensation or benefits paid to employees [53 P.S. § 6924.303(f)]. Under no circumstances should the payroll tax be deducted from the employees' wages [Pittsburgh Payroll Tax Regulations § 202(a)].

• *Conducting business*

A person is deemed to be conducting business within Pittsburgh who engages, hires, employs, or contracts with one or more individuals as employees or is self-employed and, in addition, does at least one of the following [Pittsburgh Code § 258.01(a)]:

(1) Maintains a fixed place of business within Pittsburgh.

(2) Owns or leases real property within Pittsburgh for business purposes.

(3) Maintains a stock of tangible personal property in Pittsburgh for sale in the ordinary course of business.

(4) Conducts continuous solicitation within Pittsburgh related to the business.

(5) Utilizes the streets of Pittsburgh in connection with the operation of the business (other than for the mere transportation from a site outside Pittsburgh, through the city, to a destination outside of Pittsburgh).

Rental Activities and Passive Investments

A person who, in return for rental income, rents, leases, or hires real or personal property to others is deemed to be engaged in a business. A person, however, is not deemed to be engaged in business solely by reason of the receipt of income for which no services were rendered [Pittsburgh Code § 258.01(a)].

- *Computation of tax*

General rule: The payroll amount attributable to Pittsburgh is determined by applying an apportionment factor to total payroll expenses based on that portion of payroll expense that the total number of days an employee, partner, member, shareholder, or other individual works within Pittsburgh bears to the total number of days an employee or person works within and outside of Pittsburgh [Pittsburgh Payroll Tax Regulations § 202(b); 53 P.S. § 6924.303(a)].

Alternative Apportionment Method

The regulations also indicate that apportionment can be calculated by using working hours rather than days [Pittsburgh Payroll Tax Regulations § 102(d)].

Temporary business: An employer that conducts business in Pittsburgh on a temporary, seasonal, or itinerant basis calculates the tax on the total compensation earned while in the City of Pittsburgh [Pittsburgh Payroll Tax Regulations § 202(d)]. See Example 4 below. A "temporary, seasonal, or itinerant business" means an employer whose presence in Pittsburgh is of a duration of 120 days or less [Pittsburgh Payroll Tax Regulations § 203].

Discontinuing business: Taxpayers who cease to carry on a business during any tax quarter after having paid the payroll tax for the entire quarter shall, upon making proper application on a form obtained from the Treasurer, be entitled to receive a prorated refund of the tax paid based upon the period of time the taxpayer was not in business during the tax quarter. If a taxpayer discontinues business during a tax quarter before payment of the tax becomes due for the quarter, that person may apportion the tax and pay an amount to be computed by multiplying the payroll expense for the preceding tax quarter by a fraction the numerator of which is the number of days in business during the quarter and the denominator of which is the total number of days in the quarter. The final return is due 10 days after discontinuation of business [Pittsburgh Payroll Tax Regulations § 202(3)].

Charitable organizations: Charitable organizations calculate the tax that would otherwise be attributable to Pittsburgh and file a return but pay only the tax on that portion of its payroll expense attributable to business activity for which a tax may be imposed pursuant to IRC § 511. If the charity has purchased or is operating branches, affiliates, subsidiaries, or other business entities that do not independently meet the standards of the "institutions of Purely Public Charity Act," the tax must be paid on the payroll attributable to such for-profit branches, affiliates, or subsidiaries, whether or not the employees are leased or placed under the auspices of the charity's umbrella or parent organization [Pittsburgh Payroll Tax Regulations § 202(f)]. See Example 15 below. A charitable organization may be permitted to provide services to the city in lieu of some or all of its payroll tax due [53 P.S. § 6902(a.1)].

¶4309

CAUTION: *Nonprofit vs. Charitable*

Not all not-for-profit organizations qualify as charitable organizations. Nonprofits are subject to the payroll tax unless they also qualify as a purely public charity. Purely public charities are discussed at ¶ 705. Note, also, that nonprofits remain subject to the institution and service privilege tax, discussed at ¶ 4308.

• *Registration*

Every person having an office, factory, workshop, branch, warehouse, or other place of business (including banks, schools, hospitals, nonprofits, and trade associations) located in Pittsburgh or outside Pittsburgh who, during any tax year, performs work or renders services in whole or in part in Pittsburgh, who has not previously registered, must, within 15 days, register with the Treasurer its name and address and provide such other information as the Treasurer may require [Pittsburgh Code § 258.05].

• *Returns and payment of tax*

Employers must file payroll tax returns quarterly and make quarterly payments of tax. The correctness of returns must be certified by employers, and Pittsburgh may audit, examine, or inspect the books, records, or accounts of all employers subject to the payroll tax [Pittsburgh Code § 258.04; 53 P.S. § 6924.303(c)]. The quarterly returns are calculated and due as indicated in the following table [Pittsburgh Code § 258.06; Pittsburgh Payroll Tax Regulations § 301(d)]:

Quarter	Tax Based on Payroll Expense of the Months of	Due Date
First	October, November, December of preceding year	February 28
Second	January, February, March of current year	May 31
Third	April, May, June of current year	August 31
Fourth	July, August, September of current year	November 30

• *Discontinuation of business*

An employer who discontinues business or ceases operations before December 31 of the current tax year must file and pay a return within 10 days after discontinuing business or ceasing operation [Pittsburgh Payroll Tax Regulations § 301(e)].

• *Recordkeeping and examination of books*

Records: Taxpayers and employers liable for the payroll tax are required to keep records that will enable the filing of true and accurate returns of the tax, and the records must be preserved for a period of not less than the later of three years from the filing date or due date [Pittsburgh Payroll Tax Regulations § 403].

Examination of books and records: Agents designated by the Treasurer are authorized to examine the books, papers, and records of any employer or supposed employer, or of any taxpayer or supposed taxpayer, in order to verify the accuracy of any declaration or return or, if no declaration or return was filed, to ascertain the tax due [Pittsburgh Payroll Tax Regulations § 402(a)]. Taxpayers must make these records available to the Treasurer either by producing them in a Pittsburgh location or by paying for the Treasurer's expense in traveling to the place where the records are regularly kept [Pittsburgh Payroll Tax Regulations § 402(b)].

Audits: If, as a result of an examination conducted by the Treasurer, a return is found to be incorrect, the Treasurer is authorized to assess and collect any underpayments of the payroll tax. If no return has been filed and a tax is found to be due, the tax actually due may be assessed and collected with or without the formality of obtaining a return from the taxpayer. Deficiency assessments (*i.e.*, where a taxpayer has filed a return but is found to owe additional tax) include taxes for up to three

¶4309

years prior to the date when the deficiency is assessed. Where no return was filed, there is no limit for the period of assessment [Pittsburgh Payroll Tax Regulations § 404].

● *Enforcement*

Pittsburgh may bring suit for the recovery of LST due or unpaid within the later of (1) three (3) years after the tax is due or (2) three (3) years after the return was filed [53 P.S. § 6924.303(g)]. There is no statute of limitations in the case of (1) failure to file or (2) a fraudulent return [53 P.S. § 6924.303(g)(1), (2)]. In the case of substantial understatement of tax liability of 25% or more and no fraud, suit must begin within six (6) years [53 P.S. § 6924.303(g)(3)].

● *Interest and penalties*

Interest on unpaid tax: If for any reason the tax is not paid when due, interest at the rate of 6% per annum on the amount of unpaid tax and an additional penalty of 1% of the amount of the unpaid tax for each month or fraction thereof during which the tax remains unpaid will be added and collected [Pittsburgh Code § 258.07].

Costs of collection: If suit is brought for the recovery of the tax, the employer will, in addition, be liable for the costs of collection and the interest and penalties imposed.

False statement by employer: An employer who willfully makes a false statement on the employer's return is, upon conviction, guilty of a misdemeanor of the second degree and subject to a fine of not more than $2,000 or to imprisonment for not more than two (2) years, or both [53 P.S. § 6902(I)(1)].

Refusal to appear for examination of books: A person who willfully fails or refuses to appear before the collector in person with the employer's books, records, or accounts for examination when required or willfully refuses to permit inspection of books, records, or accounts in the person's custody or control is, upon conviction, guilty of a misdemeanor and subject to a fine of not more than $500 or to imprisonment for not more than six (6) months, or both [53 P.S. § 6924.303(I)(2)].

For more information on interest and penalties, see Article V of the Pittsburgh Payroll Tax Regulations.

● *Taxpayer remedies*

Treasurer's Hearings: Any person aggrieved by an assessment by the Treasurer may (within 90 days after the date of notice of the assessment) request a Treasurer's Hearing on a form obtained from the Treasurer for that purpose. The taxpayer may be required to attend a hearing [Pittsburgh Payroll Tax Regulations § 601].

Timely Request for Treasurer's Hearing Important

If a taxpayer fails to request a Treasurer's Hearing in a timely manner, the taxpayer waives the right to contest any element of the assessment and the taxpayer's failure to challenge the Treasurer's adjudication will be construed as an admission by that party as to the propriety of the assessment [Pittsburgh Payroll Tax Regulations § 601(b)]. Note that the 90-day period for requesting a Treasurer's Hearing begins with the date of notice of the assessment, not the date received by the taxpayer.

Review of tax refund request: A taxpayer may request a Treasurer's Hearing so that a tax refund request can be reviewed [Pittsburgh Payroll Tax Regulations § 601(c)].

● *Appeals*

Any person aggrieved by the decision of the Treasurer has the right to make an appeal in accordance with the Taxpayers Bill of Rights Act (discussed at ¶ 4606). Any appeal must be commenced within 30 days of the date of the notice of the Treasurer's decision. If an appeal is not timely filed, the aggrieved party waives the right to

¶4309

contest any element of the Treasurer's adjudication, and the taxpayer's failure to challenge the Treasurer's decision will be construed as an admission by that party as to the propriety of the Treasurer's decision [Pittsburgh Payroll Tax Regulations § 602].

Hearing/Appeal Does Not Suspend Accrual of Penalty and Interest

No hearing or appeal will operate to suspend the accrual of penalty and interest from the date the tax was due to the date it is actually paid [Pittsburgh Payroll Tax Regulations § 602].

• *Payment under protest*

The Treasurer will accept payments of disputed tax amounts under protest pending appeals. However, a request for refund of payments under protest must be filed in accordance with § 604 of the Pittsburgh Payroll Tax Regulations (discussed below) [Pittsburgh Payroll Tax Regulations § 603].

• *Refunds*

A taxpayer who has overpaid the payroll tax or believes he or she is not liable for the payroll tax may file a written request on an amended tax return (ET-1) with the Department of Finance for a refund or credit of the tax. A request for refund or credit must be made within the later of (1) three years of the due date for filing the report or (2) one year after actual payment of the tax. If no report is required, the request must be made within the later of (1) three years after the due date for payment or (2) one year after actual payment [Pittsburgh Payroll Tax Regulations § 604(1)].

Amounts paid as result of notice of underpayment: For amounts paid as a result of notice asserting or informing a taxpayer of an underpayment, a written request for refund must be filed with the Department of Finance within one year of the date of the payment [Pittsburgh Payroll Tax Regulations § 604(b)].

Erroneous refund recovery: The Treasurer may sue for recovery of an erroneous refund if suit for recovery is begun two years after making the refund, except that the suit may be brought within five years if any part of the refund was induced by fraud or misrepresentation of material fact [Pittsburgh Payroll Tax Regulations § 604(c)].

• *Payroll tax examples*

The following examples, adapted from the regulations, illustrate the application of Pittsburgh's payroll tax provisions [Pittsburgh Payroll Tax Regulations § 203]:

Example 1—Payroll tax not deductible from employee salary: Babbage Company has an office in and performs work in Pittsburgh, and all of its employees' salaries are taxable. John Smith has a salary of $1,000 for the current period, all of which is subject to the Pittsburgh payroll tax. Babbage's payroll tax due on Smith's salary is $5.50 ($1,000 × 0.0055), and it cannot be deducted from Smith's salary. The entry below, which applies whether Babbage has one employee or more than one employee, illustrates the recording of Smith's salary. Note that no deduction is made for the $5.50 payroll tax imposed on the employer.

	DEBIT	CREDIT
Salary expense - John Smith	1,000.00	
Federal income tax payable		100.00
State income tax payable		28.00
City of Pittsburgh & school wage tax payable		30.00
FICA tax - employee's share		67.00
Medicare tax - employee's share		10.00
Healthcare deduction		2.00
Salary payable - John Smith		763.00

Salary expense: Payroll expense means all compensation earned by an employee, including commissions, bonuses, stock options, and incentive payments. Section 125 plans for medical or other cafeteria plan items are not allowable deductions. Deferred compensation plans (*e.g.*, 401(K) plans) are not deductible.

Employer's portion of payroll taxes: The employer's portion of payroll taxes that do not appear on the employee's W-2 (*e.g.*, employer's share of FICA, Medicare, unemployment, and payroll expense taxes) is not taxable for payroll tax purposes.

Example 2—Employer does business both inside and outside Pittsburgh: Abercrombie Company is located in Pittsburgh and performs construction work both inside and outside the city. The following information is available for Abercrombie:

Fourth-Quarter Payroll Expense	
General office staff	$90,000.00
Construction workers' expense for work in Pittsburgh	$1,000,000.00
Construction workers' expense for work outside Pittsburgh	$500,000.00

The general office staff payroll expense and the workers' expense for work performed in Pittsburgh are taxable for Pittsburgh payroll tax purposes. The construction workers' expense for work outside Pittsburgh is not taxable. Thus, the total payroll expense subject to tax is $1,090,000, and Abercrombie's payroll tax on this amount is $5,995 ($1,090,000 × 0.0055). The return for this tax is due by February 28 of the following calendar year.

Example 3—Offices both inside and outside Pittsburgh: Aberman Corporation has two offices—one in Pittsburgh and one in Philadelphia. Use the total gross payroll of the employees who work in Pittsburgh (same as Example 2) and multiply it by 0.0055 to determine Aberman's payroll tax liability. If the employees who work in the Philadelphia office do no work in Pittsburgh, their gross compensation should not be included in the tax base.

Example 4—Business in Pittsburgh for one day: Gade Company, a general contractor with an office located outside Pittsburgh, comes into Pittsburgh for a one-day job. Gade is subject to the payroll tax for this one-day job. Gade should calculate the tax on the employee's total compensation earned while in Pittsburgh and pay the tax due within 10 days.

Example 5—Nonresident general contractor: Naber Company, a nonresident general contractor, is located in Ohio. Naber renovates a building in downtown Pittsburgh. Naber is subject to the Pittsburgh payroll tax. Naber should determine the total payroll expense attributable to work done in Pittsburgh and compute the payroll tax on that amount.

Example 6—Regulated companies: Barker Bank is located in Pittsburgh. It is subject to the Pittsburgh payroll tax. Regulated businesses located in Pittsburgh (*e.g.*, banks, beer distributors, taverns, stock brokers, insurance companies) are subject to the payroll tax. Only government entities are excluded from the requirements of filing a payroll tax return.

Example 7—Starts after beginning of year: Machen Corporation began conducting business in Pittsburgh on May 15. Its first return is due August 31 and is based on the previous quarter's payroll from May 15 through June 30.

Example 8—Proration of tax: Yates Corporation goes out of business and stops conducting business in Pittsburgh on November 1. The payroll expense for July, August, and September was $30,000, and the payroll expense for October 1 through November 1 as $11,000. All of Yates's work was conducted in Pittsburgh. Yates's tax must be prorated. The numerator is 32 days (October 1 through November 1), and the denominator is 92 days (October 1 through December 1). The amount of payroll expenses subject to tax is $10,434.90 (32/92 × $30,000). The amount of tax due for the last quarter is $57.39 ($10,434.90 × 0.0055). Yates's last return is due November 11.

Example 9—Partner's draw: During the first quarter Jason Deals, a partner in JKL Partnership, made draws totaling $7,000. This draw is subject to the payroll tax. A partner's draw serves as a quasi-salary account until the partnership income is determined for the individual partners. Taxable draws are limited by the amount of draws or net income for that partner, whichever is less.

Example 10—Sole proprietor —Distribution equals net profit: Preston is a sole proprietor who operates a pizza shop. During the year Preston takes out $5,000 in the first quarter, $5,000 in the second quarter, $5,000 in the third quarter, and $15,000 in the fourth quarter. Preston's net profit for the year is $30,000. All of Preston's distributions ($30,000) are subject to the payroll tax.

Example 11—Sole proprietor —Distribution less than net profit: Quentin, a sole proprietor, takes $25,000 out of the business during the year, and his net profit was $30,000. The taxable distribution is $25,000.

Example 12—Sole proprietor —Distribution more than net profit: Royce, a sole proprietor takes $50,000 out of the business for the year, and the net profit was $30,000. Taxable distribution is $30,000.

Example 13—Medical practice outside Pittsburgh: Cardiac Surgery operates its business in an office outside Pittsburgh. Work is performed in hospitals inside Pittsburgh. Cardiac Surgery is subject to the payroll tax for the time that work is performed in Pittsburgh hospitals and/or locations. The payroll amount attributable to Pittsburgh is determined by applying an apportionment factor to total payroll expenses based on that portion of payroll that the total amount of time an employee, partner, member, shareholder, or other individual works within Pittsburgh bears to the total amount of time such employee or person works both within and outside Pittsburgh.

Example 14—Rental property: Samantha owns five rental properties located in Pittsburgh. Samantha has no employees. A person is not deemed to be engaged in business solely by reason of the receipt of income from passive investments for which no services are rendered. Samantha is not subject to the payroll tax. If, however, Samantha hires an employee, the employ's wages would be subject to the payroll tax.

Example 15—Profit center in nonprofit organization: NP Hospital (NPH) (a purely public charity) has a gift shop in which it sells shirts and other sports items. NPH pays federal taxes under IRC § 511 by filing Form 990T. The payroll expense incurred to operate the gift shop is subject to the payroll tax.

¶4310 Nonresident Sports Facility Usage Fee

Pittsburgh levies (under the authority of 53 P.S. § 6924.304) a license fee (referred to herein as "usage fee") equal to 3% of earned income upon each nonresident who uses a publicly funded facility to engage in an athletic event or otherwise render a performance for which a nonresident receives remuneration [Pittsburgh Code § 271.02]. A "publicly funded facility" is any sports stadium or arena in Pittsburgh that has been constructed or maintained (in whole or in part) through the use of public funds [Usage Fee Regulations § 101]. The usage fee is effective January 1, 2005, and is applicable to the calendar year beginning January 1 and ending December 30. Those individuals liable for the fee are exempt from any earned income tax imposed by Pittsburgh pursuant to Act 222 of 2005 (H.B. 197) and any such tax imposed under § 652.1 of the Public School Code of 1949 [53 P.S. § 6924.304; Pittsburgh Code § 271.06].

Sports Facility Usage Fee/Earned Income Tax Difference

The sports facility usage fee applies to every nonresident of the city of Pittsburgh; the earned income tax applies to nonresidents of the Commonwealth.

• *Who must file a return*

Employers: Employers who employ one or more nonresident employees who earn compensation as the result of services performed within Pittsburgh, whose services require the use of a publicly funded facility to engage in an athletic event for which a nonresident receives remuneration, are required to withhold and remit to the Treasurer (*i.e.,* the Director and/or Department of Finance) the usage fee. In the event that the employer fails, refuses, or neglects to withhold or remit the usage fee, or any portion thereof, the employer becomes personally liable for payment of the usage fee and any applicable penalty [Usage Fee Regulations § 102(a)].

Other users: Other users who engage in events held at a publicly funded facility within Pittsburgh for which the user receives compensation (*e.g.*, entertainers, performers), who are not residents of Pittsburgh, are also subject to the usage fee [Usage Fee Regulations § 102(b)].

* *Computation of usage fee*

Allocation of wages for professional sports teams' players: Nonresident players on a professional sports team are subject to the usage fee when they perform for compensation in Pittsburgh at a publicly funded facility. These include players on the professional or major league level. Those on the practice squad or the minor league level are categorized as "other employees" of a professional sports team (see below). A player's compensation attributable to Pittsburgh is determined by using a ratio of games in Pittsburgh to the total games played by the team while the player is on the roster (commonly known as the "duty day" method). Exhibition games, regular-season games, and post-season games are included in the calculation [Usage Fee Regulations § 203(a)]. The calculation of the usage fee due for a player can be expressed as follows:

Gross Wages × (Total duty days in Pittsburgh/Total duty days) × 0.03

Allocation of wages for other employees of a professional sports team: "Other employees" of a professional sports team who are not residents of Pittsburgh are subject to the usage fee when they perform for compensation in Pittsburgh in a publicly funded facility. These include (but are not limited to) players of the minor league or practice squad, coaches, trainers, medical staff, equipment managers, scouts, and announcers paid by the team. The compensation attributable to Pittsburgh is determined by using a ratio of days spent in Pittsburgh to the total days worked in the year [Usage Fee Regulations, § 203(b)]. This calculation can be expressed as follows:

Gross Wages × (Total days in Pittsburgh/Total work days) × 0.03

Allocation of wages for entertainers and other users: Other persons who are not residents of Pittsburgh (*e.g.*, entertainers, performers) are subject to the usage fee when they perform for compensation in Pittsburgh in a publicly funded facility. The gross compensation attributable to Pittsburgh is determined by the specific amount received for each performance. A schedule should be attached showing the gross earned income, date of performance, and usage fee required to be paid [Usage Fee Regulations § 203(c)].

Alternate methods of allocation: Whenever the Director and/or the Department of Finance (Treasurer) determines (either upon his own initiative or upon application by the user) that an apportionment is appropriate for a particular user, a class of users, or for the City, the Treasurer may authorize use of a method of apportionment with due regard to the nature of the business concerned [Usage Fee Regulations § 203(d)].

PITTSBURGH CITY AND SCHOOL DISTRICT TAXES

CHAPTER 44
PITTSBURGH SCHOOL DISTRICT TAXES

¶4401 Scope of Chapter

This chapter provides a brief explanation of Pittsburgh School District earnings tax and mercantile license tax. The explanation is not detailed. For details consult the statutes and regulations.

¶4402 Earned Income and Net Profits Tax

The Pittsburgh School District levies a tax on earned income and net profits under the authority of the First Class A School District Earned Income Tax Act [Act of August 24, 1961, P.L. 1135, No. 508]. The rate is increased by imposing an additional tax based on the same provisions but levied under the authority of the Public School Code of 1949 [24 P.S. § 1-101 *et seq.*]. The school district tax is adopted annually by the Board of Education. The rate for 2008 is 2% on residents only. Consult local ordinances for rates for other years. With minor exceptions, the provisions of the Pittsburgh city tax on earned income apply to the school district earned income tax. The same regulations apply to the taxes of both jurisdictions, and returns for both jurisdictions are made on a combined form [PGH-40]. The City Treasurer, who is also the School District Treasurer, administers both taxes. The city tax is levied on both residents and nonresidents, while the school district tax is levied only on residents. See discussion of the Pittsburgh city earned income and net profits tax at ¶4201 *et seq.*

¶4403 Personal Property Tax

The Pittsburgh School District levies a personal property tax. The personal property tax is explained in Chapters 34 and 35.

¶4404 Realty Transfer Tax

The Pittsburgh School District levies a realty transfer tax on the transfer of any interest in realty located within the district. The tax is 1% of the value of property transferred. It is an addition to the city tax (¶4305).

PITTSBURGH CITY AND SCHOOL DISTRICT TAXES

CHAPTER 45

ALLEGHENY COUNTY SALES, USE, AND OCCUPANCY TAX

¶4501 Scope of Chapter

This chapter provides an explanation of the Allegheny County sales, use, and occupancy tax, generally referred to as the Allegheny County sales and use tax. The term "Allegheny County sales and use tax," when used in this *Guidebook*, should be understood to include the Allegheny County occupancy tax.

¶4502 Source of Authority

The Allegheny County sales and use tax is authorized by the Second Class County Code [16 P.S. §3101 *et seq.*]. The rules and regulations promulgated under §270 are applicable to the Allegheny sales and use tax insofar as such rules and regulations are consistent with Article XV of Allegheny County Ordinance 32066 [Allegheny County Ordinance 32066, Article VI, §1(1)]. The Chief Clerk of Allegheny County is authorized to adopt any rules and regulations necessary for the implementation of the Allegheny sales and use tax [Allegheny County Ordinance 32066, Article VI, §1(3)].

¶4503 Administration

The Allegheny County sales and use tax is administered and collected by the Pennsylvania Department of Revenue. The Department of Revenue credits the tax collected, less collection costs and refunds and credits paid, to the Allegheny Regional Asset District Sales and Use Tax Fund [16 P.S. §6157-B]. The Allegheny County ordinance incorporates, by reference, all of the definitions set forth in 72 P.S. §7201, 72 P.S. §4947.3, and 72 P.S. §4751-3 [Allegheny County Ordinance 32066, Article I, §2].

¶4504 Base and Rate

The Allegheny County sales and use tax is imposed at the rate of 1% on the following transactions:

(1) Each separate sale at retail of tangible personal property or services within the boundaries of Allegheny County. The tax must be collected by the vendor from the purchaser and remitted to the Commonwealth [Allegheny County Ordinance 32066, Article IV, §1]. For purposes of this tax the word "Commonwealth" means the Department of Revenue of the Commonwealth of Pennsylvania.

(2) The use, within Allegheny County, of tangible personal property purchased at retail and on services purchased at retail. The tax must be remitted to

the Commonwealth by the person who makes the use of the taxable property or service. The use tax is not imposed on any person on any property or service for which the sales tax has been paid [Allegheny County Ordinance 32066, Article IV, § 2].

(3) The rent or consideration received by each operator of a hotel within Allegheny County from each transaction of renting a room or rooms to accommodate transients or patrons. The tax must be collected by the operator or owner of the hotel from the patron or transient and paid over to the Commonwealth [Allegheny County Ordinance 32066, Article IV, § 3].

The Allegheny County sales and use tax is levied in addition to the sales and use tax imposed by the Commonwealth.

• *Licenses*

A license for the collection of the tax is issued in the same manner as provided for in § 505 of the Pennsylvania Intergovernmental Cooperation Authority Act for Cities of the First Class. A license shall be issued pursuant to Article II of the Tax Reform Code, or a separate license may be issued by the Department of Revenue. The license or licenses are non-assignable and subject to renewal periodically when required by the Department, but in no event more frequently than once every five years. No fee is charged for either a license or a renewal. Failure of any person to obtain a license does not relieve that person of liability to pay the taxes levied, assessed, or imposed by Allegheny County Ordinance 32066 [Allegheny County Ordinance 32066, Article V].

NOTE: See ¶ 4505 for more detailed discussion of situs and collection rules.

• *Bracket system*

The law provides a bracket system for computing the tax, as follows [Allegheny County Ordinance 32066, Article IV, § 5]:

Purchase Price	Tax
$0.50 or less	No tax
$0.51 but less than $1.51	$0.01
$1.51 but less than $2.51	$0.02
$2.51 but less than $3.51	$0.03
$3.51 but less than $4.51	$0.04
$4.51 but less than $5.51	$0.05
$5.51 but less than $6.51	$0.06
$6.51 but less than $7.51	$0.07
$7.51 but less than $8.51	$0.08
$8.51 but less than $9.51	$0.09
$9.51 but less than $10.51	$0.10

For amounts more than $10, the tax is 1% of each $10 plus the above bracket amount for any fractional part of a $10 increment.

¶4505 Situs Rules

The following situs rules apply to the Allegheny County sales and use tax [Allegheny County Ordinance No. 32066, Article IV, § 6]:

(1) A sale at retail is deemed to be consummated at the place of business of the retailer unless the tangible personal property sold is delivered by the retailer or his/her agent to an out-of-state designation or to a common carrier for delivery to an out-of-state destination or the U.S. mails for delivery to an out-of-state destination.

(2) If a retailer has more than one place of business in Pennsylvania that participates in a sale, the sale is deemed to be consummated at the place of the retailer where the initial order for the tangible personal property is taken, even though the order must be forwarded elsewhere for acceptance, approval of credit, shipment, or billing.

(3) A sale by a retailer's employee (*e.g.*, traveling salesman) is deemed to be consummated at the place of business from which that employee works.

(4) Vehicle, aircraft, and motorcraft sales are deemed to take place at the address of the purchaser or user. The tax due must be paid by the purchaser or user directly to the Department of Transportation at the time of making application for a title or directly to the Department if licensing is not required or obtained.

(5) The sale of utility services (steam, natural and manufactured gas, electricity, telephone and telegraph service) is deemed to occur at the service address in the County, which is the address where the telephone equipment is located and to which the telephone number is assigned or where the telegraph originated or where the meter that registers the service is located, without regard to where the services are rendered.

(6) The *lease* of a motor vehicle, trailer, semitrailer or mobile home (as defined in 75 Pa.C.S.) or of a motorboat, aircraft or other similar tangible personal property required under either federal or state laws to be registered or licensed is deemed to have been completed or used at the address of the *lessee.* The tax shall be paid by the lessee to the lessor [72 P.S. § 7201-A(a)].

(7) The *rental* of a motor vehicle, trailer, semitrailer or mobile home (as defined in 75 Pa.C.S.) or of a motorboat, aircraft or other similar tangible personal property required under either federal or state laws to be registered or licensed is deemed to be consummated at the place of business of the retailer. The tax due is paid by the renter to the retailer [72 P.S. § 7201-A(b)].

¶4506 Disbursements

The tax is collected by the Commonwealth and paid to the State Treasurer. The amount collected by the Commonwealth, along with interest and penalties, less collection costs and refunds and credits paid is credited to the Allegheny Regional Asset District Sales and Use Tax Fund not less often than every two weeks. On or before the tenth day of every month the State Treasurer must make, out of the moneys in the fund, the following disbursements on behalf of Allegheny County [16 P.S. § 6157-B]:

(1) One-half to the District (which may not use more than 1% of the moneys received by the District for administrative expenses).

(2) One-fourth to qualified municipalities.

(3) One-fourth to Allegheny County.

The funds received by the District, County, and municipalities must be used for support of regional assets and for tax relief. See ¶ 4507 and ¶ 4508.

¶4507 Regional Assets

The Allegheny County Regional Asset District may assume the financial functions of the Allegheny County and Pittsburgh with respect to the support of regional assets vital to the quality of life within the County [Allegheny County Ordinance No. 32066, Article III]. A regional asset is a civic, recreational, library, sports, or cultural facility or project designated as such by the District. However, the County may not provide financial support for the following:

(1) Any health care facility or institution that predominantly provides elementary, secondary or higher education, or other training.

(2) Any park that contains fewer than 200 acres, except for linear parks located in more than one city, township, borough, or home rule municipality, other than the County.

(3) Any asset that fails to serve a significant number of persons who are not residents of the city, borough, or township within which the asset is located.

(4) Any library that is not a regional library resource center, a district library center, or that is not part of a library system serving multiple municipalities.

¶4508 Tax Relief

Beginning in the first full calendar year in which disbursements are received, the County and municipalities must utilize disbursements for tax relief as follows [72 P.S. §4751-1]:

(1) Allegheny County and Pittsburgh must repeal any tax imposed upon personal property, and the City of Pittsburgh must reduce to an amount not to exceed 5% the tax on admissions to places of amusement, athletic events, and motion picture theaters. Allegheny County and Pittsburgh must utilize all or a portion of revenues remaining from disbursements for tax relief for long-time senior citizen owner-occupants of personal residences.

(2) Municipalities other than Allegheny County and Pittsburgh must use at least two-thirds of the disbursements received in the first full calendar year in which disbursements are received for the reduction of local taxes and must use all or a portion of disbursements received for the implementation of programs for long-time senior citizen owner-occupants of personal residences who are eligible for property tax rebates under the Senior Citizens Rebate and Assistance Act (72 P.S. §4751-1) (see ¶3512). Municipalities in Allegheny County (other than the County and Pittsburgh) who do not levy a tax on personal property on February 20, 1994, are prohibited from imposing a tax on personal property thereafter.

PART XIX

ADMINISTRATION AND PROCEDURE

CHAPTER 46
PROCEDURES, PROTESTS, AND APPEALS

¶4601 Administration

The administration of the tax system in Pennsylvania is primarily in the hands of the Department of Revenue, but it involves the other fiscal officers of the Commonwealth. The following is an overview of the role of Commonwealth fiscal officers.

Caution: Consult Various Taxes

General administrative powers and duties are prescribed by the Fiscal Code [72 P.S. § 1 *et seq.*]. The Fiscal Code, however, does not specify the details for all Commonwealth taxes, so the statutes governing the various taxes should be consulted for details pertaining to a particular tax (*e.g.*, the personal income tax, the corporate net income tax).

• *Department of State*

The Department of State, headed by the Secretary of State, generally has an indirect role in taxation. The Department of State, however, does collect certain corporate fees, and a representative of the State Department sits on the Board of Finance and Revenue [Act of April 4, 1929, P.L. 177, Art. IV, 405]. The Secretary of State is appointed by the Governor.

• *Department of Revenue*

The Department of Revenue is the Department with primary responsibility for administration of Pennsylvania tax laws. The head of the Department of Revenue is the Secretary of Revenue, appointed by the Governor. The Department of Revenue collects taxes, enforces tax laws, and conducts administrative review of tax reports (settlement, assessment, appraisement, determination) [72 P.S. § 202].

• *Department of the Auditor General*

The head of the Department of the Auditor General is the Auditor General. The Auditor General is elected, not appointed. The primary function of the Department of the Auditor General in matters of taxation is to audit and approve all settlements and resettlements made by the Department of Revenue [72 P.S. § 401; 72 P.S. § 1102].

• *Department of Justice*

The head of the Department of Justice is the Attorney General, who is also an elected official. In tax cases before the courts, the Attorney General represents the Commonwealth.

• *Treasury Department*

In Pennsylvania the State Treasurer, who heads the Treasury Department, is an elected official. The State Treasurer is responsible for "handling" Commonwealth funds. The State Treasurer must deposit, disburse, and account for all Commonwealth monies.

• *General Counsel*

The General Counsel is appointed by the Governor as his legal advisor. They are also responsible for the appointment of Deputy Counsel for the administrative agencies of the Commonwealth.

¶4602 Administrative Review

When the Department of Revenue receives reports and payments of tax, the audit and examination process (administrative review) begins. The Department is charged with making sure taxpayers conform to the tax laws and pay the required taxes. The Department's primary tool is administrative review, in Pennsylvania called assessment, appraisement, or determination. All these terms refer to the process of reviewing returns for accuracy and compliance and "billing" taxpayers for additional tax if the Department of Revenue arrives at the conclusion that they did not pay enough.

• *Timely filing of protests*

A taxpayer is considered to have made a timely filing of a petition for resettlement, a petition for reassessment, a petition for redetermination, or any other protest relating to the assessment of tax or any other matter relating to any tax imposed by the Tax Reform Code if the letter transmitting the petition is received by the Department of Revenue or is postmarked by the U.S. Postal Service on or prior to the final day on which the petition is required to be filed [72 P.S. § 10003.6].

Review Processes

Care must be taken when considering review processes. Not only does Pennsylvania use different names, but in some cases there are different rules. In particular, one must be careful about time limitations for petitions and appeals. These differ among taxes and sometimes within the same tax.

- *Appeals*

Pennsylvania taxpayers have the right to appeal Departmental decisions (if they feel "aggrieved" by them. Petitions for reassessment are discussed at ¶ 4604; the Board of Finance and Revenue is discussed at ¶ 4605.

¶4603 Tax Assessments

CAUTION

Formerly, the Department of Revenue was required to mail notices of assessment by certified mail. Now the Department is not required to use certified mail. A taxpayer may fail to receive a notice for a number of reasons (*e.g.,* notice sent to the wrong address, notice lost in the mail). Without the certified mail requirement a taxpayer has no way of proving he or she did not receive the notice. This takes away a layer of protection the taxpayer formerly had.

Personal income tax: Assessment provisions for the personal income tax are discussed at ¶ 404.

Sales and use tax: Assessment provisions for the sales and use tax are discussed at ¶ 802.

Corporate taxes: Assessment provisions for corporate taxes are discussed at ¶ 1204.

Other taxes: All taxes, fees, additions, bonuses, costs, penalties, or charges collected by the Department that were subject to settlement or determination prior to January 1, 2008, or for which no other method for the establishment of the unpaid or unreported liability to be collected by the Department is provided by law are now assessed under the corporate provisions discussed at ¶ 1204 [72 P.S. § 10003.18]. In addition, the following are assessed under the corporate provisions:

(1) The state personal property tax.

(2) Taxes imposed by the "Co-Operative Agricultural Association Corporate Net income Tax Act."

(3) The state admissions tax.

(4) The pari-mutuel wagering tax.

The corporate assessment procedures do not apply to the following [72 P.S. § 10003.18(c)]:

(1) The procedure for collection of moneys due the Commonwealth by county or city officers as provided by the Fiscal Code.

(2) The liquid fuels and fuels tax.

(3) The motor carriers road tax.

¶4604 Petition for Reassessments and Refunds

Article XVII of the Tax Reform Code, enacted by Act 119 of 2006 (S.B. 1993), § 28 governs the procedure for petitions for reassessment of taxes assessed after January 1,

2008, and applies to all Commonwealth taxes except appeals from assessment of the bank and trust company shares tax and the title insurance companies tax (which are governed by § 1104.1 of the Fiscal Code) and protests of the appraisement and assessment of the inheritance tax [72 P.S. § 9702].

• *General rule*

A taxpayer may file a petition for reassessment with the Department of Revenue within 60 days (90 days, prior to October 30, 2017) after the mailing date of the notice of assessment [72 P.S. § 9702(a)].

• *Petition for reassessment when tax due is not increased*

A petition for reassessment under the general rule may include a petition for review of the Department's adjustment of a tax item if the adjustment did not result in a tax increase in the year of adjustment but may increase the tax due in a subsequent year. A taxpayer must file a petition for review when tax due is not increased within 60 days (90 days, prior to October 30, 2017) of the mailing date of the Department of Revenue's notice of adjustment [72 P.S. § 9702].

• *Content of petitions for reassessment*

Petition for reassessment: A petition for reassessment must state the following [72 P.S. § 9703(a)(1)]:

(1) The tax type and tax periods included within the petition.

(2) The amount of tax that the taxpayer claims to have been assessed erroneously.

(3) The basis upon which the taxpayer claims that the assessment is erroneous.

Petition for refund: A petition for refund must state the following [72 P.S. § 9703(a)(2)]:

(1) The tax type and tax periods included within the petition.

(2) The amount of tax that the taxpayer claims to have been overpaid.

(3) The basis of the taxpayer's claim for refund.

(4) The basis upon which the taxpayer claims that the adjustment of a tax item is erroneous (effective for decedents dying after June 30, 2010 and applicable to tax periods that are open on or after July 2, 2012). Importantly, an amended tax return is not a petition for refund. *Quest Diagnostics Venture, LLC v. Commonwealth*, 2015 WL 3561310.

• *Affidavit*

The petition must be supported by an affidavit by the petitioner or the petitioner's authorized representative that the petition is not made for the purpose of delay and that the facts set forth in the petition are true 72 P.S. § 9703(a)(3)].

• *Request for hearing*

Upon written request of the petitioner or when deemed necessary by the Department of Revenue, the Department will schedule a hearing to review a petition; and the petitioner will be notified of the date, time, and place where the hearing will be held [72 P.S. § 9703(b)].

• *Decision and order*

The Department will issue a decision and order disposing of a petition of such basis as it deems to be in accordance with law and provide a written explanation of the basis for any denial of relief [72 P.S. § 9703(c)].

Time limit for decision and order: The Department is required to issue a decision and order disposing of a petition within six (6) months after receipt of the petition. Petitioner and Department may agree to extend the time period for one additional

¶4604

six-month period. Notice of the Department's decision and order disposing of the petition will be issued to the petitioner [72 P.S. § 9703(d)].

Time limit exception: If at the time of the filing of a petition proceedings are pending in a court of competent jurisdiction wherein any claim made in the petition may be established, the Department, upon the written request of the petitioner, may defer consideration of the petition until the final judgment determining the question(s) involved in the petition has been decided. If consideration of the petition is deferred, the Department must issue a decision and order disposing of the petition within six (6) months after the final judgment [72 P.S. § 9703(e)].

• *Failure of the Department to take action*

Failure of the Department to dispose of a petition within the required time period will act as a denial of the petition; and notice of the department's failure to act and denial must be mailed to the petitioner [72 P.S. § 9703(f)].

• *Burden of proof*

In general, the burden of proof is upon the petitioner or appellant [72 P.S. § 9705].

• *Abatement of additions or penalties*

For petitions for reassessment or refund filed on or after January 1, 2008, additions or penalties imposed on the taxpayer may be waived or abated, in whole or in part, where the petitioners have established that they acted in good faith, without negligence, and with no intent to defraud [72 P.S. § 9706].

• *Compromise by Secretary of Revenue*

General rule: A taxpayer who has filed a petition under any statutory provision that allows for administrative tax appeal to the Department of Revenue may propose a compromise of the amount of liability for tax, interest, penalty, additions, or fees administered by the Department. The compromise offer must be submitted prior to a final decision by the Department of Revenue on the petition. An informal conference (in person or by telephone), may be conducted by the Department of Revenue with representatives of the Department and the petitioner. If the compromise offer is accepted, the Department will issue an order reflecting the compromise that shall not be subject to further appeal [72 P.S. § 9707(a)].

Bases for compromise: There are two bases for compromise [72 P.S. § 99707(b)]:

(1) Doubt as to liability.

(2) The promotion of effective tax administration.

Ineligible for compromise: The following are not eligible for compromise.

(1) A petition of denial of property tax or rent rebate claim.

(2) A petition of denial of a charitable tax exemption.

(3) A petition of the revocation of a sales tax license.

(4) A petition of jeopardy assessments.

(5) A petition arising under 4 Pa.C.S., Pt. II (relating to gaming).

¶4605 Board of Finance and Revenue

Effective April 1, 2014, Pennsylvania's Board of Finance and Revenue was reconstituted with independent voting members and other improved procedures. The Board of Finance and Revenue is a body provided for by law. It now has three members. Two are appointed by the Governor and confirmed by the Pennsylvania Senate—one initially serving a four-year term and one serving a six-year term, with all subsequent terms being six years. The State Treasurer or the Treasurer's designee fills the third seat. All such members must be either attorneys or certified public accountants with substantial knowledge of Pennsylvania tax law. All petitions filed with the Board of Finance and Revenue are accepted *only* in Harrisburg.

In addition, effective for petitions filed with the Board of Finance and Revenue on or after April 1, 2014, both the taxpayer and the Department of Revenue will be able to present oral and documentary evidence before the Board. Another important change brought about by Act 52 of 2013 is that the Board will be able to order a compromise settlement that is agreed to by the taxpayer and the Department of Revenue.

• *Review by Board of Finance and Revenue*

Within 60 days (90 days, prior to October 30, 2017) after the mailing date of the Department's notice of decision and order on a petition filed with it, a taxpayer may petition the Board to review the decision and order [72 P.S. § 9704(a)]. A petition for review may be filed with the Board 60 days (90 days, prior to October 30, 2017) after the mailing date of the Department's notice of its failure to dispose of the petition within the required time periods [72 P.S. § 9704(b)].

• *Content of petition*

Petition for review of reassessment decisions: A petition for review of the decision and order of the Department of Revenue on a petition for reassessment must state all of the following [72 P.S. § 9704(c)(1)]:

(1) The tax type and tax periods included within the petition.

(2) The amount of the tax that the taxpayer claims to have been assessed erroneously.

(3) The basis upon which the taxpayer claims that the assessment is erroneous.

Petition for review of refund decisions: A petition for review of the Department's decision and order on a petition for refund must state all of the following [72 P.S. § 9704(c)(2)]:

(1) The tax type and tax periods included within the petition.

(2) The amount of the tax that the taxpayer claims to have been overpaid.

(3) The basis of the taxpayer's claims for refund.

Establishing the basis of taxpayer's claim: A petition may satisfy the requirement of stating the basis of the taxpayer's claim that the reassessment is erroneous or the basis of the taxpayer's claims for refund may be made by incorporating by reference the petition filed with the Department in which the basis of the taxpayer's claim is specifically stated [72 P.S. § 9704(c)(3)]. A petition must be supported by an affidavit by the petitioner or the petitioner's authorized representative that the petition is not made for the purpose of delay and that the facts set forth in the petition are true [72 P.S. § 9704(d)].

Affidavit: A petition must be supported by an affidavit by the petitioner or the petitioner's authorized representative that the petition is not made for the purpose of delay and that the facts set forth in the petition are true [72 P.S. § 9704(d)].

• *Decision and order of the Board of Finance and Revenue*

The Board will issue a decision and order disposing of a petition on any basis as it deems to be in accordance with law and equity [72 P.S. § 9704(e)]. Act 52 of 2013 provides that, after April of 2013, the Board may order a compromise settlement that is agreed to by the taxpayer and the Department of Revenue. Additionally, the decisions of the Board are to be published and available for viewing by the public.

¶4605

• *Time limit*

In general, the Board must issue a decision and order disposing of a petition within six (6) months after receipt of the petition. However, if at the time of the filing of a petition proceedings are pending in a court of competent jurisdiction in which any claim made in the petition may be established, the Board, upon written request by the petitioner, may defer consideration of the petition until the final judgment determining the question(s) involved in the petition has been decided. If consideration of the petition is deferred, the Board must issue a decision and order disposing of the petition within six (6) months after the final judgment [72 P.S. § 9704(f)].

• *Failure of the Board to take action*

The failure of the Board to dispose of the petition within the required time period acts as a denial of the petition; and notice of the Board's failure to take action and the denial of the petition must be issued to the petitioner [72 P.S. § 9704(f)].

Raise Issues Here or Not at All

Taxpayers who appeal to the Commonwealth Court cannot raise any questions before the court that were not raised during settlement, resettlement, or review before the Department or Board of Finance and Revenue and set forth in the specification of objections unless the court is satisfied that the appellant was not able, by the exercise of reasonable diligence, to have raised the questions before the Department and the Board of Finance and Revenue [210 Pa. Code Rule 1571].

A taxpayer should raise every potential issue in his/her petition to the Board of Finance and Revenue. The Department of Revenue is not bound by the same rules as the taxpayer. It can raise new questions and present new facts if it gives the taxpayer 20 days, notice before the Commonwealth Court trial [210 Pa. Code Rule 1571].

It has long been believed that the Department of Revenue is not bound by the same rules with respect to raising new issues as the taxpayer. However, in Footnote 13 to *First Union National Bank v. Cmwlth.* [Pa.Commw., 867 A.2d 711 (2005); exceptions dism'd, October 20, 2005], the Commonwealth Court said the following:

The Commonwealth also makes two assertions in its brief that, admittedly, were not considered by the Board of Finance and Revenue: (1)" [C]an [North Bank] be valued as a new bank arising from the merger activities in 1998 for the purposes of the Shares Tax as of January 1, 1999?" and (2) "Is there any constitutional impediment to the Bank Shares taxation of the admittedly unitary North Bank on an apportioned basis, where [North Bank] makes no challenge to the composition of the apportionment factor?" (Commonwealth Br. at 3.) Because these arguments were not brought before the administrative agency below, they are waived on appeal. Pa. R.A.P. 1571(h).

Timely mailing treated as timely filing: A petition to the Board of Finance and Revenue is considered timely filed, regardless of when it is received by the Board, if it is mailed on or before the filing deadline and bears a U.S. Postal Service postmark [72 P.S. § 1103.1]. A receipt indicating that the petition was mailed by registered or certified mail on or before the due date is evidence of timely filing [72 P.S. § 1103.1]. When a due date falls on a Saturday, Sunday, or a legal holiday, the due date is extended to midnight of the next full business day [72 P.S. § 1103.2(a)].

Mail Box Rule

If a taxpayer uses a private postage meter or a private courier and the petition does not reach Harrisburg by the due date, he/she has not made a timely filing. It must be received within 90 days or sent by *U.S. Postal Service certified mail.* The taxpayer can, of course, hand deliver the petition to the Board in Harrisburg and if so, should have two copies date stamped, keeping one for proof of timely filing.

Extension of time to file: The Board may, on written application and for good cause shown, grant an extension of time to file a petition, but the extension cannot exceed three months [72 P.S. § 1103.2(b)].

• *Hearings*

The Board of Finance and Revenue holds monthly hearings. A taxpayer who has filed a petition with the Board will be notified of the date of his/her hearing, but specific hours are not assigned. The practice is that representatives (or taxpayers) go to Harrisburg and sign up in the morning, and cases are heard in the order in which representatives have signed up. The petitioner or an authorized representative may attend the hearing and make oral arguments or submit the petition on merits and not attend the hearing. The petitioner is, however, required to notify the Secretary of the Board whether he/she (or a representative) will attend or request the Board to act in his/her absence [61 Pa. Code § 701.5]. Only an attorney-at-law representing a petitioner or other applicant or an applicant acting in his or her own behalf is permitted to raise any legal question in any petition or application filed with the Board or to argue or discuss any legal questions at a Board hearing [61 Pa. Code § 701.6].

Before the hearing, counsels to the Board review all petitions and prepare a memorandum for the Board members, describing the tax and recommending action.

Communicate with Board Counsel

The Board of Finance and Revenue will not see a taxpayer's petition unless they specifically ask for it. Usually they do not; so communication with the Board Counsel handling the case is critical. However, *ex parte* communications are no longer permitted; therefore, counsel should notify all parties of any communication being made.

• *Video-conference hearings*

The Board of Finance and Revenue offers videoconference hearings from Pittsburgh. For more information, contact

Board of Finance and Revenue Riverfront Office Center
1101 S. Front Street
Suite 400
Harrisburg, PA 17104-2539

• *Appeal to Commonwealth Court*

A taxpayer who disagrees with the action of the Board of Finance and Revenue has 30 days from the decision of the Board to file an appeal in the Pennsylvania Commonwealth Court [210 Pa. Code Rule 1571]. This 30-day period begins to run from the later of (1) end of the six-month period in which the Board fails to act or (2) the date of entry of the order of the Board if the Board takes action. The date of entry of the order of the Board is the mailing date of the notice of the refusal of the petition if the Board makes no resettlement or the mailing date by the Department of Revenue of the certification of a resettlement if the Board has made a resettlement [210 Pa. Code Rule 1571].

Check Dates

A taxpayer has only 30 days to file an appeal with the Commonwealth Court. If the Board fails to take action on a petition for review, it will not notify the taxpayer until after the 30-day period has started running. Taxpayers should keep track of the critical dates.

¶4605

¶4606 Taxpayers' Bill of Rights

• *Highlights of Taxpayers' Bill of Rights*

The purpose of the Taxpayers' Bill of Rights is to protect the rights of Pennsylvania taxpayers and to provide guidance for solution of problems. In general, the Taxpayers' Bill of Rights applies to any tax that is administered by the Secretary. Any reference to a tax or taxes includes special assessments, fees, and other impositions that are administered by the Secretary [72 P.S. § 3310-201(a)]. The Bill provides safeguards for taxpayers but does not excuse taxpayers from compliance with the tax laws [72 P.S. § 3310-201(b)]. The explanation below covers the highlights of the bill. For more details, consult the statutes. The Taxpayers' Bill of Rights is codified at 72 P.S. § 3310-101 *et seq.*].

Local Taxpayers Bill of Rights

The Taxpayers' Bill of Rights applies to taxes imposed by the Commonwealth. The Local Taxpayers Bill of Rights applies to taxes imposed by local jurisdictions. The Local Taxpayers Bill of Rights is discussed at ¶3404.

• *Established rights*

The Taxpayers', Bill of Rights establishes the following:

(1) The right of the taxpayer to timely and accurate respond to requests for information and tax assistance.

(2) The right of the taxpayer to have tax payments applied in the following order:

(a) The tax itself.

(b) Additions to tax.

(c) Interest.

(d) Penalties.

(e) Other fees or charges.

(3) The right of the taxpayer to receive instructions (in simple, non-technical terms) about refunds, audits, or appeals of decisions of the Department of Revenue. See "*Interviews*" below.

(4) The requirement that the Department cannot raise an identical or substantially identical issue when the Board of Finance and Revenue has issued a decision in favor of a taxpayer and the Commonwealth has not appealed. This establishes legal precedence for decisions of the Board of Finance and Revenue when applied to the same taxpayer and the same fact pattern.

(5) The obligation of the Department of Revenue to provide the following explanations:

(a) Procedures for filing taxpayer complaints.

(b) Procedures the Department may use in enforcing the tax law.

(c) Rights of taxpayers with regard to interviews with the Department.

(d) Conditions under which a taxpayer may enter into written installment payment agreements.

(e) Creation of a Taxpayers' Rights Advocate to represent the interests of taxpayers with audit or collection grievances against the Department (see "*Taxpayers' Rights Advocate*," below).

(f) Abatement of interest attributable to errors and delays by the Department (see "*Abatement of interest*," below).

• *Interviews*

The taxpayer has the right to make (or have made) audio recordings of any in-person interview of him/her [72 P.S. § 3310-203(a)]. Upon written request of the taxpayer, the Department of Revenue will make an audio recording using its own equipment, but at the expense of the taxpayer. If the taxpayer makes his/her own audio recording, all parties to the interview must be notified prior to the beginning of the interview that it will be recorded. A taxpayer may be represented in interviews by an attorney, certified public accountant, or any other person with a written power of attorney from the taxpayer. A taxpayer does not have to appear in person at any interview with the Department except in the case of subpoena, writ, or other lawful process to examine and inspect books, records, or other papers of the taxpayer. The taxpayer may be notified directly if the Department believes a representative is responsible for unreasonable delay or hindrance of an examination or investigation.

• *Taxpayers' Rights Advocate*

The Taxpayers' Rights Advocate (TRA) is designated by and reports directly to the Secretary of Revenue and works to make procedures more uniform and understandable for taxpayers [72 P.S. § 3310-207]. The TRA represents the interests of taxpayers with grievances regarding audits or collections of tax. The TRA may merely provide guidance or may issue a Taxpayer Assistance Order if necessary to protect the rights of the taxpayer [72 P.S. § 3310-208]. A Taxpayer Assistance Order may require the Department of Revenue to release taxpayer's property levied by the Department, to cease any action, or to refrain from taking any action to enforce tax laws against the taxpayer until the disputed issue has been resolved. Most problems presented to the TRA are resolved with the issuance of a Taxpayer Assistance Order [*Pennsylvania Tax Update No. 102*, Pennsylvania Department of Revenue, November/December 2002]. However, the Advocate's decision whether to issue a Taxpayer Assistance Order is final. Note that the Advocate cannot issue taxpayer assistance orders for problems related to sales tax, corporation tax, motor carrier tax, liquid fuel taxes, and similar taxes [*Pennsylvania Tax Update No. 102*, Pennsylvania Department of Revenue, November/December 2002].

A taxpayer or his/her agent should contact the Advocate when any of the following has happened:

(1) The taxpayer is unable to resolve a personal income tax or inheritance tax problem through normal administrative procedures within the Department of Revenue.

(2) It has been more than 30 days since the taxpayer provided information requested from the Department of Revenue and has not received a reply.

(3) The taxpayer believes he/she may be eligible for innocent spouse relief.

The Taxpayers' Rights Advocate may be contacted through any of the following methods:

Telephone: (717) 772-9347
Fax: (717) 787-8264
E-mail: pataxadvocate@state.pa.us
Mail: PA Department of Revenue
Attn: Taxpayers' Rights Advocate
Lobby, Strawberry Square
Harrisburg, PA 17128-0101

• *Abatement of interest*

Interest attributable to errors and delays by employees of the Department of Revenue may be abated [72 P.S. § 3310-204]. Abatements will be granted only if no significant aspect of the error or delay can be attributed to the taxpayer involved and

¶ 4606

after the Department has contacted the taxpayer in writing with respect to the final determination of deficiency or tax. The Department determines what constitutes timely performance of various ministerial acts. The Department may grant abatements of penalty or excess interest due to erroneous advice furnished to the taxpayer in writing by an employee of the Department if (1) the taxpayer reasonably relied on the written advice that was a response to specific written request of the taxpayer and (2) the penalty or addition to tax or excess interest did not result from a failure by the taxpayer to provide adequate or accurate information. Administrative and judicial review of abatements is limited to a review of whether failure to abate would be widely perceived as grossly unfair.

• *Regulations*

The Pennsylvania Department of Revenue has adopted regulations relating to innocent spouse relief (effective December 11, 2010) for personal income tax purposes. The regulation clarifies the policy of the Department of Revenue, provides uniformity and guidance on innocent spouse relief, and provides instructions and examples for taxpayers regarding elections filed with the Taxpayers' Rights Advocate seeking relief from tax liability [61 Pa. Code § 119.30].

• *Innocent spouse relief*

A taxpayer who has made a joint return may elect to seek relief from liability in the circumstances described in IRC § 6015(b) or (c). This election must be filed with the Taxpayers' Rights Advocate [72 P.S. § 3310-212(a)].

Circumstances warranting relief: In general, relief is available under IRC § 6015(b) or (c) if (i) a joint return was made for a taxable year; (ii) on that return there was an understatement of tax attributable to erroneous items of one individual filing the joint return; and (ii) the other individual filing the joint return (the innocent spouse) establishes that in signing the return he or she did not know, and had no reason to know, that there was an understatement.

Action of Advocate: The Taxpayers' Rights Advocate is required to dispose of an innocent spouse relief election within six (6) months of receiving the election. If, taking into account all the facts and circumstances, it is inequitable to hold the taxpayer liable for any unpaid tax or any deficiency, and relief is not otherwise available to the taxpayer, the Taxpayers' Rights Advocate may relieve the individual of the liability. Prompt notice of the action taken must be given to the taxpayer [72 P.S. § 3310-212(b)].

Appeals: A denial of an election or a failure to notify the taxpayer of a decision with six (6) months after the date an election is filed with the Taxpayers' Rights Advocate may be appealed in the manner provided by law for appeals from actions taken on a petition for reassessment [72 P.S. § 3310-212(b)]. See discussion of reassessments at ¶ 407.

Notice: The Department of Revenue and the Board of Finance must provide adequate notice and an opportunity to become a party to an innocent spouse proceeding to a taxpayer who has filed a joint return but who does not elect to proceed under the innocent spouse provisions [72 P.S. § 3310-212(c)].

Regulations: The Department of Revenue and the Board of Finance and Revenue shall promulgate regulations necessary to implement the innocent spouse provisions [72 P.S. § 3310-212(d)].

• *Requests for innocent spouse relief*

A taxpayer who filed a joint return with his or her spouse can request relief under the innocent spouse provisions in the following ways [*Pennsylvania Tax Update No. 100*, Pennsylvania Department of Revenue, August 2002]:

(1) *Innocent spouse relief:* This form of relief is available if the understatement of tax is due to an erroneous item of one's spouse. The spouse requesting relief must establish that, at the time he or she signed the return, he or she did not know, and had no reason to know, that there was an understatement of tax, and that it would be inequitable to hold him or her liable for the understatement, taking into account all of the facts and circumstances. The spouse requesting relief does not have to be divorced or separated at the time he or she requests relief.

(2) *Relief by separation of liabilities:* This relief can be requested when a taxpayer has filed a joint return that has an understatement of tax due, in part, to an item attributable to one's spouse. This form of relief does not provide the requesting spouse with a refund, but it limits the liability to that which is allocable to the spouse requesting relief. In order to qualify for this form of relief, the requesting spouse must be (i) legally separated; (ii) divorced; or (iii) no longer a member of his or her spouse's household for an entire year before filing for relief. If the Department of Revenue demonstrates that the spouse requesting relief actually knew of the item that gave rise to the understatement, no relief is available to the extent of this knowledge.

(3) *Equitable relief:* This form of relief is available to individuals who do not qualify for innocent spouse relief or relief by separation of liabilities and provides relief where it is inequitable to hold the requesting spouse liable for an underpayment or understatement of tax, taking into account all of the facts and circumstances. Equitable relief requires that there be no transfer of assets between spouses as part of a fraudulent scheme, or for the main purpose of avoiding tax or payment of tax and that the spouses did not file their return with the intent to commit fraud. A refund may be available to some taxpayers who seek equitable relief. The requesting spouse does not have to be divorced or separated in order to qualify for equitable relief.

• *Injured spouse relief*

A taxpayer can seek a return of all or part of his or her refund when it is used to pay his or her spouse's (i) past-due child support; (ii) past-due spousal support; or (iii) past-due state income tax by requesting injured spouse relief. This form of relief requires the taxpayer (i) to file a joint return; (ii) to have received income that has been reported on the joint return; (iii) to have made tax payments; and (iv) to have had an overpayment of tax applied to the past-due obligations of the nonrequesting spouse. A taxpayer does not have to be separated or divorced to seek injured spouse relief [*Pennsylvania Tax Update No. 100,* Pennsylvania Department of Revenue, August 2002].

¶4607 Judicial Review

A taxpayer has 30 days from the decision of the Board of Finance and Revenue to appeal to the Commonwealth Court (explained at ¶4605). After the filing of an appeal to the Commonwealth Court, the taxpayer has entered the tax litigation process and needs a lawyer (if one has not been engaged before).

This is the first time the Justice Department, with the advice and counsel of the Department of Revenue, can compromise cases. Before litigation occurs, it is possible for a taxpayer's attorney to have a conference with the tax litigation unit of the Justice Department in an attempt to settle the case. Unless the matter is trivial or the chances of success are narrow, it is a good idea for the taxpayer to go at least this far. If a compromise is reached, both parties make an agreement called a stipulation to judgment, which is filed with the Commonwealth Court. The court usually approves the stipulation. Stipulated decisions are not published.

Pay the Interest

If a taxpayer compromises at this point, he/she has to pay the proportionate amount of interest due.

- *Appeal—Payment of tax or posting of bond*

This is also the first time that payment or security becomes relevant in corporate taxation. When a taxpayer files an appeal with the Commonwealth Court, he/she must either pay the tax or post a bond (usually 120% of the tax).

Filing an appeal does not automatically mean that a day in court is imminent. The appeal can sit for a long time. In the majority of the cases it is the taxpayer who starts actual proceedings, although the Department of Justice has the power to, and on occasion does, instigate actual court proceedings. Therefore, one taxpayer option is to simply file an appeal and let it sit.

Taxpayers Are Vulnerable to Resettlement

As long as an appeal is timely filed, the statute of limitations for the Department of Revenue to make a resettlement is open. A taxpayer is vulnerable to resettlement by the Department. If the taxpayer later decides to do something like sell assets (at a price that would cause the Department to resettle the valuation), he/she might want to have a lawyer pull the appeal.

If a taxpayer decides to initiate court proceedings, lawyers will prepare his/her briefs and file them with the court. A detailed explanation of the litigation process is beyond the scope of this Guidebook, but one point is extremely important. All Commonwealth Court hearings are *de novo*. This means that a new record of facts is made. However, under the rules of procedure of the Commonwealth Court, the appellant *cannot* raise new issues (although the Commonwealth can). This has implications for the way a taxpayer prepares his/her petition during the administrative review process.

Caution: Timely Filing

Timely filing during the administrative appeals process is crucial. The Commonwealth Court does not have jurisdiction if administrative appeals are not timely filed. A taxpayer (Mattice) whose appeal was received by the Board of Appeals one day after the expiration of the statutory appeal period was denied review by the Commonwealth Court [*Mattice v. Cmwlth.*, 721 A.2d 74 (Pa.Commw. 1998)].

- *Appeals from Commonwealth Court*

Appeals from decisions of the Commonwealth Court are made to the Pennsylvania Supreme Court. Before appeal to the Supreme Court the appellant *must* first file exceptions to the Commonwealth Court Decisions [210 Pa. Code Rule 1571(e)]. Unlike the U.S. Supreme Court, the Pennsylvania Supreme Court cannot refuse to hear a taxpayer's appeal. If U.S. constitutional issues are involved, a decision of the Pennsylvania Supreme Court can be appealed to the U.S. Supreme Court. Note that a taxpayer must have filed exceptions with the Commonwealth Court in order to have a case heard by the Pennsylvania Supreme Court.

- *Appeals to federal district courts*

The Federal Anti-Injunction Act will not permit a district court to enjoin, suspend, or restrain the assessment, levy, or collection of any state tax if there is a plain, speedy, and efficient remedy available in state court [28 U.S.C. § 1341]. A taxpayer who had exhausted all administrative and judicial remedies in Pennsylvania asked the district court to invalidate a local business privilege tax. The U.S. Court of Appeals for the Third Circuit held that Pennsylvania provides a plain, speedy and efficient remedy and denied the taxpayer the right to maintain an appeal in federal district court to invalidate the tax [*Lawrence J. Spielvogel, Inc. v. Township of Cheltenham*, U.S. Court of Appeals, Third Circuit, No. 95-2047 (June 13, 1996), Opinion Not Reported].

¶4608 Communication Function

The communication function refers to the process of supplying information to the Department of Revenue in the form of returns, schedules, attachments to returns, letters, documents—any information that the Department might need in any matter. It is vital to include in or with returns, in a conspicuous place, all information necessary to allow the Commonwealth to reach the most favorable (to the taxpayer) settlement. If the Department later asks for more information, it is important to give it to them as completely and expeditiously as possible, but it is better to provide the information with the return in the first place.

The communication function is critical. If all the information is not available to the Department of Revenue at the time the settlement, assessment or determination is made, the Department will resolve all doubts in favor of the Commonwealth, and the settlement may be less favorable than the taxpayer anticipated. See, for example, the Department's policy on estimated settlements discussed at ¶1203.

A taxpayer petitioning for relief of any kind—refund, resettlement, review—should remember the importance of effective communication at *every* step.

¶4609 Returns, Payment, and Collection of Tax

Filing requirements are not the same for all taxes. See individual specific taxes for filing requirements.

• *Electronic filing*

The Department of Revenue may now allow the electronic filing of any tax return or document [72 P.S. § 10003.8(a)]. For the purposes of electronic filing of returns of documents, the Department of Revenue may determine alternative methods for the signing, subscribing or verifying of a return, statement, or other document that have the same validity and consequences as the actual signing by the taxpayer [72 P.S. § 10003.8(b)].

• *Electronic funds transfer*

A payment in the amount of $20,000 or more must be remitted by a form of electronic funds transfer (EFT). The taxpayer may choose the ACH debit method or the ACH credit method [61 Pa. Code § 53.(3)]. See ¶4617 for explanation of EFT.

• *Tax Offset Program*

The Internal Revenue Service is authorized to offset state tax liabilities against federal income tax refunds [IRC § 6402(3)]. The Pennsylvania Department of Revenue has decided to use the program, which will allow the Department to forward selected personal income tax accounts to offset Internal Revenue Service tax refunds for up to 10 years [*Pennsylvania Tax Update No. 88,* Pennsylvania Department of Revenue, August 2000].

• *Administrative bank attachment for accounts of obligors to the Commonwealth*

The Department of Revenue is allowed to levy bank account of delinquent taxpayers if the amount of the delinquency is greater than $1,000 [72 P.S. § 10003.22]. This new section is a very long section. Consult the statute for details.

¶4610 Estimated Tax

• *Scope of paragraph*

This paragraph contains a discussion of estimated tax payments with respect to taxes other than the personal income tax. The estimated tax provisions for the personal income tax are discussed in Chapter 3.

• *Entities required to make payments of estimated tax*

The credits allowed against Pennsylvania taxes are explained at ¶1004—1011. The following taxpayers are required to pay estimated tax [72 P.S. § 10003.2(a)]:

    (1) Corporations subject to the corporate net income tax (see ¶918).

    (2) Corporations subject to the capital stock/franchise tax (see ¶1321).

    (3) Mutual thrift institutions subject to the mutual thrift institutions tax (see ¶2006).

    (4) Insurance companies subject to the insurance premiums tax (see ¶2208).

    (5) Taxpayers subject to the gross receipts tax (see ¶2406).

    (6) Taxpayers subject to the public utility realty tax (PURTA) surcharge (see ¶2504).

Estimated tax must be separately reported, determined, and treated [72 P.S. § 10003.2(g)].

• *Payment of estimated tax*

    (1) *Corporate net income tax:* Estimated tax paid in equal installments on or before the fifteenth day of the third, sixth, ninth, and twelfth months of the taxable year. Remaining portion of tax due, if any, is due on the date the corporate return is due without reference to any extension of time [72 P.S. § 10003.2(c)(1)].

    (2) *Capital stock/franchise tax:* Estimated tax paid in equal installments on or before the fifteenth day of the third, sixth, ninth, and twelfth months of the taxable year. Remaining portion of tax due, if any, is due on the due date of the corporate return without reference to any extension of time [72 P.S. § 10003.2(c)(2)].

    (3) *Mutual thrift institutions tax:* Estimated tax made in equal installments on or before the fifteenth day of the third, sixth, ninth, and twelfth months of the taxable year. Remaining portion due on the due date of the corporate return is due without reference to any extensions of time [72 P.S. § 10003.2(c)(3)].

    (4) *Insurance premiums tax:* Estimated tax paid in a single installment on or before March 15 of the taxable year. Remaining portion, if any, due on the returns due date without reference to any extension of time [72 P.S. § 10003.2(c)(4)].

    (5) *Gross receipts tax:* Estimated tax due on or before March 15 of the taxable year. Remaining portion, if any, due on the returns due date without reference to any extension of time [72 P.S. § 10003.2(c)(5)].

    (6) *PURTA surcharge:* Estimated tax due in a single installment on or before March 15 of the taxable year. Remaining portion, if any, due on the returns due date without reference to any extension of time [72 P.S. § 10003.2(c)(6)].

• *Underpayment of estimated tax*

In case of any underpayment of an installment of estimated tax, interest will be imposed at the established rate (see ¶4612). In the case of a substantial underpayment, interest will be at 120% of the established rate [72 P.S. § 10003.3(a)].

¶4610

Amount of underpayment: The amount of an underpayment is the excess of the cumulative amount of installments required if the estimated tax were equal to 90% of the tax shown on the report for the taxable year over the cumulative amount of installments paid on or before last due date. However, there is an exception to this rule. If the total tax exceeds the tax shown on the report by 10% or more, the amount of the underpayment is based on 90% of the amount of the total tax [72 P.S. § 10003.3(b)(1)]. If the total tax is revised, the amount of underpayment is calculated without the necessity of the filing of any petition by the Department or taxpayer [72 P.S. § 10003.3(b)(2)].

"Total Tax"

The term "total tax" is a new term added by § 29 of Act 119 of 2006 (S.B. 993) and means "the total tax liability of the taxpayer for the tax period including the tax reported by the taxpayer and settled, resettled, or assessed by the Department."

Period of underpayment: The underpayment period runs from the due date of the installment to the earlier of (1) the 15th day of the 4th month following the close of the taxable year or (2) with respect to any portion of the underpayment, the date on which it is paid [72 P.S. § 10003.3(c)].

• *Safe harbor*

Alert

Since the capital stock/franchise tax rate was retroactively increased from 1.89 mills to 2.89 mills for 2009, no estimated payments are required at the higher rate for payments due prior to January 1, 2010. There is no similar relief for the retroactive change in sales factor weighting for corporate net income tax, so a catch-up payment must be made by December 15, 2010.

Interest on underpayments will not be imposed if the total amount of all estimated tax paid on or before the due date equals or exceeds the amount that would have been required to be paid by the due date if the estimated tax were an amount equal to the tax computed at the rates applicable to the taxable year (including any minimum tax) but otherwise on the basis of the facts shown on the taxpayer's report for, and the law applicable to, the safe harbor base year, adjusted for any changes to 72 P.S. §§ 7401, 7601, 7602, and 8101 enacted for the safe harbor base year [72 P.S. § 10003.3(d)]. If the amount of estimated tax paid on or before the due date is not equal to or more than the safe harbor amount but is paid after the due date, the period of underpayment runs from the due date to the date paid.

Total tax for base year: If the total tax for the safe harbor base year is more than the tax shown on the report by 10% or more, the settled tax adjusted to reflect the current tax rate is used for the purpose of determining the safe harbor amount. In the event that the total tax for the safe harbor base year exceeds the tax shown on the report by 10% or more, interest on the underpayments will not be imposed if, within 45 days of the mailing date of assessment (settlement or resettlement prior to January 1, 2008), payments are made such that the total amount of estimated tax payments equals or exceeds the amount that would have been required based on the total [72 P.S. § 10003.3(d)].

Safe harbor base year: A taxpayer's "safe harbor base year" is the taxpayer's second preceding taxable year. If the second preceding taxable year is less than 12 months, the "safe harbor base year" means the taxpayer's annualized second preceding taxable year. If the taxpayer has filed only one previous report, the "safe harbor base year" is the first preceding taxable year. If the first preceding taxable year is less than 12 months, the "safe harbor base year" is the taxpayer's annualized first preceding taxable year [72 P.S. § 10003.1(4.4)].

¶4610

Short taxable years: If the taxable year for which estimated tax payments are made is a short taxable year, in determining the tax shown on the report or the total tax for the safe harbor base year, the tax will be reduced by multiplying it by the ratio of the number of installment payments made in the short taxable year to the number of installment payments required to be made for the full taxable year [72 P.S. § 10003.3(d)].

Federal/Commonwealth Difference

The Pennsylvania "safe harbor" rule for underpayment of estimated tax is similar to the federal safe harbor rule provided if IRC § 6655(d)(2). Note, however, that the federal safe harbor amount is computed with reference to the preceding year, whereas the Pennsylvania safe harbor amount is based on the second preceding year.

¶4611 Credits and Refunds

• *Tax credits*

See specific taxes for credits allowed. Credits allowed against Pennsylvania taxes are explained at ¶ 1004—1011.

• *Uniform refund period*

There is a uniform three-year refund period for all taxes paid on or after January 1, 1998 [72 P.S. § 10003.1(a)]. All petitions for refund, except certain Liquid Fuels Tax refunds (see ¶ 2602), are filed with the Department of Revenue (Board of Appeals).

Exception for Periods Covered by Audit

The Department of Revenue may grant a refund or credit to a taxpayer for all tax periods covered by a departmental audit. If a credit is not granted by the department in the audit report, the taxpayer must file a petition for refund within six (6) months of the mailing date of the notice of assessment, determination or settlement or within three (3) years of actual payment of the tax, whichever is later [72 P.S. § 10003.1(b)], effective July 1, 2012. Formerly a taxpayer was prohibited from asking for refunds within the audit period unless a petition was filed within six (6) months, even though the overpayments were within the normal three-year refund period.

In the case of amounts paid as a result of an assessment, determination, settlement, or appraisement, a petition for refund must be filed with the Department within six (6) months of the actual payment of the tax [72 P.S. § 10003.1(d), effective July 1, 2012)]. Formerly, the refund had to be filed within six (6) months of the mailing date of the notice of assessment, determination, settlement, or appraisement.

The Commonwealth Court denied the refund of an overpayment of slot machine tax because the claim for refund was not filed within the three-year limitations time period. The refund claim was based on an Pennsylvania Supreme Court decision, *Greenwood Gaming and Entertainment, Inc. v. Cmwlth.*, 90 A.3d 699 (2014) (*Greenwood II*), reversing a Commonwealth Court decision which held that a casino and racetrack operator was not entitled to a deduction for cash and non-cash awards distributed to casino patrons holding Players Cards in determining gross terminal revenue (GTR) for purposes of the gaming tax, and remanded the matter for determination of the refund due for tax years 2007 and 2008. The casino taxpayer subsequently filed a petition for refund of slot machine taxes based on deductions of cash and non-cash awards from January 1, 2009, through January 4, 2011. That refund claim was denied because it was filed outside the three-year period for filing refund claims mandated under 72 Pa. Stat. Ann. § 10003.1(a). The taxpayer argued that the three-year limitations period was inequitable and violated its due process rights because the prior Commonwealth Court opinion (*Greenwood Gaming and Entertainment, Inc. v. Cmwlth.*, 29 A.3d 1215 (2011) (*Greenwood I*)) was the controlling law during that three-year period. Consequently, it would have been futile and improper for the taxpayer to seek a refund during that time. However, the Pennsylvania Commonwealth Court held that a voluntary payment of taxes can be subsequently recovered only as a statute provides, and statutory time limitations must be strictly enforced. Therefore, the taxpayer's failure to file the refund request within the statutory period extinguished its right to a refund and neither the PA DOR, nor the court may rely on equitable principles to revive the taxpayer's statutory right to request a refund. Taxpayer's assertion that filing a timely refund would have subjected it to liability under sections of the Judicial Code commonly referred to as the Dragonetti Act was also rejected because those sections do not apply to taxpayers who have a reasonable belief and probable cause to initiate a judicial proceeding. *Greenwood Gaming and Entertainment, Inc. v. Cmwlth.*, Pa Commw. Ct. Dkt. No. 609 F.R. 2015, 09/06/2018 2018 BL 320987 (unreported).

¶4612 Interest

Taxpayers must pay interest on all unpaid taxes due the Commonwealth. There is no interest on penalties or fines; nor is there interest on interest [72 P.S. § 806; 61 Pa. Code § 4.3(a)]. Additional tax, additions to tax, surtax, and disallowed commissions provided by statute and not designated as penalty or interest by statute are taxes that bear interest [61 Pa. Code § 4.3(b)].

- *Rate of interest on unpaid taxes*

The annual rate of interest is the rate established by the Secretary of the Treasury of the United States under the Internal Revenue Code that is in effect on January 1 of a calendar year without regard to changes in the federal rate during the year. The Secretary will annually certify the applicable rate of interest and recommend that the certification be published in the *Pennsylvania Bulletin* and be codified in 61 Pa. Code § 4.2 [61 Pa. Code § 4.2(a)]. The annual interest rate remains in effect for a full year.

The following rates have been certified by the Secretary [61 Pa. Code § 4.2(b)]:

Year	Rate
2012	3%
2013	3%
2014	3%
2015	3%
2016	3%
2017	4%
2018	4%

- *Rate of interest on overpayments*

Overpayments of tax will bear interest rates as follows [61 Pa. Code § 4.2]:

Year	Rate on Personal Income Tax	Rate on All Other Taxes
2012	3%	1%
2013	3%	1%
2014	3%	1%
2015	3%	1%
2016	3%	1%
2017	4%	2%
2018	4%	2%

Federal/Commonwealth Difference

The Secretary of the Treasury of the United States is required to establish quarterly rates of interest to become effective for federal purposes on the first month of each calendar quarter. This federal requirement, however, does not affect Commonwealth law. The Pennsylvania Fiscal Code requires that the interest rate be established effective January 1 of each calendar year without regard to any change in the federal interest rate during the calendar year [72 P.S. § 806].

- *Initial applicable rate*

When a tax becomes due, the initial applicable interest rate is the rate in effect at the time it becomes due (without regard to subsequent extensions for filing, amendments, or alterations or subsequent resettlements, reassessments, or redeterminations) [61 Pa. Code § 4.4(a)]. The interest rate in effect when a tax becomes due remains in effect until the earlier of the date the tax is paid or the end of the calendar year. If the tax remains unpaid at the end of the calendar year, the new interest rate for that year begins to apply to the unpaid tax [61 Pa. Code § 4.4(b)]. The initial rates for unpaid taxes are determined as follows [61 Pa. Code § 4.4(a)]:

(1) *Personal income tax:* The initial rate is the rate in effect on the due date for the tax.

(2) *Withheld personal income tax:* The initial rate is the rate in effect on the date the tax is required to be reported and paid by the employer to the Commonwealth.

(3) *Sales/use tax:* The initial rate on sales/use tax is the rate in effect on the date the tax is originally required by statute to be reported and transmitted by any officer, licensee, or collector to the Department of Revenue (without regard to when the tax was collected).

(4) *Tentative tax:* The initial rate for tentative taxes required to be reported and paid in installments prior to the original due date of the annual return is the rate in effect on the due date of the prepayment (without regard to the due date of the return). The remaining portion of the tax due (if any) bears interest at the rate in effect on the due date of the annual return (without regard to extensions of time).

(5) *Corporate net income tax:* Underpayments of installments of estimated tax do not bear interest during the period of the underpayment. The initial rate on unpaid taxes is the rate in effect on the date the annual report is due.

(6) *Inheritance tax:* The initial rate is the rate in effect on the date the tax becomes delinquent.

- *Computation of interest on unpaid taxes*

Daily computation: Simple interest is computed daily (using a 365-day year), beginning on the first day of delinquency and continuing through (*i.e.,* including) the day of payment. If paid by mail, the U.S. Postal Service postmark is the date of payment [61 Pa. Code § 4.5(a)].

Extensions: Interest begins running on the date the tax is due without regard to extensions of time for filing returns. Although an extension may relieve the taxpayer from late filing or late payment additions or penalties, it does not relieve the taxpayer from the payment of interest on unpaid taxes from the due date to the date of payment [61 Pa. Code § 4.5(b)].

Underpayments due to amendments: Amended returns are considered to amend the tax liability as of the original due date of the tax for the purpose of computing interest owed the Commonwealth [61 Pa. Code § 4.5(c)]. The initial rate of interest is not affected by an amended return, but the Department of Revenue must recompute and adjust the dollar amount of interest based on the amended return [72 P.S. § 806].

Underpayments due to federal report of change: An underpayment of corporate net income tax resulting from a settlement or resettlement of tax based upon a final change or correction of federal taxable income by the IRS is considered due (for establishing the rate and for computing the amount of interest) 30 days after the corporation receives the federal report of change. Interest is computed until the additional tax is paid. The applicable interest rate is the rate established by the Secretary for the year, except for taxes originally due on or before December 31, 1981 (in which case the rate is 6%).

Personal Income Tax

> The 30-day period for federal changes does not apply to the personal income tax. Increases in personal income tax liability assessed or reassessed because of federal redetermination of federal taxable income begin to bear interest from the original due date of the return at the rate in effect on the due date (without regard to the date of the federal redetermination) [61 Pa. Code § 4.5(d)].

Underpayments resulting from application, assignment, or refund of credit: If an application, assignment, or refund of credit results in underpayment of tax due upon settlement or resettlement, interest is calculated on the amount of the credit applied, assigned, or refunded from the date it was applied, assigned, or refunded to the date of payment.

• *Interest on overpayments*

The Commonwealth must pay interest on overpayments of tax at the rate established for underpayments of the same tax for the same period [72 P.S. § 806.1(a); 61 Pa. Code § 4.6]. An overpayment of tax is a payment that is determined not to be legally due [72 P.S. § 806.1(a); 61 Pa. Code § 4.6(1)]. An overpayment of interest or penalty does not bear interest [72 P.S. § 806.1(a)(7)].

• *Date of overpayments*

Interest is paid for the period during which the Commonwealth retains an overpayment, beginning with the date of overpayment, with the following exceptions [72 P.S. § 806.1(a); 61 Pa. Code § 4.6(3)].

(1) *Withheld taxes:* Taxes that are withheld at the source are considered to be overpaid by the employee on the due date of the employee's return (without regard to extensions of time for filing). Taxes withheld by an employer are considered overpaid on the *later* of the due date for filing or actual payment date.

(2) *Installments:* Overpayments of an installment payment, tentative tax, or estimated tax are considered overpaid on the due date for filing the final return or report for the taxable year (without regard to extensions of time for filing).

(3) *Overpayments before the due date:* Overpayments made before the due date prescribed by statute for payment of the tax bear interest from the due date of the return.

(4) *Taxes collected:* Taxes collected by an officer, licensee, or collector are considered overpaid on the *later* of the first date that the tax is required by statute to be reported and transmitted to the Department of Revenue by the officer, licensee, or collector or the date the tax is actually reported and transmitted to the Commonwealth.

(5) *Administrative or appellate review procedure:* A taxpayer has the right to pay all or part of a tax claim made against her/him by the Department for the purpose of stopping the running of interest without prejudicing the right to pursue other administrative or judicial remedies provided by statute [61 Pa. Code § 4.10]. If a taxpayer initiates an administrative or appellate review procedure by claiming to have made an overpayment (or contesting the Department's refusal or denial of his/her claim), the claimed overpayment is considered to have been made on the 60th day following the date of initiation of the review or appellate procedure [72 P.S. § 806.1(a)(4)].

¶4612

- *Period of overpayment*

Overpayments shown on tax returns or reports: If an overpayment of tax is refunded or credited within 75 days after the due date of the return, no interest is allowed on the overpayment [72 P.S. §806.1(a)(5); 61 Pa. Code §4.6(4)(i)]. This is true even if the taxpayer has initiated an administrative or appellate review procedure. If a taxpayer files a late final return showing an overpayment and the overpayment is refunded or credited within 75 days after the date the final return is actually filed, no interest is allowed on the overpayment. For this purpose a final return is one filed in processible form, which means that it is filed on a prescribed form and contains the taxpayer's name, address, identification number (if applicable), the required signature, and required information sufficient to permit verification of the liability. Where a credit or payment is to be applied against a reported tax liability, required information sufficient to verify the credit or payment must be supplied. If a return or report is not received in processible form, the 75-day period begins on the date the Department of Revenue receives the required additional information.

Overpayments due to amended returns: If a taxpayer claims an amount of tax to be overpaid, and the basis for the claimed overpayment consists of additional information that constitutes an amendment of the taxpayer's original return, the date the Department receives the additional information is considered the date of filing the final return, and interest will be paid from the date of the overpayment on any portion not credited or refunded within 75 days of the date the Department received the additional information [61 Pa. Code §4.6(4)(ii)].

Overpayments due to federal report of change: If the amount of a taxpayer's federal taxable income is changed by the IRS (or by another agency or court of the United States), the corporation must make a corrected report to the Department of Revenue [72 P.S. §7406(a)]. The corrected report is considered the final return for purposes of computing interest on the overpayment [61 Pa. Code §4.6(4)(iii)].

Unidentified overpayments: The Department does not recognize as overpayments any payments made without an accompanying statement for the application of the payment. Such payments do not bear interest [61 Pa. Code §4.6(5)].

Priority of provisions: If the Department of Revenue refunds or credits overpayments within 75 days after the later of the due date of a return or the actual filing date of a return, no interest will be paid to the taxpayer, even if the taxpayer has initiated an administrative or review procedure. If a taxpayer initiates an administrative or review procedure, and the tax is not refunded or credited within 75 days of the due date or filing date, interest begins to accrue 60 days after the initiation date, without regard to the filing date [61 Pa. Code §4.6(6)].

- *Date interest stops on overpayments*

Cash refunds: If the Commonwealth pays a cash refund, interest terminates on a date not exceeding 30 days prior to the date of the Commonwealth's refund check [72 P.S. §806.1(c)(1); 61 Pa. Code §4.7(a)].

Credits: If the Commonwealth recognizes a claimed overpayment, the taxpayer is entitled to interest until the earlier of the date the Commonwealth notifies the taxpayer or the date the Commonwealth applies the credit to the taxpayer's account [72 P.S. §806.1(c)(2)]. If the amount reported on a corporation's annual report is less than the amount of taxes paid, the Department of Revenue will credit the taxpayer's account. The credit may be applied in payment of another tax liability, assigned to another taxpayer, or refunded if other obligations the Commonwealth have been paid. If the Department notifies the taxpayer of the available credit within 60 days of the filing date of the annual report, no interest is allowed on the credit [61 Pa. Code §4.7(b)(2)].

• *Application dates*

When a portion of an overpayment credit upon which interest has been allowed and paid is transferred, applied, or assigned in payment of another tax liability, the overpayment credit acquires a new effective payment date for determining the date on which interest terminates [61 Pa. Code § 4.9(a)]. Interest that has been allowed and credited is available for transfer, application, or assignment in payment of another tax liability, effective on the date the interest ceased to accrue [61 Pa. Code § 4.9(b)].

• *Refunds*

A taxpayer who receives a notice of allowance of a credit may apply to the Department of Revenue in writing for a cash refund. No formal petition is required, but the application must be in writing and signed by the person entitled to the refund (or her/his agent). The application must fully identify the taxpayer, the tax, and the amount of refund claimed. If the Department fails to make a cash refund within 90 days after receipt of a proper application for a cash refund, interest begins on the credit after 90 days and continues until a date within 30 days of the date of the Commonwealth's refund check [61 Pa. Code § 4.8].

• *Appeals*

A taxpayer who disagrees with the Department of Revenue's determination of entitlement to interest can file a petition for redetermination with the Board of Appeals within 90 days of the mailing date of the notice with which the taxpayer disagrees, specifying the reasons the taxpayer believes entitle him/her to a redetermination. Failure of the Board to act within 6 months constitutes a denial of the taxpayer's petition for redetermination. A taxpayer then has the right to review the action under normal administrative procedures [61 Pa. Code § 4.11]. See ¶ 4602 for outline of review procedures.

Due Diligence Required of Taxing Jurisdiction

In an unreported decision, the Commonwealth Court applied the doctrine of laches in ruling that the taxing jurisdiction could not collect interest and penalties on back business privilege taxes owed because of lack of due diligence on the part of the taxing jurisdiction. See *Sullivan Plumbing, Inc., Borough of Braddock and Central Tax Bureau of Pennsylvania, Inc. v.,* Pa.Commw., No. 954 C.D. 2007 (April 18, 2008). In this case Sullivan Plumbing had not filed returns of paid taxes for 1994 through 2003. The Borough and the Bureau, according to the Court, made no effort during those years to check whether Sullivan was paying the tax or was aware of its obligation to pay. Thus, Sullivan was required to pay the taxes but no interest or penalties.

¶4613 Penalties, Additions, and Fees

Remission of penalties: The Fiscal Code provides that Department of Revenue is authorized to hear and determine petitions for the remission of penalties for failure to file a tax report by the due date. If the Department is satisfied that (1) the failure to file was not willful, (2) the report was actually filed within 30 days after it was due, and (3) that the tax (exclusive of penalty) was paid within 30 days of the date it was due, the Department may strike off the penalty. A petition for remission of penalties imposed but not paid must be filed within two years after the penalty was imposed [72 P.S. § 503(c)].

Abatement of penalties: Upon the filing of a petition for reassessment or refund, penalties may be abated upon showing that the taxpayer has acted in good faith, without negligence, and with no intent to defraud [72 P.S. § 9706].

¶4613

Bureau of Audits May Offer Penalty Abatement

Taxpayers who cooperate with the Department of Revenue throughout the audit process and meet the same standards used by the Board of Appeals for penalty abatement now have the opportunity to have penalties abated at the audit level.

The Bureau of Audits will consider penalty abatement for eligible taxpayers who received audit engagement letters on or after December 1, 2011. Individuals and businesses meeting the established standards will receive a penalty petition form from Audit staff near the conclusion of the audit.

The penalty abatement procedures at the audit level will in no way limit or reduce a taxpayer's right to appeal an audit assessment.

Formerly, penalties were automatically applied at the audit level, and the taxpayer then had the right to appeal.

Bad checks and electronic funds transfers: If any check received in payment of any amount receivable under Commonwealth laws administered by the Department of Revenue is not paid upon when presented, or any electronic funds transfer as payment of any amount receivable under Commonwealth laws administered by the Department of Revenue is not credited upon transmission, the Department of Revenue will charge the person who tendered the check or electronic transmission a fee equal to 10% of the face amount plus interest and protest fees, provided that this addition is not to be more than $1,000 or less than $25 [72 P.S. § 10003.9].

• *Corporate officer penalties*

Effective October 9, 2009, corporate officers who intentionally fail to file returns for any two successive tax years has committed a misdemeanor and, upon conviction, may be subject to a fine of not less than $2,500 and not more than $5,000 [72 P.S. § 10003.20].

¶4614 Corporate Clearance Certificates

A corporate clearance certificate is a certificate evidencing payment of all taxes and charges required by law [61 Pa. Code § 151.4(a)]. A corporate clearance certificate must be obtained for certain purposes, the most common of which are dissolution, withdrawal from Pennsylvania, merger and consolidation, bulk sale, and a foreign corporation seeking the release of a public contract bond [61 Pa. Code § 151.4(b)]. A taxpayer applying for a corporate clearance certificate must comply with the requirements of § 1403 of the Fiscal Code.

• *Where to make application*

Applications for corporate clearance certificates are made to the Department of Revenue, which issues the certificates. In the case of bulk sales, applications must also be submitted to the Department of Labor and Industry (see ¶4621).

• *Application information and documentation*

The information and documentation that must be furnished to obtain a corporate clearance certificate depend on the purpose for which the certificate is sought [61 Pa. Code § 151.4(b)].

• *Dissolution*

If an application for a corporate clearance certificate is made pursuant to the Business Corporation Law [Act of May 5, 1933, P.L. 364], the following information and documentation are needed [61 Pa. Code § 151.4(b)(1)]:

(i) An application for a corporate clearance certificate (Form REV-181) executed in duplicate.

(ii) Reports for the current tax year to the date of complete divestiture.

(iii) A schedule of distribution of assets in dissolution. If distribution of assets is made in kind to stockholders, a copy of federal Form 1099 must be attached [61 Pa. Code § 151.4(b)(iii)].

(iv) A detailed schedule of capital gains exempted pursuant to IRC § 337.

- *Dissolution by Court of Common Pleas*

If an application for a corporate clearance certificate is made pursuant to a dissolution by the Court of Common Pleas, the following information and documentation must be furnished [61 Pa. Code § 151.4(b)(2)]:

(1) An application for a corporate clearance certificate executed in duplicate.

(2) A copy of the petition for dissolution that was submitted to the Court of Common Pleas.

(3) Reports for the current tax year to the date of filing the Petition for Dissolution.

(4) A schedule of distribution of assets in dissolution.

(5) A detailed schedule of capital gains exempt under IRC § 337.

- *Withdrawal from Pennsylvania*

If a foreign corporation wishes to withdraw from Pennsylvania pursuant to the Business Corporation Law [Act of May 5, 1933, P.L. 364], its application for a corporate clearance certificate must contain the following information and documentation [61 Pa. Code § 141.4(b)(3)]:

(1) An application for a corporate clearance certificate executed in duplicate.

(2) A withdrawal affidavit for a foreign corporation.

(3) Reports for the current year to the date business activities ceased and the corporation no longer employed property in Pennsylvania. An explanation of the disposition of assets located in Pennsylvania must accompany the reports.

(4) A detailed schedule of capital gains exempt under IRC § 337.

Skipping Formalities

Reporting in Pennsylvania can be terminated without going through formal dissolution or withdrawal. See ¶ 1320 for procedures when formal dissolution or withdrawal is not desired.

- *Merger or consolidation*

An application for a corporate clearance certificate with respect to a merger pursuant to the Business Corporation Law [Act of May 5, 1933, P.L. 364] must contain the following information and documentation [61 Pa. Code § 141.4(b)(4)]:

(1) An application for a corporate clearance certificate executed in duplicate.

(2) A copy of the plan of merger or consolidation.

(3) Reports for the current tax year to the proposed date of merger or consolidation.

¶4614

Consolidations

The regulations do not refer to consolidations, only to mergers. However, consolidations are controlled by the same section of the Business Corporation Law, and a taxpayer must get a clearance certificate if planning a consolidation.

• *Bulk and auction sales*

The corporate clearance certificates applicable to bulk sales and auctions are:

(1) An application for a corporate clearance certificate executed in duplicate.

(2) Reports for the current tax year to the proposed date of sale.

(3) A schedule of the assets to be sold and the resulting gains and losses.

NOTE: Bulk sales are discussed in detail at ¶ 4621.

• *Foreign corporation seeking release of public contract bond*

A foreign corporation seeking the release of a public contract bond pursuant to the Act of June 10, 1947, P.L. 493, must provide the following information and documentation [61 Pa. Code § 141.4(b)(6)]:

(1) An application for a corporate clearance certificate.

(2) Reports for the current tax year to the date on which the contract was completed.

• *Department of Labor and Industry*

The Department of Labor and Industry, Bureau of Employment Security, will receive copies of applications for corporate clearance certificate. A clearance certificate evidencing the payment of liabilities owed to the Department of Labor and Industry will be issued directly to the applicant by the Department of Labor and Industry, except when the application was for a bulk sale clearance certificate. See details at ¶ 4621. Corporate clearance certificates issued by the Department of Revenue in the case of bulk sales will include a clearance certificate issued by the Department of Labor and Industry [61 Pa. Code § 151.4(c)].

¶4615 Voluntary Disclosure Program

The Voluntary Disclosure Program (VDP) provides an opportunity for businesses and individuals who have recently become aware of their Pennsylvania tax obligations to come forward voluntarily and meet their obligations. In return for coming forward voluntarily, filing their tax returns, and clearing their tax debts, taxpayers are only responsible for the payment of tax and interest. All penalties for taxes administered by the Pennsylvania Department of Revenue will be waived when the requirements of the Voluntary Disclosure Agreement have been completed [*Pennsylvania Tax Update No. 95*, Pennsylvania Department of Revenue, September/October 2001].

• *Voluntary disclosure exposure limits*

The Pennsylvania Department of Revenue now limits the payment and filing periods of corporate taxes under the VDP to five years plus the current year. All penalties will be stricken when all requirements of the agreement have been completed. The responsibility for payment and filing of non-corporate taxes of taxpayers accepted into the VDP is limited to three years plus the current year [*Pennsylvania Tax Update No. 97*, Pennsylvania Department of Revenue, January/February 2002].

• *Eligible participants in Voluntary Disclosure Program*

Taxpayers eligible to participate are those who owe non-corporate taxes (*e.g.,* sales & use, employer withholding, individual) due after December 31, 1993. For taxpayers accepted into the VDP, the responsibility for payment and filing of non-corporate taxes is limited to the current year plus three (3) prior years. The responsibility for the payment and filing of corporate taxes of taxpayers accepted into this program is limited to five (5) years plus the current year. Participating taxpayers must file applicable returns and pay all tax and interest for the period covered in the Voluntary Disclosure Agreement. Penalties will be stricken when all requirements of the agreement have been completed.

• *Ineligible participants*

Taxpayers are not eligible to participate in the VDP if any of the following apply:

(1) Taxpayers currently registered with the Pennsylvania Department of Revenue that have not filed or are delinquent in filing tax returns for periods being requested for participation in the VDP.

(2) Foreign and domestic corporations registered with the Pennsylvania Department of State. These corporations are automatically registered with the Pennsylvania Department of Revenue and are not eligible for participation for corporate tax liabilities. This does not, however, preclude them from participating in the VDP for other types of non-corporate taxes.

(3) Taxpayers currently under investigation by the Pennsylvania Department of Revenue, Bureau of Audits, or Discovery Division.

• *Business trust fund taxes*

The exposure limitation (*i.e.,* 3 years or 5 years) does not apply to business trust fund taxes (sales and employer withholding) when the tax has been collected *but not remitted.* Taxpayer who fail to remit taxes they have collected must comply from the date the tax was collected.

• *Application for participation*

A taxpayer who would like to participate in the VDP should contact the Office of Voluntary Disclosure. The taxpayer will be assigned a case number by the liaison officer. All correspondence, telephone inquiries, and requests for the Business Activities Questionnaire, Form DAS-77, should be directed to the following:

Liaison Officer
Voluntary Disclosure Program
PA Department of Revenue
Dept. 281100
Harrisburg, PA 17128-1100
(717) 787-9832

After receiving a case number, the taxpayer will be asked to submit the following information in writing:

(1) The type(s) of tax involved and the date taxpayer's activities began in Pennsylvania.

(2) A detailed description of the taxpayer's activities in Pennsylvania and the product sold or service provided.

(3) An explanation of the taxpayer's failure to file and pay the applicable taxes in the past.

(4) A statement that the taxpayer has not been contacted previously by the Department of Revenue concerning the tax liability.

(5) A completed Business Activities Questionnaire (Form DAS-77).

¶4615

• *Voluntary disclosure agreement*

A Voluntary Disclosure Committee reviews all applications. If the application is approved by the Committee, the taxpayer/representative will receive two copies of the proposed Voluntary Disclosure agreement for signature. Both copies of the voluntary disclosure agreement received from the Voluntary Disclosure Committee must be completed and signed by the taxpayer or an authorized representative and returned to the Department of Revenue within 45 business days of the Department's original mailing date. The agreement will then be signed by the appropriate Department official; and one signed copy will be returned to the taxpayer/representative with specific instructions for filing returns on applicable forms and making payments. Applicable forms will be provided. Any modification of the agreement will render it void. Failure to comply with the terms of the agreement or other requirements of the program in a timely and accurate manner will render the agreement void, and the taxpayer will be subject to all assessment action deemed appropriate by the Department.

• *Refunds and audit*

Taxpayers participating in the Voluntary Disclosure Program must sign an agreement that states they will not petition for a refund of any taxes reported through the program. However, the Department reserves the right to audit the taxpayer. Under no condition will the Department accept prospective agreements through the VDP.

¶4616 Tax Audits

The Secretary of Revenue and the Auditor General, severally, and any agent appointed by either of them, are authorized to examine the books and papers of any corporation, association, or individual subject to tax for Pennsylvania purposes to verify the accuracy of any return or report made under any act requiring the filing of a return or report [72 P.S. § 1601].

• *General*

The Department of Revenue (or any of its authorized agents) is authorized to examine the books, papers and records of any taxpayer or other persons in order to verify the accuracy and completeness of any return or report made, or if no return or report was made, to ascertain and assess any tax or other liability owed the Commonwealth [72 P.S. § 10003.21(a)]. The Department may determine the amount of tax or other liability required to be paid and determine the liability based upon the facts contained in the return or report being audited or other information in the Department's possession [72 P.S. § 10003.21(b)]. The Department may determine the liability based upon a reasonable statistical sample or test audit if records are incomplete or if a complete audit would impose an undue burden on the Department [72 P.S. 10003.21(b)].

Audit Challenges

The taxpayer may challenge the accuracy of a statistical sample or test audit by providing clear and convincing evidence that the method used for a statistical sample or test audit is erroneous, lacks a rational basis or produces a different result when the complete records are considered [72 P.S. § 10003.21(c)]. This is a departure from the ordinary rule, which provides for *de novo* appellate review for tax matters.

• *Examination under oath*

The Department of Revenue by its duly authorized agents may also, upon reasonable notice, examine any person under oath about taxable sales or use by any taxpayer or about any other matter that relates to the enforcement or administration of the statute. For this purpose, the Department has the power to compel, through the legal process, the production of books, papers, records, or other documents, and the attendance of any person(s) (as parties or as witnesses) who it believes have knowledge of such matters [61 Pa. Code § 35.1(a)(3)]. Procedures for these hearings and examinations are conducted in the manner provided by relevant provisions of the Fiscal Code [72 P.S. § § 1—1855].

- *Retention and maintenance of records*

Records must be retained for a period not less than three years from the end of the calendar year to which they relate [61 Pa. Code § 35.1(a)(5)]. Nonresidents who maintain required records must maintain them at all times at a place within Pennsylvania, unless authorized by the Department, in writing, to maintain the records at a place outside Pennsylvania. Such authorization is conditioned upon agreement to and compliance with those requirements the Department may impose, including the assumption by the nonresident of an obligation to pay the reasonable expense of examination by the Department or its agents of records located outside Pennsylvania [61 Pa. Code § 35.1(l)(5)].

- *Effect of noncompliance*

Criminal and other sanctions imposed for failure to register or maintain required records or permit examination of relevant materials or persons are discussed in 61 Pa. Code § 35.2 [61 Pa. Code § 35.1(a)(6)].

- *Definition of terms*

The following words and terms, when used in the context of auditing regulations, have the following meanings, unless the context clearly indicates otherwise [61 Pa. Code § 8a.1]:

— *Audit period:* the period of time for which an audit is conducted.

— *Block sample:* one or more groups of transactions selected as a unit from a population (*e.g.,* invoices numbered 100 to 200 or transactions for the months of May and October).

— *Clustered sample:* statistical sample in which blocks of adjacent transactions are selected with known probability; a statistical sample of transactions within the blocks may be selected, creating a two-stage statistical sample.

— *Deviation from the mean:* the numerical difference between a single statistical observation and the mean (average) of all of the statistical observations.

— *Outlier:* a statistical observation that appears to deviate markedly from other members of the sample from which it came.

— *Population:* the total transactions during an audit period from which the sample is selected.

— *Range:* the numerical difference between the largest and smallest statistical observations in the sample.

— *Standard deviation:* the square root of the average squared deviation from the mean (*i.e.,* arithmetic average).

— *Standard error:* the standard deviation divided by the square root of the number of statistical observations in the sample.

— *Statistical estimation:* a method of estimating the numerical characteristics of a population (*e.g.,* averages, totals, or ratios) from a statistical sample and estimating the precision of the estimated characteristics.

— *Statistical sample:* a selection of transactions (observations) in which each of the transactions in the population, or a stratum from it, has a known chance of being selected (also called a probability sample).

— *Stratum:* a subdivision of the population in which the transactions within the subdivision are expected to be more uniform with respect to the characteristics being examined than the transactions across the subdivisions.

— *Taxpayer:* a person, association, fiduciary, partnership, corporation or other entity required to pay, withhold or collect any tax administered by the Department of Revenue.

— *Test audit:* an audit of sampled transactions selected by either a block sample or a statistical sample method.

— *Test period:* a time period or periods selected for the test audit (*e.g.,* the month of May).

— *Transaction:* a term that includes an entry, document, invoice or other record regardless of the method of creation or retention.

• *Types of audit*

Examination may be made by desk audit, field audit or another form of audit [72 P.S. § 10003.21(b); 61 Pa. Code § 8a.3]. The Department of Revenue is specifically authorized to use a reasonable statistical sample or test audit performed in accordance with its regulations if the individual being audited does not have complete records of transactions or if the review of each transaction or invoice would place an undue burden on the Department to conduct an audit in a timely and efficient manner [72 P.S. § 10003.21(b)].

• *Determination of audit method*

If the taxpayer does not have complete records or if the review of each transaction would be unduly burdensome for the Department, the Department will determine whether to examine all of the records of a taxpayer for an entire audit period, employ a test audit method or utilize a combination of audit methods [61 Pa. Code § 8a.5]. The following factors will be considered in determination of audit method:

— The type of tax under audit.

— The nature of the taxpayer's business.

— The number of transactions in the population (*i.e.,* the total transactions during an audit period from which the sample is selected).

— The adequacy and availability of the taxpayer's records.

— Whether the taxpayer's business is cyclical or seasonal.

— Whether significant changes in the taxpayer's business or activities occurred during the audit period (*e.g.,* discontinuing or adding a line of business).

— Other relevant factors.

Motor carriers road tax: When determining whether to employ the test audit method in an audit of a motor carriers road tax or a similar tax that may be enacted, the Department will consider the following factors [61 Pa. Code § 8a.6(4)]:

— The average fleet mileage reported by the taxpayer.

— Whether the vehicles are company-owned, permanently leased from owner-operators, or a combination of both.

— The types of vehicles in the fleet.

— The type of fuel used to power the vehicles.

— The geographical area in which the vehicles operate.

— The type of commodities hauled.

— The total number of vehicles in the fleet.

— The adequacy and availability of taxpayer records.

— Whether the taxpayer's business is cyclical or seasonal.

— Whether significant changes in the taxpayer's business or activities occurred during the audit period (*e.g.,* discontinuing or adding a line of business).

— Other relevant factors.

• *Test audit plan*

Prior to conducting a test audit, the Department of Revenue will set forth in writing a test audit plan and provide the taxpayer with an opportunity to review and comment on the plan [61 Pa. Code § 8a.8]. The plan will describe the following:

— The audit period (the period for which the audit is conducted).

— The records subject to review.

— Methods for selecting records.

— Statistical estimation procedures (see below), including the taxpayer's right to request an increased sample size.

— The manner in which any tax liability will be calculated based upon the records reviewed.

Specification of factors for sales and use tax and similar taxes: When the Department uses a test audit method in an audit of a state or local sales and use tax or hotel occupancy tax or Public Transportation Assistance Tax, or a similar tax that may be enacted, the following factors will be considered [61 Pa. Code § 8a.6(5)]:

— Average gross sales.

— Ratio of taxable sales to gross sales.

— Whether the taxpayer's business is cyclical or seasonal.

— Whether significant changes in the taxpayer's business or activities occurred during the audit period (*e.g.,* discontinuing or adding a line of business).

— The adequacy and availability of taxpayer records.

— Average gross sales.

— Ratio of taxable sales to gross sales.

— Other relevant factors.

• *Selection of sample for a test audit*

When a test audit is used, the selection of the block sample, statistical sample or clustered sample will be based on the Department's analysis of the taxpayer's business operations and records and must reasonably represent the population from which the sampled transactions are selected [61 Pa. Code § 8a.6]. The Department may use stratification levels in performing statistical sampling. When a block sample method is used, the Department will select blocks whose average is approximately equal to the estimated average of key characteristics for the audit period (*e.g.,* sales, taxable to gross sales ratio, purchases or number of transactions). Outliers will be identified and excluded from the sample.

Outliers: In determining whether to exclude the values of certain transactions from the sample, the Department will identify the transactions in the sample that are outliers. For purpose of identifying outliers, the Department will determine the transaction difference (*i.e.,* the difference between audited value and reported value) for each transaction in the sample. See 61 Pa. Code § 8a.6 for more details about transaction differences. If a transaction is confirmed to be an outlier, the following steps will be taken:

(1) The taxpayer will be notified about the outliers and requested to furnish evidence to be considered in determining the audited finding. If, after examining the further evidence, the auditor agrees that a smaller difference between reported amount and audited amount (*i.e.,* the transaction difference) is justified, the auditor will replace the original transaction by the adjusted finding.

(2) If the taxpayer does not provide sufficient evidence, the outlier will be eliminated from the sample and audited independently. The audit finding on the outlier will be computed separately, and the audit finding will be added to or, if negative, subtracted from the result of the project for the remaining sample.

(3) The sample values, adjusted for outliers, will be used for projection of the total audit finding and its standard error.

- *Statistical examination and software*

Audit results are computed by projecting the audit findings identified in the sample, as adjusted for outliers, regardless of whether the sample is a statistical sample or a block sample [61 Pa. Code § 8a.7]. When the statistical estimation method is used, a standard error of the estimate is computed from the sample observations (adjusted for outliers) to indicate the reliability of the estimated average, total or ratio. The standard error cannot be estimated when the block sampling method is used. The Department of Revenue may use software that has been designed in accordance with accepted statistical practices, and the formulas used by the software will be available for examination by the taxpayer.

Except as otherwise mutually agreed by the Department and the taxpayer, the number of observations in the sample will be chosen so that the projected sample will, on the average, yield an estimated precision within 25% of the midpoint of a 90% two-sided confidence interval. In determining the size of the sample, the Department will use the sample size selection table of 61 Pa. Code § 8a.7(4). The estimated precision of the sample selected may be less than or greater than 25%, depending upon the variability in the sample data. The standard error and estimated precision will be calculated and reviewed with the taxpayer. The sample size will be increased upon the request of the taxpayer. The process of increasing the sample size will be repeated until mutual agreement is reached between the taxpayer and the Department on an acceptable number of observations [61 Pa. Code § 8a.7(3)].

Planning for Audits

It is important that taxpayers utilize the expertise of employees or consultants with knowledge of audit sampling techniques to be prepared to interact with the Department of Revenue in determining the appropriate sample size. The taxpayer can initiate internal statistical reviews to anticipate the results of a Departmental audit and discover problems (*e.g.*, the existence of outliers that might distort results) that should be brought to the attention of the Department auditors. The taxpayer will be given the opportunity to review the audit findings, but it is important to plan for this final step in advance of receiving the Department's findings.

- *Audit findings*

At the conclusion of the audit, the audit findings and a copy of the work papers will be provided to the taxpayer [61 Pa. Code § 8a.9]. The auditor will do the following:

(1) Discuss the findings with the taxpayer.

(2) Provide the taxpayer the opportunity to comment in writing.

(3) Explain the procedures for the processing, assessing and appealing of the audit findings.

¶4617 Electronic Funds Transfer

Electronic Funds Transfer (EFT) is a program that enables taxpayers to remit certain tax payments electronically. EFT is mandatory for payments of $10,000 or more [72 P.S. § 1503]. EFT, however, is available to all taxpayers on a voluntary basis regardless of the amount of their tax liabilities.

Taxpayers remitting payments of $10,000 or more must make those payments by one of the electronic funds transfer (EFT) payment methods available (ACH Debit or ACH Credit) [61 Pa. Code § 5.3(c)]. Separate transfers must be made for each payment [61 Pa. Code § 5.3(f)]. For payments of less than $10,000, use of EFT is voluntary. This method of payment is authorized by § 9 of the Fiscal Code. A taxpayer may choose the ACH debit method or the ACH credit method. This requirement applies to payments of only the following taxes [61 Pa. Code § 5.3(d)]:

— Sales and use tax.

— Employer withholding tax.

— Liquid fuels tax.

— Fuels use tax.

— Mutual thrift institutions tax.

— Oil company franchise tax.

— Malt beverage tax.

— Motor carrier road tax.

— Corporate net income tax.

— Capital stock/franchise tax.

— Bank shares tax.

— Title insurance companies shares tax.

— Insurance premiums tax.

— Public utility realty tax (PURTA).

— Gross receipts taxes.

• *Voluntary participation*

A taxpayer not required to remit payments by EFT may, upon approval from the Secretary, use the EFT method for tax payments [61 Pa. Code § 5.4].

• *Registration*

In order to participate in the EFT program, a taxpayer must submit a completed Authorization Agreement to the Department of Revenue. Registration for the electronic transfer of funds (EFT) for all business taxes can now be done on-line through the e-TIDES web site. See ¶ 4620 for more information on e-TIDES.

The Department will each year notify a taxpayer it anticipates will be required to register on or before September 1. A taxpayer notified by the Department is required to register with the Department by October 1. A taxpayer registered with the Department for EFT payment is not required to re-register unless the taxpayer wants to change the method of payment [61 Pa. Code § 5.5].

• *Failure to make payment by EFT*

Any person who fails to make a required payment by a prescribed method shall, in addition to any other penalty, interest or addition provided by law, be liable for a penalty of 3% of the total tax due up to a maximum of $1,000 [72 P.S. § 10003.7]. Note that § 9.1 of the Fiscal Code says that this 3% additional penalty shall not exceed $500. There is no authoritative answer to the question of which section prevails. Taxpayers should be careful when dealing with this issue.

• *Late filing*

Taxpayers are required to see that EFT payments are deposited to the Commonwealth's account on or before the due date. If the due date falls on a day other than a business day, the deposit by EFT is due on the first business day thereafter. The EFT payment method does not change filing requirements or the provisions for penalties

¶4617

and interest for late filing apply as provided by law. However, if a taxpayer is unable to make a timely payment because of failures within the banking system/ACH interface that are beyond the taxpayer's control, the taxpayer will not be subject to penalties and interest for late filing. If the late filing is caused by errors made by the Treasury, the Department, or their agents, late filing penalties and interest will not be assessed. Other miscellaneous provisions can be found in 61 Pa. Code § 5.7.

• *Alternative payment method—certified or cashier's check*

The Fiscal Code requires that the Department of Revenue establish an option permitting payment by certified or cashier's check *delivered in person or by courier* to the Department of Revenue on or before the due date of the obligation in lieu of payment by EFT [72 P.S. § 9]. The Department will accept payment by a certified or cashier's check, in person or by courier with the appropriate return or deposit statement, to the Pennsylvania Department of Revenue, Bureau of Business Trust Fund Taxes, EFT Unit, Ninth Floor, Strawberry Square, Fourth & Walnut Streets, Harrisburg, PA 17128 on or before the due date of the obligation. Payments will not be accepted at other locations [61 Pa. Code § 5.3(e)].

• *Definition of terms*

The following words and terms have the following meaning within the context of EFT, unless the context clearly indicates otherwise [61 Pa. Code § 5.2]:

"ACH—Automated Clearing House": A federal reserve bank or an organization established by agreement with the National Automated Clearing House Association (NACHA) that operates as a clearing house for transmitting or receiving entries between the banks or bank accounts.

"ACH credit": A transaction in which the taxpayer, through its own bank, originates an entry crediting the Commonwealth's bank account and debiting its own bank account for the amount of the payment due. For more detail see 61 Pa. Code § 5.6.

"ACH debit": A transaction in which the Commonwealth, through its designated depository bank, originates an ACH transaction debiting the taxpayer's bank account and crediting the Department's bank account for the amount of the payment due. For more detail see 61 Pa. Code § 5.6.

"Business day": The hours set by the Department on a day other than a Saturday, Sunday or the following holidays as set by the Act of May 31, 1893 [P.L. 188, No. 138, § 11]: New Year's Day, Dr. Martin Luther King, Jr. Day, President's Day, Memorial Day, Independence Day, Labor Day, Columbus Day, Veteran's Day, Thanksgiving Day and Christmas Day. For ACH credit taxpayers, the business day will be between 9 a.m. and 5 p.m. prevailing Eastern time. For ACH debit taxpayers, the hours are specified in the instructions provided by the Department.

"EFT—Electronic Funds Transfer": A transfer of funds, other than a transaction originated by check, draft or similar paper instrument, that is initiated through an electronic terminal, telephonic instrument or computer or magnetic tape to instruct or authorize a financial institution to debit or credit an account.

"Fedwire—Federal Reserve Wire Transfer": A transaction utilizing the national electronic payment system to transfer funds through Federal Reserve Banks. Fedwire is no longer a routine payment method. It may be used in emergency situations only and with prior approval of the Department. For details, see 61 Pa. Code § 5.6.

¶4618 Tax Liens

All taxes imposed by the Commonwealth, along with interest and penalties, are a first lien against the franchises and property (both real and personal) of taxpayers unless otherwise expressly provided by law [72 P.S. § 1401].

Perfection of Tax Liens

Even though unpaid taxes create a lien against a taxpayer, the lien is not perfected until it has been filed by the Department of Revenue with a prothonotary of the Commonwealth Court and the prothonotary has docketed the lien [72 P.S. §1404; 61 Pa. Code §119.11(a)(2)]. The Commonwealth cannot take any action against a taxpayer (*e.g.*, publish the lien in the newspaper, start action to take property) until the lien is perfected. Taxpayers should be careful to comply with all requirements to contest the tax in order to prevent perfection of the lien.

• *Attachment and seizure of funds believed to hold property subject to a Commonwealth lien for tax items*

Administrative bank attachment for accounts of obligors to the Commonwealth: Provided that an obligor has not entered into and is in compliance with a deferred payment plan with the Department of Revenue, the Department may order the attachment and seizure of funds in an obligor's account that the Department reasonably believes to hold property subject to a lien in favor of the Commonwealth for tax, interest, additions, or penalties due to the Commonwealth. Upon receiving seized funds, the Department has applied the amount seized to the obligor's lien obligation [72 P.S. § 10003.22(a)]. The Department may order the attachment of funds in the obligor's account by sending a notice to the financial institution sent by an electronic format or any other reasonable manner as agreed to by the Department and the financial institution [72 P.S. § 10003.22(b)(2)]. The notice must include all the information required by 72 P.S. § 10003.22(b)(3).

CAUTION

This is a general overview of the seizure and attachment provisions. 72 P.S. § 10003.22 is a lengthy and detailed section. Consult the statute for further details.

• *Donation of property subject to tax claims*

Effective April 24, 2006 [Act 18 of 2006 (S.B. 640), §5], a county, city, borough, incorporated town, township, home rule municipality, optional plan municipality, or optional charter municipality may accept the donation of property that is subject to a claim for taxes. A donation under this provision operates to divest all liens (including penalties, interest, and fees) against the property possessed by the municipality accepting the donation, and all other local tax liens recorded prior to the date of donation [53 P.S. §7501.1(a)]. An owner who donates property under this provision is not personally liable for the amount of claims for taxes exempted to extinguished as a result of the donation [53 P.S. §7501.1(e)]. A school district or municipal authority (other than a redevelopment authority) also may accept donated property if it has designated another municipality or redevelopment authority in which the property is located to act as its agent with regard to the donation [53 P.S. §7501.1(g)].

• *Priority of tax liens*

The proceeds of a tax sale must be applied to tax liens filed by the Department of Revenue before any other judgment, mortgage, or other claim that may subsequently arise [72 P.S. §1404.1; 61 Pa. Code §119.11]. Tax liens have priority over any other obligation, judgment, claim, lien, or estate arising after the filing and docketing of the tax lien and are subordinate only to the following:

(1) Mortgages against realty or other liens existing and duly recorded before the tax lien.

(2) Cost of the writ and the judicial sale.

(3) Real estate taxes on real estate [61 Pa. Code §119.11(c), (d)].

- *Judicial sales*

When a tax lien is discharged by a judicial sale, the lien of the Commonwealth is transferred from the property sold to the fund realized from the sale, and the purchaser takes free of the Commonwealth lien, even if the fund is insufficient to pay the Commonwealth's claim. When the fund is distributed, the Commonwealth's lien is postponed in payment to the lien or liens created by or entered against the predecessor in title or other mortgagee or lien holder having priority. However, the Commonwealth's lien will not be postponed in payment to local taxes or municipal claims, except as otherwise expressly provided by law under which the Commonwealth claim arose [72 P.S. § 1401].

Judicial sales to discharge subordinate liens: When property is sold to discharge a lien that is subordinate to the Commonwealth's lien, the Commonwealth's lien continues in full force and effect to the extent it is not paid from the proceeds.

- *Release of liens*

If, after a judicial sale, all tax liens have been satisfied, the Department of Revenue will issue to the sheriff, receiver, trustee, assignee, master, or other office in charge of the sale a certificate showing that fact.

Release upon payment of proportionate share of tax: A corporation (or its owners or lien creditors) may pay its proportionate part of taxes due and request a release of a lien or liens. The Department of Revenue, with the approval of the Attorney General and Auditor General, may then release the corporation from tax liens unless the value of the real property requested to be released is less than the proportionate share of the taxes due. In that case the Department of Revenue, with the approval of the Attorney General and Auditor General, may release the corporation from tax liens after it pays the portion of the taxes due deemed equitable by the Department, which in any case cannot exceed the value of the property to be released. The Department will then furnish the person or corporation paying the tax with a certificate showing the property released, and the certificate may be recorded in the office of the recorder of deeds of the county in which the land lies [72 P.S. § 1401].

- *Request for release/subordination of liens*

The Department of Revenue has announced that it will now take requests for the release and/or subordination of a lien [*Pennsylvania Tax Update No. 98*, March/April 2002, Pennsylvania Department of Revenue]. Claims must originate with the Department of Revenue Office of Chief Counsel for recommendation purposes and must be approved by (i) the Office of Attorney General; (ii) the Auditor General (if warranted); and (iii) the Department of Revenue.

All requests for release and/or subordination of a lien must have the following supporting documentation attached:

(1) Amount of consideration offered for the release.

(2) Copy of the deed description for each parcel of property that is the subject of the lien release, including deed description of additional property that the taxpayer may have as additional collateral.

(3) Copy of all relevant tax liens with a current payoff figure for each lien as of the proposed settlement date or other relative period.

(4) Statement with respect to whether the taxpayer has other collectible Pennsylvania tax liabilities, including liened and unliened collectibles.

(5) Copies of all Corporate Officer Assessment and liens filed of record.

(6) Copy of all documents from the lending institution willing to lend the funds if the request is for subordination.

(7) Copy of all mortgages and notes with current payoff statements.

¶4618

(8) Copy of the Title Report reflecting all lien holders with the lien dates filed of record and all other supporting documents.

(9) Copy of the Agreement of Sale and Complaint for Mortgage Forfeiture (if any) along with a copy of the appraisal report reflecting current fair market value of the subject property to release and a copy of the Settlement Statement.

(10) Copy of the return receipt (if any) from the Register of Wills and the appraisal if a release is requested for inheritance taxes.

(11) Documents relative to the case if the taxpayer requesting the release is in bankruptcy. If a business if out of existence, state the date and attach a copy of the Out of Existence form.

(12) Copy of the County Tax Assessment Card and State Tax Equalization Board Assessment Factor for the year in question.

(13) Copy of a Pennsylvania liquor license or lottery license (if any), and whether the taxpayer is delinquent in any unfiled tax returns.

(14) Correspondence from the Internal Revenue Service or other lien holders that indicate they are going to release their liens or judgments for amounts less than the lien and for what consideration.

(15) Copy of a Deferred Payment Plan (if any).

(16) All related documentation if the subject property is currently up for a sheriff's sale.

Release/subordination is based on the merits of individual cases, which may require other supporting documentation in addition to the items enumerated above. For more information about the release/subordination of liens, contact the Office of Chief Counsel at 717-787-1382.

• *Redemption of property sold*

The owner of any property sold under a tax or municipal claim, their assignees, or any parties whose lien or estate has been discharged may redeem the property within nine months (one year prior to September 13, 2004) from the date of the acknowledgement of the sheriff's deed by paying the amount bid at the tax sale and other specified charges and expenses [53 P.S. §7293(a)]. For more details, see the Municipal Claims and Tax Liens Act [53 P.S. §7101 *et seq.*].

Vacant property: Notwithstanding any other provision of law to the contrary, in any township, borough, or incorporated town, vacant property cannot be redeemed by any person after the date of the acknowledgment of the sheriff's deed therefor. Property is deemed to be "vacant property" unless it was continuously occupied by the same individual or basic family unit as a residence for at least 90 days prior to the date of the sale and continues to be so occupied on the date of the acknowledgment of the sheriff's deed therefor [53 P.S. §7293(c)].

¶4619 Enterprise Registration (Form PA-100)

The Pennsylvania Enterprise Registration Form (PA-100) must be completed by enterprises to register for certain taxes and services administered by the Pennsylvania Department of Revenue and the Pennsylvania Department of Labor & Industry. For registration assistance, contact 717-787-1064, Monday through Friday, 8:00 a.m. to 4:30 p.m. (EST); service for customers with special hearing and/or speaking needs (TT only) 1-800-447-3020.

Form PA-100 is also used for the following purposes:

(1) By previously registered enterprises to (a) register for additional taxes and services; (b) reactivate a tax or service; or (c) notify both Departments that additional establishment locations have been added.

(2) To request the Unemployment Compensation Experience Record and Reserve Account Balance of a Predecessor.

- *Enterprise defined*

An enterprise is any individual or organization, sole proprietorship, partnership, corporation, government organization, business trust, association, etc., that is subject to the laws of Pennsylvania and performs at least one of the following:

(1) Pays wages to employees.

(2) Offers products or services for sale to others.

(3) Collects donations.

(4) Collects taxes.

(5) Is allocated use of tax dollars.

(6) Has a name that is intended for use and, by that name is to be recognized as an organization engaged in economic activity.

- *Establishment defined*

An establishment is an economic unit (usually at a single physical location) where one of the following occurs:

(1) Business is conducted inside Pennsylvania;

(2) Business is conducted outside Pennsylvania with reporting requirements to Pennsylvania.

(3) Pennsylvania residents are employed (inside or outside of Pennsylvania).

An enterprise and an establishment may have the same physical location. Multiple establishments exist if the following apply:

(1) Business is conducted at multiple locations.

(2) Distinct and separate economic activities involving separate employees are performed at a single location. Each activity may be treated as a separate establishment if separate reports can be prepared for (a) the number of employees, (b) wages and salaries, or (c) sales and receipts.

- *Taxes and services*

Form PA-100 is used to register for the following taxes and services:

(1) Cigarette dealer's license.

(2) Corporation taxes.

(3) Employer withholding tax.

(4) Fuels tax report.

(5) Local sales, use, hotel occupancy tax.

(6) Motor carriers road tax/IFTA.

(7) Promoter license.

(8) Public transportation assistance tax license.

(9) Sales tax exempt status.

(10) Sales, use, hotel occupancy tax license.

(11) Small games of chance license/certificate.

(12) Transient vendor certificate.

(13) Unemployment compensation.

(14) Use tax.

¶4619

(15) Vehicle rental tax.

(16) Wholesaler certificate.

(17) Workers' compensation coverage.

• *Registration options*

Enterprises now have the option of either the PA Open for Business registration process, which can be accessed at http://www.paopen4business.state.pa.us. or the on-line PA-100 form, which can be accessed at http://www.pa100.state.pa.us.

The Department of Labor & Industry has a signature requirement for the Unemployment Compensation section of the PA-100. When a user who is registering for Unemployment Compensation completes the on-line application, he or she will be prompted to print, sign, and mail the application to the Pennsylvania Department of Labor & Industry. Users' data will be processed electronically and matched with the signed copy forwarded in the mail.

Users who have questions about the on-line PA-100 can e-mail the Department of Revenue at ra-pa100reg@state.Pennsylvania.us. Responses will be given within three (3) business days [*Pennsylvania Tax Update No. 97*, Pennsylvania Department of Revenue, January/February 2002].

The PA Departments of Revenue and Labor & Industry have partnered to bring e-TIDES (*Electronic Tax Information and Data Exchange System*). E-TIDES is an Internet filing system that allows electronic filing of returns, payments and/or extension requests. Details of the e-TIDES program can be found at http://www.etides.state.pa.us/. A list of forms that may be submitted through e-TIDES can be found at http://www.etides.state.pa.us/HomePage/TaxFormInfo.htm.

¶4620 Electronic Filing of Certain Returns and Payments

• *Registration for EFT*

Taxpayers may now register for the Electronic Funds Transfer (EFT) program at the Department's e-TIDES web site at http://www.etides.state.pa.us. See ¶4617 for more information about EFT.

No Sales and Use Tax and Employer Withholding Coupon Booklets

Beginning with tax year 2004, the Department of Revenue will no longer mail Sales and Use Tax and Employer Withholding Tax coupon booklets to taxpayers registered to use e-TIDES. Should the need for paper forms arise, forms and coupon booklets can be ordered from the Department's web site at http://www.revenue.state.pa.us. Go to the web site, click on "Forms and Publications," and choose the "Business Taxes" link. Alternatively, taxpayers may call the 24-hour Forms Ordering Message Service at 1-800-362-2050 [*Pennsylvania Tax Update No. 105*, Pennsylvania Department of Revenue, July/August 2003].

¶4621 Bulk and Auction Sales

A bulk sale occurs when a corporation, joint-stock association, limited partnership, or company sells or transfers in bulk 51% or more of any stock of goods, wares or merchandise of any kind, fixtures, machinery, equipment, buildings, or real estate [72 P.S. § 1403]. A bulk sale always involves the sale or transfer of 51% or more of the goods, wares or merchandise of a kind, fixtures, machinery, equipment, buildings, or real estate. The definitions of "bulk sale" for the personal income tax, the sales and use tax, and corporate taxes, however, differ slightly. Pay close attention to the specific definition of bulk sale for the tax involved. The reporting requirements discussed below, however, are the same for all taxes involved.

The Department of Revenue has interpreted the bulk sales statute disjunctively with respect to each asset classification and as applicable only to assets located within

Pennsylvania. Therefore, a taxpayer must secure a clearance certificate when 51% or more of any of the listed assets are sold [REV-1076]. The bulk sale reporting requirements of 72 P.S. § 1403 (discussed below) also apply to the personal income tax (see ¶ 305) and to the sales and use tax (see ¶ 702).

Fiscal Code Controls

All bulk sales (whether subject to the personal tax, the sales and use tax, or corporate taxes) must comply with the requirements of § 1403 of the Fiscal Code [72 P.S. § 1403].

- *Exclusions*

    The bulk sales provisions do not apply to the following [72 P.S. § 1403(a)]:

    (1) Sales or transfers made under any order of court.

    (2) Sales or transfers made by assignees for the benefit of creditors; executors, administrators, receivers.

    (3) Any public officer in his official capacity, or by any officer of a court.

- *Estimated tax settlements*

    If it is necessary for the Department of Revenue to make an estimated tax settlement for the purpose of issuing a corporate clearance certificate the Department may strike it off when the annual report is settled [72 P.S. § 1402(a)].

- *Notice requirement*

    All taxpayers who make bulk sales must give the Department of Revenue ten (10) days' notice of the sale or transfer prior to the completion of the transfer of the property sold [72 P.S. § 1403(b)].

- *Requirement to pay taxes*

    A taxpayer making a bulk sale is required to file all state tax reports with the Department of Revenue to the date of the proposed transfer of property and pay all taxes due the Commonwealth up that date [72 P.S. § 1403(b)].

Protection for Buyer

When a taxpayer purchases assets in a bulk sale, and the seller is later found to have a sales tax liability, the buyer has assumed that liability. The way for a buyer to protect against such an unknown liability is to have a tax indemnification provision in the purchase agreement, in which the seller agrees to pay any past tax liability that may later be found to be due.

- *Bulk sale clearance certificate*

    In the case of a bulk sale, a seller or transferor is required to present to the purchaser a bulk sale clearance certificate from the Department of Revenue showing that all Pennsylvania tax reports have been filed and all Pennsylvania taxes paid up to, and including, the date of the proposed transfer. Failure on the part of purchasers to obtain a clearance certificate makes the purchasers or assignees, as well as the seller, jointly liable for all the sellers' taxes, settled and unsettled, up to and including the date of the sale or transfer [72 P.S. § 1403(a); REV-1076].

Failure to Obtain Bulk Sale Clearance Certificate

Failure to obtain a bulk sale clearance certificate in a timely manner makes the successor corporation (the purchaser) liable for unpaid tax debts of the predecessor (the seller) [*Cmwlth. v. Qwest Transmission, Inc.*, 765 A.2d 818 (Pa.Commw. 2000)]. Qwest Microwave VII, Inc. merged into Qwest Microwave Corporation, which subsequently sold all of its assets to a corporation eventually known as Qwest Transmission Corporation

¶4621

without obtaining a bulk sale clearance certificate as required by § 1403 of the Fiscal Code [72 P.S. § 1403]. Qwest Transmission therefore became liable for the unpaid taxes of Qwest Microwave VII. Citing the controlling case of *Cmwlth. v. Marros*, 431 A.2d 392 (Pa.Commw. 1981), the Commonwealth Court said that the duty imposed by § 1403 of the Fiscal Code is not overly burdensome. The timely discharge of that duty would have assured the purchasers that all taxes had been paid or, if not paid, would have notified the purchasers of the amount alleged to be due. That knowledge would then have enabled the purchasers to contest the amount of tax alleged to be due and would have given them the ability to contest the assessment. Having failed to exercise the duty imposed on the purchaser by 72 P.S. § 1403, the taxpayers cannot contest the assessment and are liable for the seller's unpaid taxes. See also *Reese's Pizza and More v. Dept. of Labor and Industry et al.*, 93 A.3d 914 (2014) (where a successor employer was liable for the unpaid unemployment compensation contributions of a predecessor employer).

• *Information and documentation required*

The following information and documentation must be submitted with an application for a corporate clearance certificate with respect to a bulk sale [61 Pa. Code § 151.4(b)(5)]:

(1) An application for a corporate clearance certificate (Form REV-181) executed in duplicate. The original is sent to the Pennsylvania Department of Revenue (PA Department of Revenue, Bureau of Compliance, Clearance & Collections Division, Attention: Business Clearance Section, Dept. 280947, Harrisburg, PA 17128-0947), and a copy is sent to the PA Department of Labor and Industry, Bureau of Employer Tax Operations, Clearance Unit, Labor and Industry Building, Room 916, 7th & Forster Streets, Harrisburg, PA 17121. The taxpayer should retain one copy for the taxpayer's records.

(2) Reports for the current tax year to the proposed date of sale. When a bulk sale occurs prior to the end of a reporting period, the Department will accept a short-period estimated tax report, supported by a pro forma income statement and a pro forma balance sheet [REV-1076]. All tax reports, schedules, and correspondence pertaining to the bulk sales clearance certificate must be submitted to the Pennsylvania Department of Revenue at the address in item (1) above.

(3) A schedule of the assets to be sold and the resulting gains and losses.

¶4622 Keystone Opportunity Zones

• *Enabling legislation*

The legislation authorizing KOZs is the "Keystone Opportunity Zone, Keystone Opportunity Expansion Zone and Keystone Opportunity Improvement Zone Act" [73 P.S. § 820.101 *et seq.*]and is referred to herein simply as the KOZ Act. The Keystone Opportunity Zone (KOZ) Act [Act 92 of 1998, H.B. 2328] authorized the creation of 12 KOZs in Pennsylvania. The goal of the KOZ Act was to promote revitalization of economically distressed urban and rural areas by establishing zones that are virtually free of state and local taxes. In 2000, the KOZ Act was amended to include economically distressed areas that did not qualify for tax relief under the 1998 act and created Keystone Opportunity Expansion Zones (KOEZs) [Act 119 of 2000, H.B. 2498]. In 2002 a provision was made for designation of deteriorated properties as Keystone Opportunity Improvement Zones (KOIZs), to be designated by the Governor [Act 217 of 2002, S.B 1478]. The KOZ Act was again amended in 2003 to provide that companies relocating into a KOZ may qualify for the benefits of the zone merely by (i) entering into a lease agreement for property within the zone for a term at least equivalent to the duration of the zone benefits and (ii) making aggregate payments under the lease in an amount at least equal to 5% of the gross revenues of the business in the immediately preceding calendar or fiscal year [Act 51 of 2003 (H.B. 521)]. Prior to the passage of this legislation, businesses relocating to a KOZ from within Pennsylvania had to either increase employment by a significant amount or make significant capital improvements to the premises. Thus, this provision makes it significantly easier for businesses to qualify for KOZ benefits. The KOZ Act is scheduled to terminate December 31, 2018 [73 P.S. § 820.1309].

• *Administration*

The KOZ Program is administered by the Department of Community and Economic Development (DCED) in partnership with the Department of Revenue (administration of state taxes) and the Department of Labor and Industry (administration of unemployment compensation taxes).

• *Keystone opportunity zones (KOZs)*

A KOZ is a defined geographic area composed of one or more political subdivisions or portions of political subdivisions designated by the Department of Community and Economic Development (DCED) [73 P.S. § 820.103]. A KOZ is composed of deteriorated property [73 P.S. § 820.301(a)]. It is the responsibility of the DCED to authorize KOZs [73 P.S. § 820.301(b)].

Subzones: The DCED designates subzones [73 P.S. § 820.301(c)]. A "subzone" is a clearly defined geographic area containing a minimum of 20 contiguous acres or a minimum of 10 contiguous acres in a rural area [73 P.S. § 320.102].

Expansion of Keystone Opportunity Zone Program

On Feb. 14, 2012 Governor Corbett signed into law Act 16 (S.B. 1237), an expansion of the Keystone Opportunity Zone program that authorizes designation of new zones, extensions of tax-benefit for certain unoccupied parcels and additional acreage for certain zones. The most notable program changes are as follows:

   • Deteriorated, underutilized or unoccupied parcels in zones that expire in 2013 and beyond may be granted tax benefits for an additional seven to 10 years, if application for extension is received within three months of a zone's expiration date.

   • Fifteen new Keystone Opportunity Expansion Zones 10 to 350 acres in size are authorized for designation, plus four unused zones authorized in 2009 may be designated.

   • Existing zones may expand by 15 acres, if expansion is expected to increase job creation or capital investment.

   • Additional reporting requirements are imposed on businesses regarding capital investment and job creation and retention data.

For additional information, please contact the Department of Community and Economic Development at 717-346-0327.

• *Keystone opportunity expansion zones (KOEZs)*

A KOEZ is a defined geographic area composed of one or more political subdivisions or portions of political subdivisions designated by the Department of Community and Economic Development (DCED) [73 P.S. § 820.103]. A KOEZ is composed of deteriorated property and cannot exceed a total of 1,500 acres [73 P.S. § 820.301a(a)]. The DCED may authorize up to 12 KOEZs in the Commonwealth [73 P.S. § 820.301a(b)]. Qualified persons and businesses within an authorized KOEZ are entitled to the tax benefits of its designation for a period of 10 or 13 years [73 P.S. § 820.301a(b)]. The KOZ program was expanded by Act 84 of 2016 to include the designation of 12 new KOEZs for up to 10 years effective January 1, 2017 to December 31, 2026. Additionally, designated parcels can be extended up 10 years for state tax benefits if the applicant meets certain job creation and capital investment requirements.

Expansion subzones: The DCED designates subzones in a KOEZ [73 P.S. § 820.301a(c)]. An "expansion subzone" is a clearly defined geographic area containing a minimum of 15 contiguous acres or a minimum of five contiguous acres in a rural area [73 P.S. § 820.103].

• *Keystone opportunity improvement zones (KOIZs)*

A KOIZ is an area composed of improvement subzones consisting of deteriorated property designated by the Governor [73 P.S. § 820.301b]. An "improvement subzone" is a clearly defined area [73 P.S. § 820.103]. The executive order specifies the period of time (not to exceed 15 years) for which the tax benefits provided by the KOZ Act may be granted [73 P.S. § 820.301b(b)]. Qualified persons and businesses within a KOIZ subzone are entitled to the tax benefits of its designation for the period for which the KOIZ subzone has been designated [73 P.S. § 820.301(d)].

"Subzone"

In this *Guidebook*, the term "subzone" is used to refer to KOZ subzones, KOEZ subzones, and KOIZ subzones, unless otherwise indicated.

• *Deteriorated property*

"Deteriorated property" is any blighted, impoverished area containing residential, industrial, commercial, or other real property that is abandoned, unsafe, vacant, undervalued, underutilized, overgrown, defective, condemned, demolished, or that contains economically undesirable land use. The term includes property adjacent to deteriorated property that is significantly undervalued and underutilized due to the proximity of the deteriorated property and property that has been designated as deteriorated property in accordance with any other act [73 P.S. § 820.103].

• *Qualified persons*

In order to qualify each year for the tax benefits provided by the KOZ Act, a person must be domiciled and must reside in a subzone for a period of 184 consecutive days during each taxable year, which may begin on the date of designation by the DCED or on the date the person first resides within the subzone [73 P.S. § 820.306]. A "person" for this purpose is a natural person [73 P.S. § 820.103]. If a person completes the residency requirements of 73 P.S. § 820.306 or if a nonresident realizes income attributable to business activity or property within a subzone on or before the end of the tax year, the person may claim the personal income tax benefits of the KOZ Act for that portion of the tax year that the person was a resident or for that portion of the tax year during which the area is designated as a subzone [73 P.S. § 820.513].

• *Qualified businesses*

A "qualified business" is a business authorized to do business in Pennsylvania that is located or partially located within a subzone and is engaged in the active conduct of a trade or business in accordance with the following requirements [73 P.S. § 820.103; 73 P.S. § 820.307(a)]:

(1) It owns or leases real property in a subzone from which it actively conducts a trade, profession, or business.

(2) It receives certification from the DCED that the business is located and is in the active conduct of a trade, profession, or business, within the subzone, expansion subzone, or improvement subzone.

(3) It obtains annual renewal of the certification from the DCED to continue to qualify.

- *Relocation*

Any business that relocates from outside a subzone into a subzone is not eligible for KOZ Act benefits unless it does one of the following [73 P.S. § 820.307(b)]:

(1) It increases full-time employment by at least 20% in the first full year of operation within the subzone, expansion subzone, or improvement subzone.

(2) It makes a capital investment in the property located within the subzone at least equivalent to 10% of the gross revenues of that business in the immediately preceding calendar or fiscal year.

(3) It enters into a lease agreement for property located within the subzone (i) for a term at least equivalent to the duration of the subzone, expansion subzone, or improvement subzone; and (ii) with aggregate payment under the lease agreement at least equivalent to 5% of the gross revenues of that business in the immediately preceding calendar or fiscal year.

Measure Separately for Each Legal Entity

The Department of Revenue takes the position that the Pennsylvania Supreme Court's decision in *Cmwlth. v. Weldon Pajamas, Inc.* [248 A.2d 204 (Pa. 1968)] requires the measurement of capital investment and increased employment to be made separately for each legal entity.

- *Applications*

In order to maintain eligibility for KOZ Act benefits, property owners, businesses, and residents must file an annual application by December 31 of the year for which they are applying for benefits [73 P.S. § 820.907]. Once the paper copy is completed, it should be forwarded to the appropriate local KOZ coordinator. A paper copy of the application may be obtained from the local KOZ coordinator. Local KOZ coordinators are listed at http://www.newpa.com/default.aspx?id=350.

- *Tax relief requirement*

No area will be authorized as a KOZ or KOEZ unless, as part of its application, each political subdivision in which the proposed zone or subzone is to be located adopts (and provides a copy of) an ordinance, resolution, or other required action from the governing body of each political subdivision that exempts or provides deductions, abatements or credits to qualified persons and qualified businesses from local taxes upon area designation as a KOZ/KOEZ [73 P.S. § 820.304(c)].

- *State tax benefits*

Qualified persons and businesses receive the following Commonwealth tax benefits:

(1) Sales and use tax exemption (for purchases consumed and used by the business in the subzone, expansion subzone, or improvement subzone) [73 P.S. § 820.511]. See ¶ 514 and ¶ 701.

(2) Personal income tax exemption [73 P.S. § 820.512]. See ¶ 201.

(3) Corporate net income tax credit [73 P.S. § 820.515]. See ¶ 1013.

(4) Capital stock/franchise tax [73 P.S. § 820.516]. See ¶ 1329.

(5) Bank and trust company shares tax [73 P.S. § 820.517]. See ¶ 1908.

(6) Mutual thrift institutions tax [73 P.S. § 820.517]. See ¶ 1908.

(7) Insurance premiums tax [73 P.S. § 820.518]. See ¶ 2213.

Expiration of benefits: Exemptions, deductions, abatements, or credits expire on the date of expiration of the subzone [73 P.S. § 820.501(a)].

¶ 4622

• *Local tax benefits*

Political subdivisions in which designated subzones are located are required to provide exemptions, deductions, abatements, or credits with respect to the following local taxes [73 P.S. §§ 820.701—820.704]:

(1) Real property tax.

(2) Earned income and net profits tax.

(3) Business gross receipts tax.

(4) Business occupancy tax.

(5) Business privilege tax.

(6) Business occupancy tax.

(7) Mercantile license tax.

• *Tax and building code compliance required*

In order to be entitled to claim any exemptions, deductions, abatements, or credits offered by the KOZ/KOEZ program, all qualified businesses and qualified persons must be in full compliance with all state and local tax laws [73 P.S. § 820.903]. Furthermore, a qualified person or business is precluded from claiming KOZ/KOEZ benefits if that person or business owns real property in a KOZ/KOEZ subzone that is not in compliance with all applicable state and local zoning, building, and housing laws, ordinances or codes [73 P.S. § 820.904].

• *Recapture of benefits*

A qualified business located with a subzone that relocates outside of the subzone within the first five years of locating there may be required to refund the benefits the business received to the state and local jurisdiction granting the benefits [73 P.S. § 820.902].

Eligibility for Other Programs

KOZ Act benefit recipients may be eligible for other programs administered by the DCED. Through one form (Single Application for Assistance) a business may apply for funding from the DCED's various funding sources. Information about the Single Application for Assistance is available at http://www.inventpa.com/default.aspx?id—127.

• *Penalties*

Taxpayers who claim KOZ/KOEZ tax benefits to which they were not entitled are liable for the tax benefits received, plus applicable interest, in addition to civil and criminal penalties under 73 P.S. § 820.1304.

¶4623 Keystone Innovation Zone

• *Overview*

The keystone innovation zone (KIZ) program is designed to provide economic assistance to KIZ companies for the purpose of improving and encouraging research and development efforts and technology commercialization efforts resulting in employment growth and revitalization of communities [12 Pa.C.S. § 3703(a)]. The Department of Community and Economic Development (DCED) may provide grants to institutions of higher learning in KIZs [12 Pa.C.S. § 3705]; and KIZ companies may claim tax credits for increased revenues attributable to activities in the KIZ. KIZ grants are beyond the scope of this Guidebook; KIZ tax credits are discussed below.

KIZ defined: Keystone innovation zones (KIZs) are clearly defined contiguous geographic areas made up of portions of one or more political subdivisions [12

Pa.C.S. §3702]. KIZs may be established in communities in which institutions of higher education are located. An institution of higher education for this purpose is a public or private institution within Pennsylvania authorized by the Department of Education to grant an associate degree or higher degree, including branch or satellite campuses of the institution [12 Pa.C.S. §3702].

Establishment of KIZs: A KIZ partnership may apply to the DCED to establish a KIZ [12 Pa.C.S. §3703(b)]. A KIZ partnership is any association or group that is made up of at least one institution of higher education and a combination of private businesses, business support organizations, commercial lending institutions, venture capital companies, angel investor networks, or foundations [12 Pa.C.S. §3702].

Administration: The DCED will administer the KIZ program.

KIZ vs. KOZ

KIZ and KOZ are similar names, but they are very different programs. The goal of KOZs is to improve the economy of blighted areas through tax benefits. See ¶4622 for discussion of KOZs. KIZs, on the other hand, are designed to encourage research and development efforts and technology commercialization efforts.

• *Application for KIZ tax credit*

A KIZ company may file an application for a KIZ tax credit with the DCED [12 Pa.C.S. §3706(b)]. A KIZ company is a for-profit business entity that is (i) located within a KIZ and (ii) has been in operation for fewer than eight years [12 Pa.C.S. §3702].

Applications must be filed by September 15 of each year for the prior taxable year, beginning September 15, 2006. The application must be submitted on a form required by the DCED and must be accompanied by a certification from the KIZ coordinator that the KIZ company falls within a targeted industry segment identified in the strategic plan adopted by the KIZ partnership. The DCED will review the application and, upon being satisfied that all requirements have been met, will issued a tax credit certificate to the KIZ company. All certificates will be awarded by December 15 of each year [12 Pa.C.S. §3706(b)]. A KIZ coordinator is a nonprofit organization that (i) is not an institution of higher education and (ii) is chosen by a KIZ partnership and agreed to by the DCED to administer the activities of a KIZ [12 Pa.C.S. §3702].

• *Amount of KIZ tax credit*

A keystone innovation zone (KIZ) company (*i.e.*, a company that is located in a KIZ and has been in existence for fewer than eight years) may claim a tax credit equal to 50% of the increase in the KIZ company's gross revenues in the immediately preceding taxable year attributable to activities in the KIZ over the KIZ company's gross revenues in the second preceding taxable year attributable to its activities in the KIZ. A tax credit for a KIZ company cannot exceed $100,000 annually. For the purposes of the KIZ tax credit, the term "gross revenues" may include grants received by the KIZ company from any source whatsoever [12 Pa.C.S. §3706(a)].

• *Limitation on tax credits*

The total amount of tax credits approved by the DCED cannot exceed $15 million for any one taxable year. If $15 million of the tax credits are not approved for any one taxable year, the unused portion will not be available for use in future taxable years. If the total amount of tax credits applied for by all taxpayers for any one taxable year exceeds $15 million, each applicant will receive its pro rata share of the $15 million [12 Pa.C.S. §3706(c)]. Prior to 2016, the cap was $25 million.

¶4623

- *Application of KIZ credits to tax liabilities*

A KIZ tax credit may be applied against a KIZ company's personal income tax liability, corporate income tax liability, and capital/stock franchise tax liability for the taxable year during which the credit is approved. If application of the credits to these liabilities do not use up the entire credit, unused KIZ tax credits may be carried forward or sold/assigned, but they may not be carried back or refunded [12 Pa.C.S. § 3706(d)].

- *Carryforward*

If the amount of tax liability owed by the KIZ company is less than the amount of the tax credit, the KIZ company may elect to carry forward the amount of the remaining tax credit for a period not to exceed four additional taxable years and to apply the credit against tax liability incurred during those years, or the KIZ company may elect to sell or assign a portion of the tax credit [12 Pa.C.S. § 3706(d)].

- *Sale or assignment of tax credit*

If a KIZ company applies to and gets the approval of the DCED, it may sell or assign, in whole or in part, the tax credit granted to it [12 Pa.C.S. § 3706(f)(1)]. The application must be on the form required by the DCED and must include or demonstrate all of the following:

(1) The applicant's name and address.

(2) A copy of the tax credit certificate previously issued by the DCED.

(3) A statement as to whether any part of the tax credit has been applied to tax liability of the applicant and the amount so applied.

(4) Any other information required by the DCED.

The DCED will review the application and, if satisfied that all requirements have been met, may approve the application and will notify the Department of Revenue [12 Pa.C.S. § 3607(f)(2)].

- *Use of sold or assigned tax credit*

The purchaser/assignee of all or a portion of a KIZ tax credit must claim the credit in the taxable year in which the purchase or assignment is made. The purchaser/assignee of a tax credit may use the tax credit against its tax liability for any of the following taxes [12 Pa.C.S. § 3706(g)]:

(1) Personal income tax.

(2) Corporate net income tax.

(3) Capital stock/franchise tax.

(4) Bank and trust company shares tax.

(5) Title insurance companies shares tax.

(6) Insurance premiums tax.

(7) Mutual thrift institutions tax.

The amount of the tax credit used cannot exceed 75% of the purchaser's/assignee's tax liability for the taxable year. The purchaser/assignee cannot carry over, carry back, obtain a refund of, or assign the KIZ tax credit. The purchaser/assignee must notify the DCED and the Department of Revenue of the seller/assignor of the KIZ tax credit in compliance with procedures specified by the DCED [12 Pa.C.S. § 3706(g)].

¶4624 Tax Amnesty

Act 84 of 2016 (H.B. 1198) establishes a Tax Amnesty Program that will run for a 60-day period set by the governor during the 2016-2017 fiscal year. The program allows delinquent taxpayers to satisfy tax liabilities without the imposition of penalties. In order to qualify for the program, a taxpayer must: (1) file a tax amnesty return, (2) pay all taxes and 50% of all interest, and (3) file complete tax returns and amended tax returns as needed for each year of delinquency. The program exempts a taxpayer from paying any penalties owed due to and prohibits the Department from pursuing administrative or judicial proceedings against a taxpayer with respect to an eligible tax disclosed on a tax amnesty return.

The program applies to any tax administered by the Department on which a taxpayer is delinquent as of December 31, 2015. Delinquent liabilities include a liability for returns not filed; liabilities according to records of the Department as of December 31, 2015; and liabilities not reported, underreported or not established, but delinquent as of December 31, 2015. Additionally, the program provides that a taxpayer with unknown liabilities reported and paid under the program and that complies with all other requirements will not be liable for any taxes of the same type due prior to January 1, 2011.

Amnesty is contingent on continued compliance and the Department may assess and collect from a taxpayer all penalties and interest waived through the program if, within two years after the end of the program, either of the following occurs: (1) the taxpayer becomes delinquent for three consecutive periods in payment of taxes due or filing of returns required on a semimonthly, monthly, quarterly or other basis and the taxpayer has not contested the tax liability through a timely valid administrative or judicial appeal; or (2) the taxpayer granted amnesty becomes delinquent and is eight or more months late in payment of taxes due or filing of returns on an annual basis and the taxpayer has not contested the liability through a timely valid administrative or judicial appeal. A taxpayer that participates in the program is not eligible to participate in a future tax amnesty program.

Voluntary Disclosure

The Voluntary Disclosure Program discussed at ¶4516 was suspended during the 2010 amnesty period, but was resumed after June 18, 2010.

¶4625 Compromise by Board of Appeals

• *General*

A taxpayer who has filed a petition for relief under any statutory provision allowing for administrative tax appeal to the Department of Revenue may propose a compromise of the amount of liability for tax, interest, penalty, additions, or fees administered by the Department of Revenue [72 P.S. § 100707(a)]. The compromise offer must be submitted prior to a final decision by the Department on the petition. An informal conference, in person or by telephone, may be conducted by the Department with representatives of the Department and the petition. If the compromise offer is accepted, the Department shall issue an order reflecting the compromise. The compromise is not subject to further appeal.

• *Bases for compromise*

There are two bases for compromise [72 P.S. § 100707(b)]:

    (1) Doubt as to liability.

    (2) The promotion of effective tax administration.

• *Items ineligible for compromise*

The following are not eligible for compromise [72 P.S. § 100707(c)]:

    (1) A petition of denial of property tax or rent rebate claim.

    (2) A petition of denial of a charitable tax exemption.

    (3) A petition of the revocation of a sales tax license.

    (4) A petition of jeopardy assessments.

    (5) A petition arising under 4 Pa.C.S. Pt. II (relating to gaming).

ADMINISTRATION AND PROCEDURE

CHAPTER 47
PENNSYLVANIA RESOURCES

Department of Revenue, 4th & Walnut, Strawberry Sq., Harrisburg, PA 17128

Individual taxpayers 717-787-8201

Business taxpayers 717-787-1064

Prerecorded answers to FAQs 1-888-PATAXES

TTY only 1-800-447-3020

Internet: www.revenue.state.pa.us

Department of Community & Economic Development, 400 North St., 4th Flr., Commonwealth Keystone Bldg., Harrisburg, PA 17120-0225

Center for Business Financing 717-787-7120

Center for Entrepreneurial Assistance 1-800-280-3801
717-783-5700

Center for Private Financing 717-783-1109

Economic Development Marketing Office 1-800-237-4363

Governor's Center for Local Government Services 1-888-223-6837

International Business Development 717-787-7190

Pennsylvania Industrial Development Authority (PIDA) 717-787-6245

Small Business Advocate 717-783-2525

Small Business Resource Center 1-800-280-3801
717-783-5700

Internet: www.inventpa.com

PART XX

UNCLAIMED PROPERTY

CHAPTER 48

UNCLAIMED PROPERTY

¶4801 Unclaimed Property

Generally, property that is unclaimed by its rightful owner is presumed abandoned after a specified period of years following the date upon which the owner may demand the property or the date upon which the obligation to pay or distribute the property arises, whichever comes first.

What is unclaimed property?

All abandoned and unclaimed property and property without a rightful or lawful owner is subject to the custody and control of the Commonwealth if:

it is tangible and physically located within the Commonwealth; or

it is intangible, and, according to the records of the holder:

the last known address of the owner is within the Commonwealth; or

the last known address of the owner is within a jurisdiction, the laws of which do not provide for the escheat or custodial taking of such property, and the domicile of the holder is within the Commonwealth; or

no address of the owner is given and the domicile of the holder is within the Commonwealth; or

no address of the owner is given and the domicile of the holder is not within the Commonwealth, but it is proved that the last known address of the owner is in the Commonwealth.

(Sec. 1301.2(a), Act of April 9, 1929, P.L. 343, [72 P.S. Sec. 1301.2(a)])

CCH Comment: Escheat is an area of potential federal/state conflict

A federal statute may preempt state escheat provisions, as for instance Sec. 514(a) of the Employee Retirement Income Security Act of 1974 (ERISA). Pursuant to this provision, the Department of Labor and Workforce Development has been of the opinion that funds of missing participants in a qualified employee benefit plan must stay in the plan despite a state escheat provision because ERISA preempts application of the state escheat laws with respect to such funds (Advisory Opinion 94-41A, Department of Labor, Pension and Welfare Benefit Administration, Dec. 7, 1994). Some states have challenged the federal position on this and similar narrowly delineated situations. In the case of federal tax refunds, IRC Sec. 6408 disallows refunds if the refund would escheat to a state.

Practitioners are thus advised that a specific situation where federal and state policy cross on the issue of escheat may, at this time, be an area of unsettled law.

What are the dormancy periods for unclaimed property?

General rule. Generally, all property, not otherwise specified, that has remained unclaimed by the owner for more than three years after it became payable or distributable and in which the owner has not indicated an interest, is presumed abandoned and unclaimed. (Sec. 1301.10, Act of April 9, 1929, P.L. 343, [72 P.S. Sec. 1301.10])

Checks and drafts. Sums payable on a check or written instrument, including drafts, are presumed abandoned three years after the date payable or from the date of issuance, if payable on demand. (Sec. 1301.3, Act of April 9, 1929, P.L. 343, [72 P.S. Sec. 1301.3])

Bank accounts. Demand, savings, or matured time deposits in a financial institution, or any funds paid toward the purchase of shares or other interest in a savings association, savings and loan or building and loan association are presumed abandoned after three years of inactivity. (Sec. 1301.3, Act of April 9, 1929, [72 P.S. Sec. 1301.3])

Property distributable in the course of demutualization or related reorganization of an insurance company. Uncollected property distributable during a demutualization or related reorganization is presumed abandoned two years after the date of the demutualization or reorganization, or two years from the date a statement to the property owner was issued and not delivered due to a postal error or incorrect address. (Sec. 1301.4, Act of April 9, 1929, P.L. 343, [72 P.S. Sec. 1301.4])

Gift certificates, gift cards and credit memos. Consideration paid for a gift certificate or a gift card (but not a qualified gift certificate that has no expiration date or postsale charge or fee) is presumed abandoned after the later of:

— two years after its redemption period has expired or the minimum period specified in the Consumer Credit Protection Act; or

— three years after the issuance date, if no redemption period is specified.

(Sec. 1301.6, Act of April 9, 1929, P.L. 343, [72 P.S. Sec. 1301.6])

Stock and other intangibles. A stock certificate or other participating right in a business association for which a certificate has been issued or is issuable but not delivered is presumed abandoned three years after the holder has lost contact with the owner, unless the owner has, within the three-year period:

— increased or decreased the principal;

— accepted payment of principal or income; or

— otherwise indicated an interest in the property or in other property of the owner that is in the possession or control of the holder.

(Sec. 1301.6, Act of April 9, 1929, P.L. 343, [72 P.S. Sec. 1301.6])

Other dormancy periods. Most states also have specified dormancy periods for:

Business association dissolutions/refunds,

Insurance policies,

IRAs/retirement funds,

Money orders,

Proceeds from class action suits,

Property held by agents-in-fact and fiduciaries,

Safe deposit boxes,

Shares in a financial institution,

Traveler's checks,

¶4801

Utilities,

Wages/salaries, and

Property held by courts/public agencies.

Is there a business-to-business exemption for unclaimed property?

Pennsylvania does not have a business-to-business exemption for unclaimed property.

What are the notice requirements for unclaimed property?

Notice by the holder to the owner of property presumed to be abandoned must be sent no more than 120 days or less than 60 days prior to the date in which the corresponding report is mailed the State Treasurer. The notice must be by first class mail or, if previously agreed to by the owner, electronic delivery. No fee or cost associated with such notice can be imposed upon an owner. (Sec. 1301.10a, Act of April 9, 1929, P.L. 343, [72 P.S. Sec. 1301.10a])

What are the reporting requirements for unclaimed property?

General requirements. Every person holding property that became subject to the custody and control of the state during the preceding year must file a report with the State Treasurer by April 15. (Sec. 1301.11(d), Act of April 9, 1929, P.L. 343, [72 P.S. Sec. 1301.11(d)])

Negative reporting. While not required, holders may file a negative report. (Pennsylvania Unclaimed Property Annual Reporting, Pennsylvania Treasury)

Minimum reporting. There is no minimum threshold reporting amount. (Pennsylvania Unclaimed Property Annual Reporting, Pennsylvania Treasury)

Aggregate reporting. Items with a value of less than $50 each may be reported in the aggregate. (Sec. 1301.11(b)2, Act of April 9, 1929, P.L. 343, [72 P.S. Sec. 1301.11(b)2])

Electronic reporting. Electronic reporting is required for 10 or more properties. (Pennsylvania Unclaimed Property Annual Reporting, Pennsylvania Treasury)

Recordkeeping. If a holder does not maintain adequate records and the records of the holder are insufficient to permit the preparation of a report, the State Treasurer may require the holder to report and pay to the State Treasurer the amount the State Treasurer reasonably estimates, on the basis of any available records of the holder or by any other reasonable method of estimation that the State Treasurer may select. While there is no specific record retention period, the Treasurer recommends 10 years. (Sec. 1301.23(f), Act of April 9, 1929, P.L. 343, [72 P.S. Sec. 1301.23(f)]; Pennsylvania Unclaimed Property Annual Reporting, Pennsylvania Treasury)

CASE TABLE

A

AL

B

BA

C

CA

F

H

I

IN

L

M

LE

N

O

P

PE

Q

Quaker Oats Co., Cmwlth. v.
  38 A.2d 325 (Pa. 1944) 1301, 1412

Quality Market, Inc. v. Cmwlth.
  514 A.2d 228 (1986), *aff'd per curiam*, 526 A.2d 357 (Pa. 1987), *cert. den.*, U.S. Sup. Ct.
  (October 19, 1987) 1405, 1501

Quest Diagnostics Venture, LLC v. Commonwealth
  2015 WL 3561310 . . . . 1207, 4604

Quill Corporation v. North Dakota
  504 U.S. 298 (1992) 722

Qwest Transmission, Inc., Cmwlth. v.
  765 A.2d 818 (Pa.Commw. 2000) 4621

R

R&R Express v. Cmwlth.
  65 A.3d 900 (Pa. 2013), *aff'g per curiam*, 37 A.3d 46 (2012) 2605

Reading Housing Authority v. Board of Assessment Appeals of Berks County
  103 A.3d 869 (2014) 3504

Reaman v. Allentown Power Center, L.P.
  74 A.3d 371 (2013) 3606

Reese's Pizza and More v. Dept. of Labor and Industry et al.
  93 A.3d 914 (2014) 2804, 4621

Rendina, Inc., v. City of Harrisburg
  No. 130 MAP 2005 (Pennsylvania. 2007), *rev'g* 859 A.2d 888 (Pa.Commw. 2004) . . . .
  3606

RHA Pennsylvania Nursing Homes, In re
  747 A.2d 1257 (Pa.Commw. 2000) 3505

Radecke v. York County Board of Assessment Appeals
  798 A.2d 265 (Pa.Commw. 2002) 3507

Rauch v. Tax Review Board of the City of Philadelphia and the City of Philadelphia
  708 A.2d 142 (Pa.Commw. 1998) 3804

Reading and Southwestern Street Railway Co., The Cmwlth. v.
  54 Dauph. 277 (1943) 913

Reddinger, Terry R., Inc. v. Cmwlth. v.
  Pa.Commw., No. 198 F.R. 1996 (April 5, 2001), *opinion not reported* 2605

Reick-McJunkin Dairy Co. v. Pittsburgh School District
  66 A.2d 295 (1949) 1603, 1605

Reiniger Brothers, Inc. v. Cmwlth.
  522 A.2d 187 (Pa.Commw. 1987) 1311

Renda, Ernest, Contracting v. Cmwlth.
  532 A.2d 416 (Pa. 1987), *rev'g* 504 A.2d 1349 (Pa.Commw. 1986) 713

Ringling, Cmwlth. v.
  509 A.2d 936 (1980) 206

Rittenhouse Square Corp., Cmwlth. v.
  62 Dauph. 49 (1952), *exceptions overruled*, 62 Dauph. 285 (1952) 1703

SA

T

SP

UN

UN

TOPICAL INDEX

References are to paragraph numbers.

CAR

KEY

QUA